Lecture Notes in Computer Science 16140

The series Lecture Notes in Computer Science (LNCS), including its subseries Lecture Notes in Artificial Intelligence (LNAI) and Lecture Notes in Bioinformatics (LNBI), has established itself as a medium for the publication of new developments in computer science and information technology research, teaching, and education.

LNCS enjoys close cooperation with the computer science R & D community, the series counts many renowned academics among its volume editors and paper authors, and collaborates with prestigious societies. Its mission is to serve this international community by providing an invaluable service, mainly focused on the publication of conference and workshop proceedings and postproceedings. LNCS commenced publication in 1973.

Daniel Garijo · Sabrina Kirrane ·
Angelo Salatino · Cogan Shimizu ·
Maribel Acosta · Andrea Giovanni Nuzzolese ·
Sebastián Ferrada · Thibaut Soulard ·
Kouji Kozaki · Hideaki Takeda ·
Anna Lisa Gentile
Editors

The Semantic Web – ISWC 2025

24th International Semantic Web Conference,
Nara, Japan, November 2–6, 2025
Proceedings, Part I

Springer

Editors
Daniel Garijo
Universidad Politécnica de Madrid
Madrid, Spain

Angelo Salatino
The Open University
Milton Keynes, UK

Maribel Acosta
Technical University of Munich
Munich, Germany

Sebastián Ferrada
Universidad de Chile
Santiago, Chile

Kouji Kozaki
Osaka Electro-Communication University
Osaka, Japan

Anna Lisa Gentile
IBM Research
San Jose, CA, USA

Sabrina Kirrane
Vienna University of Economics
and Business
Vienna, Austria

Cogan Shimizu
Wright State University
Dayton, OH, USA

Andrea Giovanni Nuzzolese
CNR - Institute of Cognitive Sciences
and Technologies
Rome, Italy

Thibaut Soulard
University of Paris-Saclay
Gif-sur-Yvette, France

Hideaki Takeda
National Institute of Informatics
Chiyoda City, Japan

ISSN 0302-9743 ISSN 1611-3349 (electronic)
Lecture Notes in Computer Science
ISBN 978-3-032-09526-8 ISBN 978-3-032-09527-5 (eBook)
https://doi.org/10.1007/978-3-032-09527-5

This Springer imprint is published by the registered company Springer Nature Switzerland AG
The registered company address is: Gewerbestrasse 11, 6330 Cham, Switzerland

Preface

The 2025 edition of the International Semantic Web Conference (ISWC) was held in Nara, Japan. I had the honor of serving as the General Chair for ISWC 2025 and working alongside a highly talented and dedicated Organizing Committee, whose efforts were instrumental in making the conference a success. I would like to extend special thanks to Kouji Kozaki, the Local Chair, for his outstanding behind-the-scenes work and unwavering support, as well as the entire Local Organizing team for their vital contributions. My gratitude also goes to the Semantic Web Science Association (SWSA), particularly its President Elena Simperl, for their invaluable guidance and support throughout the organization of ISWC 2025. Warm thanks are also due to all who contributed as Senior Program Committee members, Program Committee members, Workshop and Tutorial organizers, and Challenge organizers - their dedication played a key role in shaping the conference. ISWC 2025 ran over five days and marked a return to Japan following the 2016 edition in Kobe. The first two days were devoted to Workshops, Tutorials, Challenges, and the Doctoral Consortium, while the final three days featured presentations from the Research, Resources, In-Use, and Industry Tracks, along with Poster & Demo sessions, two Journal Sessions, Keynotes, a Panel, and more. This volume includes 60 accepted papers from the Research, Resources, and In-Use Tracks.

The Research Track of ISWC 2025 was chaired by Daniel Garijo and Sabrina Kirrane. The track received 219 abstract submissions and 171 full submissions, of which 17 were desk-rejected and 152 were sent for review. In the end, 34 articles were accepted into the proceedings, giving an acceptance rate of 20%. The 276 reviewers who conducted reviews were instrumental in the discussions and in reaching a decision about accepted papers, together with the 26 Senior Program Committee members who oversaw the review process and provided meta-reviews and recommendations to the chairs. All articles received at least three reviews in a double-anonymous process.

The Resources Track of ISWC 2025, co-chaired by Angelo Salatino and Cogan Shimizu, showcased novel artifacts pertinent to the Semantic Web research community. These encompassed benchmarks, knowledge graphs, tools, ontologies, models, and vocabularies. This year, the track saw a significant increase in popularity, more than doubling submissions from the previous edition. Out of 95 abstract submissions, 82 materialized into full submissions. Following a thorough single-anonymous peer-review process, 19 manuscripts were accepted, resulting in a 23% acceptance rate. The acceptance decisions were the result of a collaborative effort by 128 Program Committee (PC) members and 13 Senior PC (SPC) members. The reviewers were instrumental in the discussions, while the SPC members oversaw the entire review process, provided meta-reviews, and offered recommendations. Every article received at least three reviews, with 23 getting four reviews and three even receiving five.

The In-Use Track of ISWC 2025, co-chaired by Maribel Acosta and Andrea Giovanni Nuzzolese, featured innovative applications of knowledge graphs and semantic web technologies in real-world scenarios. The track focused on practical deployments with applications in a wide range of domains, including smart and power grids, life and earth sciences, government, and industry. This year, the track maintained strong interest from the community, with 26 abstracts materialising into 24 full submissions. After a rigorous single-anonymous peer-review process, 7 papers were accepted, resulting in an acceptance rate of 29%. The review process was supported by 30 Program Committee (PC) members. Each paper received at least three reviews, and final decisions were based on discussions among reviewers and the track chairs. The accepted papers provide valuable contributions, showing how semantic technologies are being translated into impactful, real-world solutions.

September 2025

Anna Lisa Gentile
Daniel Garijo
Sabrina Kirrane
Angelo Salatino
Cogan Shimizu
Maribel Acosta
Andrea Giovanni Nuzzolese
Sebastián Ferrada
Thibaut Soulard
Kouji Kozaki
Hideaki Takeda
Anna Lisa Gentile

Organization

General Chair

Anna Lisa Gentile	IBM Research, USA

Local Chair

Kouji Kozaki	Osaka Electro-Communication University, Japan

Local Co-chairs

Ken Fukuda	National Institute of Advanced Industrial Science and Technology, Japan
Ikki Ohmukai	The University of Tokyo, Japan
Hideaki Takeda	National Institute of Informatics, Japan

Research Track Chairs

Daniel Garijo	Universidad Politécnica de Madrid, Spain
Sabrina Kirrane	Vienna University of Economics and Business, Austria

Resources Track Chairs

Angelo Salatino	The Open University, UK
Cogan Shimizu	Wright State University, USA

In-Use Track Chairs

Maribel Acosta	Technical University of Munich, Germany
Andrea Giovanni Nuzzolese	Institute of Cognitive Sciences and Technologies, Italy

Workshop and Tutorials Chairs

Juan Sequeda	ServiceNow (data.world), USA
Blerina Spahiu	Università di Milano-Bicocca, Italy

Industry Track Chairs

Irene Celino	Cefriel, Italy
Oktie Hassanzadeh	IBM Research, USA

Doctoral Consortium Chairs

Abraham Bernstein	University of Zurich, Switzerland
Natasha Noy	Google, USA

Poster, Demo and Lightning Talk Chairs

Gong Cheng	Nanjing University, China
Shenghui Wang	Universiteit Twente, Netherlands

Semantic Web Challenge Chairs

Mayank Kejriwal	University of Southern California, USA
Pablo Mendez	Objective, USA

Job Fair Chair

Nandana Mihindukulasooriya	IBM Research, US

Sponsorship Chairs

Ray Atarashi	Internet Initiative Japan, Japan
Neha Keshan	Rensselaer Polytechnic Institute, USA
Armando Stellato	University of Rome Tor Vergata, Italy

Proceedings and Metadata Chairs

Sebastián Ferrada — Universidad de Chile, Chile
Thibaut Soulard — University of Paris-Saclay, France

Student Grants and Activities Chairs

Ines Akaichi — Vienna University of Economics and Business, Austria
Atsuko Yamaguchi — Tokyo City University, Japan

Web Presence and Publicity Chairs

Genet-Asefa Gesese — Karlsruhe Institute of Technology, Germany
Tetsuya Mihara — University of Tsukuba, Japan
Zequn Sun — Nanjing University, China
Jenifer Tabita Ciuciu-Kiss — Universidad Politécnica de Madrid, Spain

Research Track Senior Program Committee

Maribel Acosta — Technical University of Munich, Germany
Carlos Buil Aranda — Philip Morris International, Spain
David Chaves-Fraga — Universidade de Santiago de Compostela, Spain
Gong Cheng — Nanjing University, China
Michael Cochez — Vrije Universiteit Amsterdam, Netherlands
Oscar Corcho — Universidad Politécnica de Madrid, Spain
Julien Corman — Free University of Bozen-Bolzano, Italy
Gianluca Demartini — University of Queensland, Australia
Anastasia Dimou — KU Leuven, Belgium
Mauro Dragoni — Fondazione Bruno Kessler, Italy
Peter Haase — metaphacts, Germany
Olaf Hartig — Linköping University, Sweden
Aidan Hogan — Universidad de Chile, Chile
Laura Hollink — Centrum Wiskunde & Informatica, Netherlands
Ernesto Jiménez-Ruiz — City St George's, University of London, UK
Boris Motik — University of Oxford, UK
Terry Payne — University of Liverpool, UK
Catia Pesquita — Universidade de Lisboa, Portugal
María Poveda-Villalón — Universidad Politécnica de Madrid, Spain

Anisa Rula	University of Brescia, Italy
Hala Skaf-Molli	University of Nantes - LS2N, France
Kavitha Srinivas	IBM Research, USA
Kostas Stefanidis	Tampere University, Finland
Valentina Tamma	University of Liverpool, UK
Maria-Esther Vidal	Leibniz University Hannover, Germany
Domagoj Vrgoc	Pontificia Universidad Católica de Chile, Chile

Research Track Program Committee

Nathalie Abadie	LASTIG, Université Gustave Eiffel, IGN-ENSG, France
Alessandro Adamou	Bibliotheca Hertziana - Max Planck Institute for Art History, Italy
Shqiponja Ahmetaj	TU Wien, Austria
Mehwish Alam	Télécom Paris, France
Elvira Amador-Domínguez	Universidad Politécnica de Madrid, Spain
Amin Anjomshoaa	Vienna University of Economics and Business, Austria
Gianluca Apriceno	Fondazione Bruno Kessler, Italy
Julián Arenas-Guerrero	Universidad Politécnica de Madrid, Spain
Dörthe Arndt	TU Dresden, Germany
Carlos Badenes-Olmedo	Universidad Politécnica de Madrid, Spain
Tania Bailoni	Fondazione Bruno Kessler, Italy
Pierpaolo Basile	University of Bari, Italy
Christian Bizer	University of Mannheim, Germany
Eva Blomqvist	Linköping University, Sweden
Carlos Bobed	University of Zaragoza, Spain
Piero Bonatti	University of Naples Federico II, Italy
Pieter Bonte	KU Leuven, Belgium
Paolo Bouquet	University of Trento, Italy
Janez Brank	Jožef Stefan Institute, Slovenia
Davide Buscaldi	LIPN, Université Sorbonne Paris Nord, France
Jean-Paul Calbimonte	University of Applied Sciences and Arts Western Switzerland HES-SO, Switzerland
Pablo Calleja	Universidad Politécnica de Madrid, Spain
Cinzia Cappiello	Politecnico di Milano, Italy
Antonella Carbonaro	University of Bologna, Italy
Davide Ceolin	Centrum Wiskunde & Informatica, Netherlands
Pierre-Antoine Champin	W3C/Inria, France
Nathalie Charbel	Neo4j, France

Victor Charpenay	Mines Saint-Étienne, France
Vinay Chaudhri	Knowledge Systems Research LLC, USA
Jiaoyan Chen	University of Manchester, UK
Ioannis Chrysakis	Netcompany, Luxembourg, and ICS-FORTH, Greece
Yashrajsinh Chudasama	Leibniz University Hannover, Germany
Philipp Cimiano	Bielefeld University, Germany
Andrei Ciortea	University of St. Gallen, Switzerland
Pieter Colpaert	Ghent University – imec, Belgium
Philippe Cudre-Mauroux	University of Fribourg, Switzerland
Claudia d'Amato	University of Bari, Italy
Mathieu D'Aquin	LORIA, University of Lorraine, France
Enrico Daga	The Open University, UK
Ioannis Dasoulas	KU Leuven, Belgium
Victor de Boer	Vrije Universiteit Amsterdam, Netherlands
Stefano De Giorgis	Vrije Universiteit Amsterdam, Netherlands
Christophe Debruyne	Université de Liège, Belgium
Daniele Dell'Aglio	Aalborg University, Denmark
Elena Demidova	University of Bonn, Germany
Stefan Dietze	GESIS & Heinrich-Heine-University Düsseldorf, Germany
John Domingue	The Open University, UK
Fajar J. Ekaputra	Vienna University of Economics and Business, Austria
Basil Ell	CITEC, Universität Bielefeld and University of Oslo, Norway
Lorena Etcheverry	Universidad de la República, Uruguay
David Eyers	University of Otago, New Zealand
Daniel Faria	INESC-ID, Instituto Superior Técnico, Universidade de Lisboa, Portugal
Catherine Faron	Université Côte d'Azur, France
Anna Fensel	Wageningen University and Research, Netherlands
Holly Ferguson	University of Notre Dame, USA
Javier D. Fernández	F. Hoffmann-La Roche AG, Switzerland
Sebastián Ferrada	Universidad de Chile, Chile
Erwin Filtz	Siemens AG Österreich, Austria
Giorgos Flouris	ICS-FORTH, Greece
Ken Fukuda	National Institute of Advanced Industrial Science and Technology, Japan
Naoki Fukuta	Shizuoka University, Japan
Irini Fundulaki	ICS-FORTH, Greece
Mohamed H. Gad-Elrab	Bosch AI, Germany

Luis Galárraga	Inria, France
Fabien Gandon	Inria, France
Aldo Gangemi	Università di Bologna & CNR-ISTC, Italy
Sandra Geisler	RWTH Aachen University, Germany
Stefano Germano	University of Oxford, UK
Pouya Ghiasnezhad Omran	Australian National University, Australia
Martin Giese	University of Oslo, Norway
Rafael Gonçalves	Stanford University, USA
Simon Gottschalk	Leibniz Universität Hannover, L3S Research Center, Germany
Guido Governatori	Central Queensland University, Australia
Jorge Gracia	University of Zaragoza, Spain
Paul Groth	University of Amsterdam, Netherlands
Tudor Groza	Bioinformatics Institute, A*STAR, Singapore
Claudio Gutierrez	Universidad de Chile, Chile
José Manuel Gómez Pérez	expert.ai, Spain
Andreas Harth	Friedrich-Alexander-Universität Erlangen-Nürnberg and Fraunhofer IIS, Germany
Mounira Harzallah	LS2N, University of Nantes, France
Oktie Hassanzadeh	IBM Research, USA
Maria M. Hedblom	Jönköping University, Sweden
Daniel Hernández	University of Stuttgart, Germany
Sven Hertling	University of Mannheim, Germany
Ryohei Hisano	The University of Tokyo, Japan
Andreas Hotho	University of Würzburg, Germany
Wei Hu	Nanjing University, China
Luis Ibanez-Gonzalez	University of Southampton, UK
Ryutaro Ichise	Institute of Science Tokyo, Japan
Enrique Iglesias	Forschungszentrum L3S, Germany
Ana Iglesias-Molina	Universidad Politécnica de Madrid, Spain
Prateek Jain	The Trade Desk, Inc., USA
Jan-Christoph Kalo	University of Amsterdam, Netherlands
Timotheus Kampik	SAP, Umeå University, Sweden
Takahiro Kawamura	The University of Tokyo, Japan
Mayank Kejriwal	University of Southern California, USA
Ilkcan Keles	Booking.com, Netherlands
Elmar Kiesling	Vienna University of Economics and Business, Austria
Haridimos Kondylakis	Institute of Computer Science, FORTH, Greece
George Konstantinidis	University of Southampton, UK
Roman Kontchakov	Birkbeck, University of London, UK

Manolis Koubarakis	National and Kapodistrian University of Athens, Greece
Markus Krötzsch	TU Dresden, Germany
Tobias Käfer	Karlsruhe Institute of Technology, Germany
Jose Emilio Labra Gayo	Universidad de Oviedo, Spain
Christoph Lange	Fraunhofer Institute for Applied Information Technology and RWTH Aachen University, Germany
Davide Lanti	Free University of Bozen-Bolzano, Italy
Danh Le Phuoc	TU Berlin, Germany
Maxime Lefrançois	MINES Saint-Étienne, France
Huanyu Li	Linköping University, Sweden
Ke Liang	National University of Defense Technology, China
Pasquale Lisena	EURECOM, France
Vanessa Lopez	IBM Research Europe, Ireland
Maria Maleshkova	Helmut Schmidt University, Germany
Lorenzo Marconi	Sapienza University of Rome, Italy
Milan Markovic	University of Aberdeen, UK
Jose L. Martinez-Rodriguez	Autonomous University of Tamaulipas, Mexico
Simon Mayer	University of St. Gallen, Switzerland
Hande McGinty	Kansas State University, USA
Albert Meroño-Peñuela	King's College London, UK
Nandana Mihindukulasooriya	IBM Research AI, USA
Pascal Molli	University of Nantes - LS2N, France
Deshendran Moodley	University of Cape Town, South Africa
Summaya Mumtaz	Merkle Inc., USA
Raghava Mutharaju	IIIT Delhi, India
Hubert Naacke	Sorbonne Université, LIP6, France
María Navas-Loro	Universidad Politécnica de Madrid, Spain
Sebastian Neumaier	St. Pölten University of Applied Sciences, Austria
Axel-Cyrille Ngonga Ngomo	Paderborn University, Germany
Andriy Nikolov	AstraZeneca, UK
Werner Nutt	Free University of Bozen-Bolzano, Italy
Andrea Giovanni Nuzzolese	CNR - Institute of Cognitive Sciences and Technologies, Italy
Femke Ongenae	Ghent University - imec, Belgium
Francesco Osborne	The Open University, UK
Julian Padget	University of Bath, UK
Matteo Palmonari	University of Milano-Bicocca, Italy
Jeff Pan	University of Edinburgh, UK
Peter Patel-Schneider	USA/Canada

Evan Patton	Massachusetts Institute of Technology, USA
Heiko Paulheim	University of Mannheim, Germany
Bernardo Pereira Nunes	Australian National University, Australia
Romana Pernisch	Vrije Universiteit Amsterdam, Netherlands
Alina Petrova	Thomson Reuters Labs, UK
Rafael Peñaloza	University of Milano-Bicocca, Italy
Giuseppe Pirrò	University of Calabria, Italy
Dimitris Plexousakis	Institute of Computer Science, FORTH, Greece
Axel Polleres	Vienna University of Economics and Business, Austria
Nico Potyka	Cardiff University, UK
Nicoleta Preda	University de Versailles, France
Cédric Pruski	Luxembourg Institute of Science and Technology, Luxembourg
Disha Purohit	TIB – Leibniz Information Centre for Science and Technology and University Library in Hannover, Germany
Hemant Purohit	George Mason University, USA
Umair Qudus	University of Paderborn, Germany
Joe Raad	University of Paris-Saclay, France
David Ratcliffe	Microsoft, Australia
Juan L. Reutter	Pontificia Universidad Católica, Chile
Martin Rezk	Google, USA
Mariano Rico	Universidad Politécnica de Madrid, Spain
Philipp D. Rohde	TIB Leibniz Information Centre for Science and Technology, Germany
Edelweis Rohrer	Universidad de la República, Uruguay
Julián Rojas	Ghent University, Belgium
Oscar Romero	Universitat Politècnica de Catalunya, Spain
Marco Rospocher	Università degli Studi di Verona, Italy
Jože M. Rožanec	Jožef Stefan Institute, Slovenia
Marta Sabou	Vienna University of Economics and Business, Austria
Harald Sack	FIZ Karlsruhe, Leibniz Institute for Information Infrastructure & KIT Karlsruhe, Germany
Tomer Sagi	Aalborg Universitet, Denmark
Muhammad Saleem	University of Paderborn, Germany
Emanuel Sallinger	TU Wien, Austria
Bruno Sartini	Ludwig-Maximilians-Universität München, Germany
Marco Luca Sbodio	IBM Research, Ireland
Francois Scharffe	University of Montpellier, France
Ralf Schenkel	Trier University, Germany

Daniel Schwabe	Pontifical Catholic University of Rio de Janeiro, Brazil
Juan Sequeda	ServiceNow, USA
Patricia Serrano Alvarado	University of Nantes - LS2N, France
Kuldeep Singh	Cerence AI, Germany
Martin G. Skjæveland	University of Oslo, Norway
Sebastian Skritek	TU Wien, Austria
Blerina Spahiu	Università degli Studi di Milano-Bicocca, Italy
Steffen Staab	University of Stuttgart, Germany
Nadine Steinmetz	University of Applied Sciences Erfurt, Germany
Lise Stork	University of Amsterdam, Netherlands
Chang Sun	Maastricht University, Netherlands
Vojtěch Svátek	Prague University of Economics and Business, Czechia
Danai Symeonidou	INRAE, France
Ruben Taelman	Ghent University – imec, Belgium
Lionel Tailhardat	Orange, France
Hideaki Takeda	National Institute of Informatics, Japan
Aisling Third	The Open University, UK
Steffen Thoma	FZI Research Center for Information Technology, Germany
Ilaria Tiddi	Vrije Universiteit Amsterdam, Netherlands
Dominik Tomaszuk	University of Bialystok, Poland
Riccardo Tommasini	INSA Lyon - LIRIS, France
Cassia Trojahn	Université Grenoble Alpes, Inria, France
Raphaël Troncy	EURECOM, France
Takanori Ugai	Fujitsu Limited, Japan
Ricardo Usbeck	Leuphana University Lüneburg, Germany
Marieke van Erp	KNAW Humanities Cluster, Netherlands
Ruben Verborgh	Ghent University – imec, Belgium
Serena Villata	CNRS - Laboratoire d'Informatique, Signaux et Systèmes de Sophia-Antipolis, France
Ruijie Wang	University of Zurich, Switzerland
Shenghui Wang	University of Twente, Netherlands
Xiaxia Wang	University of Oxford, UK
Simon Werner	Trier University, Germany
Xander Wilcke	Vrije Universiteit Amsterdam, Netherlands
Josiane Xavier Parreira	Siemens AG Österreich, Austria
Fouad Zablith	American University of Beirut, Lebanon
Joseph Zalewski	Kansas State University, USA
Antoine Zimmermann	École des Mines de Saint-Étienne, France
Remzi Çelebi	Maastricht University, Netherlands

Resources Track Senior Program Committee

Philippe Cudre-Mauroux	University of Fribourg, Switzerland
Michel Dumontier	Maastricht University, Netherlands
Anna Fensel	Wageningen University & Research, Netherlands
Aidan Hogan	Universidad de Chile, Chile
Milan Markovic	University of Aberdeen, UK
Lionel Medini	Université Claude Bernard Lyon1, France
Nandana Mihindukulasooriya	IBM Research, USA
Pascal Molli	University of Nantes - LS2N, France
Tong Ruan	East China University of Science and Technology, China
Marta Sabou	Vienna University of Economics and Business, Austria
Ruben Taelman	Ghent University – imec, Belgium
Maria-Esther Vidal	Leibniz University Hannover, Germany
Xiaowang Zhang	Tianjin University, China

Resources Track Program Committee

Daniel Adam	Prague University of Economics and Business, Czechia
Mark Adamik	Vrije Universiteit Amsterdam, Netherlands
Mehdi Akbari Gurabi	Fraunhofer Institute for Applied Information Technology, Germany
Vladimir Alexiev	Graphwise.ai, Bulgaria
Jorge Álvarez Fidalgo	Universidad de Oviedo, Spain
Vito Walter Anelli	Politecnico di Bari, Italy
Simone Angioni	CNR-ISTI, Italy
Gianluca Apriceno	Fondazione Bruno Kessler, Italy
Ghislain Atemezing	European Union Agency for Railways, France
Miriam Baglioni	CNR-ISTI, Italy
Sahil Bansal	SAP, USA
Roberto Barile	University of Bari Aldo Moro, Italy
Hannah Bast	University of Freiburg, Germany
Hossein Beigi Nasrabadi	FIZ Karlsruhe, Leibniz Institute for Information Infrastructure, Germany
Germán Alejandro Braun	Universidad Nacional del Comahue, Argentina
Grégoire Burel	The Open University, UK
Diego Calvanese	Free University of Bozen-Bolzano, Italy

Miguel Ceriani	Institute for Cognitive Sciences and Technologies, Italy
Pierre-Antoine Champin	W3C and Inria, France
David Chaves-Fraga	Universidade de Santiago de Compostela, Spain
Gong Cheng	Nanjing University, China
Fiorela Ciroku	Institute of Cognitive Sciences and Technologies, Italy
Diego Conde-Herreros	Universidad Politécnica de Madrid, Spain
Oscar Corcho	Universidad Politécnica de Madrid, Spain
David Corsar	Robert Gordon University, UK
Marco Cremaschi	University of Milano-Bicocca, Italy
Claudia d'Amato	University of Bari, Italy
Jennifer D'Souza	TIB Leibniz Information Centre for Science and Technology, Germany
Jérôme David	Université Grenoble Alpes - Inria, France
Stefano De Giorgis	Vrije Universiteit Amsterdam, Netherlands
Christophe Debruyne	Université de Liège, Belgium
Stefan Decker	RWTH Aachen University, Germany
Pathirage Deelaka	Rensselaer Polytechnic Institute, USA
Caglar Demir	Paderborn University, Germany
Rohit Arunrao Deshmukh	Fraunhofer Institute for Applied Information Technology FIT, Germany
Davide Di Pierro	Université de Montpellier, France
Dimitar Dimitrov	GESIS Leibniz Institute for the Social Sciences, Germany
Daniil Dobriy	Vienna University of Economics and Business, Austria
Milan Dojchinovski	Czech Technical University in Prague, Czechia
Mauro Dragoni	Fondazione Bruno Kessler, Italy
Fajar J. Ekaputra	Vienna University of Economics and Business, Austria
Beatriz Esteves	Ghent University, Belgium
Sebastián Ferrada	Universidad de Chile, Chile
Nicolas Ferranti	Vienna University of Economics and Business, Austria
Rosa Filgueira	University of Edinburgh (EPCC), UK
Pablo Fillottrani	Universidad Nacional del Sur, Argentina
Kathrin Füllenbach	eccenca, Netherlands
Susmita Gangopadhyay	GESIS Leibniz Institute for the Social Sciences, Germany
Katerina Gkirtzou	Athena Research Center, Greece
Sergio Alejandro Gomez	Universidad Nacional del Sur, Argentina
Jorge Gracia	University of Zaragoza, Spain

Arianna Graciotti	University of Bologna, Italy
Christophe Guéret	Accenture Labs, Ireland
Xin Fan Guo	King's College London, UK
Peter Haase	metaphacts, Germany
Linyi Han	Tianjin University, China
Fatma-Zohra Hannou	EDF Recherche et Développement, France
Fabian Hoppe	Vrije Universiteit Amsterdam, Netherlands
Ana Iglesias-Molina	Universidad Politécnica de Madrid, Spain
Eleni Ilkou	TIB Leibniz Information Centre for Science and Technology University Library, Germany
Theofilos Ioannidis	National and Kapodistrian University of Athens, Greece
Antoine Isaac	Europeana, France
Nitisha Jain	King's College London, UK
Clement Jonquet	MISTEA (INRAE) and LIRMM (University of Montpellier), France
Milos Jovanovik	Vienna University of Technology, Austria
Eduard Kamburjan	IT University of Copenhagen, Denmark
Yavuz Selim Kartal	GESIS Leibniz Institute for the Social Sciences, Germany
Evgeny Kharlamov	Bosch Centre for AI, Germany, and University of Oslo, Norway
Christian Kindermann	Stanford University, USA
Tomáš Kliegr	Prague University of Economics and Business, Czechia
Jakub Klímek	Charles University, Czechia
Manolis Koubarakis	National and Kapodistrian University of Athens, Greece
Kabul Kurniawan	Universitas Gadjah Mada, Indonesia
Jose Emilio Labra Gayo	Universidad de Oviedo, Spain
Christoph Lange	Fraunhofer Institute for Applied Information Technology, and RWTH Aachen University, Germany
Nicolas Lazzari	University of Bologna, Italy
Xiaoze Liu	Purdue University, USA
Zola Mahlaza	University of Cape Town, South Africa
Andrea Mannocci	CNR-ISTI, Italy
Patricia Martín-Chozas	Universidad Politécnica de Madrid, Spain
Antonello Meloni	University of Cagliari, Italy
Eduardo Mena	University of Zaragoza, Spain
Albert Meroño-Peñuela	King's College London, UK
Cedric Möller	University of Hamburg Germany
Alba Catalina Morales Tirado	The Open University, UK

Alessandro Mosca	Institute for Cognitive Sciences and Technologies, Italy
Daham Mustafa	Fraunhofer Institute for Applied Information Technology, Germany
Lina Nachabe	LIMOS, Étienne des Mines de Saint-Étienne, France
Iman Naja	The Open University, UK
Ebrahim Norouzi	FIZ Karlsruhe, Leibniz-Institut für Informationsinfrastruktur, Germany
Louis-Félix Nothias	Université Côte d'Azur, and Institut Interdisciplinaire d'Intelligence Artificielle (3iA), France
Beatriz Olarte-Martinez	Politecnico di Milano, Italy
Sarah Rebecca Ondraszek	FIZ Karlsruhe, Leibniz Institute for Information Infrastructure, Germany
Axel Polleres	Vienna University of Economics and Business, Austria
María Poveda-Villalón	Universidad Politécnica de Madrid, Spain
Martino Mare Lakota Pulici	Bosch Centre for AI, Germany
Georg Rehm	DFKI, Germany
Maria del Mar Roldan-Garcia	Universidad de Málaga, Spain
Harald Sack	FIZ Karlsruhe, Leibniz Institute for Information Infrastructure, and KIT Karlsruhe, Germany
Henrique Santos	Rensselaer Polytechnic Institute, USA
Sonja Schimmler	Fraunhofer FOKUS, Technical University Berlin, Germany
Umutcan Serles	Onlim GmbH, Austria
Mohamed Ahmed Sherif	Paderborn University, Germany
Meilin Shi	University of Vienna, Austria
Thibaut Soulard	Paris-Saclay University, France
Blerina Spahiu	Università degli Studi di Milano-Bicocca, Italy
George Stamoulis	National and Kapodistrian University of Athens, Greece
Armando Stellato	University of Rome Tor Vergata, Italy
Vojtěch Svátek	Prague University of Economics and Business, Czechia
Mary Ann Tan	FIZ Karlsruhe, Leibniz Institute for Information Infrastructure, Germany
Aisling Third	The Open University, UK
Tabea Tietz	FIZ Karlsruhe, Leibniz Institute for Information Infrastructure, Germany
Konstantin Todorov	LIRMM/University of Montpellier, France

Dimitar Trajanov	Ss. Cyril and Methodius University - Skopje, North Macedonia
Cassia Trojahn	Université Grenoble Alpes - Inria, France
Mahsa Vafaie	FIZ Karlsruhe, Leibniz Institute for Information Infrastructure, and KIT Karlsruhe, Germany
Jörg Waitelonis	yovisto GmbH, Germany
Zhichun Wang	Beijing Normal University, China
Meng Wang	Tongji University, China
Jesse Wright	University of Oxford, UK
Tianxing Wu	Southeast University, China
Beyza Yaman	ADAPT Centre - Trinity College Dublin, Ireland
Hamada Zahera	Paderborn University, Germany
Ondřej Zamazal	Prague University of Economics and Business, Czechia
Sai Zhang	Tianjin University, China
Ningyu Zhang	Zhejiang University, China
Rui Zhao	University of Oxford, UK
Zhuoxun Zheng	Bosch Centre for AI, Germany

In-Use Track Program Committee

Luigi Asprino	CNR - Institute of Cognitive Sciences and Technologies, Italy
Nathalie Aussenac-Gilles	IRIT CNRS, University of Toulouse, France
Sahil Bansal	SAP, USA
Oliver Bensch	German Aerospace Center (DLR), Germany
Carlos Buil Aranda	Philip Morris International, Spain
Jean-Paul Calbimonte	University of Applied Sciences and Arts Western Switzerland HES-SO, Switzerland
Miguel Ceriani	University of Bari, Italy
Fiorela Ciroku	CNR - Institute of Cognitive Sciences and Technologies, Italy
Damien Graux	Huawei Technologies R&D (UK) Ltd., UK
Peter Haase	metaphacts, Germany
Lars Heling	SAP SE, Germany
Mayank Kejriwal	University of Southern California, USA
Craig Knoblock	University of Southern California, USA
Christoph Lange	Fraunhofer Institute for Applied Information Technology and RWTH Aachen University, Germany
Anna Sofia Lippolis	CNR - Institute of Cognitive Sciences and Technologies, Italy

C. Fabio Longo	CNR - Institute of Cognitive Sciences and Technologies, Italy
Michael Luggen	University of Fribourg, Switzerland
Ioanna Lytra	Graphwise, Austria
Beatrice Markhoff	Université de Tours, UMR 7324 CITERES, France
Antonello Meloni	University of Cagliari, Italy
Johannes Mäkelburg	Technical University of Munich, Germany
Declan O'Sullivan	Trinity College Dublin, Ireland
Francesco Poggi	CNR - Institute of Cognitive Sciences and Technologies, Italy
Mariano Rico	Universidad Politécnica de Madrid, Spain
Tong Ruan	East China University of Science and Technology, China
Edna Ruckhaus	Universidad Politécnica de Madrid, Spain
Alessandro Russo	CNR - Institute of Cognitive Sciences and Technologies, Italy
Mohamad Javad Saeedizade	Linköping University, Sweden
David Maria Schmidt	Bielefeld University, Germany
Tim Schwabe	Technical University of Munich, Germany

In-Use Track Additional Reviewers

Alexander Graß	RWTH Aachen University, Germany
Ashutosh Hathidara	SAP, USA
Fandel Lin	University of Southern California, USA
Ramit Pahwa	Rivian and VW Group Technologies, USA
Johannes Theissen-Lipp	RWTH Aachen University, Germany
Binh Vu	University of Southern California, USA

Sponsors

Below we list the sponsors confirmed before the preparation of the proceedings, i.e., September 2025. The full up-to-date list of sponsors is available at the ISWC 2025 Website: https://iswc2025.semanticweb.org/#/sponsorship/sponsors.

Platinum Sponsors

Gold Sponsors

Silver Sponsors

Student Support Sponsors

Artificial Intelligence
www.elsevier.com/locate/artint

SWSA
Semantic Web Science Association

Best Paper Award Sponsor

Springer

Best Student Paper Award Sponsor

Best Resource Paper Award Sponsor

JOURNAL OF WEB ENGINEERING

River Publishers

Contributors

Videolectures

Keynote Talks

Large Language Models and the AI Divide: Challenges and Pathways for Globally Equitable AI

Rachel Adams
Global Centre on AI Governance, and University of Cambridge

Large Language Models (LLMs) have become a defining technology of our time, promising to transform knowledge access, communication, and productivity. Yet, their development and governance remain concentrated in a handful of institutions and geographies, raising critical questions about equity, justice, and global power. For Africa and the wider Global Majority, LLMs present a paradox: they hold the potential to expand access to information, enable innovation in local languages, and support inclusive development, but they also risk deepening existing asymmetries of data, infrastructure, and governance.

In this talk, I will explore the limitations and challenges of LLMs as they intersect with African and Global Majority contexts. I will highlight three critical areas of concern: (1) the epistemic exclusions embedded in training data that marginalize local knowledge systems and languages; (2) the infrastructural and resource dependencies that make access costly and uneven; and (3) the governance gaps that allow external models and actors to shape socio-technical futures with limited accountability to local communities. To move beyond critique, this talk will also outline pathways for governance and intervention that can help ensure LLMs are used to empower rather than exploit. These include developing regionally grounded ethical frameworks, advancing open and locally adapted models, building public–private research collaborations, and embedding fairness and transparency into technical standards. Crucially, it calls for a re-imagining of AI governance not merely as risk mitigation, but as an opportunity to redistribute power, democratize innovation, and foreground the values of justice and dignity in technological futures.

Building Safety on Large Language Model

Satoshi Sekine
National Institute of Informatics, Japan

I will introduce the activities on AI Safety, mostly conducted at the Research and Development Center for Large Language Models, National Institute of Informatics (NII-LLMC). At our institute, we are developing LLMs from scratch (i.e., from pre-training) in order to ensure transparency through elucidation of the learning principles of generative AI models, and carry out R&D that contributes to the advancement of generative AI models. Safety is one of the most crucial components, and the technologies to embody safety will be educational for many industrial partners developing LLMs. We will introduce *AnswerCarefully*, a dataset for promoting the safety and appropriateness of Japanese LLM outputs. The dataset consists of 1,800 pairs of questions and reference answers, where the questions require special attention in answering. It covers a wide range of risk categories established in prior English language datasets, but the data samples are original in that they are manually created to reflect the socio-cultural context of LLM usage in Japan. We show that using this dataset for instruction to fine-tune a Japanese LLM led to improved output safety without compromising the utility of general responses. We also report the results of a safety evaluation of 12 Japanese LLMs using this dataset as a benchmark. Finally, we describe the latest update on the dataset, which provides English translations and annotations of the questions, aimed at facilitating the derivation of similar datasets in different languages and regions. We will also introduce other activities, including the development of a misinformation and disinformation dataset, *Jailbreak data set*, fine-tuning and DPO tuning for safety, a large human evaluation experiment, and so on.

Wikipedia and the Semantic Web - Celebrating 20 Years of Co-development, and the Future

Denny Vrandečić
Wikimedia Foundation

In 2005, the very first papers proposed integrating Semantic Web technologies in the nascent Wikipedia ecosystem. This wasn't just a convergence; it ignited two decades of mutual inspiration and benefit. From this crucible, the work in semantic wikis drew inspiration. Semantic MediaWiki particularly, which found global adoption at Google, Microsoft, NASA, and beyond. Wikipedia became the bedrock for pioneering knowledge graphs, including DBpedia, Freebase, and Yago. These pivotal experiences directly fueled the development of Google's Knowledge Graph, a term that has since found ubiquitous adoption, and, critically, Wikidata, a project that has become an indispensable, living component of Wikipedia itself. With over half a million global contributors, Wikidata stands as the world's most-edited wiki, powering one of, if not the, most widely used public SPARQL endpoint. Its software, Wikibase, has spawned a federation of knowledge graphs, serving diverse domains from museums to language preservation. Furthermore, Wikidata's evolution into lexicographic data (inspired by ontologies such as OntoLex and Lemon) laid the groundwork for projects such as Wikifunctions and Abstract Wikipedia, a vision first unveiled right here at ISWC 2018 and now an official Wikimedia Foundation project.

This takes us to the present and future: Abstract Wikipedia collaboratively confronts the inherent expressivity gap in knowledge graphs, while Wikipedia's foundational role in training and the current use of language models can not be overstated. This creates a tantalising confluence of large language models and knowledge graphs, hinting at profound opportunities - and critical challenges - for Wikipedia, the Web, and beyond. As this rich history promises many more years of co-development and mutual inspiration, we will conclude with a forward-looking sketch of open research questions and exciting upcoming opportunities.

Panel

Reimagining Knowledge: The Future and Relevance of Symbolic Representation in the Age of LLMs

As large language models (LLMs) continue to reshape the landscape of artificial intelligence, the role of symbolic representation, once central to knowledge modeling and reasoning, faces renewed scrutiny and exciting possibilities. This panel, *Reimagining Knowledge: The Future and Relevance of Symbolic Representation in the Age of LLMs*, brings together leading thinkers at the intersection of machine learning, knowledge engineering, and AI in the broader sense to explore the evolving relationship between symbolic and machine-learning paradigms. Through a multidisciplinary dialogue, panelists will examine whether symbolic structures remain essential for interpretability, reasoning, and alignment in modern AI systems or if they are being eclipsed by the impressive but opaque capabilities of LLMs.

Panel Chair

Ramanathan V. Guha Microsoft

Panelists

Ora Lassila Amazon Web Services
Natasha Noy Google
Tara Raafat Bloomberg LP
Elena Simperl Open Data Institute

Contents – Part I

Contents – Part II

In-Use Track

Research Track

CompoST: A Benchmark for Analyzing the Ability of LLMs to Compositionally Interpret Questions in a QALD Setting

David Maria Schmidt[(✉)], Raoul Schubert, and Philipp Cimiano

Semantic Computing Group, CITEC, Technical Faculty, Bielefeld University, Bielefeld, Germany
{daschmidt,cimiano}@techfak.uni-bielefeld.de, raoul.schubert@uni-bielefeld.de

Abstract. Language interpretation is a compositional process, in which the meaning of more complex linguistic structures is inferred from the meaning of their parts. Large language models possess remarkable language interpretation capabilities and have been successfully applied to interpret questions by mapping them to SPARQL queries. An open question is how systematic this interpretation process is. Toward this question, in this paper, we propose a benchmark for investigating to what extent the abilities of LLMs to interpret questions are actually compositional. For this, we generate three datasets of varying difficulty based on graph patterns in DBpedia, relying on Lemon lexica for verbalization. Our datasets are created in a very controlled fashion in order to test the ability of LLMs to interpret structurally complex questions, given that they have seen the atomic building blocks. This allows us to evaluate to what degree LLMs are able to interpret complex questions for which they "understand" the atomic parts. We conduct experiments with models of different sizes using both various prompt and few-shot optimization techniques as well as fine-tuning. Our results show that performance in terms of macro F_1 degrades from 0.45 over 0.26 down to 0.09 with increasing deviation from the samples optimized on. Even when all necessary information was provided to the model in the input, the F_1 scores do not exceed 0.57 for the dataset of lowest complexity. We thus conclude that LLMs struggle to systematically and compositionally interpret questions and map them into SPARQL queries.

Keywords: Compositionality · Large Language Models · Question Answering over Linked Data · Semantic Web

1 Introduction

In light of rapidly increasing capabilities of large language models (LLMs), some even proclaiming the "age of LLMs" [4], the question arises where the limits of current LLMs lie. One central question is whether LLMs are able to truly work

D. Garijo et al. (Eds.): ISWC 2025, LNCS 16140, pp. 3–22, 2026.
https://doi.org/10.1007/978-3-032-09527-5_1

and reason in a compositional way. For example, to cite a classic example from Zoltán G. Szabó [45], a compositional system understanding both "brown dog" and "black cat" should understand "brown cat" as well. More precisely, Szabó divides compositionality into two sub-properties, namely productivity, describing the ability to produce utterances never encountered before, and systematicity, describing the ability to understand other combinations of known constituents. As figuring out what LLMs have seen during pre-training is notoriously hard if at all possible, in this paper, we focus on a structured investigation of systematicity.

The question of whether LLMs can work in a compositional way has been investigated from different perspectives already, e.g., from a more (complexity-) theoretical point of view [8,14,29,44,55], or with focus on arithmetics [12,28] or logic puzzles [12]. Many tasks and works deal with compositionality in one way or another, either directly [12,20,37], or indirectly by exploring multi-step compositional tasks [30,40,49,53]. While some of these also investigate question answering [37], the task of mapping natural language questions into SPARQL queries (i.e., Question Answering over Linked Data, QALD) [43], to the best of our knowledge, still lacks a structured investigation of the abilities of LLMs to interpret questions in terms of a formal query language in a systematic way.

As discussed by Dziri et al. [12], many tasks do not require as much compositional behavior as it initially seems, leaving room for overfitting and shortcut learning. This raises the need for specialized datasets, testing the compositional power of LLMs in isolation for different domains. Therefore, in this paper, we present *CompoST*, a *Compositional Systematicity Test* dataset for QALD. In comparison to other datasets, this dataset allows us to test the degree of systematicity of LLM behavior in a controlled setting where irrelevant confounders are removed, so that we can focus on the assessment of the systematicity in isolation from other capabilities. In order to create a well-founded dataset, we first operationalize the concept of compositionality w.r.t. [45] and then generate a corresponding dataset to test the sub-property of systematicity. Finally, we conduct a broad set of zero-shot, few-shot and fine-tuning experiments with this dataset. More precisely, we delve into the following research questions:

RQ1. How can compositionality be operationalized for the question answering over linked data context?
RQ2. Do large language models satisfy the defined property of systematicity when using in-context learning?
RQ3. Does fine-tuning improve the abilities of large language models to work in a compositional manner?

2 Related Work

2.1 Compositional Generalization in NLP

Compositional generalization in terms of the ability to interpret new combinations of known components has emerged as a critical challenge in evaluating the generalization capacity of neural models. Datasets such as SCAN [26], CFQ [22] and COGS [25] have been designed to test this ability under controlled syntactic and semantic conditions: SCAN focuses on mapping simple commands to actions in a synthetic navigation task, CFQ tests generalization over complex SPARQL-like logical forms derived from Freebase and COGS evaluates structural generalization from surface syntax to abstract meaning representations. Unlike QALD tasks, these datasets do not require the generation of executable queries or the linking of expressions to real-world entities. In SCAN, Lake and Baroni [26] observed that RNN-based models failed to generalize compositionally, succeeding only when test sequences were very similar to those seen during training. Keysers et al. [22] found that Transformer models performed well on CFQ when trained and tested on similar compositions, but accuracy sharply declined when they were tested on structurally novel combinations. Kim and Linzen [25] reported that models trained on COGS often failed to generalize across syntactic alternations, such as the dative shift. Furrer et al. [15] showed that even models such as BERT [10] underperform on compositional generalization in Freebase-style question answering, and Dessì and Baroni [9] demonstrated similar shortcomings in convolutional architectures on synthetic symbolic tasks. These results suggest that, across architectures, including large-scale Transformer models, there remains a consistent difficulty with systematic generalization to previously unseen combinations of known elements. Recent work has proposed taxonomies and metrics to distinguish compositional generalization from mere pattern matching [20], which emphasizes the need for benchmarks that isolate compositional competence from surface-level generalization. While this work focuses on a systematicity definition similar to ours, they use an artificial language for a translation task instead of QALD as a task and do not use pre-trained LLMs.

2.2 Large Language Models and Compositionality

LLMs have shown impressive zero-shot and few-shot performance across diverse NLP tasks, however their compositional capabilities do still remain contested. Although prompt engineering and in-context learning have extended the apparent flexibility of LLMs [6,48], there are still limitations in their ability to generalize from known linguistic or logical primitives to new combinations [18,36]. For instance, Petty et al. [35] have found that increasing transformer depth yields diminishing returns for compositional generalization tasks. In a similar vein, Yang et al. [51] have observed that training LLMs on higher-order compositional instructions improves performance on simpler tasks, but not vice versa. Furthermore, Ismayilzada et al. [21] have reported that instruction-fine-tuned multilingual models struggle when it comes to morphological compositional generalization in agglutinative languages such as Turkish and Finnish, particularly when applied to novel word roots. These findings suggest a discrepancy between LLMs' surface-level fluency and their deeper semantic systematicity.

Dziri et al. [12] investigate the limits of Transformer-based architectures on compositional reasoning tasks, e.g., multiplication and logic puzzles. They demonstrate that even advanced LLMs exhibit systematic failures when faced with reasoning chains that are beyond the complexity seen during training. Although Dziri et al. also investigate the compositional abilities of LLMs, they focus on different tasks, use a set of older and less diverse models as well as a more implicit compositionality definition. Press et al. [37] propose an empirical framework for quantifying what they call the "compositionality gap" in language models. By introducing diagnostic datasets and evaluation metrics, they showcase how current models often rely on statistical heuristics rather than exhibiting true compositional understanding. They also test question answering as a task, although not QALD. Moreover, the problems tested in [37] are limited in size and complexity by mostly focusing on 2-hop question answering, together with older and less diverse tested LLMs. In contrast, our approach generalizes from that 2-hop setting to a general sub-graph-based notion for determining the parts of a question that allows to easily scale the complexity of the benchmarks.

2.3 Compositionality in QALD

QALD represents a natural way of testing for compositional generalization, as building SPARQL queries involves, among other challenges, logical composition, nesting relations, and linking entities. Previous approaches in semantic parsing have addressed these challenges by explicitly modeling the structure of SPARQL queries derived from natural language [11,34,46,47,52]. However, these systems typically require domain-specific grammars or supervision, which greatly limits their scalability. Recent investigations have focused on the capacity of LLMs to answer knowledge base questions without explicit parsing. In contrast, Schmidt et al. [41,42] aim to combine the strengths of both LLMs as well as symbolic approaches in a compositional QALD pipeline. Their system works by utilizing lexical entries and explicit meaning representations together with neural parts for, e.g., dependency parsing or selecting the most promising SPARQL query.

While LLMs perform reasonably on atomic questions (i.e., involving a single RDF triple), they do still struggle with multi-hop or nested constructions [7,17,33], which are prevalent in QALD. Recent studies suggest that these failures may stem from LLMs' limited ability to systematically map natural language inputs to the compositional structures that are required for accurate knowledge base reasoning. For instance, Chen et al. [8] demonstrate that integrating explicit knowledge graphs enhances LLM performance on multi-hop question answering tasks, at the same time indicating that LLMs alone struggle with such compositional reasoning. In a similar vein, Zhao et al. [54] find that LLMs possess the necessary knowledge components but fail to combine them effectively in novel contexts, pointing out a deficiency in systematic compositionality. As such, this paper positions itself at the intersection of these concerns: operationalizing compositionality through limited linguistic units, DBpedia-based property verbalizations, and testing whether LLMs exhibit systematic generalization w.r.t. QALD. By grounding the experimental design in a formal notion of compositionality and providing the CompoST dataset, our aim is to offer a controlled, yet scalable, approach to evaluating this dimension of model behavior.

3 Methods

3.1 Operationalization of Compositionality

For our definition of compositionality in a QALD context, we rely on work by Zoltán G. Szabó [45], where compositionality is described as consisting of two sub-properties, namely productivity and systematicity. We slightly generalize the definitions and arguments made in that work to also include generative LLMs. These definitions are also similar to the systematicity and productivity tests described in [20]. The definitions used in this work are, therefore, as follows:

Definition 1 (Productivity [45]**).** *The property of productivity is satisfied iff an agent can understand*[1] *complex expressions it never encountered before.*

Definition 2 (Systematicity [45]**).** *The property of systematicity is satisfied iff an agent that understands a number of complex expressions* $e_1, \ldots, e_n$ *also understands all other complex expressions that can be built up from the constituents of* $e_1, \ldots, e_n$ *using syntactic rules employed in building up their structures.*

As we want to operationalize compositionality and develop a benchmark dataset for LLMs, we need to think of ways to test these definitions. For Def. 1, an obvious challenge in applying it to LLMs is that i) for many models, the datasets used for pre-training are not publicly available, and ii) even if they are, e.g., for models like OLMo [31], they are huge and it is hardly verifiable whether an expression is or is not part of the training data beyond exact string matches. We therefore focus on the systematicity property as stated in Def. 2 only.

In order to operationalize Def. 2, there are multiple ways in which the term "constituents" can be interpreted in the QALD context. On the one hand, this could be interpreted as constituents w.r.t. natural language, i.e., words or sentence structures, and, on the other hand, w.r.t. SPARQL, syntax elements like triple patterns. In this paper, we focus on investigating the behavior of LLMs w.r.t. SPARQL constituents and verbalize the corresponding SPARQL queries with only slight linguistic variations. In this way, we want to test the basic abilities of LLMs to work in a compositional, i.e., systematic, manner, without having to generalize over many potential verbalizations.

3.2 CompoST Dataset Creation

For creating a dataset to test the systematicity property, we thus need pairs of questions and SPARQL queries (named "benchmark item" or just "item" in the following) such that we know that the sufficiency criterion is fulfilled, i.e.,

[1] As the original definition refers to "understand" in a human context, we use the following working definition of understanding for generative LLMs in this paper: An LLM understands a sentence w.r.t. some knowledge graph iff it can generate a correct SPARQL query for that respective sentence and knowledge graph.

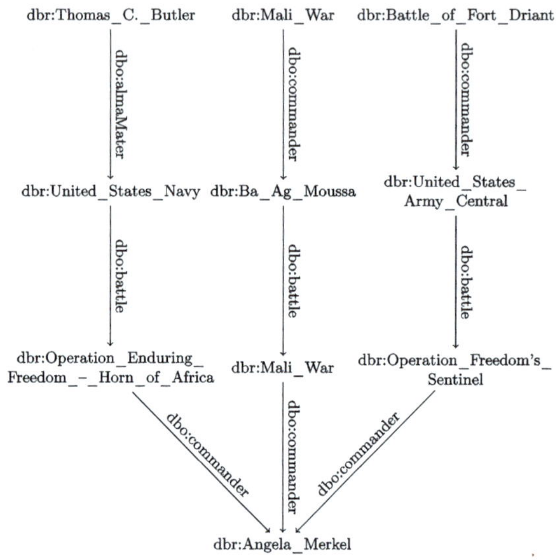

Fig. 1. RDF graph of SPARQL graph pattern instance with depth of 3 and breadth of 3 with concrete entities and properties from DBpedia.

we know whether or not a set of benchmark items contains all necessary constituents to build another specific item. This requirement also prevents us from using existing QALD datasets. QALD benchmarks typically consist of a large number of mostly different questions, but lack two aspects that are necessary to test compositional systematicity. More precisely, they a) usually do not have large numbers of different combinations of the same "basic building blocks" and b) do not have known relations between two benchmark items that would allow us to determine whether the sufficiency criterion is satisfied or not. Thus, we create a new dataset that meets these requirements. For our dataset, this is achieved by first generating graph patterns of a certain size and structure, then fetching instances of that pattern from a DBpedia snapshot from December 2022, and finally verbalizing the full pattern as well as all connected sub-patterns in the same structured fashion. For each resulting set of benchmark items, we know whether the sufficiency criterion is satisfied if the graph patterns connected to a set of items are an (exact) edge set cover of the considered other item's graph pattern. More precisely, we use "pitchfork-like"/star patterns of variable depth and breadth. An instance for depth 3 and breadth 3 is given in Fig. 1. These pattern instances as well as all connected sub-graphs of those patterns form the basis of our benchmark dataset. However, the pattern instance of Fig. 1 still needs to be translated into SPARQL queries and corresponding verbalizations. For this, we rely on 1070 hand-crafted Lemon lexical entries [27] for 147 DBpedia properties, roughly corresponding to the properties covered in QALD-9 [46]. Of these entries, 245 are `NounPPFrame` entries for verbalizing DBpedia properties and 825 are about verbalizing different `rdf:type`, `dbo:country`, `dbo:nationality` and

1. Question: Who is the spouse of Michelle Obama and parent of Malia Obama?
   SPARQL: `dbr:Michelle_Obama dbo:spouse ?result. dbr:Malia_Obama dbo:parent ?result.`
2. Question: Who is the spouse of the child of Marian Shields Robinson?
   SPARQL: `dbr:Marian_Shields_Robinson dbo:child ?v1. ?v1 dbo:spouse ?result.`

Question: Who is the spouse of the child of Marian Shields Robinson and parent of Malia Obama?
SPARQL: `dbr:Marian_Shields_Robinson dbo:child ?v1. ?v1 dbo:spouse ?result. dbr:Malia_Obama dbo:parent ?result.`

Fig. 2. Example question-query-pairs. 1 and 2 together contain all relevant information to compose the bottom query. Only triple patterns of queries shown.

⟨S⟩ ⊨ `Give me` ⟨DP⟩ (⟨CP⟩ | ϵ) ⟨PP⟩ `.`
  | `Who is` ⟨DP⟩ (⟨CP⟩ | ϵ) ⟨PP⟩ `?`
⟨VP⟩ ⊨ `is` ⟨DP⟩
  | `works` ⟨PP⟩
  | ⟨VP⟩ ⟨CP⟩
  | (⟨VP⟩ | ⟨DP⟩) `and` (⟨VP⟩ | ⟨DP⟩)
⟨DP⟩ ⊨ ⟨Det⟩ ⟨N⟩ | ⟨Det⟩ ⟨N⟩ `industry`
⟨Det⟩ ⊨ `the` | `a` | `an` | ϵ
⟨CP⟩ ⊨ `, that` ⟨VP⟩ `,`
⟨PP⟩ ⊨ ⟨P⟩ ⟨DP⟩ | ⟨PP⟩ ⟨CP⟩ | ⟨PP⟩ ⟨PP⟩ | ⟨PP⟩ `and` ⟨PP⟩
⟨N⟩ ⊨ *canonical form of lexical entry*
  | *label of corresponding DBpedia entity or literal value*
⟨P⟩ ⊨ *preposition of NounPPFrame lexical entry* | `in`

Fig. 3. EBNF [3] of the sentences generated for the CompoST dataset.

`dbo:industry` patterns, e.g., "`?v dbo:nationality dbr:Germany`" as "is German". For this, we reused and extended the lexicon of Schmidt et al. [41,42] as well as parts of the code for parsing and using the lexical entries.

A Lemon lexical entry consists of a canonical form of the respective word or phrase, the corresponding preposition (if applicable) as well as the associated DBpedia property, among other things. Based on this information, we can verbalize a given "pitchfork-like" graph pattern such that we ask for `?result`. Examples are given in Fig. 2, illustrating how a set of items can contain all necessary information to compose another item. By using the information from 1 and 2, a compositional system should be able to generate the bottom query.

As the structure of these questions and queries is quite simple and monotonous, we additionally increased the diversity of our dataset in two ways: i) inverting the direction of some triples in the pattern and ii) adding verbalizations of `rdf:type` or, e.g., `dbo:nationality` values to the query. For further details about the dataset generation process, we published the corresponding generation code in our software artifact. All in all, the generated questions can be described by the grammar in Extended Backus-Naur Form (EBNF, [3]) presented in Fig. 3. However, that grammar generates a super-set of the sentences that can actually be generated by our approach. Therefore, some additional constraints enforced during the dataset generation are omitted. For example, the choice of "works in ...", "is a", "is an" or just "is" depends on the respective canonical form, the corresponding property, as well as the specific lexical entry type.

For the final dataset, patterns with the following depth and breadth combinations of the basic pattern were used: breadth 2 & depth 2, breadth 2 & depth 3, breadth 3 & depth 2, and breadth 3 & depth 3. For each, we searched for matching pattern instances in DBpedia and, based on the instances found, generated a verbalization of those base pattern instances as well as of all connected sub-patterns of the respective instances. In cases of multiple available lexical entries for a property, we chose the entries consistently between the base pattern and its sub-patterns by seeding the random choices accordingly. Similarly, we fetched all `rdf:type`, `dbo:country`, `dbo:nationality` and `dbo:industry` objects for all entities of the instance and selected a random sample of random size of the available objects for which a corresponding lexical entry was available. This sample was then fixed for that pattern instance and verbalized as a "that" clause for all (sub-)patterns that include the respective node at an appropriate position. All those choices are necessary in order to ensure that, as Def. 2 states, all necessary constituents are present in the sub-patterns such that one should be able to compose those parts to verbalizations of larger (sub-)patterns.

The generated instances, their verbalizations and the corresponding SPARQL queries were then split equally among three datasets of varying difficulty, with every dataset having in total 75 base pattern instances as well as the corresponding sub-graphs. In total, this makes 2803 question-query-pairs per dataset. The splitting was done based on the portion of the number of pattern edges (thus, "that" clause edges were excluded from that calculation) up to which sub-patterns were added to the training split. More precisely, they were split into *easy* (sub-patterns with up to 75% of the total base pattern edges were included in the train split, e.g., for breadth 3 & depth 3 with a total of 9 edges, patterns with up to 6 edges were included in train), *medium* (50%) and *hard* (25%, with an absolute minimum of two edges to cover all phenomena, such as chaining triples or branching with "and"). For the validation and test splits, we chose the lower and upper half of the remaining data sorted by the number of base pattern edges, respectively.

Additionally, based on these datasets, we created additional variants where an edge set cover of the target pattern, i.e., all information necessary to compose the correct answer, is given in the input. In the following, these variations will be called *self-contained tasks*, as no knowledge beyond the input is necessary to solve it. Analogously, the original tasks are called *classic* tasks. The self-contained tasks were created by taking the validation items for the new train and the test items for the new test datasets together with an edge set cover of the target pattern taken from the train dataset, comprising up to 10 examples[2].

With these datasets, which together comprise CompoST, we investigate the ability of models to generalize beyond what they have seen either during prompt optimization, in the given examples or during fine-tuning. A system which is able

[2] In some cases, there were fewer than 10 smaller samples related to the target pattern and thus given in the input. For further details, please refer to our software artifact.

to truly generalize in a compositional way would be expected to show almost no performance degradation, as all necessary information is already in sub-patterns with as few as one triple, or two triples to cover combination phenomena.

4 Experiments

In the following, we describe the experiments conducted with CompoST.

Zero-Shot Prompting: As a first baseline, we consider zero-shot prompting. In order to run the experiments in a structured manner together with, e.g., prompt optimization techniques, we use the DSPy framework [23,24] for our in-context learning experiments. We evaluate a broad set of models, namely Llama 3.3 (70B) [16], Phi-4 (14B) [1], Qwen2.5-Coder (7B) [19,50], OLMo 2 (7B) [31] and GPT-4o-mini [32]. As optimization techniques, we used none, COPRO, MIPROv2 (light, medium and heavy) together with plain as well as chain of thought prompting. In each experiment, the model is given a question from the dataset and expected to generate a corresponding SPARQL query for DBpedia. Finally, the results of both queries are compared and the F_1 scores are calculated. The optimization strategies are given the training split and can optimize the prompt based on an evaluation method that calculates the F_1 score for a predicted query compared to the gold standard.

Few-Shot Prompting: As generating SPARQL queries for natural language questions is a hard task, one might argue that, besides prompt optimization, examples are necessary for the model to properly understand the task. Therefore, we use MIPROv2 (light, medium and heavy), LabeledFewShot, BootstrapFewShot and BootstrapFewShotWithRandomSearch choosing the shots given to the model, as well as (in case of MIPROv2) optimizing the prompt at the same time, again paired with plain or chain of thought prompting. In these experiments, the models are additionally given a number of examples, i.e., "shots", chosen by the respective optimization strategies. For choosing those shots, the strategies are also given the SPARQL queries for the train split and have the same information available as the zero-shot experiments. For the self-contained tasks, we evaluated MIPROv2 (light, medium and heavy) with and without chain of thought prompting, as the given shots are a fixed part of the input already.

Fine-Tuning: For particularly hard tasks, even with the most recent models, it might be necessary to apply fine-tuning when in-context learning fails. Therefore, we also conducted experiments with fine-tuned models. In particular, we fine-tuned GPT-4o-mini, OLMo 2 and Qwen2.5-Coder. Although hardware limitations were no issue for GPT-4o-mini fine-tuning because of the OpenAI API usage, we chose the two 7B parameter models OLMo 2 and Qwen2.5-Coder over Llama 3.3 and Phi-4 as this was the largest model size we could fine-tune in reasonable time with our available hardware. For the classic tasks, these models were fine-tuned on a zero-shot setting, i.e., given a basic task description[3] together with the input question and fine-tuned to output just the SPARQL query. For self-contained tasks, we fine-tuned the best-performing model of the classic tasks, namely GPT-4o-mini. In this setting, the model was additionally given the relevant edge set cover of example items. Thus, the model is fine-tuned to compose the answer based on question-query-pairs that are given to the model.

4.1 Experimental Settings

For all in-context learning experiments, we used the OpenAI API for GPT-4o-mini, evaluating the `gpt-4o-mini-2024-07-18` version, and Ollama[4] to serve all other models. More precisely, we used the default Ollama models with `Q4_K_M` quantization, i.e., Llama 3.3 with 70B parameters, Phi-4 with 14B parameters, and Qwen2.5-Coder with 7B parameters. Additionally, we used the `7b-1124-instruct-q4_K_M` version of OLMo 2. The models used for (classic) fine-tuning were GPT-4o-mini as well as Qwen2.5-Coder (`Qwen/Qwen2.5-Coder-7B-Instruct`) and OLMo 2 (`allenai/OLMo-2-1124-7B-Instruct`). For fine-tuning GPT-4o-mini, we used the OpenAI API, leaving all parameters to "auto". For the other models, we performed a hyperparameter search using Optuna [2] and fine-tuned the models using PyTorch Lightning [13] with DeepSpeed [38]. For our experiments, we had up to 10 Nvidia A40 GPUs available, utilizing nodes with up to four A40 GPUs paired with 120 CPU cores and 443GB of RAM. With quantization and DeepSpeed [38], we were able to fine-tune the given 7B models on a single node. The prompting experiments not using the OpenAI API were conducted with Ollama instances running on a single A40 GPU each, grouping experiments by models accordingly to avoid reloading.

To measure the "raw" performance, we get the results for both the gold standard, as well as the generated SPARQL query of a DBpedia snapshot from December 2022[5]. We then compare the two result sets and calculate true positives, false positives, etc. in the standard way. Based on the confusion matrix, we can then calculate F_1 scores at a macro level (calculating F_1 score per question and using the mean of the respective scores as the final score). The F_1 scores for single questions are available to the DSPy [23,24] optimizers.

Additionally, we calculate a second set of scores focusing more on the compositionality aspect, evaluating whether or not the model behaves in a compositional way. For this, we define the confusion matrix values w.r.t. expectations of compositional behavior. More precisely, this means that true positives (TP) are those correctly-answered benchmark items for which all sub-problems, i.e., all sub-patterns of the respective target graph pattern, are correctly answered as

[3] Given a natural language question about a specific entity, generate a SPARQL query that retrieves relevant information from DBpedia.

[4] https://ollama.com/.

[5] https://databus.dbpedia.org/dbpedia/collections/dbpedia-snapshot-2022-12.

Table 1. Performance of the best-performing model and optimization strategy for each category. * = self-contained tasks, BFRS = BootstrapFewShotWithRandomSearch, CoT = Chain of Thought, MIPRO: H = Heavy, M = Medium

Experiment	Best Configuration		Macro F_1			Compositionality F_1		
	Model	Optimization	Train	Validation	Test	Train	Validation	Test
Easy (75%)								
zero-shot	Llama 3.3	$MIPRO_{H+CoT}$	0.17	0.04	0.01	0.10	0.00	0.00
few-shot	Llama 3.3	$MIPRO_{M+CoT}$	0.23	0.12	0.09	0.15	0.00	0.00
fine-tuned	GPT-4o-mini	fine-tuning	0.92	0.58	0.45	0.79	0.49	0.31
few-shot*	Llama 3.3	$MIPRO_M$	0.56		0.57	0.72		0.52
fine-tuned*	GPT-4o-mini	fine-tuning	0.72		0.48	0.84		0.53
Medium (50%)								
zero-shot	Llama 3.3	$MIPRO_H$	0.19	0.03	0.01	0.14	0.00	0.16
few-shot	Llama 3.3	$BFRS_{CoT}$	0.29	0.15	0.09	0.18	0.02	0.03
fine-tuned	GPT-4o-mini	fine-tuning	0.94	0.57	0.26	0.78	0.60	0.22
few-shot*	Llama 3.3	$MIPRO_H$	0.68		0.48	0.76		0.33
fine-tuned*	GPT-4o-mini	fine-tuning	0.92		0.55	0.95		0.57
Hard (25%)								
zero-shot	Llama 3.3	$MIPRO_{H+CoT}$	0.25	0.07	0.04	0.08	0.18	0.06
few-shot	GPT-4o-mini	$MIPRO_{M+CoT}$	0.36	0.13	0.08	0.11	0.09	0.07
fine-tuned	GPT-4o-mini	fine-tuning	0.95	0.34	0.09	0.61	0.45	0.10
few-shot*	Llama 3.3	$MIPRO_M$	0.89		0.51	0.92		0.43
fine-tuned*	GPT-4o-mini	fine-tuning	0.99		0.30	0.99		0.41

well. False positives (FP) are all other correctly-answered tasks, i.e., where one or more sub-problems are wrong. Finally, false negatives (FN) are those incorrect answers for which an edge set cover of the target graph is correctly answered, but the actual question is still answered incorrectly.

$$\mathcal{I} = \mathcal{C} \cup \mathcal{W} \qquad TP = \{i \in \mathcal{C} \mid \forall i' \in \mathcal{I} \colon i' \subseteq i \Rightarrow i' \in \mathcal{C}.\} \qquad FP = \mathcal{C} \setminus TP$$

$$FN = \{i \in \mathcal{W} \mid \exists \alpha \subseteq \mathcal{C} \colon \bigcup_{i' \in \alpha} \text{edges}(i') = \text{edges}(i) \ \wedge \ \forall i' \in \alpha \colon i' \subset i..\}$$

with $\mathcal{I}$ being the set of all benchmark items (represented by their graph pattern instance), $\mathcal{C}$ the set of correctly-answered items and $\mathcal{W}$ the set of items with a wrong answer. Furthermore, edges($i \in \mathcal{I}$) returns the set of edges of the graph pattern instance of a benchmark item. Based on this, the compositionality-adjusted F_1 score is then calculated per question and aggregated as a macro F_1 score for the resulting compositionality F_1 score displayed in Table 1.

5 Results

As we conducted over 400 experiments in total, this section will only discuss the results of the best-performing models (w.r.t. overall macro F_1 score) and optimization strategies per category. As shown in Table 1, the best-performing

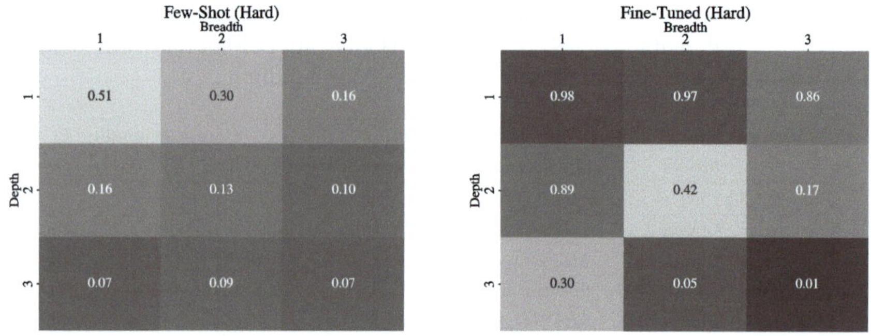

(a) Best Few-Shot Approach (b) Best Fine-Tuned Approach

Fig. 4. Macro F_1 scores of best approaches of the respective category for the *hard* dataset, grouped by graph pattern depth and breadth. Training data comprised samples up to two edges, i.e., up to breadth 2, depth 1 and depth 2, breadth 1.

models (in terms of macro F_1 score) are either Llama 3.3 or GPT-4o-mini across all categories and datasets. Additionally, for in-context learning, MIPROv2 prompt optimization works best in most cases, with *medium* few-shot being the only exception, achieving the best results for BootstrapFewShotWithRandomSearch. However, fine-tuning outperforms in-context learning in all cases in terms of macro F_1 scores for the classic tasks. For the self-contained task variants, it is slightly different. Here, few-shot experiments outperform the fine-tuned approaches for the *easy* (0.57 vs. 0.48) and *hard* (0.51 vs. 0.30) datasets. Considering the different datasets with different portions of the total edge count being present in training data, it can generally be observed that the models perform worse the more the tasks differ from their training samples. This effect is especially strong for the fine-tuned models, with, e.g., fine-tuned test macro F_1 scores degrading from 0.45 for *easy* over 0.29 for *medium* to 0.09 for *hard*. Notably, in all datasets, all relevant information is part of the training data. Thus, only the number and complexity of components that need to be composed differs.

For the compositionality F_1 score, all classic configurations show poor performance. No approach achieves a higher test score than 0.31, which even degrades to 0.22 for *medium* and 0.10 for *hard*. But also for self-contained configurations, where the models are optimized for composing the pieces already present in the input, the compositionality F_1 score does not exceed 0.57 for the test split, with just 0.43 being the best result for the hard dataset. Comparing in-context learning and fine-tuning, no clear trend is observable. For the *easy* dataset, the fine-tuned approach's compositionality F_1 score is slightly higher than for the best few-shot approach (0.53 vs. 0.52), although the macro F_1 score is lower (0.48 vs. 0.57). In contrast, the opposite is true for the *medium* and *hard* datasets.

The performance of the models depending on the depth and breadth of the given question and respective SPARQL query is further examined in Fig. 4 by the

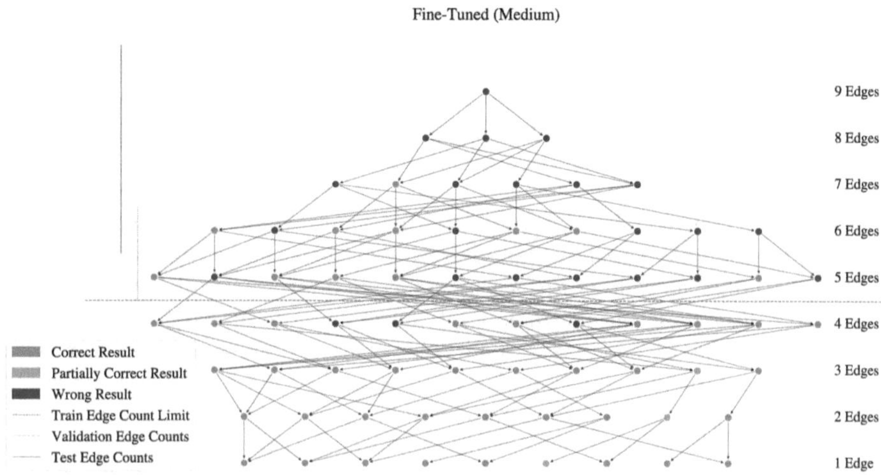

Fig. 5. Results for a depth and breadth 3 graph pattern instance and connected sub-patterns taken from the best fine-tuned *medium* approach. Arrows indicate source contains target node pattern, omitting nodes with > 1 edge difference.

example of the hard dataset. As we observed in Fig. 4a, the single-triple queries work comparably well, whereas increasing depth and breadth substantially hurts performance. The fine-tuned approach, see Fig. 4b, works almost perfectly for the training data and successfully generalizes to breadth 3, however, increasing both depth and breadth degrades performance down to 0.01 for depth and breadth 3.

Figure 5 shows all results for a single graph pattern instance of depth and breadth 3 as well as the corresponding sub-graphs from the medium dataset for the best fine-tuned approach. The illustration can be understood similarly as a Hasse diagram [5,39] for the "subset of" relation between two graphs. The nodes in the bottom line correspond to single-triple questions, e.g., "Who is the president of X?", while the second-bottom line is one triple richer, e.g., "Who is the father of the president of X?". Thus, the figure illustrates the questions that can be built from the "atomic" building blocks up to the whole pattern instance. We can observe that data that were available during training plus up to two edges work relatively well, but almost all predictions beyond that are incorrect. Similarly, most non-training results violate the systematicity property.

6 Discussion

Before we conclude to answer our research questions, we will first go through the results with the hypothesis that LLMs do work in a systematic (Def. 2) manner and see whether this view is compatible with our empirical results.

Zero-Shot Experiments: In an ideal scenario, the models have already seen sufficient amounts of data for DBpedia during pre-training, such that it only needs a suitable explanation of the task to perform well. To ensure the explanation is not the problem here, we evaluated multiple prompt optimization techniques to find the best prompt for each tested model. However, the poor results (macro F_1 between 0.01 and 0.04) suggest that our assumptions are not true and the models need more information to successfully deal with QALD.

Few-Shot Experiments: Thus, the natural next step when zero-shot prompting fails is to additionally provide examples/"shots" to the model. However, we can observe in Table 1 as well as Fig. 4 that, while it improves results, the absolute scores are still poor. Even for single-triple questions, the macro F_1 score is only 0.51 in Fig. 4a. The test compositionality scores are not much better either, with scores between 0.00 and 0.07. Similarly to the zero-shot experiments, the weak performance as well as the low compositionality scores question the hypothesis that LLMs work in a compositionally systematic manner.

Fine-Tuning Experiments: One reason that makes models struggle with the QALD task could be that, in order to construct a correct DBpedia SPARQL query for a specific question, one also needs to know how to deal with peculiarities in the mapping from natural language to DBpedia vocabulary. The peculiarities could be learned by a model through fine-tuning, as the model then has the chance to learn to connect certain entities and properties to certain natural language expressions. As all entities, properties and "atomic" natural language expressions are by design part of the training data, ambiguity problems should be minimal after fine-tuning. Although the results of (classic) fine-tuning presented in Table 1 are much better overall, there are a few trends suggesting that the model has substantial problems to generalize beyond training data. First, the macro F_1 performance degrades to almost few-shot level as the deviation of samples from the training examples grows (i.e., for *easy*, test performance jumps from 0.09 to 0.45, but for *hard* only from 0.00 to 0.00). This impression is corroborated by the results presented in Fig. 4b, where the top left three rectangles, which represent the training data, achieve almost perfect results, whereas almost all other examples slightly outside the training data already display substantial performance drops. This impression that the models lack a proper generalization is further corroborated by Fig. 5. As we can see from the green nodes in the graph, most of the training split results are correct. However, this performance severely degrades when adding edges beyond the training data size. Thus, even when adding one additional edge, the number of respective incorrect results more than doubles and continues to grow. This indicates that the models struggle to generalize on a compositional level, contradicting our hypothesis.

Self-contained Few-Shot and Fine-Tuning Experiments: Especially for the in-context learning experiments, we might discard the assumption that the models have already seen the relevant data from DBpedia such that we need to provide all necessary information in the input. This is what we did with the self-contained experiments, which contain an edge set cover of the target graph pattern, i.e., the respective questions and queries, in the input. Although this eases the task a lot and comes at the risk of overfitting during prompt optimization or fine-tuning, it also focuses the task on the core ability we want to test, namely systematicity. Thus, self-contained tasks provide almost optimal conditions for a model to show its abilities to work in a compositional way.

However, the performance improvements in Table 1 are not as large as one would expect assuming our initial hypothesis that the models indeed work in a compositional, systematic manner. The best-performing self-contained experiments in all cases outperform the classic experiments in terms of test macro F_1 scores and are less affected by the portion of edges given as training samples, i.e., the *easy*, *medium* and *hard* datasets. This might be due to the fact that all relevant information is given in the input and always with (up to) 10 shots, only with varying closeness of the given examples to the target question due to the edge portion limit. Notably, fine-tuning achieves worse results for the *easy* and *hard* datasets than the few-shot approach (0.48 vs. 0.57 and 0.30 vs. 0.51). Only for *medium* the fine-tuning approach works better (0.55 vs. 0.48). It is not clear what this deviation is caused by. One possibility would be that the fine-tuning process overfits stronger to the training dataset and thus has more problems generalizing to larger target questions, whereas for in-context learning, only the prompt is optimized, with less potential to overfit. Regarding compositionality scores, we see better overall results as well, but with slight differences between approaches. For fine-tuning, the test compositionality F_1 score is in all cases slightly higher than the "raw" macro F_1 score, whereas it is lower for few-shot prompting. This might suggest that fine-tuning leads to better compositional behavior than few-shot prompting. Nevertheless, given the discussed simplifications and all scores being no greater than 0.57 for both macro and compositionality F_1 score, this raises questions how compositionally LLMs are able to work and may indicate a fundamental weakness, especially considering the observations for higher depths, breadths, or edge counts. Overall, our results are in line with those in Dziri et al. [12], indicating fundamental weaknesses in LLMs w.r.t. compositional reasoning.

Research Questions: Considering RQ1, we presented an operationalization of compositionality in terms of systematicity in Def. 2 and Sect. 3.1. When it comes to whether or not LLMs satisfy the property defined in Def. 2 w.r.t. RQ2, our results indicate that the LLMs tested do not satisfy the property in a strict sense. Considering the merely mediocre scores even under optimal conditions, this at least heavily questions the general abilities to work in a compositional way w.r.t. the QALD domain. For RQ3, we have seen promising results that fine-tuning slightly improves the compositional behavior of LLMs, however, without achieving scores that would justify the assumption that LLMs actually satisfy systematicity in terms of Def. 2 when fine-tuned accordingly.

6.1 Limitations

Our study has multiple limitations that frame the scope and interpretation of our results. First, the dataset used is synthetic and constructed with a controlled set of lexical entries and structural templates. This therefore limits the diversity of surface verbalizations. However, we see this primarily as an advantage in the sense that by minimizing linguistic variation, we can reduce confounding factors such as paraphrasing and noise from formulation differences, thereby isolating the core ability of models to generalize compositionally. We aimed to address shortcut learning and overfitting by running diverse experiments with and without optimization/fine-tuning. If the limited linguistic diversity had a substantial impact on the (optimization) performance, this would have been visible in the results in one way or another. If the optimizations would hurt performance, this would usually be visible by experiments with non-optimized models performing better. If the optimization found an easy shortcut for the datasets, the scores would have been very high. All in all, both is not the case, such that we assume the simplicity to have a positive if any impact on the results. Secondly, it has to be highlighted that our dataset is built on a curated but ultimately limited subset of DBpedia. Although the coverage is relatively large, it does not represent the full heterogeneity of the DBpedia knowledge graph. Furthermore, DBpedia exhibits certain idiosyncrasies, particularly in its type definitions and predicate choices for particular information, that may result in generated benchmark items that appear to be "unnatural". Generalization to other knowledge bases, such as Wikidata, remains to be tested in future work. Additionally, we conducted only a limited set of fine-tuning experiments due to resource constraints. More experiments or even specialized training techniques for compositionality may yield further novel insights. Finally, we emphasize that our evaluation focuses on necessary conditions for compositionality. Success on our task does not definitively demonstrate that a model reasons compositionally in a systematic fashion. However, failure to generalize in our reduced and highly controlled setting strongly suggests a lack of compositional generalization capabilities.

7 Conclusion

In this paper, we presented the *CompoST* dataset for testing systematic compositionality for the QALD task, together with benchmark results for a diverse set of current LLMs and optimization strategies. Our results suggest that LLMs face limitations when it comes to systematic compositional behavior, with increasing performance degradations the larger the deviation from the training data is. For example, the best-performing classic experiment achieves a test macro F_1 score of 0.45 for the *easy* dataset, but only 0.09 for *hard*. Even for self-contained experiments, with all necessary information in the input, only test macro F_1 scores between 0.30 and 0.57 are achieved. All in all, our results do not justify the assumption that LLMs work in a compositional manner. Future work could further investigate whether there are more specialized training techniques not covered by this paper which might improve their ability to work in a compositional manner.

Acknowledgments. This work is partially funded by the Ministry of Culture and Science of the State of North Rhine-Westphalia under grant no NW21-059A (SAIL).

Supplemental Material Statement. Source code and dataset are available at https://doi.org/10.5281/zenodo.16312287.

Disclosure of Interests. The authors have no competing interests to declare that are relevant to the content of this article.

References

1. Abdin, M., et al.: Phi-4 technical report. arXiv:2412.08905 (2024)
2. Akiba, T., Sano, S., Yanase, T., Ohta, T., Koyama, M.: Optuna: a next-generation hyperparameter optimization framework. In: Proceedings of the 25th ACM SIGKDD International Conference on Knowledge Discovery and Data Mining (2019)
3. Backus, J.W.: The syntax and semantics of the proposed international algebraic language of the Zurich ACM-GAMM Conference. In: Information Processing, Proceedings of the 1st International Conference on Information Processing, UNESCO, Paris 15–20 June 1959, pp. 125–131. UNESCO (Paris) (1959), tex.bibsource: dblp computer science bibliography, https://dblp.org tex.timestamp: Fri, 26 Jul 2019 12:25:09 +0200
4. Birhane, A., Kasirzadeh, A., Leslie, D., Wachter, S.: Science in the age of large language models. Nat. Rev. Phys. **5**(5), 277–280 (2023). https://doi.org/10.1038/s42254-023-00581-4, https://www.nature.com/articles/s42254-023-00581-4
5. Birkhoff, G.: Lattice Theory, revised ed. In: American Mathematical Society Colloquium Publications, vol. 25 (1948)
6. Brown, T.B., et al.: Language models are few-shot learners. In: Advances in Neural Information Processing Systems, vol. 33, pp. 1877–1901 (2020)
7. Chakraborty, A.: Multi-hop question answering over knowledge graphs using large language models. arXiv:2404.19234 (2024)
8. Chen, L., Peng, B., Wu, H.: Theoretical limitations of multi-layer transformer. arXiv: 2412.02975 (2024)
9. Dessì, R., Baroni, M.: CNNs found to jump around more skillfully than RNNs: compositional generalization in Seq2seq convolutional networks. In: Proceedings of the 57th Annual Meeting of the Association for Computational Linguistics, pp. 3919–3923. Association for Computational Linguistics, Florence, Italy (2019). https://doi.org/10.18653/v1/P19-1381, https://www.aclweb.org/anthology/P19-1381
10. Devlin, J., Chang, M.W., Lee, K., Toutanova, K.: BERT: pre-training of deep bidirectional transformers for language understanding. arXiv:1810.04805 (2019)
11. Dubey, M., Banerjee, D., Abdelkawi, A., Lehmann, J.: LC-QuAD 2.0: a large dataset for complex question answering over Wikidata and DBpedia. In: Ghidini, C., et al. (eds.) The Semantic Web – ISWC 2019, vol. 11779, pp. 69–78. Springer International Publishing, Cham (2019). https://doi.org/10.1007/978-3-030-30796-7_5, https://link.springer.com/10.1007/978-3-030-30796-7_5
12. Dziri, N., et al.: Faith and fate: limits of transformers on compositionality. In: Nips 2023, Proceedings of the 37th International Conference on Neural Information Processing Systems. Curran Associates Inc., Red Hook, NY, USA (2023)
13. Falcon, W., The PyTorch Lightning team: PyTorch lightning (2019). https://doi.org/10.5281/zenodo.3828935, https://github.com/Lightning-AI/lightning

14. Feng, G., Zhang, B., Gu, Y., Ye, H., He, D., Wang, L.: Towards revealing the mystery behind chain of thought: a theoretical perspective. In: Oh, A., Naumann, T., Globerson, A., Saenko, K., Hardt, M., Levine, S. (eds.) Advances in Neural Information Processing Systems, vol. 36, pp. 70757–70798. Curran Associates, Inc. (2023). https://proceedings.neurips.cc/paper_files/paper/2023/file/dfc310e81992d2e4cedc09ac47eff13e-Paper-Conference.pdf
15. Furrer, D., Zee, M.v., Scales, N., Schärli, N.: Compositional generalization in semantic parsing: pre-training vs. specialized architectures. arXiv:2007.08970 (2021)
16. Grattafiori, A., et al.: The Llama 3 herd of models. arXiv:2407.21783 (2024)
17. He, J., Hu, N., Long, W., Chen, J., Pan, J.Z.: MINTQA: a multi-hop question answering benchmark for evaluating LLMs on new and tail knowledge. arXiv:2412.17032 (2025)
18. Herzig, J., Shaw, P., Chang, M.W., Guu, K., Pasupat, P., Zhang, Y.: Unlocking compositional generalization in pre-trained models using intermediate representations. arXiv:2104.07478 (2021)
19. Hui, B., et al.: Qwen2. 5-coder technical report. arXiv preprint arXiv:2409.12186 (2024)
20. Hupkes, D., Dankers, V., Mul, M., Bruni, E.: Compositionality decomposed: how do neural networks generalise? J. Artif. Intell. Res. **67**, 757–795 (2020). https://doi.org/10.1613/jair.1.11674, https://jair.org/index.php/jair/article/view/11674
21. Ismayilzada, M., et al.: Evaluating morphological compositional generalization in large language models. arXiv:2410.12656 (2025)
22. Keysers, D., et al.: Measuring compositional generalization: a comprehensive method on realistic data. arXiv:1912.09713 (2020)
23. Khattab, O., et al.: Demonstrate-search-predict: composing retrieval and language models for knowledge-intensive NLP. arXiv preprint arXiv:2212.14024 (2022)
24. Khattab, O., et al.: DSPy: compiling declarative language model calls into self-improving pipelines. The Twelfth International Conference on Learning Representations (2024)
25. Kim, N., Linzen, T.: COGS: a compositional generalization challenge based on semantic interpretation. arXiv:2010.05465 (2020)
26. Lake, B., Baroni, M.: Generalization without systematicity: on the compositional skills of sequence-to-sequence recurrent networks (2018)
27. McCrae, J., Spohr, D., Cimiano, P.: Linking lexical resources and ontologies on the semantic web with lemon. In: Antoniou, G., et al. (eds.) ESWC 2011. LNCS, vol. 6643, pp. 245–259. Springer, Heidelberg (2011). https://doi.org/10.1007/978-3-642-21034-1_17
28. McLeish, S., et al.: Transformers can do arithmetic with the right embeddings. In: Globerson, A., et al. (eds.) Advances in Neural Information Processing Systems, vol. 37, pp. 108012–108041. Curran Associates, Inc. (2024). https://proceedings.neurips.cc/paper_files/paper/2024/file/c35986bc1ee29b31c1011481b77fe540-Paper-Conference.pdf
29. Merrill, W., Sabharwal, A.: The parallelism tradeoff: Limitations of log-precision transformers. Trans. Assoc. Comput. Linguist. **11**, 531–545 (2023). https://doi.org/10.1162/tacl_a_00562, https://direct.mit.edu/tacl/article-pdf/doi/10.1162/tacl_a_00562/2131191/tacl_a_00562.pdf
30. Nye, M., et al.: Show your work: scratchpads for intermediate computation with language models. arXiv:2112.00114 (2021)
31. OLMo, T., et al.: 2 OLMo 2 furious. arXiv:2501.00656 (2025)

32. OpenAI, et al.: GPT-4 technical report. arXiv:2303.08774 (2024)
33. Panda, P., Agarwal, A., Devaguptapu, C., Kaul, M., Ap, P.: HOLMES: hyper-relational knowledge graphs for multi-hop question answering using LLMs. In: Proceedings of the 62nd Annual Meeting of the Association for Computational Linguistics (Volume 1: Long Papers), pp. 13263–13282. Association for Computational Linguistics, Bangkok, Thailand (2024). https://doi.org/10.18653/v1/2024.acl-long.717, https://aclanthology.org/2024.acl-long.717
34. Perevalov, A., Diefenbach, D., Usbeck, R., Both, A.: QALD-9-plus: a multilingual dataset for question answering over DBpedia and Wikidata translated by native speakers, pp. 229–234. IEEE Computer Society (2022). https://doi.org/10.1109/ICSC52841.2022.00045, https://www.computer.org/csdl/proceedings-article/icsc/2022/341800a229/1BYIptAeqty
35. Petty, J., Steenkiste, S., Dasgupta, I., Sha, F., Garrette, D., Linzen, T.: The impact of depth on compositional generalization in transformer language models. In: Duh, K., Gomez, H., Bethard, S. (eds.) Proceedings of the 2024 Conference of the North American Chapter of the Association for Computational Linguistics, Mexico City, Mexico (2024). https://doi.org/10.18653/v1/2024.naacl-long.402, https://aclanthology.org/2024.naacl-long.402/
36. Piantadosi, S.T., Hill, F.: Meaning without reference in large language models. arXiv:2208.02957 (2022)
37. Press, O., Zhang, M., Min, S., Schmidt, L., Smith, N., Lewis, M.: Measuring and narrowing the compositionality gap in language models. In: Bouamor, H., Pino, J., Bali, K. (eds.) Findings of the Association for Computational Linguistics: EMNLP 2023, pp. 5687–5711. Association for Computational Linguistics, Singapore (2023). https://doi.org/10.18653/v1/2023.findings-emnlp.378, https://aclanthology.org/2023.findings-emnlp.378/
38. Rasley, J., Rajbhandari, S., Ruwase, O., He, Y.: DeepSpeed: system optimizations enable training deep learning models with over 100 billion parameters. In: KDD 2020, Proceedings of the 26th ACM SIGKDD International Conference on Knowledge Discovery & Data Mining, pp. 3505–3506. Association for Computing Machinery, New York, NY, USA (2020). https://doi.org/10.1145/3394486.3406703, https://dl.acm.org/doi/10.1145/3394486.3406703
39. Rival, I.: The diagram. In: Rival, I. (ed.) Graphs and Order: The Role of Graphs in the Theory of Ordered Sets and Its Applications, pp. 103–133. Springer Netherlands, Dordrecht (1985). https://doi.org/10.1007/978-94-009-5315-4_3
40. Saparov, A., He, H.: Language models are greedy reasoners: a systematic formal analysis of chain-of-thought. arXiv:2210.01240 (2023)
41. Schmidt, D.M., Elahi, M.F., Cimiano, P.: Lexicalization is all you need: examining the impact of lexical knowledge in a compositional QALD system. In: Badenes-Olmedo, C., et al. (eds.) Joint Proceedings of Posters, Demos, Workshops, and Tutorials of the 24th International Conference on Knowledge Engineering and Knowledge Management (EKAW-PDWT 2024). CEUR Workshop Proceedings, vol. 3967. CEUR, Amsterdam, Netherlands (2024). https://ceur-ws.org/Vol-3967/#PD_paper_160
42. Schmidt, D.M., Elahi, M.F., Cimiano, P.: Lexicalization is all you need: examining the impact of lexical knowledge in a compositional QALD system. In: Alam, M., Rospocher, M., van Erp, M., Hollink, L., Gesese, G.A. (eds.) Knowledge engineering and knowledge management, pp. 102–122. Springer Nature Switzerland, Cham (2025). https://doi.org/10.1007/978-3-031-77792-9_7

43. Shekarpour, S., et al.: Question answering on linked data: challenges and future directions. In: Proceedings of the 25th International Conference Companion on World Wide Web (WWW), pp. 693–698 (2016)
44. Strobl, L., Merrill, W., Weiss, G., Chiang, D., Angluin, D.: What formal languages can transformers express? A survey. Trans. Assoc. Comput. Linguist. **12**, 543–561 (2024). https://doi.org/10.1162/tacl_a_00663
45. Szabó, Z.G.: The case for compositionality. In: Werning, M., Hinzen, W., Machery, E. (eds.) The Oxford Handbook of Compositionality. Oxford University Press (2012)
46. Usbeck, R., Gusmita, R.H., Ngomo, A.C.N., Saleem, M.: 9th challenge on question answering over linked data (QALD-9). In: Joint Proceedings of the 4th Workshop on Semantic Deep Learning (SemDeep-4) and NLIWoD4: Natural Language Interfaces for the Web of Data (NLIWOD-4) and 9th Question Answering Over Linked Data Challenge (QALD-9) Co-located with 17th International Semantic Web Conference (ISWC), pp. 58–64. California, United States of America (2018)
47. Usbeck, R., et al.: QALD-10 — the 10th challenge on question answering over linked data. Semantic Web (2023)
48. Wei, J., et al.: Chain-of-thought prompting elicits reasoning in large language models. In: NIPS 2022, Proceedings of the 36th International Conference on Neural Information Processing Systems, pp. 24824–24837. Curran Associates Inc., Red Hook, NY, USA (Nov 2022)
49. Welleck, S., Liu, J., Lu, X., Hajishirzi, H., Choi, Y.: NaturalProver: grounded mathematical proof generation with language models. In: Advances in Neural Information Processing Systems, vol. 35, pp. 4913–4927 (2022). https://proceedings.neurips.cc/paper_files/paper/2022/hash/1fc548a8243ad06616eee731e0572927-Abstract-Conference.html
50. Yang, A., et al.: Qwen2 technical report. arXiv preprint arXiv:2407.10671 (2024)
51. Yang, H., Lu, H., Lam, W., Cai, D.: Exploring compositional generalization of large language models. In: Proceedings of the 2024 Conference of the North American Chapter of the Association for Computational Linguistics: Human Language Technologies (Volume 4: Student Research Workshop), pp. 16–24. Association for Computational Linguistics, Mexico City, Mexico (2024). https://doi.org/10.18653/v1/2024.naacl-srw.3, https://aclanthology.org/2024.naacl-srw.3
52. Yih, W.t., Chang, M.W., He, X., Gao, J.: Semantic parsing via staged query graph generation: question answering with knowledge base. In: Proceedings of the 53rd Annual Meeting of the Association for Computational Linguistics and the 7th International Joint Conference on Natural Language Processing (Volume 1: Long Papers), pp. 1321–1331. Association for Computational Linguistics, Beijing, China (2015). https://doi.org/10.3115/v1/P15-1128, http://aclweb.org/anthology/P15-1128
53. Zhang, Y., Backurs, A., Bubeck, S., Eldan, R., Gunasekar, S., Wagner, T.: Unveiling transformers with LEGO: a synthetic reasoning task. arXiv:2206.04301 (2023)
54. Zhao, J., Tong, J., Mou, Y., Zhang, M., Zhang, Q., Huang, X.: Exploring the compositional deficiency of large language models in mathematical reasoning through trap problems. In: Proceedings of the 2024 Conference on Empirical Methods in Natural Language Processing, pp. 16361–16376. Association for Computational Linguistics, Miami, Florida, USA (2024). https://doi.org/10.18653/v1/2024.emnlp-main.915, https://aclanthology.org/2024.emnlp-main.915
55. Zubić, N., Soldá, F., Sulser, A., Scaramuzza, D.: Limits of deep learning: sequence modeling through the lens of complexity theory. arXiv: 2405.16674 (2025)

Are Quality Dimensions Correlated? An Empirical Investigation Over Linked Data

Maria Angela Pellegrino[1(✉)], Anisa Rula[2], and Gabriele Tuozzo[1]

[1] Dipartimento di Informatica, Università degli Studi di Salerno, Fisciano, Italy
{mapellegrino,gtuozzo}@unisa.it

[2] Department of Information Engineering, University of Brescia, Brescia, Italy
anisa.rula@unibs.it

Abstract. Data quality is a complex and multidimensional concept, hierarchically organized into categories, dimensions, and metrics. Although theoretical correlations among quality dimensions have been proposed, they have not yet been empirically validated. This study addresses this gap by systematically investigating whether such correlations hold in practice, comparing theoretical assumptions with empirical, data-driven insights over a five-quarter longitudinal analysis. Leveraging outputs from a freely available quality assessment tool, the findings challenge some prior assumptions, e.g., the relationship between timeliness and accuracy, while uncovering new correlations, including a positive association between interpretability and intrinsic-related dimensions. Through this empirical evidence, this work refines existing data quality models, enhances best practices for dataset management, and informs future efforts to optimize quality assessment frameworks in the Semantic Web.

Keywords: Quality dimensions · Correlations · Empirical investigation

1 Introduction

Data quality is inherently multidimensional, typically hierarchically organized into categories, dimensions, and metrics [45]. While dimensions are abstract, they can be operationalized and quantified through metrics. Although significant research has been focused on defining data quality dimensions and associated metrics [5,8,39,42,43], relatively little attention has been given to the interrelationships among these dimensions. In practice, dimensions rarely operate in isolation. Data publishers and consumers often face resource constraints and must decide which dimensions to prioritize over others. Consider a public biomedical knowledge graph, expected to be accurate, complete, and regularly updated. A data engineer may ask: if the dataset is timely and consistently structured, is it likely accurate? Conversely, can the presence of licensing information serve as an indicator of trustworthiness? Answering such questions is challenging, as the relationships among quality dimensions are complex and poorly explored.

D. Garijo et al. (Eds.): ISWC 2025, LNCS 16140, pp. 23–41, 2026.
https://doi.org/10.1007/978-3-032-09527-5_2

Understanding and quantifying the correlation between data quality dimensions carries significant implications for data quality management. Such correlations may reveal interdependencies between dimensions, enabling a deeper understanding of how data quality evolves and offering insights into underlying data-driven patterns observed over time. Understanding correlations—regardless of strength or stability—helps map the complex data quality landscape and supports more resilient and intelligent quality management systems.

Rationale and implications for estimating quality dimensions correlations are:

- **Targeted Interventions.** Persistent strong correlations may suggest intrinsic or structural linkages between dimensions. Such pairs can be jointly monitored and improved, with the expectation that gains in one will positively influence the other. While strong positive correlations between dimensions imply that improving one dimension will likely result in improvements in the other (i.e., mutual reinforcement), negative correlations between dimensions may indicate trade-offs requiring careful management.
- **Efficiency and Performance Optimization.** If strong interdependencies exist, it may be possible to streamline evaluations by measuring only a subset of dimensions and inferring others. Organizations can reduce redundancy and optimize resource use by focusing on "influential" dimensions with strong downstream effects. For example, if Dimension A is expensive to monitor but consistently correlates strongly with Dimension B (which is inexpensive to measure), B can serve as a proxy for A.
- **Predictive Insights.** Stable correlations offer reliable patterns that can be leveraged for forecasting the behavior of related dimensions, supporting proactive and informed decision-making.
- **Early Indicators.** A breakdown in the observed correlations, e.g., the weakening of a stable strong correlation, may indicate degradation, drift, or anomalies in data quality processes, prompting a timely investigation.
- **Benchmarking and Continuous Monitoring.** Identifying correlations empowers organizations to adopt a systematic and evidence-based approach to data quality management, ensuring data remains trustworthy, reliable, and fit for its intended purpose. It lays the groundwork for continuous benchmarking, offering a data-driven basis for iterative enhancement.

Previous works, including Zaveri et al. [45] and Hogan et al. [21], have theoretically hypothesized correlations among quality dimensions and metrics, but these claims have yet to be validated through empirical studies. This study addresses this gap by systematically exploring whether quality dimensions are empirically correlated, and whether these correlations align with theoretical assumptions. The research questions (RQs) guiding the investigation follow:

RQ1 - *Do data-driven correlations align with those theoretically proposed?*
RQ2 - *Are data-driven correlations time sensitive?*

To address these RQs, this study reports about an empirical analysis of 142 Linked Datasets indexed in the LOD Cloud[1] and DataHub[2]. The analysis is based on a generalizable methodology for correlation analysis using statistical methods to validate or challenge hypothesized relationships and to uncover new ones. Our findings confirm several theoretical assumptions, such as strong alignment between intrinsic dimensions, but also reveal contradictions.

The main contributions of this paper are:

- The design of a taxonomy-based framework for systematically categorizing correlations in terms of strength, direction, and temporal stability.
- An empirical, data-driven assessment of inter-dimensional data quality correlations conducted over five quarters, representing the first empirical verification of quality dimension correlations, to the best of our knowledge.
- Degree of agreement among empirically observed data quality correlations and those theoretically hypothesized.

This paper is structured as follows. Section 2 provides an overview of quality dimensions and categories and the theoretical correlations between them as outlined in the literature. Section 3 reports a reusable methodology for computing quality correlations, describes the correlation taxonomy, and overviews how the methodology has been applied in the context of this study. Section 4 presents and interprets the results [29], which are fully available online, as well as the code to reproduce the results [28]. Section 5 compares empirically observed correlations with the theoretical ones hypothesized in the literature [21,45]. The article concludes with final thoughts, limitations, and future directions.

2 Background and Related Work

This section first reports on the theoretical framework defining data quality categories and dimensions, and then overviews related work theoretically evaluating data quality dimensions correlations.

2.1 Data Quality Categories and Dimensions

Several studies have addressed the issue of data quality by proposing frameworks for its assessment [7,10,11,13,24,31–33,41]. Starting from these generic frameworks, more tailored approaches have emerged over time, specifically adapted to the structure of the data being evaluated. In the context of linked data, various frameworks have been proposed with the aim of measuring the quality of these data, which are characterized by their interconnected nature [12,43,45].

This article is grounded in the linked data quality framework proposed by Zaveri et al. [45] and its adaptation according to [27], because it underpins KGHeartBeat [27], the quality assessment tool used in this study. This framework consider the following data quality categories and related dimensions:

[1] LOD Cloud: https://lod-cloud.net.
[2] DataHub: https://old.datahub.io.

- The *accessibility* cluster involves dimensions related to the access, authenticity, and retrieval of data. It includes availability, interlinking, licensing, security, and performance.
- The *contextual* cluster involves dimensions that highly depend on the context of the task at hand, assessing the amount of data and completeness.
- The *dataset dynamicity* cluster focuses on the currency and timeliness of published data.
- The *intrinsic* cluster involves dimensions independent of the user's context, focusing on whether the information represents the real world correctly and compactly and whether the information is logically consistent. It includes semantic accuracy, consistency, and conciseness.
- The *representational* category includes dimensions that capture aspects related to the design of the data, such as representational conciseness, interoperability, interpretability, understandability, and versatility.
- The *trust* category includes dimensions focused on trustworthiness in terms of verifiability, reputation, and believability.

2.2 Related Work

Linked Data Quality Assessment. Numerous studies in the literature have investigated the assessment of linked data quality, monitoring the LOD Cloud quality [4,14,15,17,18,35,40], focusing on a limited number of datasets [16,23,38], or on domain-specific linked data [9,20,25,30,44]. Other works provide large-scale evaluations across a wide variety of datasets from multiple catalogs [2,3,22,26].

Quality dimensions are not uniformly curated. A particularly critical issue is the Accessibility category as many publicly available datasets suffer from non-functional access points or provide static access to the data through data dumps [14,17]. Moreover, licensing is often unreliable and inconsistent [4,21,26].

Correlation in Data Quality. The correlation between data quality dimensions has been widely studied, especially in the context of relational databases. Most works investigate interdependencies among dimensions such as accuracy, completeness, consistency, and timeliness. Barone et al. [6] use a Bayesian network to analyze real-world data, revealing dependencies among accuracy, completeness, and consistency. Hassany et al. [19] include timeliness in a similar analysis. De Amicis et al. [1], using an information-theoretic approach with Shannon entropy, find no correlation between syntactic accuracy and completeness, but do find links between syntactic accuracy and timeliness, and between completeness and timeliness. Scannapieco et al. [34] present a theoretical framework positing potential correlations among timeliness, accuracy, completeness, and consistency. Specifically, they hypothesize links between timeliness and accuracy, timeliness and completeness, timeliness and consistency, and between consistency and completeness. However, these hypotheses have not been empirically validated.

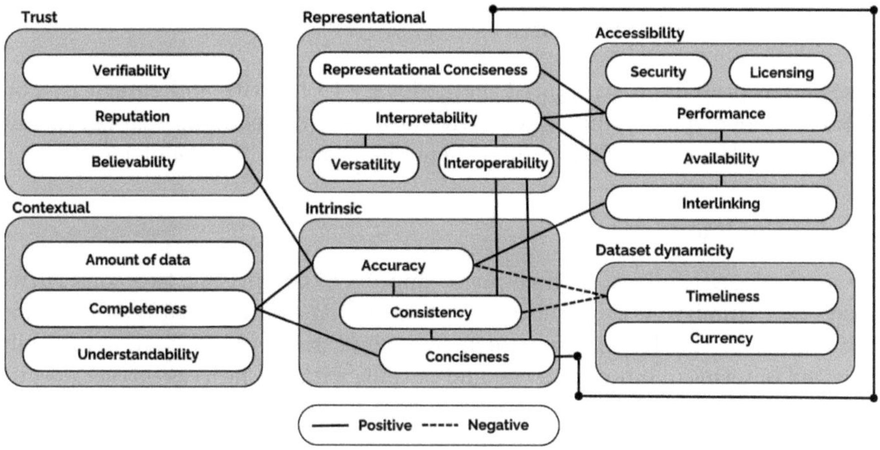

Fig. 1. KGs quality dimensions and their correlations theoretically hypothesized by Zaveri et al. [45] and Hogan et al. [21].

Correlations in Linked Data Quality. One of the earliest studies to explore correlations among quality metrics is by Hogan et al. [21]. They observed that RDF resources with a high proportion of blank nodes often have fewer dereferenceable URIs and that constructs like collections, reification, and containers, typically implemented with blank nodes, negatively impact performance by lowering throughput and increasing latency. The study also highlighted that shorter URIs improve scalability, indexing, and memory efficiency, enhancing SPARQL endpoint performance. However, while these patterns suggested quality correlations, rigorous statistical validation was limited. The study used Kendall's rank correlation only to assess whether Knowledge Graphs (KGs)' overall quality scores correlated with resource PageRank, finding a positive correlation between PageRank and both external linking and vocabulary reuse, indicating that more interconnected resources tend to be better recognized and interoperable.

A theoretical attempt to hypothesize quality dimensions correlations is proposed by Zaveri et al. [45], who emphasized that categories and dimensions are not independent of one another. They identified correlations within the dimensions of the same category and across categories.

Figure 1 illustrates all correlations theoretically identified in related work, by manually mapping metrics and dimensions to quality categories reported in Sect. 2.1. While plain lines indicate positive relationships, dashed lines represent negative ones. Although these theoretical correlations provide valuable insights, empirical analysis has not validated them. No study has conducted a rigorous statistical investigation to substantiate the proposed relationships, leaving room for empirical exploration and data-driven validation of these correlations.

3 Method and Material

This section presents a structured methodology to identify and categorize correlations among quality dimensions, the proposed correlations taxonomy, and overviews KGHeartBeat [27] to implement the proposed methodology.

3.1 Methodology

The methodology follows a three-phase approach, comprising two consecutive phases, i.e., Quality Assessment and Correlation Analysis, and a temporal loop back related to the Trend Assessment over time. Each phase is systematically organized in terms of input, process, and output, with the process further decomposed into consecutive steps. The methodology grounds on standard approaches to perform correlation analysis and it is designed to be general and reproducible, ensuring its applicability across diverse data sources and tools. The methodology itself is tool-agnostic and can be implemented with alternative quality assessment tools. Detailed descriptions of each phase follow.

Phase 1 - Quality Assessment.

- *Input.* Data and metadata at the dataset level.
- *Process.* It involves the following steps:
  1. **Dimension identification**: defining metrics, identifying best values (if available), collecting the necessary input, and calculating quality scores. In the following, the framework defined in [45] and reported in Sect. 2.1 will be used as a reference as it is the unique theoretical framework to define interplay and hypothesize correlations among dimensions.
  2. **Quality computation.** Evaluate each dataset to be assessed by computing a quality score for each dimension. While this study utilizes KGHeartBeat [27] for scoring, any quality assessment tool can be employed.
- *Output.* Quality assessment report per dataset, detailing dimension-specific scores, on a scale from 0 to 1.

Phase 2 - Correlation Analyses. This phase requires verifying the normality of the data distribution and selecting an appropriate correlation coefficient.

- *Input.* Per dataset quality assessment report.
- *Process.* It involves the following steps:
  1. **Normality Test.** Treat each quality dimension as a variable and assess its distribution using the Shapiro-Wilk test [37].
  2. **Selection of Correlation Coefficient.** If the data follows a normal distribution, compute correlations using the Pearson coefficient; otherwise, apply the Spearman coefficient.
  3. **Computation of Correlation Coefficient.** Calculate the pairwise correlation coefficient, recording the coefficient value (r) and the p-value.
- *Output.* A set of pairwise quality dimension correlation scores.

Phase 3 - Trend Analyses and Taxonomy Alignment. It is interpreted as a loop back to perform cyclically the quality assessment and the correlation analyses, monitoring the evolution and trends of correlation analysis scores over time.

- *Input.* A set of pairwise quality dimension correlation scores computed over time steps, denoted as $T_0, ..., T_n$.
- *Process.* It involves the following steps:
  1. **Correlation Analysis over-time.** Systematically compare correlation analysis results over time.
  2. **Alignment with the Correlation Taxonomy.** Estimates correlation analyses results regarding strength, direction, and temporal patterns, as described in Sect. 3.2.
- *Output.* Correlation characterization according to the proposed taxonomy.

3.2 Correlation Taxonomy

The proposed taxonomy is structured around three key dimensions, which collectively aim to systematically characterize the nature of observed correlations among data quality dimensions. This taxonomy is informed by established practices in the statistical and data quality literature, ensuring both methodological rigor and alignment with prior works. Key dimensions are defined as follows:

- **Strength:** correlation magnitude based on commonly accepted thresholds in the correlation analysis literature [36] distinguishing:
  - ***Strong*** (i.e., $|r| \geq 0.6$) indicating a substantial or strong relationship.
  - ***Moderate*** (i.e., $0.4 \leq |r| < 0.6$), indicating a moderate relationship, suggestive of a meaningful but not dominant association.
  - ***Weak*** (i.e., $|r| < 0.4$), indicating a weak or low association, where the correlation is present but may not have practical significance.
- **Direction:** sign of the correlation coefficient, distinguishing:
  - ***Positive***, where an increase in one quality dimension is associated with an increase in another;
  - ***Negative***, where an increase in one dimension corresponds to a decrease in the other.
- **Temporal Patterns.** Recognizing the dynamic nature of datasets and their evolving quality over time, we introduce this dimension to differentiate:
  - ***Stable*** correlations, where the observed relationship persists consistently across multiple temporal snapshots.
  - ***Occasional*** correlations, where the relationship appears only sporadically or in specific periods.

While those dimensions can be arbitrarily combined, we identify classes of worth monitored correlation patterns mainly guided by the role played by the time dimension. Those worth monitored patterns are significant for informing both quality assessment strategies and dataset management practices and are widely observed in data-driven exploration. They are defined as follows, along with a rationale to justify their relevance.

- **Stable correlations.** These represent dimension pairs whose correlation strength and direction remain consistent throughout the entire observation period. This category can be further refined into *stable moderate* and *stable strong*. Stable correlations indicate persistent, structural relationships between data quality dimensions, which can be used to optimize quality assessment processes. For example, the consistent co-occurrence of accuracy and consistency suggests that monitoring one dimension might give predictive insights into the status of the other, potentially reducing redundancy in assessments or informing automated monitoring rules.
- **Occasional correlations.** This category includes dimension pairs that display fluctuating correlation strengths, with observable peaks or declines during specific periods. These can be further detailed as:
  - *Isolated.* Correlation scores that are generally low or unstable but register isolated strong or moderate peaks.
  - *Emerging.* Correlations that show a clear pattern of strengthening over time, indicating that the relationship between the dimensions is becoming more significant in recent data snapshots.
  - *Disappearing.* Correlations that weaken over time, suggesting a diminishing relationship between the dimensions.

  This pattern matches important early warning signals or indicators of shifts in dataset management practices, data modeling changes, or evolving publisher behaviors. Emerging correlations potentially highlight new dependencies, while disappearing correlations might expose decaying data quality relationships or deteriorating data curation processes. Isolated peaks could signal exceptional events or data publishing anomalies that merit investigation.
- **Inverted correlations.** This class captures dimension pairs where the correlation direction reverses over the observation period, shifting from positive to negative or vice versa. Those correlations are particularly critical as they may reveal substantial shifts in data governance, modeling practices, or content evolution. These shifts could reflect changes in dataset structure, curation priorities, or external influencing factors (e.g., policy changes, system upgrades) and may require immediate corrective action. Inverted trends also signal instability, suggesting the need for closer scrutiny and possible interventions to maintain data reliability and user trust.

3.3 KGHeartBeat and Quality Assessment Input

The study leverages KGHeartBeat [27], a community-shared and open access quality assessment framework. Among similar tools such as YummyData [44] and SPARQLES [40], KGHeartBeat is chosen due to its broader coverage of quality dimensions, wider evaluated datasets and conceptual alignment with the theoretical framework established by Zaveri et al. [45], which hypothesized correlations at a theoretical level. KGHeartBeat provides automated, periodic assessments of all six quality categories reported in Sect. 2.1. It results in the coverage of 20 dimensions and 52 metrics that can be objectively computed without requiring domain-specific gold standards. Metric scores range in the range [0,1]. According to the hierarchy induced by the taxonomy proposed by Zaveri et al. [45], metrics scores are linearly merged in dimension scores. Data and metadata to compute metrics can be retrieved via the VoID file, search engine where the dataset is registered, such as the LOD Cloud, and working SPARQL endpoints. As quality scores are heavily biased by the lack of working SPARQL endpoints due to the impossibility of retrieving data and metadata, correlation analyses have been performed on datasets provided with an operational SPARQL endpoint, which return a triple when pinged. In those cases, scores correctly model the quality of data and metadata, informing patterns and analyses. It resulted in 142 datasets[3], provided with functional SPARQL endpoints in the entire observational period. The analyses have been performed using the CSV files of the five snapshots, corresponding to T_0 January 7th, 2024; T_1 April 7th, 2024; T_2 August 4th, 2024; T_3 December 1st, 2024; and T_4 April 6th, 2025. All input files are freely accessible online [28].

4 Results

This section first documents the correlation analysis results referring to the last assessment, then reports the trend analyses over the five quarters and the taxonomy alignment.

4.1 Point-in-Time Correlation Analyses

Table 1 provides the correlation matrix for 142 datasets provided with a functional SPARQL endpoint and related to the matrix obtained in T_4 April 6th, 2025, the most recent results in the longitudinal study[4]. Given the non-normal distribution of quality dimension variables obtained via KGHeartBeat, Table 1 displays Spearman's rank correlation coefficient along with the corresponding p-value. Asterisks indicate statistical significance: *** for p-values below 0.001, ** for p-values below 0.01, and * for p-values below 0.05. To enhance interpretability, the dimensions are grouped by categories, coherently with the hierarchy described in Sect. 2.1. Table 1 is rendered as a heat map, where darker shades correspond to higher correlation scores. Three gray-scale intensities are used to distinguish different correlation strengths: moderate (absolute values between 0.4 and 0.59), strong (0.6 to 0.79), and very strong correlation (0.8 to 1).

Most correlations are positive and statistically significant with a p-value less than 0.05. Intrinsic dimensions show moderate to strong correlations with one another. In particular, a **strong positive correlations** apply between accuracy and consistency. It holds that inconsistency (e.g., conflicting values across

[3] The list of monitored datasets is available online [29].

[4] The correlation analysis results per each quarter are available online [29].

Table 1. Correlation matrix on datasets provided with a working SPARQL endpoint using scores computed by KGHeartBeat in April 2025. For each correlation, Spearman's rank correlation coefficient is provided along with the corresponding p-value, with significance levels indicated by three asterisks for p-values less than 0.001, two asterisks for p-values less than 0.01, a single one for p-values less than 0.05, and empty cells otherwise.

	Availability (1)	Interlinking (2)	Licensing (3)	Performance (4)	Security (5)	Amount of data (6)	Completeness (7)	Understandability (8)	Currency (9)	Timeliness (10)	Accuracy (11)	Conciseness (12)	Consistency (13)	Interoperability (14)	Interpretability (15)	Rep. Conciseness (16)	Versatility (17)	Believability (18)	Reputation (19)	Verifiability (20)
	ACCESSIBILITY					CONTEXTUAL			DATASET DYNAMICITY		INTRINSIC			REPRESENTATIONAL				TRUST		
(1)	1	0.05	0.11	0.17	-0.20 *	-0.11	0.23 *	-0.03	0.01	-0.16	0.00	-0.10	-0.23 *	0.35 ***	0.04	0.31 **	0.54 ***	0.21 *	-0.03	-0.08
(2)	0.05	1	0.18	0.16	-0.12	0.23 *	0.24 *	0.02	0.18	0.27 **	0.24 *	-0.04	0.24 *	-0.10	0.27 **	0.11	0.16	0.34 ***	0.08	0.51 ***
(3)	0.11	0.18	1	0.23 *	-0.29 **	0.14	0.17	0.13	0.32 ***	0.14	0.15	0.41 ***	0.36 ***	-0.08	0.11	0.13	0.03	0.39 ***	0.34 ***	0.44 ***
(4)	0.17	0.16	0.23 *	1	-0.38 ***	-0.11	0.02	-0.10	0.16	0.15	0.02	0.02	0.03	0.22 *	0.08	0.28 **	0.26 **	0.35 ***	-0.08	0.35 ***
(5)	-0.20 *	-0.12	-0.29 **	-0.38 ***	1	0.15	0.07	0.27 **	-0.18	-0.09	0.06	0.04	0.01	-0.09	0.19	0.02	-0.01	-0.22 *	0.23 *	-0.14
(6)	-0.11	0.23 *	0.14	-0.11	0.15	1	0.03	0.59 ***	0.34 ***	0.45 ***	0.47 ***	0.27 **	0.62 ***	-0.63 ***	0.63 ***	0.07	-0.05	0.14	0.36 ***	0.40 ***
(7)	0.23 *	0.24 *	0.17	0.02	0.07	-0.03	1	0.03	0.02	-0.35 ***	0.12	0.00	-0.17	0.17	0.07	0.13	0.23 *	0.11	0.26 **	0.07
(8)	-0.03	0.02	0.13	-0.10	0.27 **	0.59 ***	0.03	1	0.48 ***	0.35 ***	0.49 ***	0.43 ***	0.51 ***	-0.39 ***	0.55 ***	0.32 ***	0.09	0.28 **	0.46 ***	0.34 ***
(9)	-0.01	0.18	0.32 ***	0.16	-0.18	0.34 ***	0.02	0.48 ***	1	0.35 ***	0.39 ***	0.38 ***	0.54 ***	-0.21 *	0.55 ***	0.24 *	-0.04	0.41 ***	0.28 **	0.53 ***
(10)	-0.16	0.27 **	0.14	0.15	-0.09	0.45 ***	-0.35 ***	0.35 ***	0.35 ***	1	0.59 ***	0.37 ***	0.68 ***	-0.49 ***	0.57 ***	0.12	0.12	0.20 *	0.09	0.46 ***
(11)	0.00	0.24 *	0.15	0.02	0.06	0.47 ***	0.12	0.49 ***	0.39 ***	0.59 ***	1	0.57 ***	0.65 ***	-0.25 *	0.68 ***	0.24 *	0.04	0.22 *	0.44 ***	0.21 *
(12)	-0.10	-0.04	0.41 ***	0.02	0.04	0.27 **	0.00	0.43 ***	0.38 ***	0.37 ***	0.57 ***	1	0.64 ***	-0.25 *	0.45 ***	0.16	-0.13	0.25 *	0.41 ***	0.20 *
(13)	-0.23 *	0.24 *	0.36 ***	0.03	0.01	0.62 ***	-0.17	0.51 ***	0.54 ***	0.68 ***	0.65 ***	0.64 ***	1	-0.51 ***	0.63 ***	0.07	0.10	0.25 **	0.43 ***	0.45 ***
(14)	0.35 **	-0.10	-0.08	0.22 *	-0.09	-0.63 ***	0.17	-0.39 ***	-0.21 *	-0.49 ***	-0.25 *	-0.25 *	-0.51 ***	1	-0.29 **	0.15	0.27 **	-0.06	-0.33 ***	-0.36 ***
(15)	0.04	0.27 **	0.11	0.08	0.19	0.63 ***	0.07	0.55 ***	0.55 ***	0.57 ***	0.68 ***	0.45 ***	0.63 ***	-0.29 **	1	0.39 ***	0.13	0.25 **	0.31 **	0.30 **
(16)	0.31 **	0.11	0.13	0.28 **	0.02	0.07	0.13	0.32 ***	0.24 *	0.12	0.24 *	0.16	0.07	0.15	0.39 ***	1	0.41 ***	0.40 ***	0.01	0.12
(17)	0.54 ***	0.16	0.03	0.26 **	-0.01	-0.05	0.23 *	0.09	-0.04	0.12	0.04	-0.13	-0.19	0.27 **	0.13	0.41 ***	1	0.13	-0.11	0.12
(18)	0.21 *	0.34 ***	0.39 ***	0.35 ***	-0.22 *	0.14	0.11	0.28 **	0.41 ***	0.20 *	0.22 *	0.25 *	0.25 **	-0.06	0.25 **	0.40 ***	0.13	1	0.30 **	0.55 ***
(19)	-0.03	0.08	0.34 ***	-0.08	0.23 *	0.36 ***	0.26 **	0.46 ***	0.28 **	0.09	0.44 ***	0.41 ***	0.43 ***	-0.33 ***	0.31 **	0.01	-0.11	0.30 **	1	0.35 ***
(20)	-0.08	0.51 ***	0.44 ***	0.35 ***	-0.14	0.40 ***	0.07	0.34 ***	0.53 ***	0.46 ***	0.21 *	0.20 *	0.45 ***	-0.36 ***	0.30 **	0.12	0.12	0.55 ***	0.35 ***	1

records or formats) is frequently a symptom of underlying inaccuracy. So when you resolve inconsistencies, usually accuracy improves. Moreover, many validation techniques, such as schema validation, constraint checks, and cross-source reconciliation, target both simultaneously. These processes eliminate contradictions and fix incorrect values, boosting both dimensions together.

The analysis reveals a set of strong and mutually reinforcing correlations among key data quality dimensions, notably consistency and timeliness, conciseness and amount of data, interpretability and accuracy. Consistency and timeliness, often seen as complementary, work together to ensure that data remains both coherent and up-to-date. Regular updates help catch and resolve inconsistencies, such as deprecated formats or conflicting entries, contributing to both structural integrity and temporal relevance.

Interestingly, consistency also positively correlates with conciseness, suggesting that well-curated datasets often avoid redundancy and unnecessary complexity. Concise representations can reduce the potential for conflicting information, leading to more uniform and interpretable data. This relationship indicates that minimizing superfluous content may support greater consistency by enforcing tighter control over the structure and semantics of the data.

Moreover, larger datasets show a positive correlation with both consistency and interpretability. It may reflect more rigorous data engineering practices, such as schema enforcement and validation workflows, typically adopted in large-scale or institutionally maintained datasets. The need to make extensive data accessible to diverse users also promotes more precise documentation and the adoption of standard vocabularies, enhancing interpretability.

Finally, the observed positive correlation between interpretability and accuracy underscores the importance of semantic clarity: datasets that are easier to understand tend to support more reliable use and reduce errors. Together, these trends suggest that scale, when managed with appropriate practices, can be a driver of structural and semantic data quality, while dimensions such as timeliness and conciseness support overall consistency.

Moderate positive correlations often emerge between various factors related to trust and intrinsic data quality. To name a few, verifiability and interlinking are positively correlated, perhaps because linked data from verified sources is easier to validate. Similarly, consistency and verifiability are moderately correlated, as both are vital for ensuring data reliability and accuracy. Licensing also shows a moderate positive correlation with verifiability, as both contribute to the legitimacy and trustworthiness of data.

Understandability is moderately correlated with the intrinsic category, as accurate, consistent, and concise data foster clarity and aid user comprehension. These qualities help users trust and interpret information correctly. Additionally, interpretability is positively correlated with dataset dynamicity, such as currency and timeliness, because when presented clearly, up-to-date information improves user understanding.

Negative correlations are pretty rare and all involve interoperability. Interoperability is negatively correlated with the amount of data, consistency, and timeliness, perhaps because the complexity of managing seamless communication between systems grows as the amount of data increases. Larger datasets introduce more potential points of failure, such as mismatched formats or data quality issues, making it harder to maintain smooth interoperability. Similarly, achieving consistency across systems with varying standards, data formats, or rules becomes more difficult as systems scale. The more consistent the data must be across different platforms, the more effort it requires to ensure compatibility, leading to decreased overall interoperability. Additionally, when timeliness is critical, systems need to exchange data quickly. However, ensuring timely data exchange with large volumes or diverse systems introduces delays, especially when discrepancies arise in data formats or processing speeds, further undermining interoperability. Thus, the increase in data volume, consistency requirements, and the need for timely exchanges often complicates achieving effective interoperability.

4.2 Trend Analyses and Taxonomy Alignment

The correlation matrix for datasets with a functional SPARQL endpoint has been computed for each quarter from January 2024 to April 2025, verifying how empirical correlations evolve (RQ2). While all the results are available online [29], Table 2 only reports correlations aligned with the worth mentioned classes described in Sect. 3.2 due to the lack of space. The omitted correlations are all weak positive correlations. Dimension names sort pairs.

Conciseness and Consistency, and Consistency and Timeliness are the only pairs exhibiting a consistently strong correlation throughout the observation period. These stable relationships suggest underlying structural dependencies within data pipelines that remain robust despite evolving practices or external influences. In addition, a set of moderately stable correlations also emerges, predominantly involving Understandability and Reputation. These dimensions maintain steady moderate correlations, occasionally punctuated by strong peaks, particularly in relation to Interpretability, emphasizing moments where data transparency gains heightened relevance.

Most correlations observed are positive, affirming the general alignment of data quality dimensions in enhancing overall trustworthiness and usability. However, notable negative correlations persist, especially involving Interoperability and Consistency, possibly highlighting friction between flexible integration across systems and maintaining uniform data standards.

An interesting trend is the inversion of specific correlations over time, all involving Currency. These shifts likely reflect evolving priorities, with increasing emphasis on data recency and freshness potentially compromising other quality aspects like reliability or validation.

Moreover, the number of emerging correlations—some reaching strong intensity—grows over time, especially involving the Amount of Data and Accuracy. This pattern likely points to the effects of scaling and increased sophistication in data-intensive applications, where richer datasets begin to influence precision and performance more directly. In contrast, disappearing correlations are rare and mostly concern Understandability and Representational Conciseness. It may suggest that as tools for navigating complex data improve, the

Table 2. Trend analyses results in T_0 - January 2024, T_1 - April 2024, T_2 - August 2024, T_3 - December 2024, T_4 - April 2025. Only results relevant for the taxonomy are reported, omitting occasionally moderate scores due to space constraints. Correlated Pairs are reported in alphabetic order.

Correlated Pair	T_0	T_1	T_2	T_3	T_4	Taxonomy
Accuracy ↔ Amount of Data	0.30 **	0.33 ***	0.33 ***	0.45 ***	0.47 ***	Emerging
Accuracy ↔ Conciseness	0.11	0.03	0.11	0.48 ***	0.57 ***	Emerging
Accuracy ↔ Consistency	0.33 ***	0.29 **	0.33 ***	0.68 ***	0.65 ***	Emerging & Strong
Accuracy ↔ Interpretability	0.42 ***	0.43 ***	0.44 ***	0.64 ***	0.68 ***	Emerging & Strong
Accuracy ↔ Rep. Conciseness	0.47 ***	0.45 ***	0.45 ***	0.35 ***	0.24 ***	Disappearing
Accuracy ↔ Reputation	-0.04	-0.03	0.05	0.25 **	0.44 ***	Emerging
Accuracy ↔ Timeliness	0.26 **	0.25 **	0.24 *	0.52 ***	0.59 ***	Emerging
Amount of Data ↔ Consistency	0.43 ***	0.43 ***	0.41 ***	0.62 ***	0.62 ***	Emerging
Amount of Data ↔ Interpretability	0.46 ***	0.45 ***	0.44 ***	0.64 ***	0.63 ***	Emerging & Strong
Amount of Data ↔ Interoperability	-0.15	-0.16	-0.17	-0.48 ***	-0.63 ***	Emerging, Strong & Negative
Amount of Data ↔ Understandability	0.26 **	0.24 *	0.26 **	0.61 ***	0.59 ***	Emerging & Strong
Availability ↔ Consistency	-0.14	-0.08	-0.41 ***	-0.23 **	-0.23 *	Negative with a Moderate Peak
Availability ↔ Versatility	0.49 ***	0.49 ***	0.72 ***	0.41 ***	0.54 ***	Occasionally Strong
Believability ↔ Currency	-0.27 **	-0.27 **	-0.26 **	0.23 **	0.41 ***	Inverted
Conciseness ↔ Consistency	0.63 ***	0.70 ***	0.67 ***	0.64 ***	0.64 ***	Stable Strong
Conciseness ↔ Currency	-0.34 ***	-0.43 ***	-0.41 ***	0.34 ***	0.38 ***	Inverted
Conciseness ↔ Reputation	0.43 ***	0.44 ***	0.42 ***	0.39 ***	0.41 ***	Stable Moderate
Consistency ↔ Currency	-0.46 ***	-0.45 ***	-0.42 ***	0.58 ***	0.54 ***	Inverted
Consistency ↔ Interpretability	0.58 ***	0.55 ***	0.57 ***	0.64 ***	0.63 ***	Emerging & Strong
Consistency ↔ Interoperability	-0.38 ***	-0.41 ***	-0.38 ***	-0.37 ***	-0.51 ***	Negative with Moderate Peaks
Consistency ↔ Reputation	0.40 ***	0.40 ***	0.45 ***	0.36 ***	0.43 ***	Stable Moderated
Consistency ↔ Understandability	0.68 ***	0.57 ***	0.57 ***	0.51 ***	0.51 ***	Disappearing
Consistency ↔ Timeliness	0.62 ***	0.64 ***	0.63 ***	0.66 ***	0.68 ***	Stable Strong
Currency ↔ Interpretability	-0.40 ***	-0.40 ***	-0.47 ***	0.47 ***	0.55 ***	Inverted
Currency ↔ Understandability	-0.51 ***	-0.48 ***	-0.51 ***	0.49 ***	0.48 ***	Inverted
Currency ↔ Verifiability	-0.36 ***	-0.37 ***	-0.40 ***	0.57 ***	0.53 ***	Inverted
Interlinking ↔ Rep. Conciseness	0.54 ***	0.35 ***	0.34 ***	0.12	0.11	Disappearing
Interpretability ↔ Rep. Conciseness	0.51 ***	0.49 ***	0.53 ***	0.48 ***	0.39 ***	Stable Moderate
Interpretability ↔ Understandability	0.57 ***	0.55 ***	0.61 ***	0.59 ***	0.55 ***	Stable Moderated with a Strong Peak
Interpretability ↔ Timeliness	0.60 ***	0.57 ***	0.61 ***	0.57 ***	0.57 ***	Stable Moderated with a Strong Peak
Interoperability ↔ Understandability	-0.45 ***	-0.36 ***	-0.34 ***	-0.26 **	-0.39 ***	Negative with a Moderate Peak
Interoperability ↔ Timeliness	-0.51 ***	-0.51 ***	-0.56 ***	-0.42 ***	-0.49 ***	Stable, Moderate, Negative
Reputation ↔ Understandability	0.46 ***	0.38 ***	0.40 ***	0.40 ***	0.46 ***	Stable Moderate
Understandability ↔ Verifiability	0.41 ***	0.45 ***	0.48 ***	0.45 ***	0.34 ***	Stable Moderate
Understandability ↔ Timeliness	0.57 ***	0.56 ***	0.55 ***	0.34 ***	0.35 ***	Disappearing
Verifiability ↔ Timeliness	0.29 ***	0.29 ***	0.36 ***	0.46 ***	0.46 ***	Emerging

trade-off between brevity and clarity becomes less critical, reducing their interdependence.

Together, these trends reflect a dynamic and maturing data quality landscape, where foundational relationships endure, while others adapt or evolve in response to technological advances and shifting user or system-level expectations.

5 Discussion: Theoretical vs Empirical Correlations

This section verifies the alignment between theoretically hypothesized correlations among quality dimensions (visually rendered in Fig. 1) and data-driven empirical findings reported in Sect. 4, replying to RQ1.

Correlations Confirmed by Both Theory and Empirical Evidence. When considering datasets with functioning SPARQL endpoints, both theoretical predictions and empirical observations indicate an absence of correlations within the contextual and dataset dynamicity categories. There is also agreement that the intrinsic category is the most internally correlated. For inter-category correlations, however, alignment is only partial. Confirmed interactions exist between the representational and intrinsic, contextual and intrinsic, trust and intrinsic, and dataset dynamicity and intrinsic categories. At the dimension level, several key correlations are supported by both theory and empirical findings:

- **Accuracy and Consistency**: A positive correlation between accuracy and consistency is confirmed, representing an emerging and strong correlation empirically discovered. Theoretically, Zaveri et al. [45] suggested that merging semantically accurate datasets leads to fewer inconsistencies than merging inaccurate ones. However, semantically accurate data can still be inconsistent if it fails to meet structural or logical requirements. The empirical detection of this correlation, driven by syntactic accuracy measures in KGHeartBeat, may reflect the influence of automated consistency checks, such as the identification of undeclared or deprecated classes and properties.
- **Conciseness and Consistency**: Both theoretical and empirical analyses confirm a stable, strong positive correlation between conciseness and consistency. Zaveri et al. [45] highlighted that duplicate instances negatively impact conciseness and can lead to inconsistencies. Reducing redundancy in triples empirically minimizes errors, thereby improving consistency.

Directional Discrepancies Between Theory and Empirical Observations.

- **Timeliness and Accuracy**: While Zaveri et al. [45] hypothesized a negative correlation between timeliness and accuracy, empirical findings show a moderate and increasing positive correlation instead. The theoretical assumption was that ensuring accuracy, particularly in terms of semantic correctness and completeness, requires additional time, which could reduce timeliness. However, KGHeartBeat measures accuracy based on the syntactic correctness of triples. Automated validation during data production may explain why frequently updated datasets also exhibit high syntactic accuracy, leading to a positive correlation.

– **Interoperability and Consistency**: Zaveri et al. [45] suggested that interoperability and consistency might be positively correlated because enforcing interoperability often requires reusing existing vocabularies; improper or invalid reuse can introduce inconsistencies into the data. However, empirical results contradict this claim. In practice, a negative correlation between interoperability and consistency may arise in dynamic, multi-source environments where integrating diverse systems (to improve interoperability) introduces heterogeneity that undermines consistency. When data from different sources with varying standards, formats, or quality levels is combined to enable broader interoperability, maintaining a uniform and predictable structure across all inputs becomes more difficult. For example, systems that accommodate multiple protocols or ontologies often sacrifice internal consistency to remain flexible and inclusive. This trade-off reflects a tension between broad compatibility (interoperability) and internal uniformity (consistency), particularly when no dominant standard is enforced.

6 Conclusion

This study investigates empirical correlations among data quality dimensions within the Semantic Web, offering insights that both support and challenge prior theoretical assumptions. While expected relationships—such as the positive correlation between accuracy and consistency—were confirmed, other findings diverged. For instance, timeliness and accuracy, previously thought to be negatively correlated, showed a positive link, suggesting updated datasets tend to be more accurate. Conversely, a negative correlation between interoperability and consistency highlights potential trade-offs between these dimensions.

The study also reveals novel correlations, such as between interlinking and verifiability, and between amount of data and interpretability, challenging the assumption that larger datasets are inherently less understandable. A consistent positive link between consistency and timeliness likely reflects how outdated data can introduce contradictions within the dataset.

The wide range of empirically identified dimension correlations highlights the non-trivial interplay among quality dimensions, cautioning against treating them as isolated evaluation criteria. The findings imply that quality assessment frameworks can benefit from accounting for these correlations, potentially optimizing evaluation strategies by focusing on the most informative or interdependent dimensions. The work sets a precedent for empirical, statistically grounded approaches to understanding and utilizing data quality metrics in the Semantic Web. These findings have significant implications for dataset design and quality assessment, as they suggest that improvements in one dimension may directly impact others, making it possible to optimize data quality more efficiently.

Finally, these insights call for refinements to existing theoretical data quality models, suggesting that frameworks should account for the interdependencies among dimensions rather than treating them in isolation. By integrating empirical evidence into theoretical foundations, future models can provide a more accurate and actionable representation of data quality, supporting data-driven decision-making and fostering higher standards across the Semantic Web.

Limitations and Future Directions. This study focuses on pairwise correlations among data quality dimensions, offering useful but preliminary insights. A key limitation lies in the aggregation of metrics at the dimension level, which may mask strong correlations visible at finer granularity. For example, while conciseness and number of entities correlate strongly at the metric level (r = 0.88), their dimension-level correlation drops to 0.27. This suggests that important signals may be lost when collapsing metrics into broader categories, highlighting the need for more detailed analyses and the use of clustering or dimensionality reduction methods to better capture inter-metric relationships. Additionally, the study considers only objectively measurable metrics, excluding subjective or context-specific quality factors. Including such perspectives in future work could provide a more comprehensive view of data quality.

While this work does not focus on tool comparison, preliminary heatmaps generated using other tools (Luzzu, SPARQLES, Yummy) and included in the supplementary material show that correlation patterns can vary significantly depending on how metrics are implemented. For example, both SPARQLES and Luzzu identify a positive correlation between data volume and performance, yet only Luzzu reflects a link between interoperability and interpretability. This divergence points to the need for clearer metric definitions and more harmonized quality assessment frameworks. Future studies could build on the methodology proposed here to support systematic cross-tool evaluations and explore quality dynamics across different domains. Importantly, the methodology proposed in this study remains tool-independent, making it adaptable for reuse with different tools to ensure fair and robust comparisons.

While this paper focuses on pair-wise correlations, methods such as PCA and K-means clustering might offer further insights by uncovering latent structures across metrics. Preliminary analyses available in the supplementary material suggest promising directions for future exploration of higher-order groupings and their alignment with theoretical quality dimensions.

Acknowledgments. This publication is based upon work from COST Action CA23147 GOBLIN - Global Network on Large-Scale, Cross-domain and Multilingual Open Knowledge Graphs, supported by COST (European Cooperation in Science and Technology, https://www.cost.eu) and it was partially supported by the European Alliance NEOLAiA (Project 101124794: "NEOLAiA - Transforming Regions for an Inclusive Europe").

Supplementary Material. Results are available online [29] along with the code to reproduce them [28].

References

1. Amicis, F., Barone, D., Batini, C.: An analytical framework to analyze dependencies among data quality dimensions, pp. 369–383 (2006)

2. Assaf, A., Senart, A., Troncy, R.: Towards an objective assessment framework for linked data quality: enriching dataset profiles with quality indicators. In: Information Retrieval and Management: Concepts, Methodologies, Tools, and Applications, pp. 453–478. IGI Global (2018). https://doi.org/10.4018/978-1-5225-5191-1.ch021
3. Assaf, A., Troncy, R., Senart, A.: Roomba: an extensible framework to validate and build dataset profiles. In: Gandon, F., Guéret, C., Villata, S., Breslin, J., Faron-Zucker, C., Zimmermann, A. (eds.) ESWC 2015. LNCS, vol. 9341, pp. 325–339. Springer, Cham (2015). https://doi.org/10.1007/978-3-319-25639-9_46
4. Assaf, A., Troncy, R., Senart, A.: What's up LOD cloud? In: Gandon, F., Guéret, C., Villata, S., Breslin, J., Faron-Zucker, C., Zimmermann, A. (eds.) ESWC 2015. LNCS, vol. 9341, pp. 247–254. Springer, Cham (2015). https://doi.org/10.1007/978-3-319-25639-9_40
5. Avogadro, R., Cremaschi, M., Jiménez-Ruiz, E., Rula, A.: A framework for quality assessment of semantic annotations of tabular data. In: Hotho, A., et al. (eds.) ISWC 2021. LNCS, vol. 12922, pp. 528–545. Springer, Cham (2021). https://doi.org/10.1007/978-3-030-88361-4_31
6. Barone, D., Stella, F., Batini, C.: Dependency discovery in data quality. In: Pernici, B. (ed.) CAiSE 2010. LNCS, vol. 6051, pp. 53–67. Springer, Heidelberg (2010). https://doi.org/10.1007/978-3-642-13094-6_6
7. Batini, C., Cappiello, C., Francalanci, C., Maurino, A.: Methodologies for data quality assessment and improvement. ACM Comput. Surv. **41**(3) (2009). https://doi.org/10.1145/1541880.1541883
8. Batini, C., Scannapieco, M.: Data and Information Quality. DSA, Springer, Cham (2016). https://doi.org/10.1007/978-3-319-24106-7
9. di Buono, M.P., Gonçalo Oliveira, H., Barbu Mititelu, V., Spahiu, B., Nolano, G.: Paving the way for enriched metadata of linguistic linked data. Semantic Web **13**(6), 1133–1157 (2022). https://doi.org/10.3233/SW-222994
10. Cappiello, C., Ficiaro, P., Pernici, B.: HIQM: a methodology for information quality monitoring, measurement, and improvement. In: Roddick, J.F., et al. (eds.) ER 2006. LNCS, vol. 4231, pp. 339–351. Springer, Heidelberg (2006). https://doi.org/10.1007/11908883_41
11. Carlo, B., Daniele, B., Federico, C., Simone, G.: A data quality methodology for heterogeneous data. Int. J. Database Manage. Syst. **3**, 60–79 (2011). https://doi.org/10.5121/IJDMS.2011.3105
12. Chen, H., Cao, G., Chen, J., Ding, J.: A practical framework for evaluating the quality of knowledge graph. In: Zhu, X., Qin, B., Zhu, X., Liu, M., Qian, L. (eds.) CCKS 2019. CCIS, vol. 1134, pp. 111–122. Springer, Singapore (2019). https://doi.org/10.1007/978-981-15-1956-7_10
13. Cichy, C., Rass, S.: An overview of data quality frameworks. IEEE Access **7**, 24634–24648 (2019). https://doi.org/10.1109/ACCESS.2019.2899751
14. Debattista, J., Attard, J., Brennan, R., O'Sullivan, D.: Is the LOD cloud at risk of becoming a museum for datasets? Looking ahead towards a fully collaborative and sustainable LOD cloud. In: The World Wide Web Conference, pp. 850–858. ACM (2019). https://doi.org/10.1145/3308560.3317075
15. Debattista, J., Lange, C., Auer, S., Cortis, D.: Evaluating the quality of the LOD cloud: an empirical investigation. Semantic Web **9**(6), 859–901 (2018). https://doi.org/10.3233/SW-180306
16. Färber, M., Bartscherer, F., Menne, C., Rettinger, A.: Linked data quality of DBpedia, Freebase, OpenCyc, Wikidata, and YAGO. Semant. Web **9**(1), 77–129 (2018). https://doi.org/10.3233/SW-170275

17. Gabriele, T.: Navigating the LOD Subclouds: assessing linked open data quality by domain. In: Companion Proceedings of the Web Conference. ACM (2025). https://doi.org/10.1145/3701716.3717569
18. Haller, A., Fernández, J.D., Kamdar, M.R., Polleres, A.: What are links in linked open data? A characterization and evaluation of links between knowledge graphs on the web. J. Data Inform. Qual. (JDIQ) **12**(2), 1–34 (2020). https://doi.org/10.1145/3369875
19. Hassany, P., Sidi, F., Affendey, L., Jabar, M.A., Ibrahim, H., Mustapha, A.: Discovering dependencies among data quality dimensions: a validation of instrument. J. Appl. Sci. **13**, 95–102 (2013). https://doi.org/10.3923/jas.2013.95.102
20. Hidalgo-Delgado, Y., López, Y.A., Rodríguez, J.P.F., Mederos, A.L.: Quality assessment of library linked data: a case study. In: Villazón-Terrazas, B., Ortiz-Rodríguez, F., Tiwari, S., Goyal, A., Jabbar, M.A. (eds.) KGSWC 2021. CCIS, vol. 1459, pp. 93–108. Springer, Cham (2021). https://doi.org/10.1007/978-3-030-91305-2_8
21. Hogan, A., Umbrich, J., Harth, A., Cyganiak, R., Polleres, A., Decker, S.: An empirical survey of linked data conformance. J. Web Semant. **14**, 14–44 (2012). https://doi.org/10.1016/j.websem.2012.02.001
22. Käfer, T., Abdelrahman, A., Umbrich, J., O'Byrne, P., Hogan, A.: Observing linked data dynamics. In: Cimiano, P., Corcho, O., Presutti, V., Hollink, L., Rudolph, S. (eds.) ESWC 2013. LNCS, vol. 7882, pp. 213–227. Springer, Heidelberg (2013). https://doi.org/10.1007/978-3-642-38288-8_15
23. Kontokostas, D., et al.: Test-driven evaluation of linked data quality. In: Proceedings of the 23rd international conference on World Wide Web, pp. 747–758 (2014). https://doi.org/10.1145/2566486.2568002
24. Lee, Y.W., Strong, D.M., Kahn, B.K., Wang, R.Y.: AIMQ: a methodology for information quality assessment. Inform. Manage. **40**(2), 133–146 (2002). https://doi.org/10.1016/S0378-7206(02)00043-5
25. Monaco, D., Pellegrino, M.A., Scarano, V., Vicidomini, L.: Linked open data in authoring virtual exhibitions. J. Cult. Herit. **53**, 127–142 (2022). https://doi.org/10.1016/j.culher.2021.11.002
26. Neto, C.B., Kontokostas, D., Kirschenbaum, A., Publio, G.C., Esteves, D., Hellmann, S.: IDOL: comprehensive & complete LOD insights. In: Proceedings of the 13th International Conference on Semantic Systems, pp. 49–56 (2017). https://doi.org/10.1145/3132218.3132238
27. Pellegrino, M.A., Rula, A., Tuozzo, G.: KGHeartBeat: an open source tool for periodically evaluating the quality of knowledge graphs. In: International Semantic Web Conference, pp. 40–58. Springer (2024). https://doi.org/10.1007/978-3-031-77847-6_3
28. Pellegrino, M.A., Rula, A., Tuozzo, G.: Code to enable reproducibility (2025). https://doi.org/10.5281/zenodo.16420613, https://github.com/isislab-unisa/Are-Quality-Dimensions-Correlated
29. Pellegrino, M.A., Rula, A., Tuozzo, G.: Results as supplementary material (2025). https://isislab-unisa.github.io/Are-Quality-Dimensions-Correlated/
30. Pellegrino, M.A., Scarano, V., Spagnuolo, C.: Move cultural heritage knowledge graphs in everyone's pocket. Semant. Web **14**(2), 323–359 (2023). https://doi.org/10.3233/SW-223117
31. del Pilar Angeles, M., García-Ugalde, F.: A data quality practical approach. Int. J. Adv. Softw. **2**(3) (2009). https://personales.upv.es/thinkmind/dl/journals/soft/soft_v2_n23_2009/soft_v2_n23_2009_7.pdf

32. Pipino, L.L., Lee, Y.W., Wang, R.Y.: Data quality assessment. Commun. ACM **45**(4), 211–218 (2002). https://doi.org/10.1145/505248.506010
33. Redman, T.C.: Data Quality for the Information Age. Artech House on Demand (1997)
34. Scannapieco, M., Missier, P., Batini, C.: Data quality at a glance. Datenbank-Spektrum **14**, 6–14 (2005). https://pubs.dbs.uni-leipzig.de/dc/files/Scannapieco2005DataQualityata.pdf
35. Schmachtenberg, M., Bizer, C., Paulheim, H.: Adoption of the linked data best practices in different topical domains. In: Mika, P., et al. (eds.) ISWC 2014. LNCS, vol. 8796, pp. 245–260. Springer, Cham (2014). https://doi.org/10.1007/978-3-319-11964-9_16
36. Schober, P., Boer, C., Schwarte, L.A.: Correlation coefficients: appropriate use and interpretation. Anesth. Anal. **126**(5), 1763–1768 (2018). https://doi.org/10.1213/ANE.0000000000002864
37. Shapiro, S.S., Wilk, M.B.: An analysis of variance test for normality (complete samples). Biometrika **52**(3–4), 591–611 (1965)
38. Shenoy, K., Ilievski, F., Garijo, D., Schwabe, D., Szekely, P.: A study of the quality of wikidata. J. Web Semant. **72**, 100679 (2022). https://doi.org/10.1016/j.websem.2021.100679, https://www.sciencedirect.com/science/article/pii/S1570826821000536
39. Stvilia, B., Gasser, L., Twidale, M.B., Smith, L.C.: A framework for information quality assessment. J. Am. Soc. Inform. Sci. Technol. **58**(12), 1720–1733 (2007). https://doi.org/10.1002/asi.20652
40. Vandenbussche, P.Y., Umbrich, J., Matteis, L., Hogan, A., Buil-Aranda, C.: SPARQLES: Monitoring public SPARQL endpoints. Semant. web **8**(6), 1049–1065 (2017). https://doi.org/10.3233/SW-170254
41. Wang, R.Y., Strong, D.M.: Beyond accuracy: what data quality means to data consumers. J. Manage. Inf. Syst. **12**(4), 5–33 (1996). https://doi.org/10.1080/07421222.1996.11518099
42. Wang, X., et al.: Knowledge graph quality control: a survey. Fundam. Res. **1**(5), 607–626 (2021). https://doi.org/10.1016/j.fmre.2021.09.003
43. Xue, B., Zou, L.: Knowledge graph quality management: a comprehensive survey. IEEE Trans. Knowl. Data Eng. **35**(5), 4969–4988 (2023). https://doi.org/10.1109/TKDE.2022.3150080
44. Yamamoto, Y., Yamaguchi, A., Splendiani, A.: YummyData: providing high-quality open life science data. Database **2018** (2018). https://doi.org/10.1093/database/bay022
45. Zaveri, A., Rula, A., Maurino, A., Pietrobon, R., Lehmann, J., Auer, S.: Quality assessment for linked data: a survey. Semant. Web **7**(1), 63–93 (2016). https://doi.org/10.3233/SW-150175

SAT-Based Bounded Fitting for the Description Logic $\mathcal{ALC}$

Maurice Funk[1], Jean Christoph Jung[2], and Tom Voellmer[2](✉)

[1] Leipzig University and ScaDS.AI, Leipzig, Germany
mfunk@informatik.uni-leipzig.de
[2] TU Dortmund University, Dortmund, Germany
{jean.jung,tom.voellmer}@tu-dortmund.de

Abstract. Bounded fitting is a general paradigm for learning logical formulas from positive and negative data examples, that has received considerable interest recently. We investigate bounded fitting for the description logic $\mathcal{ALC}$ and its syntactic fragments. We show that the underlying size-restricted fitting problem is NP-complete for all studied fragments, even in the special case of a single positive and a single negative example. By design, bounded fitting comes with probabilistic guarantees in Valiant's PAC learning framework. In contrast, we show that other classes of algorithms for learning $\mathcal{ALC}$ concepts do not provide such guarantees. Finally, we present an implementation of bounded fitting in $\mathcal{ALC}$ and its fragments based on a SAT solver. We discuss optimizations and compare our implementation to other concept learning tools.

Keywords: Class Expression Learning · Description Logic · SAT solving

1 Introduction

Learning *class expressions* from given data examples is an important task when working with large knowledge bases [25,26]. For the purpose of this paper, an *example* is a pair $(\mathcal{I}, a)$ where $\mathcal{I}$ is a data instance, e.g., a database or a knowledge graph, and a is some element in the instance. Moreover, a class expression C *fits* a set P of *positive examples* and a set N of *negative examples* if $\mathcal{I} \models C(a)$ for all $(\mathcal{I}, a) \in P$ and $\mathcal{I} \not\models C(a)$ for all $(\mathcal{I}, a) \in N$. We mention three applications. First, the fitting class expression may be used as an *explanation* of the separation between good and bad scenarios, described by P and N, respectively. For example, P and N could be data describing users who visited (resp., did not visit) a certain web page, and a fitting C would explain the users' behavior based on their data. Second, under the classical *query-by-example* paradigm [28,40], a human user may *reverse-engineer* a class expression by manually selecting elements they want to have returned (P) or not returned (N), and a system produces an expression satisfying the demands. Here, the intended use of the

D. Garijo et al. (Eds.): ISWC 2025, LNCS 16140, pp. 42–60, 2026.
https://doi.org/10.1007/978-3-032-09527-5_3

Input: Positive examples P, negative examples N

for $k := 1, 2, \ldots$ **do**

  if *there is* $\varphi \in \mathcal{L}$ *of size* k *that fits* P, N **then**

    return φ

Algorithm 1: Bounded Fitting for abstract logic $\mathcal{L}$.

fitting class expression is as a query. Finally, an ontology engineer may seek a definition of some class A occurring in the data instance, so they may request a class expression C separating all elements P satisfying A from those that do not (N), and add $A \equiv C$ to the ontology.

In this paper, we study the problem of learning class expressions formulated in the description logic (DL) $\mathcal{ALC}$. $\mathcal{ALC}$ can be viewed as the conceptual basis of the very expressive description logic $\mathcal{SROIQ}(\mathcal{D})$ that underlies the web ontology language OWL 2 DL [1,17] in that $\mathcal{ALC}$ provides the central logical constructors that are also available in $\mathcal{SROIQ}(\mathcal{D})$. The importance of finding fitting class expressions / description logic concepts has resulted in both foundational work [13,14,27] and implemented systems. While most systems are based on heuristic search and refinement operators [6,16,18,34,37] or, more recently, also on neural techniques [12,23], we approach the problem via bounded fitting. *Bounded fitting* is a general paradigm for fitting logical formulas to positive and negative examples that has been investigated recently for a range of logics like linear temporal logic LTL [7,30], computational tree logic CTL [32], and the description logic $\mathcal{EL}$ [9]. Algorithm 1 provides an abstract description of bounded fitting for a given logic $\mathcal{L}$. It should be clear that, if any fitting formula exists, bounded fitting always returns a fitting formula of minimal size, which is often a desirable property. From a practical perspective, human users typically prefer shorter, that is, simpler formulas in the applications described above. For instance, when class expressions are used as explanations, a shorter class expression might provide a more transparent explanation. From a theoretical perspective, this property makes bounded fitting an *Occam algorithm*, which implies that it comes with probabilistic generalization guarantees in Valiant's probably approximately correct (PAC) learning framework [4,38]. Intuitively, this means that bounded fitting needs only few examples to be able to generalize to unseen examples. A further advantage of bounded fitting is that it is *complete*: whenever there is a fitting concept bounded fitting will find one.

The basic DL $\mathcal{ALC}$ provides the logical constructors conjunction $\sqcap$, disjunction $\sqcup$, negation $\neg$, existential restriction $\exists r$, and universal restriction $\forall r$ to build complex concepts. Motivated by the fact that, depending on the application, one may not need all concept constructors, fragments $\mathcal{L}(O)$ of $\mathcal{ALC}$ have been studied which allow only a subset $O \subseteq \{\sqcap, \sqcup, \neg, \exists, \forall\}$ of the available constructors. For instance, the mentioned DL $\mathcal{EL}$ is defined by $\{\sqcap, \exists\}$ and the DL $\mathcal{FL}_0$ is defined by $\{\sqcap, \forall\}$. Bounded fitting has been studied recently for $\mathcal{EL}$, and we extend this study here to all other syntactical fragments.

Our main contributions are as follows. First, we study the *size-restricted fitting problem*: given positive examples P, negative examples N, and a size bound k, determine whether there is a concept of size at most k that fits P and N. Clearly, this is precisely the problem to be solved in Line 2 of Algorithm 1. Our main result is that size-restricted fitting for $\mathcal{L}(O)$ is NP-complete for all O that include at least $\exists$ or $\forall$. While the NP upper bound is straightforward, the lower bound is more technical and rather strong. First, surprisingly, it already applies for inputs consisting of one positive and one negative example, and thus strengthens known hardness results for $\mathcal{EL}$ [10,11]. Second, it uses only a fixed set of symbols in contrast to related hardness results for temporal logics [5,29].

Then, motivated by the ability of bounded fitting to generalize well from few examples, we discuss the generalization abilities of fitting algorithms for languages $\mathcal{L}(O)$ in Valiant's PAC learning framework. We start with observing that under reasonable complexity theoretic assumptions, *no* $\mathcal{L}(O)$ admits an *efficient* PAC learning algorithm. We then analyze the generalization ability of fitting algorithms that have favorable properties from a logical perspective in that they return fitting formulas that are most specific, most general, or of minimal quantifier depth among all fitting formulas. We show that, with one exception, all such algorithms are not *sample-efficient*, and hence do not generalize well. Similar results have been obtained for $\mathcal{EL}$ concepts [9] and also for the related query language of conjunctive queries [8].

Finally, we provide an implementation of bounded fitting for $\mathcal{ALC}$ and its fragments, that relies on a SAT solver to solve size-restricted fitting in Line 2 of bounded fitting. We describe our implementation and present several improvements in the encoding which lead to significant speed-ups. We also present an *approximation scheme*, which is an adaptation of the basic bounded fitting algorithm depicted in Algorithm 1 to be able to provide approximate solutions in case no perfect fitting was found. We then compare our implementation to other concept learning tools from the literature, both in terms of achieved accuracy, size of the returned concepts, and generalization ability.

For detailed proofs, we refer the reader to the full version [15]

2 Preliminaries

We introduce syntax and semantics of the description logic $\mathcal{ALC}$ [3]. Let $\mathsf{N_C}$ and $\mathsf{N_R}$ be mutually disjoint and countably infinite sets of *concept names* and *role names*, respectively. An $\mathcal{ALC}$ *concept* C is defined according to the syntax rule

$$C, D ::= \bot \mid \top \mid A \mid \neg C \mid C \sqcap D \mid C \sqcup D \mid \forall r.C \mid \exists r.C$$

where A ranges over concept names and r over role names. For any set $O \subseteq \{\neg, \sqcap, \sqcup, \forall, \exists\} = O_{\text{all}}$, we define $\mathcal{L}(O)$ as the set of all $\mathcal{ALC}$ concepts built only from connectives and quantifiers from O. We associate with each such set O a *dual* set $\overline{O}$ that contains precisely the symbols dual to those in O where $\neg$ is dual to itself, $\sqcap$ is dual to $\sqcup$, and $\exists$ is dual to $\forall$. The size $\|C\|$ of an $\mathcal{ALC}$ concept C is defined as the number of nodes in its syntax tree, see below for an example. A *signature* Σ is a finite set of concept and role names. The signature *of an* $\mathcal{ALC}$ *concept* C is the set of concept and role names that occur in C.

The semantics of $\mathcal{ALC}$ concepts is given as usual in terms of interpretations. An *interpretation* is a pair $\mathcal{I} = (\Delta^\mathcal{I}, \cdot^\mathcal{I})$ where $\Delta^\mathcal{I}$ is a non-empty set of elements, called *domain*, and $\cdot^\mathcal{I}$ is an interpretation function that assigns a set $A^\mathcal{I} \subseteq \Delta^\mathcal{I}$ to every $A \in \mathsf{N_C}$ and a binary relation $r^\mathcal{I} \subseteq \Delta^\mathcal{I} \times \Delta^\mathcal{I}$ to every $r \in \mathsf{N_R}$. The *extension* $C^\mathcal{I}$ of complex $\mathcal{ALC}$ concepts C is defined inductively by taking $\bot^\mathcal{I} = \emptyset$, $\top^\mathcal{I} = \Delta^\mathcal{I}$, $(\neg C)^\mathcal{I} = \Delta^\mathcal{I} \setminus C^\mathcal{I}$, $(C \sqcap D)^\mathcal{I} = C^\mathcal{I} \cap D^\mathcal{I}$, $(C \sqcup D)^\mathcal{I} = C^\mathcal{I} \cup D^\mathcal{I}$, and

$$(\exists r.C)^\mathcal{I} = \{d \in \Delta^\mathcal{I} \mid \text{there is } (d,e) \in r^\mathcal{I} \text{ with } e \in C^\mathcal{I}\}$$

and $(\forall r.C)^\mathcal{I} = (\neg \exists r.\neg C)^\mathcal{I}$.

We call an interpretation $\mathcal{I}$ *finite*, if both $\Delta^\mathcal{I}$ and the set of all concept and role names that have a nonempty extension in $\mathcal{I}$ are finite. A finite interpretation $\mathcal{I}$ corresponds to a finite set of facts

$$\{A(a) \mid A \in \mathsf{N_C}, a \in A^\mathcal{I}\} \cup \{r(a,b) \mid r \in \mathsf{N_R}, (a,b) \in r^\mathcal{I}\},$$

and can hence be viewed as a database. Conversely, every database or finite set of facts corresponds to a finite interpretation. We define an example as a pair $(\mathcal{I}, a)$ consisting of a finite interpretation $\mathcal{I}$ and some domain element $a \in \Delta^\mathcal{I}$. Let P and N be sets of examples which we will refer to as *positive* and *negative* examples. We say that an $\mathcal{ALC}$ concept C fits P, N if $a \in C^\mathcal{I}$ for each $(\mathcal{I}, a) \in C$ and $b \notin C^\mathcal{J}$ for each $(\mathcal{J}, b) \in N$. In the special case of $P = \{(\mathcal{I}, a_0)\}$ and $N = \{(\mathcal{J}, b_0)\}$ we just write that C fits $(\mathcal{I}, a_0), (\mathcal{J}, b_0)$.

The *size* of such an example $(\mathcal{I}, a)$, denoted $\|(\mathcal{I}, a)\|$, is $n+1$ where n is the cardinality of $\mathcal{I}$, viewed as set of facts. As usual, we view interpretations as node and edge labeled graphs and use graph terminology to speak about them.

We investigate the following decision problem.

Problem: SIZE-RESTRICTEDFITTING FOR $\mathcal{L}$

Given: Sets P, N of examples, integer k
Question: Is there an $\mathcal{L}$ concept C that fits P, N and has size $\|C\| \leq k$?

We study size-restricted fitting for syntactic fragments $\mathcal{L}(O)$ of $\mathcal{ALC}$, assuming that k is given in unary, which is a natural choice in the context of bounded fitting. If we drop the size restriction k from the input, we obtain the *fitting problem for* $\mathcal{L}$.

Example 1. As an example for size-restricted fitting, consider the two positive examples $P = \{(\mathcal{I}, a_1), (\mathcal{I}, a_2)\}$ and one negative example $N = \{(\mathcal{J}, b)\}$ depicted in Fig. 1. Then $P, N, k = 4$ is a yes-instance of size-restricted fitting for $\mathcal{ALC}$ with witnessing fitting concept $C = \forall r.(A \sqcup B)$ with $\|\forall r.(A \sqcup B)\| = 4$, see the syntax tree depicted in the right of Fig. 1. Indeed, we have $a_1, a_2 \in C^\mathcal{I}$ but $b \notin C^\mathcal{J}$. It can also be verified, that it is the minimal k for which there exists a fitting concept, and that there is no fitting $\mathcal{L}(\{\exists, \sqcap\})$ concept at all, hence P, N is a no-instance for the fitting problem for $\mathcal{L}(\{\exists, \sqcap\})$. ⊣

To transfer results between dual fragments of $\mathcal{ALC}$, we rely on an auxiliary lemma that relates fitting in $\mathcal{L}(O)$ to fitting in $\mathcal{L}(\overline{O})$. To formulate the lemma,

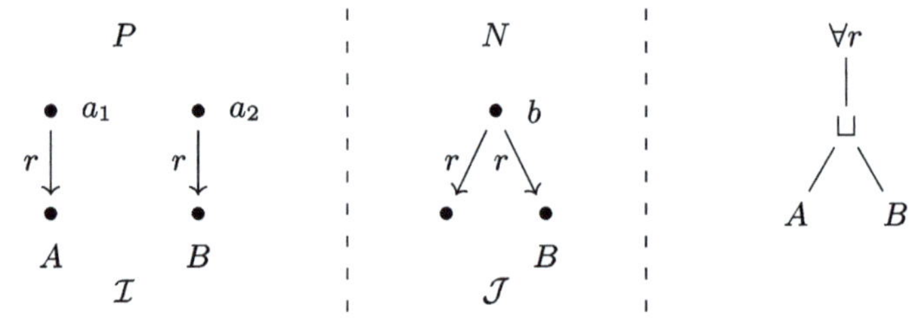

Fig. 1. Example for size-restricted fitting

we define a *duality* mapping $\overline{\cdot}$ for $\mathcal{ALC}$ concepts, interpretations and sets of examples. For an $\mathcal{ALC}$ concept C, the dual concept $\overline{C}$ is obtained from C by replacing $\top$ with $\bot$ and vice versa, replacing $\sqcap$ with $\sqcup$ and vice versa, and replacing $\exists$ with $\forall$ and vice versa. Moreover, for an interpretation $\mathcal{I}$ and a signature Σ, the interpretation $\overline{\mathcal{I}}_\Sigma$ is obtained by complementing the interpretation of the concept names in Σ, that is, $\Delta^{\overline{\mathcal{I}}_\Sigma} = \Delta^{\mathcal{I}}$,

$$A^{\overline{\mathcal{I}}_\Sigma} = \begin{cases} \Delta^{\mathcal{I}} \setminus A^{\mathcal{I}} & \text{if } A \in \mathsf{N_C} \cap \Sigma, \\ A^{\mathcal{I}} & \text{if } A \in \mathsf{N_C} \setminus \Sigma, \end{cases}$$

and keeping the interpretation of the role names, that is, $r^{\overline{\mathcal{I}}_\Sigma} = r^{\mathcal{I}}$, for all $r \in \mathsf{N_R}$. One can then show inductively that the following duality is satisfied for all signatures Σ, $\mathcal{ALC}$ concepts C with signature contained in Σ, interpretations $\mathcal{I}$, and $a \in \Delta^{\mathcal{I}}$:

$$a \in C^{\mathcal{I}} \quad \text{if and only if} \quad a \notin \overline{C}^{\overline{\mathcal{I}}_\Sigma}. \tag{1}$$

For a set of examples Ex and signature Σ, we define the set $\overline{Ex}_\Sigma = \{(\overline{\mathcal{I}}_\Sigma, a) \mid (\mathcal{I}, a) \in Ex\}$. Duality (1) is used to relate fitting in dual languages as follows:

Lemma 1. *For any signature Σ, all sets of examples P and N and $\mathcal{ALC}$ concepts C with signature contained in Σ, C fits P, N if and only if $\overline{C}$ fits $\overline{N}_\Sigma, \overline{P}_\Sigma$.*

Since for given sets of examples P, N there is a fitting $\mathcal{L}$ concept of size k if and only if there is a fitting $\mathcal{L}$ concept of size k which uses only concept and role names that occur in P, N, Lemma 1 implies the following:

Corollary 1. *For every $O \subseteq O_{all}$, there is a polynomial time reduction of size-restricted fitting for $\mathcal{L}(O)$ to size-restricted fitting for $\mathcal{L}(\overline{O})$.*

3 Complexity of Size-Restricted Fitting

We determine the complexity of size-restricted fitting as the decision problem underlying bounded fitting in all syntactic fragments $\mathcal{L}(O)$ where $O \subseteq O_{\text{all}}$ and $O \cap \{\forall, \exists\} \neq \emptyset$. Our main result states that the problem is NP-complete, for any such O. While the proof of the upper bound is straightforward, the NP-hardness proof is rather involved. Notably, it holds already for single positive and negative examples, which came as a surprise to us.

Theorem 1. *For every $O \subseteq O_{all}$ such that O contains at least one of $\exists$ and $\forall$, size-restricted fitting for $\mathcal{L}(O)$ is* NP*-complete.*

Containment in NP follows from a standard guess-and-check argument. Given P, N and k, the algorithm non-deterministically picks an $\mathcal{L}(O)$ concept C of size at most k and verifies (in polynomial time) that $a \in C^{\mathcal{I}}$ for all $(\mathcal{I}, a) \in P$ and $b \notin C^{\mathcal{J}}$ for all $(\mathcal{J}, b) \in N$. Showing hardness is more involved and proceeds in two steps. First, with the following proposition, we show NP-hardness for any O with $\exists \in O$. Then, Corollary 1 implies NP-hardness for any O with $\forall \in O$.

Proposition 1. *Size-restricted fitting for $\mathcal{L}(O)$ is* NP*-hard for any $O \subseteq O_{all}$ with $\exists \in O$. This already holds if only a single positive and a single negative example are allowed, and over a signature consisting of two role names and one concept name.*

Proof. We give a reduction of *Hitting Set* which is the problem to decide, given a collection of sets $S = \{S_1, \ldots, S_m\}$ and a size bound $k \in \mathbb{N}$, whether there exists a set H such that $|H| \leq k$ and $H \cap S_j \neq \emptyset$, for each $j \in \{1, \ldots, m\}$. The set H is called a hitting set for S.

Let (S, k) be an instance of *Hitting Set* with $S = \{S_1, \ldots, S_m\}$ a collection of sets $S_i \subseteq \mathbb{N}$ and $k \in \mathbb{N}$. Assume without loss of generality that $\bigcup_{j=1}^{m} S_j = \{1, \ldots, n\}$ for some $n \in \mathbb{N}$. We construct a positive example $(\mathcal{I}, a)$ and a negative example $(\mathcal{J}, b)$ in which we interpret only two role names r, s and a concept name A non-empty, and such that, for $P = \{(\mathcal{I}, a)\}$, $N = \{(\mathcal{J}, b)\}$, and $k' = k+n+2$,

$$S \text{ has hitting set of size } k \quad \Leftrightarrow \quad P, N \text{ admit an } \mathcal{L}(O) \text{ fitting of size } k'. \qquad (2)$$

We provide an informal description of $\mathcal{I}, \mathcal{J}$; more details can be found in the full version. The main components of both $\mathcal{I}$ and $\mathcal{J}$ are r-paths of length n, which end in an element satisfying A. To encode a subset $S' \subseteq \{1, \ldots, n\}$, such a path is extended with additional "detours" along role s. In more detail, suppose such a path consists of elements $b_0, \ldots, b_n$. We encode a subset $S' \subseteq \{1, \ldots, n\}$ as follows:

- For all $i \in \{1, \ldots, n\} \setminus S'$, there is an s-path of length 2 from b_i to b_{i+1}.
- For every b_i and role $t \in \{r, s\}$: if b_i does not have a t-successor, then make c a t-successor of b_i where c is a *sink*, which has both an r and an s self loop.

Now, $\mathcal{J}$ consists of one path for each $S_j \in S$ and an additional root node b which connects via r to the initial nodes of all the paths. The interpretation $\mathcal{I}$ is an extension of $\mathcal{J}$ with an additional component that encodes the empty set, and has root node a which connects via r to the initial nodes of all paths. Figure 2 depicts the constructed interpretations for the instance $(S, 2)$ for $S = \{\{1, 3\}, \{2, 4\}\}$. We omit the sink element c in the figure for the sake of readability. For this input, $H = \{1, 2\}$ is a hitting set of size 2.

We verify Equivalence (2) by showing that the following are equivalent:

(i) S has a hitting set of size at most k;

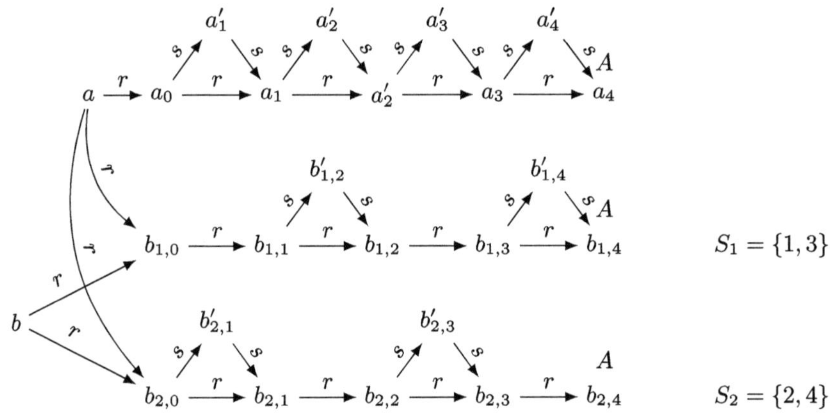

Fig. 2. Example of the interpretations $\mathcal{I}$ and $\mathcal{J}$ used in the reduction.

(ii) there is an $\mathcal{L}(\{\exists\})$ concept fitting P, N of size at most k';
(iii) there is an $\mathcal{ALC}$ concept fitting P, N of size at most k'.

We start with (i)⇒(ii). Let H be a hitting set for $S = \{S_1, \ldots, S_m\}$ with $|H| = k$. We inductively define concepts C_i, for $i = 0, \ldots, n$, by setting $C_0 = A$ and

$$C_i = \begin{cases} \exists r.C_{i-1} & \text{if } n - i + 1 \notin H \\ \exists s.\exists s.C_{i-1} & \text{otherwise,} \end{cases} \tag{3}$$

for $1 \leq i \leq n$. Thus, $\|C_n\| = n+|H|+1$ and therefore $\|\exists r.C_n\| = n+k+2 = k'$. We claim that $D = \exists r.C_n$ fits P, N. In the example in Fig. 2, the concept constructed for the hitting set $H = \{1, 2\}$ is $D = \exists r.\exists s.\exists s.\exists s.\exists s.\exists r.\exists r.A$, and it is easily verified that it fits. In general, any concept that can be obtained this way fits the positive example $(\mathcal{I}, a)$. Moreover, a concept D constructed from a hitting set H fits the negative example $(\mathcal{J}, b)$ since the construction forces the path described by D to "leave" the paths encoding the sets S_j in $(\mathcal{J}, b)$. This means that D cannot be satisfied in b, since the sink c does not satisfy A.

The direction (ii)⇒(iii) is immediate. For (iii)⇒(i), we take advantage of the structure of $(\mathcal{I}, a)$ and $(\mathcal{J}, b)$ to show that it is without loss of generality to assume that the smallest fitting is from $\mathcal{L}(\{\exists\})$ and has the shape from Equation (3). The main properties we exploit are that, except at the roots a, b, r, s are interpreted as total functions (to replace $\forall r/s$ by $\exists r/s$) and that there are single positive and negative examples (to remove disjunction and conjunction, respectively). □

4 Generalization

In this section, we investigate the generalization ability of fitting algorithms with certain properties using the well-known PAC learning framework [38], see also [2] for an introduction. Here, with a *fitting algorithm for* $\mathcal{L}$, we mean an algorithm $\mathcal{A}$ that receives as input P, N and returns an $\mathcal{L}$ concept C that fits P, N if such a concept exists. To define PAC learning, we need some additional notation.

A *probability distribution over examples* is a function $\mathbb{P}$ that maps examples $(\mathcal{I}, a)$ to a non-negative value $\mathbb{P}(\mathcal{I}, a)$ in a way such that $\sum_{(\mathcal{I},a)} \mathbb{P}(\mathcal{I}, a) = 1$. A *signature* is a finite set Σ of concept and role names. We say that $\mathbb{P}$ is *over* Σ if in examples $(\mathcal{I}, a)$ with $\mathbb{P}(\mathcal{I}, a) > 0$, the $\mathcal{I}$ contains only facts $A(a)$ and $r(a, b)$ with $A \in \Sigma$ and $r \in \Sigma$, respectively. A *sample* of $\mathbb{P}$ is a set Ex of examples drawn according to $\mathbb{P}$. *Labeling* Ex *according to a (target) concept* C_T means to split Ex into P, N by taking $P = \{(\mathcal{I}, a) \in Ex \mid a \in C_T^{\mathcal{I}}\}$ and $N = Ex \setminus P$. The *error* of a (hypothesis) concept C_H compared to C_T is defined as the probability that C_H and C_T label a random example differently, that is:

$$\text{error}_{\mathbb{P}}(C_T, C_H) = \mathbb{P}(\{(\mathcal{I}, a) \mid a \in C_T^{\mathcal{I}} \mathbin{\Delta} C_H^{\mathcal{I}}\})$$

where Δ denotes symmetric difference.

Definition 1. *Let* $O \subseteq O_{all}$. *A fitting algorithm* $\mathcal{A}$ *for* $\mathcal{L}(O)$ *is a PAC learning algorithm if there is a function* $m\colon \mathbb{R}^2 \times \mathbb{N}^3 \rightarrow \mathbb{N}$, *such that for all* $\varepsilon, \delta \in (0, 1)$, *all signatures* Σ, *all* $s, n \in \mathbb{N}$, *all probability distributions* $\mathbb{P}$ *over examples* $(\mathcal{I}, a)$ *over* Σ *with* $||(\mathcal{I}, a)|| \leq s$, *and all target concepts* $C_T \in \mathcal{L}(O)$ *over* Σ *with* $||C_T|| \leq n$, *algorithm* $\mathcal{A}$ *has the following property. If* $\mathcal{A}$ *receives* $m(\frac{1}{\delta}, \frac{1}{\varepsilon}, |\Sigma|, s, n)$ *examples* P, N *sampled from* $\mathbb{P}$ *and labeled according to* C_T, *it returns with high probability at least* $1 - \delta$ *a concept* $C_H \in \mathcal{L}(O)$ *with small* $\text{error}_{\mathbb{P}}(C_T, C_H) \leq \varepsilon$.

A PAC learning algorithm is said to be sample-efficient *if* m *is a polynomial, and* efficient *if it is sample-efficient and runs in polynomial time.*

Unfortunately, efficient PAC learnability is known to be elusive, and we confirm this to be the case here as well, under reasonable assumptions.

Theorem 2. *Let* $O \subseteq O_{all}$. *If there is an efficient PAC learning algorithm for* $\mathcal{L}(O)$, *then:*

1. NP = RP, *if* O *contains at least one of* $\exists/\forall$ *and* $\{\sqcap, \sqcup\} \not\subseteq O$;
2. *RSA encryption is polynomial time invertible, if* $\{\sqcap, \sqcup\} \subseteq O$.

Recall that RP is the class of problems for which probabilistic polynomial-time Turing machines exist that reject no-instances, and accept yes instances with probability $\frac{1}{2}$. Both NP = RP and polynomial time RSA decryption (without private key) are considered unlikely. Point 1 was known for $\mathcal{EL} = \mathcal{L}(\{\exists, \sqcap\})$ [11,22] and we show it to be the case for all other mentioned fragments. The proof relies on a well-known result due to Pitt and Valiant which roughly states that efficient PAC learnability implies (under suitable conditions) that the corresponding (not size restricted) fitting problem is in RP [31]. To show Theorem 2, we thus consider the relevant fitting problems. In the full version, we show that the fitting problem for $\mathcal{L}(\{\forall\})$, $\mathcal{L}(\{\forall, \sqcap\})$, and $\mathcal{L}(\{\forall, \exists, \sqcap\})$ is NP-hard via reduction from SAT. Applying Lemma 1 then yields the same lower bounds for all other fragments from Point 1. The same strategy fails for O as in

Point 2 as the fitting problem for such O is solvable in polynomial time. Instead, we observe that $\mathcal{L}(O)$ contains all monotone Boolean formulas and exploit that these are not efficiently PAC learnable under cryptographic assumptions [21].

Given these negative results on *efficient* PAC learning, we will analyze concrete fitting algorithms regarding their sample-efficiency. More precisely, we study algorithms that behave well from a logical perspective in that they return fitting concepts that are most specific, most general, or of minimal quantifier depth among all fitting concepts. We denote with $C \sqsubseteq D$ the fact that $C^{\mathcal{I}} \subseteq D^{\mathcal{I}}$, for all interpretations $\mathcal{I}$, and let $C \equiv D$ abbreviate $C \sqsubseteq D$ and $D \sqsubseteq C$. Recall that a concept C is a *most specific fitting* for P, N if it fits P, N and there is no concept D with $D \sqsubseteq C$ and $D \not\equiv C$ that fits. Dually, a concept C is a *most general fitting* concept for P, N if it fits P, N and there exists no D with $C \sqsubseteq D$ and $C \not\equiv D$ that fits as well. Finally, the *quantifier depth* of a concept is the nesting depth of $\exists/\forall$. Unfortunately, in most cases, logically well-behaved algorithms are not sample-efficient. The following theorem summarizes the situation.

Theorem 3. *Let $O \subseteq O_{all}$ be any set containing at least one of $\exists/\forall$ and at least one of $\sqcap/\sqcup$, and let $\mathcal{A}$ be a fitting algorithm for $\mathcal{L}(O)$. Then $\mathcal{A}$ is not a sample-efficient PAC learning algorithm, if:*

1. *$O \neq \{\exists, \sqcup\}$ and $\mathcal{A}$ always returns a most specific fitting if one exists;*
2. *$O \neq \{\forall, \sqcap\}$ and $\mathcal{A}$ always returns a most general fitting if one exists;*
3. *$\mathcal{A}$ always returns a fitting of minimal quantifier depth if some fitting exists.*

It is interesting to note that Lemma 1 plays a central role here as well. Indeed, the dualization operation preserves quantifier depth and turns most specific fittings into most general ones, and vice versa. This means that it suffices to show only one of Point 1 or Point 2; the other one follows by dualization. Theorem 3 was known for $\mathcal{L}(\{\sqcap, \exists\}) = \mathcal{EL}$ [9]. We begin with Point 3 and note that it suffices to show Lemma 2 below and then apply Lemma 1.

Lemma 2. *For any O with $\{\exists, \sqcup\} \subseteq O \subseteq O_{all}$, any fitting algorithm for $\mathcal{L}(O)$ that always returns a fitting of minimal quantifier depth if some fitting exists is not a sample-efficient PAC learning algorithm.*

Proof. Assume there is a sample-efficient PAC learning algorithm $\mathcal{A}$ with associated polynomial m that always returns a fitting $\mathcal{L}(O)$ concept of minimal quantifier depth, if some fitting exists. We choose $\varepsilon = 0.4$, $\delta = 0.5$, $\Sigma = \{r, s, t\}$, and a target concept $C_T = \exists t^{n+1}.\top$, for some n to be determined later. We consider the following interpretations $\mathcal{I}_w, \mathcal{J}_w$, for $w \in \{r, s\}^n$:

- for each $w \in \{r, s\}^n$, $\mathcal{I}_w$ is a path of length n whose edges are labeled according to w and whose start element is called a_w;
- for each $w \in \{r, s\}^n$, $\mathcal{J}_w$ is obtained from $\mathcal{I}_w$ by adding a t-path of length $n + 1$ starting from a_w.

Clearly, each $(\mathcal{J}_w, a_w)$ is a positive example, while each $(\mathcal{I}_w, a_w)$ is a negative example. Let $\mathbb{P}$ be the probability distribution that assigns $\frac{1}{2^{n+1}}$ to each of the

2^{n+1} examples $(\mathcal{I}_w, a_w), (\mathcal{J}_w, a_w)$, and 0 to all others. We choose n large enough so that the probability that a sample of size $m(\frac{1}{\delta}, \frac{1}{\varepsilon}, 3, 2n+1, n+2)$ does not contain both $(\mathcal{I}_w, a_w)$ and $(\mathcal{J}_w, a_w)$ for some $w \in \{r,s\}^n$ is at least $1-\delta$.

Let P, N be a sample of size $m(\frac{1}{\delta}, \frac{1}{\varepsilon}, 3, 2n+1, n+2)$ and suppose that it satisfies the mentioned property: for each $w \in \{r,s\}^n$, not both $(\mathcal{I}_w, a_w) \in N$ and $(\mathcal{J}_w, a_w) \in P$. Consider the $\mathcal{L}(\{\exists, \sqcup\})$ concept

$$C_0 = \bigsqcup_{(\mathcal{I}_w, a_w) \in P} C_w$$

where C_w is the concept $\exists t_1 \ldots \exists t_n.\top$ if $w = t_1 \ldots t_n$. Clearly, C_0 has quantifier depth n and fits P, N. Hence, if $\mathcal{A}$ runs on P, N, it returns a fitting $\mathcal{L}(O)$ concept C quantifier depth at most n. However, such C cannot distinguish $(\mathcal{I}_w, a_w)$ and $(\mathcal{J}_w, a_w)$, for any $w \in \{r,s\}^n$, hence $\text{error}_{\mathbb{P}}(C_T, C) = 0.5 > \varepsilon$. □

We now turn our attention to Points 1 and 2 of Theorem 3. Inspecting the proof of Point 1 for $\mathcal{EL}$ from [10, Theorem 6] reveals that it actually implies Point 1 for each fragment of $\mathcal{ALC}$ that contains $\mathcal{EL}$. Hence, it suffices to show Point 2 for $\{\exists, \sqcup\}$, $\{\exists, \sqcup, \sqcap\}$, and $\{\exists, \forall, \sqcap\}$ (note that adding negation to any of these sets leads to full $\mathcal{ALC}$). We show the first here and the latter two in the full version. Both are by non-trivial extensions of the proof for the same fact for $\mathcal{EL}$.

Lemma 3. *Any fitting algorithm for $\mathcal{L}(\{\exists, \sqcup\})$ that always returns a most general fitting concept if one exists is not sample-efficient.*

Proof. Assume towards a contradiction that there is a fitting algorithm $\mathcal{A}$ for $\mathcal{L}(\{\exists, \sqcup\})$ that always returns a most general fitting $\mathcal{L}(\{\exists, \sqcup\})$ concept and which moreover is sample-efficient with associated polynomial m. We choose $\varepsilon = \frac{1}{7}, \delta = \frac{8}{9}$, $\Sigma = \{r, s, A\}$, $C_T = A$, and n large enough such that $2^{n-1} > m(\frac{1}{\varepsilon}, \frac{1}{\delta}, 3, 2n, 1)$. We use the following interpretations $\mathcal{I}, \mathcal{J}$ and $\mathcal{I}_w$ for $w \in \{r,s\}^n$:

- $\mathcal{I}$ consists of elements $a_1, \ldots, a_n$ satisfying $a_1 \in A^{\mathcal{I}}$, $a_n \in A^{\mathcal{I}}$, and $(a_i, a_{i+1}) \in r^{\mathcal{I}}$ and $(a_i, a_{i+1}) \in s^{\mathcal{I}}$, for all $i < n$.
- $\mathcal{J}$ consists of elements $b_1, \ldots, b_n, b_{n+1}$ satisfying $b_i \in A^{\mathcal{J}}$ for all $i \in \{2, \ldots, n-1, n+1\}$ and $(b_i, b_{i+1}) \in r^{\mathcal{I}}$, $(b_i, b_{i+1}) \in s^{\mathcal{I}}$, for all $i \leq n$, and $(b_{n+1}, b_{n+1}) \in r^{\mathcal{J}}$ and $(b_{n+1}, b_{n+1}) \in s^{\mathcal{J}}$.
- For $w \in \{r,s\}^n$, $\mathcal{I}_w$ is a path of length n whose edges are labeled according to w, whose end satisfies A, and whose start element is denoted a_w.

Let $\mathbb{P}$ be the probability distribution that assigns $\mathbb{P}(\mathcal{I}, a_1) = \mathbb{P}(\mathcal{J}, b_1) = \frac{1}{3}$, $\mathbb{P}(\mathcal{I}_w, a_w) = \frac{1}{3 \cdot 2^n}$ for $w \in \{r,s\}^n$ and probability 0 to all other examples. Note that $(\mathcal{I}, a_1)$ is a positive example, and $(\mathcal{J}, b_1)$ and all $(\mathcal{I}_w, a_w)$ are negative examples for C_T.

Let P, N be a sample of size $m(\frac{1}{\varepsilon}, \frac{1}{\delta}, 3, 2n, 1)$ drawn according to $\mathbb{P}$. Then with probability at least $1-\delta$, both $(\mathcal{I}, a_1) \in P$ and $(\mathcal{J}, b_1) \in N$. We argue in the full version that $C_0 = A \sqcup \bigsqcup_{(\mathcal{I}_w, a_w) \notin N} C_w$ is the unique most general

$\mathcal{L}(\{\exists, \sqcup\})$ concept fitting P, N, where C_w is $\exists t_1 \ldots . \exists t_n.A$ in case $w = t_1 \cdots t_n$. Thus, $\mathcal{A}$ returns (a concept equivalent to) C_0 when run on P, N. However, all negative examples $(\mathcal{I}_w, a_w) \notin N$ are labeled incorrectly by C_0. The choice of n implies that there are at least 2^{n-1} such examples; thus the error is at least $\frac{1}{6} > \varepsilon$. □

It remains to discuss the exceptions mentioned in Points 1 and 2 of Theorem 3. Interestingly, bounded fitting is a counter-example for these cases:

Lemma 4. *Bounded fitting for $\mathcal{L}(\{\exists, \sqcup\})$ (resp., $\mathcal{L}(\{\forall, \sqcap\})$ returns a most specific $\mathcal{L}(\{\exists, \sqcup\})$ (resp. most general $\mathcal{L}(\{\forall, \sqcap\})$) concept, if any fitting exists.*

5 SAT-Based Bounded Fitting

Motivated by the NP-completeness of size-restricted fitting established in Theorem 1, we implemented bounded fitting for any logic $\mathcal{L}(O)$ for $O \subseteq O_{\text{all}}$ using a SAT solver to efficiently search for fitting $\mathcal{L}(O)$ concepts of a given size. In this section, we first give an overview of the reduction to SAT and describe two optimizations that improve the performance of the basic reduction. Then, we propose a variant of bounded fitting tailored towards approximate fitting. Finally, we compare our implementation with other concept learning implementations.

We describe the reduction for $\mathcal{ALC}$. Let P, N be sets of examples and $k \geq 1$. We aim to produce a propositional formula φ that is satisfiable if and only if there is an $\mathcal{ALC}$ concept C that fits P, N with $\|C\| \leq k$. We assume w.l.o.g. that all examples in P and N share a single (finite) interpretation $\mathcal{I}$. Let Σ_C and Σ_R be the set of concept and role names, respectively, that occur in $\mathcal{I}$.

The formula φ is the conjunction of two formulas $\varphi_1 \wedge \varphi_2$ whose purpose is to encode syntax trees of $\mathcal{ALC}$ concepts and to evaluate the encoded concepts over $\mathcal{I}$, respectively. For this task, φ_1 uses variables $x_{i,v}$, $y_{1,i,j}$, and $y_{2,i,j}$ for $i, j \in \{1, \ldots, k\}$ and v a node label from $\mathcal{V} = \{\top, \bot, \neg, \sqcap, \sqcup\} \cup \Sigma_\mathsf{C} \cup \{\exists r, \forall r \mid r \in \Sigma_\mathsf{R}\}$ with the following intended meaning:

- $x_{i,v}$ is true if and only if node i of the syntax tree is labeled with v,
- $y_{1,i,j}$ is true if and only if node i has the single successor j, and
- $y_{2,i,j}$ is true if and only if node i has the two successors j and $j+1$.

We treat node 1 as the root of the syntax tree. The clauses in φ_1 enforce that a satisfying assignment to these variables represents a well-formed syntax tree of an $\mathcal{ALC}$ concept. For example, to ensure that nodes that are labeled by a concept name do not have successors and that nodes labeled with $\sqcap$ have two successors, respectively, the clauses

$$x_{i,A} \rightarrow (\neg y_{1,i,j} \wedge \neg y_{2,i,j}) \qquad \text{and} \qquad x_{i,\sqcap} \rightarrow \bigvee\nolimits_{i<\ell<k} v_{2,i,\ell}$$

are included in φ_1 for each $i, j \in \{1, \ldots, k\}$ with $i < j$ and $A \in \Sigma_\mathsf{C}$. Similar clauses encode the rules for nodes labeled with other labels from $\mathcal{V}$. In case we are interested in a fragment $\mathcal{L}(O)$ of $\mathcal{ALC}$, we restrict $\mathcal{V}$ accordingly.

To evaluate the encoded $\mathcal{ALC}$ concept, φ_2 uses variables $z_{i,a}$ for $i \in \{1, \ldots k\}$, $a \in \Delta^{\mathcal{I}}$ with the intended meaning that $z_{i,a}$ is true if and only if $a \in C^{\mathcal{I}}$ where C is the concept represented by node i in the syntax tree. For example, to encode the semantics of concept names and of conjunction $\sqcap$, φ_2 contains the clauses

$$x_{i,A} \rightarrow z_{i,b}, \quad x_{i,A} \rightarrow \neg z_{i,c}, \quad x_{i,\sqcap} \wedge y_{2,i,j} \rightarrow (z_{i,a} \leftrightarrow (z_{j,a} \wedge z_{j+1,a})) \tag{4}$$

for all $i, j \in \{1, \ldots, k\}$, $A \in \Sigma_{\mathsf{C}}$, $b \in A^{\mathcal{I}}$, $c \in \Delta^{\mathcal{I}} \setminus A^{\mathcal{I}}$, and $a \in \Delta^{\mathcal{I}}$.

Finally, the fitting condition is enforced by the following formula:

$$\bigwedge\nolimits_{(\mathcal{I},a) \in P} z_{1,a} \wedge \bigwedge\nolimits_{(\mathcal{I},b) \in N} \neg z_{1,b} \tag{5}$$

Given the provided intuitions, it should be clear that we can read off a witness concept from a satisfying assignment of φ. Overall, the constructed formula φ uses $O(k^2 + k|\Sigma| + kn)$ variables, $O(nk^3|\Sigma|)$ clauses, and is of total size $O(nk^3|\Sigma|)$ where $\Sigma = \Sigma_{\mathsf{C}} \cup \Sigma_{\mathsf{R}}$ and $n = ||\mathcal{I}||$.

5.1 Optimizations

We discuss two optimizations that we implemented on top of the basic reduction described above. Similar optimizations have been implemented in [9, 33].

Taking Advantage of Types. The encoding of the semantics of concept names given in (4) produces $k \times |\Delta^{\mathcal{I}}| \times |\Sigma_{\mathsf{C}}|$ clauses. In realistic data sets, both $|\Delta^{\mathcal{I}}|$ and $|\Sigma_{\mathsf{C}}|$ tend to be large. For example, in the Carcinogenesis data set of the SML-Benchmark [39], there are 19 221 individuals and 133 concept names, resulting in more than 10 million clauses for $k = 4$, which is the majority of clauses in the encoding. To reduce the number of clauses, one can exploit that not all combinations of concept names actually occur in realistic data sets. In *carcinogenesis*, only 105 different combinations occur. This allows us to encode the semantics with fewer clauses, at the cost of introducing additional variables.

The *type* $\mathsf{type}(a)$ of an individual a in an interpretation $\mathcal{I}$ is the set $\{A \in \Sigma_{\mathsf{C}} \mid a \in A^{\mathcal{I}}\}$. Let T be the set of all types that occur in $\mathcal{I}$, that is, $T = \{\mathsf{type}(a) \mid a \in \Delta^{\mathcal{I}}\}$. For each $i \in \{1, \ldots, k\}$ and $t \in T$, we introduce an additional variable $x_{i,t}$ with the intended meaning that $x_{i,t}$ is true if and only if node i is labeled with a concept name that is contained in t. We ensure this with the clauses

$$x_{i,A} \rightarrow x_{i,t} \quad \text{and} \quad x_{i,B} \rightarrow \neg x_{i,t}$$

for each $t \in T$, $i \in \{1, \ldots, k\}$, $A \in t$ and $B \in \Sigma_{\mathsf{C}} \setminus t$. We then replace the clauses that enforce the semantics of concept names with

$$x_{i,\mathsf{type}(a)} \rightarrow z_{i,a} \quad \text{and} \quad \neg x_{i,\mathsf{type}(a)} \rightarrow \neg z_{i,a} \vee \neg \ell_i$$

for all $i \in \{1, \ldots, k\}$ and $a \in \Delta^{\mathcal{I}}$, where ℓ_i are additional variables that are true if and only if node i is labeled with a concept name. In the carcinogenesis dataset, the modified encoding produces only $4 \cdot 105 \cdot 133 + 4 \cdot 19\,221 \cdot 2 = 209\,628$ clauses.

Syntax Tree Templates. A major problem is that different models of φ_1 can represent (syntax trees of) equivalent concepts. For example, already the arguably simple concept $\exists r.A \sqcap \forall s.B$ is encoded in four different models. This phenomenon is well-known also from other domains and is called *symmetry* in the search space [35]. The problem it brings is that the SAT solver often does significant redundant work by trying symmetric solutions, which slows down the solving process, especially for unsatisfiable formulas. A solution is to *break* symmetries by introducing additional clauses to the encoding that restrict how the nodes of a syntax tree may be ordered. Similar symmetries have been observed in other SAT-based implementations of bounded fitting [9,32].

By the *topology* of the syntax tree of an $\mathcal{ALC}$ concept, we mean the binary tree that results from removing all node labels. It is clear that isomorphic topologies can represent the same set of concepts (up to commutativity of $\sqcap/\sqcup$). We thus extend φ by clauses that enforce, for each topology isomorphism equivalence class, a canonical ordering of the nodes in the syntax tree. This is achieved by enumerating all binary trees with k nodes, and through a long disjunction, demanding that the encoded syntax tree must have one of these topologies. A similar approach has been taken in [33], but instead of including the large disjunction in the encoding, there is one call of the SAT solver per topology.

Note that the number of binary trees with k nodes grows exponentially with k. To prevent a negative impact on runtime, we limit this process to topologies with at most 10 nodes, after which the topologies are only considered as *prefixes* of the topology of the encoded syntax tree. The used threshold of 10 was determined empirically; higher values resulted in a slowdown on the benchmarks.

It is worth noting that these clauses do not break all symmetries, especially many related to commutativity remain. Essentially, there will always be a trade-off between the number of clauses needed to break symmetries and the gain in avoiding symmetric solutions. In the extreme case, breaking *all* symmetries will require many clauses and thus likely not result in performance improvements. In our experience, adding some extra clauses avoiding certain syntactical patterns proved beneficial, e.g., $\top$ or $\bot$ directly below $\sqcap$ or $\sqcup$, $\neg$ directly below $\neg$, $\exists$, $\forall$, and two $\sqcap$-successors below a $\sqcap$-node, and the same for $\sqcup$.

5.2 Approximation Scheme

In practice, there may not always be a concept that perfectly fits the provided examples. In such cases, it is more realistic to view the fitting problem as an optimization problem. We address this by changing the basic bounded fitting algorithm from Algorithm 1 into the approximation scheme described in Algorithm 2. There, an extra variable m stores the best coverage of examples achieved so far. If an exact fitting concept is found (Lines 4/5), the algorithm returns it. Otherwise, m is increased (Line 7). If for the current size-bound k, m cannot be improved (test in Line 3), the algorithm moves on to the next k. Note that this approximation scheme is an *anytime algorithm* in the sense that, if it is interrupted at some point, it may return the best solution found up to this point.

Input: Positive examples P, negative examples N

$m \leftarrow 1$;
for $k := 1, 2, \ldots$ **do**
    while *there is* $\varphi \in \mathcal{L}$ *of size* k *that fits* m *examples from* P, N **do**
        if $m = |P| + |N|$ **then** // all examples covered?
            return φ
        else // try to cover more examples
            increase m;

Algorithm 2: Approximation version of Bounded Fitting.

This change in the algorithm is reflected in the interface to the SAT solver as follows. We replace clauses (5), that demand exact fitting, with *cardinality constraints*, that demand that at least m of the literals in (5) be true. We exploit the ability to solve *incrementally* provided by some SAT solvers, since the increase of m can be realized by adding clauses. However, whenever k increases, we have to produce a new propositional formula as before.

5.3 Evaluation

Our implementation uses the PySat library [19,20] to decide satisfiability of φ with the Glucose SAT solver and, if satisfiable, read off a fitting concept from a model of φ. In the following, we refer with ALC-SAT to the base implementation and with ALC-SAT$^+$ to the one with the optimized encoding.

We compared our implementation to other concept learning tools CELOE [6], SParCEL [37], and EvoLearner [16].[1] While these tools also support extensions of $\mathcal{ALC}$ such as number restrictions or data properties, we restricted all tools to $\mathcal{ALC}$ for our evaluation. We did not consider fragments in these first experiments since not all tools support them. We also did not compare our implementation against concept learning tools such as NCES2 [24] and DRILL [12], as these require a pretraining step for each data set, which makes direct performance comparison difficult. We evaluate performance in two setups: in the first, we test the ability to find exact fitting concepts on a new benchmark where fitting concepts are guaranteed to exist. In the second, we evaluate the approximation scheme from Sect. 5.2 on the standard SML benchmark [39].

For evaluating exact fitting we extracted fragments of the YAGO 4.5 knowledge base [36] by taking all facts talking about a given signature. The *family* fragment is based on signature $\{$*spouse, children, gender, Male, Female*$\}$, and the *language* fragment uses the role name *hasLanguage* and several concept names that represent languages. We handcrafted 70 $\mathcal{ALC}$ concepts of varying complexity and used them to obtain positive and negative examples by querying

[1] We use the version of CELOE from DL-Learner 1.5.0 and the version of EvoLearner from ontolearn 0.8.1. The exact learning benchmarks were run on a MacBook Pro with M3 Pro chip and 36GB RAM. The generalization benchmarks were run on a MacBook Pro with M1 Pro Chip and 32 GB RAM.

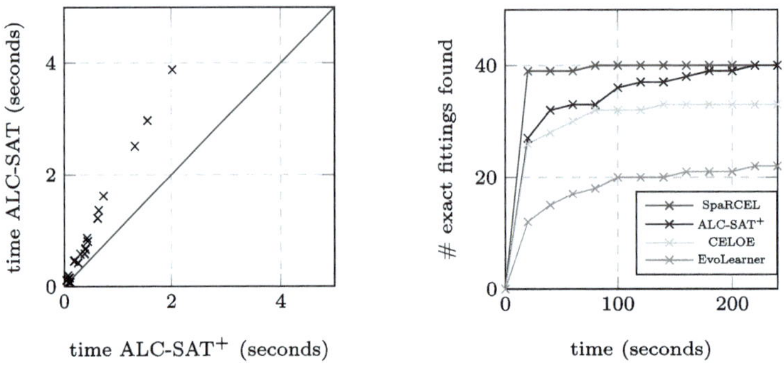

Fig. 3. Exact learning runtime

the extracted fragments. The task was then to reverse-engineer the $\mathcal{ALC}$ concept from (subsets of) the examples. For the family fragment we used concepts with high quantifier depth, for example $\exists c.(\exists c.\exists g.F \sqcap \exists c.\exists g.M)$ asking for all individuals having a child that has both a daughter (gender female) and a son (male); we use also deeper concepts, referring to grand-children and so on. For the language fragment we use shallow concepts that contain Boolean combinations of concept names under existential or universal restrictions, for example, $\exists l.(F \sqcup I \sqcup R) \sqcap \forall l.\neg G$.

We highlight the impact of our optimizations on the encoding in Fig. 3 (left). The data points stem from experiments on the 25 benchmarks over the language fragment and compare the time ALC-SAT and ALC-SAT$^+$ needed until an exact fitting was found. The data shows that we find exact fitting concepts about twice as fast with optimizations enabled. We conjecture that this is largely explained by the type encoding which is beneficial in the presence of many concept names.

We also compared the time of ALC-SAT$^+$ to find a fitting concept to that of EvoLearner, CELOE and SParCEL over the 45 benchmarks generated from the family fragment. The graph in Fig. 3 (right) displays the number of exact fittings found by each tool within a given runtime. It can be seen that ALC-SAT$^+$ finds exact fittings faster than both CELOE or EvoLearner. However, SParCEL achieves better results for smaller values for maximum runtime. Both SParCEL and ALC-SAT$^+$ find the same number of exact fittings within the timeframe displayed, however, for 5 benchmarks SParCEL was unable to find an exact fitting concept whereas ALC-SAT$^+$ was able to find exact fittings for all benchmarks, at the cost of increased execution time.

We evaluated approximate fitting of ALC-SAT$^+$ and the other tools by measuring accuracy and length of the returned concept on the SML-Benchmark using 10-fold validation. Each tool was allowed to run for 5 mins. The results are given in Table 1 where for each tool and benchmark the first row shows accuracy while the second row shows concept length, both with standard deviation. The accuracy achieved by ALC-SAT$^+$ is comparable to that of EvoLearner, except for Mammographic. The values for accuracy of CELOE and SParCEL, in

Table 1. Generalization results on SML-Benchmarks

	Carcinogenesis	Hepatitis	Lymphography	Mammographic	Mutagenesis	Nctrer
EvoLearner	0.53 ± 0.18	0.58 ± 0.01	0.81 ± 0.12	0.46 ± 0.00	0.78 ± 0.18	0.6 ± 0.04
	7.2 ± 3.52	$3.2, \pm 1.03$	19.6 ± 6.88	1.7 ± 0.48	3.5 ± 1.35	3.3 ± 0.95
CELOE	0.54 ± 0.01	0.41 ± 0.01	0.82 ± 0.11	0.46 ± 0.0	0.56 ± 0.2	0.6 ± 0.04
	3.8 ± 0.42	4.6 ± 1.26	10.8 ± 0.42	1.7 ± 2.21	6.8 ± 0.63	3.9 ± 0.32
SParCEL	0.54 ± 0.1	n/a	0.74 ± 0.13	0.55 ± 0.02	0.73 ± 0.23	0.46 ± 0.08
	860.1 ± 66.54	n/a	164.3 ± 49.48	178.2 ± 21.6	85.1 ± 9.35	65.4 ± 18.84
ALC-SAT$^+$	0.55 ± 0.2	0.58 ± 0.01	0.8 ± 0.09	0.77 ± 0.05	0.81 ± 0.26	0.63 ± 0.07
	6.4 ± 0.7	4 ± 1.7	9.9 ± 0.32	11.3 ± 2.06	9.4 ± 0.84	11.7 ± 0.95

general, are lower. For SParCEL, a possible explanation is that the length of concepts is much larger than that of concepts returned by EvoLearner, CELOE and ALC-SAT$^+$. Small concepts are known to generalize well whereas large concepts are prone to overfitting. In comparison to SParCEL, EvoLearner, CELOE, and ALC-SAT$^+$ are able to find small fitting concepts. While this is 'by design' for ALC-SAT$^+$, we conjecture that the heuristics in EvoLearner and CELOE prefer shorter concepts as well. Note, that when searching for approximate fitting concepts, ALC-SAT$^+$ returns the smallest concept with the highest accuracy found within the time limit and may thus report larger concepts than EvoLearner or CELOE.

6 Conclusion and Future Work

We investigated the bounded fitting paradigm for learning class expressions formulated in the description logic $\mathcal{ALC}$ and its fragments. We analyzed theoretical properties, and we believe that many of our results can be extended to more expressive description logics. Additionally, we provided a preliminary implementation that uses the power of a SAT solver to find good fittings, and compared it with other concept learning tools with encouraging results. From a theoretical perspective, it would be interesting to study bounded fitting in an open world setting where an ontology provides additional background knowledge.

From a practical perspective, we see three relevant avenues for future work. First, OWL 2 DL supports several practically relevant features that are not currently supported by our implementation, such as inverse roles, number restrictions, and data properties. Hence, one natural next step is to extend our implementation to be able to learn (ideally) $\mathcal{SROIQ}(\mathcal{D})$ concepts. Second, we would like to understand the syntactic shape of fittings that occur in realistic knowledge bases. While currently the shape of the sought concepts is determined by the allowed logical constructors, it would also be possible to further restrict it by bounding the number of, say, disjunctions. Finally, we would like to improve the speed of our implementation either by providing better CNF encodings or by *parallelization* relying on syntax tree templates similar to [33].

Acknowledgments. Jean C. Jung was supported by DFG grant (JU 3197/1-1).

Disclosure of Interests. The authors have no competing interests to declare.

Supplemental Material Statement. The source code of our implementation ALC-SAT^{+} and instructions on how to reproduce the benchmarks are available at https://github.com/SAT-based-Concept-Learning/ALCSAT. The full version of this paper including all proof details is available under [15].

References

1. OWL 2 web ontology language overview. https://www.w3.org/TR/2012/REC-owl2-overview-20121211/. Accessed July 24 2025
2. Anthony, M., Biggs, N.: Computational Learning Theory: An Introduction. Cambridge Tracts in Theoretical Computer Science, Cambridge University Press (1992)
3. Baader, F., Horrocks, I., Lutz, C., Sattler, U.: An introduction to description logics. Cambridge University Press (2017). https://doi.org/10.1017/9781139025355
4. Blumer, A., Ehrenfeucht, A., Haussler, D., Warmuth, M.K.: Learnability and the Vapnik-Chervonenkis dimension. J. ACM (JACM) **36**(4), 929–965 (1989). https://doi.org/10.1145/76359.76371
5. Bordais, B., Neider, D., Roy, R.: The complexity of learning LTL, CTL and ATL formulas. In: Proceedings of 42nd International Symposium on Theoretical Aspects of Computer Science, STACS. LIPIcs, vol. 327, pp. 19:1–19:20. Schloss Dagstuhl - Leibniz-Zentrum für Informatik (2025). https://doi.org/10.4230/LIPICS.STACS.2025.19
6. Bühmann, L., Lehmann, J., Westphal, P., Bin, S.: DL-Learner – structured machine learning on semantic web data. In: Companion Proceedings of the The Web Conference 2018. pp. 467–471 (2018). https://doi.org/10.1145/3184558.3186235
7. Camacho, A., McIlraith, S.A.: Learning interpretable models expressed in linear temporal logic. In: Proceedings of the Twenty-Ninth International Conference on Automated Planning and Scheduling, ICAPS, pp. 621–630. AAAI Press (2019). https://doi.org/10.1609/icaps.v29i1.3529
8. ten Cate, B., Funk, M., Jung, J.C., Lutz, C.: Fitting algorithms for conjunctive queries. SIGMOD Rec. **52**(4), 6–18 (2023). https://doi.org/10.1145/3641832.3641834
9. ten Cate, B., Funk, M., Jung, J.C., Lutz, C.: SAT-based PAC learning of description logic concepts. In: Proceedings of the Thirty-Second International Joint Conference on Artificial Intelligence, IJCAI 2023, pp. 3347–3355. ijcai.org (2023). https://doi.org/10.24963/IJCAI.2023/373
10. ten Cate, B., Funk, M., Jung, J.C., Lutz, C.: SAT-based PAC learning of description logic concepts. CoRR **abs/2305.08511** (2023). https://doi.org/10.48550/arXiv.2305.08511
11. ten Cate, B., Funk, M., Jung, J.C., Lutz, C.: On the non-efficient PAC learnability of conjunctive queries. Inf. Process. Lett. **183**, 106431 (2024). https://doi.org/10.1016/J.IPL.2023.106431
12. Demir, C., Ngonga Ngomo, A.: Neuro-symbolic class expression learning. In: Proceedings of the Thirty-Second International Joint Conference on Artificial Intelligence, IJCAI 2023, 19th-25th August 2023, Macao, SAR, China, pp. 3624–3632. ijcai.org (2023). https://doi.org/10.24963/ijcai.2023/403

13. Funk, M., Jung, J.C., Lutz, C.: Actively learning concept and conjunctive queries under $\mathcal{EL}^r$-ontologies. In: Proceedings of the Thirtieth International Joint Conference on Artificial Intelligence, IJCAI-21. pp. 1887–1893 (2021). https://doi.org/10.24963/ijcai.2021/260
14. Funk, M., Jung, J.C., Lutz, C., Pulcini, H., Wolter, F.: Learning description logic concepts: When can positive and negative examples be separated? In: Proceedings of the Twenty-Eighth International Joint Conference on Artificial Intelligence, IJCAI-19, pp. 1682–1688 (2019). https://doi.org/10.24963/ijcai.2019/233
15. Funk, M., Jung, J.C., Voellmer, T.: SAT-based bounded fitting for the description logic $\mathcal{ALC}$. CoRR arXiv:2507.21752 (2025), https://doi.org/10.48550/arXiv.2507.21752
16. Heindorf, S., et al.: EvoLearner: Learning description logics with evolutionary algorithms. In: WWW '22: The ACM Web Conference 2022, pp. 818–828. ACM (2022). https://doi.org/10.1145/3485447.3511925
17. Horrocks, I., Kutz, O., Sattler, U.: The even more irresistible SROIQ. In: Doherty, P., Mylopoulos, J., Welty, C.A. (eds.) Proceedings, Tenth International Conference on Principles of Knowledge Representation and Reasoning, Lake District of the United Kingdom, June 2-5, 2006, pp. 57–67. AAAI Press (2006), http://www.aaai.org/Library/KR/2006/kr06-009.php
18. Iannone, L., Palmisano, I., Fanizzi, N.: An algorithm based on counterfactuals for concept learning in the semantic web. Appl. Intell. **26**(2), 139–159 (2007). https://doi.org/10.1007/S10489-006-0011-5
19. Ignatiev, A., Morgado, A., Marques-Silva, J.: PySAT: A Python toolkit for prototyping with SAT oracles. In: Theory and Applications of Satisfiability Testing – SAT 2018, pp. 428–437 (2018). https://doi.org/10.1007/978-3-319-94144-8_26
20. Ignatiev, A., Tan, Z.L., Karamanos, C.: Towards universally accessible SAT technology. In: 27th International Conference on Theory and Applications of Satisfiability Testing, pp. 4:1–4:11 (2024). https://doi.org/10.4230/LIPICS.SAT.2024.16
21. Kearns, M.J., Valiant, L.G.: Cryptographic limitations on learning Boolean formulae and finite automata. J. ACM (JACM) **41**(1), 67–95 (1994). https://doi.org/10.1145/174644.174647
22. Kietz, J.: Some lower bounds for the computational complexity of inductive logic programming. In: Machine Learning: ECML-93, pp. 115–123 (1993). https://doi.org/10.1007/3-540-56602-3_131
23. Kouagou, N.J., Heindorf, S., Demir, C., Ngomo, A.N.: Neural class expression synthesis. In: The Semantic Web - 20th International Conference, ESWC 2023. Lecture Notes in Computer Science, vol. 13870, pp. 209–226. Springer (2023). https://doi.org/10.1007/978-3-031-33455-9_13
24. Kouagou, N.J., Heindorf, S., Demir, C., Ngonga Ngomo, A.: Neural class expression synthesis in *ALCHIQ(D)*. In: Machine Learning and Knowledge Discovery in Databases: Research Track - European Conference, ECML PKDD 2023. Lecture Notes in Computer Science, vol. 14172, pp. 196–212. Springer (2023). https://doi.org/10.1007/978-3-031-43421-1_12
25. Lehmann, J.: Learning OWL Class Expressions, Studies on the Semantic Web, vol. 6. IOS Press (2010). https://doi.org/10.3233/978-1-61499-340-7-i
26. Lehmann, J., Fanizzi, N., Bühmann, L., d'Amato, C.: Concept learning. In: Perspectives on Ontology Learning, pp. 71–91. AKA / IOS Press (2014), https://jens-lehmann.org/files/2014/pol_concept_learning.pdf

27. Lehmann, J., Hitzler, P.: Concept learning in description logics using refinement operators. Mach. Learn. **78**, 203–250 (2010). https://doi.org/10.1007/s10994-009-5146-2
28. Martins, D.M.L.: Reverse engineering database queries from examples: State-of-the-art, challenges, and research opportunities. Inf. Syst. **83**, 89–100 (2019). https://doi.org/10.1016/J.IS.2019.03.002
29. Mascle, C., Fijalkow, N., Lagarde, G.: Learning temporal formulas from examples is hard. CoRR **abs/2312.16336** (2023). https://doi.org/10.48550/ARXIV.2312.16336
30. Neider, D., Gavran, I.: Learning linear temporal properties. In: Proceedings of 18th Conference on Formal Methods in Computer Aided Design FMCAD, pp. 1–10. IEEE (2018). https://doi.org/10.23919/FMCAD.2018.8603016
31. Pitt, L., Valiant, L.G.: Computational limitations on learning from examples. J. ACM **35**(4), 965–984 (1988). https://doi.org/10.1145/48014.63140
32. Pommellet, A., Stan, D., Scatton, S.: SAT-based learning of computation tree logic. In: Proceedings of 12th International Joint Conference on Automated Reasoning IJCAR. Lecture Notes in Computer Science, vol. 14739, pp. 366–385. Springer (2024). https://doi.org/10.1007/978-3-031-63498-7_22
33. Riener, H.: Exact synthesis of LTL properties from traces. In: Kazmierski, T.J., von Hanxleden, R., Mak, T.S.T. (eds.) 2019 Forum for Specification and Design Languages, FDL 2019, Southampton, United Kingdom, September 2-4, 2019, pp. 1–6. IEEE (2019). https://doi.org/10.1109/FDL.2019.8876900
34. Rizzo, G., Fanizzi, N., d'Amato, C.: Class expression induction as concept space exploration: from DL-FOIL to DL-FOCL. Future Gener. Comput. Syst. **108**, 256–272 (2020). https://doi.org/10.1016/J.FUTURE.2020.02.071
35. Sakallah, K.A.: Symmetry and satisfiability. In: Handbook of Satisfiability - Second Edition, Frontiers in Artificial Intelligence and Applications, vol. 336, pp. 509–570. IOS Press (2021). https://doi.org/10.3233/FAIA200996
36. Suchanek, F.M., Alam, M., Bonald, T., Chen, L., Paris, P., Soria, J.: YAGO 4.5: A large and clean knowledge base with a rich taxonomy. In: Proceedings of the 47th International ACM SIGIR Conference on Research and Development in Information Retrieval, SIGIR 2024, pp. 131–140. ACM (2024). https://doi.org/10.1145/3626772.3657876
37. Tran, A.C., Dietrich, J., Guesgen, H.W., Marsland, S.: Parallel symmetric class expression learning. J. Mach. Learn. Res. **18**, 64:1–64:34 (2017). https://jmlr.org/papers/v18/14-317.html
38. Valiant, L.G.: A theory of the learnable. Commun. ACM **27**(11), 1134–1142 (1984). https://doi.org/10.1145/1968.1972
39. Westphal, P., Bühmann, L., Bin, S., Jabeen, H., Lehmann, J.: SML-bench - a benchmarking framework for structured machine learning. Semantic Web **10**(2), 231–245 (2019). https://doi.org/10.3233/SW-180308
40. Zloof, M.M.: Query by example. In: American Federation of Information Processing Societies: 1975 National Computer Conference, 19-22 May 1975, Anaheim, CA, USA. AFIPS Conference Proceedings, vol. 44, pp. 431–438. AFIPS Press (1975). https://doi.org/10.1145/1499949.1500034

Ontology-Enhanced Knowledge Graph Completion Using Large Language Models

Wenbin Guo[1], Xin Wang[1(✉)], Jiaoyan Chen[2(✉)], Zhao Li[1], and Zirui Chen[1]

[1] Tianjin University, College of Intelligence and Computing, Tianjin 300350, China
{wenff,wangx,lizh,zrchen}@tju.edu.cn
[2] Department of Computer Science, University of Manchester, Manchester M13 9PL, UK
jiaoyan.chen@manchester.ac.uk

Abstract. Large Language Models (LLMs) have been extensively adopted in Knowledge Graph Completion (KGC), showcasing significant research advancements. However, as black-box models driven by deep neural architectures, current LLM-based KGC methods rely on implicit knowledge representation with the concurrent dissemination of erroneous knowledge, thereby hindering their ability to produce confirmative reasoning outcomes. We aim to integrate neural-perceptual structural information with ontological knowledge, leveraging the powerful capabilities of LLMs to achieve a deeper understanding of the intrinsic logic of the knowledge. We propose an **O**ntology-enhanced **L**LM-based **KGC** method—OL-KGC. It first leverages neural perceptual mechanisms to effectively embed structural information into the textual space, and then uses an automated extraction algorithm to retrieve ontological knowledge from the knowledge graphs (KGs) that needs to be completed, which is further transformed into a textual format that can be processed by LLMs to enhance their logical capability. We conducted extensive experiments on three widely-used benchmarks—FB15K-237, UMLS, and WN18RR. The experimental results demonstrate that OL-KGC significantly outperforms existing mainstream KGC methods across multiple evaluation metrics, achieving state-of-the-art performance. The implementation of the algorithm and related data have been open-sourced.

Keywords: Knowledge Graph Completion · Ontology · Large Language Model · Neural-symbolic Integration

1 Introduction

Knowledge Graphs (KGs) [14] represent a foundational paradigm for structured knowledge representation, serving as a cornerstone in the progression from perceptual intelligence to cognitive intelligence[1]. KGs underpin numerous critical applications across diverse domains, including information retrieval [26], question answering [11], and recommendation [33]. KGs often organize real-world

[1] https://github.com/xiumu-gg/OL-KGC

D. Garijo et al. (Eds.): ISWC 2025, LNCS 16140, pp. 61–80, 2026.
https://doi.org/10.1007/978-3-032-09527-5_4

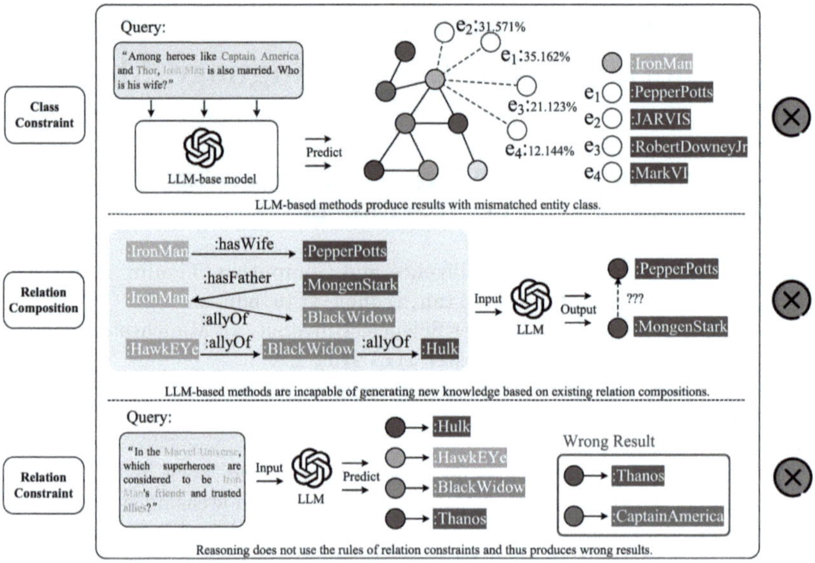

Fig. 1. LLM-based methods that fail to effectively utilize ontological knowledge.

knowledge through triples in form of (head entity, relation, tail entity), enabling the structured representation of relational facts. Their expressive power and reasoning capabilities are further augmented by the incorporation of ontological frameworks and symbolic logic reasoning methods. However, KGs often suffer from incompleteness due to various reasons. For example, algorithms designed to extract structured information from data often struggle to comprehensively capture the full spectrum of information in large datasets. The Knowledge Graph Completion (KGC) is to address this challenge by leveraging existing knowledge and structural patterns to (iteratively) infer missing knowledge [32].

Due to the powerful capabilities of Large Language Models (LLMs), the field of KGC has undergone a significant transformation. Recent LLM-based methods to KGC leverage the advanced contextual and semantic understanding capabilities of LLMs to enhance the precision and completeness of extracted entity and relation information, thereby improving the overall quality and reliability of results [3]. These methods can be broadly categorized into two approaches: 1) leveraging existing paradigms such as zero-shot reasoning [2] and instruction tuning [43] to translate structured KG predictions into LLM-based text predictions; and 2) integrating non-textual structural information from KGs into LLMs through correspondences between KG embeddings and LLM tokens. While the methods are capable of handling complex nonlinear relations, the absence of a mechanism for factual verification does not ensure the veracity and reliability of the generated content [37].

As depicted in Fig. 1, LLM-based methods often fail to effectively leverage ontological information when verifying the accuracy of test triples, primarily

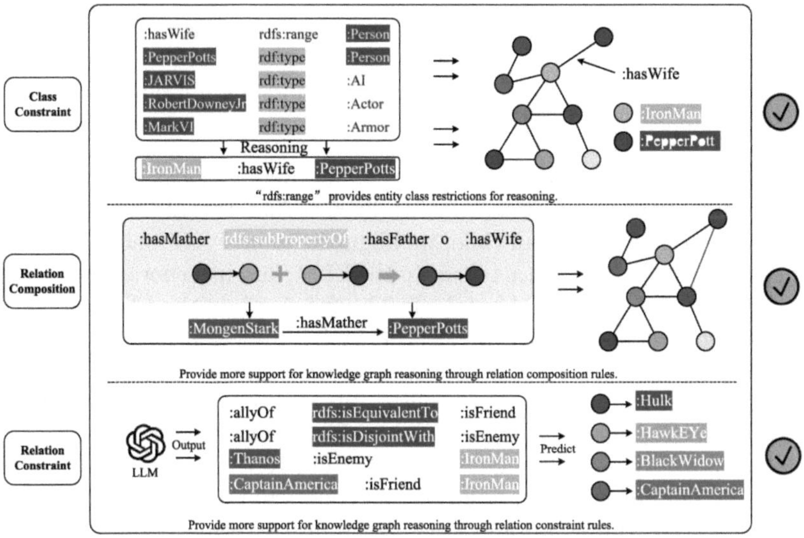

Fig. 2. The role of ontological knowledge in reasoning.

in the following three aspects. First, these methods exhibit a lack of sensitivity to entity classes, and are unable to fully utilize the constraints imposed by relation range and domain to filter out the interference from erroneous triples. Second, they are incapable of performing reasoning based on existing relational paths within the KGs, thereby failing to accurately identify newly generated triples through relation compositions. Third, these methods cannot apply complex ontological knowledge, such as equivalence and disjointness relations, and are prone to deriving conclusions that are completely contrary to the facts during the reasoning process. The underlying cause of this phenomenon is that LLMs do not incorporate an explicit symbolic reasoning mechanism during the prediction process. Instead, they rely excessively on the semantic correlation between entities, usually lacking fundamental logical reasoning capabilities. Although previous studies [40] have attempted to address this issue by injecting rules into KG embeddings and constraining the quality of rule embeddings through loss functions, the results have been unsatisfactory. Therefore, how to utilize the extensive knowledge domain covered by LLMs and their ability to capture complex data patterns to achieve a deep integration of vector space and symbolic space is the core issue of this research.

Given that a KG for completion is often short of ontological knowledge, this study first proposes an LLM-based automatic extraction algorithm to derive ontological knowledge from the KG that needs to be completed. As shown in Fig. 2, these extracted ontological knowledge cover the following key information:

- The range and domain of each relation, which can effectively validate triples according to the classes of their entities.

- The relation compositions based on existing relational paths, which can enabling the inference of new knowledge.
- Complex relation constraints beyond relation domain and range, such as relation equivalence and disjointness.

We rewrite the extracted ontological knowledge, which is originally represented as RDF triples, into text so as to ensure that the LLM can fully comprehend their semantics. Meanwhile, we align the neural KG embeddings in the vector space with the text space tokens in the LLM, and incorporate the symbolic KG structural information and ontological knowledge into the LLM based on its tuning, thereby achieving effective neural-symbolic integration. To the best of our knowledge, this work is the first to systematically integrate explicit ontological knowledge—encompassing class constraints and relation compositions—into LLMs through the joint exploitation of textual inference and structured symbolic logic. Experimental results demonstrate that OL-KGC achieves SOTA performance in the field of KGC. In addition, we conducted ablation studies to individually assess the contributions of KG structural information and ontological knowledge. Furthermore, we assessed the influence of various types of ontological knowledge on reasoning performance within the model.

The main contributions of this paper can be summarized as follows:

- We propose a novel method for integrating neural KG embeddings, and symbolic KG structural information and ontological knowledge based on LLMs and their tuning, achieving effective neural-symbolic integration and significantly enhancing LLM reasoning for KGC.
- We design an LLM-based automatic ontology extraction algorithm that can automate the ontology framework design for general KGs. This approach improves the semantic richness and the consistency and coherence of the relations and overall organization within KGs.
- Through extensive experiments, we demonstrate the performance superiority of OL-KGC in the KGC task. Additionally, we release all related code and data to provide a reproducible benchmark for future research.

2 Related Works

2.1 Traditional Embedding-Based KGC Models

Traditional KGC models often adopt geometric embedding, assuming relational consistency, where relations imply a close alignment of entity vectors through specific operations [17]. Models enhance embedding quality using various operator spaces [6], such as TransE [1], which treats relations as translations between entity vectors. Subsequent studies have leveraged advanced natural language processing techniques to model complex relational patterns, including hyperplanes [34], Riemannian spheres [22], relational mapping spaces [15], multi-mapping spaces [9], rotational spaces [29], and convolutional spaces [8,18,23].

The introduction of attention mechanisms has enhanced the flexibility and efficiency of KGC models in deep learning [5]. RelAtt refines embeddings using a relation-aware attention mechanism [28], HRAN aggregates features along relational paths [21], and KGT5 and HittER leverage Transformers for scalable and context-aware representation learning [4,27]. Despite their success, embedding-based models still struggle with distinguishing semantically similar but class-inconsistent entities [10].

2.2 PLM-Based and LLM-Based KGC Models

PLM-based KGC models leverage the implicit knowledge within Pre-trained Language Models (PLMs) which are usually encoder-based and the structured knowledge in KGs to predict missing triples [36]. KG-BERT is a pioneering work in this domain [38], which takes the textual information of triples as input and predicts the plausibility of triples through fine-tuning the BERT model. However, integrating the implicit knowledge of PLMs with KGs has always been a key challenge for such methods.

In contrast to leveraging contextual embeddings from PLMs to represent entities and relations in KGs for predicting missing triples, LLM-based KGC models exploit the more powerful and flexible text-generation capabilities of LLMs to directly generate missing triples or provide more comprehensive reasoning over KGs by generating textual explanations or intermediate steps. Recently, LLM-based KGC methods have been primarily categorized into two types [24]:

The first approach leverages paradigms like zero-shot reasoning and instruction tuning to translate structured KG information into text-based predictions via LLMs [37]. For example, MuKDC uses LLMs to generate subgraph-based questions for KGC [19], while KLR-KGC enhances LLM reasoning by retrieving analogical and subgraph knowledge from KGs [16].

The second approach incorporates structured KG information into LLMs by aligning KG embeddings with LLM tokens, improving their understanding and representation of KGs. TEA-GLM employs LLMs as zero-shot learners for graph machine learning tasks [31]. KGEditor converts paths into Chain-of-Thought prompts for multi-hop link prediction [6]. KoPA, the current state-of-the-art, introduces a knowledge prefix adapter to align structural embeddings with LLM tokens, effectively integrating KG information into LLMs [42].

2.3 Neuro-Symbolic Integration for KGC

Besides embedding and language model-based methods, there are some neuro-symbolic methods for KGC that focus on the integration of symbolic reasoning and neural networks for enhancing reasoning capabilities and interpretability, often with mutual feedback between symbolic and neural components.

Neuro-symbolic approaches leverage logical rules to expand reliable data and enhance embedding quality [20]. NeoEA aligns entity embeddings with ontological knowledge to reduce distribution discrepancies [12], while SymRITa employs symbolic rule graphs and a logical transformer to address predicate non-commutativity [25]. Other methods enforce logical constraints via loss functions, such as IterE, which integrates rules into embeddings [41]. GCR uses graph convolution networks with rule-enhanced embeddings [7], and KALE integrates embeddings and logical rules through a loss function [13].

However, these methods compromise the precision and interpretability of symbolic reasoning, facing challenges in integrating vector and symbolic spaces. The emergence of LLMs, which encapsulate extensive knowledge and complex patterns, presents new opportunities for this integration [35].

3 Notations and Preliminaries

A KG is represented as $\mathcal{G} = \{\mathcal{E}, \mathcal{R}, \mathcal{T}, \mathcal{H}, \mathcal{D}\}$, where $\mathcal{E}$ and $\mathcal{R}$ denote the sets of entities and relations, respectively, and $\mathcal{T} = \{(h, r, t) \mid h, t \in \mathcal{E}, r \in \mathcal{R}\}$ represents the set of triples. $\mathcal{H}$ refers to the ontological information, represented as a set of RDF triples. The ontological information we consider includes the following types:

- **Relation Domain and Range Constraints:** For a given entity $e \in \mathcal{E}$, the entity class constraint stipulates that e belongs to a specific class a. Furthermore, if e also belongs to a superclass class of a_s, it is denoted as a $a_s \subseteq a$, indicating that a inherits the attributes of a_s. The properties `:range` and `:domain` can be utilized to restrict the classes of the head entity h and the tail entity t of a specific relation r. For instance, for the relation `:hasWife`, the `:range` and `:domain` property can restrict the head entity h to the class `:Person` and the tail entity t to the class `:Person`. Given that the entity `:PepperPotts` belongs to the class `:Women`, which is a subclass of `:Person`, the entity `:PepperPotts` complies with the `:range` restriction of the relation `:hasWife`, thereby validating the `:range` constraint.
- **Relation Compositions:** Relation compositions enable the inference of new relations within a $\mathcal{G}$. For instance, given two RDF triples (`:MongenStark :hasFather :IronMan`) and (`:IronMan :hasWife :PepperPotts`), a new relation can be inferred through the relation composition (`:hasMother rdfs:subPropertyOf :hasFather o :hasWife`). This results in the new inference (`:MongenStark :hasMother :PepperPotts`), thereby deducing the previously unknown fact that PepperPotts is the mother of MongenStark based on the existing knowledge in the $\mathcal{G}$.
- **Complex Relation Constraints:** Complex relations, such as equivalence and disjointness relation, are employed to constrain the results of inference. For equivalence relations, the $\mathcal{G}$ is expanded. For example, given that `:allyOf` and `:isFriend` are equivalent relations, the triple (`:IronMan :allyOf :CaptainAmerica`) can be expanded to yield the new triple (`:IronMan :isFriend :CaptainAmerica`). For disjointness relations, the inference results are validated. For instance, given that `:isEnemy` and `:isFriend` are disjointness relation, if the triple (`:IronMan :isEnemy :Thanos`) is true, then the triple (`:IronMan :isFriend :Thanos`) must be false.

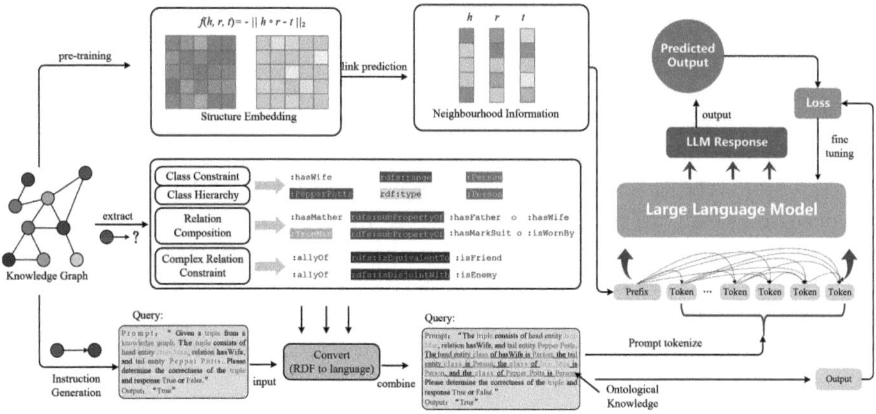

Fig. 3. The overall framework of OL-KGC.

$\mathcal{D}$ denotes the descriptive information of each entity and relation, where each entity and relation is uniquely identified in the real data. Specifically, we use $\mathcal{D}(e)$ and $\mathcal{D}(r)$ to represent the textual descriptions of each entity and relation, respectively. For example, in the widely used dataset FB15K-237, we have $\mathcal{D}(/\mathrm{m}/0\mathrm{dzlbx}) =$ "Iron Man".

We introduce an LLM $\mathcal{M}$ as the text decoder for KGC. The input sequence $\mathcal{S}$ consists of three components: the instruction prompt $\mathcal{I}$, the triple prompt $\mathcal{X}$, and the ontology prompt $\mathcal{O}$. $\mathcal{I}$ provides manual guidelines for completing the task, such as the instruction "Please help determine whether the triple (h,r,t) is a valid triple." Meanwhile, $\mathcal{X}$ contains textual descriptions of the triple symbols, represented as $\mathcal{X}(h,r,t) = \mathcal{D}(h) \oplus \mathcal{D}(r) \oplus \mathcal{D}(t)$, where (h,r,t) is the triple, and $\oplus$ denotes the concatenation. $\mathcal{O}$ represents the textual form of the ontological information, which is derived by transforming a relevant part of $\mathcal{H}$ into corresponding text.

We focus on triple classification which is a fundamental task of KGC. Following most LLM-based methods that reformulate tasks as text generation problems, we expect our LLM model $\mathcal{M}$, given a text sequence $\mathcal{S} = \mathcal{I} \oplus \mathcal{X} \oplus \mathcal{O}$ of an input triple, outputs a response of either "True" or "False" for validating this triple. Unlike text classification, the complex semantics of KGs cannot be captured by a single description. Without KG structural information, LLMs may primarily encapsulate isolated term-level knowledge, which restricts their capacity for comprehensive understanding. Despite their vast general knowledge, LLMs are prone to hallucinations due to insensitivity to fine-grained facts. Thus, effective KGC with LLMs requires vector-based methods to provide structured knowledge, enabling structure-aware reasoning.

4 Methodology

This section elucidates how OL-KGC integrates LLMs with vectorized structural and ontological knowledge. Initially, ontological knowledge is extracted in RDF format and transformed into text to serve as part of the input for the LLM. Subsequently, traditional knowledge graph embedding (KGE) algorithms are employed to extract structural information from the KG, which is then provided to the LLM in prefix form to enhance its understanding of the complex structure of the KG. Finally, the LLM integrates the vectorized structural and ontological knowledge, and the completion performance is optimized through fine-tuning using the LoRA method. The framework of OL-KGC is shown in Fig. 3.

4.1 Ontological Knowledge Integration

KGs typically store knowledge in symbolic form. For instance, in the FB15K-237 dataset, entities are represented by symbols such as /m/0dzlbx, which are not directly suitable for extracting ontological information. To address this, we uesd an automated script to map the symbols to the Freebase database, generating textual descriptions for each entity. For example, the entity /m/0dzlbx is mapped to $\mathcal{D}(/\mathrm{m}/0\mathrm{dzlbx}) =$ "Iron Man".

We further leverage the powerful generative capabilities of LLMs to automatically derive corresponding classes for each entity, generate equivalence, disjointness, and composition rules for each relation, and create class inheritance relationships for each class. Based on the output of the LLM, we designed an algorithm to automatically extract ontological knowledge represented in RDF format, denoted as $\mathcal{H}$, from its generated results. To ensure the accuracy of the extracted ontological knowledge $\mathcal{H}$, we introduced a mechanism for manual expert verification.

In addition, we constructed an RDF language mapping dictionary. For a given test triple (h, r, t), we retrieve relevant RDF triples from $\mathcal{H}$ and transform them into natural language text using predefined templates. For example, the RDF triple (`:IronMan rdf:type :Person`) is mapped to "The class of entity `:IronMan` is `:Person`." This mapping method helps the LLM understand the logical structure of the KG. The process can be represented as follows:

$$\mathcal{O} = \mathcal{B}\left(\sum_{\mathcal{H}_i \in \mathcal{H}} \mathcal{S}(\mathcal{H}_i, (h, r, t))\right) \tag{1}$$

where $\mathcal{S}(\cdot)$ is an indicator function that determines the relevance between $\mathcal{H}_i$ and the test triple by checking whether there exist entity, relation, or corresponding entity class related to the test triple within $\mathcal{H}_i$. When $\mathcal{H}_i$ is relevant to the test triple (h, r, t), $\mathcal{S}(\cdot)$ returns $\mathcal{H}_i$; otherwise, it returns nothing. $\mathcal{B}$ maps RDF triples to natural language text via a predefined dictionary. $\mathcal{O}$ is the textual description of ontological knowledge of the KG and will serve as part of the input to the LLM.

4.2 Structural Information Integration

$\mathcal{G}$ contains rich structural information, but its complexity makes it difficult to represent through explicit reasoning processes. To capture the intricate structural information within the KG, we utilize self-supervised embedding pretraining. For each entity $e \in \mathcal{E}$ and each relation $r \in \mathcal{R}$, we learn embeddings $\mathbf{e} \in \mathbb{R}^{d_e}$ and $\mathbf{r} \in \mathbb{R}^{d_r}$, where d_e and d_r represent the dimensions of the entity and relation embeddings, respectively, to represent neighborhood structure information. We evaluated existing KGC models experimentally, and the results show that using a rotational operator most effectively extracts the structural features of the KG. The scoring function is defined as:

$$f(h, r, t) = - \mid \mathbf{h} \circ \mathbf{r} - \mathbf{t} \mid_2 \tag{2}$$

where $\circ$ denotes the Hadamard product between the head entity embedding and the relation embedding, and $\mid \cdot \mid_2$ represents the l_2-norm of the complex vector. By improving the quality of embeddings $\mathbf{e}$ and $\mathbf{r}$, we are able to extract the complex structural information of the KG. As the score of the positive triples increases, the entity embeddings $\mathbf{e}$ and relation embeddings $\mathbf{r}$ are optimized, thus capturing subgraph structures and relation patterns within the KG. This approach has been demonstrated to be effective in several embedding-based KGC methods [29], which can capture classical structural information such as relation patterns and distributed entity representations.

As shown in Fig. 3, for the test triple (h, r, t), we extract its corresponding vector representation through structural embedding. The dimensionality of this vector is consistent with that of the token vectors in the LLM. To enhance the perception of the structural information in KG, we innovatively concatenate the vectors corresponding to (h, r, t) and transform the structural embedding from the vector space to the LLM token text space via a linear adapter. This transformed representation is then used as a prefix for the input to the LLM.

$$\mathbf{v}_{(h,r,t)} = \mathbf{W}_{\text{linear}}(\mathbf{v}_h \oplus \mathbf{v}_r \oplus \mathbf{v}_t) + \mathbf{b}_{\text{linear}} \tag{3}$$

there $\oplus$ denotes the concatenation operation, $\mathbf{W}_{\text{linear}}$ is the weight matrix of the linear layer, and $\mathbf{b}_{\text{linear}}$ is the bias vector. The resulting vector $\mathbf{v}_{(h,r,t)}$ serves as the prefix for the input to the LLM. This design enables the structural information to directly influence the generation process of each subsequent token, thereby providing richer semantic and structural context for the KGC. During training, the pre-trained structural embeddings are frozen, while the linear adapter is optimized to learn the mapping from structural knowledge to textual representation. This mapping can then be generalized to new triples during the inference stage.

4.3 LLM Fine Tuning

The powerful reasoning capabilities of LLMs provide a more effective tool for integrating vectorized KG structural information and ontological information.

The input to the LLM includes the instruction, the textual interpretation of the triple, and the ontological information, which can be represented as follows:

$$\mathcal{S} = \mathcal{I} \oplus \mathcal{X} \oplus \mathcal{O} \tag{4}$$

there $\mathcal{X}$ denotes the descriptive text of the triple, and $\mathcal{O}$ represents the ontological information that describes the logic within the KG. We concatenate these two types of textual information with the instruction $\mathcal{I}$ to form the input to the LLM. Additionally, the structural embedding is transformed from the vector space to the LLM token text space and serves as a prefix during the LLM's generation phase, providing structural information of the KG for each token generated in this phase.

$$\mathcal{A}_{\text{token}} = \mathbf{v}_{(h,r,t)} \oplus \text{tokenize}(\mathcal{S}) \tag{5}$$

there $\mathcal{A}_{\text{token}}$ represents the complete token sequence input to the LLM, and the tokenize($\cdot$) function denotes the process of tokenizing the text. Through unidirectional attention decoding, the LLM can perceive the structural information of the KG while generating each token, which is beneficial for prediction.

To train the large model to better predict the triples, thereby enhancing its performance in KGC, we fine-tune the model using LoRA by minimizing the following loss function:

$$\mathcal{L} = \gamma \cdot \mathcal{D}(\mathcal{M}(\mathcal{A}_{\text{token}}), Output) \tag{6}$$

where γ is a weighting factor used to adjust the intensity of the loss; $\mathcal{D}$ is a discrepancy measurement function that quantifies the difference between the output and the expected result. The model parameters are optimized through backpropagation based on this discrepancy, which helps the LLM perform more accurate KGC.

5 Experiments

We conducted experiments to verify the superiority of OL-KGC. The experiments were guided by answering the following four questions: **Q1:** What are the advantages of this method compared with various traditional KGC methods? **Q2:** What roles do the vectorized structural information and ontological knowledge play respectively? **Q3:** Are the ontological knowledge effectively incorporated into the LLM, and what is the impact of the ontological knowledge?

5.1 Experimental Settings

Datasets. We conducted experiments using three public datasets: UMLS, FB15K-237, and MN18RR. Based on the fundamental datasets, we introduced ontological information in the form of RDF triples to each dataset through

Table 1. Dataset Statistics.

Dataset	Rel	Ent	Tri	Ont	Ont-cla	Ont-rel	Ont-com
UMLS-O	46	135	6,529	165	106	13	46
FB15K-237O	237	14,541	310,116	18,763	16,073	93	2597
MN18RR-O	11	40,943	94,003	4,710	4,683	9	18

the LLM, which encompassed rules such as entity classes, relation composition, equivalence relations, and disjointness relations. This resulted in the creation of the UMLS-O, FB15K-237O, and MN18RR-O datasets. The fundamental datasets are composed in the form of symbols. For the FB15K-237 and WN18RR datasets, we extracted relevant entity description text information from Freebase and WordNet respectively. As for the UMLS dataset, we introduced the Metathesaurus ontology[2] to obtain relevant information. The enriched datasets will be publicly available[3]. Detailed information is provided in Table 1. The symbols Rel, Ent, Tri, Ont represent the quantities of relations, entities, triples, and ontological information, respectively. The ontological information is further subdivided into three distinct categories: Ont-cla, which pertains to entity classes; Ont-rel, which encompasses relation composition; and Ont-com, which represents constraints on complex relations.

For the data leakage scenario where the LLM may have directly seen or learned from the data used during testing, we have checked that our datasets FB15K-237 and WN18RR, as well as the original KGs they come from, are not used in any training stage of the GLM model which used in our experiments. LLM may have seen text with similar semantics as the structured triples, but such memorization is a key feature of LLM itself. We intentionally selected UMLS—a domain-specific biomedical dataset—to reduce the overlap with the pretraining corpora.

Baseline Methods. In the experimental section, we perform a comparative analysis across four categories of KGC models: traditional KGE models, neuro-symbolic integrated KGC models, PLM-based KGC models, and LLM-based KGC models. For traditional KGE models, we selected four baseline models: TransE [1], ComplEx [30], RotatE [29], and ConvE [8], which represent different approaches to capturing semantic relations in KGs via various scoring functions. The neuro-symbolic models IterE [41] and NeoEA [12] were also included for comparison. For PLM-based KGC models, we chose KG-BERT [38] and KnowC [36], which utilize the semantic power of PLM-based models to integrate graph structure and semantic information. Additionally, we selected high-performance LLM-based models such as KG-LLaMA [39], KoPA [42], MuKDC [19], and KGEditor [6] as baselines.

[2] https://www.nlm.nih.gov/research/umls/knowledge_sources/metathesaurus.

[3] https://github.com/xiumu-gg/OL-KGC/data.

Table 2. The experimental results for triple classification are evaluated using accuracy (Acc), precision (P), and F1-score (F1). The best results are marked in **bold**, and the second-best results are underlined. The performance metrics for the models are primarily sourced from [42]. For models without reported results in [42], we conducted local experiments to obtain the corresponding values. In cases where certain results could not be reproduced, a '-' symbol is used to indicate missing data.

Model	UMLS-O			FB15K-237O			WN18RR-O		
	Acc	P	F1	Acc	P	F1	Acc	P	F1
TransE	84.46	86.13	83.82	69.85	70.80	68.75	62.55	51.23	52.87
ComplEx	90.76	89.90	90.85	65.68	66.45	64.85	77.43	71.83	69.91
RotatE	91.95	90.14	92.15	68.82	69.43	67.10	78.61	74.82	70.06
ConvE	90.08	88.34	90.26	68.59	69.91	66.88	77.05	71.67	69.50
IterE	80.37	83.29	81.89	65.73	66.62	65.10	71.85	67.81	65.06
NeoEA	85.62	84.62	83.47	66.92	67.29	66.38	72.61	69.42	67.68
KG-BERT	77.25	70.84	80.24	55.83	53.42	67.71	58.80	57.28	64.38
KnowC	80.84	86.97	84.89	59.72	60.12	66.83	68.16	64.80	66.57
KG-LLaMA	85.68	87.77	85.30	74.77	67.40	79.27	80.85	76.83	**80.54**
KoPA	92.58	90.85	92.70	77.65	70.81	80.81	-	-	-
MuKDC	89.13	90.07	86.85	72.70	75.92	74.63	77.55	77.83	73.82
KGEditor	92.85	86.96	90.56	63.47	68.73	70.03	80.63	81.22	77.81
OL-KGC	**93.10**	**92.32**	**93.16**	**80.41**	**76.26**	**84.66**	**81.45**	**83.50**	78.65

Evaluation Metrics. Unlike conventional link prediction tasks, LLMs are not inherently suited for predicting the global ranking of specific entities. Consequently, we selected triple classification as the evaluation task for KGC models, which serves as a crucial subtask within the KGC framework. We assessed model performance with the standard suite of metrics—accuracy, precision, recall, and F1-score—defined as follows: Accuracy is defined as the ratio of correctly classified triples (both positive and negative) to the total number of evaluated triples. Precision is the ratio of correctly predicted positive triples to the total number of triples predicted as positive. Recall is the ratio of correctly predicted positive triples to the total number of ground-truth positive triples. F1 is the harmonic mean of precision and recall.

5.2 Link Prediction Results

The experimental results for triple classification are shown in Table 2. Given that the core objective of this study is to evaluate the prediction accuracy and precision of the model, and considering the limitations of page space, we did not present the results of recall in the link prediction experiment section. We believe that precision and the F1 score can more accurately reflect the value of the model. The complete experimental results report has been detailed in the supplementary material for reference by the readers.

OL-KGC achieved state-of-the-art performance on average across the three datasets, with respective performance improvements of 2.238%, 1.361%, and 2.246% on the UMLS-O, FB15K-237O, and WN18RR-O datasets. This indicates that the KGC method combining vectorized structural information and ontological information using LLM can achieve more accurate predictions. It is worth noting that the model reached state-of-the-art levels in terms of accuracy across different datasets, demonstrating its capability to accurately complete missing information. However, the model exhibited poor performance in terms of the F1 metric on the WN18RR-O dataset. In KGs, certain classes contain a significantly larger number of entities compared to others. The ontological knowledge we designed is unable to effectively constrain the prediction process, which can easily lead to the neglect of minority positive triples, thereby resulting in a relatively lower F1 metric compared to other metrics.

Compared to traditional KGE methods, LLM-based approaches achieve superior results. While PLM-based models possess complex structures, they fail to capture the structural information of triples, leading to poor performance on triple classification tasks. Traditional KGE methods are more suitable for reasoning on small datasets, and their reasoning results are more balanced across four different metrics, without the drawback of a significantly lower F1 score. LLM-based methods, on the other hand, are overall better suited for triple classification tasks, but exhibit significant disparities across different metrics.

On the small UMLS-O dataset, LLM-based methods do not exhibit overwhelming advantages, as smaller parameterized KGE models are capable of capturing sufficient structural and semantic information. However, on larger datasets, LLM-based approaches demonstrate more significant advantages. Specifically, the FB15K-237O dataset contains more relations, and OL-KGC is able to perform more accurate reasoning in KGs with a higher number of relations. In contrast, on the relatively simpler WN18RR-O dataset characterized by fewer relational patterns, OL-KGC lacks the capacity to infer richer relation-based ontological knowledge, leading to performance comparable to other current state-of-the-art LLM-based KGC methods (answering **RQ1**).

Table 3. The results of the ablation study on the FB15K-237O dataset are presented, with the best performance highlighted in **bold**.

	Acc	P	R	F1
w/o ontology	67.81	61.41	69.08	69.40
w/o structure	74.35	70.81	79.38	77.44
w/o structure & ontology	62.18	57.53	66.20	64.83
OL-KGC	**80.41**	**76.26**	**86.44**	**84.66**

5.3 Ablation Study

Structural Information and Ontological Information. The model achieved state-of-the-art performance by integrating vectorized structural information and ontological knowledge through the LLM. However, the specific contributions of the vectorized structural information and ontological knowledge to the final prediction results remain unknown. To investigate this, we conducted experiments by removing the ontological information from the input $\mathcal{S} = \mathcal{I} \oplus \mathcal{X} \oplus \mathcal{O} \oplus \mathcal{U}$ and eliminating the relevant text in the instructions to assess the impact of removing ontological knowledge (w/o ontology). We also randomized the prefixes of the neural-perceived structural information to cancel the implicit structural information influence (w/o structure). Additionally, we removed both structural information and ontological knowledge (w/o structure & ontology) to evaluate the performance of a standard LLM on the triple classification task. The results on the FB15K-237O dataset are shown in Table 3.

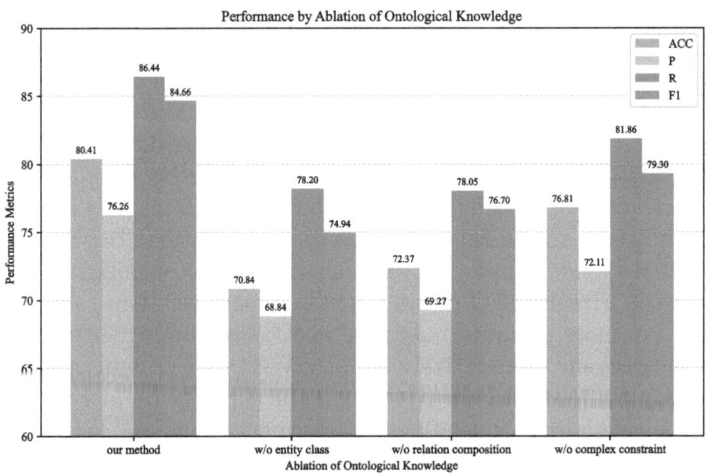

Fig. 4. The results of the ontology rule ablation experiments.

The experimental results indicate that each module of OL-KGC contributes to the final performance of the model. The impact of structural information on the final outcome is relatively minor, ranging from 7.05% to 8.50%. The performance of a standard LLM on the triple classification task is significantly inferior, with a gap of 22.77% to 24.48% compared to OL-KGC. The influence of ontological knowledge on the model lies between 15.77% and 20.08%. Given that LLMs are inherently based on a black-box architectural design, the implicit knowledge provided by vectorized structural information serves as a supplement to LLMs. Ontological knowledge, on the other hand, offers logical connections for LLM reasoning. Therefore, it is reasonable that ontological knowledge has a more substantial impact on the results.

Concrete Ontological Information. To investigate the impact of different classes of ontological information, we selectively removed distinct rules and assessed the effects of entity classes (w/o entity class), relation compositions (w/o relation composition), and complex constraints (w/o complex constraint) on the model. Specifically, for entity classes and class inheritance relations, we eliminated the RDF triples corresponding to the rules and the RDF triples that restrict the class of triples. For relation compositions, we removed all RDF rules related to relation compositions. Similarly, for complex relations, we deleted rules concerning equivalence, disjointness, and other complex relations. The results on the FB15K-237O dataset are illustrated in Fig. 4.

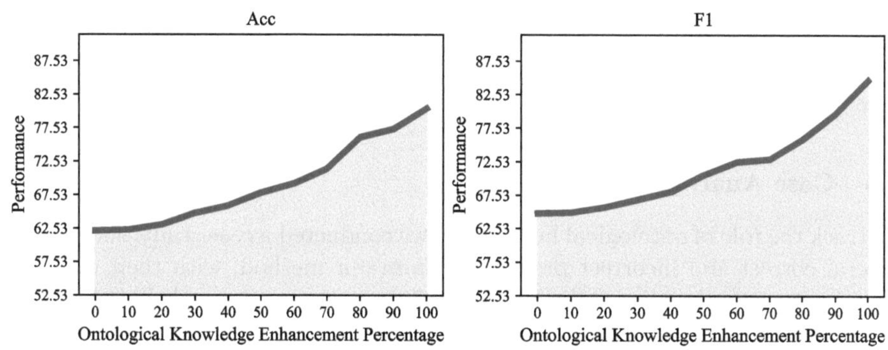

Fig. 5. The results of the ontological knowledge analysis experiment.

The experimental results indicate that OL-KGC mitigates hallucinations by injecting logical constraints derived from the underlying ontology, thereby enhancing inter-run consistency and improving inferential accuracy. Specifically, the impact of entity class rules is relatively substantial, ranging from 9.53% to 12.01%. In contrast, the influence of complex relations on the model is relatively minor, falling between 4.60% and 6.30%. We attribute the differences to the fact that specialized complex category relations are not extensively present in the KG data; they primarily serve as supplementary information to aid the LLM in reasoning. Conversely, entity classes can impose constraints on every triple (answering **RQ2**).

5.4 Ontological Knowledge Analysis Experiment

We focus specifically on the impact of ontological knowledge on model performance. By gradually increasing the application of ontology rules, we compare the ACC and F1 under constrained and unconstrained conditions. This comparison visually demonstrates the positive impact of explicit rules on model performance, thereby validating the interpretability of the model in KGC. The results on the FB15K-237O dataset are shown in Fig. 5.

The dark-colored lines indicate the performance of the model after incorporating the corresponding percentage of ontological knowledge, while the shaded areas represent the performance gains attributable to the use of such knowledge—that is, correct reasoning outcomes derived from ontological analysis. Across all evaluation metrics, model performance consistently improves as the amount of ontological knowledge increases. This trend suggests that the incremental incorporation of ontological knowledge provides the model with progressively richer semantic constraints.

Meanwhile, our approach is readily applicable to real-world KGs that embed rich ontological knowledge, with financial KGs serving as a paradigmatic example. Within these graphs, hierarchical concept taxonomies such as `:Enterprise` $\sqsupseteq$ `:SmallEnterprise` $\sqsupseteq$ `:HighRiskSmallEnterprise` enable OL-KGC to (i) infer class inheritance and (ii) verify constraint satisfaction, thereby safeguarding class-level consistency and enhancing the accuracy of downstream risk assessments (answering **RQ3**).

5.5 Case Analysis Experiment

To track the role of ontological knowledge, we conducted a case study, showcasing several correct and incorrect predictions from our method, with their explanation. In our experiments on the FB15K-237 dataset, we observed that the triple (`:LosAngeles`, `:locatedIn`, `:Country`) was incorrectly predicted as True by the LLM when no ontological knowledge was provided. This misjudgment arises from strong semantic associations between the entities, despite violating the range constraint of `:locatedIn` relation, which expects the tail entity to belong to `:Country` class (for example, entity `:America` satisfies this constraint), whereas the entity `:Country` itself does not belong to the `:Country` class. When ontological constraints—specifically domain and range information—were injected, OL-KGC correctly predicted this triple as False. Conversely, the valid triple (`:LosAngeles`, `:locatedIn`, `:Country`) was consistently predicted as True due to class consistency.

6 Conclusion

This paper introduces OL-KGC, a KGC method that leverages LLMs. By integrating vectorized structural information and ontological knowledge, the performance and reasoning capability of the KGC are effectively enhanced. We introduced various types of ontological knowledge into existing KGs and utilized LLMs to incorporate symbolic ontological knowledge into reasoning. Experimental results demonstrate that OL-KGC achieves state-of-the-art performance in the field of KGC.

Supplemental Material Statement: We have published the algorithms for introducing ontological knowledge to existing KGs using LLM on GitHub [4]*. The*

[4] https://github.com/xiumu-gg/OL-KGC/dataset-process

datasets FB15K-237O, WN18RR-O, and UMLS-O, which were constructed on FB15K-237, WN18RR, and UMLS, are also open-sourced on GitHub [5]. *The algorithmic implementations and complete experimental parameters — including per-component computational costs and detailed hardware configurations — are publicly available on GitHub*[6].

Acknowledgments. This work was supported by the National Natural Science Foundation of China (62472311), the Key Research and Development Program of Ningxia Hui Autonomous Region (2023BEG02067), and the EPSRC Project OntoEm (EP/Y017706/1).

References

1. Bordes, A., Usunier, N., Garcia-Durán, A., Weston, J., Yakhnenko, O.: Translating embeddings for modeling multi-relational data. In: Proceedings of the 26th International Conference on Neural Information Processing Systems, pp. 2787–2795. NeurIPS'13 (2013)
2. Brown, T., et al.: Language models are few-shot learners. **33**, 1877–1901 (2020)
3. Chen, J., Zhang, K., Gan, A., Tong, S., Shen, S., Liu, Q.: Enhancing knowledge graph completion with entity neighborhood and relation context. arXiv preprint arXiv:2503.23205 (2025)
4. Chen, S., Liu, X., Gao, J., Jiao, J., Zhang, R., Ji, Y.: Hitter: hierarchical transformers for knowledge graph embeddings. In: Proceedings of the 2021 Conference on Empirical Methods in Natural Language Processing, pp. 10395–10407. EMNLP'21 (2021)
5. Chen, Y., Li, S., Fang, H., Li, Y., Hu, J.: A knowledge graph completion model combining graph convolutional networks with self-attention mechanisms. In: 2024 IEEE 5th International Conference on Pattern Recognition and Machine Learning (PRML), pp. 199–203 (2024). https://doi.org/10.1109/PRML62565.2024.10779724
6. Cheng, S., Zhang, N., Tian, B., Chen, X., Liu, Q., Chen, H.: Editing language model-based knowledge graph embeddings. In: Proceedings of the AAAI Conference on Artificial Intelligence, vol. 38, pp. 17835–17843 (2024)
7. DeLong, L.N., Mir, R.F., Fleuriot, J.D.: Neurosymbolic ai for reasoning over knowledge graphs: a survey. IEEE Transactions on Neural Networks and Learning Systems (2024)
8. Dettmers, T., Minervini, P., Stenetorp, P., Riedel, S.: Convolutional 2d knowledge graph embeddings. In: Proceedings of the Thirty-Second AAAI Conference on Artificial Intelligence, pp. 1811–1818. AAAI'18 (2018)
9. Fan, M., Zhou, Q., Chang, E., Zheng, F.: Transition-based knowledge graph embedding with relational mapping properties. In: Proceedings of the 28th Pacific Asia Conference on Language, Information and Computing, pp. 328–337 (2014)
10. Feng, T., Wu, Y., Li, L.: Research on knowledge graph completion based upon knowledge graph embedding. In: 2024 9th International Conference on Computer and Communication Systems (ICCCS), pp. 1335–1342 (2024). https://doi.org/10.1109/ICCCS61882.2024.10603073

[5] https://github.com/xiumu-gg/OL-KGC/data
[6] https://github.com/xiumu-gg/OL-KGC

11. Gu, Y., et al.: Beyond iid: three levels of generalization for question answering on knowledge bases. In: Proceedings of the Web Conference 2021, pp. 3477–3488 (2021)
12. Guo, L., Zhang, Q., Sun, Z., Chen, M., Hu, W., Chen, H.: Understanding and improving knowledge graph embedding for entity alignment. In: International Conference on Machine Learning, pp. 8145–8156. PMLR (2022)
13. Guo, S., Wang, Q., Wang, L., Wang, B., Guo, L.: Jointly embedding knowledge graphs and logical rules. In: Proceedings of the 2016 Conference on Empirical Methods in Natural Language Processing. Association for Computational Linguistics (2016)
14. Hogan, A., et al.: Knowledge graphs. ACM Comput. Surv. **54**(4) (Jul 2021). https://doi.org/10.1145/3447772
15. Ji, G., He, S., Xu, L., Liu, K., Zhao, J.: Knowledge graph embedding via dynamic mapping matrix. In: Proceedings of the 53rd Annual Meeting of the Association for Computational Linguistics and the 7th International Joint Conference on Natural Language Processing pp. 687–696. ACL'15 (2015)
16. Ji, S., Liu, L., Xi, J., Zhang, X., Li, X.: KLR-KGC: Knowledge-guided LLM reasoning for knowledge graph completion. Electronics **13**(24) (2024). https://doi.org/10.3390/electronics13245037
17. Jiang, D., Wang, R., Xue, L., Yang, J.: Multisource hierarchical neural network for knowledge graph embedding. Expert Syst. Appl. **237**, 121446 (2024)
18. Jiang, X., Wang, Q., Wang, B.: Adaptive convolution for multi-relational learning. In: Proceedings of the 2019 Conference of the North American Chapter of the Association for Computational Linguistics: Human Language Technologies, Volume 1 (Long and Short Papers), pp. 978–987. NAACL'20 (2019)
19. Li, Q., Chen, Z., Ji, C., Jiang, S., Li, J.: LLM-based multi-level knowledge generation for few-shot knowledge graph completion. In: Proceedings of the Thirty-Third International Joint Conference on Artificial Intelligence, vol. 271494703 (2024)
20. Li, Z., Liu, X., Wang, X., Liu, P., Shen, Y.: Transo: a knowledge-driven representation learning method with ontology information constraints. World Wide Web **26**(1), 297–319 (2023)
21. Li, Z., Liu, H., Zhang, Z., Liu, T., Xiong, N.N.: Learning knowledge graph embedding with heterogeneous relation attention networks. IEEE Trans. Neural Netw. Learn. Syst. **33**(8), 3961–3973 (2021)
22. Nayyeri, M., Vahdati, S., Aykul, C., Lehmann, J.: 5* knowledge graph embeddings with projective transformations. In: Proceedings of the AAAI Conference on Artificial Intelligence, vol. 35, pp. 9064–9072 (2021)
23. Nguyen, D.Q., Nguyen, T.D., Nguyen, D.Q., Phung, D.: A novel embedding model for knowledge base completion based on convolutional neural network. In: Proceedings of the 2018 Conference of the North American Chapter of the Association for Computational Linguistics: Human Language Technologies, pp. 327–333. NAACL'18 (2018)
24. Pan, S., Luo, L., Wang, Y., Chen, C., Wang, J., Wu, X.: Unifying large language models and knowledge graphs: A roadmap. IEEE (2024)

25. Pan, Y., Liu, J., Zhao, T., Zhang, L., Lin, Y., Dong, J.S.: A symbolic rule integration framework with logic transformer for inductive relation prediction. In: Proceedings of the ACM Web Conference 2024, pp. 2181–2192. WWW '24, Association for Computing Machinery, New York, NY, USA (2024). https://doi.org/10.1145/3589334.3645594
26. Sanmartin, D.: Kg-rag: Bridging the gap between knowledge and creativity. arXiv preprint arXiv:2405.12035 (2024)
27. Saxena, A., Kochsiek, A., Gemulla, R.: Sequence-to-sequence knowledge graph completion and question answering. In: Proceedings of the 60th Annual Meeting of the Association for Computational Linguistics, pp. 2814–2828. ACL'22 (2022)
28. Sheikh, N., Qin, X., Reinwald, B., Miksovic, C., Gschwind, T., Scotton, P.: Knowledge graph embedding using graph convolutional networks with relation-aware attention. arXiv preprint arXiv:2102.07200 (2021)
29. Sun, Z., Deng, Z.H., Nie, J.Y., Tang, J.: Rotate: Knowledge graph embedding by relational rotation in complex space. In: Proceedings of the Seventh International Conference on Learning Representations, pp. 328–337. ICLR'19 (2019)
30. Trouillon, T., Welbl, J., Riedel, S., Gaussier, É., Bouchard, G.: Complex embeddings for simple link prediction. In: Proceedings of the 33rd International Conference on International Conference on Machine Learning, pp. 2071–2080. ICML'16 (2016)
31. Wang, D., Zuo, Y., Li, F., Wu, J.: Llms as zero-shot graph learners: Alignment of GNN representations with llm token embeddings. arXiv preprint arXiv:2408.14512 (2024)
32. Wang, Q., Mao, Z., Wang, B., Guo, L.: Knowledge graph embedding: A survey of approaches and applications. IEEE Trans. Knowl. Data Eng. **29**(12), 2724–2743 (2017)
33. Wang, X., et al.: Learning intents behind interactions with knowledge graph for recommendation. In: Proceedings of the Web Conference 2021, pp. 878–887 (2021)
34. Wang, Z., Zhang, J., Feng, J., Chen, Z.: Knowledge graph embedding by translating on hyperplanes. In: Proceedings of the Twenty-Eighth AAAI Conference on Artificial Intelligence, pp. 1112–1119. AAAI'14 (2014)
35. Xu, J., Fei, H., Pan, L., Liu, Q., Lee, M.L., Hsu, W.: Faithful logical reasoning via symbolic chain-of-thought (2024). https://arxiv.org/abs/2405.18357
36. Yang, G., Liu, Y., Zhang, L., Zhang, L., Xie, H., Mao, Z.: Knowledge context modeling with pre-trained language models for contrastive knowledge graph completion. In: Findings of the Association for Computational Linguistics ACL 2024, pp. 8619–8630 (2024)
37. Yang, L., Chen, H., Li, Z., Ding, X., Wu, X.: Chatgpt is not enough: enhancing large language models with knowledge graphs for fact-aware language modeling, pp. arXiv–2306 (2023)
38. Yao, L., Mao, C., Luo, Y.: Kg-bert: Bert for knowledge graph completion. arXiv e-prints, pp. arXiv–1909 (2019)
39. Yao, L., Peng, J., Mao, C., Luo, Y.: Exploring large language models for knowledge graph completion. arXiv preprint arXiv:2308.13916 (2023)
40. Zhang, W., Chen, J., Li, J., Xu, Z., Pan, J.Z., Chen, H.: Knowledge graph reasoning with logics and embeddings: survey and perspective. In: 2024 IEEE International Conference on Knowledge Graph (ICKG), pp. 492–499 (2024). https://doi.org/10.1109/ICKG63256.2024.00069

41. Zhang, W., et al.: Iteratively learning embeddings and rules for knowledge graph reasoning. In: The World Wide Web Conference, pp. 2366–2377. WWW '19, Association for Computing Machinery, New York, NY, USA (2019). https://doi.org/10.1145/3308558.3313612
42. Zhang, Y., Chen, Z., Guo, L., Xu, Y., Zhang, W., Chen, H.: Making large language models perform better in knowledge graph completion. In: Proceedings of the 32nd ACM International Conference on Multimedia, pp. 233–242 (2024)
43. Zhao, W.X., et al.: A Survey of Large Language Models. p. arXiv:2303.18223 (Mar 2023). https://doi.org/10.48550/arXiv.2303.18223

ProgKGC: Progressive Structure-Enhanced Semantic Framework for Knowledge Graph Completion

Zhuang Li, Yingwen Wu(✉), YaChao Yuan(✉), and Jin Wang(✉)

School of Future Science and Engineering, Soochow University, Suzhou 215222, China
20245258030@stu.suda.edu.cn, {ywwu,chao910904,wjin1985}@suda.edu.cn

Abstract. Knowledge graph completion (KGC) aims to predict missing links between entities based on known relational facts. Text-based methods typically leverage pretrained language models to extract semantic representations of entities, and some of these methods further incorporate graph structure information to enhance the representations. Despite these advances, current approaches face two significant limitations: insufficient integration of semantic and structural information, and incomplete neighborhood context representation that neglects tail-entity perspectives. In this work, we introduce a progressive semantic framework enhanced by structural signals, which is trained in stages by first establishing robust semantic representations and then gradually integrating graph attention to incorporate structural context. It also includes a bidirectional neighborhood aggregation mechanism that captures both head- and tail-entity contexts to enrich relational understanding. Experiments on two public datasets demonstrate the effectiveness of our method in improving KGC performance while keeping the architecture simple and lightweight.

Keywords: Knowledge Graph Completion · BERT · Structural Encoder · Progressive Training

1 Introduction

Knowledge graphs (KGs) provide structured representations of real-world facts by organizing entities and their relations into graph-based semantic networks [1]. They have become fundamental to a wide range of applications, including question answering [2], recommendation systems [3], and web search [4], where they support more effective reasoning and enhance overall system performance. However, the practical utility of KGs is often limited by their inherent incompleteness, arising from the dynamic nature of real-world knowledge and the high cost of manual curation. This challenge has positioned Knowledge Graph Completion (KGC) as a critical research area that aims to predict missing links in KGs—typically represented as triples (h, r, t)—by inferring the missing entity in incomplete triples such as $(h, r, ?)$ [5].

D. Garijo et al. (Eds.): ISWC 2025, LNCS 16140, pp. 81–98, 2026.
https://doi.org/10.1007/978-3-032-09527-5_5

The fundamental challenge in KGC lies in effectively capturing both the semantic meaning of entities and their structural relationships within the knowledge graph. While embedding-based methods excel at modeling graph topology through geometric operations, they often lack semantic richness and struggle with sparse graphs. Conversely, text-based methods leverage rich semantic information from entity descriptions but may inadequately incorporate the structural patterns that are crucial for accurate link prediction. The integration of these two types of information—semantic and structural—remains a significant challenge, often resulting in noisy interactions and unstable embeddings that compromise prediction accuracy.

Our work addresses these limitations through a novel progressive training framework that carefully orchestrates the integration of semantic and structural information. We propose a two-phase approach that first establishes robust semantic representations using pretrained language models, then gradually incorporates structural context through graph attention mechanisms. This progressive strategy, combined with bidirectional neighborhood aggregation from both head and tail entities, provides a more stable and comprehensive foundation for knowledge graph completion.

2 Related Work

2.1 Embedding-Based Knowledge Graph Completion

Early approaches to knowledge graph completion primarily focused on learning low-dimensional embeddings that capture the structural patterns in KGs. TransE [6] pioneered this direction by modeling relations as translations in the embedding space, where $h + r \approx t$ for a valid triple (h, r, t). This simple yet effective approach inspired numerous extensions, including TransH [7] and TransR [8], which addressed limitations in handling complex relation types.

Bilinear models represent another major category of embedding-based methods. DistMult [9] uses element-wise multiplication to score triples, while ComplEx [10] extends this to complex embeddings to better handle asymmetric relations. More sophisticated approaches like TuckER [11] employ tensor decomposition to capture higher-order interactions between entities and relations. While these methods demonstrate strong performance on well-structured graphs, they inherently lack semantic understanding and struggle with sparse graphs where structural patterns are insufficient for accurate predictions.

2.2 Text-based Knowledge Graph Completion

Recognizing the limitations of purely structural approaches, researchers have increasingly turned to text-based methods that leverage the rich semantic information available in entity descriptions and relation names. These methods typically employ pretrained language models to encode textual representations, then apply various techniques to align these representations for link prediction.

SimKGC [12] represents a seminal work in this direction, using contrastive learning to align entity representations by maximizing the similarity between matching pairs while minimizing similarity between negative pairs. This approach demonstrates significant improvements over embedding-based methods, particularly on datasets with rich textual descriptions. Building upon SimKGC, several works have focused on improving the contrastive learning process. GHN [13] addresses the challenge of generating hard negative samples, which are crucial for effective contrastive learning. MoCoSA [14] incorporates momentum contrast and self-augmentation strategies to further enhance the learning process.

To further improve text-based methods, some approaches incorporate structural information from entity neighborhoods while maintaining the text-based foundation. AttEt [15] proposes a neighborhood-attention mechanism that adaptively fuses entity attribute text and neighborhood structural information to enhance fine-grained entity typing in knowledge graphs. CAFE [16] proposes a neighborhood-aware feature engineering framework that explicitly constructs interpretable structural features—such as paths, types, and similarities—to guide knowledge graph completion. NNKGC [17] enhances entity representations by aggregating the semantic information of multi-hop structural neighbors using a BERT-based encoder, focusing on head entity neighborhoods and introducing an auxiliary link prediction task to reinforce relational reasoning.

2.3 Challenges in Current Approaches

Despite the progress made by text-based approaches, existing methods face several significant limitations that motivate our work. First, the integration of semantic and structural features can lead to noisy interactions and unstable embeddings, as these approaches fail to ensure the quality and consistency of the fused representations. For example, when the semantic encoder (e.g., BERT) has not yet fully converged, the resulting embeddings may still be noisy or inaccurate. If structural signals—such as neighbor-based aggregation—are incorporated at this early stage, the model may fuse unreliable semantic features with potentially noisy structural ones, further amplifying representation errors and leading to suboptimal performance.

Second, they predominantly focus on the head entity's neighborhood, often neglecting the crucial structural context provided by the tail entity's neighborhood. However, tail entities also reside in informative local structures that can aid in distinguishing between semantically similar candidates. Ignoring this information may lead to incomplete or biased structural representations, thus limiting prediction accuracy. A more balanced integration of both head and tail neighborhoods is therefore essential for comprehensive structural modeling.

To address these challenges, we propose a phased training strategy. In the first phase, semantic embeddings are learned using only a pretrained language model without any structural information, establishing a stable semantic foundation. In the second phase, a Graph Attention Network (GAT) [18] is applied to integrate neighborhood features from both the head and tail entities, providing a richer structural context. This design reduces noise from unreliable neighbor embeddings by ensuring high-quality base representations before gradually introducing structural information. Moreover, the bidirectional neighborhood integration significantly enriches structural context and enhances embedding robustness—especially in cases with limited entity descriptions or sparse graph structures.

3 Method

We propose a **Prog**ressive Structure-Enhanced Semantic Framework for **K**nowledge **G**raph **C**ompletion (ProgKGC), as shown in Fig. 1. Our framework integrates a textual encoder with a structure encoder through a progressive training strategy, incorporates bidirectional neighborhood aggregation, and employs contrastive learning with cosine similarity to align textual and structural representations. We define the task as follows: given an incomplete KG $\mathcal{G} = (\mathcal{E}, \mathcal{R})$, the goal is to predict the tail entity t given the head entity h and the query relation r, i.e., $(h, r, ?)$.

3.1 Textual Encoder

We utilize a pre-trained BERT [19] model to encode both entities and relations. Each entity is described by its name (*name*) and textual description (*desc*), while each relation is represented as a phrase (*rel*).

For the *head entity*, we concatenate its name and description with the relation text to form the input sequence for BERT, separated by a special token [SEP]. This allows the model to jointly consider both head entity and the relation when computing the embedding:

$$\mathbf{e}_{hr}^{\text{text}} = \text{BERT}(\texttt{name}_h \parallel \texttt{desc}_h \parallel \texttt{[SEP]} \parallel \texttt{rel}_r) \tag{1}$$

For the *tail entity*, only its name and description are provided to BERT, independently from the relation:

$$\mathbf{e}_{t}^{\text{text}} = \text{BERT}(\texttt{name}_t \parallel \texttt{desc}_t) \tag{2}$$

Here, $\mathbf{e}_{hr}^{\text{text}}$ and $\mathbf{e}_{t}^{\text{text}}$ denote the textual embeddings of the head and tail entities, respectively. This design enables the model to capture relation-aware semantics for the head entity while preserving the tail entity's contextual meaning from its standalone textual information. Meanwhile, generated entity embeddings are cached in the Embedding Cache Queue and retrieved during the second training phase for neighbor aggregation by the structural encoder.

3.2 Structural Encoder

To enhance entity representations by leveraging graph topology, we introduce a GAT to incorporate 1-hop neighborhood information. Unlike prior methods that focus solely on the head entity's neighborhood, we extend the aggregation

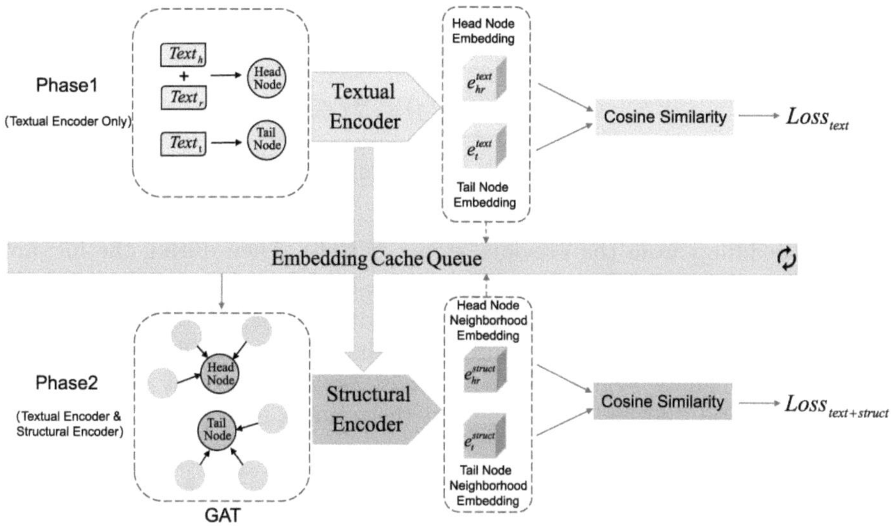

Fig. 1. ProgKGC Model Architecture. The model comprises a Textual Encoder for extracting semantic representations and a Structural Encoder for incorporating structural information. In Phase 1, the Textual Encoder encodes head entities with relation-aware inputs and tail entities with standalone textual information. In Phase 2, both encoders operate jointly, with the Textual Encoder processing texts and the Structural Encoder integrating neighborhood information of both head and tail entities via GAT. An Embedding Cache Queue stores and updates entity embeddings generated in both Phase 1 and Phase 2 throughout training. Cosine similarity-based contrastive learning optimizes entity embeddings across both phases.

strategy to both the head and tail entities, enabling bidirectional contextual encoding.

For a given triple (h, r, t), we retrieve the 1-hop neighbors $\mathcal{N}(h)$ and $\mathcal{N}(t)$ of the head and tail entities, respectively. To compute the structural-enhanced embeddings, we combine the real-time textual embedding of the target entity (generated by BERT) with the cached embeddings of its neighbors using a GAT:

$$\mathbf{e}_{hr}^{\text{struct}} = \text{GAT}\left(\left\{\mathbf{e}_{hr}^{\text{text}}\right\} \cup \left\{\mathcal{Q}_\tau(j) \mid j \in \mathcal{N}(h)\right\}\right) \tag{3}$$

$$\mathbf{e}_{t}^{\text{struct}} = \text{GAT}\left(\left\{\mathbf{e}_{t}^{\text{text}}\right\} \cup \left\{\mathcal{Q}_\tau(j) \mid j \in \mathcal{N}(t)\right\}\right) \tag{4}$$

Here, $\mathbf{e}_{hr}^{\text{text}}$ and $\mathbf{e}_{t}^{\text{text}}$ denote the current textual embeddings of the head and tail entities, respectively, produced by the Textual Encoder. The term $\mathcal{Q}_\tau(j)$ denotes the cached embedding of neighbor entity j, retrieved from the shared *Embedding Cache Queue* at the current training step τ, where each step τ corresponds to a mini-batch-level update within an epoch.

The *Embedding Cache Queue* $\mathcal{Q}$ maintains a mapping:

$$\mathcal{Q}_\tau(j) = \mathbf{e}_j^{(\tau)}, \quad \forall j \in \mathcal{E} \tag{5}$$

where $\mathbf{e}_j^{(\tau)}$ denotes the most recent embedding of entity j at training step τ. The queue is maintained across training steps as follows:

$$\mathcal{Q}_{\tau+1}(j) \leftarrow \mathcal{Q}_{\tau}(j), \quad \forall j \in \mathcal{E} \tag{6}$$

$$\mathcal{Q}_{\tau+1}(j) \leftarrow \mathbf{e}_j^{(\tau+1)} \quad \text{if } \mathbf{e}_j^{(\tau+1)} \text{ is computed at step } \tau+1 \tag{7}$$

Specifically, at the beginning of step $\tau+1$, the queue is initialized with all entity embeddings from the previous step τ (Eq. 6). Then during the forward pass at step τ+1, whenever a new embedding $\mathbf{e}_j^{(\tau+1)}$ is computed, it immediately replaces the corresponding stale embedding in the queue (Eq. 7). This progressive update mechanism ensures that the latest embeddings are always available for neighbor aggregation operations, facilitating timely access to up-to-date structural information throughout the training process.

3.3 Progressive Training

We adopt a two-phase progressive training strategy to integrate semantic and structural information. During the first phase, the model learns high-quality semantic representations through the Textual Encoder. Once these representations are established, the second phase jointly trains both the Textual and Structural Encoders, allowing the model to enhance semantic features with structural context. This phased approach improves overall training stability and ensures that structural learning builds upon a solid semantic foundation, as illustrated in Fig. 1.

3.4 Contrastive Learning

We employ a unified contrastive learning objective in both training phases. Specifically, the similarity between head and tail entity embeddings is computed using cosine similarity:

$$\text{score}(h, r, t) = \cos(\mathbf{e}_{hr}, \mathbf{e}_t) \tag{8}$$

where $\mathbf{e}_{hr}$ and $\mathbf{e}_t$ denote entity representations from the current phase—textual in the first phase and structure-enhanced in the second.

We adopt the InfoNCE loss [20] to maximize the similarity of positive triples over negatives. In the first phase, only the Textual Encoder is updated. In the second phase, gradients are propagated to both the Textual and Structural Encoders, ensuring the joint optimization of semantic and structural representations.

4 Experiment

4.1 Experimental Setup

Datasets. We evaluate our model on two widely used KGC benchmarks: FB15k-237 [21] and WN18RR [22]. FB15k-237 is a curated subset of Freebase [23], characterized by rich and diverse relations while eliminating inverse relation leakage. In contrast, WN18RR is derived from WordNet [24] and consists of lexical and hierarchical relations with a sparser structure. The two datasets vary in size and graph density, providing a comprehensive testbed for evaluating model robustness, as detailed in Table 1.

Table 1. Dataset Statistics: Avg. Len and Med. Len are the average and median token counts, and Vocab is the total number of unique tokens in all descriptions.

Dataset	#Entities	#Rel	Train/Valid/Test	Avg.Len	Med.Len	Vocab
WN18RR	40,943	11	86,835/3,034/3,134	17.1	15	18,741
FB15k-237	14,541	237	272,115/17,535/20,466	114.6	76	28,538

Evaluation Metrics. We use Mean Reciprocal Rank (MRR) and Hits@K (K = 1, 3, 10) as evaluation metrics. MRR quantifies the average reciprocal rank of the first correct answer across all test queries, computed as

$$\mathrm{MRR} = \frac{1}{N}\sum_{i=1}^{N}\frac{1}{\mathrm{rank}_i} \tag{9}$$

where higher values indicate better model performance in ranking relevant entities. Hits@K measures the proportion of test cases where the ground-truth entity is ranked within the top-k predicted candidates. Specifically, Hits@1 reflects strict precision, Hits@3 captures moderate recall, and Hits@10 provides a broader recall capability. These complementary metrics jointly evaluate both ranking quality (via MRR) and threshold-dependent retrieval performance (via Hits@K at K = 1, 3, 10), following standard information retrieval evaluation protocols in KGC tasks.

Hyperparameters. We use `bert-base-uncased` as the textual encoder and a GAT layer as the structural encoder; both have a hidden size of 768. The GAT uses 4 attention heads and a dropout rate of 0.1 applied across all submodules.

Most hyperparameters are shared across datasets, except for the learning rate, which is selected from 5e–4, 5e–5, 1e–5 via grid search. We set the temperature $\tau = 0.05$ and margin $\gamma = 0.02$, and use the AdamW [25] optimizer with linear learning rate decay. All models are trained on a single A100 GPU with a batch size of 768.

We adopt a two-phase training strategy: the structural encoder is activated from epoch 30 on WN18RR and from epoch 5 on FB15k-237. The total number of training epochs is 70 for WN18RR and 11 for FB15k-237. Further implementation details are available in our released code.

Table 2. Link prediction performance comparison on FB15k-237 and WN18RR. Bold indicates the best result for each metric. ProgKGC (Head only) uses only the neighbors of the head entity during structure enhancement; ProgKGC (Head + Tail) incorporates both head and tail entity neighbors.

	FB15k-237				WN18RR			
	MRR	H@1	H@3	H@10	MRR	H@1	H@3	H@10
Embedding-based Methods								
TransE	27.9	19.8	37.6	44.1	24.3	4.3	44.1	53.2
RotatE	47.6	42.8	49.2	57.1	33.8	24.1	37.5	53.3
DistMult	28.1	19.9	30.1	44.6	44.4	41.2	47.0	50.4
ComplEx	27.8	19.4	29.7	45.0	44.9	40.9	46.9	53.0
TuckER	35.8	26.6	39.4	54.4	47.0	44.3	48.2	52.6
Text-based Methods								
KG-BERT	–	–	–	42.0	21.6	4.1	30.2	52.4
StAR	29.6	20.5	32.2	48.2	40.1	24.3	49.1	70.9
LP-BERT	31.0	22.3	33.6	49.0	48.2	34.3	56.3	75.2
KG-S2S	33.6	25.6	37.1	49.8	57.4	53.1	59.5	66.1
GHN	33.9	25.1	36.4	51.8	67.8	59.6	71.9	82.1
SimKGC	33.6	24.9	36.2	51.1	66.6	58.7	71.7	80.5
NNKGC	33.8	25.2	36.5	51.5	67.4	59.6	72.2	81.2
ProgKGC (Head only)	34.1	**25.6**	37.2	52.1	68.1	**60.8**	72.7	81.3
ProgKGC (Head + Tail)	**34.4**	25.5	**37.5**	**52.3**	**68.2**	59.7	**73.9**	**83.4**

4.2 Main Results

Table 2 presents the link prediction performance of our model compared with both embedding-based methods (e.g., ComplEx, RotatE [26], TuckER) and text-based approaches (e.g., KG-BERT, SimKGC, KG-S2S [27]) on FB15k-237 and WN18RR. The results cover four standard metrics (MRR, Hits@1/3/10) across the two benchmarks.

Building upon the robust semantic foundation of SimKGC, the full model ProgKGC (Head + Tail) consistently improves performance, achieving +0.8% MRR on FB15k-237 and +1.6% MRR on WN18RR. In addition to the full model, we also evaluate a variant, ProgKGC (Head only), which considers only the head entity's neighbors. Both configurations outperform all embedding-based and text-based baselines across key metrics.

Compared to NNKGC, which employs head-only aggregation, our ProgKGC (Head only) variant already surpasses it across all metrics (e.g., +1.7% Hits@3, +2.2% Hits@10 on WN18RR), highlighting the effectiveness of our progressive training strategy. The full ProgKGC (Head + Tail) model further boosts performance, confirming the benefit of bidirectional neighbor aggregation. Notably, ProgKGC achieves these improvements while completing 30 epochs on WN18RR in just 150 minutes, compared to NNKGC's 180 minutes under identical settings. This efficiency demonstrates the lightweight nature of our approach, which stems from our progressive strategy that defers structural encoding until semantic representations stabilize, and employs a caching queue mechanism to avoid repeated neighbor encoding.

5 Ablation Study

We conduct ablation studies on WN18RR to assess the effectiveness of our progressive training strategy and bidirectional neighbor integration. As WN18RR is structurally sparse yet semantically rich, it serves as a suitable benchmark for validating these two components.

5.1 Progressive Training Strategy Analysis

Our progressive training strategy introduces the structural encoder only after the semantic encoder has reached a certain level of stability. To systematically evaluate the effectiveness of this approach, we design a series of experiments examining three key aspects: (1) the comparative advantage of progressive integration versus simultaneous training or complete omission of structural components; (2) the optimal timing for introducing structural information to maximize performance gains; and (3) the consistency of these patterns across varying training durations.

Effectiveness of Progressive Structural Integration. To assess the impact of progressively introducing the structural encoder, we compare three different strategies for integrating the structural encoder into the training process. Specifically, we investigate the following configurations:

- Early Structural Encoder Integration (Early): The structural encoder is introduced at the beginning of training.
- Progressive Structural Encoder Integration (Progressive): The structural encoder is introduced after the semantic encoder has become relatively stable, with both semantic and structural encoders updated throughout.
- No Structural Encoder (None): The model is trained exclusively using only the semantic encoder, without incorporating structural information.

As shown in the Fig. 2, introducing the structural encoder from the outset results in the weakest performance, while omitting it entirely performs slightly better. In contrast, our approach, which incorporates the structural encoder only after the textual encoder has stabilized, consistently achieves the best results. These findings demonstrate that deferring the integration of structural information until semantic representations are well-learned leads to a more effective fusion of structural and semantic information.

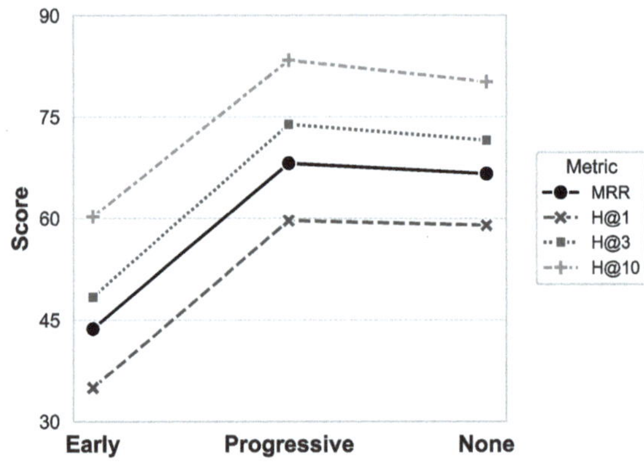

Fig. 2. Performance comparison of three structural encoder integration strategies: Early, Progressive, and None.

Optimal Timing for Structural Encoder Integration. To further explore how the integration timing of the structural encoder affects model performance, we conduct additional experiments by varying the epoch at which the encoder is introduced. Specifically, under a fixed total of 70 training epochs, we evaluate the model's performance in terms of Mean Reciprocal Rank (MRR) by enabling the structural encoder every 10 epochs, from epoch 0 to 70.

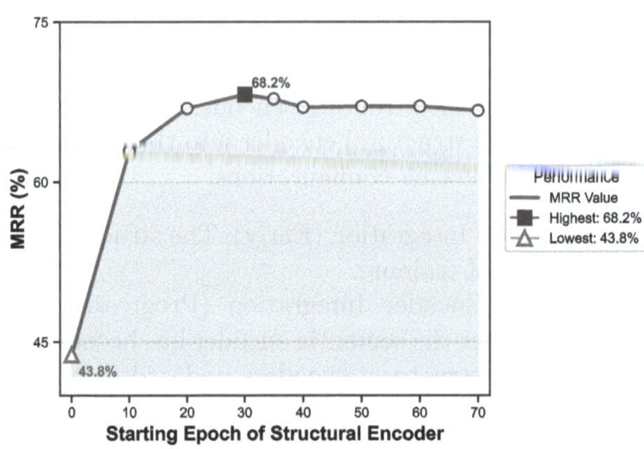

Fig. 3. MRR (%) of the model under different starting epochs for structural encoder integration.

As shown in Fig. 3, the model's performance improves as the integration point is delayed, peaking around epoch 30. After that, the gains plateau and begin to slightly decline. This trend suggests that introducing the structural encoder after the semantic encoder has reached a relatively stable state leads to better overall performance, while integrating it too early or too late can hinder model effectiveness.

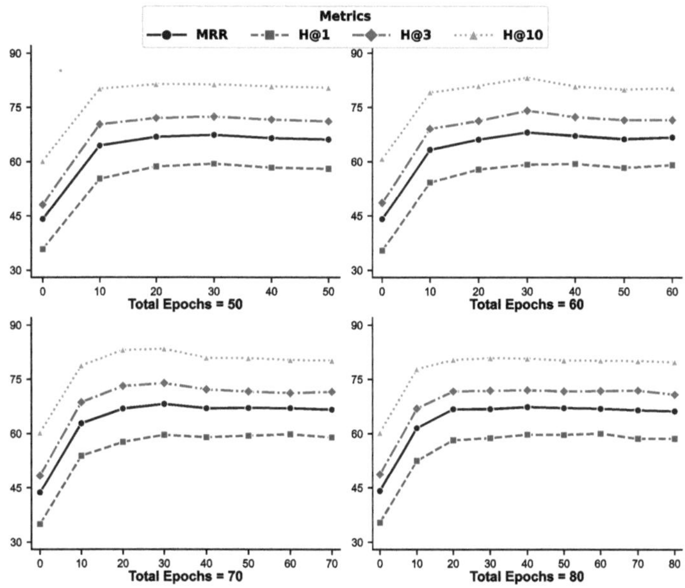

Fig. 4. Performance trends under different structural encoder start epochs across total training durations of 50, 60, 70, and 80 epochs.

Robustness to Varying Training Durations. Given that the performance of our training framework is closely related to the timing of the structural encoder integration, we further investigate how the model's performance is affected by the total number of training epochs. Specifically, we conduct experiments with total training durations of 50, 60, 70 and 80 epochs, exploring the effect of progressively introducing the structural encoder from epoch 0 to the end of training.

As shown in Fig. 4, the results exhibit a similar pattern across different training durations, with performance improving initially and stabilizing or slightly declining after reaching an optimal point. This consistency further validates the effectiveness and robustness of our framework, regardless of the training duration.

In addition, we compiled the top-performing configurations across different total training epochs, as shown in Table 3. The results indicate that the total number of training epochs has a minor effect on the final performance. The best results are typically achieved when the structural encoder is introduced at around the midpoint of the training process.

Table 3. The best performance under different training epochs.

Total Epochs	Encoder Start Epoch	MRR (%)	H@1	H@3	H@10
50	30	67.4	59.5	72.5	81.3
60	30	68.1	59.3	**74.1**	83.2
70	**30**	**68.2**	**59.7**	73.9	**83.4**
80	40	67.4	59.7	72	80.8

5.2 Bidirectional Neighbor Aggregation Analysis

Our method aggregates neighbors from both the head and tail entities to capture a more comprehensive structural context. To assess the effectiveness of this approach, we compare three different aggregation strategies, within our progressive structural-enhanced semantic framework. Additionally, we conduct a case study to further analyze performance differences, highlighting a trade-off between top-1 accuracy and overall ranking quality.

Performance Comparison Across Different Aggregation Strategies. We evaluate our framework under three distinct settings: aggregating head neighbors only, tail neighbors only, and both.

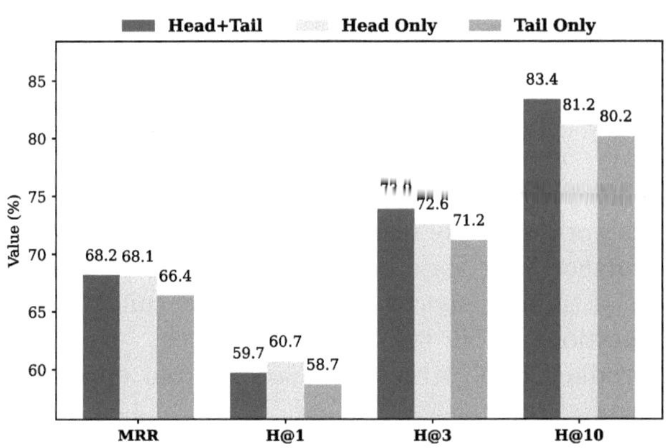

Fig. 5. Performance comparison under different neighbor aggregation strategies.

As illustrated in Fig. 5, bidirectional neighbor aggregation yields the best overall performance. Although head-only aggregation achieves competitive results in Hits@1, it falls short in other metrics. In contrast, tail-only aggregation consistently underperforms. These results confirm the advantage of incorporating structural information from both head and tail entities rather than relying on a unidirectional aggregation strategy.

Analysis of Ranking Trade-offs Between Aggregation Strategies. We observed an interesting phenomenon: integrating only head entity neighborhoods tends to yield higher Hits@1 performance, whereas incorporating both head and tail neighborhoods (i.e., bidirectional aggregation) improves broader ranking metrics, such as Hits@3 and Hits@10. To better understand this trade-off, we examined two representative cases from FB15k-237 and WN18RR, whose visualizations are shown in Figs. 6 and 7, respectively.

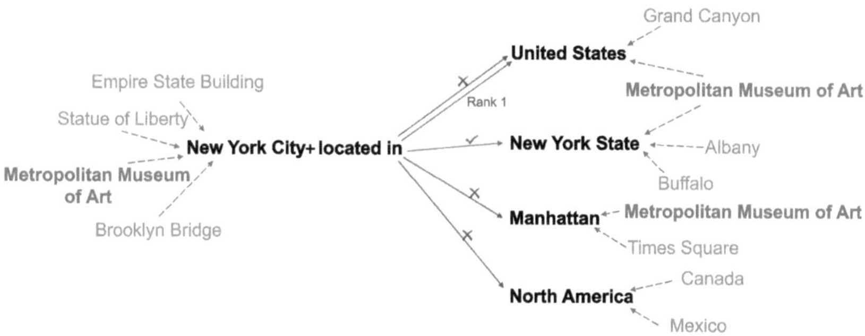

Fig. 6. Example 1 (FB15k-237): Predicting *New York State* from *New York City* via *located_in* with bidirectional neighbors. Green arrow: ground truth tail, red arrow: non-ground truth tail, blue arrow: Rank 1 prediction, dark gray: shared neighbors.

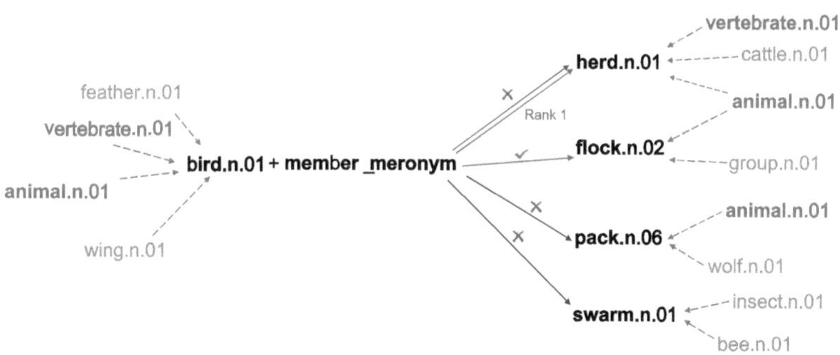

Fig. 7. Example 2 (WN18RR): Predicting *flock.n.02* from *bird.n.01* via *member_meronym* with bidirectional neighbors.

In the FB15k-237 case (*New York City*, located_in, ?) (Table 4), we find that the incorrect prediction *United States* is ranked above the correct tail *New York State*, despite both entities sharing meaningful connections with the head. Upon closer inspection, a likely reason is the presence of widely shared neighbors such as the *Metropolitan Museum of Art*, which appear not only in the head but also

Table 4. Example 1 from FB15k-237 illustrating the head entity and relation, the ground truth tail entity, and the ranked list of predicted tail entities along with their respective neighbors.

Head Entity	New York City
Relation	**located in**
Neighbors	*Metropolitan Museum of Art, Brooklyn Bridge, Statue of Liberty, Empire State Building, ...*
Ground Truth	**New York State**
Predicted Tails	
Rank 1:	United States ✗
Neighbors:	*Metropolitan Museum of Art, Grand Canyon, ...*
Rank 2:	**New York State ✓**
Neighbors:	*Metropolitan Museum of Art, Albany, Buffalo, ...*
Rank 3:	Manhattan ✗
Neighbors:	*Metropolitan Museum of Art, Times Square, ...*
Rank 4:	North America ✗
Neighbors:	*Canada, Mexico, ...*
(more predictions)	

in several candidate tails (e.g., *United States*, *New York State*, and *Manhattan*). These shared neighbors may introduce redundant or overly similar signals across candidates, making it difficult for the model to differentiate among them. In this setting, integrating tail neighbors may inadvertently amplify the confusion.

In contrast, when only the head entity's neighbors are aggregated, the model avoids integrating potentially noisy or overlapping structural information from incorrect candidate tails. This can lead to a clearer distinction between plausible and implausible candidates, thereby improving Hits@1. However, this more selective strategy also omits useful contextual cues from the correct tail, such as *New York State*'s neighbors like *Albany* and *Buffalo*, which could have strengthened its representation. As a result, its rank may be penalized in broader metrics, even if it's semantically relevant.

A similar pattern is observed in WN18RR (Table 5). In the example (*bird.n.01*, member_meronym, ?), the model incorrectly ranks *herd.n.01* above the correct tail *flock.n.02*. Again, we find considerable overlap in neighbor sets across the candidates. Both *flock.n.02* and *herd.n.01* share high-level taxonomic neighbors like *animal.n.01* and *vertebrate.n.01*, which are also present in the head. This may cause embeddings of conceptually different entities—like bird-specific and mammal-specific groups—to become overly similar. Nevertheless, thanks to bidirectional integration, the correct tail *flock.n.02* still ranks near the top (Rank 2), likely because it shares more specific neighbors such as *group.n.01* and *animal.n.01*, the latter of which is also a neighbor of the head.

These examples illustrate that while aggregating tail neighborhoods introduces valuable semantic cues that enhance ranking robustness (i.e., top-k recall), it can also lead to embedding collapse due to ambiguous neighbor signals. Conversely, aggregating only head neighbors reduces noise and sharpens candidate

Table 5. Example 2 from WN18RR illustrating the head entity and relation, the ground truth tail entity, and the ranked list of predicted tail entities along with their respective neighbors.

Head Entity	bird.n.01
Relation	**member_meronym**
Neighbors	*animal.n.01, vertebrate.n.01, wing.n.01, feather.n.01, ...*
Ground Truth	**flock.n.02**
Predicted Tails	
Rank 1:	herd.n.01 ✗
Neighbors:	*animal.n.01, vertebrate.n.01, cattle.n.01, ...*
Rank 2:	**flock.n.02 ✓**
Neighbors:	*animal.n.01, group.n.01, ...*
Rank 3:	pack.n.06 ✗
Neighbors:	*animal.n.01, wolf.n.01, group.n.01, ...*
Rank 4:	swarm.n.01 ✗
Neighbors:	*insect.n.01, bee.n.01, group.n.01, ...*
(more predictions)	

distinctions, benefiting Hits@1, but at the cost of contextual richness and overall retrieval performance.

Therefore, our observations highlight a nuanced trade-off between precision and robustness: *unidirectional aggregation favors sharper top-1 accuracy*, while *bidirectional aggregation enhances recall in top-k settings*. These insights support the use of progressive strategies that can flexibly balance the two, depending on the target application scenario (e.g., question answering vs. recommendation).

Effect of Higher-Order Neighborhoods. To further investigate the impact of neighborhood scope on structural modeling, we conduct a preliminary study by incorporating 2-hop neighbors into the aggregation process. While our default design focuses on 1-hop neighbors to maintain high relevance and reduce noise, extending to 2-hop neighbors could potentially capture broader contextual signals.

We evaluate two configurations on WN18RR: using only 1-hop neighbors and using 2-hop neighbors.

As shown in Fig. 8, incorporating 2-hop neighbors causes a modest but consistent performance drop across all metrics, suggesting added noise or weaker semantic connections.

This trend reinforces the effectiveness of focusing on high-precision 1-hop neighborhoods, and points to the need for more selective strategies when leveraging higher-order neighborhoods. We leave these directions for future work.

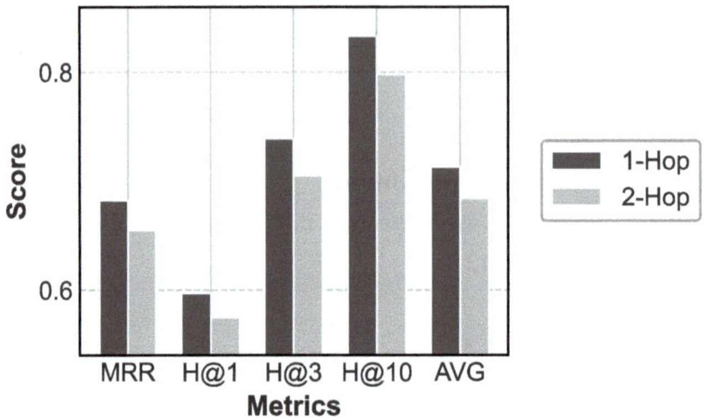

Fig. 8. Performance difference between using 1-hop and 2-hop neighbors on WN18RR.

6 Conclusion

We propose ProgKGC, a KGC framework that improves performance through progressive training and bidirectional neighbor aggregation. By first learning robust semantic representations and then progressively integrating structural context, ProgKGC enhances link prediction accuracy while maintaining model simplicity. Experimental results and ablation studies validate the effectiveness of our approach. Future work could explore advanced progressive fusion strategies and selective mechanisms for higher-order neighborhood incorporation.

Supplemental Material Statement: Source code, datasets and other details are available at https://github.com/0214ZhuangLi/ProgKGC.

Acknowledgments. This study was funded by the National Natural Science Foundation of China (grant number 72402156, 62406215 & 62072321), the China Postdoctoral Science Foundation (grant number 2025M770693), the Science and Technology Program of Jiangsu Province (grant number BZ2024062), the Natural Science Foundation of the Jiangsu Higher Education Institutions of China (grant number 22KJA520007), and Suzhou Planning Project of Science and Technology (grant number 2023ss03).

Disclosure of Interests. The authors have no competing interests to declare that are relevant to the content of this article.

References

1. Hogan, A., et al.: Knowledge graphs. ACM Comput. Surv. (Csur) **54**(4), 1–37 (2021)
2. Yasunaga, M., Ren, H., Bosselut, A., Liang, P., Leskovec, J.: Qa-gnn: reasoning with language models and knowledge graphs for question answering. arXiv preprint arXiv:2104.06378 (2021)

3. Guo, Q., et al.: A survey on knowledge graph-based recommender systems. IEEE Trans. Knowl. Data Eng. **34**(8), 3549–3568 (2020)
4. Dong, X., et al.: Knowledge vault: a web-scale approach to probabilistic knowledge fusion. In: Proceedings of the 20th ACM SIGKDD International Conference on Knowledge Discovery and Data Mining, pp. 601–610 (2014)
5. Ji, S., Pan, S., Cambria, E., Marttinen, P., Yu, P.S.: A survey on knowledge graphs: representation, acquisition, and applications. IEEE Trans. Neural Netw. Learn. Syst. **33**(2), 494–514 (2022). https://doi.org/10.1109/TNNLS.2021.3070843
6. Bordes, A., Usunier, N., Garcia-Duran, A., Weston, J., Yakhnenko, O.: Translating embeddings for modeling multi-relational data. In: Advances in Neural Information Processing Systems, vol. 26 (2013)
7. Wang, Z., Zhang, J., Feng, J., Chen, Z.: Knowledge graph embedding by translating on hyperplanes. In: Proceedings of the AAAI Conference on Artificial Intelligence, vol. 28 (2014)
8. Lin, Y., Liu, Z., Sun, M., Liu, Y., Zhu, X.: Learning entity and relation embeddings for knowledge graph completion. In: Proceedings of the AAAI Conference on Artificial Intelligence, vol. 29 (2015)
9. Yang, B., Yih, W.T., He, X., Gao, J., Deng, L.: Embedding entities and relations for learning and inference in knowledge bases. arXiv preprint arXiv:1412.6575 (2014)
10. Trouillon, T., Welbl, J., Riedel, S., Gaussier, É., Bouchard, G.: Complex embeddings for simple link prediction. In: International Conference on Machine Learning, pp. 2071–2080. PMLR (2016)
11. Balažević, I., Allen, C., Hospedales, T.M.: Tucker: tensor factorization for knowledge graph completion. arXiv preprint arXiv:1901.09590 (2019)
12. Wang, L., Zhao, W., Wei, Z., Liu, J.: Simkgc: simple contrastive knowledge graph completion with pre-trained language models. In: Proceedings of the 60th Annual Meeting of the Association for Computational Linguistics (Volume 1: Long Papers), pp. 4281–4294. ACL, Dublin, Ireland (2022). https://doi.org/10.18653/v1/2022.acl-long.295, https://aclanthology.org/2022.acl-long.295
13. Qiao, Z., Ye, W., Yu, D., Mo, T., Li, W., Zhang, S.: Improving knowledge graph completion with generative hard negative mining. In: Findings of the Association for Computational Linguistics: ACL 2023, pp. 5866–5878 (2023)
14. He, J., Liu, J., Wang, L., Li, X., Xu, X.: Mocosa: momentum contrast for knowledge graph completion with structure-augmented pre-trained language models. In: 2024 IEEE International Conference on Multimedia and Expo (ICME), pp. 1–6. IEEE (2024)
15. Zhuo, J., Zhu, Q., Yue, Y., Zhao, Y., Han, W.: A neighborhood-attention fine-grained entity typing for knowledge graph completion. In: Proceedings of the Fifteenth ACM International Conference on Web Search and Data Mining, pp. 1525–1533 (2022)
16. Borrego, A., Ayala, D., Hernández, I., Rivero, C.R., Ruiz, D.: Cafe: knowledge graph completion using neighborhood-aware features. Eng. Appl. Artif. Intell. **103**, 104302 (2021)
17. Li, I., Yang, B.: Nnkgc: improving knowledge graph completion with node neighborhoods. arXiv preprint arXiv:2302.06132 (2023)
18. Veličković, P., Cucurull, G., Casanova, A., Romero, A., Lio, P., Bengio, Y.: Graph attention networks. arXiv preprint arXiv:1710.10903 (2017)
19. Devlin, J., Chang, M.W., Lee, K., Toutanova, K.: Bert: pre-training of deep bidirectional transformers for language understanding. In: Proceedings of the 2019 Conference of the North American Chapter of the Association for Computational

Linguistics: Human Language Technologies, volume 1 (long and short papers), pp. 4171–4186 (2019)
20. Oord, A.V.d., Li, Y., Vinyals, O.: Representation learning with contrastive predictive coding. arXiv preprint arXiv:1807.03748 (2018)
21. Toutanova, K., Chen, D., Pantel, P., Poon, H., Choudhury, P., Gamon, M.: Observed versus latent features for knowledge base and text inference. In: Proceedings of the 3rd Workshop on Continuous Vector Space Models and their Compositionality, pp. 57–66 (2015)
22. Dettmers, T., Minervini, P., Stenetorp, P., Riedel, S.: Convolutional 2d knowledge graph embeddings. In: Proceedings of the AAAI Conference on Artificial Intelligence, vol. 32 (2018)
23. Bollacker, K., Evans, C., Paritosh, P., Sturge, T., Taylor, J.: Freebase: a collaboratively created graph database for structuring human knowledge. In: Proceedings of the 2008 ACM SIGMOD International Conference on Management of Data, pp. 1247–1250 (2008)
24. Miller, G.A.: Wordnet: a lexical database for english. Commun. ACM **38**(11), 39–41 (1995)
25. Loshchilov, I., Hutter, F.: Decoupled weight decay regularization. arXiv preprint arXiv:1711.05101 (2017)
26. Sun, Z., Deng, Z.H., Nie, J.Y., Tang, J.: Rotate: knowledge graph embedding by relational rotation in complex space. arXiv preprint arXiv:1902.10197 (2019)
27. Chen, C., Wang, Y., Li, B., Lam, K.Y.: Knowledge is flat: a seq2seq generative framework for various knowledge graph completion. arXiv preprint arXiv:2209.07299 (2022)

Link Prediction Under Non-targeted Attacks: Do Soft Labels Always Help?

Adel Memariani(✉), Michael Röder, Arnab Sharma, Caglar Demir, and Axel-Cyrille Ngonga Ngomo

Data Science Group (DICE), Heinz Nixdorf Institute, Paderborn University, Paderborn, Germany
{adel.memariani,michael.roeder,arnab.sharma,caglar.demir, axel.ngonga}@upb.de

Abstract. Knowledge Graph Embedding (KGE) models rely on precise factual information to learn effective representations. These learned representations support many downstream tasks, with link prediction being a primary application. However, recent studies have shown that noise in training data can compromise the effectiveness of knowledge graph embeddings. Therefore, KGEs are highly vulnerable to data poisoning attacks. Typically current attacks on KGEs are studied under targeted scenarios, where target facts and the model are assumed to be known beforehand. Yet, this information is not often available in real-world scenarios. Thus, more realistic scenarios involve non-targeted but malicious perturbations aimed at reducing the overall model performance. In this paper, we focus on enhancing the robustness of link prediction approaches in non-targeted settings. To mitigate the harmful impact of the noisy data, we explore soft-label loss functions as a strategy for reducing overconfidence in model predictions. We performed a thorough evaluation on six state-of-the-art models and five benchmark datasets, with different noise ratios introduced into each dataset. Our results show that soft labels commonly improve the robustness of KGE models across various noise ratios.

Keywords: Knowledge Graph Embeddings · Label Smoothing · Label Relaxation · Non-Adversarial Attacks · Data Poisoning

1 Introduction

Knowledge Graph Embedding (KGE) models encode factual information into dense vectors to support downstream tasks such as link prediction [1]. However, real-world knowledge graphs may contain wrong or inconsistent facts, that can arise from human curation mistakes, deficiencies in automated retrieval pipelines,

Supplementary Information The online version contains supplementary material available at https://doi.org/10.1007/978-3-032-09527-5_6.

D. Garijo et al. (Eds.): ISWC 2025, LNCS 16140, pp. 99–121, 2026.
https://doi.org/10.1007/978-3-032-09527-5_6

or even data poisoning attacks [2]. Despite the prevalence of noise in knowledge graphs, verifying the correctness of information is costly. Fact validation methods rely on a reference knowledge and are often computationally expensive due to reasoning and evidence retrieval. This poses a challenge for applying fact-checking to large-scale knowledge graphs [3–6]. Yet, unreliable facts can distort knowledge graph embeddings, which in turn, compromise the trustworthiness of link prediction methods. In addition to the noise introduced during automatic construction, knowledge graphs are at risk of data poisoning attacks that are designed to corrupt the outcomes of link prediction tasks. In this context, two broad categories of attacks exist in the literature, (i) *targeted*, where specific triples are strategically added or removed to alter particular inferences [7–11], and (ii) *non-targeted*, which introduce noisy data to degrade overall model accuracy [12,13]. Therefore, systems must be designed to remain robust even when faced with noisy or unreliable data. In fields such as healthcare, social policy, and economics, this robustness becomes even more critical because misleading data can lead to harmful consequences [14,15].

To mitigate the effects of noisy data, the machine learning community has introduced several regularization-based approaches [16–23]. Primarily, *confidence* in predictions indicates how certain a model is about its outputs, and the above-mentioned regularization techniques penalize overconfidence to help align the confidence with actual correctness, i.e., avoiding confidence in an incorrect prediction. Regularization is particularly helpful for noisy input data. Because overconfident predictions can amplify the impact of corrupted data and this leads to a biased learning [24].

Label smoothing [25] is a widely used method to address the overconfidence problem [16,26,27]. It replaces binary or *hard* labels with soft or *smoothed* labels. Therefore, it encourages the model to learn more generalizable patterns rather than memorizing potentially corrupted inputs. A subsequent work introduced label relaxation [28], as an alternative to label smoothing that provides a more flexible approach for handling uncertainty by allowing labels to vary within a predefined range. Non-targeted attacks [12,13] aim to introduce noise to disrupt model predictions without targeting specific outputs. It has already been shown that regularized loss functions can help build models that are more robust to such perturbations [29,30]. However, despite this potential, the application of such approaches in KGE, under non-targeted attack settings, remains underexplored. In this work, we study whether the robustness of KGE models against noise introduced by non-targeted attacks can be improved by using loss functions based on soft labels.

We begin by applying standard label smoothing and label relaxation techniques to KGE models, using a predefined smoothing or relaxation ratio as commonly adopted in prior studies [25,27,31–36]. However, determining the optimal smoothing or relaxation ratio is a non-trivial task, therefore, we further employ Bayesian optimization [37] to identify the optimal ratios. Although Bayesian optimization can be effective for finding more suitable smoothing or relaxation ratios, still a static ratio is applied throughout the entire training process. A static smoothing or relaxation ratio might lead to *over-smoothing*. Especially as the model begins to converge, this can weaken the discriminative power of the model and result in performance degradation [20,26,38]. Therefore, we developed a novel and adaptive smoothing approach that adjusts the smoothing ratio over the course of training by tracking the Kullback-Leibler (KL) divergence between the distribution of model outputs and the smoothed labels. We further developed an analogous approach for label relaxation, where the relaxation ratio is also adjusted during training. To summarize, our main contributions are as follows: **(1)** We study the use of soft-label loss functions considering standard approaches to improve KGE model robustness against non-targeted attacks. **(2)** We propose adaptive KL-based label smoothing, which adjusts smoothing ratios dynamically based on KL-divergence during training. We also propose an adaptive label relaxation technique. **(3)** We performed 5,760 experiments to evaluate the effectiveness of soft-label-based loss functions across state-of-the-art KGE models and benchmark datasets, supported by an additional 3,000 Bayesian optimization trials, yielding a total to 8,760 experiments.

2 Related Works

KGEs empower many downstream applications such as information retrieval [39], question answering [40], link prediction [41], and recommendation systems [1]. They also serve as *auxiliary* information to incorporate structured knowledge into many application [42–45]. The growing need for more effective KGEs has led to the use of large-scale public knowledge bases to achieve broader coverage of concepts [1,46,47]. A broader coverage can improve representations, but it brings a challenge: community-driven KGs may contain wrong or inconsistent facts, which can arise from data vandalism [47], or even adversarial or non-adversarial attacks [1,2,13,48–50]. Yet, KGE models are commonly assessed using benchmark datasets constructed from reliable facts, rather than on real-world datasets that contain noise and inconsistencies [48,51,52]. Therefore, KGE models are vulnerable to encode and produce wrong information [48,52]. Training on incorrect data results in suboptimal learning. This leads to inefficient use of computational resources, higher operational costs, and elevated carbon footprint due to the GPUs' high energy demand [53–55].

Deep neural networks rely on numerous learnable parameters to model and extract complex patterns from input data. However, this flexibility also increases their vulnerability for overfitting to even noisy patterns [56,57]. Mainly, noise occurs when the labels in the dataset do not match the actual labels. This means the observed label distribution differs from the ground truth, leading the model to learn from inaccurate signals [58–60]. Label smoothing [25] is a widely used regularization technique to improve model robustness against input noise [31–34]. It has been introduced into image classification [25,27,31–34], sequence-to-sequence [35], and language models [36].

While the original label smoothing technique allocates uniform probabilities to all non-target categories, a subsequent study suggested that these probabilities should be adjusted based on their similarity to the target category [56]. A closely related study has shown that adaptive approaches can enhance the performance of label smoothing [38]. To assess its impact, we incorporated the proposed Adaptive Conditional Label Smoothing (ACLS) [38] method into state-of-the-art KGE models. Another study proposed an untargeted adversarial attack [48] using Neural Compositional Rule Learning (NCRL) [61], to degrade KGE performance by adding or removing triples. The study also evaluated the robustness of various KGE models. However, our work focuses on *enhancing the robustness* through soft labels during training. Furthermore, a defense strategy was introduced in [62] that combines adversarial training to reduce the impact of malicious modifications with a detection mechanism to identify and remove corrupted triples during preprocessing. This approach, however, introduces extra computations by requiring additional model training and subgraph-based evaluation of candidate triples [62]. Another approach named as PTrustE [63] introduced a method for detecting noisy triples by evaluating the trustworthiness of paths between head and tail entities. This approach also introduces additional computational cost through multi-path extraction and sequential processing.

Primarily, most existing work on data poisoning in knowledge graphs has been focused on targeted attacks that manipulate specific facts through techniques such as rule-based abductive reasoning [64], gradient-based poisoning [1], and instance attribution methods [50]. Our work addresses a non-targeted setting, where the objective is to degrade the overall performance of knowledge graph embedding models. Our aim is to enhance robustness with minimal overhead compared to existing loss functions. We are focused on regularization methods to support scalability and practical use in real-world large knowledge graphs.

3 Background

We start by formalizing the knowledge graphs and the embedding models. Let $\mathcal{E}$ denote the set of entities and $\mathcal{R}$ the set of relations between these entities. Assertions about these entities are represented as triples, where a triple (h, r, t) consists of a head entity h, a tail entity t ($h, t \in \mathcal{E}$), and a relation $r \in \mathcal{R}$ that links them. We define a knowledge graph $\mathcal{G}$ as a collection of such triples $\mathcal{G} := \{(h, r, t) \mid h, t \in \mathcal{E}, r \in \mathcal{R}\}$. Let $\mathbb{V}$ be a normed-division algebra, e.g., $\mathbb{R}, \mathbb{C}, \mathbb{H}, \mathbb{O}$ [65–69]. A KGE model represents a knowledge graph via entity embeddings $\mathbf{E} \in \mathbb{V}^{|\mathcal{E}| \times d}$ and relation embeddings $\mathbf{R} \in \mathbb{V}^{|\mathcal{R}| \times d}$, where d denotes the embedding dimension [70]. Embedding vectors are represented in bold, e.g., $\mathbf{h}, \mathbf{r}, \mathbf{t}$ for entities and relations. A KGE algorithm optimizes a scoring function, primarily for link prediction [71,72], defined as: $\phi_\Theta : \mathcal{E} \times \mathcal{R} \times \mathcal{E} \rightarrow \mathbb{R}$ where Θ includes $\mathbf{E}, \mathbf{R}$, and additional parameters (e.g., affine transformations, batch normalization, convolutions). Given a triple $(h, r, t) \in \mathcal{G}$, the score $\hat{y} := \phi_\Theta(h, r, t)$ indicates its likelihood of being true [73]. Since $\mathcal{G}$ contains only assumed-true assertions, negative samples must be generated. We focus on the widely adopted K-vs-All strategy [73], frequently used in recent KGE models [65,74–77].

3.1 Knowledge Graph Poisoning

In this work, we aim to develop robust KGE models when the underlying KG is noisy. We assume that the knowledge graph is poisoned using non-targeted attacks. We consider the attack settings described in [12,13], with the assumption that there exist an *attacker* who has the following adversarial capabilities: *Access:* the attacker cannot create new entities or relations but can modify existing triplets by substituting entities or relations with others from $\mathcal{G}$. *Knowledge:* the adversary does not have access to the model's architecture, parameters, or training method. The only available information is the structure of $\mathcal{G}$. *Budget:* at most $k\%$ of triplets may be altered and duplicate triplets are not allowed. Given this attack setting, the attacker poisons $k\%$ of triples by replacing the head, tail or relation with another entity or relation sampled from the KG, based on a random value drawn from Bernoulli distribution. These modifications introduce semantic inconsistencies, causing the KGE model to learn incorrect representations, ultimately degrading the model's performance on link predictions.

3.2 Baseline

We used the commonly used Binary Cross-Entropy (BCE) loss function as the baseline for our experiments. We aim to investigate the effect of using alternative loss functions based on soft labels, instead of conventional binary labels. As the name implies, BCE operates on binary labels and encourages predictions to align with ground truth encoded as true or false. The BCE loss over all possible tails is then computed as $\mathcal{L}(\hat{y}, y) = -\frac{1}{|\mathcal{E}|}\sum_{i=1}^{|\mathcal{E}|}[y_i \log(\hat{y}_i) + (1 - y_i)\log(1 - \hat{y}_i)]$.

3.3 Soft Label Loss Functions

We train KGE models using the k-vs-All [73] approach, a common extension of the 1-vs-All classification method widely used for link prediction tasks. Instead of learning from a single positive target per training instance, k-vs-All considers multiple true tail entities for a given (h, r) pair, capturing the multi-label nature of real-world knowledge graphs. For a given pair $(h, r) \in \mathcal{E} \times \mathcal{R}$, the set of all correct tails is defined as $T_{(h,r)} = \{t \in \mathcal{E} \mid (h, r, t) \in \mathcal{G}\}$. Therefore, a training instance consists of the input pair (h, r) and a binary label vector $y \in \{0, 1\}^{|\mathcal{E}|}$ such that $y_i = 1$ if $e_i \in \mathcal{T}(h, r)$, otherwise $y_i = 0$. The model computes a score vector $z \in \mathbb{R}^{|\mathcal{E}|}$ where each element $z_i = \phi_\Theta(h, r, e_i)$ is the raw score of the triple (h, r, e_i) given the current model parameters Θ. These scores are converted into probabilities using the softmax function to obtain $\hat{y}_i = \sigma(z_i)$, for $i = 1, \ldots, |\mathcal{E}|$.

3.4 Label Smoothing (LS)

As discussed in Sects. 1 and 2, label smoothing is a strategy to prevent overconfident predictions [25]. In typical KGE settings using 1-vs-All or K-vs-All strategy, the ground truth is encoded as a binary vector where the correct tail entity receives a probability of 1 and all others receive 0. Instead of such hard labels, LS redistributes a small portion of the probability mass uniformly across all incorrect entities. Therefore, given a triple $(h, r, t) \in G$ and a smoothing parameter α, which is a real value between 0 and 1. The smoothed target distribution p_s is defined in Eq. 1, where $|\mathcal{E}|$ denotes the total number of entities. The cross-entropy loss is then computed using p_s instead of the original label y_i.

$$p_s(t \mid h, r) = \begin{cases} 1 - \alpha & \text{if } t' = t \\ \frac{\alpha}{(|\mathcal{E}|-1)} & \text{otherwise} \end{cases} \tag{1}$$

3.5 Label Relaxation (LR)

Instead of a fixed target distribution, the label relaxation [32] uses set of plausible distributions that allow for uncertainty in the ground truth. Thus, label relaxation constructs a *credal set* of distributions that are sufficiently close to the original target, accounting for possible label noise. Formally, given a triple (h, r, t) and a relaxation parameter $\alpha \in (0, 1]$, the target set is defined according to Eq. 7:

$$Q_\alpha^{(h,r,t)} = \{p' \in \mathcal{P}(Y) \mid p'(t \mid h, r) \geq 1 - \alpha\} \tag{2}$$

where $\mathcal{P}(Y)$ denotes the set of valid probability distributions over the label space Y. The model is trained to minimize the Kullback-Leibler divergence between the predicted distribution $\hat{p}$ and the most plausible distribution in the credal set: $\mathcal{L}^*(Q_\alpha, \hat{p}) = \min_{p' \in Q_\alpha} D_{\mathrm{KL}}(p' \parallel \hat{p})$. Herein, the optimal p' is selected as shown in Eq. 3.

$$p'(t' \mid h, r) = \begin{cases} 1 - \alpha & \text{if } t' = t \\ \frac{\alpha}{|\mathcal{E}|-1} & \text{otherwise} \end{cases} \tag{3}$$

3.6 Bayesian Optimized Alpha Value for LS and LR

The smoothing or relaxation ratio has typically been predefined in practice. It has not been thoroughly investigated whether the optimal smoothing ratio varies depending on the model architecture and training dataset. Therefore, we explored the use of Bayesian optimization to identify the most suitable smoothing and relaxation ratio, rather than relying on a fixed value across all settings. Below, we formally define the optimization process for choosing the optimal ratio for LS and LR. Let $\mathcal{A} \subset (0, 1]$ denote the smoothing or relaxation ratio to be tuned. The objective is to find an optimal $\alpha^* = \arg\min_{\alpha \in \mathcal{A}} \mathcal{L}_\alpha$, where $\mathcal{L}_\alpha$ quantifies model predictive performance for a given α. Bayesian optimization models the objective function $\mathcal{L}_\alpha$ as a sample from a probabilistic surrogate model, typically a Gaussian Process (GP), which maintains a posterior distribution over $\mathcal{L}_\alpha$ given the observed evaluations. At each step, the optimizer selects the next α_{next} to evaluate by maximizing an acquisition function $a(\alpha)$, which balances exploration and exploitation. Formally $\alpha_{\text{next}} = \arg\max_{\alpha \in \mathcal{A}} a(\alpha \mid \mathcal{D})$, where $\mathcal{D} = \{(\alpha_i, \mathcal{L}_{\alpha_i})\}_{i=1}^{n}$ denotes the history of evaluated parameter values and their corresponding losses. This iterative process continues until a budget is exhausted or convergence is observed, yielding the optimized smoothing or relaxation parameter α^*. We conducted 50 trials per modelâĂŞdatasetâĂŞloss combination, which led in 3000 complementary Bayesian optimization experiments to support the main experiments.

3.7 Adaptive KL-Based Smoothing (AKLS)

A static smoothing ratio is suboptimal as it fails to adapt to changing model confidence during training and can lead to under- or over-regularization at different steps. We aim to make label smoothing dynamic while avoiding the additional computational cost compared to the original label smoothing. Our adaptive approach offers a simple yet highly effective mechanism that adjusts the smoothing ratio dynamically during training. Rather than relying on a fixed smoothing ratio α, our method tracks the change in Kullback-Leibler (KL) divergence between the predicted distribution $\hat{p}$ and the smoothed target distribution p_s at successive training steps. Let $\mathcal{KL}_t$ denote the KL-divergence at training step t. We refer to the change $\mathcal{KL}_{t+1} - \mathcal{KL}_t$ as KLdiff. We define the core strategy of our approach as follows: If the KLdiff increases, the model is presumed to be becoming overconfident. Because overconfidence can amplify the effect of noise in training triples (as discussed in Sect. 1), we aim to increase the smoothing ratio α to introduce more uncertainty into the training process. On the other hand, If the KLdiff decreases, the model is likely generalizing better. In this case, we further reduce α. There are three primary motivations to always maintain lower softness ratios. First, too much softening can make it difficult for the model to learn meaningful differences between classes. Second, overly softened labels (which can be seen as a form of *over-regularization*) may slow down convergence. Third, reducing the softening ratio helps preserve the model's confidence, which is crucial for maintaining correct predictions. Therefore, we aim to determine whether further reduction is feasible. Finally, to prevent instability in the learning process, α is adjusted by a small step size $\Delta\alpha$ and kept between pre-defined minimum and maximum values, $\alpha_{\min}$ and $\alpha_{\max}$, respectively. The update rule is formalized as follows:

$$\alpha_{t+1} = \begin{cases} \min(\alpha_t + \Delta\alpha, \alpha_{\max}), & \text{if } \mathcal{KL}_{t+1} > \mathcal{KL}_t \\ \max(\alpha_t - \Delta\alpha, \alpha_{\min}), & \text{otherwise} \end{cases} \tag{4}$$

3.8 Adaptive Label Relaxation (ALR)

We further examined if a dynamically adapted relaxation ratio provides better performance compared to a fixed static relaxation during training. Therefore, analogous to adaptive label smoothing, we developed an adaptive strategy for label relaxation that dynamically updates the relaxation parameter α during training based on changes in the label relaxation loss. The loss formulation is structurally identical to LR, but adaptively tunes the relaxation α to reflect training dynamics. The update rule for the relaxation parameter α is analogous to Eq. 4 for adaptive label smoothing but is based on LR loss defined in Eq. 7 instead of KL-divergence.

3.9 Adaptive and Conditional Label Smoothing (ACLS)

We additionally explored a new label smoothing method, introduced in [38], and known as ACLS. This method tackled the overconfidence problem by combining adaptive label smoothing with Conditional Regularization(CR) [23]. ACLS selectively adjusts training labels based on the difference between the most confident class and the remaining classes, applying regularization only when this difference exceeds a predefined margin.

$$f(z_j) = \begin{cases} \lambda_1 \cdot (z_j - \min_k z_k - M), & \text{if } j = \hat{y} \\ \lambda_2 \cdot (z_{\hat{y}} - z_j - M), & \text{if } j \neq \hat{y} \end{cases} \tag{5}$$

4 Evaluation Setup

We investigated the impact of soft labels on KGE models under varying noise levels. To this end, we integrated various soft-label loss functions into different KGE state-of-the-art models and assessed their effectiveness. Our experiments were conducted on datasets that vary in graph size, density, distribution of entities and relations, and noise levels. The training configuration uses an embedding dimension of 32, a learning rate of 0.1, the Adam optimizer, 100 training epochs, a batch size of 1024, and the K-vs-All [77] training strategy. Throughout the remainder of this paper, we report the Mean Reciprocal Rank (MRR) scores, while the corresponding Hit@1, Hit@3, and Hit@10 results are provided in supplementary materials and show similar patterns.

4.1 Datasets

We used five widely used knowledge graph benchmarks, differing in size, structure, and domain. The Unified Medical Language System (UMLS) [78] provides standardized biomedical vocabularies to support the development of integrated biomedical data systems. KINSHIP [79] provides a structured representation of kinship ties among members of the Alyawarra tribe. NELL-995-h100 [80] is derived from the Never-Ending Language Learning (NELL) dataset. WN18RR [73] is a dataset derived from WordNet, which is a structured hierarchy of relationships among words [81]. FB15K-237 [82] is built upon Freebase, which is a knowledge base of real-world facts. The characteristics of the datasets are listed in Table 1. The Entity Density (ED) is defined as $\frac{2|\mathcal{T}|}{|\mathcal{E}|}$ with

Table 1. $|\mathcal{E}|$: entities, $|\mathcal{R}|$: relations, $|\mathcal{G}^{\text{Train}}|/|\mathcal{G}^{\text{Val}}|/|\mathcal{G}^{\text{Test}}|$: train/val/test triples, *ED:* Entity Density, *RD:* Relation Density, *EE:* Entity Entropy, *RE:* Relation Entropy.

Dataset	$\|\mathcal{E}\|$	$\|\mathcal{R}\|$	$\|\mathcal{G}^{Train}\|$	$\|\mathcal{G}^{Val.}\|$	$\|\mathcal{G}^{Test}\|$	*ED*	*RD*	*EE*	*RE*
UMLS [78]	135	46	5,216	652	661	48.36	141.93	6.60	4.47
KINSHIP [79]	104	25	8,544	1,068	1,074	102.75	427.44	6.70	4.24
WN18RR [73]	40,943	22	86,835	3,034	3,134	<u>2.27</u>	8454.82	14.64	<u>2.23</u>
NELL-995-h100 [80]	22,411	43	50,314	3,763	3,746	<u>2.58</u>	1344.72	12.01	4.19
FB15K-237 [82]	14,541	237	272,115	17,535	20,466	21.33	1308.51	12.72	6.55

$\mathcal{T}$ being the total number of triples. This metric reflects the overall connectivity among entities [51,66,73]. Relation Density (RD) defined as $\frac{|\mathcal{T}|}{|\mathcal{R}|}$ measures the average number of triples involved in relations [51]. Therefore, these metrics reflect the *sparsity* of the knowledge graphs. The WN18RR [73] and NELL-995-h100 [80] have much lower entity density, highlighting the sparsity of their graph structures. Furthermore, we used an entropy-based metric from [51] to analyze the distribution of entities and relations based on their probability of appearing in a randomly sampled triple. The entity entropy (EE) is defined as $-\sum_{i=1}^{n} p_i \log_2(p_i)$, where $p_i = \frac{c_i}{\sum_{j=1}^{n} c_j}$, and c_i is the number of triples in which a given entity participates in. Similarly, for relation entropy (RE), each c_i denotes the number of triples in which a particular relation appears. Hence, these metrics reflect the diversity of entities and relations across triples. High entropy indicates a balanced distribution of facts, while low entropy suggests dominance by specific entities or relations. The high EE in Table 1 indicates a diverse set of entities. The low RE for WN18RR [73] reveals a relation bias.

4.2 Models

To assess noise robustness, we incorporated each soft labeling approach (see Sect. 3.3) into six state-of-the-art knowledge graph embedding models. Fundamentally, the effectiveness of knowledge graph embedding models largely depends on their ability to capture and generalize relational patterns among entities [83]. However, most models are limited to learning only a subset of these patterns [83]. Best performing KGE models have different architectural characteristics and operate in different vector spaces, such as real numbers ($\mathbb{R}$), complex numbers ($\mathbb{C}$), and quaternions ($\mathbb{H}$). Although early models utilized the real numbers ($\mathbb{R}$), more recent studies suggest that using more expressive division algebras namely complex numbers ($\mathbb{C}$) and quaternions ($\mathbb{H}$) can yield improved performance. These algebras better capture relational patterns such as (anti)symmetry and compositionality through their mathematical structure [66].

The RESCAL [84] model is among the early and most influential knowledge graph embedding models. It represents multiple binary relations in a simple and structured way using a third-order tensor, in which entities take two dimensions of the tensor, while the other dimension represents relations. Following the Resource Description Framework (RDF) [85] formalism, each entry of the three-mode tensor is set to 1 if a (subject, predicate, object) triple exists, and 0 otherwise. This approach effectively captures different relation types; however, RESCAL has a quadratic complexity in the factorization rank, which limits its scalability on large datasets [66,86]. This approach is also likely to overfit as the number of parameters associated with each relation grows quadratically compared to the number of parameters per entity [87]. DistMult [67] addresses this by using diagonal relation matrices, offering a more efficient alternative. DistMult [67] shows strong performance on symmetric relations but has limitations in capturing antisymmetric patterns [68]. The ComplEx [68] model improves DistMult by representing entities and relations in a complex-valued vector space, enabling it to model both symmetric and antisymmetric relations. QMult [69] builds upon DistMult by incorporating hypercomplex representations in $\mathbb{H}$. The advantage of QMult becomes more noticeable with increasing size and complexity of the knowledge graph [66]. The RotateE [83] model embeds entities as complex vectors and models relations as rotation operations, allowing it to effectively capture composition, as well as inversion and (anti)symmetry relation patterns [66]. Moreover, RotatE [83] is also capable of handling large knowledge graphs efficiently, as its time and memory usage grow linearly with data size [66]. Keci [88] builds on the idea that the most suitable algebra for embedding a knowledge graph depends on the specific characteristics of the data being embedded. Therefore, Keci [88] serves as a generalization of prior approaches, including DistMult [67], ComplEx [68]. In addition to different relational patterns, knowledge graphs often have multiple hierarchical structures among entities, meaning that a single set of entities can form different hierarchies depending on the relation type. To handle these different and potentially overlapping hierarchies, the MuRE [87] model learns different parameters for each relation to transform the embeddings of the head and tail entities accordingly.

5 Results

Our investigation consists of 1,920 unique experiments, built upon the combination of 5 datasets, 6 knowledge graph embedding models, 8 loss functions, and 8 noise ratios. To mitigate the impact of random initialization in deep neural networks, we repeated each experiment three times with different random seeds. This yielded a total of 5,760 experimental runs. We then computed the mean and standard deviation for each unique experiment. The line charts in Figs. 1 and 2 show the impact of soft-label loss functions under different noise ratios. Each bar represents the average MRR computed over three runs with different random seeds. More detailed figures are provided in the supplementary materials, showing the changes in MRR compared to BCE loss and highlighting the improvements.

5.1 Key Insights

Figures 1 and 2 highlight the following notable trends: **(1)** Overall, soft labels often improve link prediction performance under varying noise ratios, as observed in models such as Keci, QMult, DistMult, ComplEx, and RotatE. However, there is one exception: MuRE does not appear to benefit from soft labels, only small improvement from fixed label smoothing approaches could be observed. We discuss potential explanations for this effect in Sect. 6. **(2)** When focusing solely on scores achieved with the BCE loss, MuRE often outperforms the other approaches (especially in UMLS). Except often being competitive with RotatE on the FB15K-237 dataset and slightly outperformed by QMult on KINSHIP especially in low noise ratios. This pattern can be observed in first row of each tile in Fig. 1 to 4 in supplementary materials, where each tile corresponds to a different noise ratio. **(3)** At lower to moderate noise ratios, soft labels enhance the performance, but this advantage fades at high noise ratios. For example, while soft labels consistently yield benefits, especially in UMLS and KINSHIP, when the noise ratio goes beyond 0.16, the effect of soft labels on the RotatE model becomes less favorable, and even hurt performance (The last row in Fig. 5 to 8 in supplementary materials. **(4)** None of the label relaxation variants (static, Bayesian-optimized, or adaptive) performed well on sparse datasets such as NELL-995-h100 and WN18RR. This pattern is evident in Fig. 1 to 4 in supplementary materials by the cells with light green background, corresponding to all variants of label relaxation on sparse datasets, particularly in 3rd, 5th, and 7th rows in each noise ratio, in the third and fourth columns (NELL-995-h100 and WN18RR). **(5)** Adaptive label smoothing consistently outperforms the non-adaptive (static) versions, with the performance gap being especially noticeable on smaller datasets such as UMLS and KINSHIP. **(6)** While QMult does not perform well on sparse datasets, its performance is notably enhanced with adaptive label smoothing (Figure Fig. 5 to 8 in supplementary materials, row 3, column 4). Similarly, while DistMult and ComplEx did not achieve the best overall performance on sparse datasets, adaptive smoothing helps improve their results. **(7)** For DistMult and Keci, label relaxation yields better performance than label smoothing on the UMLS and KINSHIP, and FB15k-237 datasets.

5.2 Statistical Significance

Beyond the quantitative improvements illustrated in Figs. 1 and 2 (together with Figs. 1 to 8 in supplementary materials), we further assessed the significance of these results through statistical testing. The Wilcoxon signed-rank test was applied to determine if soft-label based loss functions significantly outperformed the BCE baseline. A low p-value (e.g., < 0.05) indicates that the soft-label based loss function performs significantly better than BCE under the matched experimental runs. We considered 8 noise ratios across 5 datasets, resulting in 48 groups. As shown in Table 2, the proposed soft-label-based loss functions led to statistically significant improvements in link prediction performance across 41 out of 48 groups. These results highlight the effectiveness of our proposed soft-label loss functions in enhancing link prediction performance in the presence of noise.

6 Discussion

This section explores the limited effectiveness of the proposed soft-label loss functions for MuRE and offers possible explanations. We also provide a practical fix for the numerical instability we observed throughout our label relaxation experiments.

6.1 Implications of Ineffective Soft Labels in MuRE

As discussed in Sect. 4.2, in MuRE [87] model, each relation transform entity embeddings using parameters that are specific to that relation. The score function of the MuRE model is shown in Eq. 6, where $h \in \mathrm{R}$ and $t \in \mathrm{R}$ are the embedding of the head and tail entities respectively, $R \in \mathbb{R}^{d \times d}$ is a transformation matrix, $\mathbf{R}(h)$ is the transformed head entity by relation r, $\mathbf{b}_h \in \mathrm{R}$ and $\mathbf{b}_t \in \mathrm{R}$ are biases associated with the head and tail entities.

$$f(h, r, t) = -\left\|\mathbf{R}(h) - t + \mathbf{r}\right\|^2 + \mathbf{b}_h + \mathbf{b}_t \tag{6}$$

The key distinction in this score function lies in different biases for head and tail entities, which influence the geometry of the embedding space. Each bias expands the representation of an entity from a point to a *sphere of influence* centered at its embedding. Each relation modifies the placement of spheres within the embedding space such that the spheres representing related heads and tails overlap with each other [87]. The extent of overlap between spheres reflects the degree of relatedness among entities. However, the radius of the sphere, which can be seen as the decision boundary, is independent of the relation.

Therefore, one possible explanation for the limited suitability of soft labels in MuRE [87] is its use of independent biases for entities depending on whether they appear as head or tail entities. Notably, when soft labels assign probability mass to multiple plausible tails, the model is encouraged to pull the relation-transformed head into overlapping regions of multiple entity-specific spheres, which may be difficult since each tail has a unique sphere of influence.

Moreover, as discussed in Sect. 5, the MuRE [87] model already performs well compared to other models when considering the BCE loss. Indeed, the MuRE model inherently incorporates continuous and flexible decision boundaries through its entity-specific spheres and distance-based scoring. This already can mitigate overconfidence by design, and may also explain why label smoothing is not particularly helpful for MuRE: Soft labels add uncertainty that could be unnecessary due to the geometric flexibility built into MuRE.

Another possible reason for the ineffectiveness of soft labels could be the specific geometric structure the MuRE model relies on. Recent studies have shown

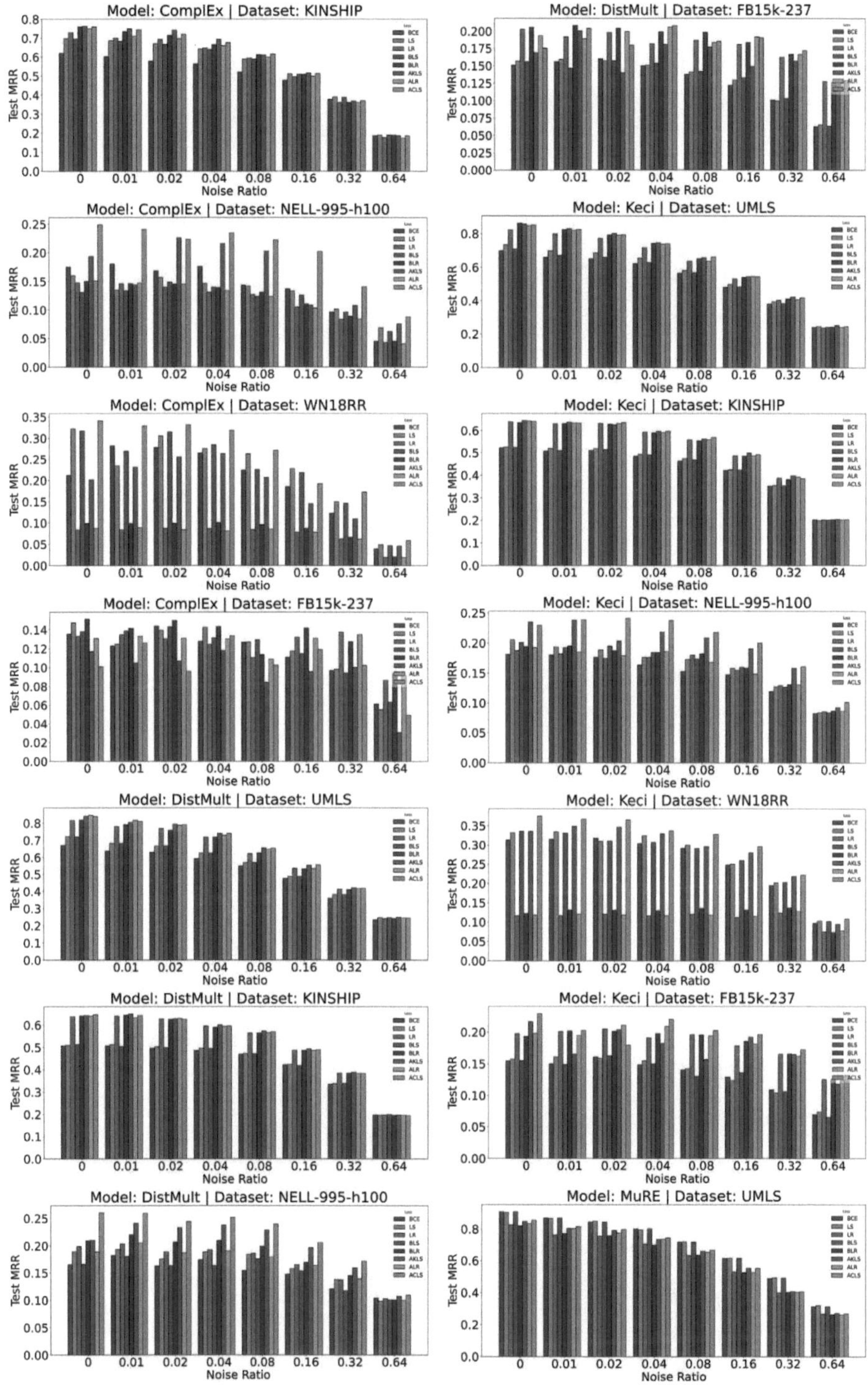

Fig. 1. Impact of soft-label loss functions on KGE models across datasets

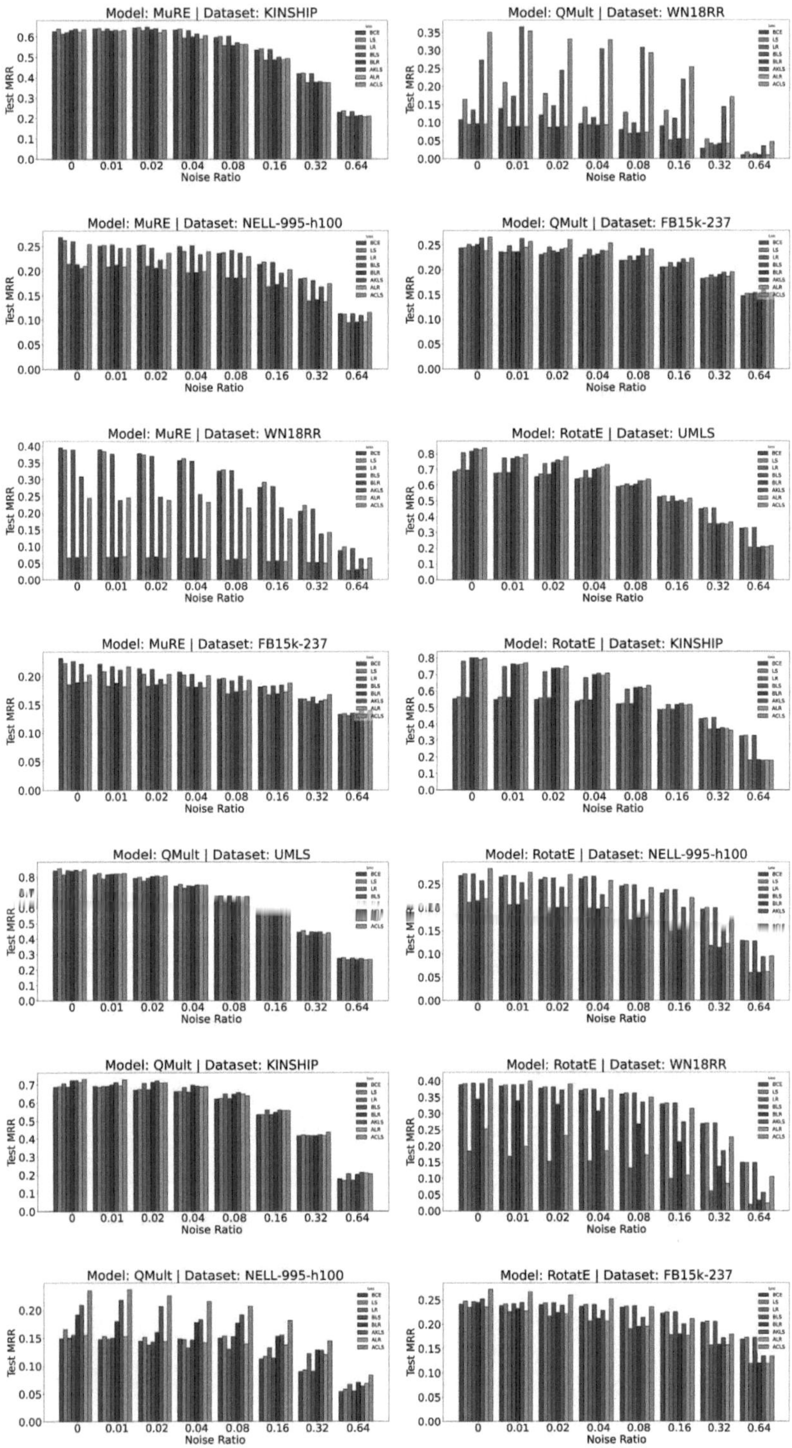

Fig. 2. Impact of soft-label loss functions on KGE models across datasets

Table 2. Wilcoxon signed-rank, $p < 0.05$, on MRR scores. Soft label-based loss functions that outperformed BCE and are statistically significant. ◆ ACLS, ● AKLS, ■ LS, ⬡ BLS, ◈ BLR

	ComplEx	**DistMult**	**Keci**	**MuRE**	**QMult**	**RotatE**
0.0	◆⬡■	◆●■	◆●⬡■		◆●⬡■	◆●⬡■
0.01	◆	◆●■	◆●⬡■		◆●⬡	◆●⬡■
0.02	◆●⬡■	◆●■	◆●		◆●■	◆⬡■
0.04	◆●	◆●	◆●⬡■		◆●■	◆⬡■
0.08	◆■	◆●⬡	◆●■		◆●⬡■	⬡■
0.16	◆⬡■	◆●	◆●⬡	■	◆●⬡■	⬡■
0.32	⬡■	◆●◈	◆●⬡■		◆●◈⬡■	⬡■
0.64	⬡		◆●	■	◆●	⬡

that label smoothing encourages the representations to cluster more tightly in embedding space [31,56,89]. This could collapse the sphere boundaries and lead to unintended overlaps between unrelated entities.

6.2 Implications of Ineffective Label Relaxation in Sparse Datasets

The WN18RR dataset is highly sparse and exhibits strong relation imbalance (see Table 1). Therefore, in K-vs-All strategy, training samples contain only a few positive labels among a large number of negatives. As shown in Sect. 5, LR achieves suboptimal performance on sparse datasets, which may be due to a high imbalance between the few positive labels and the large number of negatives.

Through our experiments, we observed that the label relaxation can become numerically unstable during training. As defined by Eq. 7, if the model prediction $\hat{\mathbf{p}}_i$ falls inside the credal set Q_i^α, the loss (shown as $\mathcal{L}_{\text{LR}}$) is 0. Here i refers to i_{th} training sample. Otherwise, loss is the KL divergence between the relaxed target distribution $\mathbf{p}_i^r$ and the predicted distribution $\hat{\mathbf{p}}_i$. The $(\mathbf{p}_i^r)_j$ in Eq. 7 assign a relaxed label to class j. Here, $\hat{p}_{i,j}$ is the predicted probability for class j (e.g., specific entity) in the i_{th} sample. If class j is the target class, then it is assigned most of the probability mass $1 - \alpha$. Otherwise, it is assigned α, scaled by the predicted probability $\hat{p}_{i,j}$ and normalized by the total predicted probability over all non-target classes, $\sum_{k \neq j} \hat{p}_{i,k}$.

$$\mathcal{L}_{\text{LR}} = \begin{cases} 0, & \text{if } \hat{\mathbf{p}}_i \in Q_i^\alpha(\tau) \\ D_{\text{KL}}\left(\mathbf{p}_i^r \parallel \hat{\mathbf{p}}_i\right), & \text{otherwise} \end{cases}, \quad (\mathbf{p}_i^r)_j = \begin{cases} 1 - \alpha, & \text{if } y_{i,j} = 1 \\ \dfrac{\alpha \hat{p}_{i,j}}{\sum_{k \neq j} \hat{p}_{i,k}}, & \text{otherwise} \end{cases} \tag{7}$$

When applying label relaxation [28], the probabilities are obtained by applying the softmax to the model's logits. The output of softmax can become *infinity* with very large inputs (overflow), or *zero* with small inputs (underflow) [90,91].

Both cases can break computations in Eq. 7. When relaxing the target, the denominator involves the sum of predicted probabilities for non-target classes. Since these probabilities are computed using softmax, extremely small values can lead zero in practice, which result in division by zero.

Moreover, as shown in Eq. 8, KL divergence involves a logarithmic term, and in case of zero values (as a result of softmax of very small logits), it leads to invalid log operation as the log(0) is undefined. Indeed, both of these issues made the training of our experiments unstable and, in some cases, caused the training process to crash as the loss diverged and yielded non-finite values. We solved these issues by simply clamping the predicted probabilities, using a very small ε value (e.g., 10^{-14}) to prevent division by zero and undefined logarithms. This ensures numerical stability, especially when predicted probabilities are close to zero. However, even with this fix, label relaxation remained ineffective on sparse datasets.

$$D_{\mathrm{KL}}(P \,\|\, Q) = \sum_{x \in \mathcal{X}} P(x) \log \left(\frac{P(x)}{Q(x)} \right) \tag{8}$$

7 Conclusion and Future Work

We addressed the challenge of noisy training triples by focusing on model overconfidence. We showed the suitability of KL divergence for label smoothing. In our proposed AKLS approach, smoothing adjustment is driven by a comparison between the predicted distribution and the dynamically smoothed target distribution. While, matching distributions does not guarantee correctness for each label, correctness of label assignments is enforced by the cross-entropy part, which includes label smoothing. This adaptive strategy helps to identify the optimal smoothing ratio for different datasets and models. This is motivated by the fact that in KGE models trained with the K-vs-All strategy, the output is often a highly imbalanced softmax over all entities in the graph. Thus, KL divergence in this context provides a way to shape the model's output distribution to align with the desired soft label distribution. We showed that while Bayesian optimization can improve performance by tuning smoothing or relaxation ratios for each model and dataset, it is computationally expensive. Alternatively, adaptive variants achieve better performance without noticeable computational overhead. Our proposed AKLS method for KGE models often performs competitively with ACLS, and is easily applicable to domains beyond knowledge graph embedding. Finally, we showed that soft labels are not effective for the MuRE model, highlighting the importance of considering embedding's geometry when applying label smoothing.

So far, we evaluated the robustness of KGE models against random noise. While random noise offers a baseline for robustness testing, it may not reflect the structured inconsistencies commonly found in practical settings. These inconsistencies often arise from systematic errors in information extraction, misalignments in ontological hierarchies, or integration of heterogeneous sources. Therefore, as a future work, we aim to study how models respond to perturbations that violate relation properties, such as (anti-)symmetry and composition. In particular, we plan to introduce noise based on ontological patterns to create semantic errors. This will allow us to examine how models handle schema and logic violations.

Acknowledgment. This work has been supported by the Ministry of Culture and Science of North Rhine-Westphalia (MKW NRW) within the project SAIL under the grant no NW21-059D, the project "WHALE" (LFN 1-04) funded under the Lamarr Fellow Network programme by the Ministry of Culture and Science of North Rhine-Westphalia (MKW NRW), and the European Union's Horizon Europe research and innovation programme under grant agreement No 101070305.

References

1. Zhang, H., et al.: Data poisoning attack against knowledge graph embedding. arXiv:1904.12052 (2019)
2. Sharma, A., Kouagou, N., Ngonga Ngomo, A.-C.: Resilience in knowledge graph embeddings. arXiv:2410.21163 (2024)
3. Qudus, U., Pekarou, F.L.T., Silva, A.A.M.d., Röder, M., Ngomo, AC.N.: FaVEL: fact validation ensemble learning. In: International Conference on Knowledge Engineering and Knowledge Management, pp. 209–225. Springer, Cham (2024). https://doi.org/10.1007/978-3-031-77792-9_13
4. Gad-Elrab, M.H., Stepanova, D., Urbani, J., Weikum, G.: Exfakt: a framework for explaining facts over knowledge graphs and text. In: Proceedings of the Twelfth ACM International Conference on Web Search and Data Mining, pp. 87–95 (2019)
5. Syed, Z.H., Srivastava, N., Röder, M., Ngomo, A.C.N.: Copaal-an interface for explaining facts using corroborative paths. In: ISWC (Satellites), pp. 201–204 (2019)
6. Huaman, E., Tauqeer, A., Fensel, A.: Towards knowledge graphs validation through weighted knowledge sources. In: Iberoamerican Knowledge Graphs and Semantic Web Conference, pp. 47–60. Springer (2021). https://doi.org/10.1007/978-3-030-91305-2_4
7. Zhang, H., et al.: Data poisoning attack against knowledge graph embedding. In: Proceedings of the Twenty-Eighth International Joint Conference on Artificial Intelligence, IJCAI (2019)
8. Pezeshkpour, P., Tian, Y., Singh, S.: Investigating robustness and interpretability of link prediction via adversarial modifications. In: 1st Conference on Automated Knowledge Base Construction, AKBC (2019)

9. Bhardwaj, P., Kelleher, J.D., Costabello, L., O'Sullivan, D.: Poisoning knowledge graph embeddings via relation inference patterns. In: Proceedings of the 59th Annual Meeting of the Association for Computational Linguistics and the 11th International Joint Conference on Natural Language Processing, ACL/IJCNLP (2021)
10. Bhardwaj, P., Kelleher, J.D., Costabello, L., O'Sullivan, D.: Adversarial attacks on knowledge graph embeddings via instance attribution methods. In: Proceedings of the Conference on Empirical Methods in Natural Language Processing, EMNLP (2021)
11. You, X., et al.: Mass: model-agnostic, semantic and stealthy data poisoning attack on knowledge graph embedding. In: Proceedings of the ACM Web Conference, WWW (2023)
12. Zhao, T., Chen, J., Ru, Y., Lin, Q., Geng, Y., Liu, J.: Untargeted adversarial attack on knowledge graph embeddings. In: Proceedings of the 47th International ACM SIGIR Conference on Research and Development in Information Retrieval, 2024, pp. 1701–1711. ACM (2024)
13. Kapoor, S., Sharma, A., Röder, M., Demir, C., Ngomo, A.C.N.: Performance evaluation of knowledge graph embedding approaches under non-adversarial attacks. CoRR abs/2407.06855 (2024)
14. Alber, D.A., et al.: Medical large language models are vulnerable to data-poisoning attacks. Nat. Med. 1–9 (2025)
15. Ong, J.C.L., et al.: Regulatory science innovation for generative AI and large language models in health and medicine: a global call for action. arXiv preprint arXiv:2502.07794 (2025)
16. Zhu, Z., Liu, T., Liu, Y.: A second-order approach to learning with instance-dependent label noise. In: IEEE Conference on Computer Vision and Pattern Recognition, CVPR 2021, virtual, June 19–25, 2021, pp. 10113–10123. Computer Vision Foundation/IEEE (2021)
17. Wei, J., Liu, Y.: When optimizing f-divergence is robust with label noise. In: 9th International Conference on Learning Representations, ICLR 2021, Virtual Event, Austria, May 3–7, 2021. OpenReview.net (2021)
18. Ding, Z., Han, X., Liu, P., Niethammer, M.: Local temperature scaling for probability calibration. In: 2021 IEEE/CVF International Conference on Computer Vision, ICCV 2021, Montreal, QC, Canada, October 10–17, 2021, pp. 6869–6879. IEEE (2021)
19. Cheng, J., Vasconcelos, N.: Calibrating deep neural networks by pairwise constraints. In: IEEE/CVF Conference on Computer Vision and Pattern Recognition, CVPR 2022, New Orleans, LA, USA, June 18–24, 2022, pp. 13699–13708. IEEE (2022)
20. Ghosh, A., Schaaf, T., Gormley, M.R.: Adafocal: calibration-aware adaptive focal loss. In: Koyejo, S., Mohamed, S., Agarwal, A., Belgrave, D., Cho, K., Oh, A. (eds.) Advances in Neural Information Processing Systems 35: Annual Conference on Neural Information Processing Systems 2022, NeurIPS 2022, New Orleans, LA, USA, November 28 – December 9, 2022 (2022)
21. Moon, J., Kim, J., Shin, Y., Hwang, S.: Confidence-aware learning for deep neural networks. In: Proceedings of the 37th International Conference on Machine Learning, ICML 2020, 13–18 July 2020, Virtual Event, volume 119 of Proceedings of Machine Learning Research, pp. 7034–7044. PMLR (2020)

22. Ma, X., Blaschko, M.B.: Meta-cal: well-controlled post-hoc calibration by ranking. In: Meila, M., Zhang, T. (eds.) Proceedings of the 38th International Conference on Machine Learning, ICML 2021, 18–24 July 2021, Virtual Event, volume 139 of Proceedings of Machine Learning Research, pp. 7235–7245. PMLR (2021)
23. Liu, B., Ayed, I.B., Galdran, A., Dolz, J.: The devil is in the margin: margin-based label smoothing for network calibration. In: IEEE/CVF Conference on Computer Vision and Pattern Recognition, CVPR 2022, New Orleans, LA, USA, June 18–24, 2022, pp. 80–88. IEEE (2022)
24. Guo, C., Pleiss, G., Sun, Y., Weinberger, K.Q.: On calibration of modern neural networks. In: Precup, D., Teh, Y.W. (eds.) Proceedings of the 34th International Conference on Machine Learning, ICML 2017, Sydney, NSW, Australia, 6–11 August 2017, volume 70 of Proceedings of Machine Learning Research, pp. 1321–1330. PMLR (2017)
25. Szegedy, C., Vanhoucke, V., Ioffe, S., Shlens, J., Wojna, Z.: Rethinking the inception architecture for computer vision. In: 2016 IEEE Conference on Computer Vision and Pattern Recognition, CVPR (2016)
26. Lee, D., Cheung, K.C., Zhang, N.L.: Adaptive label smoothing with self-knowledge in natural language generation. In: Goldberg, Y., Kozareva, Z., Zhang, Y. (eds.) Proceedings of the 2022 Conference on Empirical Methods in Natural Language Processing, EMNLP 2022, Abu Dhabi, United Arab Emirates, December 7–11, 2022, pp. 9781–9792. Association for Computational Linguistics (2022)
27. Gao, Y., Si, S.: Label smoothing for enhanced text sentiment classification. CoRR abs/2312.06522 (2023)
28. Lienen, J., Hüllermeier, E.: From label smoothing to label relaxation. In: Proceedings of the AAAI Conference on Artificial Intelligence, vol. 35, pp. 8583–8591 (2021)
29. Yang, D., Kong, I., Kim, Y.: Enhancing adversarial robustness in low-label regime via adaptively weighted regularization and knowledge distillation. In: IEEE/CVF International Conference on Computer Vision, ICCV 2023, Paris, France, October 1–6, 2023, pp. 4529–4538. IEEE (2023)
30. Yang, Y., Dan, S., Roth, D., Lee, I.: In and out-of-domain text adversarial robustness via label smoothing. In: Rogers, A., Boyd-Graber, J.L., Okazaki, M. (eds.) Proceedings of the 61st Annual Meeting of the Association for Computational Linguistics (Volume 2: Short Papers), ACL 2023, Toronto, Canada, July 9–14, 2023, pp. 657–669. Association for Computational Linguistics (2023)
31. Lukasik, M., Bhojanapalli, S., Menon, A.K., Kumar, S.: Does label smoothing mitigate label noise? In: Proceedings of the 37th International Conference on Machine Learning, ICML 2020, 13–18 July 2020, Virtual Event, volume 119 of Proceedings of Machine Learning Research, pp. 6448–6458. PMLR (2020)
32. Lienen, J., Hüllermeier, E.: Credal self-supervised learning. In: Ranzato, M., Beygelzimer, A., Dauphin, Y.N., Liang, P., Vaughan, J.W. (eds.) Advances in Neural Information Processing Systems 34: Annual Conference on Neural Information Processing Systems 2021, NeurIPS 2021, December 6–14, 2021, virtual, pp. 14370–14382 (2021)
33. Wei, J., Liu, H., Liu, T., Niu, G., Sugiyama, M., Liu, Y.: To smooth or not? when label smoothing meets noisy labels. In: Chaudhuri, K., Jegelka, S., Song, L., Szepesvári, C., Niu, G., Sabato, S. (eds.) International Conference on Machine Learning, ICML 2022, 17–23 July 2022, Baltimore, Maryland, USA, volume 162 of Proceedings of Machine Learning Research, pp. 23589–23614. PMLR (2022)

34. Lukov, T., Zhao, N., Lee, G.H., Lim, S.-N.: Teaching with soft label smoothing for mitigating noisy labels in facial expressions. In: Avidan, S., Brostow, G.J., Cissé, M., Farinella, G.M., Hassner, T. (eds.) Computer Vision - ECCV 2022 - 17th European Conference, Tel Aviv, Israel, October 23–27, 2022, Proceedings, Part XII, volume 13672 of Lecture Notes in Computer Science, pp. 648–665. Springer (2022)
35. Chorowski, J., Jaitly, N.: Towards better decoding and language model integration in sequence to sequence models. arXiv preprint arXiv:1612.02695 (2016)
36. Vaswani, A., et al.: Attention is all you need. In: Advances in Neural Information Processing Systems, vol. 30 (2017)
37. Snoek, J., Larochelle, H., Adams, R.P.: Practical bayesian optimization of machine learning algorithms. In: Advances in Neural Information Processing Systems, vol. 25 (2012)
38. Park, H., Noh, J., Oh, Y., Baek, D., Ham, B.: ACLS: adaptive and conditional label smoothing for network calibration. In: IEEE/CVF International Conference on Computer Vision, ICCV 2023, Paris, France, October 1–6, 2023, pp. 3913–3922. IEEE (2023)
39. Dalton, J., Dietz, L., Allan, J.: Entity query feature expansion using knowledge base links. In: The 37th International ACM SIGIR Conference on Research and Development in Information Retrieval (2014)
40. Ferrucci, D.A., et al.: Building watson: an overview of the deepqa project. AI Mag. **31**(3), 59–79 (2010)
41. Rossi, A., Barbosa, D., Firmani, D., Matinata, A., Merialdo, P.: Knowledge graph embedding for link prediction: a comparative analysis. ACM Trans. Knowl. Discov. Data **15**(2), 1–49 (2021)
42. Liu, X., Yang, Z., Cheng, J.: Music recommendation algorithms based on knowledge graph and multi-task feature learning. Sci. Rep. **14**(1), 2055 (2024)
43. Zhang, F., Yuan, N.J., Lian, D., Xie, X., Ma, W.-Y.: Collaborative knowledge base embedding for recommender systems. In: Proceedings of the 22nd ACM SIGKDD International Conference on Knowledge Discovery and Data Mining, pp. 353–362 (2016)
44. Ruffinelli, D., Gemulla, R.: Beyond link prediction: on pre-training knowledge graph embeddings. In: Proceedings of the 9th Workshop on Representation Learning for NLP (RepL4NLP-2024), pp. 136–162 (2024)
45. Wang, H., Zhang, F., Xie, X., Guo, M.: DKN: deep knowledge-aware network for news recommendation. In: Proceedings of the 2018 World Wide Web Conference, pp. 1835–1844 (2018)
46. Auer, S., Bizer, C., Kobilarov, G., Lehmann, J., Cyganiak, R., Ives, Z.G.: Dbpedia: a nucleus for a web of open data. In: The Semantic Web, 6th International Semantic Web Conference ISWC (2007)
47. Heindorf, S., Potthast, M., Stein, B., Engels, G.: Vandalism detection in wikidata. In: Proceedings of the 25th ACM International on Conference on Information and Knowledge Management, pp. 327–336 (2016)
48. Zhao, T., Chen, J., Ru, Y., Lin, Q., Geng, Y., Liu, J.: Untargeted adversarial attack on knowledge graph embeddings. In: Proceedings of the 47th International ACM SIGIR Conference on Research and Development in Information Retrieval, pp. 1701–1711 (2024)
49. Liu, C., Wang, Y., Cao, H., Liu, B., Jiang, D., Xu, L.: Non-targeted adversarial attacks on vision-language models via maximizing information entropy (2024)

50. Bhardwaj, P., Kelleher, J., Costabello, L., O'Sullivan, D.: Adversarial attacks on knowledge graph embeddings via instance attribution methods. arXiv preprint arXiv:2111.03120 (2021)
51. Pujara, J., Augustine, E., Getoor, L.: Sparsity and noise: where knowledge graph embeddings fall short. In: Proceedings of the 2017 Conference on Empirical Methods in Natural Language Processing, pp. 1751–1756 (2017)
52. Ma, J., et al.: Ptruste: a high-accuracy knowledge graph noise detection method based on path trustworthiness and triple embedding. Knowl.-Based Syst. **256**, 109688 (2022)
53. Budach, L., et al.: The effects of data quality on machine learning performance. arXiv preprint arXiv:2207.14529 (2022)
54. Guerra, E., Wilhelmi, F., Miozzo, M., Dini, P.: The cost of training machine learning models over distributed data sources. IEEE Open J. Commun. Soc. **4**, 1111–1126 (2023)
55. Patterson, D., et al.: Carbon emissions and large neural network training. arXiv preprint arXiv:2104.10350 (2021)
56. Zhang, C.-B., et al.: Delving deep into label smoothing. IEEE Trans. Image Process. **30**, 5984–5996 (2021)
57. Zhang, C., Bengio, S., Hardt, M., Recht, B., Vinyals, O.: Understanding deep learning requires rethinking generalization. arXiv preprint arXiv:1611.03530 (2016)
58. Angluin, D., Laird, P.: Learning from noisy examples. Mach. Learn. **2**, 343–370 (1988)
59. Scott, C., Blanchard, G., Handy, G.: Classification with asymmetric label noise: consistency and maximal denoising. In: Conference on Learning Theory, pp. 489–511. PMLR (2013)
60. Lukasik, M., Bhojanapalli, S., Menon, A., Kumar, S.: Does label smoothing mitigate label noise? In: International Conference on Machine Learning, pp. 6448–6458. PMLR (2020)
61. Cheng, K., Ahmed, N.K., Sun, Y.: Neural compositional rule learning for knowledge graph reasoning. arXiv preprint arXiv:2303.03581 (2023)
62. Zhang, Y., Chen, Q., Hao, X., Pan, H., Yu, Q., Huang, K.: Defense against adversarial attack on knowledge graph embedding. In: Emerging Trends in Cybersecurity Applications, pp. 441–461. Springer (2022). https://doi.org/10.1007/978-3-031-09640-2_20
63. Cheng, K., Zhu, Y., Zhang, M., Sun, Y.: NoiGAN: noise aware knowledge graph embedding with adversarial learning. In: ICLR 2020 Conference (2020)
64. Betz, P., Meilicke, C., Stuckenschmidt, H.: Adversarial explanations for knowledge graph embeddings. In: IJCAI, vol. 2022, pp. 2820–2826 (2022)
65. Balažević, I., Allen, C., Hospedales, T.M.: Hypernetwork knowledge graph embeddings. In: Artificial Neural Networks and Machine Learning–ICANN, 2019, pp. 553–565 (2019)
66. Demir, C., Moussallem, D., Heindorf, S., Ngomo, A.C.N.: Convolutional hypercomplex embeddings for link prediction. In: Asian Conference on Machine Learning, pp. 656–671. PMLR (2021)
67. Yang, B., Yih, W.-T., He, X., Gao, J., Deng, L.: Embedding entities and relations for learning and inference in knowledge bases. arXiv preprint arXiv:1412.6575 (2014)
68. Trouillon, T., Welbl, J., Riedel, S., Gaussier, É., Bouchard, G.: Complex embeddings for simple link prediction. In: International Conference on Machine Learning, pp. 2071–2080. PMLR (2016)

69. Zhang, S., Tay, Y., Yao, L., Liu, Q.: Quaternion knowledge graph embeddings. In: Advances in Neural Information Processing Systems, vol. 32 (2019)
70. Nickel, M., Murphy, K., Tresp, V., Gabrilovich, E.: A review of relational machine learning for knowledge graphs. Proc. IEEE **104**(1), 11–33 (2015)
71. Chami, I., Wolf, A., Juan, D.-C., Sala, F., Ravi, S., Ré, C.: Low-dimensional hyperbolic knowledge graph embeddings. arXiv preprint arXiv:2005.00545 (2020)
72. Hogan, A., et al.: Knowledge graphs. ACM Comput. Surv. (CSUR) **54**(4), 1–37 (2021)
73. Dettmers, T., Minervini, P., Stenetorp, P., Riedel, S.: Convolutional 2d knowledge graph embeddings. In: Proceedings of the AAAI Conference on Artificial Intelligence, vol. 32 (2018)
74. Balažević, I., Allen, C., Hospedales, T.M.: Tucker: tensor factorization for knowledge graph completion. arXiv preprint arXiv:1901.09590 (2019)
75. Nguyen, D.Q., Nguyen, T.D., Nguyen, D.Q., Phung, D.: A novel embedding model for knowledge base completion based on convolutional neural network. In: Proceedings of the Conference of the North American Chapter of the Association for Computational Linguistics: Human Language Technologies, vol. 2 (Short Papers) (2018)
76. Demir, C., Ngomo, A.C.N.: Convolutional complex knowledge graph embeddings. In: The Semantic Web: 18th International Conference, ESWC 2021, Virtual Event, June 6–10, 2021, Proceedings 18, pp. 409–424. Springer (2021). https://doi.org/10.1007/978-3-030-77385-4_24
77. Ruffinelli, D., Broscheit, S., Gemulla, R.: You can teach an old dog new tricks! on training knowledge graph embeddings. In: 8th International Conference on Learning Representations, ICLR. OpenReview.net (2020)
78. McCray, A.T.: An upper-level ontology for the biomedical domain. Comp. Funct. Genomics **4**(1), 80–84 (2003)
79. Denham, W.W.: The detection of patterns in Alyawara nonverbal behavior. Ph. D thesis, University of Washington (1973)
80. Xiong, W., Hoang, T., Wang, W.Y.: Deeppath: a reinforcement learning method for knowledge graph reasoning. arXiv preprint arXiv:1707.06690 (2017)
81. Miller, G.A.: Wordnet: a lexical database for English. Commun. ACM **38**(11), 39–41 (1995)
82. Toutanova, K., Chen, D.: Observed versus latent features for knowledge base and text inference. In: Proceedings of the 3rd Workshop on Continuous Vector Space Models and Their Compositionality, pp. 57–66 (2015)
83. Sun, Z., Deng, Z.-H., Nie, J.-Y., Tang, J.: Rotate: knowledge graph embedding by relational rotation in complex space. arXiv preprint arXiv:1902.10197 (2019)
84. Nickel, M., Tresp, V., Kriegel, H.-P., et al.: A three-way model for collective learning on multi-relational data. In: ICML, vol. 11, pp. 3104482–3104584 (2011)
85. Klyne, G.: Resource description framework (RDF): concepts and abstract syntax (2004). http://www.w3.org/TR/rdf-concepts/
86. Trouillon, T., Dance, C.R., Welbl, J., Riedel, S., Gaussier, É, Bouchard, G.: Knowledge graph completion via complex tensor factorization. arXiv preprint arXiv:1702.06879 (2017)
87. Balazevic, I., Allen, C., Hospedales, T.: Multi-relational poincaré graph embeddings. In: Advances in Neural Information Processing Systems, vol. 32 (2019)
88. Demir, C., Ngomo, A.C.: Clifford embeddings–a generalized approach for embedding in normed algebras. In: Joint European Conference on Machine Learning and Knowledge Discovery in Databases (2023)

89. Müller, R., Kornblith, S., Hinton, G.E.: When does label smoothing help? In: Advances in Neural Information Processing Systems, vol. 32 (2019)
90. Kloberdanz, E., Kloberdanz, K.G., Le, W.: Deepstability: a study of unstable numerical methods and their solutions in deep learning. In: Proceedings of the 44th International Conference on Software Engineering, pp. 586–597 (2022)
91. Blanchard, P., Higham, D.J., Higham, N.J.: Accurate computation of the log-sum-exp and softmax functions. arXiv preprint arXiv:1909.03469 (2019)

UpSHACL: Targeted Constraint Validation for Updates over Knowledge Graphs

Zenon Zacouris(✉), Jin Ke, and Maribel Acosta

Technical University of Munich, Munich, Germany
{zenon.zacouris,jin.ke,maribel.acosta}@tum.de

Abstract. Knowledge Graphs (KGs) evolve frequently through updates that reflect new information or corrections, but such changes can compromise data quality constraints. For KGs modelled in RDF, such constraints can be expressed with the Shapes Constraint Language (SHACL). Current SHACL engines are tailored to validating static graphs but are inefficient for KGs under updates, as they require revalidating the full graph after each update. In this paper, we present UpSHACL, an approach for efficient SHACL validation after updates. UpSHACL introduces a formal model to identify the subgraph affected by an update and constructs a reduced subgraph that can be validated using existing SHACL engines. Our algorithm, implemented with SPARQL over RDF triple stores, integrates seamlessly with Semantic Web technologies. Experimental results show that UpSHACL achieves up to 10× speedup over static full validation, with performance gains increasing on larger KGs.

Keywords. SHACL · Update · Knowledge Graph · Validation

1 Introduction

Knowledge Graphs (KGs) such as DBpedia [16] and Wikidata [19], are continuously evolving. For instance, Wikidata receives over a million updates per day [21]. Updates over KGs reflect new facts, corrections, or refinements, keeping KGs accurate and up to date. Yet, frequent changes also raise concerns about data quality. Assessing if nodes in the KG conform or not to expected constraints after updates is essential for supporting reliable downstream applications.

To address quality assurance, the W3C-recommended Shapes Constraint Language (SHACL) [15] allows for specifying constraints in RDF KGs. SHACL constraints are expressed using shapes, which describe the expected structure and values of nodes in the KG, including required properties, data types, value ranges, and cardinality restrictions. These shapes can form complex structures, including nested shapes, property paths, and references to other constraints, which define how validation propagates through the KG.

D. Garijo et al. (Eds.): ISWC 2025, LNCS 16140, pp. 122–139, 2026.
https://doi.org/10.1007/978-3-032-09527-5_7

While SHACL engines [5,8,18] are efficient for validating static graphs, validation becomes computationally expensive when applied to large or frequently evolving KGs as they re-validate the entire graph after every update. This results in redundant computations over unaffected portions of the graph, making static validation inefficient and impractical at scale. Recent work has proposed extensions such as SHACL$^+$ [2], which rewrites shapes into a language to reason about the effects of updates and check whether they preserve the validity of the graph. This approach focuses on consistency-preserving updates, i.e., determining whether a given update leaves the KG valid.

In this work, we address efficient validation of RDF graphs after updates, which may introduce new violations, even when the original graph is already invalid. To overcome the limitations of the state of the art, we introduce UpSHACL. Our approach includes a novel model that formally defines the subgraph relevant for validation against a SHACL schema and determines which portions of the KG may be affected by a given update and require re-validation. This requires analyzing how updates interact with the structure of SHACL shapes, which may involve property paths spanning long node chains or references to other shapes. Therefore, UpSHACL identifies (i) the set of nodes affected by the update, and (ii) a shape-induced subgraph rooted at these nodes. These elements are combined into a post-update validation subgraph, a reduced yet sufficient subgraph of the KG that can be validated using any standard SHACL engine for static graphs. UpSHACL also includes an algorithm that, given an RDF KG, a SHACL schema serialized as an RDF graph, and an update delta (insertions and deletions of triples), computes the reduced validation subgraph. This algorithm is implemented over a triple store and uses SPARQL queries to extract the relevant subgraph. Validation is then delegated to existing SHACL engines, making the approach easily integrable with current semantic technologies.

We empirically demonstrate the effectiveness of our approach. Our experimental evaluation is conducted on synthetic and real-world datasets with millions of triples and SHACL schemas featuring up to several hundred shapes. The results show that UpSHACL can efficiently compute the reduced post-update graph and achieves up to 10× speedup over static validation, without missing relevant validation results. Moreover, the observed speedup scales with the size of the dataset, as larger KGs contain more unchanged portions after updates that UpSHACL effectively prunes from validation.

Contributions. UpSHACL is novel in the following ways:

- introduces a formal model for identifying potentially affected graph regions after a change, based on update deltas and shape structure;
- presents an algorithm for SHACL validation that constructs a reduced validation subgraph;
- can be used with any state-of-the-art SHACL validator;
- significantly reduces validation runtime compared to full revalidation, as shown in the experimental results.

2 Related Work

Validation Over Static Graphs. Evolving KGs can be validated using SHACL engines for static graphs by materializing each set of changes as a new updated graph and passing it to the validator. Several engines currently support static SHACL validation [5,8,13,18]; some implement optimizations to reduce validation runtime for certain shapes [8], while others support ontological reasoning during validation [13,18]. Yet, validating the entire updated graph is inefficient, as these engines redundantly check parts of the graph unaffected by the update.

Validation Under Updates. The works by Ahmetaj et al. [2] and Jäger [11] focus on consistency-preserving updates over KGs, where consistency is defined by a SHACL schema. These works present a theoretical framework that first defines an update language for expressing certain changes or actions on RDF graphs. Based on this language, the authors propose an extension to SHACL, termed SHACL^+, to rewrite the shapes graph to capture changes over the data graph. Using the extended shapes and the actions, the authors define a framework to verify whether the RDF graph remains valid w.r.t. to the rewritten shapes in SHACL^+ after the updates. In contrast, our work does not focus on consistency-preserving updates, but rather on performing a validation process that reports whether the nodes conform or violate the SHACL shapes after the update. The work by Wang et al. [20] also addresses the problems of RDF validation after updates, yet our approach differs in both methodology and focus. Their method, Typed-SHACL, introduces a tailored validation strategy, whereas we build on existing SHACL validators. Moreover, our work provides a principled mechanism for identifying the affected subgraph after an update, a component that remains underspecified in their framework. As such, our contribution can complement and potentially be integrated into Typed-SHACL.

Incremental Updates in Other Data Models. Approaches beyond the RDF and SHACL are generally inapplicable to this work due to differences in data models and constraint languages. Unlike our work, the relational data model assumes that updates preserve consistency. Recent work, such as that by Kaminsky et al. [12], addresses incremental validation using auxiliary indices to track affected structures. In the case of XML, incremental validation (e.g. [4]) is comparatively simpler, as updates are typically confined to subtrees. In contrast, SHACL constraints may involve arbitrary path patterns, which makes isolating the affected subgraph significantly more challenging.

3 Preliminaries

SHACL validation requires two inputs: a *data graph* and a *SHACL schema*. We assume a triple-based model for graphs, which can be applied to RDF graphs.

Definition 1 (Data Graph). *A data graph G is a set of triples $G = \{(v, p, u)\}$. We define P_G as the set of predicates in G, i.e., $P_G = \{p \mid (v, p, u) \in G\}$. V_G is the set of nodes in G, i.e., $V_G = \{v \mid (x, p, y) \in G, x = v \vee y = v\}$. As an abbreviation, we write $v \in^\circ G$ to indicate that v is a node in G, i.e., $v \in V_G$.*

Definition 2 (SHACL Schema [1]**).** *A SHACL schema $\mathcal{S}$ is defined as a set of constraints in the form of 2-tuples $s = (sel, \varphi_s)$, where sel is a SHACL selector (Definition 3) and φ_s is a SHACL shape (Definition 5).*

The selector in a shape determines the finite set of nodes in the data graph that should be validated against a shape. Those nodes are called *focus nodes* [15].

Definition 3 (SHACL Selector [1]**).** *The grammar of a SHACL selector sel, for $p \in P_G$, and $c \in V_G$, is defined as follows:*

$$sel ::= \exists p.\top \mid \exists p^{-}.\top \mid is(c)$$

To express SHACL shapes, we rely on path expressions defined over predicates in the data graph. Next, we present the grammar of path expressions defined by Ahmetaj et al. [1] for graphs following a triple-based data model.

Definition 4 (Path Expression [1]**).** *The grammar of a path expression π, for $p \in P_G$, is defined as follows:*

$$\pi ::= p \mid \pi^{-} \mid \pi \cdot \pi \mid \pi \cup \pi \mid \pi^{*}$$

Definition 4 defines a simple path, inverse paths, path sequences, path disjunctions, and one-or-more paths. The evaluation of a path expression π over a graph G, denoted $[\![\pi]\!]^G$, is defined by Ahmetaj et al. [1] as the set of pairs of nodes $(v, u) \subseteq V \times V$ such that u and v are connected through a path π. Furthermore, SHACL shapes use path expressions to define complex constraints. The literature [1,6] provides slightly different definitions for the grammar of shapes. In this work, we mainly adopt the notation by Ahmetaj et al. [1], with two minor differences. First, we use *test*() to refer to the validation of a condition (e.g., datatype, value comparison, regular expression, etc.), denoted I in Corman et al. [6]. Second, our grammar allows for references to (potentially other) constraints in the SHACL schema [15]. In the following, we define the grammar of SHACL shapes assumed in this work.

Definition 5 (SHACL Shape [1,6]**).** *The grammar of a SHACL shape φ is defined as follows:*

$$\begin{aligned}
\varphi ::= {} & \top \mid is(c) \mid test(E) \mid && \textit{(shapes over nodes)}\\
& closed(Q) \mid eq(\pi, p) \mid disj(\pi, p) \mid && \textit{(shapes with paths)}\\
& \neg\varphi \mid \varphi \wedge \varphi \mid \varphi \vee \varphi \mid \exists^{\geq n}\pi.\varphi \mid \exists^{\leq n}\pi.\varphi \mid && \textit{(shapes with paths and shapes)}\\
& s && \textit{(shape referencing a constraint)}
\end{aligned}$$

where $\top$ is the trivial constraint, $c \in V_G$, E is a condition (e.g., datatype, value comparison, regular expression, etc.), $Q \subseteq_{fin} P_G$, π is a path expression, $p \in P_G$, n is a natural number, and s is a constraint of the form (sel, φ).

The validation of a node $v \in V_G$ in the data graph G against a SHACL shape φ is denoted $G, v \models \varphi$. Ahmetaj et al. [1] and Corman et al. [6] provide the semantics of SHACL shapes, which define the conditions when $G, v \models \varphi$ holds. Lastly, the process of SHACL validation is carried out by selecting the target nodes and validating them against each shape in the SHACL schema.

Definition 6 (SHACL Validation [1]). *Consider $s = (sel, \varphi)$ in a SHACL schema $\mathcal{S}$. A node $v \in V_G$ is a focus node of s, if v satisfies the sel condition in G, which is denoted as $G, v \models sel$. Furthermore, v is valid w.r.t. (or conforms to a shape) φ, if $G, v \models \varphi$. Lastly, a data graph G is valid w.r.t. $\mathcal{S}$, if for each $v \in V_G$ and $(sel, \varphi) \in \mathcal{S}$ it holds that:*

$$G, v \models sel \textit{ implies } G, v \models \varphi.$$

4 Our Approach

We present UpSHACL, an approach for computing the subgraph of a data graph that requires validation after an update. We begin by defining the graph relevant for validating a set of shapes (Sect. 4.1). We then extend these definitions to capture the subgraph affected by an update, effectively pruning parts of the graph that remain unchanged (Sect. 4.2). Finally, we describe an implementation of UpSHACL (Sect. 4.3). The output of our approach is a reduced graph that can be efficiently validated using off-the-shelf SHACL validators.

4.1 Validation Graph

The validation graph is a subgraph of the data graph that includes the triples necessary to perform validation, while preserving equivalent results. It is constructed by combining subgraphs induced by the shapes defined in the SHACL schema. Since these shapes are expressed through path expressions (Definition 4), we first formalize the notion of a *path-induced subgraph*, as the set of triples reachable via a given path expression from a specified node.

Definition 7 (Path-Induced Subgraph). *Let G be a data graph with the set of nodes V_G and properties P_G. For a given $v \in V_G$ and a path expression π'', the path-induced subgraph denoted $G[(v, \pi'')]$ for v is as follows:*

$$\begin{aligned}
G[(v,p)] &= \{(v,p,u) \mid (v,p,u) \in G\} \\
G[(v,\pi^-)] &= \{(u,p,v) \mid (u,p,v) \in G[(u,\pi)]\} \\
G[(v,\pi \cdot \pi')] &= \bigcup\nolimits_{(v,u) \in [\![\pi]\!]^G, G[(u,\pi')] \neq \emptyset} (G[(v,\pi)] \cap G[(u,\pi^-)] \,\cup\, G[(u,\pi')]) \\
G[(v,\pi \cup \pi')] &= G[(v,\pi)] \cup G[(v,\pi')] \\
G[(v,\pi^*)] &= G[(v,\pi)] \cup G[(v,\pi \cdot \pi)] \cup \dots
\end{aligned}$$

where $p \in P_G$, and π, π' are path expressions.

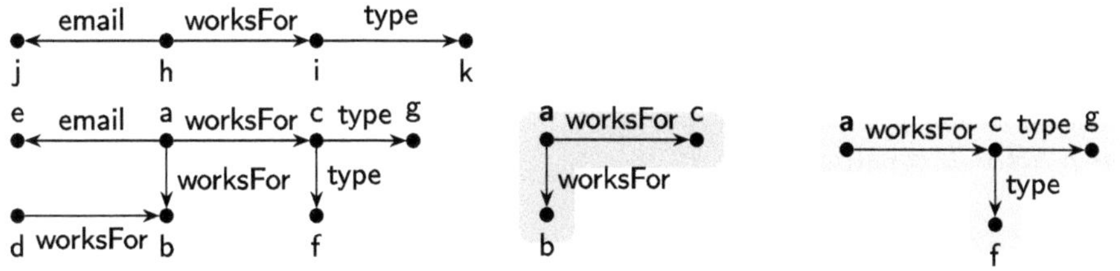

(a) Data graph G (b) $G[(\mathsf{a}, \mathsf{worksFor})]$ (c) $G[(\mathsf{a}, \mathsf{worksFor} \cdot \mathsf{type})]$

Fig. 1. Examples of path-induced subgraphs. (a) Data graph to be validated. (b) Subgraph induced by a path composed of a single edge worksFor. (c) Subgraph induced by a path where worksFor is followed by type. Following Definition 7, we obtain all intermediate nodes u reachable from a via worksFor, and retain only those for which a continuation via type exists. For each such u, we include the triples on the worksFor path from a to u (via inverse path) and the continuation from u induced by the path type.

Figure 1 shows path-induced subgraphs from the data graph G (Fig. 1a). The examples illustrate the cases of path-induced subgraphs for the simple case $G[(v, p)]$ (Fig. 1b) and a composed path $G[(v, \pi \cdot \pi')]$ (Fig. 1c). The definition of $G[(v, \pi \cdot \pi')]$ includes only those triples in $G[(v, \pi)]$ that participate in a path from v to some u with a valid continuation via π'. The use of the inverse π^- ensures that only the relevant prefix paths from v to u are selected, while $G[(u, \pi')]$ captures the continuation of the path π' starting from u.

Given a node, the *shape-induced subgraph* contains all triples necessary to validate that node against a SHACL shape. Its construction depends on the structure of the shape (Definition 5), which may include path expressions, shapes, and references to other constraints. The following definition formalizes how this subgraph is derived based on the structures of the shape.

Definition 8 (Shape-Induced Subgraph). *Let φ_s be a SHACL shape to be evaluated over a data graph G. For a given $v \in V_G$, the shape-induced subgraph for the node v denoted $G[(v, \varphi_s)]$ is defined as follows:*

$$
\begin{aligned}
G[(v, \top)] &= \emptyset \\
G[(v, is(c))] &= \emptyset \\
G[(v, test(E))] &= \emptyset \\
G[(v, closed(Q))] &= \{(v, r, u) \mid (v, r, u) \in G\} \\
G[(v, eq(\pi, p))] &= G[(v, \pi)] \cup G[(v, p)] \\
G[(v, disj(\pi, p))] &= G[(v, \pi)] \cup G[(v, p)] \\
G[(v, \neg\varphi)] &= G[(v, \varphi)] \\
G[(v, \varphi \wedge \varphi')] &= G[(v, \varphi)] \cup G[(v, \varphi')] \\
G[(v, \varphi \vee \varphi')] &= G[(v, \varphi)] \cup G[(v, \varphi')] \\
G[(v, \exists^{\geq n} \pi.\varphi)] &= G[(v, \pi)] \cup \bigcup\nolimits_{(v,u) \in [\![\pi]\!]^G} G[(u, \varphi)] \\
G[(v, \exists^{\leq n} \pi.\varphi)] &= G[(v, \pi)] \cup \bigcup\nolimits_{(v,u) \in [\![\pi]\!]^G} G[(u, \varphi)] \\
G[(v, s' = (sel', \varphi'))] &= \bigcup\nolimits_{G, u \models sel'} G[(u, \varphi')]
\end{aligned}
$$

where $\top$ *is the trivial constraint,* $c \in V_G$ *is a constant,* E *is a condition (e.g., datatype, class, value comparison, regular expression, etc.),* $Q \subseteq_{fin} P_G$*,* π *is a path expression,* $p \in P_G$*,* φ, φ' *are SHACL shapes,* n *is a natural number, and* s' *is a SHACL constraint.*

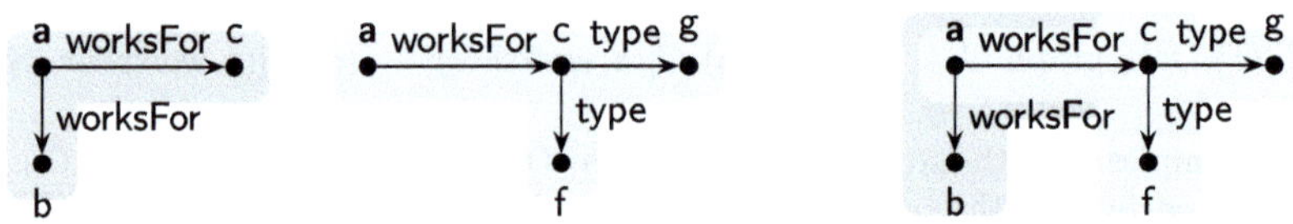

(a) $G[(\mathsf{a}, \varphi)]$ (b) $G[(\mathsf{a}, \varphi')]$ (c) $G[(\mathsf{a}, \varphi \wedge \varphi')]$

Fig. 2. Example of shape-induced subgraphs. (a) Subgraph induced for node a and the shape $\varphi = \exists^{\leq 1}\mathsf{worksFor}.\top$, which checks that a has at most one property worksFor.(b) Subgraph induced for node a and the shape $\varphi' = \exists^{\geq 1}\mathsf{worksFor} \cdot \mathsf{type}.is(\mathsf{g})$; which is constructed as $G[(\mathsf{a}, \mathsf{worksFor} \cdot \mathsf{type})]$. The shape requires that a has at least one worksFor.type path where the object satisfies $is(\mathsf{g})$. This is the graph from Fig. 1c union $G[(\mathsf{f}, is(\mathsf{g}))] \cup G[(\mathsf{g}, is(\mathsf{g}))]$. (c) Subgraph induced for node a and the shape $\varphi \wedge \varphi'$; which is the union of the graphs (a) and (b).

Following Definition 8, shapes over nodes – i.e., $\top$, $is()$, and $test()$ – induce the empty subgraph, as the relevant nodes are already retrieved via path expressions. For *closed*(Q) shapes, the induced subgraph includes all incident edges of the node to verify that only predicates in Q are used. The other shape structures involve shapes and path expressions; in these cases, the induced subgraph is formed by the union of the subgraphs induced by each component. While using the union for shape conjunctions may seem counterintuitive, the rationale is clarified in the example shown in Fig. 2.

We now define the *validation subgraph* as the union of all shape-induced subgraphs for each focus node, based on the shapes in the SHACL schema.

Definition 9 (Validation Subgraph). *Let* G *be a data graph, and* $\mathcal{S}$ *a SHACL schema. The validation subgraph denoted* $G[\mathcal{S}]$ *is obtained as follows:*

$$G[\mathcal{S}] = \bigcup_{(sel,\varphi)\in\mathcal{S}\ \wedge\ v\in V_G\ \wedge\ G,v\models sel} G[(v,\varphi)]$$

By construction, for each focus node in the data graph, the validation subgraph for a given SHACL schema produces the same results as the validation over the entire data graph.

Property 1. Given a SHACL schema $\mathcal{S}$ over a data graph G, it holds:

$$G, v \models sel \text{ implies } G, v \models \varphi \quad \Leftrightarrow \quad G, v \models sel \text{ implies } G[\mathcal{S}], v \models \varphi$$

for each $v \in V_G$ and $(sel, \varphi) \in \mathcal{S}$.

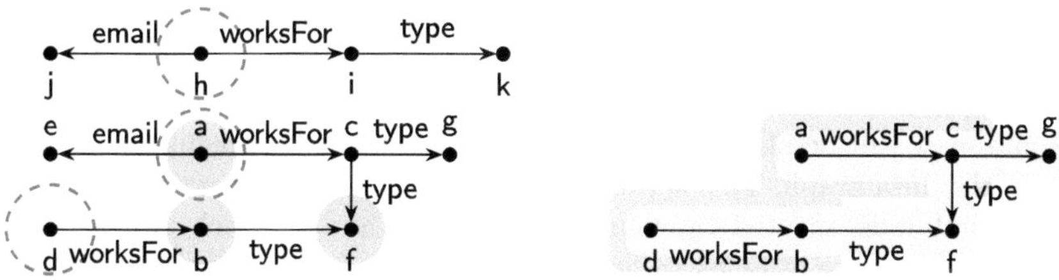

(a) Data graph G' after update $\Delta^+ = \{(\mathsf{b}, \mathsf{type}, \mathsf{f})\}$ and $\Delta^- = \{(\mathsf{a}, \mathsf{worksFor}, \mathsf{b})\}$

(b) Reduced validation graph $G'_\Delta[\mathcal{S}]$

Fig. 3. Example of post-update graphs. (a) Data graph after updating G (Fig. 1a): filled circles are updated nodes; dashed circles are focus nodes of the shapes $\varphi = \exists^{\leq 1}\mathsf{worksFor}.\top$ and $\varphi' = \exists^{\geq 1}\mathsf{worksFor} \cdot \mathsf{type}.is(\mathsf{g})$. (b) Post-update reduced validation graph w.r.t. $\mathcal{S}$ with φ, φ'.

4.2 Validation Graph After Updates

In the previous section, we formalized how to extract the subgraph required to validate a data graph against a SHACL schema. In this section, we extend this model to handle updates. Specifically, we define the post-update reduced validation subgraph, which captures the parts of the graph affected by an update. The intuition behind our approach is that only focus nodes affected by the update require "revalidation", as their validation results can change.

To reason about changes in a data graph, we formalize updates as sets of added and deleted triples. These updates capture how the graph evolves over time and serve as the basis for identifying which nodes require revalidation.

Definition 10 (Updates on Data Graphs). *Let G and G' be data graphs, where G is the original data graph and G' is obtained after adding or deleting a set of triples over G. We define the set of added and deleted triples as follows:*

$$\Delta^+ = G' \setminus G \quad \textit{(added triples)},$$
$$\Delta^- = G \setminus G' \quad \textit{(deleted triples)}.$$

We denote $\Delta = (\Delta^+, \Delta^-)$ an update operation over a data graph.

To determine which parts of the graph may be affected by an update, we define the notion of an updated node. A node is considered updated if it appears as a subject or object in any triple that is added to or deleted from the graph.

Definition 11 (Updated Nodes). *Let $v \in V_G$ be a node in the data graph G. The node v is updated by an operation Δ (denoted $v \in^\circ \Delta$, abusing notation) when the following condition holds:*

$$v \in^\circ \Delta \Leftrightarrow v \in^\circ \Delta^+ \vee v \in^\circ \Delta^-$$

Figure 3a depicts an update on the data graph from Fig. 1a and the updated nodes {a, b, f}; we assume that the focus nodes of the shape $\varphi \wedge \varphi'$ are {a, d, h}. This example shows that not all focus nodes are directly involved in an update, but some may still be affected due to their structural relationships to updated nodes in the data graph. This is the case for node d, which has not been directly updated, but it is affected by changes between b and f, which appear in the path of φ'. Therefore, a focus node is affected by an update if it either appears directly in the added or deleted triples (Definition 11), or if it is connected to an updated node through a path specified in one of the shapes. The following definition formalizes the notion of affected focus nodes by updates.

Definition 12 (Focus Nodes Affected by Updates). *Let G' be a graph after performing the update Δ, and $s = (sel, \varphi)$ a SHACL constraint. The set of focus nodes of s affected by Δ is the defined as follows:*

$$\Delta_s = \{v \mid G', v \models sel \wedge (v \in^{\circ} \Delta \vee (\exists v' \in^{\circ} \Delta)(v' \in^{\circ} G'[(v, \varphi)]))\}$$

The set of focus nodes affected by an update w.r.t. to a SHACL schema $\mathcal{S}$ is:

$$\Delta_{\mathcal{S}} = \bigcup\nolimits_{s \in \mathcal{S}} \Delta_s$$

Following the example from Fig. 3a, we obtain that nodes a and d are focus nodes affected by the update. The node a is directly affected by a triple in Δ^-, and d is indirectly affected by the triple (b, type, f) in Δ^+.

Next, we define the post-update reduced validation subgraph as the union of the shape-induced subgraphs for all focus nodes affected by the update.

Definition 13 (Post-Update Reduced Validation Subgraph). *Let G' be the resulting data graph after updating G with the operations Δ. The subgraph that requires validation of $\mathcal{S}$ after the update, termed the post-update reduced validation subgraph and denoted $G'_{\Delta}[\mathcal{S}]$, is obtained as follows:*

$$G'_{\Delta}[\mathcal{S}] = \bigcup\nolimits_{s=(sel,\varphi) \in \mathcal{S} \ \wedge \ v \in \Delta_s} G'[(v, \varphi)]$$

Figure 3b shows the resulting post-update reduced validation subgraph for our running example. Since the affected focus nodes are a and d, the reduced graph contains the shape-induced subgraphs of the corresponding shapes.

By construction, for each focus node affected by an update, the post-update reduced validation subgraph for a given SHACL schema produces the same results as the validation over the entire updated data graph.

Property 2. The validation of $\mathcal{S}$ over G' produces the same results as the validation of $\mathcal{S}$ over $G'_{\Delta}[\mathcal{S}]$ for each $v \in \Delta_{\mathcal{S}}$, and $s \in \mathcal{S}$, i.e.,

$$G', v \models sel \text{ implies } G', v \models \varphi \quad \Leftrightarrow \quad G', v \models sel \text{ implies } G'_{\Delta}[\mathcal{S}], v \models \varphi.$$

In summary, the reduced graph $G'_\Delta[\mathcal{S}]$ consists of the shape-induced subgraphs for focus nodes affected by the update. Focus nodes unaffected by the update are excluded, as their previous validation results remain the same. For example, in Fig. 3, h is a focus node but is not impacted by the update; hence, it does not require revalidation and is omitted from $G'_\Delta[\mathcal{S}]$. While this reduced graph eliminates unnecessary validation for unaffected nodes, it is not guaranteed to be *minimal*. In some cases, it may still include shape-induced subgraphs that remain unchanged before and after the update. In our example, the subgraphs $G[(\mathsf{a}, \varphi')]$ (Fig. 2b) and $G'[(\mathsf{a}, \varphi')]$ (contained in Fig. 3b) are identical, even though a and f are updated nodes. This reflects a trade-off in our approach: it safely prunes unaffected nodes but may include redundant validations when it cannot be statically guaranteed that the update has no effect.

4.3 UpSHACL Implementation

UpSHACL is designed for large-scale KGs stored in triple-stores. We considered two implementation options: (1) integration within the triple-store, and (2) external access via SPARQL. We opted for the latter. We now present an algorithm that implements the framework described in Sects. 4.1 and 4.2. UpSHACL assumes that the updated data graph G', SHACL schema $\mathcal{S}$ and updates Δ are serialized as RDF graphs, which are loaded into a triple store, and queried using SPARQL. When a SHACL schema is serialized as RDF, the shapes are specified using the SHACL vocabulary [15].[1]

Algorithm 1 shows an excerpt of our implementation to illustrate the operations carried out by UpSHACL for SHACL constraints where the focus nodes are specified using the sh:targetClass predicate from the SHACL vocabulary, and the paths are composed of single edges retrieved via sh:path. However, our actual implementation[2] also handles other SHACL features and complex paths. To be able to use complex paths, we use our library[3] to translate SHACL property paths into SPARQL queries that collect all triples included in the path.

The UpSHACL algorithm operates in three stages (Fig. 4). In the first stage, it identifies pairs of affected focus nodes and their shapes and stores them in `A`. For this, UpSHACL executes a series of SPARQL queries as shown in Algorithm 1. To check if an updated node `v` occurs in an induced subgraph, UpSHACL implements the `TraverseGraph` that traverses the `data_graph` from the `focus_node` following the shape `path` using SPARQL queries. If `v` is found, the `TraverseGraph` function has an early stop, and the pair `(focus_node, shape)` is considered affected by the update and added to `A` (line 8). In the second stage, UpSHACL constructs the reduced graph `G_red` from the `data_graph` for the elements in `A`. For this, UpSHACL implements the `BuildReducedGraph` that traverses the `data_graph` by following all the subgraphs induced by the pair `(focus_node, shape)` in `A`. The third stage, UpSHACL serializes `G_red` into an

[1] For the SHACL vocabulary, we use the prefix `sh: <http://www.w3.org/ns/shacl#>`.
[2] https://github.com/DE-TUM/UpSHACL.
[3] https://github.com/zenon-z/shacl-path-query-generator.

Algorithm 1: Excerpt of the UpSHACL Algorithm

Input: data_graph (G'), shapes_graph ($\mathcal{S}$), delta_graph ($\Delta^+ \cup \Delta^-$)
Output: G_red ($G'_\Delta[\mathcal{S}]$, reduced RDF graph)

```
// Stage 1: Compute affected node-shape pairs A
A ← ∅;
updated_nodes ← Results of executing query in Listing 1.1 (Definition 11);
pairs ← Results of executing query in Listing 1.2 (Definition 12);
foreach (focus_node, shape) in updated_nodes do
    foreach v in updated_nodes do
        path ← Results of executing query in Listing 1.3;
        // Implementation of Definition 8 using Definition 7
        if v in TraverseGraph(data_graph, focus_node, path) then
            A ← A ∪ (focus_node, shape);
            break;
// Stage 2: Construct reduced graph G_red
G_red ← ∅;
foreach (focus_node, shape) in A do
    // Implementation of Definition 13
    G_red ← G_red ∪ BuildReducedGraph(data_graph, focus_node, shape);
// Stage 3: Serialize G_red
return Serialize(G_red);
```

RDF format, so that it can be passed to any SHACL validator. This stage is optional and depends on the infrastructure where UpSHACL is deployed. For example, if the SHACL validator is integrated into the triple store, then no serialization is required.

Listing 1.1. SPARQL query to get updated nodes $v \in^\circ \Delta$

```
SELECT DISTINCT ?v
FROM <delta_graph>
WHERE {
  { ?v ?p ?o . }
  UNION
  { ?s ?p ?v . } }
```

Listing 1.2. SPARQL query to get (focus nodes, shape)

```
SELECT ?focus_node ?shape
FROM <shapes_graph>
FROM <data_graph>
WHERE {
  ?shape a sh:NodeShape ;
      sh:targetClass ?class .
  ?focus_node a ?class .}
```

Listing 1.3. SPARQL query to get simple paths p from a given shape

```
SELECT ?p
FROM <shapes_graph>
WHERE {
  %shape% a sh:NodeShape ;
      sh:property ?ps .
  ?ps sh:path ?p . }
```

Runtime Complexity. UpSHACL complexity depends on three factors: (1) the number of affected (node, shape) pairs, denoted a; (2) the shape graph structure, i.e., the number and depth of property paths; and (3) the data graph structure, captured by average out-degree b and maximum traversal depth k. The worst case runtime is $O(a * b^k)$, where a can grow to $2 * d * |\mathcal{S}|$, with $d = |\Delta^+| + |\Delta^-|$ the number of changed triples, and $|\mathcal{S}|$ the number of shapes.

Table 1. Dataset descriptions

Data Graph	Triples	Subjects	Predicates	Objects
LUBM (SKG)	1,001,716	163,701	18	122,989
LUBM (MKG)	4,258,329	693,909	18	516,901
LUBM (LKG)	34,106,115	5,549,100	18	4,125,586
DBpedia (DB50)	534,696	134,303	2,888	140,855
DBpedia (DB100)	912,108	208,836	3,463	229,587
DBpedia (DB1000)	3,382,528	490,612	5,713	767,604

Shapes Graph	Node Shapes	Property Shapes	Targeted Classes	Targeted Properties	Shape References
LUBM (Schema1)	3	12	3	10	Yes
LUBM (Schema2)	7	24	7	16	Yes
LUBM (Schema3)	14	79	14	17	Yes
DBpedia (Shape30)	30	611	30	255	No

5 Experimental Study

In the experiments, we investigate the following research questions: **(Q1)** What is the impact of UpSHACL stages in isolation? **(Q2)** How does UpSHACL compare to state-of-the-art static validation approaches in terms of runtime efficiency? **(Q3)** How does UpSHACL affect the number of constraint violations detected, compared to validating the full updated graph?

5.1 Experimental Setup

Data and Shape Graphs. We evaluate three synthetic datasets from LUBM [10] and three real-world datasets [14] from DBpedia [16]. For LUBM, the shape graphs were provided by Figuera et al. [9]; the DBpedia shapes graphs [13] are derived from a subset mined by Rabbani et al. [17]. These graphs vary in size and structural complexity, allowing us to evaluate UpSHACL under diverse conditions. In total, we run 12 data-shape combinations, summarized in Table 1.

Update Simulation. To simulate evolving RDF graphs, we apply a sequence of insertions and deletions. From each dataset, we randomly sample 6k triples: 50% is removed up front to simulate future insertions; 50% is used for deletions. Each update applies a batch of 1k insertions and 1k deletions to the current graph.

Implementation Details and Baseline. UpSHACL experiments were run in Python 3.12.8. It uses OpenLink Virtuoso v7.2.13 [7] for RDF graph storage and SPARQL query execution, and PySHACL [18] for SHACL validation. Among existing SHACL engines, we use PySHACL and Jena-SHACL [3], because they are the only engines that support all the shapes and constraints used in our experiments. To integrate these tools, both the data graph and shapes graph are loaded into main memory. All experiments were done on a 64-bit Linux server with an AMD EPYC 9224 24-core CPU (48 threads), 566 GiB RAM, and 7 TB SSD storage.

Metrics. Each experiment is executed three times. We report: (i) *Runtime* – total elapsed time (in seconds) from invocation to termination; (ii) *Violations* – number of constraint violations reported by the validator.

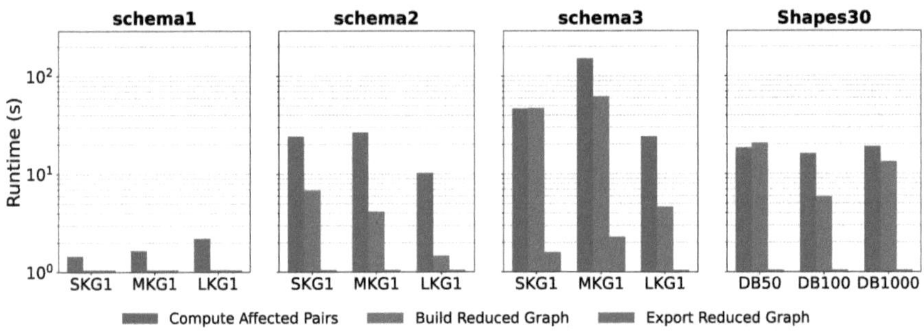

Fig. 4. UpSHACL runtime breakdown across all shapes graphs. Each subplot reports the average over 3 runs per dataset. Very small non-zero values are clipped to 1 s to remain visible on the logarithmic scale.

5.2 Impact of UpSHACL on Performance

In this study, we measure the performance of the UpSHACL stages when computing the post-update reduced graph. This experiment helps us identify performance bottlenecks and evaluate the practical overhead of our approach. The studied stages are: (1) *Affected pair computation:* determining the affected node-shape pairs after updates; (2) *Graph reduction:* constructing the reduced graph from the affected node-shape pairs; (3) *Serialization:* writing the reduced graph to a Turtle file. The last stage is optional in some architectures, e.g., when the validator is integrated into the triple store.

We evaluate six data graphs (3 DBpedia, 3 LUBM) and four shape graphs (Shapes30, Schema-1,2,3). DBpedia is validated using Shapes30, which defines simple property constraints with no nested shapes. LUBM datasets are paired with Schema-1,2,3 with high structural complexity, including use of `sh:node`. Due to stricter RDF graph parsing rules, Jena-SHACL was not able to validate any of the DBpedia datasets.

Impact of Computing Affected Pairs. The affected pairs are computed in the first phase of the UpSHACL Algorithm 1. As shown in Fig. 4, this step accounts for the majority of the total runtime in most experiments. This is expected, as it includes both the expansion of updated nodes and their matching against all relevant shapes. We observe that runtime scales more moderately with increasing LUBM data graph sizes (SKG1, MKG1, LKG1) than with increasing shape graph complexity (Schema-1,2,3). A similar pattern holds for the DBpedia datasets, where all three use the same shapes graph: runtime remains relatively stable despite large differences in data graph size. This suggests that the affected pair computation is primarily influenced by the shape graph rather than the data graph. Between Schema1 and Schema2, and again between Schema2 and Schema3, we observe roughly an order-of-magnitude increase in runtime. Since Table 1 shows a two-fold increase in property shapes from Schema1 to Schema2, and a three-fold increase from Schema2 to Schema3, this indicates a super-linear relationship. Combined with the use of `sh:node` constructs in all three schemas, we conclude that both the size and structural complexity of the shape graph – particularly nested node shapes – contribute significantly to this non-linear runtime behavior.

Impact of Graph Reduction. We observe that the time spent on reduced graph construction increases with shape graph size. This is likely due to the higher number of node-shape pairs and more complex SPARQL queries required to extract relevant subgraphs. While data graph size appears to have a smaller effect, some variation is still visible (particularly in Schema3) suggesting that the number of affected nodes also plays a role in reduction cost. The runtime increase may also be attributed to batching overhead in larger graphs.

Graph Serialization. The serialization time depends on the size of the reduced graph obtained in the previous stage. In our experiments, the serialization of the reduced graphs contributes only a small fraction to the overall pipeline runtime.

In summary, Fig. 4 shows that the execution time is dominated by affected pair computation and reduced graph construction, while serialization is consistently negligible. Increasing the data graph size has a small effect on the performance, whereas increasing shape graph size and structural complexity has a significant performance impact. In other words, UpSHACL's runtime depends on the overlap between updates and SHACL shapes; a large, irrelevant update may be faster than a small, shape-relevant one **(Q1)**.

5.3 Analyzing Performance Compared to SOTA

To evaluate the performance of UpSHACL against traditional static validation approaches, we compare the end-to-end runtime of both methods. Specifically, we run the complete UpSHACL pipeline, which takes an RDF graph as input and produces a reduced RDF graph based on change deltas. We then validate this reduced graph. As a benchmark, we perform standard SHACL validation on the full updated RDF graph. For both methods, we use PySHACL as validator

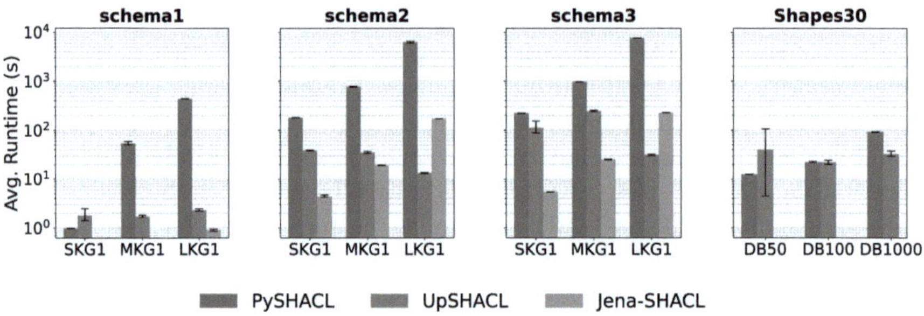

Fig. 5. Validation runtime of static validation (Full Validation) and UpSHACL. Error bars represent the min–max range over three runs. UpSHACL runtime includes the materialization time of the reduced graph (Fig. 4) and validation time.

and measure the total time taken to execute SHACL validation. We compare these results to Jena-SHACL validation. This experiment aims to assess whether UpSHACL offers a measurable runtime advantage over state-of-the-art static validation. Results are shown in Fig. 5.

Impact of Data Graph Size. The runtime for full validation for both tools increases noticeably as the data graph size grows. In contrast, the run time of the UpSHACL pipeline grows at a much slower rate, indicating better scalability. All in all, the trend suggests that UpSHACL handles larger data graphs more efficiently than the baseline. The narrow error bars for UpSHACL further highlight its consistent performance across repeated runs in most cases.

Impact of Shapes Graph Size. We observe that increasing the size and complexity of the shapes graph results in longer runtimes for all approaches. Between Schema2 and Schema3, there is minimal change in full validation runtime, whereas the difference is larger for UpSHACL. This supports the thesis that the UpSHACL runtime correlates with shape size and complexity. In the largest LUBM configurations (LKG1 with Schema2 and Schema3), UpSHACL achieves a runtime over 10× faster than PySHACL, and 5× faster than Jena-SHACL.

Overall, UpSHACL outperforms traditional full validation when using larger data graphs. These results demonstrate the effectiveness of UpSHACL in reducing validation runtime, particularly as data graph size increases **(Q2)**.

5.4 Detected Violations

To assess the correctness of UpSHACL, we compare the violations detected in the reduced graph to those introduced by graph updates. A violation is identified by the tuple (`sh:sourceConstraintComponent`, `sh:focusNode`, `sh:resultPath`, `sh:value`). We compute the set difference between validation results before and after a batch update (denoted B). Table 2 shows per dataset and batch the results of (`VG'` $\setminus$ `VG`) which are new violations, and compares

Table 2. UpSHACL validation reports. B_n is the batch $B_n \rightarrow B_{n+1}$. VG/VG' are validation reports before/after update; RG is the reduced graph report.

Dataset		VG	VG'	Diff	RG	Missing	Redundant
Schema1	lubm-skg-1 (B_1)	2047	2078	31	205	0	174
	lubm-skg-1 (B_2)	2078	2113	35	234	0	199
	lubm-mkg-1 (B_1)	5844	5841	0	26	0	26
	lubm-mkg-1 (B_2)	5841	5839	0	18	0	18
	lubm-lkg-1 (B_1)	40030	40021	4	116	0	112
	lubm-lkg-1 (B_2)	40021	40012	2	101	0	99
Schema2	lubm-skg-1 (B_1)	192065	192058	772	18158	0	17386
	lubm-skg-1 (B_2)	192058	192037	757	17503	0	16746
	lubm-mkg-1 (B_1)	798072	798840	768	9190	0	8422
	lubm-mkg-1 (B_2)	-	-	-	-	-	-
	lubm-lkg-1 (B_1)	-	-	-	-	-	-
	lubm-lkg-1 (B_2)	-	-	-	-	-	-
Schema3	lubm-skg-1 (B_1)	253792	251631	0	24849	0	24849
	lubm-skg-1 (B_2)	251631	249344	0	47328	0	47328
	lubm-mkg-1 (B_1)	-	-	-	-	-	-
	lubm-mkg-1 (B_2)	-	-	-	-	-	-
	lubm-lkg-1 (B_1)	-	-	-	-	-	-
	lubm-lkg-1 (B_2)	-	-	-	-	-	-
Shape30	EnDe-Lite50 (B_1)	26352	26349	0	836	0	836
	EnDe-Lite50 (B_2)	26349	26330	0	7215	0	7215
	EnDe-Lite100 (B_1)	48267	48205	0	1873	0	1873
	EnDe-Lite100 (B_2)	48205	48155	0	1906	0	1906

them against violations in the reduced graph (RG) to identify missing and extra violations.

As shown in Table 2, UpSHACL detects all new violations across all tested configurations, i.e., the number of missing violations is always zero. This confirms that the reduction procedure is *complete* with respect to dynamic SHACL validation. Yet, UpSHACL is not minimal, as it may revalidate unaffected nodes and re-report pre-existing violations (redundant, but correct).

In summary, Table 2 shows that UpSHACL captures all new violations while reporting fewer total violations than full validation, despite some extra ones. This demonstrates a reduction in validation effort with preserved validation report completeness **(Q3)**.

6 Conclusion and Future Work

In this work, we presented UpSHACL, an approach for computing a reduced data graph from a given set of insertions, deletions, and a shapes graph. This reduction aims to enable efficient SHACL validation over large, frequently evolving knowledge graphs. UpSHACL comprises a formal model and an algorithm that implements this formalization. Our experimental results demonstrate that applying SHACL validation to the reduced subgraph produced by UpSHACL yields significant performance improvements, achieving up to 10× speedups on large datasets, while providing correct validation results. As future work, we aim to extend our framework toward computing the *minimal* validation subgraph, further reducing redundancy in the reduced graph. Other works can explore specialized data structures (e.g., indexes) and parallelization techniques.

Acknowledgments. This work has been funded by the Deutsche Forschungsgemeinschaft (DFG, German Research Foundation) SFB 1608 – 501798263, and supported by SFB 1625 - 506711657, subproject A06.

Supplemental Material Statement. The UpSHACL source code and code to reproduce our experiments are available online: https://github.com/DE-TUM/UpSHACL. Links to download the benchmarks from the literature are included in the repository.

References

1. Ahmetaj, S., et al.: Common foundations for SHACL, ShEx, and PG-Schema. In: Proceedings of the ACM on Web Conference 2025, pp. 8–21 (2025)
2. Ahmetaj, S., Ortiz, M., Šimkus, M.: Towards SHACL validation of evolving graphs. In: Proceedings of the 16th Alberto Mendelzon International Workshop on Foundations of Data Management (AMW'2024). CEUR Workshop Proceedings, vol. 3954. CEUR-WS.org (2024)
3. Apache Software Foundation: Apache Jena (2025). https://jena.apache.org/. Accessed 31 July 2025
4. Balmin, A., Papakonstantinou, Y., Vianu, V.: Incremental validation of xml documents. ACM Trans. Database Syst. (TODS) **29**(4), 710–751 (2004)
5. Corman, J., Florenzano, F., Reutter, J.L., Savkovic, O.: SHACL2SPARQL: validating a SPARQL endpoint against recursive SHACL constraints. In: ISWC (Satellites), pp. 165–168 (2019)
6. Corman, J., Reutter, J.L., Savković, O.: Semantics and validation of recursive SHACL. In: Vrandečić, D., et al. (eds.) ISWC 2018. LNCS, vol. 11136, pp. 318–336. Springer, Cham (2018). https://doi.org/10.1007/978-3-030-00671-6_19
7. Erling, O., Mikhailov, I.: RDF support in the virtuoso DBMS. In: The Social Semantic Web 2007 – Proceedings of the 1st Conference on Social Semantic Web (CSSW), pp. 59–68. Gesellschaft für Informatik e. V., Bonn (2007)
8. Figuera, M., Rohde, P.D., Vidal, M.E.: Trav-SHACL: efficiently validating networks of SHACL constraints. In: Proceedings of the Web Conference 2021, pp. 3337–3348 (2021)
9. Figuera, M., Rohde, P.D., Vidal, M.E.: Trav-SHACL: benchmarks, experimental settings, and evaluation (2021). https://doi.org/10.25835/0035739, https://data.uni-hannover.de/dataset/25a28ec2-f9a8-412f-a6e8-6808b66ef957 [Data set]
10. Guo, Y., Pan, Z., Heflin, J.: LUBM: a benchmark for OWL knowledge base systems. J. Web Semant. **3**(2–3), 158–182 (2005)

11. Jäger, D.: SHACL validation of evolving RDF graphs. Master's thesis, Technische Universität Wien (2023)
12. Kaminsky, Y., Pena, E.H., Naumann, F.: Incremental detection of denial constraint violations. Proc. VLDB Endowment **18**(4), 1000–1012 (2024)
13. Ke, J., Zacouris, Z., Acosta, M.: Efficient validation of SHACL shapes with reasoning. Proc. VLDB Endowment **17**(11), 3589–3601 (2024)
14. Ke, J., Zacouris, Z., Acosta, M.: Efficient validation of SHACL shapes with reasoning (datasets) (2024). https://doi.org/10.5281/zenodo.12798851
15. Knublauch, H., Kontokostas, D.: Shapes constraint language (SHACL). W3C recommendation, W3C (2017). https://www.w3.org/TR/2017/REC-shacl-20170720/
16. Lehmann, J., et al.: Dbpedia - A large-scale, multilingual knowledge base extracted from wikipedia. Semant. Web **6**(2), 167–195 (2015)
17. Rabbani, K., Lissandrini, M., Hose, K.: Extraction of validating shapes from very large knowledge graphs. Proc. VLDB Endowment. **16**(5), 1023–1032 (2023)
18. Sommer, A., Car, N., Yu, J.: pySHACL (2018). https://pypi.org/project/pyshacl/0.30.1/
19. Vrandečić, D., Krötzsch, M.: Wikidata: a free collaborative knowledgebase. Commun. ACM **57**(10), 78–85 (2014)
20. Wang, Y., Wang, X., Liu, B.: Incremental validation of RDF graphs. In: International Conference on Web Information Systems and Applications, pp. 359–371. Springer (2021). https://doi.org/10.1007/978-3-030-87571-8_31
21. Wikidata contributors: Wikidata:SPARQL query service/WDQS backend update/October 2023 scaling update (2023). https://www.wikidata.org/wiki/Wikidata:SPARQL_query_service/WDQS_backend_update/October_2023_scaling_update. Accessed 12 May 2025

SHACL Validation Under Graph Updates

Shqiponja Ahmetaj[1(✉)], George Konstantinidis[2], Magdalena Ortiz[1], Paolo Pareti[2], and Mantas Simkus[1]

[1] Vienna University of Technology (TU Wien), Vienna, Austria
shqiponja.ahmetaj@tuwien.ac.at
[2] University of Southampton, Southampton, UK

Abstract. SHACL (SHApe Constraint Language) is a W3C standardized constraint language for RDF graphs. In this paper, we study SHACL validation in RDF graphs under updates. We present a SHACL-based update language that can capture intuitive and realistic modifications on RDF graphs and study the problem of static validation under such updates. This problem asks to verify whether every graph that validates a SHACL specification will still do so after applying a given update sequence. More importantly, it provides a basis for further services for reasoning about evolving RDF graphs. Using a regression technique that embeds the update actions into SHACL constraints, we show that static validation under updates can be reduced to (un)satisfiability of constraints in (a minor extension of) SHACL. We analyze the computational complexity of the static validation problem for SHACL and some key fragments. Finally, we present a prototype implementation that performs static validation and other static analysis tasks on SHACL constraints and demonstrate its behavior through preliminary experiments.

Keywords: SHACL · satisfiability · evolving graphs · static validation · updates

1 Introduction

The SHACL (SHApe Constraint Language) standard, a W3C recommendation since 2017, provides a formal language for describing and validating integrity constraints on RDF data. In SHACL we can express, for example, that instances of the class Person must have exactly one date of birth. SHACL specifications consist of a *shapes graph* that pairs *shape* constraints with *targets* specifying which nodes in a data graph must satisfy which shapes. The central service in SHACL is *validation*, that is, determining whether an RDF graph conforms to a given shape graph. SHACL is being increasingly adopted as the basic means for ensuring data quality and integrity in RDF-based applications, and the development of SHACL validators and related tools is rapidly evolving [2,13,14,21].

RDF graphs can be large and may be subject to frequent changes and updates. The development of an appropriate standard for describing these updates is an ongoing effort in which the Semantic Web community has invested

D. Garijo et al. (Eds.): ISWC 2025, LNCS 16140, pp. 140–157, 2026.
https://doi.org/10.1007/978-3-032-09527-5_8

considerable effort [20]. While there are technologies for updating RDF graphs and validating them against SHACL specifications, these two steps currently need to be handled independently: if a validated graph is updated, it has to be re-validated from scratch, which can be expensive, and if an update leads to non-validation, returning to a valid state may be difficult or even impossible. This challenge becomes even more critical in privacy-sensitive domains and systems that integrate heterogeneous data sources, where direct access to the entire data graph is either restricted or impractical. For example, in healthcare or federated knowledge graphs, data may be held by external providers or evolve independently across sources, so executing an update that results in non-validation could be highly undesirable. This motivates our study of *validation under updates*, in which we study two problems of interest. The first is to determine whether a given update to a graph will preserve the validation of a SHACL constraint, enabling users to guarantee that data quality is preserved by identifying problematic updates before they are executed. We then move to our main goal: determining whether a given update preserves certain SHACL constraints for every input data graph.

Consider a hospital management system that stores patient data and enforces the SHACL constraints: (i) every patient must be linked to at least one address, and (ii) every address must include both a city and a house number. This can be expressed in SHACL abstract syntax as the following shapes graph (C, T)

$$\begin{aligned} C =& (\mathsf{PatientShape} \leftrightarrow \exists\, hasAddress.Address, \\ & \mathsf{AddressShape} \leftrightarrow \exists\, hasCity \wedge \exists\, hasHouseNumber) \\ T =& ((Patient, \mathsf{PatientShape}), (Address, \mathsf{AddressShape})) \end{aligned}$$

Now, suppose that, as part of a privacy-preserving policy, the hospital decides to stop collecting the house numbers of patients' addresses. This is implemented as an update action that removes all *hasHouseNumber* triples in RDF from addresses linked to patients, that is all atoms of the form the $hasHouseNumber(x, y)$, where x must satisfy the shape $\exists hasAddress^{-}.Patient$ and y can be any node, and can be expressed in SHACL with $\top$. The question is whether such an update is safe: does it preserve the SHACL constraints for all input graphs? Unfortunately, in this case, the update violates the constraint for AddressShape, as the updated data would no longer contain required house numbers. This highlights a critical need for static validation; that is, before applying the update, we must verify that it will not break constraints for any valid input graph. Since data evolves frequently (e.g., hourly admissions), validating updates against every snapshot is infeasible. Static validation enables correctness guarantees across all current and future graphs, without exposing sensitive information. If an update is unsafe, one must revise either the update or the constraints (e.g., update the AddressShape to only require *hasCity*).

In our setting, the modifications to RDF graphs are described in a simple update language that captures the core fragment of SPARQL Update. It is designed to be intuitive for SHACL practitioners, in the sense that SHACL expressions can be used to select the nodes affected by the updates and as preconditions in the actions. We are not aware of other works on the preservation of SHACL constraints under updates. Some authors have examined the interaction between updates and schema information in RDF-S [11] or even ontological knowledge [6,24,25]. In the context of graph databases, Bonifati et al. have considered the joint evolution of graphs and schema, focusing on different schema languages and reasoning problems [10]. In relational databases, static validation is well-understood [12]. Particularly relevant to us is [3], which studied validation under updates in dynamic graph-structured data, using a custom description logic [7] due to the lack of a standard constraint language. With SHACL now established as a W3C standard for RDF constraint specification, we revisit these problems in the SHACL setting. Our focus is to develop a foundational framework for reasoning about SHACL validation under RDF updates: we introduce a SHACL-aware action language, leverage SHACL validation for conditional execution, and study static validation under such updates. SHACL's expressive language and specific validation semantics introduce technical challenges that require careful handling. A preliminary version of this work has been published in [5]. The main contributions of this work are:

◦ We introduce a declarative language for specifying updates on RDF graphs that uses SHACL shapes both to select affected nodes and to define preconditions for conditional updates. The language covers a large fragment of SPARQL Update and extends it with if–then–else constructs based on SHACL validation checks. To allow more expressive update actions, we also extend SHACL paths with features such as difference and more expressive targets.

◦ We adapt the *regression* method from [3] to rewrite an input shapes graph by incorporating the effects of actions 'backwards', allowing us to show that validation under updates can be reduced to standard validation in a small extension of SHACL. We prove the correctness of the method and show that the SHACL extension is necessary to capture the effects of actions on constraints accurately.

◦ We then study the problem of *static validation under updates*, which checks whether the execution of a given action preserves the SHACL constraints for every initial data graph. Using the regression technique, we show that static validation under updates can be reduced to (un)satisfiability of a shapes graph in (a minor extension of) SHACL. Since satisfiability is known to be undecidable already for plain SHACL [19], we leverage the results of [3] to identify expressive fragments for which the problem is feasible in coNExpTime and ExpTime.

◦ We provide an implementation of static verification under updates for an expressive subset of the studied action language. We provide scalability results showing that, despite its high computational complexity, static verification is feasible for medium-sized shapes graphs and large numbers of actions.

2 SHACL Validation

In this section, we introduce RDF graphs and SHACL *validation*. We follow the abstract syntax and semantics for the fragment of SHACL core studied in [4]; for more details on the W3C specification of SHACL core we refer to [1], and for details of its relation with DLs to [8,15].

RDF Graphs. We let N_N, N_C, N_P denote countably infinite, mutually disjoint sets of *nodes* (constants), *class names*, and *property names*, respectively. An RDF (data) graph G is a finite set of (ground) *atoms* of the form $B(c)$ and $p(c,d)$, where $B \in N_C$, $p \in N_P$, and $c,d \in N_N$. The set of nodes appearing in G is denoted with $V(G)$.

Syntax of SHACL. Let N_S be a countably infinite set of *shape names*, disjoint from N_N, N_C, N_P. A *shape atom* has the form $\mathsf{s}(a)$, where $\mathsf{s} \in N_S$ and $a \in N_N$. A *path expression* E is a regular expression built using the usual operators $*$, $\cdot$, $\cup$ from symbols in $N_P^+ = N_P \cup \{p^- \mid p \in N_P\}$, where p^- is the *inverse property* of p. A *(complex) shape* is an expression ϕ obeying the syntax:

$$\phi, \phi' ::= \top \mid \mathsf{s} \mid B \mid c \mid \phi \wedge \phi' \mid \neg\phi \mid \geq_n E.\phi \mid E = p \mid disj(E,p) \mid closed(P)$$

where $\mathsf{s} \in N_S$, $p \in N_P$, $B \in N_C$, $c \in N_N$, $P \subseteq N_P$, n is a positive integer, and E is a path expression. In what follows, we write $\phi \vee \phi'$ instead of $\neg(\neg\phi \wedge \neg\phi')$; $\geq_n E$ instead of $\geq_n E.\top$; $\exists E.\phi$ instead of $\geq_1 E.\phi$; $\forall E.\phi$ instead of $\neg\exists E.\neg\phi$.

A *(shape) constraint* is an expression of the form $\mathsf{s} \leftrightarrow \phi$, where $\mathsf{s} \in N_S$ and ϕ is a possibly complex shape. *Targets* in SHACL prescribe that certain nodes of the input data graph should validate certain shapes. A *target expression* is of the form (W, s), where $\mathsf{s} \in N_S$, and W takes one of the following forms: (i) constant from N_N, also called *node target*, (ii) class name from N_C, also called *class target*, (iii) expressions of the form $\exists p$ with $p \in N_P$, also called *subjects-of target*, (iv) expressions of the form $\exists p^-$ with $p \in N_P$, also called *objects-of target*. A target is any set of target expressions. A *shapes graph* is a pair (C, T), where C is a set of constraints and T is a set of targets. We assume that each shape name appearing in C occurs exactly once on the left-hand side of a constraint, and each shape name occurring in T must also appear in C. A set of constraints C is *recursive*, if there is a shape name in C that directly or indirectly refers to itself. In this work, we focus on *non-recursive* constraints.

Semantics of SHACL. The evaluation of shape expressions is given by assigning nodes of the data graph to (possibly multiple) shape names. More formally, a *(shape) assignment* for a data graph G is a set $I = G \cup L$, where L is a set of shape atoms such that $a \in V(G)$ for each $s(a) \in L$. Let $V(I)$ denote the set of nodes that appear in I. The evaluation of a complex shape w.r.t. an assignment I is given in terms of a function $[\![\cdot]\!]^I$ that maps a shape expression ϕ to a set of nodes, and a path expression E to a set of pairs of nodes as defined in Table 1. We assume that the nodes appearing in a shapes graph $\mathcal{S}$ occur in the graph G.

Let I be a shapes assignment for a data graph G. We say I is a *model* of (or satisfies) a constraint $\mathsf{s} \leftrightarrow \phi$ if $[\![\mathsf{s}]\!]^I = [\![\phi]\!]^I$; I is a model of a set of constraints C if I is a model of every constraint in C; I is a model of a target (W, s) if $[\![W]\!]^I \subseteq [\![\mathsf{s}]\!]^I$; I is a model of a target set T if I is a model of every $(W, \mathsf{s}) \in T$. Assume a SHACL shapes graph (C, T) and a data graph G such that each node that appears in C or T also appears in G. The data graph G *validates* (C, T) if there exists an assignment $I = G \cup L$ for G such that (i) I is a model of C, and (ii) I is a model of T.

Clearly, for non-recursive constraints, which is the setting we consider here, the unique assignment obtained in a bottom-up fashion, starting from G and evaluating each constraint once, is a model of C. More precisely, one can start from constraints of the form $\mathsf{s}_1 \leftrightarrow \phi_1$, where ϕ_1 has no shape names, and add to G all the atoms $\mathsf{s}_1(a)$ such that $a \in [\![\phi_1]\!]^G$; let the result be $G \cup L_1$. We then proceed with constraints of the form $\mathsf{s}_2 \leftrightarrow \phi_2$, where ϕ_2 has only shape names occurring in L_1 and add in L_2 all $\mathsf{s}_2(a)$ such that $a \in [\![\phi_2]\!]^{G \cup L_1}$; the new assignment is $G \cup L_1 \cup L_2$. By iteratively evaluating all the constraints in this manner we obtain in polynomial time a unique assignment, denoted $I_{G,C} = G \cup L_{G,C}$ that is a model of C. If $I_{G,C}$ is also a model of T, then we that G *validates* (C,T). We call a shapes graph (C,T) *satisfiable* if there exists some data graph G that validates it.

Table 1. Semantics of SHACL shape expressions

$$[\![\top]\!]^I = V(I) \qquad [\![c]\!]^I = \{c\} \qquad [\![B]\!]^I = \{c \mid B(c) \in I\}$$

$$\mathsf{s}^I = \{c \mid \mathsf{s}(c) \in I\} \qquad [\![\neg\phi]\!]^I = V(I) \setminus [\![\phi]\!]^I \qquad [\![\phi_1 \wedge \phi_2]\!]^I = [\![\phi_1]\!]^I \cap [\![\phi_2]\!]^I$$

$$[\![p]\!]^I = \{(a,b) \mid p(a,b) \in I\} \qquad [\![p^-]\!]^I = \{(a,b) \mid p(b,a) \in I\}$$

$$[\![E \cdot E']\!]^I = \{(a,b) \mid \exists d : (a,d) \in [\![E]\!]^I \text{ and } (d,b) \in [\![E']\!]^I\}$$

$$[\![E \cup E']\!]^I = [\![E]\!]^I \cup [\![E']\!]^I$$

$$[\![E^*]\!]^I = \{(a,a) \mid a \in V(I)\} \cup [\![E]\!]^I \cup [\![E \cdot E]\!]^I \cup \cdots$$

$$[\![\geq_n E.\phi]\!]^I = \{c \mid |\{(c,d) \in [\![E]\!]^I \text{ and } d \in [\![\phi]\!]^I\}| \geq n\}$$

$$[\![E = p]\!]^I = \{c \mid \forall d : (c,d) \in [\![E]\!]^I \text{ iff } (c,d) \in [\![p]\!]^I\}$$

$$[\![disj(E,p)]\!]^I = \{c \mid \nexists d : (c,d) \in [\![E]\!]^I \text{ and } (c,d) \in [\![p]\!]^I\}$$

$$[\![closed(P)]\!]^I = \{c \mid \forall p \notin P : c \notin [\![\exists p]\!]^I\}$$

Example 1. Consider the following data graph G and shapes graph (C,T):

$$\begin{aligned} G = \{ & Patient(p_1), Patient(p_2), ActivePatient(p_1), ActivePatient(p_2), \\ & Physician(Ann), Physician(Ben), Physician(Tom), \\ & treatsPatient(Ann,p_1), treatsPatient(Ben,p_1), treatsPatient(Tom,p_2)\} \\ C = \{ & \mathsf{PatientShape} \leftrightarrow ActivePatient \vee DischargePatient, \\ & \mathsf{PhysicianShape} \leftrightarrow Physician \vee \exists treatsPatient.ActivePatient\}, \\ T = \{ & (Patient, \mathsf{PatientShape}), (\exists treatsPatient, \mathsf{PhysicianShape})\} \end{aligned}$$

The data graph describes two patients, p_1 and p_2, both marked as active patients. There are three physicians: *Ann*, *Ben*, and *Tom*. *Ann* and *Ben* are assigned to treat p_1, and Tom treats p_2. The shapes graph specifies the following constraints. Every node that is a patient must also be either an active patient or a discharged patient. Every node that treats a patient (i.e., has an outgoing *treatsPatient*-edge) must either be a physician or must treat a patient who is an active patient. Clearly, G validates (C, T) since $I_{G,C}$ is a model of T, where $I_{G,C}$ contains the shape atoms $\mathsf{PatientShape}(p_1)$, $\mathsf{PatientShape}(p_2)$, $\mathsf{PhysicianShape}(Ann)$, $\mathsf{PhysicianShape}(Ben)$, $\mathsf{PhysicianShape}(Tom)$.

3 Updating RDF Graphs

In this section, we define an update language that is both expressive and tightly integrated with SHACL validation. To achieve this, we begin by extending SHACL itself. In our framework, SHACL shape graphs can serve as preconditions for actions, enabling validation checks prior to applying updates. To support richer and more practical update scenarios, we extend SHACL with richer targets, addressing a known limitation of the standard. In similar spirit, the SHACL Advanced Features Working Group[1] is addressing this limitation by proposing SPARQL-based targets as a more flexible targeting mechanism.

Moreover, we enrich path expressions by allowing constructs such as difference operators and some special type of properties, which are crucial for capturing fine-grained structural changes in RDF graphs. This extension is particularly essential for precisely capturing the impact of updates on SHACL constraints. While the expressivity required for such checks could in principle be captured by first-order logic, we opt to remain within an extended SHACL fragment, whose connection to Description Logics makes it well-suited for studying the complexity of static validation under updates for various fragments of SHACL.

Extending SHACL to Handle Updates. We propose an extension of SHACL which we denote with SHACL$^+$. The syntax of SHACL$^+$ is defined as for SHACL, with the following extensions. First, we extend path expressions from SHACL to allow in addition to the usual operators also a new *difference* operator ($\setminus$) on symbols from N_P^+ and *shape properties* of the form (ϕ_1, ϕ_2), where ϕ_1, ϕ_2 are shape expressions without shape names. More specifically, path expressions in SHACL$^+$ are of the following syntax:

$$E ::= p \mid p^- \mid (\phi_1, \phi_2) \mid E \cdot E \mid (E)^* \mid E \cup E \mid E \setminus E$$

where, $p, p^- \in N_P^+$, and ϕ_1, ϕ_2 are SHACL$^+$ shape expressions without shape names. Shape expressions are defined over such extended paths as expected. For example, $r \cdot (q \setminus (\exists r, \exists p))$ is an E-path expression; $(\exists r, \exists p)$ intuitively represents the Cartesian product of the domains of r and p. Note that a *singleton* property of the form (a, b) is a special case where $a, b \in N_N$. Target expressions are of the form (ϕ, s), where ϕ is a complex shape without shape names. Targets are any Boolean combinations of target expressions. That is, if T_1 and T_2 are targets,

[1] https://www.w3.org/TR/shacl-af/#targets.

then $T_1 \wedge T_2$, $T_1 \vee T_2$, and $\neg T_1$ are targets; we may write T_1, T_2 instead of $T_1 \wedge T_2$. The notions of shapes constraints and shapes graph are defined as for SHACL.

The evaluation of shape expressions w.r.t. an assignment I is defined as in Table 1, and we add the following two extensions for the evaluation of shape properties and path difference:

$$\begin{aligned}
[\![(\phi_1, \phi_2)]\!]^I =& \{(a, b) \mid a \in [\![\phi_1]\!]^I, b \in [\![\phi_2]\!]^I\} \\
[\![E \setminus E'^{+}]\!]^I =& \{(a, b) \mid (a, b) \in [\![E]\!]^I \text{ and } (a, b) \notin [\![E'^{+}]\!]^I\}.
\end{aligned}$$

That I is a model of a target expression (ϕ, s) is naturally defined as $[\![\phi]\!]^I \subseteq [\![\mathsf{s}]\!]^I$. For targets, the definition of satisfaction is defined as expected, that is I models T_1 and T_2 if T is of the form $T_1 \wedge T_2$; I models T_1 or T_2 if T is of the form $T_1 \vee T_2$, and I does not T_1, if T is of the form $\neg T_1$. The notion of validation is then the same as for SHACL.

SHACL-Based Update Language for RDF Graphs. We now introduce an action language for updating RDF graphs under SHACL constraints, leveraging SHACL itself to define the syntax and semantics of the language. To allow for more flexible actions and to capture a wider range of updates, we base our language on the extension SHACL$^+$. The update language is composed of two types of actions, namely *basic* and *complex* actions. Basic actions enable two core operations: (i) adding or removing nodes satisfying a shape expression from the extension of a class, and (ii) adding or removing edges (properties) between pairs of nodes connected via a path expression. Complex actions allow for composing multiple actions and conditional executions based on the outcome of SHACL$^+$ validation checks over the graph.

To make actions more flexible, we assume a countable infinite set N_V of variables disjoint from N_N, N_C, N_P, and N_S. In particular, we may allow variables in SHACL$^+$ shapes graphs in places of nodes. Path and shape expressions, targets, and shapes graphs with variables we call *path formulas*, *shape formulas*, *target formulas* and *shapes graph formulas*, respectively.

Basic actions β and *complex actions* α are defined by the following grammar:

$$\begin{aligned}
\beta &::= (B \xleftarrow{\oplus} \phi) \mid (B \xleftarrow{\ominus} \phi) \mid (p \xleftarrow{\oplus} E) \mid (p \xleftarrow{\ominus} E) \\
\alpha &::= \emptyset \mid \beta \cdot \alpha \mid (\mathcal{S}?\alpha[\alpha]) \cdot \alpha
\end{aligned}$$

where $B \in N_C$, ϕ is a SHACL$^+$ shape formula without shape names but possibly with variables, $p \in N_P$, E is a SHACL$^+$ path formula, $\emptyset$ denotes the empty action, and $\mathcal{S}$ is a SHACL$^+$ shapes graph formula.

A *substitution* is a function σ from N_V to N_N. For any formula, an action, γ, we use $\sigma(\gamma)$ to denote the result of replacing in γ every occurrence of a variable x by a constant $\sigma(x)$. An action α is ground if it has no variables, and α' is a ground instance of an action α if $\alpha' = \sigma(\alpha)$ for some substitution σ. Intuitively, an application of a ground action $(A \xleftarrow{\oplus} \phi)$ (or $(A \xleftarrow{\ominus} C)$) on a graph G stands for the addition (or deletion) of $A(c)$ to G for each c that makes ϕ true in G. Similarly, $(p \xleftarrow{\oplus} E)$ adds a p-edge whenever there is an E-path between two nodes; the case with deletion is as expected. Composition stands for successive action execution, and a conditional action $\mathcal{S}?\alpha_1[\alpha_2]$ expresses that α_1 is executed if G validates $\mathcal{S}$, and α_2 is performed otherwise. If $\alpha_2 = \emptyset$, then we have an action with a simple precondition as in classical planning languages, and write it $\mathcal{S}?\alpha_1$. The semantics of applying actions on graphs is defined only for ground actions.

Definition 1. *Let G be a data graph and α a ground action. For a basic ground action β, $up(G, \beta)$ is defined as follows:*

- $up(G, \beta) = G \cup \{B(a) \mid a \in [\![\phi]\!]^G\}$ *for* $\beta = (B \xleftarrow{\oplus} \phi)$,
- $up(G, \beta) = G \cup \{p(a, b) \mid (a, b) \in [\![E]\!]^G\}$ *for* $\beta = (p \xleftarrow{\oplus} E)$.

The case with deletion ($\xleftarrow{\ominus}$) is analogous. Then, the result $up(G, \alpha)$ of applying a ground action α on G is a graph defined recursively as follows:

- $up(G, \emptyset) = G$,
- $up(G, \beta \cdot \alpha') = up(up(G, \beta), \alpha)$ *if α is of the form $\beta \cdot \alpha'$, and*
- *if α is of the form $(\mathcal{S}?\alpha_1[\alpha_2]) \cdot \alpha'$, then $up(G, \mathcal{S}?\alpha_1[\alpha_2]) \cdot \alpha')$ is*
  - $up(G, \alpha_1 \cdot \alpha')$, *if G validates $\mathcal{S}$, and*
  - $up(G, \alpha_2 \cdot \alpha')$ *if G does not validate $\mathcal{S}$.*

We illustrate the effects of an action update on a data graph with an example.

Example 2. Consider G and (C, T) from Example 1. Now, consider the action α that discharges patient p_2, which is removed from the active patients and added to the discharged ones; the physicians treating only this patient are removed.

$$(ActivePatient \xleftarrow{\ominus} p_2) \cdot (DischargePatient \xleftarrow{\oplus} p_2) \cdot$$
$$(Physician \xleftarrow{\ominus} \forall treatsPatient.p_2)$$

After applying α to G, we obtain the graph $(G \cup \{DischargePatient(p_2))\} \setminus \{ActivePatient(p_2), Physician(Tom)\}$. The updated data graph $up(G, \alpha)$ does not validate the shapes graph (C, T) since now Tom will still have a $treatsPatient$-edge to patient p_2, but he does not satisfy the shape constraint for PhysicianShape as Tom is not a physician and does not treat an active patient.

We have not defined the semantics of actions with variables, that is non-ground actions. In our framework, variables are treated as parameters that must be instantiated with concrete nodes before execution.

Example 3. The action α_2 with variables x, y, z transfers the physician x from treating patient y to treating patient z and is as follows:

$$(\mathsf{s} \leftrightarrow Physician \wedge \exists treatsPatient.y, s' \leftrightarrow Patient), ((x, s), (y, s'), (z, s'))?$$
$$(treatsPatient \xleftarrow{\ominus} (x, y)) \cdot (treatsPatient \xleftarrow{\oplus} (x, z))$$

Under the substitution σ with $\sigma(x) = Tom$, $\sigma(y) = p_2$, $\sigma(z) = p_1$, the action α_2 first checks whether the target node Tom is an instance of the class $Physician$ and has a $treatsPatient$-property to p_2, and whether target nodes p_1 and p_2 are patients. If this is the case, the action removes the $treatsPatient$-edge between Tom and p_2 and creates a $treatsPatient$-edge between Tom and p_1.

In many scenarios, it is desirable for actions to have the ability to introduce "fresh" nodes into a data graph. Intuitively, the introduction of new nodes can be modeled in our setting by separating the domain of an assignment into the active domain and the inactive domain. The active domain consists of all nodes that occur in the data and shapes graph, whereas the inactive domain contains the remaining nodes. The inactive domain serves as a supply of fresh nodes that can be introduced into the active domain by executing actions. Since we focus on finite sequences of actions, a sufficiently large (but finite) inactive domain can always be assumed in the initial graph to provide an adequate supply of fresh constants. Likewise, node deletion can be captured by actions that move elements from the active domain back into the inactive domain.

Example 4. Consider again our running example. Consider the action

$$\alpha' = (treatsPatient \xleftarrow{\ominus} (\exists treatsPatient.p_2, p_2)),$$

which removes the *treatsPatient*-edges to p_2 from physicians treating p_2. Clearly, α' can be applied to the updated graph $up(G, \alpha)$ from Example 2 by deleting $treatsPatient(Tom, p_2)$, resulting in a valid graph. Hence, the action $\alpha \cdot \alpha'$ is such that $up(G, \alpha \cdot \alpha')$ validates (C, T).

4 Capturing Effects of Updates

In this section, we define a transformation $tr_\alpha(\mathcal{S})$ that rewrites an input SHACL shapes graph $\mathcal{S} = (C, T)$ to capture all the effects of an action α. This transformation can be seen as a form of regression, which incorporates the effects of a sequence of actions starting from the last to the first. More precisely, the transformation $tr_\alpha(\mathcal{S})$ takes a SHACL shapes graph $\mathcal{S}$ and an action α and rewrites them into a new shapes graph $\mathcal{S}_\alpha$, such that for every data graph G: $up(G, \alpha)$ validates $\mathcal{S}$ iff G validates $\mathcal{S}_\alpha$. The idea is to simply update the constraints in C and target expressions in T accordingly, namely the actions replace every class name B in C and T with $B \wedge C$ (or $B \wedge \neg C$) if the action is $B \xleftarrow{\oplus} C$ (or $(B \xleftarrow{\ominus} C)$); analogously for actions over properties. If the action is of the form $\mathcal{S}'?\alpha_1[\alpha_2]$, then we create two shapes graphs: one shapes graph $\mathcal{S}_{\alpha_1}$ if G validates $\mathcal{S}'$ and $\mathcal{S}_{\alpha_2}$ if G does not validate $\mathcal{S}'$.

Before we proceed, to capture the effects of actions, we allow for Boolean combinations of shapes graphs. That is, if $\mathcal{S}$ and $\mathcal{S}'$ are shapes graphs, then $\mathcal{S} \wedge \mathcal{S}'$, $\mathcal{S} \vee \mathcal{S}'$, and $\neg\mathcal{S}$ are shapes graphs. Clearly, the notion of validation is defined as expected. However, allowing for boolean combinations of shapes graphs is just syntactic sugar, as they can be easily transformed (in linear time) into a single equivalent shapes graph (C, T) in SHACL$^+$ that preserves validation (see Proposition 1 in Appendix).

Definition 2. *Assume a SHACL$^+$ shapes graph $\mathcal{S}$ and a ground action α. We use $\mathcal{S}_{Q \leftarrow Q'}$ to denote the new shapes graph that is obtained from $\mathcal{S}$ by replacing* *in $\mathcal{S}$ every class or property name Q with the expression Q'. Then, the transformation $tr_\alpha(\mathcal{S})$ of $\mathcal{S}$ w.r.t., α is defined recursively as follows:*

$$\begin{aligned}
tr_\epsilon(\mathcal{S}) &= \mathcal{S}\\
tr_{(B \xleftarrow{\oplus} C)\cdot\alpha}(\mathcal{S}) &= (tr_\alpha(\mathcal{S}))_{B \leftarrow B \vee C}\\
tr_{(B \xleftarrow{\ominus} C)\cdot\alpha}(\mathcal{S}) &= (tr_\alpha(\mathcal{S}))_{B \leftarrow B \wedge \neg C}\\
tr_{(p \xleftarrow{\oplus} E)\cdot\alpha}(\mathcal{S}) &= (tr_\alpha(\mathcal{S}))_{p \leftarrow p \cup E}\\
tr_{(p \xleftarrow{\ominus} E)\cdot\alpha}(\mathcal{S}) &= (tr_\alpha(\mathcal{S}))_{p \leftarrow p \setminus E}\\
tr_{(\mathcal{S}'?\alpha_1[\alpha_2])\cdot\alpha}(\mathcal{S}) &= (\neg\mathcal{S}' \vee tr_{\alpha_1\cdot\alpha}(\mathcal{S})) \wedge (\mathcal{S}' \vee tr_{\alpha_2\cdot\alpha}(\mathcal{S}))
\end{aligned}$$

The transformation correctly captures the effects of complex actions.

Theorem 1. *Given a ground action α, a data graph G and a SHACL shapes graph $\mathcal{S}$. Then, $up(G,\alpha)$ validates $\mathcal{S}$ if and only if G validates $tr_\alpha(\mathcal{S})$.*

Proof (Sketch.). We prove the claim by induction on the structure of the action α. For the base case, the claim trivially holds: $up(G,\emptyset) = G$ and $tr_\emptyset(\mathcal{S}) = \mathcal{S}$. For the step, for actions $\beta \cdot \alpha'$, for each type of basic action β it can be shown by induction on the structure of shape expressions that for every shapes graph $\mathcal{S}'$, it holds that $up(G,\beta)$ validates $\mathcal{S}'$ iff G validates $\mathcal{S}'_\beta$. For conditional actions of the form $(\mathcal{S}'?\alpha_1[\alpha_2] \cdot \alpha')$ we split the cases based on whether G validates $\mathcal{S}'$.

We illustrate the transformation above with an example.

Example 5. Consider $\mathcal{S} = (C,T)$ and α from our running example. Then, the transformation $tr_\alpha(\mathcal{S})$ is the new shapes graph (C',T), where:

$$\begin{aligned}
C' = \{&\mathsf{PatientShape} \leftrightarrow (\mathit{ActivePatient} \wedge \neg p_2) \vee (\mathit{DischargedPatient} \vee p_2),\\
&\mathsf{PhysicianShape} \leftrightarrow (\mathit{Physician} \wedge \exists \mathit{treatsPatient}.\neg p_2) \vee\\
&\qquad \exists \mathit{treatsPatient}.(\mathit{ActivePatient} \wedge \neg p_2)\},\\
T = \{&(\mathit{Patient}, \mathsf{PatientShape}), (\exists \mathit{treatsPatient}, \mathsf{PhysicianShape})\}
\end{aligned}$$

We extended SHACL to support expressive update actions, but if we restrict to sequences of basic additions using standard shape and path expressions, and deletions for shapes, the transformation stays within (almost) plain SHACL. Although targets may allow arbitrary shape expressions, these can be rewritten using only standard SHACL constructs with the minor extension of allowing $\top$. As our focus is on static validation via satisfiability checking, and in absence of SHACL satisfiability tools, we rely on first-order-logic-based tools, and strict conformance to plain SHACL is not essential; see Appendix for details.

5 Static Validation Under Updates for Arbitrary Graphs

In this section, we consider a stronger form of reasoning about updates. As shown in the previous section validation under updates can be reduced to standard validation within a minor extension of SHACL. Building on this result, we now turn to the central task of this paper: *static validation under updates*. Broadly speaking, this task asks whether a given sequence of update actions always preserves the validation of a shapes graph, independently of a concrete data graph.

Definition 3. *Let $\mathcal{S}$ be a shapes graph and let α be an action. Then, α is an* $\mathcal{S}$-preserving *action if for every data graph G and for every ground instance α' of α, we have that G validates $\mathcal{S}$ implies $up(G, \alpha')$ validates $\mathcal{S}$. The* static validation under updates *problem is:*

Given an action α and a shapes graph $\mathcal{S}$, is α $\mathcal{S}$-preserving?

Using the transformation from Definition 2, we can reduce static validation under updates to unsatisfiability of shapes graphs: an action α is not $\mathcal{S}$-preserving if and only if there is some data graph G and a ground instance α^* of α such that G validates $\mathcal{S}$ and G does not validate $tr_{\alpha^*}(\mathcal{S})$. In particular, if such a ground instance of α exists, then there exists a ground instance obtained by substituting the variables with nodes from the input or an arbitrary fresh node.

Theorem 2. *Let α be a complex action with n variables and $\mathcal{S}$ a SHACL$^+$ shapes graph. Let $\Gamma \subseteq N_N$ be the set of nodes appearing in $\mathcal{S}$ and α together with a set of n fixed fresh nodes. Then,*

(i) α is not $\mathcal{S}$-preserving, if and only if
(ii) $\mathcal{S} \wedge \neg tr_{\alpha^*}(\mathcal{S})$ is satisfiable for some ground instance α^* obtained by replacing each variable in α with a node from Γ.

Proof (Sketch). For (i) implies (ii), assume α is not $\mathcal{S}$-preserving. Then, by definition there exists a data graph and a ground instance α' of α such that if the graph validates $\mathcal{S}$, then the result of applying α' to the graph validates $\mathcal{S}$. Let G be such a graph and let σ be such a substitution of the form $x_1 \rightarrow a_1, \ldots, x_n \rightarrow a_n$ with $\sigma(\alpha) = \alpha'$. That is, G validates $\mathcal{S}$ and $up(G, \alpha')$ does not validate $\mathcal{S}$. The latter together with Theorem 1 implies that G does not validate $tr_{\alpha'}(\mathcal{S})$. Hence, G validates $\mathcal{S} \wedge \neg tr_{\alpha'}(\mathcal{S})$. Now, let σ^* be a substitution obtained from σ as follows: $x_i \rightarrow a_i$ if a_i appears in $\mathcal{S}$ or α, and $x_i \rightarrow c_i$ with c_i is a fresh node in Γ if a_i does not appear in $\mathcal{S}$ or α. Moreover, let G^* be the graph obtained by replacing in G all nodes a_i not appearing in $\mathcal{S}$ or α with c_i from Γ. Clearly, $\alpha^* = \sigma^*(\alpha)$ is a desired ground instance of α and G^* is such that G^* validates $\mathcal{S} \wedge \neg tr_{\alpha^*}(\mathcal{S})$. For (ii) implies (i), assume that $\mathcal{S} \wedge \neg tr_{\alpha^*}(\mathcal{S})$ is satisfiable. Let α^* be a ground instance of α obtained by replacing each variable in α with a node from Γ and let G be a graph that validates $\mathcal{S} \wedge \neg tr_{\alpha^*}(\mathcal{S})$. Hence, G validates $\mathcal{S}$ and G does not validate $tr_{\alpha^*}(\mathcal{S})$. By Theorem 1, the latter implies that $up(G, \alpha^*)$ does not validate $\mathcal{S}$, and therefore α is not $\mathcal{S}$-preserving.

We illustrate static validation under updates with an example.

Example 6. The action α from Example 2 is not (C, T)-preserving since G validates (C, T), but $up(G, \alpha)$ does not validate (C, T). From Example 5, we can see that G does not validate $(C', T) = tr_\alpha(C, T)$ since the model

$I_{G,C'}$ does not satisfy T. That is, $Tom \in [\![\exists treatsPatient]\!]^{I_{G,C'}}$ but $Tom \notin [\![\mathsf{PhysicianShape}]\!]^{I_{G,C'}}$ since Tom does not satisfy any of the conjuncts defining the shape PhysicianShape, and in particular $Tom \notin [\![Physician \wedge \exists treatsPatient.\neg p_2]\!]^{I_{G,C'}}$. Intuitively, nodes removed from the class *Physician* should also be removed from the *treatsPatient* property as in the $\mathcal{S}$-preserving action $\alpha^* = \alpha \cdot \alpha'$ from Example 4. By applying α^* to $\mathcal{S}$, we obtain the following transformed shapes graph $tr_{\alpha^*}(\mathcal{S})$:

$$\begin{aligned}C^* = \{&\mathsf{PatientShape} \leftrightarrow (ActivePatient \wedge \neg p_2) \vee (DischargedPatient \vee p_2),\\ &\mathsf{PhysicianShape} \leftrightarrow (Physician \wedge \exists E.\neg p_2) \vee \exists E.(ActivePatient \wedge \neg p_2)\},\\ T^* = \{&(Patient, \mathsf{PatientShape}), (\exists E, \mathsf{PhysicianShape})\}\end{aligned}$$

where E is the path expression $(treatsPatient \setminus (\exists treatsPatient.p_2, p_2))$.

The above theorem provides an algorithm for static validation under updates by converting it into satisfiability checking of shapes graphs in SHACL$^+$. While satisfiability has been shown to be undecidable already for plain SHACL in [18], better upper bounds can be obtained by restricting SHACL$^+$ to Description Logic (DL)-like fragments. Specifically, in addition to disallowing expressions of the form $E = p$, $disj(E, p)$, and $closed(P)$, we also disallow path operators $*$ and composition $\cdot$ in E, and limit shape properties in paths to singleton properties of the form (a, b) where $a, b \in N_N$. For this fragment, the co-problem of static validation can be reduced to finite satisfiability in the description logic $\mathcal{ALCHOIQ}^{br}$ – an extension of the DL $\mathcal{ALCHOIQ}$ – which has been shown in [3] to be NExpTime-complete. If we further restrict, shape expressions of the form $\geq_n E.\phi$ to only allow $n = 1$, we can reduce to $\mathcal{ALCHOI}^{br}$, for which finite satisfiability is in ExpTime. The coNExpTime-membership holds even when allowing unrestricted shape properties which can be easily captured by extending $\mathcal{ALCHOIQ}^{br}$ with pairs of arbitrary concepts in places of roles. The matching upper bound immediately follows by extending with this construct the translation of $\mathcal{ALCHOIQ}^{br}$ [3] to $\mathcal{C}^2$, the two-variable fragment of first-order predicate logic extended with counting quantifiers, where such constructs translate naturally. For the lower bounds, we reduce the NExpTime problem of finite satisfiability of $\mathcal{ALCOIQ}$ [3,23] (and ExpTime [3] of $\mathcal{ALCHOI}$) into the co-problem of static validation for SHACL under updates.

Condition (ii) of Theorem 2 requires the existence of a ground instance among potentially exponentially many options, proportional to the number of variables appearing in α. However, each shapes graph $\mathcal{S}$ can be straightforwardly translated into an equisatisfiable DL knowledge base $K_{\mathcal{S}}$ in the extended DLs $\mathcal{ALCHOI}(\mathcal{Q})^{br}$, which allows for boolean combinations of KBs. Exploiting this, we can show the following: α is not $\mathcal{S}$-preserving iff $\mathcal{S} \wedge \neg tr_{\alpha^*}(\mathcal{S})$ is satisfiable for some ground instance $\alpha^* \in \Sigma$ iff $K_{\mathcal{S}} \wedge \neg K_{tr_{\alpha^c}(\mathcal{S})}$ is finitely satisfiable, where α^c is obtained from α by replacing each variable with a fresh node not occurring in $\mathcal{S}$ and α. Note that for a sequence of basic ground actions α^*, the size of $tr_{\alpha^*}(\mathcal{S})$ may grow exponentially in the number of actions. Intuitively, if the same class or property name B is updated n times in the action, and each update action introduces another occurrence of B, then the resulting constraint may contain up to 2^n occurrences of B, leading to exponential blow-up. However, for static validation, it suffices to construct an equisatisfiable description logic knowledge base (or first-order logic formula), where we can control the size more effectively. To this end, we define a transformation $tr_{\alpha^*}(K_S)$, which introduces a fresh class or property name for each update action, along with simple equivalence axioms (e.g., $B' \equiv B \vee \varphi$) storing the effect of the action. The result of this transformation $tr_{\alpha^*}(K_S)$ is equisatisfiable to $K_{tr_{\alpha^*}}(\mathcal{S})$ but the size is linear in the input action if α^* is a sequence of basic actions. Clearly, for conditional actions, the transformation may yield a Boolean combination of exponentially many knowledge bases, but each of them will be of linear size. From the above follows that $K_\mathcal{S} \wedge \neg K_{tr_{\alpha^c}(\mathcal{S})}$ is finitely satisfiable iff $K_\mathcal{S} \wedge \neg tr_{\alpha^c}(K_\mathcal{S})$ is finitely satisfiable. It was shown in [3] that finite satisfiability of $K_\mathcal{S} \wedge \neg tr_{\alpha^c}(K_\mathcal{S})$ KBs is in NExpTime for $\mathcal{ALCHOIQ}^{br}$ and ExpTime for $\mathcal{ALCHOI}^{br}$. The proof holds also for the extension of $\mathcal{ALCHOIQ}^{br}$ that allows shape properties in places of roles.

The correctness of the following theorem immediately follows.

Theorem 3. *We obtain the following complexity results for static validation:*

- *The problem is* undecidable. *It remains undecidable also when the input shapes graph and action uses only plain SHACL.*
- *The problem is* coNExpTime*-complete, when the input uses the fragment of SHACL*$^+$ *that does not allow the operators* $*$ *and* $\cdot$ *in path expressions, and expressions of the form* $E = p$, $disj(E, p)$, *and* $closed(P)$.
- *The problem is* ExpTime*-complete if additionally shape expressions of the form* $\geq_n E.\phi$ *are restricted to only* $n = 1$ *and shape properties in paths are restricted to singleton properties.*

6 Implementation and Experiments

To implement a solver for the static validation under updates problem, given a complex action α and a shapes graph $\mathcal{S}$, we compute $\neg tr_{\alpha^*}(\mathcal{S})$ and then check whether $\mathcal{S}$ is contained in $tr_{\alpha^*}(\mathcal{S})$, as detailed in Theorem 2. Our approach is based on the translation of SHACL shape graphs into equisatisfiable FOL sentences [18]. The SHACL2FOL tool [16] performs this translation, generating such sentences in the TPTP [22] format. The TPTP file is then used by a theorem prover to determine satisfiability, enabling the SHACL2FOL tool to check both the satisfiability of individual shape graphs, and the containment problem between two shape graphs.

To enable static validation under updates, we have extended SHACL2FOL to compute the transformation of a shape graph under updates. This functionality accepts a shapes graph and a list of actions, in JSON format, as inputs. Given a shape graph $\mathcal{S}$, and its equisatisfiable FOL translation φ, and a complex action α, we have implemented the regression approach that generates a FOL translation φ_α equisatisfiable to $tr_{\alpha^*}(\mathcal{S})$. Our implementation currently supports actions in the form $p \xleftarrow{\oplus} E$ and $p \xleftarrow{\ominus} E$, where E is either a pair of shapes (ϕ_1, ϕ_2), or a SHACL property path. This implementation effectively follows the regression approach from Sect. 4, but as a direct transformation of the FOL sentence φ. The formalisation of actions in JSON format, their translation into logic expressions, and their integration into a TPTP file are novel extensions of the SHACL2FOL tool. The code for this implementation is available through the link in the Supplemental Material Statement.

```
sh:path p;              sh:path p;                          sh:path P;
sh:(equals/             sh:qualified(Min/Max)Count i;       sh:(hasValue/class) c;
    disjoint) r;        sh:qualifiedValueShape [
                          sh:(hasValue/class) c; ];
```

Fig. 1. Three constraint templates where "/" denotes an alternative, p and r are property names, P is property path, i is an integer and c is a constant.

A comprehensive benchmark of real world usages of SHACL is still missing from the literature, and for this reason our evaluation focuses on studying the effects of updates on different types of SHACL constraints. In particular, we focused on the constraint components that have been identified as the most problematic for the problem of satisfiability checking, namely: property pair equality, the qualified cardinality constraints, and sequence, alternative and transitive paths [18]. We use those constraints both to define the initial shape graph, and the updates to be performed. Our aim is not to cover all the possible interactions between constraints, but to show scalability across a wide range of constraints known for their theoretical complexity.

To generate a synthetic test case we create a shape graph consisting of a number of shapes, each one having a single target, equally divided among the four SHACL target definitions (excluding the implicit one). Each shape is initialized with a random constraint chosen from property pair equality, disjointness, a cardinality constraint (with limits from 0 to 2), or a constraint over a property path, using the constraint templates shown in Fig. 1. Whenever a node needs to be initialized, it is chosen randomly from a predefined set of constants of size double that of the number of shapes. Relations are initialized randomly from a predefined set of constants in the same way, with the exception that this set always includes the class membership relation `rdf:type`. This ratio of constants to shapes was chosen empirically to enable actions and shapes to interact through the reuse of the same constants, while also allowing for a limited number of new constants to be introduced. This is also used to create test cases where the split between true and false results of the static validation are more evenly balanced. Actions are created randomly in one of the two allowed types. Constraints and paths for actions are created in the same way as the constraints for the shapes, and draw from the same sets of node and relation constants.

We run our experiments using an Intel Core i7-9750H CPU and each datapoint shows the average over 10 randomized runs. We use the Vampire 4.9

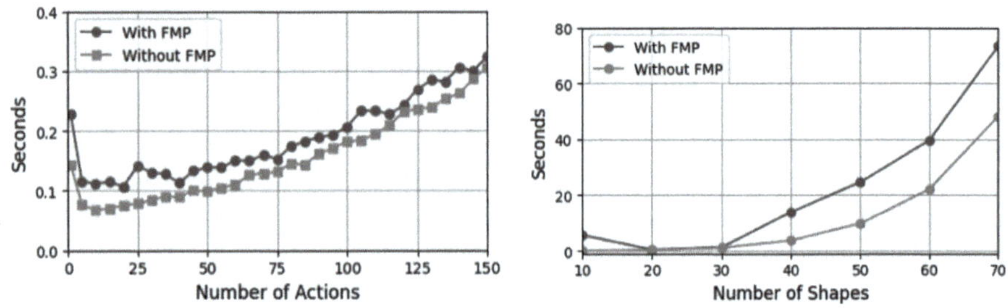

Fig. 2. Time to solve the static validation problem with 10 shapes and an increasing number of actions (left), and with 20 actions and an increasing number of shapes (right), depending on usage of Finite Model Property.

theorem prover to determine the satisfiability of the TPTP sentences, requiring finite models for satisfiability, and using the `-mode portfolio` option to enable diverse, pre-tuned strategies to increase the likelihood of quickly solving the problem. In our first experiment, we use a shape graph of fixed size 10, and we measure the time to perform the static verification test as the number of actions scales from 1 to 200. The results of this experiments, in the left plot of Fig. 2, show how the computation increases linearly with the number of actions. On average, the actions were shape preserving in 10% of the cases.

In our second experiment, we use an update list of 20 actions, and we scale the number of shapes in the original shapes graph from 10 to 70. The results of this second experiment, shown in the right plot of Fig. 2, show how the computation time increases exponentially with the number of shapes. This exponential increase is in line with the known complexity of the shape containment problem [18]. On average, the actions were shape preserving in 33% of the cases.

Across both experiments, the theorem prover failed to find a proof in 16% of the cases in the first experiment, and 8% in the second. This is to be expected, as the satisfiability of certain combinations of shape constraints is known to be undecidable. It should also be noted that the performance of our tool strongly depends on the specific theorem prover being used and on its configuration. For example, Fig. 2 shows how enabling finite model checking increases the computation time. Overall, the experiments show that the problem of static validation under updates, although complex, can be solved quickly for medium-sized shape graphs. It is important to note that the size of a shapes graph is linked with schema complexity and not data complexity, and thus it typically does not need to scale to very large numbers. The fact that the increase in computational time is linear in the number of actions is promising, showing that our regression approach could be applicable to domains involving large updates.

7 Conclusion and Future Work

We have presented a framework for formalizing updates for RDF graphs in the presence of SHACL constraints. We identified a suitable SHACL-aware update language, that can capture intuitive and realistic modifications on RDF graphs, covers a significant fragment of SPARQL updates and extends them to allow for conditional updates. We addressed an important problem: static validation under updates, which asks whether for every RDF graph that validates a SHACL shapes graph, the graph will remain valid after applying a set of updates. We showed that the latter problem can be reduced to (un)satisfiability of a shapes graph in a mild extension of SHACL and studied the complexity. We tested a prototype implementation of our regression-based method for static validation showing its potential for handling inputs of realistic size.

Toward lowering the complexity of static validation, we plan to analyze the problem for other relevant fragments of SHACL. We aim to further develop our implementation to support more action types, with the goal of creating a comprehensive tool for SHACL static analysis tasks. We will also study other basic static analysis problems such as the static type checking problem [9], which intuitively checks whether actions preserve a validation from source to target shapes graphs and problems related to planning.

Supplemental Material Statement: The code for our implementation of the regression approach, and its evaluation, is available on Zenodo [17].[2]

Acknowledgements. Ahmetaj was supported by the Austrian Science Fund (FWF) projects netidee SCIENCE [T1349-N] and the Vienna Science and Technology Fund (WWTF) [10.47379/ICT2201]. Ortiz and Simkus were supported by the FWF projects PIN8884924, P30873 and 10.55776/COE12. The contributions of Pareti and Konstantinidis were supported by the UKRI Horizon Europe guarantee funding scheme for the Horizon Europe projects UPCAST (10.3030/101093216), RAISE (10.3030/101058479) and DataPACT (10.3030/101189771).

References

1. Shapes constraint language (SHACL) (July 2017). https://www.w3.org/TR/shacl/
2. Ahmetaj, S., et al.: Common foundations for shacl, shex, and pg-schema. In: Proceedings of the ACM on Web Conference 2025, WWW 2025, Sydney, NSW, Australia, 28 April 2025- 2 May 2025, pp. 8–21. ACM (2025). https://doi.org/10.1145/3696410.3714694
3. Ahmetaj, S., Calvanese, D., Ortiz, M., Simkus, M.: Managing change in graph-structured data using description logics. ACM Trans. Comput. Log. **18**(4), 27:1–27:35 (2017). https://doi.org/10.1145/3143803
4. Ahmetaj, S., David, R., Ortiz, M., Polleres, A., Shehu, B., Simkus, M.: Reasoning about explanations for non-validation in SHACL. In: Proceedings of KR 2021, Online event, November 3-12, 2021. pp. 12–21 (2021). https://doi.org/10.24963/KR.2021/2
5. Ahmetaj, S., Ortiz, M., Simkus, M.: Towards SHACL validation of evolving graphs. In: Montoya, G., Sallinger, E., Vargas-Solar, G. (eds.) Proceedings of the 16th Alberto Mendelzon International Workshop on Foundations of Data Management

[2] The code is also available at https://github.com/paolo7/SHACL2FOL.

(AMW 2024), Mexico City, Mexico, October 2-4, 2024. CEUR Workshop Proceedings, vol. 3954. CEUR-WS.org (2024). https://ceur-ws.org/Vol-3954/paper1130.pdf
6. Ahmeti, A., Calvanese, D., Polleres, A.: Updating RDFS aboxes and tboxes in SPARQL. In: The Semantic Web - ISWC 2014. Lecture Notes in Computer Science, vol. 8796, pp. 441–456. Springer (2014). https://doi.org/10.1007/978-3-319-11964-9_28
7. Baader, F., Horrocks, I., Lutz, C., Sattler, U.: An Introduction to Description Logic. Cambridge University Press (2017). http://www.cambridge.org/de/academic/subjects/computer-science/knowledge-management-databases-and-data-mining/introduction-description-logic?format=PB#17zVGeWD2TZUeu6s.97
8. Bogaerts, B., Jakubowski, M., den Bussche, J.V.: SHACL: A description logic in disguise. In: Gottlob, G., Inclezan, D., Maratea, M. (eds.) Logic Programming and Nonmonotonic Reasoning - 16th International Conference, LPNMR. Lecture Notes in Computer Science, vol. 13416, pp. 75–88. Springer (2022). https://doi.org/10.1007/978-3-031-15707-3_7
9. Boneva, I., Groz, B., Hidders, J., Murlak, F., Staworko, S.: Static analysis of graph database transformations. In: Proceedings of the 42nd ACM SIGMOD-SIGACT-SIGAI Symposium on Principles of Database Systems, PODS, pp. 251–261. ACM (2023). https://doi.org/10.1145/3584372.3588654
10. Bonifati, A., Furniss, P., Green, A., Harmer, R., Oshurko, E., Voigt, H.: Schema validation and evolution for graph databases. In: Conceptual Modeling - 38th International Conference, ER 2019. Lecture Notes in Computer Science, vol. 11788, pp. 448–456. Springer (2019). https://doi.org/10.1007/978-3-030-33223-5_37
11. Flouris, G., Konstantinidis, G., Antoniou, G., Christophides, V.: Formal foundations for RDF/S KB evolution. Knowl. Inf. Syst. **35**(1), 153–191 (2013). https://doi.org/10.1007/S10115-012-0500-2
12. Kachniarz, J., Szałas, A.: On a Static Verification of Integrity Constraints in Relational Databases, pp. 97–109. Physica-Verlag HD, Heidelberg (2001)
13. Ke, J., Zacouris, Z.G., Acosta, M.: Efficient validation of SHACL shapes with reasoning. Proc. VLDB Endow. **17**(11), 3589–3601 (2024). https://doi.org/10.14778/3681954.3682023, https://www.vldb.org/pvldb/vol17/p3589-acosta.pdf
14. Okulmus, C., Simkus, M.: SHACL validation under the well-founded semantics. In: Proceedings of the 21st International Conference on Principles of Knowledge Representation and Reasoning, KR (2024). https://doi.org/10.24963/KR.2024/52
15. Ortiz, M.: A short introduction to SHACL for logicians. In: Logic, Language, Information, and Computation - 29th International Workshop, WoLLIC 2023. Lecture Notes in Computer Science, vol. 13923, pp. 19–32. Springer (2023). https://doi.org/10.1007/978-3-031-39784-4_2
16. Pareti, P.: SHACL2FOL: An FOL Toolkit for SHACL Decision Problems. arXiv preprint arXiv:2406.08018 (2024)
17. Pareti, P.: paolo7/SHACL2FOL: SHACL Validation under Graph Updates (July 2025). https://doi.org/10.5281/zenodo.16633178
18. Pareti, P., Konstantinidis, G., Mogavero, F.: Satisfiability and containment of recursive shacl. J. Web Semantics p. 100721 (2022). https://doi.org/10.1016/j.websem.2022.100721, https://www.sciencedirect.com/science/article/pii/S1570826822000130
19. Pareti, P., Konstantinidis, G., Mogavero, F., Norman, T.J.: SHACL satisfiability and containment. In: The Semantic Web - ISWC 2020 - 19th International Semantic

Web Conference. Lecture Notes in Computer Science, vol. 12506, pp. 474–493. Springer (2020). https://doi.org/10.1007/978-3-030-62419-4_27

20. Polleres, A., Gearon, P., Passant, A.: SPARQL 1.1 update. W3C recommendation, W3C (Mar 2013). https://www.w3.org/TR/2013/REC-sparql11-update-20130321/
21. Seifer, P., Hernández, D., Lämmel, R., Staab, S.: From shapes to shapes: Inferring SHACL shapes for results of SPARQL CONSTRUCT queries. In: Proceedings of the ACM on Web Conference 2024, WWW 2024, pp. 2064–2074. ACM (2024). https://doi.org/10.1145/3589334.3645550
22. Sutcliffe, G., Suttner, C.: The TPTP problem library. J. Autom. Reason. **21**, 177–203 (1998)
23. Tobies, S.: The complexity of reasoning with cardinality restrictions and nominals in expressive description logics. J. Artif. Intell. Res. **12**, 199–217 (2000). https://doi.org/10.1613/JAIR.705
24. Wandji, R.E., Calvanese, D.: Ontology-based update in virtual knowledge graphs via schema mapping recovery. In: Rules and Reasoning - 8th International Joint Conference, RuleML+RR. Lecture Notes in Computer Science, vol. 15183, pp. 59–74. Springer (2024). https://doi.org/10.1007/978-3-031-72407-7_6
25. Zablith, F., et al.: Ontology evolution: a process-centric survey. Knowl. Eng. Rev. **30**(1), 45–75 (2015). https://doi.org/10.1017/S0269888913000349

GLIDE: Knowledge Graph Linking Using Distance-Aware Embeddings

Alexander Becker(✉), Axel-Cyrille Ngonga Ngomo, and Mohamed Ahmed Sherif

Data Science Group (DICE), Heinz Nixdorf Institute, Paderborn University, Paderborn, Germany
beckeral@campus.upb.de, {axel.ngonga,mohamed.sherif}@upb.de
https://dice-research.org/

Abstract. The number of datasets on the web of data increases continuously. However, the knowledge contained therein cannot be fully utilized without finding links between the entities contained in these datasets. Equivalent entities cannot be identified solely by checking the equivalence of IRIs because of the different origins and naming schemes of different data providers. Yet, such equivalences can be discovered by computing the similarity of their attributes. In this paper we propose GLIDE, an approach that links entities from two different datasets by embedding a joint model of these datasets enriched by additional relations describing the similarity of literals. The joint model is embedded into a latent vector space while paying attention to juxtaposing similar literals. We evaluate our approach against state-of-the-art algorithms using real-world datasets commonly used in link discovery literature. The results show that GLIDE outperforms all baselines on 5 of 7 datasets with perfect or near-perfect accuracy. Our approach achieves its best performance on datasets that feature several literals with similarities. Our experiments indicate that researchers should not only pay attention to equal literals in knowledge graph embedding but should also be aware of the distance between similar literals.

Keywords: Knowledge graphs · Data Integration · Linked Data · Similarity Measures · Literal Matching

1 Introduction

The ever-growing number of knowledge graphs (KGs) available on the web emphasizes the need for algorithms capable of integrating these KGs in a manner that follows the 5-star linked data principles [13]. While numerous KGs remain private within industrial domains, the Linked Open Data (LOD) cloud [19] currently hosts over 1600 publicly available datasets. Integrating knowledge from diverse KGs is pivotal for downstream tasks such as fact-checking [25,32], question answering [39], and digital assistance [38]. These tasks often face challenges stemming from data heterogeneity and incompleteness [3,8,14]. By leveraging additional data through robust data integration techniques, these challenges can be mitigated, ultimately enhancing task performance

D. Garijo et al. (Eds.): ISWC 2025, LNCS 16140, pp. 158–176, 2026.
https://doi.org/10.1007/978-3-032-09527-5_9

and reliability [26]. A critical KGs integration task is discovering similar entities, a process essential for merging knowledge across diverse data sources [40]. Discovering equivalent entities across different KGs cannot rely solely on comparing IRIs. This is because data providers often adopt distinct namespaces and naming schemes in accordance with W3C recommendations for IRI assignment [36]. To address this issue, the attributes of entities are analyzed with the assumption that two entities from different KGs represent the same entity if they share identical or highly similar attributes, such as name, birth date, or address. Discovering matching entities is trivial task when entities have identical attributes and the data is free of inaccuracies. However, in real-world scenarios, KGs are often noisy and incomplete [15]. Therefore, entity pairs with similar attributes, even if there are only a few differences, should also be considered potential matches. Current link discovery frameworks address this by using link specifications (LSs) to specify the conditions necessary for linking resources [20,23]. Other approaches match instances based on word embeddings [2] or KG embeddings [37].

To assess attribute similarity, various measures have been developed, including string similarity metrics [33] such as *Levenshtein* and *Cosine* similarity, as well as phonetic measures [10] like *Soundex* and *Metaphone*. String similarity measures typically evaluate the overlap of character sequences between two strings, while phonetic measures focus on the pronunciation of words by converting different character sequences into phonetic codes. Similarity measures can be used for computing the similarity of literal attributes which can indicate likely equivalences between entities from different data sources.

In this paper, we introduce GLIDE, an approach for linking resources that is robust to attribute variations. GLIDE starts by merging two KGs into a joint KG while at the same time enriching the resulting KG by adding relations that indicate the similarity of literals. This is achieved by assigning a desired maximum latent space distance between literals based on their similarity to keep similar literals close to each other in the embedding space. During the embedding process, any resource pairs that are further apart than the allowed distance are brought closer together by assigning a penalty to the loss function based on their distance. Finally, all resource pairs that are in close proximity to each other within the latent embedding space are matched.

The rest of the paper is structured as follows: Sect. 2 introduces the basic formal definitions, followed by an overview of related work in Sect. 3. We present our approach, GLIDE, in Sect. 4, followed by our experiments to compare GLIDE with other algorithms using real-world datasets in Sect. 5. Finally, Sect. 6 summarizes our findings and future work.

2 Preliminaries

Definition 1 (Knowledge Graph). *A Knowledge Graph (KG)* $G(\mathcal{R}, \mathcal{B}, \mathcal{P}, \mathcal{L})$ *is a set of triples* $(s, p, o) \in (\mathcal{R} \cup \mathcal{B}) \times \mathcal{P} \times (\mathcal{R} \cup \mathcal{L} \cup \mathcal{B})$*, where* $\mathcal{R}$ *is the set of all resources,* $\mathcal{B}$ *is the set of all blank nodes,* $\mathcal{P}$ *is the set of all predicates, and* $\mathcal{L}$ *the set of all literals. The entities of* G *are denoted* $\mathcal{E}(G) = \{x \in \mathcal{R} : \exists (s, p, o) \in G \text{ with } x = s \vee x = o\}$.

Definition 2 (Link Discovery). *Given two knowledge graphs* G *and* G' *and a relation* r *(e.g.,* `owl:sameAs`*), the goal of the link discovery problem is to find all pairs*

$(e, e') \in \mathcal{E}(G) \times \mathcal{E}(G')$ such that $r(s,t)$ holds. The result computed by a link discovery algorithm is called a mapping*:* $M = \{(s,r,t)|s \in \mathcal{E}(G), t \in \mathcal{E}(G')\}$.

Definition 3 (Similarity Function). *A similarity function $\sigma(x,y) \in [0,1]$ returns the similarity value between two objects x and y based on a similarity measure. A value of* 0 *indicates that there is no similarity between x and y, while a value of* 1 *indicates that the two objects are identical w.r.t. the measure.*

3 Related Work

Link Discovery. Current link discovery frameworks like SILK [34] and LIMES [23] use link specifications (LSs) to formalize the conditions necessary for linking resources between KGs. LSs can either be manually specified by the user or learned by using various machine learning paradigms [22]. For instance, RAVEN [21] uses active learning which involves the user for classifying uncertain elements. WOMBAT [27] employs an upward refinement operator, leveraging positive examples exclusively in its supervised learning approach. While the previous algorithms mostly rely on string measures, [1] introduces phonetic measures into LS learning. A more complete list of LS learning algorithms can be found in [23]. VDMI [18] uses a combination of virtual document creation for representing the entities, primary candidate selection and user input for candidate refinement. VDLS [2] matches instances by creating a virtual document for all instances and comparing the similarity of word embeddings for these documents.

Embedding-Based Link Discovery. Embedding-based link discovery algorithms often focus on finding links between multilingual KGs [42] like DBP15K [29] or SRPRS [12]. JAPE [29] introduces an embedding model for jointly embedding cross-lingual entities with a focus on correlations between attributes. ITRANSE and IPTRANSE [43] iteratively align entities by mapping embeddings to a joint space based on semantic distances and match entities based on positive examples for aligned entities. BOOTEA [30] iteratively uses high probability matches as training data for bootstrapping while allowing the previously found training pairs to change their partner if the likelihood of a match between them decreases. Trisedya and Zhang [31] distinguish the embedding into structure embedding and attribute character embedding to then jointly optimize their cosine similarity. MULTIKE [41] uses multiple combination strategies to embed the view of names, relations and attributes and align entities based on a set of positive example alignments. NAEA [44] enhances entity matching by incorporating neighborhood information, aggregating embeddings of neighboring entities weighted by their features' significance, and integrating this with relation-level representations to improve matching accuracy. OTEA [24] approaches the linking problem by transforming it to an optimal transport problem for optimizing the entity-level loss and group-level loss. BLINK [4] matches blank nodes by merging two graphs and embedding the merged model including literals. Other approaches for link discovery can be found in [12,40].

Literal Embeddings. Some link prediction approaches enrich embeddings by incorporating specific types of literals [5]. For instance, LITERALE [17] introduces a new scoring function for literals that can be integrated with existing models. On the other hand, TRANSEA [37] includes numeric literals into the loss function of TransE [6]. KGA [35] discretizes numerical literals and bins values to reduce the number of distinct values.

4 Approach

GLIDE gets a similarity function σ and two KGs G and G' as input and computes the mapping $M = \{(s, \texttt{owl:sameAs}, t) \mid s \in \mathcal{E}(G), t \in \mathcal{E}(G')\}$ with the goal of mapping entities that represent the same real-world entity to each other. We assume the KGs have not been linked yet, i.e. there is no triple containing resources from both G and G'. The main idea of GLIDE is to compute geometric embeddings for a merged version G^+ of the two KGs that juxtaposes similar entities. Our approach achieves this by using the following three phases: (1) Merge the two input KGs G and G' into one KG G^+ and enrich the resulting KG with additional information about the similarity of attributes (Sect. 4.1), (2) Embed G^+ and address the absence of links between G and G'(Section 4.2), and (3) Compute the mapping M based on the distance between embedding vectors of resources in G^+ (Sect. 4.3).

4.1 Graph Merging and Similarity Computation

In the first phase of GLIDE, we tackle the challenge caused by the absence of links between the resources in G and G'. This step is critical, as the open-world assumption, a cornerstone in the domain of KGs, inherently accommodates incomplete information. However, the presence of missing facts can profoundly undermine the performance of embedding models [28], highlighting the necessity of addressing this limitation to ensure robust and reliable KGs integration. To address this, we construct the merged graph G^+ in a way that enables the embedding process to infer when resources originate from different KGs. This ensures that missing links are not penalized. Simultaneously, we aim to introduce additional links between G and G' by leveraging various similarity metrics.

Rewriting IRIs and Literal Values. We aim to leverage all available information during the embedding process, including literal values. To achieve this, each literal is assigned a unique IRI by prefixing the literal value with a symbol ▲ that does not exist in either G or G', and converting the literal to lowercase characters. After this transformation, literals are treated as named resources. In the rest of the paper, please note that all references to resources also encompass literals that have been converted to named resources via IRI assignment. To preserve the origin of each graph for all IRIs, a unique prefix representing the source graph is added to each IRI. IRIs originating from G are prefixed with ♣, while those from G' are prefixed with ♠. Similarly, literal values are prefixed with their originating graph to distinguish their source. This distinction is crucial for identifying literals that occur in one graph but not the other. Finally, we concatenate G and G' with the updated IRIs to create the merged graph G^+.

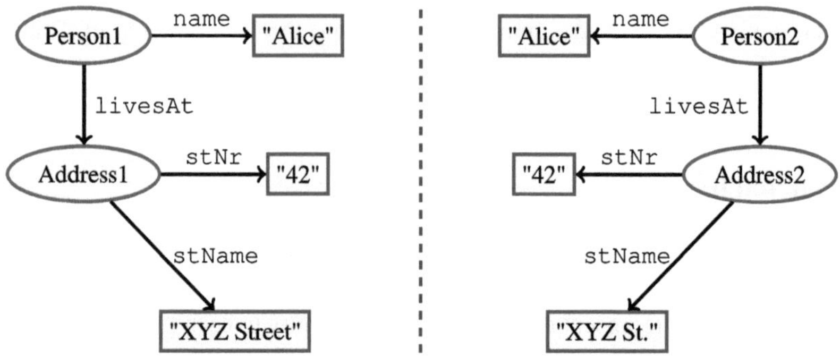

Fig. 1. Graph G (left) and G' (right) before merging.

Computing Allowed Distances Between Literals. To ensure that the embedding model positions similar literals within G^+ close to each other, we introduce a new set of relations, denoted as *allowed-dist*$_{\text{value}}$. Here, *value* represents the maximum permissible distance between two literals, l and l', in the embedding space, beyond which the loss function applies a penalty. This maximum distance is determined using an *allowed-dist* function, which is derived from the similarity measure $\sigma(l, l')$.

Given that constraining the distance between two literals to an excessively large value has negligible impact on the embedding algorithm's results, we do not generate *allowed-dist* triples for all similarity values. In particular, we introduce a hyperparameter λ that regulates how many *allowed-dist* triples are created. Our idea is that each literal should have λ *allowed-dist* relations to other literals, so that literals get pulled towards their λ most similar counterparts from the other graph. However, not all source graph literals have similar literals in the other graph (i.e., literal similarity < 0.0001), and would therefore result in impactless *allowed-dist* relations. Hence, we decide to include at least λ similarities for each literal on average. We create $\lambda \cdot max(|\mathcal{L}(G)|, |\mathcal{L}(G')|)$ *allowed-dist* triples. Taking the maximum value from the literals of G and the literals of G' ensures that even for unbalanced datasets, each literal gets on average λ other literals that it is juxtaposed with. This approach not only optimizes memory usage but also significantly reduces computational overhead during the embedding phase. Formally, let $S = [\,\sigma(l, l') \mid l \in \mathcal{L}(G),\ l' \in \mathcal{L}(G')\,]$ denote the list of all pairwise similarity scores between two literals from different graphs computed using the similarity function σ. Let t be the $(\lambda \cdot max(|\mathcal{L}(G)|, |\mathcal{L}(G')|))^{\text{th}}$ largest value in S.

$$allowed\text{-}dist(l, l', \sigma) = \begin{cases} \sigma(l, l') < t : \infty \\ otherwise : 1 - \sigma(l, l') \end{cases}$$

While including the triples for all similarity values would not negatively impact the algorithm (given an appropriate *allowed-dist* function), this decision saves memory and significantly reduces the number of computations needed for enforcing *allowed-dist* relations during the embedding phase. Figure 2 shows the result of merging the KGs G and G' in Fig. 1. Notably, due to the exact matches between the two literal nodes *"alice"* and the two literal nodes *"42"*, their respective distances in the embedding space should approach 0. In contrast, the distance between *"xyz street"* and *"xyz st."* should not exceed 0.4, reflecting their high similarity despite the absence of an exact match.

Fig. 2. The merged graph G^+ for $\lambda = 1$.

4.2 Embedding

GLIDE operates by matching resources based on their proximity in the embedding space. Consequently, our approach leverages geometric Knowledge Graph Embedding (KGE) models [7] to achieve this. Specifically, we select TransE [6] as the KGE model due to its simplicity and wide usage [26]. Nevertheless, GLIDE is flexible to utilize any geometric KGE model.

The main idea of our embedding algorithm is to split the embedding into two phases with different loss functions as we want to optimize the model for multiple objectives. On one hand, we want to minimize (e_{head} + e_{rel} - e_{tail}) for existing triples and have larger values of (e_{head} + e_{rel} - e_{tail}) for non existing triples. Because the absence of links between the two input KGs G and G', we want to ignore any missing triples from the loss. For this, we design the *intra-graph loss function*. On the other hand, we want to keep similar literal values close to each other. This will lead to similar resources from G and G' that have similar attributes being close to each other, so they can be matched based on their distance. To optimize this, we create a *inter-graph loss function*.

Intra-graph Optimization. Embedding the merged graph G^+ introduces the additional challenge regarding the loss function, as there are no links between the resources from G to the ones within G'. For example, in Fig. 1 and 2 there is no link between *Person1* and *Address2* even though the attributes of *Address1* and *Address2* are almost identical. This would severely impact the KGE models performance, as similar entities are pushed apart in the embedding space solely due to the absence of links between entities across G and G'. This issue stems from the construction of the merged KG, which fails to capture these implicit relationships.

To address this, we propose modifying the loss function to account for missing links between entities originating from G and G'. Our modifications build upon the adjustments to the loss function introduced in [4], extending them to incorporate the newly introduced links generated during our similarity-based merging stage. These changes ensure that the embedding process effectively captures similarities between entities across G and G', even in the absence of explicit links.

Our goal is to exclude all *missing* triples from the loss function calculations, ensuring that the model does not penalize the absence of any link. This approach accounts for the fact that such links, while not explicitly present in G', might exist in reality. For this, we change the target value for the neural network to be 0.5 for each triple that contains resources of both G and G' and later ignore all target values of 0.5 in the loss function. By default, using the binary cross entropy (BCE) loss, the target value $y_i = 1$ for triples that exist in the graph and $y_i = 0$ for triples that do not exist in the graph. We change this to $y_i = 0.5$ in case the subject and object do not have the same origin graph. Formally,

$$y_i(\text{head, rel, tail}) = \begin{cases} 1 & : (\text{head, rel, tail}) \in G^+ \\ 0.5 : & \text{head } \in \mathcal{E}(G) \wedge \text{ tail } \in \mathcal{E}(G') \\ 0.5 : & \text{head } \in \mathcal{E}(G') \wedge \text{ tail } \in \mathcal{E}(G) \\ 0 & : \text{otherwise} \end{cases}$$

Note that this also ignores the *allowed-dist* links. They are handled during the *inter-graph optimization* phase explained in the next section.

To exclude all triples with $y_i = 0.5$ from the target function, we modify the loss function as defined in [4]. Formally,

$$\underset{\text{intra}}{L}(y_i, \hat{y}_i) = -\sum_{i=1}^{N} \big(y_i \log(\hat{y}_i) + (1 - y_i)\log(1 - \hat{y}_i)\big) \cdot \mathbb{1}_{[y_i \neq 0.5]},$$

with $\mathbb{1}$ being an indicator function and $\hat{y}_i$ representing the output value of the neural network for each triple x_i = (head, rel, tail). The left part of this equation is the standard BCE loss, while the right part evaluates to 0 if $y_i = 0.5$ and to 1 when $y_i = 0$ or $y_i = 1$. This modification to the loss function ensures that it remains unaffected for triples that should not be ignored, while effectively neutralizing the impact of triples that are meant to be excluded from consideration.

Inter-graph Optimization. To ensure that the embedding of the IRIs of literals originating from different KGs remain close to each other, we define the *inter-graph loss function* (inter-GLF). The inter-GLF penalizes only those distances between literals that exceed the *allowed-dist* threshold specified during the merging phase (Sect. 4.1). The inter-GLF is formally defined as:

$$\underset{\text{inter}}{L}(sT) = \sum_{i=1}^{N} \Big[\big(\|e_h(sT_i) - e_t(sT_i)\| - \textit{allowed-dist}(sT_i)\big)_+\Big]^2$$

with $(x)_+$ representing the ReLU operation $max(0, x)$, sT representing the triples with the *allowed-dist* relation and e_h and e_t being the latent space vectors of the head entity and tail entity of a triple, respectively. The inter-GLF only penalizes distances between literals that are larger than the *allowed-dist* as specified in the merging phase (Sect. 4.1). The inter-GLF is incorporated in every mini-batch loss calculation to consistently enforce proximity between similar literals throughout the training process. Furthermore, the inner component of the summation within the inter-GLF is squared to impose a disproportionately higher penalty when the KGE model places highly similar literals significantly far apart. This design also ensures stability by preventing excessive gradient magnitudes for small distance values, thereby avoiding overshooting the optimal embedding configuration.

Since the penalty is applied only when the distance between literals exceeds the specified threshold, the KGE model is granted considerable flexibility. It can position the embeddings of two literals anywhere within the range, from being exactly co-located to being separated by the maximum *allowed-distance*, without incurring a penalty. For our example in Fig. 2, this would mean as missing relations between entities of different KGs are not penalized, the embedding model would be encouraged to place ♠▲*xyz st.* at the same location as ♣▲*xyz street*. However, in cases where ♣*Address1* and ♠*Address2* would have different *stNr* attributes and attached persons, then the distance between the two street names could be as big as 0.4 as this is the maximum non penalized distance between them.

Combining the Optimizations. Both the intra-graph optimization and the inter-graph optimization are done during each mini-batch computation and are combined to a single loss function. Formally,

$$L_{\text{combined}} = \alpha L_{\text{inter}} + (1 - \alpha) L_{\text{intra}}, \tag{1}$$

where the parameter $\alpha \in [0, 1]$ represents a weighting factor that balances the contributions of the inter-graph loss L_{inter} and the intra-graph loss L_{intra} to the overall loss. i.e., with α close to 1, GLIDE prioritizes L_{inter}, giving more importance to the alignment between KGs, while with α close to 0, GLIDE prioritizes L_{intra}, focusing on maintaining the internal consistency of each graph.

4.3 Matching

During the matching phase, the matches between entities from G and G' get created. Two entities, e and e', are matched when their *Euclidean distance* in the embedding space is smaller than a predefined threshold, *max-dist*. Determining an optimal value for *max-dist* is a challenging task: if the threshold is set too small, the recall will suffer, as many true matches will be missed. Conversely, if the threshold is set too large, the precision will decrease due to an increase in incorrect matches. Striking the right balance is critical to ensure that both precision and recall are at acceptable levels. While supervised approaches depend on user-provided examples to tune such parameters [21,27], GLIDE adopts a pseudo F-measure approach, aiming to achieve a mapping that approximates a 1-to-1 mapping between entities as closely as possible.

To compute our pseudo F-measure (PFM), we classify each entity based on its mapping status: Entities not mapped to any other entity are counted as one pseudo false negative (*pfn*), those mapped to at least one entity are considered one pseudo true positive (*ptp*), and entity mapped to n entities contribute $n - 1$ pseudo false positives (*pfp*) to penalize multi-mappings. Penalizing multi-mappings is essential, as their presence indicates that the original KGs incorrectly represent multiple entities for what should be a single real-world entity, deviating from the ideal structure of a well-constructed KG. Afterwards, the pseudo precision (PP) and the pseudo recall (PR) are formally defined as:

$$PP = \frac{|ptp|}{|ptp| + |pfp|}, PR = \frac{|ptp|}{|ptp| + |pfn|}.$$

The PFM is the harmonic mean of PP and PR. This method is highly efficient, especially when *max-dist* increases incrementally, requiring at most $|\mathcal{E}(G)| \cdot |\mathcal{E}(G')|$ distance computations. The optimal *max-dist* is selected based on the highest PFM, and entity pairs $(e, e' | e \in \mathcal{E}(G) \land e' \in \mathcal{E}(G'))$ are matched if $euclidean\_dist(s,t) \leq$ *max-dist.*

5 Evaluation

Research Questions. To evaluate our approach, we compare the results of GLIDE with different similarity measures combined with different *allowed-dist* functions. We also compare our approach GLIDE with state-of-the-art algorithms based on link specifications and embeddings described in Sect. 3. We aim to answer the following research questions:

Q_1. How does the shape of *allowed-dist* functions impact the performance of GLIDE?
Q_2. Is is beneficial to either weight the inter-graph loss function or intra-graph loss function higher than the other?
Q_3. How many similar literals in the source and target dataset should be considered for each literal during the embedding phase?
Q_4. How does GLIDE perform in comparison to state-of-the-art link discovery approaches?

Datasets. We evaluate GLIDE on three datasets from OAEI[1] [11]: *Person1*, *Person2* and *Restaurants*. These benchmark datasets contain two different KGs each that stem from separate sources or were manipulated as described in [11]. We also used four real-world datasets (based on their popularity in the literature [1,16,20]): three from [16], namely *Amazon-GoogleProducts*, *DBLP-ACM*, and *ABT-BUY*, and the forth was the *Drugs* dataset[2]. The dataset characteristics are summarized in Table 1, where $|\mathcal{E}(G)|$ and $|\mathcal{E}(G')|$ are the number of entities in the source and target KGs, respectively, and $|M^*|$ is the size of the perfect mappings from $\mathcal{E}(G)$ to $\mathcal{E}(G')$. Notably, the number of entities and gold-standard mapping sizes vary considerably, presenting challenges such as non-1-to-1 reference alignments and coverage gaps. This diversity ensures robust evaluation of linking methods under realistic and imbalanced conditions.

This reflects real-world KGs, where high-quality linking is essential, even for imbalanced KGs with missing equivalent entities.

[1] http://oaei.ontologymatching.org/2010.
[2] http://www4.wiwiss.fu-berlin.de/drugbank/sparql.

5.1 Experiment Setup

All experiments are conducted using the DICE embeddings library[3] [9] on a NVIDIA A100 with 40 GB memory. The training is run for 4096 epochs with a batch size

Table 1. Characteristics of the benchmark datasets.

Dataset	$\|\mathcal{E}(G)\|$	$\|\mathcal{E}(G')\|$	$\|M^*\|$
Abt-Buy	1081	1092	1097
Amazon-GP	1363	3226	1301
DBLP-ACM	2616	2294	2224
Person1	500	500	500
Person2	600	400	400
Restaurant	113	752	89
Drugs	1046	1046	1046

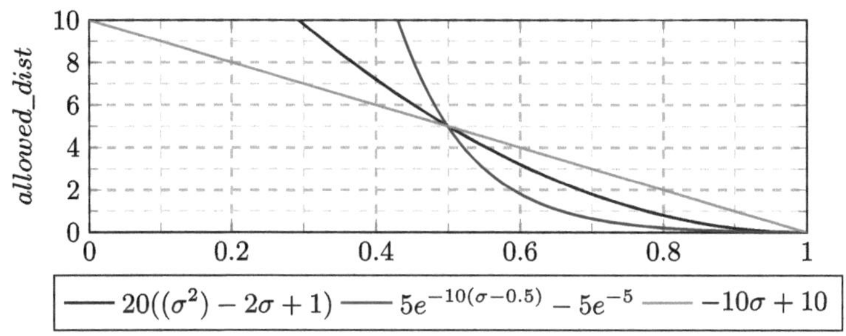

Fig. 3. The selected *allowed-dist* functions.

of 1024 and embedding dimension 32. To ensure the reproducibility, a seed value of 1 is consistently used for random number generation. We use the following values for the hyperparameters: $\alpha = \{0.1, 0.25, 0.5, 0.75, 0.9\}$ and $\lambda = \{1, 2, 4, 8\}$. As string similarity measures we use *Cosine*, *Jaccard*, *Levenshtein*, *Overlap*, *Trigrams*, and *MaxString* which is the maximum similarity value reported by the five string similarity measures. For the *Cosine* string similarity we use the definition commonly used in link discovery literature that is based on the number of shared words separated by spaces [23]. As phonetic measures we use *Caverphone1*, *Caverphone2*, *Cologne*, *DoubleMeta*, *MatchRating*, *RefinedSoundex*, *Soundex*, and *MaxPhonetic* which is the maximum similarity value reported by the seven phonetic similarity measures. To further aggregate the similarities, we also report the result for *MaxOfAll* which is the maximum similarity for all string and phonetic similarity measures.

GLIDE is compared with an unsupervised version of WOMBAT [27] using string and phonetic similarity measures [1], and their combination, referred to as WOMBAT$_S$,

[3] Version 0.1.3.2 from: https://pypi.org/project/dicee/0.1.3.2/.

WOMBAT$_P$, and WOMBAT$_H$, respectively. To benchmark GLIDE against embedding-based link discovery methods, we also evaluate: (1) Embedding of the IRIs within the KGs without literals [17] using TRANSE [6], and (2) TRANSE with identical literals constrained to juxtaposition by setting the *allowed-dist* function to be 0 for identical strings and to ∞ otherwise, dubbed as TRANSE$_{+L}$. (3) BLINK with the same configuration as in [4] where we match relation names beforehand and convert all necessary entities that should be matched to blank nodes beforehand as BLINK matches blank nodes only.

5.2 Experiments

We performed three sets of experiments to answer our research questions.

Q_1: Impact of Different Function Shapes. To answer our first research question, Q_1, we carried out three experiments with different *allowed-dist* functions.

We tested a linear function $-10x + 10$ whose results can be seen in Table 2, a quadratic function $20((x^2) - 2x + 1)$ (results in Table 3) and an exponential function $5e^{-10(x-0.5)} - 5e^{-5}$ (results in Table 4). The three functions are plotted in Fig. 3.

Our results show that the linear and exponential *allowed-dist* function performed best most of the time. In total, the linear function was equal to or better than the quadratic and exponential functions 83 times, the quadratic function was best 76 times and the exponential function was best 77 times. The other cases were ties between the functions. The linear function performed the best, as it offers the most flexibility for the embedding algorithm, allowing greater distance between moderately similar but not perfectly matching literals. In the interval $[0.8, 0.9]$ of Fig. 3, the quadratic and exponential functions only allow tiny distances between literals, even though similarity values in that range are far away from indicating almost equalities. This effect is amplified for phonetic measures as they tend to assign higher similarity scores because of their limited encoding length.

The best performing measures over all *allowed-dist* function types were *Trigram* with an average F-measure of 0.79, followed by *MaxString* with an F-measure of 0.72. The best performing phonetic measures were *Caverphone1* and *Caverphone2* with an F-measure of 0.40 and 0.39, respectively. This clearly indicates that string similarity measures outperform phonetic similarity measures on data linking tasks.

For datasets with high possible accuracy (e.g., *DBLP-ACM*, *Person1*, *Person2*, *Restaurants* and *Drugs*) and the most accurate measure (*Trigram*), the exponential function most often remained best as it forces similar literals to be placed closer than the other two functions. This answers our research question Q_1.

Q_2: Impact of Inter-Graph vs Intra-Graph Loss Weighting. To answer our second research question, we tried different values of α. If alpha is low, the *intra-graph loss* is weighted more heavily than the similarity-based *inter-graph loss* loss, and vice versa. The average results for the string similarity measures and phonetic measures are shown in Table 5.

For the datasets *Abt-Buy*, *Amazon-GoogleProducts*, *DBLP-ACM*, and *Restaurants*, the accuracy is decreasing monotonically for both string and phonetic similarity measures. For the other datasets *Person1*, *Person2*, and *Drugs*, the value of alpha does not

Table 2. Average F-measure results for the linear *allowed-dist* function over the hyperparameters specified in Sect. 5.1.

$\sigma(x, y)$	Abt-Buy	Amazon-GP	DBLP-ACM	Person1	Person2	Restaurants	Drugs
Cosine	0.01	0.08	0.89	1.00	0.94	0.71	1.00
Jaccard	0.01	0.08	0.89	1.00	0.94	0.71	1.00
Levenshtein	0.26	0.15	0.78	1.00	0.96	0.71	1.00
Overlap	0.01	0.08	0.89	1.00	0.94	0.71	1.00
Trigram	0.47	0.27	0.95	1.00	0.97	0.77	1.00
MaxString	0.30	0.17	0.86	1.00	0.96	0.71	1.00
Caverphone1	0.02	0.15	0.46	0.80	0.38	0.08	0.97
Caverphone2	0.15	0.17	0.35	0.79	0.37	0.08	0.98
Cologne	0.10	0.11	0.00	0.00	0.00	0.71	0.98
DoubleMeta	0.04	0.11	0.00	0.00	0.00	0.04	0.74
MatchRating	0.23	0.05	0.44	0.00	0.00	0.58	0.99
RefinedSoundex	0.12	0.12	0.00	0.01	0.00	0.68	0.99
Soundex	0.03	0.10	0.00	0.00	0.00	0.14	0.70
MaxPhonetic	0.03	0.08	0.42	0.00	0.00	0.07	0.57
MaxOfAll	0.03	0.08	0.42	0.00	0.00	0.07	0.58

change the outcome in a relevant way. Generally, weighting the *intra-graph loss* higher is better in terms of accuracy, however, there are some small outliers where the performance marginally increases for higher values of α.

We attribute the benefit of weighting the *intra-graph loss* higher to the fact that the *inter-graph loss* is already zero or almost zero after a few training epochs. After that the *inter-graph loss* cannot get any better but only forces similar literals to stay close to each other. The *intra-graph loss*, however, is not anywhere close to zero as in an embedding space constrained to a certain dimension, a perfect solution to placing all entities is impossible. We conclude that the main point of the embedding algorithm is still to optimize the *intra-graph loss* while the *inter-graph loss* is a (still very important) side objective. This answers our research question Q_2.

Q_3: Number of Similar Literals to Be Considered. To explore how many similarities should be considered in the embedding phase of GLIDE, we tested multiple values for λ. The hyperparameter GLIDE decides how many similarities per literal get included on average. The average results for the string similarity measures and phonetic measures are shown in Table 6. The results clearly show that care should be taken to not include too many similarities in the computation, as irrelevant similarities and similarities between literals that are not representing the same real-world entity compromise the results. This supports the intuitive idea that each literal from one dataset has one counterpart in the other dataset. For example, if a person's name is present in both datasets, then it suffices to pull the instances of the same name together and juxtaposing similar but different names is detrimental. This answers our research question Q_3.

Table 3. Average F-measure results for the quadratic *allowed-dist* function over the hyperparameters specified in Sect. 5.1.

$\sigma(x, y)$	Abt-Buy	Amazon-GP	DBLP-ACM	Person1	Person2	Restaurants	Drugs
Cosine	0.01	0.07	0.94	1.00	0.94	0.77	1.00
Jaccard	0.01	0.07	0.94	1.00	0.94	0.77	1.00
Levenshtein	0.28	0.20	0.78	1.00	0.96	0.70	1.00
Overlap	0.01	0.07	0.94	1.00	0.94	0.77	1.00
Trigram	0.52	0.31	0.97	1.00	0.98	0.81	0.99
MaxString	0.33	0.22	0.86	1.00	0.96	0.71	1.00
Caverphone1	0.02	0.14	0.43	0.80	0.38	0.08	0.97
Caverphone2	0.11	0.14	0.30	0.79	0.37	0.08	0.98
Cologne	0.12	0.14	0.00	0.00	0.00	0.71	0.98
DoubleMeta	0.04	0.11	0.00	0.00	0.00	0.04	0.76
MatchRating	0.19	0.04	0.39	0.00	0.00	0.57	0.99
RefinedSoundex	0.13	0.16	0.00	0.01	0.00	0.68	0.99
Soundex	0.03	0.10	0.00	0.00	0.00	0.14	0.68
MaxPhonetic	0.03	0.08	0.42	0.00	0.00	0.07	0.62
MaxOfAll	0.03	0.08	0.42	0.00	0.00	0.07	0.62

Q_4: Comparison Against Baselines. To answer our research question Q_4, we compared GLIDE against several baselines. As our approach uses multiple similarity measures, different *allowed-dist* functions, as well as different hyperparameters α and λ, we report the F-measure results only for the string measure with the best pseudo-F-measure and the phonetic measure with the best pseudo-F-measure.

The outcomes of this experiment are shown in Table 7. GLIDE$_S$ (i.e., GLIDE combined with the best performing string similarity) achieves the best performance among the baselines in 5 out of 7 datasets. Specifically, GLIDE$_S$ achieved a near perfect F-measure for the datasets (*DBLP-ACM*, *Person1*, *Person2*, and *Drugs*) and outperforms the baselines on *Abt-Buy* and *Restaurants*. GLIDE$_P$ (i.e., GLIDE combined with the best performing phonetic similarity) also achieving a near perfect F-measure for the *Drugs* dataset but was outperformed by GLIDE$_S$ for all other datasets. Notably, GLIDE$_P$ outperformed TRANSE$_{+L}$ on 3 datasets (*Abt-Buy*, *Amazon-GP*, and *Restaurants*), demonstrating that phonetic measures aid in discovering links among KGs. However, on their own, phonetic measures were less accurate than string measures. This supports the findings of [1] that phonetic measures alone perform worse than string measures in complex scenarios.

The *Abt-Buy* and *Amazon-GoogleProducts* are the hardest datasets from our experiments. For such complex datasets, WOMBAT performs well because of its flexibility in combining different measures to determine matches. The performance of GLIDE suffers for such datasets because they contain a lot of similar, yet different, entities that sometimes do not have a corresponding counterpart in the other dataset. For example,

Table 4. Average F-measure results for the exponential *allowed-dist* function over the hyperparameters specified in Sect. 5.1.

$\sigma(x, y)$	Abt-Buy	Amazon-GP	DBLP-ACM	Person1	Person2	Restaurants	Drugs
Cosine	0.01	0.06	0.94	1.00	0.94	0.79	1.00
Jaccard	0.01	0.06	0.94	1.00	0.94	0.79	1.00
Levenshtein	0.30	0.26	0.75	1.00	0.94	0.68	0.99
Overlap	0.01	0.06	0.94	1.00	0.94	0.79	1.00
Trigram	0.53	0.34	0.97	1.00	0.97	0.83	1.00
MaxString	0.34	0.28	0.80	1.00	0.94	0.68	0.99
Caverphone1	0.02	0.14	0.41	0.80	0.38	0.08	0.96
Caverphone2	0.07	0.12	0.25	0.79	0.37	0.08	0.92
Cologne	0.14	0.17	0.00	0.00	0.00	0.71	0.97
DoubleMeta	0.04	0.11	0.00	0.00	0.00	0.04	0.73
MatchRating	0.14	0.04	0.34	0.00	0.00	0.53	0.98
RefinedSoundex	0.15	0.18	0.00	0.01	0.00	0.68	0.98
Soundex	0.03	0.10	0.00	0.00	0.00	0.14	0.67
MaxPhonetic	0.03	0.08	0.42	0.00	0.00	0.07	0.62
MaxOfAll	0.03	0.08	0.42	0.00	0.00	0.07	0.62

Table 5. Average F-measure results for different values of α using string and phonetic similarity measures.

Type	α	Abt-Buy	Amazon-GP	DBLP-ACM	Person1	Person2	Restaurants	Drugs
String	0.10	0.23	0.19	0.92	1.00	0.95	0.76	1.00
	0.25	0.21	0.17	0.91	1.00	0.95	0.76	0.99
	0.50	0.19	0.15	0.90	1.00	0.95	0.75	1.00
	0.75	0.17	0.14	0.88	1.00	0.95	0.74	1.00
	0.90	0.15	0.13	0.85	1.00	0.95	0.72	1.00
Phonetic	0.10	0.10	0.14	0.23	0.20	0.09	0.30	0.86
	0.25	0.09	0.13	0.22	0.20	0.09	0.30	0.86
	0.50	0.08	0.11	0.21	0.20	0.09	0.30	0.86
	0.75	0.08	0.10	0.17	0.20	0.09	0.30	0.86
	0.90	0.07	0.10	0.13	0.20	0.10	0.28	0.87

product names starting with "`microsoft windows vista business`" appear two times in *Amazon* and five times in *GoogleProducts* with no identical match across datasets. They all differ in the suffix, however, because the company and product name constitutes a large part of the products name, similarity measures consider all these products very similar. As this happens often for established products, similarity measures without attention mechanisms cannot always clearly differentiate different products of the same category.

Table 6. Average F-measure results for different values of λ using string and phonetic similarity measures.

Type	λ	Abt-Buy	Amazon-GP	DBLP-ACM	Person1	Person2	Restaurants	Drugs
String	1	0.20	0.18	0.93	1.00	0.96	0.74	1.00
	2	0.20	0.16	0.91	1.00	0.95	0.76	1.00
	4	0.18	0.15	0.87	1.00	0.94	0.74	1.00
	8	0.18	0.14	0.85	1.00	0.95	0.74	1.00
Phonetic	1	0.10	0.12	0.32	0.20	0.09	0.30	0.87
	2	0.09	0.12	0.26	0.20	0.09	0.30	0.86
	4	0.07	0.12	0.11	0.20	0.09	0.29	0.86
	8	0.07	0.10	0.08	0.20	0.09	0.29	0.86

Table 7. F-measure results for baselines and GLIDE with the highest PFM for string and phonetic similarity measures. The highest scores are marked bold.

Algorithms	Abt-Buy	Amazon-GP	DBLP-ACM	Person1	Person2	Restaurants	Drugs
TRANSE	0.00	0.00	0.00	0.00	0.00	0.00	0.00
TRANSE$_{+L}$	0.01	0.04	0.91	**1.00**	0.95	0.63	**1.00**
BLINK	0.02	0.04	0.86	**1.00**	0.24	0.78	0.94
WOMBAT$_S$	0.40	0.42	0.88	0.85	0.45	0.77	0.90
WOMBAT$_P$	0.35	0.01	0.90	0.74	0.50	0.30	**1.00**
WOMBAT$_H$	0.29	**0.45**	0.91	0.87	0.54	0.46	**1.00**
GLIDE$_S$ (ours)	**0.62**	0.37	**0.98**	**1.00**	**0.99**	**0.80**	0.99
GLIDE$_P$ (ours)	0.16	0.22	0.89	0.80	0.39	0.65	0.99

The performance difference between TRANSE$_{+L}$ and our approach clearly demonstrates that an embedding algorithm incorporating literals must do more than simply include literal representations, rather it must also account for latent space distances between similar literals to effectively capture their contextual relationships. TRANSE without embedding any literals fails to produce a meaningful result because there are no shared IRIs in the tested datasets. Overall, our results show that GLIDE not only matches but also outperforms the existing state-of-the-art link discovery approaches in many cases demonstrating the effectiveness of the distance-aware embedding in link discovery; this answers Q_4.

6 Conclusion and Future Work

In this paper, we present an approach for distance-aware KG embedding based on similarity measures. We study the impact of varying parameters α and λ with different *allowed-dist* functions and their influence on similarity measures. On five out of seven datasets, GLIDE$_S$ achieves a new state-of-the-art in F-measure among all compared unsupervised methods (Table 7), including link specification systems and recent embedding-based approaches. This study underscores the importance of incorporating literal similarities into KG embeddings to enhance embedding accuracy for link discovery tasks.

In future work, we aim to enhance GLIDE's accuracy by integrating multiple similarity measures into the *allowed-dist* function and tailoring specific similarity measures to literals associated with different relations. For instance, attributes of one relation may align better using string similarities, while another may benefit from phonetic similarities for improved precision. We also plan to incorporate content-aware attention based similarity measures into our approach to improve the accuracy for product names which are part of a line of several very similar products. Furthermore, we plan to develop an algorithm for the automatic selection of an optimal *allowed-dist* function, based on the overall similarity distribution within the datasets. Additionally, we plan to devise a method for dynamically learning the optimal value of the loss-balancing factor α (Eq. 1), enabling an effective balance between the *inter-* and *intra-*graph loss functions for better linking accuracy.

Supplemental Material Statement: Source code for graph merging, similarity computations and the source code for the embedding process, datasets, unaggregated results, and entity mappings for each configuration are available from our Github[4].

Acknowledgements. This work has been supported by the Ministry of Culture and Science of North Rhine-Westphalia (MKW NRW) within the project SAIL under the grant no NW21-059D. This work has been supported within the project "WHALE" (LFN 1-04) funded under the Lamarr Fellow Network programme by the Ministry of Culture and Science of North Rhine-Westphalia (MKW NRW). This project has received funding from the European Union's Horizon Europe research and innovation programme under grant agreement No 101070305. The authors gratefully acknowledge the computing time provided to them on the high-performance computers Noctua2 at the NHR Center PC2. These are funded by the Federal Ministry of Education and Research and the state governments participating on the basis of the resolutions of the GWK for the national highperformance computing at universities (www.nhr-verein.de/unsere-partner).

References

1. Ahmed, A.F., Sherif, M.A., Ngonga Ngomo, A.C.: Do your resources sound similar? on the impact of using phonetic similarity in link discovery. In: Proceedings of the 10th International Conference on Knowledge Capture, pp. 53–60 (2019)
2. Assi, A., Mcheick, H., Karawash, A., Dhifli, W.: Context-aware instance matching through graph embedding in lexical semantic space. Knowl.-Based Syst. **186**, 104925 (2019). https://doi.org/10.1016/j.knosys.2019.104925, https://www.sciencedirect.com/science/article/pii/S0950705119303739
3. Bansal, I., Tiwari, S., Rivero, C.R.: The impact of negative triple generation strategies and anomalies on knowledge graph completion. In: Proceedings of the 29th ACM International Conference on Information & Knowledge Management, pp. 45–54. CIKM '20, Association for Computing Machinery, New York, NY, USA (2020). https://doi.org/10.1145/3340531.3412023

[4] https://github.com/becker-al/GLIDE

4. Becker, A., Sherif, M.A., Ngonga Ngomo, A.C.: Blink: Blank node matching using embeddings. In: The Semantic Web – ISWC 2024. Baltimore, USA (2024)
5. Blum, M., Ell, B., Ill, H., Cimiano, P.: Numerical literals in link prediction: a critical examination of models and datasets. In: The Semantic Web – ISWC 2024, pp. 23–46. Springer Nature Switzerland, Cham (2025)
6. Bordes, A., Usunier, N., Garcia-Duran, A., Weston, J., Yakhnenko, O.: Translating embeddings for modeling multi-relational data. In: Advances in Neural Information Processing Systems, vol. 26. Curran Associates, Inc. (2013). https://proceedings.neurips.cc/paper_files/paper/2013/file/1cecc7a77928ca8133fa24680a88d2f9-Paper.pdf
7. Cao, J., Fang, J., Meng, Z., Liang, S.: Knowledge graph embedding: a survey from the perspective of representation spaces. ACM Comput. Surv. **56**(6) (mar 2024). https://doi.org/10.1145/3643806
8. Chen, Z., Wang, Y., Zhao, B., Cheng, J., Zhao, X., Duan, Z.: Knowledge graph completion: a review. IEEE Access **8**, 192435–192456 (2020)
9. Demir, C.: Ngonga Ngomo. Hardware-agnostic computation for large-scale knowledge graph embeddings. Software Impacts, A.C. (2022)
10. Doval, Y., Vilares, M., Vilares, J.: On the performance of phonetic algorithms in microtext normalization. Expert Syst. Appl. **113**, 213–222 (2018)
11. Euzenat, J., Et al.: Results of the ontology alignment evaluation initiative 2010. In: Proceedings of the 5th International Conference on Ontology Matching - Volume 689, pp. 85–117. OM'10, CEUR-WS.org, Aachen, DEU (2010)
12. Guo, L., Sun, Z., Hu, W.: Learning to exploit long-term relational dependencies in knowledge graphs. In: International Conference on Machine Learning, pp. 2505–2514. PMLR (2019)
13. Hyland, B., Atemezing, G.A., Pendleton, M., Srivastava, B.: Linked data glossary. W3C note, W3C (Jun 2013). https://www.w3.org/TR/2013/NOTE-ld-glossary-20130627/
14. Issa, S., Adekunle, O., Hamdi, F., Cherfi, S.S.S., Dumontier, M., Zaveri, A.: Knowledge graph completeness: a systematic literature review. IEEE Access **9**, 31322–31339 (2021)
15. Ju, W., et al.: A survey of graph neural networks in real world: imbalance, noise, privacy and ood challenges. arXiv preprint arXiv:2403.04468 (2024)
16. Köpcke, H., Thor, A., Rahm, E.: Comparative evaluation of entity resolution approaches with fever. Proc. VLDB Endowment **2**(2), 1574–1577 (2009)
17. Kristiadi, A., Khan, M.A., Lukovnikov, D., Lehmann, J., Fischer, A.: Incorporating literals into knowledge graph embeddings. In: Ghidini, C., Hartig, O., Maleshkova, M., Svátek, V., Cruz, I., Hogan, A., Song, J., Lefrançois, M., Gandon, F. (eds.) ISWC 2019. LNCS, vol. 11778, pp. 347–363. Springer, Cham (2019). https://doi.org/10.1007/978-3-030-30793-6_20
18. Li, J., Wang, Z., Zhang, X., Tang, J.: Large scale instance matching via multiple indexes and candidate selection. Knowledge-Based Syst. **50**, 112–120 (2013). https://doi.org/10.1016/j.knosys.2013.06.004, https://www.sciencedirect.com/science/article/pii/S0950705113001809
19. McCrae, J.P., et al.: The linked open data cloud. Lod-cloud.net (2019)
20. Nentwig, M., Hartung, M., Ngonga Ngomo, A.C., Rahm, E.: A survey of current link discovery frameworks. Semantic Web **8**(3), 419–436 (2017)
21. Ngomo, A.C.N., Lehmann, J., Auer, S., Höffner, K.: Raven-active learning of link specifications. Ontol. Match. **2011** (2011)
22. Ngonga Ngomo, A.C., Lyko, K.: Unsupervised learning of link specifications: deterministic vs. non-deterministic. In: Proceedings of the Ontology Matching Workshop, vol. 12 (2013)
23. Ngonga Ngomo, A.C., et al.: LIMES - A framework for link discovery on the semantic web. KI - Künstliche Intelligenz, German J. Artif. Intell. (2021). https://doi.org/10.1007/s13218-021-00713-x

24. Pei, S., Yu, L., Zhang, X.: Improving cross-lingual entity alignment via optimal transport. In: Proceedings of the 28th International Joint Conference on Artificial Intelligence, pp. 3231–3237. IJCAI'19, AAAI Press (2019)
25. Qudus, U., Röder, M., Saleem, M., Ngonga Ngomo, A.C.: Hybridfc: a hybrid fact-checking approach for knowledge graphs. In: International Semantic Web Conference, pp. 462–480. Springer (2022)
26. Rossi, A., Barbosa, D., Firmani, D., Matinata, A., Merialdo, P.: Knowledge graph embedding for link prediction: a comparative analysis. ACM Trans. Knowl. Discov. Data (TKDD) **15**(2), 1–49 (2021)
27. Sherif, M.A., Ngonga Ngomo, A.C., Lehmann, J.: Wombat–a generalization approach for automatic link discovery. In: The Semantic Web: 14th International Conference, ESWC 2017, Portorož, Slovenia, May 28–June 1, 2017, Proceedings, Part I 14, pp. 103–119. Springer (2017)
28. Shi, B., Weninger, T.: Open-world knowledge graph completion. Proc. AAAI Conf. Artif. Intell. **32**(1) (Apr 2018). https://doi.org/10.1609/aaai.v32i1.11535, https://ojs.aaai.org/index.php/AAAI/article/view/11535
29. Sun, Z., Hu, W., Li, C.: Cross-lingual entity alignment via joint attribute-preserving embedding. In: d'Amato, C., et al. (eds.) ISWC 2017. LNCS, vol. 10587, pp. 628–644. Springer, Cham (2017). https://doi.org/10.1007/978-3-319-68288-4_37
30. Sun, Z., Hu, W., Zhang, Q., Qu, Y.: Bootstrapping entity alignment with knowledge graph embedding. In: Proceedings of the 27th International Joint Conference on Artificial Intelligence, pp. 4396–4402. IJCAI'18, AAAI Press (2018)
31. Trisedya, B.D., Qi, J., Zhang, R.: Entity alignment between knowledge graphs using attribute embeddings. Proc. AAAI Conf. Artif. Intell. **33**(01), 297–304 (Jul 2019). https://doi.org/10.1609/aaai.v33i01.3301297, https://ojs.aaai.org/index.php/AAAI/article/view/3798
32. Vedula, N., Parthasarathy, S.: Face-keg: fact checking explained using knowledge graphs. In: Proceedings of the 14th ACM International Conference on Web Search and Data Mining, pp. 526–534 (2021)
33. Vijaymeena, M., Kavitha, K.: A survey on similarity measures in text mining. Mach. Learn. Appl.: Int. J. **3**(2), 19–28 (2016)
34. Volz, J., Bizer, C., Gaedke, M., Kobilarov, G.: Silk-a link discovery framework for the web of data. Ldow **538**, 53 (2009)
35. Wang, J., Ilievski, F., Szekely, P.A., Yao, K.T.: Augmenting knowledge graphs for better link prediction. In: International Joint Conference on Artificial Intelligence (2022)
36. Wood, D., Lanthaler, M., Cyganiak, R.: RDF 1.1 concepts and abstract syntax. W3C recommendation, W3C (Feb 2014). https://www.w3.org/TR/2014/REC-rdf11-concepts-20140225/
37. Wu, Y., Wang, Z.: Knowledge graph embedding with numeric attributes of entities. In: Proceedings of the Third Workshop on Representation Learning for NLP, pp. 132–136. Association for Computational Linguistics, Melbourne, Australia (Jul 2018). https://doi.org/10.18653/v1/W18-3017, https://aclanthology.org/W18-3017
38. Xiang, X., Wang, Z., Jia, Y., Fang, B.: Knowledge graph-based clinical decision support system reasoning: a survey. In: 2019 IEEE Fourth International Conference on Data Science in Cyberspace (DSC), pp. 373–380. IEEE (2019)
39. Yani, M., Krisnadhi, A.A.: Challenges, techniques, and trends of simple knowledge graph question answering: a survey. Information **12**(7), 271 (2021)
40. Zeng, K., Li, C., Hou, L., Li, J., Feng, L.: A comprehensive survey of entity alignment for knowledge graphs. AI Open **2**, 1–13 (2021)
41. Zhang, Q., Sun, Z., Hu, W., Chen, M., Guo, L., Qu, Y.: Multi-view knowledge graph embedding for entity alignment. In: International Joint Conference on Artificial Intelligence (2019)

42. Zhang, R., Trisedya, B.D., Li, M., Jiang, Y., Qi, J.: A benchmark and comprehensive survey on knowledge graph entity alignment via representation learning. VLDB J. **31**(5), 1143–1168 (2022)
43. Zhu, H., Xie, R., Liu, Z., Sun, M.: Iterative entity alignment via joint knowledge embeddings. In: IJCAI, vol. 17, pp. 4258–4264 (2017)
44. Zhu, Q., Zhou, X., Wu, J., Tan, J., Guo, L.: Neighborhood-aware attentional representation for multilingual knowledge graphs. In: Proceedings of the Twenty-Eighth International Joint Conference on Artificial Intelligence, IJCAI-19, pp. 1943–1949 (7 2019). https://doi.org/10.24963/ijcai.2019/269

FastER: On-demand Entity Resolution in Property Graphs

Shujing Wang[1], Sibo Zhao[1], Shiqi Miao[1], Selasi Kwashie[2], Michael Bewong[3], Junwei Hu[1], Vincent M. Nofong[4], and Zaiwen Feng[1,5,6](✉)

[1] College of Informatics, Huazhong Agricultural University, Wuhan, China
zaiwen.feng@mail.hzau.edu.cn
[2] AI & Cyber Futures Institute, Charles Sturt University, Bathurst, Australia
[3] School of Computing, Mathematics and Engineering, Charles Sturt University, Bathurst, Australia
[4] Department of Computer Science and Engineering, University of Mines and Technology, Tarkwa, Ghana
[5] Hubei Key Laboratory of Agricultural Bioinformatics, Wuhan, China
[6] Engineering Research Center of Agricultural Intelligent Technology, Ministry of Education, Beijing, China

Abstract. Entity resolution (ER) is the problem of identifying and linking database records that refer to the same real-world entity. Traditional ER methods use batch processing, which becomes impractical with growing data volumes due to high computational costs and a lack of real-time capabilities. In many applications, users need to resolve entities for only a small portion of their data, making full data processing unnecessary—a scenario known as "ER-on-demand". This paper proposes FastER, an efficient ER-on-demand framework for property graphs. Our approach uses *graph differential dependencies* (GDD) as a knowledge-encoding language to design effective filtering mechanisms that leverage both the structural and attribute semantics of graphs. We construct a blocking graph from the filtered subgraphs to reduce the number of candidate entity pairs that require comparison. Additionally, FastER incorporates Progressive Profile Scheduling (PPS), allowing the system to incrementally produce results throughout the resolution process. Extensive evaluations on multiple benchmark datasets demonstrate that FastER significantly outperforms state-of-the-art ER methods in computational efficiency and real-time processing for on-demand tasks, without compromising quality or reliability. We make FastER publicly available at the Github link here.

Keywords: Entity Resolution · On-Demand · Progressive · Graph Differential Dependencies (GDDs) · Property Graphs

S. Wang and S. Zhao—Equal Contribution.

D. Garijo et al. (Eds.): ISWC 2025, LNCS 16140, pp. 177–195, 2026.
https://doi.org/10.1007/978-3-032-09527-5_10

1 Introduction

Entity Resolution (ER) is the problem of determining when different data records represent the same real-world entity. While critical in domains like finance, healthcare, and social networks, ER faces significant computational challenges in big data. Indeed, its quadratic time complexity means every possible entity pair must be compared in the worst case. Traditional solutions like blocking [1,2,5,6] and nearest-neighbor [4,7,8] techniques reduce comparisons by filtering unlikely matches [3]. However, these methods often struggle with graph data, where entity relationships provide crucial context for identification. For example, in social networks and knowledge graphs, understanding connections among entities is essential for accurate duplicate detection. Moreover, conventional ER approaches may not meet the performance requirements of real-time applications where immediate results are needed. This paper studies the on-demand ER problem in property graphs, illustrated in Example 1 below.

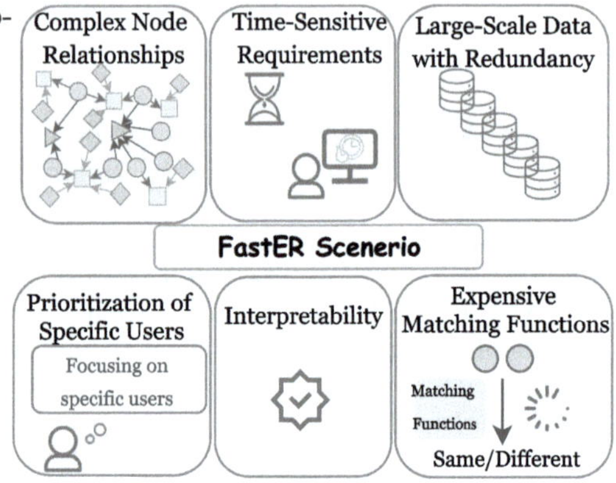

Fig. 1. On-Demand ER in Property Graphs.

Example 1 (On-Demand ER Scenario). Consider a video streaming platform modeled as a property graph, where users, devices, and videos are represented as nodes with rich attributes, and complex relationships exist among them. Figure 1 outlines six key requirements for entity resolution (ER) in this scenario. First, batch-based ER methods are inefficient, especially when dealing with large-scale data, as they require processing the entire dataset before returning results. This makes it difficult to meet the responsiveness needed in time-sensitive applications and to prioritize relevant entities (Requirements 1, 2, and 4). Matching functions, such as neural or knowledge-based models, are often computationally expensive (Requirement 6), making pre-filtering essential for reducing unnecessary invocations. Moreover, interpretability is a crucial requirement in many real-world ER applications (Requirement 5). Second, progressive ER methods struggle with the structural complexity of property graphs (Requirement 1) and are unable to focus on application-specific subgraphs (Requirement 4). Existing on-demand ER solutions [10,14,17] are primarily designed for relational data and are not well-suited to the structural needs of graph-based scenarios (Requirement 1). We propose FastER, an on-demand ER framework for property graphs that satisfies all six requirements outlined in Fig. 1. □

Contributions. We present a graph differential dependencies (GDDs) [21] based framework for on-demand entity resolution in property graphs. Our approach dynamically processes relevant subgraphs and progressively emits cleaned entities, enabling direct querying of dirty property graphs. More formally, the contributions of the paper are summarised as follows: 1) We leverage GDDs to encode users' application-relevant domain knowledge, enabling relevance filtering that utilizes both structural relationships and attribute semantics. 2) Further, we propose an efficient and effective blocking solution for ER-on-demand tasks that reduces computational overhead while maintaining recall. Our approach extends traditional rule-based filtering with a targeted blocking scheme and a progressive scheduling scheme, representing the first adaptation of on-demand ER to graph data. 3) We conduct extensive experiments on benchmark graphs and relational datasets. The empirical results show that our method achieves significant improvements in efficiency, offering superior real-time processing capabilities and reliability compared to existing solutions in ER-on-demand tasks.

Related Work. Works related to this paper fall under three groupings below. *Graph Constraints.* In recent years, graph constraints have emerged as a prominent research area due to their relevance in data quality management. For instance, graph keys (GKeys) [22] leverage graph isomorphism properties to uniquely identify entities within a graph. Graph functional dependencies [23] apply attribute-value dependencies (similar to CFDs [24]) to the topological structures of graphs, while graph entity dependencies (GEDs) [25] further integrate the semantics of both GFDs and GKeys. In this study, we adopt graph differential dependencies (GDDs) [21], an extension of GEDs. GDDs introduce similarity and matching semantics into the existing structure, making them suitable for defining declarative matching rules. This characteristic allows GDDs to better capture approximate matching relationships in graphs, thereby improving the accuracy and robustness of entity resolution (cf. [21,26,28]).

Progressive ER. Madhavan et al. [15] were among the first to implement a progressive data integration system in Google Base, demonstrating how web data can be integrated progressively under time and resource constraints. Since then, progressive methods have been widely applied to schema mapping [16,18–20] and entity resolution [9,11], especially in scenarios with limited computational capacity or time for debugging. Existing progressive ER methods employ blocking and scheduling strategies to prioritize high-probability matches for faster discovery [9,11]. However, these approaches have two key limitations. First, since result emission is not performed at the entity level, matching remains incomplete, potentially leading to incorrect intermediate results that fail to meet user requirements. Second, it lacks support for graph data structures, e.g., entity profiles generated from partial cluster matches may result in inaccurate outcomes.

On-Demand ER. The most related works to this paper are in [10,14,17]. Query-Driven Approach (QDA) [14] streamlines data cleaning by analyzing selection predicates within a block to reduce comparisons. However, its lack of progressive execution capability makes it unsuitable for real-time applications. On the other hand, BrewER [10] incrementally cleans data during SQL SP query evaluation using prioritized attribute comparisons. While similar to our approach, it has three key limitations: it requires computationally expensive Cartesian products to generate candidates, demands whole-dataset blocking preparation, and lacks support for graph relationships. QueryER [17] addresses ER in the relational data setting through user-specified queries, operating within a well-defined schema using a dedicated parser, planner, and executor. Its goal is to integrate ER capabilities into query engines. In contrast, our work presents a standalone, on-demand ER solution for property graphs, without requiring integration into query processing systems.

2 Preliminaries

This section presents relevant concepts and definitions used in the paper.

2.1 Basic Definitions and Notions

The definitions of *property graphs, graph patterns, and matches* follow [25].

A ***property graph*** is a directed graph $G = (V, E, L, FA)$, where V is a set of nodes, $E \subseteq V \times L \times V$ is a set of labeled edges, and each node $v \in V$ has a unique ID, label $L(v)$, and attributes $FA(v) = [(A_1, c_1), \ldots, (A_n, c_n)]$, where A_i are distinct attributes and c_i their values.

A ***graph pattern*** $Q[\bar{z}] = (V_Q, E_Q, L_Q)$ describes node structures and relationships: V_Q is the set of pattern nodes, E_Q the set of edges, and L_Q a labeling function that assigns labels, including the wildcard $*$, which denotes unrestricted labels. Two labels l_1 and l_2 match ($l_1 \simeq l_2$) if $l_1 = l_2$ or either is a wildcard.

A ***match*** of a graph pattern $Q[\bar{z}]$ in a graph G is a homomorphism, h, mapping Q onto the graph G, preserving labels and structure.

An ***entity profile*** for a real-world entity is a tuple $p = \langle pid, eid, type, P, R \rangle$, where pid is a unique profile identifier, eid is the (possibly unknown) real-world entity ID, and $type$ denotes its category (e.g., *person*, *location*). P is a set of attribute-value pairs (A, c), and R a list of relations $(rela, pid')$ linking the entity to other profiles. If two profiles, p_1, p_2, represent the same entity, then $p_1.eid = p_2.eid$.

Example 2 (Property graph, graph patterns, and matches). Figure 2 illustrates: a) a property graph, b) two graph patterns $Q_1[x, x', y]$ and $Q_2[x, x', y]$, and c) the matches of Q_1 in G in a pseudo-table. As an example, the pattern Q_1 represents two `user` nodes connected to the same `platform` via a `watched` relationship. Matches in G are shown in Fig. 2 c).

2.2 Graph Differential Dependency (GDD)

We present the syntax and semantics of ***graph differential dependency*** [21]. A GDD φ is a pair $(Q[\bar{u}], \Phi_X \rightarrow \Phi_Y)$, where $Q[\bar{u}]$ is a graph pattern, and Φ_X, Φ_Y are sets of distance constraints on pattern variables $\bar{u}$. GDD captures dependencies among graph entities based on similarity or matching conditions. The distance constraints are given as:

$$\delta_A(x.A, c) \leq t_A; \quad \delta_{A_1A_2}(x.A_1, x'.A_2) \leq t_{A_1A_2}; \quad \delta_{eid}(x.eid, c_e) = 0;$$
$$\delta_{eid}(x.eid, x'.eid) = 0; \quad \delta_{\equiv}(x.rela, c_r) = 0; \quad \delta_{\equiv}(x.rela, x'.rela) = 0,$$

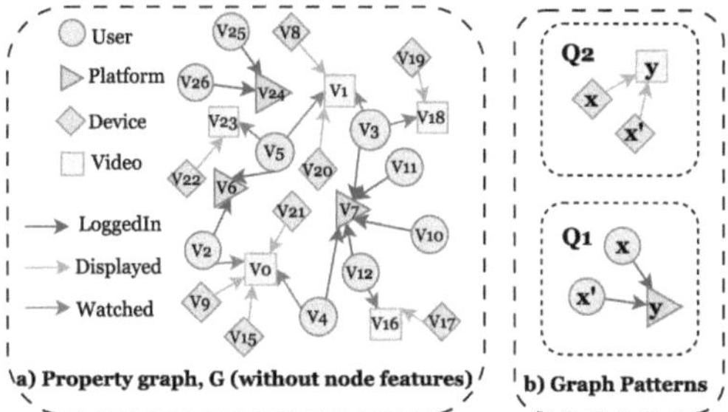

Pattern variables	x	x'	y
Matches	id	id	id
h0	V2	V5	V6
h1	V3	V4	V7
h2	V3	V10	V7
h3	V3	V11	V7
h4	V4	V10	V7
h5	V4	V11	V7

Pattern variables	x	x'	y
Matches	id	id	id
h6	V10	V11	V7
h7	V12	V3	V7
h8	V12	V4	V7
h9	V12	V10	V7
h10	V12	V11	V7
h11	V25	V26	V24

c) Matches of Graph Pattern Q1 in G (attributes omitted)

Fig. 2. Toy Example: a) Property graph G; b) Graph patterns Q_1, Q_2; c) Matches of Q_1 in G.

where $x, x' \in \bar{u}$ are pattern variables, A_i are attributes, and c is a constant. $\delta_{A_1A_2}$ depends on attribute types (e.g., arithmetic operations for numerical values, edit distance for strings). In GDD, Φ_X specifies constraints that must hold for Φ_Y to be satisfied. We use GDDs to encode user-specified and application-relevant constraints. We illustrate GDD semantics with a toy example below.

Example 3 (GDD Semantics). Consider φ : $(Q_1[x, x', y], \Phi_X \rightarrow \Phi_Y)$, where $\Phi_X = \{\delta_{Age}(x, x') \leq 3 \wedge \delta_{Ph}(x, x') = 0\}$ and $\Phi_Y = \{\delta_{eid}(x, x') = 0\}$. This states that if two `users` in Q_1 have an `Age` difference within 3 and identical `Phone` numbers, they refer to the same real-world entity. □

2.3 Problem Definition

Given a property graph, G, and a set Σ of user-specified GDDs, we seek to identify and link all Σ-relevant node pairs $v_i, v_j \in G$, that refer to the same real-world entity. A node pair $v_i, v_j \in G$ is said to be Σ-relevant iff: $v_i, v_j \in H(Q, G) \in G$, where $H(Q, G)$ is the list of matches of a pattern Q in Σ.

The user-defined GDD specification is outside the scope of our study, but existing GDD mining algorithms [21,27] can be used. We present empirical results in Sect. 4.6 to guide rule selection.

3 The FastER Framework for Property Graphs

In this section, we introduce FastER, a framework designed for candidate filtering and match scheduling, allowing the integration of any matching function of your

Algorithm 1: FastER($G, Q[\bar{z}], \delta$, threshold)

Data: Property graph G
Input: Graph pattern $Q[\bar{z}]$,distance constraints δ,edge weight threshold
Result: Matched results

```
   /* Stage 1: Graph pattern filtering */
1  H_1 ← {subgraphs | subgraphs satisfy Q[z̄]}
   /* Stage 2: Constraint-based filtering */
2  H_2 ← {s ∈ H_1 | s satisfies constraints δ}
   /* Stage 3: Blocking graph construction and PPS */
3  foreach (x, x') ∈ H_2 do
4      edgeWeight ← Σ_{r∈R} if x, x' satisfy r
5      if edgeWeight > 0 then
6          Add edge (x, x') with edgeWeight to BlockingGraph
7  SortedProfileList ← sortByEdgeWeights(BlockingGraph)
8  foreach v ∈ SortedProfileList do
9      CompareList ← getCandidates(v)
10     foreach candidate ∈ CompareList do
11         if edgeWeight(v, candidate) ≥ threshold then
12             Compare(v, candidate), updateMatchLists(v, candidate)
13             if meetsUserRequirements(v, candidate) then
14                 addToResultSet(v, candidate)
15         else
16             prune(v, candidate) ;   // Skip if edge weight is too low
17 return Final matched results
```

choice. A brief pseudo-code is presented in Algorithm 1. The FastER algorithm consists of three stages: graph pattern filtering, constraint based filtering, and blocking graph construction and Progressive Profile Scheduling(PPS). In Stage 1, it identifies candidate subgraphs $\mathcal{H}_1$ that match the graph pattern $Q[\bar{z}]$ (line 1). In Stage 2, it refines these candidates by applying the user-defined constraints δ, forming the set $\mathcal{H}_2$ (line 2). Finally, Stage 3 constructs a blocking graph from pairs in $\mathcal{H}_2$, computes edge weights based on rules satisfaction (lines 3-6), and sorts nodes to form a SortedProfileList (line 7). It iteratively processes nodes against candidate pairs, performing comparisons if their edge weight meets the specified threshold (lines 8-11), otherwise pruning the pair (line 16), the aggregated values at the entity level are validated to ensure they meet the user's demand (line 13). The algorithm returns the final matched results (line 17).

In addition, FastER offers interpretability by design. The filtering process is driven by user-defined GDD rules, which specify explicit graph patterns and attribute constraints. Each candidate match retained by the system can be traced back to the rules it satisfies, allowing users to understand and refine the matching behavior based on domain semantics.

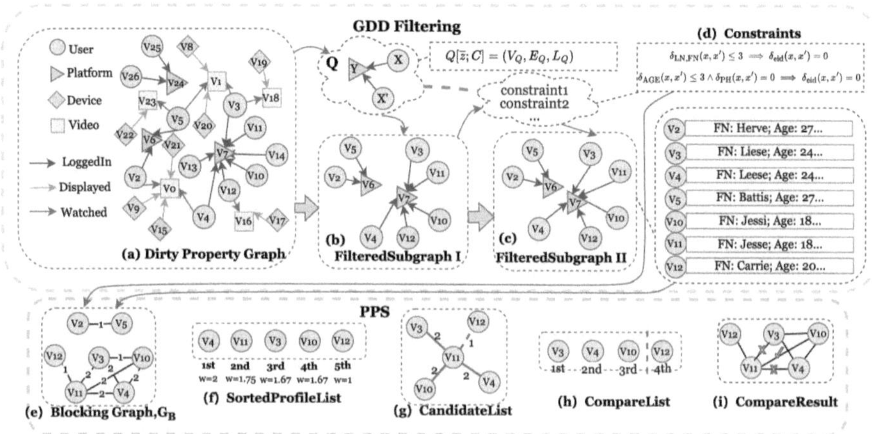

Fig. 3. The overall architecture of FastER. (a) The dirty property graph to be cleaned, (b) Subgraph obtained after graph pattern filtering, (c) Subgraph further refined by constraint-based filtering, (d)Constraints in GDD, (e) Blocking graph generated based on candidate matches and constraints, (f) The sorted profile list, (g) The neighborhood of node V11 within the same block, (h) The comparison list after processing V11 during the emission phase, (i) Comparison results of V11's related candidates.

3.1 Graph Pattern Filtering

In the first stage of graph pattern filtering, we use graph patterns of the GDDs as query inputs over the dirty property graph to extract subgraphs that satisfy the structural constraints. These graph patterns are designed to capture potential entity relationships based on the properties of nodes and the relationships between them. For example, considering the property graph shown in Fig. 3 b), let us assume that we use the graph pattern defined in $Q[z;C] = (V_Q, E_Q, L_Q)$. The pattern specifies any two user nodes, x and x', connected to the same platform node y via watch edges. Distance constraints can be defined over this pattern. For example, nodes must satisfy certain attribute requirements, such as the user's age being greater than 18, which, under the definition of an on-demand query, ensures that only matches meeting specific user requirements are selected. Based on this structure, we first extract a set of subgraph candidates from the original graph that satisfy this structural requirement. The set of matched subgraphs can be represented as: $H_1(x, x', y) = \{(v_2, v_5, v_6), (v_3, v_4, v_7), (v_3, v_{10}, v_7), (v_3, v_{11}, v_7), (v_4, v_{10}, v_7), (v_4, v_{11}, v_7), (v_{10}, v_{11}, v_7), (v_{12}, v_3, v_7), (v_{12}, v_4, v_7), (v_{12}, v_{10}, v_7), (v_{12}, v_{11}, v_7)\}$.

Compared to Fig. 2, one fewer subgraph is present due to not satisfying the user's demand (i.e., on-demand). These subgraphs, consisting of nodes and edges, satisfy the structure of user-platform relationships through "logged-in" edges,and the user-specified demand, forming the candidate subgraphs for further filtering in the next step.

3.2 Constraints-Based Filtering

Here, we apply a predefined set of distance constraints to further filter matches of the subgraphs from the first stage. These constraints, based on domain knowledge, are designed to ensure that candidate node pairs exhibit sufficient similarity, thereby retaining only the most promising matching candidates. For example, the distance constraints may require that the last names or phone numbers of two nodes be similar for them to be considered potential matches.

We define several distance constraints, which require that the differences between node pairs on certain attributes must fall within specific thresholds, such as last names, phone numbers, and ages. In this example, we define four constraints: - Lastname (LN) edit distance: $\delta_{\mathrm{LN}}(x, x') \leq 3$ - Firstname (FN) edit distance: $\delta_{\mathrm{FN}}(x, x') \leq 3$ - Phone (PH) edit distance: $\delta_{\mathrm{PH}}(x, x') \leq 3$ - Age (AGE) difference: $\delta_{\mathrm{AGE}}(x, x') = 0$. Only candidate pairs that satisfy at least one of these constraints will be retained for further processing.

After applying these filtering constraints, we obtain a more refined set of candidate pairs and their corresponding subgraphs. These subgraphs focus on nodes and edges that satisfy the similarity constraints and are therefore more likely to represent entity matches.

3.3 Blocking Graph Construction and PPS

Next, we construct a Blocking Graph based on the refined candidate list. In this graph, nodes represent entities, and edges represent potential matches based on their attributes. The weight of each edge is determined by the similarity between connected nodes. For simplicity and clarity, we assume that if two nodes satisfy one rule, the edge weight increases by one. We can define a Blocking Graph as shown in Fig. 3 e). This graph naturally divides the nodes from the original subgraph into two blocks, reducing the number of node comparisons and improving matching efficiency.

However, to improve matching accuracy, more sophisticated weighting methods can be applied. For example, the ARCS function is used to assign weights by summing the inverse cardinality of common blocks. The ARCS function assigns higher weights to pairs of entities that share smaller (i.e., more distinctive) blocks, and is defined as: $ARCS(p_i, p_j, B) = \sum_{b_k \in B_i \cap B_j} \frac{r_{p_i, p_j, b_k}}{|b_k|}$, where r_{p_i, p_j, b_k} denotes the number of rules satisfied by the entity pair (p_i, p_j) within the common block b_k. This modification ensures that pairs satisfying more rules receive proportionally higher weights while still considering the distinctiveness of smaller blocks. Similarly, other weighting functions can be applied to the Blocking Graph to assign higher weights to edges connecting nodes with strong co-occurrence patterns and lower weights to edges representing casual co-occurrences. Thus, with this weighting mechanism, the Blocking Graph not only reflects the similarity between entities more accurately, but it also adjusts the matching priorities based on the importance of different attributes, making the matching process more efficient overall.

Progressive Profile Scheduling (PPS). Once the Blocking Graph is constructed, we adopt the Progressive Profile Scheduling (PPS) technique to efficiently perform entity matching. PPS is an entity-centric scheduling method designed to prioritize nodes with the highest likelihood of matching by assessing their duplication probability.

First, within each block, nodes are sorted based on the average weight of their edges in the Blocking Graph, generating a SortedProfileList. The nodes in this list are ranked from highest to lowest, and nodes with higher average edge weights are prioritized for comparison, as they are more likely to match with other nodes. For instance, in Fig. 3 c), each node has multiple candidate nodes. We begin by comparing the node with the highest weight in the sorted list. During this process, PPS prunes unnecessary comparisons based on a predefined threshold (e.g., edge weight less than 2). For example, in the case of node v_{11}, if the edge weight between node v_{12} and v_{11} is below the threshold, this comparison is skipped, and v_{12} is removed from v_{11}'s candidate list.

By utilizing this selective pruning strategy, PPS significantly reduces the number of required comparisons, thereby improving matching efficiency. In this example, edges with a weight of 1 are ignored, leading to the removal of $v_2 \leftrightarrow v_5$ (weight 1), $v_{12} \leftrightarrow v_{11}$ (weight 1), $v_3 \leftrightarrow v_{10}$ (weight 1). The remaining comparisons are: $v_3 \leftrightarrow v_{11}$ (weight 2), $v_4 \leftrightarrow v_{11}$ (weight 2), $v_4 \leftrightarrow v_{10}$ (weight 2), $v_{11} \leftrightarrow v_{10}$ (weight 2), $v_3 \leftrightarrow v_4$ (weight 2). Consequently, the total number of comparisons is reduced from 8 to 5, as the three edges with a weight of 1 are ignored. Before publishing the final results, the aggregated values at the entity level will be validated to ensure they meet the user's demand.

Transitive Matching Optimization. In an ideal scenario, transitive relationships can be leveraged to further reduce the number of comparisons. For example, if both v_3 and v_4 match v_{11}, and v_{11} also matches v_{10}, we can infer through transitivity that v_3, v_4, v_{10}, and v_{11} all represent the same entity. As a result, redundant comparisons can be eliminated, leaving only the essential matches: $v_4 \leftrightarrow v_3$, $v_4 \leftrightarrow v_{10}$, $v_3 \leftrightarrow v_{11}$. This reduces the total number of comparisons from 5 to 3, thereby optimizing the resolution process.

3.4 Time Complexity

Let $G = (V, E)$ be a property graph with $|V| = n$ nodes and $|E| = m$ edges, and let $Q = (V_Q, E_Q)$ be a small graph pattern. Subgraph isomorphism using Cypher (the query language used by Neo4j) in Neo4j has worst-case time complexity $O(m \cdot |E_Q|)$, which reduces to $O(m)$ for constant-size patterns (as discussed in Appendix A.1, Sect. 1).

Let C be the number of candidate node pairs identified by pattern matching. Each of these undergoes d GDD constraint checks, giving $O(C \cdot d)$ time. Since d is typically constant, this simplifies to $O(C)$. After constraint filtering, only a fraction $\beta \in (0, 1)$ of the pairs remain. Let $C' = \beta C$ denote the number of valid pairs after filtering. Blocking graph construction on these C' pairs requires $O(C' \cdot r)$ for edge weight computation, where r is the number of features per edge, and $O(C' \log C')$ for sorting by similarity score. Finally, Progressive Profile Scheduling (PPS) incrementally compares each query-relevant profile (total N) to its k' most promising candidates (typically $k' \ll C'$), yielding $O(N \cdot k')$ complexity for the matching phase.

Summing the steps, the total complexity is: $O(m + \beta C + C' \log C' + N \cdot k')$. As shown in Appendix A.1, β and k' are empirically small in most cases (e.g., $\beta < 0.1$, $k' < 5$), yielding an overall complexity close to linear in the graph size m and number of target entities N.

4 Experimental Evaluation

This section empirically evaluates our proposal *w.r.t.* different SOTA solutions.

4.1 Experimental Setting

All experiments were performed on a PC with a 2.40GHz Intel Xeon Silver 4210R processor and 32GB of memory, running Linux OS. The experiments were implemented in Python 3.10 and interacted with the Neo4j graph database (version 5.19.0).

Datasets. In this study, we used five graph benchmark datasets and five relational benchmark datasets (cf. Table 1) from various domains. All datasets used in this paper are publicly available on the GitHub repository[1]. Although FastER is specifically designed for property graphs, we show it can also be applied in the relational data setting. Thus, we transformed the relational datasets in Table 1 into graph representations by leveraging their attribute relationships. The detailed conversion methods are provided in the GitHub repository. The reported values for Nodes, Edges, Node Types, and Edge Types in the relational datasets are based on their graph-transformed statistics. We apply automated GDD mining algorithms [21,27], followed by manual selection of a small number of high-quality rules to ensure interpretability and relevance. This process is detailed in Subsect. 4.6. To ensure a fair and consistent comparison across methods, all approaches use the same oracle matcher.

Methods. We categorize the examined methods into On-Demand ER, Progressive ER, and Batch ER methods. **On-Demand ER methods** include BrewER and QDA. BrewER [10] is an on-demand framework that enables direct execution of SQL SP queries on dirty data while progressively returning query results. QDA [14] is a query-driven algorithm that optimizes matches within a data block by using selective predicates to reduce unnecessary record comparisons. **Batch ER methods** include HG, RobEM, and Ditto. HG [30] employs a hierarchical graph attention transformation network for ER tasks. RobEM [29] leverages pre-trained language models (PLMs) for entity resolution, while Ditto [31] is a Transformer-based PLM approach designed for ER. **Progressive ER methods**

[1] https://github.com/Zaiwen/On_Demand_Entity_Resolution.

include PSN and I-PES. PSN [11] employs dynamic window adjustment to prioritize and resolve matching entities by initially sorting and selecting the most relevant records. I-PES [9] is an incremental ER algorithm that dynamically maintains the comparison order using a priority queue to achieve progressive resolution. All hyperparameters are set to the default values from the original papers unless otherwise specified.

Table 1. Graph and Relational Benchmark Datasets (NT: Node Types, ET: Edge Types, ND: Node Duplicates, ER: Entity Resolution

Category	Dataset	Nodes	Edges	NT	ET	ND	Domain
Graph	WWC	2.688k	15.757k	5	9	202	Sports
	GDS	8.977k	80.365k	5	5	350	Airport
	Entity Resolution (ER)	1.237k	1.819k	4	3	12	Streaming
	ArXiv	88.07k	58.515k	2	1	5.92k	Research
	CiteSeer	4.393k	2.892k	2	1	456	Citations
Relational	SIGMOD20	13.58k	12.01k	3	2	3.06k	Cameras
	Altosight	12.47k	12.44k	3	2	453	Cameras
	Fodors-Zagats (FZ)	1.69k	1.73k	3	2	112	Restaurants
	DBLP-ACM (DA)	8.70k	9.82k	3	2	2.22k	Bibliography
	Amazon-Google (AG)	4.98k	4.59k	2	1	116	Software

Evaluation Metrics. It is important to note that in our experiments, we do not directly evaluate precision or F1-score. FastER is a matcher-agnostic framework that focuses on filtering and scheduling components. Therefore, we adopt an oracle matcher—i.e., entity pairs are labeled using ground truth— to isolate the effects of the matching function and enable a fair comparison of the framework's efficiency and recall capabilities. Additionally, following standard practice in ER on-demand literature [10], the final matching confirmation stage guarantees a precision of 1. As a result, we exclude precision and F1-score from our evaluation. Instead, we focus on metrics such as query recall and error rate, which are discussed in detail later. We explore the following questions in subsequent subsections:

1. How does FastER perform in ER-on-demand scenario (Exp-1)?
2. How does FastER compare to SOTA batch processing methods (Exp-2)?
3. How well do progressive solutions perform in on-demand ER tasks? (Exp-3)
4. How does FastER perform on different components (Exp-4)?
5. How can users be guided to select appropriate rules (Exp-5)?

4.2 Exp-1: FastER vs On-demand Baselines

Since FastER is a matcher-agnostic framework, we adopt an oracle matcher across all three methods to better evaluate its performance. This matcher accurately labels all comparisons based on the known ground truth. As both BrewER and QDA are frameworks that can embed any blocking function, we employ JedAI [12,13], which is based on a completely unsupervised blocking approach. We use its standard configuration, which relies on Token Blocking and Meta-blocking [12]. This blocking method has been proven to achieve good results with BrewER and QDA.

The reported performance of BrewER in our experiments may differ from that in its original paper [10], as the original study relies on ground truth for blocking, whereas we employ the unsupervised approach JedAI to better reflect real-world scenarios. This setup ensures a fair comparison with FastER.

To comprehensively evaluate performance, we executed two queries on different datasets, each with distinct attribute constraints, and generated ground truth matching sets for each subgraph. To assess effectiveness, we introduce *query recall*, which considers only the subset of interest to the user, rather than the entire result set. It is defined as: $R_{\text{query}} = \frac{|M_{\text{query}} \cap M_{\epsilon}|}{|M_{\text{query}}|}$ where M_{query} is the ground truth matching set within the subset, and M_{ϵ} is the set of matches found by the algorithm in the same subset.

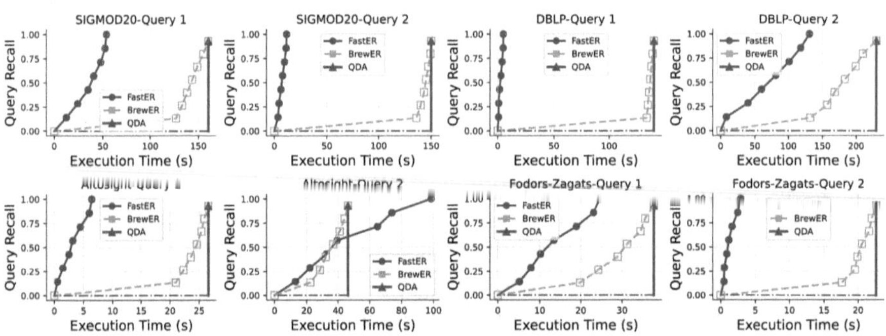

Fig. 4. FastER vs On-Demand baselines.

First, we show how FastER performs on all graph data sets in Table 1 – captured in Fig. 5. The results highlight the real-time capability of FastER. In general, graph complexity dictates efficiency as the characteristics in Table 1 bear out. Further, Fig. 4 shows the relative performance of FastER *w.r.t.* on-demand

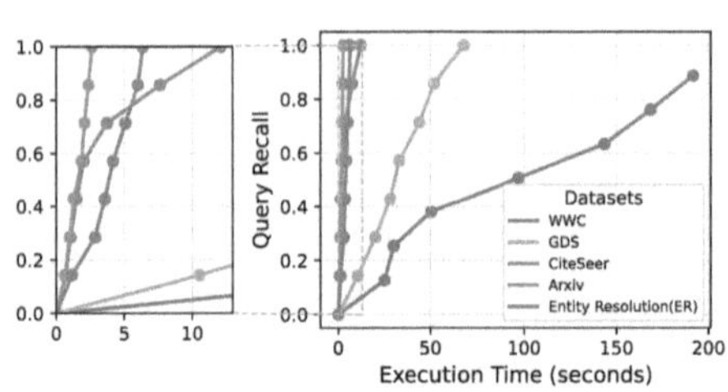

Fig. 5. Performance of FastER on Graphs.

baselines. The plots show QDA exhibits a typical stepwise execution curve because it must compare all candidate pairs before producing any output. In contrast, the recall rates of both FastER and BrewER show a gradual increase across all datasets.

Additionally, FastER generally achieves a lower execution time by performing blocking after filtering, reducing blocking overhead. In contrast, BrewER partitions the entire dataset, incurring higher preparation costs. FastER underperforms on *Altosight-Query2* because the rules fail to effectively capture candidates, leading to insufficient filtering.

4.3 Exp-2: FastER vs Batch-Query Baseline

To evaluate FastER against batch processing methods, we define "average time per matching result" (Tavg) as a fair metric for speed comparison, and we still extract a sub-ground-truth. Tavg is computed as: $T_{\text{avg}} = \frac{T_{\text{total}}}{|M_{\text{emitted}} \cap M_{\text{gt}}|}$, where T_{total} is the total query execution time, M_{emitted} is the set of entity matches that have been emitted, and M_{gt} represents the sub-ground-truth matching set.

Table 2. FastER vs Batch-Query baseline

Dataset	Recall				Tavg (k seconds)			
	HG	RobEM	Ditto	FastER	HG	RobEM	Ditto	FastER
FZ	0.954	**1.000**	**1.000**	**1.000**	2.781 ± 0.053	4.349 ± 0.076	0.917 ± 0.015	**0.553** ± 0.011
DA	0.982	0.982	0.978	**1.000**	1.440 ± 0.042	3.198 ± 0.088	0.464 ± 0.009	**0.052** ± 0.003
AG	0.654	**0.846**	0.786	0.841	1.162 ± 0.033	5.245 ± 0.121	**0.818** ± 0.018	2.910 ± 0.077
WWC	0.902	0.585	**0.927**	0.923	1.069 ± 0.029	4.270 ± 0.089	1.105 ± 0.022	**0.630** ± 0.013
GDS	0.943	0.800	0.900	**1.000**	1.817 ± 0.040	4.665 ± 0.102	0.678 ± 0.014	**0.445** ± 0.010

Table 2 compares FastER and batch-query baselines across multiple datasets, focusing on recall and average time per matching result (Tavg). FastER consistently achieves the highest recall, demonstrating the effectiveness of rule filtering in capturing matching candidates. Regarding time efficiency, batch-query baselines require full dataset traversal, whereas our approach significantly

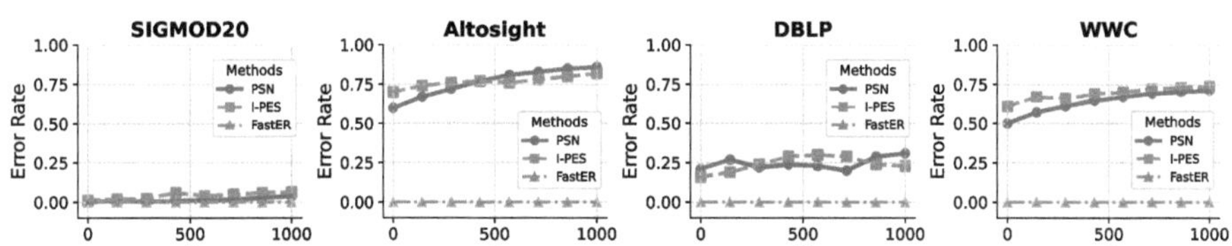

Fig. 6. FastER vs Progressive-Query baseline (error rate).

enhances practical performance. Tavg comparisons show FastER achieves substantial speed improvements across most datasets, except for Amazon-Google. The reason for this exception lies in the large intra-cluster variance of the dataset, which makes it difficult for the rules to accurately capture all matching candidates. Attempting to capture all candidates would come at the cost of introducing a large number of irrelevant matches. Therefore, users need to carefully balance and weigh their decisions when mining and selecting rules. Specific optimization suggestions will be discussed in detail in Subsect. 4.6.

4.4 Exp-3: FastER vs Progressive-Query Baselines

The most advanced progressive ER methods, such as *PSN* [11] and *I-PES* [9], rank entity pairs by matching likelihood, prioritizing the most probable matches to enhance early quality. However, new matches may alter the aggregated results, leading to inconsistencies. Unlike FastER, progressive baseline lacks a final verification mechanism to ensure strict on-demand output, contributing to its high error rate. We evaluate progressive baseline's accuracy using the error rate over the first k emitted entities, denoted as Err@k: Err@$k = \frac{\text{Errors}}{k}$. Here, an *error*

Table 3. Ablation study results on graph and relational datasets.

Graph Datasets

Method	Arxiv		CiteSeer		WWC	
	Rel. Comp.	Recall (%)	Rel. Comp.	Recall (%)	Rel. Comp.	Recall (%)
No-RF	453508.8	99.67	14659.1	99.20	117.9	99.00
No-B	10.4	98.96	29.4	[illegible]	[illegible]	89.90
No-PPS	1.6	97.78	1.4	97.09	2.3	89.20
No-T	2.9	97.68	3.0	96.42	2.2	89.20
FastER	1.0	97.68	1.0	96.42	1.0	89.20

Relational Datasets

Method	Fodors-Zagat		DBLP-ACM		Amazon-Google	
	Rel. Comp.	Recall (%)	Rel. Comp.	Recall (%)	Rel. Comp.	Recall (%)
No-RF	1210.2	100.00	11662.8	100.00	301.1	99.00
No-B	8.2	100.00	3.1	100.00	6.7	87.00
No-PPS	1.2	100.00	1.6	100.00	1.4	82.18
No-T	2.2	100.00	1.5	100.00	1.8	79.00
FastER	1.0	100.00	1.0	100.00	1.0	79.00

refers to an emitted result that does not meet user requirements, quantifying the proportion of incorrect matches in the first k outputs.

Figure 6 shows error rate variations across datasets and k values. FastER, as a precise method, consistently maintains a 0% error rate by verifying matches individually. In contrast, progressive baseline exhibits high error rates in most datasets, except for SIGMOD20, which has minimal intra-cluster variance. Thus, progressive baseline is unreliable for ER-on-demand.

4.5 Exp-4: Ablation Study

In this experiment, we conducted an ablation study on the FastER framework to evaluate the impact of different components on matching efficiency and recall across multiple graph and relational datasets. We systematically removed the key components as follows. 1) No Rules Filtering (No-RF): Since blocking relies on rules filtering, this renders the system equivalent to a pure PPS method without blocking. 2) No Blocking (No-B): Blocking partitions the matching space to minimize unnecessary comparisons. 3) No Progressive Profile Scheduling (No-PPS): PPS enables the system to incrementally generate matches and employs pruning strategies to reduce the number of comparisons. 4) No Transitivity Matching (No-T): Transitivity matching leverages existing matches to infer new ones, enhancing completeness while reducing the number of comparisons.

The results are presented in Table 3 showing the relative number of comparisons in each ensuing method with respect to FastER's number of comparison. In general, the results indicate that rules filtering is crucial for reducing the number of comparisons, as its removal significantly increases computational overhead. On datasets with low variance, eliminating rules filtering has minimal impact on recall, whereas on high-variance datasets, the effect is relatively significant. Blocking significantly affects execution time; removing it leads to a substantial increase in the number of comparisons, but has little impact on recall. PPS plays a key role in system responsiveness; its pruning mechanism effectively reduces the number of queries. Without PPS, processing time increases, though recall remains largely unaffected. Transitivity matching effectively reduces the number of comparisons without compromising recall.

4.6 Exp-5: Rules Selection Strategies for Efficient Entity Resolution

We conducted experiments on ten datasets, applying three different filtering rules to each. The specific rules used are provided in Appendix A.2.

The results (Fig. 7) show that rules with steeper slopes and higher recall are of higher quality, as they achieve superior performance within shorter execution times. Based on our findings, we summarize key principles for selecting filtering rules. First, the strictness of rules impacts execution time and recall. Looser rules increase candidate matches, leading to longer execution times, while overly strict rules reduce execution time but risk excessive filtering, lowering recall. Thus, selecting appropriate rules is essential to balance efficiency and accuracy.

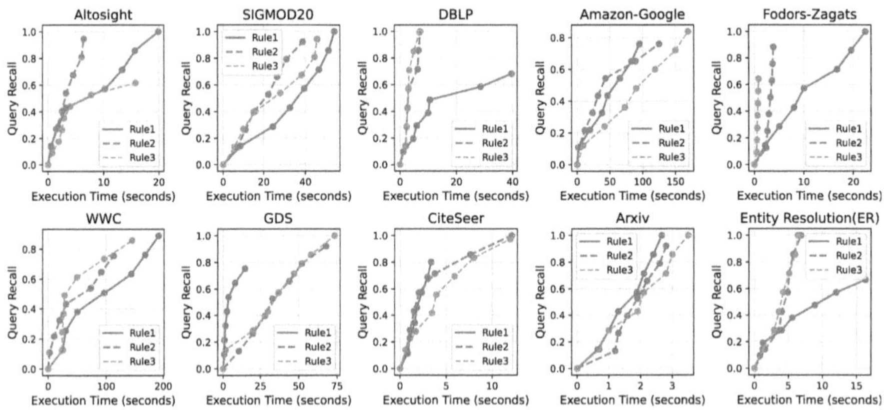

Fig. 7. Ablation study of the impact of multiple rules on filtering performance.

Moreover, as the complexity of relationships among nodes increases, the graph pattern should incorporate more nodes, and filtering rules should constrain multiple attributes to effectively capture structural dependencies.

When selecting a graph pattern, overly strict constraints should be avoided. For example: *Pattern 1*: $x \rightarrow y \rightarrow z \leftarrow y' \leftarrow x'$; *Pattern 2*: $x \rightarrow y \rightarrow z$, $x' \rightarrow y' \rightarrow z'$. Requiring node z' to be strictly identical to z may exclude many valid candidates. Instead, constraining the similarity between z and z' rather than enforcing identical entity IDs (eid) prevents over-filtering and enhances match coverage. In summary, filtering rule and graph pattern selection directly influence the trade-off between execution time and recall. Stricter rules are preferable when execution time is a priority, whereas relatively looser rules are recommended when balancing execution time and recall. FastER is designed to leverage domain-specific rules for high-precision filtering. Meanwhile, recent work has begun to explore automated strategies for rule selection in graph-based entity resolution. We provide supporting resources on our project page[2], which assist users in automatically constructing effective rules programmatically. This line of research is actively evolving and offers potential for future enhancements.

5 Conclusion

We introduce FastER, an efficient on-demand entity resolution (ER) approach for property graphs based on Graph Differential Dependencies (GDDs), addressing the six key challenges outlined in Fig. 1. FastER captures complex graph patterns for high-precision entity matching and employs Progressive Profile Scheduling (PPS) to incrementally output results and provide real-time feedback. To enhance computational efficiency, FastER applies rule-based filtering, reducing

[2] https://github.com/Zaiwen/On_Demand_Entity_Resolution.

candidate entity pairs by a factor of 10^3 to 10^5, and prioritizes user queries, focusing on user-specified subgraphs to avoid unnecessary computations. Experimental results demonstrate that FastER significantly outperforms existing ER methods in both processing time and recall. Future research could explore advanced filtering techniques for heterogeneous data sources and automated rule selection mechanisms to better handle intra-cluster variations.

Supplemental Material Statement. Our material is available at https://doi.org/10.5281/zenodo.15389843 and includes the source code and datasets used for running FastER. All details are provided in the `README.md` file. `Appendix.pdf` contains the algorithm complexity proof and Cypher queries.

Acknowledgment. The authors affiliated with institutions 1, 5 and 6 were supported in part by the National Key Research and Development Program of China under Grant No. 2023YFF1000100; the Hubei Key Research and Development Program of China under Grant Nos. 2024BBB055 and 2024BAA008; the Major Science and Technology Project of Yunnan Province under Grant No. 202502AE090003; and the Fundamental Research Funds for the Central Universities under Grant No. 2662025XXPY005.

References

1. Papadakis, G., Fisichella, M., Schoger, F., Mandilaras, G., Augsten, N., Nejdl, W.: How to reduce the search space of Entity Resolution: with Blocking or Nearest Neighbor search? arXiv preprint arXiv:2202.12521 (2022). https://arxiv.org/abs/2202.12521
2. Brinkmann, A., Shraga, R., Bizer, C.: SC-Block: Supervised Contrastive Blocking Within Entity Resolution Pipelines. In: Meroño Peñuela, A., Dimou, A., Troncy, R., Hartig, O., Acosta, M., Alam, M., Paulheim, H., Lisena, P. (eds.) The Semantic Web. LNCS, vol. 14681, pp. 121–142. Springer, Cham (2024). https://doi.org/10.1007/978-3-031-60626-7_7
3. Papadakis, G., Fisichella, M., Schoger, F., Mandilaras, G., Augsten, N., Nejdl, W.: Benchmarking filtering techniques for entity resolution. In: 39th IEEE International Conference on Data Engineering (ICDE), pp. 653–666. IEEE, Anaheim, CA, USA (2023). https://doi.org/10.1109/ICDE55515.2023.00389
4. Wang, S., et al.: *k*NN-NER: Named Entity Recognition with Nearest Neighbor Search. arXiv preprint arXiv:2203.17103 (2022). https://arxiv.org/abs/2203.17103
5. Christen, P.: Data Matching: Concepts and Techniques for Record Linkage, Entity Resolution, and Duplicate Detection. Springer, Heidelberg (2012)
6. Christen, P.: A survey of indexing techniques for scalable record linkage and deduplication. IEEE Trans. Knowl. Data Eng. **24**(9), 1537–1555 (2012). https://doi.org/10.1109/TKDE.2011.127
7. Mann, W., Augsten, N., Bouros, P.: An empirical evaluation of set similarity join techniques. Proc. VLDB Endow. **9**(9), 636–647 (2016). https://doi.org/10.14778/2947618.2947620
8. Jiang, Y., Li, G., Feng, J., Li, W.-S.: String similarity joins: an experimental evaluation. Proc. VLDB Endow. **7**(8), 625–636 (2014). https://doi.org/10.14778/2732296.2732299

9. Maciejewski, J., Nikoletos, K., Papadakis, G., Velegrakis, Y.: Progressive entity matching: a design space exploration. Proc. ACM Manag. Data **3**(1), Article 65, 25 pages (2025https://doi.org/10.1145/3709715
10. Zecchini, L., Simonini, G., Bergamaschi, S., Naumann, F.: BrewER: entity resolution on-demand. Proc. VLDB Endow. **16**(12), 4026–4029 (2023). https://doi.org/10.14778/3611540.3611612
11. Simonini, G., Papadakis, G., Palpanas, T., Bergamaschi, S.: Schema-agnostic progressive entity resolution. IEEE Trans. Knowl. Data Eng. **31**(6), 1208–1221 (2019). https://doi.org/10.1109/TKDE.2018.2852763
12. Papadakis, G., et al.: Three-Dimensional Entity Resolution with JedAI. Inf. Syst. **93**, 101565 (2020). https://doi.org/10.1016/j.is.2020.101565
13. Papadakis, G., Tsekouras, L., Thanos, E., Giannakopoulos, G., Palpanas, T., Koubarakis, M.: Domain- and Structure-Agnostic End-to-End Entity Resolution with JedAI. SIGMOD Rec. **48**(4), 30–36 (2020). https://doi.org/10.1145/3385658.3385664
14. Altwaijry, H., Kalashnikov, D.V., Mehrotra, S.: QDA: a query-driven approach to entity resolution. IEEE Trans. Knowl. Data Eng. **29**(2), 402–417 (2017). https://doi.org/10.1109/TKDE.2016.2623607
15. Madhavan, J., et al.: Web-scale Data Integration: You Can Only Afford to Pay As You Go. In: CIDR 2007, pp. 1–10. CIDR, Asilomar, CA, USA (2007)
16. De Uña, D., Rümmele, N., Gange, G., Schachte, P., Stuckey, P.J.: Machine learning and constraint programming for relational-to-ontology schema mapping. In: Proc. of the 27th International Joint Conference on Artificial Intelligence (IJCAI), pp. 1277–1283. AAAI Press, Stockholm, Sweden (2018)
17. Alexiou, G., Papastefanatos, G., Stamatopoulos, V., Koutrika, G., Koziris, N.: QueryER: a framework for fast analysis-aware deduplication over dirty data. In: Simitsis, A., Kemme, B., Queralt, A., Romero, O., Jovanovic, P., (eds.), In: Proceedings of 28th International Conference on Extending Database Technology, EDBT 2025, Barcelona, Spain, March 25-28 (2025)
18. Kimmig, A., Memory, A., Miller, R.J., Getoor, L.: A Collective, Probabilistic Approach to Schema Mapping: Appendix. arXiv preprint arXiv:1702.03447 (2017). https://arxiv.org/abs/1702.03447
19. Kimmig, A., Memory, A., Miller, R.J., Getoor, L.: A collective, probabilistic approach to schema mapping using diverse noisy evidence. IEEE Trans. Knowl. Data Eng. **31**(8), 1426–1439 (2019). https://doi.org/10.1109/TKDE.2018.2865785
20. Qian, L., Cafarella, M.J., Jagadish, H.V.: Sample-driven schema mapping. In: Proeedings of the 2012 ACM SIGMOD International Conference on Management of Data (SIGMOD), pp. 73–84. ACM, Scottsdale, Arizona, USA (2012). https://doi.org/10.1145/2213836.2213846
21. Kwashie, S., Liu, L., Liu, J., Stumptner, M., Li, J., Yang, L.: Certus: an effective entity resolution approach with graph differential dependencies (GDDs). Proc. VLDB Endow. **12**(6), 653–666 (2019)
22. Fan, W., Fan, Z., Tian, C., Dong, X.L.: Keys for Graphs. Proc. VLDB Endow. **8**(12), 1590–1601 (2015https://doi.org/10.14778/2824032.2824056
23. Fan, W., Wu, Y., Xu, J.: Functional Dependencies for Graphs. In: Proceedings of the 2016 International Conference on Management of Data (SIGMOD), pp. 1843–1857. ACM, San Francisco, CA, USA (2016https://doi.org/10.1145/2882903.2915232
24. Fan, W., Geerts, F., Jia, X., Kementsietsidis, A.: Conditional Functional Dependencies for Capturing Data Inconsistencies. ACM Trans. Database Syst. **33**(2), Article 6, 48 (2008). https://doi.org/10.1145/1366102.1366103

25. Fan, W., Lu, P.: Dependencies for graphs. ACM Trans. Database Syst. **44**(2), Article 5, 40 (2019). https://doi.org/10.1145/3287285
26. Hu, J., et al.: When GDD meets GNN: a knowledge-driven neural connection for effective entity resolution in property graphs. Inf. Syst. **132**, 102551 (2025)
27. Zhang, Y., et al.: Discovering graph differential dependencies. In: Databases Theory and Applications. Proceedings of the 34th Australasian Database Conference (ADC), pp. 259–272. Springer, Melbourne, VIC, Australia (2023). https://doi.org/10.1007/978-3-031-47843-7_18
28. Wang, S., Miao, S., Kwashie, S., Bewong, M., Hu, J., Feng, Z.: LLM-enhanced entity resolution using graph differential dependencies. In: International Conference on Intelligent Computing, pp. 125–136. Singapore, Springer Nature Singapore (2025)
29. Akbarian Rastaghi, M., Kamalloo, E., Rafiei, D.: Probing the robustness of pre-trained language models for entity matching. In: Proceedings of the 31st ACM International Conference on Information & Knowledge Management (CIKM), pp. 3786–3790. ACM, Atlanta, GA, USA (2022). https://doi.org/10.1145/3511808.3557673
30. Yao, D., Gu, Y., Cong, G., Jin, H., Lv, X.: Entity resolution with hierarchical graph attention networks. In: Proceedings of the 2022 International Conference on Management of Data (SIGMOD), pp. 429–442. ACM, Philadelphia, PA, USA (2022). https://doi.org/10.1145/3514221.3517872
31. Li, Y., Li, J., Suhara, Y., Doan, A., Tan, W.-C.: Deep entity matching with pre-trained language models. Proc. VLDB Endow. **14**(1), 50–60 (2020). https://doi.org/10.14778/3421424.3421431

FLORA: Unsupervised Knowledge Graph Alignment by Fuzzy Logic

Yiwen Peng(✉), Thomas Bonald(✉), and Fabian M. Suchanek(✉)

Télécom Paris, Institut Polytechnique de Paris, Palaiseau, France
{yiwen.peng,thomas.bonald,fabian.suchanek}@telecom-paris.fr

Abstract. Knowledge graph alignment is the task of matching equivalent entities (that is, instances and classes) and relations across two knowledge graphs. Most existing methods focus on pure entity-level alignment, computing the similarity of entities in some embedding space. They lack interpretable reasoning and need training data to work. In this paper, we propose FLORA, a simple yet effective method that (1) is unsupervised, i.e., does not require training data, (2) provides a holistic alignment for entities and relations iteratively, (3) is based on fuzzy logic and thus delivers interpretable results, (4) provably converges, (5) allows dangling entities, i.e., entities without a counterpart in the other KG, and (6) achieves state-of-the-art results on major benchmarks.

Keywords: Knowledge Graphs · Entity Alignment · Holistic Matching · Symbolic Reasoning · Fuzzy logic

1 Introduction

The task of Knowledge Graph (KG) alignment consists in matching both entities and relations in one KG to their equivalents in another. Figure 1 shows a toy example of alignment between DBpedia and Wikidata. KG alignment is useful for knowledge fusion [49,53] and thus for a wide range of downstream applications like question answering [2,12], common-sense reasoning [32], and recommender systems [5,23]. It is a challenging task for several reasons. First, KGs are generally heterogeneous and incomplete: One KG may contain information that the other one does not contain. Second, entity names can differ vastly across KGs (in Fig. 1 for instance, entities in Wikidata are represented by non-readable IDs, unlike in DBpedia). Third, training data are most often not available in practice, due to the high cost of manual annotation. Finally, the alignment of entities and relations is interdependent.

Many approaches exist for KG alignment, but most focus on the alignment of entities only. Moreover, they generally require training data [59] or assume a one-to-one entity mapping from one KG to the other (i.e., ignore dangling entities) [44]. A notable exception is PARIS [39], an approach based on the iterative computation of probabilistic equations that has been shown to outperform other methods in recent studies [29,43]. However, this approach (1) lacks convergence

D. Garijo et al. (Eds.): ISWC 2025, LNCS 16140, pp. 196–215, 2026.
https://doi.org/10.1007/978-3-032-09527-5_11

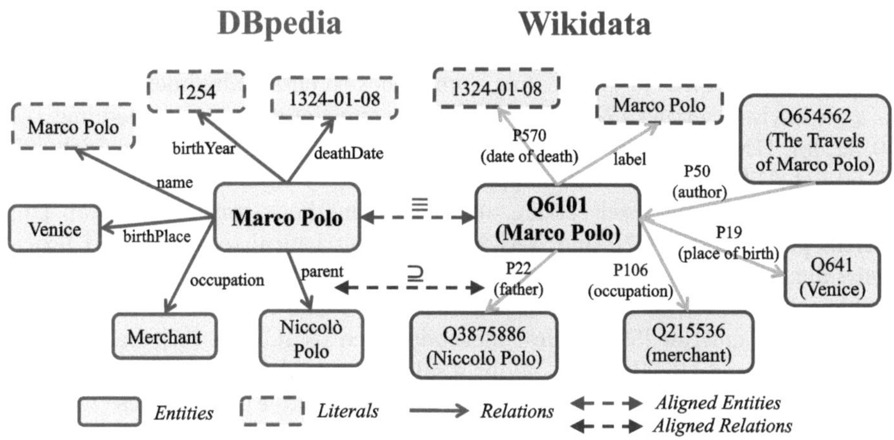

Fig. 1. An excerpt of DBpedia and Wikidata KGs. Note the asymmetric mapping of the relation *parent* to the sub-relation *father*.

guarantees, (2) does not achieve good performance when functional relations are absent, and (3) cannot see similarities between literals beyond a strict identity.

To address these shortcomings, we present FLORA[1], a novel unsupervised approach for aligning both entities and relations. FLORA formalizes the alignment in Fuzzy Logic, in a principled framework that integrates various signals, both semantic and structural, and yields human-interpretable explanations for the results. FLORA works even in the presence of dangling entities and in the absence of functional relations. It relies on an iterative algorithm that provably converges. Our contributions are the following:

- FLORA, an approach based on Fuzzy Logic for aligning entities and relations that accounts for the asymmetry of relation alignments and the incompleteness of KGs. Although unsupervised by nature, FLORA can optionally exploit training data if available.
- An iterative algorithm that provably converges towards the optimal solution of the problem, as formalized in Fuzzy Logic.
- Extensive experiments on five entity alignment datasets across four languages, as well as two KG alignment datasets from the OAEI KG Track, showing that FLORA consistently outperforms both unsupervised and supervised baselines.

In what follows, Sect. 2 reviews related work, Sect. 3 provides preliminaries, Sect. 4 introduces our Fuzzy Logic formalism, Sect. 5 presents our method, Sect. 6 shows experimental results, and Sect. 7 concludes and outlines future work. All our code and data are publicly available at https://github.com/dig-team/FLORA.

[1] Fuzzy-Logic based Object and Relation Alignment.

2 Related Work

Entity Alignment. Many existing approaches to entity alignment (EA) work in a supervised setting [59]. They use either translation-based embedding [24, 40–42,48], GNN encoders [31,33,50,51,54], or fine-tuned language models [25, 45,60,61]. Different from these approaches, FLORA does not require training data. In the unsupervised setting, non-neural methods such as LogMap [26], PARIS [39], PRASE [37], and NALA [55] exploit logical reasoning and lexical matching. Other methods transform the EA task into an optimal assignment problem [11,34,44], or leverage names, attributes and relations to improve the alignment of entities [58]. Neural methods, such as ICLEA [57], SelfKG [30], LLM4EA [8] and HLMEA [27], adopt a self-supervised setting or leverage large language models (LLMs) in a zero-shot manner. Unlike FLORA, these methods are *black-box* methods, i.e., they cannot explain why a given alignment was found. Besides, we show in our experiments that FLORA outperforms all of the above approaches on standard benchmark datasets. Moreover, FLORA aligns not just entities, but also relations at the same time.

Knowledge Graph Alignment. The task of KG alignment (also known as KG matching or holistic KG alignment) extends EA by aligning not only instances, but also classes and relations. Unlike Ontology Alignment [13], KG Alignment takes a simplistic view on classes, and typically does not consider asymmetric class subsumptions across KGs. The Ontology Alignment Evaluation Initiative (OAEI)[2] organizes a KG track tailored for KG alignment. Methods such as OLaLa [21] and SOBERT [18] align only classes. Our work, in contrast, aims at performing a holistic matching of instances, classes, and relations. Some methods like PARIS [39], LogMap [26], ATMatcher [20], and AgreementMakerLight [14] are based on lexical matching. Others, such as Wiktionary [36] or ALOD2Vec [35] incorporate external background knowledge. We can show that FLORA achieves better results than these methods without requiring additional external datasets.

Fuzzy Logic. Very few approaches use Fuzzy Logic for KG alignment. FuzzyEA [24] relies on a standard embedding approach for entity alignment and Fuzzy Logic is used only to filter candidate entity pairs. This is very different from our approach, where Fuzzy Logic is central in the alignment process, for both entities and relations. In other works [16,22,28,47], Fuzzy Logic is used for ontology alignment, but is limited to either class matching or instance matching.

3 Preliminaries

A knowledge graph $\mathcal{G}$ is based on a set of entities $\mathcal{E}$ and a set of relations $\mathcal{R}$. In this paper, in line with [6,9,49], we see a KG as a set of triples (or facts) $\mathcal{T} \subset \mathcal{E} \times \mathcal{R} \times \mathcal{E}$. Each triple $(h, r, t) \in \mathcal{T}$ represents a semantic relationship between the head entity h and the tail entity t with the relation r. We denote by $r(h, t)$ the corresponding boolean proposition, which evaluates to *true* if and

[2] https://oaei.ontologymatching.org/.

only if $(h, r, t) \in \mathcal{T}$. Without loss of generality, we assume that each relation $r \in \mathcal{R}$ has an inverse relation $r^{-1} \in \mathcal{R}$, such that $r(h,t)$ if and only if $r^{-1}(t,h)$. In this paper, the entity set $\mathcal{E}$ includes literals, instances, and classes.

Functionality. Like PARIS [39], our approach exploits the notion of functionality of a relation, i.e., the degree to which a relation tends to map the head entity to a unique tail entity. Formally, the functionality of a relation $r \in \mathcal{R}$ is:

$$fun(r) = \frac{|\{h \mid \exists t: \ r(h,t)\}|}{|\{(h,t) \mid r(h,t)\}|}$$

Note that $fun(r) \in [0,1]$ with $fun(r) = 1$ if and only if the relation r is functional: It maps any head entity to a unique tail entity. For example, the relation *hasCapital* generally assigns exactly one capital city to each country, so that $fun(hasCapital) \approx 1$. If the entities referring to *France* in each KG are aligned, the corresponding entities referring to *Paris* can then be aligned as well.

Our approach also uses the notion of *local* functionality, which is specific to the head entity h:

$$fun(r,h) = \frac{1}{|\{t \mid r(h,t)\}|}$$

Again, $fun(r,h) \in [0,1]$ with $fun(r,h) = 1$ if and only if there is a unique entity t such that $r(h,t)$ is true. The local functionality is needed to deal with relations that are globally functional, but have local exceptions. For instance, *South Africa* has three capitals, *Pretoria*, *Bloemfontein*, and *Cape Town*, so that the relation *hasCapital* is not locally functional for the head entity *South Africa*.

KG Alignment. Given two knowledge graphs $\mathcal{G} = \langle \mathcal{E}, \mathcal{R}, \mathcal{T} \rangle$, $\mathcal{G}' = \langle \mathcal{E}', \mathcal{R}', \mathcal{T}' \rangle$, entity alignment (EA) is the task of finding the set

$$\mathcal{M}_e = \{(e,e') \mid e \equiv e', e \in \mathcal{E}, e' \in \mathcal{E}'\}$$

where $e \equiv e'$ means that entity e is semantically equivalent to e'. Relation alignment is the task of finding the set

$$\mathcal{M}_r = \{(r, O, r') \mid rOr', r \in \mathcal{R}, r' \in \mathcal{R}', O \in \{\subseteq, \supseteq, \equiv\}\},$$

where $\subseteq, \supseteq, \equiv$ refer to subrelation, superrelation, or equivalence, respectively. KG alignment is the task of doing the alignment of both entities and relations at the same time.

4 Fuzzy Logic Framework

Our method, FLORA, is based on Fuzzy Logic. This allows us to integrate signals of different nature, semantic and structural, in a single principled framework. Our framework can use arbitrary aggregation functions, as long as they are continuous and non-decreasing. This distinguishes our framework from Probabilistic Soft Logic [4], which commonly requires linear aggregation functions (usually

Łukasiewicz T-norms, or Gödel T-norms for negatively weighted rules [10]), and from standard propositional Gödel logic, which uses *min* aggregation [3].

Fuzzy Inference System. A *fuzzy set* A over a universe of discourse X is given by a membership function μ_A, which maps every element of X to a value in $[0,1]$. In an often-used example, X is the range of temperatures in degrees Celsius and A is the fuzzy set that describes "hot temperatures". The membership function of A is then, for example, $\mu_A(x) = 0$ for $x \leq 10°$, $\mu_A(x) = (x - 10°)/15°$ for x between $10°$ and $25°$, and $\mu_A(x) = 1$ for $x \geq 25°$. In its simplest form, a Mamdani-style Fuzzy Rule Based Reasoning System [38], or Fuzzy Inference System (FIS), consists of a set of rules of the form

$$p_1 \textit{ is } P_1 \wedge ... \wedge p_n \textit{ is } P_n \Rightarrow c \textit{ is } C$$

Here, $p_1, ..., p_n$ are input variables (we call them *premises*), $P_1, ..., P_n$ are fuzzy sets, c is the output variable (which we call the *conclusion*), and C is a fuzzy set. For example, p_1 can be the temperature of the room in degrees Celcius, P_1 is the fuzzy set that describes "hot temperature", p_2 is the number of people in the room, P_2 is the fuzzy set of "a crowded room", c is the desired speed of the fan (say, in rotations per minute), and C is the fuzzy set of "a fast rotation". The expression "p_i *is* P_i" (for $i = 1, ..., n$) evaluates to $\mu_{P_i}(p_i)$ (in a process called *fuzzification*). In our example, a room temperature of $p_1 = 20°$ belongs to the fuzzy set P_1 of hot temperatures to a degree of $\frac{2}{3}$, and a number of people $p_2 = 10$ could belong to "a crowded room" P_2 to a degree of 0.5.

The *firing strength* of the rule is then computed by aggregating the individual fuzzified values of each premise using a custom aggregation function ϕ. Usually, ϕ is a T-norm [17], but we will not impose this restriction in this paper. A common choice for ϕ is *min*, which yields 0.5 in our example. The output of the rule is a fuzzy set for c, which is given by the membership function of C, capped at the firing strength of the rule. In our example, μ_C could assign a value of 1 to a speed of more than 60 rotations per minute, and would be capped to 0.5. If several rules have the same output variable (c in our example), their fuzzy sets (C in our example) are combined, usually using a point-wise max operation on the membership functions. This yields one final fuzzy set for the output variable, which is then *defuzzified* into a single scalar value c^*.

Simple Positive FIS. For our work, we need a simpler form of FIS, where all membership functions are identity functions, there is no negation, and defuzzification is done by the First of Maxima (FoM) method, i.e., the aggregated fuzzy set C is defuzzified into the scalar value $c^* = \min\{c|\forall x, \mu_C(c) \geq \mu_C(x)\}$. Our example rule can thus be written more simply as:

$$\textit{temperature} \wedge \textit{crowded} \Rightarrow \textit{fanspeed}$$

Here, *temperature* is a normalized value for the temperature in $[0,1]$, *crowded* is a normalized value for the degree of crowdedness in $[0,1]$, and *fanspeed* is the normalized speed of the fan in $[0,1]$. If we use *min* as aggregation, this rule means that *fanspeed* must be identical to the minimum of *temperature* and *crowdedness*.

If several rules have *fanspeed* as conclusion, then it will be the maximum of the firing strengths of the rules. More formally:

Definition 1 (Simple Positive FIS). *A Simple Positive FIS F is a set of rules of the form* $P_1 \wedge ... \wedge P_n \overset{\phi}{\Longrightarrow} C$*, where* $P_1, ..., P_n$ *are input variables (premises) that have a given value in* $[0,1]$*, C (the conclusion) is an output variable whose value is to be computed, and* $\phi : \mathbb{R}^n \rightarrow [0,1]$ *is an aggregation function. A rule of F is satisfied if the value of the conclusion is greater than or equal to the rule strength* $\phi(P_1, ..., P_n)$*. A solution of F is an assignment of each output variable to a value so that (1) all rules are satisfied, and (2) no output variable can be assigned a smaller value and still satisfy all rules.*

Recursive FIS. We now extend the Simple Positive FIS by allowing the conclusions to appear as premises of rules:

Definition 2 (Recursive FIS). *A recursive FIS is a Simple Positive FIS where the output variables can appear as premises.*

In our example, a fast-running fan may attract more people seeking chilling air:

$$\textit{fanspeed} \Rightarrow \textit{crowded}$$

The notions of rule satisfaction and solution carry over to recursive FISs.

Fixed point iteration. Algorithm 1 computes the solution of a Recursive FIS. It starts by assigning all output variables the value of zero, computes the firing strength of each rule, and updates the value of the output variable of this rule. This process is iterated until convergence.

Algorithm 1. Solve Recursive FIS

```
Require: A recursive FIS F
Ensure: The solution v of F
  v(x) ← 0 for all output variables x of F
  while no convergence do
      for rule r of F do
          strength(r) ← firing strength of r with values v
          x ← output variable of r
          v(x) ← max(v(x), strength(r))
      end for
  end while
  return v
```

Theorem 1. *If each aggregation function is continuous and non-decreasing, then Algorithm 1 converges to the solution of the input recursive FIS.*

Proof. Let K be the number of output variables. Let us see the assignment v of Algorithm 1 as a vector $\overrightarrow{v} \in [0,1]^K$, with one value per output variable. Each iteration of the algorithm corresponds to the update $\overrightarrow{v} \leftarrow f(\overrightarrow{v})$ for some mapping $f : [0,1]^K \rightarrow [0,1]^K$. A solution to the FIS must satisfy $\overrightarrow{v} \geq f(\overrightarrow{v})$ component-wise so that all rules are satisfied. Since $\overrightarrow{v} \leq f(\overrightarrow{v})$ component-wise, this means that $\overrightarrow{v} = f(\overrightarrow{v})$, i.e., $\overrightarrow{v}$ is a fixed point of f. Now since f is non-decreasing, because so are the aggregation functions involved in f, as well as the *max* operator, it follows from the Knaster-Tarski fixed point theorem [46] that the set of fixed points is a lattice and that there is a unique least fixed point. It remains to prove that Algorithm 1 converges to this least fixed point.

The algorithm computes a sequence of vectors $\overrightarrow{v_0} = 0, \overrightarrow{v_1}, \overrightarrow{v_2}, \ldots$ by applying f at each iteration. Since $\overrightarrow{v} \leq f(\overrightarrow{v})$ component-wise for any vector $\overrightarrow{v}$, we have $\overrightarrow{v_0} \leq \overrightarrow{v_1}$ component-wise. Since f is non-decreasing, we deduce that $f(\overrightarrow{v_0}) \leq f(\overrightarrow{v_1})$ component-wise, that is $\overrightarrow{v_1} \leq \overrightarrow{v_2}$. By induction, we obtain that the sequence $\overrightarrow{v_0}, \overrightarrow{v_1}, \overrightarrow{v_2}, \ldots$ is non-decreasing. Since this sequence is upper bounded by the vector of ones, it has some limit $\overrightarrow{v}^\star$ in $[0,1]^K$, showing that the algorithm converges.

To prove that $\overrightarrow{v}^\star$ is a fixed point of f, we use the continuity of f, which again follows from the fact that the aggregation functions involved in f and the *max* operator are continuous. We have:

$$f(\overrightarrow{v}^\star) = f(\lim_{t\rightarrow\infty} \overrightarrow{v_t}) = \lim_{t\rightarrow\infty} f(\overrightarrow{v_t}) = \lim_{t\rightarrow\infty} \overrightarrow{v_{t+1}} = \overrightarrow{v}^\star.$$

Finally, $\overrightarrow{v}^\star$ is the least fixed point of f because for any other fixed point of f, say $\overrightarrow{v}$, we have $\overrightarrow{v_0} = 0 \leq \overrightarrow{v}$ and thus $\overrightarrow{v_1} = f(\overrightarrow{v_0}) \leq f(\overrightarrow{v}) = \overrightarrow{v}$ component-wise. By induction, we get $\overrightarrow{v_{t+1}} = f(\overrightarrow{v_t}) \leq f(\overrightarrow{v}) = \overrightarrow{v}$ component-wise for all $t \geq 0$. Taking the limit gives $\overrightarrow{v}^\star \leq \overrightarrow{v}$ component-wise. □

Our result extends to the scenario where some or all output variables have an initial value that shall not be undercut. It suffices to add a rule of the form $c \Rightarrow x$ for each output variable x with initial value c. This allows for an alternative definition of a recursive FIS: A recursive FIS is a set of rules of the form $P_1 \wedge \ldots \wedge P_n \stackrel{\phi}{\Longrightarrow} C$, where ϕ is an aggregation function, and $P_1, \ldots, P_n$ and C are variables, each of which has an initial value in $[0,1]$. A solution is then an assignment of each variable to a value so that (1) all variables have values that are larger than or equal to their initial value, (2) all rules are satisfied, and (3) no variable can be assigned a smaller value and still satisfy all rules. Such an alternative FIS can be translated to a FIS according to Definition 2 by considering all variables that appear in conclusions as output variables, considering the others as input variables, and adding a rule $c \Rightarrow x$ for any output variable x with initial value c.

5 FLORA

We now apply our framework of Fuzzy Logic to the task of KG alignment. We first extend the notion of functionality to relation lists, which is exploited in FLORA to align entities that are objects of multiple facts.

5.1 Relation Lists

For an alphabetically sorted list $R = (r_1, \dots, r_n)$ of relations, a list of head-entities $H = (h_1, \dots, h_n)$, and a tail entity t, we define $R(H,t)$ as the boolean proposition that all corresponding facts exist:

$$R(H,t) := r_1(h_1,t) \wedge \ldots \wedge r_n(h_n,t).$$

By convention, the head entities corresponding to the same relation are sorted in alphabetic order. This ensures that there is a unique way to write $R(H,t)$ even if several relations in R are identical. We can then define the functionality of the relation list R as:

$$\mathit{fun}(R) = \frac{|\{H \mid \exists t,\ R(H,t)\}|}{|\{(H,t) \mid R(H,t)\}|}$$

For instance, the relations *BirthDateOf* and *FamilyNameOf* are themselves not functional, but their combination is, as few people have both the same birth date and family name. Similarly, the local functionality of relation list R and entity list H is defined as:

$$\mathit{fun}(R,H) = \frac{1}{|\{t \mid R(H,t)\}|}$$

We have $\mathit{fun}(R,H) = 1$ if and only if there is a unique tail entity t such that $R(H,t)$ is *true*. Again, this notion is used to cope with relation lists that are globally functional, but have local exceptions.

5.2 Alignment Rules

In order to align two KGs $\mathcal{G}$ and $\mathcal{G}'$, we construct a recursive Fuzzy Inference System. The key insight, similar to PARIS [39], is the following: If there exist facts $r(h,t)$ and $r'(h',t')$ such that entities h, h' have already been matched and r, r' are functional, then entities t, t' are matched. FLORA goes beyond PARIS by generalizing this insight to lists of relations, by embedding it in the framework of Fuzzy Logic, and by proving its convergence.

Entity alignment. For each pair of entities $t \in \mathcal{E}$ and $t' \in \mathcal{E}'$ that are not literals, and for each list of relations R and list of head entities H with $R(H,t)$ in $\mathcal{G}$, and for each list of relations R' and list of head entities H' with $R'(H',t)$ in $\mathcal{G}'$, we use:

$$\begin{aligned} &R(H,t) \wedge R'(H',t') \wedge H \equiv H' \wedge R \cong R' \\ &\quad \wedge \mathit{fun}(R) \wedge \mathit{fun}(R,H) \wedge \mathit{fun}(R') \wedge \mathit{fun}(R',H') \quad \overset{\text{min}}{\Longrightarrow} \quad t \equiv t' \end{aligned} \tag{1}$$

Here, $R(H,t)$ and $R'(H',t')$ are input variables whose value is, by construction, 1. $H \equiv H'$ is an output variable that is implied by the equivalences of each pair of head entities of H and H' through the following rule:

$$h_1 \equiv h_1' \wedge \ldots \wedge h_n \equiv h_n' \quad \overset{\text{hmean}}{\Longrightarrow} \quad H \equiv H'$$

The premises of this rule are either themselves output variables of other rules, or literals, whose similarity is computed upfront (see Sect. 5.3). The aggregation function of this rule is the harmonic mean *hmean*, which allows taking into account high evidence (which would be ignored if we used the minimum) while penalizing strong conjunctions with low evidence (unlike the arithmetic mean).

The term $R \cong R'$ is an output variable that means "R is similar to R'". It is constrained by the following rule:

$$r_1 \cong r_1' \wedge \ldots \wedge r_n \cong r_n' \quad \overset{\text{hmean}}{\Longrightarrow} \quad R \cong R'$$

Here, each statement of the form $r \cong r'$ is itself an output variable, which is implied by two rules as follows:

$$r \subseteq r' \quad \Longrightarrow \quad r \cong r'$$
$$r' \subseteq r \quad \Longrightarrow \quad r \cong r'$$

This means that two relations are considered similar if one is a subrelation of the other (and aggregation is the identity function as there is only one premise).

The functionality terms are input variables whose values correspond to the functionality or local functionality of the respective lists of relations. Note that we cannot resort to local functionality only, due to the incompleteness of KGs. For example, people generally have two parents. If one person happens to have only a single parent in one KG, and a single parent in the other, this does not entitle us to match these two parents (as one could be, e.g., the mother and the other the father). The imposition of global functionality avoids such matches. We cannot use only global functionality either, as a globally functional relationship (such as *hasCapital*) can be non-functional in some cases (such as *South Africa*).

Finally, $t \equiv t'$ is an output variable that determines to what degree t and t' are matched. We use the *min* aggregation function to make sure all premises of the rule are fulfilled (and a strong premise cannot make up for a weak one).

Subrelation alignment. To find that one relation $r \in \mathcal{R}$ is a subrelation of another relation $r' \in \mathcal{R}'$, we first build the following rule for all entities $h, t \in \mathcal{E}, h', t' \in \mathcal{E}'$ with $r(h,t), r'(h',t')$:

$$r(h,t) \wedge r'(h',t') \wedge h \equiv h' \wedge t \equiv t' \quad \overset{\text{min}}{\Longrightarrow} \quad r \equiv_{h,t} r'$$

As before, $r(h,t), r'(h',t')$ are input variables that evaluate to 1 by construction, while $h \equiv h'$ and $t \equiv t'$ are output variables of Eq. 1. Then $r \equiv_{h,t} r'$ is an output variable that says that r and r' coincide on h and t. The subrelation alignment can then be written as:

$$\bigwedge_{h,t:\, r(h,t)} r \equiv_{h,t} r' \quad \overset{\alpha\text{-mean}}{\Longrightarrow} \quad r \subseteq r' \tag{2}$$

This rule means that r is a subrelation of r' if all facts of r are also facts of r'. To make the degree of $r \subseteq r'$ reflect the proportion of facts of r that are facts of r', we use the arithmetic mean as the aggregation function. However, the arithmetic mean alone is not enough: Under the Open World Assumption, the KG $\mathcal{G}'$ can be incomplete. Thus, some facts $r'(h', t')$ might be missing, which would jeopardise our subrelation alignment. Therefore, we multiply the arithmetic mean by a constant α, which we call the *benefit of the doubt* (we show different values of α in our experiments). The aggregation function α-mean is then the arithmetic mean multiplied by α and capped to $[0, 1]$.

5.3 Algorithm

Our method for KG alignment is shown in Fig. 2. It receives as input two knowledge graphs to be matched, optionally with training data.

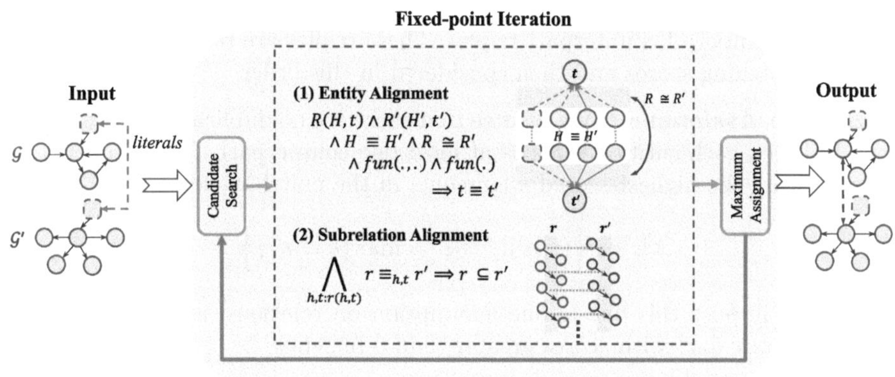

Fig. 2. Knowledge Graph Alignment with FLORA.

Initialization. We first compute the similarities between the literals of the two KGs (see details below). All literal similarity values are computed only once, belong to $[0, 1]$, and remain fixed throughout the algorithm. We integrate training data in the same way: If two entities are matched in the training data, we set their matching score to 1, and treat this match as an input variable that will never be changed. To bootstrap the rule of entity alignment of Eq. 1, relation similarities are initially set to some small value θ_r. This value is superseded by the value of the subrelation alignment of Eq. 2 in the following iterations.

Fixed Point Iteration. After initialization, the steps of entity alignment (Eq. 1) and subrelation alignment (Eq. 2) are applied alternately. If multiple rules imply the same output variable, its score is the maximum of the rule strengths, in line with Algorithm 1. Since all our aggregation functions are continuous and non-decreasing, Theorem 1 applies after the first iteration (when initial values have been set for both entity and relation alignments), proving the convergence of the iterative process to the solution of the corresponding FIS.

5.4 Implementation Details

Similarity Between Literals. The similarity between strings is computed by a (small) language model. To reduce the computational cost, we identify, for each string literal, its most similar string counterparts in the other KG by cosine similarity, and retain only those above some threshold θ_s. Dates are matched exactly, and numbers are matched with a similarity score of 1 if they are approximately equal within a relative error of 10^{-9}. While more complex matching strategies for dates are possible, experiments in Sect. 6 show that FLORA performs well even with simple exact matching.

Candidate Search. Performing a full search over all possible entity and relation combinations would be prohibitively expensive. Therefore, we first perform a candidate search to identify the most structurally similar counterpart for each entity. Specifically, we select for each entity $t \in \mathcal{E}$ those entities $t' \in \mathcal{E}'$ with the maximum number of counterpart triples. These triples are ranked in decreasing order of matching scores and then considered in this order.

Maximum Assignment. We assume that there are no duplicate entities within each KG, i.e., each entity $e \in \mathcal{E}$ has at most one counterpart $e' \in \mathcal{E}'$. Therefore, we store only the highest-scored alignments in the matching set:

$$\mathcal{M}_e \leftarrow \left\{(e, e')|e \equiv e' = \max_{e''}\{e \equiv e''\}\right\} \quad (3)$$

We do not impose this one-to-one assumption on relations, and thus store all relation pairs $r \subseteq r'$ with scores greater than 0 in $\mathcal{M}_r$.

Final Alignment. The iterations terminate when the total matching score increases by less than some threshold ε (early stopping). We keep only those entity matches that exceed a threshold $\theta_e \in [0, 1]$. The final alignment between two relations r and r' can be a subrelation $r \subseteq r'$, a superrelation $r \supseteq r'$, or an equivalence $r \equiv r'$ if both $r \subseteq r'$ and $r' \subseteq r$ holds.

6 Experiments

6.1 Experimental Setup

Datasets. We evaluate FLORA on five widely-adopted entity alignment datasets, including two monolingual datasets (D-W-15K-V1/V2) from OpenEA [43] and three cross-lingual datasets from DBP15K [40]. D-W-15K is based on DBpedia and Wikidata and comes in two versions: Sparse version (D-W-15K-V1) and Dense version (D-W-15K-V2). DBP15K consists of three cross-lingual KG pairs extracted from DBpedia: Chinese and English (DBP_{ZH-EN}), Japanese and English (DBP_{JA-EN}), French and English (DBP_{FR-EN}). For holistic evaluation, we also include two datasets from the OAEI Knowledge Graph Track [19], memoryalpha-stexpanded (Mem-ST) and starwars-swtor (Star-SWT), which have non-trivial matches for relations, classes, and instances.

Parameters. As in PARIS [39], the relation similarity of FLORA is initialized to $\theta_r = 0.1$. We choose the benefit of doubt as $\alpha = 3$ (we show other values in the ablation study). We choose $\theta_s = 0.7$ and $\theta_e = 0.1$, which maximizes the F1 value in our experiments (a smaller value favors recall, a larger value favors precision). Early stopping is set to $\varepsilon = 0.01$ (a smaller value improves precision but increases the execution time). Regarding the language models used for string similarity, we use LaBSE[3] [15] for the multilingual datasets, and PEARL[4] [7] for the monolingual datasets (because of its good performance on phrases).

Evaluation Metrics. On D-W-15K-V1/V2 and the OAEI KGs Track, we use standard classification-based metrics (Precision, Recall, F1), while on DBP15K, we follow existing EA baselines by reporting Hit@K and MRR, which measure top-K accuracy and mean reciprocal rank, respectively. To evaluate our model in ranking-based metrics, we directly output all possible entity pairs with scores instead of selecting the top-scoring ones.

Competitors. We select more than 30 competitors. For the EA task, we include the supervised methods JAPE [40], BootEA [41], RDGCN [51], OntoEA [52], PARIS+ [29], RHGN [31], GCNAlign [50], TransEdge [42], FuzzyEA [24], SelfKG [30], AttrGNN [33], TEA [60], SDEA [61], LLMEA [56], ChatEA [25] and the unsupervised methods AttrE [48], PARIS [39], PRASE [37], FGWEA [37], NALA [55], LLM4EA [8], CPL-OT [11], MultiKE [58], ICLEA [57], BERT-INT [45], HLMEA [27], and EmbMatch, a simple method using embedding similarity between entity names. For BERT-INT, which uses entity descriptions, we replace the descriptions with entity names for a fair comparison, following [61]. For holistic KG alignment, we choose classical methods LogMap [26], AML [14], and the most recent ATMatcher [20], ALOD2Vec [35], and Wiktionary [36]. We report the results available from the original papers.

6.2 Overall Results

Table 1 shows the results on monolingual EA in both unsupervised and supervised settings. FLORA achieves considerable improvements over all baselines, with and without training data. Table 2 shows the results for multi-lingual EA. FLORA consistently performs the best or the second-best across all datasets. FLORA does not beat FGWEA, which is designed for multilingual datasets and exploits the name bias present in such benchmarks [33]. Therefore, FGWEA performs worse than FLORA when entity names are incomplete, as observed in the monolingual EA datasets. FGWEA further assumes that each entity of one KG has one match in the other KG, which is not representative of real-world scenarios. Regarding ChatEA, it is supervised and additionally uses the background knowledge of LLMs to generate entity descriptions. In contrast, FLORA is unsupervised, relies solely on the given KGs data, and needs only a small language model for string similarity. Overall, the difference of FLORA to the

[3] https://huggingface.co/sentence-transformers/LaBSE.
[4] https://huggingface.co/Lihuchen/pearl_small.

Table 1. Performance comparison on the OpenEA datasets (monolingual)

Category	Method	D-W-15K-V1			D-W-15K-V2		
		Precision	Recall	F1	Precision	Recall	F1
Supervised	JAPE	0.250	0.250	0.250	0.262	0.262	0.262
	BootEA	0.572	0.572	0.572	0.821	0.821	0.821
	RHGN	0.560	0.753	0.644	-	-	-
	OntoEA	0.591	0.591	0.591	0.814	0.814	0.814
	PARIS+	0.965	0.746	0.841	0.976	0.903	0.938
	Ours	**0.967**	**0.856**	**0.908**	**0.985**	**0.966**	**0.975**
Unsupervised	EmbMatch	0.461	0.452	0.456	0.515	0.509	0.512
	AttrE	0.299	0.299	0.299	0.489	0.489	0.489
	PARIS	0.953	0.726	0.824	0.950	0.850	0.897
	PRASE	0.918	0.809	0.860	0.948	0.900	0.923
	FGWEA	0.933	0.725	0.816	0.952	0.903	0.927
	NALA	-	-	-	0.917	0.908	0.912
	LLM4EA	0.472	0.472	0.472	0.907	0.816	0.859
	Ours	**0.954**	**0.838**	**0.893**	**0.978**	**0.947**	**0.962**

best performer is less than 1% point – a price we pay for a fully transparent unsupervised algorithm that works across different scenarios.

Table 3 further shows the performance of FLORA on the KG alignment task. FLORA achieves the highest overall F1 score with an average of 96%, outperforming competitors for the alignment of classes, relations, and instances. It falls within 2% points of the best model for relation matching precision on the Star-SWT dataset. This slight drop is because FLORA finds structural matches (*apprentice* matches *padawan*, which also means apprentice) rather than the intended semantic matches (*apprentice* matches *apprentices*).

6.3 Analysis

Ablation Study. We first experimented with different values of the benefit-of-doubt parameter α (see Fig. 3). We find that setting $\alpha = 1$ is ineffective and leads to a significant reduction in performance, thus proving the necessity of $\alpha > 1$. Beyond $\alpha = 2$, the performance does not change much while computation time first decreases and then remains stable. However, a larger α does not necessarily yield better results, as the performance degrades once α goes beyond 100 (see Table 4). In practice, we set $\alpha = 3$ to balance effectiveness and efficiency. We also replaced the language model used for string similarity by simple string identity (see Table 4). This leads to an overall performance drop, especially on DBP_{ZH-EN}, where entities have very different literal values across languages. But even with identity literal initialization, the score drops by 3%

Table 2. Performance comparison on the DBP15K dataset across three language pairs (ZH-EN, JA-EN, FR-EN). Group (I) are structure-only methods, Group (II) uses both structure and entity names, Group (III) jointly uses relational triples, attribute triples, and entity names, and Group (IV) is LLM-based.

Group	Method		DBP_{ZH-EN}			DBP_{JA-EN}			DBP_{FR-EN}		
			Hit@1	Hit@10	MRR	Hit@1	Hit@10	MRR	Hit@1	Hit@10	MRR
I	GCNAlign	S	0.413	0.744	0.549	0.399	0.745	0.546	0.373	0.745	0.532
	BootEA	SS	0.629	0.848	0.703	0.622	0.854	0.701	0.653	0.874	0.731
	TransEdge	S	0.735	0.919	0.801	0.719	0.932	0.795	0.710	0.941	0.796
II	RDGCN	S	0.708	0.846	0.749	0.767	0.895	0.812	0.886	0.957	0.908
	FuzzyEA	S	0.863	0.984	0.909	0.898	0.985	0.933	0.977	0.998	0.986
	SelfKG	U	0.745	0.866	0.782	0.816	0.913	0.844	0.957	0.992	0.971
	CPL-OT	U	0.911	0.950	0.930	0.945	0.976	0.960	0.986	0.992	0.990
	SEU	U	0.900	0.965	0.924	0.956	0.991	0.969	0.988	0.999	0.992
III	AttrGNN	S	0.796	0.929	0.845	0.783	0.921	0.834	0.919	0.978	0.910
	TEA	S	0.941	0.983	0.960	0.941	0.979	0.959	0.979	0.997	0.991
	SDEA	S	0.871	0.966	0.912	0.848	0.952	0.890	0.969	0.995	0.981
	MultiKE	U	0.509	0.576	0.532	0.393	0.489	0.432	0.639	0.712	0.665
	ICLEA	U	0.884	0.972	-	0.924	0.978	-	0.991	0.999	-
	$BERT\text{-}INT_{name}$	U	0.814	0.835	0.820	0.806	0.835	0.821	0.987	0.992	0.990
	FGWEA	U	**0.976**	**0.994**	**0.983**	**0.978**	**0.992**	**0.988**	**0.997**	**0.999**	**0.998**
	Ours	U	**0.976**	0.988	0.981	0.967	0.979	0.972	0.992	0.997	0.993
IV	HLMEA	U	0.930	-	0.934	0.938	-	0.950	**0.986**	-	0.989
	LLMEA	S	0.890	0.923	-	0.911	0.946	-	0.957	0.977	-
	ChatEA	S	**0.980**	-	**0.984**	**0.985**	-	**0.993**	-	-	-

points at most, and FLORA still outperforms strong baselines such as RDGCN and SelfKG, underscoring the strength of our structural matching. Next, we restrict the list of relations in entity alignment (Eq. 1) to length 1, thereby removing the structural signal from our rules. In this setting, our system can propagate only alignment scores through flat triples, similar to PARIS [39]. This significantly degrades performance, demonstrating the importance of structural information in the absence of functional relations. Finally, using the *min* aggregation function for all inference rules significantly degrades the performance across all datasets.

Explainability. A salient feature of FLORA is that its results are interpretable by humans. For any pair of aligned entities, the corresponding rule with the highest firing strength, as given by Eq. 1, explains the alignment. In the dataset D-W-15K-V1 for instance, the entities t=*Lady Gaga* of DBPedia and t'=Q19848 of Wikidata are aligned with a value of 0.984. The rule leading to this alignment states that Lady Gaga was born on *1986-03-28* and featured in the song *3-Way*;

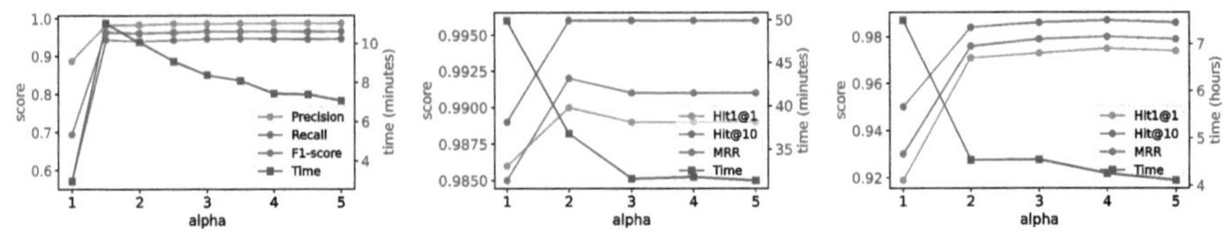

(a) D-W-15K-V2 (b) $\text{DBP}_{\text{FR-EN}}$ (c) $\text{DBP}_{\text{ZH-EN}}$

Fig. 3. Sensitivity to the benefit of doubt α

Table 3. Performance comparison on datasets from OAEI

		Class			Relation			Instance			Overall		
		Prec.	Rec.	F1	Prec.	Rec.	F1	Prec.	Rec.	F1	Prec.	Rec.	F1
Mem-ST	BaselineLabel	1.00	0.46	0.63	0.97	0.68	0.80	0.98	0.84	0.91	0.98	0.83	0.90
	LogMap	0.78	0.54	0.64	-	-	-	0.88	0.77	0.82	0.88	0.75	0.81
	AML	1.00	0.69	0.82	0.89	0.80	0.85	0.93	0.93	0.93	0.93	0.92	0.93
	ATMatcher	1.00	0.77	0.87	0.95	0.95	0.95	0.96	0.92	0.94	0.96	0.92	0.94
	ALOD2Vec	1.00	0.62	0.76	0.87	0.95	0.91	0.92	0.93	0.93	0.92	0.93	0.92
	Wiktionary	1.00	0.62	0.76	0.87	0.95	0.91	0.92	0.93	0.93	0.92	0.93	0.92
	Ours	**1.00**	**0.85**	**0.92**	**0.98**	**0.98**	**0.98**	**0.96**	**0.95**	**0.95**	**0.96**	**0.95**	**0.95**
Star-SWT	BaselineLabel	1.00	0.80	0.89	**1.00**	0.89	0.94	0.95	0.84	0.89	0.95	0.84	0.89
	LogMap	1.00	0.73	0.85	-	-	-	0.94	0.78	0.86	0.94	0.75	0.84
	AML	1.00	0.87	0.93	0.98	0.71	0.82	0.93	0.90	0.92	0.93	0.90	0.91
	ATMatcher	1.00	0.87	0.93	**1.00**	0.98	**0.99**	0.94	0.91	0.92	0.95	0.91	0.93
	ALOD2Vec	1.00	0.87	0.93	0.98	0.98	0.98	0.92	0.91	0.92	0.93	0.92	0.92
	Wiktionary	1.00	0.87	0.93	0.98	0.98	0.98	0.92	0.91	0.92	0.93	0.92	0.92
	Ours	**1.00**	**1.00**	**1.00**	0.98	**0.98**	0.98	**0.98**	**0.96**	**0.97**	**0.98**	**0.96**	**0.97**

Table 4. Ablation studies of FLORA on various datasets

Method	D-W-15K-V1			D-Y-15K-V2			$\text{DBP}_{\text{FR-EN}}$			$\text{DBP}_{\text{ZH-EN}}$		
	Prec.	Rec.	F1	Prec.	Rec.	F1	Hit@1	Hit@10	MRR	Hit@1	Hit@10	MRR
FLORA	**0.954**	**0.838**	**0.893**	**0.978**	**0.947**	**0.962**	**0.992**	**0.997**	**0.993**	**0.976**	**0.988**	**0.981**
- w/o literal similarity	0.939	0.797	0.862	0.962	0.925	0.943	0.975	0.983	0.977	0.947	0.965	0.951
- w/o list of relations	0.894	0.604	0.721	0.918	0.628	0.756	0.933	0.964	0.944	0.700	0.852	0.757
- with *min* aggregation	0.564	0.524	0.543	0.659	0.626	0.641	0.894	0.949	0.912	0.547	0.778	0.632
- with $\alpha = 100$	0.940	0.807	0.868	0.956	0.928	0.937	0.974	0.985	0.976	0.871	0.935	0.898

it is the alignment of the relations *musicalArtist* $\cong$ P175 and $birthDate^{-1} \cong$ P569^{-1}, the functionality of the corresponding relation set, and the alignment of the birth dates and of the entities *3-Way* and Q659417, that lead to the final alignment of *Lady Gaga* and Q19848.

Table 5. Performance comparison on the OpenEA 100K datasets (monolingual)

Method	Supervised	D-W-100K-V1			D-W-100K-V2		
		Precision	Recall	F1	Precision	Recall	F1
RDGCN	Yes	0.362	0.362	0.362	0.421	0.421	0.421
BootEA	Yes	0.516	0.516	0.516	0.766	0.766	0.766
PARIS	No	0.934	0.644	0.762	0.933	0.796	0.859
PRASE	No	-	-	-	0.927	0.855	0.890
NALA	No	0.732	0.732	0.732	0.919	0.919	0.919
FLORA	No	**0.937**	**0.773**	**0.847**	**0.970**	**0.929**	**0.949**

Scalability and Efficiency. Finally, we evaluate the scalability and efficiency of our approach. For scalability, we use a larger-scale entity alignment dataset from OpenEA, D-W-100K (with 100k gold alignments). As shown in Table 5, FLORA outperforms both advanced unsupervised and supervised baselines.

For efficiency, we measured the run time of FLORA on datasets of different sizes from our previous experiments, using a Linux server with an AMD EPYC 9374F CPU and 519 GB of RAM. FLORA takes approximately 7 min on D-W-15K(V1/V2) and 48 min on the larger dataset D-W-100K-V1. This is comparable to most state-of-the-art methods [43]. However, the other methods are executed in GPUs, while our approach needs only CPUs. On the DBP15K datasets, FLORA is much slower than on the D-W-15K datasets, with around 2 h on average. This is likely due to the amount of auxiliary information (i.e., attribute values), which is about five times larger in the DBP15K datasets than in the D-W-15K datasets. On the OAEI KG Track datasets, FLORA completes the alignment process in about 1h45min. This is much slower than the runtime of lexical-based methods (e.g., 4 min on average for ALOD2Vec) that has been reported by the OAEI platform on a virtual machine with 32 GB of RAM and 16 vCPUs (2.4 GHz) [1]. This is because FLORA relies more on structural reasoning, which, in turn, leads to better performance, allows for explainability, and can find not only relation equivalence but also relation subsumption.

7 Conclusion and Future Work

In this paper, we have introduced FLORA, an iterative method based on Fuzzy Logic that aligns entities and relations across knowledge graphs. FLORA provably converges to the solution of the corresponding Fuzzy Inference System. It can find subrelation matches, it can deal with dangling entities, it does not need training data, and it provides interpretable results. Comparative experiments on major EA and KG alignment benchmarks show that FLORA outperforms all competitors on nearly all datasets. Future work could extend FLORA to more complex taxonomy structures, for example, by exploring cross-KGs subclasses, computing deductive closures, and taking into account the graph structure.

Supplementary Material Statement. The dataset, source code, supplementary material, and hyperparameters are available at our GitHub repository https://github.com/dig-team/FLORA.

References

1. Abd, M., et al.: Results of the D2021 ⋆. In: Shvaiko, P., Digitale, T., Euzenat, I.J., Alpes, I..U.G., Jiménez-Ruiz, F.E., City, of London, U., SIRIUS, U.., of Oslo, U., Hassanzadeh, N.O., Research, I., Trojahn, U.C., IRIT, France (eds.) Proceedings of the 16th International Workshop on Ontology Matching co-located with the 20th International Semantic Web Conference (ISWC 2021). vol. 3063, pp. 62–108. Ceur Workshop Proceedings, Virtual conference, United States (Oct 2021). https://hal.inrae.fr/hal-05007937
2. Abi Akl, H.: PSYCHIC: A neuro-symbolic framework for knowledge graph question-answering grounding. In: ISWC 2023-International Semantic Web Conference (2023)
3. Baaz, M., Preining, N., Zach, R.: First-order gödel logics. Ann. Pure Appl. Logic **147**(1–2), 23–47 (2007)
4. Bach, S.H., Broecheler, M., Huang, B., Getoor, L.: Hinge-loss Markov random fields and probabilistic soft logic. J. Mach. Learn. Res. **18**(109), 1–67 (2017)
5. Chen, H., et al.: Macro graph neural networks for online billion-scale recommender systems. In: Proceedings of the ACM web conference 2024, pp. 3598–3608 (2024)
6. Chen, J., et al.: Learning short-term differences and long-term dependencies for entity alignment. In: Pan, J.Z., Tamma, V., d'Amato, C., Janowicz, K., Fu, B., Polleres, A., Seneviratne, O., Kagal, L. (eds.) ISWC 2020. LNCS, vol. 12506, pp. 92–109. Springer, Cham (2020). https://doi.org/10.1007/978-3-030-62419-4_6
7. Chen, L., Varoquaux, G., Suchanek, F.M.: Learning high-quality and general-purpose phrase representations (PEARL). In: EACL (2024)
8. Chen, S., Zhang, Q., Dong, J., Hua, W., Li, Q., Huang, X.: Entity alignment with noisy annotations from large language models. In: The Thirty-eighth Annual Conference on Neural Information Processing Systems (2024)
9. Chen, Z., et al.: Rethinking uncertainly missing and ambiguous visual modality in multi-modal entity alignment. In: International Semantic Web Conference (ISWC), pp. 121–139. Springer (2023)
10. Dickens, C., Augustine, E.: Negative weights in hinge-loss Markov random fields. In: Workshop on Tractable Probabilistic Modeling (TPM) (2021)
11. Ding, Q., Zhang, D., Yin, J.: Conflict-aware pseudo labeling via optimal transport for entity alignment. In: 2022 IEEE International Conference on Data Mining (ICDM), pp. 915–920. IEEE (2022)
12. Dong, J., Zhang, Q., Huang, X., Duan, K., Tan, Q., Jiang, Z.: Hierarchy-aware multi-hop question answering over knowledge graphs. In: Proceedings of the ACM web conference 2023, pp. 2519–2527 (2023)
13. Euzenat, J., Shvaiko, P.: Ontology matching. Springer (2007)
14. Faria, D., Santos, E., Balasubramani, B.S., Silva, M.C., Couto, F.M., Pesquita, C.: Agreementmakerlight. Semantic Web **16**(2), SW–233304 (2025)
15. Feng, F., Yang, Y., Cer, D., Arivazhagan, N., Wang, W.: Language-agnostic bert sentence embedding. In: Proceedings of the 60th Annual Meeting of the Association for Computational Linguistics (Volume 1: Long Papers), pp. 878–891 (2022)

16. Fernández, S., Velasco, J.R., Marsa-Maestre, I., Lopez-Carmona, M.A.: Fuzzyalign-a fuzzy method for ontology alignment. In: International Conference on Knowledge Engineering and Ontology Development. vol. 2, pp. 98–107. SciTePress (2012)
17. Fodor, J.: Left-continuous t-norms in fuzzy logic: an overview. Acta Polytechnica Hungarica **1**(2), 35–47 (2004)
18. Gosselin, F., Zouaq, A.: SORBET: a Siamese network for ontology embeddings using a distance-based regression loss and BERT. In: International Semantic Web Conference (ISWC), pp. 561–578. Springer (2023)
19. Hertling, S., Paulheim, H.: The knowledge graph track at OAEI-gold standards, baselines, and the golden hammer bias. In: The Semantic Web - 17th International Conference, ESWC (2020)
20. Hertling, S., Paulheim, H.: ATBox results for OAEI 2021. In: CEUR Workshop Proceedings. vol. 3063, pp. 137–143. RWTH Aachen (2021)
21. Hertling, S., Paulheim, H.: OLaLa: Ontology matching with large language models. In: Proceedings of the 12th Knowledge Capture Conference 2023, pp. 131–139 (2023)
22. Hnatkowska, B., Kozierkiewicz, A., Pietranik, M.: Fuzzy logic framework for ontology instance alignment. In: International Conference on Computational Science, pp. 653–666. Springer (2022)
23. Huang, S., Hu, C., Kong, W., Liu, Y.: Disentangled contrastive learning for knowledge-aware recommender system. In: International Semantic Web Conference (ISWC), pp. 140–158. Springer (2023)
24. Jiang, W., Liu, Y., Deng, X.: Fuzzy entity alignment via knowledge embedding with awareness of uncertainty measure. Neurocomputing **468**, 97–110 (2022)
25. Jiang, X., et al.: Unlocking the power of large language models for entity alignment. In: Proceedings of the 62nd Annual Meeting of the Association for Computational Linguistics (Volume 1: Long Papers), pp. 7566–7583 (2024)
26. Jiménez-Ruiz, E., Cuenca Grau, B.: LogMap: Logic-based and scalable ontology matching. In: International Semantic Web Conference (ISWC), pp. 273–288. Springer (2011)
27. Jin, X., et al.: HLMEA: Unsupervised entity alignment based on hybrid language models. In: Proceedings of the AAAI Conference on Artificial Intelligence. vol. 39, pp. 11888–11896 (2025)
28. Kozierkiewicz, A., Pietranik, M., Jankowiak, W.: Fuzzy logic framework for ontology concepts alignment. In: Asian Conference on Intelligent Information and Database Systems, pp. 170–182. Springer (2023)
29. Leone, M., Huber, S., Arora, A., García-Durán, A., West, R.: A critical re-evaluation of neural methods for entity alignment. Proc. VLDB Endowment **15**(8), 1712–1725 (2022)
30. s Liu, X., Hong, H., Wang, X., Chen, Z., Kharlamov, E., Dong, Y., Tang, J.: SelfKG: self-supervised entity alignment in knowledge graphs. In: Proceedings of the ACM Web Conference 2022, pp. 860–870 (2022)
31. Liu, X., et al.: RHGN: Relation-gated heterogeneous graph network for entity alignment in knowledge graphs. In: Findings of the Association for Computational Linguistics: ACL 2023, pp. 8683–8696 (2023)
32. Liu, Y., Wan, Y., He, L., Peng, H., Yu, P.S.: KG-BART: knowledge graph-augmented bart for generative commonsense reasoning. In: Proceedings of the AAAI Conference on Artificial Intelligence, vol. 35, pp. 6418–6425 (2021)

33. Liu, Z., Cao, Y., Pan, L., Li, J., Chua, T.S.: Exploring and evaluating attributes, values, and structures for entity alignment. In: Proceedings of the 2020 Conference on Empirical Methods in Natural Language Processing (EMNLP), pp. 6355–6364 (2020)
34. Mao, X., Wang, W., Wu, Y., Lan, M.: From alignment to assignment: frustratingly simple unsupervised entity alignment. In: Proceedings of the 2021 Conference on Empirical Methods in Natural Language Processing, pp. 2843–2853 (2021)
35. Portisch, J., Paulheim, H.: ALOD2vec matcher results for OAEI 2021. In: CEUR Workshop Proceedings. vol. 3063, pp. 117–123. RWTH Aachen (2022)
36. Portisch, J., Paulheim, H.: Wiktionary matcher results for OAEI 2021. In: CEUR Workshop Proceedings, vol. 3063, pp. 199–206. RWTH Aachen (2022)
37. Qi, Z., et al.: Unsupervised knowledge graph alignment by probabilistic reasoning and semantic embedding. In: International Joint Conference on Artificial Intelligence (2021)
38. Sabri, N.: Fuzzy inference system: Short review and design. International Review of Automatic Control (01 2013)
39. Suchanek, F.M., Abiteboul, S., Senellart, P.: PARIS: probabilistic alignment of relations, instances, and schema. Proc. VLDB Endowment **5**(3) (2011)
40. Sun, Z., Hu, W., Li, C.: Cross-lingual entity alignment via joint attribute-preserving embedding. In: International semantic web conference (ISWC), pp. 628–644. Springer (2017)
41. Sun, Z., Hu, W., Zhang, Q., Qu, Y.: Bootstrapping entity alignment with knowledge graph embedding. In: IJCAI, vol. 18 (2018)
42. Sun, Z., Huang, J., Hu, W., Chen, M., Guo, L., Qu, Y.: TransEdge: translating relation-contextualized embeddings for knowledge graphs. In: Ghidini, C., et al. (eds.) ISWC 2019. LNCS, vol. 11778, pp. 612–629. Springer, Cham (2019). https://doi.org/10.1007/978-3-030-30793-6_35
43. Sun, Z., Zhang, Q., Hu, W., Wang, C., Chen, M., Akrami, F., Li, C.: A benchmarking study of embedding-based entity alignment for knowledge graphs. Proc. VLDB Endowment **13**(11) (2020)
44. Tang, J., Zhao, K., Li, J.: A fused gromov-wasserstein framework for unsupervised knowledge graph entity alignment. In: 61st Annual Meeting of the Association for Computational Linguistics, ACL 2023, pp. 3320–3334. Association for Computational Linguistics (ACL) (2023)
45. Tang, X., Zhang, J., Chen, B., Yang, Y., Chen, H., Li, C.: BERT-INT: a bert-based interaction model for knowledge graph alignment. In: Proceedings of the Twenty-Ninth International Conference on International Joint Conferences on Artificial Intelligence, pp. 3174–3180 (2021)
46. Tarski, A.: A lattice-theoretical fixpoint theorem and its applications. Pacific J. Math. (1955)
47. Todorov, K., Hudelot, C., Popescu, A., Geibel, P.: Fuzzy ontology alignment using background knowledge. Internat. J. Uncertain. Fuzziness Knowl.-Based Syst. **22**(01), 75–112 (2014)
48. Trisedya, B.D., Qi, J., Zhang, R.: Entity alignment between knowledge graphs using attribute embeddings. In: Proceedings of the AAAI Conference on Artificial Intelligence, vol. 33, pp. 297–304 (2019)
49. Wang, Y., et al.: Facing changes: continual entity alignment for growing knowledge graphs. In: International Semantic Web Conference (ISWC), pp. 196–213. Springer (2022)

50. Wang, Z., Lv, Q., Lan, X., Zhang, Y.: Cross-lingual knowledge graph alignment via graph convolutional networks. In: Proceedings of the 2018 Conference on Empirical Methods in Natural Language Processing, pp. 349–357 (2018)
51. Wu, Y., Liu, X., Feng, Y., Wang, Z., Yan, R., Zhao, D.: Relation-aware entity alignment for heterogeneous knowledge graphs. arXiv preprint arXiv:1908.08210 (2019)
52. Xiang, Y., Zhang, Z., Chen, J., Chen, X., Lin, Z., Zheng, Y.: OntoEA: ontology-guided entity alignment via joint knowledge graph embedding. In: Findings of the Association for Computational Linguistics: ACL-IJCNLP 2021, pp. 1117–1128 (2021)
53. Xin, K., Sun, Z., Hua, W., Hu, W., Qu, J., Zhou, X.: Large-scale entity alignment via knowledge graph merging, partitioning and embedding. In: Proceedings of the 31st ACM International Conference on Information & Knowledge Management, pp. 2240–2249 (2022)
54. Xin, K., Sun, Z., Hua, W., Hu, W., Zhou, X.: Informed multi-context entity alignment. In: Proceedings of the Fifteenth ACM International Conference on Web Search and Data Mining, pp. 1197–1205 (2022)
55. Xu, C., Cheng, J., Zhang, F.: NALA: an effective and interpretable entity alignment method. In: Findings of the Association for Computational Linguistics: EMNLP 2024, pp. 13752–13772 (2024)
56. Yang, L., Chen, H., Wang, X., Yang, J., Wang, F.Y., Liu, H.: Two heads are better than one: Integrating knowledge from knowledge graphs and large language models for entity alignment. arXiv preprint arXiv:2401.16960 (2024)
57. Zeng, K., et al.: Interactive contrastive learning for self-supervised entity alignment. In: Proceedings of the 31st ACM International conference on information & knowledge management, pp. 2465–2475 (2022)
58. Zhang, Q., Sun, Z., Hu, W., Chen, M., Guo, L., Qu, Y.: Multi-view knowledge graph embedding for entity alignment. In: International Joint Conference on Artificial Intelligence (2019)
59. Zhao, X., Zeng, W., Tang, J., Wang, W., Suchanek, F.M.: An experimental study of state-of-the-art entity alignment approaches. IEEE Trans. Knowl. Data Eng. **34**(6), 2610–2625 (2020)
60. Zhao, Y., Wu, Y., Cai, X., Zhang, Y., Zhang, H., Yuan, X.: From alignment to entailment: A unified textual entailment framework for entity alignment. In: Findings of the Association for Computational Linguistics: ACL 2023 pp. 8795–8806 (2023)
61. Zhong, Z., Zhang, M., Fan, J., Dou, C.: Semantics driven embedding learning for effective entity alignment. In: 2022 IEEE 38th International Conference on Data Engineering (ICDE), pp. 2127–2140. IEEE (2022)

Proxy-Enriched Imputation on Contextually Incomplete Web Tables

Denis Nagel(✉), Jonas MeiSSner, Niklas Kiehne, and Wolf-Tilo Balke

Institute for Information Systems, TU Braunschweig, Braunschweig, Germany
{nagel,kiehne,balke}@ifis.cs.tu-bs.de, j.meissner@tu-bs.de

Abstract. Structured data in the form of Web tables and open data repositories lays the foundation for the Semantic Web.However, quality concerns are often raised, mostly with respect to accuracy and completeness. While missing value imputation is the go-to solution to fill in blanks, (1) it can only approximate known unknowns and (2) struggles if values are missing not at random. As a remedy, this paper combines semantically rich *narratives* with proven-quality *knowledge graphs* to dynamically assess the completeness of individual data sets while accounting for the user's intent, too. Having determined which values are actually missing, we leverage state-of-the-art NLP techniques to identify *functionally dependent attributes* as proxies for later value imputation. Being functionally dependent (at least to some degree), these attributes provide the necessary context in the sense of *relatedness* allowing for more sophisticated imputation techniques. As a proof of concept we demonstrate our approach's benefits in a real world setting using real-life narratives on the open data repository of the World Health Organization.

Keywords: Narrative Intelligence · Open Data · Web Tables · Imputation

1 Introduction

Currently, a growing amount of research data is made publicly available through Web tables and large-scale repositories [3,24]. This knowledge provides a valuable source of evidence for approaches in fact-checking [13,15,16] and plausibility assessment [22], where significant advances have recently been made. As a running example, consider the UNICEF narrative[1] and excerpt of a data set from the Global Health Observatory [35] of the World Health Organization (WHO) in Fig. 1. The narrative underpins a general observation regarding the recent development of the DTP3 vaccination coverage with hard facts. At the same time, the claims are embedded into a clear-cut context spatially (global/worldwide) and temporally (during the COVID-19 pandemic, i.e; 2019 - 2021). Note that the WHO-table contains a suitable indicator (*DTP3 Immunization coverage among 1-year-olds (%)*) as well as the necessary contextual information to act as evidence for the claims made throughout the narrative.

[1] https://data.unicef.org/topic/child-health/immunization/.

D. Garijo et al. (Eds.): ISWC 2025, LNCS 16140, pp. 216–234, 2026.
https://doi.org/10.1007/978-3-032-09527-5_12

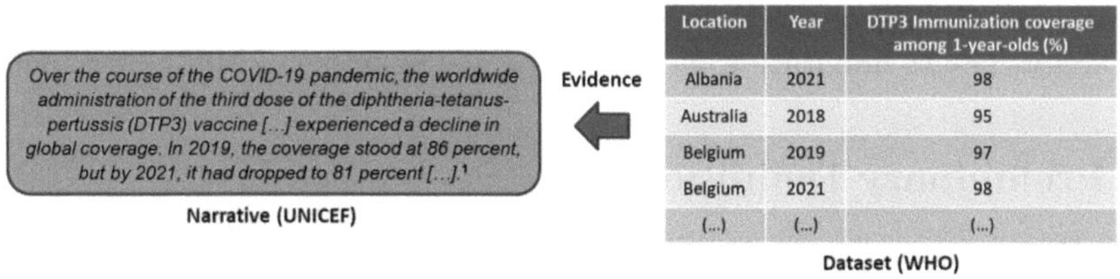

Fig. 1. The introductory narrative (left) and a data set providing evidence (right).

Since open data is often provided in large and highly heterogeneous *data lakes* [23,39], quality concerns are frequently raised about its accuracy and completeness. Although there is already a large amount of research on assessing the correctness of data sets [9,17,31], the completeness of data sets is difficult to handle, as it is bound to the particular narrative's context. For example, a data set on global DTP3 vaccination rates could lack all values, say between 2010 and 2017, and still contain all relevant information for the UNICEF narrative.

Missing values in tabular data are usually approximated using missing value imputation. However, imputation can only fill explicit gaps in a table (known unknowns), while records required to match a narrative's specific context (unknown unknowns) would need to be determined first. Moreover, imputation techniques generally perform well, whenever data is missing completely at random (MCAR). Yet, they struggle if data is missing not at random (MNAR), i.e; the chance of missing is dependent on its particular values [14]. In our example, if the table only contains those countries with coverage greater than 80%, any imputation would probably apply comparable values to the missing countries.

This paper introduces a novel approach to tackle these shortcomings. First, it relies on the rich semantics provided by established knowledge graphs to dynamically assess the completeness of Web tables with respect to some given narrative and fill in missing records. This can be achieved by computing the overlap between the contextual scope covered by a data set's records and the contextual scope described by the narrative. Once missing records have been added, our approach leverages the vast pool of indicators provided by large-scale open data repositories and the capabilities of recent NLP-tools, in particular large language models and sentence embeddings, to compute the relatedness between attributes and identify stand-in proxies that provide the necessary statistical dependencies for an effective application of missing value imputation in the MNAR-case. For our running example, suitable proxies could be the *available doses of DTP3 vaccine* or the *percentage of the population with access to health services.*

Our main contributions are (1) the application of knowledge bases to dynamically assess the degree of a data set's completeness dependent on a given narrative's contextual scope and (2) the narrative-driven identification of stand-in proxies for incomplete data sets to allow for an effective application of missing-value imputation. We evaluate the applicability of our approach on real-world narratives and data of the WHO and show that it indeed improves the quality of state-of-the-art imputation techniques on the example of MissForest [30].

2 Preliminary Definitions

2.1 Comparing Contexts

Our approach determines the completeness of a data set dynamically based on the given narrative's context. Therefore, it is necessary for us to be able to compare this given context with the contextual scope provided by a data set.

In this paper, we define a **context** *con* as a tuple consisting of multiple **context variables**, i.e; $con = (cv_1, ..., cv_n)$. Each context variable restricts the context in a different **contextual dimension** by providing a specific substitution for this dimension (e.g; the context variable *Europe* for the spatial dimension). The same contextual dimension can be substituted in different contexts in varying granularity. We say a broader context variable cv_b **covers** a more narrow context variable cv_n, written $cv_b \rhd cv_n$ if the scope of cv_b fully encompasses the scope of cv_n (e.g; $Europe \rhd Germany$). Similarly, we say that a context con_b covers a context con_n, denoted $con_b \rhd con_n$, if for each context variable $cv_i \in con_b$ there is a context variable $cv_j \in con_n$ such that $cv_i \rhd cv_j$ (e.g; $(Europe, 1970s) \rhd (Germany, 1975)$).

If a broader context variable cv_b is semantically equivalent to the union of a set of narrower context variables CV_n, we say cv_b **comprises** CV_n, denoted as $cv_b \blacktriangleright CV_n$ (e.g; *1970s* $\blacktriangleright \{1970, 1971, ..., 1979\}$). Similarly, we say that a context c_b comprises a set of contexts C_n, denoted $c_b \blacktriangleright C_n$, if c_b is semantically equivalent to the union of all contexts $c_n \in C_n$ (e.g; (France and Germany, 1970-71) $\blacktriangleright$ {(France, 1970), (France, 1971), (Germany, 1970), (Germany, 1971)}).

2.2 Narratives

A narrative is an argumentation structure consisting of several narrative claims that are embedded in a specific context. For now, we only consider isolated narrative claims that are defined as follows.

Definition 1. *We define a narrative claim as a tuple* $n = (cl_n, con_n)$ *with*

- $cl_n := (ind_n, val_n)$ *being the claim specifying a value val for the indicator ind*
- $con_n := (cv_1, cv_2, ..., cv_k)$ *being the claim's context, consisting of k context variables*

For an example, consider the narrative claim *The global DTP3 vaccination coverage in 2019 was 86%.* It consists of the claim (DTP3 vaccination coverage, 86%) and the context (Global, 2019).

2.3 Data Sets

Throughout this paper, we use the term **data set** to describe relational information stored in a tabular structure. Each table is considered a single data set that might be provided by a larger **data set repository**. Each data set column describes an **attribute** of an entity type or abstract event whose instances are represented by the rows or **records**.

Definition 2. *We define a data set d consisting of r rows and c columns as $d \subseteq Dom_1 \times ... \times Dom_c$ with*

- $A_d = \{a_1, a_2, ..., a_c\}$ *being its set of attributes with Dom_i being the value domain of a_i*
- $head_d = (cap_1, cap_2, ..., cap_c)$ *being the data set header, with cap_i being the caption of attribute a_i*
- $R_d = \{r_j := (v_{ja_1}, v_{ja_2}, ..., v_{ja_c})\}$ $(1 \leq j \leq r)$ *being its set of records, where v_{ja_i} denotes the j-th record's value for the i-th attribute*

We distinguish between two types of attributes: **indicators** and **contextual attributes**. While the indicators represent the main information provided by a data set, the contextual attributes describe the contexts in which this information is measured, i.e; indicators functionally depend on the complete set of contextual attributes in the same data set. Consider the data set in Fig. 1. Its attributes consist of a single indicator, namely *DTP3 immunization coverage among 1-year-olds (%)*, that was measured in different contexts, described by the two contextual attributes *country* and *year*. We denote the set of indicators of a data set d as $I_d \subseteq A_d$ and the set of its contextual attributes by $CA_d \subseteq A_d$.

We denote the context of a record r as $con_r = (cv_1, ..., cv_n)$. The context con_d of a data set d is the union of all its records' contexts, which is computed by forming the union of any context variables of the same dimension.

2.4 Narrative Witnesses

The information contained in a data set d might be suitable to provide evidence for a given narrative claim n. In this case, we call d a **witness** for n.

Definition 3. *Given a narrative claim $n = (cl, con)$, with $cl = (ind, val)$, we define a witness to be any data set d fulfilling the following constraints:*

- I_d *contains at least one indicator that corresponds to ind*
- *There is at least one record $r \in R_d$, such that $con_e \rhd con_r$*

Consider Fig. 1 for an intuition. The narrative contains two claims regarding the indicator *DTP3 vaccine administration*, which considers two different contexts, i.e; (global,2019) and (global,2021). The data set on the right is a witness for both claims as (1) the attribute *DTP3 immunization coverage among 1-year-olds (%)* corresponds to *DTP3 vaccine administration* (even though the attribute is more specific) and (2) the claims' contexts each cover at least one of the records' contexts, e.g; $(global, 2019) \rhd (Belgium, 2019)$ and $(global, 2021) \rhd (Albania, 2021)$.

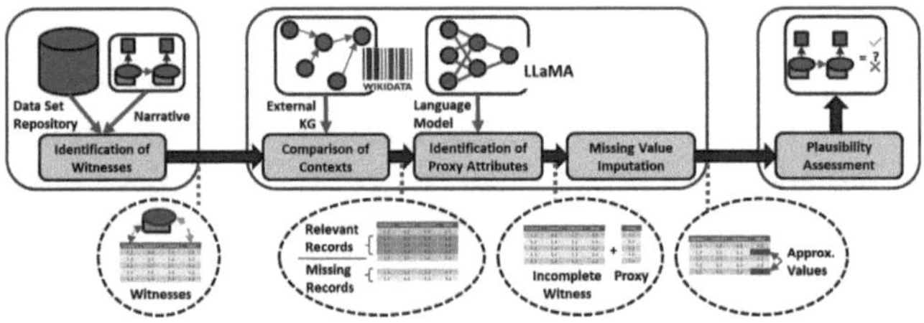

Fig. 2. Subtasks of our approach (red outline). Intermediate results are shown in dashed circles. (Color figure online)

2.5 Proxies and Functional Dependencies

Our approach centers around the idea of identifying proxies for attributes with missing values to improve the effectiveness of imputation, especially if these values are not missing at random. The idea is to allow imputation approaches to leverage statistical dependencies between the proxy and the to-be-imputed attribute for more precise approximations. In this sense, functionally dependent attributes would prove perfect proxies.

Definition 4. *Given two sets of attributes A_i and A_j, a functional dependency (FD) between A_i and A_j, denoted $A_i \rightarrow A_j$, exists iff each value for A_i is associated with exactly one value for A_j*

However, identifying FDs is a complex data profiling problem that is especially challenging in data lakes with many heterogeneous and independent data sets [4]. Additionally, demanding proxies to be truly functionally dependent is difficult to achieve. Even relaxed functional dependencies [4] are usually too restrictive. Hence, we weaken this constraint by only demanding proxies to be *related* (in the sense of functional dependencies) to the to-be-imputed attribute.

Definition 5. *Given two attributes a_i and a_j, we define the relatedness between them as a function $rel(a_i, a_j) \mapsto [0, 1]$. We say a_i is a proxy for a_j if $rel(a_i, a_j) > \theta$, with θ being a predefined threshold.*

For our approach, we analyze two different options to compute this relatedness, which we will describe in detail in Sect. 3.3.

3 Methodology

Our idea is based on two assumptions: (1) knowledge graphs contain extensive world knowledge that can be exploited to dynamically assess the completeness of a data set with respect to a narrative's context, and (2) open data repositories provide a rich selection of suitable proxies for a given attribute. Figure 2 outlines our approach. Given a narrative claim and a set of witnesses, it consists of three subtasks:

- **Comparison of Contextual Scopes:** For any witness, its degree of completeness with respect to the narrative claim's context is determined.
- **Identification of Proxy Attributes:** If the data is incomplete, proxies have to be identified in the repository and joined with the witness.
- **Missing Value Imputation:** Imputation techniques are then applied to approximate the missing data.

3.1 Preliminary Considerations

Identifying Witnesses When considering open data, there are many repositories available, each consisting of thousands of individual tables from which suitable witnesses need to be identified. As this paper is concerned with the completeness of discovered witnesses, we simply rely on established techniques.

While there has been much progress on *relevant data set selection* [25], we settle on algorithms introduced in [22] as they specifically focus on identifying relevant data sets for any contextualized indicator in a heterogeneous data environment. For our use case, we only perform the first two steps (*event* and *constraint matching*) outlined in that paper for each narrative claim n. After applying these steps, for each identified witness w, ind_n is matched against an attribute $a \in I_w$, which we call the *to-be-imputed attribute*, denoted ia_w. Additionally, each context variable $cv \in con_n$ is matched to a contextual attribute $ca \in CA_w$, denoted $ca_{cv}(w)$.

3.2 Comparing Contextual Scopes

For each claim n, the first objective is to determine whether each matched witness covers n's context or if relevant records are missing. Given a witness w, we can distinguish the following cases:

- There is no record $r \in R_w$, with $con_n \rhd con_r$
- There is a set of records $R'_w \subseteq R_w$, with $con_n \rhd con_r$ for all $r \in R'_w$ but $con_n \blacktriangleright \{con_r | r \in R'_w\}$ does not hold
- There is a set of records $R'_w \subseteq R_w$, with $con_n \blacktriangleright \{con_r | r \in R'_w\}$

In the first case, the witness provides no information relevant for the narrative's plausibility. In the second case, the witness contains records covered by the claim's context but lacks some relevant information. In the third case, the witness is complete. To distinguish between these cases, it is necessary to analyze how each record's context relates to the claim's context, which requires external world knowledge.

Here, we rely on knowledge graphs (KGs) to provide the information required for a comprehensive contextual comparison. KGs offer two main advantages: (1) They provide a vocabulary with uniquely defined concepts and (2) their taxonomies give insight into how these concepts can be sensibly combined to form broader concepts. Thus, for each witness, we apply the following three steps (an example is shown in Fig. 3):

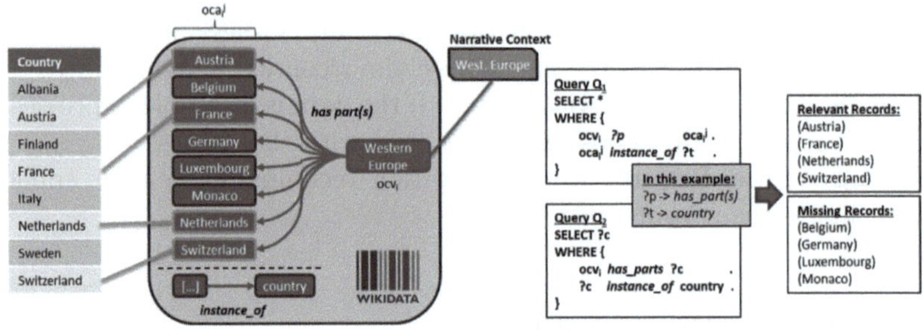

Fig. 3. Queries and simple example for the contextual comparison.

Entity Linking. Given a claim n and a witness w, we first apply entity linking (the tool used depends on the KG used) for each context variable cv_i in con_n to identify its corresponding ontological concept ocv_i. We then take the matched contextual attribute $ca_{cv_i}(w) \in A_w$ and again apply entity linking on each attribute value. This results in a set of ontological concepts $OCA_i = \{oca_i^1, oca_i^2, ...\}$, with oca_i^j being the concept linked to the entry of the j-th record. Hence, we receive a pair (ocv_i, OCA_i) for each context variable cv_i in con_n.

Using Wikidata [33], the example in Fig. 3 visualizes this step by linking the narrative context variable *Western Europe* (cv_i) to the Wikidata concept (ocv_i) of the same name (ID: Q27496). At the same time, the values of the matched contextual attribute ($ca_{cv_i}(w)$) *Country* of the witness w (on the left) are linked to concepts of the same names (oca_i^j), respectively (e.g; the value *Austria* to the concept with ID: Q40).

Contextual Comparison. Next, we need to identify for each record $r_j \in R_w$ how its context con_{r_j} relates to the claim's context con_n. For each cv_i in con_n we determine how its linked concept ocv_i relates to the concept oca_i^j linked to the entry in r_j. If $ocv_i = oca_i^j$, the context variable cv_i is covered by the record r_j. If this holds for all context variables of con_n, then it comprises con_{r_j}, i.e; $con_n \blacktriangleright \{con_{r_j}\}$, and the remaining records can be ignored. Otherwise, we need to query a KB to identify how ocv_i and oca_i^j are related. In an RDF-based triple store (e.g; Wikidata [33]), we can use the KG-agnostic query template Q_1 in Fig. 3 (the actual syntax depends on the KG used). For now, we restrict our approach to only considering direct relationships, i.e; one hop. However, this is easy to generalize by using path expressions.

If Q_1 returns no results, there is no relation between the two context variables and the record r_j can be ignored. Otherwise, assuming cv_i is correctly matched to ca_i, both variables share the same contextual dimension and the predicate substituting ?p expresses some form of part-of-relationship (the exact type of relation can differ and is determined via Q_1). As such, either $ocv_i \triangleright oca_i^j$ or vice versa. If ocv_i represents the broader context, then there should be multiple records for which Q_1 returns the same result for $?p$.

A record r_j is relevant, if for each cv_i in con_n it holds that either (1) $ocv_i = oca_i^j$ or (2) there is a triple $<ocv_i,pred,oca_i^j>$ with *pred* being the predicate substituting $?p$ in Q_1. In this case, the claim's context covers the record's context, i.e; $con_n \rhd con_{r_j}$. Hence, we can identify the set of relevant records $R'_w \subseteq R_w$.

Continuing our previous example, if $oca_i^j \in \{Austria, France, Netherlands, Switzerland\}$ query Q_1 substitutes $?p$ with the predicate *has part(s)* (ID: P527). The respective records are considered relevant. If $oca_i^j \in \{Albania, Finland, Italy, Sweden\}$, there is no relation to *Western Europe* (ocv_i) and thus Q_1 does not produce any result.

Determining Completeness. Using R'_w, we can now refer to the KG again to determine which records are missing to cover con_n. Using Q_1, we identified the type of each concept oca_i^j substituting $?t$ and the predicate connecting oca_i^j with ocv_i substituting $?p$. If a concept has multiple types, i.e; $?t$ allows for multiple substitutions, we consider the one returned for the most oca_i^j as the *main type*.

In our example, $?p$ is substituted by *has part(s)*, while dependent on oca_i^j there are multiple substitutions for ?t (e.g; if $oca_i^j = Austria$, substitutions for $?t$ are *sovereign state*, *country*, *republic*, etc.). However, only *country* (ID: Q6256) is a valid substitution for all oca_i^j.

Query Q_2 (see Fig. 3) can then be used to identify all concepts substituting $?c$ that are of the same main type and connected with ocv_i via the same predicate, i.e; all individual pieces of the same granularity that together form ocv_i. Let CC_i be the result set of query Q_2 obtained for the context variable cv_i. By forming the cross-product of the result sets for each cv_i, i.e; $CC_n = CC_1 \times CC_2 \times ... \times CC_m$, we yield the set of all subcontexts needed to cover the context con_n. Hence, by computing the set difference between this set and the set of all contexts in R'_w we obtain the set of missing contexts MC_w. In our example, $MC_w = \{Belgium, Germany, Luxembourg, Monaco\}$.

3.3 Deriving Proxy Attributes

For each claim n, we can now distinguish between complete witnesses and those that are missing some contexts, i.e; records. In the latter case, we now need to add the missing records and approximate their values.

Sophisticated imputation techniques rely on statistical dependencies between attributes to approximate missing data points. For precise approximations, related attributes are required from which missing values can be derived. If we are, for example, interested in vaccination coverage, related attributes could be the availability of vaccines, the density of health services, or the GDP of a country. Hence, our idea is to enrich each witness with suitable attributes. While open data repositories contain a vast selection of different indicators, the challenge is to identify those that can act as suitable proxies for the to-be-imputed attribute.

To assess the relatedness between indicators, we rely on state-of-the-art NLP tools, namely large language models (LLMs) and sentence embeddings (SE). The

I have two measures i and p, with the following definitions:
i: *<definition of i>*
p: *<definition of p>*
Based on these definitions, is there a strong influence from p on i?
Answer only with yes or no.

Fig. 4. Prompt template for the first stage of our proxy retrieval method. For each pair of indicator i and potential proxy p we replace the respective parts in the template with the short names of i and p, as well as their definition.

input consists of the indicator for which missing data should be approximated, denoted i, and the set of indicators available as potential proxies PI.

For the sentence embedding we simply use pre-trained tools, such as SBERT [28], to compute the cosine similarity between i and all elements in PI and then rank the results accordingly.

For the LLM (for our proof-of-concept we use a pre-trained LLaMA 2 [32] without domain-specific fine-tuning) we apply two stages. First, we query the LLM to assess whether a potential proxy could have a strong influence on the target indicator, see Fig. 4 for the prompt setup. This yields a list of suitable proxy attributes for i. Even though each of these attributes might be strongly related to i, the relatedness degree might still differ greatly between them. Thus, we implement a second stage to establish a ranking of relatedness.

Using the prompting setup shown in Fig. 5, we gather pairwise rankings of all proxies concerning their relatedness to i. The ranking process can be described as a tournament, consisting of a series of binary decisions to simplify the task and account for the input lengths that LLMs can handle. We conduct a double round robin style tournament, since language models have been shown to be susceptible to ordering-effects [29,40]. The rank of a proxy corresponds to its win-rate against other proxies.

We do not ask the LLM to directly provide proxy attributes as this approach is not scalable with respect to token/context limits. It would require the entire list of proxy candidates, including attribute descriptions, to be provided as input, thus easily exceeding the capacities of most LLMs for larger data repositories. Another drawback would be the fact that LLMs tend to forget some of the candidates in the provided ranking. A small evaluation regarding these problems can be found in our GitHub repository (see supplemental material statement).

Apart from using an LLM and embeddings we also considered other options to identify related indicators. These included (1) computing simple correlations, (2) applying data profiling techniques, or (3) using expert knowledge extracted from large document collections. However, applying any of these options has severe drawbacks. In incomplete data sets, a correlation between those values available must not necessarily imply a correlation on the missing values. While functionally dependent indicators, identified through data profiling, would prove valuable proxies, true functional dependencies rarely exist in open data. Even

I have this measure: "i: <*definition of i*>"
Now I want to know, which of these two measures has higher influence on it:
Option A
p_a: <*definition of* p_a>
Option B
p_b: <*definition of* p_b>
Which of the options has higher influence on i?
Answer "A" for p_a or "B" for p_b.

Fig. 5. Prompt template for the second stage of our proxy retrieval method.

relaxed functional dependencies [4] are too restrictive. Finally, large document collections offer extensive expert knowledge that could be exploited, e.g; by relying on the co-occurrence of concepts. However, indicators occurring in open data sets are often very specific, e.g; *Malaria prevalence in children aged <5 years (according to rapid diagnostic testing) (%)*. Hence, it proves challenging to identify suitably specific documents.

3.4 Missing Value Imputation

For each witness w we have identified the set of missing contexts MC_w to cover the claim's context and a set of proxy attributes PA_{ia_w} for the to-be-imputed attribute ia_w. The goal is now to approximate ia_w's value for each $mc \in MC_w$.

When approximating missing values in tabular data, a large selection of imputation techniques are readily available. These include everything from very simple mean/mode imputation over more sophisticated k-NN and random-forest-based approaches to deep learning techniques [8,20,30]. Many strategies rely on statistical dependencies between the individual attributes of a data set to derive missing values. Hence, by enriching incomplete witnesses with suitable proxy attributes, we aim to increase their effectiveness. Our approach can then be applied in combination with any of the aforementioned strategies.

Again, we refrained from using an LLM to fill in missing values directly due to scalability concerns (the largest table of the GHO repository, as an example, requires 5,5 million tokens, while most state-of-the-art LLMs have a token limit of 1-2 million). In addition, we ran a small evaluation, showing that LLaMA 2 failed in most cases to provide any sensible results (see our GitHub for details).

For the first step of our approach, artificial records have to be created for each missing context in MC_w and added to the data set. These records receive values for each contextual attribute according to the context they represent. The remaining cells containing the to-be-imputed values do not receive initial values. Next, the witness is joined with the data sets that contain the proxies in PA_{ia_w}. Finally, an imputation is applied on the join, filling in the missing values.

Computing joins in open data environments, where schema information is rarely available and metadata might not be very expressive, is a very challenging problem. Over the recent years, this led to an increased research interest in *join table discovery* [10,11]. However, many state-of-the-art approaches only consider the syntactic and semantic similarity of individual columns, thus ignoring the data sets' contexts and failing to ensure their compatibility.

Consider the data set in Fig. 1, denoted as d_{ex}, which stores the DTP3 vaccination coverage of a country's population. Let d_j be a similar table on the measles vaccination coverage of different countries. In addition to the attributes *country* and *year* it also includes the contextual attribute *place of residence* whose value domain consists of the set $\{rural, urban\}$. Hence, unlike d_{ex}, it distinguishes rural and urban populations. It is impossible to correctly join both tables without information about the distribution of a country's population with respect to their place of residence. Then, the values for each pair of country and year in d_j could be aggregated to match d_{ex}. While context-compatible join table discovery presents a fascinating research topic, it is out of scope for this paper.

Instead, we apply a simple join heuristic, which, while naive, is sufficient for a proof-of-concept evaluation: Two tables are joined by matching any two records that contain exactly the same context variables for each contextual dimension. If a contextual dimension is represented by multiple context variables, only the most specific context variable needs to match, e.g; a record containing a country and its region is still matched to a record containing only the country. We also keep all records of the witness having no join partner, i.e; we conduct a left outer join (instead of padding with null values, the respective fields remain empty). Then a projection is applied such that the final data set contains only the attributes of the witness and the proxy attributes.

4 Evaluation

We follow a similar setup as in [22] and evaluate the applicability of our approach on a large-scale open data repository of the World Health Organization (WHO) as a proof-of-concept (all material used is available on GitHub - see supplemental material statement). Thereby, we do not focus on comparing individual imputation techniques but rather on the effect of incorporating proxies into the imputation. In fact, while we apply MissForest in this evaluation, our approach can be applied in conjunction with any existing imputation technique.

4.1 Evaluation Setup

Data Set Repository. We evaluate our approach on the Global Health Observatory (GHO) [35], a large-scale open data repository provided by the World Health Organization (WHO). Additionally, we consider the data sets included in the Health Equity Assessment Toolkit (HEAT Plus) [36], which is also provided by the WHO. Combined, these repositories encompass 2,807 individual data sets (with the HEAT Plus Data split into one indicator per table as a preprocessing step). As in [22], the data is annotated with metadata to provide further information for the identification of witnesses.

Narratives. For our evaluation, we use 24 narratives extracted from documents published by the WHO[2], each consisting of between 1 and 6 claims (50 in total). These *data stories* describe observations that have been reported by analyzing data available in the GHO or the HEAT Plus. The data sets used for these reports are directly referenced in each document. Analogously to [22], this direct connection between narrative and supporting data can be used as a ground truth for identifying candidate witnesses in the data set repository.

Identification of Candidate Witnesses. We identify witnesses for each of the 50 claims by applying the event and constraint matching from [22], using those parameters that have been identified as striking the best balance between recall and precision ($\theta_{EM} = 0.65$ and $\theta_{PM} = 0.6$). In four cases, no witness could be identified. For the remaining 46 narrative claims, the number of witnesses varies between 1 and 48. We only consider the highest scoring witness for each claim, as a full evaluation using all witnesses would exceed the scope of this paper. This results in a set of 21 tables (if a data set is considered a witness for multiple claims, it is only counted once), denoted D_w.

4.2 Deriving Proxy Attributes and Imputation

This evaluation aims to show that (1) the availability of sensible proxy attributes improves the quality of missing value imputation on open data sets if data is missing not at random, (2) LLMs and embeddings are capable of identifying and ranking these proxy attributes effectively, and (3) having highly related proxy attributes is preferable over loosely related or randomly chosen attributes.

Ground Truth and Baseline. To assess the quality of the imputed values, we need to compare them with the actual values they approximate. Hence, we take the data sets in D_w and incorporate artificial incompleteness by removing a subset V_{del} of all the values of all to-be-imputed attributes. We apply two different missing patterns: Missing Completely At Random (MCAR) and Missing Not At Random (MNAR). MCAR has a higher probability to preserve the overall data distribution while MNAR simulates the situation in many real-life use cases in which data values are missing due to specific causes. One prominent example is the healthcare domain, where MNAR seems to be one of the most prevalent missing patterns [26]. In recommender systems and surveys MNAR can also often be observed [6,18]. In the MCAR setting, we randomly remove k% records, while in the MNAR setting, we order the records of the data set by the to-be-imputed attribute and remove the bottom k% records. The removed values are then considered as the ground truth for the subsequent missing value imputation. The reduced data sets without any proxy attributes act as a baseline to measure the impact that the addition of any proxy has on the imputation.

Proxy Identification. For each to-be-imputed attribute ia_w of a witness $w \in D_w$, we generate three lists of proxy attributes:

[2] https://www.who.int/data/stories.

- $Prox_{ia_w}^{LLM}$: all proxies p identified by a large language model (we use LLaMA 2 [32]) using the approach described in 3.3. The proxies are ranked according to a relatedness score $rel(p, ia_w)$ assigned by the language model.
- $Prox_{ia_w}^{SE}$: all proxies p identified by a sentence transformer (we use SBERT [28]). The proxies are ranked according to their assigned cosine similarity score $coSim(p, ia_w)$.
- $Prox_{ia_w}^{Rand}$: a list of randomly chosen attributes of all indicators available in the data set repository.

In two cases, the LLM was unable to identify suitable proxies. These data sets were removed from D_w. It is important to note that we use a pre-trained LLM without domain-specific fine-tuning, which could further improve the results.

Data Set Augmentation. Each witness needs to be augmented by the selected proxy attributes. For this, we compute the join between the witness and all tables containing the respective proxies using the heuristic outlined in Sect. 3.4. As the identification of proxy attributes is independent of the actual context of their data sets, these data sets might be contextually incompatible with the witness, thus resulting in a failed join. If no successful join can be achieved for a proxy attribute, it is removed from the original proxy list. We continue to select a new proxy until a join can be achieved. For two witnesses, none of the identified proxies could be joined successfully, which ultimately results in 17 data sets that are considered for imputation. If a proxy attribute occurs in multiple data sets, the union of all contextually compatible occurrences is computed.

Imputation and Metrics. For the imputation, we apply a random forest based approach, called MissForest [30]. It is widely used as an effective strategy that performs well in benchmarks, both on numerical and categorical data. The imputation results are evaluated using two measures that are commonly used to assess the quality of imputed data, namely the *root mean square error*

- $\text{RMSE} = \sqrt{\frac{1}{n}\sum_{i=1}^{n}(y_i - \hat{y}_i)^2}$

and *mean absolute error*

- $\text{MAE} = \frac{1}{n}\sum_{i=1}^{n}|y_i - \hat{y}_i|$,

where y_i refers to the series of n imputed values and $\hat{y}_i$ refers to the series of n actual values. Using both measures for evaluating imputation results is beneficial due to their complementary perspectives on error characteristics. RMSE is sensitive to large errors and outliers, highlighting when the imputation occasionally deviates significantly from the true values. In contrast, MAE provides a straightforward average of error magnitudes less influenced by extreme values.

Performance on Different Degrees of Incompleteness. As a first experiment, we run MissForest on data sets with different degrees of incompleteness. We set the size of V_{del} to be 10, 20, 30, 40 and 50%, respectively, of the to-be-imputed column. For proxy selection, we take the top-ranked proxy from each

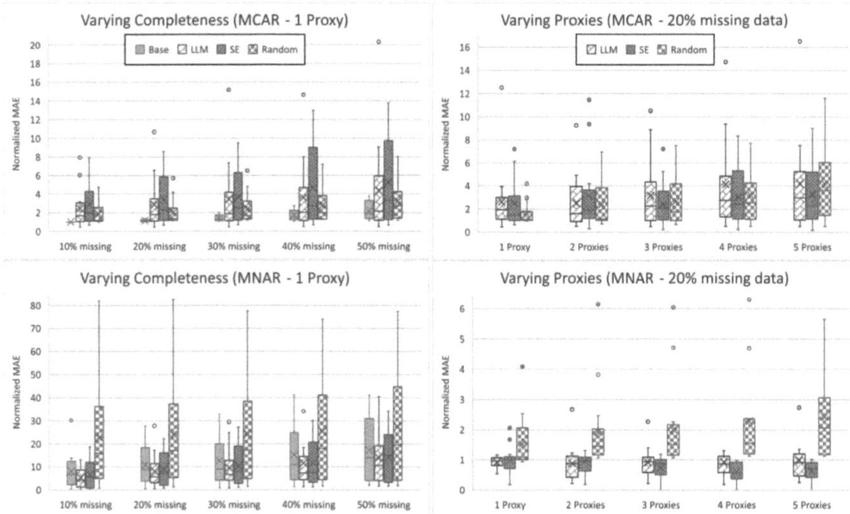

Fig. 6. MAE when varying the degrees of incompleteness of the witnesses from 10% to 50% (left) and the number of proxies from 1 to 5 (right).

proxy list, while the data sets without proxies act as a baseline. For direct comparability, we normalize the error for each data set so that the result of the baseline at 10% missing data (MCAR) equals 1. The results are shown on the left in Fig. 6 (only MAE is shown since RMSE yields similar results).

As expected, the error increases with higher percentages of missing data, when fewer information is available for the approximation. Furthermore, we see a significant difference between the two missing patterns. When data is missing completely at random, we see that the imputation deteriorates when a proxy is added to the witnesses, with randomly chosen proxy attributes performing better than those computed by the LLM and SE. While there are proxies that improve the imputation results for their witness, in the majority of cases their introduction worsens the results. A potential explanation could be that their dependency to the missing values does not contribute anything useful and instead adds unnecessary noise. When random values are missing, the overall data distribution remains largely intact, thus providing MissForest with valuable statistical information even when no proxy attributes are available. Additionally, the imputation can draw from the context attributes in each witness to approximate values in similar contexts, e.g; if a single record referencing a specific country in a specific year is removed the remaining records for the same country in different years provide an indicator for sensible value ranges.

This is not necessarily the case when values are missing not at random as all records regarding a specific context might be removed, with the proxy providing the only point of reference. Here, MissForest struggles to approximate the missing data effectively with the error being almost a magnitude higher than in the MCAR-case. However, the imputation improves significantly when a proxy is added to the witnesses, as long as the proxy is selected carefully (i.e; using the LLM and SE), in the best cases reducing the error by 90% at 10% missing data and on average still reaching a reduction of up to 26.1% at 20% missing data for the LLM and 16.7% for the SE when compared to the baseline. Contrary, the randomly chosen proxy leads to a drastic performance decrease of MissForest, on average increasing the MAE more than 2-fold in the same scenario. This increase is reduced with higher percentages of missing data, but still reaches 1.6 times the baseline when 50% of the data is removed. This shows that it is important to identify a proxy that is related to the missing data. Otherwise, spurious correlations might be introduced that negatively affect the imputation.

However, often when joining proxy attributes to a witness, there are a lot of records that do not find any join partner. This is largely due to differences in the covered contexts, e.g; the witness might cover the years 2000, 2005 and 2010, while the table containing the proxy covers the years 2000, 2001 and 2002. This might also negatively impact the imputation results.

Impact of the Quality and Number of Proxy Attributes. In the second experiment, we apply MissForest using different numbers of proxy attributes. We choose the top k attributes from each proxy list, where k ranges from 1 to 5 and set the percentage of missing values to 20%. The results are normalized so that the baseline (no proxies) is considered an error of 1. The results are shown on the right in Fig. 6 (only MAE as RMSE again yields similar overall results).

While the addition of proxies heavily affects the imputation for both missing patterns, this impact is almost exclusively negative in the MCAR case and worsens with the number of proxies. However, in the MNAR case, this depends on whether the proxies are related to the missing data. If they are related, adding proxies significantly improves the approximated results, with the transformer, in the best case, reducing the error by 99.8%. On the other hand, when using random proxies, the imputation deteriorates.

Contrary to the first experiment, the transformer outperforms the language model for higher numbers of proxies. An explanation could be that the LLM selects a higher variety of attributes as relevant proxies, whereas the SE mainly selects proxies which are linguistically similar to the incomplete indicator. Consider the indicator *PCV3 immunization coverage*. The LLM selects factors having an impact on vaccination rates such as *skilled health professionals density* and *per capita government expenditure on health* while the SE selects other vaccination rates such as for *Measles* or the *Rotavirus*. As countries having high vaccination rates for one disease usually do so for any disease, this dependency can be exploited more effectively. Thus, SE can be used to great effect if many very similar indicators are available in the repository. However, if no similar indicator is available, the LLM performs better in identifying related concepts.

5 Related Work

Recently, the task of *approximate query processing (AQP)* [5] has received a lot of interest. AQP aims to approximate query responses, either to avoid extensive execution times or to mitigate missing data, while ensuring acceptable accuracy. Zhang et al. [39] outlined an architecture to enable AQP in the context of open data to overcome the challenges posed by heterogeneous and often incomplete, noisy and unstructured data collections. While we apply a similar assessment of data completeness, our strategy to approximate missing values differs drastically.

For approximating missing data in incomplete data sets, there is already a vast selection of missing value imputation techniques available [27]. Simple statistical approaches such as mean, regression, or KNN [8] should be used with caution, as important correlations between variables might be ignored, leading to unrealistic values. Advanced methods, based on the random forest algorithm [30], discriminative or generative deep learning methods [20], variational autoencoder [2] or generative adversarial networks [38], take these correlations into account. The recent work from Mei et al. [21] introduces a method using pre-trained language models (IPM) which views imputation as a classification problem.

Alternatively, if the properties of the overall data set can be preserved, the plausibility of narratives could be assessed using representative subsets or data summarizations of relevant data sets. In the context of machine learning, data summarizations are widely used, since training with large data sets is time and resource consuming [34,37]. Popular approaches include cluster-based [1,7] and weighted graph-based approaches [19]. Advanced subset selection techniques are also capable of maintaining structural relationships among items [12].

6 Conclusion

In this paper, we propose a novel approach to mitigate the shortcomings of missing-value imputation. It integrates world knowledge provided by external knowledge bases and the capabilities of modern NLP tools to assess the completeness of relevant data sets and identify related information to approximate missing values. Our evaluation on the GHO repository of the WHO showed that proxy attributes identified by LLMs and sentence transformers can significantly improve imputation results in the MNAR scenario. This is also the most challenging scenario for state-of-the-art imputation tools, which often fail to produce precise approximations. Hence, our paper presents valuable insight to improve on a main drawback of imputation. We also showed that in an MCAR scenario, where the overall data distribution is not affected by missing values, the addition of proxy attributes might add unnecessary noise, thus impairing the effectiveness of imputation algorithms. However, state-of-the-art imputation already performs well in MCAR scenarios. Finally, we outlined multiple open questions, such as computing context-compatible joins, which we plan to address in future work.

Supplemental Material Statement. The code, including all data sets and narratives, can be found on https://github.com/ProxyImputation/ProxyImputation.

References

1. Angelidakis, H., Kurpisz, A., Sering, L., Zenklusen, R.: Fair and fast k-center clustering for data summarization. In: International Conference on Machine Learning, vol. 162, pp. 669–702. ICML . Proceedings of Machine Learning Research. PMLR, Baltimore, 17-23 July (2022)
2. Boquet, G., Vicario, J.L., Morell, A., Serrano, J.: Missing data in traffic estimation: a variational autoencoder imputation method. In: ICASSP 2019-2019 IEEE International Conference on Acoustics, Speech and Signal Processing (ICASSP). IEEE (2019)
3. Brickley, D., Burgess, M., Noy, N.: Google dataset search: building a search engine for datasets in an open web ecosystem. In: The World Wide Web Conference, pp. 1365–1375. WWW '19, Association for Computing Machinery, New York (2019)
4. Caruccio, L., Deufemia, V., Naumann, F., Polese, G.: Discovering relaxed functional dependencies based on multi-attribute dominance. IEEE Trans. Knowl. Data Eng. **33**(9), 3212–3228 (2021)
5. Chaudhuri, S., Ding, B., Kandula, S.: Approximate query processing: No silver bullet. In: Proceedings of the 2017 ACM International Conference on Management of Data, SIGMOD Conference 2017, pp. 511–519, Chicago, May 14-19. ACM (2017)
6. Chen, J., Xu, Y., Wang, P., Yang, Y.: Deep generative imputation model for missing not at random data. In: Proceedings of the 32nd ACM International Conference on Information and Knowledge Management, CIKM 2023, pp. 316–325, Birmingham, October 21-25. ACM (2023). https://doi.org/10.1145/3583780.3614835
7. Chen, X., Fain, B., Lyu, L., Munagala, K.: Proportionally fair clustering. In: Proceedings of the 36th International Conference on Machine Learning, vol. 97, pp. 1032–1041, ICML 2019, 9-15 June 2019, Long Beach. Proceedings of Machine Learning Research. PMLR (2019)
8. Domeniconi, C., Yan, B.: Nearest neighbor ensemble. In: 17th International Conference on Pattern Recognition, pp. 228–231, ICPR 2004, Cambridge, August 23-26, 2004. IEEE Computer Society (2004)
9. Dong, X.L., et al.: Knowledge-based trust: estimating the trustworthiness of web sources. Proc. VLDB Endow. **8**(9), 938–949 (2015)
10. Dong, Y., Takeoka, K., Xiao, C., Oyamada, M.: Efficient joinable table discovery in data lakes: a high-dimensional similarity-based approach. In: 37th IEEE International Conference on Data Engineering, pp. 456–467, ICDE 2021, Chania, Greece, April 19-22, 2021. IEEE (2021)
11. Dong, Y., Xiao, C., Nozawa, T., Enomoto, M., Oyamada, M.: Deepjoin: joinable table discovery with pre-trained language models. Proc. VLDB Endow. **16**(10), 2458–2470 (2023)
12. Elhamifar, E., Kaluza, M.C.D.P.: Subset selection and summarization in sequential data. In: Advances in Neural Information Processing Systems 30: Annual Conference on Neural Information Processing Systems 2017, pp. 1035–1045, December 4-9, 2017, Long Beach (2017)
13. Hassan, N., et al.: Claimbuster: the first-ever end-to-end fact-checking system. Proc. VLDB Endowment **10**, 1945–1948 (2017)
14. Heymans, M.W., Twisk, J.W.: Handling missing data in clinical research. J. Clin. Epidemiol. **151**, 185–188 (2022). https://doi.org/10.1016/j.jclinepi.2022.08.016, https://www.sciencedirect.com/science/article/pii/S0895435622002189

15. Jo, S., et al.: Verifying text summaries of relational data sets. In: Proceedings of the 2019 International Conference on Management of Data, pp. 299–316. SIGMOD '19, Association for Computing Machinery, New York (2019)
16. Karagiannis, G., Saeed, M., Papotti, P., Trummer, I.: Scrutinizer: fact checking statistical claims. Proc. VLDB Endowment **13**(12), 2965–2968 (2020)
17. Li, Q., Li, Y., Gao, J., Zhao, B., Fan, W., Han, J.: Resolving conflicts in heterogeneous data by truth discovery and source reliability estimation. In: Proceedings of the 2014 ACM SIGMOD International Conference on Management of Data, pp. 1187–1198. SIGMOD '14, Association for Computing Machinery, New York (2014)
18. Ma, C., Zhang, C.: Identifiable generative models for missing not at random data imputation. In: Advances in Neural Information Processing Systems 34: Annual Conference on Neural Information Processing Systems 2021, NeurIPS 2021, pp. 27645–27658, December 6-14, 2021, virtual (2021). https://proceedings.neurips.cc/paper/2021/hash/e8a642ed6a9ad20fb159472950db3d65-Abstract.html
19. Mall, R., Jumutc, V., Langone, R., Suykens, J.A.K.: Representative subsets for big data learning using k-NN graphs. In: 2014 IEEE International Conference on Big Data (IEEE BigData 2014), pp. 37–42, Washington, October 27-30. IEEE Computer Society (2014)
20. Mattei, P., Frellsen, J.: MIWAE: deep generative modelling and imputation of incomplete data sets. In: Proceedings of the 36th International Conference on Machine Learning, ICML 2019, 9-15 June 2019, Long Beach, California. Proceedings of Machine Learning Research, PMLR (2019)
21. Mei, Y., Song, S., Fang, C., Yang, H., Fang, J., Long, J.: Capturing semantics for imputation with pre-trained language models. In: 37th IEEE International Conference on Data Engineering, ICDE 2021, Chania, Greece, April 19-22, 2021. IEEE (2021)
22. Nagel, D., Affeldt, T., Voges, N., Güntzer, U., Balke, W.T.: Binding data narrations - corroborating the plausibility of scientific narratives by open research data. In: 2023 ACM/IEEE Joint Conference on Digital Libraries (JCDL). Santa Fe (2023)
23. Nargesian, F., Zhu, E., Miller, R.J., Pu, K.Q., Arocena, P.C.: Data lake management: challenges and opportunities. Proc. VLDB Endow. **12**(12), 1986–1989 (2019)
24. Nargesian, F., Zhu, E., Pu, K.Q., Miller, R.J.: Table union search on open data. Proc. VLDB Endow. **11**(7), 813–825 (2018)
25. Paton, N.W., Chen, J., Wu, Z.: Dataset discovery and exploration: a survey. ACM Comput. Surv. **56**(4) (2023)
26. Pereira, R.C., Abreu, P.H., Rodrigues, P.P., Figueiredo, M.A.: Imputation of data missing not at random: Artificial generation and benchmark analysis. Expert Syst. Appl. **249**, 123654 (2024). https://doi.org/10.1016/j.eswa.2024.123654, https://www.sciencedirect.com/science/article/pii/S0957417424005207
27. Psychogyios, K., Ilias, L., Askounis, D.: Comparison of missing data imputation methods using the framingham heart study dataset. In: IEEE-EMBS International Conference on Biomedical and Health Informatics, BHI 2022, pp. 1–5, Ioannina, Greece, September 27-30, 2022. IEEE (2022)
28. Reimers, N., Gurevych, I.: Sentence-BERT: Sentence embeddings using siamese BERT-networks. CoRR abs/1908.10084 (2019)
29. Robinson, J., Wingate, D.: Leveraging large language models for multiple choice question answering. In: The Eleventh International Conference on Learning Representations, ICLR 2023, Kigali, Rwanda, May 1-5, 2023. OpenReview.net (2023)
30. Stekhoven, D.J., Bühlmann, P.: Missforest - non-parametric missing value imputation for mixed-type data. Bioinform. **28**(1), 112–118 (2012)

31. Tabibian, B., Valera, I., Farajtabar, M., Song, L., Schölkopf, B., Gomez-Rodriguez, M.: Distilling information reliability and source trustworthiness from digital traces. In: Proceedings of the 26th International Conference on World Wide Web, pp. 847–855. WWW '17, International World Wide Web Conferences Steering Committee, Republic and Canton of Geneva, CHE (2017)
32. Touvron, H., et al.: Llama 2: Open foundation and fine-tuned chat models (2023)
33. Vrandečić, D., Krötzsch, M.: Wikidata: a free collaborative knowledgebase. Commun. ACM **57**(10), 78–85 (2014)
34. Wei, K., Iyer, R.K., Bilmes, J.A.: Submodularity in data subset selection and active learning. In: Proceedings of the 32nd International Conference on Machine Learning, ICML 2015, Lille, France, 6-11 July 2015 (2015)
35. World Health Organization: Global health observatory (2023). https://www.who.int/data/gho
36. World Health Organization: Health equity assessment toolkit (2023). https://www.who.int/data/inequality-monitor/assessment_toolkit
37. Wang, Y., Francesco Fabbri, M.M.: Fair and representative subset selection from data streams. In: WWW '21: The Web Conference 2021, Virtual Event / Ljubljana, Slovenia, April 19-23, 2021 (2021)
38. Yoon, J., Jordon, J., van der Schaar, M.: GAIN: missing data imputation using generative adversarial nets. In: Proceedings of the 35th International Conference on Machine Learning, ICML 2018, Stockholmsmässan, vol. 80, pp. 5675–5684, Stockholm, July 10-15, 2018. Proceedings of Machine Learning Research. PMLR (2018)
39. Zhang, M., Mundra, P., Chikweze, C., Nargesian, F., Weikum, G.: Approximate query answering over open data. In: Proceedings of the Workshop on Human-In-the-Loop Data Analytics, HILDA 2023, pp. 11:1–11:3, Seattle, 18 June 2023. ACM (2023)
40. Zheng, C., Zhou, H., Meng, F., Zhou, J., Huang, M.: Large language models are not robust multiple choice selectors. In: The Twelfth International Conference on Learning Representations, ICLR 2024, Vienna, May 7-11, 2024. OpenReview.net (2024)

A Domain-Independent Approach for Semantic Table Interpretation

Binh Vu(✉), Craig A. Knoblock, and Fandel Lin

Information Sciences Institute and Department of Computer Science, University of Southern California, Marina del Rey, CA 90292, USA
{binhvu,knoblock,fandelli}@isi.edu

Abstract. Understanding the semantic structure of tabular data is essential for data integration and discovery. Specifically, the goal is to annotate columns in a tabular source with types and relationships between them using classes and predicates of a target ontology. Previous work either requires trained labeled data or exploits the overlapping data between the table data and a knowledge graph to predict types and relationships. However, these approaches cannot be used in a new domain with limited labeled data. To address this issue, we propose a novel domain-independent approach to estimate a score reflecting the semantic relatedness between a table column and an ontology class or property using the table metadata and data. Our empirical evaluation demonstrates that our approach significantly outperforms strong baselines based on large language models.

Keywords: Semantic Models · Semantic Descriptions · Data Integration · Knowledge Graphs · Semantic Web

1 Introduction

The semantic modeling problem, also known as semantic table interpretation, involves annotating the types and relationships of columns using classes and predicates from an ontology. The resulting annotation, called a semantic description, enables tabular data to be mapped to a common ontology, a key step in many data integration pipelines. This problem has become increasingly important in today's world, where machine learning applications, analytics, and predictive workflows rely on large volumes of high-quality, well-structured data.

Existing approaches to semantic modeling generally fall into two categories. The first group leverages overlapping data between the input tables and a target knowledge graph (KG) [8,17,19,23,24,29,30,33,45]. These methods typically identify column types and relationships by matching entities and their associated properties across columns. However, it is well known that KGs are incomplete and there are domains where KGs have very little data. The second category uses supervised learning techniques that rely on labeled data sources for training [11,37,40]. These methods do not require a target KG and can be applied

D. Garijo et al. (Eds.): ISWC 2025, LNCS 16140, pp. 235–252, 2026.
https://doi.org/10.1007/978-3-032-09527-5_13

to different ontologies as long as sufficient labeled data is available. However, manual annotation is costly, and thus such methods frequently suffer from the cold-start problem in a new domain.

Instead of relying on overlapping data or labeled data sources, which are often unavailable in new domains, we can use textual descriptions and a few examples from the target ontology to identify appropriate ontology classes and properties for each table column, similar to how humans approach the task. This semantic relatedness function can be learned through distant supervision using automatically generated labels from Wikipedia tables.

In this paper, we present a novel domain-independent approach for learning the semantic descriptions of tables without overlapping data with KGs. Our method is trained with distant supervision to estimate a score reflecting the semantic relatedness between a table column and an ontology class or property. For each column, we predict top K classes and properties. Then, the candidate classes and properties are combined to create the final semantic description. The empirical evaluation shows that our approach significantly outperforms strong baselines based on large language models. Our contribution is a novel method for the semantic modeling problem in domains with limited background knowledge and no labeled tables. Our method can be applied to domain ontologies that differ from those used during training, an important setting that has not been adequately addressed by the previous methods.

2 Example of Constructing a Semantic Description

In this section, we provide a real-world example to explain how information in the table and ontology can help create the semantic description of a table of soccer players, as shown in Fig. 1.

Scenario 1 (Using Table Data): We assume that each class and property in the ontology comes with a set of example values. For example, the class *association football position (Q4611891)* includes examples such as *goalkeeper (Q201330)* and *defender (Q336286)*, whereas the class *position (Q4164871)* contains examples like *president (Q30461)* and *senator (Q15686806)*. When examining the *position* column, we find that its values such as midfielder and goalkeeper are very similar to examples of the correct class *association football position (Q4611891)* and are different from examples of *position (Q4164871)*. These example values help disambiguate between candidate classes.

Scenario 2 (Using Table Metadata): For the *player* column, we do not find any cell values in the set of examples of the correct class *Q5 human*. Nonetheless, the column's header *player* strongly suggests that the column refers to people rather than places or organizations. This demonstrates how textual cues from the table header can guide semantic interpretation, even when the data values alone are insufficient.

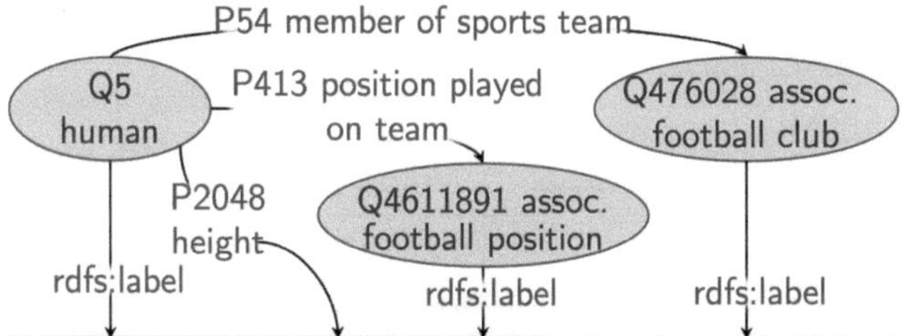

player	height	position	team
Tom Aldred	1.88	Defender	Brisbane Roar
Shae Cahill	1.71	Midfielder	Brisbane Roar
Macklin Freke	1.93	Goalkeeper	Brisbane Roar

Fig. 1. Excerpt of a table of association football players with its semantic description on top. Green circle nodes are ontology classes; blue cells on the first table row represent columns. (Color figure online)

3 Approach

In this section, we explain our approach for the semantic modeling task, which is formally defined as follows:

Definition 1. ***(Semantic Modeling Problem).*** *Given a target ontology $\mathcal{O}$ and a table $s(c_1, c_2, ..., c_n)$, where each c_i is a column, predict the semantic description $sm(s)$ of the table. The semantic description $sm(s)$ is a graph whose nodes represent table columns, ontology classes, and literal values, and whose edges are ontology properties that capture semantic relationships between nodes.*

Figure 2 shows an overview of our approach, which consists of three main steps. First, we predict candidate classes and properties for each column in the input table. Second, we construct a candidate graph that encodes possible types and relationships among the columns. Finally, we apply a Steiner tree algorithm [20] to select a coherent subgraph that forms the final semantic description.

3.1 Column Concept Prediction

In this step, we identify candidate classes and properties for each table column. For conciseness, in this section, we refer to an ontology class or ontology property as a concept. For example, the column *position* in Fig. 1 has the top 3 concepts followed by their scores: *association football position (Q4611891)*: *0.87*, *position played on team (P413)*: *0.72*, and *position held (P39)*: *0.39*. If a column is an entity column, the predicted property will be the incoming relationship to the class associated with the column as shown in Fig. 1.

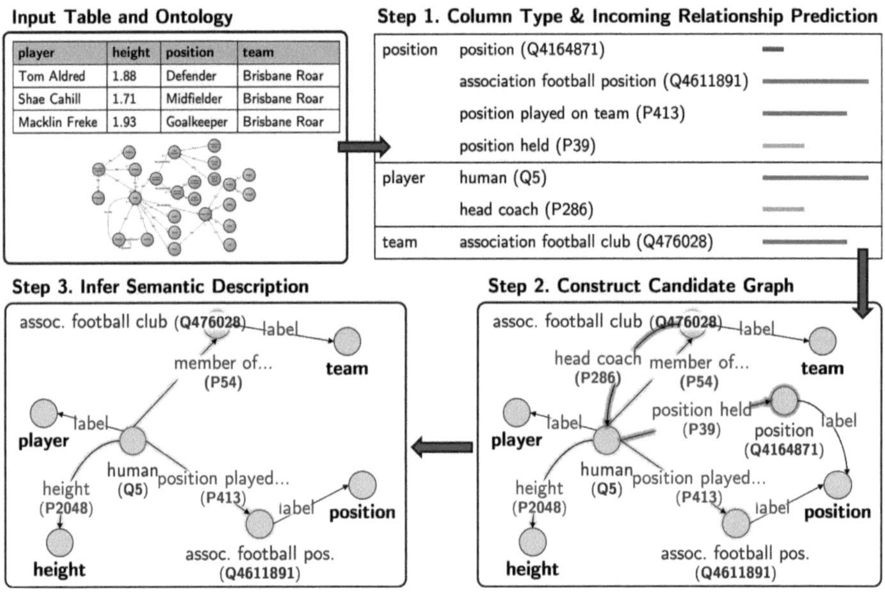

Fig. 2. Given an input table and a target ontology, we first predict candidate classes and incoming properties for each column. Next, we construct a candidate graph that encodes the possible types and relationships among the columns. Finally, we infer the semantic description by selecting a coherent subgraph that best represents the table's meaning.

Note that our goal differs from the traditional semantic labeling task [32]. The semantic labeling task predicts semantic types of a column, where a semantic type is a pair of a class and a property. In contrast, our goal is to predict a single class or a single property. Semantic labeling is more complex and may not be ideal for three reasons. First, we observe that many columns primarily express a property without an explicit associated class. For example, a column *capacity* may store the maximum capacity of stadiums, parks, restaurants, or vehicles. The correct class (e.g., *stadium*) is implicit and often requires a holistic view of the entire table to infer. This makes learning semantic types more difficult and can lead to ambiguity, especially when the same property is valid for many classes, thereby crowding out the top-K predictions with redundant combinations. The second reason is that predicting semantic types may leave out significant information that could be used in later processing steps. For example, the correct semantic type of a column *author* in Wikidata is ⟨*human (Q5)*, *rdfs:label*⟩, which fails to capture that the column contains authors (represented by the incoming *author (P50)* property). Finally, the number of possible class and property combinations can be enormous, as many properties are defined without strict domain constraints. For instance, the property *location (P276)* is broadly applicable and can be associated with a wide range of classes. As a result, predicting class and property pairs can be computationally expensive and may not scale well to large ontologies.

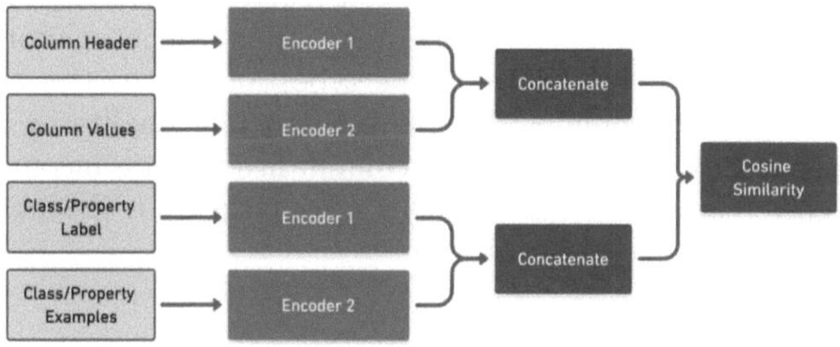

Fig. 3. Architecture of our neural network model to estimate a similarity score between a column and a concept.

To find the candidate concepts of a column, we learn to estimate the similarity score between the column and a concept based on the textual description and example values of the concept. This approach has two implications. First, we assume that a small set of example values is available for each class and property in the target ontology. In many cases, such examples can be retrieved automatically when classes or properties are linked (e.g., via *owl:sameAs*) to well-known concepts in public knowledge graphs. Second, we compute the similarity score for every concept in the ontology. While feasible for small or domain-specific ontologies, this becomes computationally impractical for large-scale ontologies like Wikidata, which include millions of classes and thousands of properties. One possible solution is to first classify the domain of a table, then cluster the concepts by domain or topic, and finally only compare concepts within the predicted domain. While promising, this direction is beyond the scope of the paper and is left for future work. For simplicity, in our evaluation, we limit the set of concepts to only the classes and properties that appear in the ground truth annotations.

Figure 3 shows the overall architecture of our neural network (NN) model for this task. First, it encodes a column name, column values, the name of a concept, and examples of the concept using encoders. Our encoders comprise a pre-trained transformer-based model[1] and a linear fully-connected layer. For data that are a list, such as column values or semantic label examples, we concatenate the data to create a sentence before feeding it to our encoders.

Our model is trained using a triplet loss [34]:

$$\mathcal{L}(\mathbf{x}, \mathbf{c}^+, \mathbf{c}^-) = \max(0, \text{dis}(\mathbf{x}, \mathbf{c}^+) - \text{dis}(\mathbf{x}, \mathbf{c}^-) + \epsilon)$$

where dis is the distance function between a column and a concept $\mathbf{c}$, $\mathbf{c}^+$ and $\mathbf{c}^-$ are the correct and incorrect concepts of the column, respectively, and the margin parameter ϵ is configured as the minimum offset between distances of similar vs

[1] We use BAAI/bge-m3 [4] in our experiment.

dissimilar pairs. In our experiment, we use $\text{dis}(a, b) = 1 - \text{cosine\_similarity}(a, b)$ and $\epsilon = 0.1$.

Our model is trained on the automatically labeled Wikipedia tables introduced by Vu et al. [41]. This dataset is constructed by linking table cells to Wikidata entities using Wikipedia hyperlinks, from which column types and relationships are inferred by matching the types and properties of associated entities across different columns. To improve labeling quality, a block list is applied to filter out examples where the column headers are incompatible with the inferred types (e.g., the column name is *soccer team*, but the labeled column type is *country (Q6256)*).

3.2 Semantic Description Prediction

Using the predicted concepts from the previous section, we perform two sub-tasks to construct the final semantic description of a table: column type prediction and column relationship prediction.

For column type prediction, we first identify entity columns using the entity column recognition algorithm introduced by [30]. This algorithm detects the types of individual cells (e.g., numbers, currency, dates), and considers a column to be an entity column if the majority of its cells are named entities. For each identified entity column, we assign the ontology class with the highest predicted score from the previous step as its correct type.

For column relationship prediction, we first construct a candidate graph that captures possible relationships among the columns in the table. Then, we employ a Steiner tree algorithm to select relationships that maximize the average likelihood as our final prediction.

Constructing Candidate Graphs. Algorithm 1 outlines the steps for constructing a candidate graph. It uses tuples of ⟨source class, property, qualifier, target class, frequency⟩, referred to as meta edges, as a guideline to discover relationships between classes and columns (lines 5 - 18). If the target ontology is a KG ontology, meta edges can be automatically extracted by grouping and counting property co-occurrences. Otherwise, they can be mined from Linked Open Data [38] or derived from domain and range constraints specified in the ontology.

The algorithm consists of two main steps. In the first step (lines 5 - 13), for each predicted property of a column, we use the meta edges to determine its source classes. Then, for each node associated with one of these source classes, we add a corresponding edge to the graph, but only if the domain and range constraints are satisfied. For example, if the predicted property is *author*, but the target column's predicted types are *company* and *publisher*, which do not appear in the range of *author*, then the property is rejected and no edge is added to the graph.

In the second step (lines 13 - 18), we iterate over each pair of source and target classes, identify the columns predicted to belong to those classes, and add edges between columns that contain properties capable of connecting the

Algorithm 1: CONSTRUCT CANDIDATE GRAPH

```
   Input: the input table T,
          columns' concepts: ℂ = {c_i : {class or property : score, ...}},
          indexes of entity columns,
          list of meta edges: { ⟨ source class, property, qualifier, target class,
          frequency⟩, ... },
          top K classes tkc,
          top K properties tkp
   Output: the candidate graph G
 1 G ← empty graph
 2 add columns in the table T as nodes to G
 3 keep maximum top tkc classes and tkp properties for each column in ℂ
 4 class2nodes ← a mapping from each ontology class to associated columns based
     on ℂ
   // add relationships between classes and columns
 5 for column_index, col_classes, col_props ← ℂ do
 6     for label, score ← col_props do
 7         candidate_edges ← meta edges used label
 8         for candidate_edge ← candidate_edges do
 9             if domains and ranges of candidate_edge do not satisfy then
10                 continue
11             for node ← class2nodes do
12                 if node.column_index ≠ column_index then
13                     add candidate_edge between node and column_index to G
   // add relationships between classes
14 for source_class, source_nodes ← class2nodes do
15     for target_class, target_nodes ← class2nodes do
16         candidate_edges ← meta edges between source_class and target_class
17         for candidate_edge ← candidate_edges do
18             add candidate_edge between pairs of source_nodes and
                 target_nodes to G
19 return G
```

two classes. To limit the graph size and reduce potential noise, we consider only top-K predicted classes and top-K predicted properties for each column (K = 5 in our experiment) in the algorithm (line 3).

Finding the Steiner Tree. To identify the correct relationships from the candidate graph, we use a modified version of the BANKS algorithm [3], as adapted by [41], to compute a Steiner tree. The algorithm works by performing upward traversals from the terminal nodes (which represent table columns) until they converge at common roots. Candidate Steiner trees are then constructed by merging possible paths from each root to all terminal nodes. Since the number of possible combinations grows exponentially, the algorithm uses beam search to find the tree with the highest average likelihood.

This algorithm requires assigning a likelihood score to each edge in the graph. We compute these scores as follows. Let

- $e = \langle u, v, p \rangle$ be an edge representing the relationship p between nodes u and v,
- $\mathrm{f}(v, c)$ be the predicted likelihood of the concept c for column v,
- $\mathrm{sou\_f}(e)$ and $\mathrm{tar\_f}(e)$ be the predicted likelihood of source and target class connected by e,
- $g(e)$ be the relative frequency of the property p being used to connect the source and target classes of e. The relative frequency is computed from the input meta edges.

We calculate the likelihood of e for different cases as follows. If e is a data property, then $\mathrm{score}(e) = f(v,p) * \mathrm{sou\_f}(e)$. If e is an object property, then $\mathrm{score}(e) = \mathrm{sou\_f}(e) * \mathrm{tar\_f}(e) * (f(v,p) * \alpha + g(e) * \beta)$, where α and β are hyper-parameters to balance the predicted likelihood by our model and the property popularity mined from the knowledge graph. Finally, if v is a statement node, then $\mathrm{score}(e = \langle u, v, p \rangle) = \max_{t,p'}(\mathrm{score}(e' = \langle v, t, p' \rangle))$.

4 Evaluation

Data. We evaluate our approach on the 250WT and T2Dv2 [33] datasets. We use the automatically labeled Wikipedia tables introduced by [41] to train our model. Both the training dataset and 250WT use the Wikidata ontology while T2Dv2 uses the DBpedia ontology. Table 1 shows statistics of these datasets. For the 250WT dataset, approximately 58% of classes and 66% of properties do not appear in the training dataset.

Metrics. We assess the performance on two tasks: column type annotation (CTA) and column relationship annotation (CPA) using the approximate precision, recall, and F1 metrics defined by the SemTab challenge [1]. These approximate metrics extend their exact version by giving partial credit when a prediction is close to the correct class or property, such as predicting a parent or child in the ontology hierarchy. Specifically, let $d(x)$ denote the shortest path from the predicted item x (a class or property) to the ground truth (GT). If x matches

Table 1. Statistics of datasets used in the evaluation

	train dataset	250WT	T2Dv2
#tables	18261	250	224
#classes	326	155	36
#properties	104	112	103

the ground truth exactly, or is its immediate parent or child, then $d(x) = 0$ or 1, respectively. The score for x is computed as follows: $\text{score}(x) = 0.8^{d(x)}$ if $d(x) \leq 5$ and x is a correct annotation or an ancestor of GT; $\text{score}(x) = 0.7^{d(x)}$ if $d(x) \leq 3$ and x is a descendant of GT; otherwise, $\text{score}(x) = 0$. For simplicity, we refer to these approximate scores as just precision, recall, or F_1.

Baselines. We developed several baselines to verify the effectiveness of our approach. The first baseline, named DSL-SM, uses DSL [32] to generate semantic types of columns of a table, then uses a frequent pattern mining method proposed by Taheriyan et al. [38] to combine the semantic types and create the semantic description of the table. The remaining baselines are based on large language models (LLM) that are trained and fine-tuned to follow textual instructions and to answer given questions. TableLlama [44] fine-tuned a Llama 2 (7B) model on 1.24 million tables for 11 tasks including CTA and CPA. We also compared with two recent LLM open-source models Llama 3.1-8B Instruct [13] and OLMo 2 [31]. For both models, we provide the table along with a list of ontology classes and properties as context, then ask the LLMs a series of questions to determine the types[2] of the columns and the relationships[3] between the columns.

Model Training. Our neural network model for column concept prediction is trained using AdamW [27] with a learning rate of 5e−5 for 5 epochs on an A5000 GPU. We also use 150 examples per target ontology class and property.

4.1 Overall Performance

Table 2 shows the performance of our method versus the baselines on the two datasets: 250WT and T2Dv2. On the 250WT dataset, our method outperforms the best-performing baseline, Llama 3.1-8B Instruct, on this dataset by 36.4% and 13.59% in F_1 scores on the CPA and CTA tasks, respectively. The baselines do not perform well on this hard dataset due to many classes and properties. Also, the precisions of LLM baselines are much lower than their recalls because they cannot predict if two columns have a relationship or not. Our gains in performance come from two sources. First, distant supervised training helps our method to better distinguish between candidate classes and properties. Second, finding the Steiner tree enables us to eliminate incorrect predictions to achieve high precision results.

All baselines achieve higher performance on the T2Dv2 dataset, as it is considerably simpler: each table is annotated with only one ontology class, and the target ontology (DBpedia) is less complex than the Wikidata ontology used

[2] Question's template: *What is the best class in the list above to describe the column {COLUMN}? Please keep your answer short with only the class or N/A if there is no suitable class. Also please wrap your answer with backticks. For example, {EXAMPLES}.*

[3] Question's template: *What is the best property in the list above to describe the relationship between the column {COLUMN1} and the column {COLUMN2}? Please keep your answer short with only the property or N/A if there is no suitable property. Also, please wrap your answer with backticks. For example, {EXAMPLE}.*

Table 2. Performance comparison between our method and the baselines on the CPA and CTA tasks. AP, AR, and AF_1 are macro-average approximate precision, recall, and F_1 in percentage, respectively

Dataset	Method	CPA			CTA		
		AP	AR	AF_1	AP	AR	AF_1
250WT	DSL-SM	19.53	22.03	19.71	27.76	27.97	27.37
	LLama 3.1- 8B Instruct	24.47	58.47	33.73	63.78	64.53	63.83
	OLMo 2	19.49	45.04	25.69	48.75	48.93	48.38
	TableLlama	23.06	29.79	21.20	41.00	35.65	35.73
	Our method	**76.12**	**67.38**	**70.13**	**77.36**	**78.35**	**77.42**
T2Dv2	DSL-SM	51.14	48.57	48.69	80.26	88.94	82.95
	LLama 3.1- 8B Instruct	56.99	55.95	56.01	70.53	67.85	67.85
	OLMo 2	63.29	60.99	61.50	91.22	89.44	89.44
	TableLlama	54.75	39.22	40.42	90.47	79.31	79.31
	Our method	**82.02**	**77.70**	**78.42**	**92.95**	**92.95**	**92.95**

in the 250WT dataset. Our method outperforms the strongest baseline on this dataset, OLMo 2, by 16.92% and 3.51% in F_1 score on the CPA and CTA tasks, respectively. These results demonstrate the effectiveness of our approach across different domains, despite using a significantly smaller model (0.5 billion versus 8 billion parameters). The performance gap of DSL-SM between the T2Dv2 and 250WT datasets further highlights the challenge of the traditional semantic labeling task in Wikidata, where the large number of classâĂŞproperty combinations greatly increases ambiguity and complexity.

Finally, TableLlama underperforms the other LLM baselines, even though it was fine-tuned for the CTA and CPA tasks. This is primarily because it tends to predict classes and properties seen in its training data, rather than selecting from those provided in the context.

4.2 Runtime

We evaluate the efficiency of our method by measuring the average runtime per table on the 250WT and T2Dv2 datasets. The experiment is conducted on a machine with an eight-core CPU and an A5000 GPU. Table 3 reports the results, comparing our method with two LLM baselines: Llama 3.1-8B Instruct and OLMo 2.

Our method is substantially faster than the LLM baselines on both datasets. On 250WT, our method processes a table in only 0.63 s on average, while Llama 3.1-8B Instruct and OLMo 2 require 32.93 and 35.74 s, respectively. Similarly, on T2Dv2, our method runs in just 0.28 s per table, compared to 8.28 s for Llama 3.1-8B Instruct and 6.88 s for OLMo 2. These results highlight the scalability and efficiency of our approach, making it suitable for large-scale table processing scenarios.

Table 3. Average runtime (in seconds) per table for the evaluated systems on the 250WT and T2Dv2 datasets

Method	250WT (sec.)	T2Dv2 (sec.)
Our method	0.63	0.28
Llama 3.1-8B Instruct	32.93	8.28
OLMo 2	35.74	6.88

4.3 Ablation Study

To assess the contribution of different input signals to overall performance, we conduct an ablation study by removing either the column header or the column values from the input. Table 4 reports the accuracy of each variant on the 250WT and T2Dv2 datasets.

The results reveal that both the column header and column values are important for accurate concept prediction. Removing either signal leads to a substantial drop in performance across both datasets. On the 250WT dataset, excluding the column header reduces the CTA F_1 score from 77.42% to 61.26%, while excluding the column values lowers it to 69.11%. A similar trend is observed for CPA. On T2Dv2, removing the header results in a 7.55-point drop in the CTA F_1 score and nearly a 25-point drop in the CPA F_1 score. Removing the values causes the CTA F_1 score to fall from 92.95% to 71.48%, and the CPA F_1 score to drop by 7.59 points.

An interesting observation is that, in many cases, the column values alone are sufficiently informative to identify the correct class or property. This is particularly evident in the T2Dv2 dataset, where using only the column values still yields a high CTA F_1 score of 85.40%. Upon examining examples from both datasets, we found that 50% of the columns have zero overlap with the provided examples of target concepts based on exact matching, and the average overlap is only around 13%. These results suggest that our approach effectively captures and leverages semantic similarity between the column values and the concept examples, even in the absence of direct matches. Futhermore, we found that the surrounding context of a table—such as the topic of the web page—can also play a crucial role. For instance, a table with just two columns, *year* and *title*, may have *title* values that resemble both books and films. While the column values alone may not clearly distinguish between the two, knowing that the table appears on a page about movies makes *film* the correct class. Incorporating such contextual signals is an interesting direction for future work.

5 Related Work

Prior research on the semantic modeling task falls into two broad categories: supervised methods designed for custom domain ontologies [8,9,11,36,37,40], and methods that leverage KGs [8,17,19,23,24,29,30,33,41,45].

Table 4. Performance of our method when (i) using only the column header, (ii) using only the column values, and (iii) using both (default). AP, AR, and AF_1 are macro-average approximate precision, recall, and F_1 in percentage, respectively

Dataset	Method	CPA			CTA		
		AP	AR	AF_1	AP	AR	AF_1
250WT	Our method	76.12	67.38	70.13	77.36	78.35	77.42
	- column headers	66.19	59.10	61.03	61.32	61.81	61.26
	- column values	63.54	59.36	60.39	69.16	69.84	69.11
T2Dv2	Our method	82.02	77.70	78.42	92.95	92.95	92.95
	- column headers	62.59	52.74	53.76	85.40	85.40	85.40
	- column values	74.48	70.83	71.03	71.48	71.48	71.48

Supervised approaches typically require two inputs: a target ontology and a set of tables annotated with their corresponding semantic descriptions. Taheriyan et al. [37] generate a semantic description by identifying a Steiner Tree that maximizes the coherence and frequency of classes and properties observed in the training data. Expanding on this idea, Vu et al. [40] propose a probabilistic graphical model (PGM) to estimate the likelihood of a semantic description and use it as a scoring function to guide the search for the most probable one. Feng et al. [11] enhance this line of work by incorporating a domain-specific KG in a post-processing step to further improve the accuracy of the predictions. More recent approaches based on transformer architectures, such as TURL [9], DODUO [36], and TorchicTab-Classification [8], frame the semantic modeling problem as a supervised classification task. In this setting, the model is trained to predict types for specific columns or relationships between given pairs of columns. However, this formulation is more constrained, as it assumes that the target columns are known in advance, an assumption that often does not hold in practice. Moreover, these methods require a huge amount of labeled training data. For example, TURL and DODUO are trained on a modified version of WikiGS [10], in which Wikipedia tables are labeled automatically with Freebase ontology. TorchicTab-Classification extends DODUO with a sub-table sampling strategy to work for large tables and is trained on SOTAB [22], a dataset constructed automatically from microdata embedded in websites. While supervised approaches offer flexibility in supporting arbitrary target ontologies, they suffer from the cold-start problem: the system requires a substantial number of labeled data sources to perform well. This limitation is even more pronounced for large ontologies, where extensive training data is needed to cover the wide range of classes and properties. In contrast, our approach does not require retraining to be applied to a new domain. Although it relies on example values for each ontology class or property, these examples can typically be obtained with minimal effort. For instance, we can reuse values from similar classes or properties in a knowledge graph, or prompt a large language model to generate them. Furthermore, performance on new domains can be further improved by simply adding relevant example values to the target table.

Methods that leverage existing knowledge in KG are typically unsupervised. However, some of them can incorporate labeled data to fine-tune their parameters. These approaches generally follow a common pipeline: they begin by linking table cells to KG entities (Entity Linking, or EL), and then use the properties associated with those entities to infer column types (CTA) and column relationships (CPA). Limaye et al. [24] and Mulwad et al. [29] are among the first works to solve the three tasks (EL, CTA, and CPA) jointly using probabilistic graphical models. However, their methods are limited to entity columns and do not accommodate columns containing literal values. Subsequent research shifted toward iterative approaches and expanded the scope to include literal columns. Ritze et al. [33] proposed an iterative method that begins by identifying the subject (entity) column of a table, followed by generating candidate relationships between the subject and the remaining columns. The method then refines both the candidate entities and relationships over multiple iterations until convergence. Zhang et al. [45] further improved this process by refining entity linking outputs to be consistent with both the predicted column types and the overall table domain, which is estimated using a bag-of-words approach. More recent systems that achieved top performance in the SemTab challenges [1,7,15,21], such as MTab [30], DAGOBAH [19], and others KGCode-Tab [23], LinkingPark [6], BBW [35], TorchicTab-Heuristic [8], and SemTex [17] also follow the iterative paradigm. These systems introduce improvements at various stages of the pipeline, such as more accurate candidate entity retrieval and enhanced scoring mechanisms for ranking annotations. GRAMS [42] extends the semantic modeling task to the full setting, supporting the prediction of n-ary relationships and missing context values in Wikipedia tables. Specifically, they construct a candidate graph of potential relationships and use a Probabilistic Soft Logic [2] to rank the edges and select the most likely subgraph that represents the table's semantics. GRAMS+ [41] further generalizes this framework to handle non-Wikipedia tables by automatically generating labeled data from Wikipedia to train models that score candidate entities and candidate relationships. Compared to our approach, methods that rely on knowledge graphs are constrained to tables that contain overlapping data with the target KG and can only map to the KG's ontology. In contrast, our method does not depend on such overlap and can be applied to a wide range of domains and ontologies without retraining.

Finally, there is some previous work on table understanding that has different or restricted settings compared to the semantic modeling task in this paper [25]. For example, DSL [32], ColNet [5], JellyFish [43], Sherlock [18] focus on only annotating the column types in the tables. Tab2KG [12]'s core idea is to address the semantic labeling task similar to DSL using features such as histograms, average text length extracted from data in a target knowledge graph. However, after mapping columns to pairs of ontology classes and properties, Tab2KG constructs the final semantic description by assigning object properties to class pairs without resolving ambiguities (i.e., treating all candidate relationships equally without disambiguation). Luzuriaga et al. [28] focus on generating triples of relationships between columns for Wikipedia tables. The Metadata-to-KG track in the SemTab 2024 challenge [16] focuses on mapping a given column to an ontology property using only the table header. Adwan [39], the winning system in this track, employs an LLM with a retrieval-augmented generation (RAG) approach to first retrieve candidate properties and then rerank them. The dataset used in the first round is a subset of the T2Dv2 dataset, and the system achieves an accuracy of 62%. The authors also present an alternative method that achieves higher accuracy (75%) by retrieving properties from the LLM parametric memory rather than from the context. This is motivated by findings that top-performing LLMs are often pretrained on DBpedia data [26].

6 Conclusion

In this paper, we presented a novel, domain-independent method for semantic table interpretation that does not rely on overlapping data with a knowledge graph. Using distant supervision, our method learns to identify the top-K most relevant classes and properties for each table column and constructs semantic descriptions based on these candidates. Our evaluation demonstrates that the approach achieves strong performance across different ontologies, including those in unseen domains. This makes the method especially effective in scenarios where labeled data is scarce or unavailable.

Our approach is also particularly well-suited for semi-automated systems for publishing tables to knowledge graphs, such as Karma [14]. Since our method produces the top-K candidate classes and properties for each column, it can assist users in correcting errors introduced by the automated semantic modeling process. Moreover, because our method does not require retraining to incorporate newly annotated tables, it enables more efficient and incremental updates, an important feature for interactive systems where retraining may be time-consuming.

7 Future Work

There are several promising directions for extending this work. First, while our method computes similarity scores between a table column and every class and property in the target ontology, this becomes computationally expensive for large ontologies such as Wikidata, which contains millions of entities and thousands of relations. A potential solution is to first classify the domain of a table and then identify the subset of ontology concepts that are relevant to that domain based on their usage in the knowledge graph. This strategy could significantly reduce the number of concepts that need to be considered, making the approach more scalable to large and heterogeneous ontologies.

Second, we believe that the performance of the column concept prediction component (Sect. 3.1) can be further improved with models that better leverage the surrounding context of the table. One approach we experimented with involves fine-tuning a Llama model that is given the full table, a candidate concept (including its textual description and example values), and prompted with a yes/no question asking whether the concept correctly describes the given column. The similarity score is then computed by applying a softmax over the logits corresponding to the *Yes* and *No* responses. While preliminary results showed lower overall performance compared to our current model, this LLM-based approach achieved a notable 8.43% improvement in CPA F_1 score (86.85%) on the T2Dv2 dataset. However, the main drawback is its high inference cost, due to the large number of combinations between columns and candidate concepts. Specifically, prediction took 93 h (22 minutes per table) for the 250WT dataset and 26 h (7 minutes per table) for the T2Dv2 dataset. Finding efficient strategies to reduce the cost would be an important step toward making this approach practical at scale.

Finally, many real-world tables contain auxiliary or uninformative columns that may not correspond to any class or property in the target ontology. Introducing an "unknown" concept, augmented with previously seen column headers and cell values, could help our concept prediction component identify and filter out such columns. This capability would not only improve the robustness of semantic labeling but also enhance overall performance by reducing noise during prediction.

Acknowledgments. This material is based upon works supported by the Defense Advanced Research Projects Agency (DARPA) under Agreement No. HR00112390132 and Contract No. 140D0423C0093. Any opinions, findings and conclusions or recommendations expressed in this material are those of the authors and do not necessarily reflect the views of DARPA or its Contracting Agent, the U.S. Department of the Interior.

The first author is grateful for the support of the Vietnam Education Foundation (VEF) Fellowship, which provided funding during the early stages of this research.

Supplemental Material Statement. The source code for our approach is publicly available at https://github.com/binh-vu/iswc25.

References

1. Abdelmageed, N., et al.: Results of semtab 2022. In: Semantic Web Challenge on Tabular Data to Knowledge Graph Matching (SemTab 2022). CEUR Workshop Proceedings, vol. 3320. CEUR (2022). https://openaccess.city.ac.uk/id/eprint/29744/, 2022 Copyright for this paper by its authors. Use permitted under Creative Commons License Attribution 4.0 International (CC BY 4.0)
2. Bach, S.H., Broecheler, M., Huang, B., Getoor, L.: Hinge-loss markov random fields and probabilistic soft logic. J. Mach. Learn. Res. **18**(109), 1–67 (2017)
3. Bhalotia, G., Hulgeri, A., Nakhe, C., Chakrabarti, S., Sudarshan, S.: Keyword searching and browsing in databases using BANKS. In: Proceedings 18th International Conference on Data Engineering, pp. 431–440 (2002). https://doi.org/10.1109/ICDE.2002.994756

4. Chen, J., Xiao, S., Zhang, P., Luo, K., Lian, D., Liu, Z.: Bge m3-embedding: multi-lingual, multi-functionality, multi-granularity text embeddings through self-knowledge distillation (2024)
5. Chen, J., Jiménez-Ruiz, E., Horrocks, I., Sutton, C.: ColNet: embedding the semantics of web tables for column type prediction. AAAI **33**(01), 29–36 (2019)
6. Chen, S., et al.: LinkingPark: an integrated approach for semantic table interpretation. https://ceur-ws.org/Vol-2775/paper7.pdf?ref=https://githubhelp.com, Accessed 6 Oct 2023
7. Cutrona, V., et al.: Results of semtab 2021. In: 20th International Semantic Web Conference. vol. 3103, pp. 1–12. CEUR Workshop Proceedings (2022). https://openaccess.city.ac.uk/id/eprint/28056/, copyright 2021 for the individual papers by the papers' authors. This volume and its papers are published under the Creative Commons License Attribution 4.0 International (CC BY 4.0)
8. Dasoulas, I., Yang, D., Duan, X., Dimou, A.: TorchicTab: semantic table annotation with wikidata and language models. In: CEUR Workshop Proceedings, pp. 21–37. CEUR Workshop Proceedings (2023)
9. Deng, X., Sun, H., Lees, A., Wu, Y., Yu, C.: TURL: table understanding through representation learning (2020)
10. Efthymiou, V., Hassanzadeh, O., Rodriguez-Muro, M., Christophides, V.: Matching web tables with knowledge base entities: from entity lookups to entity embeddings. In: The Semantic Web – ISWC 2017, pp. 260–277. Springer International Publishing (2017). https://doi.org/10.1007/978-3-319-68288-4_16
11. Feng, Z.W., et al.: Automatic semantic modeling for structural data source with the prior knowledge from knowledge graph (2021)
12. Gottschalk, S., Demidova, E.: Tab2kg: semantic table interpretation with lightweight semantic profiles. Semantic Web **13**(3), 571–597 (2022)
13. Grattafiori, A., et al.: The llama 3 herd of models. arXiv preprint arXiv:2407.21783 (2024)
14. Gupta, S., Szekely, P., Knoblock, C.A., Goel, A., Taheriyan, M., Muslea, M.: Karma: a system for mapping structured sources into the semantic web. In: Extended Semantic Web Conference, pp. 430–434. Springer (2012)
15. Hassanzadeh, O., et al.: Results of semtab 2023. In: CEUR Workshop Proceedings vol. 3557, pp. 1–14 (2023)
16. Hassanzadeh, O., et al.: Proceedings of the Semantic Web Challenge on Tabular Data to Knowledge Graph Matching co-located with the 23rd International Semantic Web Conference (ISWC 2024), Baltimore, USA, November 13, 2024, CEUR Workshop Proceedings, vol. 3889. CEUR-WS.org (2025). https://ceur-ws.org/Vol-3889
17. Henriksen, E.G., et al.: Semtex: A hybrid approach for semantic table interpretation (2023)
18. Hulsebos, M., Hu, K., et al.: Sherlock: a deep learning approach to semantic data type detection. In: Proceedings of the 25th ACM SIGKDD International Conference on Knowledge Discovery & Data Mining, pp. 1500–1508. KDD '19, Association for Computing Machinery, New York (2019)
19. Huynh, V.P., Chabot, Y., Labbé, T., Liu, J., Troncy, R.: From heuristics to language models: a journey through the universe of semantic table interpretation with DAGOBAH. Semantic Web Challenge on Tabular Data to Knowledge Graph Matching (SemTab) (2022)
20. Hwang, F.K., Richards, D.S.: Steiner tree problems. Networks **22**(1), 55–89 (1992)

21. Jimenez-Ruiz, E., Hassanzadeh, O., Efthymiou, V., Chen, J., Srinivas, K., Cutrona, V.: Results of semtab 2020. CEUR Workshop Proc. **2775**, 1–8 (2020). http://ceur-ws.org/Vol-2775/, copyright 2020 for this paper by its authors
22. Korini, K., Peeters, R., Bizer, C.: Sotab: the wdc schema. org table annotation benchmark. In: CEUR Workshop Proceedings. vol. 3320, pp. 14–19. RWTH Aachen (2022)
23. Li, X., et al.: KGCODE-Tab results for SemTab 2022. https://ceur-ws.org/Vol-3320/paper5.pdf, Accessed 6 Oct 2023
24. Limaye, G., Sarawagi, S., Chakrabarti, S.: Annotating and searching web tables using entities, types and relationships. In: Proceedings of the VLDB Endowment. vol. 3, pp. 1338–1347. VLDB Endowment (2010)
25. Liu, J., Chabot, Y., Troncy, R., Huynh, V.P., Labbé, T., Monnin, P.: From tabular data to knowledge graphs: a survey of semantic table interpretation tasks and methods. J. Web Semantics **76**, 100761 (2023)
26. Lo, P.C., Tsai, Y.H., Lim, E.P., Hwang, S.Y.: On exploring the reasoning capability of large language models with knowledge graphs. arXiv preprint arXiv:2312.00353 (2023)
27. Loshchilov, I., Hutter, F.: Decoupled weight decay regularization. In: International Conference on Learning Representations (2019). https://openreview.net/forum?id=Bkg6RiCqY7
28. Luzuriaga, J., Munoz, E., Rosales-Mendez, H., Hogan, A.: Merging web tables for relation extraction with knowledge graphs. IEEE Trans. Knowl. Data Eng., 1–1 (2021)
29. Mulwad, V., Finin, T., Joshi, A.: Semantic Message Passing for Generating Linked Data from Tables. In: Alani, H., et al., (eds.) ISWC 2013. LNCS, vol. 8218, pp. 363–378. Springer, Heidelberg (2013). https://doi.org/10.1007/978-3-642-41335-3_23
30. Nguyen, P., Yamada, I., Kertkeidkachorn, N., Ichise, R., Takeda, H.: SemTab 2021: tabular data annotation with MTab tool. http://ceur-ws.org/Vol-3103/paper8.pdf, Accessed 6 Oct 2023
31. OLMo, T., et al.: 2 olmo 2 furious. arXiv preprint arXiv:2501.00656 (2024)
32. Pham, M., Alse, S., Knoblock, C.A., Szekely, P.: Semantic labeling: a domain-independent approach. In: Groth, P., Simperl, E., Gray, A., Sabou, M., Krötzsch, M., Lecue, F., Flöck, F., Gil, Y. (eds.) ISWC 2016. LNCS, vol. 9981, pp. 446–462. Springer, Cham (2016). https://doi.org/10.1007/978-3-319-46523-4_27
33. Ritze, D., Lehmberg, O., Bizer, C.: Matching HTML tables to DBpedia. In: Proceedings of the 5th International Conference on Web Intelligence, Mining and Semantics, pp. 1–6. No. Article 10 in WIMS '15, Association for Computing Machinery, New York (2015)
34. Schroff, F., Kalenichenko, D., Philbin, J.: FaceNet: a unified embedding for face recognition and clustering. In: Proceedings/CVPR, IEEE Computer Society Conference on Computer Vision and Pattern Recognition. IEEE Computer Society Conference on Computer Vision and Pattern Recognition, pp. 815–823 (2015). https://doi.org/10.1109/CVPR.2015.7298682, https://www.cv-foundation.org/openaccess/content_cvpr_2015/html/Schroff_FaceNet_A_Unified_2015_CVPR_paper.html
35. Shigapov, R., Zumstein, P., Kamlah, J., Oberlander, L., Mechnich, J., Schumm, I.: bbw: matching CSV to wikidata via meta-lookup. https://madoc.bib.uni-mannheim.de/57386/3/paper2.pdf, Accessed 6 Oct 2023

36. Suhara, Y., et al.: Annotating columns with pre-trained language models. In: Proceedings of the 2022 International Conference on Management of Data, New York. ACM (2022)
37. Taheriyan, M., Knoblock, C.A., Szekely, P., Ambite, J.L.: Learning the semantics of structured data sources. J. Web Semantics **37–38**, 152–169 (2016)
38. Taheriyan, M., Knoblock, C.A., Szekely, P., Ambite, J.L.: Leveraging linked data to discover semantic relations within data sources. In: Lecture Notes in Computer Science, pp. 549–565. Lecture notes in computer science, Springer International Publishing, Cham (2016). https://doi.org/10.1007/978-3-319-46523-4_33
39. Vandemoortele, N., Steenwinckel, B., Hoecke, S., Ongenae, F.: Scalable table-to-knowledge graph matching from metadata using LLMS (2024)
40. Vu, B., Knoblock, C., Pujara, J.: Learning semantic models of data sources using probabilistic graphical models. In: The World Wide Web Conference, pp. 1944–1953. WWW '19, Association for Computing Machinery, New York (2019)
41. Vu, B., Knoblock, C.A., Shbita, B., Lin, F.: Exploiting distant supervision to learn semantic descriptions of tables with overlapping data. In: International Semantic Web Conference, pp. 116–134. Springer (2024)
42. Vu, B., Knoblock, C.A., Szekely, P., Pham, M., Pujara, J.: A Graph-Based Approach for Inferring Semantic Descriptions of Wikipedia Tables. In: Hotho, A., et al., (eds.) ISWC 2021. LNCS, vol. 12922, pp. 304–320. Springer, Cham (2021). https://doi.org/10.1007/978-3-030-88361-4_18
43. Zhang, H., Dong, Y., Xiao, C., Oyamada, M.: Jellyfish: a large language model for data preprocessing. arXiv preprint arXiv:2312.01678 (2023)
44. Zhang, T., Yue, X., Li, Y., Sun, H.: Tablellama: towards open large generalist models for tables. arXiv preprint arXiv:2311.09206 (2023)
45. Zhang, Z.: Effective and efficient semantic table interpretation using TableMiner+. Semant. Web **8**(6), 921–957 (2017)

Neuro-Symbolic Adaptive Query Processing over Knowledge Graphs

Chang Qin[1,2(✉)] and Maribel Acosta[1]

[1] Technical University of Munich, Munich, Germany
maribel.acosta@tum.de

[2] Fraunhofer-Institue für Intelligente Analyse- und Informationssysteme IAIS, Sankt Augustin, Germany
chang.qin@iais.fraunhofer.de

Abstract. In adaptive query processing (AQP), the query plan is adjusted based on actual execution conditions. AQP has proven effective in dynamic querying environments, such as knowledge graphs (KGs) on the web. The technique known as eddies enables tuple-wise adaptivity by dynamically reordering query operators at runtime. Eddies operate under a predefined symbolic routing policy, which determines the next operator to process each tuple. Although various routing policies have been proposed, their effectiveness varies across queries, and choosing a suboptimal policy can significantly degrade performance. To address this challenge, we propose a neuro-symbolic AQP approach that combines representation learning and supervised learning to predict the optimal routing policy for a given query. Experimental results on synthetic and real-world KGs demonstrate that our method achieves high precision in predicting optimal policies, is efficient to train and use at inference time, and generalizes well to queries with constants not seen during training.

Keywords: Adaptive Query Processing · Query Optimization · Neuro-Symbolic System · GNN · Tree-LSTM · MLP · Knowledge Graphs

1 Introduction

Adaptive Query Processing (AQP) [6] is a paradigm designed to overcome the limitations of the traditional optimize-then-execute approach to query execution, where a single static query plan is generated before execution begins and followed regardless of runtime conditions. AQP enables query engines to dynamically adapt execution strategies, improving performance in the presence of unpredictable data distributions, network latencies, or intermediate result sizes.

Among the AQP techniques from the literature, *eddies* [4] allow for seamlessly adapting the query plan on the fly, without the need of re-invoking the optimizer. Eddies operate at a tuple-at-a-time level, dynamically selecting the next physical operator for each intermediate tuple based on a routing policy. Originally proposed for relational databases, eddies have been successfully adapted

D. Garijo et al. (Eds.): ISWC 2025, LNCS 16140, pp. 253–270, 2026.
https://doi.org/10.1007/978-3-032-09527-5_14

to SPARQL query processing over RDF knowledge graphs in the nLDE query engine [1]. In nLDE, routing policies guide the evaluation of SPARQL queries over Triple Pattern Fragment (TPF) servers, where execution involves numerous requests and intermediate result transfers – both of which are highly sensitive to network delays and suboptimal query planning.

However, the effectiveness of eddy-based systems such as nLDE is limited by their reliance on manually defined and fixed routing policies. In practice, only a small set of predefined policies are used uniformly across all queries, which may lead to suboptimal performance due to the varying structures and selectivities of SPARQL queries. Selecting a suboptimal policy can degrade query performance significantly [2], making the choice of routing strategy a critical factor in eddy-based AQP.

In this work, we tackle the challenge of automatically selecting the optimal routing policies for a given query from a pool of candidate policies. We frame this as a multi-label classification problem and we propose a Neuro-Symbolic AQP system (NSAQP) that integrates symbolic routing policies with neural models. First, we extend the pool of candidate routing policies from the state of the art. Second, we devise a suitable SPARQL query representation such that NSAQP can effectively learn to map a query to its most suitable routing policy. Traditional query representations often rely on rule-based methods to capture structural similarities in queries [3,10,22], yet, these lack flexibility when dealing with complex or diverse query structures. In contrast, we investigate two complementary architectures: the first models query graphs with Graph Neural Networks (GNNs) [16], and the second represents query plans using Tree Long Short-Term Memory networks (Tree-LSTMs) [7]; these architectures have shown remarkable results in other query optimization tasks. Lastly, NSAQP includes a Multi-Layer Perceptron (MLP) [14] that predicts query-specific routing policies in a supervised setting, using the learned representations of queries and plans as inputs and the symbolic policy labels as targets.

We show through experiments that our approach effectively selects optimal routing policies with 0.90 precision in LUBM, and 0.81 in YAGO. In addition, NSAQP exhibits efficient training behavior and achieves high precision even with a fraction of the training data. The NSAQP models also introduce negligible overhead at inference time, requiring from 0.02 to 20 milliseconds for a prediction. Lastly, our experiments show that NSAQP can still achieve high precision when handling SPARQL queries that contain IRIs and literals that were not seen by the model during training. All these results show that NSAQP can be integrated into eddy-based AQP engines, leading to improved query performance compared to fixed-policy baselines with low training effort.

In summary, the contributions of our work are:

1. We introduce novel symbolic routing policies for eddies.
2. We design a novel and effective Neuro-Symbolic Adaptive Query Processing system (NSAQP), enabling query-specific decision-making for optimal routing policies.

3. We investigate two neural architectures GNN and Tree-LSTM, based on query graphs and optimized query plans, respectively, to learn an effective SPARQL query representation for NSAQP.
4. Our experiments show that NSAQP achieves high precision in predicting query-specific optimal routing policies.

2 Related Work

Routing Policies for Eddies. Eddies rely on a *routing policy* to select the next operator to send a tuple to. A variety of routing policies have been proposed to optimize tuple, broadly categorized into two approaches: Source-Based Routing (SBR) and Content-Based Routing (CBR) [5]. SBR makes routing decisions based on the performance metrics of each operator, treating all tuples from the same stream uniformly. The key operator performance metrics used for routing strategies include queue length [4,19], selectivity [1,4,13,19], and processing cost [19]. These metrics serve as critical criteria for optimizing the routing decisions. In contrast, CBR integrates the content of tuples into the decision-making process, exploiting correlations between tuple attributes and operator performance metrics. For instance, Bizarro et al. [5] proposed a CBR approach that partitions the data into distinct classes with similar statistical properties by identifying correlations between tuple content and operator selectivities. Then, the eddies apply tailored routing plans to each data class. While several routing policies have been proposed, the most recent studies [1] show that the selection of the best performing policy varies can greatly vary from query to query.

Eddies Framework. The original eddies [4] framework was designed for centralized query processing, focusing on dynamically reordering operators to overcome optimization errors. Yet, as data sizes grew and distributed systems became more prevalent, eddies were adapted to handle distributed and decentralized environments in relational query processing [19] and SPARQL query processing [1] in RDF-based systems. In the context of RDF, nLDE [1] introduces eddies into SPARQL query processing against Triple Pattern Fragment [21] servers. nLDE primarily employs SBR strategies and leverages metadata such as triple pattern cardinality and routing policies to address data transfer delays and skewed data distributions, demonstrating improvements in continuous performance [1]. Despite its contributions, nLDE faces two key limitations. Firstly, it relies solely on two reordering policies: selectivity and random routing, restricting its ability to fully optimize query execution. Secondly, nLDE applies a (manually) preselected policy across all queries, without tailoring its approach to the diverse structures and requirements of different SPARQL queries.

Machine Learning for Eddies. The routing policies used by eddies are based on performance metrics, which can be represented symbolically. For instance, some policies prioritize selective operators (which produce a low rate of answers), while others prefer operators with low input-output latency. Rather than specifying a routing policy manually, reinforcement learning-based eddies [20] instead

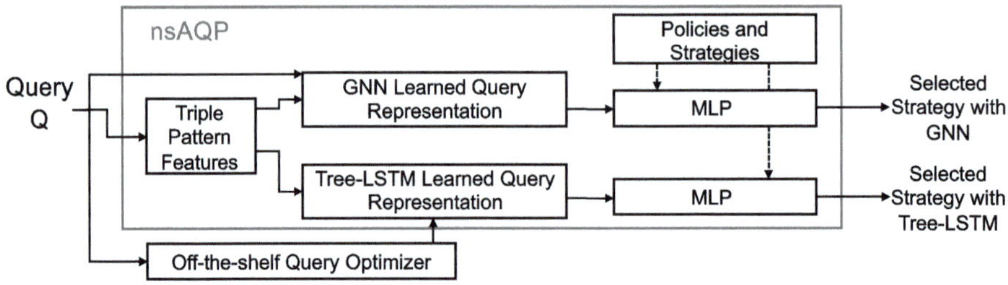

Fig. 1. Overview of the nsAQP architecture. Given an input query Q, the system generates vector representations that are processed by two alternative neural models. A GNN learns from the query graph, while a Tree-LSTM encodes the initial execution plan produced by an off-the-shelf query optimizer. Each representation is then fed into a MLP, which uses predefined policies as labels to predict the optimal routing strategy.

learn a policy on-the-fly for a given query workload by observing operator performance and execution rewards, aiming to discover an optimal routing policy through exploration. In contrast, we propose a supervised ML approach that efficiently selects an optimal routing policy from a given set of candidate policies.

3 Our Approach: nsAQP

We propose a neuro-symbolic adaptive query processing (nsAQP) approach in eddies, where the goal is to predict the most effective routing policy for a given query. Traditional eddies rely on fixed symbolic routing policies to guide the routing of intermediate tuples. While effective in some scenarios, a fixed policy may underperform in some queries. To overcome this, nsAQP is equipped with a neural model to predict the best routing policy based on query characteristics.

Figure 1 shows an overview of nsAQP. In this work, we design new routing policies and strategies (Sect. 3.1) that can outperform traditional ones for specific query types. Next, we devise vector representations that serve as input to the neural model. As a basis, we describe how terms and triple patterns are represented as vectors using knowledge graph embeddings (Sect. 3.2). Then we investigate two alternative query representations. The first learns a vector directly from the query structure using a Graph Neural Network (Sect. 3.3). The second, using Tree-LSTM (Sect. 3.4), learns a vector from the plan generated by the query optimizer, which reflects the system's initial execution state before adaptivity takes effect. The query representation is then fed into a Multi-Layer Perceptron (Sect. 3.5), which outputs the best routing strategy for the query. The selected routing policy fully maintains the tuple-at-a-time adaptivity as in the original Eddy model (Table 2).

Table 1. Definitions of operator priority under different routing policies.

Routing Policy	Priority Definition for $o \in \mathcal{O}$
Selectivity Routing [1]	$priority(o) = 1 - \frac{T_{\text{output}}(o)}{T_{\text{input}}(o)}$ Prioritizes operators with fewer output tuples.
Productivity Routing	$priority(o) = \frac{T_{\text{output}}(o)}{T_{\text{input}}(o)}$ Prioritizes operators that produce more output.
Load Balancing Routing	$priority(o) = \frac{1}{1+T_{\text{output}}(o)}$ Balances workload by prioritizing low-output operators.
No Policy	$priority(o) = d(o)$ Prioritizes operators based on their depth $d(.)$ in the plan.

Table 2. Routing rules for under constrained and unconstrained conditions.

Constraint	**Routing Rule**
With Constraint [1]	$o^* = \begin{cases} \arg\max_{o \in \mathcal{O}_t \cap \mathcal{O}_{\text{S}}} priority(o) & \text{if } \mathcal{O}_t \cap \mathcal{O}_{\text{S}} \neq \emptyset, \\ \arg\max_{o \in \mathcal{O}_t \cap \mathcal{O}_{\text{NS}}} priority(o) & \text{if } \mathcal{O}_t \cap \mathcal{O}_{\text{S}} = \emptyset. \end{cases}$
Without Constraint	$o^* = \arg\max_{o \in \mathcal{O}_t} priority(o)$

3.1 Routing Policies and Strategies

Routing policies are symbolic reasoning units defined in terms of the operators' performance metric to determine the *priority* of operator. In this way, tuples are routed to the operator with the highest priority. To start, the operator priority is initialized following the optimized plan – the operators with highest depth $d(.)$ are executed first –, and these priorities are updated at runtime according to the routing policy. Let $\mathcal{O}$ denote the set of all operators in a query plan. The performance of a given operator $o \in \mathcal{O}$ can be measured at runtime by the number of tuples it consumes and produces, denoted as $T_{\text{input}}(o)$ and $T_{\text{output}}(o)$, respectively. In addition to the selectivity policy of nLDE [1], we introduce three complementary routing policies, as described in Table 1.

Besides the priority, routing policies can also adhere to *constraints* that enforce routing rules to ensure high-performance. For instance, a default constraint states that tuples are only routed to operators that share variables in common [1]. This ensures that no Cartesian products are unnecessarily introduced into the plan. Another constraint refers to the type of plan operators. Let $\mathcal{O}_t \subset \mathcal{O}$ be the set of operators where a tuple t that can be routed to, $\mathcal{O}_{\text{NS}} \subset \mathcal{O}$ be the set of non-symmetric operators (e.g., Nested Loop join), and $\mathcal{O}_{\text{S}} = \mathcal{O} \setminus \mathcal{O}_{\text{NS}}$ be the set of symmetric operators (e.g., Symmetric Hash join). nLDE implements a constraint where tuples cannot be routed to non-symmetric operator if there are other available symmetric operators. In this work, we eliminate this constraint to study its effect on query performance. We denote the former and modified strategies as *With Constraint* and *Without Constraint*, respectively, as shown in

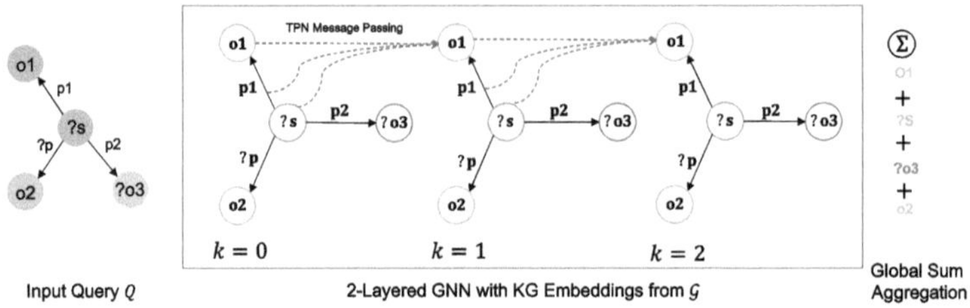

Fig. 2. GNN-based model. A SPARQL query is represented using entity and predicate embeddings, along with the connectivity between these components. For clarity, the TPN aggregation process is illustrated for a single node. After the aggregation, the entire query graph is represented by the sum of all node embeddings [16].

Table 2. The combination of a routing policy and constraints is termed a *routing strategy*, which decides how tuples are dynamically assigned to operators.

3.2 Triple Pattern Features

Triple patterns are the atomic units of SPARQL queries and serve as the foundation and initial representation for learning both query graph (Sect. 3.3) and tree plan (Sect. 3.4) representations. By using the same featurization of triple patterns across models, we ensure that any differences in performance arise from structural distinctions rather than from variations in the initial representation.

In this work, we use the triple pattern featurization by Schwabe et al. [16], which distinguishes between *bound terms* (such as IRIs or literals) and *variable terms* in a triple pattern. For a term x, its feature vector $\mathbf{x}$ is as follows:

$$\mathbf{x} := \begin{cases} \mathit{rdf2vec}(x) \parallel \mathit{occ}(x), & \text{if } x \text{ is a bound term,} \\ \mathrm{ID}(x), 1, 1, \ldots, 1, & \text{if } x \text{ is a variable term.} \end{cases} \tag{1}$$

where *rdf2vec(x)* is the RDF2Vec [15] embedding of x, and occ(x) is the count of x in the KG, and ID is a randomly assigned number for a variable in the query.

Lastly, we define the feature vector $\mathbf{t}$ of a triple pattern $t = (s, p, o)$ as:

$$\mathbf{t} := \mathbf{s} \parallel \mathbf{p} \parallel \mathbf{o} \tag{2}$$

This featurization provides two major advantages. First, using RDF2Vec embeddings [15] allows for capturing semantic relationships among entities. In this process, all terms – nodes (IRIs or literals) and predicates – are treated as nodes in random walks, producing embeddings that support every type of term atom within the KG. We compute embeddings only for entities and predicates observed during training, so the entire dataset is not required locally, and NSAQP remains effective even in inductive settings where unseen IRIs or literals appear (see Sect. 4.5). Second, by encoding the triple pattern in this way, the position of the subject, predicate, and object is also implicitly captured within the concatenated feature vector. This ensures that the structural role of each

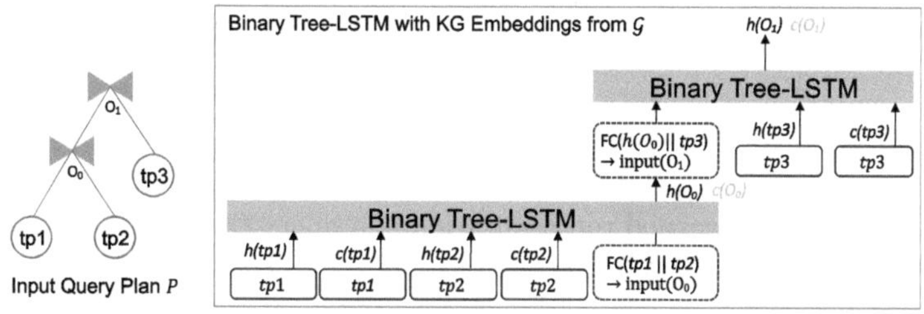

Fig. 3. Architecture of the binary Tree-LSTM model. Each triple pattern is represent by embeddings and processed to produce hidden states $h(\cdot)$ and cell states $c(\cdot)$. Internal nodes O_0 and O_1 are constructed by concatenating child node features and applying a fully connected (FC) layer. The final representation of plan is $h(O_1)$.

term within the triple pattern is encoded alongside its semantic and contextual information.

3.3 Learned Query Representation: GNN-Based Model

In this representation, we treat a SPARQL query Q as a graph $G = (V, E)$, where V are the subject and objects of triple patterns, and E are the directed edges connecting the nodes. We denote $\mathbf{Q}_G$ the learned representation of a query Q with its graph G. This representation is learned with GNCE [16] , i.e., $\mathbf{Q}_G = \text{GNCE}(G, \mathbf{X})$, where $\mathbf{X}$ is the matrix of the initial features of each term x (Eq. 1) that occurs in the query. We chose GNCE over alternative architectures, as it has demonstrated superior performance in other query optimization-related tasks.

The GNCE model leverages a GNN with Message-Passing Layers, as follows:

$$\mathbf{H}^{(k)} = \text{GNN}^{(k)}(G, \mathbf{H}^{(k-1)}), \quad \text{with } \mathbf{H}^{(0)} = \mathbf{X} \tag{3}$$

The GNN then applies two rounds of Message Passing ($k = 2$) to aggregate information across the graph, where each Message-Passing Layer computes updated node embeddings by aggregating representations from neighboring nodes using the connections in E. GNCE includes a custom Message Passing function called Triple Pattern Network (TPN) based on *GINECONV* [11] to preserve structural information from both incoming and outgoing edges (see Fig. 2).

After the Message-Passing Layers, the resulting node embeddings are aggregated using Global Sum Aggregation to generate a single vector representation of the entire query graph, as follows:

$$\mathbf{Q}_G = \sum_{x \in V} \mathbf{h}_x^{(k)}, \quad \text{with } \mathbf{h}_x^{(k)} \text{ the } x^{\text{th}} \text{ column in } \mathbf{H}^{(k)} \tag{4}$$

3.4 Learned Plan Representation: Tree-LSTM Model

This representation is learned from a query plan as shown in Fig. 3. Given a SPARQL Q, a plan P (devised by a query optimizer) is a tree where the leaf nodes are triple patterns, and the intermediate nodes are query operators (i.e., joins) in Q. We denote $\mathbf{Q}_P$ the learned representation of a query Q using the plan P. This representation is learned with Tree-LSTM [18], i.e., $\mathbf{Q}_P = \text{Tree-LSTM}(P, \mathbf{X})$.

Initial Plan Representation. Each node in P contains an ID, a type (leaf or parent), a triple pattern (for leaf nodes), and a cardinality value. Each leaf node corresponds to a triple pattern $j = (s_j, p_j, o_j)$, which we encode following Eq. 2, yielding a feature vector $x_j := \mathbf{t}_j$. Each parent node is a join operator that references its left and right child nodes. We do not transform or combine child features at this stage but only record node connections. To build a hierarchical structure from these nodes, the plan P is traversed using depth-first search (DFS), resulting in an initial representation of the query plan.

Model Definition. On the initial plan representation, we apply a binary Tree-LSTM [18] to compute hidden and cell states at each node. This approach extends the standard Tree-LSTM to handle exactly two children per parent (left and right), reflecting the structure of SPARQL join operations.

Leaf Node States. For each node j, we begin with its input feature vector x_j. Two learnable transformations are then applied, each followed by a tanh activation, to produce the initial hidden state h_j and the cell state c_j. Each learnable transformation allows the model to flexibly adapt how it encodes leaf nodes during training and learn which parts of the input are important for downstream tasks.

Parent Node States. The input of the parent node x_j is constructed by concatenating the feature vectors of its left and right child nodes. Since this concatenation may double the dimension, we apply a fully connected (FC) layer to project it back to the required size:

$$x_j = \texttt{FC}\big(x_{\text{left},j} \parallel x_{\text{right},j}\big). \tag{5}$$

We then compute the binary Tree-LSTM gates and update the tree representation as follows [18]:

$$\begin{aligned}
h_{\text{cat},j} &= h_{\text{left},j} \parallel h_{\text{right},j}, \\
i_j &= \sigma(W_i x_j + U_i h_{\text{cat},j} + b_i), \\
f_{\text{left},j} &= \sigma(W_f x_j + U_f h_{\text{cat},j} + b_f), \\
f_{\text{right},j} &= \sigma(W_f x_j + U_f h_{\text{cat},j} + b_f), \\
o_j &= \sigma(W_o x_j + U_o h_{\text{cat},j} + b_o), \\
\tilde{c}_j &= \tanh(W_c x_j + U_c h_{\text{cat},j} + b_c), \\
c_j &= i_j \odot \tilde{c}_j \ + \ f_{\text{left},j} \odot c_{\text{left}} \ + \ f_{\text{right},j} \odot c_{\text{right}}, \\
h_j &= o_j \odot \tanh(c_j).
\end{aligned} \tag{6}$$

Here, σ is the sigmoid function, and W, U, and b are learnable parameters. Subscripts i, f, o, and c denote the input gate, forget gates, output gate, and candidate cell state, respectively.

Depth-First Search for State Computation. DFS is applied recursively to compute (h_j, c_j) from the leaves to the root. Since the tree is already built, DFS traverses it again to compute Tree-LSTM states. At each leaf node, we apply the transformations aforementioned, and at each parent node, we retrieve the children's states, form x_j, and apply the Tree-LSTM equations (Eq. 6).

Final Representation. When DFS reaches the root node, it returns $(h_{\text{root}}, c_{\text{root}})$. The hidden state h_{root} is a comprehensive representation of the query plan P. Therefore, the final representation of the plan P with Tree-LSTM is as follows:

$$\mathbf{Q}_P = h_{\text{root}} \tag{7}$$

3.5 Routing Strategy Prediction: MLP

To automatically select the best routing strategy for a given query, we employ a Multi-Layer Perceptron (MLP) to model the prediction task. Our MLP is a two-layer fully connected neural network. Let S denote the set that represents the routing strategy space. For a query Q, multiple strategies may achieve the best performance; we denote this as $S_Q^* \subseteq S$. We define the label vector $y \in \{0,1\}^{|S|}$, s.t., $y_i = 1$ if $S_i \in S_Q^*$, and $y_i = 0$ otherwise.

We formulate the routing strategy prediction as a multi-label classification task, and train a model f based on a MLP architecture to perform this classification. The model takes as input a learned representation of the query, denoted by $\mathbf{Q}$. This query representation can be either $\mathbf{Q}_G$ (Eq. 4), obtained through a Graph Neural Network (GNN), or $\mathbf{Q}_P$ (Eq. 7), computed using a Tree-LSTM. The prediction $\hat{y}$ is then given by:

$$\hat{y} = f(\mathbf{Q}) = \sigma(W\mathbf{Q} + b) \tag{8}$$

where σ is the element-wise sigmoid activation function, and W, b are learnable parameters of the MLP. We use the sigmoid activation function to produce independent probabilities for each class, following Maxwell et al. in *Deep Learning* [14]. The function $f(\mathbf{Q})$ outputs a probability distribution over multiple policy labels for a query Q, thereby estimating $\hat{y} \approx y$. Each probability indicates the likelihood of a specific routing policy being the best for Q.

Ground Truth. We identify the best strategies S_Q^* based on two performance metrics: execution time and number of answers. A strategy S_i that completes the query execution before a given timeout T_{timeout} is considered optimal, if its execution time T_i is close to the minimal execution time $T_{\min}$, i.e., $T_i - T_{\min} \leq \epsilon \cdot T_{\min}$. We introduce a tolerance margin $\epsilon \in (0, 1]$ to account for minor timing variations due to factors like system load. When all strategies exceed the timeout limit T_{timeout} for a query, we focus on number of answers to identify optimal strategies. In this case, a strategy S_i is considered optimal if their number of answers C_i are within a predefined margin δ of the maximum number of answers $C_{\max}$ produced by another strategy, i.e., $C_{\max} - C_i \leq \delta \cdot C_{\max}$. The margin $\delta \in (0, 1]$ ensures that selected policies produce results close to the maximum number of answers while accounting for variability in system performance.

Loss Function. The training process aims to minimize the difference between the predicted probabilities $\hat{y}$ and the ground truth y. To achieve this, we use the Binary Cross-Entropy (BCE) loss [8] for each label independently and sum these losses across all L classes (routing strategies) and N samples (queries):

$$\min_{\hat{y}} \frac{1}{N \times L} \sum_{n=1}^{N} \sum_{k=1}^{L} [-y_{nk} \log(\hat{y}_{nk}) - (1 - y_{nk}) \log(1 - \hat{y}_{nk})] \tag{9}$$

where y_{nk} is the ground truth for the routing strategy k of query n, and $\hat{y}_{nk}$ is the corresponding prediction.

4 Experiments

In our experimental evaluation, we investigate the following questions: **(Q1)** How effective are the newly proposed routing strategies? **(Q2)** What are the capabilities of NSAQP to predict an optimal routing strategy for a given query? **(Q3)** How do GNN and Tree-LSTM compare in terms of training efficiency? **(Q4)** How do GNN and Tree-LSTM compare in terms of prediction time? **(Q5)** What is the precision of NSAQP when new queries contain unseen constants? Our experimental configuration is as follows:

Datasets and Queries. Following other works that use ML for query processing [16], we choose LUBM [9], a synthetic KG in the university domain, and YAGO [17], a large, real-world, cross-domain KG. For each dataset, we generate SELECT queries composed of basic graph patterns (BGPs), reflecting the optimization challenges of conjunctive queries in RDF, where cost-based methods often fail due to skewed data distributions [1]. The number of queries and their cardinality ranges are reported in Table 3, along with dataset statistics. Queries were shuffled randomly, with 80% allocated for training and 20% for evaluation. KGs were loaded into a TPF server (Linked Data Fragments Server, version 2.2.4), and queries were executed with nLDE [1](Python 2.7) as it implements AQP with eddies.

Table 3. Dataset [16] and query characteristics.

KG	Triples	Entities	Preds	Classes	Typed	Queries	Card.
LUBM	2.69M	664K	18	15	66%	48,872	$[e^0, e^6]$
YAGO	58M	13M	92	19K	84%	34,849	$[e^0, e^8]$

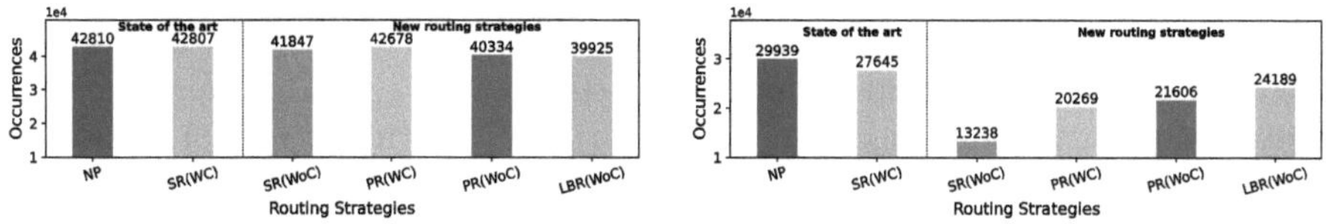

(a) LUBM (b) YAGO

Fig. 4. Occurrences of optimal routing strategies in S^*. The studied strategies: NP (NoPolicy), Selectivity Routing (SR), Productivity Routing (PR), and Load-Balancing Routing (LBR), with constraints (WC) and without constraints (WoC).

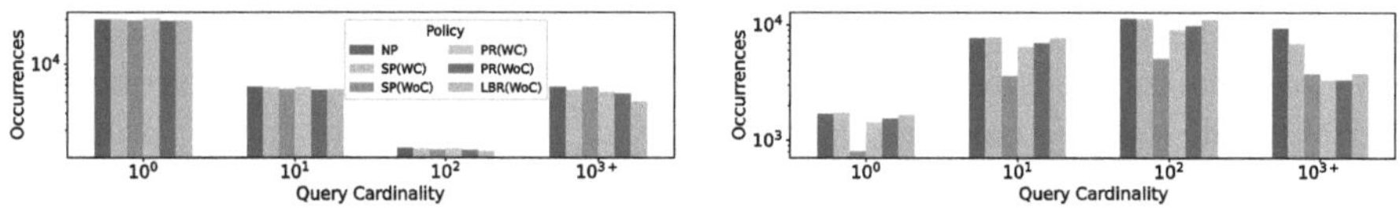

(a) LUBM (b) YAGO

Fig. 5. Distribution of optimal routing policies across different query cardinality ranges.

Implementation Details. We compute the RDF2Vec embeddings with a dimensionality of 100 using the implementation by Schwabe et al. [16], and train the RDF2Vec model for 10 epochs, using 5 random walks per entity with a maximum depth of 4.

In NSAQP, both the GNN and Tree-LSTM models are implemented using Python 3.10. The experiments were conducted on a MacBook Pro (16-inch, 2023) equipped with an Apple M2 Max chip, utilizing its 12-core CPU and 32 GB of RAM. Due to the computational efficiency of the GNN, it was trained solely on the CPU. In contrast, the more computationally demanding Tree-LSTM model was trained using Apple's Metal Performance Shaders.

Model Training. We train all models with a batch size of 100 and for 100 epochs. For optimization of the GNN model, we use the Adam optimizer [12] with an initial learning rate of e^{-3}. The Tree-LSTM model also uses the Adam optimizer with the same initial learning rate, and we apply a ReduceLROnPlateau scheduler that automatically halves the learning rate if no improvement in the training loss is observed for three consecutive epochs.

4.1 Efficiency of the Routing Policies

Combining the routing policies (Table 1) with the constraints (Table 2), we obtain six routing strategies. Next, we compute the ground truth S^* with the best routing strategies for each query by executing each query with the different strategies. To determine S^*, NSAQP relies on (hyper)parameters T_{timeout}, ϵ and δ (cf. Section 3.5). To account for the large variance in query runtimes—where small absolute differences in short queries correspond to large relative differences—we set ϵ as a function of $T_{\min}$ rather than using a fixed threshold.

After empirical tests, we set up these values to $T_{\text{timeout}} = 60\,s$, $\epsilon = 0.3$ for *fast queries* (s.t. $T_{\min} \leq 5\,s$), and $\epsilon = \max(0.30 - 0.005 \times T_{\min}, 0.05)$ for *long-running queries*, where ϵ is proportional to the total runtime of the query. For queries in which all routing strategies timed out, we set $\delta = 0.1$, as these queries typically produce large result counts (often exceeding 10,000).

We analyse the occurrence of routing strategies in S^* (Fig. 4). First, we observe that the state-of-the-art strategies cover a large portion of the queries in both datasets. For example, No Policy (NP) is one of the best policies for 42,810 out of the 48,872 ($\sim$ 88%) LUBM queries. Similar results for YAGO, where NP covers $\sim$ 86% of the queries. Still, our proposed strategies are competitive to the state of the art, and behave differently across datasets. For example, Load-Balancing without Constraints (LBR(WoC)) is the least frequent in LUBM, while it is the most frequent strategy in YAGO from the newly proposed ones. The lower occurrence of optimal policies in YAGO reflects intrinsic differences between the datasets. LUBM's simpler and more homogeneous query patterns allow various routing strategies to perform similarly well, whereas YAGO's larger size and real-world complexity introduce greater query heterogeneity, making specific strategies optimal only for certain query types. This highlights the importance of adaptive, query-specific routing approaches.

Next, we study whether query cardinality influences the performance of routing strategies. Figure 5a shows that the occurrences of strategies are, in general, equally distributed across queries with different cardinalities. In Fig. 5b, PR and LBR are not the best policies for queries with more than 10^3 results, but have an equal distribution in the other queries, like the other proposed strategies.

To further quantify the overall overhead of NSAQP, we compared the end-to-end execution time (inference + execution) of NSAQP against the NoPolicy baseline per-query on average on the same hardware. Table 4 shows that on LUBM, NSAQP introduces only minimal overhead, whereas on YAGO it actually yields substantial speedups compared to NoPolicy. These results demonstrate that NSAQP not only maintains near-baseline efficiency on synthetic workloads but even outperforms the static NoPolicy on more complex, real-world data.

Table 4. End-to-end time difference per-query on average in milliseconds.

KG	GNN based	Tree LSTM
LUBM	+2.65	+24.09
YAGO	−1004.90	−696.20

Lastly, we inspect in how many queries, S^* only included our newly proposed strategies and none of the state-of-the-art strategies. In LUBM, 3,423 ($\sim$ 7%) are executed more efficiently with our policies, and 1,721 ($\sim$ 5%) for YAGO. These results show that in certain query workloads, some queries require alternative strategies to the ones proposed in the state of the art **(Q1)**.

4.2 NSAQP Prediction Quality

The NSAQP MLP (Sect. 3.5) produces a prediction $\hat{y}_i$ per strategy s_i (or class) that corresponds to the likelihood that s_i is optimal for a given query. In Fig. 6,

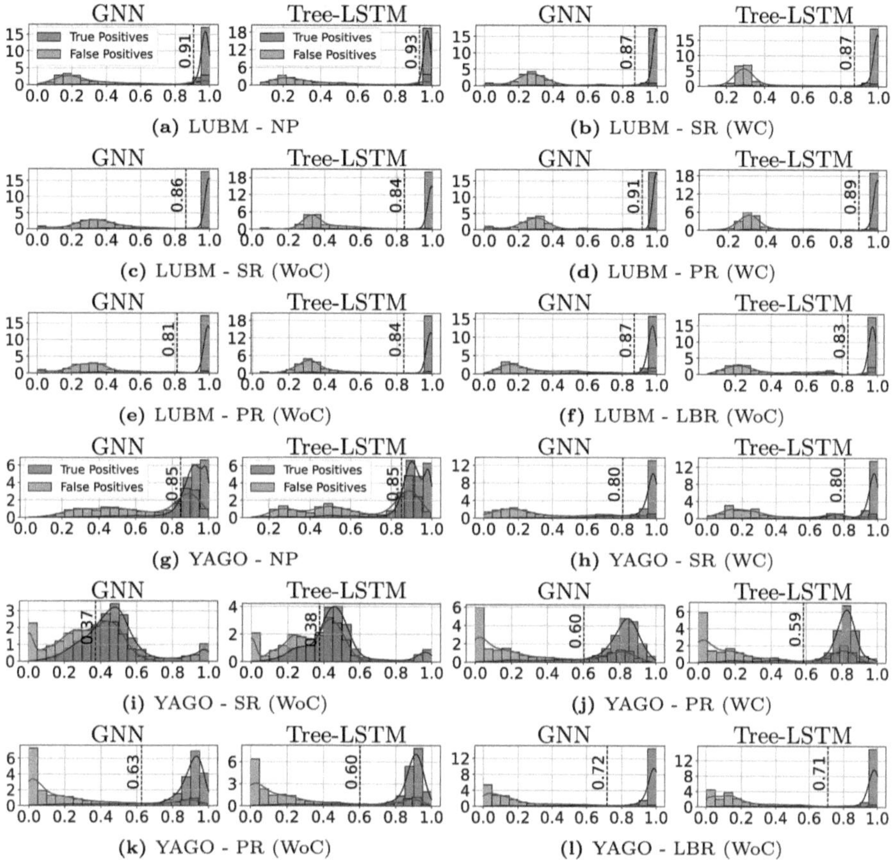

Fig. 6. Predicted routing policy scores $\hat{y}_i$ distributions, optimal strategy (blue), non-optimal strategy (red), and thresholds θ_i (vertical line) using GNN and Tree-LSTM models for the LUBM and YAGO datasets.(Color figure online)

we compare the distribution of $\hat{y}_i$ values for the training set with the ground truth. Ideally, optimal policies should have high $\hat{y}_i$ values and, conversely, non-optimal policies low $\hat{y}_i$ values. In LUBM (Fig. 6 (a)-(f)), the MLP produces $\hat{y}_i$ values that can very well distinguish optimal from non-optimal strategies, and only a few non-optimal strategies are assigned high $\hat{y}_i$ values. For YAGO (Fig. 6 (g)-(l)), the MLP cannot distinguish well when the strategies No Policy, SR (WoC), and PR (WC), are optimal or not. Still, the distribution for both models (GNN and Tree-LSTM) are very similar, indicating that both query and tree representations produce similar predictions.

NSAQP treats the problem of routing strategy selection as a multi-label classification setting. Therefore, we calculate a class-specific threshold θ_i, such that if $\hat{y}_i \geq \theta_i$, then s_i is classified as optimal. The values of θ_i (shown in Fig. 6) are determined with the predictions on the training set, to maximize the number of optimal strategies to be predicted as optimal. Then, in the test set, we apply these values of θ_i to determine if a strategy is predicted to be optimal for a given query. After thresholding, we calculate the precision of the model. Here, we distinguish two types of predictions: empty and non-empty predictions. We define an *empty prediction* ($\varnothing$) as a prediction where all $\hat{y}_i < \theta_i$; for empty predictions, we choose the strategy s_i with the highest $\hat{y}_i$ value as the predicted optimal strategy. We define a *non-empty prediction* ($\neg\varnothing$) as a prediction where at least a $\hat{y}_i \geq \theta_i$. Next, we calculate precision as the proportion of optimal strategies correctly predicted out of all predicted strategies.

Table 5. NSAQP prediction quality with GNN-based and Tree-LSTM representations. Prediction denotes the portion of optimal strategies correctly predicted, over *all* queries in the test set, queries with *empty predictions* ($\varnothing$), and with *non-empty predictions* ($\neg\varnothing$). The number of queries with their prediction types are also shown.

	Prediction Precision						**Number of Queries**				
	GNN-based			**Tree-LSTM**				**GNN-based**		**Tree-LSTM**	
KG	All	$\varnothing$	$\neg\varnothing$	All	$\varnothing$	$\neg\varnothing$	**Test set**	$\varnothing$	$\neg\varnothing$	$\varnothing$	$\neg\varnothing$
LUBM	0.898	0.431	0.980	0.899	0.448	0.979	9775	1454	8321	1458	8317
YAGO	0.811	0.479	0.861	0.816	0.465	0.861	6970	905	6065	792	6178

Table 5 presents the precision results. Overall, GNN-based and Tree-LSTM achieve very similar performance in the test set in both KGs; this means that the behavior observed for the training set (Fig. 6) is consistent in the test set. The models achieved a precision of 0.90 for LUBM and 0.81 for YAGO over *all* the test queries. We attribute this small difference to the KG characteristics. LUBM being smaller and more structured, benefits both models. In contrast, YAGO's larger size and real-world complexity presents greater challenges for the models.

Next we compare the performance for $\varnothing$ and $\neg\varnothing$ predictions. Overall, we see a drop in precision for $\varnothing$ predictions; this indicates that when the MLP is not "confident enough" in the predictions (low values of $\hat{y}_i$ in all strategies), selecting the strategy with the highest $\hat{y}_i$ value only works in $\sim$ 44% of the queries. On the positive side, both models produce empty prediction for a small portion of the queries (12% to 15% of the test set). Notably, Tree-LSTM produces fewer empty predictions, suggesting better handling of YAGO's structural complexity. Lastly, for $\neg\varnothing$ predictions, both models achieve very high precision in LUBM (0.98), clearly outperforming the NP baseline (optimal in $\sim$ 88% of queries), and high precision (0.86) in YAGO. Although NP is also optimal for about 86% of YAGO queries, the remaining "hard" cases dominate latency and often exceed the 60*s* timeout. NSAQP learned policy specifically optimizes these expensive queries, improving execution times and system responsiveness despite comparable overall precision.

In general, these results indicate that both models are effective in identifying optimal routing starting strategies for a large portion of queries **(Q2)**.

4.3 NSAQP Training Efficiency

We study the time required to train both NSAQP variants using 80% of the queries over 100 epochs. Figure 7 shows the average runtime per epoch and the total training time, which reflect the intrinsic computational characteristics of the model architecture. The GNN-based model requires significantly less training time than the Tree-LSTM model. Per epoch, the GNN runs in 4–6 seconds, while the Tree-LSTM needs roughly 23–33 minutes. This is because the Tree-LSTM model requires recursive computation to construct hierarchical query trees.

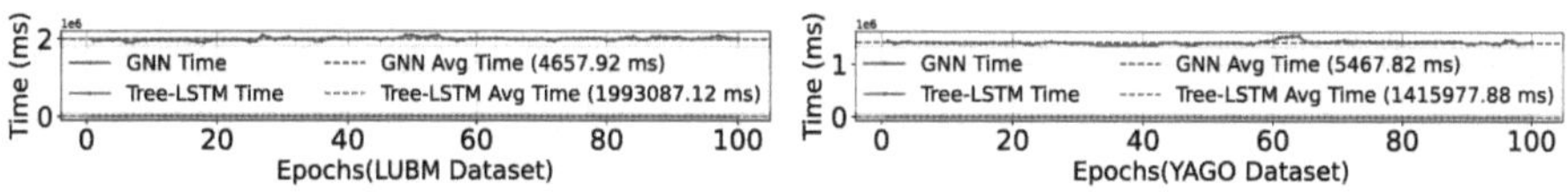

Fig. 7. NSAQP training time in milliseconds: GNN with MLP, and Tree-LSTM with MLP. Both NSAQP variants were trained for 100 epochs.

Next, we investigate the precision of the NSAQP variants at different epochs (Fig. 8) and training set sizes. This will help to determine whether NSAQP can be trained in fewer epochs and fewer queries. Although the Tree-LSTM model requires significantly more time to train compared to the GNN model, it achieves higher precision with fewer epochs and even with reduced training data, particularly on complex and imbalanced datasets like YAGO. On the YAGO dataset, training the Tree-LSTM model on only one-fourth of the queries for 50 epochs yields a precision that visibly surpasses the GNN model trained on all queries for 100 epochs. This indicates that despite the higher computational cost, Tree-LSTM remains effective for handling datasets with greater complexity and imbalance.

These results show that NSAQP can be trained efficiently on diverse query workloads **(Q3)**, while achieving high performance in terms of precision.

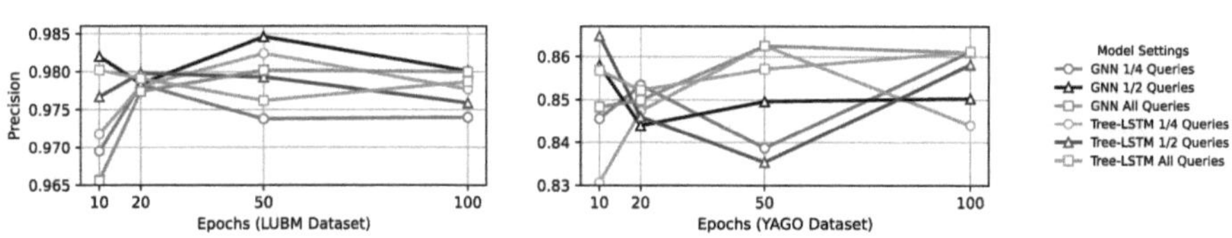

Fig. 8. NSAQP precision across training epochs. Each curve represents a different training set size (1/4 queries, 1/2 queries, and all queries).

4.4 NSAQP Prediction Time

Since the neural component is invoked at query runtime to predict the most suitable routing strategy, its inference must be highly efficient to avoid introducing significant overhead into the query execution process. Table 6 reports the average per-query inference time of the NSAQP models, computed by dividing the total batch inference time by the number of test queries.

Table 6. NSAQP average per-query inference time in milliseconds (ms).

KG	GNN-based	Tree-LSTM
LUBM	0.027	19.68
YAGO	0.058	19.83

Overall, the GNN model is noticeably faster (less than 0.1ms) on both datasets. The higher inference time on YAGO with both learning models than that of LUBM is the result of the greater complexity and imbalance present within the YAGO dataset. Still, these results show that NSAQP introduces a very small overhead, and it can be integrated into real-time query processing **(Q4)**. For very short queries, however, the overhead of the Tree-LSTM may not pay off if the No Policy strategy already performs well. In practice, the GNN model is viable for all query types, offering negligible inference time even on complex datasets.

4.5 Inductive Case: NSAQP Quality Under Unseen Constants

Section 4.2 shows the precision of NSAQP in query workloads, where terms of the test queries are seen by the models during training. In the *inductive case*, we assess the NSAQP performance for queries where their constants (IRIs and literals) in the subject/object position have not been seen during training. Note that this represents the worst-case scenario for inductivity, as typically some entities will have been observed, leading to improved practical performance.

We conducted this experiment by training and evaluating both models on mutually exclusive training and test datasets. The results are shown in Table 7. The GNN consistently achieves higher precision than Tree-LSTM on both datasets. This indicates that the simpler architecture of GNNs is able to generalize better to queries with unseen constants. Furthermore, the drop in precision is larger for the YAGO dataset, indicating that, for KGs with complex structures (many predicates and classes), the inductive capabilities of the models are affected. In general, these results demonstrate that NSAQP can be applied effectively in the inductive case with new constants, without the need for frequent retraining **(Q5)**.

Table 7. NSAQP avg. precision at 20 epochs under (un)seen constants.

	GNN-based		Tree-LSTM	
KG	Seen	Unseen	Seen	Unseen
LUBM	0.977	0.954	0.979	0.872
YAGO	0.850	0.816	0.852	0.629

5 Conclusion and Future Work

In this work, we address routing strategy prediction in adaptive query processing (AQP) over knowledge graphs as a multi-label classification task. We present a neuro-symbolic approach, NSAQP, which leverages Graph Neural Networks (GNNs) and Tree-LSTMs to capture structural and hierarchical aspects of queries and plans. These representations are used to predict optimal symbolic routing strategies via a Multi-Layer Perceptron. Experiments show that NSAQP achieves high precision on both synthetic and real-world KGs. The GNN-based variant offers efficient training and negligible inference time, while the Tree-LSTM variant trades efficiency for robustness to complex and imbalanced data. Moreover, NSAQP generalizes to unseen queries without retraining, making it suitable for production AQP systems. Although implemented over a TPF infrastructure, NSAQP applies to any SPARQL engine using triple pattern access.

Future work could improve precision in low-confidence outputs (empty predictions), and explore fine-tuning techniques to enhance inductive performance with minimal retraining. Furthermore, the strategy space could be expanded with novel symbolic policies, enabling more options for adaptivity at runtime. Finally, NSAQP could also be extended to more complex queries, identifying distinct policies per BGP while respecting the overall query structure.

Acknowledgement. This work has been supported by the Deutsche Forschungsgemeinschaft (DFG, German Research Foundation) - SFB 1625 - 506711657, project A06.

Supplemental Material. The source code for NSAQP and the queries used in Sect. 4 are available at https://github.com/changqin26/nsAQP_publication.

References

1. Acosta, M., Vidal, M.-E.: Networks of linked data eddies: an adaptive web query processing engine for RDF data. In: Arenas, M., et al. (eds.) ISWC 2015. LNCS, vol. 9366, pp. 111–127. Springer, Cham (2015). https://doi.org/10.1007/978-3-319-25007-6_7
2. Acosta, M., Vidal, M.E., Sure-Vetter, Y.: Diefficiency metrics: measuring the continuous efficiency of query processing approaches. In: International Semantic Web Conference, pp. 3–19. Springer (2017)
3. Amat, D.A.C., Buil-Aranda, C., Valle-Vidal, C.: A neural networks approach to Sparql query performance prediction. In: 2021 XLVII Latin American Computing Conference (CLEI), pp. 1–9. IEEE (2021)
4. Avnur, R., Hellerstein, J.M.: Eddies: Continuously adaptive query processing. In: Proceedings of the 2000 ACM SIGMOD International Conference on Management of data, pp. 261–272 (2000)
5. Bizarro, P., Babu, S., DeWitt, D., Widom, J.: Content-based routing: Different plans for different data. In: Proceedings of the 31st International Conference on Very Large Data Bases, pp. 757–768 (2005)
6. Deshpande, A., Ives, Z., Raman, V., et al.: Adaptive query processing. Found. Trends® Databases **1**(1), 1–140 (2007)

7. Eschauzier, R., Taelman, R., Morren, M., Verborgh, R.: Reinforcement learning-based Sparql join ordering optimizer. In: European Semantic Web Conference, pp. 43–47. Springer (2023)
8. Goodfellow, I., Bengio, Y., Courville, A.: Deep Learning. MIT Press (2016). http://www.deeplearningbook.org
9. Guo, Y., Pan, Z., Heflin, J.: Lubm: a benchmark for owl knowledge base systems. J. Web Seman. **3**(2–3), 158–182 (2005)
10. Hasan, R., Gandon, F.: A machine learning approach to Sparql query performance prediction. In: 2014 IEEE/WIC/ACM International Joint Conferences on Web Intelligence (WI) and Intelligent Agent Technologies (IAT), vol. 1, pp. 266–273. IEEE (2014)
11. Hu, W., et al.: Strategies for pre-training graph neural networks. arXiv preprint arXiv:1905.12265 (2019)
12. Kingma, D.P.: Adam: A method for stochastic optimization. arXiv preprint arXiv:1412.6980 (2014)
13. Madden, S., Shah, M., Hellerstein, J.M., Raman, V.: Continuously adaptive continuous queries over streams. In: Proceedings of the 2002 ACM SIGMOD International Conference on Management of Data, pp. 49–60 (2002)
14. Maxwell, A., et al.: Deep learning architectures for multi-label classification of intelligent health risk prediction. BMC Bioinform. **18**, 121–131 (2017)
15. Ristoski, P., Paulheim, H.: Rdf2vec: RDF graph embeddings for data mining. In: InterNational Semantic Web Conference, pp. 498–514. Springer (2016)
16. Schwabe, T., Acosta, M.: Cardinality estimation over knowledge graphs with embeddings and graph neural networks. Proc. ACM on Manag. Data **2**(1), 1–26 (2024)
17. Suchanek, F.M., Kasneci, G., Weikum, G.: Yago: a large ontology from Wikipedia and wordnet. J. Web Seman. **6**(3), 203–217 (2008)
18. Tai, K.S., Socher, R., Manning, C.D.: Improved semantic representations from tree-structured long short-term memory networks. arXiv preprint arXiv:1503.00075 (2015)
19. Tian, F., DeWitt, D.J.: Tuple routing strategies for distributed eddies. In: Proceedings 2003 VLDB Conference, pp. 333–344. Elsevier (2003)
20. Tzoumas, K., Sellis, T., Jensen, C.S.: A reinforcement learning approach for adaptive query processing. History, pp. 1–25 (2008)
21. Verborgh, R., et al.: Querying datasets on the web with high availability. In: Mika, P., Tudorache, T., Bernstein, A., Welty, C., Knoblock, C., Vrandečić, D., Groth, P., Noy, N., Janowicz, K., Goble, C. (eds.) ISWC 2014. LNCS, vol. 8796, pp. 180–196. Springer, Cham (2014). https://doi.org/10.1007/978-3-319-11964-9_12
22. Zhang, W.E., Sheng, Q.Z., Qin, Y., Taylor, K., Yao, L.: Learning-based Sparql query performance modeling and prediction. World Wide Web **21**(4), 1015–1035 (2018)

GRASP: Generic Reasoning And SPARQL Generation Across Knowledge Graphs

Sebastian Walter(✉) and Hannah Bast

University of Freiburg, 79100 Freiburg im Breisgau, Germany
{swalter,bast}@cs.uni-freiburg.de

Abstract. We propose a new approach for generating SPARQL queries on RDF knowledge graphs from natural language questions or keyword queries, using a large language model. Our approach does not require fine-tuning. Instead, it uses the language model to explore the knowledge graph by strategically executing SPARQL queries and searching for relevant IRIs and literals. We evaluate our approach on a variety of benchmarks (for knowledge graphs of different kinds and sizes) and language models (of different scales and types, commercial as well as open-source) and compare it with existing approaches. On Wikidata we reach state-of-the-art results on multiple benchmarks, despite the zero-shot setting. On Freebase we come close to the best few-shot methods. On other, less commonly evaluated knowledge graphs and benchmarks our approach also performs well overall. We conduct several additional studies, like comparing different ways of searching the graphs, incorporating a feedback mechanism, or making use of few-shot examples.

Keywords: Question Answering · SPARQL · Knowledge Graphs

1 Introduction

More and more datasets are available as RDF, one of the standard data models for knowledge graphs.[1] Early examples are DBpedia [4] and Freebase [12], followed by Wikidata [45], and more recently UniProt [18], OpenStreetMap [8] (OSM), and DBLP [1]. The standard query language for RDF data is SPARQL, which can be powerful but also very challenging for multiple reasons. For example, consider the following question on Wikidata: "Who was the Governor of Ohio by the end of 2011?".[2] Here is a SPARQL query that answers the question:[3]

[1] Whenever we speak of knowledge graphs, we mean RDF knowledge graphs.
[2] This is a question very similar to one from our benchmarks in Sect. 4.1.
[3] See www.wikidata.org for the PREFIX definitions for *p:*, *ps:*, *wd:*, *pq:*, and *xsd:*.

D. Garijo et al. (Eds.): ISWC 2025, LNCS 16140, pp. 271–289, 2026.
https://doi.org/10.1007/978-3-032-09527-5_15

```
SELECT ?result WHERE {
  ?result p:P39 ?m .
  ?m ps:P39 wd:Q17989863 ; pq:P580 ?start .
  OPTIONAL { ?m pq:P582 ?end . }
  FILTER(?start <= "2011-12-31"^^xsd:date &&
         (!BOUND(?end) || ?end >= "2011-12-31"^^xsd:date))
}
```

Let us go through the many challenges of formulating this SPARQL query:

1. One has to know the basic syntax of SPARQL.
2. One has to know that in Wikidata, the information about which person holds which position is modeled by the property *P39* ("position held").
3. One has to know how the quaternary information about the position (person, position, start, end) is modeled in Wikidata and that the IRIs of the respective predicates are *p:P39*, *ps:P39*, *pq:580*, and *pq:P582*.
4. One has to know that there is an own entity for "governor of Ohio" (as opposed to separate entities for "governor" and "Ohio") and that its IRI is *wd:Q17989863*.
5. One has to realize that the person might still be in office, so that the end date has to be OPTIONAL.
6. One has to translate "in office at the end of 2011" to a logical expression that states that the term started on or before the last day of 2011, and ended after that or is still ongoing.
   Based on our own extensive experience with SPARQL users, let us briefly discuss how a casual SPARQL user, an expert SPARQL user, and an unassisted large language model (LLM) will perform at this task. All three of them know 1.

Both the expert and the LLM will know 2 and 3 because that is a common construct in Wikidata queries. Both the casual and the expert user will have to do some research to find out how "governor of Ohio" is expressed in Wikidata and with which IRI.[4] An unassisted LLM will hallucinate an IRI and almost certainly get it wrong. The casual user might miss 5, the expert user will know this, for the LLM it can go either way. The casual and the expert user will eventually find out 6, but with some trial and error. The unassisted LLM will often get it wrong without feedback. Also note that in practice, LLMs act probabilistically, and the generated query varies widely between attempts, even for the exact same prompt. For the question above, the query produced by an unassisted LLM is never 100% correct, but sometimes more and sometimes less wrong.

More generally, an LLM requires two kinds of assistance to be able to formulate SPARQL queries for arbitrary given questions: (1) it needs help to find the right IRIs and literals, and (2) it needs help with the finer points of formulating the query. Let us briefly discuss the challenges of both of these.

Issue (1) is hard because of the sheer size of many knowledge graphs. For example, Wikidata contains 1.2 B distinct literals and 2.2 B subjects. It would

[4] For this, an autocompletion mechanism is typically used; see [10] for an overview.

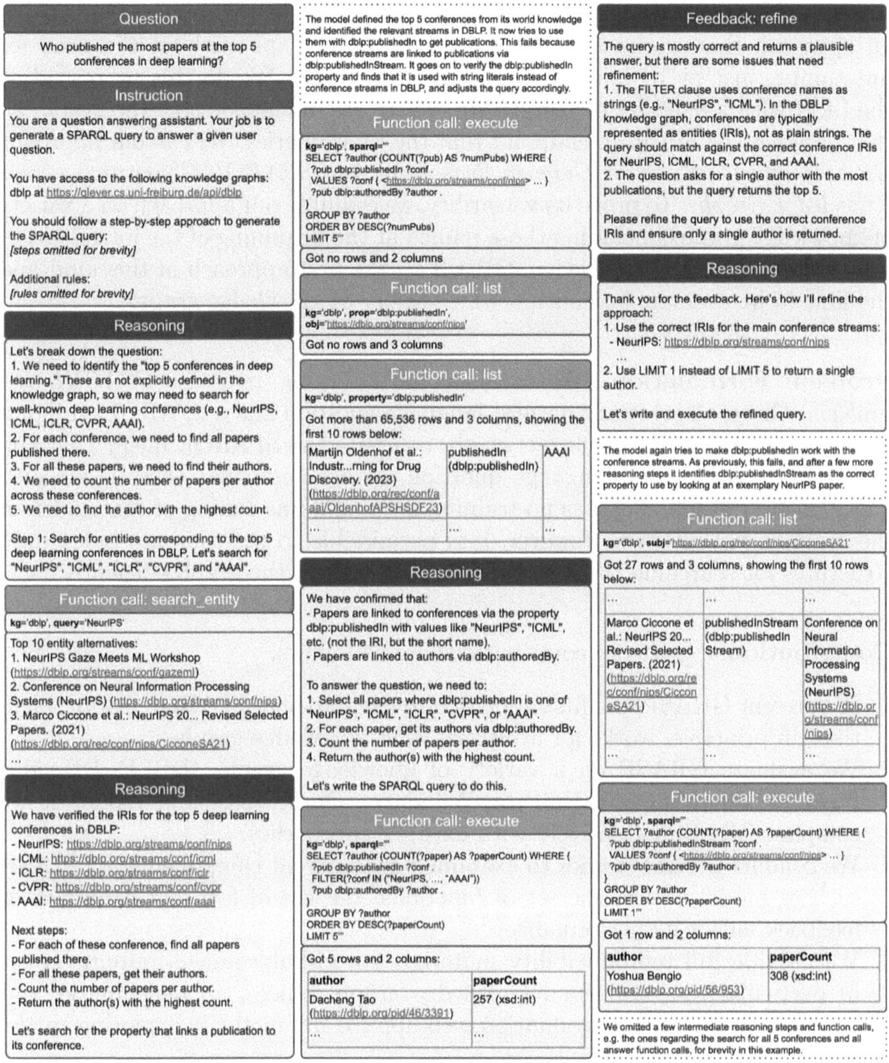

Fig. 1. Overview over GRASP with feedback using the question "Who published the most papers at the top 5 conferences in deep learning?" as a running example.

require a gargantuan LLM to memorize these and even if that was achieved, it would be a waste of resources. A more reasonable approach would be to either post-process the query by replacing hallucinated IRIs and literals by the matching ones or to store the IRIs and literals externally and provide a means for the LLM to query them. Regarding (2), one could fine-tune the LLM to learn frequently used query patterns and then hope for the best. Or one could provide some feedback mechanism to let the LLM reason and let it know whether it is on the right track.

We explore and evaluate a variety of approaches in this paper. Our goal is an approach that works for *any* given knowledge graph without the need for fine-tuning, just by dynamically exploring the graph. We do this by providing the LLM with a fixed set of ***functions***. These are independent of the graph; all that differs is the SPARQL endpoint that the LLM queries. We call our approach *GRASP*, which stands for *Generic Reasoning And SPARQL Generation across Knowledge Graphs*. To prove its versatility, we evaluate our approach on a variety of knowledge graphs, including those named at the beginning of the introduction. To be the best of our knowledge, GRASP is the first approach of this kind and the first to be evaluated on such a wide variety of knowledge graphs.

Problem Formulation. We consider the following *zero-shot SPARQL QA problem*: Given an arbitrary natural-language question and a SPARQL endpoint for an arbitrary RDF knowledge graph, compute the SPARQL query that corresponds to the natural-language question, or conclude that there is no such query on that graph. There is no training data, and fine-tuning of the model on the graph is not allowed. However, it is permissible to pre-compute index data structures for searching the set of IRIs and literals in the graph efficiently.[5]

Contributions. Our core contributions are as follows:

1. We present GRASP, the first approach to the zero-shot SPARQL QA problem that, in principle, works for arbitrary RDF knowledge graphs.
2. We evaluate GRASP on a variety of knowledge graphs (DBLP, DBpedia, Freebase, ORKG, OSM, UniProt, Wikidata). On Freebase and Wikidata, we compare GRASP extensively with existing approaches.
3. We conduct several studies to examine how different components of GRASP, such as model choice, the set of functions, the use of few-shot examples or feedback, affect its performance.
4. We provide full reproducibility materials via github.com/ad-freiburg/grasp, in particular: our code and knowledge graph indices, all benchmarks and model outputs, and an evaluation web app for interactively exploring model results.

2 Related Work

Our zero-shot SPARQL QA problem is closely related to the more general problem of knowledge graph question answering (KGQA), which allows answers to questions to be found through other ways than by generating SPARQL queries. We divide KGQA methods into three categories.

[5] Specifically, for each of the knowledge graphs we investigate in this paper, we have written a SPARQL query that extracts the label and optional additional information for each IRI; see Sect. 3.4. This is query-independent and the SPARQL query could, in principle, also be found by our approach itself.

In the first category are methods that fine-tune on a particular benchmark for a particular knowledge graph. Examples for such methods are DeCAF [51], RoG [30], ChatKBQA [29], and many more [2,17,20,26,27,37,47]. State-of-the-art on KGQA benchmarks is typically achieved by such methods because they can adapt to the peculiarities of the benchmark and knowledge graph and exploit similarities between training and test sets.

In the second category are methods that do not fine-tune on a particular benchmark dataset but still have access to benchmark specific information in-context during inference, most often in the form of exemplary question-SPARQL pairs or input-output examples for submodules. Examples in this category are KB-BINDER [35], Pangu [20], DoG [31], KELDaR [25] and Interactive-KBQA [46]. They achieve good performance, sometimes even close to fine-tuned methods, but they either use a large number of examples (100 for KB-BINDER, 1000 for Pangu, 10/10/1 for different modules in DoG, 40/6/10/4 for different modules in KELDaR) or few extensive ones (full generation processes for Interactive-KBQA). Interactive-KBQA is similar to our approach, but with different functions, some optimized for specific knowledge graphs (e.g. *SearchGraphPatterns* for CVT structures in Freebase), and tailored instructions with hints for each graph.

In the third category are zero-shot methods that work without fine-tuning or examples. StructGPT [23] finds answer entities starting from a given topic entity by moving along edges and stopping once it assesses the newly discovered entities suitable to answer the question. Similarly, ToG [38] explores the knowledge graph starting from topic entities along edges and nodes, and always keeps track of the overall best paths so far. SPINACH [28] is similar to our approach and equips a LLM with functions to search in and execute queries over a knowledge graph. However, they only focus on Wikidata and use the Wikidata API to implement their search functionality, limiting transferability to other knowledge graphs. They also structure the generation process differently, with separate prompts for different subtasks, like language detection, action generation, output generation, SPARQL extraction, and the pruning of Wikidata entries, for which they use two Wikidata-specific examples in context. In contrast, our approach works with a single instruction that is the same across all knowledge graphs and a single-context continuous generation process from question to SPARQL query.

3 Approach

We introduce our overall approach as well as its different components in the following. For all SPARQL-related functionality, such as retrieving data from and executing queries over knowledge graphs, we use the public SPARQL endpoints at qlever.cs.uni-freiburg.de [9] because of QLever's superior performance for hard queries compared to alternatives like Blazegraph or Virtuoso.

3.1 GRASP

With GRASP, the generation of SPARQL queries relies on a LLM that interacts with a knowledge graph autonomously by interleaving function calls to search or query the knowledge graph with reasoning about previous and future steps. Note, that this is in style similar to ReAct prompting [49], though we also allow multiple successive reasoning steps or function calls. Starting point of a generation is the GRASP instruction, which contains the name and endpoint of all available knowledge graphs, details about the step-by-step approach, and additional rules to be followed. Note, that this instruction is generic and does not contain any graph-specific information other than their names and endpoints. Optionally, few-shot examples (see Sect. 3.5) and a feedback mechanism for refining the output (see Sect. 3.6) can be added. See Fig. 1 for an overview over GRASP's approach by means of an example for DBLP.

3.2 Functions

In the following we define all functions that we use for interaction between model and knowledge graph. Each function has a `kg` parameter for dynamically specifying the knowledge graph. The model can thus choose the most suitable graph itself. This mechanism even allows federated queries across multiple graphs. We give every function a three-letter mnemonic and denote optional and enum arguments with `?` and `|` respectively.

`ANS: answer(kg: str, sparql: str, answer: str)`
Provides the final SPARQL query, the knowledge graph to execute it on, and a human-readable answer to the question. Calling this function stops the generation process.

`CAN: cancel(expl: str, best_attempt: {sparql: str, kg: str}?)`
If no satisfactory SPARQL query can be found, calling this function allows to give an explanation for that and an optional best attempt at the SPARQL query. It also stops the generation process.

`EXE: execute(kg: str, sparql: str)`
Execute a SPARQL query over the knowledge graph and retrieve its results as a table in the case of success, and an error message otherwise. If the result table has more than 10 rows or columns, we only show the first five and last five rows or columns respectively. The client-side query timeout is set to 60 s.[6]

`LST: list(kg: str, subj: str?, prop: str?, obj: str?)`
List triples from the knowledge graph according to the given constraints on the subject, property, and object positions. It returns at most 10 triples and makes sure that the returned ones are relevant and diverse.[7] For example, we prefer entities and properties with high scores and avoid multiple occurrences of the same entities and properties.

`SEN: search_entity(kg: str, query: str)`

[6] We consider 10 rows and 10 columns to be enough to get a sense of the query result. Larger timeouts didn't improve results significantly.

[7] A larger number of triples costs more tokens, but did not improve results significantly.

Search for entities in the specified knowledge graph with the query. Uses a prefix-keyword-index internally.
`SPR: search_property(kg: str, query: str)`
Search for properties in the specified knowledge graph with the query. Uses a similarity index internally.
`SPE: search_property_of_entity(kg: str, query: str, ent: str)`
Same as `SPR`, but restricts the search to properties that exist for the given entity in the knowledge graph.
`SOP: search_object_of_property(kg: str, query: str, prop: str)`
Similar to `SEN`, but restricts the search to entities and literals that exist for the given property in the knowledge graph at the object position.
`SAC: search_autocomplete(kg: str, query: str, sparql: str)`
Search for items in the knowledge graph with the query in a context-sensitive way. The given SPARQL query must be a SELECT query with a variable *?search* in its body. The search is then restricted to items that fit at the variable's position.
`SCN: search_constrained(kg: str, query: str, pos: subj|prop|obj, constraints: {subj: str?, prop: str?, obj: str?})`
Search for triple items at the specified position in the knowledge graph with the query. If there are further constraints specified, they are used to limit the search space to matching triples accordingly.
All search functions return the top 10 search results, which we consider to be enough in most scenarios.
`FSE: find_similar_examples(kg: str, question: str)`
Find question-SPARQL-pairs over the specified knowledge graph that have questions similar to the given one. It returns the three most similar pairs based on a pre-computed similarity index. In this work, the index is built from the training set of the respective benchmark we evaluate on, if available.
`FEX: find_examples(kg: str)`
Like `FSE` but the returned examples are selected randomly.
Note, that the two functions above are only used for few-shot evaluations.

3.3 Function Sets

We evaluate different variants of our approach, where each variant has a particular subset of the functions from Sect. 3.2 available. We call such a subset a ***function set***. We start with the basic function set $\boldsymbol{B} = \{\texttt{ANS}, \texttt{CAN}, \texttt{EXE}\}$, which allows the model to interact with the knowledge graph solely by executing SPARQL queries. For the other functions sets, we build upon $\boldsymbol{B}$ and add `LST` to enable the model to retrieve RDF triples, and one or more search functions to enable the model to search the knowledge graph. We use `SEN` and `SPR` for the function set $\boldsymbol{S}$, `SAC` for the function set $\boldsymbol{S_A}$ and `SCN` for the function set $\boldsymbol{S_C}$. In theory, the model can perform the most sophisticated searches with `SAC`, followed by `SCN`, and then the search functions in $\boldsymbol{S}$. The first two can dynamically constrain searches to subgraphs, with `SAC` providing even more flexibility than `SCN` because it allows for full-blown SPARQL queries as constraining element rather than a single RDF triple. However, during initial experiments with these functions, we noticed that the model often struggles to use them properly, or only uses them in their most basic form for unconstrained search. Therefore, we introduce the $\boldsymbol{S_E}$ function set to strike a balance between ease of use and functionality. This function set builds upon the function set $\boldsymbol{S}$ but contains additional specialized functions for the two most common types of searches a human expert performs when writing SPARQL queries: `SPE` to look for properties of a given entity, and `SOP` to look for entities and literals reachable by a given property. For few-shot evaluations we also add one of `FSE` or `FEX` to each function set. See Sect. 3.5 for more details. See Table 1 for an overview over all function sets.

Table 1. The function sets and which functions they include. The `FSE` and `FEX` functions are only added for few-shot evaluations.

Set	ANS	CAN	EXE	LST	SEN	SPR	SPE	SOP	SAC	SCN	FSE	FEX
$\boldsymbol{B}$	✓	✓	✓								(✓)	(✓)
$\boldsymbol{S}$	✓	✓	✓	✓	✓	✓					(✓)	(✓)
$\boldsymbol{S_E}$	✓	✓	✓	✓	✓	✓	✓	✓			(✓)	(✓)
$\boldsymbol{S_A}$	✓	✓	✓	✓					✓		(✓)	(✓)
$\boldsymbol{S_C}$	✓	✓	✓	✓						✓	(✓)	(✓)

3.4 Search Indices

The search functions are all based on pre-computed index data structures, which we describe in the following. See Table 3 for details about all used indices.

Data. The data for the index data structures comes from two SPARQL queries per knowledge graph, one for entities and one for properties. They compute one row per item with five columns each: IRI, label, score, synonyms, and additional information. The IRI is unique and besides it only the label is required. The rows are ordered by descending score, with a higher score corresponding to more popular or more commonly used items.[8] Synonyms define alternative labels that are indexed like the main label.[9] The additional information is not indexed but can help to disambiguate similarly labeled items. See Table 2 for example data.[10]

Prefix-Keyword Index. Our prefix-keyword index scores and ranks entities by the number of exact and prefix matches between the entity keywords and a keyword query. For example, given the query "Albert E" and entities {*Peter*

[8] In the indices the score is used to resolve tie-breaks between equally ranked items.
[9] When querying an index, labels and synonyms of each IRI are ranked separately, but the highest-ranked one determines the IRI's final rank.
[10] See the corresponding SPARQL query at qlever.cs.uni-freiburg.de/wikidata/InnqDm.

Table 2. Index data for four example Wikidata entities.

IRI	Label	Score	Synonyms	Infos
wd:Q9047	Gottfried Wilhelm Leibniz	202	Gottfried Wilhelm; Leibniz; Gottfried Wilhelm von Leibniz; Leibnitz; Freiherr Gottfried Wilhelm von Leibniz; ...	archivist; jurist; zoologist; philosopher of law; writer; ...
wd:Q5202	Almazán	167	Almazan	municipality in the province of Soria, Castile and León, Spain
wd:Q12117	cereal grain	147	cereal; cereals	fruits (grains) of cereal crops used for food and agricultural products
wd:Q9950	Q	142	q	letter of Latin alphabet

Falk, *Carlos Alberto*, *Albert Einstein*, *Albert Finney*} our index will return the ranked list [*Albert Einstein*, *Albert Finney*, *Carlos Alberto*].[11]

Similarity Index. Our similarity index scores and ranks properties by the cosine-similarity between search query embedding and property embeddings. For vector search on the pre-computed property embeddings we use FAISS [15]. For

Table 3. Details about the size of our indices for various knowledge graphs. We use prefix-keyword indices for entities and similarity indices for properties. # refers to the number of indexed items, while Data and Index refer to the disk space occupied by the data from the SPARQL queries and index data structures respectively. * The Open Research Knowledge Graph (ORKG) indices are based on an old version from 2023 [5], that is needed to evaluate on SciQA [3].

KG	Entities			Properties		
	#	Data	Index	#	Data	Index
DBLP [1]	141M	13GB	11GB	67	12kB	280kB
DBpedia [4]	19M	3GB	906MB	54k	3MB	213MB
Freebase [12]	47M	6GB	2GB	21k	3MB	82MB
*ORKG [22]	180k	16MB	8MB	7k	440kB	27MB
OSM [8]	106M	7GB	4GB	101K	8MB	397MB
UniProt [18]	4M	343MB	317MB	237	24kB	960kB
Wikidata [45]	85M	12GB	6GB	12k	2MB	134MB

[11] *Albert Einstein* has one exact and one prefix match, *Albert Finney* one exact match, and *Carlos Alberto* one prefix match. *Peter Falk* is excluded because it has no match.

our embedding model we use *mxbai-embed-large-v1* [24] within the Sentence Transformers library [36].

3.5 Few-Shot Examples

Our focus with GRASP is zero-shot inference, but we are still interested in whether providing a few question-SPARQL examples in context can improve performance. For a given knowledge graph and question, the few-shot examples are retrieved from the training set of the corresponding benchmark (if one exists) at the beginning of the generation process, either randomly or by similarity to the question. This is implemented via the functions `FSE` and `FEX`.

3.6 Feedback

We also investigate how providing feedback on calls of `ANS` or `CAN` can help the model produce better outputs. We do this especially to improve rule following for the rules specified in the GRASP instruction, because this typically suffers in long generation traces. Importantly, the feedback model is the same as the SPARQL generating one but receives only the `ANS` or `CAN` arguments and the SPARQL rules from the GRASP instruction as input, not the full generation history. The feedback consists of a status `done|refine|retry` and a general feedback message. If the status is `done`, we stop ultimately. Otherwise, we add the feedback to the history and continue the generation process until the next `ANS` or `CAN` call. We allow at most two intermediate feedback loops.

4 Evaluation

In this section, we present our evaluation results. We start by describing the evaluation setup, such as the benchmarks and metric used, as well as the different model configurations we look at. Unless stated otherwise, we use the S_E function set. We call the variant of our approach with feedback enabled GRASP-F.

4.1 Benchmarks and Metric

In the following, we introduce the main benchmark datasets we evaluate on in this work. We chose them because they are either widely used in the research community or very relevant to our work. We also evaluate our approach on more knowledge graphs and benchmarks, see Sect. 4.3 and Table 9 for details.

Benchmarks. WebQuestionsSP (WQSP) annotates the WebQuestions dataset [11] with SPARQL queries over Freebase [50]. ComplexWebQuestions (CWQ) extends WQSP with automatically generated, more complex SPARQL queries, and annotates them with corresponding natural language questions [39]. QALD-7 [43] is the first QALD edition involving Wikidata. QALD-10 [44] then focuses on Wikidata, with a new large test set with real-world questions and expert-annotated SPARQL queries. SPINACH is created from real-world SPARQL queries in Wikidata's "Request a query" forum, annotated with natural language questions [28]. WikiWebQuestions (WWQ) adapts WQSP to Wikidata [47].

Metric. All models are evaluated using the F_1-score averaged across samples. We adopt SPINACH's modification, which permits additional columns (e.g., labels) in the predicted results without penalty.[12] Samples with empty groundtruth are excluded. If the predicted query is an ASK query and the groundtruth is a SELECT query (or vice versa), we assign a score of 1 if their results are semantically equivalent. To save compute and money, we evaluate on 200 random samples for each benchmark, which for QALD-7 and SPINACH is still the whole test set. For the component studies in Sect. 4.3, we use a subset of the benchmarks for the same reasons.[13] Wherever we have access to the original predictions from previous work, we re-evaluate them with our metric and, for a fair comparison, only use those samples present in both our and their evaluation.

4.2 Results

Table 4 shows our zero-shot and few-shot results for GRASP and GRASP-F on the main Wikidata and Freebase benchmarks using GPT-4.1 models [32]. In the zero-shot setting we reach very good performance overall. The GPT-4.1 variant sets a new state-of-the-art on all Wikidata benchmarks, while coming close to or surpassing the best few-shot approaches on Freebase. The inclusion of feedback improves performance across the board: it thus helps if the model gets the chance to reassess and refine its own outputs once in a while. In the few-shot setting we only evaluate GPT-4.1 mini due to cost. As expected, adding examples improves performance even further, with few-shot GRASP using GPT-4.1 mini surpassing zero-shot GRASP-F using GPT-4.1 on 3 out of 5 benchmarks. Interestingly, feedback does not seem to help as much in the few-shot setting, probably because the in-context examples already provide sufficient information in this case.

4.3 Various Studies

Model Provider Study. Table 5 shows the results for GRASP using various base models. We find that open-source models like Qwen2.5 72B and Qwen3 32B [48] can reach performance equal to or better than commercial models like Gemini 2.0 Flash [19]. Most commercial models still outperform the open-source models, with GPT-4.1 and o4-mini [33] at the top. The reasoning models do not significantly outperform non-reasoning models, probably because we explicitly instruct GRASP to "think" before and after each step, which leads to reasoning-like behavior.

[12] For results exceeding 1,024 rows, we revert to the standard exact F_1-score due to the computational cost of row-wise assignment.

[13] Except for the function set study, were full coverage is key for a clear picture.

Table 4. Comparison of our approach with previous work. * marks previous work where we re-evaluated the original predictions on the same sample set and with the same exact metric as our models. All other results are taken from the respective papers. † marks results taken from SPINACH [28]. Results in [brackets] report Hits@1 instead of F_1-score. Few-shot results on SPINACH are missing because this benchmark does not provide a dedicated train set. Our best and second best models per benchmark are bold and underlined respectively.

Approach	**Freebase**		**Wikidata**			
	CWQ	WQSP	QALD-10	QALD-7	SPINACH	WWQ
Fine-tuned						
DeCAF [51]	[70.4]	78.8	-	-	-	-
Pangu [20]	-	79.6	-	-	-	-
FlexKBQA [26]	-	60.6	-	-	-	-
ChatKBQA [29]	77.8	79.8	-	-	-	-
RGR-KBQA [17]	76.6	80.7	-	-	-	-
RoG [30]	56.2	70.8	-	-	-	-
RwT [37]	66.7	79.7	-	-	-	-
SymAgent [27]	48.3	57.1	-	-	-	-
LightPROF [2]	[59.3]	[83.8]	-	-	-	-
WikiSP [47]	-	-	-	-	7.1†	71.9
Few-shot						
KB-BINDER [35]	-	74.4	-	-	-	-
Interactive-KBQA [46]	49.1	71.2	-	-	-	-
Pangu [20]	-	68.3	-	-	-	-
KELDaR-rel [25]	[44.2]	[76.7]	-	-	-	-
DoG [31]	[58.2]	[91.0]	-	-		
Zero-shot						
StructGPT [23]	-	[72.6]	-	-	-	-
ToG [38]	[69.5]	[82.6]	[54.7]	-	7.2†	-
SPINACH [28]	-	-	69.5	74.6	45.3	70.3
*SPINACH [28]	-	-	71.0	72.9	39.2	68.3
Zero-shot						
GRASP GPT-4.1 mini	23.5	46.1	66.7	66.2	32.1	71.5
GRASP-F GPT-4.1 mini	32.2	52.1	69.5	68.6	35.4	71.3
GRASP GPT-4.1	44.2	52.1	**72.5**	<u>79.4</u>	<u>40.8</u>	75.3
GRASP-F GPT-4.1	58.5	62.2	<u>70.6</u>	**81.5**	**42.6**	75.2
Few-shot using GPT-4.1 mini						
GRASP similar 3-shot	<u>63.7</u>	**71.0**	68.1	74.5	-	**79.7**
GRASP-F similar 3-shot	**65.6**	<u>67.9</u>	67.4	73.0	-	<u>78.3</u>

Table 5. Comparison of GRASP when using different base models. Reasoning models are evaluated on 100 samples to save costs and compute. The best and second best models per benchmark are bold and underlined respectively.

Model	Freebase	Wikidata	
	WQSP	QALD-10	WWQ
Using non-reasoning models			
Gemini 2.0 Flash	41.4	58.5	62.6
Qwen2.5 72B	40.8	61.7	68.7
GPT-4.1 mini	46.1	66.7	<u>71.5</u>
GPT-4.1	<u>52.1</u>	<u>72.5</u>	**75.3**
Using reasoning models			
Qwen3 32B	39.2	50.3	61.3
Gemini 2.5 Flash	47.4	62.7	68.6
o4-mini	**59.2**	**82.3**	65.2

Function Set Study. We run Qwen2.5 72B on all benchmarks with each of our function sets. As expected, we find that the base function set $\boldsymbol{B}$ without explicit search functions performs worst across all benchmarks. This is because the builtin search functionality in SPARQL on literals is limited compared to our search indices, often leads to errors due to high memory usage or timeouts, and is harder to use for the model. We find that overall the $\boldsymbol{S_E}$ function set performs the best. We hypothesize that this is because it is easier to use than $\boldsymbol{S_A}$ or $\boldsymbol{S_C}$ while still allowing constrained search unlike $\boldsymbol{S}$. See Table 6 for full results.

Table 6. Comparison of GRASP when using different function sets. The best and second best models per benchmark are bold and underlined respectively.

Set	Freebase		Wikidata			
	CWQ	WQSP	QALD-10	QALD-7	SPINACH	WWQ
Using Qwen2.5 72B						
$\boldsymbol{B}$	6.5	19.8	43.8	52.6	17.3	55.7
$\boldsymbol{S}$	<u>23.9</u>	36.8	<u>63.3</u>	<u>73.0</u>	27.4	**68.7**
$\boldsymbol{S_A}$	16.2	<u>40.3</u>	60.1	70.8	**27.9**	<u>68.4</u>
$\boldsymbol{S_C}$	23.1	38.1	**67.0**	68.7	24.1	67.5
$\boldsymbol{S_E}$	**29.9**	**40.8**	61.7	**73.5**	<u>27.6</u>	**68.7**

Model Size Study. The Qwen2.5 and Qwen3 model families provide a range of different model sizes which we use to determine how model size affects performance with GRASP. As expected, we find that performance increases with model size. There also seems to be quite a jump in performance between the 7 B and 14 B models for Qwen2.5 and between the 4 B and 8 B models for Qwen3. The best model overall is Qwen2.5 72 B , though a model of comparable size is missing for Qwen3. See Table 7 for full results.

Few-Shot and Feedback Study. In addition to the results from Table 4, we also run GPT-4.1 mini with random few-shot examples. As mentioned in Sect. 4.2, our results show that feedback generally improves performance if no examples are given but does not help as much, and sometimes even hurts, if there are examples. Also as expected, in most cases both types of examples improve performance, with similar examples helping more than random examples, especially on benchmarks with more similar train and test splits. We validate these findings with a separate set of evaluations using Qwen2.5 72B and observe similar patterns there. As a rule of thumb, one should generally use feedback for best performance, but it can be disabled if there are examples available, especially if they are known to be similar to expected future questions. See Table 8 for full results.

Knowledge Graph Study. To show that our approach also generalizes to other, less commonly evaluated knowledge graphs, we collect or create benchmarks for DBLP, DBpedia, ORKG, OSM, and UniProt, and add two more benchmarks for Wikidata and one for Freebase. We evaluate GRASP-F using GPT-4.1 on all of them and show the results in Table 9. Our approach performs well overall, except on OSM and UniProt (for reasons partly explained next).

4.4 Error Analysis

We manually inspect a random subset of the results of our best variant (GRASP-F using GPT-4.1) for each benchmark. For almost all queries, the model performs sensible function calls, which are suited to lead to the correct query. There is no dominant source of error across graphs, but each graph has some quirks that are hard for the model to handle. Here are three examples:
1. Wikidata potentially contains the same information in different ways. Sometimes, a complex information is captured by a single IRI, such as *Mayor of Germasogeia Municipality Elections (wd:Q93306595)*. Sometimes, such information uses a highly non-trivial combination of properties like *p:2139, psv:P2139, pq:P585*. Our model sometimes commits to the wrong alternatives, which then gives suboptimal or no results. This is a hard problem, also for expert users.
2. Several of the DBLP queries involve citations. However, there is no triple that directly connects the DBLP ID for a paper with a cited or citing paper or with an object that represents a citation. Instead, there is a predicate *dblp:omid* that

Table 7. Comparison of GRASP for different model sizes with Qwen2.5 (non-reasoning) and Qwen3 (reasoning). The best and second best models per benchmark are bold and underlined respectively.

Size	Freebase	Wikidata	
	WQSP	QALD-10	WWQ
Using Qwen2.5 models			
7B	24.1	39.3	37.0
14B	38.2	51.6	60.2
32B	29.9	<u>59.8</u>	58.7
72B	**40.8**	**61.7**	**68.7**
Using Qwen3 models			
4B	25.2	25.4	35.3
8B	33.6	46.2	51.5
14B	24.4	45.7	50.7
32B	<u>39.2</u>	50.3	<u>61.3</u>

Table 8. Effect of feedback and few-shot examples on performance. Models using three similar examples are marked as *sim*, while models using three random examples are marked as *rand*. The best and second best models per benchmark are bold and underlined respectively.

Variant	Freebase	Wikidata	
	WQSP	QALD-10	WWQ
Using GPT-4.1 mini			
GRASP	46.1	66.7	71.5
GRASP-F	52.1	<u>69.1</u>	71.3
GRASP *rand*	57.4	**70.8**	70.5
GRASP-F *rand*	59.0	67.3	71.2
GRASP *sim*	**71.0**	67.8	**79.7**
GRASP-F *sim*	<u>67.9</u>	67.1	<u>78.3</u>
Using Qwen2.5 72B			
GRASP	40.8	61.7	68.7
GRASP-F	47.6	64.1	64.6
GRASP *rand*	45.0	65.1	66.4
GRASP-F *rand*	57.0	62.5	63.2
GRASP *sim*	65.9	65.0	76.2
GRASP-F *sim*	66.5	68.0	70.4

connects the DBLP ID to another kind of ID (called OMID), which in turn is connected to an object representing a citation. Our models desperately look for this connection but don't find it. This, too, is hard for experts.
3. Several of the OSM examples involve finding members of OSM ways or relations. The obvious predicate *ogc:sfContains* does not work, instead the predicates *osmrel:member* and *osmway:member* are needed. Our models do encounter these predicates during their search, but do not follow through with them. In general, the OSM and UniProt queries are considerable more complex.
Independently of the graph, our model tends to forgo the property search and hallucinate properties, despite unsuccessful query executions. We tried to mitigate this behavior by returning error messages to the model if it uses IRIs within `EXE` that were not part of a prior function call result, and got some initial positive results that this indeed helps; exploring this further is an interesting direction for future work. Another kind of error are ambiguous questions, where ground truth and generated SPARQL query are both reasonable but different. Similarly, ground truth and generated query sometimes only differ in the LIMIT clause. In both cases, the model gets an unfairly low F_1-score. It would be desirable to develop metrics that are more robust against such errors.

Table 9. Performance of GRASP-F on other knowledge graphs and benchmarks. We evaluate on 50 randomly selected samples per benchmark.

KG	Benchmark	F_1-score	Description
Using GPT-4.1			
DBLP	DBLP-QuAD	51.0	KGQA benchmark over DBLP [7]
DBLP	Examples	50.3	Examples for the RDF version of DBLP [1,13]
DBpedia	SimpleQ	53.5	Migration of Freebase SimpleQ to DBpedia [6]
DBpedia	LC-QuAD	48.6	Template-based SPARQL queries over DBpedia [40]
DBpedia	QALD-7	60.3	English DBpedia subset of QALD-7 [43]
DBpedia	QALD-9	65.2	English subset of QALD-9 [42]
Freebase	SimpleQ	59.8	Questions answerable by a single triple [21]
ORKG	SciQA	52.2	KGQA benchmark over ORKG [3]
OSM	Examples	17.3	Examples from the OSM website [34]
UniProt	Examples	20.7	Examples from the UniProt website [41]
Wikidata	SimpleQ	67.6	Migration of Freebase SimpleQ to Wikidata [14]
Wikidata	LC-QuAD 2.0	62.1	Wikidata variant of the LC-QuAD successor [16]

5 Conclusion

We present GRASP, a new approach for zero-shot generation of SPARQL queries over arbitrary knowledge graphs. In an extensive evaluation across many graphs, GRASP performs well across the board. On Wikidata, it achieves state-of-the-art in the zero-shot setting, and comes close to few-shot or fine-tuned models on Freebase. We investigated GRASP's individual components (function set, language model, feedback mechanism, example incorporation) in detail. It turns out that search functions that are both context-sensitive and easy to use work best. GRASP works well with both commercial and open-source models, with a slight edge for GPT-4.1. Both examples and feedback help to improve performance.

Supplemental Material Statement: All of our code and data (e.g. knowledge graph indices, benchmarks, model outputs, etc.) is openly available via github.com/ad-freiburg/grasp. This includes a web app for evaluating and comparing models.

Acknowledgments. Funded by the Deutsche Forschungsgemeinschaft (DFG, German Research Foundation) Project-ID 499552394 SFB 1597.

References

1. Ackermann, M.R., Bast, H., Beckermann, B.M., Kalmbach, J., Neises, P., Ollinger, S.: The DBLP knowledge graph and SPARQL endpoint. TGDK **2**(2), 3:1–3:23 (2024). https://doi.org/10.4230/TGDK.2.2.3

2. Ao, T., et al.: LightPROF: a lightweight reasoning framework for large language model on knowledge graph. In: AAAI, pp. 23424–23432. AAAI Press (2025)
3. Auer, S., et al.: The SciQA scientific question answering benchmark for scholarly knowledge. Sci. Rep. **13**(1), 7240 (2023)
4. Auer, S., Bizer, C., Kobilarov, G., Lehmann, J., Cyganiak, R., Ives, Z.: DBpedia: a nucleus for a web of open data. In: Aberer, K., Choi, K.-S., Noy, N., Allemang, D., Lee, K.-I., Nixon, L., Golbeck, J., Mika, P., Maynard, D., Mizoguchi, R., Schreiber, G., Cudré-Mauroux, P. (eds.) ASWC/ISWC -2007. LNCS, vol. 4825, pp. 722–735. Springer, Heidelberg (2007). https://doi.org/10.1007/978-3-540-76298-0_52
5. Auer, S., et al.: SciQA benchmark: dataset and RDF dump (2023)
6. Azmy, M., Shi, P., Lin, J., Ilyas, I.F.: Farewell freebase: migrating the simplequestions dataset to DBpedia. In: COLING, pp. 2093–2103. Association for Computational Linguistics (2018)
7. Banerjee, D., Awale, S., Usbeck, R., Biemann, C.: DBLP-QuAD: a question answering dataset over the DBLP scholarly knowledge graph. In: BIR@ECIR. CEUR Workshop Proceedings, vol. 3617, pp. 37–51. CEUR-WS.org (2023)
8. Bast, H., Brosi, P., Kalmbach, J., Lehmann, A.: An efficient RDF converter and SPARQL endpoint for the complete OpenStreetMap data. In: SIGSPATIAL/GIS, pp. 536–539. ACM (2021)
9. Bast, H., Buchhold, B.: QLever: A query engine for efficient SPARQL+Text search. In: CIKM, pp. 647–656. ACM (2017)
10. Bast, H., Kalmbach, J., Klumpp, T., Kramer, F., Schnelle, N.: Efficient and effective SPARQL autocompletion on very large knowledge graphs. In: CIKM, pp. 2893–2902. ACM (2022)
11. Berant, J., Chou, A., Frostig, R., Liang, P.: Semantic parsing on Freebase from question-answer pairs. In: EMNLP, pp. 1533–1544. ACL (2013)
12. Bollacker, K.D., Evans, C., Paritosh, P.K., Sturge, T., Taylor, J.: Freebase: a collaboratively created graph database for structuring human knowledge. In: SIGMOD Conference, pp. 1247–1250. ACM (2008)
13. DBLP GitHub: Wiki page for TGDK 2024 paper. https://github.com/dblp/kg/wiki/Paper-TGDK-2024. Accessed 07 May 2025
14. Diefenbach, D., Tanon, T.P., Singh, K.D., Maret, P.: Question answering benchmarks for Wikidata. In: ISWC (Posters, Demos & Industry Tracks). CEUR Workshop Proceedings, vol. 1963. CEUR-WS.org (2017)
15. Douze, M., et al.: The Faiss library (2024)
16. Dubey, M., Banerjee, D., Abdelkawi, A., Lehmann, J.: LC-QuAD 2.0: a large dataset for complex question answering over Wikidata and DBpedia. In: Ghidini, C., Hartig, O., Maleshkova, M., Svátek, V., Cruz, I., Hogan, A., Song, J., Lefrançois, M., Gandon, F. (eds.) ISWC 2019. LNCS, vol. 11779, pp. 69–78. Springer, Cham (2019). https://doi.org/10.1007/978-3-030-30796-7_5
17. Feng, T., He, L.: RGR-KBQA: generating logical forms for question answering using knowledge-graph-enhanced large language model. In: COLING, pp. 3057–3070. Association for Computational Linguistics (2025)
18. Garcia, L., et al.: FAIR adoption, assessment and challenges at UniProt. Sci. Data **6**(1), 175 (2019)
19. Google DeepMind: Introducing Gemini 2.0: our new AI model for the agentic era (2024). https://blog.google/technology/google-deepmind/google-gemini-ai-update-december-2024/. Accessed 11 May 2025
20. Gu, Y., Deng, X., Su, Y.: Don't generate, discriminate: a proposal for grounding language models to real-world environments. In: ACL (1), pp. 4928–4949. Association for Computational Linguistics (2023)

21. He, X., Golub, D.: Character-level question answering with attention. In: EMNLP, pp. 1598–1607. The Association for Computational Linguistics (2016)
22. Jaradeh, M.Y., et al.: Open research knowledge graph: next generation infrastructure for semantic scholarly knowledge. In: K-CAP, pp. 243–246. ACM (2019)
23. Jiang, J., Zhou, K., Dong, Z., Ye, K., Zhao, X., Wen, J.: StructGPT: a general framework for large language model to reason over structured data. In: EMNLP, pp. 9237–9251. Association for Computational Linguistics (2023)
24. Lee, S., Shakir, A., Koenig, D., Lipp, J.: Open source strikes bread - new fluffy embedding model (2024). https://www.mixedbread.ai/blog/mxbai-embed-large-v1
25. Li, Y., et al.: A framework of knowledge graph-enhanced large language model based on question decomposition and atomic retrieval. In: EMNLP (Findings), pp. 11472–11485. Association for Computational Linguistics (2024)
26. Li, Z., et al.: FlexKBQA: A flexible LLM-powered framework for few-shot knowledge base question answering. In: AAAI, pp. 18608–18616. AAAI Press (2024)
27. Liu, B., Zhang, J., Lin, F., Yang, C., Peng, M., Yin, W.: SymAgent: a neural-symbolic self-learning agent framework for complex reasoning over knowledge graphs. In: WWW, pp. 98–108. ACM (2025)
28. Liu, S., Semnani, S.J., Triedman, H., Xu, J., Zhao, I.D., Lam, M.S.: SPINACH: SPARQL-based information navigation for challenging real-world questions. In: EMNLP (Findings), pp. 15977–16001. Association for Computational Linguistics (2024)
29. Luo, H., et al.: ChatKBQA: a generate-then-retrieve framework for knowledge base question answering with fine-tuned large language models. In: ACL (Findings), pp. 2039–2056. Association for Computational Linguistics (2024)
30. Luo, L., Li, Y., Haffari, G., Pan, S.: Reasoning on graphs: Faithful and interpretable large language model reasoning. In: ICLR, OpenReview.net (2024)
31. Ma, J., et al.: Debate on graph: a flexible and reliable reasoning framework for large language models. In: AAAI, pp. 24768–24776. AAAI Press (2025)
32. OpenAI: Introducing GPT-4.1 in the API (2025). https://openai.com/index/gpt-4-1/. Accessed 11 May 2025
33. OpenAI: OpenAI o3 and o4-mini system card. Technical report, OpenAI (2025). https://cdn.openai.com/pdf/2221c875-02dc-4789-800b-e7758f3722c1/o3-and-o4-mini-system-card.pdf. Accessed 11 May 2025
34. OpenStreetMap Website: QLever example queries. https://wiki.openstreetmap.org/wiki/QLever/Example_queries. Accessed 07 May 2025
35. Patidar, M., Sawhney, R., Singh, A.K., Chatterjee, B., Mausam, Bhattacharya, I.: Few-shot transfer learning for knowledge base question answering: Fusing supervised models with in-context learning. In: ACL (1), pp. 9147–9165. Association for Computational Linguistics (2024)
36. Reimers, N., Gurevych, I.: Sentence-BERT: sentence embeddings using siamese BERT-networks. In: Proceedings of the 2019 Conference on Empirical Methods in Natural Language Processing. Association for Computational Linguistics (2019). https://arxiv.org/abs/1908.10084
37. Shen, T., Wang, J., Zhang, X., Cambria, E.: Reasoning with trees: faithful question answering over knowledge graph. In: COLING, pp. 3138–3157. Association for Computational Linguistics (2025)
38. Sun, J., et al.: Think-on-graph: deep and responsible reasoning of large language model on knowledge graph. In: ICLR, OpenReview.net (2024)

39. Talmor, A., Berant, J.: The web as a knowledge-base for answering complex questions. In: NAACL-HLT, pp. 641–651. Association for Computational Linguistics (2018)
40. Trivedi, P., Maheshwari, G., Dubey, M., Lehmann, J.: LC-QuAD: a corpus for complex question answering over knowledge graphs. In: d'Amato, C., Fernandez, M., Tamma, V., Lecue, F., Cudré-Mauroux, P., Sequeda, J., Lange, C., Heflin, J. (eds.) ISWC 2017. LNCS, vol. 10588, pp. 210–218. Springer, Cham (2017). https://doi.org/10.1007/978-3-319-68204-4_22
41. UniProt Website: SPARQL example queries. https://sparql.uniprot.org/.well-known/sparql-examples. Accessed 07 May 2025
42. Usbeck, R., Gusmita, R.H., Ngomo, A.N., Saleem, M.: 9th challenge on question answering over linked data (QALD-9) (invited paper). In: Semdeep/NLIWoD@ISWC. CEUR Workshop Proceedings, vol. 2241, pp. 58–64. CEUR-WS.org (2018)
43. Usbeck, R., Ngomo, A.-C.N., Haarmann, B., Krithara, A., Röder, M., Napolitano, G.: 7th open challenge on question answering over linked data (QALD-7). In: Dragoni, M., Solanki, M., Blomqvist, E. (eds.) SemWebEval 2017. CCIS, vol. 769, pp. 59–69. Springer, Cham (2017). https://doi.org/10.1007/978-3-319-69146-6_6
44. Usbeck, R., et al.: QALD-10 – the 10th challenge on question answering over linked data: shifting from DBpedia to Wikidata as a KG for KGQA. Semantic Web **15**(6), 2193–2207 (2024)
45. Vrandecic, D., Krötzsch, M.: Wikidata: a free collaborative knowledgebase. Commun. ACM **57**(10), 78–85 (2014)
46. Xiong, G., Bao, J., Zhao, W.: Interactive-KBQA: multi-turn interactions for knowledge base question answering with large language models. In: ACL (1), pp. 10561–10582. Association for Computational Linguistics (2024)
47. Xu, S., et al.: Fine-tuned LLMs know more, hallucinate less with few-shot sequence-to-sequence semantic parsing over Wikidata. In: EMNLP, pp. 5778–5791. Association for Computational Linguistics (2023)
48. Yang, A., et al.: Qwen2.5 technical report. arXiv preprint arXiv:2412.15115 (2024)
49. Yao, S., et al.: ReAct: Synergizing reasoning and acting in language models. In: ICLR. OpenReview.net (2023)
50. Yih, W., Richardson, M., Meek, C., Chang, M., Suh, J.: The value of semantic parse labeling for knowledge base question answering. In: ACL (2). The Association for Computer Linguistics (2016)
51. Yu, D., et al.: DecAF: Joint decoding of answers and logical forms for question answering over knowledge bases. In: ICLR. OpenReview.net (2023)

ReFactX: Scalable Reasoning with Reliable Facts via Constrained Generation

Riccardo Pozzi[1,3(✉)], Matteo Palmonari[1], Andrea Coletta[2], Luigi Bellomarini[2], Jens Lehmann[3,5,7], and Sahar Vahdati[3,4,5,6]

[1] University of Milano-Bicocca, Milano, Italy
riccardo.pozzi@unimib.it
[2] Banca d'Italia, Roma, Italy
[3] Institute for Applied Informatics (InfAI), Leipzig, Germany
[4] TIB Leibniz Information Centre for Science and Technology, Hannover, Germany
[5] ScaDS.AI Dresden/Leipzig, Technische Universität Dresden, Dresden, Germany
[6] Data Science Institute, Leibniz University Hannover, Hannover, Germany
[7] Amazon, Dresden, Germany

Abstract. Knowledge gaps and hallucinations are persistent challenges for Large Language Models (LLMs), which generate unreliable responses when lacking the necessary information to fulfill user instructions. Existing approaches, such as Retrieval-Augmented Generation (RAG) and tool use, aim to address these issues by incorporating external knowledge. Yet, they rely on additional models or services, resulting in complex pipelines, potential error propagation, and often requiring the model to process a large number of tokens. In this paper, we present ReFactX, a scalable method that enables LLMs to access external knowledge without depending on retrievers or auxiliary models. Our approach uses constrained generation with a pre-built prefix-tree index. Triples from Wikidata are verbalized in textual facts, tokenized, and indexed in a prefix tree for efficient access. During inference, to acquire external knowledge, the LLM generates facts with constrained generation which allows only sequences of tokens that form an existing fact. We evaluate our proposal on Question Answering and show that it scales to large knowledge bases (800 million facts), adapts to domain-specific data, and achieves effective results. These gains come with minimal generation-time overhead.

ReFactX code is available at https://github.com/rpo19/ReFactX.

1 Introduction

Large Language Models (LLMs) have demonstrated a variety of capabilities, ranging from natural language understanding and generation to reasoning, especially when enhanced with techniques like Chain-of-Thought (CoT) prompting [28]. However, LLMs are prone to hallucinations [20] and their internal

R. Pozzi—This work was done while Riccardo Pozzi was visiting InfAI and TU Dresden.
A. Coletta and L. Bellomarini—The opinions expressed are personal and should not be attributed to Banca d'Italia.
J. Lehmann—This work was done outside of Amazon.

D. Garijo et al. (Eds.): ISWC 2025, LNCS 16140, pp. 290–308, 2026.
https://doi.org/10.1007/978-3-032-09527-5_16

knowledge remains limited to their training data [5,18]. This complicates their application to knowledge-intensive tasks such as Question Answering (QA), especially when these tasks necessitate accessing information beyond the parametric knowledge of LLMs, including time-sensitive data or confidential corporate information.

Retrieval-Augmented Generation (RAG) [16,30] and tool-use [15,27,31] represent two prominent families of solutions. They enable LLMs to consult external knowledge bases (KBs) or execute external tools to enrich their responses with grounded information. We will refer to these methods as Knowledge-Enhanced QA (KE-QA). They often rely on additional components such as retrievers, entity linking systems, or auxiliary models, which are orchestrated in information processing pipelines. However, such pipeline-based or service-based solutions have a number of drawbacks. They require the optimization of a larger number of parameters and make it difficult to effectively back-propagate supervision signals to early components of the pipeline [34]. These approaches are susceptible to error-propagation [14], and knowledge updates may be complex to propagate to all the different components (e.g., to QA and entity linking knowledge bases).

An interesting technique that may overcome such limitations is constrained generation [4,23], which restricts the model's output space during decoding to sequences that satisfy predefined structural, syntactic, or semantic constraints. A few recent approaches have applied constrained generation to KE-QA, achieving promising results [17,19]. However, as the application of this technique to KE-QA is quite novel, there is an important research challenge to address to advance these techniques: the scalability to large knowledge bases. Can these approaches be applied to large KBs such as Wikidata[1]? In this paper, we present Reliable Fact eXtractor (ReFactX), an approach that addresses this challenge and poses itself as an alternative to pipeline-based solution. ReFactX allows LLMs to integrate external knowledge without depending on additional models or external retrievers, but relying solely on constrained generation, supported by a pre-built prefix-tree index, designed to facilitate and speed-up fact retrieval.

At inference time, the LLM is instructed via In-Context Learning (ICL) [7] to invoke the *Fact* command when external facts are required. Once the command is recognized, constrained generation is activated: the model produces tokens only along valid paths in the prefix tree, guaranteeing that the output matches a fact from the knowledge base, which is derived from Wikidata. Once an entire KB fact is generated, the decoding mechanism reverts back to normal. It is important to note that every generated token is selected based on LLM's probability estimates. Constrained generation only narrows the vocabulary to the tokens that form an existing fact in the KB, but always leaves the final choice to the LLM.

Motivating Example. We illustrate our approach in Fig. 1, by depicting an example with the question *"When was the director of Slumdog Millionaire born?"*. The model is instructed to first reason on how to reach the correct answer, and then it starts to acquire facts. Once the *Fact* command is called, we enable constrained generation (underlined in blue) and we guide the model to generate

[1] https://www.wikidata.org.

an existing fact. This way the model is able to first find that "Danny Boyle" is the director of "Slumdog Millionaire", then to find his birth date, and finally to answer the question correctly.

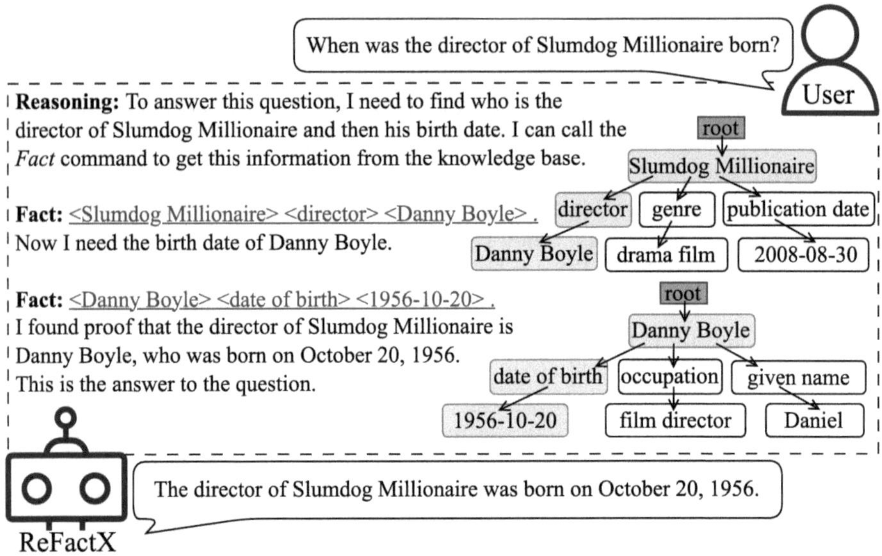

Fig. 1. ReFactX answering an open-domain question. The LLM sketches a plan, makes two *Fact* calls, and—with constrained generation (blue underline)—inserts valid facts from a Wikidata-based prefix tree before giving the final answer.

We can summarize the main contributions of this work as follows

- **ReFactX**: a generic, constrained-generation system that enables any LLM to access very large KBs, with no external retrievers or pipelines.
- **Efficiency and scalability**: a disk-backed prefix tree capable of holding up to 800 million facts, adding only ~1% latency.
- **Empirical validation**: insights on four QA datasets suggest that ReFactX can achieve competitive results, with accuracy gains exceeding 20% points at over 90% precision on certain benchmarks—compared to LLMs answering only with their parametric knowledge.

2 Related Work

Several approaches have been proposed to incorporate external knowledge into LLMs [8]. In our work, we focus on Question Answering (QA)—more specifically, on **Knowledge-Enhanced QA (KE-QA)**, where a model acquires external knowledge for answering questions.

Most of approaches can be classified as **input-based KE-QA**. They rely on external tools, such as search engines or dense retrievers [13], which can be arranged in pipeline-based workflows [16,30] or actively called by LLMs [15,22,31]. These approaches usually feed external knowledge as input (either in plain text or with dense embeddings) to the LLMs. Input-based KE-QA approaches, while effective in reducing hallucinations [25], require additional models or services for retrieving external information that can introduce delays, especially when calling remote APIs, increase training complexity [26], and raise substantially the number of input tokens [11], leading to higher response time and resource usage.

Other approaches can be classified as **memory-based KE-QA**. They propose memory modules, separated from model parameters, which make the models' internal mechanisms interact with external knowledge, e.g., by using cross-attention to incorporate external vectors [11,29]. While memory-based KE-QA approaches fuse external knowledge into LLMs' generation process more deeply, they typically require architectural modifications, complicating the use of pre-trained LLMs.

Constrained generation [4,23], described in detail in Sect. 3.1, is a promising technique to avoid the drawbacks of input-based and memory-based KE-QA approaches. It has been successfully applied to various tasks, including code generation [23], guaranteeing that the model produces syntactically correct code, as well as entity linking [4] and information retrieval [2]. It has also been applied to instruction-following LLMs for several tasks that require the LLM to produce a specifically structured output, such as entity disambiguation [9].

Two recent studies [17,19] proposed **constrained generation for KE-QA**, especially for guiding LLMs through paths from a knowledge graph (KG). However, they do not address the problem of accessing facts from large knowledge bases in a scalable way (800 million facts, in our case), and still rely on entity linking systems for extracting question entities, similarly to input-based approaches. A first approach, *Decoding on Graphs (DoG)* [17], generates triples from a knowledge graph in a reasoning process similar to CoT [28] but grounded on KG knowledge, also allowing the model to alternate the constrained generation of triples and the reasoning with normal generation. A second approach, *Graph-Constrained Reasoning (GCR)* [19] generates entire paths from a KG using a fine-tuned LLM to find answer hypotheses, and then asks a top-tier language model to give a final answer based on the paths.

3 ReFactX: Enabling LLMs to Access Large-Scale KBs

ReFactX allows LLMs to efficiently access large KBs at inference time with constrained generation, generating valid facts, and weave them into chain-of-thought reasoning. In this work we construct our KB from Wikidata. The three subsections below walk through (i) the decoding mechanism, (ii) the scalable Wikidata index, and (iii) how both pieces plug into a QA workflow.

3.1 Constrained Fact-Generation Mechanism

The mechanism of constrained generation alters the autoregressive next-token generation process, in which the LLM parameterized by θ, iteratively estimates the probability of each token $P(t)$ from the vocabulary V to be the chosen as the next-token, given the current sequence $t_0..t_k$:

$$P_\theta(t|t_0..t_k) \forall t \in V \tag{1}$$

The next-token t_{k+1} can be chosen according to different sampling strategy; in greedy decoding the most probable token is chosen as follows:

$$t_{k+1} = \text{argmax}_{t \in V} P_\theta(t|t_0..t_k) \tag{2}$$

Intuitively, to constrain this process for generating only existing facts, we need to restrict V to only allow tokens that can form a fact from the KB. We define $V^A_{t_0..t_k}$, which contains all the tokens that can lead to an existing fact if added to the sequence $t_0..t_k$. Considering the example in Fig. 2, at step t_{k+1}, when $t_0..t_k =$ "<Danny Boyle> <", $V^A_{t_0..t_k} =$ {"date","given"}.

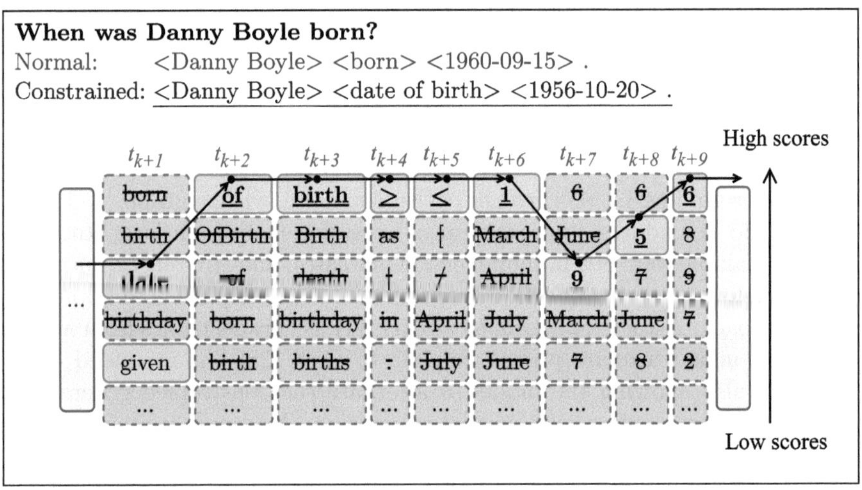

Fig. 2. Constrained decoding steers the LLM toward the correct fact. At each step, the constrained decoding mechanism chooses the highest-probability token that still completes a Wikidata fact, avoiding invalid branches and yielding "<Danny Boyle> <date of birth> <1956-10-20> .".

Next, we define the *next tokens* function NT_{KB} that, given $t_0..t_k$, obtains $V^A_{t_0..t_k}$ for the considered KB. Consequently, the token selection formula from Eq. 2 is updated to:

$$t_{k+1} = \text{argmax}_{t \in V^A_{t_0..t_k}} P_\theta(t|t_0..t_k), \text{ where } V^A_{t_0..t_k} = NT_{KB}(t_0..t_k). \tag{3}$$

However, the same result can be achieved by altering the probability distribution, setting the probability of all forbidden tokens to zero—without modifying the vocabulary:

$$P_\theta^c(t|t_0..t_k) = \begin{cases} P_\theta(t|t_0..t_k) & \text{if } t \in V^A_{t_0..t_k}, \\ 0 & \text{otherwise.} \end{cases} \tag{4}$$

By using P_θ^c, instead of P_θ, we achieve constrained generation, relying on the assumption that the sampling strategy (Eq. 2) would never choose any $t_{k+1}|P^c(t_{k+1}) = 0$. In practice, since at implementation level the models use log-probabilities, we directly set the log-probabilities of forbidden tokens to $-\infty$[2]:

$$\log P_\theta^c(t|t_0..t_k) = \begin{cases} \log P_\theta(t|t_0..t_k) & \text{if } t \in V^A_{t_0..t_k}, \\ -\infty & \text{otherwise.} \end{cases} \tag{5}$$

Figure 2 illustrates the application of constrained generation. It shows a fact produced by the same LLM in response to the question *"When was Danny Boyle born?"*—first using normal (unconstrained) generation, highlighted in red, and then using constrained generation, underlined in blue. While, the fact generated in normal mode is not correct, with constrained generation we are able to guide the LLM to the correct fact. The lower part of the figure details the mechanism of constrained generation. For each decoding step, allowed tokens are displayed in green boxes, whereas forbidden tokens are displayed in red boxes with dashed borders and a strikethrough. Tokens t_k are arranged in ascending order according to $P_\theta(t_k)$, from bottom to top.

Starting from the sequence $t_0..t_k$ = "<Danny Boyle> <", normal generation would generate $t_{k+1} = \text{argmax}_{t \in V} P_\theta(t|t_0..t_k)$ = "born", leading to an incorrect fact, while with constrained generation $t_{k+1} = \text{argmax}_{t \in V} P_\theta^c(t|t_0..t_k)$ = "date". This happens because in the KB there is no fact starting with "<Danny Boyle> <born". Subsequently, when generating t_{k+7}, the constrained generation mechanism guides the model to select "9" that leads to the correct birth year of Danny Boyle "<Danny Boyle> <born> <1956", avoiding the model to generate "<Danny Boyle> <born> <16" or "<Danny Boyle> <born> <196", both leading to incorrect information. This mechanism is additionally improved by beam search [12] which allows the model to explore multiple paths in the prefix tree in parallel.

3.2 Scaling to 800 Million Facts from Wikidata

We use the Wikidata truthy dump (Wikidata's highest-confidence statements, excluding qualifiers[3]) of the triples[4]. To filter out uninformative facts we retain only triples whose subject and relation have Wikidata identifiers. For the object,

[2] We use Hugging Face Transformers LogitsProcessor to alter the log-probabilities.
[3] https://www.wikidata.org/wiki/Wikidata:Database_download/en#RDF_dumps.
[4] We use the dump from 11 December 2024.

we allow entities with Wikidata identifiers, English literals, numbers, dates, and literals with no language. Then, for each entity, we obtain a meaningful textual label (as Wikidata IDs lack meaning for LLMs) corresponding to the Wikipedia title if the entity is described in English Wikipedia[5]. Otherwise we use the template `rdf-schema#label (schema.org/description)`, e.g., "Jane Hajduk (American actress)", since the label alone is not unique. With this process we obtain more than 800 million facts like the ones underlined in Fig. 1.

Now we tokenize the facts and we index them in a prefix tree for efficient access. Additionally, while creating the tree, we calculate the number of reachable leaves from each node to avoid that LLMs generate the same fact repeatedly, a behavior we witnessed during preliminary experiments.

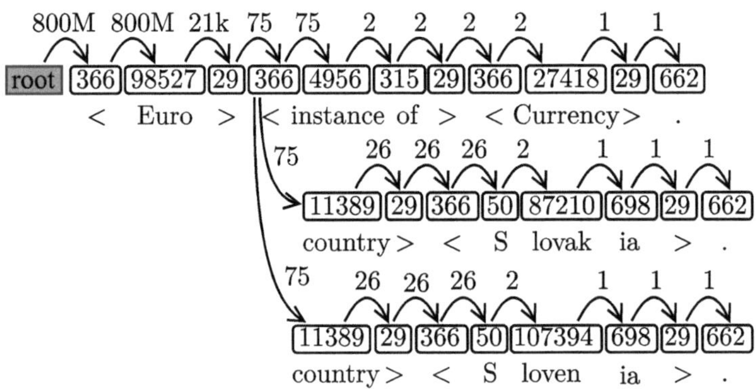

Fig. 3. Generating facts from the fact tree. Token ids are surrounded by rounded rectangles. The arrows $S \xrightarrow{n} t_{k+1}$ represent the selection of the next token t_{k+1} from the current sequence $S = t_0 \dots t_k$ and n is the number of leaves reachable from S.

Duplicate fact generation is prevented as follows. Consider the prefix X = "<Euro> <country> <S" in Fig. 3, where the number or reachable leaves is $numleaves(X) = 2$. After generating "<Euro> <country> <Slovakia> .", this number is decreased to 1 and from X the model is only allowed to select "lovenia> .". At this point, all leaves reachable from X have been generated, thus generating "S" from X' = "<Euro> <country> <" is forbidden by constrained generation. From X' the LLM can generate one of the remaining $numleaves(X') - 2 = 24$ facts (e.g., "<Euro> <country> <Italy> .").

While relatively small trees can be kept in memory, e.g., using Python dictionaries, when dealing with bigger trees, such as the 800-million-fact tree derived from Wikidata, this is often impossible. Therefore, we rely on solid relational database software. We use PostgreSQL[6] (version 17.2) and design the fact-tree table to ensure that all the information required for token generation is efficiently

[5] https://en.wikipedia.org/.
[6] https://www.postgresql.org/.

available. Given a prefix X, this includes the allowed next tokens $T = t^0..t^n$, the number of leaves reachable from X, and the number of reachable leaves if choosing t, for each $t \in T$ (to avoid selecting 0-leaves tokens and generating a fact twice). In Table 1, they are depicted respectively as *Next Tokens* and *#Lv. (number of leaves)*, and *Child.#Lv.*.

However, this tree-representation schema can quickly grow in disk space usage, as a single path of length L requires storing $L - 1$ rows. To reduce the disk space requirements, we apply two additional measures. First, after a certain prefix length L_c we stop adding rows and instead directly save the Python subtree in Pickle format[7], as shown in the last row of Table 1. In this way, during inference, subtrees that are manageable in size are directly loaded in memory (e.g., with $L_c = 7$, 99% of the subtrees use less than 116 KB). Secondly, we represent single-leaf sequences in a single row, as visible at the fourth row in Table 1, saving the rest of the sequence in *Child.#Lv.* (the token 29 comes after 694, and 662 is the last in the sequence). List items are saved as PostgreSQL arrays, while Pickle data is saved in *BYTEA*. For fast access, the *Prefix* is indexed with a B-Tree[8] index that provides logarithmic search time [6].

The ingestion process consists of creating the tree in-memory and then persisting it in the database. Nevertheless, hardware memory limits do not allow keeping the entire tree in-memory. So we perform this process in batches, constructing a limited-size tree, ingesting it, and then proceeding with the next one. This method, however, results in duplicated prefix rows, as identical prefixes from different batches are stored as different rows and must be merged during inference. The maximum number of duplicates corresponds to the number of batches used. With this mechanisms we are able to index the 800 million facts using 95 GB. Note that the index, storing token ids, depends on the LLM vocabulary, thus LLMs using distinct vocabularies require separate indexes.

At the implementation level, the functions NT_{KB} and *numleaves* access the prefix tree to obtain, respectively, the set of allowed next tokens and the number of reachable leaves for a given prefix. This information is acquired either through a SQL query to the database or from the in-memory subtree when the prefix length exceeds L_c.

Table 1. PostgreSQL table content. *#Lv.* stands for "number of leaves".

Prefix	Next Tokens	#Lv.	Child.#Lv.	Subtree
{root}	{366,1134,...}	5M	{5M,3,...}	
{root}	{366,8730,...}	5M	{5M,9,...}	
{root,366}	{537,7350,...}	2M	{2M,7,...}	
{root,694}	{29,...,662}	1	{}	
{root,366,...}	{21538,4168}	7	{4,3}	\x804

[7] https://docs.python.org/3/library/pickle.html.

[8] https://www.postgresql.org/docs/current/btree.html.

3.3 Embedding ReFactX into Question-Answering Workflows

You are a helpful question-answering assistant that bases its answers on facts from a knowledge base and always respects the prompt.

The process to answer questions:

You receive an input question.

You determine the reasoning path needed to answer the question based on the information available.

You determine the kind of answer you are asked. It can be a yes/no, a single entity, or a list of entities. Pay attention to the questions whose answer is a list of entities (e.g. Which countries share a border with Spain?): you need to find all the answer entities and include them all in the final answer.

You get relevant facts with the **"Fact:"** command. You can rely on these facts and use them a proof for your answer. While getting facts you continue the reasoning explaining it step by step.

Often description or short description may be useful for answering questions.

You conclude with a concise answer that depending on the question can be a yes/no, a single entity, or a list of entities. Pay attention to the questions whose answer is a list of entities.

The answer MUST be based on the proofs you found with **"Fact:"**.

If you didn't find proofs with **"Fact:"** that support an answer you stop and you reply: "I don't know.".

If the question requires to find proof that an event happen and you didn't find any proof, you can assume that event didn't happen.

In case you are taking too long for answering (e.g., you already generated ten facts that are not useful for the question), you stop and you answer based on the proofs you acquired to that point.

You must always follow these instructions precisely and ensure your responses adhere strictly to this prompt.

Fig. 4. System prompt for the Wikidata KB. The prompt instructs the LLM to reason step-by-step, issue *Fact* calls to access facts from the Wikidata fact tree, and deliver an answer only after evidence is gathered—otherwise respond "I don't know."

ReFactX relies on In-Context Learning (ICL) [7] for instructing the model to access external knowledge. Our prompt, shown in Fig. 4, instructs the LLM to, first, determine the reasoning path needed for answering, then to use the *Fact* command for getting relevant facts from the KB, and finally to answer based on the proofs acquired with the *Fact* command. Additionally, we instruct the model to determine which kind of answer is required, to respond "I don't know" when no useful facts have been found, to understand when it is not able to find useful facts and stop, to strictly adhere to the prompt, and to be aware of the description predicate (often useful with the Wikidata KB). At the end of this prompt, we add two examples to better guide the model behavior. While two examples are not sufficient to represent all the possible types of questions, increasing the number of few-shot example may reduce the efficiency of our approach. Therefore, a two-shot prompt is used throughout this paper.

During inference, we detect when the LLM generates the sequence of tokens corresponding to the *Fact* command and we activate constrained generation; at this point, the model is forced to generate an existing fact. After an entire fact is generated, we switch the model back to normal generation, allowing it to continue reasoning, to call again the *Fact* command, or to answer. An example of ReFactX in action is illustrated in Fig. 1.

4 Experimental Setup

Underlying Models. We evaluate ReFactX on the QA task with the following models: *meta-llama/Llama-3.3-70B-Instruct* [21], *microsoft/phi-4* [1], *Qwen/Qwen2.5-72B-Instruct*, and *Qwen/Qwen2.5-7B-Instruct* [21] with the 800-million-fact tree derived from Wikidata indexed in PostgreSQL (see Sect. 3.2).

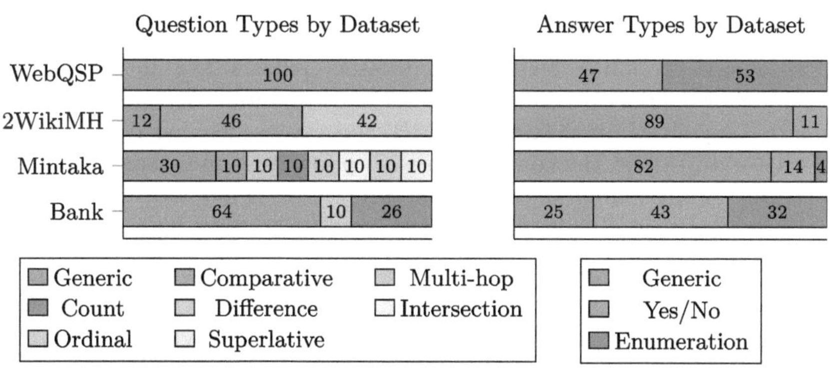

Fig. 5. Question and answer type distribution across the four evaluation datasets. Stacked bars show how each benchmark (Bank, Mintaka, 2WikiMH, WebQSP) varies in its mix of question categories (generic, comparative, multi-hop, and others) and answer forms (generic, yes/no, enumeration).

Datasets. We evaluate our approach on three public benchmark datasets—Mintaka [24], 2WikiMultiHopQA [10], WebQSP [32]—and on an anonymized proprietary financial dataset, referred to as *Bank*. Mintaka [24] is a multilingual dataset containing nine question types annotated by crowdworkers with

Wikidata IDs; in this work, we only consider eight question types, and only English questions. This dataset allows us to analyze ReFactX's performance across diverse question types. We treat *Yes/No*—which is considered a question type in Mintaka—as an answer type, alongside *Generic* and *Enumeration*. Figure 5 shows the distribution of questions and answer types across all datasets.

2WikiMultiHopQA [10], to which we refer as 2WikiMH, is composed of multi-hop, comparative, and generic questions derived from Wikipedia and Wikidata. For this dataset, we evaluate on the *dev* set, as the ground truth for the test set is not publicly available. WebQSP [32] contains generic questions annotated with Freebase [3]. These two dataset are used by the existing KE-QA approaches based on constrained generation [17,19], providing insights into ReFactX's performance relative to prior work. For computational efficiency, we consider a limited sample of 200 questions for each public dataset, stratifying by question type.

The proprietary *Bank* dataset comes from Banca d'Italia[9], a large European central bank. It covers the financial domain and allows us to study how ReFactX adapts to domain-specific data. It includes 278 template questions derived from an anonymized corporate knowledge graph containing approximately 10,000 triples and nine relations, such as ownership and control. In this setting, we can evaluate LLMs while minimizing data contamination issues, as the models are unlikely to have been exposed to this data during training. We verbalize the triples, also adding inverted facts, so that ReFactX can use tail-to-head reasoning. Finally we build an in-memory prefix-tree index. Since in this dataset each relation is considered independent from the other ones, we add specific instructions in the prompt to consider each relation independently.

The choice of public benchmark datasets reflects two main considerations. First, we prioritized datasets that natively use only or also include Wikidata—namely Mintaka and 2WikiMH. Second, we included WebQSP, based on Freebase, to extend the comparison with prior work on constrained generation [17,19]. Additionally, we include the proprietary *Bank* dataset to evaluate on data free from any data contamination.

Metrics. We evaluate on *Accuracy* (A) and *Precision* (P), to study, respectively, the overall correctness of our approach and its reliability when it provides an answer.

$$A = \frac{|\text{Correct Answers}|}{|\text{Questions}|}, \quad (6a) \qquad P = \frac{|\text{Correct Answers}|}{|\text{Given Answers}|}. \quad (6b)$$

Accuracy (A) corresponds to the ratio of questions answered correctly. Precision (P), instead, is normalized on the number of given answers, excluding "I don't know" and answers not given when the allowed maximum number of new tokens have been reached.

Precision and accuracy are calculated in two settings: (i) Exact Match: comparing the predicted answer with the ground truth with case-insensitive string

[9] https://www.bancaditalia.it/.

equality; (ii) LLM-as-a-Judge [33]: we ask Llama3.3-70B in 16-bit precision whether the predicted answer is correct and complete with respect to the ground truth.

Reference Approaches. We first evaluate the same LLMs used with ReFactX without constrained generation. In this setting, referred as *LLM-only*, we use the same settings and prompts, so that models generates not-grounded facts based solely on their parametric-knowledge, giving us clues on how important is to access external knowledge and, furthermore, on how much each dataset can be answered using only the LLM's internal knowledge.

Then, we compare against KE-QA methods that use constrained generation, specifically Decoding on Graphs (DoG) [17] and Graph-Constrained Reasoning (GCR) [19]. Additionally, we include Hybrid-QA (HQA) [15]—an input-based KE-QA approach. For these approaches, we report the results from the respective papers. HQA is evaluated on a 200-question sample of Mintaka, DoG and GCR evaluate on larger subsets of 2WikiMH and WebQSP: for 2WikiMH DoG uses 6,964 questions; for WebQSP respectively DoG and GCR consider 1,542 and 1,628 questions (filtered during preprocessing).

HQA [15] achieves state-of-the-art results on Mintaka [24]. Given a question, HQA first selects a limited set of few-shot examples maximizing their relevance for the question and the diversity between the examples, then, via ICL [7] with the selected few-shot examples, instructs the LLM to acquire external information with tools, such as a Wikipedia search engine and a Wikidata SPARQL query engine, and finally answers the question.

DoG [17] and GCR [19] are both based on constrained generation, while they consider smaller question-based prefix trees with respect to ReFactX. DoG [17], incorporates constrained generated triples from a KG inside a reasoning process similar to CoT [28], instructing the model with ICL [7], and alternating normal and constrained generation. The KG, composed of up to 120 triples, is constructed for each question, from the triples within 2-4 hops from question entities. Then, at inference time, a query-centric subgraph of the KG is obtained from the triples containing the question entities (extracted with an entity linking system). The model is allowed to generate only the triples from this query-centric subgraph, and at each generation, the subgraph is expanded with all the adjacent triples, allowing the model to form a reasoning path from question entities to the answer.

GCR [19], instead, considers a pre-built subgraph of Freebase [3] of 8 million triples containing the entities mentioned in the evaluation questions, then for each questions it constructs a smaller prefix tree from the paths obtained with breadth first search within 2-hops from question entities (obtained with entity linking). At this point an LLM, fine-tuned for the task, generates multiple reasoning paths from the prefix tree with constrained decoding and an answer hypothesis for each path. Finally, a powerful LLM, such as GPT-4o-mini, receives all the paths and the hypotheses answers and gives the final answer.

DoG and HQA use accuracy in the evaluation, while GCR calculates *Hit* and *F1*. Considering *enumeration* answer (containing a list of items), *Hit* counts a prediction as correct whenever any item of the ground truth matches the prediction, whereas *F1* is the average of the *F1* of the single predictions. These measures are equivalent to accuracy for generic answers (not for enumerations).

In our experiments, we use beam search [12] with number of beams = 3 (GCR uses 10 beams, DoG 3), disable sampling, and set the maximum number of new tokens to generate to 1,000.

5 Results and Discussion

Generation-Time Overhead. We compare ReFactX's KB-guided constrained generation time with unconstrained *LLM-only* generation time. Figure 6 plots the token generation times calculated in the two settings. The time overhead added by constrained generation is very limited: the total time for generating 4,000 tokens increases by only 1.3%, from 300.14 s to 303.89.

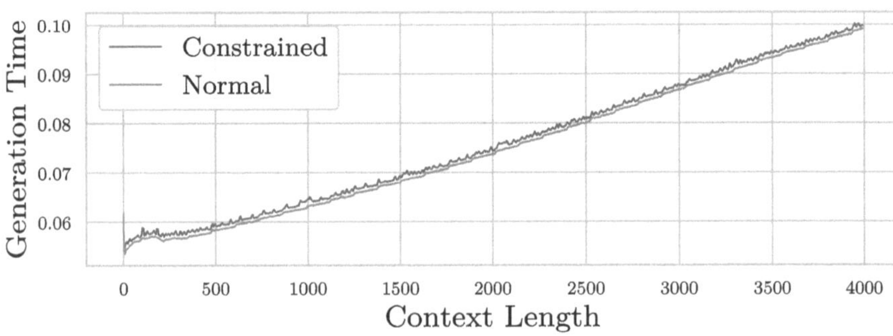

Fig. 6. Measured token generation time (in seconds). Results on 4,000 tokens using Qwen2.5-3B with PostgreSQL running on the same machine, with key-value caching enabled, using one NVIDIA Tesla T4. We apply a moving average with a 10-tokens window to reduce noise.

Performance Analysis. Table 2 shows ReFactX results on benchmark datasets, compared to *LLM-only*. The gap between Exact Match and LLM-as-a-Judge results likely derives from string comparison: correct answers with different date formats or item orders are counted as errors under Exact Match.

Compared to *LLM-only* models, ReFactX consistently achieves higher precision in the LLM-as-a-Judge evaluation. In terms of accuracy, ReFactX performs worse than *LLM-only* on the Mintaka and WebQSP datasets. This reveals these datasets are largely covered by the models' parametric knowledge—reaching 82.0% and 80.5% accuracy respectively. Instead with 2WikiMH, whose questions seem harder for the LLM parametric knowledge, ReFactX improves both accuracy and precision by more than 20% with respect to *LLM-only* models.

Table 2. Comparison between ReFactX and *LLM-only* across four datasets, considering four different LLMs (details in Sect. 4). We report Precision (P) and Accuracy (A), calculated using Exact Match (left) and LLM-as-a-Judge (right).

	Exact Match								LLM-as-a-Judge							
	Bank		Mintaka		2WikiMH		WebQSP		Bank		Mintaka		2WikiMH		WebQSP	
	P	A	P	A	P	A	P	A	P	A	P	A	P	A	P	A
ReFactX																
$\text{Llama}^{3.3}_{70B}$	**40.8**	36.0	**66.4**	40.5	**74.4**	64.0	**22.8**	17.0	50.0	**42.8**	**91.8**	56.0	93.6	81.0	85.2	63.5
$\text{Qwen}^{2.5}_{72B}$	39.9	**37.1**	43.8	28.0	71.9	**69.0**	18.5	14.0	46.1	**42.8**	82.8	55.5	**96.4**	**92.5**	84.8	65.5
Phi^{4}_{14B}	35.8	29.9	33.0	19.0	62.2	46.0	15.4	10.5	**51.3**	41.7	88.7	51.0	92.6	69.5	**89.7**	61.0
$\text{Qwen}^{2.5}_{7B}$	24.7	20.9	48.5	24.5	58.5	46.5	17.0	12.0	44.8	35.3	78.2	39.5	91.2	73.0	78.7	55.5
LLM-only																
$\text{Llama}^{3.3}_{70B}$	23.1	18.3	60.7	**59.5**	46.7	43.0	19.9	**19.5**	23.1	18.3	83.7	**82.0**	61.4	56.5	82.1	**80.5**
$\text{Qwen}^{2.5}_{72B}$	30.0	29.9	52.3	51.5	35.7	35.5	13.6	13.5	30.0	29.9	81.2	80.0	45.2	45.0	73.7	73.0
Phi^{4}_{14B}	21.8	20.1	43.6	42.5	25.5	24.0	14.4	14.0	25.7	23.7	76.9	75.0	41.5	39.0	75.3	73.0
$\text{Qwen}^{2.5}_{7B}$	21.7	18.0	45.3	41.0	21.6	18.0	10.9	10.5	28.1	21.9	65.7	60.0	35.9	30.0	66.7	64.0

The Bank dataset proved especially challenging, with ReFactX achieving precision up to 51.3% and accuracy up to 42.8%. However, a type-wise analysis reveals good results on generic Yes/No questions achieving precision (P) of 85.2% and accuracy (A) of 78.9 (using LLM-as-a-Judge) with Qwen2.5-72B while with Llama3.3-70B we achieve $P = 77.8\%$ and $A = 70.6\%$. Our approach is, instead, particularly suffering with count questions: both models achieve less than 10% accuracy on these questions. Similarly, enumeration questions pose difficulties, with correct answers achieved in only 30% of cases on the Bank dataset.

On the Mintaka dataset, ReFactX struggles especially with superlative and count questions, with Llama3.3-70B achieving 14.3% and 55.0% accuracy, respectively. Qwen2.5-72B shows a contrasting pattern, achieving higher accuracy on superlatives (47.6%) but lower on counts (35.0%). On comparative and multi-hop questions, instead, Qwen2.5-72B achieves 52.4% and 57.9% accuracy, respectively, while Llama3.3-70B reaches 66.7% and 73.7%, still below the performance levels in 2WikiMH, composed mostly by comparative and multi-hop questions.

On WebQSP, enumeration answers prove particularly difficult in terms of precision for ReFactX with both Llama3.3-70B and Qwen2.5-72B, while when using Phi-4 it maintains consistent precision across all answer types.

Results from Table 3, showing ReFactX with reference approaches, suggest our approach can achieve competitive results. In fact, compared to DoG on 2WikiMH—although evaluated on different dataset samples—ReFactX, even if considering a large KB, achieves 73.0% accuracy with Qwen2.5-7B and 92.5% with Qwen2.5-72B, while DoG stands in the middle with 84.2%.

Discussion. The generation-time overhead measurements along with the results on the benchmark QA datasets demonstrate that LLMs with constrained gen-

Table 3. Insights from comparison with related work on Precision (P) and Accuracy (A). Results for related work are taken from their papers. ReFactX is evaluated using LLM-as-a-Judge†, HQA via manual annotation‡. DoG and GCR use exact match*. GCR results are calculated with different metrics§ (see Sect. 4).

	Mintaka		**2WikiMH**		**WebQSP**	
	P	A	P	A	P	A
ReFactX Llama$^{3.3}_{70B}$ †	91.8	56.0	93.6	81.0	85.2	63.5
ReFactX Qwen$^{2.5}_{72B}$ †	82.8	55.5	96.4	**92.5**	84.8	65.5
ReFactX Qwen$^{2.5}_{7B}$ †	78.2	39.5	91.2	73.0	78.7	55.5
DoG[17]* Qwen$^{2.5}_{7B}$	–	–	–	84.2	–	**92.7**
GCR[19]* Llama$^{3.1}_{8B}$ + GPT$^{4o\text{-}mini}$	–	–	–	–	92.2§	74.1§
HQA[15] GPT$^{3.5}$‡	–	85.9	–	–	–	–
HQA[15] GPT^{4}‡	–	**95.9**	–	–	–	–

eration and a prefix tree can effectively access external knowledge without any additional model, retriever, or external service. Additionally, by storing the prefix tree on disk using a database service, we are able to scale to a large knowledge base of 800 million facts derived from Wikidata. These advantages come with only a ~1% increase in generation time.

In particular, ReFactX shows greater effectiveness on the 2WikiMH dataset. This can be explained by the nature of the dataset, which requires only simple answers and contains only generic, comparative, and multi-hop questions (see Fig. 5), easier to address with our approach. Indeed, answering these question types generally requires fewer facts with respect to count or enumeration questions. While for Mintaka multi-hop questions, we notice that in some cases they require ordinal reasoning, such as *"Where was the 16th president of the United States born?"*, making them harder for ReFactX.

On Mintaka and WebQSP, the datasets widely covered by the internal knowledge of the tested LLMs, when comparing ReFactX behavior with *LLM-only* on the same questions, ReFactX still demonstrates interesting reasoning patterns. In some cases, it uses facts to prove an answer coming from LLM parametric knowledge. In others, e.g., for *"Where did Rick Santorum attend high school?"*, in which *LLM-only* fails, ReFactX is able to acquire correct facts which lead to correcting model parametric knowledge.

However, ReFactX has some intrinsic limitations. The main one derives from the autoregressive left-to-right nature of LLMs. Indeed, ReFactX requires left-to-right facts, that start with known-information and lead to desired information. Furthermore, while we believe ReFactX is particularly useful to access point-wise factual information, count questions like *"How many movies have been directed by Danny Boyle?"* or *"Which NHL team has the most Stanley Cup wins?"* are particularly challenging, because they require ReFactX to enumerate a large list of facts and to understand when all the required facts have been generated.

This limitation likely explains why our approach is obtaining worse performance on count and superlative question types. Such question types could be better handled by using additional tools like SPARQL engines, which support counts or other set operations, or by investigating mechanisms to control ReFactX generation similarly as we did for preventing fact repetition.

The obtained results are particularly promising considering that we did not fine-tune the models to improve their ability to leverage ReFactX during reasoning. We plan to address this limitation in future work.

6 Conclusion and Future Work

In this work, we presented ReFactX, a generic knowledge-base-constrained decoding system that can be integrated with any autoregressive LLM and large knowledge bases (KB) of textual facts. In our experiments, using a 800-million-fact KB derived from Wikidata, ReFactX injects evidence during generation via constrained decoding. This mechanism permits only continuations that lead to valid KB facts and is highly efficient. Leveraging a disk-backed prefix tree, it stores 800 million facts in 95 GB, adding only 1.3% latency at generation time. On certain benchmarks, it improves question answering accuracy with gains exceeding 20% points at over 90% precision—compared to relying solely on the LLM's internal knowledge. ReFactX is thus a lightweight, easy-to-integrate solution for question answering with an external KB.

We plan to explore fine-tuning to enhance the reasoning capabilities of LLMs with ReFactX and to extend it to cover counts, long enumerations, and other set operations. To achieve higher accuracy in these cases, the model may first explore using ReFactX and then leverage additional tools—such as a SPARQL engine. We leave this extension for future work.

7 Supplemental Material Statement

Source code for using ReFactX and reproducing our work is available from GitHub at https://github.com/rpo19/ReFactX.

Acknowledgments. This work was supported by the German Federal Ministry of Education and Research (BMBF, SCADS22B) and the Saxon State Ministry for Science, Culture and Tourism (SMWK) by funding the competence center for Big Data and AI "ScaDS.AI Dresden/Leipzig". Additional support came from the EU Horizon Europe programme (grants No. 101189771—DataPACT and No. 101070284—enRichMyData), the European Community – Next Generation EU via the Italian Ministry of Justice, and the Italian PRIN project Discount Quality for Responsible Data Science (202248FWFS). The authors also acknowledge the computing resources provided by the NHR Center at TU Dresden, funded by the German Federal Ministry of Education and Research and participating state governments (www.nhr-verein.de/unsere-partner).

References

1. Abdin, M., Aneja, J., Behl, H., Bubeck, S., Eldan, R., Gunasekar, S., et al.: Phi-4 technical report (2024). https://doi.org/10.48550/arXiv.2412.08905
2. Bevilacqua, M., Ottaviano, G., Lewis, P., Yih, S., Riedel, S., Petroni, F.: Autoregressive search engines: Generating substrings as document identifiers. In: Advances in Neural Information Processing Systems. vol. 35, pp. 31668–31683. Curran Associates, Inc. (2022)
3. Bollacker, K., Evans, C., Paritosh, P., Sturge, T., Taylor, J.: Freebase: a collaboratively created graph database fozr structuring human knowledge. In: Proceedings of the 2008 ACM SIGMOD International Conference on Management of Data, pp. 1247–1250. SIGMOD '08, Association for Computing Machinery (2008). https://doi.org/10.1145/1376616.1376746
4. Cao, N.D., Izacard, G., Riedel, S., Petroni, F.: Autoregressive entity retrieval. In: International Conference on Learning Representations (2021)
5. Cheng, J., Marone, M., Weller, O., Lawrie, D., Khashabi, D., Durme, B.V.: Dated data: tracing knowledge cutoffs in large language models. In: First Conference on Language Modeling (2024)
6. Cormen, T.H., Leiserson, C.E., Rivest, R.L., Stein, C.: Introduction to algorithms. MIT press (2022)
7. Dong, Q., Li, L., Dai, D., Zheng, C., Ma, J., Li, R., et al.: A survey on in-context learning. In: Proceedings of the 2024 Conference on Empirical Methods in Natural Language Processing, pp. 1107–1128 (2024). https://doi.org/10.18653/v1/2024.emnlp-main.64
8. Gao, Y., et al.: Retrieval-augmented generation for large language models: a survey (2024). arXiv preprint arXiv:2312.10997
9. Geng, S., Josifoski, M., Peyrard, M., West, R.: Grammar-constrained decoding for structured NLP tasks without finetuning. In: Proceedings of the 2023 Conference on Empirical Methods in Natural Language Processing, pp. 10932–10952. Association for Computational Linguistics (2023). https://doi.org/10.18653/v1/2023.emnlp-main.674
10. Ho, X., Duong Nguyen, A.K., Sugawara, S., Aizawa, A.: Constructing a multi-hop QA dataset for comprehensive evaluation of reasoning steps. In: Proceedings of the 28th International Conference on Computational Linguistics. pp. 6609–6625. International Committee on Computational Linguistics (2020). https://doi.org/10.18653/v1/2020.coling-main.580
11. Hongkang Yang, H.Y., et al.: Memory^3: Language modeling with explicit memory. J. Mach. Learn. **3**(3), 300–346 (2024). https://doi.org/10.4208/jml.240708
12. Hu, X., Li, W., Lan, X., Wu, H., Wang, H.: Improved beam search with constrained softmax for NMT. In: Proceedings of Machine Translation Summit XV: Papers (2015)
13. Karpukhin, V., Oguz, B., Min, S., Lewis, P., Wu, L., Edunov, S., et al.: Dense passage retrieval for open-domain question answering. In: Proceedings of the 2020 Conference on Empirical Methods in Natural Language Processing (EMNLP), pp. 6769–6781. Association for Computational Linguistics (2020). https://doi.org/10.18653/v1/2020.emnlp-main.550
14. Lê, M., Fokkens, A.: Tackling error propagation through reinforcement learning: a case of greedy dependency parsing. In: Proceedings of the 15th Conference of the European Chapter of the Association for Computational Linguistics: Volume 1, Long Papers, pp. 677–687 (2017)

15. Lehmann, J., Bhandiwad, D., Gattogi, P., Vahdati, S.: Beyond boundaries: a human-like approach for question answering over structured and unstructured information sources. Trans. Assoc. Comput. Linguist. **12**, 786–802 (06 2024). https://doi.org/10.1162/tacl_a_00671
16. Lewis, P., Perez, E., Piktus, A., Petroni, F., Karpukhin, V., Goyal, N., et al.: Retrieval-augmented generation for knowledge-intensive NLP tasks. In: Advances in Neural Information Processing Systems, vol. 33, pp. 9459–9474. Curran Associates, Inc. (2020)
17. Li, K., Zhang, T., Wu, X., Luo, H., Glass, J., Meng, H.: Decoding on graphs: Faithful and sound reasoning on knowledge graphs through generation of well-formed chains (2024). https://doi.org/10.48550/arXiv.2410.18415
18. Li, M., Zhao, Y., Deng, Y., Zhang, W., Li, S., Xie, W., et al.: Knowledge boundary of large language models: a survey (2024). https://doi.org/0.48550/arXiv.2412.12472, arXiv preprint arXiv:2412.12472
19. Luo, L., Zhao, Z., Gong, C., Haffari, G., Pan, S.: Graph-constrained reasoning: Faithful reasoning on knowledge graphs with large language models. In: Forty-second International Conference on Machine Learning (2025)
20. Maynez, J., Narayan, S., Bohnet, B., McDonald, R.: On faithfulness and factuality in abstractive summarization. In: Proceedings of the 58th Annual Meeting of the Association for Computational Linguistics, pp. 1906–1919 (2020). https://doi.org/10.18653/v1/2020.acl-main.173
21. Qwen, Yang, A., Yang, B., Zhang, B., Hui, B., Zheng, B., et al.: Qwen2.5 technical report (2025). https://doi.org/10.48550/arXiv.2412.15115, arXiv preprint arXiv:2412.15115
22. Schick, T., Dwivedi-Yu, J., Dessi, R., Raileanu, R., Lomeli, M., Hambro, E., et al.: Toolformer: Language models can teach themselves to use tools. In: Advances in Neural Information Processing Systems. vol. 36, pp. 68539–68551. Curran Associates, Inc. (2023)
23. Scholak, T., Schucher, N., Bahdanau, D.: PICARD: Parsing incrementally for constrained auto-regressive decoding from language models. In: Proceedings of the 2021 Conference on Empirical Methods in Natural Language Processing, pp. 9895–9901. Association for Computational Linguistics (2021). https://doi.org/10.18653/v1/2021.emnlp-main.779
24. Sen, P., Aji, A.F., Saffari, A.: Mintaka: A complex, natural, and multilingual dataset for end-to-end question answering. In: Proceedings of the 29th International Conference on Computational Linguistics, pp. 1604–1619. International Committee on Computational Linguistics (2022)
25. Shuster, K., Poff, S., Chen, M., Kiela, D., Weston, J.: Retrieval augmentation reduces hallucination in conversation. In: Findings of the Association for Computational Linguistics: EMNLP 2021, pp. 3784–3803. Association for Computational Linguistics (2021). https://doi.org/10.18653/v1/2021.findings-emnlp.320
26. Sun, H., Qiao, Z., Guo, J., Fan, X., Hou, Y., Jiang, Y., et al.: Zerosearch: Incentivize the search capability of llms without searching (2025). https://doi.org/10.48550/arXiv.2505.04588, arXiv preprint arXiv:2505.04588
27. Thoppilan, R., Freitas, D.D., Hall, J., Shazeer, N., Kulshreshtha, A., Cheng, H.T., et al.: Lamda: Language models for dialog applications (2022). https://doi.org/10.48550/arXiv.2201.08239, arXiv preprint arXiv:2201.08239
28. Wei, J., Wang, X., Schuurmans, D., Bosma, M., Ichter, B., Xia, F., et al.: Chain-of-thought prompting elicits reasoning in large language models. In: Advances in Neural Information Processing Systems, vol. 35, pp. 24824–24837. Curran Associates, Inc. (2022)

29. Wu, Y., Zhao, Y., Hu, B., Minervini, P., Stenetorp, P., Riedel, S.: An efficient memory-augmented transformer for knowledge-intensive NLP tasks. In: Proceedings of the 2022 Conference on Empirical Methods in Natural Language Processing, pp. 5184–5196. Association for Computational Linguistics (2022). https://doi.org/10.18653/v1/2022.emnlp-main.346
30. Xu, P., Ping, W., Wu, X., McAfee, L., Zhu, C., Liu, Z., et al.: Retrieval meets long context large language models. In: The Twelfth International Conference on Learning Representations (2023)
31. Yao, S., et al.: React: Synergizing reasoning and acting in language models (2023). https://doi.org/10.48550/arXiv.2210.03629, arXiv preprint arXiv:2210.03629
32. Yih, W.t., Richardson, M., Meek, C., Chang, M.W., Suh, J.: The value of semantic parse labeling for knowledge base question answering. In: Proceedings of the 54th Annual Meeting of the Association for Computational Linguistics (Volume 2: Short Papers), pp. 201–206. Association for Computational Linguistics (2016). https://doi.org/10.18653/v1/P16-2033
33. Zheng, L., Chiang, W.L., Sheng, Y., Zhuang, S., Wu, Z., Zhuang, Y., et al.: Judging LLM-as-a-judge with MT-bench and chatbot arena. In: Advances in Neural Information Processing Systems, vol. 36, pp. 46595–46623. Curran Associates, Inc. (2023)
34. Zhou, J., Chen, L.: Openrag: optimizing rag end-to-end via in-context retrieval learning (2025). https://doi.org/10.48550/arXiv.2503.08398, arXiv preprint arXiv:2503.08398

Parallel Reasoning in Sequoia

Alexander Furmston[1], David J. Tena Cucala[2(✉)], Jieying Chen[3], and Bernardo Cuenca Grau[1]

[1] University of Oxford, Oxford, England
{alexander.furmston,bernardo.cuencagrau}@cs.ox.ac.uk
[2] Royal Holloway, University of London, London, England
david.tenacucala@rhul.ac.uk
[3] Vrije Universiteit Amsterdam, Amsterdam, The Netherlands
j.y.chen@vu.nl

Abstract. Description Logic (DL) ontologies underpin many Semantic Web applications. Consequence-based reasoning, which integrates techniques from hypertableau and resolution, has proved effective for tasks such as consistency checking and classification in both lightweight and expressive DLs. However, existing reasoners often fall short when applied to large, complex ontologies commonly found in domains such as healthcare and industry. In this paper, we extend the state-of-the-art consequence-based reasoner *Sequoia* [13] to support parallel reasoning, improving its scalability by leveraging system architectures with multiple cores. We explore and evaluate two parallelisation strategies for consequence-based reasoners: message passing and thread pools, and demonstrate their application within the Sequoia reasoner. Our extensive empirical evaluation shows that thread pool-based implementations achieve superior performance and resource efficiency, offering up to 2.62x speedup over the baseline on hard ontologies. We also explore the effect of increasing the number of available cores or restricting the expressivity of the ontology in the performance of our implementations.

1 Introduction

Ontologies enable the representation of structured, machine-readable knowledge on the Semantic Web. With the deployment of large-scale ontologies such as SNOMED CT [37], Wikidata [45], and the EU's Publications Office ontologies [32], efficient Description Logic (DL) reasoning has become essential to enable important tasks such as classification, consistency checking, and query answering. As a result, DL reasoners such as HermiT [14], FaCT++ [43], and Pellet [36] have become integral tools in the Semantic Web community, powering both research and production systems. These tools are embedded in widely used ontology editors like Protégé [38], and they support key Semantic Web standards, including the OWL 2 Web Ontology Language.

However, as ontologies grow in size and expressivity, the scalability of current reasoning technologies becomes a limiting factor. Large ontologies with rich log-

D. Garijo et al. (Eds.): ISWC 2025, LNCS 16140, pp. 309–327, 2026.
https://doi.org/10.1007/978-3-032-09527-5_17

ical structure pose significant computational challenges, especially in scenarios requiring frequent or real-time reasoning.

Consequence-based (CB) reasoning [4] is a promising approach to DL reasoning which combines features of (hyper)tableau [8,14,15,36,40,43] and resolution-based [17,19,22,30] algorithms. On the one hand, similarly to resolution, CB calculi derive formulae entailed by the ontology (thus avoiding the explicit construction of large models), and they are typically worst-case optimal. On the other hand, CB calculi organise clauses into *contexts* arranged as a graph structure reminiscent of that used for model construction in (hyper)tableau; this prevents CB calculi from drawing many unnecessary inferences and yields a nice goal-oriented behaviour. Furthermore, in contrast to both resolution and (hyper)tableau, CB calculi can verify multiple subsumptions in a single execution, allowing for one-pass classification. CB calculi are widely used in practice. Leading lightweight DL reasoners like ELK [21] and Snorocket [26] are CB-based, while CB reasoners for more expressive DLs like Sequoia [7] and Avalanche [44] also show competitive performance.

Sequoia is a CB reasoner for the description logic $\mathcal{SROIQ}$ that underpins OWL 2 DL [13]. It supports core reasoning tasks (such as consistency, subsumption, and classification) and uniquely offers pay-as-you-go performance. Evaluation results show that it nicely complements (hyper-)tableau reasoners by handling challenging ontologies that they struggle with.

In CB reasoning, most of the reasoning workload is carried out through small, independent contexts, making it naturally suited for parallelisation. However, despite its performance potential, Sequoia currently has no parallel implementation. We address this challenge by presenting two parallelised versions of Sequoia based on message passing and thread pooling, respectively. Our approach is, however, not tied to Sequoia's specific calculus and can be generalised to any CB calculus based on contexts—including, for instance, the calculus underpinning ELK [20]. In this paper, we demonstrate its application using Sequoia as a representative system for expressive DLs. Furthermore, we evaluate the impact of parallelisation on performance using a diverse set of benchmark ontologies. Our main contributions are as follows:

- A systematic implementation and evaluation of two parallelisation strategies for consequence-based reasoning, i.e., message passing and thread pools, demonstrated through their application to the Sequoia reasoner.
- Strong evidence that thread pools outperform message passing approaches, which face scalability issues due to excessive threading overhead.
- An empirical evaluation across 799 ontologies (Oxford Ontology Corpus [1]) showing measurable performance gains with our thread pool-based implementation.

2 Background

In this section we recapitulate basic definitions of first-order logic and Description Logics, and then we outline the classification algorithm of Sequoia and the CB calculus for $\mathcal{ALCHOIQ}+$ that underpins it. A complete description of the classification algorithm, the calculus, and their properties, can be found in [13].

2.1 First-Order Clauses

A *signature* consists of two disjoint, countable sets of *predicates* and *function symbols*, respectively. Each predicate and function symbol has a nonnegative integer *arity*. Function symbols of arity 0 are called *constants*. For a term t and a function symbol f, a term of the form $f(t)$ is called an f*-successor* of t, and t is its *predecessor*. We also consider a countably infinite set of *variables* disjoint with the predicates and function symbols. A *term* is defined inductively as a variable, a constant, or an expression of the form $f(t_1, \ldots, t_n)$ where f is a function symbol of arity n and each t_i with $i \in \{1, \ldots, n\}$ is a term.

An *equality* is an expression of the form $t_1 \approx t_2$, where t_1 and t_2 are terms. An *inequality* $t_1 \not\approx t_2$ is the negation of an equality $t_1 \approx t_2$. An *atom* is an expression of the form $A(t_1, \ldots, t_n)$, where A is a predicate of arity n, and (if $n > 0$) t_i for each $i \in \{1, \ldots, n\}$ is a term. A *literal* is either an equality, an inequality, or an atom; it is *positive* if it is either an equality or an atom.

A *clause* is an expression of the form $\forall x_1, \ldots, x_n. (\Gamma \to \Delta)$ where the *body* Γ is a finite conjunction of positive literals, the *head* Δ is a finite disjunction of literals, and $x_1, \ldots, x_n$ are the variables occurring in $\Gamma \to \Delta$. The quantifier $\forall x_1, \ldots, x_n$ in clauses is omitted for brevity. Conjunctions and disjunctions are treated as sets (i.e., they are unordered and without repetitions) and we use set operations to manipulate them. The empty conjunction and the empty disjunction are represented as $\top$ and $\bot$, respectively. We consider standard definitions of model, satisfiability, and entailment for a finite set of clauses.

A set N of clauses *contains a clause* $\Gamma \to \Delta$ *up to redundancy* (u.t.r.) if and only if (i) Δ contains an equality of the form $s \approx s$ for s an arbitrary term, (ii) Δ contains both literals $s \approx t$ and $s \not\approx t$ for arbitrary terms s and t, or (iii) there exists a clause $\Gamma' \to \Delta' \in N$ that *subsumes* it, i.e. $\Gamma' \subseteq \Gamma$ and $\Delta' \subseteq \Delta$.

2.2 $\mathcal{ALCHOIQ}+$ Ontologies

The Description Logic $\mathcal{ALCHOIQ}+$ supports all Boolean connectives, role inclusion, nominals, inverse roles, quantified number restrictions, reflexivity, and disjointness axioms [5]. $\mathcal{ALCHOIQ}+$ ontologies can be transformed into first-order DL clauses while preserving satisfiability [28], using Skolemisation for existentials and (in)equalities for nominals and number restrictions.

DL clauses use a signature with a set $\mathbf{B}$ of unary predicates (*atomic concepts*), a set $\mathbf{R}$ of binary predicates (*atomic roles*) disjoint with $\mathbf{B}$, and a set of $\mathbf{O}$ of constants (*named individuals*). DL clauses use only terms of the form x, $f_i(x)$, z_i and $o \in \mathbf{O}$, where $i \in \mathbb{N}$, each f_i is a distinct function symbol, and each z_i is a distinct variable. Moreover, literals are either equalities or inequalities between these terms, or atoms of the form $B(t)$, $R(x,t)$, and $R(t,x)$, for $B \in \mathbf{B}$, $R \in \mathbf{R}$, and t a term of the aforementioned form. For example, the DL axiom

$A \sqsubseteq \geq 2R.B$, expressing that instances of A are connected to at least two distinct instances of B via role R, is rewritten into the following DL clauses:

$$A(x) \rightarrow B(f_1(x)) \qquad A(x) \rightarrow R(x, f_1(x)) \qquad A(x) \rightarrow f_1(x) \not\approx f_2(x)$$
$$A(x) \rightarrow B(f_2(x)) \qquad A(x) \rightarrow R(x, f_2(x))$$

In what follows, an $\mathcal{ALCHOIQ}+$ *ontology* is a set of DL clauses; we use standard notions of model, instance, and satisfiability (see [13] for further details).

2.3 Sequoia's Calculus for $\mathcal{ALCHOIQ}+$

Sequoia supports the DL $\mathcal{SROIQ}$ [18], which extends $\mathcal{ALCHOIQ}+$ with complex role inclusion axioms, by eliminating transitivity and complex role inclusion axioms using well-known transformations [28]. Then, it applies the reasoning calculus for $\mathcal{ALCHOIQ}+$ until saturation, constructing in the process a *context structure* [13], which we briefly outline next.

Context Structures. A context structure is a "summary" of all models of a given ontology. It is an annotated graph where each vertex (a *context*) has an associated *core*, a conjunction of atoms of the form $B(x)$, $R(x, y)$, or $R(y, x)$—for B and R unary and binary predicates, respectively—where variable x is universally quantified and variable y represents the predecessor of x. A context represents all elements of models of the ontology that satisfy the context's core. For example, in Fig. 1, context v with core $A(x)$ represents the instances of A in all models of $\mathcal{O}$. In Sequoia's implementation, no two contexts share the same core, and so a core uniquely determines its context. The edges of the context structure are labelled by function symbols, capturing relationships between the elements represented by both contexts. For example, edge (v, w) in Fig. 1 labelled with function symbol f indicates that, in each model of $\mathcal{O}$, each element represented by context v has an f-successor represented by w.

Each context v is labelled by a set $\mathcal{S}_v$ of *context clauses*: Skolemised first-order clauses without nested function symbols. These clauses use only variables x and y, which receive a special treatment: x ranges only over elements satisfying the context core and y represents x's predecessor, if it exists. Context clauses express "local" logical consequences for the elements represented by the context. For

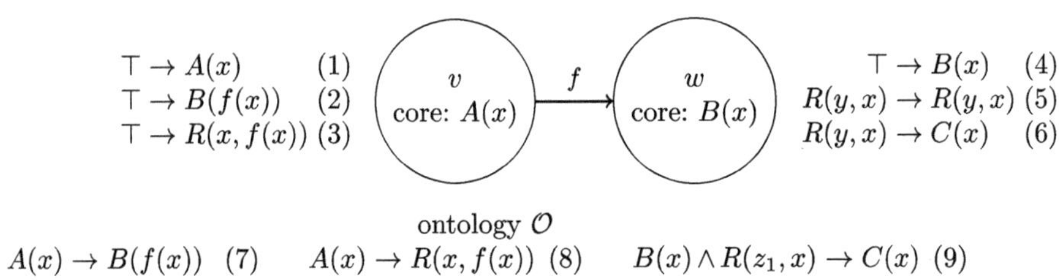

Fig. 1. A simple context structure constructed for ontology $\mathcal{O}$. Context clauses (1)–(3) are attached to v, and (4)–(6) are attached to w.

example, in Fig. 1, in context w with core $B(x)$, context clause $R(y,x) \rightarrow C(x)$ represents that each instance of B in a model of $\mathcal{O}$ whose predecessor exists and is connected to it via role R is also an instance of C.

Inference Rules. The calculus incorporates two types of inference rules. *Intra-context rules* are triggered by conditions holding *within a single context*, and their effect is to add clauses to or remove clauses from the same context. Examples of intra-context inference rules include:

- Rule Core: for A an atom in the context's core, if the context does not contain u.t.r. the clause $\top \rightarrow A$, then this clause is added to the context. In Fig. 1, this rule introduces clause (1) in v and (4) in w.
- Rule Hyper applies a hyperresolution [6] step using context clauses as side premises and a clause in the ontology as main premise. For example, in Fig. 1, it can be applied to ontology clause (7) and context clause (1) to produce context clause (2) in v; similarly, it produces (3) from (1) and (8). Inferences by Hyper can only unify variable x in $\mathcal{O}$ with variable x in context clauses, thus preventing the occurrence of nested functional terms.

Inter-context rules are triggered by conditions holding in two neighbouring contexts; their effect is to propagate clauses between them. For example, rule Succ detects atoms with function terms of the form $f(x)$ in a context v_1, seeks another context v_2 representing f-successors of elements in v_1, and propagates the atoms as function-free clauses to v_2. This enables new inferences for these atoms without introducing nested function symbols. For example, in Fig. 1, it detects atoms $B(f(x))$ and $R(x, f(x))$ in v, identifies w as a suitable context, then it draws an f-labelled edge between v and w, and adds clause (5) to w; clause $B(x) \rightarrow B(x)$ should also be added to w, but this is unnecessary since it is already contained u.t.r. due to (4). Clauses such as (5) are tautologies, but they highlight atoms that may be relevant to trigger new inferences. For example (5) triggers a new inference by Hyper in w, deriving (6) from (4), (5), and (9).

See [13] for a full description of all the rules of the calculus.

3 Parallelisation Strategies for CB Reasoning

Consequence-based reasoners such as Sequoia are amenable to parallelisation because much of their reasoning workload, especially the derivation of clauses via the Hyper rule, can be performed in each context independently of the others. In this paper, we consider two distinct approaches to parallelisation. Sequoia is used as a concrete showcase for exploring how parallelisation can be effectively applied to consequence-based reasoning.

Message Passing is a well-established approach to concurrency where independent execution units communicate by sending messages to each other rather than by sharing memory [42]. Each unit processes its internal clauses sequentially, reacting to messages through a dedicated input queue. Units that have performed all required operations enter an idle state awaiting further messages.

Thread Pooling manages concurrency by queuing tasks and assigning them to reusable threads, avoiding the overhead of frequent thread creation/destruction. Limiting threads to the number of CPU cores also prevents context switching.

We describe our implementation of Sequoia based on message passing in Sect. 3.1, and the version based on thread pools in Sect. 3.2.

3.1 Message Passing

Sequoia naturally fits message passing, with contexts as independent concurrent units communicating via messages. We considered three approaches: *(1)* Java threads (c.f. Platform Threads in [31]) where each context is implemented as a thread; *(2)* CSO (Communicating Scala Objects) [41] where contexts are represented as fibres—more lightweight than threads; and *(3)* Akka actors [24] where each context is represented as an actor running a thread or fibre behind the scenes and communicating with other actors through asynchronous messages.

The approach based on Java threads is conceptually the simplest, but experiments showed frequent crashes due to OS thread limits. The CSO approach also proved problematic due to severe library inefficiencies when handling many concurrent contexts. In contrast, the Akka library scales to millions of actors, which is critical since Sequoia often creates tens of thousands of contexts. Preliminary tests showed encouraging results; thus, we developed a full implementation of message passing using Akka actors, referred to as `AkkaSequoia`.

`AkkaSequoia` is based on Algorithm 1a (which abstracts away many technical details). The algorithm takes as input an $\mathcal{ALCHOIQ}+$ ontology $\mathcal{O}$, a set *cores* of context cores—i.e. conjunctions with atoms of the form $B(x)$, $R(x,y)$, $R(y,x)$—and a set *queries* of clauses that mention only variable x; then, it returns the subset of *queries* that logically follow from $\mathcal{O}$. The inputs *cores* and *queries* are determined by the reasoning task. For example, for classification, *cores* is the set of one-atom conjunctions of the form $B(x)$, for B a concept name, and *queries* contains the clause $B(x) \to C(x)$ for each pair B, C of concept names.

The algorithm keeps an initially empty mapping *contextStructure* (line 1) indexing the contexts by their core. Edges between contexts are not stored here but locally within each context: this duplicates some information but reduces the number of messages exchanged between contexts. The algorithm also keeps a variable *activeCount* counting incoming messages to be processed by a context. The initialisation of the context structure creates a context for each core in *cores* (lines 2-10). Contexts are created as independent actors, and launched upon creation (line 5). Lines 6-9 implement the Core rule, initialising the set of context clauses in each context.

The main thread then idles until a request is received or all contexts become saturated (lines 11-27). It provides three methods that contexts can access asynchronously. Methods IncreaseCount (line 12) and DecreaseCount (line 13) update *activeCount*. Method GetContext(*core*) (lines 14-26) can be called by any context to propagate clauses to a distinct context with core *core*, returning (a reference to) such context and creating it first if it did not already exist (lines

Algorithm 1a: CLASSIFY($\mathcal{O}$, *cores*, *queries*), for $\mathcal{O}$ an $\mathcal{ALCHOIQ}$+ ontology, *cores* a set of cores, and *queries* a set of clauses over variable x

```
1: contextStructure, activecount := ∅
2: for core ∈ cores do
3:    context := new executable actor CONTEXT(core)
4:    contextStructure(core) := context
5:    fork(context)
6:    for A ∈ core do
7:       activeCount := activeCount + 1
8:       send (core, ⊤ → A) to context.incoming
9:    end for
10: end for
11: while activeCount > 0 do
12:    synchronized on INCREASECOUNT(): activeCount := activeCount + 1
13:    synchronized on DECREASECOUNT(): activeCount := activeCount − 1
14:    synchronized function GETCONTEXT(core)
15:       if core is a key in contextStructure
16:          return contextStructure(core)
17:       else
18:          context := new executable actor CONTEXT(core)
19:          contextStructure(core) := context
20:          fork(context)
21:          for A ∈ core
22:             activeCount := activeCount + 1
23:             send (core, ⊤ → A) to context.incoming
24:          end for
25:          return context
26:       end if
27: end while
28: return {Γ → Δ ∈ queries | ⊤ → Δ ∈ contextStructure(Γ).processed}
```

18-25). When $activeCount = 0$, all contexts are saturated. The algorithm reads the saturated context structure and returns the relevant result (line 28).

Algorithm 1b describes the concurrent process realised by each context. A context keeps a queue *incoming* for messages received from other contexts, and two sets of clauses: *unprocessed* and *processed*, initially empty. It also keeps a data structure *neighbourhood* representing contexts connected to it by an edge (line 1)—but not their clauses. The context remains idle until receiving a message from another context (lines 2-22). Each message includes a clause C and the core *C_core* from which this clause has been propagated. On receiving it, the context will update its neighbourhood (line 5) if required—for example, it might add an incoming edge from the context with core *C_core* labelled by

Algorithm 1b: CONTEXT(*core*), an executable actor that creates and maintains a context with core *core*

```
1: incoming, unprocessed, processed, neighbourhood := ∅
2: while true do
3:   if incoming ≠ ∅ then
4:     (C, C_core) := pop an element from incoming
5:     use (C, C_core) to update neighbourhood if needed
6:     add C to unprocessed
7:     while unprocessed is not empty do
8:       C := remove a clause from unprocessed
9:       for (C′, core′) in APPLYRULES(C, processed, neighbourhood) do
10:        if core = core′ then
11:          add C′ to unprocessed and processed
12:          remove from unprocessed and processed clauses subsumed by C′
13:        else
14:          context′ := GETCONTEXT(core′)
15:          INCREASECOUNT()
16:          send (C′, core) to context′.incoming
17:        end if
18:      end for
19:    end while
20:    DECREASECOUNT()
21:  end if
22: end while
```

a function symbol f appearing in C—and then it will add clause C to the set *unprocessed* of clauses that must be processed by the inference rules (line 6).

The context then enters a loop where it applies the inference rules using a premise from *unprocessed* (line 8) and possibly one or more premises from *processed* or the ontology $\mathcal{O}$; the rules can also use information in *neighbourhood* to check whether some preconditions are satisfied without sending additional messages to other contexts. The result of applying the rules is a list of pairs of the form $(C', core')$ where C' is a newly derived clause and $core'$ is the core of the context where the clause should be derived in (line 9). Clauses that must be derived in this context are simply added to both *unprocessed* and *processed* (line 11), followed by a redundancy check (line 12). However, if a clause C' must be added to a distinct context, the method GETCONTEXT($core'$) is used to get (a reference to) the context with $core'$ (line 13), and then a message is sent to propagate the clause C' to that context (line 15). A call to INCREASECOUNT (line 14) ensures that the main method is aware that a new message has been queued. When there are no more clauses in *unprocessed* (line 19), this round of derivation has ended, and so DECREASECOUNT is called (line 20) to update *activeCount* in the main method.

Algorithm 2a: $\textsc{Classify}(\mathcal{O}, \mathit{cores}, \mathit{queries})$, for $\mathcal{O}$ an $\mathcal{ALCHOIQ}+$ ontology, *cores* a set of cores, and *queries* a set of clauses over variable x

1: $\mathit{contextStructure} := \mathit{contextQueues} := \emptyset$
2: *threadPool* := initialise a thread pool with a fixed number of threads
3: **for** $\mathit{core} \in \mathit{cores}$ **do**
4:    *context* := initialise a fresh context with core *core*
5:    $\mathit{contextStructure}(\mathit{core}) := \mathit{context}$
6:    $\mathit{contextQueues}(\mathit{core}) := \textsc{ContextQueue}(\mathit{core})$
7:    **for** $A \in \mathit{core}$ **do**
8:       **send** $\textsc{Saturate}(\mathit{context}, \mathit{core}, \top \rightarrow A)$ **to** $\mathit{contextQueues}(\mathit{core})$
9:    **end for**
10: **end for**
11: **while** *contextQueues* is not empty and *threadPool* is not idle **do**
12:    **synchronized function** $\textsc{getContext}(\mathit{core})$
13:       **if** *core* is a key in *contextQueues*
14:          **return** as reference $(\mathit{contextStructure}(\mathit{core}), \mathit{contextQueues}(\mathit{core}))$
15:       **else**
16:          *context* := initialise a fresh context with core *core*
17:          $\mathit{contextStructure}(\mathit{core}) := \mathit{context}$
18:          $\mathit{contextQueues}(\mathit{core}) := \textsc{ContextQueue}(\mathit{core})$
19:          **for** $A \in \mathit{core}$
20:             **send** $\textsc{Saturate}(\mathit{context}, \mathit{core}, \top \rightarrow A)$ **to** $\mathit{contextQueues}(\mathit{core})$
21:          **end for**
22:          **return** as reference $(\mathit{context}, \mathit{contextQueues}(\mathit{core}))$
23:       **end if**
24: **end while**
25: **return** $\{\Gamma \rightarrow \Delta \in \mathit{queries} \mid \top \rightarrow \Delta \in \mathit{contextStructure}(\Gamma).\mathit{processed}\}$

A key challenge in parallelising logical reasoning systems lies in handling race conditions. These occur when multiple threads modify shared data concurrently without proper synchronisation, leading to unpredictable behaviour. Our implementation prevents race conditions because most of the reasoning workload is performed in independent units that do not share memory. The completeness of Sequoia's calculus—i.e. the fact that the saturated context structure contains all elements of *queries* that follow from the ontology (see [13] for details)—can only be put at risk in this implementation if context v terminates reasoning while simultaneously receiving new messages from another context. Observe, however, that no information in *neighbourhood* is deleted during execution, and clauses are only removed if they are made redundant; hence, no information triggering non-redundant inferences is lost at any point of the execution. Furthermore, the loop from line (11) ensures that any new message received by a context always triggers checks for applicability of all inference rules, and a new round of rule applications where appropriate. As a result, completeness is not affected.

Algorithm 2b: CONTEXTQUEUE(*core*)

```
queue := a fresh queue
while true do
    if queue is not empty and threadPool is not running a task for core then
        task := pop an element from queue
        send task to threadPool
    end if
    if task is received then
        append task to queue
    end if
end while
```

Algorithm 2c: SATURATE(*context*, *core*, *clause*)

```
use (clause, core) to update context.neighbourhood if needed
add clause to context.unprocessed
while context.unprocessed is not empty do
    C := remove a clause from context.unprocessed
    for (C', core') in
    APPLYRULES(C, context.processed, context.neighbourhood) do
        if core = core' then
            add C' to context.unprocessed, context.processed
            remove clauses subsumed by C' in context.unprocessed, context.processed
        else
            context', queue' := GETCONTEXT(core')
            send SATURATE(context', core, C') to queue'
        end if
    end for
end while
```

The soundness of the calculus—i.e. the fact that each derived context clause expresses a logical consequence of the ontology [13]—is also not compromised: if the premises of a rule are satisfied at some point in time, this means that the ontology has certain logical consequences, which cannot be retracted, so the conclusion of the rule remains logically sound at any future point in time.

3.2 Thread Pool-Based Models

In the thread pool-based algorithm for Sequoia, contexts do not correspond to threads. Instead, the algorithm constructs a context structure by performing small steps called *tasks*. Each task is sent to a thread pool queue, where it awaits assignment to an available thread. A task typically consists of checking applicability of the inference rules in a context and applying them until saturation; it is triggered by the addition of a new clause to the context. If, during the execution of a task, new clauses are generated that must be propagated to other contexts, new tasks will be created and sent to the thread pool queues.

We initially considered an implementation with a single queue for the thread pool, which we call `SQESequoia`. However, preliminary tests revealed that some threads in the pool remained unused (even for very large ontologies) because different tasks involving the same context were being sent to the thread pool at similar times. These tasks, however, cannot be executed concurrently without the risk of incurring race conditions. Therefore, once a thread is assigned a task for context v, all other tasks in the queue involving v are blocked, effectively stalling the entire queue.

To prevent this, we developed `MQESequoia`, a multi-queue implementation of the thread pool model that maintains a separate queue for each context. Tasks are put in the queue for the context they target instead of being passed on directly to the thread pool. Tasks remain in their context-specific queue until the preceding task completes execution. This ensures, on the one hand, that only one task per context runs in the thread pool (guaranteeing correctness) and, on the other hand, that unused threads remain available for other contexts' tasks.

The pseudocode for `MQESequoia` is presented in Algorithm 2a. The structure is similar to Algorithm 1a, so we highlight the differences. First, contexts are created directly in the main thread, which maintains a *contextStructure* with all the contexts and a list *contextQueues* of all context queues (line 1). Each new context triggers the creation of a dedicated queue (line 6). Rather than sending direct messages to a context to apply the Core rule, the corresponding tasks are sent to the relevant queue (line 8). A key difference with Algorithm 1a is that the main thread does not keep track of the number of active contexts and can simply wait until all queues are empty and the thread pool is idle (line 11). As in Algorithm 1a, a synchronised method can be used to create new contexts (lines 12-23). The structure of each context queue is shown in Algorithm 2b. The queue accumulates all tasks it receives (lines 7-9) and sends a task to the thread pool only if no thread is already running a task for the same context (lines 3-6). Finally, Algorithm 2c specifies the context saturation task mirroring Algorithm 1b but clause propagation to other contexts occurs via the thread pool (line 11).

The single queue thread pool implementation of Sequoia is similar to Algorithms 2a-2c, except that there is a single queue for all contexts instead of a queue per context. The soundness and completeness arguments for both algorithms are analogous to the message passing version, since the same considerations apply.

4 Evaluation

We evaluated the performance of our parallel implementations of Sequoia using the *Oxford Ontology Corpus* [1]: 799 ontologies varying in size (from 1 KB to 1 GB) and expressivity (from $\mathcal{EL}$ to $\mathcal{SROIQ}$). We attempted to classify each ontology with a 10-minute timeout. This evaluation was designed to explore the following research questions: (1) Do parallel approaches—message passing and thread pools—improve performance compared to the original single-threaded

Sequoia, and which strategy is most effective? (2) Within thread pool-based models, does a multi-queue scheduling strategy provide measurable advantages over a single-queue strategy? (3) How does the number of contexts generated by Sequoia influence the effectiveness of parallelisation? (4) Which features of ontologies most strongly correlate with performance gains from parallel reasoning?

The original single-threaded implementation of Sequoia (denoted `STSequoia`) is our baseline, as it has been extensively benchmarked against other state-of-the-art reasoners over the same corpus [13] demonstrating competitive performance. Although reasoners HermiT and Konclude were able to classify around 10% more ontologies, Sequoia complemented them nicely by efficiently classifying several ontologies that were very challenging for these reasoners. Furthermore, Sequoia exhibited a distinctive pay-as-you-go behaviour in practice, offering performance on lightweight ontologies comparable to that of dedicated reasoners such as ELK.

To ensure consistency in performance measurements, all experiments were conducted on a dedicated server with two Intel Xeon E5-2640 v3 CPUs, each featuring 8 cores and supporting hyper-threading for a total of 32 threads. The system is equipped with 512GB of RAM and operates on Fedora 33. All Java-based implementations were executed using the OpenJDK 1.8.0 distribution.

Message Passing vs. Thread Pool-Based Models. We conducted an initial experiment using `STSequoia` (single-threaded baseline), `AkkaSequoia` (actor-based message passing), and `SQESequoia` (single-queued thread pool) to determine the most promising parallelisation approach. We randomly selected 49 ontologies among those classified by `STSequoia` in less than 10 min.

`SQESequoia` consistently outperformed the other versions, achieving a median speedup of 2.27× over `STSequoia`, whereas `AkkaSequoia` achieved a median speedup of 1.71× over `STSequoia`. The limited improvements achieved by `AkkaSequoia` can be attributed to coordination overheads and thread exhaustion from excessive actor creation, particularly for large ontologies with many contexts. These results indicate that thread pool-based models may be more effective than message passing approaches for parallelising consequence-based reasoning, consistent with prior findings in the literature [11]. Hence, all subsequent experiments were conducted exclusively using thread pool-based models.

This conclusion, however, should be interpreted with caution. On the one hand, it is unclear how much it depends on the specific design choices of our libraries; Akka's actor model is renowned for being lightweight, but languages or frameworks with a stronger emphasis on message passing, such as Erlang or Go, might produce better results. This line of enquiry is a promising direction for future work. On the other hand, message passing may be more effective in scenarios requiring strong fault tolerance, as it naturally isolates actor states, facilitating error recovery. Furthermore, message passing paradigms are often better suited to distributed systems, where tasks must be coordinated across multiple servers or nodes. Evaluating Sequoia's performance in fault-tolerant or distributed environments remains a topic for future work.

Table 1. Classification time, speedup factor, and timeout count per category for different Sequoia variants. Speedup is computed relative to `STSequoia` (baseline). Classification time is calculated only on 702 ontologies that were successful for all variants.

Variant	All Time (s)	Easy ($\leq$ 1 s)		Medium (110 s)		Hard ($\geq$ 10 s)		Timeout Count		
		Time (s)	Speedup	Time (s)	Speedup	Time (s)	Speedup	Easy	Medium	Hard
`STSequoia`	6.0 $\pm$ 27.1	0.28	1.00	2.65	1.00	51.96	1.00	**515**	117	78
`SQESequoia`	**2.5 $\pm$ 9.8**	0.26	**1.01**	1.70	**1.74**	19.85	**2.62**	546	**112**	56
`MQESequoia`	2.8 $\pm$ 12.3	0.28	0.96	1.61	1.60	22.44	2.50	539	118	**54**

Comparing Thread Pool-Based Models. For this experiment, we grouped ontologies by `STSequoia` classification time into easy ($\leq$ 1 s), medium (1 s-10 s), and hard ($\geq$ 10 s). As shown in Table 1, for the easy group, both parallel variants performed similarly to the baseline with marginal speedups. For the medium group, `SQESequoia` achieved a speedup of 1.74$\times$ and `MQESequoia` 1.60$\times$. The largest gains were observed in the hard group: `SQESequoia` achieved a speedup of 2.62$\times$, and `MQESequoia` a speedup of 2.50$\times$ over the baseline. Both thread pool variants also led to fewer timeouts. `STSequoia` timed out on 210 ontologies, whereas `SQESequoia` timed out on 56 ontologies and `MQESequoia` only on 54.

These results indicate that parallelisation based on thread pools is a powerful strategy for improving the efficiency and scalability of ontology reasoning. While the benefits for easy ontologies are minimal due to the overhead, the improvements for more complex ontologies can be substantial.

Impact of Core Count. We conducted experiments to evaluate the scalability of our multi-queue thread pool-based implementation `MQESequoia` with different thread counts. We used the entire Oxford Corpus and the same methodology as in the previous sections. We gathered results for 1, 2, 4, 8, 16, and 32 as the maximum number of threads in the pool. Figure 3 shows that speedup increases logarithmically with the number of cores. The equation of the line of best fit was $y = 0.02 \times \log(x) + 1.02$ for easy ontologies, $y = 0.26 \times \log(x) + 1.32$ for medium ontologies, and $y = 0.65 \times \log(x) + 1.18$ for hard ontologies. This indicates that, while performance improves with more cores, returns diminish logarithmically (Fig. 2).

Ontology Features vs. Parallel Speedup. We further investigated which ontology-level features most influence the speedup achieved through parallelisation. Our results identify the number of contexts created during classification as the most significant factor. Figure 3 presents a detailed analysis of the relationship between the number of contexts created during classification and the resulting speedup achieved by thread pool-based models. The left plot shows a clear trend: as the number of contexts increases, so does the speedup. Ontologies that generate a small number of contexts (e.g., $\leq$ 10) show little to no speedup, and in some cases, even slight slowdowns. This is expected, as parallelisation introduces overhead, and its benefits only become apparent when there is enough work to effectively distribute across multiple threads. In contrast, ontologies producing

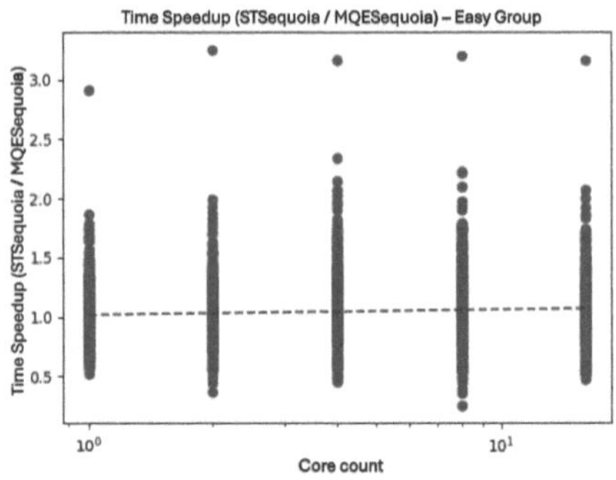

(a) Easy (≤ 1s)

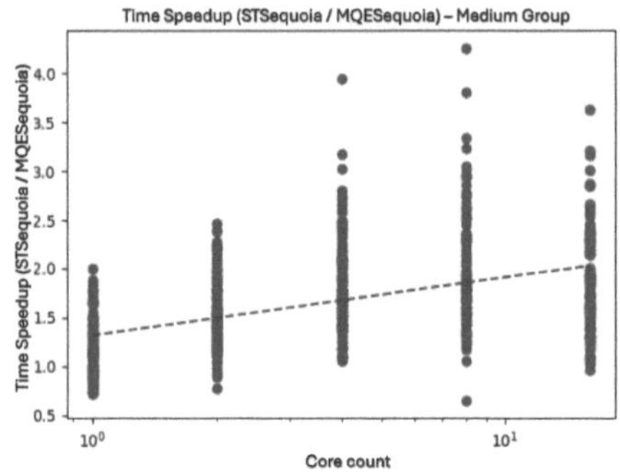

(b) Medium (1–10s)

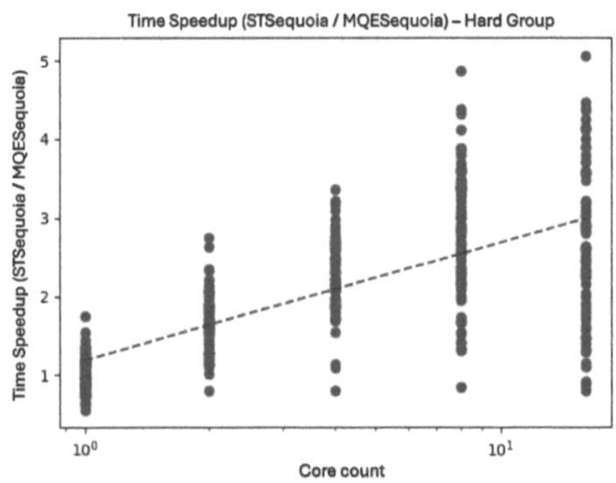

(c) Hard (≥ 10s)

Fig. 2. Scatter plots of speedup for easy, medium, and hard ontologies versus number of threads (1, 2, 4, 8, 16). A speedup greater than 1 indicates that our multi-queue thread pool-based implementation `MQESequoia` outperformed the single-threaded baseline `STSequoia`. Ontologies that timed out with `STSequoia` were excluded to avoid skewing hard-case results. The x-axis uses a logarithmic scale.

thousands or even hundreds of thousands of contexts achieve significant speedup, up to 10× in some extreme cases. Together, the plots in Fig. 3 confirm a strong correlation: ontologies with more contexts benefit more from parallelisation, as independent context saturation yields better workload distribution.

Horn ontologies exhibited slightly higher average speedups compared to non-Horn. This, however, was not the case for hard ontologies, suggesting that the Horn nature of an ontology is not a reliable predictor of parallelisation gains. Additionally, the presence of nominals was found to moderately reduce the effectiveness of parallelisation, decreasing the average speedup from 1.32× to 1.22×. This can be attributed to the fact that reasoning with nominals requires using a single, special context known as the *root context* [13] to perform a significant part of the reasoning work. This inherently limits opportunities for parallelisation.

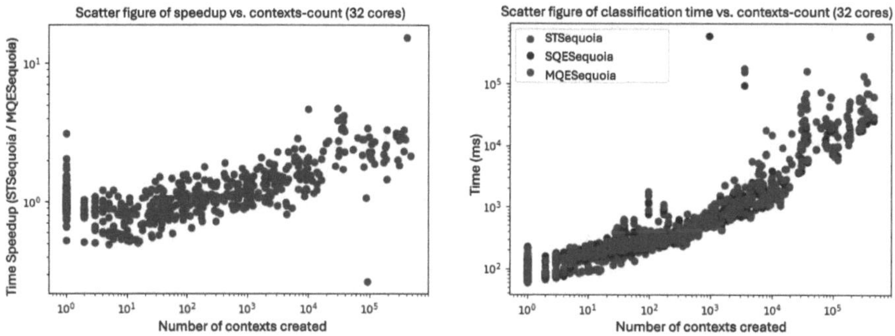

Fig. 3. Left: scatter plot comparing speedup and number of contexts created per ontology for our multi-queue thread pool-based implementation `MQESequoia`. Right: scatter plot comparing classification time (in miliseconds) with the number of contexts created for the single-threaded baseline `STSequoia`, and both our single-queue and multi-queue thread pool implementations, `SQESequoia` and `MQESequoia`, respectively.

Overall, we observe that the number and independence of contexts is the primary driver of parallel performance. Ontologies with loosely coupled contexts enable efficient distribution of work amongst threads, while those dominated by a few contexts offer limited parallelism regardless of size or expressivity.

5 Related Work

A number of reasoning systems, such as RDFox [27,29] and VLog [12] support RDF and knowledge graph applications. They are based on Datalog-based materialisation, offering fast and scalable reasoning for diverse data sources. However, they do not support the full expressivity of OWL 2 DL, such as nominals, inverse roles, and number restrictions, and thus cannot perform classification tasks targeted by DL reasoners like Sequoia. Our work focuses on consequence-based reasoning for expressive DLs, which differs fundamentally in both goal and capability. While RDFox and VLog demonstrate effective parallelisation for rule-based inference, our contributions address a different reasoning paradigm and are specifically tailored to the challenges posed by highly expressive ontologies.

Existing approaches to parallel DL reasoning include parallel structural reasoning algorithms [9], tableau-based procedures that concurrently explore non-deterministic choices [10,23,25,46], and concurrent resolution calculi such as the $\mathcal{ALCHIQ}$ reasoner where inferences are exchanged between distributed workers [33]. Methods for classification where multiple serial OWL reasoners concurrently check relevant subsumptions have been explored [2,3]; while promising, they still require further practical evaluation to confirm their benefits.

Several parallelisation strategies specifically target lightweight ontology languages. A prominent example is the ELK reasoner [21] for OWL 2 EL, which we discuss below. Distributed MapReduce-based algorithms for $\mathcal{EL}^+$ [35] have also been proposed; however, they require thorough empirical validation [34]. Parallel saturation-based reasoning has also been explored for languages like RDFS [16], highlighting alternative platforms such as multiple-core GPUs, which present unique challenges related to memory management and efficient parallelisation.

Comparison to Existing Parallel DL Reasoners. Both ELK and Konclude [40] implement parallelisation, albeit very differently from our approach.

ELK uses a persistent worker model where threads pull contexts from a shared global queue [21]. While effective for OWL 2 EL, this design suffers from contention—multiple threads trying to access or modify the same task simultaneously—and lock overhead when handling expressive ontologies with many contexts. In contrast, our work replaces this monolithic loop with micro-tasks dispatched via a work-stealing thread pool. A key innovation is context-aware gating: each context has a private queue, and only one task per context is active, eliminating global "hot spot" queues where all threads compete for tasks.

Konclude is a tableau-based reasoner and parallelises via model construction over ABox assertions [39]. Threads operate on disjoint sets of individuals and synchronise through a shared cache. While powerful for instance-heavy tasks, the applicability of this approach to TBox classification remains unclear.

Sequoia targets consequence-based reasoning and we parallelise at the level of context saturation. This approach is optimised for ontologies leading to the generation of large numbers of contexts, achieving robust performance and scalability for both lightweight and expressive ontology languages. Our empirical results demonstrate that our parallelisation can yield significant performance gains, approximately 2×3× higher speedups on large ontologies with many contexts, compared to actor-based or ELK-style worker-loop approaches.

6 Conclusion and Future Work

We presented a comprehensive exploration of parallelisation strategies for Sequoia, a consequence-based reasoner for expressive Description Logics. We implemented and compared multiple parallel architectures based on message passing and thread pooling. Our evaluation suggests that thread pool-based architectures significantly outperform message passing approaches, particularly on medium and hard ontologies. `MQESequoia`, in particular, achieves scalable parallelism by combining fine-grained task decomposition and context-aware scheduling, leading to an average speedup of up to 2.62× on hard ontologies.

Our work demonstrates that modern thread pool-based architectures provide a scalable and effective foundation for parallelising consequence-based reasoning. These insights could further guide the development of next-generation reasoners capable of handling increasingly large and complex ontologies. A promising direction for future research is to explore use cases in which message-passing parallelisation retains an advantage. We will also investigate intra-context parallelism to better exploit multi-core CPU architectures and increase inference throughput. Moreover, extending Sequoia to support distributed environments and heterogeneous compute platforms—such as GPU-based systems—represents a promising avenue for achieving scalable reasoning over very large ontologies.

Supplemental Material Statement The codebase for all versions of Sequoia is available at https://github.com/davala-9/sequoia. The repository includes detailed instructions for running the experiments in a README file and all experimental results referenced in the paper.

Acknowledgements. This work is partially funded by project ZORRO number KICH1.ST02.21.003 of the research programme Key Enabling Technologies, financed by the Dutch Research Council (NWO). This work was also supported by Samsung Research UK, and EPSRC projects UKFIRES (EP/S019111/1) and ConCur (EP/V050869/1).

References

1. Oxford ontology corpus. https://www.cs.ox.ac.uk/isg/ontologies/
2. Aslani, M., Haarslev, V.: Parallel TBox classification in description logics - first experimental results. In: 19th European Conference on Artificial Intelligence. Frontiers Artificial Intelligence and Applications, vol. 215, pp. 485–490. IOS Press (2010)
3. Aslani, M., Haarslev, V.: Concurrent classification of OWL ontologies - an empirical evaluation. In: Proceedings of the 2012 International Workshop on Description Logics, DL-2012, Rome, Italy, June 7-10, 2012. CEUR Workshop Proceedings, vol. 846. CEUR-WS.org (2012)
4. Baader, F., Brandt, S., Lutz, C.: Pushing the $\mathcal{EL}$ Envelope. In: Proceedings of the Nineteenth International Joint Conference on Artificial Intelligence (2005)
5. Baader, F., Calvanese, D., McGuinness, D.L., Nardi, D., Patel-Schneider, P.F.: The Description Logic Handbook: Theory, Implementation, and Applications. Cambridge University Press (2003)
6. Bachmair, L., Ganzinger, H.: Resolution theorem proving. In: Handbook of Automated Reasoning, vol. I, chap. 2. MIT (2001)
7. Bate, A., Motik, B., Cuenca Grau, B., Tena Cucala, D., Simancik, F., Horrocks, I.: Consequence-based reasoning for description logics with disjunctions and number restrictions. J. Artif. Intell. Res. **63**, 625–690 (2018)
8. Baumgartner, P., Furbach, U., Niemelä, I.: Hyper Tableaux. In: Fifth European Workshop on Logics in Artificial Intelligence, pp. 1–17. No. 1126 in LNAI, Springer, Évora, Portugal (1996)
9. Bergmann, F.W., Quantz, J.J.: Parallelizing description logics. In: Wachsmuth, I., Rollinger, C.-R., Brauer, W. (eds.) KI 1995. LNCS, vol. 981, pp. 137–148. Springer, Heidelberg (1995). https://doi.org/10.1007/3-540-60343-3_32
10. Bozzato, L., Homola, M., Serafini, L.: Towards more effective tableaux reasoning for CKR. In: Proceedings of the 2012 International Workshop on Description Logics. CEUR Workshop Proceedings, vol. 846. CEUR-WS.org (2012)
11. Calciu, I., et al.: Message passing or shared memory: evaluating the delegation abstraction for multicores. In: Baldoni, R., Nisse, N., van Steen, M. (eds.) OPODIS 2013. LNCS, vol. 8304, pp. 83–97. Springer, Cham (2013). https://doi.org/10.1007/978-3-319-03850-6_7
12. Carral, D., Dragoste, I., González, L., Jacobs, C., Krötzsch, M., Urbani, J.: VLog: a rule engine for knowledge graphs. In: Ghidini, C., et al. (eds.) ISWC 2019. LNCS, vol. 11779, pp. 19–35. Springer, Cham (2019). https://doi.org/10.1007/978-3-030-30796-7_2

13. Cucala, D.T., Grau, B.C., Horrocks, I.: Pay-as-you-go consequence-based reasoning for the description logic SROIQ. Artif. Intell. **298**, 103518 (2021)
14. Glimm, B., Horrocks, I., Motik, B., Stoilos, G., Wang, Z.: HermiT: An OWL 2 reasoner. J. Autom. Reasoning **53**(3), 245–269 (2014)
15. Haarslev, V., Hidde, K., Möller, R., Wessel, M.: The RacerPro knowledge representation and reasoning system. Semantic Web **3**(3), 267–277 (2012)
16. Heino, N., Pan, J.Z.: RDFS reasoning on massively parallel hardware. In: Cudré-Mauroux, P., Heflin, J., Sirin, E., Tudorache, T., Euzenat, J., Hauswirth, M., Parreira, J.X., Hendler, J., Schreiber, G., Bernstein, A., Blomqvist, E. (eds.) ISWC 2012. LNCS, vol. 7649, pp. 133–148. Springer, Heidelberg (2012). https://doi.org/10.1007/978-3-642-35176-1_9
17. Hitzler, P., Vrandecic, D.: Resolution-based approximate reasoning for OWL DL. In: ISWC, pp. 383–397 (2005)
18. Horrocks, I., Kutz, O., Sattler, U.: The even more irresistible $\mathcal{SROIQ}$. In: Tenth International Conference on Principles of Knowledge Representation and Reasoning (2006)
19. Hustadt, U., Schmidt, R.A.: Issues of decidability for description logics in the framework of resolution. In: Automated Deduction in Classical and Non-Classical Logics. LNCS, vol. 1761. Springer (2000)
20. Kazakov, Y., Krötzsch, M., Simančík, F.: Concurrent classification of el ontologies. In: The Semantic Web – ISWC 2011, pp. 305–320. Springer Berlin Heidelberg (2011)
21. Kazakov, Y., Krötzsch, M., Simančík, F.: The incredible ELK. J. Autom. Reason. **53**(1), 1–61 (2014)
22. Kazakov, Y., Motik, B.: A resolution-based decision procedure for $\mathcal{SHOIQ}$. J. Autom. Reason. **40**(2–3), 89–116 (2008)
23. Liebig, T., Müller, F.: Parallelizing tableaux-based description logic reasoning. In: On the Move to Meaningful Internet Systems, pp. 1135–1144. Springer Berlin Heidelberg (2007)
24. Lightbend: Akka - build, operate, and secure distributed applications (2024). https://akka.io/
25. Meissner, A.: A simple parallel reasoning system for the $\mathcal{ALC}$ description logic. In: Semantic Web, Social Networks and Multiagent Systems, First International Conference. Lecture Notes in Computer Science, vol. 5796, pp. 413–424. Springer (2009)
26. Metke-Jimenez, A., Lawley, M.: Snorocket 2.0: Concrete Domains and Concurrent Classification. In: OWL Reasoner Evaluation Workshop. CEUR, vol. 1015, pp. 32–38 (2013)
27. Motik, B., Nenov, Y., Piro, R., Horrocks, I., Olteanu, D.: Parallel materialisation of datalog programs in centralised, main-memory rdf systems. In: Proceedings of the AAAI Conference on Artificial Intelligence vol. 28(1) (2014)
28. Motik, B., Shearer, R., Horrocks, I.: Hypertableau reasoning for description logics. J. Artif. Intell. Res. **36**, 165–228 (2009)
29. Nenov, Y., Piro, R., Motik, B., Horrocks, I., Wu, Z., Banerjee, J.: Rdfox: a highlyscalable RDF store. In: 14th International Semantic Web Conference. Lecture Notes in Computer Science, vol. 9367, pp. 3–20. Springer (2015)
30. de Nivelle, H., Schmidt, R.A., Hustadt, U.: Resolution-based methods for modal logics. Logic J. IGPL **8**(3), 265–292 (2000)
31. Oracle: Virtual threads. https://docs.oracle.com/en/java/javase/21/core/virtual-threads.html#GUID-BEC799E0-00E9-4386-B220-8839EA6B4F5C

32. Publications Office of the European Union: Eu cellar document repository. https://publications.europa.eu/resource/cellar/369859bb-3611-11eb-b27b-01aa75ed71a1.0001.01/DOC_1
33. Schlicht, A., Stuckenschmidt, H.: Peer-to-peer reasoning for interlinked ontologies. Int. J. Semantic Comput. **04**(01), 27–58 (2010)
34. Schlicht, A., Stuckenschmidt, H.: MapResolve. In: Web Reasoning and Rule Systems - 5th International Conference. Lecture Notes in Computer Science, vol. 6902, pp. 294–299. Springer (2011)
35. Simančík, F.: Elimination of complex RIAs without automata. In: 25th International Workshop on Description Logics (2012)
36. Sirin, E., Parsia, B., Cuenca Grau, B., Kalyanpur, A., Katz, Y.: Pellet: a practical OWL-DL reasoner. J. Web Semantics **5**(2), 51–53 (2007)
37. SNOMED International: Snomed ct. https://www.snomed.org/
38. Stanford Center for Biomedical Informatics Research: Protégé ontology editor. https://protege.stanford.edu
39. Steigmiller, A., Glimm, B.: Parallelised ABox reasoning and query answering with expressive description logics. In: Verborgh, R., Hose, K., Paulheim, H., Champin, P.-A., Maleshkova, M., Corcho, O., Ristoski, P., Alam, M. (eds.) ESWC 2021. LNCS, vol. 12731, pp. 23–39. Springer, Cham (2021). https://doi.org/10.1007/978-3-030-77385-4_2
40. Steigmiller, A., Liebig, T., Glimm, B.: Konclude: system description. J. Web Semantics **27**, 78–85 (2014)
41. Sufrin, B.: Communicating scala objects (2016 revision) (2016). https://www.cs.ox.ac.uk/people/bernard.sufrin/personal/CSO/cpa2008-cso-2016revision.pdf
42. Tanenbaum, A.S., van Steen, M.: Distributed systems - principles and paradigms, 2nd Edition. Pearson Education (2007)
43. Tsarkov, D., Horrocks, I.: FaCT++ Description logic reasoner: system description. In: IJCAR. LNAI, vol. 4130, pp. 292–297. Springer (2016)
44. Vlasenko, J., Daryalal, M., Haarslev, V., Jaumard, B.: A saturation-based algebraic reasoner for $\mathcal{ELQ}$. In: 5th Workshop on Practical Aspects of Automated Reasoning. CEUR, vol. 1635, pp. 110–124 (2016)
45. Wikimedia Foundation: Wikidata. https://www.wikidata.org/
46. Wu, K., Haarslev, V.: Exploring parallelization of conjunctive branches in tableau-based description logic reasoning. In: Informal Proceedings of the 26th International Workshop on Description Logics. CEUR Workshop Proceedings, vol. 1014, pp. 1011–1023. CEUR-WS.org (2013)

HypKG: Hypergraph-Based Knowledge Graph Contextualization for Precision Healthcare

Yuzhang Xie, Xu Han, Ran Xu, Xiao Hu, Jiaying Lu, and Carl Yang(✉)

Emory University, Atlanta, GA, USA
{yuzhang.xie,andy.han,ran.xu,xiao.hu,jiaying.lu,j.carlyang}@emory.edu

Abstract. Knowledge graphs (KGs) are important products of the semantic web, which are widely used in various application domains. Healthcare is one of such domains where KGs are intensively used, due to the high requirement for knowledge accuracy and interconnected nature of healthcare data. However, KGs storing general factual information often lack the ability to account for important contexts of the knowledge such as the status of specific patients, which are crucial in precision healthcare. Meanwhile, electronic health records (EHRs) provide rich personal data, including various diagnoses and medications, which provide natural contexts for general KGs. In this paper, we propose HypKG, a framework that integrates patient information from EHRs into KGs to generate contextualized knowledge representations for accurate healthcare predictions. Using advanced entity-linking techniques, we connect relevant knowledge from general KGs with patient information from EHRs, and then utilize a hypergraph model to "contextualize" the knowledge with the patient information. Finally, we employ hypergraph transformers guided by downstream prediction tasks to jointly learn proper contextualized representations for both KGs and patients, fully leveraging existing knowledge in KGs and patient contexts in EHRs. In experiments using a large biomedical KG and two real-world EHR datasets, HypKG demonstrates significant improvements in healthcare prediction tasks across multiple evaluation metrics. Additionally, by integrating external contexts, HypKG can learn to adjust the representations of entities and relations in KG, potentially improving the quality and real-world utility of knowledge.

Keywords: Contextualized Knowledge graph · Hypergraph · Knowledge graph representation · Healthcare application of semantic webs

1 Introduction

Knowledge graphs (KGs) are important products of the semantic web, organizing and linking entities such as people, places, and objects along with their

D. Garijo et al. (Eds.): ISWC 2025, LNCS 16140, pp. 328–348, 2026.
https://doi.org/10.1007/978-3-032-09527-5_18

relationships, in graph structures [27]. They provide a powerful method for representing factual knowledge about the real world [8,69], and have found broad applications across various domains. Healthcare is one of the domains where KGs are extensively utilized, driven by the need for highly accurate knowledge and the inherently interconnected nature of healthcare data [1]. In the healthcare domain, KGs capture specialized knowledge about medical concepts, including drugs, diseases, genes, and symptoms [74]. In recent years, there has been significant growth in the development of large-scale healthcare KGs, such as UMLS [6], Concept5.5 [47], and iBKH [48]. These healthcare KGs provide rich factual knowledge, enhancing clinical research, decision-making, and healthcare delivery [13].

However, KGs storing general facts often fail to account for important contextual information about the knowledge, such as patients' statuses (e.g., demographics, medical conditions, lifestyles), which can lead to inaccuracies in the knowledge they provide. To ensure the accuracy and relevance of knowledge, it is essential to consider contexts from other data sources. In the healthcare domain, a natural consideration is to utilize KGs together with patient-specific contexts, which is crucial for precision healthcare. For instance, a patient's health status can significantly affect the relevance of drug-disease relationships retrieved from a KG. While a general KG may indicate that aspirin can be used for heart disease prevention [19], this recommendation may be inappropriate for patients with conditions such as gastrointestinal issues or bleeding disorders, where aspirin could cause adverse effects [15]. Another example involves the patient's medication context. A KG might provide information about commonly prescribed medications for depression, but these recommendations may not be suitable for patients taking other medications that could interact with antidepressants [57]. Without incorporating data about a patient's existing prescriptions, the KG might suggest treatments that could result in harmful drug interactions.

In the healthcare domain, a natural way to provide context for knowledge in KGs is to use patient information such as data from Electronic Health Records (EHRs). EHRs are widely recognized as valuable assets for comprehensive patient health analysis and informed decision-making [67]. They are usually constructed from a wide range of patients' digital medical information, including tabular data, clinical notes, medical images, genomics data, and other essential patient data types [2,49,59,63,64]. By consolidating this diverse data, EHRs facilitate a deep understanding of patients' health statuses, enabling more precise medical interventions. Moreover, EHR data often include rich contextual details, such as diagnosis, prescriptions, medication histories, admission and discharge times, and even demographic information like age and gender [38].

Motivated by the lack of context modeling in KGs for real-world applications like healthcare, and the rich contextual information found in EHRs, we propose HypKG, a novel framework to integrate patients' context information from EHR with extracted knowledge from KG, as exemplified in Fig. 1. On one hand, the background knowledge extracted from KGs can serve as a valuable complement to the detailed patient data found in EHRs. This background knowledge can

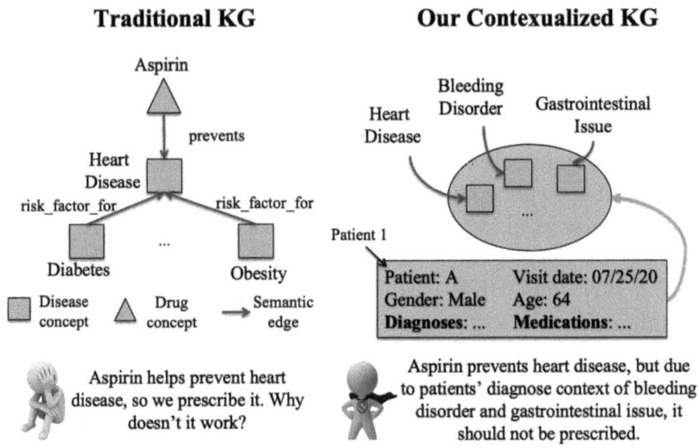

Fig. 1. A toy example of KG contextualization. *Left:* traditional KG. *Right:* our proposed contextualized KG.

provide general medical information, such as common drug-disease interactions and treatment guidelines, which EHR alone may not explicitly capture. On the other hand, the rich context provided by EHRs, such as patient diagnoses, medication histories, lab results, and personal attributes, can inform the selection of the most relevant knowledge from large-scale KGs, tailoring it to the individual patient's specific needs. This integration of EHR and KG enriches the existing knowledge with patient-specific contexts, which could serve as a foundation for a wide range of downstream healthcare applications.

To combine KG knowledge with relevant context information, several challenges must be addressed. The first challenge is **how to connect knowledge and external contexts**. For example, there may be discrepancies in the entity naming conventions used in different sources [28]– a KG may refer to a disease as "Ellis-Van Creveld syndrome", while an EHR may refer to the same disease as "Chondroectodermal dysplasia". To address this challenge of biomedical entity linking, researchers have proposed many methods using crafted string-matching rules [16], constructed thesauri [4], and pre-trained language models [55]. In our approach, we leverage the prior knowledge and semantic understanding embedded in advanced *language models* to facilitate the linking process. Through this process, we robustly enable the KG to be linked with patient-specific context information from the EHR.

Another noteworthy challenge lies in **how to jointly model knowledge and contexts**. While researchers have proposed various models for EHR data, including feature engineering [72], deep neural networks (DNNs) [11], and graph neural networks (GNNs) [33,41], these methods cannot be directly applied to incorporate additional relational knowledge from KGs. In this work, we employ a more flexible and unified graph-based data structure of *hypergraphs* [66,75], where we model EHR attributes and KG entities with nodes and model patient contexts with hyperedges. Unlike standard graphs where edges connect two nodes, hypergraphs allow hyperedges to connect multiple nodes simultaneously, enabling us to directly model the patient-attribute (context-entity) relationships [25,30]. Additionally, the many-to-many connections in hypergraphs also allow flexible capturing of entity-entity relationships within each patient context, as well as the context-context relationships for each entity.

The third challenge is **how to learn a model that properly integrates knowledge and contexts**. The foundation of this process involves jointly generating entity representations (embeddings) from large-scale KGs and context (patient) representations from EHRs. For KGs alone, many KG embedding methods have been proposed [70], popular ones including TransE [7], ComplEx [51], and CompGCN [52]. These techniques compute compact embedding vectors that capture the entity relationships. We utilize the extensively studied KG embedding methods to capture knowledge in the original KG, and use them to initialize the node features in the hypergraph model. Then we incorporate patient context into the model by utilizing *hypergraph transformers* [10] to directly model the explicit entity-context relationships, and fully learn the entity-entity and context-context relationships from EHR data. We utilize *downstream prediction tasks* to guide the whole training process of hypergraph transformers. This approach enables the KG information to be combined with the rich, patient-specific context from EHRs. The final outcomes are patient-specific representations as well as contextualized KG representations that integrate the strengths of both data sources.

Overall, the core novelty of HypKG lies in its unified, hypergraph-based framework that integrates patient-specific contexts from EHRs directly into a general biomedical KG, rather than treating KG embeddings and EHR features separately or constructing isolated "personalized" KGs. Unlike prior related work that either (a) embeds KGs without patient-specific contextualization, (b) uses only one-hot or simple pooled KG vectors for patients, or (c) builds small per-user graphs, HypKG (1) leverages an LLM-augmented entity-linking pipeline to align EHR medical attributes with KG entities; (2) represents both KG concepts and patient visits as nodes and hyperedges in a single hypergraph, capturing high-order relations; and (3) employs hypergraph transformers supervised by downstream healthcare tasks to jointly learn contextualized embeddings.

In our experiments, we utilize the large-scale public KG, iBKH [48], as the foundational KG dataset. We enhance this KG by contextualizing it with patient-specific context information from two widely used EHR datasets: MIMIC-III [24] and PROMOTE [62]. The experimental results reveal that HypKG significantly improves KG representation, with an average relative performance gain of 12.15% on MIMIC-III and 9.66% on PROMOTE across multiple evaluation metrics. HypKG also outperforms the traditional baselines that directly model the high-dimensional sparse EHR attributes without using KGs. These results highlight the effectiveness of HypKG in integrating patient-specific context into KG representations, enabling more accurate and tailored predictions in healthcare applications. Additionally, case studies show that by integrating external contexts, HypKG can learn to adjust the representations of entities and relations in KG, potentially improving the quality and real-world utility of the KG.

2 Related Work

2.1 Biomedical Entity Linking

Linking entities is a crucial part of building comprehensive healthcare knowledge graphs and is essential for entity predictions. Researchers have proposed conventional methods focusing on setting string-matching rules [16] and leveraging constructed thesauri [4], and machine learning-based methods [22,55,65,73] transforming biomedical concepts from raw text into embeddings which are then used to compute similarity scores via distance functions (*e.g.* cosine similarity), and rerank the candidate entities. Recently, some works have explored large language models (LLMs) for biomedical entity linking [61] due to their unprecedentedly rich prior knowledge as well as language capabilities [5,34,46,60]. Building on these advances, we incorporate entity linking techniques into a unified hypergraph framework for downstream predictive tasks.

2.2 KG Representations

There are many methods aiming to embed entities and relations into vector spaces in a specific dimension. TransE tries to generate embeddings that minimize the distance between the head and the tail entities in a relation, which is one of the easiest methods to train [7]. The ComplEx embedding uses the Hermitian dot product to produce the embeddings and seperates the embeddings into imaginary and real number parts to handle a large variety of binary relations [51]. Composition-based Multi-Relational Graph Convolutional Network (CompGCN) extends the traditional Graph Convolutionary Network to include the relations between entities during the message-passing process. The embeddings are generated by aggregating the neighboring entities as well as the relations between entities [52]. These models effectively learn static embeddings over KGs, but none incorporate external patient contexts during embedding learning; our method advances KG representation by embedding both KG structure and patient-specific information within the same hypergraph.

2.3 Personalized KG for Healthcare

Our contextualized KGs are distinct from personalized KGs in several ways. Unlike personalized KGs that focus on creating various small KGs to support the information needs of different users [23] [9,18,50,68,71], through knowledge contextualization, we add external contexts into KG while still modeling it as a whole. This approach can achieve the following unique effects distinct from personalized KGs: (1) it enables global modeling of interactions between knowledge and contexts, allowing learning to happen across users; (2) it utilizes the contexts to adjust knowledge representations in the whole KG, improving the quality and utility of knowledge that can potentially benefit other related KG applications; (3) it leverages knowledge in the whole KG to improve the modeling of contexts and subsequently improve the modeling of specific users. Due to the often different application scenarios of personalized KGs compared to our approach, as well as the often complicated and ad hoc processes of creating personalized KGs, we do not empirically compare with personalized KGs in this work and leave this direction as future work. Whereas personalized KGs isolate subgraphs per user, our unified hypergraph contextualization preserves KG coherence and enables collective learning across patients, demonstrating clear methodological and practical advantages.

3 Method

3.1 Preliminaries

Notations. All mathematical notations used in this paper are summarized in a comprehensive table in Section A of the Supplemental Materials.

Knowledge Graph. A knowledge graph is a multi-relational graph $\mathcal{KG} = (X, R, RT)$, where X denotes the set of entities (nodes), R denotes the set of relations (edges), and $RT \in X \times R \times X$ denotes the relational triples in the KG. In other words, knowledge in $\mathcal{KG}$ is stored as a collection of relational triples RT. For example, the relation triple *(Melatonin, Cause, Dry skin)* indicates the fact that melatonin can cause dry skin.

Knowledge Graph Representation. The objective of KG representation learning is to create the mapping functions $\mathcal{F}_X : X \mapsto \mathcal{Z}_X \in \mathbb{R}^{d_{KG}}$ and $\mathcal{F}_R : R \mapsto \mathcal{Z}_R \in \mathbb{R}^{d_{KG}}$ that transform the entities and relations in $\mathcal{KG}$ into a low-dimensional vector space. These representations, $\mathcal{Z}_X$ and $\mathcal{Z}_R$, are designed to capture and preserve the structural and attribute details of the original graph $\mathcal{KG}$, ensuring that the knowledge within the graph is retained.

Contextualizing KG Representation with EHR for Precision Healthcare. We study the KG contextualization problem in the context of patient EHR data. Let p represent a patient, and the associated EHR data can be represented as a sequence of time-stamped medical records: $\rho_p = \{r_1, r_2, \ldots, r_\tau\}$, where r_i represents the i-th record associated with the patient, and τ is the total number of events for the patient. Each medical record r_i can be described as a tuple: $r_i = (t_i, a_i, lt_i)$, where $t_i \in \mathbb{R}^+$ is the timestamp of the record (*i.e.* when the record is charted), a_i is the medical attribute (*e.g.* diagnosis such as heart failure, prescription such as desmopressin), and lt_i is the optional literal value of a_i (*e.g.* N/A for heart failure, 0.05mg for desmopressin). The medical attribute a_i of r_i can be linked to one entity X_k in $\mathcal{KG}$ using entity linking methods. Using the knowledge graph representation learning method $\mathcal{F}_X$, we can obtain the KG representations $(Z_{X_1}, \cdots, Z_{X_\tau})$ of a patient's related KG entities

$(X_1, \cdots, X_\tau)$. Consequently, a patient's overall representation Z_p is defined as $Z_p = \mathcal{F}_\mathcal{Z}(Z_{X_1}, \cdots, Z_{X_\tau})$, where $\mathcal{F}_\mathcal{Z}$ is the contextualization function that contextualizes the general factual KG representation into patient-specific knowledge representation.

Hypergraph. A hypergraph $\mathcal{HG} = \{V, E\}$ consists of a finite set of vertices (nodes) V and hyperedges E, where each hyperedge $e \in E$ is a non-empty subset of the vertex set V. Unlike regular graphs where edges connect two vertices, hyperedges can connect any number of vertices (*e.g.* $e_1 = \{v_2, v_4, v_7\}$). The size of a hyperedge e is the number of vertices it connects, while the degree deg_v of a vertex v is the number of hyperedges it participates in. In our HypKG framework, we use hypergraphs to model patient contexts and knowledge, with hyperedges representing patient visits and vertices representing medical attributes.

3.2 HypKG Framework

HypKG is a framework designed to contextualize KG representation with patient-specific context for precision healthcare, and the pipeline is described in Fig. 2. First, HypKG connects KG entities with relevant context information from EHR by linking medical entities between them (described in Sect. 3.3). Then, HypKG jointly represents KG knowledge and contextual information from EHR in a hypergraph structure, capturing key relationships between patients, features, and other patients (described in Sect. 3.4). Finally, the node and hyperedge embeddings in the hypergraph structure are learned and optimized for downstream precision healthcare tasks (described in Sect. 3.5). This framework

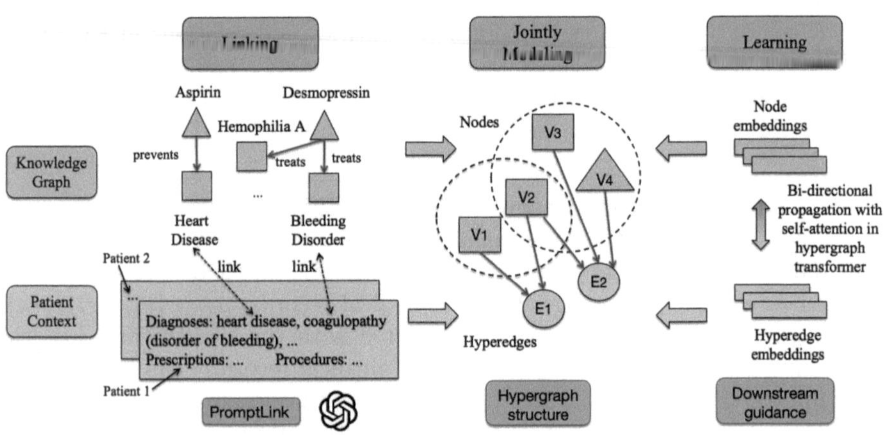

Fig. 2. Overview of HypKG framework. *Left:* Linking knowledge and contexts. *Middle:* Jointly modeling knowledge (e.g., node V_1) and contexts (e.g., hyperedge E_1, which includes nodes V_1 and V_2; hyperedge E_2, which includes nodes V_2, V_3, and V_4). *Right:* Learning to integrate knowledge and contexts.

requires the availability of contextual data such as EHRs, reliable mappings between patients and their clinical features, and a robust embedding or entity linking model to initialize node representations effectively. These components ensure that context is accurately integrated into the KG and can be leveraged for improved predictive performance.

3.3 Linking Knowledge and External Contexts

To connect KG-extracted knowledge with relevant patient context, we leverage the advanced LLM-based entity-linking technique - PromptLink [61], to accurately link patient-specific context from EHR with KG entities. The process begins with preprocessing the contextual medical attribute a in EHR ρ_p (*e.g.* diagnosis names, medication names, procedure names) by lowercasing and removing punctuation, ensuring uniformity across both EHR and KG entities. We then leverage a pre-trained language model (SAPBERT [32]) to generate embeddings $Z_{lm,a} \in \mathbb{R}^{d_{lm}}$ for EHR entity a and $Z_{lm,X_k} \in \mathbb{R}^{d_{lm}}$ for KG entity X_k. Next, we compute the cosine similarity $SIM \in [0,1]$ between the embeddings $Z_{lm,a}$ and Z_{lm,X_k}, identifying the top-LC candidates (where $LC = 10$) with the highest similarity scores as potential matches for further analysis. At the final stage, we employ a LLM (GPT-4), to establish the entity linking by analyzing the semantic meanings of the candidates. Using both the embeddings and the biomedical knowledge stored in the LLM, we generate final predictions for linking LK (between KG entities X_k and EHR medical attribute a). This multi-step approach, combining deep embeddings and LLM-based reasoning, ensures accurate entity linking, thereby enabling the integration of patient-specific data into the KG for contextualized healthcare applications. The process can be formalized as:

$$LK(a, X_k) = \text{PromptLink}(a, X_k). \tag{1}$$

3.4 Jointly Modeling Knowledge and Contexts

After connecting KG knowledge and contextual information from EHR, HypKG jointly represents them in a hypergraph structure. In this hypergraph model, medical attributes such as diagnosis and medications are treated as nodes V. A patient's individual visit ρ_p (*i.e.* single encounter) is represented as a hyperedge e, which connects the relevant nodes corresponding to the medical attributes from that visit. The collection of these hyperedges forms the hyperedge set E within the hypergraph. Unlike standard graphs that link only two nodes, hypergraphs allow hyperedges to connect multiple nodes at once, making it easier to model the relationship within the patient context. This hypergraph-based approach effectively represents the rich contextual information in EHR data and captures high-order interactions between patients and medical features, providing a more structured and comprehensive representation.

3.5 Learning to Integrate Knowledge and Contexts

HypKG learns to integrate knowledge and contexts. To facilitate this process, we initialize node embeddings within the hypergraph to incorporate KG information and patient context. For each node v, associated with an EHR attribute a and connected to a KG entity X_k, the initial node embedding $\mathcal{Z}_v^0 \in \mathbb{R}^{d_{KG}}$ is derived from the corresponding KG representation.

We design the learning process inspired by hypergraph transformers [10,31,66]. The structures consist of L layers for message passing. In each layer, the embeddings are updated as follows: hyperedge embeddings $\mathcal{Z}_e^l$ of layer l are obtained by aggregating node information from layer $l-1$ within each hyperedge e using aggregation function $f_{V\rightarrow E}$, and then the node embeddings $\mathcal{Z}_v^l$ are updated by aggregating information from hyperedges connected to the node v using aggregation function $f_{E\rightarrow V}$. These message-passing processes are iteratively applied across layers:

$$\mathcal{Z}_e^l = f_{V\rightarrow E}(\mathcal{Z}_v^{l-1}), \quad \mathcal{Z}_v^l = f_{E\rightarrow V}(\mathcal{Z}_e^l) \tag{2}$$

Additionally, in the first layer, the hyperedge embedding is aggregated using the initial node embedding $\mathcal{Z}_v^0$.

To implement the message-passing functions $f_{V\rightarrow E}$ and $f_{E\rightarrow V}$, we apply multi-head attention. Here we use notation S to represent a set, which can be a hyperedge or a node. Specifically, if S represents a hyperedge, the set S consists of its connected nodes, and then the embedding Z_S is updated using the embeddings of its connected nodes from the previous layer. Conversely, if S represents a node, the set S consists of its connected hyperedges, and its embedding Z_S is updated using the embeddings of its connected hyperedges from the previous layer. Given an embedding matrix $\mathcal{Z}_S \in \mathbb{R}^{|S|\times d_{hi}}$, the calculation of output $\mathcal{Z}'_S$ is defined as:

$$\mathcal{Z}'_S = \|_{i=1}^{H} \text{Attention}_i(Z_S), \tag{3}$$

$$\text{Attention}_i(Z_S) = \text{softmax}\left(\frac{W_{Q,i}^l (Z_S.W_{K,i}^l)^\top}{\sqrt{d_{hi}/H}}\right) Z_S.W_{V,i}^l, \tag{4}$$

where $W_{Q,i}^l \in \mathbb{R}^{1\times\lfloor d_{hi}/H\rfloor}$, $W_{K,i}^l \in \mathbb{R}^{d_{hi}\times\lfloor d_{hi}/H\rfloor}$, $W_{V,i}^l \in \mathbb{R}^{d_{hi}\times\lfloor d_{hi}/H\rfloor}$ are learnable weight matrices in layer l, H is the number of attention heads, and d_{hi} is the hidden layer dimension.

It is crucial to capture three key relationships within the patient context: (1) Patient-Attribute Relations – linking patients to their respective attributes; (2) Attribute-Attribute Relations – illustrating how attributes influence each other within a patient; and (3) Patient-Patient Relations – identifying similarities between patients with comparable medical histories or conditions. Our HypKG, which utilizes a hypergraph structure with patient-level hyperedges and attribute-level nodes, facilitates the capture of Patient-Attribute Relations through node-to-hyperedge and hyperedge-to-node propagation, as described in Eq. 2. Additionally, the multi-head attention mechanism, defined in Eqs. 3 and

4, enables the model to measure Attribute-Attribute Relations via attention between nodes within a hyperedge, and Patient-Patient Relations through attention between hyperedges connected to a common node.

To guide learning, we define downstream tasks ($\mathcal{TA}$) and divide the hypergraph data into training, validation, and test sets for robust evaluation. During training, KG information is contextualized using patient data, capturing intricate relationships like patient-attribute, attribute-attribute, and patient-patient relations. The resulting final representation, $\mathcal{Z}_{final}$, incorporates both patient-specific context and KG-derived knowledge, and can then be utilized in various healthcare applications. Since we leverage supervised classification tasks for guidance, the final representation $\mathcal{Z}_{final}$ is passed to a two-layer fully-connected layer (with size d_{final}=48) and the loss function is the binary cross-entropy.

4 Experiments

4.1 Experimental Settings

KG Dataset. We use a large-scale public knowledge graph, iBKH [48], as the primary KG dataset. iBKH integrates data from various biomedical knowledge bases, offering a comprehensive resource with 2,384,501 entities across 11 categories, including drugs, diseases, symptoms, genes, and pathways. Moreover, with over 48 million relation triples, iBKH facilitates deeper insights into complex biological interactions. More details about how we utilize the KG dataset to generate embeddings are described in Section D of Supplemental Materials.

EHR Datasets. We contextualize the knowledge graph by integrating patient-specific data from two EHR datasets: MIMIC-III [24] and PROMOTE [62]. Overview of the two EHR datasets are described in Table 1. MIMIC-III, a public dataset, includes over 53,000 patient records from critical care units at Beth Israel Deaconess Medical Center between 2001 and 2012. From MIMIC-III, we follow the settings of Xu et al. [66], to keep 12,353 patient visits (*i.e.* encounters) with 7,423 key medical attributes, including 846 diagnoses, 4,525 prescriptions, and 2,032 procedures. For the MIMIC-III dataset, we perform phenotyping prediction, framed as a multi-label classification task. This involves predicting the presence of 25 acute health conditions (e.g., chronic kidney disease) during a patient's future visits based on their current ICU stay records. PROMOTE is a private dataset containing records of 7,780 stroke patients treated from 2012 to 2021. For this dataset, we extract 2,595 medical attributes, including 1,480 ICD-10 diagnosis codes and 1,115 prescribed medications recorded up to the patients' discharge after their index stroke. For the PROMOTE dataset, we use the occurrence of post-stroke cognitive impairment (PSCI) as the label and define it as a binary classification task. More details about the two EHR datasets are described in Section C of Supplemental Materials.

Table 1. Overview of the EHR datasets. Dx denotes diagnosis, Rx denotes prescriptions, and Px denotes procedures.

EHR Dataset	Patient Encounter Count	List of Features	Task Count
MIMIC-III	12,353	Dx, Rx, Px	25
PROMOTE	7,780	Dx, Rx	1

Evaluation Metrics. In our experiments, we evaluate model performance using key metrics for classification tasks: Accuracy, Area Under the Receiver Operating Characteristic Curve (AUROC), Area Under the Precision-Recall Curve (AUCPR), and the Macro-F1 score. For the binary classification performance on PROMOTE, we follow the default way to compute these metrics. For the multilabel classification performance on MIMIC-III, all metrics are macro-averaged to ensure that performance is evaluated equally across all labels. The model's final performance is determined based on the highest AUROC score achieved on the validation set, as AUROC is a comprehensive metric for evaluating the classification model's effectiveness, and the corresponding test set performance from that epoch is then reported. To ensure robustness, we repeat the experiments five times and report the average performance across these runs. These metrics provide a thorough assessment of the model's predictive capabilities.

Baseline Methods. In our experiments, we compare the downstream risk prediction performance of the following embedding approaches, all of which are patient representations for downstream prediction tasks:

- Binary Embedding: This is a traditional patient risk factor encoding approach [37,53,58] that represents patients using one-hot binary embeddings for each medical attribute. This results in a high dimensional binary embedding with over one thousand dimensions (7423 for MIMIC-III and 2595 for PROMOTE), where each dimension indicates the presence or absence of a specific medical attribute during a patient's visit.
- KG Embedding: This method leverages KG information by mean-pooling KG representations based on the linked patient's medical attributes during a visit. While we use PromptLink [61] to perform the entity linking between EHR attributes and KG entities, our approach extends beyond PromptLink by generating and aggregating the KG embeddings into patient-level representations. The resulting 128-dimensional vector captures the patient's relevant KG context in a compact form, offering a lower-dimensional alternative to traditional high-dimensional binary feature embeddings.
- HypKG Embedding: This 128-D embedding is generated using our proposed method HypKG, which integrates patient-specific contextual information with the KG information.

Each of these embeddings is evaluated using several machine learning methods: Logistic Regression (LR), Support Vector Machine (SVM), Multi-layer Perceptron (MLP), Random Forest (RF), and XGBoost (XGB). Additionally, for the HypKG embedding, we also assess the performance during the training process using the patient context integration structure - hypergraph transformer (Hypergraph), since the contextualization process itself also uses the same downstream prediction task. These models allow us to thoroughly assess the effectiveness of the different embeddings in capturing the relevant features for healthcare tasks. The experiments for downstream prediction (Sect. 4.2) are designed to demonstrate that contextualizing KG embeddings with patient data yields substantially better risk-prediction performance. Moreover, our ablation studies (Sect. 4.3) show that HypKG remains robust under variations in hypergraph construction, entity-linking strategies, and other design choices.

Implementation Details. Implementation details of the experiments are described in Section D of Supplemental Materials. These details include the KG embedding generation method, hypergraph modeling hyperparameters, and baseline ML models' hyperparameter configurations.

4.2 Performance on Downstream Prediction

Table 2. Performance comparison of different embeddings on the downstream risk prediction task. For each evaluation metric, the best performance is highlighted in bold, and the second-best result is underlined.

Embedding	Method	MIMIC-III				PROMOTE			
		Accuracy(%)	AUROC(%)	AUCPR(%)	Macro-F1(%)	Accuracy(%)	AUROC(%)	AUCPR(%)	Macro-F1(%)
Binary Embedding	LR	78.58 ± 0.18	81.23 ± 0.14	68.22 ± 0.32	45.79 ± 0.44	74.08 ± 0.69	60.56 ± 1.96	30.67 ± 1.91	53.84 ± 1.37
	SVM	80.41 ± 0.10	83.21 ± 0.23	71.29 ± 0.37	41.77 ± 0.04	77.42 ± 0.69	63.13 ± 1.20	33.48 ± 1.61	44.28 ± 0.26
	MLP	76.05 ± 0.11	78.09 ± 0.22	63.74 ± 0.25	44.21 ± 0.22	69.30 ± 0.58	57.04 ± 1.13	28.22 ± 1.92	53.46 ± 0.71
	RF	77.17 ± 0.25	81.22 ± 0.11	67.45 ± 0.40	23.60 ± 0.21	77.40 ± 0.11	64.73 ± 1.33	32.77 ± 1.55	43.80 ± 1.12
	XGB	79.62 ± 0.20	82.72 ± 0.15	70.83 ± 0.21	49.06 ± 0.34	77.11 ± 0.91	65.01 ± 1.70	33.30 ± 2.42	49.84 ± 1.17
KG Embedding	LR	77.72 ± 0.22	80.66 ± 0.09	66.20 ± 0.36	35.80 ± 0.34	77.40 ± 0.82	61.62 ± 1.70	29.79 ± 2.41	44.08 ± 0.34
	SVM	78.38 ± 0.22	80.84 ± 0.19	67.49 ± 0.39	35.40 ± 0.30	77.49 ± 0.83	54.97 ± 1.39	24.49 ± 0.94	43.78 ± 0.26
	MLP	72.08 ± 0.21	73.12 ± 0.21	53.79 ± 0.54	42.47 ± 0.39	68.77 ± 1.11	57.64 ± 1.55	24.05 ± 6.48	53.39 ± 1.81
	RF	76.57 ± 0.17	78.98 ± 0.16	64.36 ± 0.56	25.13 ± 0.95	77.59 ± 0.83	56.49 ± 1.69	25.79 ± 1.53	43.75 ± 0.26
	XGB	75.35 ± 0.13	77.27 ± 0.19	61.77 ± 0.51	38.65 ± 0.49	77.48 ± 0.87	59.04 ± 1.31	28.95 ± 1.63	46.21 ± 0.84
HypKG Embedding	LR	80.32 ± 0.29	83.98 ± 0.45	72.84 ± 0.91	46.28 ± 0.54	77.62 ± 0.74	66.97 ± 0.51	35.65 ± 1.56	47.58 ± 0.95
	SVM	80.51 ± 0.16	83.07 ± 0.35	71.59 ± 0.62	42.83 ± 0.24	**77.70 ± 0.90**	58.07 ± 1.22	28.49 ± 1.93	44.06 ± 0.54
	MLP	74.61 ± 0.18	77.10 ± 0.30	62.15 ± 4.47	46.91 ± 0.62	69.17 ± 1.32	58.72 ± 1.59	32.19 ± 1.61	**54.60 ± 1.52**
	RF	80.54 ± 0.23	84.01 ± 0.22	72.80 ± 0.47	41.72 ± 0.29	74.26 ± 7.92	63.74 ± 1.15	32.19 ± 1.92	46.98 ± 4.74
	XGB	78.86 ± 0.21	81.89 ± 0.61	69.25 ± 0.63	**47.12 ± 0.63**	77.02 ± 0.52	64.22 ± 1.28	32.65±2.85	49.43±0.82
	Hypergraph	**80.86 ± 0.17**	**84.26 ± 0.17**	**73.12 ± 0.37**	45.30 ± 0.49	77.06 ± 0.62	**67.37 ± 1.02**	**35.74 ± 1.67**	53.28 ± 1.54

Table 2 summarizes the downstream risk prediction results on the two datasets to show the impact of contextualization. In this table, our proposed contextualized HypKG Embedding consistently outperforms other baseline methods. Across various evaluation metrics on both datasets, the HypKG Embedding consistently achieves the best and second-best performance. This performance gain demonstrates the effectiveness of integrating KG information with patient context to generate richer, more representative embeddings. Notably, the hypergraph model within the HypKG framework achieves the strongest results across most metrics. This finding suggests that the HypKG model alone is powerful enough to provide robust representations and the hypergraph model has a strong modeling ability, eliminating the need to extract embeddings and apply them to external machine learning models.

The advantages of contextualization within HypKG are further emphasized when compared with the KG Embedding. Across all evaluation metrics and on both datasets, the HypKG Embedding consistently achieves better results, demonstrating the effectiveness of incorporating contextual information and KG information. Moreover, we observe an average relative improvement of 12.15% on MIMIC-III and 9.66% on PROMOTE by comparing all methods utilizing HypKG Embedding and those using KG Embedding. This improvement highlights the significant impact of contextualization, allowing for a deeper understanding of patient information and stronger performance in downstream tasks.

In comparison to HypKG, the other two methods, Binary Embedding and KG Embedding, show comparable performance in certain models, such as Binary Embedding with SVM. However, both embeddings suffer from significant limitations. Binary Embedding, a traditional approach for generating patient representations in healthcare tasks, faces the curse of dimensionality, especially in medical datasets where the number of attributes can exceed 1,000. This leads to an exponential increase in computational complexity. For instance, when using SVM with Binary Embedding on the MIMIC-III dataset, the computation time exceeded 10 h—a time cost that is over 20 times longer than the time required by HypKG for the same task with SVM. This inefficiency highlights the unsustainable nature of Binary Embedding for large-scale applications. On the other hand, KG Embedding reduces the representation size and also incorporates patient information with KG information. However, the method used for combining them (simple mean-pooling) lacks the sophistication required to capture the intricate relationships between the knowledge graph and patient contexts. As a result, the performance of KG Embedding lags behind that of both Binary Embedding and HypKG Embedding. The main limitation here is that the KG information is not sufficiently contextualized, leading to a less effective representation. This is where HypKG excels, as it effectively integrates KG and contextual information, modeling intricate relations between them and producing better global representations efficiently for downstream applications.

4.3 Ablation Studies

HypKG consists of three key components: linking, joint modeling, and learning, leveraging EHR data to contextualize KG representations. To validate its design, we conduct comprehensive ablation studies. These studies evaluate the impact of entity linking (Supplemental Materials Section E), KG embedding generation (Supplemental Materials Section F), joint modeling of KG and EHR (Supplemental Materials Section G), hypergraph design (Supplemental Materials Section H), and learning hyperparameters (Supplemental Materials Section I). These ablation studies confirm the effectiveness of HypKG's implementation.

Entity Linking Methods. We evaluate the impact of different entity linking methods on HypKG, comparing PromptLink with BM25, BioBERT, and shuffled embeddings. Results show that PromptLink consistently achieves the best performance. Meanwhile, HypKG remains robust with only minor performance drops when using simpler or noisier linking methods. This highlights both the effectiveness of PromptLink and the resilience of HypKG to linking errors in real-world settings. Details of the experiments are described in Section E of Supplemental Materials.

KG Embedding Generation Methods. We evaluate the impact of different KG embedding methods on HypKG's performance. Details of the experiments are described in Section F of Supplemental Materials. Results show that our default setting (ComplEx + Large) achieves the best overall performance, while alternative methods like TransE and CompGCN perform slightly worse. Overall, HypKG remains robust across different embedding configurations, highlighting its adaptability and efficiency in practical applications.

Jointly Modeling EHR and KG. To assess the importance of jointly modeling EHR and KG information, we compare HypKG against two ablation baselines: KG Only and EHR Only, as demonstrated in Section G of Supplemental Materials. Results across both datasets show that HypKG significantly outperforms the baselines, demonstrating the complementary value of KG embeddings and EHR-derived hypergraph structures. This confirms the effectiveness of our joint modeling design in enhancing contextualization and predictive accuracy.

Hypergraph Design. We evaluate HypKG's hypergraph design by comparing it with state-of-the-art hypergraph models and alternative message-passing strategies. Details and results are described in Section H of Supplemental Materials. In experiments, HypKG consistently outperforms baselines across key metrics, demonstrating its effectiveness in integrating structural and semantic information from both EHRs and KGs. These results validate our contextualization approach and highlight HypKG's superior scalability and domain-specific design for precision healthcare.

Hyperparameter Studies. We conduct a comprehensive hyperparameter study to assess the impact of key settings on HypKG's performance, as described in Section I of Supplemental Materials. Results on both MIMIC-III and PROMOTE datasets show that our selected configurations achieve strong and stable outcomes, with learning rate, hypergraph transformer depth, hidden size, and attention heads all influencing performance. Among these, the learning rate plays the most critical role in balancing model optimization.

4.4 Case Studies on Knowledge Representation

To demonstrate that the representations generated by HypKG are effectively contextualized, we compare the knowledge embeddings before and after training. For each KG medical entity pair (Entity A, Entity B), we analyze them from three key perspectives: (1) Similarity: We compute the cosine similarity between the knowledge representations of each entity pair both before and after training. By comparing these values, we observe an increase in similarity after the application of HypKG for most pairs (more details analyzed in Section K of Supplemental Materials), indicating that the contextual relationships between entities are better captured. From this analysis, we identify twenty top entity pairs (including pairs of diagnosis and prescription) that show a great increase in representation similarity within both the MIMIC-III and PROMOTE datasets for a case study. Since the cosine similarity values are within the range $[-1, 1]$, the increases in similarity for these listed pairs are significant as they approach 1. (2) Occurrence and Prevalence: We further investigate the frequency with which each entity pair co-occurs in the same patient context. Additionally, we determine the prevalence of each entity in these contexts by dividing the number of co-occurrences by the total number of occurrences for each entity individually (i.e., Prevalence A and Prevalence B). This allows us to understand how common it is for both entities to appear together and how strongly their occurrence is correlated within a patient's data. (3) Relation Analysis: To provide further insights into the relationships between the entities, we consult with clinicians for qualitative assessments and cite relevant resources.

Table 3. Case studies on knowledge representation. "Increase" denotes the increase in similarity between entity pairs after applying HypKG. "Occurrence" indicates the number of times the entity pair co-occurs in the same patient context. "Prevalence A" and "Prevalence B" represent the ratio of co-occurrences to the total occurrences for each entity individually. "References" denote existing literature that discusses the relationship between the entity pairs.

Dataset and Pair	ID	Entity A	Entity B	Increase	Occurrence	Prevalence A	Prevalence B	References
MIMIC-III Diagnosis	I	Benign neonatal seizures	Pneumonia	1.08	25	67.57%	40.98%	[44]
	II	Benign neonatal seizures	Congenital hemolytic anemia	1.01	30	81.08%	34.88%	[17]
	III	Upper extremity deep vein thrombosis	Limb injury	1.01	4	57.14%	100.00%	[45]
	IV	Congenital hemolytic anemia	Pneumonia	1.00	38	44.19%	62.30%	[29]
	V	Closed fracture of bones, unspecified	Pneumothorax	0.99	43	36.44%	78.18%	[3]
MIMIC-III Prescription	VI	Starter PN D5	Heparin sodium	1.21	7	53.85%	58.33%	[40]
	VII	Insulin	Acetaminophen	1.13	5566	75.34%	69.38%	[36]
	VIII	Drug withdrawal syndrome neonatal	Indomethacin sodium	1.12	9	36.00%	81.82%	[35]
	IX	Syringe (Neonatal)	Indomethacin sodium	1.11	11	44.00%	84.62%	[54]
	X	Urethral stricture	Pulmonary tuberculosis	1.11	19	79.17%	63.33%	[39]
PROMOTE Diagnosis	XI	Respiratory system disease	Medical device complication	1.09	1043	66.01%	68.21%	[43]
	XII	Human immunodeficiency virus infectious disease	HIV infection	1.07	95	75.40%	84.07%	[20]
	XIII	Symptoms of nervous & musculoskeletal systems	Long term (current) drug therapy	1.06	2990	72.89%	55.12%	[12]
	XIV	Essential hypertension	Chronic fatigue syndrome	1.02	2966	44.37%	89.61%	[21]
	XV	Essential hypertension	Cerebrovascular disease	0.99	4282	64.06%	87.57%	[56]
PROMOTE Prescription	XVI	Isopropyl alcohol	Lancets	0.92	95	98.96%	50.00%	[26]
	XVII	Blood glucose	Lancets	0.87	181	88.73%	95.26%	[26]
	XVIII	Emtricitabine & Tenofovir disoproxil fumarate	Ritonavir	0.87	12	75.00%	66.67%	[42]
	XIX	Mycophenolate mofetil	Tacrolimus	0.83	59	71.08%	74.68%	[14]
	XX	Blood glucose	Isopropyl alcohol	0.76	86	54.78%	89.58%	[26]

The case study results are described in Table 3. Overall, HypKG enhances the similarity between entity pairs that are similar in patient contexts, even when their relationships are not explicitly captured by the KG, showing the power of our contextualization. For instance, in Case I, "Benign neonatal seizures" and "Pneumonia" are two distinct diagnostic conditions that, according to the KG, have no direct causal link. However, in the EHR context, these dignoses are associated with the medical attributes "Convulsions in newborn" and "Pneumonia", which often co-occur in newborns. Pneumonia, for example, may indirectly contribute to neonatal seizures by causing physiological stress that makes seizures more likely in affected infants [44]. While the KG might not capture this indirect relationship, the contextual co-occurrence in patient data suggests a meaningful association. Another example is seen in Case VII, which involves the prescription entity pair of Insulin and Acetaminophen. These two drugs do not have a direct pharmacological interaction, as insulin is primarily used to manage blood sugar levels in diabetic patients, while acetaminophen is typically prescribed for pain or fever relief. However, they are linked to their corresponding medical attributes within the EHR context and frequently co-occur. This can be explained by the phenomenon that patients with diabetes often require both medications—insulin for managing their condition and acetaminophen to alleviate common symptoms like pain or fever [36]. Although the KG does not reflect a direct connection between these drugs, their frequent co-prescription in clinical practice highlights a contextual relationship, which HypKG is able to capture. In summary, this case study analysis demonstrates that HypKG contextualizes the KG knowledge and generates better representations.

5 Conclusion

In this study, we propose HypKG, a novel framework that addresses the critical need for contextualized knowledge representations for precision healthcare by integrating context-specific information from EHRs with general knowledge from KGs. In this framework, we first use entity-linking techniques to connect general KG knowledge with patient contexts from EHRs, and then apply a hypergraph model to contextualize the knowledge via hyperedges. Finally, we employ hypergraph transformers guided by downstream prediction tasks to jointly learn contextualized representations for both KG and patients, leveraging the combined knowledge. In experiments, HypKG shows significant improvements in healthcare prediction tasks across multiple evaluation metrics. Additionally, by integrating external contexts, HypKG can learn to adjust the representations of entities and relations in KG, potentially improving the quality and real-world utility of knowledge. The application of HypKG allows for the effective contextualization of knowledge and advances precision healthcare, capturing the intricate relationships between patient data and general knowledge in a way that traditional KGs fail to do.

Supplemental Material Statement

The source code and dataset download instructions are available on the GitHub page: https://github.com/constantjxyz/HypKG. Additional resources—including the notation table, algorithm descriptions, dataset details, implementation notes, and ablation studies—are provided in the Supplementary Materials of the extended manuscript available on arXiv: https://arxiv.org/abs/2507.19726.

References

1. Abu-Salih, B., Al-Qurishi, M., Alweshah, M., Al-Smadi, M., Alfayez, R., Saadeh, H.: Healthcare knowledge graph construction: a systematic review of the state-of-the-art, open issues, and opportunities. J. Big Data **10**(1), 81 (2023)
2. Abul-Husn, N.S., Kenny, E.E.: Personalized medicine and the power of electronic health records. Cell **177**(1), 58–69 (2019)
3. Amer, K.M., Congiusta, D.V., Suri, P., Choudhry, A., Otero, K., Adams, M.: Clavicle fractures: associated trauma and morbidity. J. Clin. Orthopaedics Trauma **13**, 53–56 (2021)
4. Aronson, A.R., Lang, F.M.: An overview of metamap: historical perspective and recent advances. J. Am. Med. Inform. Assoc. **17**(3), 229–236 (2010)
5. Bhasuran, B., et al.: Preliminary analysis of the impact of lab results on large language model generated differential diagnoses. NPJ Digit. Med. **8**(1), 166 (2025)
6. Bodenreider, O.: The unified medical language system (UMLS): integrating biomedical terminology. Nucl. Acids Res. **32**(suppl_1), D267–D270 (2004)
7. Bordes, A., Weston, J., Collobert, R., Bengio, Y.: Learning structured embeddings of knowledge bases. In: Proceedings of the AAAI Conference on Artificial Intelligence, vol. 25, pp. 301–306 (2011)
8. Cao, J., Fang, J., Meng, Z., Liang, S.: Knowledge graph embedding: a survey from the perspective of representation spaces. ACM Comput. Surv. **56**(6), 1–42 (2024)
9. Carvalho, R.M., Oliveira, D., Pesquita, C.: Knowledge graph embeddings for ICU readmission prediction. BMC Med. Inform. Decis. Mak. **23**(1), 12 (2023)
10. Chien, E., Pan, C., Peng, J., Milenkovic, O.: You are allset: a multiset function framework for hypergraph neural networks. arXiv preprint arXiv:2106.13264 (2021)
11. Choi, Y., Chiu, C.Y.I., Sontag, D.: Learning low-dimensional representations of medical concepts. AMIA Summits Transl. Sci. Proc. **2016**, 41 (2016)
12. Clauw, D.J.: Diagnosing and treating chronic musculoskeletal pain based on the underlying mechanism (s). Best Pract. Res. Clin. Rheumatol. **29**(1), 6–19 (2015)
13. Cui, H., et al.: A review on knowledge graphs for healthcare: resources, applications, and promises. J. Biomed. Inf. 104861 (2025)
14. Dalal, P., Shah, G., Chhabra, D., Gallon, L.: Role of tacrolimus combination therapy with mycophenolate mofetil in the prevention of organ rejection in kidney transplant patients. Int. J. Nephrol. Renovascular Diseas. 107–115 (2010)
15. De Berardis, G., et al.: Association of aspirin use with major bleeding in patients with and without diabetes. JAMA **307**(21), 2286–2294 (2012)
16. D'Souza, J., Ng, V.: Sieve-based entity linking for the biomedical domain. In: Proceedings of the 53rd Annual Meeting of the Association for Computational Linguistics and the 7th International Joint Conference on Natural Language Processing (Volume 2: Short Papers), pp. 297–302 (2015)

17. Gallagher, P.G.: Anemia in the pediatric patient. Blood J. the Am. Soc. Hematol. **140**(6), 571–593 (2022)
18. Gao, Y., et al.: Leveraging a medical knowledge graph into large language models for diagnosis prediction. arXiv preprint arXiv:2308.14321 (2023)
19. Gasparyan, A.Y., Watson, T., Lip, G.Y.: The role of aspirin in cardiovascular prevention: implications of aspirin resistance. J. Am. Coll. Cardiol. **51**(19), 1829–1843 (2008)
20. German Advisory Committee Blood (Arbeitskreis Blut), S.A.o.P.T.b.B.: Human immunodeficiency virus (HIV). Transf. Med. Hemotherapy **43**(3), 203–222 (2016)
21. Hulens, M., Rasschaert, R., Vansant, G., Stalmans, I., Bruyninckx, F., Dankaerts, W.: The link between idiopathic intracranial hypertension, fibromyalgia, and chronic fatigue syndrome: exploration of a shared pathophysiology. J. Pain Res. 3129–3140 (2018)
22. Ji, Z., Wei, Q., Xu, H.: Bert-based ranking for biomedical entity normalization. AMIA Summits Transl. Sci. Proc. **2020**, 269 (2020)
23. Jiang, P., Xiao, C., Cross, A.R., Sun, J.: Graphcare: enhancing healthcare predictions with personalized knowledge graphs. In: The Twelfth International Conference on Learning Representations (2024)
24. Johnson, A.E., et al.: Mimic-III, a freely accessible critical care database. Sci. Data **3**(1), 1–9 (2016)
25. Johnson, R., Li, M.M., Noori, A., Queen, O., Zitnik, M.: Graph artificial intelligence in medicine. Ann. Rev. Biomed. Data Sci. **7** (2024)
26. Jońca, M., Krótki, F., Tomasik, P.: The effect of disinfecting procedure on the glucose concentration using a personal glucose meter. Prim. Care Diabetes **15**(5), 848–852 (2021)
27. Kejriwal, M.: Knowledge graphs: a practical review of the research landscape. Information **13**(4), 161 (2022)
28. Kohane, I.S., et al.: What every reader should know about studies using electronic health record data but may be afraid to ask. J. Med. Internet Res. **23**(3), e22219 (2021)
29. Kurugol, Z., Onen, S.S., Koturoglu, G.: Severe hemolytic anemia associated with mild pneumonia caused by mycoplasma pneumonia. Case Rep. Med. **2012**(1), 649850 (2012)
30. Lee, G., Bu, F., Eliassi-Rad, T., Shin, K.: A survey on hypergraph mining: patterns, tools, and generators. arXiv preprint arXiv:2401.08878 (2024)
31. Lee, J., Lee, Y., Kim, J., Kosiorek, A., Choi, S., Teh, Y.W.: Set transformer: a framework for attention-based permutation-invariant neural networks. In: International conference on machine learning. pp. 3744–3753. PMLR (2019)
32. Liu, F., Shareghi, E., Meng, Z., Basaldella, M., Collier, N.: Self-alignment pretraining for biomedical entity representations. arXiv preprint arXiv:2010.11784 (2020)
33. Liu, Z., Wang, X., Wang, B., Huang, Z., Yang, C., Jin, W.: Graph odes and beyond: a comprehensive survey on integrating differential equations with graph neural networks. arXiv preprint arXiv:2503.23167 (2025)
34. Lu, J., Shen, J., Xiong, B., Ma, W., Staab, S., Yang, C.: HiproMPT: few-shot biomedical knowledge fusion via hierarchy-oriented prompting. In: 46th International ACM SIGIR Conference on Research and Development in Information Retrieval - Short Paper (2023)
35. Lucas, S.: The pharmacology of indomethacin. Headache J. Head Face Pain **56**(2), 436–446 (2016)
36. Maahs, D.M., et al.: Effect of acetaminophen on CGM glucose in an outpatient setting. Diabetes Care **38**(10), e158–e159 (2015)

37. Manikandan, R., Kuwelkar, S., Sivakumar, R.: An hybrid technique for optimized clustering of EHR using binary particle swarm and constrained optimization for better performance in prediction of cardiovascular diseases. Measur. Sens. **25**, 100577 (2023)
38. Murali, L., Gopakumar, G., Viswanathan, D.M., Nedungadi, P.: Towards electronic health record-based medical knowledge graph construction, completion, and applications: a literature study. J. Biomed. Inform. **143**, 104403 (2023)
39. Naeem, M., et al.: Imaging manifestations of genitourinary tuberculosis. Radiographics **41**(4), 1123–1143 (2021)
40. Novick, K., Cober, M.P.: Evaluation of inpatient starter parenteral nutrition use in the neonatal intensive care unit. J. Pediat. Pharmacol. Therapeut. **27**(6), 524–528 (2022)
41. Ochoa, J.G.D., Mustafa, F.E.: Graph neural network modelling as a potentially effective method for predicting and analyzing procedures based on patients' diagnoses. Artif. Intell. Med. **131**, 102359 (2022)
42. Reynes, J., et al.: Lopinavir/ritonavir combined with raltegravir or tenofovir/emtricitabine in antiretroviral-naive subjects: 96-week results of the progress study. AIDS Res. Hum. Retroviruses **29**(2), 256–265 (2013)
43. Samore, M.H., et al.: Surveillance of medical device-related hazards and adverse events in hospitalized patients. JAMA **291**(3), 325–334 (2004)
44. Schüssler, S.C., et al.: Seizures in preterm infants with germinal-matrix-intraventricular hemorrhage (GM-IVH): a retrospective monocentric study on predictors and neurodevelopmental outcome. Eur. J. Paediatr. Neurol. (2025)
45. Singh, O., Juneja, D.: Upper extremity deep vein thrombosis: an intensivist's perspective. World J. Crit. Care Med. **12**(3), 130 (2023)
46. Singhal, K., et al.: Large language models encode clinical knowledge. Nature **620**(7972), 172–180 (2023)
47. Speer, R., Chin, J., Havasi, C.: Conceptnet 5.5: an open multilingual graph of general knowledge. In: Proceedings of the AAAI Conference on Artificial Intelligence, vol. 31 (2017)
48. Su, C., et al.: Biomedical discovery through the integrative biomedical knowledge hub (iBKH). iScience **26**(4) (2023)
49. Sun, W., Cai, Z., Li, Y., Liu, F., Fang, S., Wang, G.: Data processing and text mining technologies on electronic medical records: a review. J. Healthcare Eng. **2018** (2018)
50. Theodoropoulos, C., Mulligan, N., Stappenbeck, T., Bettencourt-Silva, J.: Representation learning for person or entity-centric knowledge graphs: an application in healthcare. In: Proceedings of the 12th Knowledge Capture Conference 2023, pp. 225–233 (2023)
51. Trouillon, T., Welbl, J., Riedel, S., Gaussier, É., Bouchard, G.: Complex embeddings for simple link prediction. In: International Conference on Machine Learning, pp. 2071–2080. PMLR (2016)
52. Vashishth, S., Sanyal, S., Nitin, V., Talukdar, P.: Composition-based multi-relational graph convolutional networks. In: International Conference on Learning Representations
53. Vasiljeva, I., Arandjelović, O.: Diagnosis prediction from electronic health records using the binary diagnosis history vector representation. J. Comput. Biol. **24**(8), 767–786 (2017)
54. Walker, S.E., Gray, S., Schmidt, B.: Stability of reconstituted indomethacin sodium trihydrate in original vials and polypropylene syringes. Am. J. Health Syst. Pharm. **55**(2), 154–158 (1998)

55. Wang, B., et al.: Pre-trained language models in biomedical domain: a systematic survey. ACM Comput. Surv. **56**(3), 1–52 (2023)
56. Webb, A.J., Werring, D.J.: New insights into cerebrovascular pathophysiology and hypertension. Stroke **53**(4), 1054–1064 (2022)
57. Wolff, J., et al.: Pharmacotherapy, drug-drug interactions and potentially inappropriate medication in depressive disorders. PLoS ONE **16**(7), e0255192 (2021)
58. Wu, J., Roy, J., Stewart, W.F.: Prediction modeling using EHR data: challenges, strategies, and a comparison of machine learning approaches. Med. Care **48**(6), S106–S113 (2010)
59. Wu, Y., et al.: Prediction of post-stroke AF in ESUS patients is enhanced by combining expert-derived predictors and embedding of full diagnostic codes using pre-trained hypergraph neural networks. In: STROKE. vol. 56. Lippincott Williams & Wilkins Two Commerce SQ, 2001 Market ST, Philadelphia ... (2025)
60. Xie, Y., et al.: KERAP: a knowledge-enhanced reasoning approach for accurate zero-shot diagnosis prediction using multi-agent LLMs. arXiv preprint arXiv:2507.02773 (2025)
61. Xie, Y., Lu, J., Ho, J., Nahab, F., Hu, X., Yang, C.: Promptlink: leveraging large language models for cross-source biomedical concept linking. In: Proceedings of the 47th International ACM SIGIR Conference on Research and Development in Information Retrieval, pp. 2589–2593 (2024)
62. Xie, Y., et al.: Abstract wp175: predicting post-stroke cognitive impairment (PSCI) using multiple machine learning approaches. Stroke **56**(Suppl_1), AWP175–AWP175 (2025)
63. Xie, Y., Niu, G., Da, Q., Dai, W., Yang, Y.: Survival prediction for gastric cancer via multimodal learning of whole slide images and gene expression. In: 2022 IEEE International Conference on Bioinformatics and Biomedicine (BIBM), pp. 1311–1316. IEEE (2022)
64. Xie, Y., et al.: Improving diagnosis and outcome prediction of gastric cancer via multimodal learning using whole slide pathological images and gene expression. Artif. Intell. Med. **152**, 102871 (2024)
65. Xu, D., Zhang, Z., Bethard, S.: A generate-and-rank framework with semantic type regularization for biomedical concept normalization. In: Proceedings of the 58th Annual Meeting of the Association for Computational Linguistics, pp. 8452–8464 (2020)
66. Xu, R., Ali, M.K., Ho, J.C., Yang, C.: Hypergraph transformers for EHR-based clinical predictions. AMIA Summits Transl. Sci. Proc. **2023**, 582 (2023)
67. Xu, R., Yu, Y., Zhang, C., Ali, M.K., Ho, J.C., Yang, C.: Counterfactual and factual reasoning over hypergraphs for interpretable clinical predictions on EHR. In: Machine Learning for Health, pp. 259–278. PMLR (2022)
68. Xu, Y., et al.: Seqcare: sequential training with external medical knowledge graph for diagnosis prediction in healthcare data. In: Proceedings of the ACM Web Conference 2023, pp. 2819–2830 (2023)
69. Yang, H., Lin, Z., Zhang, M.: Rethinking knowledge graph evaluation under the open-world assumption. Adv. Neural. Inf. Process. Syst. **35**, 8374–8385 (2022)
70. Yang, Y., Huang, C., Xia, L., Li, C.: Knowledge graph contrastive learning for recommendation. In: Proceedings of the 45th International ACM SIGIR Conference on Research and Development in Information Retrieval, pp. 1434–1443 (2022)
71. Ye, M., Cui, S., Wang, Y., Luo, J., Xiao, C., Ma, F.: Medpath: augmenting health risk prediction via medical knowledge paths. In: Proceedings of the Web Conference 2021, pp. 1397–1409 (2021)

72. Yu, Y., Zuo, S., Jiang, H., Ren, W., Zhao, T., Zhang, C.: Fine-tuning pre-trained language model with weak supervision: a contrastive-regularized self-training approach. In: Proceedings of the 2021 Conference of the North American Chapter of the Association for Computational Linguistics: Human Language Technologies, pp. 1063–1077 (2021)
73. Zhang, S., et al.: Knowledge-rich self-supervision for biomedical entity linking. In: Findings of the Association for Computational Linguistics: EMNLP 2022, pp. 868–880 (2022)
74. Zhang, Y., et al.: HKGB: an inclusive, extensible, intelligent, semi-auto-constructed knowledge graph framework for healthcare with clinicians' expertise incorporated. Inf. Process. Manag. **57**(6), 102324 (2020)
75. Zhang, Z., Cui, H., Xu, R., Xie, Y., Ho, J.C., Yang, C.: TACCO: task-guided co-clustering of clinical concepts and patient visits for disease subtyping based on EHR data. In: Proceedings of the 30th ACM SIGKDD Conference on Knowledge Discovery and Data Mining, pp. 6324–6334 (2024)

Graph Querying or Similarity Search? Both!

Vicente Calisto[1], Sebastián Ferrada[1,2,5(✉)], Gonzalo Navarro[1,3], Juan L. Reutter[1,4], Juan Pablo Sánchez[1,4], and Domagoj Vrgoč[1,4]

[1] Millennium Institute for Foundational Research on Data (IMFD), Santiago, Chile
vicente.calisto@imfd.c@uc.cl
[2] IDIA, Universidad de Chile, Santiago, Chile
{sebastian.ferrada,gnavarro}@uchile.cl
[3] DCC, Universidad de Chile, Santiago, Chile
[4] Pontificia Universidad Católica de Chile, Santiago, Chile
jreutter@ing.puc.cl, {jpsanchez,vrdomagoj}@uc.cl
[5] National Center for Artificial Intelligence Research (CENIA), Santiago, Chile

Abstract. Extracting information from knowledge graphs is a significant algorithmic challenge, especially when dealing with multimodal knowledge graphs that integrate images, text, and/or videos. While current graph management systems can efficiently evaluate graph queries, they struggle with multimedia data. To address this, systems rely on metadata, such as vector embeddings, for similarity search. While both graph pattern evaluation and similarity search work well independently, real-world applications often require their combination to retrieve media based on both the graph structure and specific similarity criteria.

This paper studies the problem of querying multimodal knowledge graphs by combining graph patterns with similarity constraints. We formalize this as an extraction task where some nodes in the graph pattern are filtered by similarity, and then the results must be ordered by a similarity score. While a straightforward approach is to evaluate the graph pattern first and then sort by similarity, we introduce alternative algorithms that evaluate both tasks jointly, leveraging indices for efficient similarity computation. Our implementation employs an approximate version of these indices, and our experiments show that graph database systems can efficiently integrate semantic similarity constraints into their queries.

1 Introduction

Similarity search plays a crucial role in Information Retrieval, Machine Learning, and Retrieval-Augmented Generation (RAG). It involves finding objects in a dataset that are *similar* to a given query, which is essential for document retrieval [7], recommendation systems [1], and pattern recognition [41] tasks. In RAG, similarity search enables the retrieval of knowledge relevant to the query to enhance generative models, leading to more accurate and contextually informed outputs [32]. Further, with the rise of vector representations of text, images, and

D. Garijo et al. (Eds.): ISWC 2025, LNCS 16140, pp. 349–368, 2026.
https://doi.org/10.1007/978-3-032-09527-5_19

```
SELECT ?tower ?img ?dist WHERE {
?tower wdt:P31/wdt:P279* wd:Q12518; wdt:P17 ?country; wdt:P18 ?img. ?country wdt:P361 wd:Q18.
wd:Q151356 :hasVector ?vector.
?img proc:hnswIterator ("vectorIndex" ?vector ?dist)
} LIMIT 10
```

Fig. 1. Query to get the S. American towers most similar to the Berlin TV Tower.

other media, the quest for efficient similarity search has become increasingly relevant for querying large-scale, high-dimensional data [8,13,22,26,55].

Knowledge Graphs (KGs) are structured representations of information where entities are connected through relationships. KGs facilitate complex queries, reasoning, and inferences [30]. KGs are used in semantic search [56], recommendation systems [24], and natural language processing [46], etc. In this work, we focus on Multimodal Knowledge Graphs (MKGs), where the base data remains in RDF, and other data modalities (such as images, text, or videos) are incorporated into the graph via precomputed vector embeddings. These embeddings are treated as additional attributes associated with RDF entities, allowing for more nuanced and expressive queries, where users may wish to retrieve subgraphs that satisfy structural constraints and exhibit similarity in vector spaces. Consequently, supporting similarity-aware querying in MKGs requires novel query semantics and evaluation strategies that go beyond traditional graph pattern matching or vector retrieval in isolation. Examples of MKGs include TIVA-KG [53], Richpedia [52], and IMGpedia [20].

In this paper, we investigate the problem of how to efficiently evaluate a graph pattern query Q over an MKG G while also imposing a similarity-based restriction on the results. Specifically, the query results $Q(G)$ must be sorted by the distance of the vectors associated with the bindings of a fixed variable in Q and an input vector or with the vector associated with a given entity $a \in G$. We are mostly interested in the case when the k best answers are wanted. The integration of graph pattern matching with similarity search introduces new computational challenges, including efficiently combining the two tasks and leveraging existing indices for optimization, presenting new opportunities for improving query evaluation strategies in MKGs. Furthermore, such techniques have broader applications, such as improving KG-based RAG [39] by incorporating both graph structure and similarity constraints into the retrieval process.

For instance, consider combining Wikidata [48], a large KG with structured information about various domains, and IMGpedia [20], an MKG that links Wikimedia Commons images and their corresponding embeddings to Wikidata entities. Suppose we want to retrieve images of communication towers in South America that are visually similar to an image of the Berlin TV Tower. To achieve this, we first construct a graph pattern query Q that identifies entities classified as "tower" (`wd:Q12518`) and located in South America (`wd:Q18`). Next, we apply a similarity condition to the images of these towers, requiring them to be among the 10-nearest neighbors of the Berlin TV Tower's image in Wikimedia Commons (`wd:Q151356`) based on their embeddings from IMGpedia. This approach

Index	0	1	2	3	4	5	6	7	8	9	10
?image											
?sim	1.0	0.763	0.727	0.727	0.722	0.717	0.710	0.708	0.708	0.703	0.702

Fig. 2. Results of evaluating the query from Fig. 1 over Wikidata.

```
SELECT ?pact (COUNT(?twt) AS ?nb) (AVG(?dist) AS ?mean) WHERE {
 ?member telar:hasAccount ?account ;
      telar:politicalGroupConvention ?pact.
 ?twt telar:postedBy ?account ; telar:createdAt ?date .
 FILTER(?date>="2022-02-17T02:51:20"
     && ?date<="2022-02-17T14:51:20")
 telar:twp_1494142390663360512 :hasVector ?vector
 ?twt proc:hsnwIterator ( "tweets_sbert" ?vector ?dist )
} GROUP BY ?pact
```

?pact	?nb	?mean
Frente Amplio	95	0.50
Partido Comunista	41	0.51
Vamos por Chile	27	0.64
UDI	11	0.68

Fig. 3. Query searching for polarization on opinions about regionalization.

allows us to retrieve 254 images of towers that match the graph pattern and, from them, the 10 most similar to the Berlin TV Tower. Fig. 1 illustrates how we express this example query using our own SPARQL extension with similarity indices and vectors. In our solution, RDF triplestores are extended with a special vector literal with a datatype that appears in the object position. The similarity part of the query is expressed using the `proc:hnswIterator` clause, which must receive as input the vector embedding of the image of the Berlin TV Tower (`wd:Q151356`), which is achieved through the predicate `:hasVector`. This clause mandates that similar items are to be extracted through an HNSW vector index [33] Fig. 2 contains the final 10 images of the answer.

Our setting also allows for similarity searches w.r.t. an input vector instead of a node in the KG. This problem appears continuously in the context of RAG. For example, consider a user searching for political discourses in Congress, asking for a summary of interventions on climate change. Using a RAG-based approach, we can store the vector embedding of each discourse in Congress at indexing time and use the same embedding model to embed the query "summary of discussions about climate change" at query time. Then, we retrieve the 10 most similar interventions and passed them to an LLM for summarization. Now, suppose the user asks for a "summary of discussions about climate change by congresspeople over 60." Here, a standard RAG approach might not work as intended since it could retrieve interventions from younger members of Congress. By leveraging a KG, we could first filter members of Congress over 60, ensuring only their interventions are considered. Then, we can retrieve the 10 most similar discourses from this filtered set, refining the search before passing the results to the LLM.

As a final example, we use TelarKG [2], an MKG of the Chilean constitutional process enriched with S-BERT [44] embeddings for convention members' social media posts and interventions. We query it to retrieve the members' opinions on regionalization, based on a seed neutral tweet, and compute their average similarity by political pact. The query combines graph patterns (linking members, posts, and pacts) with vector similarity over text. Figure 3 shows the query and select results, revealing the expected ideological polarization of opinions.

In this paper, we design algorithms to evaluate these queries jointly. We compare our algorithms to a *query-and-select* baseline, which first evaluates the graph pattern and then selects the results with the shortest distances. Notably, our algorithms offer theoretical guarantees in a combined setting: they are worst-case optimal in the number of results and range-optimal in distance computations. We also provide a complete implementation of our approach on top of an existing open-source SPARQL engine [35]. Experiments show that our algorithms significantly accelerate MKG query answering with broad applicability.

Before detailing our algorithms (Sects. 5–6), we cover related work (Sect. 2), preliminaries (Sect. 3), and the problem statement (Sect. 4). Implementation and evaluation are in Sects. 7–8, and conclusions in Sect. 9.

2 Related Work

The problem of retrieving objects based on nearest neighbors has recently received a lot of attention in the context of Vector Databases, which are systems built specifically for obtaining the nearest neighbors of (embeddings of) objects. For more information on the latest advances in the area, we refer to the survey by Pan et al. [38]. Notably, some of these systems allow for *filtered similarity search*, wherein users can input certain filter conditions together with the input vector, and the system retrieves only the nearest neighbors that satisfy the filter conditions [19,23,25,40,51]. Further, ChromaDB [15], a popular vector database, has specified a formal language to carry out these operations: here documents have JSON metadata, and filter conditions refer to the presence of certain values in this metadata. For example, one writes `{gender: female}` to ask only for documents where the `gender` metadata corresponds to `female`. We note that our problem is more general, as filter conditions can be expressed as triple patterns over KGs, but complex graph queries cannot be transferred to filter conditions unless precomputed at indexing time, which is not compatible with the idea that systems should support evaluating any possible pattern with similarity. Moreover, Vector Databases normally use a version of one of our algorithms (Iterate-and-Query, see Algorithm 3) to evaluate filtered similarity search, and hence studying other options for solving filtered similarity search should also be of interest to Vector Databases implementing this feature.

We are aware of only two systems that support answering graph queries based on similarity conditions of an arbitrary vector, which is the focus of this paper: MillenniumDB [49,50], the database system we use as the framework to experiment with, and pgvector [42], a Vector Database built as a PostgreSQL component that allows answering a subset of SQL queries based on similarity constraints. Using the formalization of the problem that we provide in this paper, we see that these systems evaluate queries using the baseline that we present in Sect. 5. Interestingly, the need for more efficient algorithms to answer queries based on similarity conditions has already been stated by contributors of pgvector [17]. We expect our work to guide future contributions to these systems and pave the path for more systems supporting similarity search in MKGs.

Lastly, Arroyuelo et al. study query answering where patterns feature similarity conditions between variables [3]. This work relies on precomputed indices for processing similarity conditions and hence does not support querying for arbitrary input vectors. Likewise, previous work on MKGs (e.g., [20,52,53]) does not efficiently support queries with arbitrary vectors not present in the KG.

3 Preliminaries

RDF and SPARQL. RDF [16] is the standard graph data model for the Semantic Web. RDF terms can be either IRIs ($\mathcal{I}$), literal values ($\mathcal{L}$), or blank nodes ($\mathcal{B}$). An RDF triple is a tuple $(s, p, o) \in \mathcal{IB} \times \mathcal{I} \times \mathcal{IBL}$. An RDF Graph is a finite set of RDF triples. The fundamental querying primitives in SPARQL [27] are Basic Graph Patterns (BGPs). Let $\mathcal{V}$ be a universe of variables disjoint from $\mathcal{IBL}$. A BGP Q is a set of triple patterns $(x, y, z) \in \mathcal{IV} \times \mathcal{IV} \times \mathcal{ILV}$. The output $Q(G)$ of the BGP when evaluated in a graph G is a set of solution mappings μ, where $\mu : \mathcal{V} \cup \mathcal{I} \to \mathcal{I}$ is an assignment such that for each triple pattern $(x, y, z) \in Q$, it holds that $(\mu(x), \mu(y), \mu(z)) \in G$, where $\mu(x) = x$ for all $x \in \mathcal{I} \cup \mathcal{L}$. We denote as $\mathsf{vars}(Q)$ the set of variables appearing in the triple patterns of Q.

Worst-Case-Optimal Joins. The *AGM bound* [5] establishes the maximum output size of a join query. This bound can also be applied to graph patterns by regarding each triple pattern as a relation formed by the triples matching its constants [31]. Formally, the AGM bound of a query Q over a graph database G, denoted as $Q^*(G)$, or just Q^* if G is understood from context, is the maximum size $Q(G')$ could have over any database instance G' with at most the number of edges in G. An algorithm to process queries is *worst-case optimal (wco)* if it has a running time in $\tilde{O}(Q^*)$, where $\tilde{O}$ ignores polylogs and data-independent factors. In this paper, we use Leapfrog TrieJoin (LTJ), which was shown to be worst-case optimal for any join query, including graph patterns, by Veldhuizen [47].

Similarity Search. Similarity search over a set of objects $\mathcal{D}$ from a universe $\mathcal{U}$ relies on a similarity score, the higher the score, the more similar the objects are. Similarity scores are often measured as distances. Given a *distance function* $\delta : \mathcal{U} \times \mathcal{U} \to \mathbb{R}_0^+$, smaller distances indicate greater similarity.

A common similarity task is the search for the k *nearest neighbors* in $\mathcal{D}$ of a query object $q \in \mathcal{U}$, which are k elements of $\mathcal{D}$ that are closest to q w.r.t. distance δ. Formally, the problem is to find the set k-NN(q) such that $q \notin k$-NN(q), $|k\text{-NN}(q)| = k$, and $\forall x \in k\text{-NN}(q), \forall y \in \mathcal{D} \setminus k\text{-NN}(q), y \neq q$, $\delta(q, x) \leq \delta(q, y)$.

A naive search algorithm computes the distance from q to all $x \in \mathcal{D}$; computing $n = |\mathcal{D}|$ distances. To reduce the cost, objects in $\mathcal{D}$ can be *indexed* to prune objects that are too far from q without computing their distance to q. In *metric spaces*, the triangle inequality $\delta(x, y) \leq \delta(x, q) + \delta(q, y)$ is used to prune distance computations, so that if we compute $\delta(q, x)$ and the index knows a bound $\delta(x, y) \geq d$, we know that $\delta(q, y) \geq d - \delta(q, x)$ and might avoid computing it. Some relaxations of the triangle inequality can be used for non-metric spaces.

Several indices exist for metric spaces [45,55], including the particular case where the space is $\mathbb{R}^d$ and the distance function is an L_p metric, where a famous example is the R-tree [26], which works well for low values of d; its analogous for general metric spaces is the M-tree [13]. Most indices are designed to solve *range queries*, which, given $q \in \mathcal{U}$ and $r > 0$, return all $x \in \mathcal{D}$ such that $\delta(q, x) \leq r$. k-NN queries can be solved on those indices in various ways, for example, with a sequence of range searches with increasing values of r until k or more elements are retrieved. There are also solutions that backtrack on the index, looking for the k elements closest to q. We call those solutions *KNN indices*.

A well-known technique [28,29] that works on hierarchical indices (like the R-tree) keeps a *priority queue* with the maximal nodes of the hierarchy yet to be traversed, sorted by a lower bound on the distance from q to any object in the node. The algorithm iterates, extracting the first node from the queue and reinserting its children in the queue; leaves of the index insert objects in the queue, computing their distance to q. Objects extracted from the queue are reported at once; it can be seen that the first k reported objects are k-NN(q).

An important property of this technique is that it is *range-optimal*. It finds k-NN(q) with the same number of distance computations the index would use to compute a range search that retrieves those k objects. Further, this method is *incremental*: it successively retrieves the next closest element to q, so we obtain k-NN(q) by stopping after k objects are retrieved, but we can also use it as an iterator that yields the next closest element to q. We call this operation $next_{\mathcal{D}}(q)$, and call *INN* those indices supporting this incremental search.

On *high-dimensional* spaces (where the histogram of δ is very concentrated), indices may fail to avoid performing many distance computations. This is called the *curse of dimensionality*. A way to measure the *intrinsic* dimensionality of a dataset in a metric space is $\mu^2/(2\sigma^2)$, where μ and σ^2 are the mean and variance of the histogram of δ [11], which is $\Theta(d)$ on random vectors in the $(\mathbb{R}^d, L_p)$ metric space. An extreme example is the distance $\delta(x, x) = 0$ for all x and $\delta(x, y) = 1 + \epsilon(x, y)$ for all $y \neq x$, where $\epsilon(x, y) \ll 1$ is a random value; it is impossible to save any distance computation in this space. In general, an intrinsic dimension over 20 is considered to be intractable.

In those high-dimensional spaces, finding an *approximation* to k-NN(q) may be acceptable because modeling similarity with distance functions is already an approximation to the desired answers. A good approximation may offer much lower search costs at the expense of a small difference between the correct and the returned set k-NN(q). There exist various algorithms to compute k-NN(q) approximately on L_p metrics, with various sorts of guarantees [4,43,54], as well as with no approximation guarantees but performing well in practice [8,22]. Some techniques for general metric spaces offer probabilistic approximation guarantees [12,14], while others offer no guarantees but perform well in practice [10].

Cost Model. In range or nearest-neighbor searches, the number of evaluations of the distance δ dominates all the other CPU costs; thus, it is customary to count only the number of evaluations of δ. This is not the case in our problem: solving graph patterns involves a significant CPU cost, which can be superlinear on the database size, whereas the number of evaluations of δ is at most linear. For this reason, we describe the time complexities of algorithms as a pair $\langle c, e \rangle$, where e is the number of evaluations of δ and c includes all other CPU costs.

4 Top-*k* Graph Similarity Search

Let us now formally introduce the problem we study in the paper. We assume our MKG G includes a vector store τ, which assigns vector embeddings to some (or all) nodes in G. For a node b in G, $\tau(b)$ represents its vector embedding. We assume a distance function δ to measure the similarity among the vectors in τ. Additionally, τ is indexed to support incremental search for the nearest neighbors of a given vector t, which we denote as $\text{next}_\tau(t)$.

With these definitions, we want to allow users to add a similarity clause to graph patterns. Recall that $Q(G)$ denotes the evaluation of a graph pattern Q over an MKG G. Let $x \in \mathsf{vars}(Q)$ be a fixed variable. We call (Q, x) a graph similarity pattern. Note that we can write the tuples in $Q(G)$ as $(\bar{a}, b)$, where b is the element bound to x and $\bar{a}$ are the elements bound to the variables in $\mathsf{vars}(Q) \setminus \{x\}$. Now, we select the tuples from $Q(G)$ that have the lowest value for $\delta(t, \tau(b))$: the distance from an input vector t to $\tau(b)$. Particularly, we want the k-best answers from $Q(G)$ (handling ties in any way). The problem Top-k Graph Similarity Search (or k-GSS) consists of finding such k best answers to an arbitrary graph similarity pattern w.r.t. their distance to an arbitrary vector:

Top-k Graph Similarity Search (k-GSS)	
Given:	Graph G, distance function δ, vector store τ.
Input:	Graph pattern (Q, x) with similarity, vector t and integer k.
Output:	k best answers $(\bar{a}, b) \in Q(G)$, ordered by $\delta(t, \tau(b))$

Revisiting the query from Fig. 1, the input graph pattern is stated in a `WHERE` clause. The last triple pattern sets `?img` as the variable that is subject to similarity, and the vector bound to `?vector` is given as the embedding of node `wd:Q151356`. `?dist` is the fresh variable to which the distance from the vector of `?img` and `?vector` is bound. As discussed in Sect. 7, the `proc:hsnwIterator` function supports both user-provided vectors (`type:tensorFloat` constants) and vectors retrieved from the MKG (e.g., the embedding of a given node).

5 A First Baseline: Query-and-Select

A naive algorithm for k-GSS is to (1) evaluate Q over G, (2) compute $\delta(t, \tau(b))$ for each $(\bar{a}, b) \in Q(G)$, and (3) select those with the k shortest distances.

Algorithm 1. Baseline k-GSS via query-and-select

Require: Graph G, distance δ, vector store τ, Query (Q, x), vector t and integer k
Ensure: Top k answers $(\bar{a}, b) \in Q(G)$, ordered by $\delta(t, \tau(b))$
  Ans $\leftarrow Q(G)$ ▷ using some wco algorithm
  for $(\bar{a}, b)$ in **Ans** **do**
    associate with $(\bar{a}, b)$ the value $dist = \delta(t, \tau(b))$.
  end for
  $d \leftarrow$ the kth smallest $dist$ value in **Ans**
  OAns $\leftarrow$ k tuples $(\bar{a}, b) \in$ **Ans** with $dist \leq d$
  Return OAns

This procedure is outlined in Algorithm 1. The computation of d can be done with any classic linear-time algorithm for computing quantiles. If there are ties in the distances, the k tuples are selected as follows: in a first pass over **Ans**, we report the tuples $(\bar{a}, b)$ with $dist < d$. Say we reported $k' < k$ tuples in this pass; then, in a second pass, we report the first $k - k'$ tuples with $dist = d$.[1]

This algorithm can be pipelined using a max-priority queue P with the k tuples $(\bar{a}, b)$ with the smallest $dist$ values seen so far. For each new tuple $(\bar{a}, b)$ found by the wco algorithm, we compute $dist = \delta(t, \tau(b))$ and, if $dist < \max(P)$, we extract the maximum of P (if $|P| = k$) and insert $(\bar{a}, b)$. Despite the $O(\log k)$ extra CPU time per tuple in $Q(G)$, this version likely performs better in practice.

Overall, this query-and-select algorithm takes time $\tilde{O}(Q^*)$ to compute $Q(G)$, then it performs $|Q(G)|$ distance computations, and finally it spends $O(|Q(G)|) \subseteq O(Q^*)$ (or $O(|Q(G)| \log k) \subseteq \tilde{O}(Q^*)$ if pipelined) time to compute d and find the k smallest distances. Its time complexity, using our model, is then $\langle \tilde{O}(Q^*), |Q(G)| \rangle$.

An advantage of this algorithm is its simplicity, not needing any KNN index. However, it must find *all* the results in $Q(G)$, which may be prohibitive for queries with many results. Further, it requires computing the distance of the vector t to *every* query result. Notably, its time complexity is essentially independent of k, unlike most KNN indices that perform better on smaller k.

Throughout the paper, we assume the use of a wco join algorithm for the graph query evaluation to analyze the theoretical cost of our methods. We acknowledge that such algorithms are not currently adopted in many existing graph database systems. Nevertheless, we emphasize that our algorithms are compatible with other join strategies as well; while doing so may forgo the theoretical guarantees, the usefulness of the algorithms is preserved.

Next, we explore algorithms that compute k-GSS faster, especially for small values of k. We also consider combining the wco algorithm with approximate KNN indices to further speed up queries at the cost of slight result degradation.

[1] Even if all the distances to t are distinct, there can be many tuples $(\bar{a}, b)$ for the same value of b, and they will all appear in **Ans**.

Algorithm 2. k-GSS via query-and-iterate

Require: Graph G, distance d and indexed vector store τ, $next_\tau()$
Require: Query (Q, x), vector t and integer k
Ensure: Top k answers $(\bar{a}, b) \in Q(G)$, ordered by $\delta(t, \tau(b))$

```
Ans ← Q(G)                                              ▷ using some wco algorithm
H ← dictionary of tuples (ā, b) ∈ Ans with b acting as key
OAns ← ∅
for each next element b = next_τ(t) do
    if b is a key in H then
        Add to OAns every tuple of the form (ā, b) ∈ Ans
        if |OAns| ≥ k then
            Return OAns capped to the first k tuples
        end if
    end if
end for
Return OAns                                             ▷ if less than k results
```

6 Combining Wco and KNN Search

In this section, we provide alternatives to the query-and-select algorithm. These alternatives combine a wco algorithm for the graph pattern with INN indices that support incremental KNN searches from t in our vector store τ via the iterator $next_\tau(t)$ described in the Preliminaries. Both searches are integrated into a single algorithm. For the analysis, we assume the INN algorithm is range-optimal.

6.1 Query-and-Iterate

The first algorithm we explore uses an INN to reduce the $|Q(G)|$ distance evaluations computed by query-and-select. It is most useful when the number of answers to the query, $|Q(G)|$, is large. As before, we first compute $Q(G)$, but instead of probing each result, we repeatedly use $next_\tau(t)$ to find the next neighbor of t. Each such neighbor is looked up in $Q(G)$ until k of them are found. Lookup can be implemented, for example, with a hash table for tuples $(\overline{a}, b) \in Q(G)$, with b acting as the hash key. This method is described in Algorithm 2.

Let d be the distance to the k-th nearest neighbor of t that occurs in $Q(G)$, we define $R(d) = \{b \mid \delta(t, \tau(b)) \leq d\}$ as the set of elements in the vector store up to the farthest element to t we answer. A range-optimal INN computes the required distances (for the specific index) to find $R(d)$; we call this number $D(d) \leq |Q(G)|$. Let us assume its CPU cost is within $\tilde{O}(D(d)) \subseteq \tilde{O}(Q^*)$, which is mostly the case. This includes the hash table search time.[2] Then, we immediately obtain:

Proposition 1. *the complexity of Algorithm 2 is* $\langle \tilde{O}(Q^*), D(d) \rangle$

[2] To obtain worst-case search times, we can use instead binary search on a sorted array, whose construction and searches are still within $\tilde{O}(|Q(G)|) \subseteq \tilde{O}(Q^*)$.

Algorithm 3. Approximate k-GSS via Iterate-and-query

Require: Graph G, distance d and indexed vector store τ, $next_\tau()$
Require: Query (Q, x), vector t and integer k
Ensure: Top k answers $(\bar{a}, b) \in Q(G)$, ordered by $\delta(t, \tau(b))$

```
OAns ← ∅
for each next element b = next_τ(t) do
    Ans(b) ← Q_{x=b}(G)                      ▷ using some wco algorithm
    Add Ans(b) to OAns
    if |OAns| ≥ k then
        Return OAns capped to the first k tuples
    end if
end for
Return OAns                                   ▷ if less than k results
```

This is a considerable reduction in the number of distance evaluations w.r.t. the query-and-select algorithm.

6.2 Iterate-and-Query

Our second proposal aims to reduce CPU time by working the other way around: we begin by iterating over $next_\tau(t)$ to retrieve the next-nearest neighbor of t. For each such neighbor b, we run a restricted query $Q_{x=b}$, where the variable x is replaced with the constant b. This method is detailed in Algorithm 3. It is most useful when the query Q is complex and produces many results.

Let us define $Q_{x \in R(d)}(G) \subseteq Q(G)$ as the set of answers in $Q(G)$ where x is restricted to be in $R(d)$. We show:

Proposition 2. *The time complexity of Algorithm 3 is* $\langle \tilde{O}(Q^*_{x \in R(d)}), D(d) \rangle$

Proof. The worst-case size of the output satisfies $Q^*_{x \in R(d)} \leq Q^*$. A wco algorithm that handles the query $Q' = Q \bowtie U$, where U is a unary relation with the attribute x and the rows $R(d)$, works in time $\tilde{O}(Q^*_{x \in R(d)})$. We do not proceed in this way but instead invoke the wco algorithm with $Q_{x=b}$ for each $b \in R(d)$. By Friedgut's inequality [36] it holds that: $Q^*_{x \in R(d)} \geq \sum_{b \in R(d)} Q^*_{x=b}$. The time complexity of this algorithm is then $\langle \tilde{O}(Q^*_{x \in R(d)}), D(d) \rangle$.

Although worst-case time complexities always favor iterate-and-query over query-and-iterate, actual wco algorithms may require more work to compute $Q_{x=b}(G)$ for many values of b than to compute the whole $Q(G)$. Which way works better in practice depends on this relation. A tradeoff can be obtained by evaluating in batches: for each batch $B = b_1, \ldots b_\ell$ of consecutive near neighbors returned by $next_\tau(t)$, we run the query $Q_{x \in B}$, by treating B as a unary relation associated with variable $x \in \mathsf{vars}(Q)$. The worst-case analysis stays as for the non-batched version, except that we may extract up to $R(d) + \ell$ elements from the INN (in exchange for packing the candidates into fewer queries).

7 Implementation

Algorithm 1 can be implemented on top of any existing graph database system that has a vector store by defining a new operator allowing the computation of distances to a fixed vector. In contrast, implementing Algorithms 2 and 3 requires the coordination of two components: a graph database management system with support for vectors and an INN. Practical applications such as RAG impose considerable strain on the query throughput, so we resort to ANN indices, which are faster (though less precise) and widely available in popular vector databases. We use MillenniumDB [35] for both components, a multimodal graph database supporting RDF/SPARQL which extends RDF with a vector datatype allowing to store vectors as literals. In MillenniumDB we store vectors as literals in triples, using a special datatype to denote it is a vector. Regarding queries, the engine uses Leapfrog Trie-Join (LTJ) [47] as the wco algorithm to compute the answers of graph patterns, and HNSW [33] to implement the ANN index. Naturally, these two components work independently, and thus, another implementation may use other approaches for query processing or for vector retrieval. All storage and retrieval of data is achieved through the standard disk-buffer architecture, meaning that the database is fully persistent.

Query-and-Select. Implementation of Algorithm 1 in MillenniumDB uses LTJ. As results are produced, we compute the distance to the specified vector t and keep a priority queue of size k, storing the most similar results seen so far. After evaluating Q, the queue contains the final output as described in Sect. 5.

Query-and-Iterate. For Algorithm 2, the dictionary H used to probe for query tuples is built using extendable hashing [21] (which is buffered to disk as needed). LTJ populates this table as it produces results. We also build an iterator on top of MillenniumDB's ANN index by extending the classical top-k querying for HNSW [33] with the ability to iterate over all the vectors in decreasing order of similarity to a fixed vector. As we iterate through the elements most similar to our query vector t, we probe H until the k most similar results are found.

Iterate-and-Query. To implement Algorithm 3, we modify the variable ordering of Leapfrog Trie-Join so that it starts with variable x (which is the one subject to similarity search). When instantiating this variable, we iterate over all possible assignments for it using the ANN index instead of using the database indices in MillenniumDB. Our implementation explicitly alters the variable ordering of LTJ, which is known to be important for performance [37]. As we assume $R(d)$ to be much smaller than the number of nodes in the graph, it should be the case that starting with variable x leads to a better performance.

Query Language. MillenniumDB fully supports SPARQL. We designed and implemented a SPARQL extension in MillenniumDB to add similarity search clauses. Our extension offers support for the following four new capabilities:

1. *Vector datatype.* As already mentioned, we implement a vector datatype that can be used in RDF triples. A sample syntactic specification of a vector of length 3 is `"[1,2,3]"^^type:tensorFloat`.
2. *Distance functions.* We implement special functions to calculate similarity between vectors using common distance functions. For example, the function call `fn:manhattanDistance(?vector, "[1,2,3,4]"^^type:tensorFloat)` computes the Manhattan distance between the vector stored in `?vector` and the vector `[1,2,3,4]`. We currently support several standard distance functions, such as the Manhattan and Euclidean metrics.
3. *HNSW iterators.* To support iterative algorithms, we also extend the HNSW index with the ability to return all the vectors in the vector store sorted by (approximate) distance from a fixed vector. For this, we implement the procedure: `proc:hnswIterator("index" vector ?distance)`. This procedure returns *graph nodes* in decreasing order of distance to `vector` in the HNSW index called `index` and binds this distance to `?distance`. In contrast to traditional HNSW iterators [33], which only return top-k nodes, to support our algorithms, we need to potentially iterate over all the nodes in the graph.

We now illustrate how to use these capabilities. Let us say we wish to retrieve 100 people most similar to Geoffrey Hinton, who also won a Turing Award. The following query expresses this using the HNSW iterator from item 3 above. Note that the nodes returned by `proc:hnswIterator` are bound to variable `?person`.

```
SELECT ?person ?dist WHERE {
  ?person :won :Turing_Award . :Geoffrey_Hinton :hasVector ?vector.
  ?person proc:hnswIterator("indexName" vector ?dist)
} LIMIT 100
```

Our language also supports the Query-and-Select algorithm, and also the classical HNSW method to retrieve the top-k most similar nodes. For space reasons we do not show the corresponding SPARQL queries, but they will be made avaliable as part of the documentation of our code.

8 Experimental Results

In this section, we see how our algorithms perform against the Query-and-Select baseline. Regarding query time, we expect to confirm the hypothesis that Algorithms 2 and 3 are better suited than the baseline for computing top-k queries for small k. Furthermore, we also expect our variants to thrive on queries with high selectivity, especially when running over limited time constraints. We also believe it is important to study the selectivity thresholds that mandate when to use one algorithm over the others, as this has a direct impact on the development of fully-fledged query engines looking for the best plan to evaluate each query.

In our implementation, we focus on speed by relying on ANN indices. Hence, as we cannot guarantee the retrieval of all the nearest neighbors of a vector, another natural question is how our alternatives compare to the baseline regarding the quality of the answers retrieved by the approximate methods. In summary, in this section, we use our experiments to answer the following questions:

Q1: How much faster can Algorithms 2 and 3 be for solving k-GSS in practice?
Q2: For increasing values of k, when does the baseline become a better algorithm? Regarding the number of answers, what is the selectivity range where our alternatives perform better?
Q3: How does the ANN version of Query-and-Iterate and Iterate-and-Query compare to the baseline in terms of the quality of the answers?

8.1 Data

For our experiments, we used the combined RDF graphs of Wikidata and IMGpedia. IMGpedia is an MKG that provides embeddings for 15 million images from Wikimedia Commons and also links each image to its related entities in Wikidata [20]. We use a truthy dump of Wikidata containing 617,065,092 triples.

Regarding queries, we mine them from a Wikidata query log [9,34]. We select all queries with nonempty results that involve an image (e.g., by using predicate `wdt:P18`) that has an available embedding in IMGpedia. We extract only the BGPs in these queries. Each of these real-world BGPs is transformed into a similarity pattern by selecting a random variable in the BGP that we know (from Wikidata's ontology) must be mapped to an image, selecting a random node from the answer of this BGP, and constructing a similarity clause for this variable and the vector of this node. We produced 200 queries.

In terms of similarity, we sampled a million random pairs of vectors from the HOG vectors in IMGpedia (192 dimensions). We obtain an estimated mean Manhattan (L_1) distance of 42.6, and a standard deviation of 8.1. This gives us an intrinsic dimensionality of 13.8, which is at the higher end of the tractable range, further justifying the choice of ANNs for our implementation.

8.2 Setup

We use the implementation described in Sect. 7 (see [35]). The experiments were run on a commodity server (Intel(R) Xeon(R) Silver 4110 CPU @ 2.10 GHz and 118 GB of RAM, Devuan Chimaera 4.0). MillenniumDB used 48 GB of RAM for buffering and single-threaded execution. OS caches were cleared between the algorithm versions, but remained hot within the runs. This means that each batch of queries is run in succession for a specific algorithm and similarity restriction, but caches are cleaned when switching versions. Queries have a timeout of 1 min; only results found within that time are reported. The HNSW index [33] was built with $m = 48$ edges and $efConstruction = 256$.

8.3 Query Evaluation Time

Figure 4 shows the average execution time over all queries in our benchmark. As expected, the smaller the value of k, the better our algorithms perform. On average, Query-and-Iterate shows only a slight advantage for top-1 queries, while Iterate-and-Query shows an advantage for up to top-50 queries. This already gives a direct answer to **Q1**, as Iterate-and-Query seems an obvious alternative to use in cases where $k < 50$. However, the running time of our algorithms depends heavily on the selectivity of these queries, so we look into this.

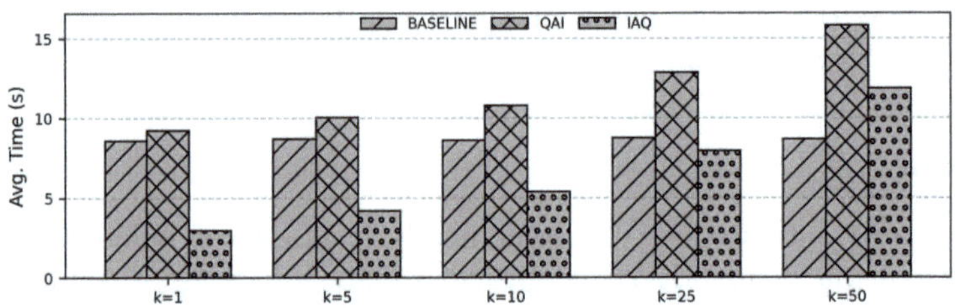

Fig. 4. Running time of Query-and-Select (baseline), Query-and-Iterate (QAI) and Iterate-and-Query (IAQ). Average overall queries in the benchmark.

From our analysis on selectivity, an important shortcoming of the Query-and-Select baseline is that it requires computing the distances between all the $|Q(G)|$ answers of the pattern and the input vector, whereas both Query-and-Iterate and Iterate-and-Query require an optimal (when using INNs) number of computations, which we call $R(d)$. Hence, the larger the number of answers, the more unnecessary computations are made by the baseline. Further, we also expect Iterate-and-Query to use far less processing time (compared to the baseline) when $R(d)$ is smaller than $|Q(G)|$: this is because we are specifically starting LTJ with the variable subject to similarity. This is a good idea if $R(d)$ is small compared to the selectivity of other variables, but it can be a poor choice if other variables provide much stricter selectivity. This fact does not show up in the wco bounds, and hence, it was not predicted by the theory.

To verify these claims experimentally, we partition the 200 queries in the benchmark into deciles w.r.t. the number of answers of the underlying graph pattern in each query and compute the proportion of time taken by Iterate-and-Query and Query-and-Select, as well as Query-and-Iterate and the baseline. Results in Table 1 show a striking difference in the running time of algorithms depending on the selectivity of the graph patterns. For queries with low selectivity (i.e., **D8–D10**), Iterate-and-Query can be up to 50x faster than the baseline. On the other hand, this is reversed in the higher-selectivity deciles, with fewer answers ($< 4,000$). In these cases, it is conceivable that the database is better off computing these 4,000 answers and then ordering them by similarity than traversing the index. This analysis also explains why Query-and-Iterate exhibits the worst performance on average: in **D8–D10**, where these algorithms shine the most, Query-and-Iterate still has the overhead of processing hundreds of thousands of tuples into a hash join, which slows down the process. With this experiment, we answer **Q2**: for the settings in our server, the selectivity threshold of queries for using Iterate-and-Query is over 248,000 expected answers.

One important observation from Table 1 is that query selectivity in our dataset is highly skewed, with 7 deciles having fewer than 4000 answers. Remarkably, even though 70% of queries are extremely selective, the running time of Iterate-and-Query (IAQ) remains competitive up to $k = 25$. This highlights the inefficiency of Query-and-Select under low selectivity. Assuming an oracle that predicts the decile of each query, combining Query-and-Select and IAQ would reduce the average running time for $k = 25$ to around 2.5 s, a 66% improvement over IAQ alone, currently the best option (see Fig. 4).

On average, the baseline takes 0.1 s for queries in **D1–D7** and up to 130 min for queries in **D8–D10**. IAQ is slightly slower on smaller queries (0.8s on **D1–D7**), but remains fast as size grows (8s on **D8–D10**).

Table 1. Proportion of median time taken by Query-and-Select (baseline), Query-and-Iterate (QAI), and Iterate-and-Query (IAQ), grouped over deciles of 20 queries, sorted by number of answers. **MNA** is the median number of answers to the queries in each decile.

		Time: IAQ/baseline					Time: QAI/baseline				
D.	MNA	$k = 1$	$k = 5$	$k = 10$	$k = 25$	$k = 50$	$k = 1$	$k = 5$	$k = 10$	$k = 25$	$k = 50$
1	459	16.31	132.38	302.82	861.22	1438.98	19.22	115.97	254.32	761.39	1219.95
2	793	6.84	23.19	37.82	58.12	130.14	7.13	20.33	33.45	49.12	106.28
3	976	5.90	17.48	35.34	107.01	173.68	6.78	12.22	15.16	36.86	71.53
4	1,303	9.05	19.55	25.51	80.80	216.00	9.79	18.62	22.85	70.08	178.57
5	1,606	26.62	47.63	84.57	174.20	248.96	24.05	38.22	68.28	141.47	195.50
6	2,095	45.99	64.58	80.71	189.45	333.63	42.45	55.39	69.84	164.54	293.63
7	3,186	17.10	44.34	79.40	145.64	291.32	16.98	39.58	73.97	124.71	242.92
8	248,004	**0.79**	1.08	1.67	2.76	4.59	1.01	1.48	2.70	3.38	3.21
9	2,572,812	**0.02**	**0.02**	**0.02**	**0.02**	**0.02**	**0.91**	**0.91**	**0.91**	**0.87**	1.08
10	7,625,570	**0.03**	**0.03**	**0.03**	**0.03**	**0.03**	1.20	1.17	1.21	1.19	1.19

8.4 Quality of the Approximated Methods

In this section, we answer **Q3** by measuring the distance between the answers retrieved by our (ANN-based) implementation of Algorithms 2 and 3 and the ground truth baseline. We remark that these results mostly depend on the choice of ANN index: the more precise the index, the better the quality of the answers. Nevertheless, the results we obtain for the HNSW index in MillenniumDB reveal a trend that should be common to any implementation that uses similar indices [6].

To evaluate the quality of the answers of our algorithms, we measure the percentage of correct k-NN objects found relative to the baseline. In this context, this percentage reflects both precision and recall. Figure 5 presents the precision distribution per algorithm and per value of k. QAI has a mean average precision (MAP) of 27.5%, while IAQ reaches 28.5%. As shown in the figure, precision increases with larger values of k, which is expected since, for smaller k, a single

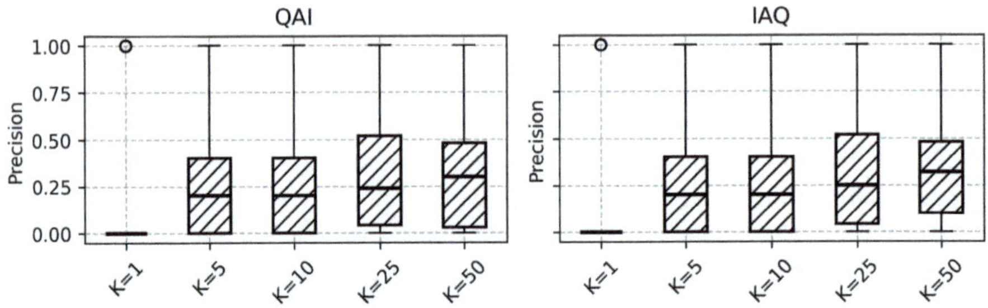

Fig. 5. Precision of Query-and-Iterate (QAI) and Iterate-and-Query (IAQ).

wrong answer has a larger impact. The figure also shows a high variance in precision, averaging 31%. These results reflect the inherent tradeoff between query evaluation time and precision [6]. We leave improving the precision metrics for future work, possibly with parameter tuning or by incorporating more sophisticated ANN indices. Moreover, for cases where precision is most important, one can always resort to deterministic non-approximated INN indices.

9 Concluding Remarks

In this paper, we formalize and study efficient algorithms for the k-GSS problem. Our theoretical analysis makes a case for Iterate-and-Query as the algorithm of choice, especially when k is small and the number of answers to patterns is large. We confirm this fact through an experiment using IMGpedia [20], an MKG that incorporates image embeddings into Wikidata. We believe our paper will pave the way for implementing k-GSS in graph databases, especially in those that currently feature vector stores, such as Neo4j or Amazon Neptune.

Improved Query Algorithms. So far, we have considered plug-and-play combinations between LTJ and an INN algorithm, but more involved arrangements may yield improved results. For example, we can enhance the LTJ algorithm so that the similarity condition is incorporated at the time of variable binding. This can be done in the style of Query-and-Select (i.e., generate all the values of a variable x that survive Leapfrog's intersection, sort them by distance to t, and then bind the values $x = b$ in that order), Query-and-Iterate (generate the values for x as before, then use the INN index to produce the neighbors of t sorted by distance, and bind the values $x = b$ that are found in the intersection), or Iterate-and-Query (generate the consecutive neighbors with the INN, and check each one to see if it survives the intersection of LTJ).

More Similarity Conditions. Both algorithms and the query language can be extended to support more similarity conditions. Assume we have a graph G, a distance δ, and a vector store τ. For query patterns, we can now fix several of its variables, which are to be compared with several individual vectors. To see how answers are sorted, suppose we have such a pattern query $(Q, x_1, \ldots, x_n)$, vectors $t_1, \dots t_n$, and an aggregation function $F : \mathbb{R}^n \rightarrow \mathbb{R}$. Then each answer $(\bar{a}, b_1, \dots, b_n)$ is ordered according to the value of $F(b_1, \dots, b_n)$. For the query-and-select baseline, we compute F at the time answers are retrieved and keep the set of best-k answers seen so far in a priority queue. For the other algorithms, we replace the $next_{\mathcal{T}}(t)$ iterator with a top-1 variant of the Threshold Algorithm [18] using $next_{\mathcal{T}}(t)$ to separately explore candidates in each dimension of F.

Supplemental Material Statement: All sources and scripts available at [35].

Acknowledgments. This work was funded by ANID – Millennium Science Initiative Program – Code ICN17_002. S. Ferrada was supported by Fondecyt Grant 11251322; by CENIA FB210017, Basal ANID; and by the Vicerrectoría de Investigación y Desarrollo (VID) of U. de Chile, project code UI-016/24. G. Navarro was supported by Fondecyt Grant 1-230755. J. L. Reutter and D. Vrgoč were supported by Fondecyt Grant 1221799. D. Vrgoč was also supported by Fondecyt Grant 1240346.

References

1. Amer, A.A., Abdalla, H.I., Nguyen, L.: Enhancing recommendation systems performance using highly-effective similarity measures. Knowl.-Based Syst. **217**, 106842 (2021). https://doi.org/10.1016/j.knosys.2021.106842
2. Angles, R., et al.: TelarKG: a knowledge graph of Chile's constitutional process. In: Proceedings of the 7th Joint Workshop on Graph Data Management Experiences & Systems (GRADES) and Network Data Analytics (NDA), Santiago AA Chile, pp. 1–5. ACM (2024). https://doi.org/10.1145/3661304.3661899
3. Arroyuelo, D., Bustos, B., Gómez-Brandón, A., Hogan, A., Navarro, G., Reutter, J.: Worst-case-optimal similarity joins on graph databases. Proc. ACM Manag. Data **2**(1), 1–26 (2024)
4. Arya, S., Mount, D., Netanyahu, N., Silverman, R., Wu, A.: An optimal algorithm for approximate nearest neighbor searching in fixed dimension. In: Proceedings of the 5th ACM-SIAM Symposium on Discrete Algorithms (SODA'94), pp. 573–583 (1994)
5. Atserias, A., Grohe, M., Marx, D.: Size bounds and query plans for relational joins. SIAM J. Comput. **42**(4), 1737–1767 (2013)
6. Aumüller, M., Bernhardsson, E., Faithfull, A.: ANN-benchmarks: a benchmarking tool for approximate nearest neighbor algorithms. Inf. Syst. **87**, 101374 (2020). https://doi.org/10.1016/j.is.2019.02.006
7. Baeza-Yates, R., Ribeiro-Neto, B., et al.: Modern Information Retrieval, vol. 463. ACM Press, New York (1999)
8. Bawa, M., Condie, T., Ganesan, P.: LSH forest: self-tuning indexes for similarity search. In: Proceedings 14th International Conference on World Wide Web (WWW), p. 651. ACM Press (2005). https://doi.org/10.1145/1060745.1060840
9. Bonifati, A., Martens, W., Timm, T.: Navigating the maze of Wikidata query logs. In: The World Wide Web Conference, pp. 127–138 (2019)
10. Chávez, E., Figueroa, K., Navarro, G.: Effective proximity retrieval by ordering permutations. IEEE Trans. Pattern Anal. Mach. Intell. **30**(9), 1647–1658 (2008)
11. Chávez, E., Navarro, G., Baeza-Yates, R., Marroquin, J.L.: Searching in metric spaces. ACM Comput. Surv. **33**(3), 273–321 (2001)

12. Ciaccia, P., Patella, M.: PAC nearest neighbor queries: approximate and controlled search in high-dimensional and metric spaces. In: Proceedings 16th International Conference on Data Engineering (ICDE), pp. 244–255 (2000)
13. Ciaccia, P., Patella, M., Zezula, P.: M-tree: an efficient access method for similarity search in metric spaces. In: Proceedings of the 23rd International Conference on Very Large Data Bases (VLDB), pp. 426–435 (1997)
14. Clarkson, K.L.: Nearest neighbor queries in metric spaces. Discrete Comput. Geometry **22**(1), 63–93 (1999)
15. Core, C.: Chroma - the open-source embedding database (2024). https://github.com/chroma-core/chroma
16. Cyganiak, R., Wood, D., Lanthaler, M., Klyne, G., Carroll, J.J., McBride, B.: RDF 1.1 Concepts and Abstract Syntax. W3C Recommendation, W3C (2014)
17. Discussion on the pgvector project. https://github.com/pgvector/pgvector/issues/259
18. Duong, Q.H., Liao, B., Fournier-Viger, P., Dam, T.L.: An efficient algorithm for mining the top-k high utility itemsets, using novel threshold raising and pruning strategies. Knowl.-Based Syst. **104**, 106–122 (2016)
19. Engels, J., Landrum, B., Yu, S., Dhulipala, L., Shun, J.: Approximate nearest neighbor search with window filters. arXiv preprint arXiv:2402.00943 (2024)
20. Ferrada, S., Bustos, B., Hogan, A.: IMGpedia: a linked dataset with content-based analysis of Wikimedia images. In: d'Amato, C., et al. (eds.) ISWC 2017. LNCS, vol. 10588, pp. 84–93. Springer, Cham (2017). https://doi.org/10.1007/978-3-319-68204-4_8
21. Garcia-Molina, H., Ullman, J., Widom, J.: Database Systems: The Complete Book. Pearson Education India (2008)
22. Gionis, A., Indyk, P., Motwani, R.: Similarity search in high dimensions via hashing. In: VLDB'99, Proceedings of 25th International Conference on Very Large Data Bases, September 7-10, 1999, Edinburgh, Scotland, UK, pp. 518–529. Morgan Kaufmann (1999). http://www.vldb.org/conf/1999/P49.pdf
23. Gollapudi, S., et al.: Filtered-diskann: graph algorithms for approximate nearest neighbor search with filters. In: Proceedings of the ACM Web Conference 2023, pp. 3406–3416 (2023)
24. Guo, Q., et al.: A survey on knowledge graph-based recommender systems. IEEE Trans. Knowl. Data Eng. **34**(8), 3549–3568 (2022). https://doi.org/10.1109/TKDE.2020.3028705
25. Guo, R., et al.: Manu: a cloud native vector database management system. arXiv preprint arXiv:2206.13843 (2022)
26. Guttman, A.: R-trees: a dynamic index structure for spatial searching. In: Proceedings of the 1984 ACM SIGMOD International Conference on Management of Data - SIGMOD '84, Boston, Massachusetts, p. 47. ACM Press (1984). https://doi.org/10.1145/602259.602266
27. Harris, S., Seaborne, A., Prud'hommeaux, E.: SPARQL 1.1 Query Language (2013). https://www.w3.org/TR/sparql11-query
28. Hjaltason, G.R., Samet, H.: Distance browsing in spatial databases. ACM Trans. Database Syst. **24**(2), 265–318 (1999)
29. Hjaltason, G.R., Samet, H.: Incremental similarity search in multimedia databases. Technical report CS-TR-4199, University of Maryland, Computer Science Department (2000)
30. Hogan, A., et al.: Knowledge Graphs. No. 22 in Synthesis Lectures on Data, Semantics, and Knowledge, Springer (2021). https://doi.org/10.2200/S01125ED1V01Y202109DSK022, https://kgbook.org/

31. Hogan, A., Riveros, C., Rojas, C., Soto, A.: A worst-case optimal join algorithm for SPARQL. In: Proceedings of the 18th International Semantic Web Conference (ISWC), pp. 258–275 (2019)
32. Lewis, P., et al.: Retrieval-augmented generation for knowledge-intensive NLP tasks. In: Proceeding 34th International Conference on Neural Information Processing Systems, Red Hook, NY, USA. Curran Associates Inc. (2020)
33. Malkov, Y.A., Yashunin, D.A.: Efficient and robust approximate nearest neighbor search using hierarchical navigable small world graphs. IEEE Trans. Pattern Anal. Mach. Intell. **42**(4), 824–836 (2018)
34. Malyshev, S., Krötzsch, M., González, L., Gonsior, J., Bielefeldt, A.: Getting the most out of Wikidata: semantic technology usage in Wikipedia's knowledge graph. In: Vrandečić, D., et al. (eds.) ISWC 2018, Part II. LNCS, vol. 11137, pp. 376–394. Springer, Cham (2018). https://doi.org/10.1007/978-3-030-00668-6_23
35. Millennium Institute for Foundational Research on Data: MillenniumDB. The link to the repository can be found at: https://anonymous.4open.science/r/WCO-SimilaritySearch-2025
36. Ngo, H.Q.: Worst-case optimal join algorithms: Techniques, results, and open problems. In: Proceedings of the 37th ACM SIGMOD-SIGACT-SIGAI Symposium on Principles of Database Systems (PODS), pp. 111–124 (2018)
37. Nguyen, D., Aref, M., Bravenboer, M., Kollias, G., Ngo, H.Q., Ré, C., Rudra, A.: Join processing for graph patterns: an old dog with new tricks. In: Proceedings of the 3rd International Workshop on Graph Data Management Experiences and Systems (GRADES), pp. 2:1–2:8 (2015)
38. Pan, J.J., Wang, J., Li, G.: Survey of vector database management systems. VLDB J. **33**(5), 1591–1615 (2024)
39. Pan, S., Luo, L., Wang, Y., Chen, C., Wang, J., Wu, X.: Unifying large language models and knowledge graphs: a roadmap. IEEE Trans. Knowl. Data Eng. **36**(7), 3580–3599 (2024)
40. Paraschakis, D., Ros, R., Borg, M., Runeson, P.: Fuserank (demo): filtered vector search in multimodal structured data. In: Joint European Conference on Machine Learning and Knowledge Discovery in Databases, pp. 404–408. Springer, Cham (2024). https://doi.org/10.1007/978-3-031-70371-3_29
41. Pelillo, M., Hancock, E.R. (eds.): Similarity-Based Pattern Recognition, LNCS, vol. 7005. Springer, Heidelberg (2011). https://doi.org/10.1007/978-3-642-24471-1
42. PostgreSQL Global Development Group: pgvector - open-source vector similarity search for postgres (2024). https://github.com/pgvector/pgvector
43. Prokhorenkova, L., Shekhovtsov, A.: Graph-based nearest neighbor search: from practice to theory. In: Proceedings of the 37th International Conference on Machine Learning, (ICML). Proceedings of Machine Learning Research, vol. 119, pp. 7803–7813 (2020)
44. Reimers, N., Gurevych, I.: Sentence-BERT: sentence Embeddings using Siamese BERT-Networks (2019). https://doi.org/10.48550/ARXIV.1908.10084
45. Samet, H.: Foundations of Multidimensional and Metric Data Structures. Morgan Kaufmann (2006)
46. Schneider, P., Schopf, T., Vladika, J., Galkin, M., Simperl, E., Matthes, F.: A decade of knowledge graphs in natural language processing: a survey. In: Proceedings of the 2nd Conference of the Asia-Pacific Chapter of the Association for Computational Linguistics and the 12th International Joint Conference on Natural Language Processing, vol. 1, pp. 601–614 (2022)

47. Veldhuizen, T.L.: Triejoin: a simple, worst-case optimal join algorithm. In: Proceedings of the 17th International Conference on Database Theory (ICDT), pp. 96–106 (2014)
48. Vrandečić, D., Krötzsch, M.: Wikidata: a free collaborative knowledgebase. Commun. ACM **57**(10), 78–85 (2014)
49. Vrgoč, D., et al.: MillenniumDB: an open-source graph database system. Data Intell. **5**(3), 560–610 (2023). https://doi.org/10.1162/dint_a_00229, https://direct.mit.edu/dint/article/5/3/560/117375/MillenniumDB-An-Open-Source-Graph-Database-System
50. Vrgoč, D., et al.: MillenniumDB: a multi-modal, multi-model graph database. In: Companion of the 2024 International Conference on Management of Data. SIGMOD '24, New York, NY, USA, pp. 496–499. Association for Computing Machinery (2024). https://doi.org/10.1145/3626246.3654757
51. Wang, J., et al.: Milvus: a purpose-built vector data management system. In: Proceedings of the 2021 International Conference on Management of Data, pp. 2614–2627 (2021)
52. Wang, M., Wang, H., Qi, G., Zheng, Q.: Richpedia: a large-scale, comprehensive multi-modal knowledge graph. Big Data Res. **22**, article 100159 (2020)
53. Wang, X., Meng, B., Chen, H., Meng, Y., Lv, K., Zhu, W.: TIVA-KG: a multimodal knowledge graph with text, image, video and audio. In: Proceeding of the 31st ACM International Conference on Multimedia, pp. 2391–2399 (2023)
54. Yianilos, P.: Locally lifting the curse of dimensionality for nearest neighbor search. In: Proceeding of the 11th ACM-SIAM Symposium on Discrete Algorithms (SODA), pp. 361–370 (2000)
55. Zezula, P., Amato, G., Dohnal, V., Batko, M.: Similarity Search - The Metric Space Approach, Advances in Database Systems, vol. 32. Kluwer (2006)
56. Zheng, W., Zou, L., Peng, W., Yan, X., Song, S., Zhao, D.: Semantic SPARQL similarity search over RDF knowledge graphs. Proc. VLDB Endowment **9**(11), 840–851 (2016). https://doi.org/10.14778/2983200.2983201

Formalizing Repairs for Wikidata Constraint Violations: A Taxonomy and Empirical Analysis

Nicolas Ferranti[1(✉)], Dayane Guimarães[3], Jairo Francisco de Souza[3], and Axel Polleres[1,2]

[1] Vienna University of Economics and Business, Vienna, Austria
nicolas.ferranti@wu.ac.at
[2] Complexity Science Hub Vienna, Vienna, Austria
[3] LApIC Research Group, Federal University of Juiz de Fora, Juiz de Fora, Brazil

Abstract. Collaboratively maintained knowledge graphs like Wikidata rely on property constraints to detect data inconsistencies. This paper systematically formalizes potential repairs for Wikidata constraint violations, presenting a comprehensive taxonomy of repair strategies encompassing both instance-level (A-box) and terminological-level (T-box) changes. T-box repairs, which alter constraint definitions or Wikidata's class hierarchy, can simultaneously address multiple violations and, to the best of our knowledge, have not been investigated in detail before. We observe repairs over time and evaluate how specific patterns within our taxonomy are applied in practice. Our analysis of historical data reveals insights into the prevalence of repair patterns in Wikidata's collaborative environment. The results indicate that T-box repairs are particularly relevant for certain constraint types and the overall consolidation of Wikidata, where modifying constraint definitions can reduce the number of recurring violations.

Keywords: Knowledge Graphs · Wikidata · Data Quality · Constraints · Knowledge Graph Refinement

1 Introduction

Knowledge Graphs (KGs) [9] power applications such as search engines, reasoning, and data integration [2]. They model real-world knowledge as graphs, with entities as nodes and relationships as edges. Despite their versatility, commonsense KGs like Wikidata often suffer from data quality issues, undermining their usefulness. Their large scale and collaborative nature make ensuring data correctness a performance and scalability challenge [1,6,21].[1]

This work was funded by the Austrian Science Fund (FWF) [10.55776/COE12].

[1] As of July 2025, Wikidata contained approximately 118 million items and 2 billion edits. Source: https://www.wikidata.org/wiki/Wikidata:Statistics. A full RDF serialization of Wikidata amounts to over 14b triples [6].

D. Garijo et al. (Eds.): ISWC 2025, LNCS 16140, pp. 369–387, 2026.
https://doi.org/10.1007/978-3-032-09527-5_20

This paper focuses on RDF-based KGs [3] exported from Wikibase, such as Wikidata (WD) [24] and the EU Knowledge Graph [4]. These graphs rely on so-called property constraints, a common mechanism for detecting inconsistencies by enforcing or prohibiting specific data patterns [16,21]. Broadly, *completeness* constraints *require* certain information (e.g., "an item used as place of birth also *must* be of type location"), while *consistency* constraints *prohibit* specific conflicting statements (e.g. explicitly forbidding certain items to be used as country of citizenship). Items violating these constraints are considered *violations*.

Shape Expressions (ShEx) [26] and the W3C standard Shapes Constraint Language (SHACL) [25] are the primary languages for expressing constraints in RDF KGs. However, Wikidata established its own property constraint model – developed within the Wikibase ecosystem – prior to the development of these standards. Although not fully expressible in SHACL [6], WD's property constraints have been formally studied using SPARQL [6] and MAPL [12]. These constraint types have also been adopted by other Wikibase-based KGs, such as the EU Knowledge Graph, highlighting the relevance of research on their properties and repairs. Previous work [2,21] has explored instance (A-box) repairs based on a simplified Description Logics (DL) formalization, but did not address repairs involving modifications to constraint definitions or Wikidata's foundational "ontology axioms". Building upon these efforts, this paper formally defines both A-box and T-box repair patterns for WD property constraints, leveraging existing formalizations in MAPL [12] and SPARQL [6]. Furthermore, we analyze the impact of T-box repair patterns, which offer the potential to fix multiple violations at once, contrasting with individual A-box repairs.

Our main contributions are as follows: (1) A complete formalization of possible repair patterns covering both A-box and T-box repairs – to the best of our knowledge, this is the first work to analyze T-box repairs in Wikidata; (2) A systematic analysis of these repair patterns based on historical edits; (3) Additionally, we provide an accompanying dataset of historical repairs performed by the Wikidata community from Jun-2019 to May-2023 for further use, cf. the *Supplementary Material* statement in the end of the paper.

The rest of the paper is structured as follows: Sect. 2 covers the Wikidata data model and its constraint representation. Section 3 defines constraint violations. Section 4 presents our formalization of Wikidata constraint repairs, covering both A-box and T-box, with general and constraint-specific repair patterns. Section 5 details our experiments on Wikidata, tracking data evolution, violations, and repair patterns. Section 6 explores data quality in KGs, including inconsistency detection and formal constraint representation. Finally, Sect. 7 summarizes the findings and future directions.

2 Preliminaries

Wikidata's KG consists of two primary components: items and properties. Items represent concrete or abstract entities, e.g. Messi, Chemistry, or California. Properties denote relationships between items, such as date of birth or country of citizenship. These relations are used to create *direct claims*, i.e., subject-property-value triples, which we will also write as property(subject,value) predicates. Here, the subject is an item and a value can be either an item or a literal. Items and properties are identified by alphanumeric IDs, where item IDs are of the form Qx (e.g. Q615 for Messi) and property IDs of the form Px (e.g. P27 for country of citizenship). Figure 1 illustrates WD's RDF data model in two layers: single-lined edges depict *direct claims* as item- property-value triples, while the double-lined edges incorporate a mechanism to add so-called *statement qualifiers* for ranks, references and other metadata, using WD's reification mechanism, such as the date (*start time* property) on which an individual's citizenship became effective (*country of citizenship* property), for enhanced description. Further details can be found in [6], which also explains the respective distinct namespaces used for direct claims (wdt:) and qualifier statements (p:, ps:, pq:, etc.).

While Wikidata does not separate between A-Box and T-Box, we borrow from this abstraction commonly made in Description Logics, to distinguish "assertional" data (A-Box), i.e., statements made about individual instance entities, from "terminology" definitions (T-Box), i.e., axioms about classes and properties, such as Wikidata's subclass hierarchy and property constraint definitions.[2]

A-Box. In analogy with standard RDF ontologies, we will call direct claims as well as statement qualifiers related to these (depicted as single and double line edges with ▲-tips in Fig. 1), the WD **A-Box**.

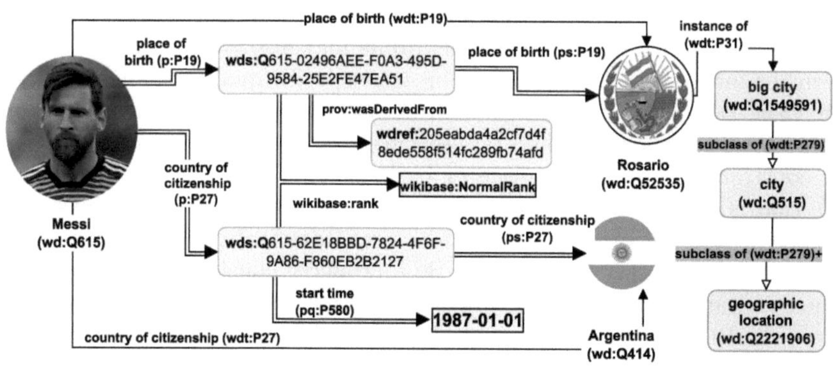

Fig. 1. Wikidata data model: single-line arrows indicate direct A-box (▲-tips) and T-box (△-tips) claims, respectively. Double line arrows denote A-box statement qualifiers, i.e., contextual information.

T-Box. Similar, but slightly different to standard RDFS and OWL ontologies, the parts of Wikidata's *terminology* (or T-Box) relevant for property constraint

[2] subproperties are not covered herein, because these are not considered by/relevant for any Wikidata property constraint definitions.

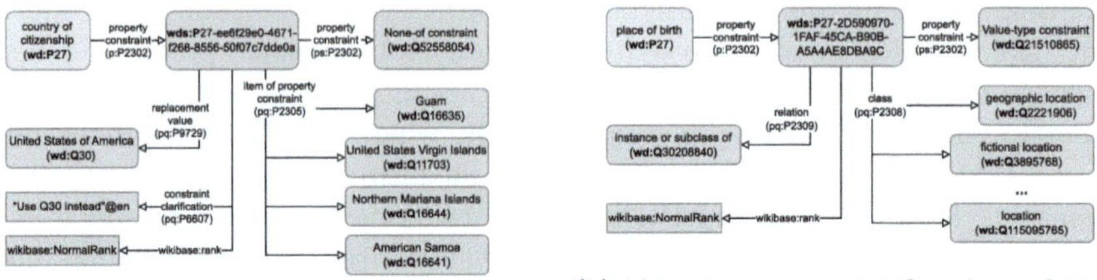

(a) None-of constraint for country of citizenship. Since the listed items are US territories, US citizenship should be used instead.

(b) Value-type constraint for place of birth. There must be at least one value that is an instance or subclass of one of the items listed in the class qualifier.

Fig. 2. Examples of WD property constraint definitions (part of the T-Box)

evaluation are described by special statements about *classes* and *properties* using a particular vocabulary: (1) items used in instance of (P31) A-box claims form a *class hierarchy*: that is, we count all subclassOf (P279) direct claims (some of which are illustrated in the righthand side of Fig. 1) part of the T-Box.

The second part of what we call WD's T-Box herein are (2) *property constraint definitions*, as illustrated in Fig. 2, which shows property constraints on the properties country of citizenship and place of birth: each such definition comprises a qualified property constraint (pc) type (P2303) statement along with additional, constraint-type specific qualifiers: Fig. 2a shows a None-of constraint, stating that none of the four item of property constraint (iopc) should be used when describing citizenship. Such constraints may also contain hints for repairing, in the form of additional constraint type specific qualifiers, such as replacement value (P9729): since the prohibited entities are US territories, the value United States of America should be used instead. Figure 2b exemplifies a Value-type constraint for property place of birth, where there must be at least one value that is an instance or subclass of one of the listed class values. Other constraint types for instance include Item-requires-statement (IRS) or Value-requires-statement (VRS) constraints; overall, 30+ property constraint types have been defined and are constantly evolving in WD.[3] We herein selected 13 constraint types – the 10 analyzed by Tanon et al. [21] and included three constraint types not previously covered: the complement of One-of, which we refer to as None-of, and two qualifier-based constraint types, Required qualifier and Allowed qualifiers, which shall show the complementary aspects of our analysis with regards to earlier works.

The A-Box data in Fig. 1 complies to the *consistency constraint* in Fig. 2a, as the single country of citizenship claim has none of the forbidden values. Likewise, the A-Box claim place_of_birth(Messi, Rosario) shown in Fig. 1 conforms to the *completeness constraint* in Fig. 2b since the additional claim instance_of (Rosario, big city) *exists* and there is a subclass path from big city to geographic

[3] https://www.wikidata.org/wiki/Help:Property_constraints_portal.

location; i.e., we see that for compliance checking of property constraints also the subclass hierarchy part of the T-Box is relevant.

3 Defining Violations with Witness Patterns

We formally define constraint violations before discussing repairs. Here, we focus on the constraint types used in earlier works and try to generalize, building on these earlier formalizations [6,12,14,21].

Marx et al. [14] have introduced Multi-Attributed Relational Structures (MARS), especially as a formal data model for generalized Property Graphs like WD. They also developed Multi-Attributed Predicate Logic (MAPL) for expressing semantic knowledge within these structures. MAPL extends First-Order Logic (FOL) to support multi-valued attributes via *set terms*. Specifically, MAPL enhances the standard components of FOL (constants, terms, atoms, and formulae) as follows [12], where we only use binary predicates herein:

1. A *set term* is either a *set variable* or a set of attribute-value pairs $\{a_1 : b_1, ..., a_n : b_n\}$, where each a_i, b_i is an *object term*. Object terms are the usual basic terms of FOL, and can be either constants or *object variables*.
2. A relational atom is written as $p(a, b)@S$, where p is a binary predicate, a, b are object terms and S is a set term. Herein, we also allow SPARQL property path expressions for p.[4]
3. A set atom is an expression $(a : b) \in S$, where a, b are object terms and S is a set term.

For further details, on the syntax and semantics of MAPL formulae, including basic concepts such as models, entailment, satisfaction and consistency, we refer to [14]. In the following, constants are denoted in a serifless font (e.g. location, country_of_citizenship, etc.), object variables use lower case letters (e.g., $x, y, z, ...$), and set variables are denoted by uppercase letters (e.g., $S, Q, ...$).

To illustrate how we can use MAPL to formalize the semantics of particular property constraint (pc) types, consider the None-of constraint from [12]:

$$\mathsf{pc}(p, \mathsf{None\text{-}of})@CQ \land (\mathsf{iopc} : v) \in CQ \rightarrow \neg\exists s.p(s, v)$$

This MAPL rule states that if a property p is constrained by a None-of constraint, specified by constraint qualifiers CQ, and CQ includes the value v as an item of the property constraint, then there should not exist any subject s that has the value v for property p. As the rule ensures data consistency, its logical negation, easily derivable via logical equivalences and De Morgan's laws, can be formulated as a conjunction reading all variables as existential to define what we call a *violation witness pattern*:

[4] This slight extension of MAPL can be seen as a form of syntactic shorthand for (linearly recursive) rules used to represent path expressions. See, for example, [19] and rule (3) in [15].

Table 1. Witness patterns in MAPL and SPARQL

Constr. Type	Witness Pattern	SPARQL Pattern
One-of (Q21510859)	$\underline{p(s,v)} \wedge \mathbf{pc}(p, \textbf{One-of})@CQ$ $\wedge(\textbf{iopc} : v) \notin CQ$	[wikibase:directClaim ?P; p:P2302 ?CQ]. ?S ?P ?V. ?CQ ps:P2302 wd:Q21510859. FILTER NOT EXISTS {?CQ pq:P2305 ?V.}
None-of (Q52558054)	$\underline{p(s,v)} \wedge \mathbf{pc}(p, \textbf{None-of})@CQ$ $\wedge(\textbf{iopc} : v) \in CQ$	[wikibase:directClaim ?P; p:P2302 ?CQ]. ?S ?P ?V. ?CQ ps:P2302 wd:Q52558054. ?CQ pq:P2305 ?V.
IRS (Q21503247) *(no value)*	$\mathbf{pc}(p, \textbf{IRS})@CQ \wedge (\textbf{property} : p_C) \in CQ$ $\wedge\underline{p(s,v)} \wedge \neg\exists v_C . p_C(s, v_C)$ $\wedge\neg\exists v_{cq} . (\textbf{iopc} : v_{cq}) \in CQ$	[wikibase:directClaim ?P; p:P2302 ?CQ]. ?S ?P ?V. ?CQ ps:P2302 wd:Q21503247. ?CQ pq:P2306 []. FILTER NOT EXISTS {?CQ pq:P2305 [].} FILTER NOT EXISTS { ?CQ pq:P2306/wikibase:directClaim ?PC. ?S ?PC ?VC.}
IRS (Q21503247) *(with value)*	$\mathbf{pc}(p, \textbf{IRS})@CQ \wedge (\textbf{property} : p_C) \in CQ$ $\wedge\underline{p(s,v)} \wedge \neg\exists v_C . (p_C(s, v_C) \wedge$ $(\textbf{iopc} : v_C) \in CQ)$	[wikibase:directClaim ?P; p:P2302 ?CQ]. ?S ?P ?V. ?CQ ps:P2302 wd:Q21503247. ?CQ pq:P2306/wikibase:directClaim ?PC. ?CQ pq:P2305 []. FILTER NOT EXISTS { ?S ?PC ?VC. ?CQ pq:P2305 ?VC.}
VRS (Q21510865) *(no value)*	$\mathbf{pc}(p, \textbf{VRS})@CQ \wedge (\textbf{property} : p_C) \in CQ$ $\wedge\underline{p(s,v)} \wedge \neg\exists v_C . p_C(v, v_C)$ $\wedge\neg\exists v_{cq} . (\textbf{iopc} : v_{cq}) \in CQ$	[wikibase:directClaim ?P; p:P2302 ?CQ]. ?S ?P ?V. ?CQ ps:P2302 wd:Q21510865. ?CQ pq:P2306 []. FILTER NOT EXISTS {?CQ pq:P2305 [].} FILTER NOT EXISTS {?CQ pq:P2306/wikibase:directClaim ?PC. ?V ?PC ?VC}
VRS (Q21510865) *(with value)*	$\mathbf{pc}(p, \textbf{VRS})@CQ \wedge (\textbf{property} : p_C) \in CQ$ $\wedge\underline{p(s,v)} \wedge \neg\exists v_C . (p_C(v, v_C) \wedge$ $(\textbf{iopc} : v_C) \in CQ)$	[wikibase:directClaim ?P; p:P2302 ?CQ]. ?S ?P ?V. ?CQ ps:P2302 wd:Q21510865. ?CQ pq:P2306/wikibase:directClaim ?PC. ?CQ pq:P2305 []. FILTER NOT EXISTS {?V ?PC ?VC. ?CQ pq:P2305 ?VC.}
Inverse (Q21510855)	$\mathbf{pc}(p, \textbf{Inverse})@CQ \wedge (\textbf{property} : p_C) \in CQ$ $\wedge\underline{p(s,v)} \wedge \neg p_C(v, s)$	[wikibase:directClaim ?P; p:P2302 ?CQ]. ?S ?P ?V. ?CQ ps:P2302 wd:Q21510855. ?CQ pq:P2306/wikibase:directClaim ?PC. FILTER NOT EXISTS {?V ?PC ?S}
Symmetric (Q21510862)	$\mathbf{pc}(p, \textbf{Symmetric})@CQ \wedge \underline{p(s,v)} \wedge \neg p(v, s)$	[wikibase:directClaim ?P; p:P2302 ?CQ]. ?S ?P ?V. ?CQ ps:P2302 wd:Q21510862. FILTER NOT EXISTS {?V ?P ?S}
Conflicts-with (Q21502838) *(no value)*	$\mathbf{pc}(p, \textbf{Conflicts-with})@CQ \wedge (\textbf{property} : p_C) \in CQ$ $\wedge\neg\exists v_{cq} . (\textbf{iopc} : v_{cq}) \in CQ$ $\wedge\underline{p(s,v)} \wedge p_C(s, v_C)$	[wikibase:directClaim ?P; p:P2302 ?CQ]. ?S ?P ?V. ?CQ ps:P2302 wd:Q21502838. ?CQ pq:P2306/wikibase:directClaim ?PC . FILTER NOT EXISTS {?CQ pq:P2305 []}. ?S ?PC ?VC.
Conflicts-with (Q21502838) *(with value)*	$\mathbf{pc}(p, \textbf{Conflicts-with})@CQ \wedge (\textbf{property} : p_C) \in CQ$ $\wedge(\textbf{iopc} : v_C) \in CQ$ $\wedge\underline{p(s,v)} \wedge p_C(s, v_C)$	[wikibase:directClaim ?P; p:P2302 ?CQ]. ?S ?P ?V. ?CQ ps:P2302 wd:Q21502838. ?CQ pq:P2306/wikibase:directClaim ?PC . ?CQ pq:P2305 ?VC. ?S ?PC ?VC.
Distinct-values (Q21502410)	$\mathbf{pc}(p, \textbf{Distinct-values})@CQ$ $\wedge\underline{p(s,v)} \wedge p(s_C, v) \wedge s \neq s_C$	[wikibase:directClaim ?P; p:P2302 ?CQ]. ?S ?P ?V. ?CQ ps:P2302 wd:Q21502410. ?SC ?P ?V. FILTER (?S != ?SC).
Single-value (Q19474404) *(no seperator)*	[illegible]$)@CQ$ $\wedge\neg\exists q . (\textbf{separator} : q) \in CQ$ $\wedge\underline{p(s,v)} \wedge p(s, v_C) \wedge v \neq v_C$	[wikibase:claim ?PSQ; p:P2302 ?CQ.] ?S ?PSQ ?SQ,?SQC. FILTER(str(?SQ) != str(?SQC)) ?CQ ps:P2302 wd:Q19474404. FILTER NOT EXISTS {?CQ pq:P4155 []}
Single-value (Q19474404) *(with separator)*	$\mathbf{pc}(p, \textbf{Single-value})@CQ \wedge (\textbf{separator} : q) \in CQ$ $\wedge\underline{p(s,v)}@SQ \wedge p(s, v_C)@SQ_C \wedge (v \neq v_C) \wedge$ $\neg\exists v_q, v_{qc} . (\underline{\underline{(q : v_q) \in SQ}} \wedge (q : v_{qc}) \in SQ_C \wedge v_q \neq v_{qc})$	[wikibase:claim ?PSQ; p:P2302 ?CQ.] ?S ?PSQ ?SQ,?SQC. FILTER(str(?SQ) != str(?SQC)) ?CQ ps:P2302 wd:Q19474404. ?CQ pq:P4155 []. FILTER NOT EXISTS { ?SQ ?Q ?VQ. ?SQC ?Q ?VQC. ?CQ pq:P4155/wikibase:qualifier ?Q. FILTER (?VQ != ?VQC) }
Required qualifier (Q21510856)	$\mathbf{pc}(p, \textbf{Required qualifier})@CQ$ $\wedge(\textbf{property} : q) \in CQ$ $\wedge\underline{p(s,v)}@SQ \wedge \neg\exists v_q . (\underline{\underline{(q : v_q) \in SQ}})$	[wikibase:claim ?PSQ; p:P2302 ?CQ]. ?S ?PSQ ?SQ. ?CQ ps:P2302 wd:Q21510856. ?CQ pq:P2306/wikibase:qualifier ?Q. FILTER NOT EXISTS { ?SQ ?Q [] }
Allowed qualifiers (Q21510851)	$\mathbf{pc}(p, \textbf{Allowed qualifiers})@CQ$ $\wedge\underline{p(s,v)@SQ}$ $\wedge\underline{\underline{(q : v_q) \in SQ}} \wedge (\textbf{property} : q) \notin CQ)$	[wikibase:claim ?PSQ; p:P2302 ?CQ]. ?S ?PSQ ?SQ. ?SQ ?Q []. ?CQ ps:P2302 wd:Q21510851. FILTER NOT EXISTS { ?CQ pq:P2306/wikibase:qualifier ?Q }
Type$_{rel}$ (Q21503250)	$\underline{p(s,v)} \wedge \mathbf{pc}(p, \textbf{Type})@CQ$ $\wedge(\textbf{relation} : rel) \in CQ$ $\wedge\neg\exists c. \ ((\textbf{class} : c) \in CQ \wedge PATH_{rel}(s, c))$	[wikibase:directClaim ?P; p:P2302 ?CQ]. ?S ?P ?V. ?CQ ps:P2302 wd:Q21503250. ?CQ pq:P2309 wd:Q_{rel}. FILTER NOT EXISTS { ?CQ pq:P2308 ?C. ?S $PATH_{rel}$?C.}
Value-type$_{rel}$ (Q21510865)	$\underline{p(s,v)} \wedge \mathbf{pc}(p, \textbf{Value-type})@CQ$ $\wedge(\textbf{relation} : rel) \in CQ$ $\wedge\neg\exists c. \ ((\textbf{class} : c) \in CQ \wedge PATH_{rel}(v, c))$	[wikibase:directClaim ?P, p:P2302 ?CQ]. ?S ?P ?V. ?CQ ps:P2302 wd:Q21510865. ?CQ pq:P2309 wd:Q_{rel}. FILTER NOT EXISTS { ?CQ pq:P2308 ?C. ?V $PATH_{rel}$?C.}

Table 2. Relation paths for Type and Value-type constraints described in Table 1.

rel	$PATH_{rel}$ (MAPL)	$PATH_{rel}$ (SPARQL)	Q_{rel}
instance_of	$\text{P31}(v, v_c) \wedge \text{P279}*(v_c, c)$	(wdt:P31/wdt:P279*)	Q21503252
subclass_of	$\text{P279}*(v, c)$	(wdt:P279*)	Q21514624
instance_or_subclass_of	$(\text{P31}(v, v_c) \wedge \text{P279}*(v_c, c)) \vee (\text{P279}*(v, c))$	(wdt:P31?/wdt:P279*)	Q30208840

$$p(s, v) \wedge \text{pc}(p, \text{None-of})@CQ \wedge (\text{iopc} : v) \in CQ$$

In MAPL, A WD statement $p(s, v)@SQ$ extends the basic $p(s, v)$ claim by incorporating statement qualifiers and references (SQ). To further analyze constraint violations, we will distinguish between: (1) the *base statement*, $p(s, v)@SQ$, which directly violates a property constraint, and (2) a *context statement*, denoted as $p_c(s, v_c)@SQ_c$ or $p_c(v, v_c)@SQ_c$, which is an additional statement that provides supporting information about the subject s or value v of the *base statement*, thereby aiding in violation identification. For example, identifying a Conflicts with constraint violation requires the presence of a prohibited specific *context statement* using a prohibited context property within the constraint definition qualifiers. Likewise, for the Value-type constraint, a supporting instance of (P31) statement may be required.

Definition 1 (Constraint Violation). *A statement* $p(s, v)@SQ \in \mathcal{A}$ *is considered a* constraint violation *if it satisfies at least one witness pattern defined in Table 1.*

Table 1 shows the complete list of witness patterns for all analyzed constraint types, including their Wikidata IDs, with Table 2 further explaining different relational paths for subtypes of Type and Value-type constraints. We "mark" different A-Box components within MAPL witness patterns with underlining, while non-underlined elements represent T-Box (constraint definition) components:

___ *base statement* (S) ═══ *base statement qualifier* (SQ)
- - - *context statement* (S_c) ≡ *context statement qualifier* (SQ_c)

Additional Note: Truthy Statements. As a notational shortcut in MAPL formulas used within Table 1, we use $p(s, v)$ (or $p_c(s, v_c)$) without the $@SQ$ (or analogously, $@CQ$) suffix, as a shorthand for wikidata:directClaims, which denote "truthy" statements of the form $p(s, v)@SQ$. The omission of SQ indicates that SQ contains an active rank attribute (i.e., rank:preferredRank, or, resp., rank:normalRank without the existence of any other rank:preferredRank claims). Only these truthy statements are accessible in Wikidata's RDF serialization through property IDs qualified by the wdt:-namespace.

By exploiting the introduced notational conventions, all MAPL witness patterns can also be directly translated into SPARQL queries to detect constraint violations [6], e.g., for the None-of running example:

`[wikibase:directClaim ?P; p:P2302 ?CQ].`	Retrieve constraint definition node and base statement property `?P`.
`?S ?P ?V.`	Select the base statement using `?P`.
`?CQ ps:P2302 wd:Q52558054.`	Filter for None-of constraint type.
`?CQ pq:P2305 ?V.`	Match forbidden values.

The unified MAPL (object and set) variable names and SPARQL variable names in Tables 1+2 illustrate the corresponding semantics. That is, the queries presented in Table 1 resemble those introduced by [6] but have been adapted in this paper to use a more uniform and standardized variable naming scheme aligned with their corresponding witness pattern roles. However, the original semantics are preserved.

We note the following for further explanation of the SPARQL queries: whereas a pattern using wikibase:directClaim points to the direct claim's wdt:-prefixed predicate p, a blank node pattern using wikibase:claim yields the p:-prefixed property that links entities to wds:-prefixed statement nodes representing SQ, just as the variable $?CQ$ is bound (via p:P2302) to a wds:-prefixed statement node representing the constraint CQ; for further details, please refer to Figs. 1 and 2 or the more in-depth explanations of Wikidata's custom RDF reification model in [6].

4 Formalizing Repairs

Completeness violation witness patterns check for the *non-existence* of required information, which results in negated conjuncts in MAPL or FILTER NOT EXISTS clauses in SPARQL, as for the Value-type constraint test. On the contrary, witness patterns for *consistency* violations result in conjunctive queries with only positive conjunctions to match *existence* of prohibited information. This straightforwardly suggests a definition of repairs by the following insights:

1. Consistency violations can be repaired by deletions of statements or qualifiers mentioned in positive MAPL witness pattern conjuncts (or, resp. `SPARQL NOT EXISTS` patterns).
2. Completeness violations can be repaired by additions of statements or qualifiers mentioned in MAPL witness pattern conjuncts under a $\neg$ (negated) scope, or, resp. within `SPARQL NOT EXISTS` patterns.

Based on this idea, we can further classify repairs by the (underlined vs. non-underlined) components of witness patterns affected by such additions and deletions, which we introduced in the previous section, distinguishing between A-Box and T-Box repairs:

A-Box Repairs encompass modifications of the base statement (S), context statement (S_C), or their respective qualifiers (SQ, SQ_c), falling into the following repair types:

S^- – **Base statement deletion**: the deletion of the base statement obviously fixes *any* constraint violation, since the base statement $\underline{p(s,v)}$ appears positively in each witness pattern in Table 1.

S_c^- – **Context Statement deletion**(s): the deletion of a "witnessing" context statement $\underline{p_c(s, v_c)}$ fixes any consistency constraints which contain a positive context statement in their witness pattern, i.e., this potentially affects Conflicts-with, Distinct-values, and Single-Value constraints.

S_c^+ – **Context Statement addition**(s): likewise, the addition of a "missing" context statement fixes any completeness violations which contain a negated context statement, i.e., IRS, VRS, Inverse, and Symmetric constraints, but also includes instance of (P31) additions for Type and Value-Type constraint violations, cf. Table 2.

SQ^- – **Base qualifier deletion**: the deletion of a "witnessing" base statement qualifier fixes any consistency violations for witness patterns with a positive, $\underline{\underline{(q : v_q) \in SQ}}$ qualifier in Table 1, i.e., a removal of a non-Allowed qualifiers.

SQ^+ – **Base qualifier addition**: likewise, the addition of a "missing" base statement qualifier fixes witness patterns with a negated, $\underline{\underline{(q : v_q) \in SQ}}$ qualifier, i.e., a separator addition for Single-Value, or an addition of a Required qualifier.

SQ_c^+ – **Context qualifier addition** - the addition of a "missing" context statement qualifier fixes consistency violations that contain a negated, $\underline{\underline{(q_c : v_{qc}) \in SQ_c}}$ qualifier, i.e., specifically this applies to the addition of a separator for Single-Value (on the context statement).

Since no context statement qualifiers appear positively in witness patterns, SQ_c^- is not a repair category in the discussed WD constraint types. We note here that Tanon et al.'s work [21] (i) only considers A-Box modifications in terms of base and context statement additions/deletions but not wrt. qualifiers, and (ii) strictly distinguishes between consistency and completeness constraints. As for (i), we additionaly consider *qualifier repairs*; and as for (ii), in our more general considerations also considering qualifiers, we see that certain constraint types could be viewed as both consistency or completeness constraints. For instance, the Single-value constraint may be either fixed by removing a conflicting value or by adding a separator (qualifier). Thus, we will rather than classifying single constraint types as consistency or completeness constraints, distinguish "repair goals" as consistency repairs by deleting (or deactivating) conflicting information or completeness repairs by adding (or activating) missing information.

T-Box repairs (not considered in [21]) concern changes in constraint definitions and/or WD's class hierarchy, i.e. concerning all the non-underlined parts in the witness patterns of Table 1:

C^- – **Constraint deletion**: the removal of the constraint definition, i.e. the qualified statement property constraint (P2302) CQ (within the "parent" property definition) obviously fixes all constraint violations of this constraint instance.

CQ^+ – **Constraint Qualifiers Addition**: the addition of a constraint qualifier matching a negated atom $(q : v) \in CQ$ within a witness pattern could affect several constraint types, i.e. Allowed qualifiers, One-of, Type, and Value-Type. Note that there might be less obvious cases, for instance where an addition fixes a violation of an IRS or VRS constraint by adding (iopc : v_c) $\in CQ$, which in turn might "activate" a priorly non-matching context statement.

CQ^- – **Constraint Qualifiers deletion**: the removal of a "required" constraint qualifier fixes any constraint violations which contain a positive constraint qualifier, i.e. for instance, Inverse, Conflicts-with, None-of, Required Qualifier.

$\subseteq^+$ – **Class Hierarchy addition**: as per Table 2, subclass Of additions can lead to repairs of a prior violation witness of Value-Type and Type constraints.

4.1 "Indirect" Repairs: Re-ranking, Exceptions, and Replacements

Note that the discussion above streamlined and simplified the consideration of repairs in some sense, wrt. leaving out to further, "indirect" repairs.

Re-ranking. First, we did not explicitly consider *re-ranking*. Changes on the rank of a statement (especially to rank:deprecatedRank) might implicitly remove or even add direct claims related to matching truthy statements: as such, we may view such rerankings as synonymous for additions/deletions, respectively, and count them in the repair categories defined above. Extending our SPARQL patterns to only consider truthy statements is straightforward, but would bloat the patterns in Table 1 – we left this out for readability.

As an exception, we explicitly considered a very common type of re-ranking that significantly impacted repairs in our experiments: *constraint deprecations* (denoted C^d), which can also be viewed as a special form of constraint deletion.

Constraint Exceptions. WD allows adding base statement subject items s as exceptions using the exception_to_constraint (P2303) constraint qualifier in constraint definitions: while this is in some sense a T-Box addition, marking instance items as exceptions might intuitively be rather seen as part of the A-Box: as such, we do not report these repairs as CQ^+ in our experiments, but rather define an own category e^+ for exceptions.

Value Replacements. So far we have classified all repairs as either additions and deletions: yet, based on the Wikidata UI, value changes of triples (statements or qualifiers) that can be done in one edit may rather be considered as a single change, combining a deletion with an addition.

In many cases, constraint types can be fixed by a *base statement value replacement* (S^r), for instance One-of, None-of, but also VRS (by implicitly changing the context statements to be considered).

Likewise, violations of Conflicts-with constraints with *values* can be fixed by a *context statement value replacement* (S_c^r).

Single-Value constraint violations, may be fixable by a *base statement qualifier value replacement* (SQ^r) for the separator qualifier.

Finally, on the T-Box level, constraint qualifier replacements (CQ^r) may induce repairs: i.e., (Value-)Type constraint violations could be fixed by changes in the relation type or class qualifiers. Also, similar to the CQ^+ example above, changing to (property : p_{new}) $\in CQ$ by replacing the constrained property p_{old}

may fix an IRS constraint, by "activating" priorly "missing" context statements. While we could classify such a repair as CQ^-, arguably the mere addition of the new property p_{new} – indirectly – would be sufficient to repair the violation.

Summarizing, repairs that are the effect of a statement or qualifier (value) *replacements* will be marked as S^r, S^r_c, SQ^r, and CQ^r, respectively.

5 Experiments

We evaluated our repair patterns by analyzing historical Wikidata constraint violations using the experimental setup described in this section. Figure 3 outlines the process.

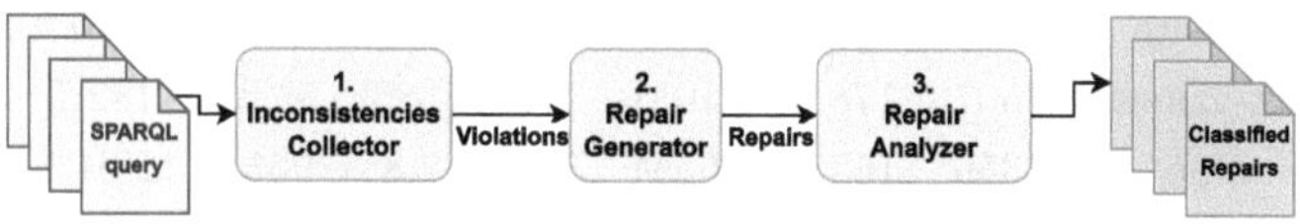

Fig. 3. Three steps experiment pipeline.

The experiment involved three steps: first, using the witness patterns, we extracted constraint violations from both 2019 and 2023 Wikidata HDT [5], denoted as $V_{ct,2019}$, and $V_{ct,2023}$ resp., per constraint type ct. Here, $V_{ct,year}$ should be understood as the set of variable bindings for the SPARQL queries in Table 1. Secondly, we identified historical repairs by comparing the violations detected on both snapshots, i.e., the set of repairs $R_{ct} = V_{ct,2019} - V_{ct,2023}$ includes those violations present in 2019 but no longer observed in 2023. Conversely, new violations are identified as $N_{ct} = V_{ct,2023} - V_{ct,2019}$. Thirdly, we developed Python scripts to analyze the repair types introduced in Sect. 4.

Table 3 summarizes the general statistics of our experiment. For constraint types also analyzed by Tanon et al. [21], we also observe a significant increase in data since 2018, reflected in the growing number of data items and detected violations over time.[5]

Table 4 represents the share of each repair type, detected to fix constraint violations between 2019 and 2023, distinguishing between T-Box, A-Box repairs, and added exceptions, respectively. We note that the shares per row do not necessarily add up to 100%, since some repairs might "overlap", in the sense that different actions might effect in repairing the same violation.

A-Box Repairs. The high share of A-Box repairs for None-of (92%) and Symmetric (95%) constraints shows that deletions or reranks were frequently made to the data by the community itself to correct violations. Value-type saw 52% of repairs involve adding missing type statements, reflecting how evolving knowledge in

[5] Note that column $\#R_{ct}$ is not comparable, since [21] does not count the total numbers of repairs.

Table 3. **#constr**: total constraints per type. $\#S$: base statements using properties with this constraint type. $\#V_{ct,2019}/\#V_{ct,2023}$: number of violations 2019 vs. 2023. $\#R_{ct}$: identified corrections 19–23. Growth compared to columns **#constr**, **#triples**, **#violations** of Table 3 in [21] is indicated by ↑%.

Name in WD	#constr.		$\#S$		$\#V_{ct,2019}/\#V_{ct,2023}$		$\#R_{ct}$
One-of	173	↑66.3%	23M	↑538%	4.3k/202k	↑4950%	2.9k
None-of	432	-	314.5M	-	1.9k/508k	-	1.1k
IRS	11051	↑256.2%	522M	↑51%	5.4M/16.7M	↑350%	3.7M
VRS	352	↑44.8%	470M	↑452%	2.5M/4.7M	↑249%	1.3M
Inverse	118	↑13%	9.8M	↑200%	322k/338k	↑44%	256k
Symmetric	47		8.2M		3.7M/253k		3.7M
Conflicts-with	2052	↑241.4%	685M	↑52%	175k/1.8M	↑1167%	117k
Distinct-values	7607	↑178.8%	210M	↑275%	386k/533k	↑182%	259k
Single-value	7356	↑165.3%	265M	↑211%	2.8M/95M	↑28K%	675k
Required qualifier	477	-	11M	-	2M/4M	-	612k
Allowed qualifiers	853	-	1B41M	-	321k/6.8M	-	222k
Type	7056	↑174%	994M	↑299%	3.1M/34.3M	↑889%	2.6M
Value-type	1090	↑56.6%	246M	↑267%	636k/27.6M	↑801%	517k

Wikidata often requires adding additional type-level information to maintain consistency.

Following the line of adding missing statements, the Inverse constraint saw 81% of repairs consisting of adding the required inverse properties to statements. Similarly, VRS witnessed the addition of required statements in 85% of the repairs. As both constraint types had small sets of constraint deletions, this may indicate that most constraint instances of those types are mature and that an effort to fix the A-box statements is in progress.

T-Box Repairs. Despite the significant number of A-Box repairs, T-Box repairs, which have been mostly ignored in prior works, play an equally critical role. These repairs indicate that the constraints are evolving alongside the data. Whether it involves adding qualifiers, adjusting property hierarchies, or deleting outdated constraints, T-Box repairs are vital for ensuring the knowledge graph remains flexible and up-to-date with changes in both structure and terminology.

As we can see, T-Box repairs are quite significant for certain constraints, reflecting how Wikidata's terminology and understanding of the schema have evolved. For instance, for the Conflicts-with constraint, 74% of the constraints were deleted, and 80% involved removing a forbidden property or value (iopc), indicating a major revision of constraints related to property conflicts. Similarly, for the Allowed qualifiers constraint, 70% of the constraints were deleted, and 19% saw qualifiers being added to the constraint definitions, which shows that the terminology itself was refined to allow for a broader range of qualifiers.

Table 4. Share of repairs by type (cf. Sect. 4) in %. Values <0.01% shown as 0

Name in WD	A-Box Repairs			T-Box Repairs			
	S^-/S^r	$S_c^+/S_c^-/S_c^r$	$SQ^+/SQ^-/SQ_c^+$	C^-/C^d	$CQ^+/CQ^-/CQ^r$	$\subseteq^+$	e^+
One-of	31/10	–/–/–	–/–/–	12/69	10/–/–	–	0
None-of	92/0	–/–/–	–/–/–	11/0	–/11/–	–	3
IRS	5/–	61/–/–	–/–/–	39/10	–/–/3.3	–	0
VRS	13/0	85/–/–	–/–/–	8/3	–/1.5/62	–	0
Inverse	40/–	81/–/–	–/–/–	2/28	–/–/0.05	–	0
Symmetric	95/–	4/–/–	–/–/–	0/0.01	–/–/–	–	0
Conflicts-with	17/–	–/12/2	–/–/–	74/3	–/80/–	–	0
Distinct-values	44/–	–/35/–	–/–/–	16/8	–/–/–	–	0.08
Single-value	24/–	–/16/–	0.9/–/2	73/5	7/–/0	–	0.04
Required qualifier	22/–	–/–/–	20/–/–	3/0.2	–/66/–	–	0
Allowed qualifiers	6/–	–/–/–	–/38/–	70/0	19/–/–	–	0
Type	4/–	12/–/–	–/–/–	0.9/0	31/–/63	35	0
Value-type	14/–	52/–/–	–/–/–	0.4/0	12/–/38	37	0

The Single-value constraint also highlights significant T-Box repair activity, with 73% of the violations being fixed by constraint deletions and 7% involving additions of separators, reflecting gradual refinement of constraints incl. qualifiers during their evolution/adoption. Some constraints indicate an ongoing effort to refine how value-related constraints are interpreted, e.g. 62% of repairs of VRS violations involve a change in the required value(s) at the T-Box level.

Lastly, also class hierarchy additions ($\subseteq^+$) seem to play a significant role, contributing to roughly one-third of repairs for (Value-)Type constraints.

These overall trends seem to suggest that the meaning of WD's terminology – in particular through property constraints – observably evolves in tandem with the data itself, ensuring that the graph's semantics better align with the A-Box data as it grows and changes.

Our method, as opposed to Tanon et al.'s [21] which tracks all historical knowledge graph states from WD's start, rather analyzes repairs between two snapshots. While this makes it challenging to pinpoint the exact order in which edits that led to repairs occurred, we can confidently assert that the identified patterns were executed between the two timestamps and might have contributed to the observed repairs. While Tanon et al.'s method offers finer-grained change tracking, our two-snapshot approach is expected to be more resource-efficient and scalable for large knowledge graphs like WD, as also confirmed by [21] results, not reporting, for instance the actual total numbers of repairs. However, further experiments are needed to validate the efficiency of this approach. In particular, for the identification of *single edit* value replacements, so far we do not really track these down to single edits, as we do not analyze the whole edit history,[6] rather following a best effort approach: while this is also just an approximation, we can identify statements with changed values having the same wds: statement

[6] Note that [21] also consider such *replacements*, but – based on personal communication – do also not explicitly distinguish between "single edit" replacements or combinations of additions and deletions.

nodes in the graph but different values, when computing the set R_{ct} (with slightly expanded SPARQL patterns as opposed to Table 1 also returning those nodes).

5.1 Analysing Most Impactful T-Box Bulk Repairs and New Violations

While having analyzed T-Box changes on a coarse level, we would like to have a closer look at two further aspects concerning "most impactful" changes, as well as possible "side effects" of T-Box changes: note that we emphasize that T-box changes could also induce new violations. To assess such effects of T-box "bulk" repairs in more detail, we have also analyzed the top-3 constraint types (with the highest share of T-box-related repairs) (Conflicts with, Required Qualifier, and VRS), in an attempt to identify schema changes behind historical repairs on particular properties and examining newly emerged violations.

For Conflicts with constraints, out of the 80% CQ^- T-box repairs, most of those constraints where eventually deleted (i.e. overlapping with the 74% C^- repairs; interestingly, almost half of those (48%) were related to only two Conflicts-with constraints (both later deleted) on the properties located in the administrative territorial entity (P131) and headquarters location (P159). New Conflicts with violations largely stemmed from new constraints introduced post-2019 (8 of top 10), totaling 701k.

In Required qualifier constraints, T-box repairs mainly involved qualifier removal (CQ^-), but hardly any constraint deletions (C^-). Notably, here 375k repairs (93% of these repairs) stemmed from removal of the point in time (P585) qualifier from the required qualifiers for position held (P39). Conversely, we note that the addition of the language of work or name (P407) qualifier to a new Required qualifier constraint for official website (P856) and described at URL (P973) properties after 2019 led to over 1.8 million new violations.

In VRS repairs, the two constrained properties most affected by T-box-based repairs (cast member (P161) and director (P57)) also accounted for the highest number of new violations between 2019 and 2023. Both require an additional occupation (P106) statement. Changes in the list of allowed occupations (14 added and 2 removed) for cast member caused 396k repairs, but 863k new violations. Likewise, the VRS constraint on occupations for director saw 288k repairs, but also 236k new violations from 8 added and 1 removed occupation.

Overall, our findings also indicate that the community frequently deletes constraints that cause many violations, and most new violations stem from newly created constraints. Developing approaches to help the community refine constraints could reduce deletions, preserve historical evolution, and simplify the assessment of constraint changes over time. This would support a more sustainable and informed constraint management and schema evolution process.

6 Related Works and Discussion

WD's constraint system arose from practical needs, not formal logic, with property constraints remaining the most used mechanism due to their broader coverage [6]. Other constraint mechanisms in WD include, for instance, entity schemas[7] and WShEx [7].

In general, there is a lack of systematic, longitudinal analyses of practical KGs' evolution [18], which we address by analyzing and classifying repairs over time, adding a focus on schema/T-Box repairs and evolution. Other related works have derived suggestions for repairs: in addition to their partial formalization of WD A-Box repairs, Tanon et al. [21] propose a method based on rule mining to correct A-box constraint violations. Similarly, Chen et al. [2] presented a general correction framework combining lexical matching, semantic embedding, soft constraint mining, and semantic consistency checks to correct entity/literal assertions in DBpedia. Beyond correction methods, Shenoy et al. [20] proposed quality indicators based on removed statements, deprecated statements, and constraint violations in WD. While we rely mostly on "vanilla" SPARQL, Tanon et al. [21] used a quad store to manipulate a sample of WD's edit history, and Shenoy et al. [20] used the Knowledge Graph ToolKit[8] to compute deprecation and deletion metrics.

Regarding WD *constraint formalization*, Tanon et al. [21] use DL to describe 10 different constraint types; however, as mentioned, the consideration of qualifiers and T-Box repairs is missing. Therefore, as we show, some constraints were tested without their full meaning. Martin and Patel-Schneider [12,13] were the first to use MAPL to express property constraints, which we build upon to express violations (and repairs) more comprehensively. Lastly, Ferranti et al. [6] similarly have deployed SHACL as well as SPARQL queries as a declarative approach to capture constraint violations through a WD RDF export for all the 32 constraint types, noting that DL is insufficient to express e.g. Single-Value constraints with separators. We put Martin et al.'s approach to use MAPL, and Ferranti et al.'s SPARQL formalizations side by side, systematically naming the relevant components of WD's property constraint "language" to classify repairs. SPARQL, which has already been deployed in earlier, use-case-specific works on constraint checking in WD [23], also turns out to be computationally efficient enough to compute constraint violations and repairs at scale in our experiments. While SHACL has also been operationalized recently, e.g. by efficient compilation techniques to SQL for usage on large KGs [10], this is not sufficient to express all current property constraint types in WD, as noted by [6].

As for expressivity of WD's property constraints, let us remark an interesting observation: WD's current property constraints seem inherently insufficient to express all constraints checked in WD's UI: for instance, particular constraint types, such as IRS constraints are restricted to having exactly one context property qualifier,[9] whereas several context property qualifiers are allowed for Allowed qualifiers constraint type definitions.[10] As opposed to other constraint checks in WD's UI, that seem to be backed up by property constraint definitions, these

[7] https://www.wikidata.org/wiki/Wikidata:WikiProject_Schemas.

[8] https://usc-isi-i2.github.io/kgtk/.

[9] At time of writing, this was flagged as violation in WD's UI, cf. https://www.wikidata.org/w/index.php?title=Property:P582&oldid=2345339934.

[10] cf. https://www.wikidata.org/w/index.php?title=Property:P1476&oldid=2342178751.

ones seem to be checked/enforced independently in WD's UI, and are clearly not expressible as property constraints; discrepancies between property constraint definitions and WD's UI violation checks have already been reported earlier [6].

As for further related areas, works on pinpointing to (minimal sets of) axioms responsible for justifying (unwanted) consequences in OWL DL [11,16], which could also be useful for finding repairs, are not directly related to what we are doing here. Our work is about analyzing and understanding repairs under constraints rather than finding repairs under deductive inference. Likewise, T-box repair methods for ontologies exploring minimal axiom weakening [22] do not play a significant role in this setting: WD's constraints are designed for validation without additional inference. Therefore, while these approaches offer conceptual parallels, they would require adaptation to WD's specific framework. Here, attempts to map WD's properties to OWL [8] could be a potential, though disputed starting point, as WD deliberately does not adopt DL or a predefined formal ontology [17].

7 Conclusions

In this work, we have systematically formalized and analyzed property constraint violations and subsequent repairs in Wikidata (WD), comparing snapshots of the knowledge graph at two different points in time. We were not only able to categorize the types of repair patterns most commonly applied, but could also draw valuable insights on how both instance data (A-Box) repairs but also T-Box repairs, i.e. changes of WD's constraint definitions and class hierarchy, determine the consolidation of WD's terminology and its usage. To the best of our knowledge, we are the first to systematically consider such T-Box repairs, and additionally investigate the effects of qualifier changes at the A-Box level, by separately considering the roles of statement changes, qualifier changes, property constraint definitions, and changes in WD's class hierarchy.

In comparison to earlier works, our analysis also shows a significant increase in the adoption and repair activities related to property constraints in WD; in some cases, the number of constraint violations is growing faster than the number of triples added to WD properties instantiating the constraints. This trend underscores the importance of tracking historical repairs to develop semi-automatic refinement approaches to assist the Wikidata community in managing and evolving its data. To this end, our fine-grained analysis of repairs offers a comprehensive tool now not only to descriptively investigate past repairs, but – as a next step – shall also help to derive recommendations for repairs, as we can now systematically observe the effects of how data and schema evolve alongside. By doing so, we hope to support the improvement of WD's quality over time, strengthening its role as a reliable and ever-growing knowledge base.

Our work is fully reproducible and extensible: as for future work, a more comprehensive coverage of all 30+ current and evolving constraint types – which we had to leave out also for space restrictions – is on our agenda. Also, we plan to extend our current, illustrative investigation of two concrete WD snapshots

(2019 vs. 2023), towards a regular, constant monitoring tool, for longitudinal analyses tracing WD's historic development periodically, or based on the full edit history, as it evolves.

Supplemental Material Statement: source code, queries and datasets used for our evaluations are available at https://github.com/nicolasferranti/wikidata-repairs, with the exception of historical WD HDT [5] snapshots.[11]

References

1. Angles, R., Buil-Aranda, C., Hogan, A., Rojas, C., Vrgoc, D.: WDbench: a Wikidata graph query benchmark. In: Sattler, U., et al. (eds.) ISWC 2022. LNCS, vol. 13489, pp. 714–731. Springer, Cham (2022). https://doi.org/10.1007/978-3-031-19433-7_41
2. Chen, J., Chen, X., Horrocks, I., Myklebust, E.B., Jiménez-Ruiz, E.: Correcting knowledge base assertions. In: Huang, Y., King, I., Liu, T., van Steen, M. (eds.) WWW '20: The Web Conference 2020, Taipei, Taiwan, April 20–24, 2020, pp. 1537–1547. ACM/IW3C2 (2020). https://doi.org/10.1145/3366423.3380226
3. Cyganiak, R., Wood, D., Lanthaler, M.: RDF 1.1 Concepts and Abstract Syntax (2014). https://www.w3.org/TR/rdf11-concepts/
4. Diefenbach, D., Wilde, M.D., Alipio, S.: Wikibase as an infrastructure for knowledge graphs: the EU knowledge Graph. In: Hotho, A., et al. (eds.) ISWC 2021. LNCS, vol. 12922, pp. 631–647. Springer, Cham (2021). https://doi.org/10.1007/978-3-030-88361-4_37
5. Fernández, J.D., Martınez-Prieto, M.A., Gutiérrez, C., Polleres, A., Arias, M.: Binary RDF representation for publication and exchange (HDT) **19**(2) (2013). https://doi.org/10.1016/j.websem.2013.01.002
6. Ferranti, N., De Souza, J.F., Ahmetaj, S., Polleres, A.: Formalizing and validating Wikidata's property constraints using SHACL and SPARQL. Semant. Web **15**(6), 2333–2380 (2024). https://doi.org/10.3233/SW-243611
7. Gayo, J.E.L.: Wshex: a language to describe and validate Wikibase entities. In: Kaffee, L., Razniewski, S., Amaral, G., Alghamdi, K.S. (eds.) Proceedings of the 3rd Wikidata Workshop 2022 co-located with the 21st International Semantic Web Conference (ISWC2022), Virtual Event, Hanghzou, China, October 2022. CEUR Workshop Proceedings, vol. 3262. CEUR-WS.org (2022). https://ceur-ws.org/Vol-3262/paper3.pdf
8. Haller, A., Polleres, A., Dobriy, D., Ferranti, N., Méndez, S.J.R.: An analysis of links in Wikidata. In: Groth, P., et al. (eds.) ESWC 2022, LNCS, vol. 13261, pp. 21–38. Springer, Cham (2022). https://doi.org/10.1007/978-3-031-06981-9_2
9. Hogan, A., Blomqvist, E., Cochez, M., d'Amato, C., de Melo, G., Gutierrez, C., Kirrane, S., Gayo, J.E.L., Navigli, R., Neumaier, S., Ngomo, A.N., Polleres, A., Rashid, S.M., Rula, A., Schmelzeisen, L., Sequeda, J.F., Staab, S., Zimmermann, A.: Knowledge graphs. ACM Comput. Surv. **54**(4), 71:1–71:37 (2022). https://doi.org/10.1145/3447772
10. Jakubowski, M., den Bussche, J.V.: Compiling SHACL into SQL. In: Demartini, G., Hose, K., Acosta, M., Palmonari, M., Cheng, G., Skaf-Molli, H., Ferranti, N.,

[11] available at https://www.rdfhdt.org/datasets/.

Hernández, D., Hogan, A. (eds.) The Semantic Web - ISWC 2024 - 23rd International Semantic Web Conference, Baltimore, MD, USA, November 11-15, 2024, Proceedings, Part II. Lecture Notes in Computer Science, vol. 15232, pp. 59–77. Springer (2024). https://doi.org/10.1007/978-3-031-77850-6_4

11. Kalyanpur, A., Parsia, B., Horridge, M., Sirin, E.: Finding all justifications of OWL DL entailments. In: Aberer, K., Choi, K., Noy, N.F., Allemang, D., Lee, K., Nixon, L.J.B., Golbeck, J., Mika, P., Maynard, D., Mizoguchi, R., Schreiber, G., Cudré-Mauroux, P. (eds.) The Semantic Web, 6th International Semantic Web Conference, 2nd Asian Semantic Web Conference, ISWC 2007 + ASWC 2007, Busan, Korea, November 11-15, 2007. Lecture Notes in Computer Science, vol. 4825, pp. 267–280. Springer (2007). https://doi.org/10.1007/978-3-540-76298-0_20
12. Martin, D.L., Patel-Schneider, P.F.: Wikidata constraints on MARS. In: Kaffee, L., Tifrea-Marciuska, O., Simperl, E., Vrandecic, D. (eds.) Proceedings of the 1st Wikidata Workshop (Wikidata 2020) co-located with 19th International Semantic Web Conference(OPub 2020), Virtual Conference, November 2-6, 2020. CEUR Workshop Proceedings, vol. 2773. CEUR-WS.org (2020), https://ceur-ws.org/Vol-2773/paper-12.pdf
13. Martin, D.L., Patel-Schneider, P.F.: Wikidata constraints on MARS (extended technical report) (2020). https://doi.org/10.48550/arXiv.2008.03900
14. Marx, M., Krötzsch, M., Thost, V.: Logic on MARS: ontologies for generalised property graphs. In: Sierra, C. (ed.) Proceedings of the Twenty-Sixth International Joint Conference on Artificial Intelligence, IJCAI 2017, Melbourne, Australia, August 19-25, 2017, pp. 1188–1194. ijcai.org (2017). https://doi.org/10.24963/IJCAI.2017/165
15. Patel-Schneider, P.F., Martin, D.: Wikidata on MARS (2020). https://doi.org/10.48550/arXiv.2008.06599
16. Peñaloza, R.: Axiom pinpointing. In: Cota, G., Daquino, M., Pozzato, G.L. (eds.) Applications and Practices in Ontology Design, Extraction, and Reasoning, Studies on the Semantic Web, vol. 49, pp. 162–177. IOS Press (2020). https://doi.org/10.3233/SSW200042
17. Piscopo, A., Simperl, E.: Who models the world?: collaborative ontology creation and user roles in wikidata. Proc. ACM Hum. Comput. Interact. **2**(CSCW), 141:1–141:18 (2018). https://doi.org/10.1145/3274410
18. Polleres, A., et al.: How does knowledge evolve in open knowledge graphs? TGDK **1**(1), 11:1–11:59 (2023). https://doi.org/10.4230/TGDK.1.1.11
19. Polleres, A., Wallner, J.: On the relation between SPARQL1.1 and answer set programming. Journal of Applied Non-Classical Logics (JANCL) **23**(1–2), 159–212 (2013). https://doi.org/10.1080/11663081.2013.798992, special issue on Equilibrium Logic and Answer Set Programming
20. Shenoy, K., Ilievski, F., Garijo, D., Schwabe, D., Szekely, P.A.: A study of the quality of wikidata. J. Web Semant. **72**, 100679 (2022). https://doi.org/10.1016/J.WEBSEM.2021.100679
21. Tanon, T.P., Bourgaux, C., Suchanek, F.M.: Learning how to correct a knowledge base from the edit history. In: Liu, L., et al. (eds.) The World Wide Web Conference, WWW 2019, San Francisco, CA, USA, May 13-17, 2019, pp. 1465–1475. ACM (2019). https://doi.org/10.1145/3308558.3313584
22. Troquard, N., Confalonieri, R., Galliani, P., Peñaloza, R., Porello, D., Kutz, O.: Repairing ontologies via axiom weakening. In: McIlraith, S.A., Weinberger, K.Q. (eds.) Proceedings of the Thirty-Second AAAI Conference on Artificial Intelligence, (AAAI-18), the 30th innovative Applications of Artificial Intelligence (IAAI-18),

and the 8th AAAI Symposium on Educational Advances in Artificial Intelligence (EAAI-18), New Orleans, Louisiana, USA, February 2-7, 2018. pp. 1981–1988. AAAI Press (2018). https://doi.org/10.1609/AAAI.V32I1.11567

23. Turki, H., et al.: Using logical constraints to validate statistical information about disease outbreaks in collaborative knowledge graphs: the case of COVID-19 epidemiology in wikidata. PeerJ Comput. Sci. **8**, e1085 (2022). https://doi.org/10.7717/peerj-cs.1085
24. Vrandecic, D., Krötzsch, M.: Wikidata: a free collaborative knowledgebase. Commun. ACM **57**(10), 78–85 (2014). https://doi.org/10.1145/2629489
25. W3C: SHACL Core Specification 1.0 (2017). https://www.w3.org/TR/shacl/
26. W3C: Shape Expressions (ShEx) 2.1 Specification (2020). https://shexspec.github.io/spec/

Beyond Manual Labels: Unsupervised Graph-Based Explanations for Error Analysis in Image Classifiers

Youmna Ismaeil[1,2](✉), Jan-Hendrik Metzen[3], Trung-Kien Tran[2], Hendrik Blockeel[1], and Daria Stepanova[2]

[1] KU Leuven, Leuven, Belgium
hendrik.blockeel@kuleuven.be
[2] Bosch Center for Artificial Intelligence, Renningen, Germany
{Youmna.ismaeil,trung-kien.tran,daria.stepanova}@de.bosch.com
[3] IPAI Aleph Alpha Research, Aleph Alpha, Heidelberg, Germany
janhendrik.metzen@aleph-alpha-ip.ai

Abstract. Training datasets often contain subtle but irrelevant patterns that bias image classifiers and limit their generalization. Prior research has focused on detecting biases in misclassified data using manually defined dimensions, such as age or gender. However, since these approaches rely on manually predefined dimensions, they are labor-intensive and bound to be limited in terms of their coverage. Moreover, existing methods overlook biases present in correctly classified data. To address these issues, we propose an unsupervised framework that leverages commonsense knowledge graphs and open-source foundation models to automatically derive semantic dimensions and their values, identifying biases that influence correct and incorrect classifications of data. Using these dimensions and values, we construct scene graphs and identify distinctive graph patterns for correctly and incorrectly classified data, uncovering how combinations of semantic dimensions impact classifier decisions. Evaluations confirm that our scene graphs are of high quality, as they include information from manual annotations while being denser and more informative than manually constructed graphs. Moreover, our framework demonstrates high predictive accuracy, effectively identifying patterns responsible for correct and incorrect classifications, with F1 scores ranging from 0.72 to 0.96. It also proves effective for error analysis and proactive bias detection in datasets.

Keywords: Explainable AI · Scene Graphs · Bias Detection · Knowledge Graphs

1 Introduction

Neural networks achieve impressive classification performance through high-quality training data, but their ability to generalize weakens when the data is biased. For instance, a classifier trained on classrooms with green desks may fail to generalize to

J.-H. Metzen—This work was done while at Bosch Center for Artificial Intelligence.

D. Garijo et al. (Eds.): ISWC 2025, LNCS 16140, pp. 388–406, 2026.
https://doi.org/10.1007/978-3-032-09527-5_21

other desk colors. Such biases are prevalent in datasets like CelebA [29], where blond females dominate certain labels. Exploring and understanding failures of image classifiers is challenging and has been addressed in several works [4,16,22,26,31,38]. These studies typically rely on manually predefined dimensions (e.g., age or gender), which are labor-intensive and restrict bias analysis to fixed dimensions and failure cases only that may not encompass the full spectrum of possible bias causes.

To address these shortcomings, we propose an unsupervised framework that combines commonsense knowledge graphs (CSKGs), foundation models, and graph mining techniques to extract patterns from automatically extracted dimensions, uncovering learned bias. This approach enables the discovery of complex patterns that go beyond limited predefined labels by generating detailed, task-agnostic scene descriptions. These descriptions include object attributes (e.g., shape, color), environmental settings (e.g., dark, cloudy, rainy), and visual styles (e.g., blurry, high or low contrast), addressing gaps left by previous scene description methods [5,32,47,52]. The descriptions are structured as scene graphs and analyzed using graph mining techniques to uncover patterns that emulate classifier behavior, revealing how input components influence predictions. E.g., a pattern can state that images correctly classified as classrooms often feature green desks and wooden chairs; at the same time, another pattern might indicate that incorrectly classified images typically depict blue desks and metal chairs.

Additionally, we utilize insights from the CSKG and extracted patterns to predict potential failures, enhancing the robustness of image classifiers and helping avoid failures due to low or no coverage of specific scenarios in the training data. For example, if a pattern shows that classrooms with blue desks and metal chairs are often misclassified, collecting more such images for retraining could improve classifier performance. We also make use of the extracted patterns to help in understanding and justifying failures made by an image classifier. The main contributions of this work are:

- An unsupervised framework that extracts **graph-based patterns** from automatically extracted semantic dimensions, enabling the discovery of complex success and failure patterns learned by an image classifier.
- An unsupervised scene descriptor that uniquely utilizes CSKGs and foundation models to create detailed scene graphs for images.
- A novel use of sub-graph mining to extract patterns for analyzing failure cases in image classifiers, providing structured insights into their behavior.
- A novel application of the framework to predict and explain failure cases using structured graph explanations for systematic error analysis.

2 Framework

Before delving into the details of our framework, we introduce the notations used throughout this work.

- A Knowledge Graph (KG) denoted as $\mathcal{KG}$ comprises triples in the form (s, r, o), where s (subject) and o (object) are entities or concepts and r denotes the relationship between them. For example, the triple *(desk, is, blue)* indicates that the desk is

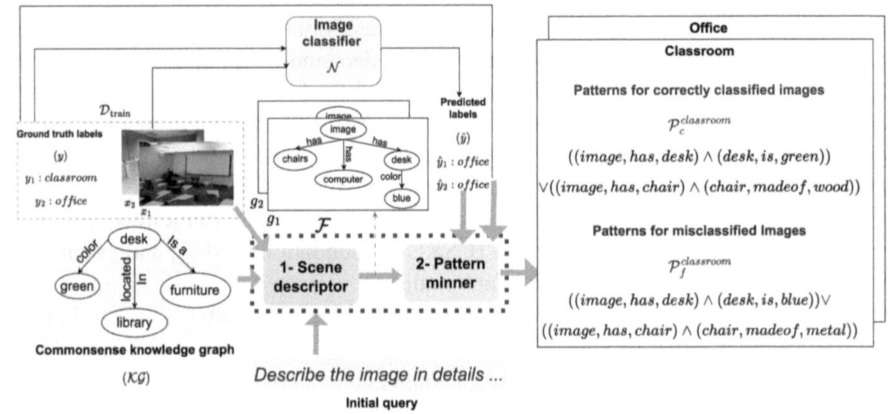

Fig. 1. Illustration of the proposed framework for pattern extraction. The framework features an unsupervised scene descriptor for generating scene graphs, and a pattern miner that identifies common graph patterns among scene graphs for correctly and misclassified images per class.

blue. In this work, we utilize ConceptNet 5.5 [40], a commonsense knowledge graph known for its high coverage and open access, though other CSKGs can also be used in our framework.
- $\mathcal{D} = \{(x_i, y_i)\}_{i=1}^m$ represents the dataset composed of image-label pairs, where x_i is the ith image, y_i its corresponding class label and m denotes the total number of images. The dataset is divided into 3 subsets: training ($\mathcal{D}_{\text{train}}$), validation ($\mathcal{D}_{\text{valid}}$), and testing ($\mathcal{D}_{\text{test}}$).
- $\mathcal{N}$ denotes the image classifier trained on $\mathcal{D}_{\text{train}}$ to predict the label $\hat{y}$ from the input image x.

Our framework $\mathcal{F}$, shown in Fig. 1, takes $\mathcal{KG}$ and $\mathcal{D}_{\text{train}}$ as input and outputs patterns reflecting distinguishing commonalities among correctly classified images (w.r.t. falsely classified ones), and separately, patterns for falsely classified images (w.r.t. correctly classified images) for each class k. To extract these patterns for each class, our framework includes two main modules: a scene descriptor that gathers detailed information from images in $\mathcal{D}_{\text{train}}$, and a pattern extractor that identifies recurring patterns in the scene descriptions. In the following sections, we explain our framework in detail.

2.1 Scene Descriptor

The scene descriptor (see Fig. 2) takes the images $\{x_1, \ldots, x_q\}$ from $\mathcal{D}_{\text{train}}$, and a CSKG $\mathcal{KG}$ as input and outputs a set of graphs $\{g_1, \ldots, g_q\}$, with each graph thoroughly describing a single image. To generate these graphs, we propose to rely on a foundation model. In principle, any foundational model suitable for visual and textual question answering could be suited for this task. In our experiments we relied on the open-source LLaVA v1.5 model [27], which is pre-trained for visual and textual question answering, allowing us to generate scene descriptions without additional fine-tuning.

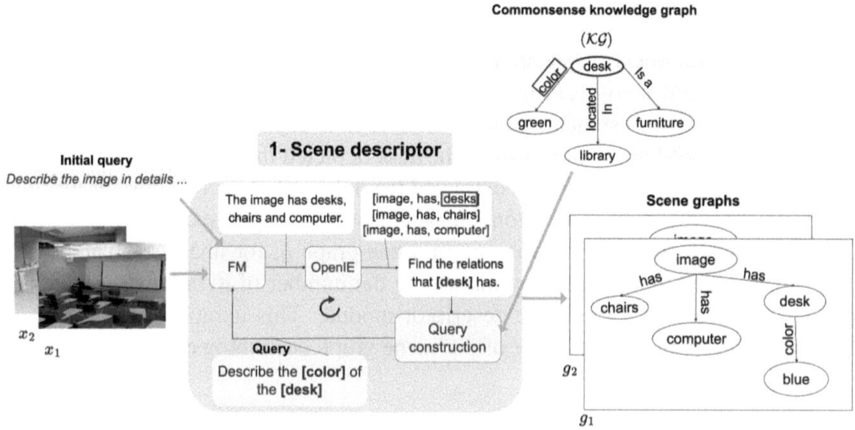

Fig. 2. The scene descriptor leverages $\mathcal{KG}$ and foundation models (FM) to generate scene graphs g_i for images x_i in an unsupervised fashion.

You are given an image, and your task is to write a paragraph describing the image in details. The description should be detailed enough to draw and paint the image again without seeing it. Provide reasoning why you think that the image has specific features. Answer in short, simple, full sentences. Stick to the image; do not mention information that is not in the image.

Describe the [relation] of the [node]. Your Answer has to be with respect to the image. If the object is not in the image or is not clear, skip the question. Answer in complete sentences. Do not answer with a single word. Do not answer with yes/no. Answer in short, simple, full sentences.

Fig. 3. On the left: details of the initial query (*"Describe the image in detail .."*) given to LLaVA for each image x_i. On the right: instructions given to LLaVA along with the question *"Describe the [relation] of the [node]."*

First, we prompt FM with an initial query asking it to generate a detailed description of a given image, including specific instructions on the desired level of detail, as outlined in Fig. 3. We then extract triplets from the foundation model's responses using OpenIE [1], an unsupervised method that does not require the fine-tuning typically needed by foundation models for triplet extraction [36]. Then we pass the triplets extracted from the answer of the initial query along with the $\mathcal{KG}$ to the query construction module that identifies proper semantic dimensions that each concept might have to ask relevant questions about them. If a concept is not in the CSKG, we extract the relations of its most similar concept based on embeddings computed using MiniLM [45], a task-agnostic, lightweight model. We treat the node's relation labels in the CSKG as semantic dimensions and then use the template *"Describe the [relation] of the [node]"* as a query to the FM, along with the image, to extract visual insights about the node and its attributes.

For example, if *writing desk* is one of the nodes in the triplets extracted from the answer to the initial query, we search for a similar node to *writing desk* in the CSKG. Based on the embedding of *writing desk*, the closest node in the CSKG is *desk*, which is associated with several semantic dimensions, such as *color*. Leveraging this relationship, we query the FM about the *color* of the *desk* depicted in the image. This process is repeated for each node in the triplets extracted from the initial query's answer for image x_i, enabling the extraction of additional triplets from the responses.

These triplets form a level in the output scene graph g_i for image x_i. The depth of the scene graph can be increased by increasing the number of iterations, n, which is a tunable parameter within the scene descriptor module. This iterative approach allows us to control the level of granularity of the scene graph describing each image.

2.2 Pattern Miner

Once we obtain the scene graphs for each image in the form of triplets, we extract the common sub-graph patterns among images that are correctly classified for each class as well as the falsely classified images. To achieve this, we use cgSpan [37], which efficiently extracts frequent closed subgraph patterns from a set of graphs and a node-to-label mapping, providing compact representations without redundancies. We use a node-to-label mapping to ensure that cgSpan finds patterns among semantically similar but differently named nodes, such as *desk* and *writing desk*. This allows it to identify sub-graph patterns involving nodes with different names that belong to the same class.

To construct this mapping, we compute node embeddings using MiniLM [45], a task-agnostic, lightweight embedding model, and consider nodes with a cosine similarity of at least 0.8 to be similar. To prepare the input for cgSpan, we group the scene graphs by class and split them into graphs for correct and incorrect classifications based on the ground truth labels vs predicted labels. For example, as shown in Fig. 4 for $k = classroom$, g_1 and g_3 belong to images that were correctly classified by $\mathcal{N}$ as classroom, while g_2 and g_4 are scene graphs for misclassified images.

For each class, we pass the group of graphs for correctly classified images, along with the node-to-label mapping, to cgSpan to extract the most frequent closed sub-graph patterns, denoted as $\mathcal{P}_c^k$. We repeat this process for the graphs of images with the ground truth label that were misclassified to obtain $\mathcal{P}_f^k$. Each set of patterns $\mathcal{P}_c^k$ is composed of a disjunction of patterns (i.e., $\mathcal{P}_c^k = p_1 \vee \ldots \vee p_j$), where each pattern p_j is a conjunction of triplets, as all the triplets in p_j are crucial for forming the pattern. The pattern can be composed of only one triplet, and the same applies to $\mathcal{P}_f^k$. We then exclude the common sub-graph patterns between $\mathcal{P}_f^k$ and $\mathcal{P}_c^k$ from both sets, as shared patterns are uninformative.

CgSpan also returns a frequency score f_j for each extracted pattern p_j that can be used to filter patterns. We consider patterns appearing in at least 50% of input image graphs, balancing quality and quantity while ensuring that no patterns are returned if the model is poorly trained or performing randomly. The parameter settings and runtime details are discussed in Sect. 3.4.

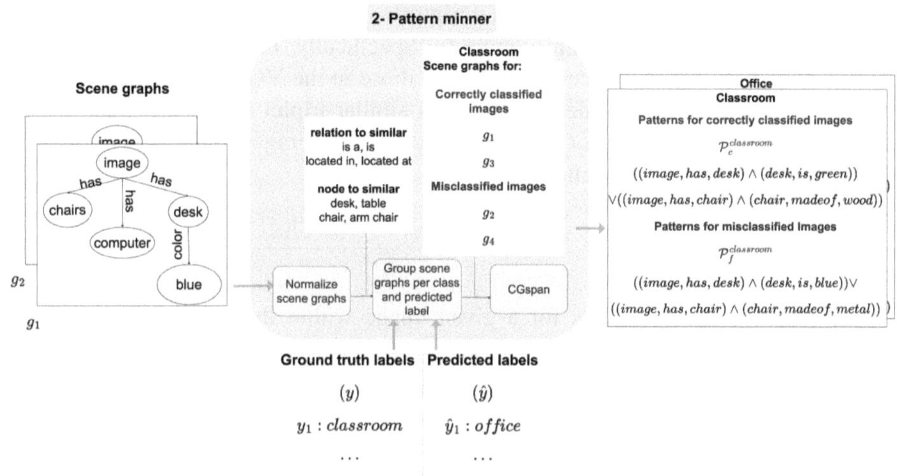

Fig. 4. The pattern miner extracts the common patterns between the scene graphs created by the scene descriptor.

3 Experiments and Results

In this section, we evaluate the scene graphs from the scene descriptor and patterns from the pattern miner using ResNet18 [15] as the classifier.

3.1 Scene Descriptor Evaluation

First, we evaluate the quality of scene graphs generated using our method by comparing them to those constructed based on manual annotations. In what follows, we set n, the parameter responsible for the number of iterations of the scene descriptor, to 2.

Dataset

We evaluate the scene descriptor using the *Visual Genome (VG)* dataset [23], which contains scene graphs created from manual annotations with an average of 35 objects, 26 attributes, and 21 relationships per image. For the evaluation of the scene graphs, we randomly select 100 images and their corresponding scene graphs.

Baseline

As a baseline for the scene descriptor, we utilized our framework with $n = 1$ and used the initial query *"Describe the image in details"*, without additional instructions. We use the following questions to assess the performance of the scene descriptor:

• Do scene graphs generated by the scene descriptor cover the aspects represented in scene graphs constructed based on human annotations?

This experiment evaluates graph quality by comparing the similarity between graphs generated by the scene descriptor and those derived from manual annotations. To handle lexical differences between the scene descriptor's output and the VG, we use embeddings for each triplet to measure similarity. Specifically, cosine similarity between triplet embeddings from our scene graphs and those in the VG is calculated. For each image triplet in the VG, we identify the most similar triplet within the graph generated by our scene descriptor for the same image. The average similarity score is then computed using the formula defined in Eq. 1.

$$S(\hat{g}_i, g_i) = \frac{\sum_{\hat{\tau} \in \hat{g}_i} \max_{\tau \in g_i} (\mathrm{Sim}(\xi(\tau), \xi(\hat{\tau})))}{|\hat{g}_i|} \tag{1}$$

where, $\hat{g}_i$ is the list of triplets for a given image within the VG dataset, while g_i represents the set of triplets for the same image generated by the scene descriptor. $\mathrm{Sim}(\xi(\tau), \xi(\hat{\tau}))$ is the cosine similarity. The triplet embedding ξ is computed as the concatenation of embeddings: for triple $\tau = (s, r, t)$ we have $\xi(\tau) = [\mathrm{Embedding}(s), \mathrm{Embedding}(r), \mathrm{Embedding}(t)]$, where embeddings are computed using MiniLM. The same applies to $\xi(\hat{\tau})$. While triplet embeddings could in principle be derived from node embeddings generated by knowledge graph embedding models [2,13,43], these models generally focus on learning node embeddings from the graph structure and node neighborhoods, rather than the semantic meanings of the node labels.

Our findings show that the triplets in the VG dataset have comparable counterparts in the outputs generated by our scene descriptor, with an observed average similarity score of 0.79. This is noteworthy compared to the baseline similarity score of 0.48. These results validate the scene descriptor and its sub-components, LLaVA & OpenIE, in replicating the quality of manually annotated graphs and extracting high-quality triplets, showcasing its potential for detailed, unsupervised scene graph construction.

• Does the scene descriptor produce richer graphs than graphs obtained from manual annotations?

To investigate this, we compare the level of detail captured by our scene descriptor against the VG dataset. This is achieved by performing a comparative analysis focusing on the following five key components: triplets, relations, nodes, node clusters, and relation clusters. Our analysis evaluates the total number of nodes and relations as well as the diversity within these elements. We specifically examine cluster counts to determine whether variations in nodes (e.g., *desk* versus *writing desk*) or relation phrases (e.g., *has* versus *has a*) contribute to the differences in graph statistics. For that, we use HDBSCAN [30], which determines the optimal number of clusters based on data density, with a minimum cluster size of 2 and cluster selection $\epsilon = 0.1$.

Figure 5 shows the overall number for each component. One can observe that graphs generated by our scene descriptor are denser compared to those from the VG dataset based on all five components. Further evidence is provided in Table 1 (with more examples from additional experimental results available in the supplementary material), where it is further confirmed that the VG graphs often contain less details about the scenes compared to the graphs generated by our scene descriptor. Indeed, as one can see in Table 1, the scene graphs constructed by our method contain such specific information as the dogs' color and species, the background, and the surfing board color in the 1st row, as well as the towel color and the exact placement of the toilet and

Table 1. VG graph vs. our scene descriptor graph for the same image, showcasing the richer details captured by our method.

Image	**VG graph** ($\hat{g}$)	**Scene descriptor graph** (g)
	(boats, are on, ocean), (ship, on, water)	(fighter jets, flying in, formation), (fighter jets, flying in, coordinated pattern), (planes, synchronize, movement), (planes, are shaped like rockets), (planes, is, military), (altitude flyby, is, low), (primary, impressive aerial display of, military), (smoke, is coming from, planes), (smoke, is, white), (smoke, is, trailing), (smoke, high into, sky), (navy ship, are, multiple), (navy ship, are on, ocean), (navy ships, including, battleship), (scene, is, dynamic), (ocean, is in, background), (two cruise ships, are in, background), (island, is, background), (view, is, up-close), (event, is, outdoor), (exercises, are, military), ...
	(dogs, have, shirts), (dogs, on, surfboard), (surfboard, on, water), (woman, in, water), (words, on, chest), (hat, on, head)	(dogs, are wearing, shirts), (dogs, wear, bandanas), (dogs, are, brown), (dogs, are on, surfboard), (dogs, are, labrador retrievers), (surfboard, is in, water), (surfboard, is, blue), (woman, is, old), (woman, is on, surfboard in water), (water, is, blue), (woman, wearing, pink hat), (custom, is with, reality rally), (scene, is, unusual), (day, is, sunny), (sky, is, clear), (apron, is, white), ...
	(towel set, hanging on, holder), (tile, on, floor)	(towel, is, black), (towels, are, hung), (floor, is, black tiled), (natural light, enter, bathroom), (toilet, is, white), (toilet, is, in the corner against the wall), (toilet, is by, sink), (tub, under, window)

bathtub in the 2nd row. These findings underscore the superior descriptive power and comprehensiveness of our scene descriptor, demonstrating its potential to enrich data in automated scene graph generation.

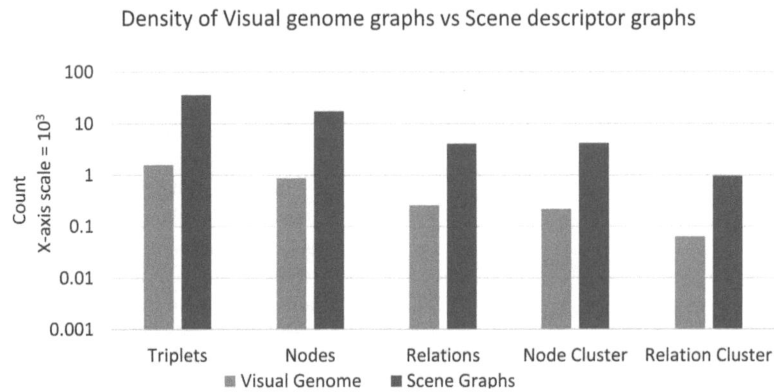

Fig. 5. A plot in logarithmic scale reflecting the total number of triplets, nodes, relations, node clusters, and relation clusters found in VG graphs vs. our scene graphs ($n = 2$).

3.2 Pattern Evaluation

In this section, we evaluate the quality of the extracted patterns using datasets with (1) known patterns and (2) unknown patterns. Our experiments aim to verify the framework's accuracy in detecting patterns recognized by image classifiers and to assess the quality of patterns in datasets lacking predefined patterns. In the experiments evaluating the pattern miner, the parameter n of our framework is set to 2 unless stated otherwise.

Datasets

For evaluation, we utilize the following datasets:

• **Biased CelebA**

CelebA [29] is a large facial attributes dataset annotated with 40 attributes. Following [35], we constructed Biased CelebA with 1000 *female* images with *blond hair* and 1000 *male* images with *dark hair*. The data was split in a 3:2 ratio for training and validation. For testing, we selected 2000 additional images with swapped attributes, where all *females* have *dark hair* and all *males* have *blond hair*.

• **Waterbirds**

The Waterbirds dataset [35] classifies images into *waterbird* and *landbird* categories. *Waterbirds* typically appear in images with *aquatic* backgrounds, and *landbirds* in images with *terrestrial* backgrounds respectively. We selected 500 images per class, splitting the 1000 images in 3:2 for training and validation. For testing, we chose 1000 additional images where the background context is swapped—*landbirds* have *aquatic* backgrounds, while *waterbirds* have *terrestrial* backgrounds.

• **MIT Indoor**

To challenge the classifier, we selected six visually similar classes (*bakery, deli, classroom, office, kitchen, and pantry*) from the MIT Indoor dataset [34]. This subset includes 2,662 images, stratified into a 3:2 ratio for training and testing.

Table 2. F1 scores of ResNet18 trained from scratch on various datasets.

Dataset	training F1	validation F1	test F1
CelebA	0.71	0.71	0.52
Waterbirds	0.76	0.77	0.47
Indoor	0.55	-	0.49

Table 3. Patterns extracted from the ResNet18 trained on the biased CelebA and Waterbirds datasets, sorted by frequency.

Dataset	Class	Patterns from correct predictions ($\mathcal{P}_c^k$)
Biased CelebA	female	(fair, is, complexion) ∨ (hair, is with, blonde)
	male	(hair, is, darkness)
Waterbirds	landbird	((small, is, bird) ∧ (bird, has, position in branch) ∧ (bird, is focus of, image)∧ (trees, in, image)) ∨ ((background, is in, forest)∧ (bird, has, bright coloration), ...
	waterbird	(bird, is, seagull) ∨ ((bird, in, image) ∧ (bird, on, water) ∧ (large, is, bird) ∧ (bird, is, black),...)

Model

For the image classifier, we trained a ResNet18 model with parameter tuning similar to [35] for the CelebA and Waterbirds datasets. Evaluation was conducted on the validation split, which exhibits patterns different from those present in the training split, to ensure the model captures dataset patterns. This is verified if the model trained on a biased data split performs better on a validation split with the same bias than on a test split with a different bias. For the MIT Indoor dataset, the model was trained for 20 epochs with a learning rate of 0.001. As the patterns in this dataset are unknown, we report F1 scores on the training and test splits.

Baseline

Given the novelty and fundamental difference of our structured graph pattern-based explanations from explanations provided in prior methods (see Sect. 4 for discussion), which rely on single-label explanations or visual illustrations, direct comparisons with earlier proposed methods is infeasible. Therefore, as a baseline, we use our framework with $n = 1$, i.e., we do not utilize the iterations to extract more information about the images, which also means that we do not use the CSKG to create scene graphs.

Relying on the introduced datasets and models we address the following questions:

• Can our framework identify known pattern bias in an image classifier?

To answer this question, we assess the quality of the patterns extracted by our framework both qualitatively and quantitatively.

Qualitative Evaluation

Table 2 shows the F1 score of ResNet18 on training and validation splits that share the same bias, as well as on a test set with a different bias. The performance of ResNet18 on the CelebA and Waterbirds biased data sets indicates its capacity to capture specific patterns. This is evidenced by high F1 scores in the training and validation splits, which share the same patterns, but lower performance on test splits that present different patterns. Upon achieving this, we extract and compare patterns from the classifier's correct and incorrect predictions against known dataset biases. For example, the bias detected in the patterns extracted from ResNet18 trained on the CelebA dataset (Table 3) align with its lack of generalization on the CelebA test set (Table 2) and the known patterns in the biased dataset [35], confirming the effectiveness of our framework in identifying biases contributing to classifier errors. This procedure was similarly applied to the Waterbirds dataset, with findings (Table 3) aligning with those observed in the biased CelebA dataset.

Quantitative Evaluation

When the dataset patterns learned by the classification neural network $\mathcal{N}$ are unknown, we evaluate the effectiveness of the extracted patterns in replicating $\mathcal{N}$'s predictive behavior. This assessment is carried out using a pattern-based classifier, denoted as PC. The classifier PC operates by taking a scene graph g_i constructed by our scene descriptor and the patterns mined by the pattern miner for different classes. It then predicts a class $\dot{y}_i$ for each image x_i by evaluating the similarity between the triplets in the scene graph g_i for x_i and the extracted patterns for each class $\mathcal{P}_j^k$, where j can be c (correctly classified) or f (falsely classified), and $\mathcal{P}_c^k$ represents the set of patterns associated with images correctly classified under the class k. More formally, PC relies on the scores computed by Eq. 2 to predict the class k of an image x_i with scene graph g_i.

$$score_{j^k}(g_i, \mathcal{P}_j^k) = \frac{\sum_{p_a \in \mathcal{P}_j^k} f_a \cdot S(g_i, p_a)}{|\mathcal{P}_j^k|} \tag{2}$$

where p_a is a subgraph pattern, f_a is the cgSpan frequency score of p_a, and $S(g_i, p_a)$ is the average similarity between the scene graph g_i and the sub-graph pattern p_a (see Eq. 1). For convenience, in Eq. 2 each pattern $\mathcal{P}$ is treated as a set of conjunctions and a conjunction p as a set of triplets. After computing $score_{j^k}$ for $j \in \{c, f\}$ for each image x_i and each class k, we apply the softmax function to these scores to obtain the probability of each $\mathcal{P}_j^k$ and select the pattern with the highest probability. For example, if $\mathcal{P}_c^{office}$ has the highest probability, then the PC classifier outputs *office*. Following prior work [19], we compute the alignment score between the predictions of PC and the predictions of $\mathcal{N}$. However, unlike previous work, we use a weighted F1 score instead of percentage to better account for the varying number of images correctly and incorrectly classified by the neural network $\mathcal{N}$.

The weighted F1 alignment score measures the coherence between the predictions made by $\mathcal{N}$ and PC with respect to the ground truth labels. For each image x_i, let y_i be the ground truth label, $\hat{y}_i$ the prediction made by $\mathcal{N}$, and $\dot{y}_i$ the prediction by PC. The alignment score is computed as the weighted F1 score between two binary sequences: one indicating whether each $\hat{y}_i$ matches y_i (1 if $\hat{y}_i = y_i$, 0 otherwise), and the other indicating whether each $\dot{y}_i$ matches y_i (1 if $\dot{y}_i = y_i$, 0 otherwise). The score is the

Table 4. Weighted F1 alignment scores comparing $\mathcal{N}$'s predictions on the test set with labels generated by three variants of PC: (1) a baseline model, (2) an FM-only model that replaces CSKG with FM for attribute extraction, and (3) our full framework that combines CSKG and FM (with $n = 2$).

Dataset	Baseline	FM Only PC	(CSKG & FM) - PC (Ours)
Biased CelebA	0.64	0.66	0.80
Waterbirds	0.90	0.93	0.96
Indoor	0.67	0.63	0.72

Table 5. Weighted F1 alignment score for different values of n for different datasets.

n	Waterbirds	CelebA	Indoor
1	0.90	0.64	0.67
2	0.96	0.80	0.72

highest when both models make correct predictions ($\hat{y}_i = \dot{y}_i = y_i$) or both make the same error ($\hat{y}_i \neq y_i$ and $\dot{y}_i \neq y_i$).

Table 4 presents the weighted F1 alignment scores for patterns extracted using different frameworks. The results indicate that patterns generated by our framework outperform those from both the baseline and the FM-only variant, where CSKG is replaced by FM for dimensions extraction. These patterns more effectively and reliably predict whether $\mathcal{N}$ will correctly classify or misclassify an unseen image from the test set. This highlights the importance of incorporating CSKGs with iterative refinement in generating informative scene graphs, which, in turn, enables the extraction of patterns that more closely align with $\mathcal{N}$'s predictions.

To assess whether the observed weighted F1 alignment scores could have occurred by chance, we performed a bootstrapped statistical significance test [11] comparing the weighted F1 scores of our proposed PC (using CSKG & FM) and $\mathcal{N}$. Bootstrapping was chosen for its flexibility and robustness in estimating p-values. Under the null hypothesis—assuming that the observed agreement between the two models' predictions is no greater than what would be expected by chance alone—the resulting p-values were found to be less than 0.001 across all datasets. This provides strong evidence that the alignment between the models is statistically significant and not attributable to random variation.

In Table 5, we present the results reflecting the effect of the parameter n on the granularity of the constructed scene graphs. We observe that larger values of n naturally result in more detailed graphs and yield better F1 alignment scores with the image classifier $\mathcal{N}$. When evaluated on the CelebA and Indoor datasets, our method benefits from two iterations of the scene graph computation, which provide richer information about the considered scene. In contrast, a single iteration is sufficient to achieve a weighted F1 alignment score of 0.9 on the simpler Waterbirds dataset. The impact of increasing the number of iterations n depends on the dataset complexity.

• Can the CSKG in our framework be replaced by a foundation model?
To address this question, we replaced the CSKG with a foundation model (LLaVA). Instead of using the CSKG to extract the respective dimensions, we instructed the LLaVA model to propose possible dimensions for an object by using the following prompt "*Return the list of properties that [node] has.*" Subsequently, we inquired about the values of the returned properties one by one. We call this variant of PC FM only PC. The results in Table 4 show that our framework, which utilizes CSKG for extracting semantic dimensions, is more effective in identifying patterns that mirror the behavior of $\mathcal{N}$ than the variant that replaces the CSKG with a foundation model. These results are consistent with prior findings [17,32,42,51,53], which show that multimodal foundation models often struggle with deep structured visual understanding when used alone, frequently overlooking objects' dimensions.

Fig. 6. Left: Top 3 images from the MIT Indoor dataset, manually labeled as *deli* but misclassified as *bakery* due to red-highlighted bakeries found in the extracted graph patterns for both the correct patterns of the *bakery* class and the false patterns of the *deli* class. Bottom 3 images are *deli* examples misclassified as *bakery*, due to the frequently occurring display cases and baked goods, identified by the graph-patterns in the false patterns of *deli* and correct patterns of *bakery*. Right: For reference, 6 *bakery* images from the same dataset, manually labeled as *bakery*. One can note the visual similarity to the *deli* images on the left, further demonstrating the validity and effectiveness of the insights uncovered by our patterns.

3.3 Use Cases

Our framework's extracted patterns have versatile applications. We highlight two: explaining the image classifier's errors and proactively detecting bias in datasets.

Error Analysis
Confusion matrices are useful to understand which classes are often confused with each other, but they do not explain *why* this happens. Our framework can address this limitation. When an image classifier frequently misclassifies instances of class A as class B, patterns in $(\mathcal{P}_c^A \cap \mathcal{P}_f^B)$ reveal likely reasons. For instance, in the MIT Indoor dataset, the

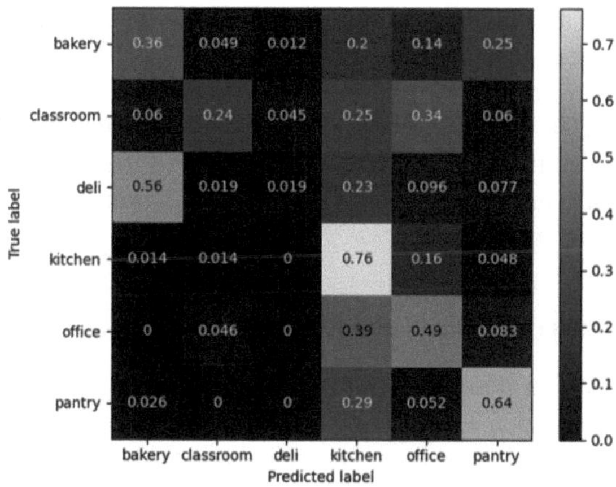

Fig. 7. Confusion matrix from evaluating the ResNet18 network trained on the Indoor dataset on the test split, showing that the model confuses images belonging to the class *deli* with images of *bakery* more than 50% of the time.

confusion matrix in Fig. 7 shows that *deli* is misclassified as *bakery* 56% of the time. Our framework reveals that the pattern *(goods, are, baked)*∨*(items, in, display case)* appears both in correctly classified images of *bakeries* and in images misclassified as *delis*. This suggests that *delis*, like *bakeries*, have baked goods; or perhaps there are images of *bakeries* that are mistakenly labeled as *delis* in the training dataset.

Looking at some actual images reveals that both scenarios hold: *deli* images often have bread, as highlighted in red in the first row of *deli* images in Fig. 6. There are annotation errors within the training dataset, as highlighted in the second row of images for *deli*, where the images feature only baked goods and are more likely to be identified by humans as *bakery* rather than *deli* but were labeled in the dataset as *deli*. This overlap leads to noisy data, complicating the training process and contributing to the misclassification of similar images across different classes.

Proactive Bias Detection

Our framework can be utilized to identify potential misclassification candidates by using patterns extracted from correctly classified images, denoted as $\mathcal{P}_c^k$. This can be done by leveraging CSKGs to extract antonyms for each node in $\mathcal{P}_c^k$ and then generate all possible antonym pattern combinations. For instance, consider $\mathcal{P}_c^{female} = ((hair, is, long) \land (hair, is, blond))$ from CelebA dataset. Based on the CSKG, while *hair* has no antonym, *long* and *blond* have antonyms *short* and *brunette*, respectively. This yields the following antonym patterns: $((hair, is, short) \land (hair, is, blond)) \lor ((hair, is, long) \land (hair, is, brunette)) \lor ((hair, is, short) \land (hair, is, brunette))$.

Images with these antonym patterns are more likely to be misclassified by the image classifier, especially if these patterns are rare or absent in the training data and, therefore, not present in the extracted patterns. This approach was applied to the CelebA and Waterbirds datasets, revealing that the derived antonym patterns align with the filtering used to create unbiased test splits. These test splits often include images that a non-robust classifier misclassifies, as reflected in the low test accuracies in Tab. 2. This underscores the value of using patterns from correctly classified images to identify gaps in the classifier's knowledge.

Additionally, our framework can be used to identify spurious patterns in the dataset before training by setting predicted labels to the ground truth. The extracted patterns can then be manually inspected for biases, serving as a proactive measure to develop fairer and more robust models.

3.4 Model Parameters, Settings and Runtime

This paper employs several models with carefully selected parameters:

• **LLaVA-v1.5-7b**, an open-source multi-modal model, was used without fine-tuning via the Hugging Face implementation, generating up to 300 tokens per output;

• **OpenIE**, an unsupervised extraction tool from the Stanza library (v1.7.0), was configured with affinity probability (1/3) to reduce noise, maximum entailments per clause (2) to ensure relevance, coreference resolution (*True*) for accuracy, and triple all nominals (*True*) to capture nominal relations;

• **CgSpan (v0.2.2)**, applied to mine frequent closed subgraph patterns, used a 50% minimum support threshold and minimum subgraph size of one edge (no maximum), balancing pattern complexity and frequency, with other parameters at default, using the authors' original code.

• The parameter n in our framework is set to $n = 2$. Based on our evaluation (see Table 5) increasing n from 1 to 2 substantially enhances both pattern quality and classifier alignment. This choice offers a practical trade-off between granularity and computational efficiency.

All experiments were run on an NVIDIA Tesla V100-SXM2-32GB GPU under Red Hat Enterprise Linux 8.9, providing up to 31.33 TFLOPS (FP16), with runtimes averaging 2 s per LLaVA query, circa 100 ms per OpenIE extraction, and under 1 min per class-level graph processed by cgSpan depending on dataset and settings.

4 Related Work

Systematic Error Analysis

Recent research has focused extensively on identifying systematic errors in neural networks [4,7,12,16,22,31,38]. Traditional methods use manually defined dimensions, such as gender, ethnicity, or object labels, to identify causes of failure. For instance, [38] relies on object labels to identify correlations between objects and model predictions, while [4] examines biases in facial analysis algorithms based on predefined phenotypes. Other approaches manipulate dimensions like blurriness to evaluate robustness [16] or analyze rare subgroups [7,31]. In contrast, our framework dynamically extracts dimensions and their values in an unsupervised fashion, eliminating manual efforts. It also extracts patterns from these dimensions for correct and incorrect predictions.

While [10] uses image captions to identify commonalities across image groups without fixed dimensions, captions fail to capture detailed structural relationships, which our scene descriptors provide. Captions have also been used to generate failure-inducing images [3,44], but these methods often miss critical scene details. Additionally, clustering misclassified images in latent spaces [9,20,39,46] often leads to incoherent groups, complicating caption associations and corrective evaluations [14].

Scene Graphs
The goal of scene graph generation is to parse an image to create a structured representation, ultimately aiming for a complete understanding of visual scenes. The following two approaches are typically used: (1) a two-stage method that first detects objects and then recognizes relationships [5,6,32,33,47,49,50,52], which gained significant attention with the release of the VG dataset; and (2) a one-stage method that simultaneously detects and recognizes objects and relations [8,25,28,41]. A comprehensive review of scene graph generation methods was conducted in [54]. Existing work focuses primarily on detecting objects and their relationships, often lacking detailed object descriptions (e.g., color, shape) and contextual information (e.g., weather, lighting, image mode, etc.) that could be the cause of model bias. Our unsupervised scene descriptor fills this gap by offering crucial details for a deeper understanding of the visual scene.

Frequent Sub-Graph Mining
Frequent sub-graph mining is a field within data mining dedicated to identifying common sub-graphs across graph datasets. Numerous studies have contributed to this field, [18,24,37,48] (see [21] for an extensive review). We chose cgSpan [37] for our work as it identifies frequent closed sub-graphs, ensuring that there are no supergraphs with the same frequency. This provides a compact, efficient representation of all frequent sub-graphs, reducing redundancy and offering faster processing than methods that enumerate all frequent sub-graphs.

5 Conclusion

We introduced a dynamic, unsupervised framework that generates graph-based patterns, offering deeper and more comprehensive explanations for better understanding of classifier behavior compared to the shallow, manually predefined dimensions used in previous work. The framework comprises two components: a novel scene descriptor that generates detailed and adaptable scene graphs for images, and a pattern extractor that identifies key patterns distinguishing between correct and incorrect classifications. Empirical evaluations demonstrate the robustness and effectiveness of our approach. Our scene graphs are richer and more detailed compared to manual annotations from VG. The pattern miner achieves high F1 scores in predicting classifier behavior, with extracted patterns proving valuable for error analysis and bias detection, fostering fairer and more robust models. This work presents the first approach for generating detailed graph-based explanations for image classifiers in an unsupervised fashion, surpassing prior efforts that rely on simplistic, manually annotated data. In future work we plan to extend our framework to utilize different foundation models and to provide explainability on models pretrained on unknown data.

Supplemental Material Statement: The supplementary material, available at: https://doi.org/10.6084/m9.figshare.29690348.v2, includes a link to code and data. TechnicalAppendix.pdf stores additional information regarding the paper and experimental results.

Acknowledgment. This work was partially funded by the European Union's programme under grant agreement No.101092908 (SMARTEDGE).

References

1. Angeli, G., Johnson, M., Manning, C.D.: Leveraging linguistic structure for open domain information extraction. In: Annual Meeting of the Association for Computational Linguistics (2015)
2. Bordes, A., Usunier, N., García-Durán, A., Weston, J., Yakhnenko, O.: Translating embeddings for modeling multi-relational data. In: NeurIPs, pp. 2787–2795 (2013)
3. Boreiko, V., Hein, M., Metzen, J.H.: Identifying systematic errors in object detectors with the scrod pipeline. ICCVW **2023**, 4092–4101 (2023)
4. Buolamwini, J., Gebru, T.: Gender shades: intersectional accuracy disparities in commercial gender classification. In: Conference on Fairness, Accountability and Transparency, FAT 2018, 23-24 February 2018, New York, NY, USA. Proceedings of Machine Learning Research, vol. 81, pp. 77–91. PMLR (2018)
5. Chen, G., Li, J., Wang, W.: Scene graph generation with role-playing large language models. In: Proceedings of the 38th International Conference on Neural Information Processing Systems (NeurIPS), pp. 4203–4231. Curran Associates Inc., Red Hook (2025)
6. Chen, T., Yu, W., Chen, R., Lin, L.: Knowledge-embedded routing network for scene graph generation. In: 2019 CVPR, pp. 6156–6164 (2019)
7. Collevati, M., Eiter, T., Higuera, N.: Leveraging neurosymbolic AI for slice discovery. In: NeSy 2024, vol. 14979, pp. 403–418 (2024)
8. Cong, Y., Yang, M.Y., Rosenhahn, B.: Reltr: Relation transformer for scene graph generation. IEEE Trans. Pattern Anal. Mach. Intell. **45**, 11169–11183 (2022)
9. d'Eon, G., d'Eon, J., Wright, J.R., Leyton-Brown, K.: The spotlight: a general method for discovering systematic errors in deep learning models. ACM FAccT 2022 (2022)
10. Dunlap, L., et al.: Describing differences in image sets with natural language. ArXiv abs/2312.02974 (2023)
11. Efron, B.: Bootstrap methods: another look at the jackknife. Ann. Stat. **7**, 1–26 (1979)
12. Fontanesi, M., Micheli, A., Podda, M.: Explaining graph classifiers by unsupervised node relevance attribution. In: xAI (2024)
13. Galkin, M., Denis, E.G., Wu, J., Hamilton, W.L.: Nodepiece: compositional and parameter-efficient representations of large knowledge graphs. In: ICLR 2022 (2022)
14. Gao, I., Ilharco, G., Lundberg, S.M., Ribeiro, M.T.: Adaptive testing of computer vision models. ICCV **2023**, 3980–3991 (2023)
15. He, K., Zhang, X., Ren, S., Sun, J.: Deep residual learning for image recognition. In: CVPR 2016, pp. 770–778 (2016)
16. Hendrycks, D., et al.: The many faces of robustness: a critical analysis of out-of-distribution generalization. In: 2021 ICCV, pp. 8320–8329. IEEE (2021)
17. Herzig, R., Mendelson, A., Karlinsky, L., Arbelle, A., Feris, R.S., Darrell, T., Globerson, A.: Incorporating structured representations into pretrained vision & language models using scene graphs. ArXiv abs/2305.06343 (2023)

18. Inokuchi, A., Washio, T., Motoda, H.: An apriori-based algorithm for mining frequent substructures from graph data. In: European Conference on Principles of Data Mining and Knowledge Discovery (2000)
19. Ismaeil, Y., Stepanova, D., Tran, T.K., Saranrittichai, P., Domokos, C., Blockeel, H.: Towards neural network interpretability using commonsense knowledge graphs. In: International Workshop on the Semantic Web (2022)
20. Jain, S., Lawrence, H., Moitra, A., Madry, A.: Distilling model failures as directions in latent space. ArXiv abs/2206.14754 (2022)
21. Jiang, C., Coenen, F., Zito, M.A.A.: A survey of frequent subgraph mining algorithms. Knowl. Eng. Rev. **28**, 75–105 (2012)
22. Kim, B., et al.: Interpretability beyond feature attribution: Quantitative testing with concept activation vectors (TCAV). In: Proceedings of the 35th International Conference on Machine Learning, ICML 2018, Stockholmsmässan, Stockholm, Sweden, July 10-15, 2018. Proceedings of Machine Learning Research, vol. 80, pp. 2673–2682. PMLR (2018)
23. Krishna, R., et al.: Visual genome: connecting language and vision using crowdsourced dense image annotations. IJCV **123**, 32–73 (2016)
24. Kuramochi, M., Karypis, G.: Finding frequent patterns in a large sparse graph. Data Min. Knowl. Disc. **11**, 243–271 (2004)
25. Li, R., Zhang, S., He, X.: Sgtr: end-to-end scene graph generation with transformer. CVPR **2022**, 19464–19474 (2022)
26. Li, Z., Xu, C.: Discover the unknown biased attribute of an image classifier. In: 2021 ICCV, pp. 14950–14959 (2021)
27. Liu, H., Li, C., Li, Y., Lee, Y.J.: Improved baselines with visual instruction tuning. In: CVPR 2024, pp. 26296–26306 (2024)
28. Liu, H., Yan, N., Mortazavi, M.S., Bhanu, B.: Fully convolutional scene graph generation. In: CVPR 2021, pp. 11541–11551 (2021)
29. Liu, Z., Luo, P., Wang, X., Tang, X.: Deep learning face attributes in the wild. In: ICCV 2015, pp. 3730–3738 (2015)
30. McInnes, L., Healy, J., Astels, S.: hdbscan: hierarchical density based clustering. J. Open Source Softw. **2**, 205 (2017)
31. Metzen, J.H., Hutmacher, R., Hua, N.G., Boreiko, V., Zhang, D.: Identification of systematic errors of image classifiers on rare subgroups. In: ICCV 2023, pp. 5041–5050 (2023)
32. Mitra, C., Huang, B., Darrell, T., Herzig, R.: Compositional chain-of-thought prompting for large multimodal models. ArXiv abs/2311.17076 (2023)
33. Qi, M., Li, W., Yang, Z., Wang, Y., Luo, J.: Attentive relational networks for mapping images to scene graphs. In: 2019 CVPR, pp. 3952–3961 (2019)
34. Quattoni, A., Torralba, A.: Recognizing indoor scenes. In: 2009 CVPR, pp. 413–420 (2009)
35. Sagawa, S., Koh, P.W., Hashimoto, T.B., Liang, P.: Distributionally robust neural networks. In: ICLR (2020)
36. Sainz, O., García-Ferrero, I., Agerri, R., de Lacalle, O.L., Rigau, G., Agirre, E.: GoLLIE: annotation guidelines improve zero-shot information-extraction. In: The Twelfth International Conference on Learning Representations (2024). https://openreview.net/forum?id=Y3wpuxd7u9
37. Shaul, Z., Naaz, S.: cgspan: closed graph-based substructure pattern mining. In: 2021 IEEE International Conference on Big Data (Big Data), pp. 4989–4998 (2021)
38. Singh, K.K., Mahajan, D., Grauman, K., Lee, Y.J., Feiszli, M., Ghadiyaram, D.: Don't judge an object by its context: Learning to overcome contextual bias. In: 2020 CVPR, pp. 11067–11075. Computer Vision Foundation / IEEE (2020)
39. Sohoni, N.S., Dunnmon, J.A., Angus, G., Gu, A., Ré, C.: No subclass left behind: fine-grained robustness in coarse-grained classification problems. ArXiv abs/2011.12945 (2020)

40. Speer, R., Chin, J., Havasi, C.: Conceptnet 5.5: an open multilingual graph of general knowledge. In: AAAI Conference on Artificial Intelligence (2016)
41. Teng, Y., Wang, L.: Structured sparse r-cnn for direct scene graph generation. 2022 IEEE/CVF Conference on Computer Vision and Pattern Recognition (CVPR), pp. 19415–19424 (2021)
42. Thrush, T., Jiang, R., Bartolo, M., Singh, A., Williams, A., Kiela, D., Ross, C.: Winoground: probing vision and language models for visio-linguistic compositionality. In: 2022 CVPR, pp. 5228–5238 (2022)
43. Vashishth, S., Sanyal, S., Nitin, V., Talukdar, P.P.: Composition-based multi-relational graph convolutional networks. In: ICLR 2020 (2020)
44. Vendrow, J., Jain, S., Engstrom, L., Madry, A.: Dataset interfaces: diagnosing model failures using controllable counterfactual generation. ArXiv abs/2302.07865 (2023)
45. Wang, W., Wei, F., Dong, L., Bao, H., Yang, N., Zhou, M.: Minilm: deep self-attention distillation for task-agnostic compression of pre-trained transformers. ArXiv abs/2002.10957 (2020)
46. Wiles, O., Albuquerque, I., Gowal, S.: Discovering bugs in vision models using off-the-shelf image generation and captioning. ArXiv abs/2208.08831 (2022)
47. Xu, B., Liao, R., Sigal, L.: Self-supervised relation alignment for scene graph generation. In: 2024 IEEE/CVF Winter Conference on Applications of Computer Vision (WACV), pp. 1328–1338 (2023)
48. Yan, X., Han, J.: gspan: graph-based substructure pattern mining. In: Proceedings of the 2002 IEEE International Conference on Data Mining, 2002, pp. 721–724 (2002)
49. Yang, X., Liu, Y., Wang, X.: Reformer: the relational transformer for image captioning. In: Proceedings of the 30th ACM International Conference on Multimedia (2021)
50. Yao, Y., et al.: Visual distant supervision for scene graph generation. In: ICCV 2021, pp. 15796–15806 (2021)
51. Yuksekgonul, M., Bianchi, F., Kalluri, P., Jurafsky, D., Zou, J.Y.: When and why vision-language models behave like bags-of-words, and what to do about it? ArXiv **abs/2210.01936** (2022)
52. Zhao, S., Xu, H.: Less is more: toward zero-shot local scene graph generation via foundation models (2023)
53. Zhao, T., Zhang, T., Zhu, M., Shen, H., Lee, K., Lu, X., Yin, J.: VL-checklist: Evaluating pre-trained vision-language models with objects, attributes and relations. ArXiv abs/2207.00221 (2022)
54. Zhu, G., et al.: Scene graph generation: a comprehensive survey. Neurocomputing **566**, 127052 (2022)

Query-Aware Dynamic Representation Learning for Temporal Knowledge Graph Reasoning

Juan Chen[1,2], Yanbo J. Wang[3,4], Wei Zhang[5], Zixuan Li[1,2], Xinchao Zhao[6], Xuan Yang[3,4], Yuhan Li[5], and Yuanzhuo Wang[1,2](✉)

[1] University of Chinese Academy of Sciences, Beijing, China
[2] State Key Laboratory of AI Safety, Institute of Computing Technology, Chinese Academy of Sciences, Beijing, China
{chenjuan,lizixuan,wangyuanzhuo}@ict.ac.cn
[3] National University of Uzbekistan named after Mirzo Ulugbek, Tashkent, Uzbekistan
{wangyanbo,yangxuan}@lyzdfintech.com
[4] Longying Zhida (Beijing) Technology Co., Ltd., Beijing, China
[5] National University of Defense Technology, ChangSha, China
{zhangwei23,liyuhan}@nudt.edu.cn
[6] Zhongke Academy of Big Data, Zhengzhou, China
zhaoxinchao@datafountain.cn

Abstract. Temporal Knowledge Graph (TKG) reasoning, which predicts future queries based on historical facts, has garnered significant attention. Existing methods learn dynamic representations of entities and then predict queries based on these representations. However, they primarily learn these representations from historical facts without considering the information in the queries. Actually, queries can highlight relevant historical facts, thereby enabling the model to learn more task-specific and accurate dynamic representations. Moreover, concurrent queries often exhibit structural dependencies and can facilitate more precise and coherent predictions. Motivated by these, we propose a Query-aware Dynamic Representation Learning (QDRL), a method that adaptively incorporates query information into the dynamic representation learning process. Specifically, to capture the structural dependencies among concurrent queries, QDRL employs a CNN-based query encoder to generate query representations, which are subsequently integrated into the dynamic entity representations via a Transformer-based temporal encoder. In addition, acknowledging that some static background knowledge of entities is not explicitly represented in TKG, we leverage Large Language Models (LLMs) to construct a comprehensive background knowledge graph. By modeling this graph, QDRL generates more informative initial representations of entities, leading to improved dynamic representations. TKG reasoning experiments on five benchmark datasets demonstrate the significant improvement of the proposed QDRL method, with up to 5.41% and 16.96% performance improvement in MRR on entity and relation prediction tasks, respectively, compared to the state-of-the-art baselines. The code and data are released here: https://github.com/vzhang-mm/QDRL.

Keywords: Temporal Knowledge Graph · Large Language Models · Knowledge Representation · Knowledge Graph Reasoning

D. Garijo et al. (Eds.): ISWC 2025, LNCS 16140, pp. 407–424, 2026.
https://doi.org/10.1007/978-3-032-09527-5_22

1 Introduction

A Temporal Knowledge Graph (TKG) can be viewed as a sequence of timestamped Knowledge Graph (KG) snapshots [22–24,40,41], each containing a set of temporal facts represented as a quadruple: (subject, relation, object, timestamp). The TKG reasoning task aims to predict future queries based on temporal facts at historical timestamps. This task is typically divided into two subtasks, i.e., entity prediction and relation prediction. The former involves predicting the missing entity in a query of the form (subject, relation, ?, timestamp), while the latter focuses on predicting the missing relation in a query of the form (subject, ?, object, timestamp). TKG reasoning has attracted growing interest in recent years due to its critical role in real-world applications such as natural disaster forecasting, sports outcome prediction, and financial trend analysis [33,39,43].

Existing methods for TKG reasoning can be broadly categorized into two types: query-based methods and snapshot-based methods. Query-based methods (e.g., ReNet [13], CyGNet [44], TITer [31], CRAFT [42] aim to capture query-specific information by modeling partial historical facts centered on a single query. However, these methods often overlook other historical facts that have implicit associations with the query, and thus do not model the historical information comprehensively. To address this limitation, snapshot-based methods (e.g., REGCN [21], TiRGN [18], HiSMatch [20], LogCL [4], RETIA [26]) first learn dynamic representations of all entities across timestamps using entire KG snapshots. Then they predict answers based on these learned representations and query information. This facilitates global interactions among all historical facts in the TKG and allows for comprehensive history modeling. However, they typically injects query information only at the decoding stage, limiting the model's ability to learn accurate and query-specific dynamic representations.

Based on the above observations, it is a key challenge for snapshot-based methods to integrate historical context and query information. From the query perspective, multiple queries occurring simultaneously at a given prediction timestamp often exhibit structural dependencies, which can enhance prediction accuracy. For example, consider two concurrent queries: *(A, criticize, ?)* and *(A, make positive comment, ?)*. Due to the semantic contrast between the relations, it is evident that their answers should not refer to the same entities. As for the historical context, although all historical facts influence their associated entities, their relevance to specific queries can vary significantly. A key question, therefore, is how to distinguish the varying influence of historical facts in light of query structures from the view of KG snapshots. Overall, both the structural dependencies among concurrent queries and the query-sensitive relevance of historical facts are crucial for learning dynamic representations that are both accurate and tailored to the specific query.

Motivated by this, we propose a Query-aware Dynamic Representation Learning (QDRL) method for TKG reasoning. To model the structural dependencies of concurrent queries, QDRL adopts a CNN-based Query encoder (Q-encoder) to capture the structural dependencies among concurrent queries into query embeddings. To integrate history and query information comprehensively, QDRL adopts a transformer-based Temporal encoder (T-encoder) to learn dynamic representations of entities with the above query embeddings considered. Specifically, Q-encoder first clusters queries by their head entities. For each group of queries, it adopts a Convolutional Neural Network (CNN) to obtain the cluster-specific embeddings. These embeddings are then appended to the input sequence of the T-encoder and provide the final dynamic representations of entities. In addition, the static background knowledge of entities provides crucial contextual information for TKG reasoning. To effectively incorporate this dimension, we employ Large Language Models (LLMs) to construct a comprehensive static background knowledge graph. By modeling this graph, QDRL generates more informative initial representations of entities, leading to improved dynamic representations. Our contributions are summarized as follows:

- We propose a novel Query-aware Dynamic Representation Learning (QDRL) method for TKG reasoning tasks. QDRL explicitly models structural dependencies among queries and integrates both the query information and history information into the dynamic representation learning of entities.
- We leverage an LLM to construct a comprehensive static knowledge graph, which further enhances the dynamic representations of entities by introducing background knowledge information.
- We conduct extensive experiments on five benchmark datasets and achieve state-of-the-art performance on both entity prediction and relation prediction tasks. Especially, QDRL achieves up to 5.41% and 16.96% performance improvement in MRR on entity and relation prediction tasks, respectively, compared to the state-of-the-art baselines.

2 Related Work

TKG reasoning can be broadly categorized into two settings: interpolation and extrapolation. The former [6, 10, 16] attempts to infer missing facts at the historical timestamps. The latter [18, 19, 21, 26], which this paper focuses on, attempts to predict new facts at future timestamps based on historical ones. This study focuses on the extrapolation settings and will introduce the related work in the following subsections.

2.1 Query-Based Methods for TKG Reasoning

Query-based methods for TKG reasoning focus on modeling query-related history, which aims to capture query-specific information. For example, RE-Net [13] leverages a recurrent neural network to model the historical evolution of a query entity's one-hop neighbors, thereby capturing query-specific local temporal signals. CyGNet [44] focuses on repeated events involving the same subject–relation pair in the past, using a copy mechanism to enhance reasoning over recurring patterns. TITer [31] adopts a reinforcement learning framework to search for multi-hop evidence paths in the temporal graph, connecting the query entity to candidate answers. This enables the model to capture long-range temporal dependencies and provides interpretable reasoning chains. CRAFT [42] further advances this line of work by constructing a distinct historical context for each candidate entity. It combines multi-hop relational paths from the query to the candidate with local frequency-based signals, allowing for more fine-grained scoring. However, despite their strengths in capturing query-specific patterns, their narrow focus may result in the omission of important historical facts that have implicit associations with the query, whose absence results in an incomplete modeling of historical information. Besides, these methods predict the queries one by one, and thus overlook the structural dependencies among concurrent queries.

2.2 Snapshot-Based Methods for TKG Reasoning

Snapshot-based methods for TKG reasoning adopt a global perspective by modeling the historical evolution of all entities across the KG snapshots. For example, RE-GCN [21] learns unified evolutional representations for all entities and answers queries based on these representations. This global view not only improves predictive accuracy by capturing broader context, but also enables boosting training efficiency. Following RE-GCN, TiRGN [18] extends this idea by employing dual encoders to separately model local temporal dependencies and global repetitive historical patterns. LogCL [4] leverages query information to enhance historical fact representations, but overlooks the structural dependencies among concurrent queries and fails to model dependencies between historical facts, limiting its effectiveness. RETIA [26] employs a twin-interaction module that jointly updates entity and relation embeddings within one unified framework, preserving a shared relational context across time. Snapshot-based methods facilitate global interactions among all historical facts in TKG and allow for comprehensive history modeling. However, it typically injects query information only at the decoding stage, limiting the model's ability to learn accurate and query-specific dynamic representations.

2.3 Pretrained Language Models for TKG Reasoning

With the advancement of Pretrained Language Models (PLMs), their application to TKG reasoning has attracted increasing attention. SToKE [9] formulates TKG reasoning as a masked prediction task, transforming graph structures into text-like sequences to help PLMs, such as BERT [8], understand structural and temporal contexts for accurate inference. With LLMs emerging [1,35], researchers have explored LLM-based TKG reasoning. CoH [38] incrementally incorporates historical information and performs staged reasoning, enhancing temporal inference. As a plug-and-play module, CoH can also integrate with graph embedding models to improve reasoning performance. To enhance efficiency, GenTKG [25] extracts query-relevant logical rules from TKGs, converting historical triples into natural language sentences while preserving structural and temporal patterns for LLMs' interpretation. This method achieves strong performance, demonstrating LLMs' potential in TKG reasoning. Additionally, LLM-DA [37] dynamically extracts and updates temporal logical rules from historical data, revealing time-dependent patterns in knowledge graphs for interpretable reasoning. Although LLMs excel in contextual processing, it is hard to transform the entire KG snapshot into a token sequence. Thus, these methods all focus on query-related history modeling and have the same problems as query-based methods.

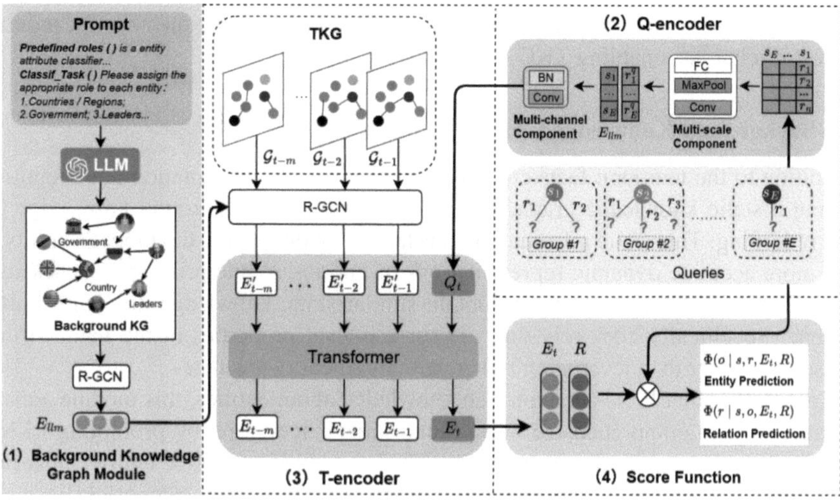

Fig. 1. An illustrative diagram of the proposed QDRL method for TKG reasoning at timestamp t.

3 Methodology

3.1 Notations and Definitions

A TKG $\mathcal{G} = \{\mathcal{G}_0, ..., \mathcal{G}_t, ..., \mathcal{G}_T\}$ consists of a sequence of KG snapshots. Each snapshot $\mathcal{G}_t = (\mathcal{E}, \mathcal{R}, \mathcal{F}_t)$, where $\mathcal{E}$ is the set of entities, $\mathcal{R}$ is the set of relations, $\mathcal{F}_t$ is the set of facts occurring at timestamp t. Each fact is represented as a quadruple (s, r, o, t), where s, o $\in \mathcal{E}$ denote the subject and object entities, $r \in \mathcal{R}$ is the relation, and t is the timestamp of occurrence. The TKG reasoning task aims to predict queries at a future timestamp t, based on a sequence of historical KG snapshots. For the entity prediction task, the query is in the form of $(s, r, ?, t)$. For the relation prediction task, the query is in the form of $(s, ?, o, t)$. For each fact in TKG, we add the inverse quadruple (o, r^{-1}, s, t) into TKG, correspondingly (Fig. 1).

3.2 Overview

The proposed QDRL method consists of four parts: (1) Background knowledge graph module: This module uses an LLM to construct a background knowledge graph and adopts R-GCN [28] to encode the structural dependencies of the constructed background knowledge graph into the initial entity representations $\mathbf{E}_{llm}$; (2) Q-encoder: It encodes all queries at the prediction timestamp t into query structure embeddings $\mathbf{Q}_t$; (3) T-encoder: T-encoder aims to integrate the historical information and the query information to produce query-aware dynamic representations. Taking the learned initial entity representations $\mathbf{E}_{llm}$, query embedding $\mathbf{Q}_t$, and the most recent m historical KG snapshots as inputs, T-encoder outputs a sequence of dynamic representations of entities $\{\mathbf{E}_{t-m}, ..., \mathbf{E}_{t-1}, \mathbf{E}_t\}$. (4) Score Functions: Finally, with the dynamic representations at the prediction timestamp, i.e., $\mathbf{E}_t$ and the learnable relation representations $\mathbf{R}$, as input, score functions compute the matching scores between the query and candidate entities or relations, enabling TKG reasoning.

3.3 Background Knowledge Graph Module

In addition to the temporal facts contained in TKGs, static information about entities, forming a static knowledge graph, can serve as valuable background knowledge for TKG reasoning. This static information is valuable for enhancing the model's ability to learn more accurate dynamic representations of entities. While prior approaches such as RE-GCN [28] have attempted to obtain similar static knowledge, they are limited in scope. Specifically, they rely only on surface-level properties in the name strings themselves, rather than leveraging richer, structured entity attributes.

Considering that LLMs contain rich knowledge about entities, this module aims to construct a more comprehensive background knowledge graph by prompting LLMs. Specifically, this module first prompts an LLM to generate a set of entity categories, denoted as C, to ensure comprehensive coverage of diverse entity categories. Each element in C represents a distinct entity category (e.g., Country/Region, Social Groups, Government, Political Figures, Business, Media). It then assigns each entity in TKG a single category label selected from this set. As a result, static triples of the form $(e, \text{Instance of}, c) \in \mathcal{F}_{bkg}$ are generated, where e denotes an entity, $c \in C$ represents the corresponding category label, and $\mathcal{F}_{bkg}$ is the set of triples in the background knowledge graph. These triples are then organized into a directed graph, where entities are connected to their assigned categories through typed edges, forming the LLM-based background knowledge graph.

Then, as shown in Eq. 1, R-GCN [28] is applied to capture the structural dependencies in this background knowledge graph. With the learnable entity representations $\mathbf{E}_{bkg} \in \mathbb{R}^{E\times D}$ and $\mathbf{R}_{bkg} \in \mathbb{R}^{R\times D}$ as input, this module outputs the background entity representations, denoted as $\mathbf{E}_{llm} \in \mathbb{R}^{E\times D}$, and the relation representations $\mathbf{R}_{llm} \in \mathbb{R}^{R\times D}$. E is the number of entities, R is the number of relations in background knowledge graph, and D is the dimension number.

$$
\begin{aligned}
\mathbf{E}_{llm}, \mathbf{R}_{llm} &= \mathrm{RGCN}(s, r, o) \\
&= \sigma\left(\frac{1}{c_o} \sum_{(s,r,o)\in\mathcal{F}_{bkg}} \mathbf{W}_1(\boldsymbol{s}+\boldsymbol{r}) + \mathbf{W}_2\boldsymbol{o}\right),
\end{aligned} \tag{1}
$$

where s denotes the head entity, r denotes the relation in the background knowledge graph, and o denotes the category of the entity. $\boldsymbol{s}$, $\boldsymbol{r}$, and $\boldsymbol{o}$ correspond to the learnable embeddings of the head entity, relation, and entity category from $\mathbf{E}_{bkg}$ and $\mathbf{R}_{bkg}$, respectively. $\mathbf{W}_1$ and $\mathbf{W}_2$ are learnable weight matrices. c_o is a normalization constant corresponding to the degree of entity o, and $\sigma(\cdot)$ denotes the RReLU [11] activation function.

3.4 Query Encoder

To capture the dependencies among concurrent queries at the prediction timestamp, we design the CNN-based Query encoder (Q-encoder). First, Q-encoder groups queries sharing the same head entity into a substructure. For each substructure, Q-encoder generates a unified query structure embedding preserving multi-relation semantics. Specifically, the Q-encoder consists of two 1D convolutional components, i.e., a multi-scale convolutional component and a multi-channel convolutional component.

For a query entity s_t at timestamp t, its concurrent query relations are denoted as $\{r^1, ..., r^n\}$. The multi-scale convolutional component processes a variable-length set of corresponding relation embeddings $\{\boldsymbol{r}^1, ..., \boldsymbol{r}^n\}$ from the learnable relation representation $\mathbf{R}$, by applying 1D convolutions with multiple kernel sizes $k \in \mathcal{K}$, extracting features at different granularities. After the MaxPooling layer, the outputs from different kernels are concatenated, which is passed through a Fully Connected (FC) layer to produce a unified relation embedding $\boldsymbol{r}^q \in \mathbb{R}^D$, as shown in Eq. 2.

$$\boldsymbol{r}^q = \mathrm{FC}\left(\bigoplus_{k\in\mathcal{K}} \mathrm{Conv}_k([\boldsymbol{r}^1, ..., \boldsymbol{r}^n]^T)\right). \tag{2}$$

Next, the multi-channel convolutional network takes the concatenation of the subject entity embedding $\boldsymbol{s}_t \in \mathbb{R}^D$ from $\mathbf{E}_{llm}$ and the relation embedding $\boldsymbol{r}^q$, and applies multiple filters to capture local interaction patterns, resulting in the final query structure embedding $\boldsymbol{q}^{str} \in \mathbb{R}^D$. If an entity does not have any query relations at the current prediction timestamp, its representation is set to a zero vector. In this way, we construct the query structure embedding matrix for all entities at the prediction timestamp t, $\mathbf{Q}_t \in \mathbb{R}^{E\times D}$, as shown in Eq. 3.

$$\begin{aligned} \boldsymbol{q}^{str} &= \begin{cases} \mathrm{Conv}_1\left([\mathbf{s}_t, \mathbf{r}^q]\right), & \text{if the entity has a query} \\ \mathbf{0}, & \text{otherwise} \end{cases} \\ \mathbf{Q}_t &= \left[\boldsymbol{q}_1^{str}, \boldsymbol{q}_2^{str}, \ldots, \boldsymbol{q}_E^{str}\right]^\top \end{aligned} \tag{3}$$

where $\bigoplus$ denotes the concatenation operation, Conv_k denotes a 1D convolution with kernel size k, and FC is a fully connected layer that aligns the output to dimension D.

3.5 Temporal Encoder

The T-encoder models the evolution of all historical facts across the graphs and captures their interactions with the current queries, producing query-aware evolving representations. The encoder first selects the most recent m KG snapshots and uses the RGCN to obtain the representations of entities $\{\mathbf{E}'_{t-m}, ..., \mathbf{E}'_{t-1}\}$. Taking timestamp $t-1$ for example, the representations of entities and relations are calculated as Eq. 4.

$$\mathbf{E}'_{t-1}, \mathbf{R}'_{t-1} = \mathrm{RGCN}(s_{t-1}, r_{t-1}, o_{t-1}), \tag{4}$$

where s_{t-1}, r_{t-1}, and o_{t-1} denote the subject entity, relation, and object entity at time $t-1$, respectively, and $\mathbf{E}'_{t-1}, \mathbf{R}'_{t-1} \in \mathbb{R}^{E\times D}$ represents the graph representation at time $t-1$. Notably, all entity embeddings are initialized using $\mathbf{E}_{llm}$ and all the relation embeddings are initialized using $\mathbf{R}$.

Subsequently, the query structure embedding $\mathbf{Q}_t$, output from the Q-encoder, is appended to the entity representation sequence $\{\mathbf{E}_{t-m}^{'}, ..., \mathbf{E}_{t-1}^{'}\}$, forming a new combined sequence $\{\mathbf{E}_{t-m}^{'}, ..., \mathbf{E}_{t-1}^{'}, \mathbf{Q}_t\}$, thereby introducing query semantics into the sequence. In addition, positional embedding is added to preserve temporal order, which is crucial for sequential modeling. Finally, the Transformer [36] is applied, allowing $\mathbf{Q}_t$ to interact with all historical facts and learn their temporal dependencies. The updated $\mathbf{Q}_t$ serves as the final dynamic representations of entities and relations at timestamp t,

$$\mathbf{E}_t = \text{Transformer}(\{\mathbf{E}_{t-m}^{'}, ..., \mathbf{E}_{t-1}^{'}, \mathbf{Q}_t\})_t, \tag{5}$$

where $(\cdot)_t$ denotes the output at the last position.

3.6 Score Function and Optimization

Previous studies [4,20] have shown that ConvTransE [30] performs well on reasoning tasks. Therefore, we adopt it as the score function (i.e., decoder), which computes the dot-product similarity between the query and all candidate entities to quantify the likelihood of each candidate entity being the tail entity, as shown in Eq. 6. Where $\Phi(o \mid s, r, \mathbf{E}_t, \mathbf{R})$ denotes the probability of predicting entity o as the tail given the query (s, r) at time t; $f(\cdot)$ denotes the softmax function; $\boldsymbol{s} \in \mathbb{R}^D$ and $\boldsymbol{r} \in \mathbb{R}^D$ represent the embeddings of s and r in $\mathbf{E}_t$ and $\mathbf{R}$, respectively.

$$\Phi(o \mid s, r, \mathbf{E}_t, \mathbf{R}) = f\left(\text{ConvTransE}(\boldsymbol{s}, \boldsymbol{r}, \mathbf{E}_t, \mathbf{R})\right). \tag{6}$$

Entity prediction tasks can be viewed as multi-label prediction tasks, where the goal of the model is to minimize the cross-entropy loss, as is shown in Eq. 7. Where T denotes the number of timestamps, F_t is the set of facts occurring at timestamp t, $\mathcal{E}$ is the set of all entities. $y_t^e \in \{0, 1\}$ indicates whether entity e is the correct answer (1 for correct, 0 for incorrect).

$$\mathcal{L} = \sum_{t=0}^{T-1} \sum_{(s,r,o) \in F_t} \sum_{e \in \mathcal{E}} y_t^e \log \Phi(o \mid s, r, \mathbf{E}_t, \mathbf{R}). \tag{7}$$

4 Experimental Settings

4.1 Datasets

We evaluate our model on five benchmark datasets for TKG Reasoning. ICEWS14 [10], ICEWS05-15 [10], and ICEWS18 [13] are subsets extracted from the Integrated Crisis Early Warning System [2] (ICEWS), which contains a large number of political events with specific timestamps. YAGO [27] is a more comprehensive dataset sourced from multiple databases, including Wikipedia, WordNet, and GeoNames. GDELT is a subset of the Global Database of Events, Language, and Tone [17] (GDELT), containing 20 distinct event types such as "Make a public statement," "Appeal", and "Consult." We follow the data preprocessing strategy of previous works and split all datasets into training, validation, and test sets with a ratio of 80%/10%/10%. The statistics for each dataset are shown in Table 1.

Table 1. Details of the TKG Datasets.

Dataset	ICEWS14	ICEWS05-15	ICEWS18	GDELT	YAGO
Entities	6,869	10,094	23,033	7,691	10,623
Relations	230	251	256	240	10
Training	74,845	368,868	373,018	1,734,399	161,540
Validation	8,514	46,302	45,995	238,765	19,523
Test	7,371	46,159	49,545	305,241	20,026
Time Gran.	24 h	24 h	24 h	15 mins	1 year
Snapshots	365	4017	365	2975	188

4.2 Evaluation Metrics

We adopt Mean Reciprocal Rank (MRR) and Hits@k (k = 1, 3, 10) as evaluation metrics, which are widely used to assess the effectiveness of TKG reasoning methods. MRR computes the average reciprocal rank of the true answers across all queries, measuring the overall ranking performance of the model. Hits@k represents the proportion of correct entity candidates appearing in the top k ranks, evaluating the prediction accuracy of the model. Recent studies [4,20] have pointed out that traditional static filtering (filtered) evaluation settings are not suitable for TKG extrapolation tasks, as they ignore the temporal dimension of facts. In fact, only facts occurring at the same time as the query should be filtered. Therefore, we use a time-aware filtered evaluation setting, which only filters out quadruples occurring at the query time, and this approach has been widely used in recent studies.

4.3 Implementation Details

In all experiments, the embedding dimensions of entities and relations is set to 256, with the number of layers in the R-GCN set to 2. QWQ-plus [34] is used to construct the background knowledge graph. The Q-encoder includes a multi-scale convolutional component with two parallel 1D convolution layers, using kernel sizes of 2 and 3 ($\mathcal{K}$ = 2), each with 256 output channels. The max-pooled outputs are concatenated into a 512-dim vector and then projected to 256-dim via a fully connected (FC) layer. It also includes a multi-channel convolutional component that comprises two 1D convolutional layers with 32 and 1 filters, both using a kernel size of 3 ($\mathcal{K} = 1$). The T-encoder's self-attention network has a hidden dimension of 512, with 4 attention heads and 2 layers, and a dropout rate of 0.2. For the ConvTransE model, the number of kernels is set to 50, and the kernel size is 2×3. The optimizer is Adam [14]. The learning rate is set to 0.0005. All experiments were conducted on A800 GPUs.

4.4 Baselines

We selected several TKG reasoning methods for comparison, categorized as follows: Static Models: ConvE [7], ConvTransE [30], and RotatE [32]. These models ignore temporal information and focus solely on modeling triples. Interpolation Models: TTransE

[16], TA-DistMult [10], and TNTComplEx [15]. These approaches incorporate temporal information into knowledge graph embeddings to enhance modeling capabilities for temporal data. Temporal Reasoning Models: RE-NET [13], CyGNet [44], TITer [31], RE-GCN [21], TiRGN [18], HisMatch [20], RETIA [26], LogCL [4], CRAFT [42] and NEDA [3]. These models utilize Graph Neural Networks (GNNs) or a sequence model (e.g., GRU, LSTM [5,12]) to capture the evolutional temporal patterns of a sequence of historical KG snapshots. LLM-based Models: COH [38], GENTKG [25], and LLM-DA [37]. These methods leverage LLMs for reasoning, offering general reasoning capabilities and the ability to incorporate external knowledge.

5 Experimental Results and Analysis

5.1 Results on Entity Prediction

Extensive TKG reasoning experiments on five benchmark datasets demonstrate the effectiveness of our approach, as shown in Tables 2 and 3. QDRL achieves MRR improvements of 2.90%, 2.06%, 5.41%, and 5.00% on the ICEWS14, ICEWS18, GDELT, and YAGO datasets, respectively, outperforming state-of-the-art baselines.

Key observations from the experiments are as follows: 1) Models based on static embeddings or interpolation struggle to capture the temporal dynamics of entities and relations, resulting in inferior performance; 2) RE-NET, CyGNet, TITer, and CRAFT focus exclusively on query-relevant local history and may overlook broader contextual signals that are often crucial for accurate reasoning; 3) RE-GCN, TiRGN, and RETIA model all entities across the entire graph but fail to capture query-specific evolutionary patterns, which limits their ability to make fine-grained predictions; 4) HisMatch and LogCL simultaneously pay attention to both global KG evolution patterns and query-relevant local information. Nevertheless, they still fall short in fully modeling the dependencies between historical facts and the specific query, restricting their potential. In contrast, QDRL explicitly injects query information throughout the entire graph evolution process, producing query-specific evolving representations and achieving remarkable performance improvements; 5) NEDA segments the TKG into multiple patches and models them to capture long-range, asynchronous dependencies, making it more suitable for datasets with extended temporal spans. Despite this, our proposed QDRL achieves the second-best MRR on ICEWS05-15 and outperforms all baselines in Hits@1, highlighting the effectiveness of incorporating query information into the representation learning process. 6) LLM-based methods (e.g., COH, LLM-DA) primarily rely on the reasoning capabilities of LLMs, but their performance is often suboptimal. In contrast, QDRL explicitly leverages the rich background knowledge provided by LLMs and achieves significant improvements, offering a novel paradigm for applying LLMs in knowledge graph reasoning tasks.

5.2 Results on Relation Prediction

In this setting, the query is defined as $(s, ?, o)$, and the graph representation G_t is used to compute scores between the query and all candidate relations. Since most existing methods do not support relation prediction, due to their lack of relation embedding

Table 2. Entity prediction results using MRR and Hits@1/3/10 as evaluation metrics on ICESW14, ICEWS05-15 and ICEWS18. The best results are shown in bold, and the second-best results are underlined.

Model	ICEWS14				ICEWS05-15				ICEWS18			
	MRR	H@1	H@3	H@10	MRR	H@1	H@3	H@10	MRR	H@1	H@3	H@10
ConvE (2018)	35.09	25.23	39.38	54.68	33.81	24.78	39.00	54.95	24.51	16.23	29.25	44.51
ConvTransE (2018)	33.80	25.40	38.54	53.99	33.03	24.15	38.07	54.32	22.11	13.94	26.44	42.28
RotatE (2019)	21.31	10.26	24.35	44.75	24.71	13.22	29.04	48.16	12.78	4.01	14.89	31.91
TTransE (2018)	13.72	2.98	17.70	35.74	15.57	4.80	19.24	38.29	8.31	1.92	8.56	21.89
TA-DistMult (2018)	25.80	16.94	29.74	42.99	24.31	14.58	27.92	44.21	16.75	8.61	18.41	33.59
TNTComplEx (2020)	34.05	25.08	38.50	50.92	27.54	9.52	30.80	42.86	21.23	13.28	24.02	36.91
GENTKG (2023)	\	36.85	47.95	53.5	\	\	\	\	\	24.25	37.25	42.1
COH (2024)	43.94	33.07	49.64	64.90	49.71	38.01	56.40	71.25	32.98	21.83	37.79	54.92
LLM-DA (2024)	47.1	36.9	52.6	67.1	52.1	41.6	58.6	72.8	\	\	\	\
RE-NET (2020)	36.93	26.83	39.51	54.78	43.32	33.43	47.77	63.06	28.81	19.05	32.44	47.51
CyGNet (2021)	35.05	25.73	39.01	53.55	36.81	26.61	41.63	56.22	24.93	15.90	28.28	42.61
TITer (2021)	40.87	32.28	45.45	57.10	47.69	37.95	52.92	65.81	29.98	22.05	33.46	44.83
RE-GCN (2021)	40.39	30.66	44.96	59.21	48.03	37.33	53.85	68.27	30.58	21.01	34.34	48.75
TiRGN (2022)	44.04	33.83	48.95	63.84	50.04	39.25	56.13	70.71	33.66	23.19	37.99	54.22
HisMatch (2022)	46.42	35.91	51.63	66.84	52.85	42.01	59.05	73.28	33.99	23.91	37.90	53.94
RETIA (2023)	45.29	34.60	50.88	66.06	52.17	40.21	59.42	73.98	34.16	22.97	39.27	55.96
LogCl (2023)	48.87	37.76	54.71	70.26	57.04	46.07	63.72	77.87	35.67	24.53	40.32	57.74
CRAFT (2024)	45.71	35.05	51.83	65.21	50.14	39.56	56.18	70.09	34.21	23.96	38.53	54.11
NEDA (2024)	50.51	39.42	56.54	**73.46**	**60.19**	46.23	63.75	**82.76**	36.84	25.55	41.70	59.16
QDRL(ours)	**51.98**	**40.83**	**58.22**	73.25	58.48	**47.66**	65.32	78.63	**37.60**	**26.31**	**42.50**	**59.94**

Table 3. Entity prediction results using MRR and Hits@1/3/10 as evaluation metrics on GDELT and YAGO. The best results are shown in bold, and the second-best results are underlined.

Model	GDELT				YAGO			
	MRR	H@1	H@3	H@10	MRR	H@1	H@3	H@10
ConvE (2018)	16.55	11.02	18.88	31.60	41.22	\	47.03	59.90
ConvTransE (2018)	16.20	10.85	18.38	30.86	46.67	\	52.22	62.52
RotatE (2019)	13.45	6.95	14.09	25.99	42.08	\	46.77	59.39
TTransE (2018)	5.50	0.47	4.94	15.25	26.10	\	36.28	47.73
TA-DistMult (2018)	12.00	5.76	12.94	23.54	44.98	\	50.64	61.11
TNTComplEx (2020)	19.53	12.41	20.75	33.42	\	\	\	\
GENTKG (2023)	\	13.9	22.55	30.45	\	\	\	\
COH (2024)	\	\	\	\	\	\	\	\
LLM-DA (2024)	\	\	\	\	\	\	\	\
RE-NET (2020)	19.62	12.42	21.00	34.01	46.81	\	52.71	61.93
CyGNet (2021)	18.48	11.52	19.57	31.98	46.72	\	52.48	61.52
TITer (2021)	15.46	10.98	15.61	24.31	64.97	\	74.80	87.44
RE-GCN (2021)	19.64	12.42	20.90	33.69	63.07	\	71.17	82.07
TiRGN (2022)	21.67	13.63	23.27	37.60	64.71	\	74.17	87.01
HisMatch (2022)	22.01	14.45	23.80	36.61	\	\	\	\
RETIA (2023)	\	\	\	\	67.58	\	78.42	**88.06**
LogCl (2023)	23.75	14.64	25.60	42.33	72.42	67.28	74.68	82.33
CRAFT (2024)	23.78	15.38	26.23	40.15	\	\	\	\
NEDA (2024)	23.07	14.71	25.03	40.12	\	\	\	\
QDRL(ours)	**25.60**	**16.12**	**27.88**	**44.94**	**76.04**	**70.85**	**78.73**	85.75

modeling, we select the most recent methods that are capable of performing relation prediction [18,21,26,29,30] as baselines and conduct experiments on five benchmark datasets using MRR as the evaluation metric. The results are summarized in Table 4.

As shown in the results, QDRL achieves MRR improvements of 16.96%, 6.64%, 14.29%, 6.33%, and 0.91% on the ICEWS14, ICEWS05-15, ICEWS18, GDELT, and YAGO datasets, respectively, consistently outperforming state-of-the-art baselines. This demonstrates that our proposed method is not only effective for entity prediction but also well-suited for relation prediction tasks. These results further validate the effectiveness and generalizability of the QDRL framework. Notably, all methods perform better on the YAGO dataset than on the others, which can be attributed to its relatively small number of relation types. Nevertheless, our method still achieves the best overall performance.

Table 4. Relation prediction results using MRR as the evaluation metric.

Model	ICEWS14	ICEWS05-15	ICEWS18	GDELT	YAGO
ConvTransE (2018)	38.40	38.26	38.00	18.97	90.98
RGCRN (2018)	38.04	38.37	37.14	20.99	90.18
RE-GCN (2021)	41.06	40.63	40.53	21.47	97.74
TiRGN (2022)	42.57	42.12	41.78	\	93.58
RETIA (2023)	42.05	43.19	41.78	\	98.91
QDRL (ours)	**49.79**	**46.06**	**47.75**	**22.83**	**99.81**

5.3 Ablation Study

To evaluate the effectiveness of the Q-encoder module and the LLM-based background knowledge graph, we conducted ablation studies. The results are shown in Tables 5 and 6. The results demonstrate that both components significantly contribute to model performance, and removing either one leads to a performance drop. Two settings are considered: 1) QDRL-w/o-Q: The Q-encoder is removed, and a randomly initialized learnable vector is used to aggregate historical information as the evolving representation. 2) QDRL-w/o-E_{llm}: The background knowledge graph is removed, and entity embeddings are initialized using learnable vectors.

Entity prediction results show that removing the Q-encoder leads to a significant performance drop, as the model lacks query guidance and fails to focus on relevant historical facts. On the YAGO dataset, however, the impact is smaller due to the limited number of relation types (only 10), which reduces the expressiveness of query semantics. Removing E_{llm} also degrades performance, as the lack of static semantics of entities impairs the model's ability to capture implicit reasoning patterns grounded in real-world knowledge.

Relation prediction results show a more significant performance drop after removing E_{llm}, in contrast to the entity prediction task. The background knowledge graph provides structured semantic information that reflects real-world associations between entities, enabling the model to directly infer plausible relations (e.g., "government" and "country" are often connected by relations such as governs), without relying solely on historical interactions.

Table 5. Ablation studies and detailed analyses for entity prediction.

Model	ICEWS14			ICEWS05-15			ICEWS18			GDELT			YAGO		
	H@1	H@3	H@10	H@1	H@3	H@10	H@1	H@3	H@10	H@1	H@3	H@10	H@1	H@3	H@10
QDRL-w/o-Q	30.45	46.19	61.81	33.03	49.01	65.17	20.49	34.72	50.66	11.73	19.38	31.53	70.53	78.64	85.26
QDRL-w/o-E_{llm}	36.42	53.58	68.24	46.04	63.34	76.78	24.03	39.61	56.44	15.81	27.39	44.36	66.29	73.89	81.06
QDRL-Q_{OneHot}	37.93	56.06	71.50	44.40	64.76	78.33	24.80	42.46	60.43	14.66	26.13	43.56	69.15	77.18	84.10
QDRL-G_{static}	39.59	57.21	71.97	47.30	65.01	78.48	23.82	41.58	59.63	15.56	27.14	44.23	\	\	\
QDRL (ours)	**40.83**	**58.22**	**73.25**	**47.66**	**65.32**	**78.63**	**26.31**	**42.50**	**59.94**	**16.12**	**27.88**	**44.94**	**70.85**	**78.73**	**85.75**

Table 6. Ablation studies and detailed analyses for relation prediction.

Model	ICEWS14			ICEWS15			ICEWS18			GDELT			YAGO		
	H@1	H@3	H@10	H@1	H@3	H@10	H@1	H@3	H@10	H@1	H@3	H@10	H@1	H@3	H@10
QDRL-w/o-Q	33.15	49.86	72.64	30.36	48.04	70.30	31.11	48.53	72.51	10.74	21.07	43.82	99.54	99.91	99.99
QDRL-w/o-E_{llm}	28.19	45.17	68.17	26.19	39.86	56.75	20.93	35.42	54.78	9.58	21.03	42.07	99.14	99.67	99.92
QDRL-Q_{OneHot}	**38.12**	54.26	74.56	34.14	50.67	71.41	33.05	51.51	**73.75**	10.33	22.58	45.99	99.68	99.93	99.99
QDRL-G_{static}	33.06	49.58	71.29	27.91	43.76	63.91	24.91	41.14	63.64	10.05	22.78	47.19	\	\	\
QDRL (ours)	37.65	**55.00**	**75.84**	**34.43**	**53.77**	**76.03**	**33.81**	**51.90**	73.37	**10.89**	**23.67**	**47.86**	**99.68**	**99.94**	**1**

5.4 Analyses on Different Query Embedding Methods

To investigate the impact of different query modeling strategies on model performance, we conduct experiments under two configurations, as shown in Tables 5 and 6. QDRL-Q_{OneHot}: which constructs a sparse one-hot vector to represent the presence of relations and uses a fully connected linear layer to align the dimensionality, generating the query embedding. QDRL: the default setting, which employs the Q-encoder to encode the subject entity and its associated relations, producing the query embedding.

Experimental results show that: 1) The Q-encoder adaptively processes varying numbers of relational inputs to generate a semantically rich query embedding. The query embedding enables the model to attend to historical information that is most relevant to the current group of queries, thereby enhancing the accuracy of temporal reasoning. 2) The One-Hot approach also achieves strong performance, suggesting that structural cues from entity-relation patterns can effectively support query representation. These findings highlight the critical importance of capturing query-relevant historical information in TKG extrapolation tasks.

5.5 Analyses on LLM-Based Background Knowledge Graph

To evaluate the effectiveness of our LLM-based background knowledge graph, we conduct experiments under different configurations, with the results summarized in Tables 5 and 6. Specifically, we compare the following two settings: QDRL-G_{static} uses only a static graph constructed based on entity naming conventions. Following [21], for example, for the entity *Citizen_(Nigeria)*, a triple *(Citizen_(Nigeria), isA, Nigeria)* is added to the static graph; QDRL: integrates both the static graph described above and the LLM-based background graph constructed in this work.

From the results, we observe the following: 1) Both QDRL-G_{static} and QDRL significantly outperform the baseline without background graph (QDRL-w/o-E_{llm}), demonstrating the importance of incorporating external background information in TKG reasoning. 2) QDRL achieves the best performance, suggesting that LLM-based background knowledge graphs provide complementary information beyond the static graph. 3) On the YAGO dataset, the lack of dataset-specific naming conventions makes it difficult to construct static background graphs. In contrast, our LLM-based method does not rely on these conventions and generalizes well across datasets, showing stronger cross-domain adaptability.

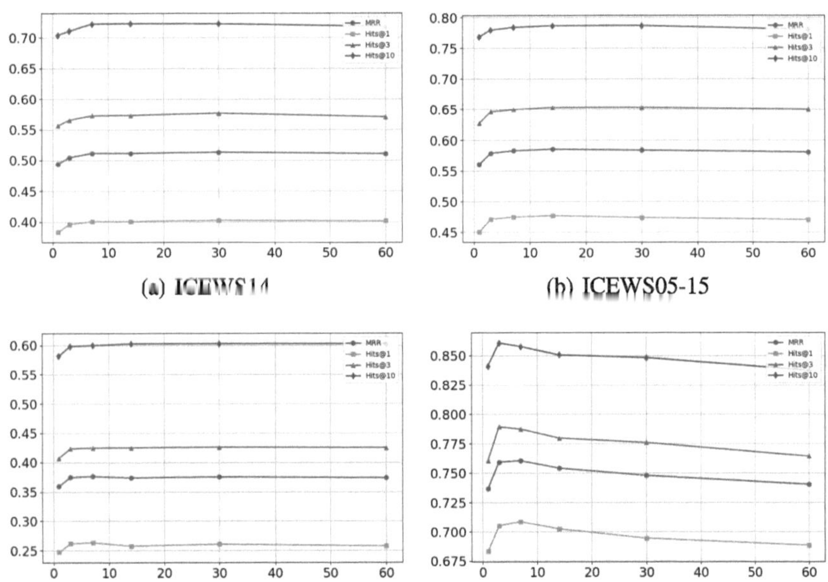

(a) ICEWS14 (b) ICEWS05-15

(c) ICEWS18 (d) YAGO

Fig. 2. Entity prediction performance under different sliding window sizes on ICESW14, ICEWS05-15, ICEWS18, and YAGO.

5.6 Analyses on Historical Window Size

To investigate how the number of KG snapshots m used as historical context affects model performance, we conduct experiments under varying temporal window sizes, as shown in Fig. 2. Specifically, when the window size is small (e.g., m = 1 or 3), the lack of contextual information hinders the modeling of entity evolution and temporal patterns, leading to a significant performance drop. As the window size increases, the model's performance improves. The optimal results are achieved when m = 7 on ICEWS14, ICEWS18, and YAGO, and when m = 14 on ICEWS18, suggesting that a moderate historical context is sufficient for most datasets. However, using overly large windows (e.g., $m \geq 30$) may introduce redundant or noisy information, which can negatively affect model performance.

6 Conclusion

In this paper, we proposed a Query-aware Dynamic Representation learning (QDRL) method for TKG reasoning. Unlike previous approaches that decouple query processing from representation learning, QDRL explicitly integrates query structure information into the historical modeling process. This design enables the model to dynamically capture query-specific temporal signals and improve reasoning accuracy. Furthermore, by constructing a semantically enriched background knowledge graph using LLMs, our method enhances the expressiveness of entity representations with external high-level semantics. Extensive experiments on five benchmark TKG datasets demonstrate that QDRL consistently outperforms state-of-the-art methods in both entity and relation prediction tasks. Ablation studies further confirm the effectiveness of both the query-aware mechanism and the LLM-based background knowledge. These findings highlight the potential of QDRL as a general and robust framework for TKG reasoning and open new directions for integrating LLMs into knowledge graph tasks.

Acknowledgments. This work is supported by National Natural Science Foundation of China (NSFC) under Grants No. 62441229.

Supplemental Material Statement. Source code and data can be found at: https://github.com/vzhang-mm/QDRL.

References

1. Achiam, J., et al.: Gpt-4 technical report. arXiv preprint arXiv:2303.08774 (2023)
2. Boschee, E., Lautenschlager, J., O'Brien, S., Shellman, S., Starz, J., Ward, M.: ICEWS coded event data (2015). https://doi.org/10.7910/DVN/28075
3. Chen, B., Xiao, C., Zhou, F.: Natural evolution-based dual-level aggregation for temporal knowledge graph reasoning. In: Al-Onaizan, Y., Bansal, M., Chen, Y.N. (eds.) Findings of the Association for Computational Linguistics: EMNLP 2024. Association for Computational Linguistics, Miami, Florida, USA, November 2024. https://aclanthology.org/2024.findings-emnlp.543/

4. Chen, W., Wan, H., Wu, Y., Zhao, S., Cheng, J., Li, Y., Lin, Y.: Local-global history-aware contrastive learning for temporal knowledge graph reasoning (2023). https://arxiv.org/abs/2312.01601
5. Cho, K., van Merriënboer, B., Gulcehre, Ç., Bahdanau, D., Bougares, F., Schwenk, H., Bengio, Y.: Learning phrase representations using rnn encoder-decoder for statistical machine translation. arXiv preprint arXiv:1406.1078 (2014)
6. Dasgupta, S.S., Ray, S.N., Talukdar, P.: Hyte: hyperplane-based temporally aware knowledge graph embedding. In: Proceedings of the 2018 Conference on Empirical Methods in Natural Language Processing, pp. 2001–2011 (2018)
7. Dettmers, T., Minervini, P., Stenetorp, P., Riedel, S.: Convolutional 2d knowledge graph embeddings. In: Proceedings of the AAAI Conference on Artificial Intelligence, vol. 32 (2018)
8. Devlin, J., Chang, M.W., Lee, K., Toutanova, K.: Bert: pre-training of deep bidirectional transformers for language understanding. arXiv preprint arXiv:1810.04805 (2019)
9. Gao, Y., He, Y., Kan, Z., Han, Y., Qiao, L., Li, D.: Learning joint structural and temporal contextualized knowledge embeddings for temporal knowledge graph completion. In: Findings of the Association for Computational Linguistics: ACL 2023, pp. 417–430 (2023)
10. García-Durán, A., Dumančić, S., Niepert, M.: Learning sequence encoders for temporal knowledge graph completion. arXiv preprint arXiv:1809.03202 (2018)
11. He, K., Zhang, X., Ren, S., Sun, J.: Delving deep into rectifiers: Surpassing human-level performance on imagenet classification. In: Proceedings of the IEEE International Conference on Computer Vision (ICCV), pp. 1026–1034 (2015)
12. Hochreiter, S., Schmidhuber, J.: Long short-term memory. Neural Comput. **9**(8), 1735–1780 (1997)
13. Jin, W., Qu, M., Jin, X., Ren, X.: Recurrent event network: autoregressive structure inference over temporal knowledge graphs (2020). https://arxiv.org/abs/1904.05530
14. Kingma, D.P., Ba, J.: Adam: a method for stochastic optimization. arXiv preprint arXiv:1412.6980 (2014)
15. Lacroix, T., Obozinski, G., Usunier, N.: Tensor decompositions for temporal knowledge base completion. arXiv preprint arXiv:2004.04926 (2020)
16. Leblay, J., Chekol, M.W.: Deriving validity time in knowledge graph. In: Companion Proceedings of the the Web Conference 2018, pp. 1771–1776 (2018)
17. Leetaru, K., Schrodt, P.A.: Gdelt: Global data on events, location, and tone, 1979–2012. In: ISA Annual Convention, vol. 2, pp. 1–49. Citeseer (2013)
18. Li, Y., Sun, S., Zhao, J.: Tirgn: time-guided recurrent graph network with local-global historical patterns for temporal knowledge graph reasoning. In: Proceedings of the Thirty-First International Joint Conference on Artificial Intelligence, IJCAI 2022, Vienna, Austria, 23-29 July 2022, pp. 2152–2158 (2022)
19. Li, Z., et al.: Complex evolutional pattern learning for temporal knowledge graph reasoning. arXiv preprint arXiv:2203.07782 (2022)
20. Li, Z., Hou, Z., Guan, S., Jin, X., Peng, W., Bai, L., Lyu, Y., Li, W., Guo, J., Cheng, X.: Hismatch: Historical structure matching based temporal knowledge graph reasoning (2022). https://arxiv.org/abs/2210.09708
21. Li, Z., et al.: Temporal knowledge graph reasoning based on evolutional representation learning (2021). https://arxiv.org/abs/2104.10353
22. Liang, K., et al.: Mgksite: multi-modal knowledge-driven site selection via intra and intermodal graph fusion. IEEE Trans. Multimed. (2024)
23. Liang, K., Meng, L., Li, H., Wang, J., Lan, L., Li, M., Liu, X., Wang, H.: From concrete to abstract: multi-view clustering on relational knowledge. IEEE Trans. Pattern Anal. Mach. Intell., 1–18 (2025). https://doi.org/10.1109/TPAMI.2025.3582689

24. Liang, K.,et al.: Learn from relational correlations and periodic events for temporal knowledge graph reasoning. In: Proceedings of the 46th International ACM SIGIR Conference on Research and Development in Information Retrieval, pp. 1559–1568 (2023)
25. Liao, R., Jia, X., Li, Y., Ma, Y., Tresp, V.: Gentkg: Generative forecasting on temporal knowledge graph with large language models. arXiv preprint arXiv:2310.07793 (2023)
26. Liu, K., Zhao, F., Xu, G., Wang, X., Jin, H.: Retia: relation-entity twin-interact aggregation for temporal knowledge graph extrapolation. In: 2023 IEEE 39th International Conference on Data Engineering (ICDE), pp. 1761–1774. IEEE (2023)
27. Mahdisoltani, F., Biega, J., Suchanek, F.M.: Yago3: A knowledge base from multilingual wikipedias. In: CIDR (2013)
28. Schlichtkrull, M., Kipf, T.N., Bloem, P., van den Berg, R., Titov, I., Welling, M.: Modeling relational data with graph convolutional networks. In: Gangemi, A., et al. (eds.) ESWC 2018. LNCS, vol. 10843, pp. 593–607. Springer, Cham (2018). https://doi.org/10.1007/978-3-319-93417-4_38
29. Seo, Y., Defferrard, M., Vandergheynst, P., Bresson, X.: Structured sequence modeling with graph convolutional recurrent networks. In: Cheng, L., Leung, A.C.S., Ozawa, S. (eds.) ICONIP 2018. LNCS, vol. 11301, pp. 362–373. Springer, Cham (2018). https://doi.org/10.1007/978-3-030-04167-0_33
30. Shang, C., Tang, Y., Huang, J., Bi, J., He, X., Zhou, B.: End-to-end structure-aware convolutional networks for knowledge base completion. In: Proceedings of the AAAI Conference on Artificial Intelligence, vol. 33, pp. 3060–3067 (2019)
31. Sun, H., Zhong, J., Ma, Y., Han, Z., He, K.: Timetraveler: reinforcement learning for temporal knowledge graph forecasting. arXiv preprint arXiv:2109.04101 (2021)
32. Sun, Z., Deng, Z.H., Nie, J.Y., Tang, J.: Rotate: Knowledge graph embedding by relational rotation in complex space. arXiv preprint arXiv:1902.10197 (2019)
33. Tao, S., Cao, Q., Shen, H., Huang, J., Wu, Y., Cheng, X.: Single node injection attack against graph neural networks. In: Proceedings of the 30th ACM International Conference on Information & Knowledge Management, CIKM '21, pp. 1794–1803. ACM, October 2021. https://doi.org/10.1145/3459637.3482393
34. Team, Q.: Qwq-32b: embracing the power of reinforcement learning, March 2025. https://qwenlm.github.io/blog/qwq-32b/
35. Touvron, H., et al.: Llama: Open and efficient foundation language models. arXiv preprint arXiv:2302.13971 (2023)
36. Vaswani, A., et al.: Attention is all you need. Advances in neural information processing systems **30** (2017)
37. Wang, J., et al.: Large language models-guided dynamic adaptation for temporal knowledge graph reasoning. Adv. Neural. Inf. Process. Syst. **37**, 8384–8410 (2024)
38. Xia, Y., Wang, D., Liu, Q., Wang, L., Wu, S., Zhang, X.: Chain-of-history reasoning for temporal knowledge graph forecasting. arXiv preprint arXiv:2402.14382 (2024)
39. Xiang, S., Cheng, D., Shang, C., Zhang, Y., Liang, Y.: Temporal and heterogeneous graph neural network for financial time series prediction. In: Proceedings of the 31st ACM International Conference on Information & Knowledge Management, CIKM '22. ACM, October 2022. https://doi.org/10.1145/3511808.3557089
40. Zhang, M., Xia, Y., Liu, Q., Wu, S., Wang, L.: Learning latent relations for temporal knowledge graph reasoning. In: Proceedings of the 61st Annual Meeting of the Association for Computational Linguistics (Volume 1: Long Papers), pp. 12617–12631 (2023)
41. Zhang, M., Xia, Y., Liu, Q., Wu, S., Wang, L.: Learning long-and short-term representations for temporal knowledge graph reasoning. In: Proceedings of the ACM Web Conference 2023, pp. 2412–2422 (2023)

42. Zhang, S., Wei, W., Huang, R., Xie, W., Chen, D.: Modeling historical relevant and local frequency context for representation-based temporal knowledge graph forecasting. In: Al-Onaizan, Y., Bansal, M., Chen, Y.N. (eds.) Findings of the Association for Computational Linguistics: EMNLP 2024, pp. 7675–7686. Association for Computational Linguistics, Miami, Florida, USA, November 2024. https://doi.org/10.18653/v1/2024.findings-emnlp.451
43. Zhang, W., Peng, L., Ge, X., Yang, L., Chen, L., Li, W.: Spatio-temporal knowledge graph-based research on agro-meteorological disaster monitoring. Remote Sensing **15**(18) (2023)
44. Zhu, C., Chen, M., Fan, C., Cheng, G., Zhan, Y.: Learning from history: modeling temporal knowledge graphs with sequential copy-generation networks (2021). https://arxiv.org/abs/2012.08492

Compact Answers to Temporal Path Queries

Muhammad Adnan, Diego Calvanese, Julien Corman(✉), Anton Dignös, Werner Nutt, and Ognjen Savković

Free University of Bozen-Bolzano, Bolzano, Italy
corman@inf.unibz.it

Abstract. We study path-based graph queries that, in addition to navigation through edges, also perform navigation through time. This allows asking questions about the dynamics of networks, like traffic movement, cause-effect relationships, or the spread of a disease. In this setting, a graph consists of triples annotated with validity intervals, and a query produces pairs of nodes where each pair is associated with a binary relation over time. For instance, such a pair could be two airports, and the temporal relation could map potential departure times to possible arrival times. An open question is how to represent such a relation in a compact form, and maintain this property during query evaluation. To address this, we investigate four compact representations of answers to a such queries. We discuss their respective advantages and drawbacks, in terms of conciseness, uniqueness, and computational cost. Notably, the most refined encoding guarantees that query answers over dense time can be finitely represented.

Keywords: graph databases · temporal databases · regular path queries

1 Introduction

Temporal databases [5] have traditionally focused on computing relations where each tuple is annotated with a *set* of time points (or a set of intervals) for validity. In comparison, little attention has been paid to the case where each tuple is annotated with a *relation* over time points, which indicates how different events are related temporally. This is the focus of this paper, more precisely *binary* relations over time points.

One application is linking potential departure times of a road trip to their corresponding arrival times, e.g. considering uncertainties like traffic. Such a relation maps each departure time to a range of possible arrival times (or equivalently each arrival time to possible departures). Another example is modelling cause-effect scenarios with uncertain delays. For instance, one may compute the relation that associates (in time) the potential malfunction a component in an

D. Garijo et al. (Eds.): ISWC 2025, LNCS 16140, pp. 425–442, 2026.
https://doi.org/10.1007/978-3-032-09527-5_23

airplane to the subsequent malfunction of another component. A third application of binary temporal relations, which we will use as a running example (inspired by [2]), is modeling the spread of phenomena such as messages or diseases. For instance, in epidemiology, the latency and infectiousness periods of a virus induce a temporal relation that maps potential infection times to possible subsequent transmissions, which allows modeling disease propagation within a population.

These examples suggest at least three elementary operations that one may want to perform over binary temporal relations: *(i) filtering* such a relation (based on some knowledge about events that took place), *(ii) combining* two such relations, and *(iii) composing* them (e.g. to model transitive cause-effect or spread). Or in database terms, selection, union and join respectively. These operations can be seen as a natural generalization of their counterparts in classical temporal databases (if we abstract away from non-temporal data). Indeed, in these systems, the set of time points associated to a fact (for validity) can be viewed as a unary relation over time, which we generalize here to a binary one.

However, prior to performing such operations, a fundamental question is how to *represent* their input and output. This is the main problem addressed in this paper. Precisely, how to represent a binary temporal relation in a compact way (or even finitely over dense time), and ensure that compactness (resp. finiteness) is preserved by selection, union and/or join. To our knowledge, this has not been addressed in the literature, and as we will see, the answer to this (apparently simple) question is not trivial. In particular, such a relation cannot be represented as a set of intervals, as opposed to the sets of time points (a.k.a. unary relations) that temporal databases traditionally focus on.

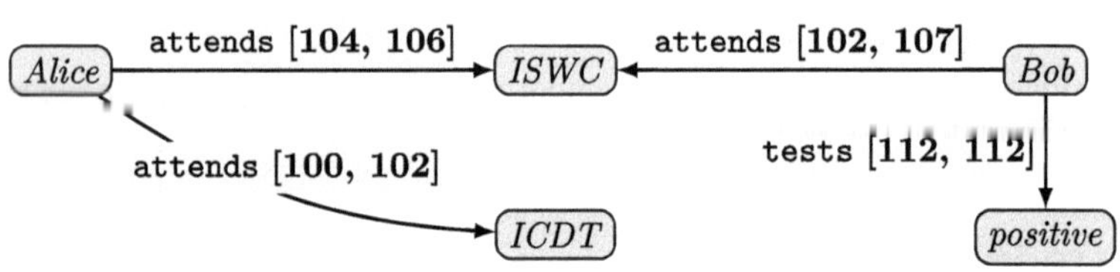

Fig. 1. A temporal graph

Concretely, we focus on the query language recently introduced in [2], which computes and performs operations on binary temporal relations, along with a graph data model used to filter such relations. To our knowledge, this is the first query language that manipulates such relations. For presentation purposes, we simplify this language and data model to a fragment that is essentially Regular Path Queries (RPQs)[1] extended with a temporal navigation operator, and evaluated over a time-labeled graphs. RPQs are used to navigate through the graph, whereas the temporal operator enables navigation in time, by a certain *range*.

[1] RPQs are a central building block of navigational graph query languages such as Cypher [15] and SPARQL [17].

An RPQ q is a regular expression, and a pair $\langle n_1, n_2 \rangle$ of nodes is an answer to q over a graph G if there exists a path from n_1 to n_2 in G whose concatenated labels match this regular expression. The language of [2], called *Temporal RPQs* (TRPQs), extends RPQs with a temporal operator that allows navigation from one node at a certain time to the same node in past or future moments. Accordingly, an answer is a pair $\langle \langle n_1, t_1 \rangle, \langle n_2, t_2 \rangle \rangle$, where n_1 and n_2 are each associated with a time point, which mark the starting and arrival time of the temporal navigation respectively.

More precisely, this temporal operator, which we denote as $\mathbf{T}_\delta$ here, allows navigation in time within the range specified as the interval δ. For instance, the latency and infectiousness periods of a virus may imply that a person can only become infectious at least three days after the infection time t, and remain infectious at most five days after t. If $\mathcal{T}$ is our temporal domain, this induces a binary temporal relation

$$R = \{(t, t + d) \mid t \in \mathcal{T} \text{ and } d \in [3, 5]\}.$$

Accordingly, if $\mathcal{N}_G$ is the set of nodes in the queried graph G, then the query $\mathbf{T}_{[3,5]}$ outputs all pairs $\langle \langle n, t_1 \rangle, \langle n, t_2 \rangle \rangle$ such that $n \in \mathcal{N}_G$ and $(t_1, t_2) \in R$. This output can be joined and filtered based on events registered in G, effectively restricting the initial temporal relation R, and associating each returned time point with a meaningful node. For instance, the graph of Fig. 1 represents data about attendance at a conference, where each fact is a labelled edge, annotated with an interval for validity. We can extend our query as follows

$$q_1 = \mathrm{T}_{[3,5]}/\texttt{attends}/\texttt{attends}^-.$$

This query outputs all pairs $\langle \langle n_1, t_1 \rangle, \langle n_2, t_2 \rangle \rangle$ such that n_1 and n_2 attended a same event, and n_1 may have transmitted the virus to n_2 (during this event) at time t_2 if n_1 got infected at time t_1. These include the two pairs $\langle \langle \mathit{Alice}, 100 \rangle, \langle \mathit{Bob}, 104 \rangle \rangle$, and $\langle \langle \mathit{Alice}, 100 \rangle, \langle \mathit{Bob}, 105 \rangle \rangle$, meaning that if Alice contracted the virus on day 100, then she may have transmitted it to Bob during day 104 or day 105 (among other possibilities). In this query, the "/" operator is a join, and the subqueries `attends` and `attends`$^-$ act as filters on our initial temporal relation R, restricting it based on the time intervals contained in the graph. We can further restrict this relation by requiring that person n_2 tested positive at most a week after the possible transmission, with

$$q_2 = q_1/?\Big(\mathrm{T}_{[0,7]}/\texttt{tests}/(= \mathit{positive})\Big).$$

In this query, the operator $?q$ acts as an existential quantifier: it only requires the existence of a match for the subquery q, so that the output of q_2 is a subset of the output of q_1.

As we have seen above, the initial temporal relation R can be easily represented in a compact way, using the temporal domain $\mathcal{T}$ for the set of initial infection points, and a single interval of temporal distances [3, 5] that indicates by how much each initial time point can be shifted. This holds regardless of whether $\mathcal{T}$ is discrete or continuous. However, this does not hold anymore for the outputs of our queries. For instance, the temporal relation induced by the answers to q_2 (which all have *Alice* and *Bob* as first and second node respectively) is uneven: over discrete time (and with a granularity of one day), 100 is associated with a single day 105, whereas 101 is associated with both 105 and 106. Moreover, without a compact representation of query answers, altering the time granularity (e.g. from days to hours) may significantly increase the number of output tuples (exponentially in the size of the input, assuming that interval boundaries are encoded in binary). Besides, even in the case where the output of a query can be represented compactly, computing all answers before summarizing them may be prohibitive, because the number of intermediate results may impact the performance of (worst-case quadratic) join operations. Hence the need to not only represent answers in a compact way, but also maintain compactness during query evaluation. This is even a necessity over dense time, where the lack of a finite representation may forbid query evaluation. To our knowledge, these are still open questions (in particular, left open in [2]), which effectively rule out arbitrary selection, union and joins over binary temporal relations.

Contributions and Organization. In this work, we propose four alternative compact representations of answers to TRPQs. In Sect. 2, we provide an informal, graphical overview of each of them. In Sect. 3, we define the syntax and semantics of the query language that we study. In Sect. 4, we formally define and study our four representations: first, in Sect. 4.1, we present the two simpler ones, which aggregate tuples along a single temporal dimension, either starting points or distances; then, in Sect. 4.2, we present the two more complex representations, which aggregate tuples along both dimensions. We analyze the respective advantages and drawbacks of each representation in terms of finiteness (over dense time), compactness (when finite), uniqueness, and the computational cost of query answering and minimizing a set of tuples. Notably, the fourth (more complex) representation guarantees that compactness and finiteness are maintained throughout query evaluation. In Sect. 5, we discuss related work. An extended version of this paper, with full definitions and proofs, is available at https://arxiv.org/abs/2507.22143.

2 Overview

This section provides a high-level overview of the four compact representations of answers to TRPQs defined and studied in this article. As a running example, the following query q_3 outputs all pairs $\langle\langle n_1, t_1\rangle, \langle n_2, t_2\rangle\rangle$ such that, if Alice got infected at time t_1 while attending event n_1, then she may have transmitted the virus at time t_2 while attending event n_2:

$$q_3 = \texttt{attends}^- /(= \textit{Alice})/\mathbf{T}_{[3,5]}/\texttt{attends}.$$

Over discrete time, with days as temporal granularity, evaluating q_3 over the graph G of Fig. 1 outputs a set $[\![q_3]\!]_G$ of 7 pairs, each of the form $\langle\langle ICDT, t_1\rangle, \langle ISWC, t_2\rangle\rangle$. Since the two nodes ($ICDT$ and $ISWC$) are identical for all answers, we can focus on the binary temporal relation induced by these, i.e. the relation $R = \{(t_1, t_2) \mid \langle\langle ICDT, t_1\rangle, \langle ISWC, t_2\rangle\rangle \in [\![q_3]\!]_G\}$. Each pair $(t_1, t_2) \in R$ can equivalently be represented as the pair $(t_1, t_2 - t_1)$, where the second component is the temporal distance between t_1 and t_2. Accordingly, Fig. 2a displays these 7 pairs over the Euclidean plane of (discrete) time per distance.

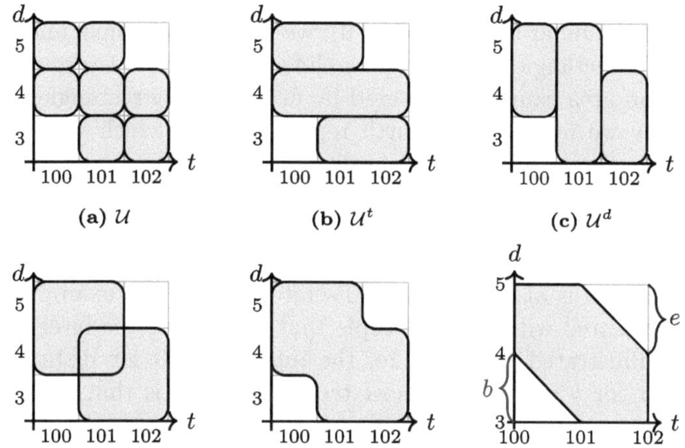

(a) $\mathcal{U}$ **(b)** $\mathcal{U}^t$ **(c)** $\mathcal{U}^d$

(d) $\mathcal{U}^{td}$ **(e)** $\mathcal{U}^c$ **(f)** $\mathcal{U}^c$ **over dense time**

Fig. 2. Alternative representations of the answers to Query q_3, in the plane of time per distance

Each of the four compact representations that we study in this article is an alternative way to reduce the number of such pairs. The first representation, which we call $\mathcal{U}^t$, groups these pairs by distance (i.e. horizontally in our figure), while aggregating time points as intervals. In this example, this yields three compact answers, namely $([100, 101], 5)$, $([100, 102], 4)$, and $([101, 102], 3)$. Each of these is a rectangle with height 1 in our plane, as illustrated with Fig. 2b, and their union is indeed the area of interest. The second representation, called $\mathcal{U}^d$, is symmetric, in the sense that it groups results by time points and aggregates distances, so that compact answers are now rectangle with width 1, as illustrated with Fig. 2c. The first representation $\mathcal{U}^t$ ensures that the number of compact answers is independent of the size of the intervals present in the graph. However, this number is linear in the size of the intervals used in the query (via the temporal navigation operator). And conversely for $\mathcal{U}^d$.

A third natural attempt (which we call $\mathcal{U}^{td}$) consists in aggregating tuples along both dimensions, representing our binary relation R as a set of pairs of intervals, one of time points, the other of distances. These correspond to arbitrary rectangles in our plane. As can be seen on Fig. 2d, two such rectangles are still needed to cover the whole area (or three if we forbid overlapping rectangles). Besides, some desirable properties of the first two representations are lost: the most compact representation (i.e. smallest set of rectangles needed to cover the area) is not unique anymore (e.g. if the area is an "L"-shaped polygon), and minimizing the number of answers (i.e. finding a minimal set of such rectangles) becomes intractable (if we allow rectangles to overlap).

Moreover, for all three representations, the number of tuples needed to aggregate all answers to q_3 may grow with a change of time granularity. This can once again be seen in Fig. 2a: if we adopt hours rather than days, then the number of "steps" (bottom left and top right of the area) gets multiplied by 24. At the limit (i.e. when granularity approaches 0), we reach dense time, and the area to cover becomes a rectangle cropped by two lines with slope -1 (drawn in Fig. 2f). Clearly, such an area cannot be covered by finitely many rectangles.

This is why we introduce a fourth representation, which we call $\mathcal{U}^c$. Over dense time, a tuple in $\mathcal{U}^c$ precisely stands for an area like the one of Fig. 2f, by means of two intervals (one for times, the other for distance), which intuitively represent the rectangle to be cropped, together with two values b and e that specify where the two cropping lines intersect respectively with this rectangle. This representation is also useful over discrete time: in our example, the whole area can be captured with a single tuple that consists of the interval $[100, 102]$ for times, as illustrated with Fig. 2e, the interval $[3, 5]$ for distance, and the values 1 and 1 for b and e. Our most technical result is that binary relations that can be represented as such geometric shapes are closed under composition. As a consequence, a TRPQ can only produce a union of such shapes. So this last format $\mathcal{U}^c$ overcomes the limitations of the previous ones, in the sense that answers to a TRPQ can always be represented in a finite way. This is also the most compact of these four representations. However, as for $\mathcal{U}^{td}$, minimizing a set of tuples under this view is intractable, and the most compact representation of a set of answers is not unique.

Our main findings about each of the four representations are summarized at the end of the dedicated section, in Fig. 6. As a brief summary, only the fourth representation ($\mathcal{U}^{td}$) guarantees that query answers remain finite and independent of the sizes of the input intervals. In comparison, the two first representations $\mathcal{U}^t$ and $\mathcal{U}^d$ benefit from a unique compact representation of query answers, and the fact that computing it (out of a non-compact one) is tractable. However, these can only be used over discrete time, and if the size of the input query (resp. graph) intervals remains small.

3 Preliminaries

Temporal Graphs. For maximal generality (and readability), we use a very simple graph data model, where each fact is a labelled edge, annotated with a set of time intervals for validity. Formally, we assume two infinite sets $\mathcal{N}$ of nodes and $\mathcal{E}$ of edge labels. As is conventional (e.g. in RDF), we represent a fact as a triple $(s, p, o) \in \mathcal{N} \times \mathcal{E} \times \mathcal{N}$ (where s, p and o intuitively stand for "subject", "property" and "object" respectively). In addition, for the temporal dimension of our data, we assume an underlying temporal domain $\mathcal{T}$ that may be either discrete or dense. For simplicity, we will use $\mathbb{Z}$ in the former case, and $\mathbb{Q}$ in the latter. We also use $\mathsf{intv}(\mathcal{T})$ for the set of nonempty intervals over $\mathcal{T}$.

In our model, a database instance simply assigns (finitely many) intervals of validity to (finitely many) triples. Precisely, a *temporal graph* $G = \langle \mathcal{T}_G, \mathcal{F}_G, \mathsf{val}_G \rangle$ consists of a bounded *effective temporal domain* $\mathcal{T}_G \in \mathsf{intv}(\mathcal{T})$, a finite set of triples $\mathcal{F}_G \subseteq \mathcal{N} \times \mathcal{E} \times \mathcal{N}$, and a function $\mathsf{val}_G \colon \mathcal{F}_G \to 2^{\mathsf{intv}(\mathcal{T}_G)}$ that maps a triple to a finite set of intervals over $\mathcal{T}_G$. For instance, in Fig. 1, val_G assigns the (singleton) set of intervals $\{[104, 106]\}$ to the triple $(\mathit{Alice}, \mathtt{attends}, \mathit{ISWC})$.

Temporal Regular Path Queries. We adopt the query language introduced in [2], but in a simpler form, made possible by the simplified data model defined above. We emphasise that this is without loss of expressivity.

A *Temporal Regular Path Query* (TRPQ) is an expression for the symbol "trpq" in the following grammar:

$$\mathsf{trpq} ::= \mathsf{edge} \mid \mathsf{node} \mid \mathbf{T}_\delta \mid (\mathsf{trpq}/\mathsf{trpq}) \mid (\mathsf{trpq} + \mathsf{trpq}) \mid \mathsf{trpq}[m, n] \mid \mathsf{trpq}[m, \_]$$
$$\mathsf{edge} ::= \mathit{label} \mid \mathsf{edge}^-$$
$$\mathsf{node} ::= \mathit{pred} \mid \leq k \mid (?\mathsf{trpq}) \mid \neg\ \mathsf{node}$$

with $\mathit{label} \in \mathcal{E}$, $k \in \mathcal{T}, \delta \in \mathsf{intv}(\mathcal{T})$, $m, n \in \mathbb{N}^+$, and $m \leq n$.

Here, edge and node are filters on edges and nodes respectively. The terminal symbol *pred* stands for a Boolean predicate that can be evaluated locally for one node n, which we write $n \models \mathit{pred}$ (for instance, in Fig. 1, the node *positive* satisfies the predicate $(= \mathit{positive})$). Similarly, the Boolean predicate $\leq k$ evaluates whether a time point is less than or equal to k. The expression $(?\mathsf{trpq})$ filters the nodes that satisfy trpq, and $\neg$ represents logical negation. The temporal navigation operator $\mathbf{T}_\delta$ stands for navigation in time by any distance in the interval δ, and the remaining operators are regular path query (RPQ) operators: / stands for join, + for union, and $\mathsf{trpq}[m, n]$ for the "repetition" of trpq from m to n times. In particular, $\mathsf{trpq}[0, \_]$ represents Kleene closure (equivalent to the $*$ operator in regular expressions).

The formal semantics of TRPQs is provided in Fig. 3, where $[\![q]\!]_G$ is the evaluation of a TRPQ q over a temporal graph G. In this definition, we use q^i for the TRPQ defined inductively by $q^1 = q$ and $q^{j+1} = q^j/q$. For convenience, we represent (w.l.o.g.) an answer as two nodes together with a time point and a distance, rather than two nodes and two time points, i.e. we use tuples of the form $\langle n_1, n_2, t, d \rangle$ rather than $\langle \langle n_1, t \rangle, \langle n_2, t + d \rangle \rangle$. We also use $\mathcal{N}_G$ to denote the set of nodes that intuitively appear in G, i.e. all n such that the triple (n, p, o) or (s, p, n) is in $\mathcal{F}_G$ for some s, p and o.

Operations on intervals. For two intervals $\alpha, \beta \in \mathsf{intv}(\mathcal{T})$, we use $\alpha \oplus \beta$ (resp. $\alpha \ominus \beta$) to denote the interval $\{a + b \mid a \in \alpha \text{ and } b \in \beta\}$ (resp. $\{a - b \mid a \in \alpha \text{ and } b \in \beta\}$). We also use $\alpha + b$ (resp. $\alpha - b$) for $\alpha \oplus [b, b]$ (resp. $\alpha \ominus [b, b]$).

4 Compact Answers

In this section, we define and study the four representations of answers to a TRPQ sketched in Sect. 2. Let $\mathcal{U}$ denote the universe of all tuples that may be output by TRPQs, i.e. $\mathcal{U} = \mathcal{N} \times \mathcal{N} \times \mathcal{T} \times \mathcal{T}$. Then each of our four representations can be viewed as an alternative format to encode subsets of $\mathcal{U}$. We specify each of these four formats as a set of admissible tuples, denoted $\mathcal{U}^t$, $\mathcal{U}^d$, $\mathcal{U}^{td}$ and $\mathcal{U}^c$ respectively.

$$
\begin{aligned}
[\![label]\!]_G &= \{\langle n_1, n_2, t, 0\rangle \mid t \in \tau \text{ for some } \tau \in \mathsf{val}_G(n_1, label, n_2)\}\\
[\![\mathsf{edge}^-]\!]_G &= \{\langle n_2, n_1, t, 0\rangle \mid \langle n_1, n_2, t, 0\rangle \in [\![\mathsf{edge}]\!]_G\}\\
[\![pred]\!]_G &= \{\langle n, n, t, 0\rangle \mid n \models pred \text{ and } t \in \mathcal{T}_G\}\\
[\![\leq k]\!]_G &= \{\langle n, n, t, 0\rangle \mid n \in \mathcal{N}_G, t \in \mathcal{T}_G \text{ and } t \leq k\}\\
[\![\mathbf{T}_\delta]\!]_G &= \{\langle n, n, t, d\rangle \mid n \in \mathcal{N}_G, t \in \mathcal{T}_G, d \in \delta \text{ and } t + d \in \mathcal{T}_G\}\\
[\![?\mathsf{trpq}]\!]_G &= \{\langle n, n, t, 0\rangle \mid \langle n, n', t, d\rangle \in [\![\mathsf{trpq}]\!]_G \text{ for some } n' \in \mathcal{N} \text{ and } d \in \mathcal{T}\}\\
[\![\neg\mathsf{node}]\!]_G &= (\{\langle n, n\rangle \mid n \in \mathcal{N}_G\} \times \mathcal{T}_G \times \{0\}) \setminus [\![\mathsf{node}]\!]_G\\
[\![\mathsf{trpq}_1/\mathsf{trpq}_2]\!]_G &= \{\langle n_1, n_3, t, d_1 + d_2\rangle \mid\\
&\qquad \exists n_2 \colon \langle n_1, n_2, t, d_1\rangle \in [\![\mathsf{trpq}_1]\!]_G \text{ and } \langle n_2, n_3, t + d_1, d_2\rangle \in [\![\mathsf{trpq}_2]\!]_G\}\\
[\![\mathsf{trpq}_1 + \mathsf{trpq}_2]\!]_G &= [\![\mathsf{trpq}_1]\!]_G \cup [\![\mathsf{trpq}_2]\!]_G\\
[\![\mathsf{trpq}[m, n]]\!]_G &= \bigcup_{k=m}^{n} [\![\mathsf{trpq}^k]\!]_G\\
[\![\mathsf{trpq}[m, \_]]\!]_G &= \bigcup_{k \geq m} [\![\mathsf{trpq}^k]\!]_G
\end{aligned}
$$

Fig. 3. Semantics of TRPQs

Definition 1 (Unfolding, compact set of tuples, finite representation). *Let $\mathcal{U}^x$ be one of $\mathcal{U}^t$, $\mathcal{U}^d$, $\mathcal{U}^{td}$ or $\mathcal{U}^c$. A tuple* $\mathbf{u}$ *in $\mathcal{U}^x$ represents a subset of $\mathcal{U}$, which we call the* unfolding *of* $\mathbf{u}$. *And the unfolding of a set $U \subseteq \mathcal{U}^x$ of such tuples is the union of the unfoldings of the elements of U. We say that U is* compact *if it is finite and if no strictly smaller (w.r.t. cardinality) subset of $\mathcal{U}^x$ has the same unfolding. A set $V \subseteq \mathcal{U}$ can be* finitely represented *(in $\mathcal{U}^x$) if there is a finite $U \subseteq \mathcal{U}^x$ with unfolding V.*

4.1 Folding Time Points ($\mathcal{U}^t$) or Distances ($\mathcal{U}^d$)

Each of our two first compact representations aggregates tuples in $\mathcal{U}$ along one dimension: either the time point associated to the first node, or the distance between times points associated to each node. The corresponding universes $\mathcal{U}^t$ and $\mathcal{U}^d$ of tuples are $\mathcal{N} \times \mathcal{N} \times \mathsf{intv}(\mathcal{T}) \times \mathcal{T}$ and $\mathcal{N} \times \mathcal{N} \times \mathcal{T} \times \mathsf{intv}(\mathcal{T})$ respectively. The unfolding of a tuple $\langle n_1, n_2, \tau, d\rangle \in \mathcal{U}^t$ is $\{\langle n_1, n_2, t, d\rangle \mid t \in \tau\}$, and analogously $\{\langle n_1, n_2, t, d\rangle \mid d \in \delta\}$ for a tuple $\langle n_1, n_2, t, \delta\rangle \in \mathcal{U}^d$.

Inductive Representation. In order to understand when the answers $[\![q]\!]_G$ to a TRPQ q over a temporal graph G can be finitely represented in $\mathcal{U}^t$ or

$\mathcal{U}^d$, and what the size of such representations may be, we define by structural induction on q two (not necessarily compact) representation of $[\![q]\!]_G$ in $\mathcal{U}^t$ and $\mathcal{U}^t$, noted $\llparenthesis q \rrparenthesis_G^t$ and $\llparenthesis q \rrparenthesis_G^d$ respectively (these representations also pave the way for implementing query evaluation). For instance, in the case where q is of the form *pred*, we define $\llparenthesis pred \rrparenthesis_G^t$ as $\{\langle n, n, \mathcal{T}_G, 0\rangle \mid n \models pred\}$.

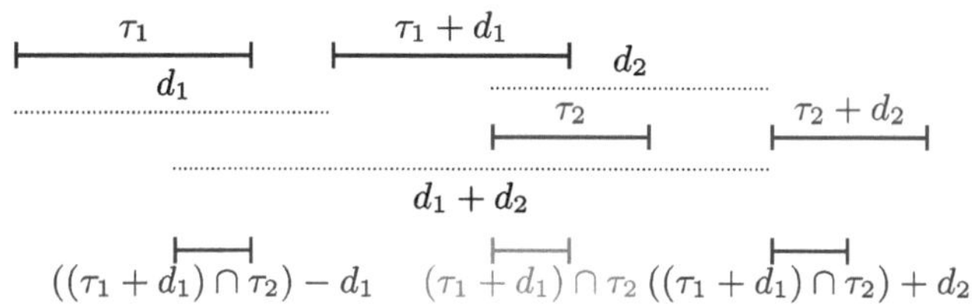

Fig. 4. Join of two tuples $\langle n_1, n_2, \tau_1, d_1\rangle$ and $\langle n_2, n_3, \tau_2, d_2\rangle$ in $\mathcal{U}^t$. Each tuple is depicted as two intervals τ_i and $\tau_i + d_i$. The two corresponding intervals τ_o and $\tau_o + d_o$ for the output tuple $\langle n_1, n_3, \tau_o, d_o\rangle$ are in violet.

Due to space limitations, we only provide the full definition of $\llparenthesis q \rrparenthesis_G^t$ and $\llparenthesis q \rrparenthesis_G^d$ in the extended version of this paper (together with proofs of correctness). We highlight here the least obvious operators. The first one is the temporal join $\mathsf{trpq}_1/\mathsf{trpq}_2$, which intuitively composes temporal relations. If we assume (by induction) that the answers to each operand (trpq_1 and trpq_2) are represented in $\mathcal{U}^t$, then the representation of $\mathsf{trpq}_1/\mathsf{trpq}_2$ in $\mathcal{U}^t$ can be computed as a regular join together with simple arithmetic operations on interval boundaries, as follows:

$$\llparenthesis \mathsf{trpq}_1/\mathsf{trpq}_2 \rrparenthesis_G^t = \Big\{\langle n_1, n_3, ((\tau_1 + d_1) \cap \tau_2) - d_1, d_1 + d_2\rangle \mid \exists n_2\colon \\ \langle n_1, n_2, \tau_1, d_1\rangle \in \llparenthesis \mathsf{trpq}_1 \rrparenthesis_G^t, \langle n_2, n_3, \tau_2, d_2\rangle \in \llparenthesis \mathsf{trpq}_2 \rrparenthesis_G^t \text{ and } (\tau_1 + d_1) \cap \tau_2 \neq \emptyset \Big\}.$$

This observation also holds for $\mathcal{U}^d$, but with different operations on interval boundaries:

$$\llparenthesis \mathsf{trpq}_1/\mathsf{trpq}_2 \rrparenthesis_G^d = \Big\{\langle n_1, n_3, t_1, t_2 - t_1 + \delta_2\rangle \mid \exists n_2\colon \langle n_1, n_2, t_1, \delta_1\rangle \in \llparenthesis \mathsf{trpq}_1 \rrparenthesis_G^d, \\ \langle n_2, n_3, t_2, \delta_2\rangle \in \llparenthesis \mathsf{trpq}_2 \rrparenthesis_G^d \text{ and } t_2 - t_1 \in \delta_1\Big\}.$$

The less obvious of these two operations is $\llparenthesis \mathsf{trpq}_1/\mathsf{trpq}_2 \rrparenthesis_G^t$, which we illustrate with Fig. 4).

Another case of interest is the temporal navigation operator $\mathbf{T}_\delta$, for the second representation $\mathcal{U}^d$ (the case of $\mathcal{U}^t$ is trivial). Consider a query of the form $q/\mathbf{T}_\delta$ (or symmetrically $\mathbf{T}_\delta/q$). If the subquery $\mathbf{T}_\delta$ is evaluated independently, then the output of this subquery may be infinite over dense time, which rules out in practice an inductive evaluation:

$$\llparenthesis \mathbf{T}_\delta \rrparenthesis_G^d = \{\langle n, n, t, ((\delta + t) \cap \mathcal{T}_G) - t\rangle \mid n \in \mathcal{N}_G, t \in \mathcal{T}_G, (\delta + t) \cap \mathcal{T}_G \neq \emptyset\}.$$

However, if $(\!|q|\!)^d_G$ is finite, then the output of the whole query $q/\mathbf{T}_\delta$ can be represented finitely, and effectively computed as follows:

$$(\!|q/\mathbf{T}_\delta|\!)^d_G = \{\langle n_1, n_2, t, (\delta' \oplus \delta) \cap \mathcal{T}_G\rangle \mid \langle n_1, n_2, t, \delta'\rangle \in (\!|q|\!)^d_G, (t + (\delta' \oplus \delta)) \cap \mathcal{T}_G \neq \emptyset\}.$$

Finiteness Over Dense Time. Over discrete time, trivially, $[\![q]\!]_G$ can be finitely represented in $\mathcal{U}$,[2] therefore as well in any of our four compact representations. But over dense time, this is not always possible. For instance, if q_t is the query $(= \mathit{positive})/\texttt{tests}^-/\mathbf{T}_{[-7,0]}$, and if the graph G of Fig. 1 is interpreted over dense time, then $\langle \mathit{positive}, \mathit{Bob}, 112, d\rangle \in [\![q_t]\!]_G$ for every rational number d in $[-7, 0]$. And no tuple in $\mathcal{U}^t$ can represent more than one of these tuples. From the definition of $(\!|q|\!)^t_G$, the only possible source of non-finiteness for $\mathcal{U}^t$ is the temporal navigation operator $\mathbf{T}_\delta$, and only if δ is not a singleton interval (i.e., if it specifies a certain *range* rather than a fixed distance).

Similarly, if q_d is the query $(= \mathit{Bob})/\texttt{attends}$, then $\langle \mathit{Bob}, \mathit{ISWC}, t, 0\rangle \in [\![q]\!]_G$, for every rational number t in $[102, 107]$, and no tuple in $\mathcal{U}^d$ can represent more than one of these.

Compactness. If $[\![q]\!]_G$ can be finitely represented in $\mathcal{U}^t$ or $\mathcal{U}^d$, then a natural requirement on these representations is conciseness. It is easy to see that a finite set $U \subseteq \mathcal{U}^t$ is compact iff all time intervals for the same n_1, n_2 and d within U are coalesced. Formally, let $\sim$ denote the binary relation over $\mathcal{U}^t$ defined by $\langle n_1, n_2, \tau_1, d_1\rangle \sim \langle n_3, n_4, \tau_2, d_2\rangle$ iff $\langle n_1, n_2, d_1\rangle = \langle n_3, n_4, d_2\rangle$ and $\tau_1 \cup \tau_2 \in \mathsf{intv}(\mathcal{T})$. Then U is compact iff $\mathbf{u}_1 \not\sim \mathbf{u}_2$ for all $\mathbf{u}_1, \mathbf{u}_2 \in U$ s.t. $\mathbf{u}_1 \neq \mathbf{u}_2$. More, there is a unique way to coalesce a finite set of intervals. Therefore if $V \subseteq \mathcal{U}$ can be finitely represented in $\mathcal{U}^t$, then V also has a unique compact representation in $\mathcal{U}^t$. A symmetric observation holds for a set $U \subseteq \mathcal{U}^d$, where we coalesce distance intervals rather than time intervals.

Coalescing a set of intervals is known to be in $O(n \log n)$, and efficient implementations have been devised (see Sect. 5). For this reason, coalescing intermediate results in $(\!|q|\!)^t_G$ or $(\!|q|\!)^d_G$ may be an interesting query evaluation strategy. For instance, this could reduce the size of the operands of a (worst-case quadratic) temporal join.

Size of Compact Answers. Our two representations $\mathcal{U}^t$ and $\mathcal{U}^d$ exhibit an interesting symmetry when it comes to the size of compact answers to a query, intuitively growing with the size of the intervals present in q in the case of $\mathcal{U}^t$, and the intervals present in G in the case of $\mathcal{U}^d$. This suggests that $\mathcal{U}^t$ is be better suited to large graphs intervals and small temporal navigation intervals, and conversely for $\mathcal{U}^d$.

Unfortunately, this does not hold for arbitrary queries. Indeed, the size of a compact representation of $[\![q]\!]_G$ may be affected by the size of the effective temporal domain $\mathcal{T}_G$ alone, even if all time intervals in the query and graph are singletons, as soon as q contains an occurrence of the closure operator $[m, \_]$, as illustrated with the following example:

[2] Recall that we assume the effective temporal domain $\mathcal{T}_G$ of G to be bounded.

Example 1. Consider a temporal graph G s.t. $\mathsf{val}_G(n_1, e, n_2) = \{[0,0]\}$ and consider the query $q = e/(\mathrm{T}_{[2,2]})[1, \_]$. The compact representation of $[\![q]\!]_G$ is $\{\langle n_1, n_2, [0,0], d\rangle \mid d \in D\}$ in $\mathcal{U}^t$, and $\{\langle n_1, n_2, 0, [d,d]\rangle \mid d \in D\}$ in $\mathcal{U}^d$, where $D = \{d \in \mathcal{T}_G \cap \mathbb{N}^+ \mid d \bmod 2 = 0\}$. □

However, for queries without closure operator, which we call *closure-free*, the symmetry sketched above holds. To formalize this, we introduce a notation that we will reuse for the other two representations.

Definition 2 (Size of compact answers to closure-free queries). *Let $\mathcal{U}^x$ be one of $\mathcal{U}^t$, $\mathcal{U}^d$, $\mathcal{U}^{td}$ or $\mathcal{U}^c$. Consider a temporal graph G and a closure-free query q, such that $[\![q]\!]_G$ can be finitely represented in $\mathcal{U}^x$. We fix G and q, with the exception of $\mathcal{T}_G$, and either* (i) *the intervals present in G, or* (ii) *the intervals present in q (with the requirement that $[\![q]\!]_G$ can still be finitely represented in $\mathcal{U}^x$). In case (i), let n be the cumulated length of the intervals in G, and let V be a compact representation of $[\![q]\!]_G$ in $\mathcal{U}^x$. We use $\#\mathsf{answers}^\tau(\mathcal{U}^x)$ for the function that maps n to the the cardinality of V. In case (ii), we use $\#\mathsf{answers}^\delta(\mathcal{U}^x)$ with an identical meaning, but where n is the cumulated size of the intervals in q.*

The following results says that the size of the compact representation of $[\![q]\!]_G$ in $\mathcal{U}^t$ (when it exists) may be affected by the size of the intervals present in q, but not the ones used to label triples in G, and conversely for $\mathcal{U}^d$

Proposition 1. *In the worst case,*[3]

(fixed query intervals)	*(fixed graph intervals)*
$\#\mathsf{answers}^\tau(\mathcal{U}^t) = O(1)$	$\#\mathsf{answers}^\delta(\mathcal{U}^t) = \Omega(n)$
$\#\mathsf{answers}^\tau(\mathcal{U}^d) = \Omega(n)$	$\#\mathsf{answers}^\delta(\mathcal{U}^d) = O(1)$

Complexity of Query Answering. Let $\mathcal{U}^x$ be one of $\mathcal{U}^t$, $\mathcal{U}^d$, $\mathcal{U}^{td}$ or $\mathcal{U}^c$. We formulate a decision problem analogous to the classical boolean query answering problem (for atemporal databases), in such a way that it remains defined even if $[\![q]\!]_G$ does not admit a finite representation in $\mathcal{U}^x$. We say that a tuple $\mathbf{u}$ in $\mathcal{U}^x$ is a *compact answer* to q over G if its unfolding is a subset of $[\![q]\!]_G$ and is maximal among the tuples in $\mathcal{U}^x$ that satisfy this condition. We can now define our (four) problems (where x is either t, d, td or c):

CompactAnswer^x
Input: temporal graph G, TRPQ q, tuple $\mathbf{u} \in \mathcal{U}^x$
Decide: $\mathbf{u}$ is a compact answer to q over G

Complexity for these problems is (partly) driven by the size of the input time intervals, and there is no reason a priori to assume that intervals in the graphs are larger than the ones in the query. This is why we do not focus on data complexity (where the query is fixed), but instead on combined complexity,

[3] We write "wort case" here to clarify that this is for the worst possible inputs with size n (as opposed to average size for instance).

where the size of the query and data may vary (we leave for future work a finer-grained analysis). We show in the extended version of this paper that the results proven in [3] for answering TRPQs in $\mathcal{U}$ immediately transfer to $\mathcal{U}^t$ (resp. $\mathcal{U}^d$), even in the case where $[\![q]\!]_G$ cannot be finitely represented in $\mathcal{U}^t$ (resp. $\mathcal{U}^d$):

Proposition 2.
CompactAnswer^t and CompactAnswer^d are PSpace-complete.

We also observe that hardness can be proven with a graph of fixed size, with the exception of the effective temporal domain $\mathcal{T}_G$. However, the number of operators of the query used in this reduction is not fixed.

4.2 Folding Time Points and Distances ($\mathcal{U}^{td}$ and $\mathcal{U}^c$)

Each of the two compact representations $\mathcal{U}^t$ and $\mathcal{U}^d$ defined above aggregates tuples in $\mathcal{U}$ along one dimension (either time points or distances), and both may fail to represent the answers to a query compactly (or even finitely over dense time). So a first natural attempt to address this limitation consists in aggregating tuples along both dimensions. Accordingly, we define the universe $\mathcal{U}^{td}$ as $\mathcal{N} \times \mathcal{N} \times \mathsf{intv}(\mathcal{T}) \times \mathsf{intv}(\mathcal{T})$, and the unfolding of $\langle n_1, n_2, \tau, \delta \rangle \in \mathcal{U}^{td}$ as $\{\langle n_1, n_2, t, d \rangle \mid t \in \tau, d \in \delta\}$.

This representation is more compact than the two previous ones, since unfolding a tuple in $\mathcal{U}^t$ or $\mathcal{U}^d$ yields a subset of some unfolded tuple of $\mathcal{U}^{td}$. However, as we will see below, minimizing the cardinality of a set of query answers becomes intractable. Besides, maybe surprisingly, this new format may also fail to represent query answers in a compact fashion (or finitely over dense time). To see this, observe that for two fixed nodes, a tuple in $\mathcal{U}^{td}$ has a natural representation as a rectangle in the Euclidean plane P of times per distances. The following example shows a query whose output, depicted in Fig. 5b, cannot be represented (over dense time) as a finite set of rectangles in P. This example also provides insight about the formalization of our fourth representation (below).

Example 2. Consider a temporal graph G with two edges such that $\mathsf{val}_G(n_1, e_1, n_2) = \{[0, 2]\}$ and $\mathsf{val}_G(n_2, e_2, n_3) = \{[1, 3]\}$ Let q be the query $e_1/\mathbf{T}_{[0,2]}/e_2$. Then $[\![q]\!]_G = \{\langle n_1, n_2, t, d \rangle \mid t \in [0, 2], d \in [0, 2] \text{ and } t + d \in [1, 3]\}$. So for an answer $\langle n_1, n_2, t, d \rangle \in [\![q]\!]_G$, we have

$$1 \leq t + d \leq 3, \quad \text{that is,} \quad 1 - t \leq d \leq 3 - t.$$

Besides, from the query q, we get $0 \leq d \leq 2$. Therefore

$$\max(1 - t, 0) \leq d \leq \min(3 - t, 2).$$

This observation gives us an interval

$$\delta_t = [\max(1 - t, 0), \min(3 - t, 2)]$$

of admissible distances for each $t \in [0, 2]$, so that $[\![q]\!]_G = \{\langle n_1, n_2, t, d \rangle \mid t \in [0, 2] \text{ and } d \in \delta_t\}$. Extending this kind of reasoning to the general case, we derive the formula (1) presented below for δ_t. □

As shown in Fig. 5b, the area covered by the output of this query can be viewed as a rectangle cropped by two parallel lines, each with slope -1. These cropped rectangles turn out to have an essential property: if two temporal relations have such a shape, then their composition also does. As a consequence, associating each tuple with such a cropped rectangle (as opposed to a regular rectangle in $\mathcal{U}^{td}$) allows us to solve our initial problem: compute inductively the output of a TRPQ q over a graph G in such a way that the number of output tuples remains independent of the size of the intervals present in either q or G. To represent these cropped rectangles, we introduce a fourth format, which we call $\mathcal{U}^c$ (where "c" stands for "cropped"), where each tuple carries, in addition to a time interval τ and a distance interval δ (a.k.a. a rectangle), the two values $b, e \in \mathcal{T}$ depicted in Fig. 5b, which intuitively indicate where the cropping lines intersect the rectangle induced by τ and δ. For each time point $t \in \mathcal{T}$, these define a specific range of distances $\delta_t \subseteq \delta$, as

$$\delta_t = \ {}_{\delta}\lfloor\ b_\delta + \max(0, b - t)\ ,\ e_\delta - \max(0, t - e)\ \rfloor_\delta \tag{1}$$

where ${}_{\delta}\lfloor$ and $\rfloor_\delta$ stand for the left and right delimiters of δ, and b_δ and e_δ for its left and right boundaries For instance, if $\delta = [2, 6)$, then ${}_{\delta}\lfloor$ is "[", b_δ is 2, e_δ is 6 and $\rfloor_\delta$ is ")".

Accordingly, a tuple $\langle n_1, n_2, \tau, \delta, b, e\rangle \in \mathcal{N} \times \mathcal{N} \times \mathsf{intv}(\mathcal{T}) \times \mathsf{intv}(\mathcal{T}) \times \mathcal{T} \times \mathcal{T}$ is in $\mathcal{U}^c$ iff δ_t is nonempty for every $t \in \tau$. And the unfolding of this tuple is $\{\langle n_1, n_2, t, d\rangle \mid t \in \tau, d \in \delta_t\}$.

Inductive Representation. As we did for our first two representations, we define (in the extended version of this paper) by structural induction on q two representations $(\!|q|\!)^{td}_G$ and $(\!|q|\!)^{c}_G$ of $[\![q]\!]_G$ in $\mathcal{U}^{td}$ and $\mathcal{U}^c$ respectively. Our most technical result is correctness of this definition for the join operator in $\mathcal{U}^c$ (and to a lesser extent the temporal navigation operator).

We reproduce these definitions here to make apparent the fact these can be computed by means of simple arithmetic operations on time points and interval boundaries (together with a regular join on nodes for the join operator). The inductive evaluation $(\!|\mathsf{trpq}_1/\mathsf{trpq}_2|\!)^c_G$ in $\mathcal{U}^c$ of the query $\mathsf{trpq}_1/\mathsf{trpq}_2$ is defined as:

$$\{\mathbf{u}_1 \bowtie \mathbf{u}_2 \mid \mathbf{u}_1 \in (\!|\mathsf{trpq}_1|\!)^c_G, \mathbf{u}_2 \in (\!|\mathsf{trpq}_2|\!)^c_G, \mathbf{u}_1 \sim \mathbf{u}_2\}$$

where $\mathbf{u}_1 \sim \mathbf{u}_2$ and $\mathbf{u}_1 \bowtie \mathbf{u}_2$ are defined as follows.
For $\mathbf{u}_1 = \langle n_1, n_2, \tau_1, \delta_1, b_1, e_1\rangle$ and $\mathbf{u}_2 = \langle n_3, n_4, \tau_2, \delta_2, b_2, e_2\rangle$, let

$$\begin{aligned}&\delta'_1 = {}_{\delta_1}\lfloor\ b_{\delta_1} + \max(0, b_1 - b_{\tau_1}), e_{\delta_1} - \max(0, e_{\tau_1} - e_1)\ \rfloor_{\delta_1}, \text{ and}\\ &\tau = (((\tau_1 \oplus \delta'_1) \cap \tau_2) \ominus \delta'_1) \cap \tau_1.\end{aligned}$$

Then the relation $\sim \subseteq \mathcal{U}^c \times \mathcal{U}^c$ is defined as $\mathbf{u}_1 \sim \mathbf{u}_2$ iff $n_2 = n_3$ and $\tau \neq \emptyset$. And if $\mathbf{u}_1 \sim \mathbf{u}_2$, then $\mathbf{u}_1 \bowtie \mathbf{u}_2$ is defined as $\langle n_1, n_4, \tau, \delta_1 \oplus \delta_2, b, e\rangle$, with $b = \max(b_1, b_2 - b_{\delta_1})$ and $e = \min(e_1, e_2 - e_{\delta_1})$.

Similarly, if $b_{\mathcal{T}_G}$ and $e_{\mathcal{T}_G}$ are the boundaries of the interval $\mathcal{T}_G$, then $(\!|\mathbf{T}_\delta|\!)^c_G$ is defined as

$$\{\langle n, n, \mathcal{T}_G, \delta, b_{\mathcal{T}_G}, e_{\mathcal{T}_G}\rangle \bowtie \langle n, n, \mathcal{T}_G, [0,0], b_{\mathcal{T}_G}, e_{\mathcal{T}_G}\rangle \mid n \in \mathcal{N}_G\}.$$

Finiteness Over Dense Time. We already illustrated in Fig. 5b why $[\![q]\!]_G$ may not be finitely representable in $\mathcal{U}^{td}$. In contrast, $[\![q]\!]_G$ can be finitely represented in $\mathcal{U}^c$, as a direct consequence of the (correctness of the) inductive definition of $(\![q]\!)^c_G$, which produces finitely many tuples (notably, the operator $\mathsf{trpq}_1/\mathsf{trpq}_2$ produces at most one tuple per pair $(\mathbf{u}_1, \mathbf{u}_2) \in (\![\mathsf{trpq}_1]\!)^c_G \times (\![\mathsf{trpq}_2]\!)^c_G)$.

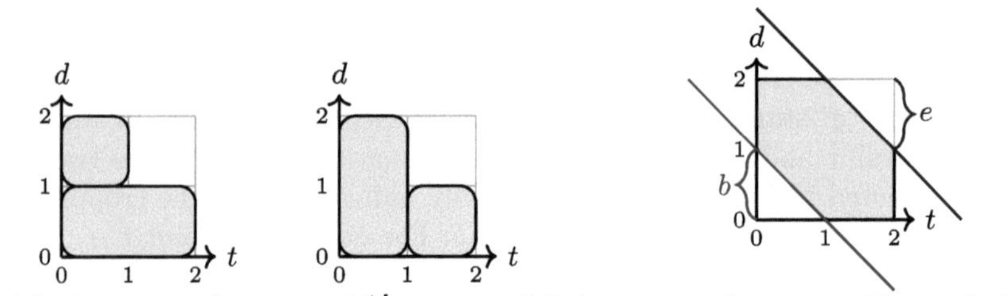

(a) Two minimal covers in $\mathcal{U}^{td}$ **(b)** Answers to the query of Example 2

Fig. 5. **(a)** Two minimal covers in $\mathcal{U}^{td}$ **(b)** Answers to the query of Example 2

Compactness. Let $U \subseteq \mathcal{U}^{td}$ and $V \subseteq \mathcal{U}$ be two sets of tuples that share the same nodes n_1 and n_2. Then U unfolds as V iff they intuitively cover the same area in the Euclidean plane of times per distances, i.e. if

$$\bigcup\{\tau \times \delta \mid \langle n_1, n_2, \tau, \delta\rangle \in U\} = \{(t,d) \mid \langle n_1, n_2, t, d\rangle \in V\}.$$

There may be several compact representations in $\mathcal{U}^{td}$ for the same $V \subseteq \mathcal{U}$. For instance, the minimal number of rectangle needed to cover an "L"-shaped polygon is two, and there are several such covers, as illustrated with Fig. 5a. This argument easily generalizes to discrete time.

Besides, minimizing the representation of $[\![q]\!]_G$ in $\mathcal{U}^{td}$ (i.e. computing a minimal set of tuples in $\mathcal{U}^{td}$ with unfolding $[\![q]\!]_G$) is intractable. To see this, we first observe that computing such a set is harder than deciding whether there exists one with size k (for a given k). Next, the following problem is known to be NP-complete: given a rectilinear polygon r and a number k, decide whether there is a set of at most k (possibly overlapping) rectangles that exactly cover r [4,9]. This problem reduces to ours, observing that for any rectilinear polygon r, a query q (with only unions) and graph G can be constructed in polynomial time so that $[\![q]\!]_G$ covers exactly r. This hardness result also immediately translates to $\mathcal{U}^c$: a rectangle is a specific case of a cropped rectangle, therefore the same reduction can be used, and if there is a minimization with at most k tuples in $\mathcal{U}^{td}$, then there is also one in $\mathcal{U}^c$.

An important difference though between these two representations and the two previous ones ($\mathcal{U}^t$ and $\mathcal{U}^d$) is that a compact set U of answers in $\mathcal{U}^{td}$ or $\mathcal{U}^c$ may be *redundant*, meaning that two tuples $\mathbf{u}_1$ and $\mathbf{u}_2$ in U may have overlapping unfoldings. This can for instance be seen in Fig. 2a, for $\mathcal{U}^{td}$. If we require tuples to be non-redundant, then the representations of answers to a query is in general

	Finite (dense time)	Unique	Size (closure-free q) graph intervals	query intervals	Minimization	Query answering
$\mathcal{U}^t$	no	yes	$O(1)$	$\Omega(n)$	$O(n \log n)$	PSPACE-c
$\mathcal{U}^d$	no	yes	$\Omega(n)$	$O(1)$	$O(n \log n)$	PSPACE-c
$\mathcal{U}^{td}$	no	no	$O(1)$	$\Omega(n)$	NP-h / $O(n^{2.5})$	PSPACE-c
$\mathcal{U}^c$	yes	no	$O(1)$	$O(1)$	NP-h	PSPACE-h

Fig. 6. Summary of results. For applications with discrete time and short intervals in the query (resp. graph), $\mathcal{U}^t$ (resp. $\mathcal{U}^d$) provides an efficient solution. $\mathcal{U}^{td}$ is more compact than both, and therefore potentially more efficient. However, minimizing the number of query answers is more expensive, which makes it less suitable for applications requiring aggregation. For applications with dense time or long intervals in both the graph and the query, $\mathcal{U}^c$ is the only viable option.

less concise. But it may be better suited for downstream tasks, such as aggregation. Besides, tractability of minimization in $\mathcal{U}^{td}$ is regained, because finding a cover with a minimal number of non-overlapping rectangles is tractable [14,20]. However, uniqueness is not regained, as shown in Fig. 5a.

Size of Compact Answers. If $V \subseteq \mathcal{U}$ can be finitely represented in $\mathcal{U}^{td}$, then trivially, a compact representation of V in $\mathcal{U}^{td}$ must be smaller than the compact representation of V in $\mathcal{U}^t$ (resp. $\mathcal{U}^d$), if the latter exists. So compact answers under this representation must be smaller than under the two previous ones. However, the size of a compact representation may still be affected by the size of time intervals in q (for a closure-free q already). In contrast, for $\mathcal{U}^c$, immediately from the definition of $(\!|q|\!)^c_G$, the number of tuples in $(\!|q|\!)^c_G$ (for a closure-free q) is independent of the size of the intervals in G or q (even though $(\!|q|\!)^c_G$ is not necessarily compact).

Proposition 3. *In the worst case,*

(fixed query intervals)	(fixed graph intervals)
$\#\mathsf{answers}^{\tau}(\mathcal{U}^{td}) = O(1)$	$\#\mathsf{answers}^{\delta}(\mathcal{U}^{td}) = \Omega(n)$
$\#\mathsf{answers}^{\tau}(\mathcal{U}^{c}) = O(1)$	$\#\mathsf{answers}^{\delta}(\mathcal{U}^{c}) = O(1)$

Complexity of Query Answering. The hardness results of [3] over $\mathcal{U}$ can also be lifted to $\mathcal{U}^{td}$ and $\mathcal{U}^c$, and this bound is tight for $\mathcal{U}^{td}$:

Proposition 4.
CompactAnswer^{td} is PSpace-complete, CompactAnswer^c is PSpace-hard.

5 Related Work

In temporal relational databases, tuples (or attributes) are most commonly associated with a *single* time interval that represents either validity or transaction time [5]. Intervals are commonly used instead of time points as a compact representation. To maintain a compact and unique representation through operations, the *coalescing operator*, which merges value-equivalent tuples over consecutive or overlapping time intervals, has received a lot of attention. Böhlen et al. [6] showed that coalescing can be implemented in SQL, and provided a comprehensive analysis of various coalescing algorithms. Al-Kateb et al. [1] investigated coalescing in the attribute timestamped CME temporal relational model and the work of [12] defines coalescing for temporal multi-set relations. Zhou et al. [23] exploited SQL:2003's analytical functions for the computation of coalescing, which to date, is the state-of-the-art technique and can be computed efficiently in $\mathcal{O}(n \log n)$. In our first two representations $\mathcal{U}^t$ and $\mathcal{U}^d$, which use a single interval, coalescing can be used to achieve a compact representation. However, this is not applicable for $\mathcal{U}^{td}$ and $\mathcal{U}^c$. Bitemporal databases [18] use two intervals (or rectangles) as a compact representation for two time points, typically one for validity and one for transaction times. Our third representation $\mathcal{U}^{td}$ also uses two intervals. but both are used for (a generalized form of) validity (we are not modeling transaction times). In bitemporal databases, coalescing does not provide a unique representation [22] and, since it is designed as a non-redundant operation, may not provide the most compact representation.

Also relevant to our work is the efficient computation of temporal joins over intervals. There has been a long line of research on temporal joins [16], ranging from partition-based [8,10], index-based [13,19], and sorting based [7,21] techniques. Recently, in [11] it has been shown that a temporal join with the overlap predicate can be transformed into a sequence of two range joins. Our inductive representations of answers require temporal joins and range joins (e.g. for $\mathcal{U}^t$ and $\mathcal{U}^d$ respectively).

Finally, this paper builds upon the original proposal made in [2] to extend regular path queries over property graphs with a temporal navigation operator—effectively allowing selection, join, and union of binary temporal relations. Our work focuses on producing compact answers that are finite even in the case of continuous time, a problem that was left open in [2].

6 Conclusions

We investigated how to compactly represent answers to queries over binary temporal relations in the TRPQ setting, where both data and queries may include time intervals for validity and temporal navigation, respectively. To our knowledge, this question was previously open. We defined and analyzed four alternative representations of compact answers to TRPQs, varying in conciseness and potential use. Notably, the fourth representation ensures that query answers are always finitely representable, and that their number is independent of the length of the input (graph and query) intervals. We see this as a useful step towards integrating temporal navigation into database systems. An open question is whether non-redundancy is tractable under this fourth representation, in particular whether tractability for minimizing compact answers is regained.

Acknowledgments. This research has been partially supported by the HEU project CyclOps (GA n. 101135513), by the Province of Bolzano and FWF through project OnTeGra (DOI 10.55776/PIN8884924), by the Province of Bolzano and EU through projects ERDF-FESR 1078 CRIMA and ERDF-FESR 1047 AI-Lab, by MUR through the PRIN project 2022XERWK9 S-PIC4CHU, and by the EU and MUR through the PNRR project PE0000013-FAIR.

Supplemental Material Statement. An extended version with proofs of our results is available online, at https://arxiv.org/abs/2507.22143.

References

1. Al-Kateb, M., Mansour, E., El-Sharkawi, M.E.: CME: a temporal relational model for efficient coalescing. In: Proc. of the 12th Int. Symp. on Temporal Representation and Reasoning (TIME), pp. 83–90. IEEE Computer Society (2005)
2. Arenas, M., Bahamondes, P., Aghasadeghi, A., Stoyanovich, J.: Temporal regular path queries. In: Proc. of the 38th IEEE Int. Conf. on Data Engineering (ICDE), pp. 2412–2425. IEEE Computer Society (2022)
3. Arenas, M., Bahamondes, P., Stoyanovich, J.: Temporal regular path queries: Syntax, semantics, and complexity. CoRR Technical Report arXiv:2107.01241, arXiv.org e-Print archive (2021). https://arxiv.org/abs/2107.01241
4. Aupperle, L., Conn, H.E., Keil, J.M., O'Rourke, J.: Covering Orthogonal Polygons with Squares. Johns Hopkins University, Department of Computer Science (1988)
5. Böhlen, M.H., Dignös, A., Gamper, J., Jensen, C.S.: Temporal data management – an overview. In: Tutorial Lectures of the 7th European Summer School on Business Intelligence and Big Data (eBISS). Lecture Notes in Business Information Processing, vol. 324, pp. 51–83. Springer (2017)
6. Böhlen, M.H., Snodgrass, R.T., Soo, M.D.: Coalescing in temporal databases. In: Proc. of the 22nd Int. Conf. on Very Large Data Bases (VLDB), pp. 180–191 (1996)
7. Bouros, P., Mamoulis, N., Tsitsigkos, D., Terrovitis, M.: In-memory interval joins. Very Large Database J. **30**(4), 667–691 (2021)
8. Cafagna, F., Böhlen, M.H.: Disjoint interval partitioning. Very Large Database J. **26**(3), 447–466 (2017)
9. Culberson, J.C., Reckhow, R.A.: Covering polygons is hard. J. Algorithms **17**(1), 2–44 (1994)
10. Dignös, A., Böhlen, M.H., Gamper, J.: Overlap interval partition join. In: Proc. of the 35th ACM Int. Conf. on Management of Data (SIGMOD), pp. 1459–1470 (2014)
11. Dignös, A., Böhlen, M.H., Gamper, J., Jensen, C.S., Moser, P.: Leveraging range joins for the computation of overlap joins. Very Large Database J. **31**(1), 75–99 (2022)
12. Dignös, A., Glavic, B., Niu, X., Gamper, J., Böhlen, M.H.: Snapshot semantics for temporal multiset relations. Proc. VLDB Endowment **12**(6), 639–652 (2019)
13. Enderle, J., Hampel, M., Seidl, T.: Joining interval data in relational databases. In: Proc. of the 25th ACM Int. Conf. on Management of Data (SIGMOD), pp. 683–694 (2004)
14. Eppstein, D.: Graph-theoretic solutions to computational geometry problems. In: Revised Papers the 35th Int. Workshop on Graph-Theoretic Concepts in Computer Science (WG). LNCS, vol. 5911, pp. 1–16 (2009)

15. Francis, N., et al.: Cypher: An evolving query language for property graphs. In: Proc. of the 39th ACM Int. Conf. on Management of Data (SIGMOD), pp. 1433–1445 (2018)
16. Gao, D., Jensen, C.S., Snodgrass, R.T., Soo, M.D.: Join operations in temporal databases. Very Large Database J. **14**(1), 2–29 (2005)
17. Harris, S., Seaborne, A.: SPARQL 1.1 query language. W3C Recommendation, World Wide Web Consortium, March 2013. http://www.w3.org/TR/sparql11-query
18. Jensen, C.S., Snodgrass, R.T.: Bitemporal relation. In: Encyclopedia of Database Systems, 2nd edn. Springer (2018)
19. Kaufmann, M., et al.: Timeline index: a unified data structure for processing queries on temporal data in SAP HANA. In: Proc. of the 34th ACM Int. Conf. on Management of Data (SIGMOD), pp. 1173–1184 (2013)
20. Keil, J.M.: Minimally covering a horizontally convex orthogonal polygon. In: Proc. of the 2nd Annual ACM SIGACT/SIGGRAPH Symposium on Computational Geometry (SCG), pp. 43–51 (1986)
21. Piatov, D., Helmer, S., Dignös, A.: An interval join optimized for modern hardware. In: Proc. of the 32th IEEE Int. Conf. on Data Engineering (ICDE), pp. 1098–1109. IEEE Computer Society (2016)
22. Toman, D.: Point-based temporal extensions of SQL and their efficient implementation. In: Etzion, O., Jajodia, S., Sripada, S. (eds.) Temporal Databases: Research and Practice. LNCS, vol. 1399, pp. 211–237. Springer, Heidelberg (1998). https://doi.org/10.1007/BFb0053704
23. Zhou, X., Wang, F., Zaniolo, C.: Efficient temporal coalescing query support in relational database systems. In: Bressan, S., Küng, J., Wagner, R. (eds.) DEXA 2006. LNCS, vol. 4080, pp. 676–686. Springer, Heidelberg (2006). https://doi.org/10.1007/11827405_66

Language Models as Ontology Encoders

Hui Yang[1(✉)], Jiaoyan Chen[1], Yuan He[2,4], Yongsheng Gao[3], and Ian Horrocks[4]

[1] The University of Manchester, Manchester, UK
{hui.yang-2,jiaoyan.chen}@manchester.ac.uk
[2] Amazon, Palo Alto, California, USA
lawhy@amazon.com
[3] SNOMED International, London, UK
yga@snomed.org
[4] University of Oxford, Oxford, UK
Ian.Horrocks@cs.ox.ac.uk

Abstract. OWL (Web Ontology Language) ontologies which are able to formally represent complex knowledge and support semantic reasoning have been widely adopted across various domains such as healthcare and bioinformatics. Recently, ontology embeddings have gained wide attention due to their potential to infer plausible new knowledge and approximate complex reasoning. However, existing methods face notable limitations: geometric model-based embeddings typically overlook valuable textual information, resulting in suboptimal performance, while the approaches that incorporate text, which are often based on language models, fail to preserve the logical structure. In this work, we propose a new ontology embedding method OnT, which tunes a Pretrained Language Model (PLM) via geometric modeling in a hyperbolic space for effectively incorporating textual labels and simultaneously preserving class hierarchies and other logical relationships of Description Logic $\mathcal{EL}$. Extensive experiments on four real-world ontologies show that OnT consistently outperforms the baselines including the state-of-the-art across both tasks of prediction and inference of axioms. OnT also demonstrates strong potential in real-world applications, indicated by its robust transfer learning abilities and effectiveness in real cases of discovering new axioms in SNOMED CT construction. Data and code are available at https://github.com/HuiYang1997/OnT.

Keywords: Ontology Embedding · Language Models · Description Logic · Web Ontology Language · Hyperbolic Space

1 Introduction

Ontologies of Web Ontology Language (OWL) can represent explicit, formal, and shared knowledge of a domain, supporting complex knowledge by incorpo-

This work is funded by the EPSRC projects OntoEm (EP/Y017706/1) and ConCur (EP/V050869/1).

Y. He—Work done prior to joining Amazon.

D. Garijo et al. (Eds.): ISWC 2025, LNCS 16140, pp. 443–461, 2026.
https://doi.org/10.1007/978-3-032-09527-5_24

rating Description Logic (DL) axioms [5,11]. These ontologies have become indispensable in domains requiring precise semantic representations; typical examples include the Gene Ontology (GO) [2] in bioinformatics and SNOMED CT [10] in healthcare. With the emergence of neural representation learning techniques [6], there has been growing interests in developing embedding approaches for ontologies that can encode their entities (which include concepts, roles and instances) as numerical vectors while effectively preserving their structural and semantic properties within the vector space for supporting different downstream tasks of prediction, (approximate) inference, retrieval and so on, usually in combination with other machine learning and statistical methods [9,20].

Despite significant advancements, the current methods—which can be divided into two types: *geometric model-based* and *language model-based*—still have distinct shortcomings.

1. *Geometric Model-Based Methods:* These methods represent ontology entities as geometric objects, such as instances as points and concepts as areas, to construct a geometric model of the target ontology [9]. For example, the early method ELEM [19] represents concepts as balls, while more recent methods like BoxEL [33], Box^{2}EL [18], and TransBox [35] represents concepts as boxes. Geometric model-based methods preserve logical relationships by translating DL operators into geometric operations—such as representing concept subsumption as area inclusion and conjunction as intersection—thereby supporting reasoning in the vector space. However, they mostly neglect valuable textual information, such as entity labels that are common in real-world ontologies. This results in suboptimal performance in ontology learning tasks such as axiom prediction, and an inability to embed new entities that are unseen during training—a critical limitation when dealing with dynamic and transfer scenarios.
2. *Language-Model-Based Methods:* These methods, exemplified by OPA2Vec [29] and OWL2Vec* [8], focus on encoding the textual information of ontologies, often following a pipeline which first transforms the axioms and the graph structure into sentences and then tunes a language model to learn entity representations from the sentences [9]. They incorporate both text and formal semantics in the embeddings, which can lead to higher similarities between more related entities [20], but ignore the preservation of logical relationships, which limits their effectiveness in inference. Moreover, most methods generate ontology embeddings using traditional non-contextual word embedding models like Word2Vec, with limited exploration towards the more recent Transformer-based PLMs, which produce layer-specific contextual embeddings rather than general representations. Recently, HiT [17] has been proposed to bridge this gap by training a PLM with geometric modeling for embedding both concept hierarchies and labels. However, HiT is designed for taxonomies, and does not support complex concepts and logical relationships beyond concept subsumption in OWL ontologies.

To address these limitations, we propose **On**tology **T**ransformer encoder (OnT), which integrates the strengths of PLM for contextual text embedding, and geometric modeling in a hyperbolic space for logical structure embedding. OnT enables the preservation of logical relationships of Description Logic $\mathcal{EL}$, thus augmenting axiom inference in the vector space. It effectively incorporates more kinds of semantics for better performance in axiom prediction, and supports the embedding of new entities.

OnT mainly consists of two steps: (1) Complex concepts (denoted as C, D) and roles (denoted by r) are embedded into vector representations using a PLM. The embeddings of complex concepts are derived from a verbalization process that generates textual descriptions for these concepts, while roles are represented as transition functions operating within the space of concept vectors. (2) General Concept Inclusion (GCI) axioms of the form $C \sqsubseteq D$ are represented by regarding them as a hierarchical pre-order $C \prec D$, which is then encoded in a Poincaré ball. Moreover, to effectively capture the logical patterns associated with the existential qualifier (i.e., $\exists r.$) and conjunction (i.e., $\sqcap$), OnT incorporates two specialized loss functions that leverage role embeddings in conjunction with concept embeddings.

Through extensive experiments on real-world ontologies of GALEN [28], Gene Ontology (GO) [2], and Anatomy (Uberon) [25], we demonstrate that our method OnT outperforms current state-of-the-art geometric-model or language-model based approaches in both prediction and inference tasks. Notably, in terms of the Mean Rank metric, OnT achieves up to a sevenfold improvement over existing methods, as observed in the prediction task on the GO dataset. Moreover, it exhibits strong transfer learning capabilities, successfully identifying missing and incorrect direct subsumptions in the SNOMED use case, which highlights the practical potential of our approach for real-world ontology applications.

2 Related Work

Geometric model-based methods encode ontologies by representing their concepts and instances as geometric objects in vector spaces and their roles (i.e., binary relations) as specific geometric relationships between these objects. These methods construct an (approximate) geometric model of the ontology, interpreting logical relationships as geometric meanings. For example, the subsumption of concepts can be understood as the set-inclusion of corresponding geometric objects. Various geometric representations have been explored for representing concepts, including boxes (TransBox [35], Box^{2}EL [18], BoxEL [33], ELBE [27]), balls (ELEM [19], EMEM++ [24]), cones [13,37], and fuzzy sets [30]. The most common way of representing relations is using transition functions defined by the addition of a given vector. Among these approaches, box-based methods have gained prominence due to their closure under intersection—the intersection of two boxes yields another box—enabling them to naturally capture concept conjunctions through geometric operations. In contrast, other geometric representations lack this crucial property, limiting their expressiveness for certain logical operations. The majority of existing methods focus on $\mathcal{EL}$-family ontologies, with notable exceptions of catE [37] and FALCON [30], which provide embeddings for $\mathcal{ALC}$-ontologies.

Language model-based methods originated from early approaches utilizing word embeddings like Word2Vec (which are widely regarded as a kind of neural language models), such as OPA2Vec [29] and OWL2Vec* [8]. They generate embeddings for ontology entities by fine-tuning a word embedding model with the ontology's information, and then apply these embeddings to downstream tasks via an additional, separated prediction model such as a binary classifier. More recently, inspired by the rapid advancement of PLMs based on Transformer architectures [31], a variety of PLM-based approaches such as SORBET and BERTSubs [1,7,14,15,23] have been developed for ontology-related tasks, particularly in the context of ontology completion and alignment. However, these methods jointly fine-tune a PLM and an additional layer that is specific to a downstream task. Thus they do not yield general embeddings that are applicable across different tasks. Furthermore, all language model-based methods—whether based on Word2Vec or transformers—fail to capture logical structures such as the transitivity of subsumption relationships, thereby preventing direct inference within the vector space.

Recently, He et al. proposed HiT [17]—a method that combines language models with hierarchical embedding techniques in hyperbolic spaces to embed taxonomies that consist of hierarchical structures of named concepts. However, this approach overlooks role embeddings and the logical operations that construct complex concepts from basic ones, which are prevalent in real-world ontologies. In this work, we address this limitation with role embeddings and specialized loss functions that capture the logical operators used to build complex concepts from fundamental ones.

We exclude work on Knowledge Graphs such as KG-BERT [36] and KEPLER [32], as our focus is on OWL ontologies, which use Description Logic to model conceptual knowledge—fundamentally different from relational fact-based Knowledge Graphs.

3 Preliminary

3.1 Ontology

OWL ontologies employ sets of statements, known as axioms, to represent and reason about concepts (unary predicates) and roles (binary predicates). In this work, we focus on $\mathcal{EL}$-ontologies, which are investigated by most existing geometric embedding methods. These ontologies strike a balance between expressivity and reasoning efficiency, making them widely applicable [4]. Consider the disjoint sets $\mathsf{N_C} = \{A, B, \ldots\}$, $\mathsf{N_R} = \{r, t, \ldots\}$, and $\mathsf{N_I} = \{a, b, \ldots\}$, representing *concept names* (a.k.a. *atomic or named concepts*), *role names*, and *individual names*, respectively. $\mathcal{EL}$*-concepts* (complex concepts) are defined recursively from these elements as $\top \mid \bot \mid A \mid C \sqcap D \mid \exists r.C \mid \{a\}$. An $\mathcal{EL}$*-ontology* is a finite collection of TBox axioms like $C \sqsubseteq D$, and ABox axioms like $A(a)$ and $r(a, b)$. Note that, through the paper, we denote by atomic concepts as A, B, and any $\mathcal{EL}$-concepts as C, D.

Example 1. Given atomic concepts *Teacher*, *Student*, *Class*, roles *teach*, *hasClass* and *study*, and individuals *Dr.Smith*, *Emma*, there is a small $\mathcal{EL}$-ontology composed of TBox axioms: $Person \sqcap \exists teach.Class \sqsubseteq Teacher$, $Person \sqcap \exists study.Class \sqsubseteq Student$, and ABox axioms: $Teacher(Dr.Smith)$, $hasClass(Emma, Math101)$.

Normalization of $\mathcal{EL}$-Ontology. In this work, we focus on the TBox part. Note that Abox axioms can be transformed into equivalent TBox axioms by treating instances as classes [18]. An $\mathcal{EL}$-ontology $\mathcal{O}$ is normalized if all its (TBox) axioms are of one of the following forms:

$$A \sqsubseteq B, \quad A_1 \sqcap A_2 \sqsubseteq B, \quad A \sqsubseteq \exists r.B, \quad \exists r.B \sqsubseteq A. \tag{1}$$

For simplicity, we refer to these four types of normalized axioms as NF1-NF4 (where NF denotes normalized form), respectively. It is worth noting that most existing geometric embedding methods are exclusively applicable to normalized ontologies. Any $\mathcal{EL}$-ontology can be transformed into a set of normalized axioms [3] by introducing new atomic concepts along with corresponding names, as illustrated in the following example.

Example 2. To normalize the axiom $Person \sqcap \exists teach.Class \sqsubseteq Teacher$ from Example 1, we introduce a new atomic concept $N_1 \equiv \exists teach.Class$. This transfers the original axiom into three normalized axioms:

$$Person \sqcap N_1 \sqsubseteq Teacher, \quad N_1 \sqsubseteq \exists teach.Class, \quad \text{and} \quad \exists teach.Class \sqsubseteq N_1.$$

Here, the newly introduced concept N_1, derived from $\exists teach.Class$, can be informally interpreted as "Something that teaches some Class."

Inference An *interpretation* $\mathcal{I} = (\Delta^{\mathcal{I}}, \cdot^{\mathcal{I}})$ comprises a non-empty set $\Delta^{\mathcal{I}}$ and a function $\cdot^{\mathcal{I}}$ that maps each $A \in \mathsf{N_C}$ to $A^{\mathcal{I}} \subseteq \Delta^{\mathcal{I}}$, each $r \in \mathsf{N_R}$ to $r^{\mathcal{I}} \subseteq \Delta^{\mathcal{I}} \times \Delta^{\mathcal{I}}$, and each $a \in \mathsf{N_I}$ to $a^{\mathcal{I}} \in \Delta^{\mathcal{I}}$, with $\bot^{\mathcal{I}} = \emptyset$, $\top^{\mathcal{I}} = \Delta^{\mathcal{I}}$, and $\{a\}^{\mathcal{I}} = a^{\mathcal{I}}$. This function extends to any $\mathcal{EL}^{++}$-concepts as follows:

$$(C \sqcap D)^{\mathcal{I}} = C^{\mathcal{I}} \cap D^{\mathcal{I}}, \quad (\exists r.C)^{\mathcal{I}} = \left\{a \in \Delta^{\mathcal{I}} \mid \exists b \in C^{\mathcal{I}} : (a,b) \in r^{\mathcal{I}}\right\},$$

An interpretation $\mathcal{I}$ *satisfies* a TBox axiom $X \sqsubseteq Y$ if $X^{\mathcal{I}} \subseteq Y^{\mathcal{I}}$ for X, Y being two concepts or two role names, or X being a role chain and Y being a role name. It satisfies an ABox axiom $A(a)$ if $a^{\mathcal{I}} \in A^{\mathcal{I}}$ and it satisfies $r(a,b)$ if $(a^{\mathcal{I}}, b^{\mathcal{I}}) \in r^{\mathcal{I}}$. Finally, $\mathcal{I}$ is a *model* of $\mathcal{O}$ if it satisfies every axiom in $\mathcal{O}$. An ontology $\mathcal{O}$ *entails* an axiom α, denoted $\mathcal{O} \models \alpha$, if α is satisfied by all models of $\mathcal{O}$.

3.2 Hyperbolic Space

A d-dimensional *manifold* [21], denoted $\mathcal{M}$, can be regarded as a hypersurface embedded in a higher n-dimensional Euclidean space $\mathbb{R}^n$, which is locally equivalent to $\mathbb{R}^d$ around each point $\mathbf{x} \in \mathcal{M}$. A *Riemannian manifold* $\mathcal{M}$ is a manifold equipped with a Riemannian metric, enabling the definition of a distance function $d_{\mathcal{M}}(\mathbf{x}, \mathbf{y})$ for $\mathbf{x}, \mathbf{y} \in \mathcal{M}$. *Hyperbolic space*, denoted $\mathbb{H}^n$, is a Riemannian manifold with a constant negative curvature of $-\kappa$ ($\kappa > 0$) [22], which can be represented by the Poincaré ball model whose points are defined by a "ball" with radius $1/\sqrt{\kappa}$: $B^n = \{\mathbf{x} \in \mathbb{R}^n : \|\mathbf{x}\| < 1/\sqrt{\kappa}\}$, and the hyperbolic distance between $\mathbf{x}, \mathbf{y} \in B^n$ are defined as

$$d_\kappa(\mathbf{x}, \mathbf{y}) = \frac{1}{\sqrt{\kappa}} \operatorname{arcosh}\left(1 + \frac{2\kappa\|\mathbf{x} - \mathbf{y}\|^2}{(1 - \kappa\|\mathbf{x}\|^2)(1 - \kappa\|\mathbf{y}\|^2)}\right). \tag{2}$$

In the Poincaré ball model, the scaling $k \in R$ of a point $\mathbf{x} \in B^n$ is defined as

$$k \odot \mathbf{x} = \tanh(k \cdot \tanh^{-1}(||\mathbf{x}||)) \cdot \frac{\mathbf{x}}{||\mathbf{x}||} \tag{3}$$

4 Methodology

In this section, we present our method, OnT, for embedding a given $\mathcal{EL}$-ontology. OnT consists mainly of three parts:

1. Embedding any $\mathcal{EL}$-concepts (atomic or complex ones) as points in hyperbolic spaces using PLMs and verbalizations (Sect. 4.1);
2. Embedding roles as rotations over hyperbolic spaces (Sect. 4.2), which allows OnT for capturing the logical structures of existential qualifications $\exists r$ (Proposition 1) and demonstrates improved performance as evidenced by evaluations on real-world ontologies;
3. Training the embeddings using the Poincaré ball model (Sect. 4.3) by regarding the axioms as hierarchical relationships between complex concepts.

It is worth noting that the role embedding component can be omitted to yield a simplified variant, referred to as OnT(w/o r).

4.1 Verbalisation-Based Concept Embedding

Given an ontology $\mathcal{O}$, we assume that each atomic concept A and role r occurring in $\mathcal{O}$ is associated with a textual description, typically its name or definition, denoted as $\mathcal{V}(A)$ and $\mathcal{V}(r)$, respectively. For instance, we may have $\mathcal{V}(A)$ = "Father" and $\mathcal{V}(r)$ = "is parent of".

Based on these descriptions of atomic concepts and roles, we systematically generate a natural language description for each complex concept C appearing in the ontology $\mathcal{O}$, denoted as $\mathcal{V}(C)$. For $\mathcal{EL}$-ontologies, we generate these descriptions according to the following compositional rules:

$$\mathcal{V}(C \sqcap D) = \text{"}\mathcal{V}(C) \text{ and } \mathcal{V}(D)\text{"}, \quad \mathcal{V}(\exists r.C) = \text{" something that } \mathcal{V}(r) \text{ some } \mathcal{V}(C)\text{"}.$$

For example, we will have $\mathcal{V}$(Person $\sqcap$ Student) = "person and student", and $\mathcal{V}$($\exists$isParentOf.Person) = "something that is parent of some person".

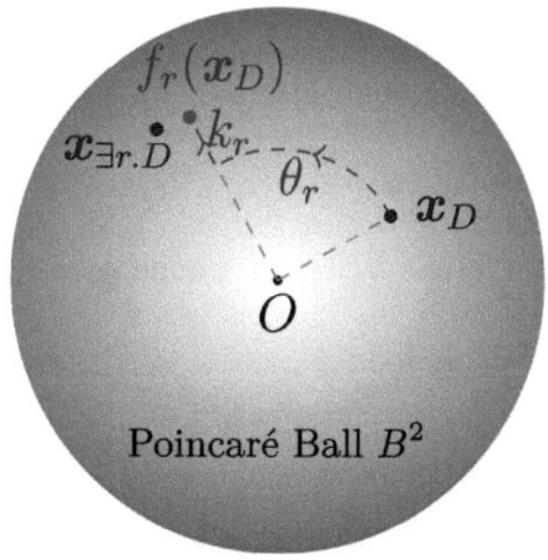

Fig. 1. Illustration of f_r in a two-dimensional hyperbolic space.

With the verbalization approach described above, we can embed any complex $\mathcal{EL}$-concept C by applying language models to its textual description $\mathcal{V}(C)$ and mapping the result to a point in hyperbolic space as in HiT [17]. Specifically, this is achieved by encoding sentences using a BERT model with mean pooling, after which the resulting embeddings are re-trained in hyperbolic space. The final embedding of C is denoted as $\boldsymbol{x}_C$.

4.2 Logic-Aware Role Embedding

In the above verbalization process, the role semantics is integrated into the concept verbalizations. However, this do not provide individual roles embeddings, which could restrict the capability of handling logical patterns involving roles and impairing the reasoning. For instance, we can not guarantee the preservation of deductive patterns such as the monotonicity of existential restrictions: if $A \sqsubseteq B$, then $\exists r.A \sqsubseteq \exists r.B$.

To address these limitations, we propose to explicitly incorporate role embeddings by interpreting a role r as a function f_r over hyperbolic space. In details, for each complex concept of the form $\exists r.D$, OnT introduces an alternative representation: $f_r(\boldsymbol{x}_D)$, which complements the verbalization-based embedding $\boldsymbol{x}_{\exists r.D}$. Here, f_r is a role-specific transformation function. We will encourage the two embeddings $f_r(\boldsymbol{x}_D)$ and $\boldsymbol{x}_{\exists r.D}$ to be identical by introducing an extra loss term in the training process.

In our implementation, we define f_r as a composition of rotations and scaling operations in hyperbolic space. Specifically, the f_r is defined by (see Fig. 1 for an illustration):

$$f_r(\mathbf{v}) = k_r \odot (R(\Theta_r) \cdot \mathbf{v}), \tag{4}$$

where $k_r \in \mathbb{R}$ is a role-specific scaling factor, $\Theta_r = (\theta_r^1, \theta_r^2, \ldots, \theta_r^m) \in \mathbb{R}^m$ is a role-specific rotation angle, and $\mathbf{v} \in \mathbb{H}^{2m}$ is a point in hyperbolic space. Here, the $\odot$ operation represents the scaling product over hyperbolic space $\mathbb{H}^{2m}$, which ensures the scaled embeddings are still in hyperbolic space. However, for rotations, we could directly apply the same rotations as the Euclidean space as we

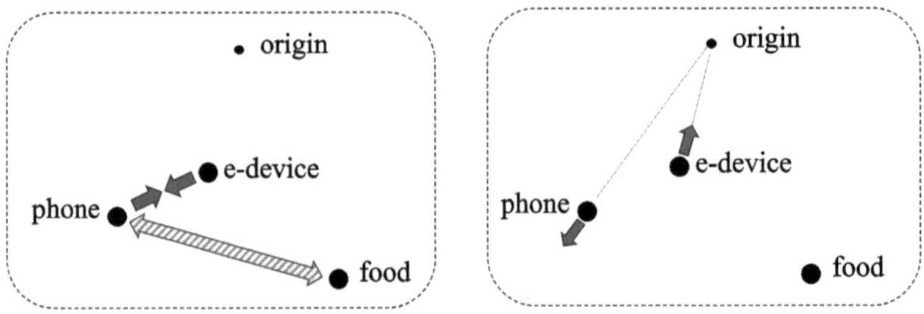

(a) Hierarchical Contrastive Loss (b) Centripetal Loss

Fig. 2. Illustration of impact of hierarchy Loss $\mathcal{L}_{\prec}$ during training.

use the Poincaré ball models for the representation of hyperbolic space. Specifically, we use the rotation matrix $R(\Theta_r) \in \mathbb{R}^{2m\times 2m}$ over the space $\mathbb{H}^{2m}$ defined as a product of two-dimensional rotations of the following form:

$$R(\Theta_r) = \begin{bmatrix} R(\theta_r^1) & \mathbf{0} & \cdots & \mathbf{0} \\ \mathbf{0} & R(\theta_r^2) & \cdots & \mathbf{0} \\ \vdots & \vdots & \ddots & \vdots \\ \mathbf{0} & \mathbf{0} & \cdots & R(\theta_r^m) \end{bmatrix}, \text{ where } R(\theta_r) = \begin{bmatrix} \cos(\theta_r) & -\sin(\theta_r) \\ \sin(\theta_r) & \cos(\theta_r) \end{bmatrix}.$$

4.3 Training

Hierarchy Loss. We interpret subsumption axioms $C \sqsubseteq D$ in the ontology $\mathcal{O}$ as partial-order relationships between their embeddings: $\boldsymbol{x}_C \prec \boldsymbol{x}_D$. Then, following the approach of HiT [17], we encode these partial-order relationships using a Poincaré embedding model [26] using a hierarchical loss defined by the hyperbolic distance. The loss function $\mathcal{L}_{\prec}(\boldsymbol{x}_C \prec \boldsymbol{x}_D)$ consists of two parts.

1. *Hierarchical Contrastive Loss*: This loss encourages embeddings of related concepts to be closer to each other than to negative samples:

$$\mathcal{L}_{contrast}(\boldsymbol{x}_C \prec \boldsymbol{x}_D) = \max(0, d_\kappa(\boldsymbol{x}_C, \boldsymbol{x}_D) - d_\kappa(\boldsymbol{x}_C, \boldsymbol{x}_{D_{\text{neg}}}) + \alpha),$$

   where D_{neg} represents a randomly sampled concept that composes a negative example with C and α is a margin hyperparameter.
2. *Centripetal Loss*: This loss enforces that parent concepts are embedded closer to the origin than their children in the hyperbolic space. Let $\|\boldsymbol{x}\|_\kappa$ denote the hyperbolic distance from a point $\boldsymbol{x} \in \mathbb{H}^n$ to the origin (also known as the hyperbolic norm). The centripetal loss is defined as:

$$\mathcal{L}_{centri}(\boldsymbol{x}_C \prec \boldsymbol{x}_D) = \max(0, \|\boldsymbol{x}_D\|_\kappa - \|\boldsymbol{x}_C\|_\kappa + \beta),$$

   where β is a margin hyperparameter. This constraint geometrically reinforces the hierarchical structure by positioning more general concepts (parents) closer to the center of the hyperbolic space.

The overall hierarchy loss is defined as the sum of these two loss components:

$$\mathcal{L}_{\prec}(\boldsymbol{x}_C \prec \boldsymbol{x}_D) = \mathcal{L}_{contrast}(\boldsymbol{x}_C \prec \boldsymbol{x}_D) + \mathcal{L}_{centri}(\boldsymbol{x}_C \prec \boldsymbol{x}_D). \quad (5)$$

The effect of the hierarchy loss on embedding updates is illustrated in Fig. 2, where the positive pair is $C =$ *"phone"* and $D =$ *"e-device"*, and the negative example is $D_{\text{neg}} =$ *"food"*. The contrastive loss encourages the embeddings of C and D to be close, while pushing C and D_{neg} farther apart, as shown in Fig. 2a. On the other hand, in in Fig. 2b, the centripetal loss pulls the parent concept D toward the origin, while pushing the child concept C away from it.

Loss for Role Embeddings. The loss for role embeddings aims to align the embeddings of $\boldsymbol{x}_{\exists r.D}$ with $f_r(\boldsymbol{x}_D)$. However, as shown by our preliminary experiments, it is not a good choice to directly align the embeddings such as introducing a loss defined by their Euclidean distance or hyperbolic, i.e., $||\boldsymbol{x}_{\exists r.D} - f_r(\boldsymbol{x}_D)||$ or $d_\kappa(\boldsymbol{x}_{\exists r.D}, f_r(\boldsymbol{x}_D))$. Instead, we would reuse the hierarchical loss above by interpreting the equivalence $\boldsymbol{x}_{\exists r.D} \equiv f_r(\boldsymbol{x}_D)$ as two partial-order $\boldsymbol{x}_{\exists r.D} \prec f_r(\boldsymbol{x}_D)$ and $f_r(\boldsymbol{x}_D) \prec \boldsymbol{x}_{\exists r.D}$. Formally, the loss is defined as:

$$\mathcal{L}_r(\exists r.D) = \frac{1}{2}\Big(\mathcal{L}_{\prec}(\boldsymbol{x}_{\exists r.D} \prec f_r(\boldsymbol{x}_D)) + \mathcal{L}_{\prec}(f_r(\boldsymbol{x}_D) \prec \boldsymbol{x}_{\exists r.D})\Big) \quad (6)$$

Loss for Conjunction. This loss is introduced to capture the logical properties of the conjunction $\sqcap$, specifically, a universally valid axiom $C \sqcap D \sqsubseteq C$. It is enough to use the following loss based on the hierarchy loss $\mathcal{L}_{\prec}$:

$$\mathcal{L}_{\sqcap}(C \sqcap D) = \frac{1}{2}\Big(\mathcal{L}_{\prec}(\boldsymbol{x}_{C\sqcap D} \prec \boldsymbol{x}_C) + \mathcal{L}_{\prec}(\boldsymbol{x}_{C\sqcap D} \prec \boldsymbol{x}_D)\Big). \quad (7)$$

Training. The final train loss is defined as the sum of the losses defined by Eqs. (5), (6), and (7) for all axioms $C \sqsubseteq D$, concept $\exists r.D$, and conjunctions $C \sqcap D$ appeared $\mathcal{O}$, respectively.

Finally, with a well-trained OnT model, we evaluate a new axiom $C \sqsubseteq D$ using the following score with a higher value indicates a higher confidence of the given axioms, which is defined as a weighted sum of distances:

$$s(C \sqsubseteq D) \equiv s(\boldsymbol{x}_C \prec \boldsymbol{x}_D) := -(d_\kappa(\boldsymbol{x}_C, \boldsymbol{x}_D) + \lambda(\|\boldsymbol{x}_D\|_\kappa - \|\boldsymbol{x}_C\|_\kappa)) \quad (8)$$

where the weight λ is determined based on the model's performance on the validation set, higher scores indicate a stronger predicted subsumption relationship between concepts.

We have the following proposition that allows us to control the difference between scores $s(f_r(\boldsymbol{x}_C) \prec f_r(\boldsymbol{x}_D))$ and $s(\boldsymbol{x}_C \prec \boldsymbol{x}_D)$ using the scaling factor k_r, and thus, capturing the deductive pattern $A \sqsubseteq B \Rightarrow \exists r.A \sqsubseteq \exists r.B$.

Proposition 1. *For any $\mathbf{x}, \mathbf{y} \in \mathbb{H}^{2m}$ and rotation matrix $R(\Theta_r) \in \mathbb{R}^{2m\times 2m}$ as defined in Eq. (4), we have $\|\boldsymbol{x}_C\|_\kappa = \|R(\Theta_r)\cdot \boldsymbol{x}_C\|_\kappa$ and $d_\kappa(\mathbf{x}, \mathbf{y}) = d_\kappa(R(\Theta_r)\cdot \mathbf{x}, R(\Theta_r)\cdot \mathbf{y})$. Moreover, we have $s(f_r(\boldsymbol{x}_C) \prec f_r(\boldsymbol{x}_D)) = s(\boldsymbol{x}_C \prec \boldsymbol{x}_D)$ when $k_r = 1$.*

Proof. The hyperbolic distance $d_\kappa(\mathbf{x}, \mathbf{y})$ depends only on the Euclidean norms $\|\mathbf{x}\|$ and $\|\mathbf{y}\|$, as per Eq. (2). Since the rotation $R(\Theta_r)$ preserves Euclidean norms, it follows that $\|R(\Theta_r) \cdot \mathbf{z}\| = \|\mathbf{z}\|$ for $\mathbf{z} = \mathbf{x}, \mathbf{y}$. Therefore, $d_\kappa(\mathbf{x}, \mathbf{y}) = d_\kappa(R(\Theta_r) \cdot \mathbf{x}, R(\Theta_r) \cdot \mathbf{y})$. By definition, we have $\|\mathbf{x}\|_\kappa = d_\kappa(\mathbf{x}, \mathbf{0})$. Applying this with $\mathbf{y} = \mathbf{0}$, we obtain: $\|\mathbf{x}\|_\kappa = \|R(\Theta_r) \cdot \mathbf{x}\|_\kappa$.

Since the score is defined by $d_\kappa(\mathbf{x}, \mathbf{y})$, $\|\mathbf{x}\|_\kappa$, and $\|\mathbf{y}\|_\kappa$, and given $f_r(\mathbf{z}) = R(\Theta_r) \cdot \mathbf{z}$ when $k_r = 1$, we conclude that $s(f_r(\boldsymbol{x}_C) \prec f_r(\boldsymbol{x}_D)) = s(\boldsymbol{x}_C \prec \boldsymbol{x}_D)$ when $k_r = 1$. This completes the proof.

5 Evaluation

5.1 Experiment Setting

The evaluation is mainly concentrated on two tasks: axiom prediction (Sect. 5.2) and inference (Sect. 5.3). The prediction and inference tasks focus on identifying missing axioms; however, the prediction task addresses arbitrary axioms, while the inference task focuses specifically on axioms that can be logically derived from the given ontologies. We also evaluate the performance of our method in different scenarios such as transfer learning, ablation study, and over real cases in Sect. 5.4.

Datasets. We adopt three real-world ontologies—GALEN [28], the Gene Ontology (GO) [2], and Anatomy (Uberon) [25]. Following the prior research [18,35], we keep only the $\mathcal{EL}$ part and use their normalized versions. For the prediction task, the training, validation, and testing data are generated by a random 80/10/10 split of the ontology axioms. For the inference task, we use the whole ontology as the training data, and all the inferred axioms of NF1 as the testing data, and 1000 randomly selected inferred NF1 subsumptions as validation data. The data statistics are shown in Table 1. Note that we developed our own ontology normalization implementation rather than using the existing implementation in ELEM [19], mOWL [38], and DeepOnto [16] as it (1) does not name the concepts introduced during normalization, and (2) sometimes produces logically inconsistent axioms[1] due to some bug in calling the jcel normalizer.

Baselines. Our study systematically compares our proposed methods with established approaches that provide general ontology embeddings, with particular emphasis on geometric embedding methods, including Box²EL [18], BoxEL [33], TransBox [35], ELBE [27], and ELEM [19]. We exclude catE and FALCON as catE cannot handle unseen complex concepts that appear in our experimental settings, and FALCON's implementation is not publicly available. Additionally, we benchmark against HiT [17], a language model-based method limited to taxonomic structures (i.e., NF1 axioms), and two classic none contextual word embedding-based methods—OPA2Vec [29] and OWL2Vec* [8]. We

[1] For example, among the normalized axioms of GALEN, we find the axiom $\exists_{hasQuantity}$ *BNFSection13_3* $\sqsubseteq$ *Tobacco*, which contradicts the original ontology where *BNFSection13_3* appears only in *BNFSection13_3* $\sqsubseteq$ *BNFChapter13Section*.

Table 1. Normalized Dataset Statistics (Train/Val/Test for prediction task).

Axioms	GALEN	GO	ANATOMY
NF1	25,610/3,200/3,203	116,751/14,593/14,596	41,764/5,220/5,222
NF2	11,679/1,459/1,462	24,097/3,011/3,014	12,336/1,542/1,543
NF3	25,299/3,161/3,165	238,899/29,861/29,865	39,766/4,970/4,972
NF4	6,287/785/788	81,948/10,243/10,245	7,586/947/951
Total	68,875/8,605/8,618	461,695/57,708/57,720	101,452/12,679/12,688
Inferred(NF1)	335,002	1,184,380	225,330

also include a simplified version of OnT, denoted as OnT(w/o r), which omits role embeddings and is trained using only the loss of Eq. 5. We ignored other PLM fine-tuning-based methods like BERTSub [7] whose embeddings are coupled to a task-specific layer without generality towards different tasks.

Evaluation Metrics. Consistent with the established literature [18,19,27,33, 35], we evaluate ontology embedding performance using various ranking-based metrics on the testing set. We rank candidates according to the score function defined in Eq. 8, where higher scores indicate more probable candidates. To comprehensively assess different methods, we track the rank of correct answers and report performance through several standard metrics: Hits@k (H@k) for $k \in \{1, 10, 100\}$, mean reciprocal rank (MRR), and mean rank (MR).

Experimental Protocol. We mainly use all-MiniLM-L12-v2 (33.4M) as the underlying language model for OnT and HiT. The influence of different language models is presented in Sect. 5.4. We trained OnT and HiT for 1 epoch, and with 1 negative sample for each given axiom, as we found that it would be enough to get good performance in the pre-test. The embedding vectors for each concept is obtained by performing an average pooling over features of the final layer of the language model. For obtaining the vector for $\Theta(r), k_r$ for a given role r, we apply an extra linear transformation on the embedding of r. The margins α, β and learning rate γ are fixed as default in HiT as $3.0, 0.5, 10^{-5}$, respectively. The weight $\lambda \in \{0, 0.1, \ldots, 1\}$ of the score function in Eq. 8 is selected based on the best performance on the validation set.

OWL2Vec* and OPA2Vec utilize fine-tuned word embeddings (https://tinyurl.com/word2vec-model) with the Random Forest classifier for superior performance, except for GO ontology inference tasks, where Logistic Regression is employed due to computational constraints. Due to dataset modifications, we also re-implemented all the other geometric embedding models (BoxEL, TransBox, ELBE and ELEM) based on the framework developed by Box^{2}EL [18] and TransBox [35]. For our implementation, we utilized embedding dimensions $d = 200$, explored margin values $\gamma \in \{0, 0.05, 0.1, 0.15\}$ and learning rates $l_r \in \{0.0005, 0.005, 0.01\}$, and trained each model for 5,000 epochs. Optimal hyperparameters were selected based on validation set performance.

Table 2. Overall performance of the prediction task across datasets. Values for H@k and MRR are percentages. $k = 1/10/100$ for H@k.

	GALEN			GO			ANATOMY		
Method	H@k	MRR	MR	H@k	MRR	MR	H@k	MRR	MR
ELEM	14/**50**/68	26	2,715	4/35/68	14	11,764	10/53/78	24	1,588
ELBE	9/37/55	18	4,661	10/30/43	18	10,236	9/41/66	20	2,672
BoxEL	0/0/2	0	13,824	0/0/2	0	65,846	1/2/4	2	12,257
Box^{2}EL	12/38/58	21	4,593	8/43/64	19	7,975	11/39/65	20	2,828
TransBox	11/41/62	22	2,972	8/43/67	19	7,092	9/49/73	22	1,299
OPA2Vec	0/1/4	1	13,547	0/1/4	0	18,493	0/5/17	2	9,537
OWL2Vec*	0/1/5	1	13,660	0/0/2	0	19,523	0/3/11	2	10,309
HiT	**25**/47/62	33	2,349	36/60/73	44	15,080	19/54/78	31	722
OnT(w/o r)	**26**/46/64	33	1,546	**38**/66/79	**48**	2,209	**22**/52/79	31	628
OnT	**25/50/69**	**34**	**792**	37/**67/81**	46	**1,121**	**22/57/82**	**33**	**475**

5.2 Prediction Task

The comprehensive evaluation results are presented in Table 2 for GALEN, GO, and Anatomy, respectively. Our method OnT consistently outperforms existing approaches across all datasets. While some geometric model-based methods achieve comparable performance in terms of H@k, such as ELEM in the GALEN dataset, they typically exhibit substantially lower average performance, which is evidenced by the significant gap between MRR and MR values. For instance, the best-performing geometric-based method on GO, Transbox, yielded MR values approximately 7 times worse and MRR values twice as poor as OnT. This indicates that OnT has overall fewer extreme worst cases (i.e., correct answers with extremely large ranks) and also better cases (i.e., lower rankings). This phenomenon occurs consistently across all three ontologies.

For language model-based methods, we observe that OPA2Vec and OWL2Vec* demonstrate limited performance, which is reasonable given their reliance on word embeddings and random forest classifiers for capturing subsumptions. It is important to note that, in our evaluation, ranking is performed over all atomic concepts as candidates—unlike the original OWL2Vec settings [8], which consider only around 50 candidates—making metrics such as Hits@k not directly comparable. In contrast, by employing more advanced BERT-based language models and geometric embeddings based on hyperbolic spaces, HiT achieved significantly better performance. By further incorporating the logical constraints of complex concepts, our method OnT outperformed HiT, especially in terms of average performance as indicated by MR values. Specifically, OnT achieved approximately 14 times better MR values than HiT in the GO dataset, suggesting that OnT could more effectively avoid extremely poor cases while also improving performance on other metrics such as H@k and MRR. Moreover, we can see that, in most cases, adding role embeddings and extra loss for logical constraints of ∃ and ⊓ lead to better performance by comparing the OnT(w/o r) and OnT.

Table 3. Performance of the inference task across datasets. Values for H@k and MRR are percentages. $k = 1/10/100$ for H@k.

	GALEN			GO			ANATOMY		
Method	H@k	MRR	MR	H@k	MRR	MR	H@k	MRR	**MR**
ELEM	0/3/9	1	8,639	0/3/17	1	18,377	0/4/22	2	4,990
ELBE	0/4/20	**2**	2,999	0/3/15	1	4,021	0/6/39	2	979
BoxEL	0/0/3	0	11,328	0/0/0	0	18,186	0/0/0	0	8,169
Box^{2}EL	0/3/15	1	5,530	0/1/7	1	11,801	0/1/7	1	11,801
TransBox	0/2/6	1	7,111	0/2/9	1	4,449	0/5/27	2	749
OPA2Vec	0/0/1	0	12,722	3/5/6	3	95,755	**2**/6/15	**3**	5,143
OWL2Vec*	0/0/1	0	12,647	3/7/8	**5**	88,614	1/5/14	**3**	5,441
HiT	0/4/26	**2**	953	0/1/4	0	44,253	0/6/**44**	**3**	**441**
OnT(w/o r)	0/4/20	1	1,047	0/5/39	2	**824**	0/**7**/40	**3**	499
OnT	0/**5**/**28**	**2**	**913**	0/**10**/**40**	3	832	0/6/41	**3**	458

5.3 Inference Task

The overall results are summarized in Table 3. We can see that OnT clearly outperforms existing geometric model-based embedding methods across all datasets. In particular, on the GO dataset, our method achieves approximately 3 times better H@10 and H@100, and 5 times better MR. This improvement may reflect the advantages of hyperbolic embeddings, as HiT also shows strong results in the GALEN and ANATOMY datasets. However, HiT performs poorly on the GO dataset. This suggests that the information encoded in NF2–NF4 axioms, which are more prominent in GO than in other datasets, plays a crucial role. Since HiT does not incorporate this information during training, its performance suffers; such trend has also been reflected in the MR metrics on the prediction task. Furthermore, we observe that in most cases, incorporating role embeddings and losses for logical constraints allows OnT(w/o r) to achieve even better performance than both OnT and HiT.

The overall performance of OPA2Vec and OWL2Vec* is lower than that of most other methods. This is expected, as both OPA2Vec and OWL2Vec* are prediction-based approaches that evaluate axioms using a binary classifier. Such methods struggle to capture complex logical relationships—like the transitivity of SubClassOf relations—which limits their effectiveness in inference tasks.

Table 4. Ablation study for prediction and inference tasks on GALEN.

Task	Method	Language Model	H@1	H@10	H@100	MRR	MR
Prediction	OnT(w/o r)	all-MiniLM-L6-v2	26	47	64	33	1,972
		all-MiniLM-L12-v2	26	46	64	33	1,546
		all-MPNet-base-v2	26	43	63	32	979
	OnT	all-MiniLM-L6-v2	26	**51**	69	35	1,131
		all-MiniLM-L12-v2	25	50	69	34	792
		all-MPNet-base-v2	**27**	50	**72**	**34**	**630**
Inference	OnT(w/o r)	all-MiniLM-L6-v2	0	**5**	23	2	1,062
		all-MiniLM-L12-v2	0	4	20	1	1,047
		all-MPNet-base-v2	0	2	13	1	1,148
	OnT	all-MiniLM-L6-v2	0	3	26	2	923
		all-MiniLM-L12-v2	0	**5**	28	2	913
		all-MPNet-base-v2	0	4	**34**	2	**630**

5.4 Other Results

Ablation Study. To evaluate the impact of different language models and loss functions, we follow the methodology of [17] and experiment with two additional top-performing pre-trained models from the Sentence Transformers library: all-MiniLM-L6-v2 (22.7M parameters) and all-mpnet-base-v2 (109M parameters), in addition to the all-MiniLM-L12-v2 model (33.4M parameters) used in our main experiments. From Table 4, we can see that the performance differences among these models are relatively small. While the larger model consistently shows better average performance, as indicated by improved MR values, it does not always outperform the smaller models across all evaluation metrics.

Transfer Learning. We evaluated the OnT and HiT models in a transfer learning paradigm, where each model was trained and evaluated on a source dataset, then tested on a distinct target dataset, using three different datasets in the prediction task. The overall transfer learning performance of OnT and HiT using MiniLM-L12-v2 is illustrated by Fig. 3. We can see that OnT and HiT both achieve good transfer abilities, while OnT performance better, indicated by the consistently lower MR value, and the higher H@100 or MRR value in most of cases. Especially for the cases from GO to GALEN or ANATOMY.

Case Study. In our case study, we evaluate real-world scenarios encountered during the construction of ontologies, particularly in the development of a new anatomy ontology derived from SNOMED CT. The following two cases, summarized in Fig. 4, illustrate the potential of our model as a valuable tool in ontology construction.

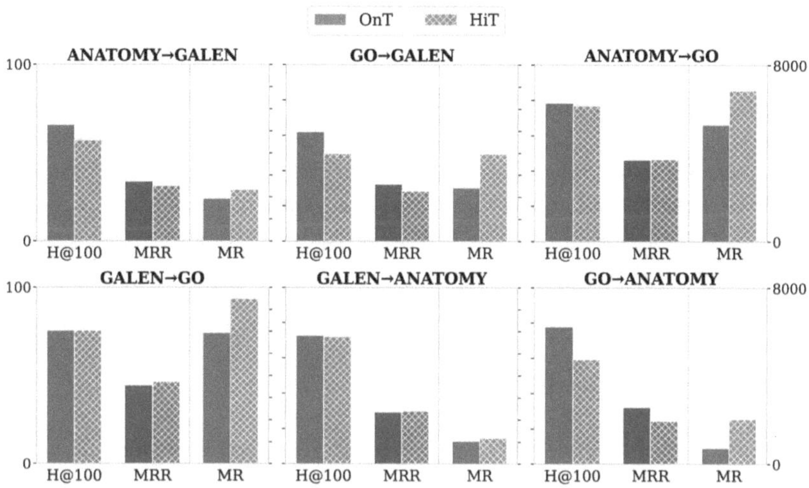

Fig. 3. Transfer learning results of OnT and HiT with MiniLM-L12-v2.

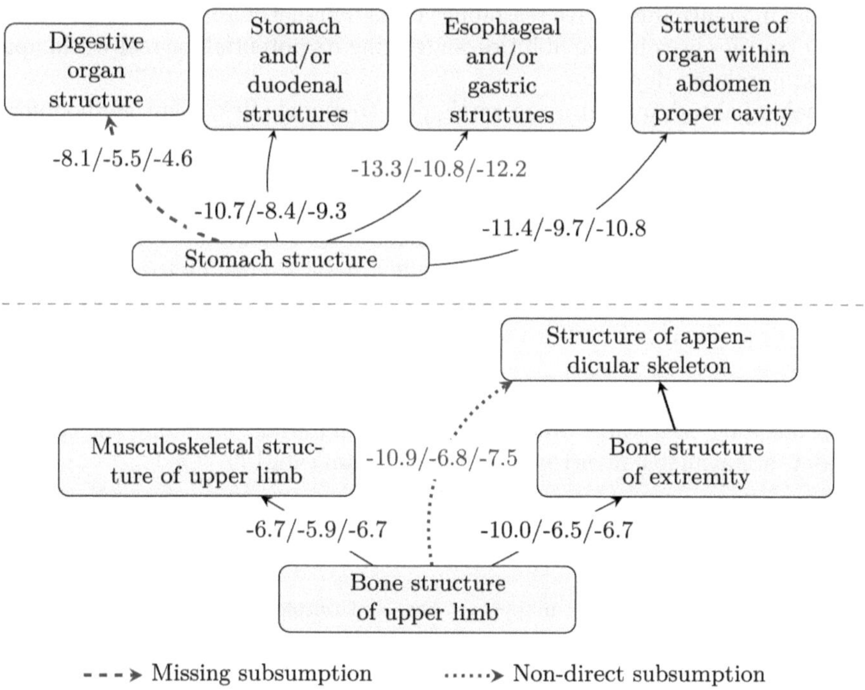

Fig. 4. Case Study: Arrows $C \rightarrow D$ represent subsumption $C \sqsubseteq D$ with scores from Eq. 8. Each arrow shows three scores from three OnT models trained on GALEN/GO/ANATOMY ontologies, respectively. A higher score indicates a more likely subsumption. Blue/red highlights indicate the highest/lowest scores for all subsumptions with the same subclass.

1. *Missing Subsumptions:* In the manually constructed ontology of SNOMED CT, a direct subsumption is overlooked: "Stomach structure $\sqsubseteq$ Digestive organ structure". Our method is proven effective in identifying this missing subsumption, consistently assigning it a higher score than other existing superclasses of the "Stomach structure" within the constructed ontology.
2. *Erroneous (Direct) Subsumptions:* We detect an incorrect direct Superclass of "Bone structure of upper limb" as "Structure of appendicular skeleton", which is incorrect as "Bone structure of extremity" should have such a parent. Our model effectively identifies this erroneous relationship by consistently assigning it the lowest score among all existing superclasses.

6 Conclusion and Future Work

In this study, we introduce OnT, which integrates geometric models with language models to derive ontology embeddings for concepts and roles. Through extensive experiments on real-world ontologies, we demonstrate that our approach achieves state-of-the-art performance in both prediction (inductive reasoning) and inference (deductive reasoning) tasks. Furthermore, our method exhibits strong transfer learning capabilities, suggesting its potential for real-world applications in related domains.

Looking ahead, our future research aims to merge our current methodologies with other hierarchical embedding techniques, such as [12,34]. Additionally, we are keen to extend our methods to more complex ontology languages, such as extending to $\mathcal{ALC}$ with the negation logical operator $\neg$, or delve deeper into the logical patterns of roles using the role embeddings generated by OnT, including investigating role inclusion axioms. It would also be interesting to conduct a more thorough analysis of our model, such as exploring the impact of verbalization quality or performance across a wider range of ontologies beyond those currently utilized.

Supplementary Materials. All supplementary materials, including the code and dataset, are available at https://github.com/HuiYang1997/OnT.

References

1. Amir, M., et al.: Truveta mapper: a zero-shot ontology alignment framework. In: Shvaiko, P., Euzenat, J., Jiménez-Ruiz, E., Hassanzadeh, O., Trojahn, C. (eds.) Proceedings of the 18th International Workshop on Ontology Matching co-located with the 22nd International Semantic Web Conference (ISWC 2023), Athens, Greece, November 7, 2023. CEUR Workshop Proceedings, vol. 3591, pp. 1–12. CEUR-WS.org (2023). https://ceur-ws.org/Vol-3591/om2023_LTpaper1.pdf
2. Ashburner, M., et al.: Gene ontology: tool for the unification of biology. Nat. Genet. **25**(1), 25–29 (2000)

3. Baader, F., Brandt, S., Lutz, C.: Pushing the EL envelope. In: Kaelbling, L.P., Saffiotti, A. (eds.) IJCAI 2005, Proceedings of the Nineteenth International Joint Conference on Artificial Intelligence, Edinburgh, Scotland, UK, 30 July - 5 August 2005, pp. 364–369. Professional Book Center (2005), http://ijcai.org/Proceedings/05/Papers/0372.pdf
4. Baader, F., Gil, O.F.: Extending the description logic EL with threshold concepts induced by concept measures. Artif. Intell. **326**, 104034 (2024)
5. Baader, F., Horrocks, I., Sattler, U.: Description logics as ontology languages for the semantic web. In: Hutter, D., Stephan, W. (eds.) Mechanizing Mathematical Reasoning. LNCS (LNAI), vol. 2605, pp. 228–248. Springer, Heidelberg (2005). https://doi.org/10.1007/978-3-540-32254-2_14
6. Bengio, Y., Courville, A., Vincent, P.: Representation learning: a review and new perspectives. IEEE Trans. Pattern Anal. Mach. Intell. **35**(8), 1798–1828 (2013)
7. Chen, J., He, Y., Geng, Y., Jiménez-Ruiz, E., Dong, H., Horrocks, I.: Contextual semantic embeddings for ontology subsumption prediction. World Wide Web (WWW) **26**(5), 2569–2591 (2023)
8. Chen, J., Hu, P., Jiménez-Ruiz, E., Holter, O.M., Antonyrajah, D., Horrocks, I.: Owl2vec*: embedding of OWL ontologies. Mach. Learn. **110**(7), 1813–1845 (2021)
9. Chen, J., Mashkova, O., Zhapa-Camacho, F., Hoehndorf, R., He, Y., Horrocks, I.: Ontology embedding: a survey of methods, applications and resources. arXiv preprint arXiv:2406.10964 (2024)
10. Donnelly, K., et al.: Snomed-ct: the advanced terminology and coding system for ehealth. Stud. Health Technol. Inform. **121**, 279 (2006)
11. Fitz-Gerald, S.J., Wiggins, B.: Staab, s., studer, r. (eds.), handbook on ontologies, series: International handbooks on information systems, second ed., vol. XIX (2009), 811 p., 121 illus., hardcover £164, ISBN: 978-3-540-70999-2. Int. J. Inf. Manag. **30**(1), 98–100 (2010). https://doi.org/10.1016/J.IJINFOMGT.2009.11.012
12. Ganea, O., Bécigneul, G., Hofmann, T.: Hyperbolic entailment cones for learning hierarchical embeddings. In: Dy, J.G., Krause, A. (eds.) Proceedings of the 35th International Conference on Machine Learning, ICML 2018, Stockholmsmässan, Stockholm, Sweden, 10-15 July 2018. Proceedings of Machine Learning Research, vol. 80, pp. 1632–1641. PMLR (2018). http://proceedings.mlr.press/v80/ganea18a.html
13. Garg, D., Ikbal, S., Srivastava, S.K., Vishwakarma, H., Karanam, H.P., Subramaniam, L.V.: Quantum embedding of knowledge for reasoning. In: Wallach, H.M., Larochelle, H., Beygelzimer, A., d'Alché-Buc, F., Fox, E.B., Garnett, R. (eds.) Advances in Neural Information Processing Systems 32: Annual Conference on Neural Information Processing Systems 2019, NeurIPS 2019, 8-14 December 2019, Vancouver, BC, Canada, pp. 5595–5605 (2019). https://proceedings.neurips.cc/paper/2019/hash/cb12d7f933e7d102c52231bf62b8a678-Abstract.html
14. Gosselin, F., Zouaq, A.: SORBET: A siamese network for ontology embeddings using a distance-based regression loss and BERT. In: Payne, T.R., et al.(eds.) The Semantic Web - ISWC 2023 - 22nd International Semantic Web Conference, Athens, Greece, November 6-10, 2023, Proceedings, Part I. LNCS, vol. 14265, pp. 561–578. Springer (2023). https://doi.org/10.1007/978-3-031-47240-4_30
15. He, Y., Chen, J., Antonyrajah, D., Horrocks, I.: Bertmap: A bert-based ontology alignment system. In: Thirty-Sixth AAAI Conference on Artificial Intelligence, AAAI 2022, Thirty-Fourth Conference on Innovative Applications of Artificial Intelligence, IAAI 2022, The Twelveth Symposium on Educational Advances in Artificial Intelligence, EAAI 2022 Virtual Event, 22 February - 1 March 2022, pp. 5684–5691. AAAI Press (2022). https://doi.org/10.1609/AAAI.V36I5.20510

16. He, Y., et al.: Deeponto: A python package for ontology engineering with deep learning. Semantic Web **15**(5), 1991–2004 (2024)
17. He, Y., Yuan, M., Chen, J., Horrocks, I.: Language models as hierarchy encoders. In: Globersons, A., et al. (eds.) Advances in Neural Information Processing Systems 38: Annual Conference on Neural Information Processing Systems 2024, NeurIPS 2024, Vancouver, BC, Canada, 10 - 15 December 2024 (2024). http://papers.nips.cc/paper_files/paper/2024/hash/1a970a3e62ac31c76ec3cea3a9f68fdf-Abstract-Conference.html
18. Jackermeier, M., Chen, J., Horrocks, I.: Dual box embeddings for the description logic el^{++}. In: Chua, T., Ngo, C., Kumar, R., Lauw, H.W., Lee, R.K. (eds.) Proceedings of the ACM on Web Conference 2024, WWW 2024, Singapore, 13-17 May 2024, pp. 2250–2258. ACM (2024).https://doi.org/10.1145/3589334.3645648
19. Kulmanov, M., Liu-Wei, W., Yan, Y., Hoehndorf, R.: EL embeddings: geometric construction of models for the description logic EL++. In: Proceedings of the Twenty-Eighth International Joint Conference on Artificial Intelligence, pp. 6103–6109. International Joint Conferences on Artificial Intelligence Organizatiohttps://doi.org/10.24963/ijcai.2019/845, https://www.ijcai.org/proceedings/2019/845
20. Kulmanov, M., Smaili, F.Z., Gao, X., Hoehndorf, R.: Semantic similarity and machine learning with ontologies. Briefings Bioinform. **22**(4), bbaa199 (2021)
21. Lee, J.: Introduction to Smooth Manifolds. Graduate Texts in Mathematics. Springer Science & Business Media (2013)
22. Lee, J.M.: Riemannian manifolds: an introduction to curvature, vol. 176. Springer Science & Business Media (2006)
23. Li, N., Bailleux, T., Bouraoui, Z., Schockaert, S.: Ontology completion with natural language inference and concept embeddings: an analysis. CoRR abs/arXiv: 2403.17216 (2024). https://doi.org/10.48550/ARXIV.2403.17216
24. Mondal, S., Bhatia, S., Mutharaju, R.: Emel++: embeddings for EL++ description logic. In: Martin, A., Hinkelmann, K., Fill, H., Gerber, A., Lenat, D., Stolle, R., van Harmelen, F. (eds.) Proceedings of the AAAI 2021 Spring Symposium on Combining Machine Learning and Knowledge Engineering (AAAI-MAKE 2021), Stanford University, Palo Alto, California, USA, March 22-24, 2021. CEUR Workshop Proceedings, vol. 2846. CEUR-WS.org (2021). https://ceur-ws.org/Vol-2846/paper19.pdf
25. Mungall, C.J., Torniai, C., Gkoutos, G.V., Lewis, S.E., Haendel, M.A.: Uberon, an integrative multi-species anatomy ontology. Genome Biol. **13**, 1–20 (2012)
26. Nickel, M., Kiela, D.: Poincaré embeddings for learning hierarchical representations. In: Guyon, I., et al. (eds.) Advances in Neural Information Processing Systems 30: Annual Conference on Neural Information Processing Systems 2017, 4-9 December 2017, Long Beach, CA, USA. pp. 6338–6347 (2017). https://proceedings.neurips.cc/paper/2017/hash/59dfa2df42d9e3d41f5b02bfc32229dd-Abstract.html
27. Peng, X., Tang, Z., Kulmanov, M., Niu, K., Hoehndorf, R.: Description logic EL++ embeddings with intersectional closure. http://arxiv.org/abs/2202.14018
28. Rector, A.L., Rogers, J.E., Pole, P.: The galen high level ontology. In: Medical Informatics Europe 1996, pp. 174–178. IOS Press (1996)
29. Smaili, F.Z., Gao, X., Hoehndorf, R.: Opa2vec: combining formal and informal content of biomedical ontologies to improve similarity-based prediction. Bioinform. **35**(12), 2133–2140 (2019)
30. Tang, Z., Hinnerichs, T., Peng, X., Zhang, X., Hoehndorf, R.: Falcon: faithful neural semantic entailment over alc ontologies. arXiv preprint arXiv:2208.07628 (2022)

31. Vaswani, A., et al.: Attention is all you need. In: Guyon, I., von Luxburg, U., Bengio, S., Wallach, H.M., Fergus, R., Vishwanathan, S.V.N., Garnett, R. (eds.) Advances in Neural Information Processing Systems 30: Annual Conference on Neural Information Processing Systems 2017, 4-9 December 2017, Long Beach, CA, USA, pp. 5998–6008 (2017), https://proceedings.neurips.cc/paper/2017/hash/3f5ee243547dee91fbd053c1c4a845aa-Abstract.html
32. Wang, X., et al.: KEPLER: a unified model for knowledge embedding and pre-trained language representation. Trans. Assoc. Comput. Linguistics **9**, 176–194 (2021). https://doi.org/10.1162/TACL_A_00360
33. Xiong, B., Potyka, N., Tran, T.K., Nayyeri, M., Staab, S.: Faithiful embeddings for EL++ knowledge bases. https://arxiv.org/abs/2201.09919v2
34. Yang, H., Chen, J.: Regd: hierarchical embeddings via distances over geometric regions. arXiv preprint arXiv:2501.17518 (2025)
35. Yang, H., Chen, J., Sattler, U.: Transbox: EL^{++}-closed ontology embedding. In: The Web Conference (2025)
36. Yao, L., Mao, C., Luo, Y.: KG-BERT: BERT for knowledge graph completion. CoRR abs/ arXiv: 1909.03193 (2019). http://arxiv.org/abs/1909.03193
37. Zhapa-Camacho, F., Hoehndorf, R.: Cate: Embedding alc ontologies using category-theoretical semantics (2023)
38. Zhapa-Camacho, F., Kulmanov, M., Hoehndorf, R.: mowl: python library for machine learning with biomedical ontologies. Bioinformatics **39**(1), btac811 (2023)

Parameter-Efficient Federated Knowledge Graph Embedding Learning and Unlearning

Xiangrong Zhu[1], Yuexiang Xie[2], Yang Liu[1], Yaliang Li[2], and Wei Hu[1(✉)]

[1] State Key Laboratory for Novel Software Technology, Nanjing University, Nanjing 210023, China
xrzhu.nju@gmail.com, yliu20.nju@gmail.com, whu@nju.edu.cn
[2] Alibaba Group, Hangzhou 310023, China
{yuexiang.xyx,yaliang.li}@alibaba-inc.com

Abstract. Knowledge graph (KG) embedding aims to learn vector representations for entities and relations. To support distributed and secure training, federated KG embedding collaboratively learns an embedding model among multiple organizations without directly sharing raw data. A federated KG embedding framework should be capable of incorporating both learning and unlearning paradigms, due to the dynamic nature of KGs and the potential need for visibility adjustment by KG owners. However, there are still several challenges in developing a federated KG embedding framework, including overcoming the communication and computation overhead caused by the huge number of entities and controlling the scope of influence when unlearning. In this paper, we propose a novel parameter-efficient federated KG embedding learning and unlearning framework, named PFLU. Specifically, we incorporate an anchor-based federated KG embedding technique to reduce computation and communication overhead when transferring knowledge. We address the anchor selection problem by formulating it as a maximum coverage problem and designing a greedy strategy for its resolution. Besides, to achieve a desirable balance between propagation and retention of unlearning effects, we adopt a two-stage mechanism combining structural and semantic unlearning. Extensive experiments on widely-used datasets show the superior parameter efficiency of PFLU over several baselines in both federated KG embedding learning and unlearning. Furthermore, we provide empirical evidence and discussions to show the effectiveness of the proposed anchor selection strategy.

Keywords: Federated learning · Knowledge graph embedding · Machine unlearning

X. Zhu—This work was done during an internship at Alibaba Group.

D. Garijo et al. (Eds.): ISWC 2025, LNCS 16140, pp. 462–480, 2026.
https://doi.org/10.1007/978-3-032-09527-5_25

1 Introduction

Knowledge graphs (KGs) [1,2,18] store a vast amount of real-world entities and their relations in the form of triplets, i.e., entity-relation-entity. With the help of KG embedding [3,19,29,33,40], these entities and relations can be mapped into a continuous vector space, supporting various downstream knowledge-driven applications, such as recommender systems [15,30] and question answering [16,25]. As more and more organizations begin to collaboratively learn KG embeddings based on local KGs, the need for distributed training with privacy protection motivates the recent studies on federated KG embedding [10,11,27,46].

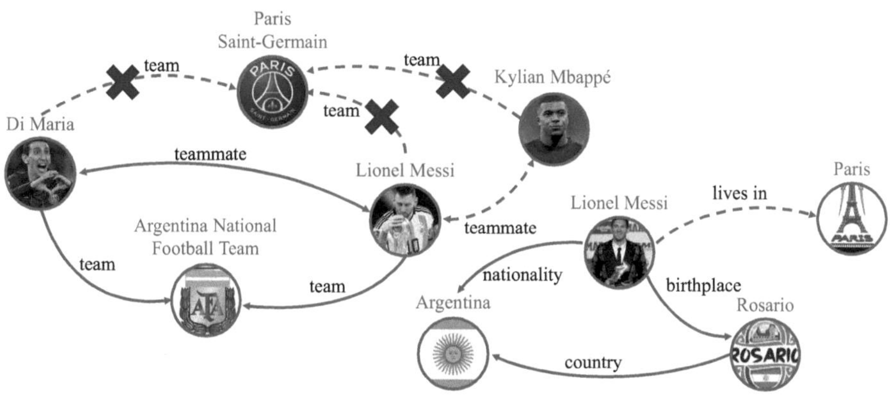

Fig. 1. An example shows complementary knowledge about football player *Lionel Messi* in multiple KGs. Forgetting target knowledge necessitates propagation to related knowledge and retention of unrelated knowledge.

Federated KG embedding is a typical cross-silo scenario in federated learning (FL) [17,21,23,34,36,37,42,45], where each client locally maintains a KG and shares the learned embeddings for knowledge transfer. When developing a federated KG embedding framework, it is essential to account for both learning and unlearning paradigms for two primary reasons. Firstly, triplets in KGs are subject to constant updates and changes, making it necessary for the embedding model to unlearn outdated triplets. Secondly, organizations need to adjust the visibility of certain triplets and perform knowledge removal to comply with privacy regulations or address conflicts of interest. An example is illustrated in Fig. 1, which shows two KGs that describe the career knowledge and basic information of football star *Lionel Messi*, respectively, complementing and supporting each other. The information related to nationality, team affiliation, and residence describes diverse aspects of *Lionel Messi*, enabling the collaborative learning of more effective KG embedding models. Unlearning must not only remove the target knowledge, but also adaptively propagate changes to semantically related facts to avoid inconsistency. Meanwhile, unrelated knowledge should be retained to preserve the model's overall utility and prevent performance degradation.

Despite the notable progress that has been made [8,10,11,27,45,46], several challenges persist in the development of federated KG embedding frameworks. Firstly, the huge number of entities can lead to excessive computation and communication overhead during the learning and unlearning processes of KG embeddings. Previous studies [10,11,27,46] propose to exchange the learned knowledge by sharing entity embeddings among clients and performing federated aggregation during the learning process, which can bring unaffordable computation and communication costs that are directly proportional to the number of entities. Besides, the unlearning process demands additional communication resources to mitigate the influence of target triplets, which poses challenges to the scalability and efficiency of unlearning. As a result, it becomes crucial to propose parameter-efficient approaches for federated KG embedding learning and unlearning.

Secondly, achieving a balance between the measures of *propagation* and *retention* is essential yet challenging, as it involves effectively controlling the scope of influence during the unlearning process [12,31]. Specifically, unlearning in federated KG embedding entails more than simply forgetting the target triplets, as the interrelated nature of triplets within knowledge graphs complicates this process. On one hand, triplets that have strong associations with the target triplets, such as those derived from the target triplets, should be erased simultaneously. We refer to this process as *propagation*. For example, when *Messi* no longer plays for *PSG*, the knowledge regarding his teammate relationship with *Mbappé* in one KG and his residence in *Paris* in another KG should be forgotten concurrently[1]. On the other hand, the unlearning process should not disturb the memory of unrelated triplets, a concept we refer to as *retention*. For example, although *Messi* and *Di Maria* are no longer teammates at *PSG*, they still collaborate in the *Argentina national football team*. Therefore, simply erasing the target triplets can inevitably disrupt entity embeddings, potentially leading to the loss of knowledge that should not be affected.

In this study, we propose a novel **P**arameter-efficient **F**ederated KG embedding **L**earning and **U**nlearning framework, called **PFLU**, to tackle the aforementioned challenges. To be more specific, PFLU incorporates an anchor-based KG embedding technique, allowing clients only to share the embeddings of selected entities (referred to as *anchors* [9,14]) for collaboration while keeping the remaining entities and relations locally. We formulate the anchor selection as a maximum coverage problem to ensure the effectiveness of learning and unlearning, and provide an approximate solution to this problem via a greedy strategy. By focusing on these anchor entities, PFLU significantly reduces the communication and computational costs associated with the large number of entities in knowledge graphs during the learning and unlearning processes.

To achieve a good balance between propagation and retention in the unlearning process, the proposed framework suggests a two-stage unlearning mechanism that integrates both structural and semantic unlearning. Structural unlearning

[1] The actual propagation sets in our experiments are strictly derived from rule-based reasoning, not from co-occurrence assumptions.

serves as a rapid local deletion procedure for updating the hard-encoded graph structure according to knowledge updates, while semantic unlearning accurately modifies the anchor embeddings to effectively propagate the influence of unlearning. By combining structural and semantic unlearning, the proposed framework efficiently removes related knowledge while preserving unrelated information.

We conduct a series of experiments on the widely-used FB15k-237 benchmark dataset [32,46] to compare the proposed framework and several baseline methods, demonstrating the advancements of PFLU in terms of both effectiveness and efficiency. The experimental results show that the two-stage unlearning mechanism enables PFLU to effectively forget target and related knowledge while retaining unrelated information. Furthermore, we provide empirical evidence that the anchor selection strategy employed in PFLU outperforms other strategies [7,14], highlighting the specific improvements achieved.

2 Related Work

Federated KG Embedding. Federated learning (FL) [22,24,26,41] is an innovative distributed machine learning paradigm in which dispersed clients collaboratively train models without directly sharing raw data. Due to the need for privacy protection, recent studies [10,11,27,46] propose federated KG embedding for training better models across multiple distributed KGs. For example, FedE [10] implements the adaptation of FL to KG embedding; FedEC [11] introduces an embedding-contrastive regularization term in local optimization to tackle data heterogeneity; FedLU [46] decouples the global and local embeddings and transfers knowledge through mutual distillation at the cost of a larger parameter size. While existing frameworks struggle with high computation and communication costs, PFLU addresses federated KG embedding with extremely low computation and communication costs.

KG Embedding Unlearning. Different from naive machine unlearning [4,6,38] that aims to erase the knowledge of specific data from a trained model, KG embedding unlearning needs to forget both the graph structure and the semantic knowledge from the embedding model simultaneously. FedLU [46] designs an approximate unlearning algorithm tailored for KG embedding, which performs gradient ascent on the triplets that need to be forgotten. The embedding model is then finetuned to restore its performance. However, FedLU only focuses on forgetting target triplets and does not consider the impact of unlearning on closely related triplets in KGs.

3 Methodology

3.1 Overview

The overall architecture of the proposed PFLU, as illustrated in Fig. 2, shows the process of federated KG embedding learning and unlearning. To facilitate this process, clients are suggested to select a subset of entities (referred to as "**anchors**") from their local KGs for sharing learned knowledge. Each client locally maintains the anchor embeddings, distance embeddings, relation embeddings, and an entity encoder. The anchor embeddings are trained to encode the shared knowledge across multiple KGs for global aggregation, while the entity encoder and the relation embeddings are utilized to preserve client-specific knowledge. With the help of hard-encoded anchor mapping and relation mapping tables, the embeddings of all entities in KGs can be constructed for learning and unlearning, as depicted in the figure. The **hard-encoded mappings** refers to precomputed mappings from each entity to its anchors and relations, stored as lookup tables. These static mappings enable consistent embedding and forgetting operations across clients.

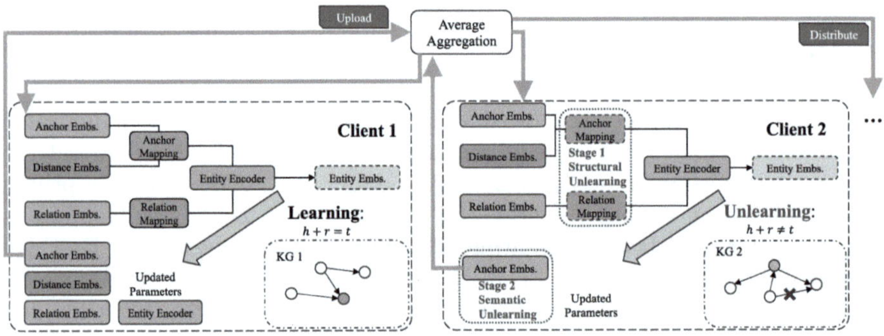

Fig. 2. Overall architecture of PFLU

PFLU designs a two-stage unlearning mechanism. In the first stage, clients who store the triplets to be unlearned perform structural unlearning by modifying the local KGs and updating the hard-encoded anchor mapping and relation mapping tables accordingly. For semantic unlearning, the second stage involves propagating the influence of unlearning to related triplets within the local KGs by fine-tuning the anchor embeddings. This influence is further disseminated to other clients through the federated aggregation of the shared anchor embeddings, resulting in a challenging inference for target triplets.

The remaining part of this section delves into a detailed description of PFLU, including federated KG embedding learning in Sect. 3.2 and federated KG embedding unlearning in Sect. 3.3. Moreover, in Sect. 3.4, we formulate the anchor selection problem and provide a greedy strategy to address it.

3.2 Federated KG Embedding Learning

The architecture of PFLU is composed of a central server and a set of dispersed clients $\mathcal{K}$. Each client $k \in \mathcal{K}$ owns a private KG, denoted by $\mathcal{G}_k = \{(h, r, t) \mid h, t \in \mathcal{E}_k, r \in \mathcal{R}_k\}$, where $\mathcal{E}_k$ and $\mathcal{R}_k$ are the entity and relation sets of client k, respectively. An anchor set $\mathcal{A}_k \subseteq \mathcal{E}_k$ is selected by client k for knowledge sharing. Following the federated KG embedding settings [10,11,46], we assume that there exist overlapping entities among these local KGs, i.e., $\forall i \in \mathcal{K}, \exists j \in \mathcal{K}, i \neq j, \mathcal{E}_i \cap \mathcal{E}_j \neq \emptyset$.

Before the training begins, the server initializes the global anchor embeddings, denoted by $\mathbf{A}^0$. Then, at the t-th training round, the server produces local anchor embeddings based on the global anchor embeddings $\mathbf{A}^t$ and broadcasts them to clients accordingly, which can be formally given as:

$$\mathbf{A}_k^t = \mathbf{M}_k \times \mathbf{A}^t, \tag{1}$$

where $\mathbf{M}_k$ is the permutation matrix from the global anchor embeddings to the local anchor embeddings for client k. The permutation matrices are calculated by the server through privacy-preserving schema matching [28].

Besides the local anchor embeddings $\mathbf{A}_k$,[2] client k locally maintains distance embeddings $\mathbf{D}_k$, relation embeddings $\mathbf{R}_k$, and an entity encoder, as shown in Fig. 2. The entity embeddings, denoted by $\mathbf{E}_k$, are constructed by the entity encoder. Specifically, for each entity $e_i \in \mathcal{E}_k$, m-nearest anchors $\mathcal{A}_{k,i}$ and n-related relations $\mathcal{R}_{k,i}$ are recorded in the anchor mapping table and relation mapping table, respectively. m and n are fixed hyper-parameters for anchors and relations per entity, respectively. The anchor information of entity e_i is composed of m-nearest anchors and respective distances as follows:

$$\mathbf{e}_{i,\text{anchor}} = \frac{\sum_{1 \leq j \leq m} \mathbf{a}_{i,j} \odot \mathbf{d}_j}{m}, \tag{2}$$

where $\mathbf{a}_{i,j}$ is the embedding of the j-th nearest anchor $a_{i,j} \in \mathcal{A}_{k,i}$ of entity e_i and $\odot$ is the element-wise multiplication of vectors. To encode the entity e_i, its m-nearest anchors are sorted by distance and number of connected paths. The ranking value j of the m-nearest anchors corresponds to the j-th vector $\mathbf{d}_j$ in the distance embeddings $\mathbf{D}_k \in \mathbb{R}^{m \times d_{\text{entity}}}$, which are initialized by the client k. The anchor embeddings are combined with the distance embeddings as the weight instead of concatenation, reducing the parameter size of the entity encoder. Distance embeddings $\mathcal{D}_k$ are learnable vectors used to weight the contribution of each anchor based on its structural proximity (e.g., shortest path) to the target entity, which enable the model to emphasize more relevant anchors. The relation information of entity e_i is calculated as follows:

$$\mathbf{e}_{i,\text{relation}} = \frac{\sum_{1 \leq j \leq n} \mathbf{r}_{i,j}}{n}, \tag{3}$$

where $\mathbf{r}_{i,j}$ is the embedding of relation $r_{i,j} \in \mathcal{R}_{k,i}$. The entity embedding of e_i is calculated by aggregating the anchor and relation information from neighborhood entities $\mathcal{N}_{k,i}$ as follows:

$$\mathbf{e}_i = \text{ReLU}\left(\mathbf{W}_k\left(\sum_{e_j \in \mathcal{N}_{k,i}} \mathbf{W}_a \cdot \mathbf{e}_{j,\text{anchor}} + \mathbf{W}_r \cdot \mathbf{e}_{j,\text{relation}}\right)\right), \tag{4}$$

[2] For the sake of simplicity, we omit the superscript t (used to denote the t-th training round) when it does not lead to any confusion.

where $\mathbf{W}_k \in \mathbb{R}^{d_{\text{entity}} \times d_{\text{entity}}}$, $\mathbf{W}_a \in \mathbb{R}^{d_{\text{entity}} \times d_{\text{entity}}}$, $\mathbf{W}_r \in \mathbb{R}^{d_{\text{entity}} \times d_{\text{relation}}}$ are all Linear layers, and $\text{ReLU}(\cdot)$ is the activation function [44].

After the construction of entity embeddings, client k updates the parameters including $\mathbf{A}_k^t$ based on its local KG. We take a widely-used scoring function of TransE [3] as an instance, given as:

$$S_{\text{TransE}} = \sum_{(h,r,t) \in \mathcal{G}_k} - || \mathbf{h} + \mathbf{r} - \mathbf{t} ||, \tag{5}$$

where $\mathbf{h}$ and $\mathbf{t}$ are the embeddings of head and tail entities h and t, respectively, and $\mathbf{r}$ is the embedding of relation r. Finally, client k uploads the updated anchor embeddings $\hat{\mathbf{A}}_k^t$ to the server, and the server performs federated aggregation to produce the global anchor embeddings as follows:

$$\mathbf{A}^{t+1} = \left(\mathbb{1} \oslash \sum_{k \in \mathcal{K}} \mathbf{v}_k \right) \otimes \sum_{k \in \mathcal{K}} \mathbf{M}_k^\top \hat{\mathbf{A}}_k^t, \tag{6}$$

where $\mathbb{1}$ is all-one vector, $\mathbf{v}_k$ is an existing vector indicating which anchors exist in client k, $\mathbf{M}_k^\top$ is the transpose of $\mathbf{M}_k$, and $\oslash$ and $\otimes$ are respectively element-wise division for vectors and element-wise multiplication with broadcasting.

3.3 Federated KG Embedding Unlearning

To satisfy the need for unlearning, PFLU designs a two-stage mechanism combining structural and semantic unlearning. During the structural unlearning stage, the memory to target triplets is thoroughly eliminated by modifying the entity mapping and relation mapping tables, which is computationally efficient. In the semantic unlearning stage, the influence of unlearning is propagated to related triplets by fine-tuning the anchor embeddings and further passed to other clients through aggregation.

The design of the structural unlearning stage is inspired by exact unlearning [4–6] to transform the model into a variant that facilitates rapid and efficient retraining. As PFLU adopts an anchor-based KG embedding technique, the pre-computed and hard-encoded anchor mapping and relation mapping tables are used to record the graph structure and relational information, respectively. For each entity e_i in client k, we find its adjacent anchors $\mathcal{A}_{k,i} \subseteq \mathcal{A}_k$ within p-hop with breadth-first search (BFS), and then record the corresponding path $path_{i,j}$ for each anchor $a_j \in \mathcal{A}_{k,i}$, which denotes the triplets connecting e_i and a_j. To generate the relation mapping, we traverse the KG and form the associated relation set $\mathcal{R}_{k,i} \subseteq \mathcal{R}_k$ for entity e_i in client k. Given the subgraph to be forgotten $\Delta\mathcal{G}_k \subseteq \mathcal{G}_k$ and the remaining triplet set $\mathcal{G}'_k = \mathcal{G}_k - \Delta\mathcal{G}_k$, the anchor mapping and relation mapping of entity e_i are respectively updated for unlearning as follows:

$$\begin{aligned} \mathcal{A}'_{k,i} &= \{a_j \,|\, a_j \in \mathcal{A}_{k,i}, path_{i,j} \cap \Delta\mathcal{G}_k = \emptyset\}, \\ \mathcal{R}'_{k,i} &= \{r_j \,|\, (e_i, r_j, e_j) \in \mathcal{G}'_k\}. \end{aligned} \tag{7}$$

During this stage, the structural information of target triplets is thoroughly eliminated from the anchor mapping table and relation mapping table without modifying the embeddings, which is computationally efficient.

The semantic unlearning stage complements the structural unlearning. Anchors serve as the foundation for constructing entity embeddings and the bridge connecting potentially related entities. Therefore, we propagate the influence of unlearning to related local triplets by manipulating the anchor embeddings. The parameters of the relation embeddings, distance embeddings, and entity encoder are frozen. Given the subgraph $\Delta\mathcal{G}_k$ to be forgotten, the anchor embeddings $\mathbf{A}_k$ of client k are fine-tuned with the unlearning scoring function as follows:

$$U_{\text{TransE}} = \sum_{(h,r,t)\in\Delta\mathcal{G}_k} \| \mathbf{h} + \mathbf{r} - \mathbf{t} \|, \tag{8}$$

which treats the target triplets as negative and performs gradient ascent on them. The impact of forgetting spreads to strongly related triplets via the anchor embeddings, thereby achieving propagation. The fine-tuned anchor embeddings $\hat{\mathbf{A}}_k^{'}$ of client k are sent to the server for aggregation, and the influence of unlearning is passed to other clients. As each entity is encoded by multiple anchors with the anchor mapping matrices preserved locally, the unlearning of a triplet affects multiple anchor embeddings and it is difficult to infer the forgetting triplets from the updates of anchor embeddings.

3.4 Anchor Selection

Drawing inspiration from subword tokenization techniques utilized in natural language processing, anchor-based KG embedding methods [9,14] encode and embed entities with a fixed-size anchor and relation vocabulary. Each entity is encoded by the embeddings of m-nearest anchors and n-related relations. To handle varying mapping lengths, the anchor and relation mapping matrices are truncated or padded accordingly. The anchor and relation embeddings capture the common and personalized semantics respectively.

To ensure the quality of the KG embeddings produced based on the anchors, the selection process must fulfill the following two requirements. The first is **Localized Encoding Constraint**, which requires that an entity in a KG should only be encoded by the anchors within its p-hop neighborhood to guarantee structural and semantic relevance. The second is **Sufficient Coverage Requirement**, which requires that each entity should be associated with an adequate number of anchors to guarantee comprehensive coverage of common knowledge. Considering the requirements, we formulate the anchor selection as a maximum coverage problem.

Definition 1 (Anchor Selection). *Let $\mathcal{E}_k$ be an entity set, $\mathcal{D} = \{dist(e_i, e_j) \,|\, e_i,\ e_j \in \mathcal{E}_k\}$ be a set of the distance between each entity pair, p be the threshold of maximum distance from anchor to entity, m be the threshold of required anchor number for each entity, and q be the number of anchors. For*

Algorithm 1: Anchor Selection Algorithm

Input: client k, local KG $\mathcal{G}_k = \{(h, r, t) \mid h, r \in \mathcal{E}_k, r \in \mathcal{R}_k\}$, distance set $\{dist(e_i, e_j) \mid e_i, e_j \in \mathcal{E}_k, e_i \neq e_j\}$, distance threshold p, anchor number q, and anchor mapping threshold m

Output: anchor set $\mathcal{A}_k$, $AnchorMapping_k$

$Neigh \leftarrow dict()$; ▷*Stores p-hop neighbors for each entity*

$Profit \leftarrow dict()$; ▷*Stores coverage gain for each entity*

$Anchor \leftarrow dict()$; ▷*Records anchor assignments*

foreach $e_i \in \mathcal{E}_k$ **do**

  transverse p-hop neighbor subgraph $\mathcal{G}_{k,i} \subseteq \mathcal{G}_k$ of e_i;

  $Neigh[e_i] \leftarrow \{(e_j, dist(e_i, e_j), path_{i,j}) \mid e_j \in \mathcal{E}_k, dist(e_i, e_j) \leq p\}$;

  $Profit[e_i] \leftarrow |Neigh[e_i]|$; ▷*Initial gain: number of reachable neighbors*

  $AnchorMapping_k[e_i] \leftarrow set()$;

for $1 \leq j \leq q$ **do**

  $a_j \leftarrow \arg\max_{e_i \in \mathcal{E}} Profit[e_i]$; ▷*Select entity with highest gain*

  $Profit[a_j] \leftarrow 0$; ▷*Avoid reselection*

  $\mathcal{A}_k.add(a_j)$;

  foreach $(e_i, dist(a_j, e_i), path_{j,i}) \in Neigh[a_j]$ **do**

    $AnchorMapping_k[e_i].add((a_j, dist(a_j, e_i), path_{j,i}))$;

    if $|AnchorMapping_k[e_i]| = m$ **then**

      foreach $(e_l, dist(e_i, e_l), path_{i,l}) \in Neigh[e_i]$ **do**

        $Profit[e_l] \leftarrow Profit[e_l] - 1$; ▷*Avoid over-coverage*

return $\mathcal{A}_k, AnchorMapping_k$;

a candidate anchor set $\mathcal{A}_k$, we define the p-hop reachable anchor set for entity e_i as follows:

$$A_{k,i} = \{a_j \mid a_j \in \mathcal{A}_k, dist(e_i, a_j) \leq p\}. \tag{9}$$

The coverage profit for entity e_i is defined as follows:

$$z_i = \frac{\min\left(m, |\mathcal{A}_{k,i}|\right)}{m}. \tag{10}$$

We define the anchor selection problem for client k as follows:

$$\max_{\mathcal{A}_k \subseteq \mathcal{E}_k} \sum_{e_i \in \mathcal{E}_k} z_i, \quad s.t. \quad |\mathcal{A}_k| = q. \tag{11}$$

The anchor selection problem is an instance of the well-defined maximum coverage problem (MCP) [39]. MCP, aiming to find a fixed-size subset that maximizes the coverage on the target set, is a known NP-hard challenge. Equation (9) satisfies the Localized Encoding Constraint by filtering the candidates within a distance threshold. Equation (10) is an optimal term for anchor selection, which satisfies the Sufficient Coverage Requirement. It indicates that if an entity is not

Table 1. Statistics of adopted datasets

Datasets	#Clients	#Relations	#Entities	#Triplets
FB15k-237-C3	3	79	6,226	103,372
FB15k-237-C5	5	47	5,119	62,023
FB15k-237-C10	10	24	2,177	21,012

linked to a sufficient number of anchors, finding suitable anchors for it remains an optimization objective. Conversely, when an entity is adequately connected to enough anchors, the priority shifts. PFLU devises a greedy algorithm with the optimal term to address the anchor selection problem.

We design Algorithm 1, a $(1 - \frac{1}{e})$-approximation greedy algorithm [13] with a time complexity of $O(q \times |\mathcal{E}_k|^2)$, the same as the standard greedy solution to MCP. Algorithm 1 needs an auxiliary space of $O(|\mathcal{E}_k|^2)$. The optimal term defined in Eq. (10) corresponds to Lines 15-17 in the pseudo-code. Thanks to the dynamic adjustment of the optimal term, Algorithm 1 consistently aims to enrich the anchor mapping of the entities that have not been not adequately encoded, thereby improving the overall effectiveness of learning and unlearning.

We provide more discussions and empirical evidence of the proposed anchor selection strategy in Sect. 4.4, which highlights its specific improvements compared to other strategies.

4 Experiments

4.1 Settings

We conduct a series of experiments to compare PFLU with several baseline methods including FedE [10], FedEC [11] and FedLU [46], facilitated with the representative KG embedding model TransE [3]. Additionally, we also report the results of local training using the anchor-based KG embedding technique, denoted by "PFLU (Local)". Three heterogeneous datasets are used for evaluation, including FB15k-237-C3/C5/C10 [32,46]. The statistics of these datasets are summarized in Table 1.

For the evaluation metrics, we adopt the average Hits@N ($N = 1, 3, 10$) and mean reciprocal rank (MRR) of all clients under the filtered setting to evaluate the performance of the entity (head and tail) link prediction task. We calculate the average parameter size $\#P$ of each client and the average communication cost $\#C$ during each iteration to evaluate the parameter and communication efficiency of each federated KG embedding framework. The unit M for parameter size $\#P$ and communication cost $\#C$ is omitted in the tables for simplicity.

4.2 Implementation Details

The batch size is set to 1,024 and the negative sampling [43] size is set to 256 in local training. The hidden dimension of the entity and relation embeddings is set

Table 2. Link prediction performance with TransE

Methods		#P	#C	Hits@1	Hits@3	Hits@10	MRR
FB15k-237-C3	FedE	1.61	1.59	20.25	39.19	56.18	32.66
	FedEC	1.61	1.59	20.65	39.36	56.44	32.99
	FedLU	3.21	1.59	20.94	39.71	56.89	33.30
	PFLU (Local)	0.38	-	17.64	34.26	51.67	29.12
	PFLU (Random)	0.38	0.16	17.71	33.60	50.61	28.74
	PFLU (Standard)	0.38	0.16	18.80	35.40	53.19	30.31
	PFLU	0.38	0.16	**22.75**	**41.57**	**59.15**	**35.14**
FB15k-237-C5	FedE	1.32	1.31	20.66	39.78	57.12	33.23
	FedEC	1.32	1.31	21.11	39.90	57.42	33.54
	FedLU	2.63	1.31	21.38	40.58	57.96	33.98
	PFLU (Local)	0.34	-	18.59	35.31	52.75	30.04
	PFLU (Random)	0.34	0.13	17.25	32.61	49.16	27.93
	PFLU (Standard)	0.34	0.13	18.58	35.16	52.74	30.05
	PFLU	0.34	0.13	**22.73**	**41.09**	**58.31**	**34.88**
FB15k-237-C10	FedE	0.56	0.56	19.86	38.15	55.82	32.10
	FedEC	0.56	0.56	20.02	38.67	56.27	32.42
	FedLU	1.12	0.56	20.53	39.21	56.82	32.95
	PFLU (Local)	0.26	-	18.10	34.55	52.17	29.53
	PFLU (Random)	0.26	0.06	17.57	33.29	50.37	28.56
	PFLU (Standard)	0.26	0.06	18.02	34.58	52.39	29.54
	PFLU	0.26	0.06	**22.12**	**40.40**	**58.00**	**34.25**

The best results are marked with **bold**.

to 256. We initialize the anchor/relation embeddings with uniform distribution following previous work [46]. We employ the Adam [20] optimizer with a learning rate of 0.001. For federated learning experiments, clients conduct local training for 5 epochs within each communication round. The maximum communication round is set to 100. We evaluate the performance of the embedding models after each communication round. The early stopping strategy is applied with a patience value of 5 bad validations to avoid overfitting. Some hyper-parameters such as the contrastive temperature in FedEC [11] and the distillation weight in FedLU [46] are set according to their original papers. For anchor selection in anchor-based KG embedding, the anchor ratio is set to 10%. The distance threshold p from anchor to entity is set to 2. To encode entities, the anchor number m and the relation number n for each entity is set to 20 and 15, respectively. For reproducibility, we set the random seed to 111213. We conducted all experiments on a server equipped with 48 Intel Xeon Platinum 8163 CPUs, 512 GB of memory, and four NVIDIA Tesla V100 GPUs.

Table 3. Link prediction performance with DistMult

Methods		#P	#C	Hits@1	Hits@3	Hits@10	MRR
C3	FedE	1.61	1.59	20.45	39.00	56.02	32.26
	FedEC	1.61	1.59	20.81	39.17	55.92	32.43
	FedLU	3.21	1.59	21.08	39.75	56.37	33.03
	PFLU	0.38	0.16	**22.60**	**41.50**	**59.08**	**35.20**
C5	FedE	1.32	1.31	20.70	39.26	57.09	33.02
	FedEC	1.32	1.31	21.23	39.95	57.44	33.25
	FedLU	2.63	1.31	22.98	40.42	58.02	34.09
	PFLU	0.34	0.13	**23.16**	**41.47**	**58.68**	**35.44**
C10	FedE	0.56	0.56	19.98	37.96	55.76	32.01
	FedEC	0.56	0.56	20.32	39.57	56.28	34.02
	FedLU	1.12	0.56	21.05	39.23	58.00	33.95
	PFLU	0.26	0.06	**22.06**	**41.03**	**58.37**	**34.94**

The best results are marked with **bold**.

Table 4. Convergence analysis according to early stop

Communication rounds	FedE	FedEC	FedLU	PFLU
FB15k-237-C3	100	100	75	39
FB15k-237-C5	100	100	80	58
FB15k-237-C10	100	100	86	65

4.3 Results and Analysis

Federated KG Embedding Learning. The experimental results of PFLU and baselines on FB15k-237-C3/C5/C10 with TransE are shown in Table 2. We conduct a comprehensive comparison between PFLU and baselines regarding the average parameter size, average communication cost, and link prediction performance. The following observations can be made based on these results: (i) PFLU achieves superior performance in federated KG embedding learning to FedE but with only 10% (i.e., the anchor ratio) communication cost. PFLU also generates better collaborative embeddings compared to PFLU (Local), which demonstrates that common knowledge is effectively transferred through the anchor embeddings. (ii) PFLU achieves comparable performance to FedLU, with a smaller parameter size and 10% communication cost of FedLU. (iii) Thanks to a fixed-size entity encoder to construct entity embeddings, PFLU significantly reduces the trainable parameter size. To further demonstrate model-agnostic applicability, we apply PFLU to DistMult. The results, reported in Table 3, show consistent improvements over FedLU.

We evaluate communication and time efficiency by recording: (1) average trainable parameters per client, (2) transmitted parameters per round, and (3)

Table 5. Ablation study of distance and relation encoding

Methods	#P	#C	Hits@1	Hits@3	Hits@10	MRR
PFLU	0.38	0.16	22.75	41.57	59.15	35.14
w/o distance	0.37	0.16	21.42	38.79	56.74	33.21
w/o relation	0.25	0.16	21.15	39.58	57.20	33.31

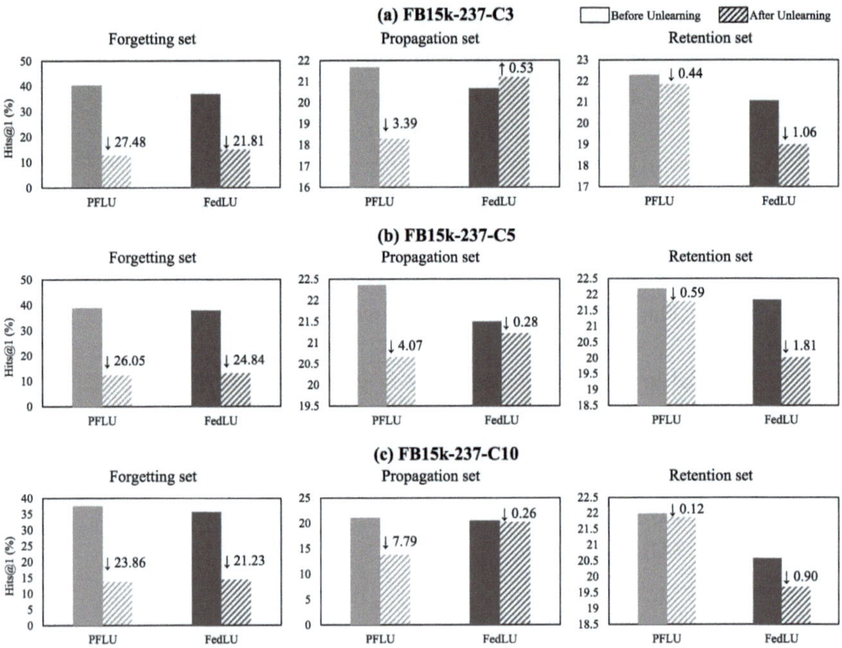

Fig. 3. Hits@1 on the forgetting/propagation/retention sets of FB15k-237-C3/C5/C10 with TransE. Larger decreases on forgetting/propagation set and smaller decreases on retention set are better.

convergence rounds to reach optimal performance. Table 4 depicts the communication rounds until convergence on validation sets (maximum 100 rounds). The table shows that PFLU converges faster than baselines during learning. During unlearning, both FedLU and PFLU fine-tune the entity/anchor embeddings for 10 epochs. Moreover, FedLU retrains the entity embeddings on the retaining set (the whole dataset except the unlearning triplets) for two more epochs to recover the performance, while PFLU does not need to. From the above analysis, we can conclude that PFLU needs much less computational resources regarding time cost in both learning and unlearning.

Further, an ablation study is conducted to investigate the effects of applying distance and relation embeddings in constructing entity embeddings, as shown in Table 5. From the table, we can observe that the proposed PFLU outperforms "PFLU w/o distance" and "PFLU w/o relation" by a noticeable margin in link prediction, which confirms the contributions of incorporating distance and relation information in constructing entity embeddings. Besides, the size of the fixed distance embeddings is relatively small, yet it provides similar improvements in entity encoding as the relation embeddings. Incorporating distance information is a favorable choice when encoding entities with anchor embeddings.

Federated KG Embedding Unlearning. Following FedLU [46], we perform unlearning of triplets. Unlearning entities can be transformed to unlearning all triplets connected to the entities. When more than one client needs to perform unlearning, PFLU handles well one by one. For comprehensive evaluation, we compare the link prediction performance of each client's embedding model before and after unlearning on the forgetting set, propagation set, and retention set, respectively. **A larger decrease on the forgetting/propagation sets indicates more effective unlearning, while a smaller decrease on the retention set suggests a more precise scope of unlearning influence.**

We follow the splitting of the forgetting set in previous work [46] to ensure a fair comparison. Propagation refers to the extent to which the forgetting process affects closely related triplets. We traverse the test set and constitute the propagation set with the following triplets: (i) Triplets that have identical head and tail entities as the target forgetting triplets; (ii) Triplets that have symmetric head and tail entities to the target triplets; and (iii) Triplets that can be derived from the target triplets. Retention, on the other hand, evaluates whether the model retains the memory of triplets that are unrelated to the target triplets. The retention set consists of the remaining triplets in the test set, excluding the propagation set.

Figure 3 presents the comparisons of the unlearning effects between PFLU and FedLU on FB15k-237-C3/C5/C10 with TransE embedding. From the results, we draw the following observations: (i) Although FedLU achieves a notable decrease in Hits@1 on the forgetting set, it struggles to forget the propagation set. This implies that FedLU is unable to unlearn related knowledge, which is especially important in KG embedding unlearning. (ii) PFLU shows a significant decrease in Hits@1 on the forgetting/propagation sets while retaining the memory to the retention set effectively. These findings demonstrate that PFLU achieves a desirable balance between propagation and retention, effectively controlling the influence scope of unlearning.

Table 6. Ablation study of structural/semantic unlearning

Hits@1	Unlearned		
	Forgetting	Propagation	Retention
PFLU	12.78	18.29	21.86
w/o structural unlearning	37.45	20.02	22.11
w/o semantic unlearning	29.16	19.34	22.08

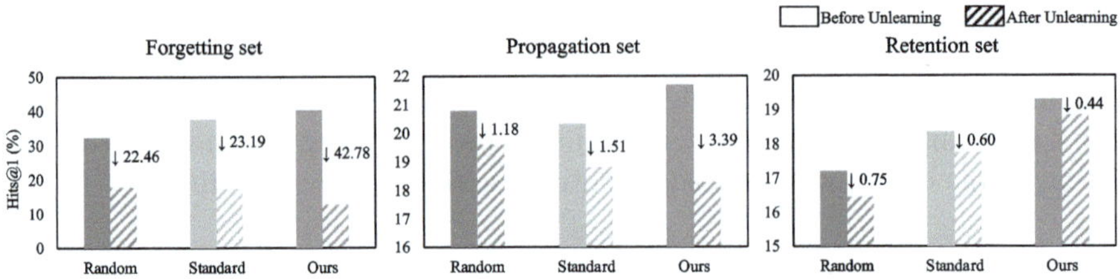

Fig. 4. Hits@1 with different anchor selection strategies on FB15k-237-C3. Larger decreases on forgetting/propagation set and smaller decreases on retention set are better.

Moreover, we conduct an ablation study to investigate the effects of the structural and semantic unlearning stages in PFLU. Table 6 compares the unlearning results of PFLU, "PFLU w/o structural unlearning" and "PFLU w/o semantic unlearning" on the FB15k-237-C3 with TransE embedding. From the table, we can observe that both the structural and semantic unlearning stages contribute to the unlearning of the forgetting and propagation set while causing minimal impact on the retention set. The structural unlearning stage exhibits a significant effect on unlearning the forgetting set, showing the effectiveness of PFLU in extracting knowledge through the anchor and relation mappings for targeted, rapid and thorough unlearning. By combining both structural and semantic unlearning stages, PFLU effectively controls the influence scope of unlearning.

4.4 Further Discussions

Different Anchor Selection Strategies. We formulate the anchor selection as MCP in Sect. 3.4 and design a greedy solution in Algorithm 1 to resolve it. Experiments are conducted to validate the rationality of the definition and the effectiveness of the strategy. For comparison, we adopt random anchors [14] (denoted by "Random") and the standard solution to the maximum coverage problem [7] (denoted by "Standard") as two baselines. Table 2 shows the link prediction performance of PFLU on FB15k-237-C3/C5/C10 with TransE. It is observed from the tables that PFLU achieves the best link prediction performance with the proposed anchor selection strategy compared to "PFLU (Random)" and "PFLU (Standard)". Additionally, we observe that PFLU (Random) and PFLU (Standard) sometimes perform worse than PFLU (Local), indicating that a good anchor selection strategy serves as the guarantee for collaborative learning of better embeddings.

In Fig. 4, we summarize the unlearning performance of PFLU on FB15k-237-C3 with TransE embedding of different anchor selection strategies. It can be observed that our anchor selection strategy significantly outperforms baselines, further confirming the effectiveness of the proposed anchor selection strategy in controlling the influence scope of unlearning precisely.

Table 7. Link prediction performance on FB15k-237-C3 under different rates of noise

Noise	Hits@1	Hits@3	Hits@10	MRR
0%	22.75	41.57	59.15	35.14
1%	22.32	41.30	58.85	34.60
5%	22.05	40.78	57.78	33.83

Robustness and Privacy. In PFLU, each entity is represented by several anchor embeddings, which provide robustness against low-quality anchor embeddings. The impact of the low-quality anchor embeddings is "smoothed" by other high-quality anchor embeddings. We perform additional experiments with Gaussian noise $X \sim N(0, 0.1)$ added to 1% and 5% of the anchors respectively on FB15k-237-C3 with TransE. Table 7 shows that several low-quality anchor embeddings would not greatly influence the modeling of target entities, thus validating the robustness of PFLU.

PFLU does not bring additional privacy concerns compared to previous studies, although it is more focused on the communication cost and propagation/retention of federated unlearning. First, the federated learning framework provides fundamental protection that the raw data would not be directly shared. Second, PFLU adopts an anchor-based method, which significantly reduces the shared parameters to 10%. Besides, PFLU is compatible with algorithms such as differential privacy [35] to enhance privacy protection.

5 Conclusion

In this paper, we propose PFLU, a novel parameter-efficient federated KG embedding learning and unlearning framework. Towards handling the computation and communication overhead brought by the huge number of entities in real-world KGs, PFLU incorporates an anchor-based KG embedding technique to transfer knowledge during the learning process and propagate the influence during the unlearning process. Notably, the anchor selection is critical to the proposed PFLU, thus we formulate it as a maximum coverage problem to ensure the quality of the encoded entities and further design a greedy strategy to address it. Besides, the proposed PFLU combines structural and semantic unlearning, which provides the ability to effectively control the scope of unlearning influence when certain triplets need to be unlearned from the model. The experiments are conducted on three heterogeneous datasets constructed from FB15k-237, which demonstrates that PFLU achieves efficiency and effectiveness in both federated KG embedding learning and unlearning. The ablation study on distance/relation encoding and structural/semantic unlearning confirm their contribution to the proposed PFLU, and some empirical evidence is provided to show the superior performance of our anchor selection strategy compared to baselines.

Acknowledgments. This work is supported by National Natural Science Foundation of China (No. 62272219).

Supplemental Material Statement. Source code and datasets are released at https://github.com/nju-websoft/PFLU.

References

1. Auer, S., Bizer, C., Kobilarov, G., Lehmann, J., Cyganiak, R., Ives, Z.: DBpedia: a nucleus for a web of open data. In: Aberer, K., et al. (eds.) ASWC/ISWC -2007. LNCS, vol. 4825, pp. 722–735. Springer, Heidelberg (2007). https://doi.org/10.1007/978-3-540-76298-0_52
2. Bollacker, K.D., Cook, R.P., Tufts, P.: Freebase: a shared database of structured general human knowledge. In: AAAI, pp. 1962–1963. AAAI Press, Vancouver, BC, Canada (2007)
3. Bordes, A., Usunier, N., García-Durán, A., Weston, J., Yakhnenko, O.: Translating embeddings for modeling multi-relational data. In: NIPS, pp. 2787–2795. Curran Associates, Inc., Lake Tahoe, NV, USA (2013)
4. Bourtoule, L., et al.: Machine unlearning. In: SP, pp. 141–159. IEEE, San Francisco, CA, USA (2021)
5. Brophy, J., Lowd, D.: Machine unlearning for random forests. In: ICML, pp. 1092–1104. PMLR, Virtual (2021)
6. Cao, Y., Yang, J.: Towards making systems forget with machine unlearning. In: SP, pp. 463–480. IEEE, San Jose, CA, USA (2015)
7. Chandu, D.P.: Big step greedy heuristic for maximum coverage problem. Inter. J. Comput. Appli. **125**(7), 19–24 (2015)
8. Chen, D., Zhu, H., Gu, J., Chen, R., Xie, M.: Unaligned federated knowledge graph embedding. In: ISWC, pp. 180–198. Springer, Baltimore, MD, USA (2024). https://doi.org/10.1007/978-3-031-77844-5_10
9. Chen, M., et al.: Entity-agnostic representation learning for parameter-efficient knowledge graph embedding. In: AAAI, pp. 1–9. AAAI Press, Washington, DC, USA (2023)
10. Chen, M., Zhang, W., Yuan, Z., Jia, Y., Chen, H.: FedE: embedding knowledge graphs in federated setting. In: IJCKG, pp. 80–88. ACM, Virtual (2021)
11. Chen, M., Zhang, W., Yuan, Z., Jia, Y., Chen, H.: Federated knowledge graph completion via embedding-contrastive learning. Knowl.-Based Syst. **252**, 109459 (2022)
12. Cheng, J., Dasoulas, G., He, H., Agarwal, C., Zitnik, M.: GNNDelete: a general unlearning strategy for graph neural networks. In: ICLR, pp. 1–22. OpenReview.net, Kigali, Rwanda (2023)
13. Cohen, R., Katzir, L.: The generalized maximum coverage problem. Inf. Process. Lett. **108**(1), 15–22 (2008)
14. Galkin, M., Denis, E.G., Wu, J., Hamilton, W.L.: NodePiece: compositional and parameter-efficient representations of large knowledge graphs. In: ICLR, pp. 1–25. OpenReview.net, Virtual (2022)
15. Guo, Q., et al.: A survey on knowledge graph-based recommender systems: extended abstract. In: ICDE, pp. 3803–3804. IEEE, Anaheim, CA, USA (2023)
16. Huang, X., Zhang, J., Li, D., Li, P.: Knowledge graph embedding based question answering. In: WSDM, pp. 105–113. ACM, Melbourne, Australia (2019)
17. Huang, Y., et al.: Personalized cross-silo federated learning on Non-IID data. In: AAAI, pp. 7865–7873. AAAI Press, Virtual (2021)

18. Ji, S., Pan, S., Cambria, E., Marttinen, P., Yu, P.S.: A survey on knowledge graphs: representation, acquisition, and applications. IEEE Trans. Neural Netw. Learn. Syst. **33**(2), 494–514 (2021)
19. Jin, L., Yao, Z., Chen, M., Chen, H., Zhang, W.: A comprehensive study on knowledge graph embedding over relational patterns based on rule learning. In: ISWC, pp. 290–308. Springer, Athens,Greece (2023). https://doi.org/10.1007/978-3-031-47240-4_16
20. Kingma, D.P., Ba, J.: Adam: a method for stochastic optimization. In: ICLR, pp. 1–15. OpenReview.net, San Diego, CA, USA (2015)
21. Konečný, J., McMahan, H.B., Ramage, D., Richtárik, P.: Federated optimization: distributed machine learning for on-device intelligence. arXiv **1610.02527** (2016)
22. Li, Q., He, B., Song, D.: Model-contrastive federated learning. In: CVPR, pp. 10713–10722. IEEE, Virtual (2021)
23. Li, Q., et al.: A survey on federated learning systems: vision, hype and reality for data privacy and protection. IEEE Trans. Knowl. Data Eng. **35**(4), 3347–3366 (2023)
24. Li, T., Sahu, A.K., Zaheer, M., Sanjabi, M., Talwalkar, A., Smith, V.: Federated optimization in heterogeneous networks. In: MLSys, pp. 429–450. mlsys.org, Austin, TX, USA (2020)
25. Liu, L., Chen, Y., Das, M., Yang, H., Tong, H.: Knowledge graph question answering with ambiguous query. In: WWW, pp. 2477–2486. ACM, Austin, TX, USA (2023)
26. McMahan, B., Moore, E., Ramage, D., Hampson, S., y Arcas, B.A.: Communication-efficient learning of deep networks from decentralized data. In: AISTATS, pp. 1273–1282. PMLR, Fort Lauderdale, FL, USA (2017)
27. Peng, H., Li, H., Song, Y., Zheng, V.W., Li, J.: Differentially private federated knowledge graphs embedding. In: CIKM, pp. 1416–1425. ACM, Queensland, Australia (2021)
28. Scannapieco, M., Figotin, I., Bertino, E., Elmagarmid, A.K.: Privacy preserving schema and data matching. In: SIGMOD, pp. 653–664. ACM, Beijing, China (2007)
29. Sun, Z., Deng, Z., Nie, J., Tang, J.: RotatE: knowledge graph embedding by relational rotation in complex space. In: ICLR, pp. 1–18. OpenReview.net, New Orleans, LA, USA (2019)
30. Sun, Z., Yang, J., Zhang, J., Bozzon, A., Huang, L.K., Xu, C.: Recurrent knowledge graph embedding for effective recommendation. In: RecSys, pp. 297–305. ACM, Vancouver, BC, Canada (2018)
31. Tan, J., Sun, F., Qiu, R., Su, D., Shen, H.: Unlink to unlearn: simplifying edge unlearning in gnns. In: WWW Companion, pp. 489–492. ACM, New York, USA (2024)
32. Toutanova, K., Chen, D.: Observed versus latent features for knowledge base and text inference. In: CVSC, pp. 57–66. ACL, Beijing, China (2015)
33. Wang, Q., Mao, Z., Wang, B., Guo, L.: Knowledge graph embedding: a survey of approaches and applications. IEEE Trans. Knowl. Data Eng. **29**(12), 2724–2743 (2017)
34. Wang, Z., et al.: FederatedScope-GNN: towards a unified, comprehensive and efficient package for federated graph learning. In: KDD, pp. 4110–4120. ACM (2022)
35. Wei, K., et al.: Federated learning with differential privacy: algorithms and performance analysis. IEEE Trans. Inf. Forensics Secur. **15**, 3454–3469 (2020)
36. Wu, H., Zhu, X., Hu, W.: A blockchain system for clustered federated learning with peer-to-peer knowledge transfer. Proc. VLDB Endowment **17**(5), 966–979 (2024)

37. Xie, Y., et al.: FederatedScope: a flexible federated learning platform for heterogeneity. Proc. VLDB Endowment **16**(5), 1059–1072 (2023)
38. Xu, H., Zhu, T., Zhang, L., Zhou, W., Yu, P.S.: Machine unlearning: a survey. ACM Comput. Surv. **56**(1), 1–36 (2023)
39. Yakovlev, S., Kartashov, O., Podzeha, D.: Mathematical models and nonlinear optimization in continuous maximum coverage location problem. Computation **10**(7), 119 (2022)
40. Yang, B., Yih, W., He, X., Gao, J., Deng, L.: Embedding entities and relations for learning and inference in knowledge bases. In: ICLR, pp. 1–12. OpenReview.net, San Diego, CA, USA (2015)
41. Yang, Q., Liu, Y., Chen, T., Tong, Y.: Federated machine learning: concept and applications. ACM Trans. Intell. Syst. Technol. **10**(2), 12:1–12:19 (2019)
42. Yang, Q., Liu, Y., Cheng, Y., Kang, Y., Chen, T., Yu, H.: Federated learning. Synthesis Lect. Artifi. Intell. Mach. Learn. **13**(3), 1–207 (2019)
43. Yao, N., Liu, Q., Yang, Y., Li, W., Bai, Q.: Entity-relation distribution-aware negative sampling for knowledge graph embedding. In: ISWC, pp. 234–252. Springer, Athens, Greece (2023)
44. Yarotsky, D.: Error bounds for approximations with deep relu networks. Neural Netw. **94**, 103–114 (2017)
45. Zhang, X., Zeng, Z., Zhou, X., Niyato, D., Shen, Z.: Personalized federated knowledge graph embedding with client-wise relation graph. Appl. Intell. **55**(4), 318 (2025)
46. Zhu, X., Li, G., Hu, W.: Heterogeneous federated knowledge graph embedding learning and unlearning. In: WWW, pp. 2444–2454. ACM, Austin, TX, USA (2023)

Measuring the Impact of Narrative Complexity on Knowledge Graph Embeddings

Inès Blin[1,2(✉)], Ilaria Tiddi[2], and Annette ten Teije[2]

[1] Sony Computer Science Laboratories-Paris, Paris, France
ines.blin@sony.com
[2] Vrije Universiteit Amsterdam, Amsterdam, The Netherlands
{i.tiddi,annette.ten.teije}@vu.nl

Abstract. In this work, we study how semantic narrative enrichment and syntactic encoding affect the performance of knowledge graph embedding models. Narratives are central to human understanding, yet their structured representation in knowledge graphs remains challenging due to their semantic and structural complexity. Although traditional knowledge graphs use binary relations, they struggle to capture richer narrative elements, such as *roles* and *causality*. More complex knowledge graph syntaxes such as rdf-star, reification, singleton or n-ary properties offer greater modeling flexibility, but their impact on downstream tasks such as link prediction remains unclear. We define a six-level categorization of narrative semantics and use it to construct a suite of structured knowledge graphs using four syntactic representations. Using different embedding models, we evaluate how semantic and syntactic factors influence the embedding quality. We find that *semantic* features such as properties and subevents generally enhance performance, while roles tend to have a detrimental effect. On the *syntactic* side, although differences were not statistically significant across all metrics, *reification* and *rdf-star* achieved the strongest results on average.

1 Introduction

Narratives are central to human understanding [11]. They serve not only as the main means of communication between humans, but also as cognitive constructs for organizing knowledge and providing coherence to otherwise fragmented data. Narratives thus capture information that goes beyond isolated facts in multiple domains such as legal [29] or historical [60]. Modeling such complex information poses substantial challenges, for instance, with knowledge graphs (KGs). The benefit of representing narratives in a structured format such as KGs lies in their ability to support semantic layering, maintain data lineage, and enable fine-grained reasoning over events, entities, and their interrelations [47].

KGs are widely used to structure factual information through entities and their relations [15,37], but most KGs rely on binary relations, which limit their

D. Garijo et al. (Eds.): ISWC 2025, LNCS 16140, pp. 481–501, 2026.
https://doi.org/10.1007/978-3-032-09527-5_26

ability to capture the semantic depth and internal structure of narratives. Narrative features like *roles* or *causal* links often go beyond what standard formalisms like *rdf* can express [9]. More complex extensions such as *reification* [58], *blank nodes* [20], *singleton properties* [61], and *rdf-star* [35] introduce support for statements about statements. Consider the sentence: "Federer won the match after breaking Nadal's serve in the final set." This narrative encodes not just the *outcome*, but *temporal* order (after), a key *subevent* (breaking serve), and participant *roles* (Federer as winner, Nadal as opponent). Capturing such structure in a KG requires modeling both events and their relations, such as causation and temporal sequence, across multiple semantic layers.

Despite this added expressiveness, modeling narratives with these syntaxes remains difficult: resulting graphs are often large, complex, and hard to query or reason over directly [4,36]. Embedding methods offer a promising alternative by projecting symbolic structures into continuous vector spaces, facilitating scalable reasoning and prediction [13,90]. Yet, an open question remains: *to what extent can these embeddings preserve the semantics of rich narrative representations?*

While previous work has addressed narrative representation and construction in KGs [29,52,60,63], there remains limited insight into how varying levels of narrative complexity and the syntactic choices used to encode them impact downstream tasks such as embedding-based inference. Building on existing work outlining narrative-specific requirements for KGs [9], we model this variation through a six-layer categorization (*base, properties, subevents, text, roles* and *causal relationships*), incrementally adding semantic depth and syntactic richness. This categorization guides the construction of narrative KGs and the evaluation of semantic and syntactic effects on embedding performance. Our investigation centers on two key research questions:

RQ1 (Semantics): How does increasing the semantic richness of narrative representations affect the performance of KG embeddings?
RQ2 (Syntax): How do different KG syntactic constructs, such as *reification* or *rdf-star*, impact embedding performance?

For each of the research questions, we hypothesize the followings:

RQ1 (Semantics): Increasing semantic richness will improve performance, but gains might diminish as complexity increases, suggesting limits in model capacity to leverage rich narrative features.
RQ2 (Syntax): More complex constructs like *rdf-star* will outperform simpler encodings in scenarios with complex semantics, due to their ability to natively represent structured relationships. However, this benefit may come at the cost of higher computational overhead.

This paper makes the following contributions:

- We introduce a categorization for modeling narratives in KGs, capturing increasing levels of semantic and syntactic complexity;
- We construct a comprehensive suite of narrative KGs across diverse representation strategies and semantic layers;

- To our knowledge, this is the first empirical study to systematically examine the impact of narrative semantics and KG syntactic constructs on embedding performance, addressing a gap in the existing literature.

2 Knowledge Representation Models

We outline several KG representation models that extend *rdf* to support statements about statements. We first recall the standard definition of a KG.

Definition 1 (Knowledge Graph). A knowledge graph ($\mathcal{KG}$) is an *rdf* graph where the nodes represent entities (subjects or objects) and literals (objects), and the edges represent the relationships (predicates) between these entities and literals. Formally, $\mathcal{KG} = \{(s,p,o)|s \in \mathcal{E}, o \in \mathcal{E} \cup \mathcal{L}, p \in \mathcal{R}\}$, where $\mathcal{E}$ is the set of entities (nodes) in the KG, $\mathcal{L}$ is the set of literals in the KG, and $\mathcal{R}$ is the set of predicates (edges) representing relationships in the KG.

To illustrate the differences between different representations, we consider a simple scenario. Roger Federer and Rafael Nadal play a match in which Federer wins and assumes the "happy" role, while Nadal loses and takes the "sad" role. Figure 1 shows how this main statement can be encoded using five syntactic models: *rdf*, *blank node*, *reification*, *singleton property*, and *rdf-star*. Each model provides a distinct mechanism for attaching additional contextual information.

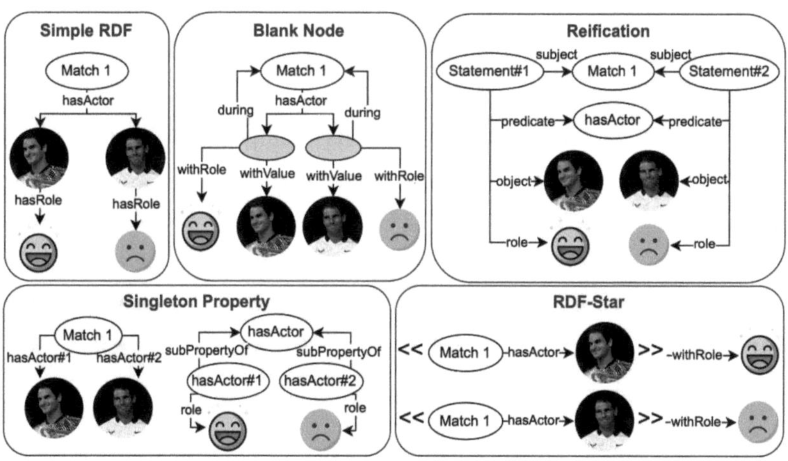

Fig. 1. Examples of existing syntactic representations.

Simple RDF (*rdf*) [20] represents facts as atomic triples (s, p, o), where a single predicate links a subject and object. It is widely used for its simplicity, but lacks built-in mechanisms for attaching metadata to statements.

Blank Nodes (*bn*) [20] are anonymous resources that group related information without global identifiers. While they offer flexibility for modeling composite structures, they can complicate querying and provenance tracking.

Reification (*reification*) [58] creates a statement node that connects to the subject, predicate, and object of a triple using *rdf*'s built-in vocabulary. This allows metadata attachment but increases verbosity and complexity.

Singleton Property (*sp*) [61] generates uniquely identified predicates (e.g., `hasActor#1`) for each triple, allowing metadata annotation.

RDF-Star (*rdf-star*) [35] extends *rdf* by embedding triples as subjects or objects in other triples, offering a compact way to represent metadata without auxiliary nodes or properties.

Table 1 outlines key syntactic properties of each KG representation, including their impact on triples, entities, and properties. We define five qualitative criteria and introduce a scoring system from 1 (low) to 3 (high) to evaluate them. The criteria are: *Modelling* (ease of information encoding), *Queryability* (ease of querying), *Compactness* (graph size efficiency), *Richness* (semantic depth and expressiveness), and *Tooling Support* (availability of practical libraries and tools). Scores are derived from our synthesis of insights in documentation and prior literature [3–5,21,38,40,44,62].

Table 1. Comparison of KG Syntax Constructs. t: triples, e: entities, and p: properties. Blank Nodes include two additional blank nodes.

Syntax	#t	#e	#p	Modelling	Queryability	Compactness	Richness	Support
rdf	4	5	2	★★★	★★★	★★☆	★☆☆	★★★
bn	8	5	4	★★☆	★☆☆	★★☆	★★★	★★☆
reification	8	8	4	★☆☆	★☆☆	★☆☆	★★★	★★☆
sp	6	8	5	★★☆	★☆☆	★★☆	★★★	★★☆
rdf-star	2	5	2	★★★	★★★	★★★	★★★	★☆☆

3 Related Work

We review three key areas relevant to our study: inductive KG embeddings, models designed to capture complex syntactic structures beyond *rdf*, and the impact of KG syntax on embedding performance.

Inductive Knowledge Graph Embeddings. Earlier methods primarily addressed transductive settings, where all entities are seen during training. In contrast, inductive models generalize to unseen entities, making them better suited for narratives with emerging entities and evolving contexts. Therefore, we focus on inductive models in this work and our comparisons. GRAIL [66] is an inductive embedding model that uses graph neural networks to learn relational representations based on entity interactions, enabling generalization to unseen entities but not relations. NBFNet [96] incorporates the Bellman-Ford algorithm for path-based reasoning, A*Net [95] learns a priority function to guide efficient path exploration, RED-GNN [91] applies attention over relational digraphs, and AdaProp [92] introduces adaptive propagation to filter irrelevant entities. More recent work, such as InGram [48] and TRIX [93], extends inductive reasoning to both entities and relations via relation graphs and expressive triple encodings. Universal models like ULTRA [31] and KG-ICL [19] aim for generalization across heterogeneous KGs without retraining, and RMPI [32] enables direct message passing across relations. For a comprehensive taxonomy, see recent survey [51].

Complex KG Embeddings. Recent advances in KG embeddings have moved beyond binary triples to better capture complex semantics [6,43,45,51,65,79]. We focus on three relevant directions: *hyper-relational embeddings* support statements about statements, typically to a single level, while *rdf-star* allows recursive nesting which most models do not yet exploit; *hypergraph embeddings* generalize edges to n-ary relations, enabling constructs such as *bn*; and *text-based embeddings* enrich semantic representation by incorporating textual descriptions of nodes and relations. Many of these models are transductive, yet they offer valuable insights for modeling semantically rich, structurally complex narrative graphs. Table 2 lists, to the best of our knowledge, all existing models that support extended KG representations falling into one of these three categories. Most target single-entity link prediction, though some diverge: RAE [88] performs multi-entity prediction, DHNE [67], HyperGCN [83], and Hyper-SAGNN [89] address multi-class classification, and BLP [22] also supports entity classification and retrieval. We highlight inductive methods in the table due to space constraints. Text-based inductive models include SimKGC [69], StATIK [59], and BLP [22], which leverage pretrained language models to encode textual features. MetaNIR [75] applies meta-learning to hyper-relational inductive prediction, and [1] explores joint modeling of structure and text in hyper-relational settings. In this work, we draw on these approaches to analyze how different syntactic constructs and text-enriched representations affect embedding performance.

Impact of Syntax on Embedding Performance. While *rdf* representations are widely adopted, their syntactic variants pose challenges and trade-offs [39,40]. Recent work has begun to assess how *rdf*, *reification*, *n-ary* relations, or *rdf-star* affect downstream tasks like link prediction. [44] compare several syntaxes across tasks such as querying and graph completion, finding that *rdf-star* and Wikidata formats aid usability, while *reification* performs more consistently in embedding tasks despite its verbosity. Other studies [38] focus on Wikidata, noting the complexity of *sp*, IoT KGs [73] or research suggestions [2]. Comparisons between *rdf* and Property Graphs also show *rdf*'s advantages in query efficiency [3,21] and

Table 2. Overview of methods handling complex semantics, categorized by modeling paradigm: Translational (distance-based), Tensor (bilinear/multilinear), NN (neural network-based), Hyperbolic (non-Euclidean geometry), Transformer (attention-based), Walk (random-walk sampling), VAE (variational autoencoders), and GloVe+CNN (textual embeddings). HR: hyper-relational, HG: hypergraph. †: paper not available, ‡: code not available. inductive, and nested.

Data	Type	Systems
HR	translational	m-TransH [77] ; RAE‡ [88] ; HSimplE, HypE [28]
HR	tensor	GETD [53] ; S2S‡ [23], RAM [54]
HR	NN	DHNE‡ [67] ; NaLP†‡ [34], HyperGCN [83] ; StarE [30], HINGE [64], NeuInfer‡ [33], G-MPNN [82] ; [87], Ali et al. [1], GRAN [71] ; HAHE [56], ShrinkE [81], HyperFormer [41] ; MetaRH [74], sHINGE‡ [55] ; MetaNIR‡ [75]
HR	hyperbolic	HYPER2‡ [85]
HR	transformer	HyNT [18]
HR	walk	RDFStar2Vec [25]
HG	NN	Hyper-SAGNN‡ [89] ; NHP†‡ [84] ; HyConvE‡ [68], RD-MPNN [94], Att-ImpGCN‡ [70], PosKHG‡ [17] ; HJE‡ [50], NestE [80], RHKH‡ [72], SLR†‡ [14], HCNet [42]
HG	tensor	LHP‡ [86]
HG	hyperbolic	H2seqRec [49]
HG	VAE	HeteHG-VAE†‡ [27] ; HyperMLN [16]
Text	GloVe + CNN	DKRL [78]
Text	transformer	BLP [22] (2021) ; SimKGC [69], StATIK [59]

interoperability [4,5]. [26] survey SPARQL query relaxation techniques across various syntaxes, and [12] examine OWL-based event modeling. [24] directly evaluate *reification*, *sp*, and *rdf-star* for link prediction in hyper-relational KGs. Most relevant to our work are [44] and [24]. The former targets consumer use cases, without narrative content or support for *rdf-star* or singleton property embeddings. The latter examine formal models for link prediction in hyper-relational KGs, while we focus on semantically layered narrative KGs and compare diverse embedding approaches, including text-augmented methods.

4 Narrative Semantics in Knowledge Graphs

Narratives are multi-layered constructs that vary in complexity based on their semantic richness and depth. Building on the narrative requirements from [9], we propose a six-level categorization to systematically capture these layers, and *examples* related to the Wimbledon Championship (WC):

1. Base: fundamental elements (e.g. events, actors, locations)
   2006 WC (event), Federer (actor), Wimbledon (location)
2. Properties: simple binary relations between base elements
   (WC, location, Wimbledon)
3. Subevents: complex, recursive event structures
   (2006 WC final, subEventOf, 2006 WC)
4. Text: natural language descriptions providing contextual information
   "Federer wins his fourth consecutive title."
5. Roles: higher-level semantics linking objects
   The roles described in Sect. 2
6. Causal relationships: higher-level semantics between events
   "Their rivalry pushed both players to elevate their games."

We assume all KGs include the "base" layer by default. The remaining five layers can be selectively activated to control the semantic richness of a narrative representation. We formalize this selective activation using a configuration vector η, defined as a tuple of Boolean variables, where each component of η toggles a narrative layer, enabling systematic control over the semantic KG complexity:

$$\eta = (\texttt{prop}, \texttt{subevent}, \texttt{text}, \texttt{role}, \texttt{causation}) \in \{0,1\}^5$$

Levels 1–4 are expressible in standard *rdf*, though level 4's textual literals pose challenges for embedding models. Levels 5 and 6 require higher-order semantics like statement about statement, demanding more expressive syntaxes such as *sp*, *reification*, *bn*, and *rdf-star*. To capture this distinction, we define the set of valid syntactic representations as a function of the configuration vector η:

$$\sigma(\eta) = \begin{cases} \{\textit{rdf, sp, reification, bn, rdf-star}\} & \text{if } \texttt{role} = 1 \text{ or } \texttt{causation} = 1 \\ \{\textit{rdf}\} & \text{otherwise.} \end{cases}$$

To construct KGs, we take as input a semantic configuration, a corresponding syntactic representation, an event, and DBpedia as the input KG. The process unfolds in two stages. First, an intermediate, *rdf* KG is built based on the configuration and event. This involves extracting relevant components based on ChronoGrapher [10]: **(1) base** relations are SEM-centric outgoing links; **(2) properties** are outgoing links from the DBpedia ontology; **(3) subevents** are filtered up to two-hop events surrounding the input; **(4) text** comes from `dbo:abstract` and `dbp:result`; **(5) roles** and **(6) causal** outcomes are obtained via frame-based information extraction from textual sources. In the second stage, this intermediate graph is converted into a target KG according to the specified syntactic representation.

Figure 2 illustrates an example where the selected narrative layers include **subevents** and **causal outcomes**, in addition to the **base** layer. This corresponds to a configuration vector $\eta = (0, 1, 0, 0, 1)$, with syntactic options

$\sigma(\eta) = \{rdf, sp, reification, bn, rdf\text{-}star\}$. We choose *rdf-star* as the target syntax and use the *2006 World Cup Final* as the input event. On the left, the figure highlights how each narrative layer is sourced from different parts of the background KG. The center shows the intermediate graph, which integrates extracted textual information and introduces auxiliary nodes to capture provenance. On the right, the final output KG combines standard and *rdf-star* triples.

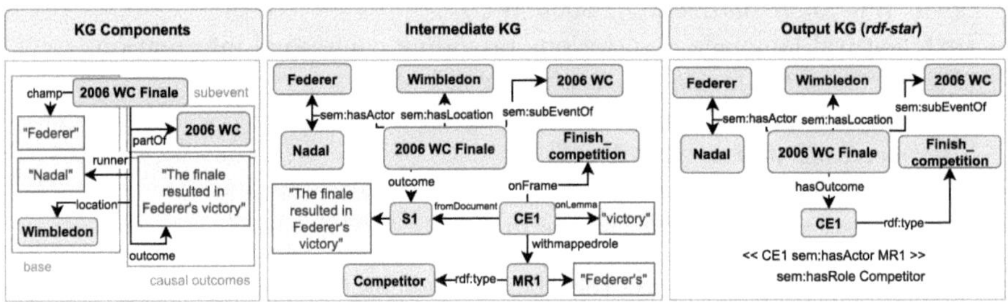

Fig. 2. Example KG construction for the 2006 WC Finale using the configuration $\eta = (0, 1, 0, 1, 1)$ and *rdf-star* syntax.

5 Experimental Setup

We present our experimental protocol, covering the embedding methods used (Sect. 5.1), dataset preparation (Sect. 5.2), and training strategy (Sect. 5.3).

5.1 Embedding Methods

Given the variety of narrative configurations and syntactic encodings, we focus on three representative, openly available embedding methods, each selected for its compatibility with specific features:

- **ULTRA** [31] is a GNN-based model designed for entity-rich graphs, and supports *rdf*, *reification*, and *sp* syntax.
- **SimKGC** [69] incorporates textual descriptions into KG embeddings, and supports *rdf*, *reification*, and *sp* syntax.
- **ILP** [1][1] is designed for handling hyper-relational forms, and is thus suited for *rdf-star* up to depth 1. It also integrates textual descriptions.

We selected SimKGC due to its recent state-of-the-art performance, ILP as the only publicly available method supporting hyper-relational data, and ULTRA for its recency and general-purpose design across heterogeneous KGs. We exclude *bn* encodings and n-ary relationships from the core experiments due

[1] The system in [1] does not have a specific name, so we use this notation hereafter.

to the absence of open-source inductive embedding methods for these formalisms, which we identify as a valuable direction for future work. We evaluate models using the standard link prediction task: given a triple with one missing element, either the tail $(h, r, ?)$ or the head $(?, r, t)$, the model must predict the correct missing entity by ranking all possible candidates.

5.2 Data Preparation

We focus on events classified as *revolutions* in DBpedia [7], as they are complex, multi-layered phenomena involving key actors, causes and consequences, making them suitable for narrative modeling. We extracted 366 entities of type `dbc:yago/Revolution107424109`[2], retaining the 204 (56%) that include both start and end dates. For each revolution and each semantic (see Sect. 4 for the 6 narrative layers) and syntactic (see Sect. 5.1 for the retained models) variant, we build a KG following the method described in Sect. 4, and precompute and store all resulting KG variants.

We apply a time-based split: revolutions are sorted chronologically, with 70% assigned to training, 15% to validation, and 15% to test. For instance, the *French Revolution* (late 18th century) is included in the training set, while the *Arab Spring* (early 21st century) appears in the test set. We ensure no triple leakage across splits and restrict the test set to novel facts not seen in training or validation. This setup reflects real-world inference scenarios, especially in historical or policy contexts where future or ongoing events must be interpreted based only on prior knowledge.

For models requiring contextual inference graphs (ULTRA [31], ILP [1]), we enrich the narrative KGs with external ontological triples and isolate all `rdf:type` predicates within the inference graph. This design emphasizes relational and event-level dynamics (e.g., who did what, when, and why) over type-based classification. We further partition validation and test KGs per predicate: 60% for context (inference graph), 40% for prediction (target graph). For models using text-based inputs (SimKGC [69], ILP [1]), we follow [1] and extract entity and relation descriptions (labels and abstracts) from DBpedia. Table 3 summarizes the average number of statements produced per configuration. On average, *reification* yields 3.6x more statements than *rdf*, compared to 1.5x for *rdf-star* and 1.0x for *sp*.

5.3 Training Strategy and Constraints

We began with pre-experiments using ULTRA and 40 datasets, the only method supporting both zero-shot and fine-tuning setups. Due to the large size of some constructed graphs, we encountered frequent memory issues when processing configurations involving narrative *roles*. A strong correlation (Pearson $\rho = 0.8$, $p << 0.05$) was found between unsuccessful runs and the presence of *roles* in the semantic layer. We conducted our experiments on two Ubuntu machines with

[2] `dbc` is the prefix for http://dbpedia.org/class/.

Table 3. Number of statements for each dataset

prop	*subevent*	*role*	*causation*	*rdf*	*reification*	*sp*	*rdf-star*
0	0	0	0	2,287	–	–	–
0	0	0	1	5,548	8,889	5,925	7,551
0	0	1	0	253,130	615,713	255,082	353,043
0	0	1	1	256,306	622,110	258,259	357,24
0	1	0	0	11,718	–	–	–
0	1	0	1	21,560	43,506	22,177	29,39
0	1	1	0	889,351	3,780,103	891,648	1,450,97
0	1	1	1	899,006	3,811,473	901,304	1,465,40
1	0	0	0	16,949	–	–	–
1	0	0	1	20,210	23,551	20,587	22,21
1	0	1	0	922,681	3,425,791	925,026	1,489,804
1	0	1	1	925,848	3,432,177	928,193	1,493,98
1	1	0	0	67,165	–	–	–
1	1	0	1	77,007	98,953	77,624	84,839
1	1	1	0	2,509,871	20,672,753	2,512,421	5,598,016
1	1	1	1	2,519,516	20,704,111	2,522,066	5,612,425

Table 4. Hyperparameters used for the three embedding methods: ULTRA, SimKGC and ILP. *lr*: learning rate, *bs*: batch size, *bpes*: batches per epoch.

Method	*lr*	*bs*	*epoch*	*bpes*
ULTRA (zero-shot)	–	$\{8\}$	$\{0\}$	–
ULTRA (fine-tune)	–	$\{16, 64\}$	$\{1, 3, 5\}$	$\{100, 1000, 2000, 4000\}$
ULTRA (train)	–	$\{16, 64\}$	$\{5, 10\}$	$\{1000, 2000\}$
SimKGC	$\{1^{-5}, 3^{-5}, 5^{-5}\}$	$\{128, 256, 512, 1024\}$	$\{1, 10\}$	–
ILP	$\{1^{-3}, 2^{-3}, 1^{-4}, 5^{-4}\}$	{192,256,896,960}	$\{1000\}$	–

comparable configurations, each equipped with 40 CPU cores and 314376GiB of RAM. The first machine has two GTX 1080Ti GPUs (11GiB), and the second has an A40 (46GiB) and an RTX A6000 (49GiB). Preliminary experiments were run on the second machine. Consequently, we limited the evaluation to configurations without *roles*, resulting in 16 datasets for SimKGC, and 4 for ILP.

For all methods, we adhered to the original parameter and hyperparameter settings from the respective publications. In cases with excessive parameters, we selected the best-performing models based on the reported results. For SimKGC, we used the *bert-based-uncased* pretrained model[3] as in the original paper [69], and for ILP, we focused on the only inductive model available, StarE [30].

Table 4 summarizes the hyperparameter configurations used for each method. For ULTRA, both zero-shot and fine-tuning experiments were conducted using the existing pretrained variants: *ultra_3g*, *ultra_4g*, and *ultra_50g*. ILP models

[3] https://huggingface.co/google-bert/bert-base-uncased.

were trained with embedding dimensions of $\{160, 192, 224\}$, with a maximum of 1000 epochs and early stopping based on validation performance.

6 Results

For RQ1 on the impact of narrative semantic richness on embedding performance, we analyze model performance across narrative layers of increasing complexity (Sect. 6.1). For RQ2 on the impact of syntax on embedding performance, we compare results across *rdf*, *reification*, *sp*, and *rdf-star* (Sect. 6.2).

6.1 Impact of Semantic Richness on Embedding Performance (RQ1)

ULTRA. ULTRA is the only method evaluated across all semantic layers, including the most complex narrative elements, such as *roles*. This is possible because ULTRA supports both fine-tuning and zero-shot inference, making it more memory-efficient compared to other models that require full training.

We ran a total of 3,320 ULTRA experiments. Of these, 1,226 runs (37%) completed successfully without exceeding memory limits. Among the successful runs: 106 (8.6%) used zero-shot inference, 1,008 (82.2%) involved fine-tuning, and 112 (9.1%) were trained from scratch. Only 59 of the successful runs included the *roles* layer, all of which used zero-shot inference. We observed a strong positive correlation between the inclusion of properties and performance ($\rho_{\text{MRR}} = 0.78$, $p << 0.05$), suggesting that binary simple relations help structure the narrative and benefit embedding learning. Please note that the properties refer to triples commonly used in large-scale domain embeddings, such as those from DBpedia, which typically yield strong performance. In contrast, more complex elements such as *roles* ($\rho_{\text{MRR}} = -0.30$, $p << 0.05$), *sub-events* ($\rho_{\text{MRR}} = --0.23$, $p << 0.05$), and *causal links* ($\rho_{\text{MRR}} = -0.09$, $p < 0.05$) were negatively correlated with performance, indicating the challenges of embedding semantically dense and structurally complex graphs.

Table 5 presents the best evaluation metrics achieved by ULTRA. Each row represents a unique combination of narrative layers, with relative performance changes (δ) compared to the simplest baseline (i.e., base elements only). The table highlights that adding *properties* consistently results in large performance gains, while including *roles* or *causation* often degrades results, especially when combined with other layers.

SimKGC. We ran 8 configurations and 78 experiments in total. *Subevents* showed a consistent and statistically significant positive correlation with all evaluation metrics (e.g., MRR: $\rho = 0.50$, Hits@1: $\rho = 0.48$, all with $p << 0.05$), indicating their positive impact on ranking performance in SimKGC. In contrast, *properties* and *causation* had negligible or inconsistent effects, with correlations near zero and non-significant p-values across metrics.

Table 5. Best metrics for each dataset run with ULTRA

prop	subevent	role	causation	MRR↑	δMRR	H@1↑	δH@1	H@3↑	δH@3	H@10↑	δH@10
0	0	0	0	0.23	0.0	0.2	0.0	0.2	0.0	0.3	0.0
0	0	0	1	0.25	0.02	0.22	0.02	0.24	0.04	0.3	−0.0
0	0	1	0	0.24	0.01	0.22	0.02	0.24	0.04	0.27	−0.03
0	0	1	1	0.24	0.0	0.22	0.02	0.24	0.04	0.27	−0.03
0	1	0	0	0.22	−0.01	0.18	−0.02	0.22	0.02	0.27	−0.03
0	1	0	1	0.24	0.01	0.21	0.01	0.24	0.04	0.28	−0.02
0	1	1	0	0.05	**−0.18**	0.03	**−0.17**	0.05	**−0.15**	0.08	**−0.22**
0	1	1	1	0.05	**−0.18**	0.03	**−0.17**	0.05	**−0.15**	0.08	**−0.22**
1	0	0	0	0.7	**0.47**	0.67	**0.47**	0.73	**0.53**	0.73	**0.43**
1	0	0	1	0.31	0.08	0.28	0.08	0.31	**0.11**	0.36	0.06
1	0	1	0	0.25	0.02	0.24	0.04	0.25	0.05	0.27	−0.03
1	0	1	1	0.25	0.02	0.24	0.04	0.25	0.05	0.27	−0.03
1	1	0	0	0.68	**0.45**	0.65	**0.45**	0.71	**0.51**	0.74	**0.44**
1	1	0	1	0.35	**0.12**	0.3	**0.1**	0.37	**0.17**	0.45	**0.15**
1	1	1	0	0.05	**−0.19**	0.03	**−0.17**	0.05	**-0.15**	0.07	**−0.23**
1	1	1	1	0.05	**−0.19**	0.03	**−0.17**	0.05	**-0.15**	0.07	**−0.23**

Table 6 shows the best scores per configuration and their improvements over the base KG. Configurations with *subevents*, especially when paired with *properties*, achieved the highest gains. In contrast, including all narrative layers led to performance drops, suggesting that excessive complexity may introduce noise that SimKGC's contrastive learning struggles to manage. Overall, *subevents* proved most beneficial, while *properties* and *causation* had limited impact.

ILP. We focused on configurations involving *causation*, as this narrative layer produces nested statements. While *roles* also introduce nesting, they were excluded based on preliminary experiments. As a result, we only consider configurations with causation and ran 192 experiments in total. Both *properties* and *subevents* contributed meaningfully to model performance. *Properties* correlated strongly with improvements across all metrics, including Hits@1 ($\rho = 0.72$), MRR ($\rho = 0.66$), and AMR ($\rho = -0.64$, all $p < 0.05$). *Subevents* notably improved AMR ($\rho = -0.33$, $p < 0.05$). The Adjusted Mean Rank (AMR) [8] is a recently proposed metric that contextualizes mean rank by comparing it to the expected rank of a random scoring model, that was computed with ILP.

These findings highlight that *properties* and *subevents* help enhancing performance in hyper-relational settings. Table 7 presents the top-performing configurations, with the best overall results (MRR = 0.32, Hits@10 = 0.48) achieved when both *properties* and *subevents* were included.

Table 6. Best metrics for each dataset run with SimKGC

prop	subevent	role	causation	MRR↑	δMRR	H@1↑	δH@1	H@3↑	δH@3	H@10↑	δH@10
0	0	0	0	0.43	0.0	0.34	0.0	0.47	0.0	0.67	0.0
0	0	0	1	0.46	0.03	0.35	0.01	0.52	0.05	0.67	0.01
0	1	0	0	0.45	0.01	0.32	-0.02	0.51	0.04	0.72	0.06
0	1	0	1	0.42	-0.02	0.31	-0.03	0.47	-0.0	0.63	-0.03
1	0	0	0	0.24	-0.2	0.15	**-0.19**	0.25	**-0.22**	0.43	**-0.24**
1	0	0	1	0.32	**-0.12**	0.25	-0.09	0.35	**-0.12**	0.46	**-0.21**
1	1	0	0	0.34	-0.09	0.26	-0.08	0.37	**-0.1**	0.52	**-0.15**
1	1	0	1	0.33	-0.1	0.24	-0.1	0.36	**-0.11**	0.51	**-0.15**

Table 7. Best metrics for each dataset run with ILP

prop	subevent	role	causation	AMR↓	MRR↑	H@1↑	H@3↑	H@10↑
0	0	0	1	0.09	0.23	0.14	0.27	0.4
0	1	0	1	0.07	0.25	0.15	0.29	0.43
1	0	0	1	0.04	0.29	0.19	0.34	0.46
1	1	0	1	0.03	0.32	0.24	0.34	0.48

Lastly, to provide a comparative overview of model behavior across shared configurations, Table 8 reports MRR scores for ULTRA, SimKGC, and ILP over the common subset of narrative configurations. It is a standard metric in KG embedding that reflects how highly the correct entity is ranked, providing a robust summary of model performance. The results highlight complementary strengths: ULTRA benefits most from properties (e.g., 0.70 MRR with properties alone, v.s. 0.24 for SimKGC), while SimKGC performs better with *causation* and *subevent* (e.g., 0.46 MRR with causation alone, v.s 0.25 for ULTRA). ILP, evaluated only on configurations involving *causation*, generally underperforms compared to other models. However, its performance improves when both *properties* and *subevents* are included, reaching a peak MRR of 0.32.

To answer RQ1, our findings show that semantic narrative enrichment has a measurable but uneven impact on embedding performance. *Properties* improved results in ULTRA and ILP, but had little effect in SimKGC. *Subevents* boosted performance in text-based models (SimKGC and ILP) but reduced it in ULTRA. *Roles* consistently degraded performance (based on ULTRA) and were excluded from other models for feasibility. *Causation* showed no consistent effect. Aggregating top-performing configurations, we found a significant positive correlation between textual inputs and performance (e.g., MRR: $\rho = 0.45$, $p < 0.05$), indicating that textual enrichment benefits models that can leverage it. Still, overall scores remain modest, underscoring the difficulty of encoding complex narrative semantics in current embedding frameworks.

Table 8. MRR↑ metrics comparison across three methods

prop	subevent	role	causation	ULTRA	SimKGC	ILP
0	0	0	0	0.23	0.43	–
0	0	0	1	0.25	0.46	0.23
0	1	0	0	0.22	0.45	–
0	1	0	1	0.24	0.42	0.25
1	0	0	0	0.7	0.24	-
1	0	0	1	0.31	0.32	0.29
1	1	0	0	0.68	0.34	–
1	1	0	1	0.35	0.33	0.32

6.2 Impact of Syntax on Embedding Performance (RQ2)

We evaluated how syntactic representation affects embedding quality, focusing on configurations involving *roles* or *causation*, features expressed across multiple syntactic forms. For each method and configuration, we retained only the best-performing variant (based on MRR) to ensure fair comparison.

Table 9 reports the average performance across four syntactic strategies. *reification* and *rdf-star* achieved the highest scores across metrics. A Kruskal-Wallis test [46] confirmed a significant effect of syntax on Hits@1 ($\chi^2 = 8.51, p = 0.037$). Follow-up pairwise Mann-Whitney U tests [57] revealed that *reification* outperformed both the *sp* and *rdf* syntaxes with significance prior to Holm-Bonferroni correction [76], but these differences did not remain statistically significant after correction. No other comparisons showed significant differences.

Table 9. Averaged metrics for the different syntaxes

syntax	MRR↑	H@1↑	H@3↑	H@10↑
reification	0.28	0.25	0.29	0.34
rdf-star	0.27	0.18	0.31	0.44
rdf	0.18	0.13	0.19	0.27
sp	0.17	0.12	0.18	0.26

To answer RQ2, we find that the choice of syntactic representation does influence embedding performance, particularly for configurations involving *roles* or *causation*. Surprisingly, in terms of intuition, *reification* yielded the highest average performance across half of the metrics, despite its known verbosity and structural complexity. We hypothesize that models may mitigate this syntactic overhead by leveraging contextual patterns and additional features within the expanded structure. *rdf-star* also performed well, suggesting that more structured encodings help models capture complex relationships more effectively.

However, the overall differences between syntaxes were moderate, indicating that while syntax plays a role, its impact is likely mediated by model architecture and input configuration.

7 Discussion

Our findings offer valuable insights into how narrative complexity and KG syntax affect embedding performance, but also point to several avenues for future work. While we focused on revolutions as a narrative domain, expanding the KG construction pipeline to other event types or external datasets could strengthen the generalizability of the results. Although we adopted hyperparameters from prior work, our KG configurations differ from standard benchmarks, which may introduce biases or favor certain models. The use of *properties* introduces challenges in controlling the information content, and both *roles* and *causation* were extracted from the same textual sources, raising potential concerns about data leakage. Moreover, both SimKGC and ILP rely on textual features, which limits their applicability in settings with noisy or absent text. Lastly, uneven KG completeness may affect the quality of semantic layers, particularly for higher-order constructs.

Another consideration is that performance metrics are computed over test sets that vary across configurations due to differences in KG construction. While trends across methods and representations are informative, the metrics do not reflect performance on a fixed set of triples, making it difficult to isolate the impact of semantic or syntactic variations based solely on numerical scores. To address this, future work could explore the use of downstream tasks, such as question-answering with large language models, which may help decouple the effects of semantic and syntactic changes from dataset construction, providing a more flexible evaluation of embedding quality.

8 Conclusion

We examined the impact of semantic narrative levels and syntactic representations on three inductive KG embedding methods. We found that certain semantic dimensions, particularly *properties* and *subevents*, can enhance performance, though their effects depend on the model. For example, *subevents* improved results in text-based models but hindered performance in ULTRA, suggesting interactions with textual context. *Roles* consistently reduced performance, while *causation* showed no clear advantages. In terms of syntax, while hyper-relational *rdf-star* offers flexibility, *reification*, despite its verbosity, achieved the best performance. We hypothesize this is due to advanced models compensating with richer contextual encodings.

Supplemental Material Statement: Source code for KG construction and data preparation[4], and extended systems[5] are available on Github. Sample KGs are included in the main repository and all the KGs are available on Zenodo[6].

Acknowledgements. We thank Daniel Daza for fruitful discussions, and Giulio Prevedello for valuable insights and numerous conversations on statistical testing and problem formulation. We are also grateful to the anonymous reviewers for their constructive and insightful feedback.

References

1. Ali, M., et al.: Improving inductive link prediction using hyper-relational facts. In: Hotho, A., et al. (eds.) ISWC 2021. LNCS, vol. 12922, pp. 74–92. Springer, Cham (2021). https://doi.org/10.1007/978-3-030-88361-4_5
2. Alivanistos, D., van der Bijl, S., Cochez, M., van Harmelen, F.: The Effect of Knowledge Graph Schema on Classifying Future Research Suggestions. In: International Workshop on Natural Scientific Language Processing and Research Knowledge Graphs. pp. 149–170. Springer Nature Switzerland Cham (2024)
3. Alocci, D., Mariethoz, J., Horlacher, O., Bolleman, J.T., Campbell, M.P., Lisacek, F.: Property graph vs RDF triple store: a comparison on glycan substructure search. PLoS One **10**(12) (2015)
4. Angles, R., Thakkar, H., Tomaszuk, D.: RDF and property graphs interoperability: status and issues. In: Alberto Mendelzon Workshop on Foundations of Data Management, vol. 2369, pp. 1–11 (2019)
5. Angles, R., Thakkar, H., Tomaszuk, D.: Mapping RDF databases to property graph databases. IEEE Access **8**, 86091–86110 (2020)
6. Antelmi, A., Cordasco, G., Polato, M., Scarano, V., Spagnuolo, C., Yang, D.: A survey on hypergraph representation learning. ACM Comput. Surv. **56**(1), 1–38 (2023)
7. Auer, S., Bizer, C., Kobilarov, G., Lehmann, J., Cyganiak, R., Ives, Z.: DBpedia: a nucleus for a web of open data. In: Aberer, K., et al. (eds.) ASWC/ISWC -2007. LNCS, vol. 4825, pp. 722–735. Springer, Heidelberg (2007). https://doi.org/10.1007/978-3-540-76298-0_52
8. Berrendorf, M., Faerman, E., Vermue, L., Tresp, V.: Interpretable and Fair Comparison of Link Prediction or Entity Alignment Methods. In: International Joint Conference on Web Intelligence and Intelligent Agent Technology, pp. 371–374. Institute of Electrical and Electronics Engineers (2020)
9. Blin, I., ten Teije, A., van Harmelen, F., Tiddi, I.: Structured representations for narratives. In: International Conference on Knowledge Engineering and Knowledge Management, pp. 133–154. Springer (2024)
10. Blin, I., Tiddi, I., van Trijp, R., ten Teije, A.: ChronoGrapher: Event-centric Knowledge Graph Construction via Informed Graph Traversal. SWJ (2025)
11. Bruner, J.: The narrative construction of reality. Crit. Inq. **18**(1), 1–21 (1991)

[4] KG construction and data preparation.
[5] ULTRA, SimKGC and ILP.
[6] https://zenodo.org/records/16094768.

12. Butkienė, R., Šukys, A., Ablonskis, L., Butleris, R.: Influence of event specialization strategy on some aspects of natural language querying interfaces to ontologies. IEEE Access (2024)
13. Cao, J., Fang, J., Meng, Z., Liang, S.: Knowledge graph embedding: a survey from the perspective of representation spaces. ACM Comput. Surv. **56**(6), 1–42 (2024)
14. Chai, L., Tu, L., Wang, X., Su, Q.: Hypergraph modeling and hypergraph multi-view attention neural network for link prediction. Pattern Recogn. **149**, 110292 (2024)
15. Chaudhri, V., et al.: Knowledge graphs: introduction, history and perspectives. AI Mag. **43**(1), 17–29 (2022)
16. Chen, Z., Wang, X., Wang, C., Li, J.: Explainable link prediction in knowledge hypergraphs. In: CIKM, pp. 262–271 (2022)
17. Chen, Z., Wang, X., Wang, C., Li, Z.: PosKHG: a position-aware knowledge hypergraph model for link prediction. Data Sci. Eng. **8**(2), 135–145 (2023). https://doi.org/10.1007/s41019-023-00214-x
18. Chung, C., Lee, J., Whang, J.J.: Representation learning on hyper-relational and numeric knowledge graphs with transformers. In: KDD. pp. 310–322 (2023)
19. Cui, Y., Sun, Z., Hu, W.: A prompt-based knowledge graph foundation model for universal in-context reasoning. NeurIPS **37**, 7095–7124 (2024)
20. Cyganiak, R., Wood, D., Lanthaler, M., Klyne, G., Carroll, J.J., McBride, B.: RDF 1.1 Concepts and Abstract Syntax. W3C Recommendation (Feb 2014). https://www.w3.org/TR/rdf11-concepts/
21. Das, S., Srinivasan, J., Perry, M., Chong, E.I., Banerjee, J.: A tale of two graphs: property graphs as RDF in oracle. In: Extending Database Technology, pp. 762–773 (2014)
22. Daza, D., Cochez, M., Groth, P.: Inductive entity representations from text via link prediction. In: WWW, pp. 798–808 (2021)
23. Di, S., Yao, Q., Chen, L.: Searching to Sparsify Tensor Decomposition for N-ary Relational Data. In: WWW., pp. 4043–4054 (2021)
24. Egami, S., Matsushita, K., Ugai, T., Fukuda, K.: Comparison of Metadata Representation Models for Knowledge Graph Embeddings. arXiv preprint arXiv:2503.21804 (2025)
25. Egami, S., Ugai, T., Oota, M., Matsushita, K., Kawamura, T., Kozaki, K., Fukuda, K.: RDF-star2Vec: RDF-star graph embeddings for data mining. IEEE Access **11**, 142030–142042 (2023)
26. Fakih, G., Serrano-Alvarado, P.: A Survey on sparql query relaxation under the lens of RDF reification. SWJ **15**(6), 2507–2554 (2024)
27. Fan, H., et al.: Heterogeneous hypergraph variational autoencoder for link prediction. IEEE Trans. Pattern Anal. Mach. Intell. **44**(8), 4125–4138 (2021)
28. Fatemi, B., Taslakian, P., Vazquez, D., Poole, D.: Knowledge hypergraphs: prediction beyond binary relations. In: IJCAI, pp. 2191–2197 (2021)
29. Filtz, E., Navas-Loro, M., Santos, C., Polleres, A., Kirrane, S.: Events matter: extraction of events from court decisions. In: Legal Knowledge and Information Systems, pp. 33–42. IOS Press (2020)
30. Galkin, M., Trivedi, P., Maheshwari, G., Usbeck, R., Lehmann, J.: Message passing for hyper-relational knowledge graphs. In: EMNLP, pp. 7346–7359 (2020)
31. Galkin, M., Yuan, X., Mostafa, H., Tang, J., Zhu, Z.: Towards foundation models for knowledge graph reasoning. In: New Frontiers in Graph Learning @NeurIPS (2023)

32. Geng, Y., et al.: Relational message passing for fully inductive knowledge graph completion. In: International Conference on Data Engineering, pp. 1221–1233. Institute of Electrical and Electronics Engineers (2023)
33. Guan, S., Jin, X., Guo, J., Wang, Y., Cheng, X.: NeuInfer: knowledge inference on N-ary Facts. In: ACL, pp. 6141–6151 (2020)
34. Guan, S., Jin, X., Wang, Y., Cheng, X.: Link Prediction on N-ary relational data based on relatedness evaluation. In: WWW, pp. 583–593 (2019)
35. Hartig, O.: Foundations of RDF∗ and SPARQL∗ (an alternative approach to statement-level metadata in RDF). In: Alberto Mendelzon International Workshop on Foundations of Data Management and the Web, vol. 1912. Juan Reutter, Divesh Srivastava (2017)
36. Hartig, O., Thompson, B.: Foundations of an Alternative Approach to Reification in RDF. arXiv preprint arXiv:1406.3399 (2014)
37. Heist, N., Hertling, S., Ringler, D., Paulheim, H.: Knowledge Graphs on the Web - an Overview. Knowledge Graphs for eXplainable Artificial Intelligence: Foundations, Applications and Challenges pp. 3–22 (2020)
38. Hernández, D., Hogan, A., Krötzsch, M.: Reifying RDF: what works well with wikidata? In: International Workshop on Scalable Semantic Web Knowledge Base Systems @ISWC, vol. 457, pp. 32–47 (2015)
39. Hogan, A.: The semantic web: two decades on. SWJ **11**(1), 169–185 (2020)
40. Hogan, A., et al.: Knowledge graphs. ACM Comput. Surv. **54**(4), 1–37 (2022)
41. Hu, Z., Gutiérrez-Basulto, V., Xiang, Z., Li, R., Pan, J.Z.: HyperFormer: enhancing entity and relation interaction for hyper-relational knowledge graph completion. In: CIKM, pp. 803–812 (2023)
42. Huang, X., Orth, M.R., Barcelo, P., Bronstein, M.M., Ceylan, I.I.: Link prediction with relational hypergraphs. Trans. Mach. Learn. Res. (2024)
43. Hubert, N., Monnin, P., Paulheim, H.: Beyond Transduction: A Survey on Inductive, Few Shot, and Zero Shot Link Prediction in Knowledge Graphs. arXiv preprint arXiv:2312.04997 (2023)
44. Iglesias-Molina, A., Ahrabian, K., Ilievski, F., Pujara, J., Corcho, O.: Comparison of knowledge graph representations for consumer scenarios. In: ISWC, pp. 271–289. Springer (2023). https://doi.org/10.1007/978-3-031-47240-4_15
45. Kim, S., Lee, S.Y., Gao, Y., Antelmi, A., Polato, M., Shin, K.: A survey on hypergraph neural networks: an in-depth and step-by-step guide. In: KDD, pp. 6534–6544 (2024)
46. Kruskal, W.H., Wallis, W.A.: Use of Ranks in One-Criterion Variance Analysis. J. Am. Statist. Assoc., 583–621 (1952)
47. Lecue, F.: On the role of knowledge graphs in explainable AI. SWJ **11**(1), 41–51 (2020)
48. Lee, J., Chung, C., Whang, J.J.: InGram: inductive knowledge graph embedding via relation graphs. In: ICML, pp. 18796–18809. PMLR (2023)
49. Li, Y., et al.: Hyperbolic hypergraphs for sequential recommendation. In: CIKM, pp. 988–997 (2021)
50. Li, Z., Wang, C., Wang, X., Chen, Z., Li, J.: HJE: joint convolutional representation learning for knowledge hypergraph completion. IEEE Trans. Knowl. Data Eng. **36**(8), 3879–3892 (2024)
51. Liang, X., Si, G., Li, J., Tian, P., An, Z., Zhou, F.: A survey of inductive knowledge graph completion. Neural Comput. Appl. **36**(8), 3837–3858 (2024)
52. Liu, X., et al.: PatientEG Dataset: Bringing Event Graph Model with Temporal Relations to Electronic Medical Records. arXiv preprint arXiv:1812.09905 (2018)

53. Liu, Y., Yao, Q., Li, Y.: Generalizing tensor decomposition for N-ary relational knowledge bases. In: WWW, pp. 1104–1114 (2020)
54. Liu, Y., Yao, Q., Li, Y.: Role-aware modeling for N-ary relational knowledge bases. In: WWW, pp. 2660–2671 (2021)
55. Lu, Y., Yang, D., Wang, P., Rosso, P., Cudre-Mauroux, P.: Schema-aware hyper-relational knowledge graph embeddings for link prediction. IEEE Trans. Knowl. Data Eng. **36**(6), 2614–2628 (2023)
56. Luo, H., et al.: HAHE: hierarchical attention for hyper-relational knowledge graphs in global and local level. In: ACL (Long Papers), pp. 8095–8107 (2023)
57. Mann, H.B., Whitney, D.R.: On a test of whether one of two random variables is stochastically larger than the other. Annals Math. Statist. 50–60 (1947)
58. Manola, F., Miller, E.: RDF Primer: W3c Recommendation. Decision Support Systems (2004)
59. Markowitz, E., Balasubramanian, K., Mirtaheri, M., Annavaram, M., Galstyan, A., Ver Steeg, G.: StATIK: structure and text for inductive knowledge graph completion. In: Carpuat, M., de Marneffe, M.C., Meza Ruiz, I.V. (eds.) Findings of NAACL, pp. 604–615. Association for Computational Linguistics, Seattle, United States (Jul (2022). https://doi.org/10.1007/s00521-023-09286-2
60. Meroño-Peñuela, A., et al.: Semantic technologies for historical research: a survey. SWJ **6**(6), 539–564 (2015)
61. Nguyen, V., Bodenreider, O., Sheth, A.: Don't like RDF reification? making statements about statements using singleton property. In: WWW, pp. 759–770 (2014)
62. Ontotext: What Is RDF-star? (2025). https://www.ontotext.com/knowledgehub/fundamentals/what-is-rdf-star/
63. Rospocher, M., et al.: building event-centric knowledge graphs from news. JWS **37**, 132–151 (2016)
64. Rosso, P., Yang, D., Cudré-Mauroux, P.: Beyond triplets: hyper-relational knowledge graph embedding for link prediction. In: WWW, pp. 1885–1896 (2020)
65. Sardina, J., Kelleher, J.D., O'Sullivan, D.: A Survey on Knowledge Graph Structure and Knowledge Graph Embeddings. arXiv preprint arXiv:2412.10092 (2024)
66. Teru, K., Denis, E., Hamilton, W.: Inductive relation prediction by subgraph reasoning. In: ICML, pp. 9448–9457. PMLR (2020)
67. Tu, K., Cui, P., Wang, X., Wang, F., Zhu, W.: Structural deep embedding for hyper-networks. In: AAAI, vol. 32 (2018)
68. Wang, C., Wang, X., Li, Z., Chen, Z., Li, J.: HyConvE: a novel embedding model for knowledge hypergraph link prediction with convolutional neural networks. In: WWW, pp. 188–198 (2023)
69. Wang, L., Zhao, W., Wei, Z., Liu, J.: SimKGC: simple contrastive knowledge graph completion with pre-trained language models. In: ACL (Long Papers).,pp. 4281–4294. Association for Computational Linguistics (May 2022)
70. Wang, P., Chen, J., Su, L., Wang, Z.: N-ary relation prediction based on knowledge graphs with important entity detection. Expert Syst. Appl. **221**, 119755 (2023)
71. Wang, Q., Wang, H., Lyu, Y., Zhu, Y.: Link prediction on n-ary relational facts: a graph-based approach. in: findings of acl, pp. 396–407 (2021)
72. Wang, Y., He, J., Wang, H.: RHKH: relational hypergraph neural network for link prediction on N-ary knowledge hypergraph. In: International Conference on Multimedia, pp. 8759–8767 (2024)
73. van der Weerdt, R., de Boer, V., Daniele, L., Siebes, R., van Harmelen, F.: Representation Learning on IoT Knowledge Graphs. In: Conference on Metadata and Semantics Research, pp. 44–57. Springer (2024). https://doi.org/10.1007/978-3-031-81974-2_4

74. Wei, J., Guan, S., Jin, X., Guo, J., Cheng, X.: Few-shot link prediction on hyper-relational facts. In: LREC-COLING, pp. 7196–7207 (2024)
75. Wei, J., Guan, S., Jin, X., Guo, J., Cheng, X.: Inductive link prediction in N-ary knowledge graphs. In: Rambow, O., Wanner, L., Apidianaki, M., Al-Khalifa, H., Eugenio, B.D., Schockaert, S. (eds.) COLING, pp. 8885–8896. Association for Computational Linguistics, Abu Dhabi, UAE (Jan 2025). https://aclanthology.org/2025.coling-main.595/
76. Weisstein, E.W.: Bonferroni Correction (2004). https://mathworld.wolfram.com/BonferroniCorrection.html
77. Wen, J., Li, J., Mao, Y., Chen, S., Zhang, R.: On the representation and embedding of knowledge bases beyond binary relations. In: IJCAI, pp. 1300–1307 (2016)
78. Xie, R., Liu, Z., Jia, J., Luan, H., Sun, M.: Representation learning of knowledge graphs with entity descriptions. In: AAAI, vol. 30 (2016)
79. Xiong, B., Nayyeri, M., Daza, D., Cochez, M.: Reasoning beyond triples: recent advances in knowledge graph embeddings. In: CIKM, pp. 5228–5231 (2023)
80. Xiong, B., Nayyeri, M., Luo, L., Wang, Z., Pan, S., Staab, S.: NestE: modeling nested relational structures for knowledge graph reasoning. In: AAAI, vol. 38, pp. 9205–9213 (2024)
81. Xiong, B., Nayyeri, M., Pan, S., Staab, S.: Shrinking embeddings for hyper-relational knowledge graphs. In: ACL (Long Papers), pp. 13306–13320 (2023)
82. Yadati, N.: Neural message passing for multi-relational ordered and recursive hypergraphs. NeurIPS **33**, 3275–3289 (2020)
83. Yadati, N., Nimishakavi, M., Yadav, P., Nitin, V., Louis, A., Talukdar, P.: HyperGCN: a new method of training graph convolutional networks on hypergraphs. NeurIPS **32** (2019)
84. Yadati, N., Nitin, V., Nimishakavi, M., Yadav, P., Louis, A., Talukdar, P.: NHP: neural hypergraph link prediction. In: CIKM, pp. 1705–1714 (2020)
85. Yan, S., Zhang, Z., Sun, X., Xu, G., Jin, L., Li, S.: HYPER2: Hyperbolic embedding for hyper-relational link prediction. Neurocomputing **492**, 440–451 (2022)
86. Yang, Y., Li, X., Guan, Y., Wang, H., Kong, C., Jiang, J.: LHP: logical hypergraph link prediction. Expert Syst. Appl. **222**, 119842 (2023)
87. Yu, D., Yang, Y.: Improving Hyper-Relational Knowledge Graph Completion. arXiv preprint arXiv:2104.08167 (2021)
88. Zhang, R., Li, J., Mei, J., Mao, Y.: Scalable instance reconstruction in knowledge bases via relatedness affiliated embedding. In: WWW, pp. 1185–1194 (2018)
89. Zhang, R., Zou, Y., Ma, J.: Hyper-SAGNN: a self-attention based graph neural network for hypergraphs. In: ICLR (2019)
90. Zhang, W., Chen, J., Li, J., Xu, Z., Pan, J.Z., Chen, H.: Knowledge graph reasoning with logics and embeddings: survey and perspective. In: International Conference on Knowledge Graph, pp. 492–499. Institute of Electrical and Electronics Engineers (2024)
91. Zhang, Y., Yao, Q.: Knowledge graph reasoning with relational digraph. In: WWW, pp. 912–924 (2022)
92. Zhang, Y., Zhou, Z., Yao, Q., Chu, X., Han, B.: AdaProp: learning adaptive propagation for graph neural network based knowledge graph reasoning. In: KDD, pp. 3446–3457 (2023)
93. Zhang, Y., Bevilacqua, B., Galkin, M., Ribeiro, B.: TRIX: a more expressive model for zero-shot domain transfer in knowledge graphs. In: Learning on Graphs Conference (2025)
94. Zhou, X., Hui, B., Zeira, I., Wu, H., Tian, L.: Dynamic relation learning for link prediction in knowledge hypergraphs. Appl. Intell. **53**(22), 26580–26591 (2023)

95. Zhu, Z., et al.: A*Net: a scalable path-based reasoning approach for knowledge graphs. NeurIPS **36**, 59323–59336 (2023)
96. Zhu, Z., Zhang, Z., Xhonneux, L.P., Tang, J.: Neural bellman-ford networks: a general graph neural network framework for link prediction. NeurIPS **34**, 29476–29490 (2021)

Large Language Models Assisting Ontology Evaluation

Anna Sofia Lippolis[1,2(✉)], Mohammad Javad Saeedizade[3(✉)], Robin Keskisärkkä[3], Aldo Gangemi[1,2], Eva Blomqvist[3], and Andrea Giovanni Nuzzolese[2]

[1] University of Bologna, Bologna, Italy
{annasofia.lippolis2,aldo.gangemi}@unibo.it
[2] ISTC-CNR, Bologna, Italy
andrea.nuzzolese@cnr.it
[3] Linköping University, Stockholm, Sweden
{javad.saeedizade,robin.keskisarkka,eva.blomqvist}@liu.se

Abstract. Ontology evaluation through functional requirements—such as testing via competency question (CQ) verification—is a well-established yet costly, labour-intensive, and error-prone endeavour, even for ontology engineering experts. In this work, we introduce **OE-Assist**, a novel framework designed to assist ontology evaluation through automated and semi-automated CQ verification. By presenting and leveraging a dataset of 1,393 CQs paired with corresponding ontologies and ontology stories, our contributions present, to our knowledge, the first systematic investigation into large language model (LLM)-assisted ontology evaluation, and include: (i) evaluating the effectiveness of a LLM-based approach for automatically performing CQ verification against a manually created gold standard, and (ii) developing and assessing an LLM-powered framework to assist CQ verification with Protégé, by providing suggestions. We found that *automated* LLM-based evaluation with o1-preview and o3-mini perform at a similar level to the average user's performance. Through a user study on the framework with 19 knowledge engineers from eight international institutions, we also show that LLMs can assist *manual* CQ verification and improve user accuracy, especially when suggestions are correct. Additionally, participants reported a marked decrease in perceived task difficulty. However, we also observed a reduction in human performance when the LLM provided incorrect guidance, showing a critical trade-off between efficiency and accuracy in assisted ontology evaluation.

Keywords: Large Language Models · Ontology Evaluation · Ontology Engineering

A. S. Lippolis and M. J. Saeedizade—Equal contribution.

D. Garijo et al. (Eds.): ISWC 2025, LNCS 16140, pp. 502–520, 2026.
https://doi.org/10.1007/978-3-032-09527-5_27

1 Introduction

Competency questions [18] (CQs), explicit questions an ontology should be able to answer, have long been considered essential functional requirements in the ontology engineering lifecycle, especially in iterative ontology development frameworks such as eXtreme Design [25]. Functional ontology testing through CQ verification, e.g., by formulating the question as a SPARQL query as suggested in [11], has been applied in knowledge engineering for more than a decade (e.g. [13,23,24,27,33,34]). In this way, it is possible to capture actual inferential capability and the ontology's alignment with its design goals. Despite its many advantages, the evaluation of ontologies through CQ verification poses several challenges. First, the process is both time- and resource-intensive, as it requires different kinds of expertise and is entirely manual. Second, it is highly dependent on the complexity, domain-specificity, and ambiguity of the terms used, as standardizing and interpreting ontological concepts is often difficult. Recent interest in applying large language models (LLMs) to knowledge engineering underscores their potential role in automating different steps of the ontology engineering lifecycle, such as formulating or retrofitting CQs [3,5,6,33] and generating ontologies from CQs and user stories [20,23,27]. For what concerns ontology generation, the lack of consistency in evaluation measures makes it difficult to establish a standardised framework for assessing ontology generation. Furthermore, no study has yet explored LLMs' potential for functional evaluation of ontologies through direct CQ verification, especially in a semi-automated setting that includes human-in-the-loop.

To fill this gap, our work presents **OE-Assist**, a novel framework designed to automate the functional evaluation of ontologies through CQ verification. The ultimate goal of our approach is to provide the end users with LLM-based suggestions to verify the modelling of ontologies according to requirements. The CQ verification method is particularly well-suited for LLM assistance as: (1) CQs are expressed in natural language, aligning with LLMs' core capabilities; (2) the verification process involves reasoning about the semantic alignment between requirements and implementation; and (3) the translation between CQs and SPARQL queries represents precisely the kind of symbolic-natural language boundary that LLMs are designed to navigate. Our method involves using an LLM to generate, for a given ontology, both verification labels (YES/NO) and a SPARQL query that motivates the label, confirming whether a CQ has been correctly modelled.

Expanding on a dataset of LLM-generated ontologies from previous work [23], we developed a dataset of 1,393 CQs, stories, and corresponding ontologies for ontology evaluation, whose assessment was cross-checked by two ontology engineers. This resource was used to investigate the performance of an LLM-based evaluation approach, against annotations in the dataset (the gold standard). Furthermore, based on this larger dataset, we derived a balanced dataset to test the efficacy of an interface prototype. It provides LLM-based suggestions to 19 ontology engineers of varying expertise and affiliation during CQ verification of an ontology with Protégé[1], with and without suggestions. This paper aims to answer the following research questions:

- **RQ1.** To what extent can LLMs evaluate ontologies using CQ verification?
- **RQ2.** To what extent can LLMs assist ontology engineers in evaluating ontologies through CQ verification, and what are the benefits and drawbacks of a hybrid approach combining LLM suggestions with expert validation compared to traditional human-only methods?

The remainder of the paper is organized as follows: Sect. 2 reviews relevant literature; Sect. 3 describes the OntoEval dataset; Sect. 4 shows our research methodology and describes our experimental setup; Sect. 6 presents our findings; Sect. 7 discusses the implications of the results. Finally, Sect. 8 summarizes the main findings.

2 Related Work

The first mention of CQs for ontology development cycles can be traced back to 1996, where Uschold and Gruninger described CQs as ontology requirements bridging the gap between informal questions and formal queries [31]. Later, Vrandečić and Gangemi [32] proposed the treatment of ontology requirements as unit tests, according to which each CQ should be turned into a query whose results on the ontology can be checked against expected outcomes. This work introduced CQ-driven validation as a distinct evaluation dimension (termed *functional evaluation*), related to the intended use of an ontology and separate from structural analysis [16]. The importance of CQs was further cemented in main agile ontology engineering methodologies like METHONTOLOGY [15] and eXtreme Design [10], which included CQs as part of the requirement specification and verification phases. Building on this foundation, Blomqvist et al. [11] proposed a methodology for ontology testing that uses CQs as requirements. They showed that reformulating CQs into SPARQL queries effectively identifies mistakes. In fact, CQ verification has been used for over a decade in several projects [13,23,24,27,33,34]. At the same time, manually writing these queries is perceived as tedious work, pointing directly to the automation opportunity our work addresses.

With the advent of LLMs, several approaches have emerged to assist various ontology engineering tasks. LLMs have been employed to generate domain-specific CQs, as demonstrated by Di Nuzzo et al. [14], who integrated GPT-4 with knowledge graphs to automatically generate domain-specific CQs and then used an LLM to judge their quality on criteria such as relevance, clarity, and depth. While promising, this work lacked comprehensive qualitative evaluation on a larger dataset (and comparison between LLM-generated metrics and human judgements) involving human engineers—a limitation our approach aims to overcome. In another work, Tüfek et al. [30] reported using GPT-4 to automatically

[1] https://protege.stanford.edu/.

convert CQs and other textual requirements into SPARQL queries for ontology validation. Similarly, Alharbi et al. [4] mentioned as a future direction of the work that LLMs could assist in determining whether a CQ truly aligns with an ontology's knowledge scope by translating CQs into SPARQL queries.

Researchers have also begun exploring LLMs for ontology conceptualization evaluation. Tsaneva et al. [29] tested GPT-4 in the chat interface as an evaluator for ontology axioms compared to human experts. However, this kind of ontology evaluation is structural, not functional, and was carried out on one toy ontology only. Benson et al. [8] investigated GPT-4's ability to generate and evaluate ontology class definitions in the chat interface, following the Basic Formal Ontology. Despite suggesting that human-in-the-loop refinement shows potential for using GPTs as productivity tools for ontology-related tasks, the work was not tested on a larger-scale benchmark, but rather on selected example classes. Furthermore, the paper addresses structural correctness but not functional evaluation.

Thus, despite promising results, the use of LLMs for ontology evaluation, especially functional adequacy, remains underdeveloped. In this context, Garijo et al. [17] leave the categorisation of existing resources on LLM use for ontology evaluation blank, highlighting this gap.

Furthermore, current evaluation approaches for LLM-generated ontologies face significant methodological challenges. Lippolis et al. [23] proposed a comprehensive evaluation method, structural and functional, for LLM-generated ontologies that still, similar to Alharbi et al. [2], relies heavily on manual components requiring the intervention of a domain expert. Similarly, Da et al. [28] developed LLM-based ontology generation techniques that depend on manual verification processes.

Rebboud et al. [26] propose evaluation criteria including accuracy, completeness, and conciseness of generated ontologies measured against a ground truth. However, these criteria introduce two critical limitations: (i) they necessitate either a gold reference taxonomy or a comprehensive domain corpus—resources that are so far unavailable or incomplete, and (ii) they fail to explicitly incorporate ontology requirements in the evaluation process.

Also, a fundamental tension exists between expecting LLM evaluation to provide definitive answers versus using it as a decision support tool to assist human judgment. This distinction becomes crucial when establishing evaluation methodologies that balance automation with human-in-the-loop oversight.

Another important aspect in this field concerns the quality of requirements that seems to significantly impact ontology generation success [22]. Therefore, methods to evaluate ontologies against their intended functional requirements need to account for the quality of those requirements, especially when derived from multiple projects. To sum up, using LLMs as evaluators in ontology engineering is only now beginning to emerge. However, current LLM-based studies on ontology generation still rely on ad-hoc methods or measures requiring intense manual effort when performing a functional evaluation.

3 The OntoEval Dataset

This section describes the OntoEval dataset—annotated for ontology evaluation using CQ verification—by detailing its construction methodology and reporting its principal descriptive statistics. We then introduce OntoEval-small, a carefully curated subset of OntoEval designed for the semi-automatic ontology evaluation experiment with ontology engineers.

3.1 Dataset Creation

Our primary OntoEval dataset consists of 1,393 ontologies, both human-curated ones from European projects (57) and LLM-generated ontologies (1,336), each paired with a corresponding CQ, user story and annotations. Including potentially imperfect, LLM-generated ontologies is intentional: real-world evaluation tools must handle noisy or partially correct models, and such ontologies can provide controlled but realistic variation. OntoEval ontologies, stories and CQs are mostly derived from multiple recent works [22,23,27], in which ontologies were manually annotated for their evaluation with respect to the CQ Verification method into three labels: YES, NO, and NO MINOR. The latter refers to the definition by [23,27] and indicates that only a single property is missing from the ontology to achieve complete CQ verification. In the automatic evaluation of this work, we treat NO MINOR as NO. Furthermore, CQs were assigned a difficulty rating on a binary scale, SIMPLE or COMPLEX, based on the presence of at most two classes and one object property for the SIMPLE label, otherwise it was considered COMPLEX. For instance, "Who built and/or renovated an organ?" is classified as SIMPLE as it involves two classes (`Person`, `Organ`) and one object property (`built/renovated`): $\exists x, y : \text{Person}(x) \wedge \text{Organ}(y) \wedge (\text{built}(x, y) \vee \text{renovated}(x, y))$. Conversely, "What was the disposition of the organ at a specific point in time?" is COMPLEX due to multiple classes and properties: $\exists x, y, z : \text{Organ}(x) \wedge \text{Parthood}(y) \wedge \text{TimeInterval}(z) \wedge \text{isWholeIncludedIn}(x, y) \wedge \text{hasTimeInterval}(y, z)$. Ontologies and their requirements were drawn from multiple sources to ensure a variety of domains and modelling patterns, and in particular, four large-scale European projects, one educational project with three ontologies, and three LLM-generated ontologies from recently peer-reviewed work:

1. *Polifonia Project* (domains: Music and Events) [9];
2. *WHOW Project* (domains: Water and Health) [21];
3. *Onto-DESIDE Project*[2] (domain: Circular Economy);
4. IKS (Interactive Knowledge Stack for content management platforms)[3];
5. "SemanticWebCourse", used in Saeedizade and Blomqvist [27] and Lippolis et al. [23], consisting of three ontology stories about the music, theatre and hospital domain and 15 CQs each;
6. AcquaDiva (domains: Microbe Habitat and Carbon and Nitrogen Cycling) [1];
7. LLM generated ontologies in the works by [22,23,27].

[2] https://ontodeside.eu.

[3] https://cordis.europa.eu/project/id/231527.

The LLM-generated ontologies were generated by the following LLMs: GPT-4 family (versions: GPT-4-0613, GPT-4-1106, GPT-4-Turbo 2024-04-09, GPT-4-2024-05-13), Llama-3.1-405B-instruct, o1-preview, and DeepSeek-V3. In these works, a sample was evaluated, among other measures, by a panel of expert ontology engineers who found that while LLMs introduce distinctive modelling patterns, they do not necessarily underperform compared to novice human modellers. These ontologies were thus designed specifically to allow a controlled comparison between human-generated and LLM-generated artefacts using the same input requirements.

3.2 OntoEval-Small

From the OntoEval corpus, we constructed a balanced subset for controlled experimentation, *OntoEval-small*. To achieve this, we employed a combination of hard and soft constraints. As hard filters, we excluded ontology models addressing only minor issues (i.e., resulting in a binary YES/NO annotation) to make sure labels were unambiguous. Additionally, we retained only the CQs rated as COMPLEX to have a more challenging evaluation. To ensure domain diversity, we limited the selection to a maximum of three CQs per project. LLM correctness served as a soft filter, meaning this filter was used as a sampling guide rather than a strict rule, such that the small dataset would have statistics similar to that of the full dataset with respect to correct and incorrect LLM predictions. We also sampled an approximately equal number of LLM-generated and human-curated ontologies and made sure that the LLM-generated ontologies were generated by different LLMs. Lastly, we selected a similar number of CQs that were modelled and not modelled. To facilitate user evaluation, each original story was condensed into a single-line summary using OpenAI's o1-preview model in a few-shot setting.

3.3 Dataset Statistics

Table 1 summarises key descriptive statistics for *OntoEval* and *OntoEval-small*. For each dataset, we report the total number of CQs and the number of correctly modelled CQs. Most CQs in OntoEval are modelled and therefore the dataset is imbalanced (1,204 YES and 189 NO). We also include the number of CQs classified as SIMPLE and COMPLEX according to the criteria outlined in Sect. 3.1, along with the domain coverage of the ontologies and their provenance. The "not modelled CQs" were not generated by automated negative-sampling techniques but were instead drawn from planned EU project deliverables or manually annotated by ontology experts. Furthermore, the ontologies are of different sizes, which are computed by the number of axioms in OntoMetrics [19], ranging from 15 to 567 axioms (mean: 132 axioms, median: 44 axioms, STD: 164 axioms).

Table 1. Comparison of the full *OntoEval* corpus for automatic ontology evaluation and the *OntoEval-small* subset for semi-automated evaluation.

Metric	OntoEval	OntoEval-small
Total CQs	1,393	20
Modelled CQs	1,204	10
Difficulty: SIMPLE	725	0
Difficulty: COMPLEX	135	20
Domains	33	6

4 Methodology and Experimental Setup

In this section, we outline our dual-phase OE-Assist methodology—comprising both fully automatic and semi-automatic approaches—along with the corresponding experimental configurations, as shown in Fig. 1.

4.1 Overall Methodology

OE-Assist—structured around semi-automatic and complementary automatic setups with ontology engineers—aims both to determine whether integrating AI-assisted suggestion can improve quality assessment and to explore the extent to which LLMs can independently evaluate ontologies as standalone agents. In this section, we describe the methodology of automatic ontology evaluation and the semi-automatic method.

Automatic Ontology Evaluation. The automatic evaluation is designed as a label-based assessment mechanism. In this phase, a prompt is introduced to an LLM to analyse whether a CQ is adequately modelled within a given ontology and an ontology story. The evaluation is structured to classify ontology coverage without human intervention. The components of the prompt are the task description, CQs, a user story, and an ontology. The expected outputs are a binary class (YES: CQ is modelled, NO: CQ is not modelled) and a SPARQL query for CQ verification.

Semi-automatic Ontology Evaluation. In the semi-automatic evaluation, we investigate the extent to which LLMs can support ontology engineers in the ontology evaluation process. This phase employs the same inputs and expected outputs as the automatic approach. The LLM's suggested label (YES or NO) and the SPARQL query are provided to the user as suggestions. Given an ontology, its ontology story, and the LLM's suggestions, the user is responsible for determining whether each CQ has been accurately modelled within the ontology or not.

4.2 Prompt Design

We propose a prompt[4] that (i) describes the ontology-evaluation task, (ii) provides some examples (out of the OntoEval-small dataset, cf. Sect. 3.3) in a few-shot style, with both positive (YES) and negative (NO) cases, (iii) includes the user story, CQ, and ontology, and (iv) instructs the model to: (a) return a Boolean label (YES or NO) indicating whether the CQ is correctly modelled, and (b) generate a SPARQL query to verify the CQ. If the model returns NO, it is also instructed to supply a partial SPARQL query highlighting the available portions of the ontology related to the CQ.

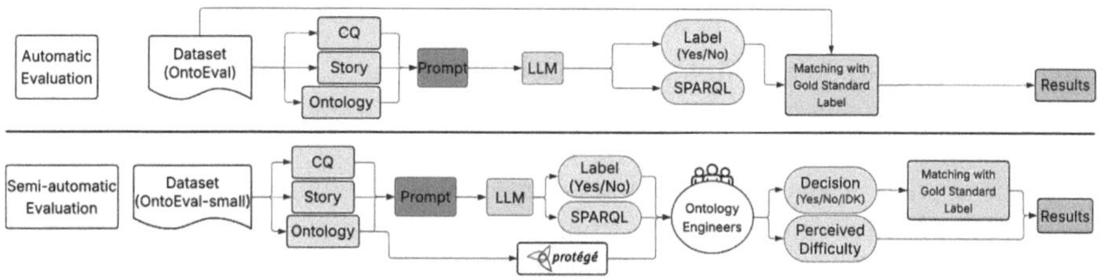

Fig. 1. Overview of OE-Assist: (i) Automatic: predicted labels are compared to gold standards to compute performance metrics. (ii) Semi-automatic: Users aided by LLM suggestions assess whether a CQ is modelled.

4.3 Automatic Ontology Evaluation

We automatically assess the correctness of each ontology using a set of three different LLMs on the OntoEval dataset and comparing the LLM YES/NO judgments against the gold standard.

Models Under Test. We run the prompt through three different LLMs: OpenAI o1-preview, GPT-4o-0513, and OpenAI o3-mini to represent a range of model capabilities and architectures. o1-preview was included as it is a state-of-the-art reasoning model with advanced capabilities for complex tasks. GPT-4o-0513 is a widely-used foundation model with established performance across knowledge-intensive tasks. o3-mini was included to test whether smaller, more efficient models could perform adequately on ontology evaluation tasks. Each model is run three times, except o1-preview on the full OntoEval dataset and accessed via Azure API, with at least five hours between each run to avoid caching, using the default hyperparameters for o1-preview. Temperature and penalty are set to 0, along with keeping default hyperparameters, for others.

Answer Extraction. Although the prompt requests both the SPARQL query and the binary label, for this evaluation, we parse only the label to compute Macro-F1 and Accuracy by comparing it to the gold standard.

[4] Due to space constraints, the full prompt specification is available on GitHub: https://github.com/dersuchendee/OE-Assist/tree/main/prompts.

4.4 Semi-automatic Ontology Evaluation

This section presents the semi-automatic evaluation of ontologies. In this study, each participant was assigned 20 ontology evaluation tasks in a limited time. Half of these tasks included suggestions generated by an LLM, whereas the remaining tasks did not feature such assistance. The order of the tasks was changed between participants to mitigate the impact of learning effects on the results. The ontology stories, CQs, and the LLM-generated suggestions (if present) were shown using a basic user interface where ontology engineers could select a final assessment decision. A second screen provided access to the Protégé application with the ontology connected with the task pre-loaded.

Participants. Nineteen ontology engineers participated in this evaluation. They were recruited through academic networks and represented roles ranging from research assistants to professors and affiliated with eight different international institutions with industrial or academic experience in semantic web technologies. Participants were divided into two experience groups (*non-expert* vs. *expert*) with professors—including assistant and associate professors—classified as *experts*, and all others as *non-experts*. While we acknowledge this distinction tends to simplify expertise, we opted for professors as a conservative and externally verifiable criterion over self-reported years of experience, which could yield inconsistent groupings. Seven participants completed the evaluation in an online setting, while the remaining twelve participated in person.

LLM Selection. The LLM employed to generate suggestions (label and SPARQL) was o1-preview as it was the best performing one in the automatic ontology evaluation phase of the experiment.

Interface. A prototype of a web-based interface was developed to present LLM suggestions and requirements along with the ontology, as illustrated in Fig. 2. The interface was made available online for the duration of the experiment and was displayed side-by-side with Protégé to facilitate comparison. On the left, participants could browse the OWL ontology file in Protégé, while on the right they interacted with the evaluation interface. The interface displayed, for a given ontology, the current CQ and story, optional LLM suggestions, and response controls to answer if a CQ is modelled or not with the perceived difficulty on a Likert scale from 1 to 5. In this way, participants could carry out ontology evaluation in two modes: An assisted mode (with LLM suggestions) and an unassisted mode (without LLM suggestions).

Procedure. Participants completed two different sets of tasks (20 in total) under both conditions *Assisted* (10) and *Unassisted* (10) in a single session of approximately one hour. Prior to the main task, each participant completed a 10-minute brief tutorial, which included worked examples intended to familiarise them with the dual-window setup and the response workflow. Time was allotted for clarifying questions. Each condition utilised a dual-screen setup—Protégé and the interface—and was assigned a maximum time window of 20 min; CQs remaining at the end of this interval were recorded as skipped. Where participants were uncertain about a particular CQ, they could skip it by selecting "I don't know" (IDK) via the interface. They could also skip each question if it was too difficult or if they could not understand a CQ. The expected sequence of actions was as follows: (i) participants were to open the ontology file in Protégé (without any plugins) and, CQ, the ontology story, and the suggestions (if available), (ii) they would select their answer (either "Yes", "No", or "IDK") and finally, (iii) indicate how difficult they found the task using a 1–5 Likert scale, as shown in Fig. 2a (assisted) and Fig. 2b (unassisted). Upon reaching the time limit or completing all tasks, participants switched to the alternate condition and proceeded with the remaining 10 questions. The sole distinction between conditions was the availability of LLM suggestions in the assisted setup. A think-aloud protocol was applied throughout the session, encouraging the participants to explain and comment on their actions and thoughts, to facilitate observational note-taking by the experiment observers. To conclude, participants completed a 10-item survey adapted from the System Usability Scale (SUS) [12].

In our setup, we recognise that each ontology evaluation task could have different difficulty, so we made sure each CQ appeared equally in the assisted mode and unassisted mode. Also, the order of assisted mode and unassisted mode, whether it appears in the first half of the experiment or the second, is changed between participants to maintain a balanced distribution.

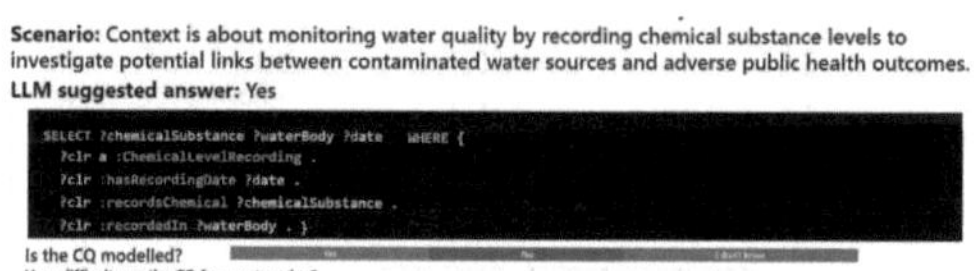

(a) Assisted version in the interface.

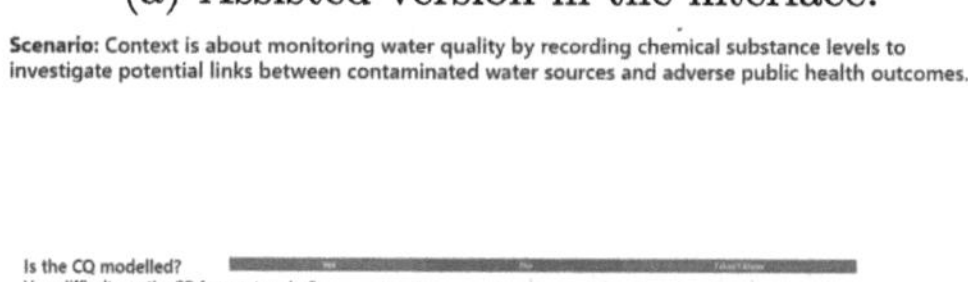

(b) Unassisted version of the interface.

Fig. 2. Comparison of assisted and unassisted settings in the interface.

5 Evaluation

In this section, we discuss evaluation metrics for both automatic and semi-automatic ontology evaluation.

Automatic Ontology Evaluation. For OntoEval, we report macro-averaged F1, which balances the majority (YES) and minority (NO) classes; for OntoEval-small, which is balanced, we report Accuracy and compare all LLMs with a uniform-random baseline (Acc = 0.50, F1 = 0.42).

Semi-automatic Ontology Evaluation. To assess the semi-automatic evaluation, we define each user's accuracy in setup (assisted vs not assisted) m as $\text{Acc}_{u,m} = C_{u,m}/(C_{u,m} + I_{u,m})$, where $C_{u,m}$ and $I_{u,m}$ are the counts of correct and incorrect answers ("IDK" ones are not counted here). We then compute the overall mode accuracy by averaging over N users: $\text{Acc}_{\textbf{setup}} = \frac{1}{N}\sum_{u=1}^{N} \text{Acc}_{u,\textbf{setup}}$, and define $\Delta\text{Accuracy} = \text{Acc}_{\textbf{assisted}} - \text{Acc}_{\textbf{unassisted}}$. We also report the standard deviation of $\text{Acc}_{u,m}$ in each setup. To further analyse the relationship between LLM assistance and task correctness, we conduct a chi-square test of independence. Since each CQ was attempted multiple times by different users across both assisted and unassisted modes, we treat each answer as an independent observation and construct a 2×2 contingency table of assistance condition (present vs. absent) and answer correctness (correct vs. incorrect).

We used paired two-tailed t-tests to compare each user's accuracy (and separately perceived difficulty) in the assisted vs. unassisted conditions, reporting the t-statistic and p-value. We assessed the relationship between perceived difficulty and accuracy using Pearson's correlation coefficient, testing significance at $\alpha = 0.05$. Where relevant, we computed Cohen's d to quantify the magnitude of paired differences (e.g. in perceived difficulty or accuracy) [7].

Finally, to investigate the potential impact of LLMs' correctness on user decision-making, we subdivide the reported results based on whether the LLM provides a correct suggestion or an incorrect suggestion. This approach allows us to discern how the varying degrees of LLMs' accuracy affect the overall effectiveness of the semi-automatic ontology evaluation methodology.

6 Results

In this section, we present the results of the automatic and semi-automatic ontology evaluation. We start with the automatic ontology evaluation on OntoEval and then select the best performing model to be used in the semi-automatic setting, assessing the users' performance in the various settings.

6.1 Automatic Ontology Evaluation

For the automatic evaluation of ontologies, as shown in Table 2, o1-preview overall outperforms the other LLMs on both datasets. The only weakness of o1-preview was over human-curated ontologies, resulting in 0.05 lower score than o3-mini. Since all LLMs have a low standard deviation (STD) and the cost of running the experiment on o1-preview is high, we ran this model only once.

Table 2. Performance of LLMs in the automatic ontology evaluation, compared to the random-guess baseline. Bold shows the best score on each column.

Model	Macro-F_1 (on OntoEval)			Accuracy (on OntoEval-small)
	EU projects,	LLM Generated,	All	All
Random baseline	0.41	0.42	0.43	0.50
GPT-4o-0513	0.34 ±0.02	0.48 ±0	0.48 ±0	0.55 ±0
o3-mini	**0.51** ±0.02	0.56 ±0.01	0.58 ±0.01	0.72 ±0.02
o1-preview	0.46	**0.66**	**0.66**	**0.75** ±0.05

6.2 Semi-automatic Ontology Evaluation

In this section, we present the results for the semi-automatic ontology evaluation, focusing on the differences in accuracy and perceived difficulty in the assisted compared to the unassisted mode. We also examine how the presence of suggestions from LLMs—whether correct or incorrect—shape these outcomes. In addition, we evaluate the relationship between perceived difficulty and correctness. Finally, we discuss the observed learning curve and the questionnaire that users filled in, highlighting how their responses inform the broader evaluation of ontologies and the role of LLMs within this process.

Accuracy in the Assisted Compared to the Unassisted Setting. Using the metrics described in Sect. 5, we calculated accuracy in both the assisted and unassisted settings. We then computed the difference (ΔAccuracy) for each condition, taking into account whether the suggestion provided was correct or not. By analysing the relationship between these variables, we assessed whether the presence of LLM suggestions had a statistically significant effect on correctness.

As accuracy scores are illustrated in Fig. 3a, when the LLM provided correct suggestions, we observed a significant average improvement of +13% (from 70.46% to 83.18%), supported by a paired t-test (t = 2.04, p = 0.047). However, when the LLM suggestions were incorrect in the same task, performance significantly declined with an average change of -28% (from 71.93% to 43.86%), confirmed by a t-test (t = –2.09, p = 0.043). Since correct LLM suggestions occurred more frequently overall, there was a total improvement of +0.04% (0.72 to 0.76) for LLM-assisted users (see Fig. 3b). However, this difference was not statistically significant. In addition, o3-mini and o1-preview have a similar accuracy to users' performance in both modes.

Using a chi-squared test, we found statistically significant associations for both correct (χ^2 = 4.12, p = 0.042) and incorrect (χ^2= 4.61, p = 0.0318) LLM suggestions. These findings underscore that the presence of LLM input, within the experimental setup, for each CQ, indeed affects decision outcomes.

Perceived Difficulty in Assisted Compared to Unassisted Mode. Participants judged the tasks as slightly less difficult when LLM suggestions were

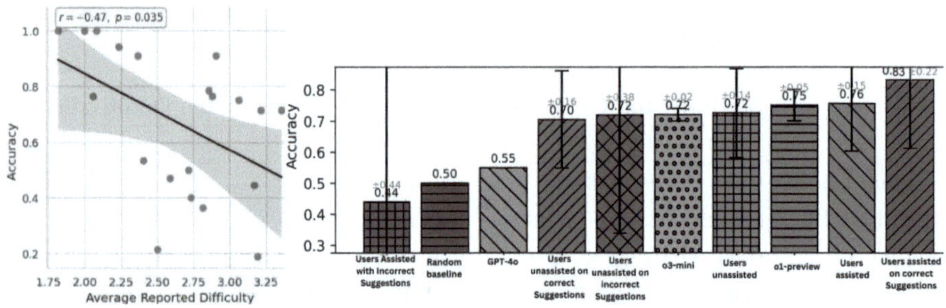

(a) Difficulty vs Accuracy. (b) Accuracy of LLMs and users on different parts.

Fig. 3. Results overview. a) Relationship between difficulty and accuracy: easier perceived tasks are solved more accurately; (b) Comparative accuracy of the LLMs (orange) and human evaluators (green: assisted and blue: unassisted), with user responses further stratified by LLM correctness. STD is in grey (Color figure online)

present (mean difficulty = 2.52, STD = 0.56) compared to when they were absent (mean difficulty = 2.75, STD = 0.46), where mean difficulty represents the average difficulty rating across all CQs on a Likert scale, and STD indicates how much those ratings varied from one CQ to another. This difference is small (Cohen's $d \approx 0.22$), indicating a modest effect size; in behavioral research, d values around 0.2 typically reflect small but meaningful differences. Note that this reflects variation across CQ-level averages rather than individual tasks.

As expected, experts consistently rated tasks as easier than novices, with the average difficulty dropping by 9% for experts (from 2.67 to 2.44) and 5% for novices (from 2.84 to 2.69) when assisted. Thus, both groups experienced slightly lower perceived difficulty with suggestions, but the expert group consistently found the tasks easier overall. For what concerns "I don't know" responses, users settled on "I don't know" almost exclusively when they perceived the question as hard (mean difficulty=3.9 vs 2.4 for other responses). Furthermore, if the accuracy of the CQ was low, there was also a higher number of "I don't know" responses. Instead, ontology size in terms of number of axioms does not play a role in pushing people towards being undecided (r = 0.01, p = 0.8).

Relationship Between Perceived Difficulty and Accuracy. Figure 3a depicts Pearson's correlation between perceived difficulty and accuracy in our setup. There is a moderate negative correlation (r = -0.47, p = 0.035) between perceived difficulty and accuracy, indicating that as users perceived tasks to be harder, their accuracy tended to decrease. This correlation seems to be explained by the tasks in which the LLM gave incorrect suggestions—users found those tasks harder and were also less likely to solve them correctly. Furthermore, when the tasks were analysed separately by the correctness of the LLMs' suggestions, the difficulty–accuracy link was no longer significant (LLM correct: r = –0.23, p = 0.44; LLM incorrect: r = +0.21, p = 0.69).

Learning Effect Curve by Expertise. As participants progressed, they rated each successive task as easier, indicating a learning effect. Participants who began in the assisted mode showed almost no change when they later switched to the unassisted mode (–0.04 accuracy), whereas those who began unassisted improved substantially after switching to assistance (+0.17 accuracy). Expertise further modulated this pattern: non-experts gained little when assisted first, yet improved modestly without assistance (+0.06). In contrast, experts improved sharply in the unassisted block (+0.29) and only slightly with assistance (+0.06). Across all users, accuracy rose in the second half for 40% of CQs solved without LLM support but for just 15% with support. A paired-samples test approached significance ($p \approx 0.08$), and the effect size (Cohen's $d \approx 0.45$) indicates a medium learning advantage in the unassisted condition—but definitive statistical confirmation requires a larger sample.

Questionnaire. In the post-task questionnaire, 63% of the participants strongly agreed that the LLM suggestions were useful in solving the task, 74% felt they could learn to use the system setup quickly, and, 21% found either the suggestions, the suggested label, or the SPARQL queries distracting.

7 Discussion

This section discusses our key findings and situates them within the broader context of automated and semi-automated ontology evaluation.

Automatic Ontology Evaluation. From our results, GPT-4o hover around the random baseline, whereas o1-preview delivers +0.23 F1 over random on automatically generated ontologies and +0.15 on human curated ones. Similar improvement was seen for o3-mini, suggesting that these reasoning LLMs can be helpful for ontology evaluation, especially given the steady upward trend in LLM performance. These results imply that o1-preview and o3-mini can already serve as an automated first-pass layer flagging potential errors before human review; for instance, they could accelerate curation in large, rapidly updated ontologies.

Semi-automatic Ontology Evaluation. Our findings show that while LLM-assisted ontology evaluation improves the accuracy by 13% when the suggestions are correct, the approach exhibits a significant decline when the user is supplied with incorrect suggestions. Overall however, these opposing effects largely cancelled each other out, resulting in no statistically significant net change in overall accuracy. Given that the o1-preview model's suggestions used in the experiment had a 70% accuracy, we speculate that future LLMs—with higher suggestion accuracy rates—will enable end users to realize a correspondingly greater enhancement in task performance. One may also consider other ways to mitigate the effects of wrong LLM suggestions, such as pre-checking suggested SPARQL queries against the ontology before showing the suggestion to the user, or including some kind of confidence assessment of the suggestions.

Also, LLM suggestions reduced the perceived difficulty (mean = 2.52 vs. 2.75). One downside of the assisted condition, however, is that it may hinder learning over time. The modest learning gains in unassisted settings suggest that task complexity from the user's point of view is higher without automated support (accuracy improved of 40% for CQs without LLM suggestions in the second half of the experiment vs. 15% with suggestions). This learning effect was shaped by task order: users who started with assistance received early support and thus performed equally well in the later unassisted phase as those who learned through doing. As a result, overall learning gains appear neutralised—since early assistance seems to substitute the effort that would otherwise lead to similar improvement.

Ontologies contained in OntoEval-small had different sizes. However, we found there is no correlation between the size of ontologies in terms of axiom number and incorrect answers. However, we note that even the largest ontology used is small by real-world standards. Taken together, these results imply that LLM support seems to be valuable mainly when its precision is high and that future versions of the prototype should pair assistance with dedicated safeguards—and perhaps dedicated learning phases—to avoid over-reliance on LLMs and preserve users' skill growth, but also that in realistic scenarios, automated suggestions could become even more valuable.

Feedback During the Experiment. Looking at users' behaviour performing the tasks revealed that when working with the assisted setting many users started the evaluation from the SPARQL queries, to find and match the named classes and properties with the ones mentioned in the CQ. A second group of users operated in reverse: first exploring the ontology through Protégé to establish a conceptual understanding, and only after that they proceeded to study the suggested SPARQL query. These contrasting workflows suggest different methods of problem-solving—one favoring a code-first approach that uses the ontology as confirmation, and another prioritizing conceptual understanding before proceeding with CQ verification. In line with these strategies, in the questionnaire feedback, users who took the code-first path appear to have leaned heavily on the system's inline suggestions to speed-check query fragments—an affinity that helps explain why 63% strongly agreed the suggestions were useful. Where the two groups converged was on the final decision aid. Only 32% endorsed the binary YES/NO recommendation. Indeed, user feedback revealed challenges with the lack of labels and comments in some ontologies, unclear CQs, domain-specific content, and flawed LLM-generated hierarchies, all of which required extra effort to interpret and evaluate. These findings highlight the need for adaptable AI interfaces that support both code-first and concept-first user strategies, while emphasizing the importance of providing transparent, context-rich justifications in addition to binary recommendations.

Quality of Requirements. User comments and the varying wording of the CQs show that inconsistent, under-specified, or overly domain-specific requirements impede reliable evaluation. When the wording or granularity of the questions shifted from one task to the next, participants reported uncertainty about how to assess the related ontology. Domain specificity created an additional hurdle: evaluators who lacked subject-matter expertise could judge structural soundness but not semantic correctness, showing LLM suggestions seem to not be helpful in these cases.

Limitations and Risks. While our findings indicate that LLMs hold considerable promise for user-based functional ontology evaluation, future work should involve a broader group of ontology engineers and a wider range of LLMs to validate these results, since our group included only five participants with expert qualification level. Additionally, some participants had worked on the ontologies several years earlier, so even though they reported remembering little, residual familiarity could still have influenced their answers. Finally, our study highlights the need to improve the quality of the requirements and to integrate the workflow into widely used tools, such as Protégé, in order to enhance overall usability. For dataset leakage, we did not find ontologies and their CQ annotations co-located online, so direct memorisation by the LLM is unlikely. Still, because pre-training data are opaque, we cannot rule out partial leakage. Running a full automated evaluation with o1-preview cost approximately $851. By contrast, a single run with gpt-4o cost about $40, and o3-mini just $25, so we only ran o1-preview once. These differences highlight a trade-off between model strength and budget that must be considered when selecting engines or planning multiple runs.

8 Conclusion

In this work, we have introduced the first end-to-end framework using LLMs for functional ontology evaluation via CQ verification through both automatic and semi-automatic methods. We also introduced OntoEval, a benchmark of 1,393 ontology–CQ pairs across 33 domains, annotated by ontology engineers. In response to RQ1, "To what extent can LLMs evaluate ontologies using CQ verification?", in automatic experiments, the o1-preview model achieved 0.66 macro-F1, outperforming other LLMs. Hence, we conclude that newer LLMs perform on par with human users. To evaluate practical impact of the semi-automated methodology, and explore RQ2 ("To what extent can LLMs assist ontology engineers in evaluating ontologies through CQ verification, and what are the benefits and drawbacks of a hybrid approach combining LLM suggestions with expert validation compared to traditional human-only methods?"), we ran a controlled study with 19 ontology engineers from eight institutions. When o1-preview's suggestions were correct, average user accuracy improved by 13% and perceived task difficulty decreased. However, incorrect suggestions caused a 28% drop in accuracy; resulting in the same overall accuracy as unassisted mode since correct suggestions outnumbered incorrect ones. We conclude that the usefulness of LLM assistance heavily depends on the suggestion accuracy, and users are easily influenced by erroneous suggestions, while still perceiving the overall approach as useful. As LLMs improve, these results bode well for reasoning-powered ontology evaluation tools.

Reproducibility Statement: Code, data, and supplementary material used in this paper are available on GitHub: https://github.com/dersuchendee/OE-Assist.

Acknowledgments. This project has received funding from the European Union's Horizon Europe research and innovation programme under grant agreements no. 101058682 (Onto-DESIDE) and 101070588 (HACID), and is supported by the strategic research area Security Link. Financial support to this project was also provided by NextGenerationEU under NRRP Grant agreement n. MUR IR0000008 - FOSSR (CUP B83C22003950001) and by the PhD scholarship "Discovery, Formalisation and Re-use of Knowledge Patterns and Graphs for the Science of Science", funded by CNR-ISTC through the WHOW project (EU CEF programme - grant agreement no. INEA/CEF/ICT/A2019/2063229). We thank OpenAI's Researcher Access Program Grant for the API credits. Finally, we deeply thank all participants of the experiments.

References

1. Algergawy, A., Hamed, H., Thiel, S., König-Ries, B.: Towards semantic annotation for scientific datasets. In: European Semantic Web Conference, pp. 164–167. Springer (2024)
2. Alharbi, R., et al.: Exploring the role of generative AI in constructing knowledge graphs for drug indications with medical context. In: 15th International Semantic Web Applications and Tools for Healthcare and Life Sciences (SWAT4HCLS 2024) (to appear) (2024)
3. Alharbi, R., Tamma, V., Grasso, F., Payne, T.: An experiment in retrofitting competency questions for existing ontologies. In: Proceedings of the 39th ACM/SIGAPP Symposium on Applied Computing, pp. 1650–1658 (2024)
4. Alharbi, R., Tamma, V., Grasso, F., Payne, T.R.: Investigating open source LLMs to retrofit competency questions in ontology engineering. In: Proceedings of the AAAI Symposium Series, vol. 4, pp. 188–198 (2024)
5. Alharbi, R., Tamma, V., Grasso, F., Payne, T.R.: A review and comparison of competency question engineering approaches. In: International Conference on Knowledge Engineering and Knowledge Management, pp. 271–290. Springer (2024)
6. Antia, M.J., Keet, C.M.: Automating the generation of competency questions for ontologies with agocqs. In: Iberoamerican Knowledge Graphs and Semantic Web Conference, pp. 213–227. Springer (2023)
7. Becker, L.A.: Effect size (es) (2000)
8. Benson, C., Sculley, A., Liebers, A., Beverley, J.: My ontologist: evaluating bfo-based ai for definition support. arXiv preprint arXiv:2407.17657 (2024)
9. de Berardinis, J., et al.: The Polifonia ontology network: Building a semantic backbone for musical heritage. In: International Semantic Web Conference, pp. 302–322. Springer (2023)
10. Blomqvist, E., Presutti, V., Daga, E., Gangemi, A.: Experimenting with extreme design. In: International Conference on Knowledge Engineering and Knowledge Management, pp. 120–134. Springer (2010)
11. Blomqvist, E., Seil Sepour, A., Presutti, V.: Ontology testing-methodology and tool. In: Knowledge Engineering and Knowledge Management: 18th International Conference, EKAW 2012, Galway City, Ireland, 8–12 October 2012. Proceedings 18, pp. 216–226. Springer (2012)

12. Brooke, J., et al.: Sus-a quick and dirty usability scale. Usability Eval. Ind. **189**(194), 4–7 (1996)
13. Carriero, V.A., et al.: ArCo: the Italian cultural heritage knowledge graph. In: Ghidini, C., et al. (eds.) ISWC 2019. LNCS, vol. 11779, pp. 36–52. Springer, Cham (2019). https://doi.org/10.1007/978-3-030-30796-7_3
14. Di Nuzzo, D., Vakaj, E., Saadany, H., Grishti, E., Mihindukulasooriya, N.: Automated generation of competency questions using large language models and knowledge graphs. In: SEMANTiCS Conference (2024)
15. Fernández-López, M., Gómez-Pérez, A., Juristo Juzgado, N.: Methontology: from ontological art towards ontological engineering (1997)
16. Gangemi, A., Catenacci, C., Ciaramita, M., Lehmann, J.: Modelling ontology evaluation and validation. In: European Semantic Web Conference, pp. 140–154. Springer (2006)
17. Garijo, D., Poveda-Villalón, M., Amador-Domínguez, E., Wang, Z., García-Castro, R., Corcho, O.: Llms for ontology engineering: a landscape of tasks and benchmarking challenges (2022)
18. Grüninger, M., Fox, M.S.: The role of competency questions in enterprise engineering, pp. 22–31. Springer US, Boston, MA (1995). https://doi.org/10.1007/978-0-387-34847-6_3
19. Lantow, B.: Ontometrics: putting metrics into use for ontology evaluation. In: KEOD, pp. 186–191 (2016)
20. Lippolis, A.S., Ceriani, M., Zuppiroli, S., Nuzzolese, A.G.: Ontogenia: ontology generation with metacognitive prompting in large language models. In: European Semantic Web Conference, pp. 259–265. Springer (2024)
21. Lippolis, A.S., Lodi, G., Nuzzolese, A.G.: The water health open knowledge graph. Sci. Data **12**(1), 274 (2025)
22. Lippolis, A.S., Saeedizade, M.J., Keskisarkka, R., Gangemi, A., Blomqvist, E., Nuzzolese, A.G.: Assessing the capability of large language models for domain-specific ontology generation. In: European Semantic Web Conference, pp. 321–341. Springer Nature Switzerland, Cham (2025)
23. Lippolis, A.S., et al.: Ontology generation using large language models. arXiv preprint arXiv:2503.05388 (2025)
24. Litovkin, D., Dontsov, D., Anikin, A., Sychev, O.: Suitability of object-role modeling diagrams as an intermediate model for ontology engineering: Testing the rules. In: Brain-Inspired Cognitive Architectures for Artificial Intelligence: BICA* AI 2020: Proceedings of the 11th Annual Meeting of the BICA Society, vol. 1310, p. 188. Springer (2020)
25. Presutti, V., Daga, E., Gangemi, A., Blomqvist, E.: Extreme design with content ontology design patterns. In: Proceedings of Workshop on Ontology Patterns, pp. 83–97. CEUR-WS (2009)
26. Rebboud, Y., Lisena, P., Tailhardat, L., Troncy, R.: Benchmarking llm-based ontology conceptualization: a proposal. In: The Semantic Web – ISWC 2024: 23rd International Semantic Web Conference, Baltimore, MD, USA, 11–15 November 2024, Proceedings (2024)
27. Saeedizade, M.J., Blomqvist, E.: Navigating ontology development with large language models. In: Meroño Peñuela, A., et al. (eds.) The Semantic Web, pp. 143–161. Springer Nature Switzerland, Cham (2024)
28. da Silva, L.M.V., Kocher, A., Gehlhoff, F., Fay, A.: Toward a method to generate capability ontologies from natural language descriptions. In: 2024 IEEE 29th International Conference on Emerging Technologies and Factory Automation (ETFA), pp. 1–4. IEEE (2024)

29. Tsaneva, S., Vasic, S., Sabou, M.: Llm-driven ontology evaluation: verifying ontology restrictions with chatgpt. In: The Semantic Web: ESWC Satellite Events, vol. 2024 (2024)
30. Tufek, N., et al.: Validating semantic artifacts with large language models. In: European Semantic Web Conference, pp. 92–101. Springer (2024)
31. Uschold, M., Gruninger, M.: Ontologies: principles, methods and applications. Knowl. Eng. Rev. **11**(2), 93–136 (1996)
32. Vrandečić, D., Gangemi, A.: Unit tests for ontologies. In: OTM Confederated International Conferences "On the Move to Meaningful Internet Systems", pp. 1012–1020. Springer (2006)
33. Zhang, B., et al.: Ontochat: a framework for conversational ontology engineering using language models. In: Proceedings of the ESWC2024 Special Track: Large Language Models for Knowledge Engineering (to appear) (2024)
34. Zhang, B., Koutsiana, E., Zhao, Y., Meroño-Peñuela, A., Simperl, E.: Trustworthy knowledge graphs: practices and approaches. In: Handbook on Neurosymbolic AI and Knowledge Graphs, pp. 363–384. IOS Press (2025)

Controlled Query Evaluation Under Epistemic Dependencies: Algorithms and Experiments

Lorenzo Marconi(✉), Flavia Ricci, and Riccardo Rosati

Sapienza University of Rome, Rome, Italy
{marconi,rosati}@diag.uniroma1.it, ricci.1883245@studenti.uniroma1.it

Abstract. We investigate Controlled Query Evaluation (CQE) over ontologies, where information disclosure is regulated by epistemic dependencies (EDs), a family of logical rules recently proposed for the CQE framework. In particular, we combine EDs with the notion of optimal GA censors, i.e. maximal sets of ground atoms that are entailed by the ontology and can be safely revealed. We focus on answering Boolean unions of conjunctive queries (BUCQs) with respect to the intersection of all optimal GA censors—an approach that has been shown in other contexts to ensure strong security guarantees with favorable computational behavior. First, we characterize the security of this intersection-based approach and identify a class of EDs (namely, full EDs) for which it remains safe. Then, for a subclass of EDs and for DL-Lite$_{\mathcal{R}}$ ontologies, we show that answering BUCQs in the above CQE semantics is in AC^0 in data complexity by presenting a suitable, detailed first-order rewriting algorithm. Finally, we report on experiments conducted in two different evaluation scenarios, showing the practical feasibility of our rewriting function.

Keywords: Description Logics · Ontologies · Confidentiality Preservation · Query Answering · Data Complexity · Epistemic Dependencies

1 Introduction

The ever-growing volume of structured and semantically rich data has created new challenges for knowledge management and data security. Several modern applications in domains like healthcare and finance rely on ontologies to establish shared vocabularies and formal semantics, facilitating effective data organization and retrieval. While these tools provide sophisticated querying and inference, they also raise critical concerns about unintended information disclosure: apparently harmless queries can reveal sensitive data when combined with ontological knowledge. *Controlled Query Evaluation* (CQE) [4,5,7,18] is a framework that addresses these concerns by mediating access to data in such a way that only

D. Garijo et al. (Eds.): ISWC 2025, LNCS 16140, pp. 521–538, 2026.
https://doi.org/10.1007/978-3-032-09527-5_28

information compliant with a formal *data protection policy*—expressed in logical terms—is accessible through queries.

We applyCQE to ontologies based on Description Logics (DLs)[1] [2], where knowledge is structured into a TBox, containing intensional axioms, and an ABox, containing extensional facts. The pivotal notion in CQE is the one of *censor*, a set of logical formulas that are logically implied by the ontology and comply with the policy. Specifically, we are interested in *GA censors* [15], which consist of ground atoms, hence structurally resembling ABoxes or relational databases.

Usually, CQE policies are defined using *denials*, i.e. expressions of the form $(\exists \mathbf{x}\, \gamma(\mathbf{x})) \rightarrow \bot$, where $\exists \mathbf{x}\, \gamma(\mathbf{x})$ is a *Boolean conjunctive query* (BCQ). Denials are used to specify information that must remain undisclosed: the system must prevent users from inferring that the formula $\exists \mathbf{x}\, \gamma(\mathbf{x})$ holds in the ontology. The recent work [12] proposed an extension for such a language of rules, called *epistemic dependencies* (EDs) [16], which are logical implications between two (possibly open) conjunctive queries, each within the scope of an epistemic operator K, though adopting a notion of censor that differs from the one considered in the current paper.

Example 1. The policy of a company stipulates that all salaries of employees must be kept confidential, except those of managers. In addition, the existence of consensual personal relationships between managers and their employees must remain undisclosed.

In logical terms, such a policy can be defined as the following set of EDs:

$$\begin{aligned}\mathcal{P} = \{\, & \forall x, y\, (K\mathsf{salary}(x, y) \rightarrow K\mathsf{manager}(x)),\\ & K\exists x, y\, (\mathsf{managerOf}(x, y) \wedge \mathsf{consRel}(x, y)) \rightarrow K\bot\,\}\end{aligned}$$

where manager is a unary predicate and salary, consRel and managerOf are binary predicates with the intuitive meaning. In the second ED, the usage of the existential quantifier indicates that, for every manager (resp., employee), the very existence of a consensual relationship with any employee (resp., manager) of hers must not be revealed—not merely the identities of the individual involved.

Moreover, suppose that the company ontology consists of:

- A TBox $\mathcal{T} = \{\exists\mathsf{managerOf} \sqsubseteq \mathsf{manager}, \mathsf{manager} \sqsubseteq \exists\mathsf{respDept}\}$, meaning that everyone who manages another individual is a manager, and managers are such only if they are responsible for some department.
- An ABox $\mathcal{A} = \{\mathsf{managerOf}(\mathsf{lucy}, \mathsf{tom}), \mathsf{consRel}(\mathsf{lucy}, \mathsf{tom}), \mathsf{salary}(\mathsf{lucy}, \mathsf{150k}), \mathsf{salary}(\mathsf{tom}, \mathsf{75k})\}$, meaning that Lucy is Tom's manager, they have a consensual relationship, and their salary is \$150,000 and \$75,000, respectively.

A censor consisting only of ground atoms must remove at least one of the facts $\mathsf{managerOf}(\mathsf{lucy}, \mathsf{tom}), \mathsf{consRel}(\mathsf{lucy}, \mathsf{tom})$ from $\mathcal{A}$ and, at the same time, must remove the fact $\mathsf{salary}(\mathsf{tom}, \mathsf{75k})$ (because Tom is not a manager). By contrast, any optimal GA censor can safely include the facts $\mathsf{manager}(\mathsf{lucy})$ and $\mathsf{salary}(\mathsf{lucy},$

[1] For an up-to-date overview of CQE in the context of DLs, we refer the reader to [6, 13].

150k), because Lucy's managerial status follows from the ontology and knowing that she is a manager (and her salary) does not violate the policy. ■

Our main objective is to evaluate queries under a formal entailment semantics that maximizes data disclosure while remaining compliant with the policy. Thus, we call *optimal GA censors* the GA censors that are maximal w.r.t. set inclusion, and focus on the problem of checking whether a *Boolean union of conjunctive queries* (BUCQ) is entailed by the TBox and the intersection of all the optimal GA censors. This task, known as *IGA-entailment*, has been shown to be *FO-rewritable* when the TBox is expressed in DL-Lite$_{\mathcal{R}}$ and the policy consists of denials [14]. That is, in the above setting, IGA-entailment of a BUCQ q can be decided by rewriting q into a new FO query q_r that only depends on the TBox and the policy and, in a second moment, evaluating q_r over the ABox. This property guarantees a nice computational behaviour at a theoretical level, as the task enjoying it has the same complexity as evaluating an SQL query over a database. However, it still needs to be empirically validated through a practical implementation. In the case based on denials, a working prototype was provided in [11], within the ontology-based data access framework.

We aim to extend this scenario to accommodate policies defined using EDs while preserving the *FO-rewritability* property. First, we prove that the class of *full EDs* and *linear EDs* enjoy a desirable property related to security. We exclude, however, the possibility that IGA-entailment remains FO-rewritable for such classes of dependencies, by proving coNP- and NL-hardness results for the related decision problem, respectively. We thus identify a condition for full EDs for which we are able to prove the FO-rewritability. For two classes of EDs that respect such a condition, namely the linear full and the acyclic full EDs, we finally conducted experiments to test the practical feasibility of our rewriting algorithm. Specifically, we implemented a tool that rewrites a SPARQL BUCQ into a new query q_r solely based on the given TBox and policy, and then evaluates q_r over an SQL database containing the ABox. Since our theoretical results are related to the logic DL-Lite$_{\mathcal{R}}$, we adopted the OWL 2 QL ontology of the OWL2Bench benchmark [26] as our testbed. Two distinct evaluation scenarios demonstrate that our method is not only theoretically sound but also practically feasible, with most rewritten queries running within acceptable time bounds.

The paper is structured as follows. Section 2 provides the necessary theoretical background. Section 3 describes the framework and the problem studied. Section 4 introduces a key property that helps identify interesting subclasses of EDs. Section 5 presents lower bounds that exclude FO-rewritability in the general case. Section 6 defines the subclass of EDs we target and presents a detailed FO-rewriting algorithm. Section 7 reports our experimental findings. Finally, Sect. 8 concludes the paper.

2 Preliminaries

In this paper, we refer to standard notions of function-free first-order (FO) logic and Description Logics (DL). We use countably infinite sets of symbols Σ_C, Σ_R,

Σ_I and Σ_V, containing respectively unary predicates (called *concepts*), binary predicates (called *roles*), constant symbols (also called *individuals*) and variables. An *atom* is a formula of the form $P(\mathbf{t})$, where P is a (either unary or binary) predicate and $\mathbf{t}$ is a sequence of terms, i.e. variables or constants.

Given a set of FO formulas Φ, we denote by $vars(\Phi)$ and $pred(\Phi)$, the sets of variables and predicates occurring in Φ, respectively. Given any FO formula ϕ, we use the notation $\phi(\mathbf{x})$ when we want to emphasize its free variables $\mathbf{x}$, and we overload $vars(\cdot)$ to work with FO formulas, with the same meaning. If $\phi(\mathbf{x})$ is closed (that is, $\mathbf{x}$ is empty), then it is called a *sentence*; Furthermore, if $vars(\phi) = \emptyset$, then ϕ is said to be *ground*. In particular, ground atoms are also called *facts*. If $\mathcal{F}$ is a set of facts, we say that an FO sentence ϕ evaluates to true in $\mathcal{F}$ to actually mean that it is true in the Herbrand model of $\mathcal{F}$.

In this work, we also refer to specific classes of domain-independent FO formulas, such as the class of *conjunctive queries* (CQs), i.e. formulas of the form $\exists \mathbf{x}\,(\gamma)$, where $\mathbf{x} \subseteq vars(\gamma)$ and γ is a conjunction of atoms. A disjunction of CQs sharing the same free variables is called *union of conjunctive queries* (UCQ), which sometimes we also treat as a set of CQs. As customary, closed CQs and UCQs are said to be *Boolean* and referred to as BCQs and BUCQs, respectively. Given any CQ q, we indicate by $QA(q)$ the set of atoms of q.

We call *substitution* any function $\sigma : \Sigma_V \rightarrow \Sigma_V \cup \Sigma_I$. Given a CQ q and a substitution σ of (a subset of) its variables, we write $\sigma(q)$ to denote the result of applying σ to q. A substitution of variables is said to be *ground* if its image is contained in Σ_I. Moreover, given a set of facts $\mathcal{F}$, an *instantiation* for q in $\mathcal{F}$ is a ground substitution σ of the variables of q such that $QA(\sigma(q)) \subseteq \mathcal{F}$. If such an instantiation σ exists, the set $QA(\sigma(q))$ is called *image* of q in $\mathcal{F}$. Given a UCQ q, an *image of q in $\mathcal{F}$* is any image of q' in $\mathcal{F}$, for any $q' \in q$.

We resort to DL ontologies as a formal way of representing structured knowledge about a given domain. Ontologies are usually partitioned into two sets used, respectively, for representing intensional and extensional knowledge. More formally, given a DL $\mathcal{L}_\mathcal{T}$, an $\mathcal{L}_\mathcal{T}$ *ontology* is a finite set $\mathcal{T} \cup \mathcal{A}$, where $\mathcal{T}$ (called $\mathcal{L}_\mathcal{T}$ TBox) is a set of axioms expressible in $\mathcal{L}_\mathcal{T}$, and $\mathcal{A}$ (called ABox) is a set of ground atoms. In particular, our complexity results hold for ontologies expressed in DL-Lite$_\mathcal{R}$ [10], which is the logic underpinning OWL 2 QL, one of the three OWL 2 profiles [17,23] that is specifically designed for efficient query answering. The axioms of a DL-Lite$_\mathcal{R}$ TBox $\mathcal{T}$ take the form $B \sqsubseteq B'$, $R \sqsubseteq R'$, $B \sqsubseteq \neg B'$, or $R \sqsubseteq \neg R'$, where B and B' (resp., R and R') are of the form A, $\exists S$ or $\exists S^-$ (resp., of the form S or S^-), with $A \in \Sigma_C$, $S \in \Sigma_R$ and S^- the inverse of S. The unqualified existential restriction $\exists S$ (resp., $\exists S^-$) represents the set of individuals occurring as the first (resp., second) argument of S.

Moreover, we denote with $\mathsf{cl}_\mathcal{T}(\mathcal{A})$ the *closure* of $\mathcal{A}$ w.r.t. $\mathcal{T}$, i.e. the set of all the ground atoms that are logical consequences of $\mathcal{T} \cup \mathcal{A}$. We also refer to the rewriting function $\mathsf{AtomRewr}$, for which the following property has been demonstrated in [15, Lemma 6].

Proposition 1 ([15]). *Let $\mathcal{T} \cup \mathcal{A}$ be a consistent DL-Lite$_{\mathcal{R}}$ ontology, and let ϕ be an FO sentence. Then, ϕ evaluates to true in $\mathsf{cl}_{\mathcal{T}}(\mathcal{A})$ if and only if* $\mathsf{AtomRewr}(\phi, \mathcal{T})$ *evaluates to true in $\mathcal{A}$.*

Finally, Sect. 5 requires the reader to be familiar with basic notions of computational complexity theory [24]. Indeed, decision problems solvable through FO-rewriting are known to be in AC^0 in data complexity [1], and we refer to the complexity classes NL and coNP (both of which are known to be strict supersets of AC^0) for showing scenarios in which the studied problem is not FO-rewritable.

3 Framework

In the spirit of [12], we adopt as *protection policy* (or simply *policy)* a finite set of epistemic dependencies, which are a special case of EQL-Lite(CQ) [9] sentences, and are defined as follows.

Definition 1. *An* epistemic dependency (ED) *is a sentence τ of the form:*

$$\forall \mathbf{x}_1, \mathbf{x}_2 \, (K q_b(\mathbf{x}_1, \mathbf{x}_2) \rightarrow K q_h(\mathbf{x}_2)) \quad (1)$$

where $q_b(\mathbf{x}_1, \mathbf{x}_2)$ is a CQ with free variables $\mathbf{x}_1 \cup \mathbf{x}_2$, $q_h(\mathbf{x}_2)$ is a CQ with free variables $\mathbf{x}_2$, and K is an epistemic operator. Given an ED τ, we refer to the CQs q_b and q_h with $\mathsf{body}(\tau)$ *and* $\mathsf{head}(\tau)$*, respectively.*

We say that an FO theory Φ *satisfies* an ED τ (in symbols $\Phi \models_{\mathsf{EQL}} \tau$) if, for every ground substitution σ for the free variables of $\mathsf{body}(\tau)$, if $\Phi \models \sigma(\mathsf{body}(\tau))$ then $\Phi \models \sigma(\mathsf{head}(\tau))$. If all the EDs of a policy $\mathcal{P}$ are satisfied by Φ, then we say that Φ *satisfies* $\mathcal{P}$ (in symbols $\Phi \models_{\mathsf{EQL}} \mathcal{P}$). Intuitively, EDs express the disclosure rules that should govern the publication of data. For every ground substitution σ of the universal variables of an ED τ, if the ontology entails $\sigma(\mathsf{body}(\tau))$, then this information may only be disclosed if $\sigma(\mathsf{head}(\tau))$ can also be disclosed. In the special case in which $\mathsf{head}(\tau) = \bot$, the ED acts as a denial constraint, i.e. its body must not be revealed under any instantiation of its free variables.

The input to our framework is a triple $\langle \mathcal{T}, \mathcal{P}, \mathcal{A} \rangle$, called *CQE instance* (or $\mathcal{L}$ *CQE instance*, if $\mathcal{T} \cup \mathcal{A}$ is expressed in a given DL $\mathcal{L}$), where $\mathcal{T}$ is a DL TBox, $\mathcal{P}$ is a policy and $\mathcal{A}$ is an ABox such that $\mathcal{T} \cup \mathcal{A}$ is consistent. Given a CQE instance $\langle \mathcal{T}, \mathcal{P}, \mathcal{A} \rangle$, it may be the case that $\mathcal{T} \cup \mathcal{A} \not\models_{\mathsf{EQL}} \mathcal{P}$, i.e. the policy is not satisfied by the ontology $\mathcal{T} \cup \mathcal{A}$. For hiding the part of information that should be protected, we rely on the following notion of GA censor [15].

Definition 2 (GA censor). *Given a CQE instance $\mathcal{E} = \langle \mathcal{T}, \mathcal{P}, \mathcal{A} \rangle$, a* ground atom (GA) censor *for $\mathcal{E}$ is any subset $\mathcal{C}$ of $\mathsf{cl}_{\mathcal{T}}(\mathcal{A})$ such that $\mathcal{T} \cup \mathcal{C} \models_{\mathsf{EQL}} \mathcal{P}$. A GA censor $\mathcal{C}$ of $\mathcal{E}$ is* optimal *if no GA censor $\mathcal{C}'$ of $\mathcal{E}$ exists such that $\mathcal{C}' \supset \mathcal{C}$.*

Informally, an optimal GA censor is a maximal (w.r.t. set inclusion) portion of $\mathsf{cl}_{\mathcal{T}}(\mathcal{A})$ that can be safely disclosed without violating the given policy. Among the possibly many GA censors for a CQE instance, we are particularly interested in the information that is common to all optimal GA censors, which represents the maximal amount of facts that can be safely revealed in every scenario where policy satisfaction is preserved. Based on this idea, we now introduce the central notion of IGA-entailment, which formalizes query answering under the intersection of all optimal GA censors.

Definition 3 (IGA-entailment). *Given a CQE instance* $\mathcal{E} = \langle \mathcal{T}, \mathcal{P}, \mathcal{A} \rangle$ *and a BUCQ* q*, we say that* $\mathcal{E}$ IGA-entails q *(in symbols* $\mathcal{E} \models_{\mathsf{IGA}} q$*) if* $\mathcal{T} \cup \mathcal{C}_{\mathsf{IGA}} \models q$*, where* $\mathcal{C}_{\mathsf{IGA}}$ *is the intersection of all the optimal GA censors of* $\mathcal{E}$*.*

Example 2. Consider the CQE instance $\mathcal{E} = \langle \mathcal{T}, \mathcal{P}, \mathcal{A} \rangle$, where $\mathcal{T}$, $\mathcal{P}$ and $\mathcal{A}$ are as in Example 1. In this case, we have only two optimal censors, i.e.:

$$\mathcal{C}_1 = \{\mathsf{managerOf}(\mathsf{lucy}, \mathsf{tom}), \mathsf{manager}(\mathsf{lucy}), \mathsf{salary}(\mathsf{lucy}, \mathsf{150k})\},$$
$$\mathcal{C}_2 = \{\mathsf{consRel}(\mathsf{lucy}, \mathsf{tom}), \mathsf{manager}(\mathsf{lucy}), \mathsf{salary}(\mathsf{lucy}, \mathsf{150k})\}.$$

Now, we have that a BCQ like $q_1 = \exists x, y\, \mathsf{consRel}(x, y)$ is not IGA-entailed by $\mathcal{E}$, because the extension of consRel is empty in $\mathcal{C}_{\mathsf{IGA}} = \mathcal{C}_1 \cap \mathcal{C}_2$ and no relevant conclusions can be drawn from the intensional axioms. Conversely, the BCQ $q_2 = \exists x, y\, (\mathsf{respDept}(x, y) \wedge \mathsf{salary}(x, \mathsf{150k}))$ is IGA-entailed by $\mathcal{E}$, because the facts $\mathsf{manager}(\mathsf{lucy})$ and $\mathsf{salary}(\mathsf{lucy}, \mathsf{150k})$ belong to the intersection $\mathcal{C}_{\mathsf{IGA}}$. ■

It is worth noting that an alternative, more expressive kind of entailment has been proposed in the literature, i.e., the skeptical entailment over all the optimal GA censors. However, such an approach has already been shown to be computationally intractable (specifically, coNP-hard in data complexity) even for BCQs and for policies restricted to sets of denial constraints [15, Thm. 6].

Although the above definitions apply to any CQE instance, our complexity analysis focuses on specific classes of EDs, which are defined below. First, borrowing the terminology from the literature on both databases and existential rules (see e.g. [3,8]), an ED τ is called *full* if no existential variable occurs in its head, and is called *linear* if $|\mathcal{QA}(\mathsf{body}(\tau))| = 1$. A policy is *full* (resp., *linear*) if all its EDs are full (resp., linear). Then, following the paper [12] that introduced EDs for CQE, we define the notion of acyclicity as follows. Given a policy $\mathcal{P}$ and a TBox $\mathcal{T}$, consider the graph G whose nodes are the predicates of $\mathcal{T} \cup \mathcal{P}$, and whose edges are of two kinds: T-edges, which connect two nodes A and B of G if they occur, respectively, on the left- and right-hand side of a concept or role inclusion of $\mathcal{T}$; analogously P-edges connect two nodes A and B of G if they occur, respectively, in the body and head of an ED of $\mathcal{P}$. Then, $\mathcal{P}$ is said to be *acyclic for* $\mathcal{T}$ if G contains no cycle involving a P-edge.

We finally define the decision problem that we focus on, called IGA-ENT, as the problem of checking whether a BUCQ is entailed under the IGA semantics.

4 Security of the Intersection of GA Censors

Before delving into the complexity analysis of the IGA-ENT problem, it is natural to ask whether the intersection of all optimal GA censors constitutes in turn a valid censor, i.e. whether it satisfies the given policy.

Actually, the above property does not hold, in general, even in the case when the TBox is empty, as shown by the following example.

Example 3. Consider the CQE instance $\mathcal{E} = \langle \mathcal{T}, \mathcal{P}, \mathcal{A} \rangle$, where $\mathcal{T}$ is empty and

$$\mathcal{P} = \{\, \tau_1 : K(B(1) \wedge B(2)) \rightarrow K\bot, \qquad \mathcal{A} = \{C(0), B(1), B(2)\,\}.$$
$$\tau_2 : \forall x\, (KC(x) \rightarrow K\exists y\, B(y))\,\},$$

We observe that $\mathcal{C}_1 = \{C(0), B(1)\}$ and $\mathcal{C}_2 = \{C(0), B(2)\}$ are the only two optimal GA censors for $\mathcal{E}$, and so their intersection $\mathcal{C}_{\mathsf{IGA}}$ is $\{C(0)\}$. Then, one can see that $\mathcal{T} \cup \mathcal{C}_{\mathsf{IGA}} \not\models_{\mathsf{EQL}} \tau_2$, which implies that $\mathcal{C}_{\mathsf{IGA}}$ is not a censor. ■

Notice that the policy employed in Example 3 is acyclic for the coupled (empty) TBox. However, it is possible to demonstrate that it is safe to refer to the intersection of the optimal GA censors when considering the classes of linear EDs and full EDs, which we focus on in the next section.

Theorem 1. *For every CQE instance $\mathcal{E} = \langle \mathcal{T}, \mathcal{P}, \mathcal{A} \rangle$ such that $\mathcal{P}$ is either full or linear, the set $\mathcal{C}_{\mathsf{IGA}} = \bigcap_{\mathcal{C} \in \mathsf{optCens}(\mathcal{E})} \mathcal{C}$ is a GA censor of $\mathcal{E}$.*

Proof. To be a GA censor of $\mathcal{E}$, $\mathcal{C}_{\mathsf{IGA}}$ must be a subset of $\mathsf{cl}_{\mathcal{T}}(\mathcal{A})$ and be such that $\mathcal{T} \cup \mathcal{C}_{\mathsf{IGA}} \models_{\mathsf{EQL}} \mathcal{P}$. The first condition always follows by construction of $\mathcal{C}_{\mathsf{IGA}}$. Then, for both the cases have just to prove the second one.

We first focus on full policies. To prove the thesis, let us consider any $\tau \in \mathcal{P}$ and any ground substitution σ of the universal variables of τ such that $\mathcal{T} \cup \mathcal{C}_{\mathsf{IGA}} \models \sigma(\mathsf{body}(\tau))$, and let us show that $\mathcal{T} \cup \mathcal{C}_{\mathsf{IGA}} \models \sigma(\mathsf{head}(\tau))$. If $\mathcal{T} \cup \mathcal{C}_{\mathsf{IGA}} \models \sigma(\mathsf{body}(\tau))$, then by monotonicity, it follows that $\mathcal{T} \cup \mathcal{C} \models \sigma(\mathsf{body}(\tau))$ for every $\mathcal{C} \in \mathsf{optCens}(\mathcal{E})$. However, for every such $\mathcal{C}$, since τ is full, then $\sigma(\mathsf{head}(\tau))$ is a ground conjunction of atoms, and since $\mathcal{C}$ is optimal, then all such ground atoms belong to it. Consequently, all the ground atoms of $\sigma(\mathsf{head}(\tau))$ belong to $\mathcal{C}_{\mathsf{IGA}}$, which immediately implies that $\mathcal{T} \cup \mathcal{C}_{\mathsf{IGA}} \models \sigma(\mathsf{head}(\tau))$.

We now turn our attention to linear policies. Notice that, if every ED is linear, then only one optimal GA censor $\mathcal{C}$ for $\mathcal{E}$ exists. Such a GA censor can indeed be deterministically computed by iteratively (until a fixpoint is reached) checking whether there exists an atom $\alpha \in \mathcal{C}$, an ED $\tau \in \mathcal{P}$ and an assignment σ of the free variables of $\mathsf{body}(\tau)$ such that $\mathcal{T} \cup \{\alpha\} \models \sigma(\mathsf{body}(\tau))$ but $\mathcal{T} \cup \mathcal{C} \not\models \sigma(\mathsf{head}(\tau))$ and, in such a case, remove α from $\mathcal{C}$. Thus, the intersection coincides with such a censor, i.e. $\mathcal{C}_{\mathsf{IGA}} = \mathcal{C}$, which implies $\mathcal{T} \cup \mathcal{C}_{\mathsf{IGA}} \models_{\mathsf{EQL}} \mathcal{P}$ by Definition 2. □

5 Negative Results

As anticipated in the Introduction, we aim to find a class of dependencies for which IGA-entailment is FO-rewritable. Starting from the results obtained in the previous section, a natural first choice would be the classes of full and linear EDs. The following property, however, excludes the possibility of FO-rewritability of IGA-entailment for the class of linear epistemic dependencies.

Theorem 2. *There exist a policy consisting of linear EDs, and a query consisting of a single atom for which* IGA-ENT *is NL-hard in data complexity, even in the case the TBox is empty.*

Proof (sketch). We prove the thesis through a logspace reduction from the restriction of st-connectivity to directed acyclic graphs (DAGs), which is known to remain NL-hard [22]. Given a DAG $\mathcal{G} = \langle V, E\rangle$ and two nodes $s, t \in V$, such a problem consists of checking whether there exists a path from s to t in $\mathcal{G}$.

First, let $\mathcal{P} = \{\forall u\, (K\exists v\, \mathit{reachableVia}(v, u) \rightarrow K\exists w\, \mathit{reachableVia}(u, w))\}$, and let $\mathcal{G}' = \langle V, E'\rangle$ be such that $E' = E \cup \{(t, s)\}$. Let also $\mathcal{T} = \emptyset$ and

$$\mathcal{A} = \{\mathit{reachableVia}(v, u) \mid (u, v) \in E'\} \cup \{\mathit{reachableVia}(s, s)\}.$$

Note that $\mathcal{A}$ (we ignore the TBox, as it is empty) does not necessarily satisfy the policy, but the set $\{\mathit{reachableVia}(s, s)\}$ does. Intuitively, the policy $\mathcal{P}$ states that, for every pair of nodes $v, u \in V$, v is reachable from s via u only if u is reachable from s via another node $w \in V$. Also, the ABox states that every node is reachable from s via all its predecessors in $\mathcal{G}'$ (which is not necessarily true), plus the fact that s is reachable via itself. Also, since $\mathcal{P}$ is linear, then exactly one optimal GA censor for $\mathcal{E} = \langle \mathcal{T}, \mathcal{P}, \mathcal{A}\rangle$ exists, which then coincides with $\mathcal{C}_{\mathsf{IGA}}$.

One can then verify that $\mathcal{G}$ contains a path from s to t iff the BCQ $q = \exists u\, \mathit{reachableVia}(t, u)$ is IGA-entailed by $\mathcal{E}$. □

We now show that the scenario is even worse for full dependencies, as the decision problem under consideration is even intractable in data complexity.

Theorem 3. *There exist a policy consisting of full EDs, and a query consisting of a ground atom for which* IGA-ENT *is coNP-hard in data complexity, even in the case the TBox is empty.*

Proof (sketch). We prove the thesis by reduction from 3-CNF. We define the TBox $\mathcal{T} = \emptyset$ and the following full policy:

$$\begin{array}{c}
\forall i, j, p, v\ (K\,(S(i) \wedge N(j, i) \wedge V_1(i, p) \wedge P_1(i, v) \wedge T(p, v)) \rightarrow K\,S(j))\\
\forall i, j, p, v\ (K\,(S(i) \wedge N(j, i) \wedge V_2(i, p) \wedge P_2(i, v) \wedge T(p, v)) \rightarrow K\,S(j))\\
\forall i, j, p, v\ (K\,(S(i) \wedge N(j, i) \wedge V_3(i, p) \wedge P_3(i, v) \wedge T(p, v)) \rightarrow K\,S(j))\\
\forall x\ (K\,(T(x, 0) \wedge T(x, 1)) \rightarrow K\,U(0))
\end{array}$$

Now, given a 3-CNF formula φ with m clauses, the ABox $\mathcal{A}$ contains the facts:

- $N(i-1, i)$ for every $1 \leq i \leq m$, meaning that c_i is the next clause of c_j (note that $N(0, 1)$ is included);
- $V_j(i, p)$ if p is the j-th propositional variable in the i-th clause;
- $P_j(i, 0)$ (resp., $P_j(i, 1)$) if the polarity of the j-th literal in the i-th clause is negative (resp., positive);
- $T(p, 0)$ and $T(p, 1)$ for every propositional variable p occurring in φ;
- $S(1), S(2), \ldots, S(m)$.

We can prove that φ is unsatisfiable iff $S(m)$ is IGA-entailed by $\mathcal{E}$. □

6 A FO-Rewritable Class of EDs

In this section, we identify a condition for full EDs that, in the case of DL-Lite$_\mathcal{R}$ TBoxes, enables solving IGA-entailment through an FO-rewriting technique. We start by defining when a given set $\mathcal{F}$ of facts is disclosable. Intuitively, this happens when we can expose it via at least one optimal GA censor.

Definition 4 (Disclosability). *Given a CQE instance $\mathcal{E}$, we say that a set of facts $\mathcal{F}$ is* disclosable in $\mathcal{E}$ *if there exists a subset $\mathcal{F}'$ of $\mathsf{cl}_\mathcal{T}(\mathcal{A})$ such that $\mathcal{F} \subseteq \mathcal{F}'$ and $\mathcal{T} \cup \mathcal{F}' \models_{\mathsf{EQL}} \mathcal{P}$.*

For technical purposes, we make use of the notion of *tuple-generating dependency* (TGD) [1], i.e. FO expressions of the form $\forall \mathbf{x}_1, \mathbf{x}_2 \, (q_b(\mathbf{x}_1, \mathbf{x}_2) \rightarrow q_h(\mathbf{x}_2))$, where both $q_b(\mathbf{x}_1, \mathbf{x}_2)$ and $q_h(\mathbf{x}_2)$ are CQs. We say that a set Σ of TGDs is *UCQ-rewritable* if, given any CQ $q(\mathbf{x})$, there exists a UCQ $\mathsf{UCQRew}(q, \Sigma)$ such that, for every set $\mathcal{F}$ of facts and for every ground substitution σ of the free variables of q, $\Sigma \cup \mathcal{F} \models \sigma(q)$ iff $\mathcal{F} \models \sigma(q_r)$ for some $q_r(\mathbf{x}) \in \mathsf{UCQRew}(q, \Sigma)$). In this regard, we refer to [3], which establishes a sufficient condition for UCQ rewritability (generalizing acyclicity and linearity), and to [20], which provides a suitable rewriting algorithm .[2]

Now, given a policy $\mathcal{P}$, let us denote by $TGD(\mathcal{P})$ the following set of TGDs:

$$\{\forall \mathbf{x}_1, \mathbf{x}_2 \, (q_b(\mathbf{x}_1, \mathbf{x}_2) \rightarrow q_h(\mathbf{x}_2)) \mid \forall \mathbf{x}_1, \mathbf{x}_2 \, (K q_b(\mathbf{x}_1, \mathbf{x}_2) \rightarrow K q_h(\mathbf{x}_2)) \in \mathcal{P}\}.$$

Moreover, given a DL-Lite$_\mathcal{R}$ TBox $\mathcal{T}$, let us denote by $TGD(\mathcal{T})$ the set of TGDs obtained from $\mathcal{T}$ in the natural way.

UCQ-rewritability is a well-established property of DL-Lite$_\mathcal{R}$ TBoxes [10]:

Proposition 2. *Let $\mathcal{T}$ be a DL-Lite$_\mathcal{R}$ TBox. Then, $TGD(\mathcal{T})$ is UCQ-rewritable.*

For the sake of readability, when referring to DL-Lite$_\mathcal{R}$ TBoxes $\mathcal{T}$, we write $\mathsf{UCQRew}(q, \mathcal{T})$ instead of $\mathsf{UCQRew}(q, TGD(\mathcal{T}))$.

Furthermore, let us indicate with $\mathcal{P}^+$ the policy containing every ED in $\mathcal{P}$ whose head does not contain $\bot$, and with $\Sigma(\mathcal{P}, \mathcal{T})$ the set of TGDs $TGD(\mathcal{P}^+) \cup TGD(\mathcal{T})$. We say that $\mathcal{P}$ is *expandable* w.r.t. $\mathcal{T}$ if $\Sigma(\mathcal{P}, \mathcal{T})$ is UCQ-rewritable. Then, from the results in [20], we directly have what follows:

Proposition 3. *Let $\mathcal{T}$ be a DL-Lite$_\mathcal{R}$ TBox, and let $\mathcal{P}$ be a policy that is either linear or acyclic for $\mathcal{T}$. Then, $\mathcal{P}$ is expandable w.r.t. $\mathcal{T}$.*[3]

We can now introduce Algorithm 1, which takes as input a DL-Lite$_\mathcal{R}$ TBox $\mathcal{T}$ and a policy $\mathcal{P}$ expandable w.r.t. $\mathcal{T}$ and returns a new policy $\mathcal{P}'$ obtained in the following way. For each ED $\tau \in \mathcal{P}$, it computes the rewriting of the body of τ w.r.t. $\Sigma(\mathcal{P}, \mathcal{T})$ and builds one new ED for every BCQ $q(\mathbf{x})$ occurring in such

[2] Actually, that paper focuses on BCQs. Anyway, as also stated by the authors, the algorithm provided is easily extendable to open CQs.

[3] It is not hard to see that this property is preserved in the case the policy also contains denials. Thus, our technique applies to a generalization of the case of denials.

Algorithm 1: PolicyExp

input : A DL-Lite$_\mathcal{R}$ TBox $\mathcal{T}$, a policy $\mathcal{P}$ expandable w.r.t. $\mathcal{T}$

$\mathcal{P}' \leftarrow \emptyset$;
foreach $\tau \in \mathcal{P}$ **do**
  foreach $q(\mathbf{x}) \in \mathsf{UCQRew}(\mathsf{body}(\tau), \Sigma(\mathcal{P}, \mathcal{T}))$ **do**
    $\mathcal{P}' \leftarrow \mathcal{P}' \cup \{\forall \mathbf{x}(Kq(\mathbf{x}) \rightarrow K\mathsf{head}(\tau))\}$;
return $\mathcal{P}'$

rewriting. In particular, it uses each of these $q(\mathbf{x})$ as the body of the new ED, it leaves the head unchanged, and it universally quantifies the free variables of q. Note that every such ED has the same universally quantified variables as the original ED τ.

Algorithm 1 realizes the function $\mathsf{PolicyExp}(\cdot, \cdot)$, which exhibits the following important property.

Lemma 1. *Let $\mathcal{E} = \langle \mathcal{T}, \mathcal{P}, \mathcal{A} \rangle$ be a DL-Lite$_\mathcal{R}$ CQE instance such that $\mathcal{P}$ is full and expandable w.r.t. $\mathcal{T}$, and let $\mathcal{F}$ be a set of facts. Then, $\mathcal{F}$ is disclosable in $\mathcal{E}$ iff both the following conditions hold:*

(i) $\mathcal{F} \subseteq \mathsf{cl}_\mathcal{T}(\mathcal{A})$;
(ii) for every $\tau \in \mathsf{PolicyExp}(\mathcal{P}, \mathcal{T})$ *and every ground substitution σ of the free variables of* $\mathsf{body}(\tau)$, $\mathcal{F} \models \sigma(\mathsf{body}(\tau))$ *implies that* $\mathcal{T} \cup \mathcal{A} \models \sigma(\mathsf{head}(\tau))$.

In the following, given a CQ q and a set of atoms $\mathcal{Z}$, we say that q is *mappable to $\mathcal{Z}$ via μ* if there exists a substitution μ replacing the variables of $\mathcal{Z}$ and the free variables of q with terms of $\mathcal{Z}$ and constants of q, in such a way that there exists a substitution μ' of the existential variables of q such that $\mu'(\mu(QA(q))) \subseteq \mu(\mathcal{Z})$. We indicate as $\mathsf{map}(q, \mathcal{Z})$ the set of all the substitutions μ such that q is mappable to $\mathcal{Z}$ via μ. E.g. if $\mathcal{Z} = \{R(x, y), R(z, w)\}$ and $q(v, u) = \exists t\, R(v, 1) \wedge R(u, t)$, then both $\{v \mapsto x, y \mapsto 1, u \mapsto z\}$ and $\{v \mapsto z, w \mapsto 1, u \mapsto x\}$ belong to $\mathsf{map}(q, \mathcal{Z})$.

Definition 5. *Given a DL-Lite$_\mathcal{R}$ TBox $\mathcal{T}$, a policy $\mathcal{P}$ expandable w.r.t. $\mathcal{T}$, and a set $\mathcal{Z}$ of atoms (we assume w.l.o.g. that every $x \in vars(\mathcal{Z})$ does not occur in* $\mathsf{PolicyExp}(\mathcal{P}, \mathcal{T})$*), we define the formula* $\mathsf{isDiscl}(\mathcal{Z}, \mathcal{T}, \mathcal{P})$ *as follows:*

$$\mathsf{AtomRewr}(\mathsf{conj}(\mathcal{Z}), \mathcal{T}) \wedge \bigwedge_{\substack{\tau \in \mathsf{PolicyExp}(\mathcal{P}, \mathcal{T})\, \wedge \\ \mu \in \mathsf{map}(\mathsf{body}(\tau), \mathcal{Z})}} \Big(\mathsf{eq}(\mu, \mathcal{Z}) \rightarrow \mathsf{UCQRew}(\mu(\mathsf{head}(\tau)), \mathcal{T})\Big)$$

where:

- $\mathsf{conj}(\mathcal{Z}) = \bigwedge_{\alpha \in \mathcal{Z}} \alpha$, *for every set $\mathcal{Z}$ of atoms;*
- $\mathsf{eq}(\mu, \mathcal{Z}) = \bigwedge_{\substack{x \mapsto t \in \mu\, \wedge \\ x \in vars(\mathcal{Z})}} x = t$ *(with true in place of the empty conjunction).*

Intuitively, for every ground substitution σ of its free variables, the FO sentence $\sigma(\mathsf{isDiscl}(\mathcal{Z}, \mathcal{T}, \mathcal{P}))$ encodes the two conditions of Lemma 1. More formally:

Lemma 2. *Let $\mathcal{E} = \langle \mathcal{T}, \mathcal{P}, \mathcal{A} \rangle$ be a DL-Lite$_\mathcal{R}$ CQE instance such that $\mathcal{P}$ is full and expandable w.r.t. $\mathcal{T}$. Then, for every set of atoms $\mathcal{Z}$ and for every ground substitution σ of the variables of $\mathcal{Z}$, $\sigma(\mathsf{isDiscl}(\mathcal{Z}, \mathcal{T}, \mathcal{P}))$ evaluates to true in $\mathcal{A}$ iff $\sigma(\mathcal{Z})$ is disclosable in $\mathcal{E}$.*

Then, given a DL-Lite$_\mathcal{R}$ TBox $\mathcal{T}$, a policy $\mathcal{P}$ expandable w.r.t. $\mathcal{T}$, a set $\mathcal{Z}$ of atoms, and a CQ $q(\mathbf{x})$ without existential variables (we assume w.l.o.g. that $\mathbf{x} \cap \mathit{vars}(\mathcal{Z}) = \emptyset$), we define the FO formula $\mathsf{Clash}(\mathcal{Z}, q, \mathcal{T}, \mathcal{P})$ as follows:

$$\mathsf{Clash}(\mathcal{Z}, q, \mathcal{T}, \mathcal{P}) = \exists \mathbf{y} \left(\mathsf{isDiscl}(\mathcal{Z}, \mathcal{T}, \mathcal{P}) \wedge \neg \mathsf{isDiscl}(\mathcal{Z} \cup QA(q), \mathcal{T}, \mathcal{P})\right),$$

where $\mathbf{y}$ is a tuple containing all the variables occurring in $\mathcal{Z}$. Note that the variables of $\mathbf{x}$ are free. In words, by existentially closing the formula $\mathsf{Clash}(\mathcal{Z}, q, \mathcal{T}, \mathcal{P})$ and then evaluating it over an ABox $\mathcal{A}$ it is possible to check whether there exists a common instantiation σ for all the atoms of $\mathcal{Z}$ and q such that (i) the set $\sigma(\mathcal{Z})$ is disclosable (and thus it is part of some censor) and (ii) it is no longer disclosable when we add the atoms of q. Intuitively, if there exists an instantiation of the variables of q for which the above does not occur for any $\mathcal{Z}$, then q is entailed by $\mathcal{E}$ under the IGA semantics.

In order to obtain a proper FO-rewriting algorithm, it remains to show that the size of $\mathcal{Z}$ can be upper-bounded by a certain integer k that is independent of $\mathcal{A}$. To this aim, given a set of predicates $\Pi = \{p_1, \ldots, p_m\}$ and a positive integer k, we define the following set of atoms:

$$\mathit{Atoms}(\Pi, k) = \{p(\mathbf{x}_i) \mid p \in \Pi \text{ and } i \in \{1, \ldots, k\}\},$$

where each $\mathbf{x}_i$ is a sequence of h fresh variables, if h is the arity of p.

We are now ready to provide the following FO-rewriting function.

Definition 6. *Let $\mathcal{T}$ be a DL-Lite$_\mathcal{R}$ TBox, let $\mathcal{P}$ be a policy expandable w.r.t. $\mathcal{T}$, and let q be a BUCQ. Then $\mathsf{IGA\text{-}Ent}(q, \mathcal{T}, \mathcal{P})$ is the sentence:*

$$\mathsf{IGA\text{-}Ent}(q, \mathcal{T}, \mathcal{P}) = \bigvee_{\exists \mathbf{x}\, \gamma(\mathbf{x}) \in q_r} \exists \mathbf{x} \Bigg(\gamma \wedge \bigwedge_{\substack{\mathcal{Z} \subseteq \mathit{Atoms}(\mathit{pred}(\mathcal{P} \cup \mathcal{T}), k) \\ \wedge |\mathcal{Z}| < k}} \neg \mathsf{Clash}(\mathcal{Z}, \gamma, \mathcal{T}, \mathcal{P})\Bigg).$$

where $q_r = \mathsf{UCQRew}(q, \mathcal{T})$ and $k = \max_{\tau \in \mathsf{PolicyExp}(\mathcal{P}, \mathcal{T})} |QA(\mathsf{body}(\tau))|$.

It is possible to prove that, for every DL-Lite$_\mathcal{R}$ CQE instance $\mathcal{E} = \langle \mathcal{T}, \mathcal{P}, \mathcal{A} \rangle$, the sentence $\mathsf{IGA\text{-}Ent}(q, \mathcal{T}, \mathcal{P})$ evaluates to true in $\mathcal{A}$ iff $\mathcal{E} \models_{\mathsf{IGA}} q$. Such an FO-rewritability property implies the next theorem.

Theorem 4. IGA-ENT *is FO-rewritable and hence in* AC^0 *in data complexity in the case of DL-Lite$_\mathcal{R}$ TBoxes and policies that are full and expandable w.r.t. the coupled TBox.*

Proof (sketch). Let ϕ be the i-th disjunct of $\mathsf{IGA\text{-}Ent}(q, \mathcal{P}, \mathcal{T})$ and let γ be the BCQ occurring in its left-hand side. First, by Lemma 2, we can prove that $\sigma(\mathsf{Clash}(\mathcal{Z}, cnj, \mathcal{T}, \mathcal{P}))$ evaluates to true in $\mathcal{A}$ iff there exists an instantiation σ' of $\mathsf{conj}(\mathcal{Z})$ in $\mathcal{A}$ such that $\sigma'(\mathcal{Z})$ is disclosable in $\mathcal{E}$ and $\sigma'(\mathcal{Z}) \cup \sigma(QA(\gamma))$ is not. Then, we can show that the integer k defined as in Definition 6 is sufficient for checking, in a sound and complete way, whether there exist a set $\mathcal{Z}$ and a substitution σ such that $\sigma(\mathcal{Z})$ is disclosable in $\mathcal{E}$ and $\sigma(\mathcal{Z}) \cup M$ is not, for every image M of γ in $\mathcal{A}$. This leads us to prove that $\mathcal{T} \cup \mathcal{C}_{\mathsf{IGA}} \models q$ iff $\mathsf{IGA\text{-}Ent}(q, \mathcal{T}, \mathcal{P})$ evaluates to true in $\mathcal{A}$, which in turn proves the thesis. □

Example 4. Recalling Example 2, let us verify that $\mathcal{E} \not\models_{\mathsf{IGA}} q_1$ by rewriting it and then evaluating it over the ABox. First, observe that $\mathsf{UCQRew}(q_1, \mathcal{T}) = q_1$, i.e. the TBox does not affect the entailment of q_1 in this case, and that the unique instantiation of q_1 in $\mathcal{A}$ is $\sigma = \{x \mapsto \mathsf{lucy}, y \mapsto \mathsf{tom}\}$. In addition, since $k = 2$, all sets $\mathcal{Z}$ of Definition 6 are singletons. In particular, for the set $\mathcal{Z} = \{\mathsf{managerOf}(x', y')\}$ one can see that, under the assignment $\sigma' = \sigma \cup \{x' \mapsto \mathsf{lucy}, y' \mapsto \mathsf{tom}\}$, the sentence $\sigma'(\mathsf{Clash}(\mathcal{Z}, q_1, \mathcal{T}, \mathcal{P}))$ evaluates to true in $\mathcal{A}$. Therefore, the whole sentence $\mathsf{IGA\text{-}Ent}(q_1, \mathcal{T}, \mathcal{P})$ evaluates to false in $\mathcal{A}$.

For q_2, we have $\mathsf{UCQRew}(q_2, \mathcal{T}) = \{q_2, \exists x, z(\mathsf{managerOf}(x, z) \wedge \mathsf{salary}(x, \mathsf{150k})), \exists x\,(\mathsf{manager}(x) \wedge \mathsf{salary}(x, \mathsf{150k}))\}$. In particular, one can verify that for the last BCQ there exists no set $\mathcal{Z}'$ analogous to the above set $\mathcal{Z}$ for query q_1, which implies that q_2 is IGA-entailed by $\mathcal{E}$. ■

7 Experiments

In this section, we describe the experiments that we conducted to test the feasibility of our approach. We evaluated our queries on a standard laptop with an Intel i7 @1.8 GHz processor and 16GB of RAM.

We refer to the OWL2Bench benchmark for OWL ontologies [26], which models the university domain and includes a tool for generating ABoxes of customizable size (measured in number of universities). For our experiments, we tested all the ten SPARQL queries [27] for OWL 2 QL against the $\mathsf{o2b}_5$ and $\mathsf{o2b}_{10}$ ABoxes, which store data about 5 and 10 universities (i.e. ~325k and ~710k ABox assertions), respectively. We removed the data properties from the input ontology (as they are not part of DL-Lite$_\mathcal{R}$), and added the definition of the `knows` object property and the `Woman` class in the TBox[4] for OWL 2 QL, as both such predicates occur in the generated ABoxes. The ABoxes were stored in an SQL database, as the FO query produced by our rewriting algorithm can be naturally translated into SQL. We were thus able to delegate the evaluation of queries on the ABox to the SQL system.

As for the reasoner, we employed the tree-witness query rewriter for OWL2 QL ontologies[5] [19,25]. It can be used as an actual implementation of the

[4] https://github.com/kracr/owl2bench/blob/master/UNIV-BENCH-OWL2QL.owl.
[5] https://titan.dcs.bbk.ac.uk/~roman/tw-rewriting/.

UCQRew abstract rewriting function when its second argument is a DL-Lite$_\mathcal{R}$ TBox.

The two cases on which we focused our experiments are the ones in which the policy is either full and linear or full and acyclic for the coupled TBox. More precisely, for the first case we define a slightly more restricted language of EDs (defined below), which we call *binary EDs*. The correspondence of such dependencies with DL-Lite$_\mathcal{R}$ axioms allows us to exploit the tree-witness rewriter in place of UCQRew for rewriting the EDs' bodies. For the case of acyclic policies, instead, we implemented a specific version of UCQRew from scratch.

Although Theorem 4 constitutes a remarkable theoretical result, from a practical point of view, the size of the rewritten formula IGA-Ent may have a severe impact on the evaluation time. For this reason, we made several intensional optimizations in our implementation to obtain a simpler yet semantically equivalent rewriting. The most important are the following ones.

- Instead of generating a Clash subformula for every possible $\mathcal{Z}$ set defined in IGA-Ent, we can only consider those sets that, for a fixed $q \in q_r$, can match at least one body of the expanded policy.
- In the isDiscl subformula, the atoms of the query can be omitted from $\mathsf{conj}(\mathcal{Z})$ (at this point of the evaluation, we know that their rewriting is satisfied). Then, since the two $\mathsf{AtomRewr}(\mathcal{Z}, \mathcal{T})$ in Clash become syntactically equal, they can only be evaluated once, that is, outside the two isDiscl.
- For its specific purpose, the output of the map function can be optimized in terms of specificity of the substitutions. Specifically, we do not use a substitution μ such that q is mappable to $\mathcal{Z}$ via μ if we also use a substitution μ' that is more generic than μ and such that q is mappable to $\mathcal{Z}$ via μ'.

Furthermore, while our results only deal with Boolean queries, the implementation of the query rewriting technique is also able to natively process non-Boolean queries (without any pre-processing). This is obtained through a simple extension of the presented technique: it is indeed sufficient to apply Definition 6 without existentially quantifying the free variables of the input query.

7.1 Binary EDs

We now define the fragment of binary EDs, a subclass of linear EDs which has a correspondence with DL-Lite$_\mathcal{R}$.

Definition 7. *A* binary ED *is an ED of one of the following forms:*

$$\forall x\,(KB_1 \to KB_2) \qquad (2) \qquad\qquad \forall x, y\,(KS_1 \to KS_2) \qquad (3)$$

where $B_1, B_2 \in \{A(x), \exists y\, R(x,y), \exists y\, R(y,x)\}$, $S_1, S_2 \in \{R(x,y), R(y,x)\}$, $A \in \Sigma_C$, *and* $R \in \Sigma_R$.

We now define the function $DL(\cdot)$ as follows:

$$DL(A(x)) = A \qquad DL(\exists y\, R(y,x)) = \exists R^- \qquad DL(R(x,y)) = R$$
$$DL(\exists y\, R(x,y)) = \exists R \qquad DL(R(y,x)) = R^-$$

Then, given a binary ED τ of the form (2), we define $DL(\tau)$ as the DL-Lite$_\mathcal{R}$ concept inclusion $DL(B_1) \sqsubseteq DL(B_2)$, and given a binary ED τ of the form (3), we define $DL(\tau)$ as the DL-Lite$_\mathcal{R}$ role inclusion $DL(S_1) \sqsubseteq DL(S_2)$. Finally, if $\mathcal{P}$ is a set of binary EDs, we define $DL(\mathcal{P})$ as the DL-Lite$_\mathcal{R}$ TBox $\bigcup_{\tau\in\mathcal{P}} DL(\tau)$.

As said above, this kind of policy enabled us not to re-implement a rewriting function UCQRew of Algorithm 1 for linear EDs. Formally, when $\mathcal{P}$ is a binary policy, instead of $\mathsf{UCQRew}(\mathsf{body}(\tau), \Sigma(\mathcal{P}, \mathcal{T}))$, we computed $\mathsf{UCQRew}(\mathsf{body}(\tau), DL(\mathcal{P}^+) \cup \mathcal{T})$ by exploiting the tree-witness rewriter also for this purpose.

One may wonder whether this restriction is sufficient to get back FO-rewritability. However, the kind of policy used in the proof of Theorem 2 immediately rules out this possibility. Hence, we restrict our attention to the case of *full* binary EDs, which is FO-rewritable by Theorem 4.[6]

7.2 Policy Definition

We ran our experiments using an acyclic policy $\mathcal{P}_\mathrm{a}$ (consisting of 6 EDs) and a binary policy $\mathcal{P}_\mathrm{b}$ (consisting of 11 EDs), namely (we removed the universally quantified variables for improving their readability):

$$
\begin{aligned}
\{\, & K\,\exists x\, \mathsf{isAdvisedBy}(x,y) \to K\,\mathsf{Woman}(y),\\
& K\,\exists x\, (\mathsf{hasAlumnus}(x,y) \land \mathsf{hasMasterDegreeFrom}(y,x) \to K\,\mathsf{FullProfessor}(y),\\
& K\,(\mathsf{takesCourse}(x,y) \land \mathsf{Student}(x)) \to K\,\bot,\\
& K\,(\mathsf{hasCollaborationWith}(x,y) \land \mathsf{Student}(x)) \to K\,\bot,\\
& K\,\mathsf{isAdvisedBy}(x,y) \land \mathsf{hasMasterDegreeFrom}(x,z) \to K\,\mathsf{hasMajor}(x,\mathsf{ComputerScience}),\\
& K\,(\mathsf{teachesCourse}(x,y) \land \mathsf{FullProfessor}(x)) \to K\,\mathsf{hasDoctoralDegreeFrom}(x,\mathsf{U2})\,\},\\
\{\, & K\,\mathsf{isAffiliatedOrganizationOf}(x,y), \mathsf{hasCollegeDiscipline}(x,\mathsf{FineArts}) \to K\,\bot,\\
& K\,\mathsf{Professor}(x) \to K\,\mathsf{Woman}(x),\\
& K\,\mathsf{teachesCourse}(x,y) \to K\,\mathsf{FullProfessor}(x),\\
& K\,\mathsf{isVisitingProfessorOf}(x,y) \to K\,\bot,\\
& K\,\mathsf{takesCourse}(x,y) \to K\,\mathsf{ElectiveCourse}(y),\\
& K\,\mathsf{Person}(x) \to K\,\mathsf{Employee}(x),\\
& K\,\mathsf{hasAlumnus}(x,y) \to K\,\mathsf{hasMasterDegreeFrom}(y,x),\\
& K\,\mathsf{hasCollaborationWith}(x,y) \to K\,\mathsf{Professor}(x),\\
& K\,\mathsf{hasSameHomeTownWith}(x,y) \to K\,\mathsf{Employee}(x),\\
& K\,\mathsf{knows}(x,y) \to K\,\mathsf{Professor}(x),\\
& K\,\mathsf{knows}(x,y) \to K\,\mathsf{Professor}(y)\,\}.
\end{aligned}
$$

We also defined $\mathcal{P}_\mathrm{a}^-$ as a reduced version of $\mathcal{P}_\mathrm{a}$, containing its last 3 EDs, and $\mathcal{P}_\mathrm{b}^-$ as a reduced version of $\mathcal{P}_\mathrm{b}$, containing its last 6 EDs.

7.3 Results

The results of our experiments are reported in Table 1. The symbol $\mathcal{P}_\emptyset$ indicates the absence of a policy: this is the configuration that we used as a baseline.

The main indications provided by these results are the following:

[6] We recall that the restriction to a single atom in the head does not actually decrease the expressiveness of full EDs (and thus of full binary EDs).

- In most cases, the evaluation time t_e is acceptable (it remains on the order of seconds). The only critical query is the seventh one, which takes several minutes to execute.
- The time t_r necessary for computing the rewritten query is always less than or equal to 3 s. As expected, for both o2b$_5$ and o2b$_{10}$, such rewriting times are very close, as they do not depend on the ABox.
- For both acyclic and binary policies, the values of t_r corresponding to smaller and larger policies are of comparable magnitude.
- Observe that binary policies tend to remove more tuples than acyclic ones. This could be explained by the fact that EDs with fewer atoms in their body are more likely "activated" by the query.

Table 1. All the evaluation results. Each entry reports the rewriting time (t_r) and evaluation time (t_e) expressed in milliseconds, plus the number of returned tuples (#).

Query		o2b$_5$					o2b$_{10}$				
		$\mathcal{P}_\emptyset$	$\mathcal{P}_a^-$	$\mathcal{P}_a$	$\mathcal{P}_b^-$	$\mathcal{P}_b$	$\mathcal{P}_\emptyset$	$\mathcal{P}_a^-$	$\mathcal{P}_a$	$\mathcal{P}_b^-$	$\mathcal{P}_b$
q_1	t_r	19	19	20	53	63	15	20	28	51	63
	t_e	513	526	547	683	958	822	560	964	1394	1085
	#	9228	9228	9228	1367	334	19782	19782	19782	2948	730
q_2	t_r	50	249	336	476	511	65	243	386	873	553
	t_e	81	8688	7335	174	206	269	39426	51181	876	402
	#	18872	18736	14829	5957	5957	44190	43889	33193	13009	13009
q_3	t_r	25	41	42	40	109	38	32	43	62	112
	t_e	4	8	6	2	4	8	5	9	5	6
	#	34	34	34	34	28	75	75	75	75	64
q_4	t_r	21	40	35	52	133	33	33	49	68	97
	t_e	6	7	2	4	3	7	5	7	5	3
	#	0	0	0	0	0	0	0	0	0	0
q_5	t_r	21	554	473	250	319	29	482	917	451	334
	t_e	17	30699	29679	1823	1003	44	110763	124305	5056	1283
	#	3574	2020	2020	952	264	6564	3676	3676	1696	394
q_6	t_r	18	114	115	161	116	25	148	109	263	193
	t_e	59	60661	28564	81	230	235	283020	141173	333	282
	#	16236	15834	7811	0	0	35889	35075	17481	0	0
q_7	t_r	75	2029	1976	1378	1847	88	2205	2244	2222	1801
	t_e	66	198641	187908	403	496	334	993701	1119538	1343	812
	#	5489	5489	5091	5489	3292	11969	11969	10971	11969	7241
q_8	t_r	22	52	48	257	263	21	49	44	399	272
	t_e	62	75	63	615	647	186	112	143	1548	963
	#	17904	17904	17904	14668	14668	39278	39278	39278	32350	32350
q_9	t_r	135	1711	2302	1765	3430	195	1778	2290	2877	3144
	t_e	31	1412	1313	137	129	93	10230	10944	598	332
	#	1698	1539	1539	0	0	3434	3196	3196	0	0
q_{10}	t_r	22	1243	1220	184	337	32	1351	1433	380	477
	t_e	78	676	3	110	159	297	4753	3	478	270
	#	642	122	0	642	144	1413	258	0	1413	335

8 Conclusions

In this work, we investigated CQE under policies expressed via epistemic dependencies (EDs), focusing on the use of ground atom (GA) censors for safe information disclosure. We investigated IGA-entailment, a semantic relation based on the intersection of all optimal GA censors, and analyzed its data complexity in the presence of ED-based policies when the TBox is expressed in DL-Lite$_\mathcal{R}$. Our results show that the intersection remains safe for full EDs, a subclass of particular interest. We established that IGA-entailment is not FO-rewritable in general, which led us to the definition of the subclass of full and expandable EDs for which FO-rewriting is feasible, and we introduced a rewriting algorithm that works for DL-Lite$_\mathcal{R}$ ontologies. We validated our approach through a prototype implementation evaluated using the OWL2Bench benchmark, showing its practical feasibility in diverse evaluation scenarios.

As for future work, we are currently working on the definition of practical algorithms for some of the non-FO-rewritable cases of IGA-entailment analyzed in the paper. Another interesting research direction is towards extending the FO-rewritable cases identified by our analysis: in particular, we would like to focus either on further subclasses of EDs, or on (subclasses of) policy languages that go beyond the expressiveness of EDs. In addition, it would be interesting to study the complexity of CQE under EDs for TBoxes expressed in DLs different from DL-Lite$_\mathcal{R}$. Finally, it would be of practical importance to extend the present approach to the framework of ontology-based data access (OBDA).

Supplemental Material Statement: The complete proofs of Theorems 2, 3 and 4, along with the proofs of Lemmas 1 and 2, are reported in the full version of this paper available on arXiv [21]. As for the software:

- Our system's source code can be downloaded from https://github.com/anonymous-iswc25/iga-ed-rewriter/blob/main/iga-ed-rewriter.zip.
- The benchmark we used is available at https://github.com/kracr/owl2bench.

The software required to run the evaluation tests is: Java 8+, MySQL, Python 3 (needed to create new ABoxes from scratch), and possibly Apache Maven (only to build the project from the source code).

Acknowledgments. This work was partially supported by: projects FAIR (PE0000013) and SERICS (PE00000014) under the MUR National Recovery and Resilience Plan funded by the EU - NextGenerationEU; the MUR PRIN 2022LA8XBH project Polar (POLicy specificAtion and enfoRcement for privacy-enhanced data management); and by the EU under the HORIZON.2.1.5 project dAIbetes (grant id. 101136305).

References

1. Abiteboul, S., Hull, R., Vianu, V.: Foundations of Databases. Addison Wesley Publ, Co (1995)

2. Baader, F., Calvanese, D., McGuinness, D., Nardi, D., Patel-Schneider, P.F. (eds.): The Description Logic Handbook: Theory, Implementation and Applications. Cambridge University Press, 2nd edn. (2007)
3. Baget, J., Leclère, M., Mugnier, M., Salvat, E.: On rules with existential variables: walking the decidability line. Artif. Intell. **175**(9–10), 1620–1654 (2011)
4. Biskup, J.: For unknown secrecies refusal is better than lying. Data Knowl. Eng. **33**(1), 1–23 (2000)
5. Biskup, J., Bonatti, P.A.: Controlled query evaluation for enforcing confidentiality in complete information systems. Int. J. Inf. Sec. **3**(1), 14–27 (2004)
6. Bonatti, P.A.: A false sense of security. Artif. Intell. **310**(103741) (2022)
7. Bonatti, P.A., Sauro, L.: A confidentiality model for ontologies. In: Alani, H., et al. (eds.) ISWC 2013. LNCS, vol. 8218, pp. 17–32. Springer, Heidelberg (2013). https://doi.org/10.1007/978-3-642-41335-3_2
8. Calì, A., Gottlob, G., Lukasiewicz, T.: A general Datalog-based framework for tractable query answering over ontologies. J. Web Semantics **14**, 57–83 (2012)
9. Calvanese, D., De Giacomo, G., Lembo, D., Lenzerini, M., Rosati, R.: EQL-lite: effective first-order query processing in description logics. In: Proceedings of the 20th International Joint Conference on Artificial Intelligence (IJCAI), pp. 274–279. Morgan Kaufmann Publishers Inc. (2007)
10. Calvanese, D., De Giacomo, G., Lembo, D., Lenzerini, M., Rosati, R.: Tractable reasoning and efficient query answering in description logics: the DL-lite family. J. Autom. Reason. **39**(3), 385–429 (2007)
11. Cima, G., Lembo, D., Marconi, L., Rosati, R., Savo, D.F.: Controlled query evaluation in ontology-based data access. In: Pan, J.Z., et al. (eds.) ISWC 2020. LNCS, vol. 12506, pp. 128–146. Springer, Cham (2020). https://doi.org/10.1007/978-3-030-62419-4_8
12. Cima, G., Lembo, D., Marconi, L., Rosati, R., Savo, D.F.: Enhancing controlled query evaluation through epistemic policies. In: Proceedings of the 33th International Joint Conference on Artifical Intelligence (IJCAI), pp. 3307–3314. International Joint Conference on Artificial Intelligence Organization, August 2024
13. Cima, G., Lembo, D., Marconi, L., Rosati, R., Savo, D.F.: A gentle introduction to controlled query evaluation in DL-Lite ontologies. Springer Nat. Comput. Sci. **5**(4), 335 (2024)
14. Cima, G., Lembo, D., Marconi, L., Rosati, R., Savo, D.F.: Indistinguishability in controlled query evaluation over prioritized description logic ontologies. J. of Web Semantics **84**, 100841 (2025)
15. Cima, G., Lembo, D., Rosati, R., Savo, D.F.: Controlled query evaluation in description logics through consistent query answering. Artif. Intell. **334**, 104176 (2024)
16. Console, M., Lenzerini, M.: Epistemic integrity constraints for ontology-based data management. In: Proceedings of the 34th AAAI Conference on Artificial Intelligence (AAAI), pp. 2790–2797. AAAI Press (2020)
17. Cuenca Grau, B., Horrocks, I., Motik, B., Parsia, B., Patel-Schneider, P., Sattler, U.: OWL 2: the next step for OWL. J. Web Semantics **6**(4), 309–322 (2008)
18. Cuenca Grau, B., Kharlamov, E., Kostylev, E.V., Zheleznyakov, D.: Controlled query evaluation over OWL 2 RL ontologies. In: Proceedings of the 12th International Semantic Web Conference (ISWC), pp. 49–65 (2013)
19. Kikot, S., Kontchakov, R., Zakharyaschev, M.: Conjunctive query answering with OWL 2 QL. In: Proceedings of the 13th International Conference on the Principles of Knowledge Representation and Reasoning (KR), AAAI Press (2012)

20. König, M., Leclère, M., Mugnier, M., Thomazo, M.: Sound, complete and minimal UCQ-rewriting for existential rules. Semantic Web J. **6**(5), 451–475 (2015)
21. Marconi, L., Ricci, F., Rosati, R.: CQE under epistemic dependencies: algorithms and experiments (extended version) (2025), https://arxiv.org/abs/2507.17487
22. van Melkebeek, D.: Deterministic and randomized bounded truth-table reductions of P, NL, and L to sparse sets. J. Comput. Syst. Sci. **57**(2), 213–232 (1998)
23. Motik, B., Cuenca Grau, B., Horrocks, I., Wu, Z., Fokoue, A., Lutz, C.: OWL 2 web ontology language profiles (second edition). W3C Recommendation, World Wide Web Consortium, December 2012, http://www.w3.org/TR/owl2-profiles/
24. Papadimitriou, C.H.: Computational Complexity. Addison Wesley Publisher, Co (1994)
25. Rodríguez-Muro, M., Kontchakov, R., Zakharyaschev, M.: Ontology-based data access: *Ontop* of databases. In: Alani, H., et al. (eds.) ISWC 2013. LNCS, vol. 8218, pp. 558–573. Springer, Heidelberg (2013). https://doi.org/10.1007/978-3-642-41335-3_35
26. Singh, G., Bhatia, S., Mutharaju, R.: OWL2Bench: a benchmark for OWL 2 reasoners. In: Pan, J.Z., et al. (eds.) ISWC 2020. LNCS, vol. 12507, pp. 81–96. Springer, Cham (2020). https://doi.org/10.1007/978-3-030-62466-8_6
27. Singh, G., Bhatia, S., Mutharaju, R.: OWL2Bench SPARQL queries, May 2020, https://zenodo.org/records/3838735

Efficient Updates for Worst-Case Optimal Join Triple Stores

Alexander Bigerl(✉), Nikolaos Karalis, Liss Heidrich, and Axel-Cyrille Ngonga Ngomo(✉)

Data Science Group (DICE), Heinz Nixdorf Institute, Paderborn University, Paderborn, Germany
{alexander.bigerl,nikolaos.karalis,liss.heidrich, axel.ngonga}@uni-paderborn.de

Abstract. It has been recently shown that worst-case optimal joins can significantly speed up query processing in RDF triple stores, especially in analytical workloads. However, this increase in query speed comes at the expense of updates being slow or not supported at all. We see this limited compatibility with updates as a key reason for the slow adoption of worst-case optimal joins in triple stores. In this paper, we address this challenge by presenting a fast, incremental insertion and deletion algorithm for the hypertrie, a worst-case optimal join data structure. This update algorithm can be used for offline bulk updates as well as online updates. Our evaluation on realistic update loads from DBpedia and scaling update sizes on Wikidata shows that the online performance of our algorithm is comparable to or better than that of traditional triple stores.

Keywords: SPARQL update · worst-case optimal join · graph database · data structure · indexing

1 Introduction

Approaches based on worst-case optimal joins (WCOJs) for SPARQL query processing [2,5,6,11,16] have recently been shown to significantly outperform traditional methods using binary joins. For example, triangle queries—which are common in SPARQL—can be answered asymptotically faster with WCOJs compared to binary joins [3]. WCOJs rely on extensive indexing to efficiently evaluate SPARQL queries [2,5,6,11]. However, a key limitation is the inefficiency of updates in these underlying indices [2].

In this paper, we address the challenge of supporting efficient updates in WCOJ-enabled RDF triple stores by proposing a fast incremental update algorithm for the hypertrie, a state-of-the-art index for WCOJs. The algorithm supports offline bulk updates at rates of up to 150k triples per second and online

D. Garijo et al. (Eds.): ISWC 2025, LNCS 16140, pp. 539–555, 2026.
https://doi.org/10.1007/978-3-032-09527-5_29

updates at up to 33k triples per second.[1] To evaluate the efficiency of the proposed update mechanisms, we conduct a thorough comparison of our approach's update performance with other triple stores. To achieve this goal, we use two benchmarks on real-world datasets: (i) DBpedia (680×10^6 triples) with updates derived from actual change logs and (ii) Wikidata (5.5×10^9 triples) with synthetic updates sampled from the dataset. Our results demonstrate that the proposed algorithm achieves update performance comparable to or better than that of conventional systems based on binary joins both in terms of update runtime and triples processed per second, thus solving the update bottleneck problem associated with WCOJs.

The rest of the paper is structured as follows. The related work in update support for WCOJ-enabled triple stores is reviewed in Sect. 2. Section 3 introduced RDF related notation. In Sect. 4, we provide an overview of the hypertrie data structure. The proposed update algorithm for efficient insertion and deletion operations on the hypertrie is detailed in Sect. 5 and its evaluation is discussed in Sect. 6. Finally, we conclude and discuss future directions in Sect. 7.

2 Related Work

WCOJ algorithms [15] are a class of multi-way join algorithms that eliminate a variable at a time instead of a triple pattern at a time like binary joins when applied in SPARQL [6]. WCOJs eliminate the influence of intermediate results from binary joins on the runtime complexity and are bound only by worst-case result size. For example, using binary joins to evaluate triangle query[2] where the triple patterns have n solutions is bound by $\mathcal{O}(n^2)$ whereas a WCOJs reduce the complexity to $\mathcal{O}(n^{1.5})$. For more details about WCOJs in triplestores we refer the reader to [1,2,11,13,14].

The Ring[2] is an indexing data structure designed to store graphs with minimal memory overhead. It is a monolithic datastructure that supports WCOJs without relying on additional indices. However, the Ring does not support incremental updates, as any modification to the data requires a complete rebuild of the structure. To avoid rebuilding the Ring on every update the authors suggest to collect changes in a classical index and rebuild periodically. The hypertrie [5,6] is another indexing data structure with native support for WCOJs, described in more detail in Sect. 4. While the versions presented in [5,6] only provide basic loading capabilities similar to the Ring, this paper extends the hypertrie with full support for incremental updates. In contrast to the monolithic solutions Ring and hypertrie, triple stores like MillenniumDB [16] and Jena-LFJ [11] use multi-indexing approaches to enable WCOJs. MillenniumDB pre-materializes only four collation orders, falling back to binary joins when a WCOJ would require a different index. Jena-LFJ, on the other hand, materializes all possible collation orders to maximize query performance. Both systems leverage B-trees

1 We refer to online updates when a HTTP SPARQL endpoint is live, and to offline updates otherwise.

2 E.g., `SELECT * WHERE {?a :knows ?b . ?b :knows ?c . ?c :knows ?a}`.

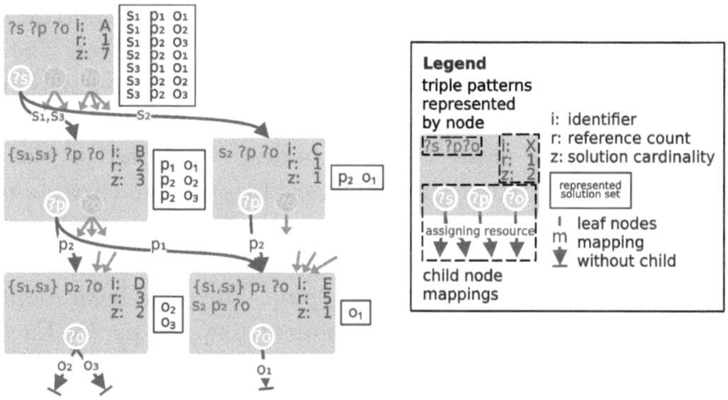

Fig. 1. Example hypertrie. For better readability, all figures show only nodes for collation order SPO. The represented graph is equivalent to solution of the triple pattern in the root node.

for indexing. Although these approaches with multiple indices enable updates, they require a considerable amount of storage for the additional indices and the updates take longer as all indices have to be updated.

3 RDF Notation

We assume a basic familiarity with RDF and SPARQL. This section introduces the core terms and notation used throughout the paper [8,10]. Let I denote the set of IRIs, L the set of literals, B the set of blank nodes, and V the set of variables. The set of RDF resources is $R = I \cup L \cup B$. An RDF triple is a tuple $(s, p, o) \in (I \cup B) \times I \times R$, where s is the subject, p the predicate, and o the object. A triple pattern is a tuple $(s, p, o) \in (I \cup B \cup V) \times (I \cup V) \times (R \cup V)$. A triple pattern's solution, or simply solution, is a partial function $\mu : V \rightharpoonup R$ that assigns resources to variables. We write solutions as sets of pairs, e.g., $\{(\texttt{?s}, \texttt{ex:Alice}), (\texttt{?p}, \texttt{ex:knows})\}$. A single assignment pair in a solution is referred to as a binding, e.g., $(\texttt{?s}, \texttt{ex:Alice})$. A triple (s, p, o) matches a triple pattern (s', p', o') if each position in the pattern is either a variable or equal to the corresponding component of the triple. The resulting solution μ binds each variable in the pattern to the matching RDF term from the triple. Given a triple pattern tp and an RDF graph G, matching tp to G yields the set of solutions that is derived from triples in G that match tp. For simplicity, we consistently use `?s`, `?p`, and `?o` as variable names for subject, predicate, and object, respectively. This does not limit generality, as the paper does not consider joins that rely on shared variable names.

4 Hypertrie

The *hypertrie* [5,6] is a data structure designed to support WCOJs over RDF knowledge graphs. To this end, the hypertrie organizes triple patterns and their solutions hierarchically in a directed acyclic graph.[3] Each hypertrie node represents one or more triple patterns that share the same solution set. The cardinality of a hypertrie node refers to the cardinality of the solution set it represents. An example is given in Fig. 1.

A hypertrie consists of three levels of nodes, organized by the number of unbound components (i.e., the number of variables) in the corresponding triple pattern. The root (depth-3) node represents the fully unbound pattern `?s ?p ?o`. Its children (depth-2 nodes) correspond to patterns with two unbound components, such as $\mathtt{s_1}$ `?p ?o`, `?s` $\mathtt{p_1}$ `?o`, or `?s ?p` $\mathtt{o_1}$. The third level (depth-1 nodes) contains patterns with one unbound component, e.g., $\mathtt{s_1}$ $\mathtt{p_2}$ `?o`. Each hypertrie node maintains a mapping for each unbound variable occurring in its associated triple pattern. For a given unbound variable v in a triple pattern tp, this mapping assigns each valid binding b of v a child node whose pattern is obtained by instantiating v in tp with b, while keeping the other positions unchanged. For example in Fig. 1, in the root node's (associated with `?s ?p ?o`) variable mapping `?s` we assign $\mathtt{s_1}$ to a depth-2 node that represents the triple pattern $\mathtt{s_1}$ `?p ?o`. In depth-1 nodes, where only one variable remains unbound, the mapping reduces to the set of valid bindings for that variable. Following SPARQL semantics, the solution set of a child node consists of those solutions of the parent node in which the mapping variable v is bound to b, with v removed from the solution. Thus, each child node represents a projection of a filtered subset of its parent's solutions.

To reduce redundancies and storage overhead in the hypertrie, [5] introduced three optimizations. (i) *Node deduplication via homomorphic hashing*: Nodes representing triple patterns with identical solution sets are deduplicated reducing the total number of nodes in the structure. For example in Fig. 1 that uses this optimization, for variable mapping `?s` both $\mathtt{s_1}$ and $\mathtt{s_3}$ are assigned to the same node because the triple patterns $\mathtt{s_1}$ `?p ?o` and $\mathtt{s_3}$ `?p ?o` have the same solution set. For the deduplication each node is assigned an *identifier* (i in Fig. 1) that is a hash of its solution set. Homomorphic hashing enables incremental updates to the identifier as the solution set changes, avoiding the need to sort and rehash the entire set on each update of a node. It is also used to look up if the node resulting from a update exists already. Since a single node may now be reachable from multiple parents, reference counting (r in Fig. 1) is used to manage node sharing and deletion. The reference count of the root node defaults to 1, as it spans the entire hypertrie. (ii) *Singleton depth-2 nodes*: If a depth-2 node represents only a single solution, it is stored as a lightweight single entry node without any children. (iii) *Singleton depth-1 nodes*: If a depth-1 node would contain only a single solution, that solution is stored in-place in the parent node's variable mapping.[4] Unless stated otherwise, figures in this paper apply only the first

[3] Note that this applies only to triple patterns that do not contain a particular variable multiple times. Such triple patterns are handled in query processing. We are not aware of any triplestore that maintains an index for such patterns.

[4] This relies on the fact that the memory slot used for the reference to a child node is large enough to store the payload of a singleton depth-1 node.

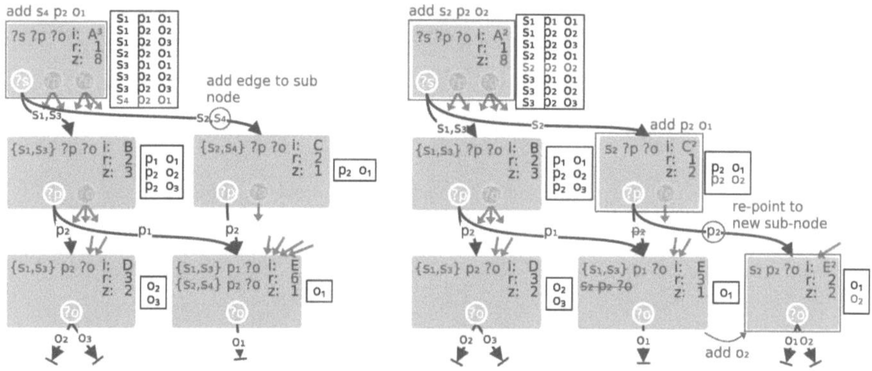

(a) Adding a triple that adds a new assignment for **?s** in the root node.

(b) Adding a triple that extends an existing assignment for **?s** in the root node.

Fig. 2. Inserting single triples into the hypertrie of Fig. 1. All insertions and deletions in subsequent figures operate on the same hypertrie instance. Executed changes are highlighted in all figures in orange.

optimization (node deduplication) to simplify the representation but our update algorithm takes all optimization into account.

5 Hypertrie Updates

This section presents our approach for performing insertions and deletions on the hypertrie. We begin by introducing the update mechanism for individual triples, followed by the creation and deletion of nodes, which together form the conceptual basis for bulk updates. We then describe how bulk updates are scheduled and executed efficiently. This includes reference count management and the deletion of unreferenced nodes. Finally, we discuss how singleton node optimizations are integrated into the update process. Each update operation consists exclusively of either insertions or removals.[5] Updates that include both must be split into two separate operations and executed consecutively.[6] All examples focus on the collation order SPO; the remaining collation orders are handled analogously. The required changes for all collation orders are collected in the same structures. This eliminates overhead for equivalent operations required multiple times for the same or different collation orders and ensures that each unique operation is executed only once.

5.1 Updates Using a Single Triple

Insertion. We begin by considering the insertion of a single triple. The process starts at the root node, where the inserted triple contributes a new solution to

[5] We assume only new triples are inserted and only existing ones are removed.
[6] This is in accordance with the SPARQL 1.1 Update specification [10].

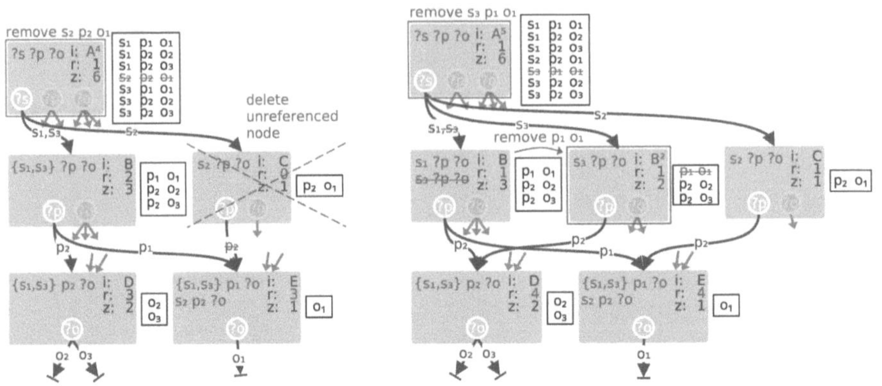

(a) Triple deletion results in an assignment removal from ?s in the root node.

(b) Triple deletion results in a reduction of a child node ?s mapping in the root node.

Fig. 3. Deleting single triples

the fully unbound triple pattern ?s ?p ?o. Consequently, each variable mapping of the root node needs to be updated by either adding a new assignment between a resource and a child node (see Fig. 2a) or update the child node of an existing assignment (see Fig. 2b).

The first scenario is illustrated in Fig. 2a. Here, inserting the triple s_4 p_2 o_1 adds the solution $\{(?s, s_4), (?p, p_2), (?o, o_1)\}$. This requires to add the assignment for s_4 in the root node's mapping of ?s, since it was not previously a solution for ?s. s_4 is assigned a hypertrie node representing the remaining part of the solution, i.e., $\{(?p, p_2), (?o, o_1)\}$. Such a node already exists in the hypertrie, since the triple pattern s_2 ?p ?o has the same solution set. Consequently, we increment the reference count of the now shared node. Since the the node's variable mappings are not modified, no further propagation is necessary.

In Fig. 2b, the subject resource s_2 of the inserted triple s_2 p_2 o_2 is assigned in the root node's mapping of ?s. Since the assigned child node is referenced no where else, we can update that node directly by adding the remaining part of the solution $\{(?p, p_2), (?o, o_2)\}$. Again, updating the node for s_2 ?p ?o requires updating its variable mappings. For variable ?p, the node assigned to p_2 must be updated. However, since that node for the triple pattern s_2 p_2 ?o is still referenced elsewhere, this time we create and reference a copy instead of modifying it in place. Since the node is a leaf node, the update is completed afterward.

Deletion. The deletion of a single triple also requires distinguishing two cases, depending on the effect it has on the hypertrie's structure. In particular, to reflect the removed solution an assignment for a variable mapping is either fully removed (see Fig. 3a) or the assigned child is reduced (see Fig. 3b).

In the first case, the triple to be removed contains a resource that will no longer be a valid binding for one of the variables in the affected triple pattern.

This is illustrated in Fig. 3a for the triple s_2 p_2 o_1. In the root node, the subject s_2 was assigned the hypertrie node representing s2 ?p ?o. Since the triple being removed is the only solution with subject s_2, this child node would now represents an empty solution set. As a result, the assignment for s_2 is removed from the root node's mapping for variable ?s, and the now-unreferenced child node is deleted. Deleting the node for s2 ?p ?o, propagates reference count decreases that are applied to its child nodes. As its previous child node with identifier E is still referenced by other nodes, it is not deleted.

In the second case, the removed triple reduces the number of solutions in a child node with multiple solutions, such that the resulting child retains at least one solution. This is illustrated in Fig. 3b, where the triple s_3 p_1 o_1 is removed. The subject s_3 remains a valid binding for ?s, so its assignment in the root node's mapping for variable ?s is preserved but the assigned child needs to be reduced. Note, that the s_3 and s_1 were orignially both assigned to the same child node with identifier B. Consequently, node B is still referenced and thus must not be modified in place; instead, a copy is created and updated to reflect the removal. Specifically, its assignment for predicate p_1 is removed to form the new node B^2. For all assignments of that remain unchanged between B and B^2—e.g., the assignment p_2 node's mapping for variable ?p—the reference counts of its corresponding child nodes are incremented to reflect the additional reference from their newly created parent node. The update terminates once all leaf nodes have been updated accordingly.

To summarize, updates to the hypertrie for a single triple alter the root node's mapping for variable—either by introducing a new assignment (insertion), removing an existing one (deletion), or modifying child node an assignment refers to (insertion or deletion). Updates are propagated recursively to child nodes. When modifying a child node, a copy-on-write mechanism is applied to preserve sharing: if the node is still referenced elsewhere, it is copied before modification; otherwise, it can be edited in place. Reference counts are adjusted to reflect node creation, deletion, and changes in variable mappings.

5.2 Creating and Deleting Nodes

As shown in Sect. 5.1, adding or removing variable mappings may trigger the creation or deletion of depth-2 and depth-1 nodes. This section briefly outlines the steps required for creating and deleting such nodes. These steps are used for both update operations using single triples and bulk updates (Sect. 5.3). The same mechanism also applies when creating or deleting the root node. Figure 4a illustrates the process of creating a node from a set of triple pattern solutions. The creation proceeds in three steps: (1) If an equivalent node already exists, it is reused by incrementing its reference count and the process terminates. (2) If such a node does not exist, a new node is allocated. For each variable of the solutions, a variable mapping is populated assigning the unique resources for the respective variable to child nodes. (3) To ensure that all assigned child nodes exist and that they have correct reference counts, their creation is triggered recursively as described in Sect. 4. Figure 4b illustrates the process of deleting a

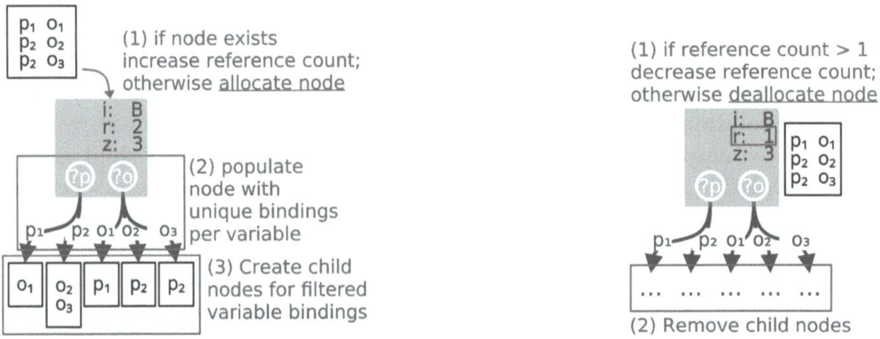

(a) Creating a node from a set of triple pattern solutions.

(b) Removing a node.

Fig. 4. Creating and deleting of nodes.

node, which is carried out in two steps: (1) If the reference count of the node is greater than one, it is decremented and the process terminates. (2) Otherwise, the node is deallocated. The deletion is then recursively propagated to all child nodes referenced by the removed node.

5.3 Bulk Updates

Database indices often suffer from write amplification when applying numerous small updates [7]. In the hypertrie, for example, each update requires modifications to each variable mapping in the root node. By applying insertions or deletions in bulk, this overhead is incurred only once, thereby reducing write amplification. We generalize the single-triple update mechanism to handle multiple inserted or deleted triples at once. Technically, these triple modifications translate to solution modifications applied to the root node and recursively propagated changes to child nodes. The core idea is to group modified solutions in the same way that variable mappings are organized in the hypertrie, and to use these groups to update the variable mappings and child nodes. Specifically, the following steps are taken for each variable v that is found in the triple patterns of a hypertrie node. First, the solutions are grouped by their binding value b for v, forming a group U for each unique resource b. Since the group U will be used to create, delete, or update a child node, the binding for v is removed from its solutions. For example, given the variable ?p and the solutions $\{\{(?\mathtt{p}, \mathtt{p}_1), (?\mathtt{o}, \mathtt{o}_1)\}, \{(?\mathtt{p}, \mathtt{p}_1), (?\mathtt{o}, \mathtt{o}_2)\}, \{(?\mathtt{p}, \mathtt{p}_2), (?\mathtt{o}, \mathtt{o}_1)\}\}$, the solutions for the grouping keys $\mathtt{p}_1$ and $\mathtt{p}_2$ are solutions $\{\{(?\mathtt{o}, \mathtt{o}_1)\}, \{(?\mathtt{o}, \mathtt{o}_2)\}\}$ and $\{\{(?\mathtt{o}, \mathtt{o}_1)\}\}$, respectively. Bulk insertions work similarly to insertions involving a single triple. If a resource b is not yet assigned for variable mapping v, a new assignment is added that points to a newly created node initialized with group U. If b is already assigned to a node X, a new node X^1 is created by adding U to X, and b is reassigned to X^1. For deletions, the outcome depends

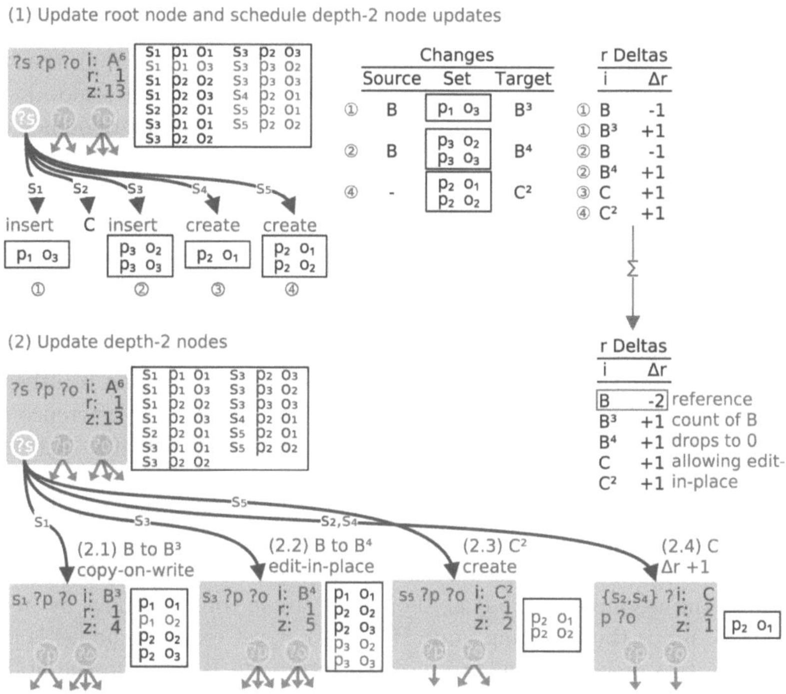

Fig. 5. Example of a bulk insertion execution. The steps shown include updating the root node, scheduling changes to depth-2 nodes, and applying those changes. Further recursive propagation is omitted from the figure.

on how many solutions are removed. If the number of solutions in U equals the total number of solutions in the child node X assigned to b (i.e., $|U| = |X|$), the assignment is removed and child node deleted. Otherwise, a new node X^2 is created by removing U from X, and b is reassigned to X^2. Our algorithm proceeds in a level-wise manner: for each node at the current level, it updates the variable mappings and collects the resulting update requests for its child nodes. Once all nodes at a particular level have been processed, the collected updates for the level below are applied.

Planning and Scheduling Changes. Planning changes targets two main objectives: (1) cache-conscious execution by applying updates originating from the same node consecutively, and (2) reduction of memory overhead by reusing nodes that become unreferenced.

To this end, we collect a set of changes. Each change consists of a source node identifier, a set of affected solutions, and a target node identifier, which is computed from the source node identifier and the set of affected solutions. In parallel, reference count deltas are collected per change. For each change, a decrement is recorded for the source node and an increment for the target node. For insertions and removals that reduce but do not delete a child node, all three change components are recorded. If a node is newly created, the source node identifier is omitted from the change. Node deletions and removals of all solutions from a node are not recorded as changes, but only as reference count decrements. Furthermore, if the target node already exists or is scheduled for creation by another change, no change is recorded and only the corresponding reference count deltas are collected. Once the collection is completed, changes are scheduled as follows. Changes are executed grouped by their source node, and reference count increments for target nodes are applied alongside each change. The reference count decrement for a source node is applied with the final change in its group. If the reference count of a source drops to zero, the source node is modified in place since that is considered cheeper than copying it; otherwise, changes are applied using copy-on-write. Finally, any remaining reference count deltas are applied. If a reference count drops to zero as a result of this, the respective node is deleted.

Figure 5 illustrates the planning and execution of a bulk insertion. The insertion begins by adding solutions to the root node. For variable ?s, this involves updating the child nodes associated with s_1 and s_3, as well as creating new associations for the resources s_4 and s_5. For s_1, a single solution must be inserted into node B. Since the resulting node B^3 does not yet exist, a change is scheduled. For s_3, two new solutions are inserted into node B creating the node B^4. Both scheduled changes contribute a decrement to the reference count of B, and an increment to the target nodes B^3 and B^4, respectively. For s_4, a node C is required. However, since C already exists, no new change is scheduled—only a reference count increment is recorded. In contrast, for s_5, the required node C^2 does not yet exist. A change is recorded with no source node (indicating creation), and a reference count increment is added for C^2. In the next phase, the changes to the depth-2 nodes are applied. The first change inserts into node B, yielding node B^3. Since further operations use B as a source, the insertion is performed via copy-on-write. The next change also inserts into B, producing node B^4, and is the last one with B as its source. As applying the reference count delta drops B to zero, it is modified in place. Node C^2 is created from scratch. The reference count increments for B^3, B^4, and C^2 are applied immediately during their respective executions. Finally, the remaining reference count deltas for nodes not involved in any scheduled change—here, only C—are applied. Further recursive propagation into scheduling and applying depth-1 changes takes place in the actual update process but is not shown in this example.

Figure 6 illustrates the planning and execution of a bulk removal. The process begins by deleting solutions from the root node. For the variable mapping of ?s, this affects the assignments for s_1, s_2, and s_3. For s_1, a single solution is removed from child node B. Since the resulting node B^2 does not yet exist, a change is scheduled. For s_3, two solutions are removed from node B, producing the node B^5. Both scheduled changes contribute a decrement to the reference count of B, and an increment to the reference counts of B^2 and B^5, respectively. In the case of s_2, all solutions are removed from node C and, as a result, the assignment

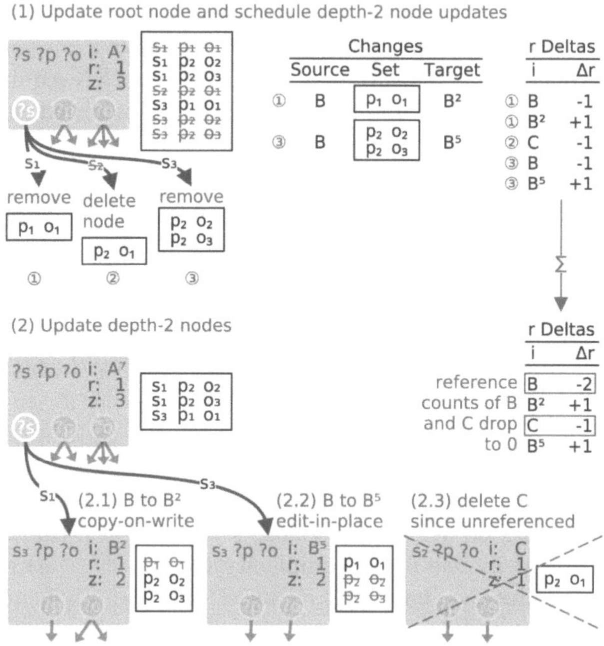

Fig. 6. Example of a bulk removal execution. The steps shown include updating the root node, scheduling changes to depth-2 nodes, and applying those changes. Further recursive propagation is omitted from the figure.

is removed. Ultimately, for node C, a reference count decrement is recorded; however, no change is scheduled. In the next phase, the changes to the depth-2 nodes are applied. The first change removes a solution from B and creates node B^2 via copy-on-write, as B is still needed for the next operation. The following change also removes solutions from B, producing node B^5, and is the last one with B as its source. Since the reference count of B drops to zero after this change, it is edited in place to become B_5. The reference count increments for B^2 and B^5 are applied immediately during their respective executions. Finally, the remaining reference count deltas for nodes not involved in any scheduled change—here, only C—are applied. As node C becomes unreferenced, it is deleted. Again, the further recursive propagation is omitted from the example.

Handling Singleton Optimizations. The application of singleton node optimizations—namely, single entry nodes (SENs) for depth-2 and in-place storage for depth-1—requires minor adjustments in both change planning and execution. In the following we refer to regular hypertrie nodes, which have been covered above, as full nodes (FNs) in contrast to SENs or in-place stored nodes.

Unlike FNs, which can be modified to represent different sets of solutions, SENs can only be created or deleted. Accordingly, SEN creation and reference count tracking are handled separately. Whenever a change involves both a FN and a SEN, it is split into two self-contained operations: a FN change, and a SEN-specific operation consisting of a reference count delta and, if necessary, a planned SEN creation. For example, transitioning from a SEN to a FN requires adding the SEN's single solution to the change set for the FN. The recorded change is then a creation, i.e., the source identifier is omitted. Conversely, transitioning from a FN to a SEN involves computing the remaining single solution and scheduling the creation of a new SEN from it. This is necessary since SEN changes are scheduled after FN changes so the FN might not be available any more by the time the SEN is actually created. As with FNs, a SEN is deleted when its reference count drops to zero. Handling singleton depth-1 nodes follows the same principles as SENs in relation to FNs. However, since singleton depth-1 nodes are not shared, they can be created and deleted immediately, without requiring change scheduling or reference counting.

Runtime Complexity. A depth-d the hypertrie encoding a set of z tuples with all optimizations from [5] requires $\mathcal{O}(z \cdot 2^{d-1} \cdot d)$ space. The runtime complexity of applying (inserting or deleting) a changeset set Δ of d-tuples to a depth-d hypertrie is bound by the space complexity $\mathcal{O}(|\Delta| \cdot 2^{d-1} \cdot d)$ of a surrogate hypertrie that encodes the change set changeset Δ. The proofs are provided in the supplementary material.

5.4 Comparison to the Baseline and Implementation

Our algorithm builds on the hypertrie implementation from [5], which includes an insertion procedure not described in the paper, but lacks support for deletions. While that insertion algorithm also follows a top-down approach, it does not separate phases making it unsuitable for extension to support removals. In our algorithm, changes are planned first based on the previous state of the hypertrie context and then executed without further consulting the hypertrie context. This allows to re-use common sub-routines for insertion and deletion in the implementations and makes it easier to follow as it is dividing it into clearly separated steps.

Our implementation TENTRIS-ID includes our extended hypertrie implementation and the necessary changes in TENTRIS to support updates, i.e., adding support for SPARQL `INSERT/DELETE DATA` update queries and implementing a reader-writer lock on the hypertrie to ensure atomicity and isolation during updates. We used the latest code versions from the repositories referenced in [5]. Since the publication of [5], the code was updated, most notably by enhancing RDF support through the rdf4cpp[7] library, and by moving from in-memory to persistent disk-based indexing by leveraging the Metall allocator [12].

6 Evaluation

For our evaluation, we focus on pure online update performance and hence solely use `INSERT/DELETE DATA` queries. We use a real-world scenario based on

[7] https://github.com/tentris/rdf4cpp.

DBpedia changelogs and a scenario based on Wikidata that tests the benchmarked systems' behavior with increasing update sizes. All experiments were executed on a Debian 11 Server with an AMD EPYC 7713 CPU, 1TB DDR4 octa-channel RAM at 2933MT/s and a 15.36TB KIOXIA CD6-R SSD with an ext4 filesystem. The supplementary material includes benchmarking results confirming that TENTRIS and TENTRIS-ID have equivalent bulk-loading performance and storage efficiency.

6.1 Systems and Experimental Setup

We compare the performance of our implementation (TENTRIS-ID) with the following triple stores that are freely available for benchmarking:

(i) Fuseki 5.2.0, (ii) GraphDB 10.6.2 (free version), (iii) Virtuoso 7.2.12, and (iv) Oxigraph 0.4.7. MilleniumDB [16] and QLever [4] were excluded since they failed or crashed on most of the updates. Jena-LFJ [11] was excluded from the evaluation because it relies on Fuseki's TDB backend with additional indices enabled, which inevitably makes it slower than Fuseki. Our experiments were carried out over HTTP, according to SPARQL's protocol "update via POST directly" [9]. Before each experiment, the triple stores went through a warmup phase for which we sent the queries from the benchmarks of [5].

6.2 DBpedia Update Logs

We start with a snapshot of DBpedia from October 2015 with 860M triples which we date stamped to October 1st, 2015 and execute the updates reported in the official DBpedia changelogs from October 2015. Based on the triples inserted and deleted in each changelog entry, one `INSERT DATA` and one `DELETE DATA` are created, resulting in a total of 15,086 updates. Figure 7 shows the update performance of the evaluated triplestores. The top row plots the update time per triple against the update size, while the bottom row summarizes the runtime distribution, total runtime, and failed updates.

Overall, TENTRIS-ID and Oxigraph are the fastest, followed by Fuseki. GraphDB shows longer update durations, particularly for smaller update sizes, but improves with larger updates. All triplestores but Virtuoso perform better with larger update sizes, likely due to the amortization of HTTP and transactional overheads. Virtuoso's performance is comparable to that of Fuseki for update sizes up to 100 triples but slows down considerably for larger updates. Additionally, Virtuoso rejected[8] all updates exceeding 1,359 triples, resulting in 11,090 (73%) rejected updates. Oxigraph rejected 18 queries (0.12%). In terms of mean update time, TENTRIS-ID consistently outperforms or matches the other systems with a mean($\pm$ standard derivation) runtime of 0.067 ($\pm$0.081) seconds (s). Oxigraph performs similarly with 0.074 ($\pm$0.049)s. The other triplestores are slower, with Virtuoso at 0.12 ($\pm$0.12)s (not comparable due to 73% rejected

[8] Its SPARQL-to-SQL mapping has a hard-coded limit (see https://github.com/openlink/virtuoso-opensource/blob/34c367/libsrc/Wi/sparql2sql.h#L1031).

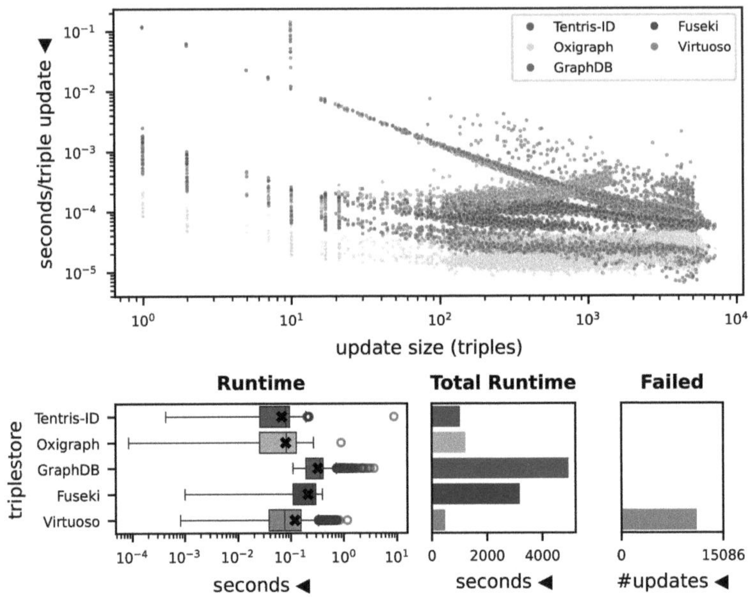

Fig. 7. The triple stores' runtime performance at replaying DBpedia's official update logs. Lower values are better on all subplots as indicated by the ◀. The top plot shows the update size versus the time spent per updated triple. The bottom row provides summary statistics: The left panel is a standard boxplot on the update runtimes with an additional cross for the mean. The middle panel compares the total cumulative runtime and the right panel shows the number of failed updates per system.

updates), Fuseki at 0.21 ($\pm$0.11)s, and GraphDB at 0.33 ($\pm$0.15)s. For total runtime see Fig. 7.

6.3 Wikidata

In our second evaluation, we assess scalability with update sizes up to 10^6 triples using the larger Wikidata trusty dataset (November 11, 2020), which contains 5.5B triples. For this scenario, SPARQL updates were generated from randomly sampled triples. We generated batches of 500 insert and 500 delete updates of sizes 10^1, 10^2, 10^3 and 10^4. For the larger update sizes, we created 100 batches of size 10^5 and 10 batches of size 10^6 for both insert and delete updates. The triples from the insert queries were removed from the dataset before it was loaded into the triple stores. Like in our first experiment, the queries were executed alternating between insert and delete.

The top plot of Fig. 8 shows the mean update time per triple as a function of the update size. Consistent with the findings from the DBpedia scenario, all systems benefit from update sizes. However, this improvement plateaus, for update sizes exceeding 10^3 in Oxigraph, 10^4 in Fuseki and 10^5 in GraphDB and Tentris-ID. Virtuoso[8] is again unable to process updates larger than 10^3.

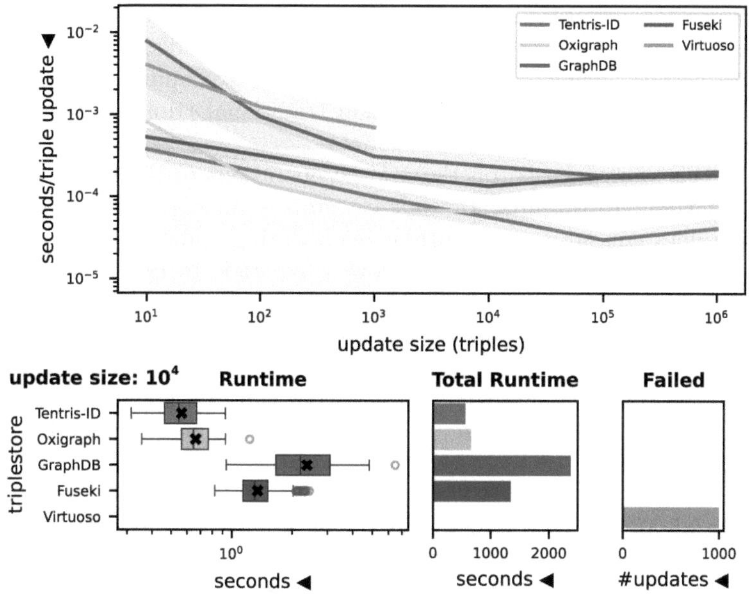

Fig. 8. The triple stores' runtime performance at applying updates to Wikidata with 5.5B triples. The top plot shows scaling update size from 10^1 to 10^6 triples, bands represent one standard deviation. For missing Virtuoso data see Footnote 8. The bottom row provides summary statistics for the batch of updates of size 10^4. For a detailed descriptions of the row layout see Fig. 7.

TENTRIS-ID achieves the overall best performance of all systems for update sizes of 10^4 or more. In particular, it is more than 5.6 times faster than Fuseki and GraphDB on updates of size 10^5 and 10^6. For small and large updates (sizes 10, 10^5 and 10^6) TENTRIS-ID performs about 2 times faster than Oxigraph. For middle-sized updates (sizes 10^3, 10^4 and 10^5), both systems perform similar within a 30% range. We further compare TENTRIS-ID with the second-best performing systems Oxigraph by measuring the performance of both systems during the warmup phase, which executed 495 SPARQL `SELECT` queries. In our experiments, this took Oxigraph over 9 h where as TENTRIS-ID finished in 43 min. Notably, Oxigraph's storage footprint is also 25–54% larger than that of TENTRIS-ID. Hence, we conclude that our extension of the hypertrie with updates leads to the first WCOJ-enabled data structure that outperforms the state of the art both on `SELECT` (as shown in [5,6]) and `INSERT/DELETE` queries.

7 Conclusion and Future Work

We present the first, to the best of our knowledge, efficient online update algorithm for RDF triplestores that fully support worst-case optimal joins (WCOJs). Our solution enables both insertion and deletion of triples while preserving the performance benefits of WCOJs, achieving a crucial milestone in making WCOJs viable for production-ready triple stores. Our evaluation demonstrated that the proposed methods deliver update performance on live updates—scaling up to 1M triples—comparable to or better than traditional triple store systems on large graphs such as DBpedia and Wikidata.

While this work focused on the update operations of the hypertrie, future work should aim to optimize the update process further. The current implementation does not support concurrent reads during updates. In the future, we plan to investigate approaches that allow a hypertrie to remain accessible for reads while updates generate a new version. A possible direction that we plan to explore is deferred materialization where nodes track deltas relative to other hypertrie nodes, thus enabling incremental updates with minimal disruption to ongoing reads. Further, a systematic study of runtime under specific update patterns, e.g., different insertion orders, could be executed to identify possible performance pitfalls.

Supplemental Material Statement: Source code for our modified version of the hypertrie and TENTRIS-ID are available from Github[9]. Raw benchmarking results, bulk-loading performance and storage efficiency results, a technical report for the implemented algorithm, scripts to setup and run the benchmarks, and scripts to generate the figures are available from GitHub[10].

Acknowledgements. This work has been supported within the project "TENTRIS" (03EFNW0356) funded under the EXIST Transfer of Research programme by the German Federal Ministry for Economic Affairs and Energy (BMWE) and co-financed by the European Social Fund. This work has been supported by the German Federal Ministry of Research, Technology and Space (BMFTR) within the project NEBULA under the grant no 13N16364. This project has received funding from the European Union's Horizon Europe research and innovation programme under grant agreement No 101070005.

References

1. Aberger, C.R., Tu, S., Olukotun, K., Ré, C.: Old techniques for new join algorithms: A case study in RDF processing. In: 2016 IEEE 32nd International Conference on Data Engineering Workshops (ICDEW), pp. 97–102 (2016)
2. Arroyuelo, D., Hogan, A., Navarro, G., Reutter, J.L., Rojas-Ledesma, J., Soto, A.: Worst-case optimal graph joins in almost no space. In: Proceedings of the 2021 International Conference on Management of Data, pp. 102–114 (2021)
3. Atserias, A., Grohe, M., Marx, D.: Size bounds and query plans for relational joins. In: Proceedings of the 2008 49th Annual IEEE Symposium on Foundations of Computer Science, pp. 739–748. FOCS '08, IEEE Computer Society, USA (2008)

[9] https://github.com/dice-group/hypertrie and https://github.com/dice-group/tentris-research-project.

[10] https://github.com/dice-group/tentris-wcoj-with-updates.

4. Bast, H., Buchhold, B.: Qlever: A query engine for efficient sparql+text search. In: Proceedings of the 2017 ACM on Conference on Information and Knowledge Management, pp. 647–656. CIKM '17, Association for Computing Machinery, New York, NY, USA (2017)
5. Bigerl, A., Conrads, L., Behning, C., Saleem, M., Ngonga Ngomo, A.C.: Hashing the hypertrie: Space- and time-efficient indexing for sparql in tensors. In: Sattler, U., et al. (eds.) The Semantic Web - ISWC 2022, pp. 57–73. Springer International Publishing, Cham (2022)
6. Bigerl, A., Conrads, L., Behning, C., Sherif, M.A., Saleem, M., Ngonga Ngomo, A.C.: Tentris - a tensor-based triple store. In: Pan, J.Z., et al. (eds.) The Semantic Web - ISWC 2020, pp. 56–73. Springer International Publishing, Cham (2020)
7. Brodal, G.S., Fagerberg, R.: Lower bounds for external memory dictionaries. In: Proceedings of the Fourteenth Annual ACM-SIAM Symposium on Discrete Algorithms, pp. 546–554. SODA '03, Society for Industrial and Applied Mathematics, USA (2003)
8. Cyganiak, R., Wood, D., Lanthaler, M., Klyne, G., Carroll, J.J.: RDF 1.1 Concepts and Abstract Syntax. https://www.w3.org/TR/rdf11-concepts/ (Feb 2014), w3C Recommendation
9. Feigenbaum, L., Williams, G., Clark, K., Torres, E.: SPARQL 1.1 Protocol. https://www.w3.org/TR/sparql11-protocol/ (Mar 2013), w3C Recommendation
10. Harris, S., Seaborne, A., Prud'hommeaux, E., Feigenbaum, L.: SPARQL 1.1 Query Language. https://www.w3.org/TR/sparql11-query/ (Mar 2013), w3C Recommendation
11. Hogan, A., Riveros, C., Rojas, C., Soto, A.: A worst-case optimal join algorithm for SPARQL. In: Ghidini, C., et al. (eds.) ISWC 2019. LNCS, vol. 11778, pp. 258–275. Springer, Cham (2019). https://doi.org/10.1007/978-3-030-30793-6_15
12. Iwabuchi, K., Youssef, K., Velusamy, K., Gokhale, M., Pearce, R.: Metall: a persistent memory allocator for data-centric analytics. Parallel Comput. **111**, 102905 (2022)
13. Karalis, N., Bigerl, A., Demir, C., Heidrich, L., Ngonga Ngomo, A.C.: Evaluating negation with multi-way joins accelerates class expression learning. In: Bifet, A., Davis, J., Krilavičius, T., Kull, M., Ntoutsi, E., Žliobaitė, I. (eds.) Machine Learning and Knowledge Discovery in Databases. Research Track. pp. 199–216. Springer Nature Switzerland, Cham (2024)
14. Karalis, N., Bigerl, A., Heidrich, L., Sherif, M.A., Ngonga Ngomo, A.C.: Efficient evaluation of conjunctive regular path queries using multi-way joins. In: Meroño Peñuela, A., et al. (eds.) The Semantic Web, pp. 218–235. Springer Nature Switzerland, Cham (2024)
15. Ngo, H.Q., Porat, E., Ré, C., Rudra, A.: Worst-case optimal join algorithms. J. ACM, pp. 16:1–16:40 (2018)
16. Vrgoč, D., et al.: MillenniumDB: an open-source graph database system. Data Intell. **5**(3), 560–610 (2023)

Leveraging Open Path from Pruned Graph for Link Prediction on Knowledge Graphs

Xingyu Liu, Yuyin Lu, and Yanghui Rao(✉)

School of Computer Science and Engineering, Sun Yat-sen University, Guangzhou, China
{liuxy356,luyy37}@mail2.sysu.edu.cn, raoyangh@mail.sysu.edu.cn

Abstract. Real-world Knowledge Graphs (KGs) are inherently incomplete, necessitating effective link prediction to infer missing facts and enhance their utility in knowledge-driven applications. While embedding-based methods falter in inductive scenarios with unseen entities, Graph Neural Network (GNN)-based link predictors sacrifice interpretability despite their expressive power. Path-based alternatives address these limitations through transparent reasoning patterns, yet conventional implementations relying on Closed Paths (CPs) between entity pairs face severe path scarcity in sparse KGs. To overcome this bottleneck, we propose Open Path from Pruned Graph enhanced Link Predictor (OPPGLP), a novel framework that integrates GNN-derived relational patterns with path-based reasoning. By converting GNN's latent features into semantically meaningful paths, our approach achieves both explainable and accurate link prediction. Comprehensive evaluations across three public datasets demonstrate state-of-the-art performance of our OPPGLP in 5 out of 6 transductive and inductive settings.

Keywords: Knowledge Graph · Link Prediction · Reasoning Path

1 Introduction

Given the inherent incompleteness of real-world KGs, link prediction plays a crucial role in enhancing KG utility by inferring missing connections between entities [16] , underpinning numerous applications such as logical query answering [13] and drug-disease prediction [34]. Traditional link prediction research primarily focuses on the transductive setting, which assumes all entities are known during training. However, novel entities frequently emerge in practical deployments. Inductive link prediction addresses this more challenging and valuable task, aiming to generalize beyond the entities encountered in training to entirely unseen testing graphs, as illustrated in Fig. 1.

Contemporary link predictors can be broadly categorized into three paradigms: embedding-based, GNN-based, and path-based methods [1]. Embedding-based methods [3,9,10,24,26] learn distributed representations of

D. Garijo et al. (Eds.): ISWC 2025, LNCS 16140, pp. 556–574, 2026.
https://doi.org/10.1007/978-3-032-09527-5_30

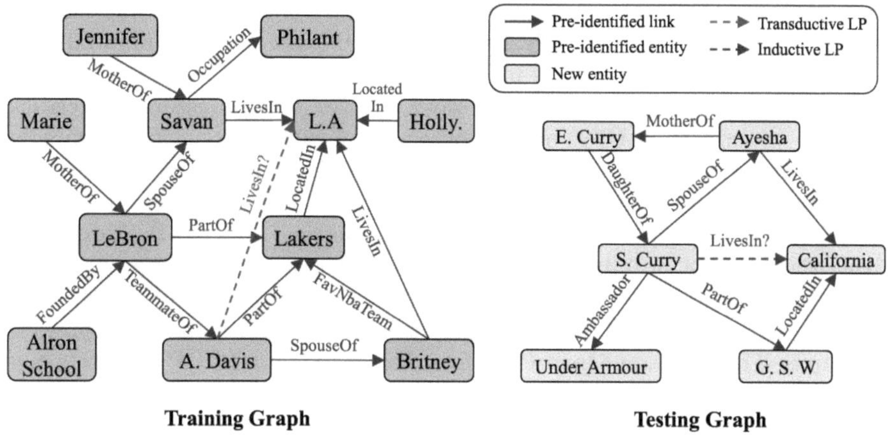

Fig. 1. An example of transductive and inductive link prediction.

entities and relations, achieving strong performance in transductive link prediction on static entities. However, these methods struggle to provide a meaningful approach to deal with new entities in inductive scenarios. Graph Neural Network (GNN)-based methods [7,14,18,23,25] mitigate this constraint by encoding topological dependencies through message passing and neighborhood aggregation mechanisms, thereby enabling inductive generalization to unseen entities. Yet the opaque decision-making processes inherent to GNNs compromise model interpretability. Oppositely, path-based methods [8,20,21,28,30,31] infer links between entities through explicit multi-hop relational path analysis, establishing an interpretable foundation for inductive reasoning. For instance, these methods can extract transferable pattern $(x, \text{LivesIn}, y) \leftarrow (x, \text{PartOf}, v) \wedge (v, \text{LocatedIn}, y)$ from the training graph and predict the missing fact (S.Curry, LivesIn, California) based on an intelligible evidence trail (S.Curry, PartOf, G.S.W.) $\wedge$ (G.S.W., LocatedIn, California).

Despite the above advantages, most path-based methods [20,28,30] critically depend on Closed Paths (CPs), which originate from the head entity and terminate at the tail entity. Due to the inherent incompleteness of KGs, CPs exhibit exponential scarcity under constrained search depths, severely limiting the generalization capacity of these path-based methods. In contrast, Open Paths (OPs) that radiate from head/tail entities without terminal constraints present a theoretically rich supplementary resource due to their combinatorial abundance. Unfortunately, the raw OPs suffer from severe quality variance. For example, for the missing triplet (A. Davis, LivesIn, L. A.), some OPs like (A. Davis, TeammateOf, LeBron) $\wedge$ (LeBron, PartOf, Lakers) encode semantically meaningful patterns, while many degenerate into low-signal sequences, such as (A. Davis, TeammateOf, LeBron) $\wedge$ (LeBron, FoundedBy^{-1}, Alron School). Current solutions like APST [21] employ static statistical filters (e.g., path frequency thresholds) to prune irrelevant OPs. However, their non-parametric nature inherently limits their capacity to capture global structural contexts and identify nuanced relational patterns. Consequently, even filtered OPs often retain suboptimal relevance, ultimately bottlenecking model performance.

Under these considerations, this work focuses on addressing the critical challenge of enhancing OPs' quality by simultaneously preserving meaningful patterns while suppressing noisy sequences. Unlike prior heuristic statistical approaches for OP refinement, we leverage a GNN (M_G) to identifies reasoning-critical edges through head entity-conditioned message passing. Besides, recognizing the inherent opacity of standard GNNs [29], we introduce a parametric probe (M_P) inspired by interpretable architectures like GraphMask [19], which transforms the latent patterns learned by M_G into sparse, human-interpretable subgraphs. The resultant **O**pen **P**ath from **P**runed **G**raph **(OPPG)** component consisting of M_G and M_P serves as a trainable OP refinement solution.

To maximize the compression of redundant edges while mitigating the inherent information loss caused by sparsification, we also design a constrained optimization paradigm that progressively tightens density constraints during M_P's training. By minimizing prediction variation between the original graph and the pruned graph while iteratively reducing target density, our method achieves controlled edge removal. This progressive density reduction strategy enables OPPG to maintain semantic fidelity while extracting compact OP subsets.

Building upon these core components, we propose **OPPG**-enhanced **L**ink **P**redictor **(OPPGLP)**, a novel link prediction framework that first extracts high-quality OPs using OPPG, and then employs a Transformer-based encoder to jointly process unobserved triplets alongside their corresponding CPs and OPs for accurate and interpretable inference. The main contributions of our paper are summarized as follows:

- We introduce OPPGLP, a novel link prediction model that effectively bridges the gap between GNN expressiveness and path-based interpretability.
- We propose a progressive density reduction strategy during OPPG training, balancing the sparsity and informativeness of refined OPs.
- Our method achieves state-of-the-art performance in 5 out of 6 transductive and inductive experimental settings.

2 Related Work

2.1 Embedding-Based Methods

Embedding-based methods project discrete entities and relations into a continuous vector space, where the relationship between entities can be expressed as measurable operations (e.g., translation, rotation, or linear transformation). The existing embedding-based methods (e.g., TransE [3], TransH [26], TransD [9], TransR [10], ComplEx [24], ConvE [5], and TuckER [2]) learn embeddings by optimizing certain scoring functions, which are used to capture the relationships between entities. Embedding-based methods offer the advantage of efficient computation and the ability to capture complex relationships between entities in a compact representation. However, they struggle with the generalization to unseen entities. Additionally, such methods are often non-explainable because the low-dimensional vectors are not comprehensible to humans.

2.2 GNN-Based Methods

GNN-based methods leverage GNNs to capture high-order relational patterns in KGs through message passing and node updating on the graph. Since these methods leverage graph structures as intrinsic features without dependence on specific entity-level information, they inherently generalize to the inductive scenarios. Notable GNN-based link predictors include R-GCN [18], CompGCN [25], GRAIL [23], Link-MoE [14], and UniLP [7]. As a classic and effective method, GRAIL [23] performs message passing over the local subgraph of the target triplet, followed by a linear layer applied to the resulting embeddings for score prediction. Link-MoE [14] utilizes various GNNs as experts and strategically selects the appropriate expert for each node pair based on various types of pairwise information. UniLP [7] leverages In-context Learning on graphs to dynamically adjust to various target graphs based on contextual demonstrations. However, GNN-based methods make black-box predictions without providing explanations, hindering their deployment in risk-sensitive scenarios [33].

2.3 Path-Based Methods

Path-based methods identify reasoning paths over KGs to infer missing links between entities. These multi-hop paths explicitly represent logic rules as entity-relation sequences, thereby providing interpretable predictions. With the development of deep neural architectures, recent methods leverage Pre-trained Language Models (PLMs) [6,11,17] to encode the semantic information of these paths for link prediction. Subsequent works focus on enhancing the quality of these paths, as well as exploring more effective ways to leverage path-based features. For instance, KG-BERT [28] and BERTRL [30] extract Closed Paths (CPs) between head and tail entities, and then leverage PLMs to encode textual descriptions of triplets or paths into embeddings. KRST [20] further introduces relational attention to weight path contributions. Considering the scarcity of CPs, APST [21] proposes statistical filtering to obtain refined Open Paths (OPs), which enhances link prediction through broader path coverage. Paths2Pair [8] incorporates meta paths with meta information of entity types. While contemporary path-based methods provide inherent interpretability advantages, their performance is limited by the quality of the extracted reasoning paths, highlighting significant opportunities for further methodological refinement.

3 Methodology

3.1 Prerequisites

Knowledge Graphs (KGs) represent and store facts through graph-structured data, where each fact is formally expressed as a triplet. Specifically, a KG is defined as $\mathcal{G}(\mathcal{E},\mathcal{R}) \subseteq \{(u,r,v)|u \in \mathcal{E}, r \in \mathcal{R}, v \in \mathcal{E}\}$, with $\mathcal{E}$ and $\mathcal{R}$ denoting the entity set and relation set, respectively. $\mathcal{G}(\mathcal{E},\mathcal{R})$ is hereafter abbreviated as $\mathcal{G}$.

Link Prediction aims at inferring missing triplets in real-world KGs, thereby enhancing KG utility. The core task involves predicting missing entities for queries formulated as $(u,r,?)$ or $(?,r,v)$. Given the logical equivalence between $(?,r,v)$ and $(v,r^{-1},?)$ via inverse relation transformation, our work focuses on the unified formulation $(u,r,?)$ without loss of generality.

Transductive and Inductive settings are two distinct scenarios of link prediction on KGs. Given a training graph $\mathcal{G}_\text{s}$ and a testing graph $\mathcal{G}_\text{t}$, the transductive setting assumes that no unseen entities exist during testing, i.e., $\mathcal{E}_s \equiv \mathcal{E}_t$. While this assumption conflicts with real-world KG dynamics, the inductive setting defines that $\mathcal{G}_\text{s} \neq \mathcal{G}_\text{t}$ with $\mathcal{E}_\text{t} \cap \mathcal{E}_\text{s} = \emptyset$, requiring link predictors to generalize to entirely novel entity sets in the testing graph. This open-world scenario better reflects practical deployment conditions where systems must process unseen entities. In summary, we can formalize link prediction on KGs as a binary classification task as follows: Given a query $(u,r,?)$ and a candidate set $\mathcal{V} \subseteq \mathcal{E}_\text{t}$, the link predictor determines $y \in \{0,1\}$ indicating whether (u,r,v') holds for each candidate entity $v' \in \mathcal{V}$. Hereafter, we use $\mathcal{G}$ to denote either $\mathcal{G}_s$ or $\mathcal{G}_t$.

Path-based Link Predictor extracts semantically relevant paths from $\mathcal{G}$ as reasoning evidence for the query $(u,r,?)$ and the candidate entity v', thereby computing prediction scores for the target triplet $q = (u,r,v')$. An n-hop path is formalized as a connected sequence $p = t_1 \wedge t_2 \wedge \cdots \wedge t_n$, where each $t_i = (u_i, r_i, v_i) \in \mathcal{G}$ is an observed triplet, and consecutive triplets satisfy $v_i \equiv u_{i+1}$. CPs and OPs for (u,r,v') are formally defined as:

$$\begin{aligned} \mathcal{P}_C(u,v') &= \{p(u,v') \mid u_1 \equiv u \wedge v_n \equiv v'\}, \\ \mathcal{P}_O(u,v') &= \{p(u) \mid u_1 \equiv u\} \cup \{p(v') \mid v_n \equiv v'\}. \end{aligned} \tag{1}$$

Then, path-based link predictors compute the prediction score $s_q \in \mathbb{R}$ for q, formalized as follows:

$$s_q = \text{PLP}\left((u,r,v'); \mathcal{P}_C(u,v'), \mathcal{P}_O(u,v')\right). \tag{2}$$

3.2 Overall Workflow

This work develops the **Open Path from Pruned Graph enhanced Link Predictor (OPPGLP)**, which provides an effective and interpretable solution for link prediction in both transductive and inductive settings. As illustrated in Fig. 2, given a KG $\mathcal{G}$, OPPGLP infer whether a candidate entity v' is the answer for the query $(u,r,?)$ through four steps:

1. **Closed Path Extraction:** OPPGLP employs Breadth-First Search (BFS) to extract CPs $\mathcal{P}_C(u,v')$ connecting the head entity u and candidate tail entity v' within $\mathcal{G}$.
2. **Open Path Refinement:** The OPPG module dynamically generates high-quality OPs $\mathcal{P}_O(u,v')$ originating from u or terminating at v' through adaptive graph sparsification.

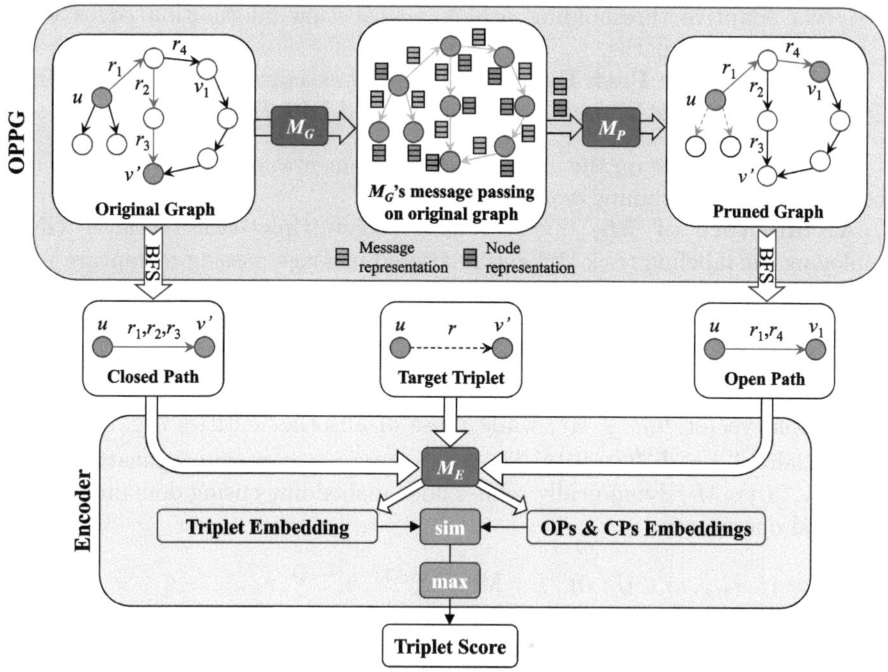

Fig. 2. The inference pipeline of the proposed OPPGLP.

3. **Evidence Integration:** The Transformer-based encoder M_E processes the textual sequence of the target triplet (u, r, v') as well as obtains CPs $\mathcal{P}_C(u, v')$ and OPs $\mathcal{P}_O(u, v')$, deriving embeddings of the triplet and paths.
4. **Interpretable Scoring:** OPPGLP computes cosine similarity between the triplet embedding and each path embedding. The maximum similarity score determines the final prediction confidence, while the corresponding path provides explainable evidence.

3.3 OPPG

To get high-quality OPs in a parametric way, we propose the OPPG component. The key idea of OPPG is to generate a subgraph $\mathcal{G}_q \subseteq \mathcal{G}$ by removing edges that are unnecessary for answering the given query $q = (u, r, ?)$ from the original graph $\mathcal{G}$. As depicted in the OPPG module of Fig. 2, our OPPG module integrates an L-layer GNN encoder M_G with a differentiable graph probe M_P, operating through the following three stages:

1. **Target-Specific Message Passing:** M_G performs target triplet-conditioned message propagation over $\mathcal{G}$ and generates node embeddings.
2. **Adaptive Edge Pruning:** Given the L-layer messages and node embeddings, M_P computes edge importance scores and generates a sparse subgraph

$\mathcal{G}_q$ via adaptive thresholding, which removes low-information edges while retaining critical paths.
3. **Evidence-Aware Path Extraction:** OPPG executes BFS originating from u or terminating at v' on $\mathcal{G}_q$, obtaining refined OPs $\mathcal{P}_O(u, v')$.

Next, we elaborate on the architectural implementation of M_G and M_P, and then introduce the training workflow of OPPG.

Architecture of M_G operates as a target triplet-aware L-layer GNN, employing the labeling trick [32] and relational message passing to capture task-specific structural patterns. Unlike GNN-based link predictors, M_G is not dedicated to generating link prediction results. Instead, its core objective is to identify and extract edges that exhibit strong correlations with potential link predictions.

Specifically, the embedding of head entity u is randomly initialized as a d-dimensional vector $\boldsymbol{h}_u^{(0)} \in \mathbb{R}^d$, while those of all other entities $e \in \mathcal{E}/\{u\}$ are zero-initialized, i.e., $\boldsymbol{h}_e^{(0)} \in \{0\}^d$. Through successive message propagation layers ($k \in \{1 \dots L\}$), M_G dynamically refines node embeddings using domain-adapted relational operators:

$$\text{For } (u, r_{u,v}, v) \in \mathcal{G} : \boldsymbol{m}_{u,v}^{(k)} = \text{Msg}(\boldsymbol{h}_u^{(k-1)}, \boldsymbol{h}_v^{(k-1)}, \boldsymbol{r}_{u,v}), \tag{3}$$

$$\text{For } \mathcal{N}(v) = \{u \mid (u, r_{u,v}, v) \in \mathcal{G}\} : \boldsymbol{h}_v^{(k)} = \text{Agg}(\{\boldsymbol{m}_{u,v}^{(k)} : u \in \mathcal{N}(v)\}), \tag{4}$$

where $\boldsymbol{r}_{u,v} \in \mathbb{R}^d$ is the representation of relation between nodes u and v, and $\mathcal{N}(v)$ is the set of neighbourhood nodes of v. The message function $\text{Msg}(\cdot)$ can be defined as the relational operators in embedding methods, e.g., TransE [3], DistMult [27], and RotatE [22]. We use the message function from Distmult and for each observed triplet (u, r, v):

$$\boldsymbol{m}_{u,v}^{(k)} = \boldsymbol{h}_u^{(k-1)} \odot \boldsymbol{r}_{u,v}. \tag{5}$$

The aggregation function $\text{Agg}(\cdot)$ supports flexible pooling operations, including mean, sum, or max pooling. In M_G, we deliberately select the DistMult+Max combination, with the rationale for this choice detailed in Sect. 4.1. At the final layer L, the representation of any entity e undergoes non-linear transformation through a feedforward scoring network $\text{FFN}(\cdot) : \mathbb{R}^d \mapsto \mathbb{R}$:

$$s_e = \text{FFN}(\boldsymbol{h}_e^{(L)}). \tag{6}$$

Architecture of M_P is a differentiable graph probe that operates on multi-scale representations from M_G to enable adaptive edge pruning. Specifically, our M_P employs three specialized feedforward networks to aggregate multi-layer representations from M_G:

$$\boldsymbol{m}_{u,v} = \text{FFN}_m(\oplus_{k=1}^{L} \boldsymbol{m}_{u,v}^{(k)}), \tag{7}$$

$$\boldsymbol{h}_u = \text{FFN}_u(\oplus_{k=1}^{L} \boldsymbol{h}_u^{(k)}), \tag{8}$$

$$\boldsymbol{h}_v = \text{FFN}_v(\oplus_{k=1}^{L} \boldsymbol{h}_v^{(k)}), \tag{9}$$

where $\oplus$ denotes vector concatenation across L layers, and the feedforward networks $\text{FFN}_m(\cdot), \text{FFN}_u(\cdot), \text{FFN}_v(\cdot) : \mathbb{R}^{L\times d} \mapsto \mathbb{R}^d$ learn layer-wise importance through parametric projection. The retaining logit $\lambda_{u,v} \in \mathbb{R}$ for the edge $(u, r_{u,v}, v)$ is computed via:

$$\lambda_{u,v} = \text{FFN}\left(\frac{1}{3}(\boldsymbol{m}_{u,v} + \boldsymbol{h}_u + \boldsymbol{h}_v)\right). \tag{10}$$

To transform the edge retaining logit $\lambda_{u,v}$ into a binary gate $g_{u,v} \in \{0,1\}$, we utilize the Hard Concrete gate mechanism following GraphMask [19]. Intuitively, it creates a continuous probability distribution over gates during training through stretch-and-clamp operations on sigmoid outputs. This allows gradients to flow through the sampling process via the reparameterization trick [12]. Formally, the distribution defines a random variable $\boldsymbol{c}$ over the interval $(l = -0.2, r = 1)$ as:

$$a \sim \mathcal{U}(0,1), \quad c_{u,v} = \sigma((\log a - \log(1-a) + \lambda_{u,v})/\tau), \tag{11}$$

$$z_{u,v} = \min(1, \max(0, r + (l-r)\cdot c_{u,v}), \tag{12}$$

where $\sigma(x) = (1+e^{-x})^{-1}$ is the sigmoid function. $\lambda_{u,v}$ acts as a location parameter skewing the probability mass toward 0 (pruning) or 1 (retaining), and τ is a learnable temperature parameter. Here, $z_{u,v} \in [0,1]$ represents the continuous relaxation of $g_{u,v}$ during training. When M_P is applied to M_G, the original message in the kth layer $\boldsymbol{m}_{u,v}^{(k)}$ is transformed into $\tilde{\boldsymbol{m}}_{u,v}^{(k)}$:

$$\tilde{\boldsymbol{m}}_{u,v}^{(k)} = z_{u,v} \odot \boldsymbol{m}_{u,v}^{(k)}. \tag{13}$$

At inference, we use a predefined threshold γ to obtain the binary $g_{u,v}$ from $z_{u,v}$, with $g_{u,v} = 1$ indicating the retention of edge (u,r,v) in the subgraph $\mathcal{G}_q$:

$$g_{u,v} = \mathbb{I}\left[z_{u,v} > \gamma\right], \tag{14}$$

$$\mathcal{G}_q = \{(u,r,v) \mid (u,r,v) \in \mathcal{G} \wedge g_{u,v} = 1\}, \tag{15}$$

where $\mathbb{I}(\cdot)$ is an indication function.

Training Workflow of OPPG starts by optimizing M_G on the training graph $\mathcal{G}_s$. For each observed triplet $(u,r,v^+) \in \mathcal{G}_s$, the model parameters of M_G are optimized by minimizing the Binary Cross-Entropy (BCE) loss:

$$\mathcal{L}_{M_G} = \log\sigma(s_{v^+}) + \frac{1}{|\mathcal{NS}|}\sum_{v^-\in\mathcal{NS}} \log\left(1-\sigma(s_{v^-})\right), \tag{16}$$

where $\mathcal{NS} \subseteq \mathcal{E}_s/\{v^+\}$ denotes the negative sample set derived by uniform sampling over $\mathcal{E}_s/\{v^+\}$.

With the pretrained and frozen M_G, the training objective of M_P is maintaining the output variation of M_G, and minimizing the density of the pruned subgraph, as illustrated in Fig. 3. Intuitively, a smaller output variation indicates more principled edge removal. For each existential triplet pattern $\exists x$:

$(u, r, x) \in \mathcal{G}_s$, we define the positive sample as $v^+ = \arg\max_{e \in \mathcal{E}_s} s_e$, where $s_e = M_G(u, e; \mathcal{G}_s)$ denotes M_G's predictive score for entity e on the original graph $\mathcal{G}_s$, and derive negative samples $\mathcal{NS} \subseteq \mathcal{E}_s / \{v^+\}$ via uniformly sampling. Then M_P is optimized via BCE loss:

$$\mathcal{L}_{M_P,1} = \log \sigma(\tilde{s}_{v^+}) + \frac{1}{|\mathcal{NS}|} \sum_{v^- \in \mathcal{NS}} \log\left(1 - \sigma(\tilde{s}_{v^-})\right), \tag{17}$$

where $\tilde{s}_{v^\pm} = M_G(u, v^\pm; \mathcal{G}_{sq})$ denotes M_G's predictive score for entity $v^\pm$ on the subgraph $\mathcal{G}_{sq}$ pruned from $\mathcal{G}_s$ via M_P, as defined in Eq. (13).

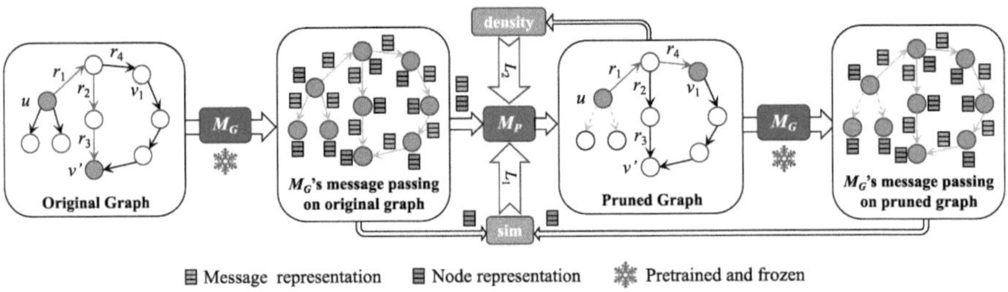

Fig. 3. The training pipeline of M_P, where M_G is pretrained and frozen.

To enforce controlled sparsity in the subgraph $\mathcal{G}_{sq}$, we first consider a baseline approach using L_2 regularization on subgraph density, formally defined as

$$\mathcal{L}'_{M_P,2} = d_c^2, \quad d_c = \frac{1}{|\mathcal{G}_s|} \sum_{(u,r,v) \in \mathcal{G}_s} z_{u,v}. \tag{18}$$

However, empirical analysis reveals this naïve regularization fails to balance the dual objectives of edge reduction and prediction fidelity preservation ($\mathcal{L}_{M_P,1}$), often resulting in insufficient sparsity (ref. Sect. 4.4). To address this limitation, we design a novel loss based on a progressively decaying target density $d_t \in \mathbb{R}^+$, formalized as

$$\mathcal{L}_{M_P,2} = (\frac{d_c - d_t}{d_t})^2. \tag{19}$$

The target density undergoes exponential decay scheduling:

$$d_t^{(i)} = d_t^{(0)} \cdot \zeta^{\lfloor \frac{i}{E} \rfloor}, \tag{20}$$

where $d_t^{(0)}$ is a predefined initial target density, $\zeta \in (0, 1)$ is the decay rate, $d_t^{(i)}$ represents the target density at epoch i, and $\lfloor \frac{i}{E} \rfloor$ indicates that the decay occurs every E epochs. In other words, as the training progresses, d_t is updated to smaller values, imposing higher requirements on the sparsity of the subgraph.

To this end, the overall loss of M_P is a weighted sum of $\mathcal{L}_{M_P,1}$ and $\mathcal{L}_{M_P,2}$ with an adaptive weight α:

$$\mathcal{L}_{M_P} = \mathcal{L}_{M_P,1} + \alpha \cdot \mathcal{L}_{M_P,2}. \tag{21}$$

3.4 Encoder M_E

Functionally, M_E generates embeddings for (1) the target triplet $q = (u, r, v')$, (2) its CPs $\mathcal{P}_C(u, v')$ from the original graph $\mathcal{G}$, and (3) its OPs $\mathcal{P}_O(u, v')$ from the pruned graph $\mathcal{G}_q$ processed by M_P. These embeddings are then compared through similarity metrics to identify the most relevant paths, which collectively determine the final prediction score. Next, we detail M_E's architecture and training protocol.

Architecture of M_E operates as a Transformer-based encoder. Following APST [21], we structure each target triplet $q = (u, r, v')$ and its associated paths $\mathcal{P}_C(u, v') \cup \mathcal{P}_O(u, v')$ into a sequential input format for M_E, which generates embeddings for both the triplet and individual paths:

$$\text{For triplet } q: \quad \text{Seq}(q) = [u][D_u][r][v'][D_{v'}], \tag{22}$$

$$\text{For CP } p(u, v') \in \mathcal{P}_C(u, v'): \quad \text{Seq}\left(p(u, v')\right) = [u][D_u][r_1][e_1] \ldots [v'][D_{v'}], \tag{23}$$

$$\text{For OP } p(u) \in \mathcal{P}_O(u, v'): \quad \text{Seq}\left(p(u)\right) = [u][D_u][r_1][r_2] \;\ldots\; [t][D_t], \tag{24}$$

$$\text{For OP } p(v') \in \mathcal{P}_O(u, v'): \quad \text{Seq}\left(p(v')\right) = [h][D_h][r_1][r_2] \;\ldots\; [v'][D_{v'}], \tag{25}$$

$$\text{For } x \in \{q\} \cup \mathcal{P}_C(u, v') \cup \mathcal{P}_O(u, v'): \quad \boldsymbol{v}_x = M_E\left(\text{Seq}(x)\right), \tag{26}$$

where $[D_u]$ denotes the textual description of the entity u and $\text{Seq}(\cdot)$ denotes a textual sequence for either the triplet or a path. t and h are the endpoints of $p(u)$ and $p(v')$, respectively. $\boldsymbol{v}_q, \{\boldsymbol{v}_{p(u,v')}\}, \{\boldsymbol{v}_{p(x)}\}$ are the embeddings of the triplet q, the CPs $\mathcal{P}_C(u, v') = \{p(u, v')\}$, and the OPs $\mathcal{P}_O(u, v') = \{p(x)\}$, respectively.

Finally, we compute the cosine similarity between the triplet embedding $\boldsymbol{v}_q$ and each of the path embeddings $\boldsymbol{v}_p \in \{\boldsymbol{v}_{p(u,v')}\} \cup \{\boldsymbol{v}_{p(x)}\}$, selecting the highest score as the probability for the triplet being true, with the corresponding path serving as the reasoning evidence. This is formulated by:

$$s_q = \max_{\boldsymbol{v}_p} \; cos(\boldsymbol{v}_p, \boldsymbol{v}_q). \tag{27}$$

Training Workflow of M_E: During training, the loss function of M_E is designed to decrease the scores of sampled negative triplets $\mathcal{NS} = \{q^- \mid q^- \notin \mathcal{G}_s\}$ and increase the scores of positive triplet $q^+ \in \mathcal{G}_s$, which is formulated as follows:

$$\mathcal{L}_{M_E} = \sum_{\boldsymbol{v}_{p^+}} \left(1 - cos(\boldsymbol{v}_{p^+}, \boldsymbol{v}_{q^+})\right) + \sum_{q^- \in \mathcal{NS}} \sum_{\boldsymbol{v}_{p^-}} \max(0, cos(\boldsymbol{v}_{p^-}, \boldsymbol{v}_{q^-}) - m), \tag{28}$$

where $m \in (-1, 1)$ is a predefined margin, which is set to 0 following APST [21].

Overall, the complete training and inference workflow of our OPPGLP is shown in Algorithm 1.

Algorithm 1: Complete workflow of OPPGLP

Input: Training graph $\mathcal{G}_s$, testing graph $\mathcal{G}_t$, testing triplets $\{q = (u, r, v')\}$
Output: Prediction scores $\{s_q\}$ for $\{q = (u, r, v')\}$
Training Phase begin
  Train M_G on triplets $(u_s, r_s, v_s) \in \mathcal{G}_s$ by Eq. (16);
  Train M_P on triplets $(u_s, r_s, v_s) \in \mathcal{G}_s$ by Eq. (21);
  Derive the pruned graph $\mathcal{G}_{sq} \leftarrow \mathcal{G}_s$ by Eq. (15);
  Obtain CPs $\mathcal{P}_C(u_s, v_s)$ by BFS on $\mathcal{G}_s$;
  Obtain OPs $\mathcal{P}_O(u_s, v_s)$ by BFS on $\mathcal{G}_{sq}$;
  Train M_E on $(u_s, r_s, v_s) \in \mathcal{G}_s$, $\mathcal{P}_C(u_s, v_s)$, and $\mathcal{P}_O(u_s, v_s)$ by Eq. (28).
end
Inference Phase begin
  Freeze M_G, M_P, and M_E;
  Derive the pruned graph $\mathcal{G}_{tq} \leftarrow \mathcal{G}_t$ by Eq. (15);
  foreach *test query* $q = (u, r, v')$ **do**
    Obtain CPs $\mathcal{P}_C(u, v')$ by BFS on $\mathcal{G}_t$;
    Obtain OPs $\mathcal{P}_O(u, v')$ by BFS on $\mathcal{G}_{tq}$;
    Infer $s_q \leftarrow M_E((u, r, v'), \mathcal{P}_C(u, v'), \mathcal{P}_O(u, v'))$ by Eq. (26) and Eq. (27);
    Yield s_q.
  end
end

4 Experiment

4.1 Experiment Setup

Datasets: We conduct experiments on three widely-used link prediction datasets, i.e., WN18RR, FB15k-237, and NELL-995 introduced by Teru et al. [23]. Each dataset comprises transductive and inductive settings. The statistics of datasets are provided in Table 1. Consistent with the setup of BERTRL [illegible], each test query is associated with a candidate set of 50 entities, including exactly one correct answer.

Evaluation Metrics: We rank the candidate entities based on the prediction scores from our OPPGLP and baseline link predictors and evaluate their performance using the Mean Reciprocal Rank (MRR) and Hits@1 metrics. MRR calculates the average reciprocal rank of the correct answer across all queries:

$$\text{MRR} = \frac{1}{|Q|} \sum_{i=1}^{|Q|} \frac{1}{\text{rank}_i}, \tag{29}$$

where $|Q|$ is the total number of test queries and rank_i is the ranking of the correct answer for the test query $q_i \in Q$. The Hits@1 metric measures the percentage of queries where the correct answer ranks first:

$$\text{Hits@1} = \frac{1}{|Q|} \sum_{i=1}^{|Q|} \mathbb{I}(\text{rank}_i = 1). \tag{30}$$

Table 1. Statistics of datasets. $|\mathcal{R}|$, $|\mathcal{E}|$, $|\mathcal{G}|$, and $|Q|$ denote the number of relations, entities, triplets, and test queries, respectively.

		WN18RR				FB15k-237				NELL-995			
		$\lvert\mathcal{R}\rvert$	$\lvert\mathcal{E}\rvert$	$\lvert\mathcal{G}\rvert$	$\lvert Q\rvert$	$\lvert\mathcal{R}\rvert$	$\lvert\mathcal{E}\rvert$	$\lvert\mathcal{G}\rvert$	$\lvert Q\rvert$	$\lvert\mathcal{R}\rvert$	$\lvert\mathcal{E}\rvert$	$\lvert\mathcal{G}\rvert$	$\lvert Q\rvert$
$\mathcal{G}_s$		9	2,746	6,670	–	180	1,594	5,223	-	88	2,564	10,063	–
$\mathcal{G}_t$	Trans	9	2,746	6,670	638	180	1,594	5,223	492	88	2,564	10,063	968
	Ind	8	922	1,991	188	142	1,093	2,404	205	79	2,086	5,521	476

Table 2. Hyperparameter settings.

Notation	d	L	γ	$d_t^{(0)}$	m
Description	Dimension of M_G	Layers in M_G	Threshold of M_P	Initial target density of M_P	Margin of M_E
Value	32	6	0.5	0.6	0

Baselines: Since our method is a path-based link predictor, we primarily benchmark it against path-based methods, including RuleN [15], MINERVA [4], KG-BERT [28], BERTRL [30], KRST [20], and APST [21]. APST is the state-of-the-art path-based method. For methodological completeness and comparative fairness, we further report results from TuckER [2], a representative embedding-based baseline with strong empirical performance, and GRAIL [23], a widely adopted GNN-based inductive link prediction model.

Implementation: We select Distmult and Max for M_G based on validation set performance: (1) DistMult outperforms TransE/RotatE by +1% MRR scores on average due to its strong relational inductive bias. (2) Max aggregation outperforms alternatives by preserving only the most salient neighborhood signals, critically amplifying key edges for downstream pruning.

The experimental hyperparameter settings are summarized in Table 2. Our hyperparameters are selected through: (1) Referencing established configurations in related work (γ [19], m [21]); (2) Grid search on the validation set (L, d); (3) Analysis of the training process ($d_t^{(0)}$). More details and validation results are available in the *Supplemental Material.*

For a fair comparison, we use the same sentence encoder (all-mpnet-base-v2[1]) as in APST [21]. The experiments are conducted on four NVIDIA Tesla V100 GPUs (16GB memory each).

4.2 Main Results

Table 3 reports the MRR and Hits@1 scores on transductive and inductive link prediction tasks, where "–" indicates the method is inapplicable in a specific

[1] https://huggingface.co/sentence-transformers/all-mpnet-base-v2.

Table 3. Results of transductive and inductive link prediction.

		Transductive			Inductive		
		WN18RR	FB15k-237	NELL-995	WN18RR	FB15k-237	NELL-995
MRR	RuleN	0.669	0.674	0.736	0.780	0.462	0.710
	GRAIL	0.676	0.597	0.727	0.799	0.469	0.675
	MINERVA	0.656	0.572	0.592	–	–	–
	TuckER	0.646	0.682	0.800	–	–	–
	KG-BERT	0.642	0.790	0.757	0.547	0.500	0.419
	BERTRL	0.683	0.695	0.781	0.792	0.605	**0.808**
	KRST	0.899	0.720	0.800	0.890	0.716	0.769
	APST	0.902	0.774	0.801	0.908	0.764	0.769
	OPPGLP	**0.938**	**0.863**	**0.824**	**0.917**	**0.783**	0.782
Hits@1	RuleN	0.646	0.603	0.636	0.745	0.415	0.638
	GRAIL	0.644	0.494	0.615	0.769	0.390	0.554
	MINERVA	0.632	0.534	0.553	–	–	–
	TuckER	0.600	0.615	0.729	–	–	–
	KG-BERT	0.434	0.691	0.628	0.436	0.341	0.244
	BERTRL	0.655	0.620	0.686	0.755	0.541	**0.715**
	KRST	0.835	0.639	0.694	0.809	0.600	0.649
	APST	0.839	0.694	0.698	0.837	0.643	0.663
	OPPGLP	**0.892**	**0.793**	**0.735**	**0.851**	**0.692**	0.674

setting. Notably, our method achieves state-of-the-art performance in 5 out of 6 experimental benchmarks, demonstrating improvements with a large margin over the strongest path-based baseline APST. These results validate that our OPPG module outperforms APST's heuristic statistical approach in generating high-quality OPs. While BERTRL marginally outperforms OPPGLP in the inductive setting on NELL-995 (first-ranked vs. second-best), its heavy reliance on CPs leads to severe cross-dataset instability. In contrast, OPPGLP delivers robust and superior performance across all benchmarks, by strategically combining CPs and OPs.

4.3 Ablation Study

To further investigate the effectiveness of key modules in OPPGLP, we conduct ablation studies on all three datasets under both transductive and inductive settings. The results are presented in Table 4, where **w/o OPPG** refers to the ablated version of OPPGLP that excludes the OPPG module, i.e., using only CPs for inference. $\mathbf{M_G}$ **only** represents the model that uses M_G alone for link prediction, i.e., the prediction score for a target triplet $q = (u, r, v')$ is computed by $s_q = s_{v'}$, as defined in Eq. (6). Notably, the ablated models exhibit varying

Table 4. Results of ablation analysis.

		Transductive			Inductive		
		WN18RR	FB15k-237	NELL-995	WN18RR	FB15k-237	NELL-995
MRR	OPPGLP	**0.938**	**0.863**	**0.824**	**0.917**	**0.783**	**0.782**
	w/o OPPG	0.895	0.842	0.802	0.890	0.739	0.757
	$\mathrm{M_G}$ only	0.780	0.737	0.781	0.850	0.493	0.563
Hits@1	OPPGLP	**0.892**	**0.793**	**0.735**	**0.851**	**0.692**	**0.674**
	w/o OPPG	0.823	0.774	0.704	0.814	0.639	0.641
	$\mathrm{M_G}$ only	0.735	0.679	0.690	0.793	0.395	0.410
Acc	$\mathrm{M_G}$ only	0.987	0.990	0.991	0.989	0.961	0.985

degrees of performance degradation. On one hand, these results validate the importance of OPs for link prediction. On the other hand, while the performance of $\mathbf{M_G}$ **only** shows a significant drop compared to OPPGLP, it still outperforms GNN-based method GRAIL on most metrics.

Additionally, we further analyze the contribution of M_G to OPPGLP. The Acc metric shows M_G's performance on both known and unknown edges in terms of Hits@1, demonstrating that M_G can accurately learn the structural information of the observed graph. This enables M_G to work with M_P in extracting high-quality OPs. In other words, the OPPG module, composed of M_P and M_G, focuses on extracting path-based logical rules from the observed graph, which assists the highly generalized M_E module in performing link prediction.

4.4 Analysis of M_P's Training Strategy

In this section, we conduct an in-depth analysis to explore the critical role of the proposed training strategy for M_P defined by Eq. (19) (denoted as **w** d_t). Specifically, we adopt the $\mathrm{L_2}$ normalization defined in Eq.(18) (denoted as **w/o** d_t) as the baseline. We evaluate the resulting M_P by measuring the variation in M_G's MRR performance (ΔMRR) and the density of the pruned subgraph (d_c).

Figure 4 (a) shows that both cases maintain M_G's output variations within the maximum allowance (see *Supplemental Material* for sensitivity analysis), ensuring model fidelity preservation. Figure 4 (b) reveals that the density curve of **OPPGLP w** d_t drops rapidly, achieving subgraph density around 3% before epoch 30, while the unconstrained training shows slower convergence, only reaching approximately 30% density after around 70 epochs. This clear contrast highlights the significant impact of incorporating the proposed progressive density reduction strategy in M_P's training process.

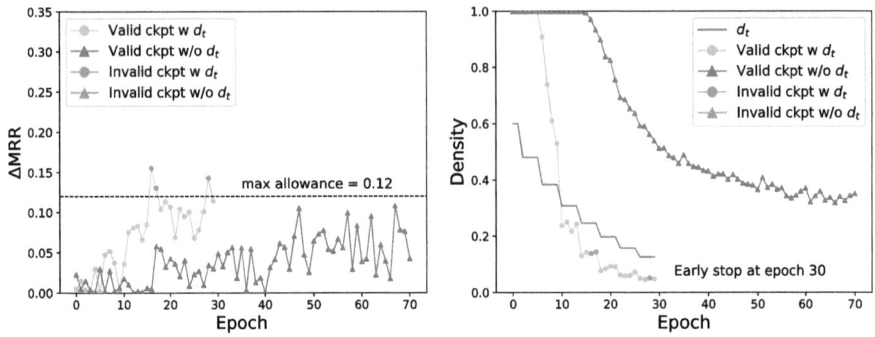

(a) Output variation during training (b) Subgraph density during training

Fig. 4. Visualization of M_P's training process.

4.5 Complexity and Scalability Analysis

This section analyzes the computational complexity of OPPGLP in terms of the KG's size (i.e., the number of triplets, denoted as $|\mathcal{G}|$) and density (defined as the average node degree, $D = |\mathcal{G}|/|\mathcal{E}|$).

For M_G with dimension d_G, the time complexity for L_G-layer message passing (DistMult) and aggregation (Max) is $O(|\mathcal{G}| \times L_G \times d_G)$ and $O(|\mathcal{E}| \times D \times L_G \times d_G)$, respectively.

For M_P with dimension d_P, the complexity of pruning a KG is $O(|\mathcal{G}| \times L_P \times d_P^2)$. The resulting subgraph exhibits significantly reduced size ($|\mathcal{G}_q| \ll |\mathcal{G}|$) and density ($D_q \ll D$). Our empirical results on the FB15k-237 dataset (inductive) demonstrate that $|\mathcal{G}_q| \approx 0.03|\mathcal{G}|$ and $D_q \approx 0.03D$.

For path search, the complexity of the BFS performed per target triplet is $O(D_q^n)$, where n denotes the length of reasoning paths.

For M_E, the time complexity of encoding a target triplet and its associated paths depends on the length of its textual descriptions, but remains independent of both the KG's size and density.

In summary, our method scales linearly with the KG's size ($|\mathcal{G}|$). The effective edge pruning yields a subgraph with substantially reduced density ($D_q \ll D$), which dramatically improves path search efficiency for a given path length k. Consequently, our approach demonstrates strong scalability to larger and denser KGs. For experimental runtime and hardware specifications, please refer to our repository which will be specified in the *Supplemental Material Statement.*

4.6 Case Study

To demonstrate the validity of the OPs refined by OPPG, we conduct a case study, as shown in Table 5. The given positive triplet t states that the nominees for an award include actresses for their performance in the film Fargo. For this triplet, a BFS on the original graph G identifies 33 OPs, many of which

Table 5. A case study on the FB15k-237 dataset on inductive setting.

BFS	OPPG	ID	t =(AwardForActress, NominatedFor, Fargo)
√		OP_1	(MeanGirls, FilmLanguage $\wedge$ FilmLanguage^{-1}, Fargo)
√		OP_2	(CarterBurwell, FilmMusic^{-1}, Fargo)
√	√	OP_3	(FrancesMcDormand, NominatedFor, Fargo)
√	√	OP_4	(FrancesMcDormand, AwardWinner^{-1}, Fargo)

are irrelevant and provide little value in answering the query. For instance, OP_1 connects Fargo to Mean Girls via a two-hop relationship, indicating that both films share the same language. However, this linguistic similarity offers no meaningful insight into the award-related status of Fargo. Similarly, OP_2 shows that Carter Burwell composed the soundtrack for Fargo, which is also unrelated to the query's focus on award nominations.

After applying the trained probe M_P to prune 95% of irrelevant edges from $\mathcal{G}$, the resulting sparse subgraph $\mathcal{G}_q$ contains only 5 OPs, all of which are highly relevant to the query. For instance, OP_3 and OP_4 indicate that the actress Frances McDormand was nominated for and won awards for her role in Fargo. These paths not only carry direct award-related information but also feature an actress as the head entity-conceptually aligned with the award category in triplet t. Such paths have high informational value and serve as strong supporting evidence for the correctness of t. By eliminating irrelevant edges, the OPPGLP framework is less affected by noisy or misleading information, enabling more accurate link prediction.

5 Conclusion and Future Work

This work proposes OPPGLP, a novel path-based link predictor that consists of an OPPG component and a Transformer-based encoder. The OPPG component obtains OPs with high quality by interpreting the latent structural patterns captured by GNNs, and the encoder projects the given triplets and their refined paths into the same embedding space. Based on their embeddings, triplets are scored and candidate answers are ranked for link prediction task. Comprehensive experiments confirm the effectiveness of our method.

However, our approach has a limitation that deserves future research. Compared to other path-based methods, OPPGLP introduces additional computational cost primarily from M_P training, whose time complexity scales linearly with KG size, leading to increased overall runtime. To address this limitation, future work should develop more efficient probe training strategies for large-scale KGs. Particularly, future improvements to this method can be explored in two directions: (1) Optimize path feature extraction: Current path embeddings encoded by PLMs could be further refined by path-specific training objectives; (2) Explore meta information: Beyond CPs and OPs, meta information like entity ontologies holds promise for improving reasoning capabilities. We also plan to explore such information in future work.

Supplemental Material Statement: The implementation of OPPGLP, along with all adopted datasets and detailed experimental reports, is publicly available in our repository: https://github.com/starrlee356/OPPGLP.

Acknowledgments. This work (corresponding author: Yanghui Rao) was supported by the National Natural Science Foundation of China (62372483).

References

1. Arrar, D., Kamel, N., Lakhfif, A.: A comprehensive survey of link prediction methods. J. Supercomput. **80**(3), 3902–3942 (2024)
2. Balazevic, I., Allen, C., Hospedales, T.: Tucker: tensor factorization for knowledge graph completion. In: Proceedings of the 2019 Conference on Empirical Methods in Natural Language Processing and 9th International Joint Conference on Natural Language Processing, pp. 5184–5193 (2019)
3. Bordes, A., Usunier, N., Garcia-Durán, A., Weston, J., Yakhnenko, O.: Translating embeddings for modeling multi-relational data. In: Proceedings of the 27th International Conference on Neural Information Processing Systems, pp. 2787–2795 (2013)
4. Das, R., et al.: Go for a walk and arrive at the answer: reasoning over paths in knowledge bases using reinforcement learning. In: International Conference on Learning Representations (2018)
5. Dettmers, T., Minervini, P., Stenetorp, P., Riedel, S.: Convolutional 2d knowledge graph embeddings. In: Proceedings of the AAAI Conference on Artificial Intelligence, pp. 1811–1818 (2018)
6. Devlin, J., Chang, M.W., Lee, K., Toutanova, K.: Bert: pre-training of deep bidirectional transformers for language understanding. In: Proceedings of the 2019 Conference of the North American Chapter of the Association for Computational Linguistics: Human Language Technologies, pp. 4171–4186 (2019)
7. Dong, K., Mao, H., Guo, Z., Chawla, N.V.: Universal link predictor by in-context learning on graphs. arXiv preprint arXiv:2402.07738 (2024)
8. Hang, J., et al.: Paths2pair: meta-path based link prediction in billion-scale commercial heterogeneous graphs. In: Proceedings of the 30th ACM SIGKDD Conference on Knowledge Discovery and Data Mining, pp. 5082–5092 (2024)
9. Ji, G., He, S., Xu, L., Liu, K., Zhao, J.: Knowledge graph embedding via dynamic mapping matrix. In: Proceedings of the 53rd Annual Meeting of the Association for Computational Linguistics and the 7th International Joint Conference on Natural Language Processing, pp. 687–696 (2015)
10. Lin, Y., Liu, Z., Sun, M., Liu, Y., Zhu, X.: Learning entity and relation embeddings for knowledge graph completion. In: Proceedings of the AAAI Conference on Artificial Intelligence, pp. 2181–2187 (2015)
11. Liu, Y., et al.: Roberta: a robustly optimized bert pretraining approach. arXiv preprint arXiv:1907.11692 (2019)
12. Louizos, C., Welling, M., Kingma, D.P.: Learning sparse neural networks through l_0 regularization. In: International Conference on Learning Representations (2018)

13. Lu, Y., Chen, H., Rao, Y., Yu, J., Hua, W., Li, Q.: An efficient fuzzy system for complex query answering on knowledge graphs. IEEE Trans. Knowl. Data Eng. **37**(9), 4962–4976 (2025). https://doi.org/10.1109/TKDE.2025.3581959
14. Ma, L., et al.: Mixture of link predictors on graphs. arXiv preprint arXiv:2402.08583 (2024)
15. Meilicke, C., Fink, M., Wang, Y., Ruffinelli, D., Gemulla, R., Stuckenschmidt, H.: Fine-grained evaluation of rule-and embedding-based systems for knowledge graph completion. In: Proceedings of the 17th International Semantic Web Conference, pp. 3–20 (2018)
16. Peng, C., Xia, F., Naseriparsa, M., Osborne, F.: Knowledge graphs: opportunities and challenges. Artif. Intell. Rev. **56**(11), 13071–13102 (2023)
17. Radford, A., Narasimhan, K.: Improving language understanding by generative pre-training (2018). https://api.semanticscholar.org/CorpusID:49313245
18. Schlichtkrull, M., Kipf, T.N., Bloem, P., Van Den Berg, R., Titov, I., Welling, M.: Modeling relational data with graph convolutional networks. In: Proceedings of the 15th International Conference on the Semantic Web, pp. 593–607 (2018)
19. Schlichtkrull, M.S., De Cao, N., Titov, I.: Interpreting graph neural networks for nlp with differentiable edge masking. arXiv preprint arXiv:2010.00577 (2020)
20. Su, Z., Wang, D., Miao, C., Cui, L.: Multi-aspect explainable inductive relation prediction by sentence transformer. In: Proceedings of the AAAI Conference on Artificial Intelligence, pp. 6533–6540 (2023)
21. Su, Z., Wang, D., Miao, C., Cui, L.: Anchoring path for inductive relation prediction in knowledge graphs. In: Proceedings of the AAAI Conference on Artificial Intelligence, pp. 9011–9018 (2024)
22. Sun, Z., Deng, Z.H., Nie, J.Y., Tang, J.: Rotate: knowledge graph embedding by relational rotation in complex space. arXiv preprint arXiv:1902.10197 (2019)
23. Teru, K., Denis, E., Hamilton, W.: Inductive relation prediction by subgraph reasoning. In: International Conference on Machine Learning, pp. 9448–9457 (2020)
24. Trouillon, T., Welbl, J., Riedel, S., Gaussier, É., Bouchard, G.: Complex embeddings for simple link prediction. In: International Conference on Machine Learning, pp. 2071–2080 (2016)
25. Vashishth, S., Sanyal, S., Nitin, V., Talukdar, P.: Composition-based multi-relational graph convolutional networks. arXiv preprint arXiv:1911.03082 (2019)
26. Wang, Z., Zhang, J., Feng, J., Chen, Z.: Knowledge graph embedding by translating on hyperplanes. In: Proceedings of the AAAI Conference on Artificial Intelligence, pp. 1112–1119 (2014)
27. Yang, B., Yih, W.t., He, X., Gao, J., Deng, L.: Embedding entities and relations for learning and inference in knowledge bases. arXiv preprint arXiv:1412.6575 (2014)
28. Yao, L., Mao, C., Luo, Y.: Kg-bert: bert for knowledge graph completion. arXiv preprint arXiv:1909.03193 (2019)
29. Yuan, H., Yu, H., Gui, S., Ji, S.: Explainability in graph neural networks: a taxonomic survey. IEEE Trans. Pattern Anal. Mach. Intell. **45**(5), 5782–5799 (2022)
30. Zha, H., Chen, Z., Yan, X.: Inductive relation prediction by bert. In: Proceedings of the AAAI Conference on Artificial Intelligence, pp. 5923–5931 (2022)
31. Zhang, C., Liu, X.: Inductive link prediction in knowledge graphs using path-based neural networks. In: International Joint Conference on Neural Networks, pp. 1–9 (2024)
32. Zhang, M., Li, P., Xia, Y., Wang, K., Jin, L.: Labeling trick: a theory of using graph neural networks for multi-node representation learning. In: Proceedings of the 35th Conference on Neural Information Processing Systems, pp. 9061–9073 (2021)

33. Zhang, S., et al.: Page-link: path-based graph neural network explanation for heterogeneous link prediction. In: Proceedings of the ACM Web Conference, pp. 3784–3793 (2023)
34. Zhang, Y., et al.: A comprehensive large-scale biomedical knowledge graph for ai-powered data-driven biomedical research. Nat. Mach. Intell. 1–13 (2025)

Revisiting Link Prioritization for Efficient Traversal in Structured Decentralized Environments

Ruben Eschauzier(✉), Ruben Taelman, and Ruben Verborgh

Department of Electronics and Information Systems, Ghent University – imec, Ghent, Belgium
ruben.eschauzier@ugent.be

Abstract. Decentralized environments distribute personal data across numerous small, independent data sources; a necessity driven by legal and socio-economic constraints that prevent the technologically more convenient central aggregation. Link Traversal-based Query Processing (LTQP) is a query technique that respects these constraints by iteratively discovering and accessing data sources while enabling fine-grained access control. Unfortunately, current LTQP implementations are slow due to limited prior knowledge of queried data and the high volume of HTTP requests required. Prioritizing data sources likely to lead to query-relevant data can improve query result arrival times. However, while link prioritization algorithms have been studied for Linked Open Data (LOD), their performance in structured decentralized environments remains untested. Evaluating this performance is essential to establish a baseline as a reference point for improving future implementations. We formally define the R^3 metric to measure prioritization performance, extend it to continuous efficiency, and account for real-world scenarios. Furthermore, we provide modular and open-source implementations of the prioritization algorithms from the literature. Finally, using the R^3 metric with existing metrics from the literature, we benchmark these link prioritization algorithms in a simulated Solid environment. In this paper, we report the benchmark results, provide a thorough analysis, and lessons learned for future work. We find that existing prioritization algorithms fail to improve performance in structured decentralized environments, with no non-oracle method outperforming the look-up order produced by a FIFO queue. We conclude that prioritization algorithms have little benefit in a structured decentralized environment, and recommend that research shift to pruning irrelevant links or improving the query plan.

Keywords: Link Traversal-based Query Processing · Benchmarking · Link Prioritization

D. Garijo et al. (Eds.): ISWC 2025, LNCS 16140, pp. 575–593, 2026.
https://doi.org/10.1007/978-3-032-09527-5_31

1 Introduction

While centralizing data can benefit query engine performance, it is often infeasible due to privacy and access control constraints. Decentralized platforms like Solid [30] and Mastodon [28] promote storing data across many small sources with agreed-upon structures, emphasizing user control over personal data. This shift introduces technical challenges for query engines, which must discover and query numerous small data stores, each with its own access policies.

Centralized querying requires collecting large amounts of personal data, which is restricted by fine-grained access controls. Traditional *federated* approaches [18,31,33] support decentralization but assume a small number (10–100) of known, uniformly accessible sources [7]. Enforcing fine-grained access control policies [10] on such large sources with expressive interfaces significantly impacts performance [25].

In contrast, other decentralized environments involve a large number (thousands) of pre-partitioned permissioned sources that use a wider range of data interfaces consisting of generic HTTP resources [39]. Due to the scale of decentralization, these resources may not all be known at query time. While this does not offer clients the increased flexibility of an expressive query language such as SPARQL, the lower per-resource generation cost makes granular access control less costly. Such interfaces require a federation approach that can query many data sources and interfaces, possibly discovered at runtime, without prior centralization.

Link Traversal-based Query Processing (LTQP) meets these needs by discovering new documents during execution via URIs found in earlier results. Starting from seed documents (user-provided or query-derived), it follows links asynchronously using a FIFO queue. LTQP enables federation at the granularity of the environment, naturally supporting fine-grained access control.

However, the iterative discovery of documents during LTQP makes efficient query processing difficult. Discovering sources on the fly challenges the *optimize-then-execute* query paradigm, as it relies on prior knowledge of the queried data, which is absent in this context. Improving LTQP query optimization and thus performance is critical for enabling more interactive decentralized applications.

Link prioritization algorithms aim to reorder link dereferencing using a priority queue instead of FIFO. By dereferencing links likely to yield query-relevant documents earlier, these algorithms can significantly reduce the time to first result [17] on Linked Open Data, improving perceived performance. This enables interactive applications to display partial results quickly and improve user experience through incremental loading [3,37].

Prioritization algorithms can improve responsiveness in decentralized applications. However, their behavior in structured decentralized environments remains unstudied. Prior work focused on the Linked Open Data (LOD) Cloud, a large, unstructured, and open environment lacking consistent data organization. In contrast, structured decentralized environments enforce predefined schemas, changing the topology of the data web and influencing the performance of the algorithms [17].

In this work, we define structured decentralized environments as decentralized systems where data is organized according to predefined schemas, protocols, or container models, enabling consistent access and reasoning across nodes. For instance, the Solid ecosystem provides structure through the use of Linked Data Platform containers and Type Indexes, allowing clients to make assumptions about data completeness and discoverability. These structural properties are important for effective source selection and query optimization [35]. While our experiments focus on Solid, similar structural properties may arise in other decentralized initiatives that enforce standardized data organization (e.g., ActivityPub [40]).

Evaluating existing prioritization algorithms in structured decentralized environments is essential for identifying their strengths and limitations, providing a baseline for comparison, and ensuring that new methods are built on a clear understanding of what works and what doesn't in these settings. An effective baseline provides a reliable and meaningful standard for comparison. To support robust evaluation, it should also be easily reproducible and built with a modular implementation, enabling ablation studies and facilitating comparisons across different engines and environments. Furthermore, future research on prioritization benefits from modular baseline implementations, facilitating their reuse, extension, and improvement.

Currently, prioritization algorithm implementations in the literature are tied to the SQUIN engine [14], which is no longer maintained and therefore unreliable as a baseline. Moreover, the reported results for these algorithms [17] are influenced by the specific query engine used, its implementation details [11], and other unrelated optimization strategies [13]. As a result, comparing these results to those of new prioritization algorithms implemented in a different engine introduces confounding factors, undermining the validity of the comparison.

To address this, we re-implement existing algorithms as modular packages in Comunica [34], including necessary system changes for (adaptive) prioritization in its iterator-based architecture. These implementations enable fair benchmarking in structured decentralized environments using established metrics and a standard benchmark [35].

To ensure this baseline facilitates performance comparisons across engines and provides deeper insights into the marginal performance of prioritization algorithms, we extend the R^3 metric [9]. The R^3 metric evaluates the marginal performance of prioritization algorithms in an implementation-independent manner, enabling cross-engine comparisons and offering a clearer understanding of prioritization performance without confounding noise.

We build on the previously introduced R^3 metric [9] by formally defining and extending the metric, and then using it in our experiment to measure the marginal performance of prioritization algorithms from the literature. We thereby aim to evolve the metric from a proof-of-concept to a rigorously validated tool for prioritization researchers.

In summary, this paper makes the following contributions:

- **Formal Definition of Link Prioritization Metrics** We mathematically define the R^3 metric introduced in prior work and extend it with alternative versions to account for real-world factors, including weighted dereference events and continuous efficiency.
- **Modular Design and Implementation of Prioritization Algorithms**: We reproduce existing link prioritization algorithms using a modular, iterator-based architecture in a state-of-the-art LTQP engine designed for structured decentralized environments. In addition, we include a new environment-specific prioritization algorithm.
- **Benchmarking and Evaluation of Link Prioritization in Structured Decentralized Environments**: We evaluate the implementation of prioritization algorithms using the decentralized benchmark SolidBench [35], analyzing their performance with existing metrics and newly defined variations of the R^3 metric.

2 Related Work

2.1 Link Traversal-Based Query Processing

The seminal work on Link Traversal-based Query Processing (LTQP) [14,15] introduces a method for dynamically expanding and querying a local RDF dataset by recursively dereferencing URIs found in previously dereferenced data. The approach employs an iterator-based pipelining architecture to produce query results continuously. In this framework, each physical operator is implemented as an iterator that consumes input from its predecessor iterators. Before an iterator can process an intermediate result, all URIs contained in that result must be dereferenced and their corresponding RDF data integrated into the local dataset. To avoid blocking query execution during URI lookups, the iterators are designed to defer the processing of intermediate results for which the required URIs have not been dereferenced and instead continue with the next input. Finally, to prevent the dereferencing of an intractable number of URIs, reachability criteria [16] are used to filter out likely irrelevant URIs. A widely adopted criterion, cMatch, restricts traversal to URIs that match a triple pattern in the query, reducing the number of links followed.

The next iteration of LTQP [17] introduces three operator types: a *data retrieval operator (DR-operator)*, a *dispatcher*, and *triple pattern operators (TP-operators)*, one for each query pattern. The DR-operator dereferences URIs, forwarding matching triples to their corresponding TP-operators. TP-operators, inspired by Eddies [1], maintain an internal index of matching triples and probe it for intermediate join results. Once a result has passed through all TP-operators, it is output as a final result. This design enables flexible, adaptive query processing by dynamically adjusting the execution order of TP-operators.

Recent advancements in LTQP for structured decentralized environments [35] combine the iterator-based pipelining architecture with the DR-operator while using structural cues from the target environment. This approach extracts links from structure-indicating predicates, regardless of standard reachability criteria, and employs TypeIndexes [38] to identify URIs pointing to specific resources, such as comments or posts. This effectively implements structurally informed link prioritization. In the context of Solid, these predicates indicate the Linked Data Platform (LDP) [22] structure used in Solid Pods.

2.2 Metrics for Link Traversal-Based Query Processing

Database benchmarks have traditionally employed a variety of metrics to evaluate query engine performance, measuring aspects such as query execution efficiency and result correctness. This section examines metrics relevant to query execution performance, specifically metrics usable for measuring link prioritization effectiveness. Table 1 summarizes commonly used benchmark metrics across three key attributes:

Continuous indicates whether the metric evaluates the continuous result production performance of an engine, as opposed to the performance of an engine at a single point.

Algorithm-bound indicates whether the metric isolates the performance of a specific algorithm within a system or evaluates the combination of all algorithms in a system.

Implementation-independent indicates whether the metric reflects performance independent of implementation-specific details and optimizations, rather than being influenced by how an algorithm is implemented.

The Query Response Time metric, commonly used in benchmarks like LUBM [12], measures the total time to complete a query from the moment it is issued. The Berlin SPARQL Benchmark (BSBM) [4] extends this by assessing metrics such as the number of query mixes or specific query types executed per second, along with minimum and maximum query execution times [24]. Diefficiency metrics [2], on the other hand, evaluate continuous query engine performance by calculating the area under the result arrival distribution curve within a specified interval, effectively capturing the result arrival rate, where a higher rate indicates faster result production.

For link traversal engines, metrics such as the time to retrieve the *first*, *last*, and *half of all results* have been widely used [35,39]. Since LTQP delivers results incrementally through its iterator-based approach, optimizing result arrival times is crucial for improving usability. To assess the impact of prioritization algorithms in LTQP, researchers compare the *relative result arrival time* of these algorithms against the *total query execution* time [17], as prioritization primarily affects result arrival rates rather than overall execution time. From Table 1, we observe that these metrics capture both point-in-time and continuous system performance, as well as the behavior of individual algorithms. However, they lack implementation-independence, making direct comparisons across different systems challenging.

Table 1. Existing metrics tend to assess point-in-time rather than *continuous performance* (**Cont.**) of an entire engine rather than *isolated algorithms* (**Alg.**) of specific implementations rather than being *implementation-independent* (**Indep.**). None capture the desired combination of all three, which our proposal addresses.

Cont.	Alg.	Indep.	Metric
			Query Response Time [12]
			Queries per Second [4]
			Query Mixes per Hour [4]
			Min/Max Query Execution time [4,24]
			Overall Runtime [4]
			Time until First/Last Result [17,35]
	✓		Relative Time Until First/Last Result [17]
✓			Diefficiency [2]
	✓	✓	R^3 [9]
✓	✓	✓	R^3Cont [proposed]

3 Method

This section provides a formal mathematical definition of the R^3 metric [9], previously only introduced informally. It also extends the metric to a novel weighted version and introduces a new metric, R^3Cont, to measure continuous prioritization efficiency. Lastly, we outline the prioritization algorithms used for benchmarking.

3.1 Preliminaries

SPARQL is a pattern-matching query language designed to query the RDF data model. The RDF data model defines triples that describe statements. These triples are formed from three disjoint sets B (blank nodes), L (Literals), and U (URIs), and are of the form $(s, p, o) \in (B \cup U) \times U \times (B \cup L \cup U)$. A triple uses an object o to make a statement about subject s through predicate p. A finite collection of triples forms a labeled directed graph called an RDF graph [27,32]. The simplest form of SPARQL query is a Basic Graph Pattern (BGP) which is defined as a finite set $P = \{tp_1, \ldots tp_n\}$ of triple patterns $tp_i \in (V \cup L \cup U) \times (U \cup V) \times (V \cup L \cup U)$, where V is a set of variables. To evaluate SPARQL queries over RDF data, the concept of solution mappings plays a central role. A solution mapping is a partial function $\mu : v \rightarrow (U \cup L)$, where v is the set of variables appearing in the BGP of query Q. Solution mappings associate variables with RDF terms, enabling the identification of matches for the query's graph patterns in the RDF graph.

In the context of Link Traversal, query execution involves dereferencing URIs to retrieve the RDF graphs D embedded in these URIs. From the triples in these graphs, new URIs are extracted based on a reachability criterion c. A reachability criterion is a function $c : T \times U \times \mathcal{B} \rightarrow \{true, false\}$, where T denotes the infinite set of all possible data triples and $\mathcal{B}$ the infinite set of possible BGPs and U as defined above. Reachability criteria determine whether a URI should be considered reachable for a given BGP. An example of a reachability criterion is *cAll*, which is true for all triples [16].

3.2 Relevant Traversal Path

During LTQP, the engine must dereference all documents contributing to the query result set to complete the query. However, during the traversal, the engine could dereference query-irrelevant documents that contain no triples required to answer the query. By defining the traversal path taken by the engine to dereference all query-relevant documents, we can formally define a metric that measures the efficiency of the path taken by the engine.

First, we must compute the where-provenance [5], the set of URIs to dereference to obtain all data required to answer the query, of each solution mapping μ_n produced by conjunctive query $\mathcal{Q}_c^{P,S}$, with P a BGP, and S a finite set of seed URIs. The evaluation of query $\mathcal{Q}_c^{P,S}$ depends on the subset of *reachable* data during traversal. This *reachable sub-web* $W_c^{S,P}$ [16] denotes the set of discoverable URIs given a reachability criterion, seed URI, and BGP. The evaluation of $\mathcal{Q}_c^{P,S}$ on $W_c^{S,P}$ produces the solution mapping $\mathcal{Q}_c^{P,S}(W)$.

Given where-provenance annotations D_{μ_n} with $\mu_n \in \mathcal{Q}_c^{P,S}(W)$, we can define the set of URIs required to be dereferenced to produce the result as

$$D_{\mathcal{T}} = \bigcup_{\mu_n \in \mathcal{Q}_c^{P,S}(W)} D_{\mu_n}. \tag{1}$$

During query execution, URIs are sequentially dereferenced and added to the queried data. This produces a traversal order of URIs $(W_c^{S,P}, \preceq)$, a totally ordered set with order

$$\forall d_a, d_b \in W_c^{S,P} : d_a \preceq d_b \Leftrightarrow t(d_a) < t(d_b). \tag{2}$$

With $t(d_a)$ the timestamp when the engine finished dereferencing URI d_a. Assuming deterministic HTTP request times, this ordering is produced by applying a traversal order algorithm during query execution. Using this ordering, we define the totally ordered set

$$R_{\mathcal{T}} = (D_{\mathcal{T}}, \preceq) \tag{3}$$

as the query-relevant documents ordered by their dereference time. We use this to define the minimal set of dereferenced documents required to dereference all query-relevant documents:

$$O_{\mathcal{T}} = \{d_i \in (W_c^{S,P}, \preceq) \mid t(d_i) < max\{t(d) \mid d \in D_{\mathcal{T}}\}\}. \tag{4}$$

This set includes all documents with a dereference timestamp smaller than the maximal timestamp among the query-relevant documents. In simpler terms, it represents the traversal path followed by the engine to retrieve all documents necessary for answering the query.

3.3 Optimal Traversal Path for Induced Sub-Web

To compare the performance of link traversal algorithms with an optimal *oracle algorithm* we will first introduce the notion of a traversed topology during LTQP. During query execution, the engine traverses the sub-web $W_c^{(S,P)}$ of documents belonging to URIs. While the engine will only dereference a URI once, multiple documents can contain references to the same URI. Thus, the engine's traversal path produces a directed (possibly cyclic) unweighted graph $T_{W_c^{(S,P)}}$ with sources S.

In this formulation, we can consider the set $D_{\mathcal{T}}$ to be a set of terminals in $T_{W_c^{(S,P)}}$, then finding the optimal traversal path for the engine is similar to finding the minimum directed Steiner tree.

The Steiner tree problem in directed graphs is defined as follows [6,19]. For a directed graph $G = (V, A)$, with $c(a)$ the cost of arc $a \in A$, root node $r \in V$, and terminals $T \subseteq V$, the objective is to find the minimum cost sub-graph starting at r and spanning all vertexes T.
The cost for such a sub-graph $X = (V', A')$ in a directed graph is given as

$$C(X) = \sum\nolimits_{a \in A'} c(a), \tag{5}$$

where $c(a) = 1$ for all $a \in A$. The topology needs a singular root node to formulate traversed topologies as a Steiner tree for directed graph problem. However, topologies can have multiple root nodes corresponding to the seed documents supplied to the query. So, we can add a new root node $\hat{r}$ to our traversed topology and create arcs $\{(\hat{r}, s) \mid s \in S\}$ with costs 0. So, for our problem, we have to find a directed Steiner tree for directed graph $T_{W_c^{(S,P)}}$, root $\hat{r}$, and terminals $D_{\mathcal{T}}$.

3.4 Relevant Retrieval Ratio R^3

Building on the optimal traversal path X and the realized minimal engine traversal path $O_{\mathcal{T}}$ introduced earlier, we now provide the *first formal definition* of the R^3 metric. Unlike the previous definition [9] that relies on informal intuition, our definition mathematically defines the relative performance of the engine compared to the optimal approach. R^3 is formally defined as:

$$R^3 = \frac{C(X)}{\mid O_{\mathcal{T}} \mid} \tag{6}$$

For this metric, higher is better, as this signifies that the traversal path generated by the engine is closer to optimal. Figure 1 illustrates an example topology, the optimal traversal path, and the selected traversal path. For these paths, the R^3 metric is calculated as $R^3 = \frac{3}{6} = 0.5$, indicating that the cost of the selected path is twice that of the optimal path.

The R^3 metric captures the traversal path followed during query execution over the Linked Data Web. This path is largely determined by the engine's prioritization and traversal strategy, rather than by engine-specific optimizations or query planning algorithms. As a result, even if execution times vary across engines, R^3 still reveals the relative performance of traversal strategies, enabling fair comparison across different engine implementations.

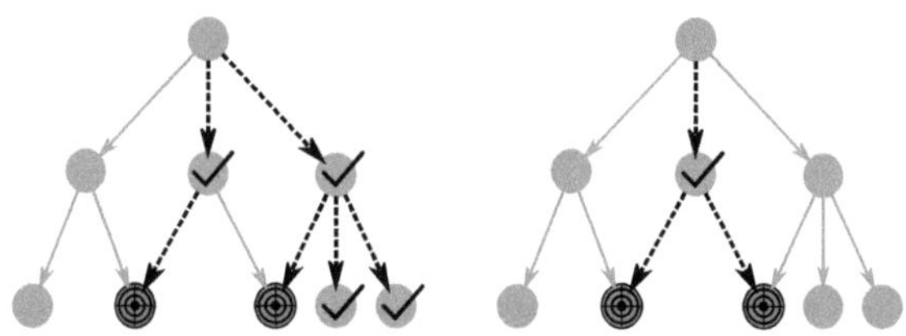

Fig. 1. The traversal on the left follows an inefficient dereference path (checkmarks) to the target documents (green), compared to the optimal path on the right. The R^3 metric captures this inefficiency. (Color figure online)

3.5 Weighted Relevant Retrieval Ratio R^3

The previous formulation of the R^3 metric assumes equal costs for each traversal step. However, this approach overlooks real-world factors that impact query execution, such as HTTP request time, which can be influenced by server congestion or significant physical distance between the client and server.

To account for these differences in the traversed topology graph we propose to weigh edges by factors influencing the real-world notion of optimal traversal, like HTTP request time. The optimal sub-graph found by Steiner tree solvers then reflects the real-world costs of traversal. We define the *weighted* R^3 **metric** as follows:

$$\hat{R}^3 = \frac{C(X)}{C(O_\mathcal{T})} \tag{7}$$

Figure 2 shows how this weighted $\hat{R}^3$ metric can alter the optimal path. In this example, one node experiences a significant delay in responding to an HTTP request. Consequently, the optimal path changes to a route with more hops but a shorter overall HTTP request time. Due to the change in weights, the previously optimal path, which had $R^3 = 1$, now has $\hat{R}^3 = \frac{1+1+3+3}{5+3+3} = 0.73$.

As is often the case, there is no universally optimal method for weighting; the choice depends on the specific optimization target. For instance, minimizing the size of HTTP request responses becomes crucial in environments with limited bandwidth.

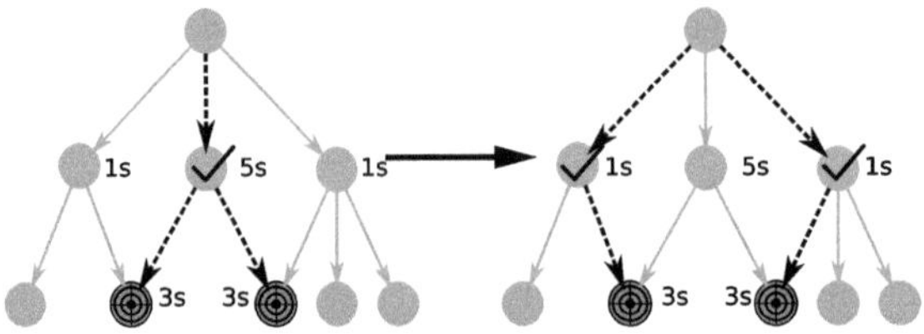

Fig. 2. By considering HTTP request latency, the weighted R^3 metric ensures that the computed traversal path corresponds to the real-world optimum.

3.6 Continuous Efficiency of Link Prioritization Algorithms

In earlier sections, we examined metrics evaluating the overall performance of prioritization algorithms against the optimal approach. However, since LTQP produces results incrementally as they become available, it is important to assess the algorithm's continuous performance during query execution.

To achieve this, we propose adapting the diefficiency metrics [2], which measure the area under the answer distribution function to assess the continuous efficiency of query engines. This function is constructed using an answer trace, defined as a sequence of pairs $A_r = (t_1, \mu_1), \ldots, (t_n, \mu_n)$, where each pair records the timestamp t_i when the i-th answer is produced, for $1 \leq i \leq n$. For non-blocking approaches like LTQP, the answer distribution function represents the number of results produced over time, with linear interpolation applied between arrivals.

We modify the answer trace to evaluate the continuous efficiency of link prioritization algorithms in retrieving documents required for query answers. The new trace, $A_d = (t_1, d_i), \ldots, (t_n, d_n)$, instead records the timestamps when the required documents for a new answer are dereferenced. Based on this trace, we calculate the new R^3Cont at k results metric as

$$R^3Cont@k = \int_0^{t_k} A_d(x)dx, \tag{8}$$

where t_k denotes the time when the documents needed for the first k results are retrieved. Note that this function is analogous to the *Dief@k* metric [2]. Thus, $R^3Cont@k$ measures the continuous efficiency of the traversal phase of the LTQP engine, with lower values being better

3.7 Existing Link Prioritization Algorithms

This paper establishes a baseline for link prioritization algorithms in structured decentralized environments. We implement existing algorithms [17] in Comunica [34] and release them as modular, user-friendly packages. Unlike the TP-operator-based model [17], our implementation uses the more widely adopted iterator-based model [14,20,23,35]. To enable adaptive prioritization, we wrap each iterator produced during query execution with an event-driven statistics emitter, which feeds into the prioritization strategy. Adopting this model facilitates comparisons across query engines and promotes broader applicability.

We briefly explain the implemented algorithms, with detailed descriptions available in the original paper [17].

Non-Adaptive Non-adaptive algorithms use a pre-defined prioritization strategy. These algorithms include *depth-first* and *breadth-first* prioritization. Additionally, *random* prioritization assigns a random priority between 0 and 10 to each new link. Finally, we include an implementation of a theoretical *oracle* algorithm that uses the result contribution counter of each document. This counter is propagated across all nodes along the shortest path from the root to the query-relevant document.

Graph-based For graph-based prioritization, the engine iteratively builds a directed traversed topology graph $G = (V, E)$, representing the queried sub-web. Links are prioritized by applying vertex scoring algorithms to this topology. We examine two such algorithms: the first sets the priority of links equal to their *in-degree*, the second uses the vertex's *PageRank* score [26].

Result-based Result-based prioritization uses the traversed topology of graph-based prioritization methods. The engine tracks the why-provenance of results and increments the result contribution counter (RCC) of the associated documents whenever a new result is produced. Based on these RCC values, [17] introduces vertex scoring functions using the first- and second-degree in-neighborhoods of documents, defined as:

$$\text{in}^1(v) = \{v' \in V \mid \langle v', v\rangle \in E\}, \tag{9}$$

$$\text{in}^2(v) = \text{in}^1(v) \cup (\bigcup\nolimits_{v' \in \text{in}^1(v)} \text{in}^1(v')). \tag{10}$$

For a vertex v with an RCC score of $rcc(v)$, four vertex scoring functions are defined for $k \in 1, 2$:

$$\text{rcc-k}(v) = \sum\nolimits_{v' \in \text{in}^k(v)} \text{rcc}(v'), \tag{11}$$

$$\text{rel-k}(v) = \mid \{v' \in \text{in}^k(v) \mid rcc(v') > 0\} \mid . \tag{12}$$

The prioritization approaches based on these scoring functions are referred to as *rcc1*, *rcc2*, *rel1*, and *rel2*, respectively.

Intermediate result-based Whereas the previous approach relies on full solutions, intermediate solutions can also guide prioritization decisions. The methods *IS* and *ISdcr* first determine the number of triple patterns satisfied by an intermediate result, storing this count as *cnt*. They then iterate over each binding in the intermediate result. If a bound value corresponds to an IRI in the look-up queue with a priority lower than *cnt*, its priority is updated to *cnt*. For *IS*, initial priorities are set to 0, whereas for *ISdcr*, they are initialized to one less than the final priority of the parent document.

Hybrid Approaches Hybrid prioritization approaches combine RCC-based and intermediate solution-based methods. For each vertex in the traversed topology, these methods track both the RCC and the *IS*-score. The priority for a vertex is then calculated by multiplying its *IS*-score with the RCC-based score, depending on the specific RCC scoring method used. The resulting approaches are named *is-rcc1*, *is-rcc2*, *is-rel1*, and *is-rel2*.

TypeIndex-based Finally, we introduce a simple approach to prioritize links in a *TypeIndex* [38], which points to files containing resources of a specific type. Listing 1.1 shows an example of a TypeIndex pointing to the location of Comments. This algorithm is an example of prioritization based on environment-specific attributes of a structured decentralized environment.

Listing 1.1. Example TypeIndex Content

```
<#bq1r5e> a solid:TypeRegistration;
  solid:forClass <http://example.org/Comment>;
  solid:instanceContainer </public/comments/>.
```

4 Evaluation

This section outlines the experiments used to evaluate link prioritization. We measure time to first and last result, excluding total execution time, since prioritization doesn't affect overall workload. Metrics include $R^3\mathit{Cont}@k$ and $\mathit{Dief}@k$ (with k as total results), as well as both unweighted and HTTP time-weighted R^3 scores. In addition, we compare result counts relative to breadth-first prioritization to account for timeouts, which can cause fewer results to be produced. The goals are to assess the effectiveness of link prioritization in structured decentralized settings, provide a baseline of prioritization performance, and isolate algorithmic performance from implementation overhead. Experiments are run on a dual Hexacore Intel E5645 (2.4 GHz) with 8 GB allocated to Node.js.

4.1 Benchmark

We use the SolidBench benchmark [35], the state-of-the-art benchmark for structured decentralized environments, to evaluate the prioritization algorithms. SolidBench simulates a social network application, including users, posts, comments, forum posts, and more. The benchmark uses a single ontology to describe the relations. Furthermore, data is fragmented to represent Solid pods, where all data related to a specific user is stored in a single pod. Using the default settings, the benchmark generates 158,233 RDF files distributed across 1,531 data vaults, containing a total of 3,556,159 triples.

The benchmark provides three query template types: *discover*, *short*, and *complex*. In this paper, we focus on the *discover* queries, as all complex queries exceed the timeout threshold, and short queries either do not traverse to new pods or time out. Discover queries primarily test various query engine bottlenecks [35], such as n hop link-traversal, irrelevant HTTP request filtering, and heterogeneous within-pod data fragmentation strategies. The timeout is set to 180 s, and each query is executed 15 times in our experiment to ensure the reliability and repeatability of the results.

4.2 Results

We report the relative arrival times of the first and last results (*1st* and *Cmpl*) and the R^3 metric. Additionally, we show the number of results produced relative to the breadth-first baseline. Figure 3 presents *1st*, *Cmpl*, and R^3 for 17 algorithms across four representative query templates; the full results are provided in the supplementary material. Overall, no algorithm consistently outperforms the baseline on *1st* or *Cmpl*. Apparent gains for templates interactive-discover 7 and 8 are due to timeouts leading to fewer results, skewing the metrics. The only exception is the oracle, which shows slight improvements in result arrival times.

Table 2 reports the percentage of queries performing 10% better or worse than breadth-first traversal. Overall, *1st* and *Cmpl* are generally worse for the prioritization algorithms compared to the baseline. As seen from the figure, the oracle is the only algorithm to improve on the baseline.

Table 2. Percentage of queries for which a prioritization algorithm performs at least 10% better or worse than the breadth-first baseline. Most algorithms do not consistently improve point-in-time or continuous result arrival times. This limitation is underscored by the R^3 metrics, which show the limited effectiveness of prioritization algorithms even when decision-making overhead is excluded.

	1st		*Cmpl*		R^3		$\hat{R}^3$ *Http*		*Dief*		R^3 *Cont*	
	better	worse	better	worse	better	worse	better	worse	better	worse	better	worse
depth-first	15.7	17.1	14.3	17.1	7.5	12.5	7.5	25.0	25.0	27.5	25.0	30.0
random	4.3	68.6	5.7	74.3	15.0	15.0	25.0	17.5	32.5	35.0	27.5	25.0
in-degree	15.7	27.1	11.4	24.3	5.0	12.5	15.0	20.0	30.0	22.5	27.5	20.0
pagerank	12.9	27.1	11.4	24.3	7.5	7.5	10.0	20.0	32.5	25.0	25.0	17.5
rcc-1	10.0	41.4	10.0	40.0	12.5	10.0	12.5	20.0	25.0	22.5	22.5	35.0
rcc-2	7.1	45.7	7.1	50.0	10.0	15.0	15.0	17.5	30.0	25.0	17.5	42.5
rel-1	10.0	44.3	12.9	44.3	7.5	7.5	12.5	10.0	30.0	27.5	20.0	40.0
rel-2	7.1	45.7	8.6	47.1	10.0	15.0	15.0	22.5	27.5	32.5	25.0	37.5
is	11.4	35.7	12.9	31.4	10.0	**2.5**	20.0	**7.5**	17.5	35.0	32.5	35.0
isdcr	2.9	32.9	5.7	28.6	12.5	15.0	12.5	22.5	25.0	32.5	17.5	62.5
is-rcc-1	4.3	57.1	5.7	60.0	7.5	5.0	10.0	17.5	25.0	27.5	15.0	50.0
is-rcc-2	5.7	62.9	8.6	68.6	12.5	5.0	20.0	17.5	25.0	27.5	12.5	52.5
is-rel-1	7.1	64.3	5.7	61.4	12.5	12.5	17.5	25.0	32.5	**15.0**	20.0	40.0
is-rel-2	5.7	61.4	7.1	64.3	12.5	5.0	17.5	17.5	**37.5**	27.5	17.5	50.0
type-index	15.7	18.6	10.0	15.7	12.5	20.0	15.0	25.0	27.5	30.0	35.0	35.0
oracle	**18.6**	**11.4**	**18.6**	**12.9**	**25.0**	**2.5**	**32.5**	12.5	30.0	30.0	**72.5**	**10.0**

We use the R^3 metric to analyze why prioritization algorithms fail to improve performance. As shown in Fig. 3 and Table 2, most approaches do not signifi-

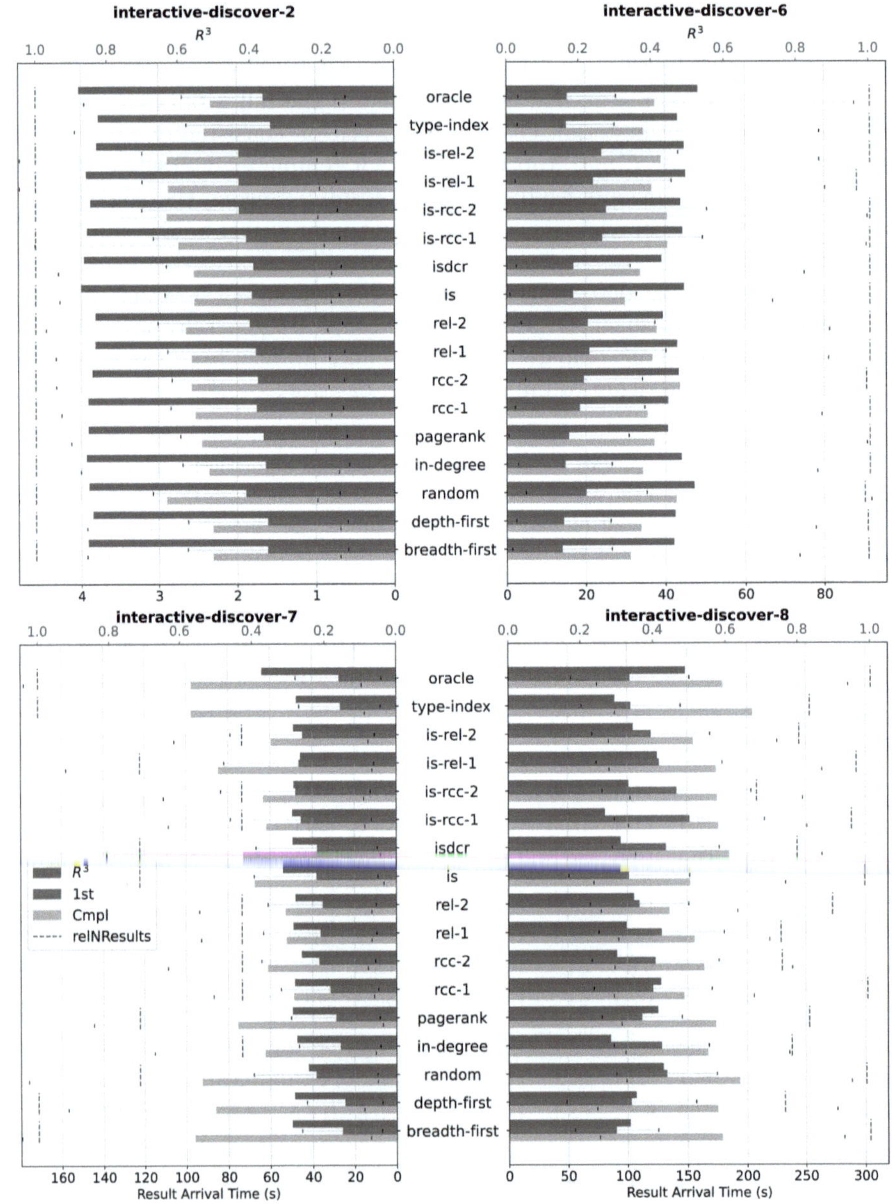

Fig. 3. Result arrival times (first/last), their standard deviations, R^3 scores (higher is better), and result counts relative to breadth-first prioritization. Link prioritization yields no meaningful improvement, often performing 0–20% worse, with similar R^3 values across methods.

cantly change the engine's traversal efficiency; fewer than 25% of queries show notable differences in unweighted R^3. While the HTTP-weighted $\hat{R}^3$ shows greater variation, this is largely due to noise from our simulated network environment. When traversal paths remain unchanged, prioritization adds overhead without benefit, leading to reduced performance. The oracle improves traversal in 25% of queries and continuous retrieval in 72.5%, but this rarely translates to faster result arrival in practice. This points towards the bottleneck of result production lying elsewhere for LTQP. Overall, even a theoretically optimal prioritization has a limited effect in structured decentralized settings like Solid.

Further investigation identifies three key factors influencing these findings:

Query Scope and Structure Many queries, such as discover 1 to 6, target data related to a single individual (and thus a single pod). In such cases, TypeIndexes [35], which act as an index for a pod by directly linking to potentially relevant data, efficiently direct the engine to the correct file containing relevant data, minimizing traversal complexity. These TypeIndexes are found in the seed document in the query, so their links are naturally added early to the queue. As a consequence, TypeIndex prioritization has little effect. We expect similar behavior for any other indexes present in a Solid pod, like a shape index [36]. While queries exist that target multiple pods, these often time out and are thus difficult to analyze.

Solid Environment Design Link prioritization largely focuses on identifying the appropriate LDP container for a query within the Solid environment. Since related data is typically grouped within a single LDP container, the presence of a correctly configured TypeIndex reduces the need for traversing the entire pod to find the relevant data LDP container, simplifying the prioritization problem even when multiple pods are involved in the query.

Link Queue Dynamics During discover queries [8], the link queue is often emptied quickly. Even when an algorithm assigns the correct priority to a link, its impact is negligible if no alternative links are available in the queue for concurrent dereferencing.

Query Plan Bottleneck Previous research [35] shows that link traversal join plans are suboptimal. In cases where the query execution time is dominated by result processing, link prioritization will have a negligible impact on result arrival times.

These findings suggest that link prioritization has a limited impact on link traversal performance in structured, decentralized environments. Even when prioritization is nearly optimal, it yields only modest performance gains. Therefore, efforts to optimize the traversal phase of LTQP should instead focus on strategies such as pruning irrelevant data sources [36]. To rigorously evaluate these strategies, a broader set of feasibly executable queries that traverse multiple pods is required. The short and complex queries of SolidBench do not satisfy these requirements, as their complexity makes them unfeasible to execute. Such benchmarks would help researchers improve their algorithms step by step, without treating performance as simply a matter of timing out or completing the query.

5 Conclusion

In this paper, we provided modular implementations of link traversal prioritization algorithms from the literature, enabling researchers to extend these approaches with minimal effort. Additionally, we benchmarked these algorithms in a previously unexplored context: structured decentralized environments. To further solidify this benchmark as a baseline for future research, we formally introduced, extended, and tested the R^3 metric.

Our findings show that prioritization algorithms do not significantly improve result arrival times compared to the baseline in structured decentralized environments. The only measured improvement came from a theoretical oracle algorithm, but even those gains were small. Therefore, future optimization efforts in LTQP should focus on strategies that either improve the query plan or prune irrelevant data sources. To evaluate these approaches more effectively, a broader set of executable queries spanning multiple pods is needed to better benchmark system performance when traversing many links.

Acknowledgements. This research was supported by SolidLab Vlaanderen (Flemish Government, EWI and RRF project VV023/10). Ruben Taelman is a postdoctoral researcher at the Research Foundation – Flanders (FWO).

Supplemental Material Statement. The main repository with links to all code needed to replicate the results is available on GitHub: https://github.com/RubenEschauzier/r3-metric-data-processor. The raw experimental data and full version of the paper's figure can be found on Zenodo: https://zenodo.org/records/15372999. The query templates used to benchmark the algorithms are found on GitHub: https://github.com/SolidBench/SolidBench.js/tree/master/templates/queries.

References

1. Acosta, M., Vidal, M.-E.: Networks of linked data eddies: an adaptive web query processing engine for RDF data. In: Arenas, M., et al. (eds.) ISWC 2015. LNCS, vol. 9366, pp. 111–127. Springer, Cham (2015). https://doi.org/10.1007/978-3-319-25007-6_7
2. Acosta, M., Vidal, M.-E., Sure-Vetter, Y.: Diefficiency metrics: measuring the continuous efficiency of query processing approaches. In: d'Amato, C., et al. (eds.) ISWC 2017. LNCS, vol. 10588, pp. 3–19. Springer, Cham (2017). https://doi.org/10.1007/978-3-319-68204-4_1
3. Aniebo, O.C.: Quantitative Assessment of the Relationship between e/m-Commerce Site Access Speed and Consumer Adoption-Retention Rate. PhD thesis, Northcentral University (2020)
4. Bizer, C., Schultz, A.: The berlin sparql benchmark. Int. J. Semant. Web Inf. Syst. (IJSWIS) **5**(2), 1–24 (2009)
5. Buneman, P., Khanna, S., Wang-Chiew, T.: Why and where: a characterization of data provenance. In: Van den Bussche, J., Vianu, V. (eds.) ICDT 2001. LNCS, vol. 1973, pp. 316–330. Springer, Heidelberg (2001). https://doi.org/10.1007/3-540-44503-X_20

6. Charikar, M., Chekuri, C., Cheung, T.-Y., Dai, Z., Goel, A., Guha, S., Li, M.: Approximation algorithms for directed steiner problems. J. Algor. **33**(1), 73–91 (1999)
7. Dang, M.H., Aimonier-Davat, J., Molli, P., Hartig, O., Skaf-Molli, H., Crom, Y.L.: Fedshop: a benchmark for testing the scalability of sparql federation engines. In: International Semantic Web Conference, pp. 285–301. Springer, Heidelberg (2023)
8. Eschauzier, R., Taelman, R., Verborgh, R.: How does the link queue evolve during traversal-based query processing? In: QuWeDa/MEPDaW@ ISWC, pp. 26–33 (2023)
9. Eschauzier R., Taelman, R., Verborgh, R.: The r3 metric: measuring performance of link prioritization during traversal-based query processing. In: Proceedings of the 16th Alberto Mendelzon International Workshop on Foundations of Data Management (2024)
10. Esteves, B., Pandit, H.J., Rodríguez-Doncel, V.: Odrl profile for expressing consent through granular access control policies in solid. In: 2021 IEEE European Symposium on Security and Privacy Workshops (EuroS&PW), pp. 298–306. IEEE (2021)
11. Fourment, M., Gillings, M.R.: A comparison of common programming languages used in bioinformatics. BMC Bioinf. **9**, 1–9 (2008)
12. Guo, Y., Pan, Z., Heflin, J.: Lubm: a benchmark for owl knowledge base systems. J. Web Semant. **3**(2–3), 158–182 (2005)
13. Hartig, O.: Zero-knowledge query planning for an iterator implementation of link traversal based query execution. In: Antoniou, G., et al. (eds.) ESWC 2011. LNCS, vol. 6643, pp. 154–169. Springer, Heidelberg (2011). https://doi.org/10.1007/978-3-642-21034-1_11
14. Hartig, O.: Squin: a traversal based query execution system for the web of linked data. In: Proceedings of the 2013 ACM SIGMOD International Conference on Management of Data, pp. 1081–1084 (2013)
15. Hartig, O., Bizer, C., Freytag, J.-C.: Executing SPARQL queries over the web of linked data. In: Bernstein, A., et al. (eds.) ISWC 2009. LNCS, vol. 5823, pp. 293–309. Springer, Heidelberg (2009). https://doi.org/10.1007/978-3-642-04930-9_19
16. Hartig, O., Freytag, J.C.: Foundations of traversal based query execution over linked data. In: Proceedings of the 23rd ACM Conference on Hypertext and Social Media, pp. 43–52 (2012)
17. Hartig, O., Özsu, M.T.: Walking without a map: ranking-based traversal for querying linked data. In: Groth, P., et al. (eds.) ISWC 2016. LNCS, vol. 9981, pp. 305–324. Springer, Cham (2016). https://doi.org/10.1007/978-3-319-46523-4_19
18. Heling, L., Acosta, M.: Federated sparql query processing over heterogeneous linked data fragments. In: Proceedings of the ACM Web Conference, vol. 2022, pp. 1047–1057 (2022)
19. Karp, R.M.: Reducibility among combinatorial problems. In: Jünger, M., Liebling, T.M., Naddef, D., Nemhauser, G.L., Pulleyblank, W.R., Reinelt, G., Rinaldi, G., Wolsey, L.A. (eds.) 50 Years of Integer Programming 1958-2008, pp. 219–241. Springer, Heidelberg (2010). https://doi.org/10.1007/978-3-540-68279-0_8
20. Ladwig, G., Tran, T.: SIHJoin: querying remote and local linked data. In: Antoniou, G., et al. (eds.) ESWC 2011. LNCS, vol. 6643, pp. 139–153. Springer, Heidelberg (2011). https://doi.org/10.1007/978-3-642-21034-1_10
21. Le, W., Kementsietsidis, A., Duan, S., Li, F.: Scalable multi-query optimization for sparql. In: 2012 IEEE 28th International Conference on Data Engineering, pp. 666–677. IEEE (2012)

22. Le Hors, A.J., Speicher, S.: The linked data platform (ldp). In: Proceedings of the 22nd International Conference on World Wide Web, pp. 1–2 (2013)
23. Miranker, D.P., Depena, R.K., Jung, H., Sequeda, J.F., Reyna, C.: Diamond: a sparql query engine, for linked data based on the rete match. In: AImWD 2012, p. 7 (2012)
24. Montoya, G., Vidal, M.-E., Corcho, O., Ruckhaus, E., Buil-Aranda, C.: Benchmarking federated SPARQL query engines: are existing testbeds enough? In: Cudré-Mauroux, P., et al. (eds.) ISWC 2012. LNCS, vol. 7650, pp. 313–324. Springer, Heidelberg (2012). https://doi.org/10.1007/978-3-642-35173-0_21
25. Padia, A., Finin, T., Joshi, A., et al.: Attribute-based fine grained access control for triple stores. In: 3rd Society, Privacy and the Semantic Web-Policy and Technology workshop, 14th International Semantic Web Conference (2015)
26. Page, L.: The pagerank citation ranking: Bringing order to the web. Technical report (1999)
27. Pérez, J., Arenas, M., Gutierrez, C.: Semantics and complexity of sparql. ACM Trans. Datab. Syst. (TODS) **34**(3), 1–45 (2009)
28. Raman, A., Joglekar, S., De Cristofaro, E., Sastry, N., Tyson, G.: Challenges in the decentralised web: the mastodon case. In: Proceedings of the Internet Measurement Conference, pp. 217–229 (2019)
29. Saleem, M., Khan, Y., Hasnain, A., Ermilov, I., Ngomo, A.C.N.: A fine-grained evaluation of sparql endpoint federation systems. Semant. Web **7**(5), 493–518 (2016)
30. Sambra, A.V., et al.: Solid: a platform for decentralized social applications based on linked data. MIT CSAIL & Qatar Computing Research Institute, Technical Report (2016)
31. Schmidt, M., Görlitz, O., Haase, P., Ladwig, G., Schwarte, A., Tran, T.: FedBench: a benchmark suite for federated semantic data query processing. In: Aroyo, L., et al. (eds.) ISWC 2011. LNCS, vol. 7031, pp. 585–600. Springer, Heidelberg (2011). https://doi.org/10.1007/978-3-642-25073-6_37
32. Schmidt, M., Meier, M., Lausen, G.: Foundations of sparql query optimization. In: Proceedings of the 13th International Conference on Database Theory, pp. 4–33 (2010)
33. Schwarte, A., Haase, P., Hose, K., Schenkel, R., Schmidt, M.: FedX: optimization techniques for federated query processing on linked data. In: Aroyo, L., et al. (eds.) ISWC 2011. LNCS, vol. 7031, pp. 601–616. Springer, Heidelberg (2011). https://doi.org/10.1007/978-3-642-25073-6_38
34. Taelman, R., Van Herwegen, J., Vander Sande, M., Verborgh, R.: Comunica: a modular SPARQL query engine for the web. In: Vrandečić, D., et al. (eds.) ISWC 2018. LNCS, vol. 11137, pp. 239–255. Springer, Cham (2018). https://doi.org/10.1007/978-3-030-00668-6_15
35. Taelman, R., Verborgh, R.: Link traversal query processing over decentralized environments with structural assumptions. In: International Semantic Web Conference, pp. 3–22. Springer, Heidelberg (2023). https://doi.org/10.1007/978-3-031-47240-4_1
36. Tam, B.E., Taelman, R., Colpaert, P., Verborgh, R.: Opportunities for shape-based optimization of link traversal queries. arXiv preprint arXiv:2407.00998 (2024)
37. Tarafdar, M., Zhang, J.: Determinants of reach and loyalty—a study of website performance and implications for website design. J. Comput. Inf. Syst. **48**(2), 16–24 (2008)

38. Turdean, T: Type indexes. Solid (2022). https://solid.github.io/type-indexes/
39. Verborgh, R., et al.: Triple pattern fragments: a low-cost knowledge graph interface for the web. J. Web Semant. **37**, 184–206 (2016)
40. W3C. Activitypub: A decentralized social networking protocol. https://www.w3.org/TR/activitypub/. W3C Recommendation (2018)

AdaGCRAG: Adaptive Graph-Chunk Retrieval for Lightweight RAG

Yanqiu Zhang[1,2], Zhen Xu[1,2(✉)], DongDong Huo[1,2], Xiaokun Guo[1,2], Qihui Zhou[1], and Yan Zhang[1,2]

[1] Institute of Information Engineering, Chinese Academy of Sciences, Beijing, China
{zhangyanqiu,xuzhen,huodongdong,guoxiaokun,zhouqihui,zhangyan}@iie.ac.cn
[2] School of Cyber Security, University of Chinese Academy of Sciences, Beijing, China

Abstract. Retrieval-Augmented Generation (RAG) mitigates hallucinations of Large Language Models (LLMs) and improves factual accuracy by incorporating external knowledge during inference. However, existing RAG approaches face critical limitations in resource-constrained environments: (1) dense retrieval often introduces irrelevant or redundant content due to semantic overlap in vector space, and (2) graph-based methods still depend on sophisticated reasoning capabilities that exceed the capacity of Small Language Models (SLMs). To address these challenges, we propose **Ada**ptive **G**raph-**C**hunk RAG (**AdaGCRAG**), a lightweight, local, and query-adaptive RAG framework that integrates chunk-level retrieval with graph-structured reasoning. AdaGCRAG categorizes each input into *Simple Specific Question (Simple SQ)*, *Complex Specific Question (Complex SQ)*, or *Abstract Question (Abstract Q)* and adaptively controls the retrieval granularity and reasoning depth. It leverages Qwen3's dual-mode reasoning to minimize computation for simple tasks while enabling graph-based multi-hop inference for complex ones. A triple-level reranking module filters noisy subgraphs before fusion with dense retrieval results. AdaGCRAG runs efficiently on a single RTX 3070 GPU, making it suitable for personal agents and offline assistants. Experiments across five Question Answering (QA) benchmarks show consistent improvements over state-of-the-art lightweight RAG systems, achieving improvements of 9.5%, 6.9%, and 6.8% on HotpotQA, MultihopRAG, and MuSiQue, respectively, demonstrating its effectiveness under limited-resource settings. Our implementation is available at https://anonymous.4open.science/r/AdaGCRAG.

Keywords: Retrieval-Augmented Generation · Knowledge Graph · Large Language Model

1 Introduction

Large Language Models (LLMs) like GPT-4 [1], Llama 3.1 [7] and Qwen3 [23] have shown remarkable capabilities across a wide range of natural language processing tasks. However, their reliance on parametric memory inevitably leads to

D. Garijo et al. (Eds.): ISWC 2025, LNCS 16140, pp. 594–610, 2026.
https://doi.org/10.1007/978-3-032-09527-5_32

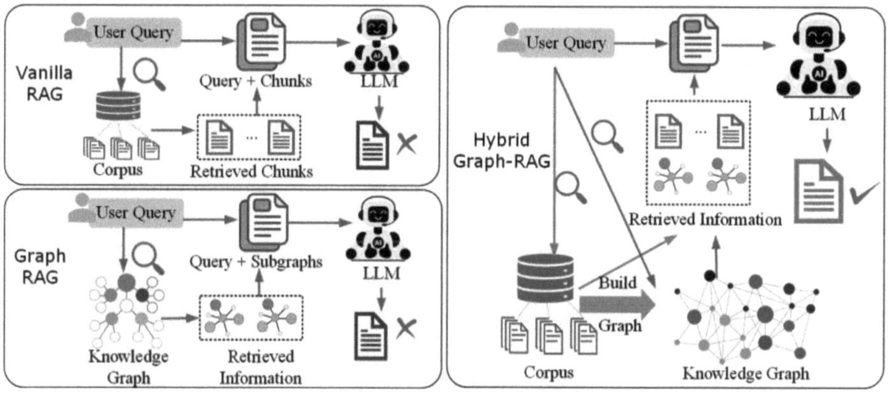

Fig. 1. The general workflow of various RAGs.

factual inaccuracies and hallucinations when dealing with knowledge-intensive questions [12]. Retrieval-Augmented Generation (RAG) has emerged as a powerful framework that enables LLMs to retrieve relevant external knowledge during inference, thereby enhancing answer faithfulness and up-to-date accuracy [4], as shown in Fig. 1. While conventional RAGs, which rely solely on dense vector similarity for document retrieval, like Vanilla RAG, often introduce irrelevant or redundant content and lack interpretability. As an improved solution, Graph-based RAGs, like LightRAG [9] and GraphRAG [5] incorporate structured Knowledge Graph (KG), representing information as graphs to capture relationships between entities. However, Graph-RAG architectures typically rely on LLMs with strong comprehension and reasoning abilities for effective query understanding, semantic alignment, and multi-hop inference, making them difficult to adapt to Small Language Models (SLMs) that lack such capabilities. This mismatch leads to sharp performance drops or complete system failure in lightweight settings [10,29].

Towards this issue, MiniRAG [6] is a lightweight RAG designed for SLMs, utilizing semantic-aware heterogeneous graph indexing and topology-enhanced retrieval. However, its performance depends on accurate entity and relation extraction to construct the KG. Given that SLMs have limited capabilities in this area, MiniRAG's real-world effectiveness may be compromised. In fact, not all queries require complex retrieval. Simple questions [27] can be answered with just a few documents, and using graph-based retrieval in such cases adds unnecessary noise and resource consumption. Therefore, hybrid approaches that selectively use chunk-based or graph-based retrieval based on query complexity can be considered an effective way to improve retrieval efficiency in SLM scenarios. However, existing hybrid methods, like HybridRAG [19], have successfully integrated knowledge from multiple sources, they still lack the capability to selectively retrieve or execute reasoning processes based on the type of query. While some systems use intent analysis models [8] to assess the query before executing RAG, this introduces additional model storage and computational overhead.

In short, existing RAGs suffer from: 1) Irrelevant or redundant information from retrieval; 2) Poor performance of graph-based RAG with SLMs; 3) Existing SLM-based RAG still heavily rely on high-quality KGs; 4) Hybrid methods lacking selective retrieval or reasoning based on query complexity, causing inefficiency. To address these limitations, we propose AdaGCRAG, a local, lightweight, and query-adaptive hybrid RAG framework that unifies dense chunk retrieval with graph-structured reasoning.

Unlike prior systems that treat all queries uniformly, AdaGCRAG categorizes each question into *Simple SQ*, *Complex SQ*, or *Abstract Q* using few-shot prompting. This classification guides both retrieval and reasoning. We adopt Qwen3 [23] models for their controllable reasoning modes: *non-thinking* for efficiency and *thinking* for complex tasks. For *Simple SQ*, AdaGCRAG performs chunk-level retrieval with reasoning disabled. *Complex SQ* adds graph-level evidence without reasoning. *Abstract Q* triggers both multi-hop graph expansion and Qwen3's *thinking* mode. To reduce subgraph noise, triple-level reranking selects the most relevant triples before merging with chunks for final generation.

Our AdaGCRAG is optimized for local deployment and runs efficiently on consumer-grade hardware such as a single RTX 3070 GPU, making it highly suitable for personal agents and offline knowledge assistants. In addition to its modular and lightweight design, AdaGCRAG outperforms MiniRAG [6], a leading SLM-oriented RAG system, on all evaluated QA benchmarks. Specifically, it achieves a 6.9% accuracy gain on MultihopRAG [22], 9.5% on HotpotQA [27], and 6.8% on MuSiQue [24], demonstrating consistent improvements in both simple and complex reasoning tasks. These results highlight AdaGCRAG's robustness and practical value in resource-constrained settings.

In summary, our main contributions are as follows:

- We introduce AdaGCRAG, a lightweight RAG framework that seamlessly combines chunk-based and graph-based retrieval, supporting efficient and accurate question answering in on-device or resource-limited settings.
- We propose a query-aware hybrid retrieval mechanism that adaptively modulates retrieval granularity and reasoning depth based on query complexity, balancing relevance with computational cost.
- We present a SLM-based RAG inference architecture that utilizes Qwen3's dual-mode reasoning capabilities to intelligently balance the trade-off between speed and accuracy.
- We demonstrate superior performance across five diverse QA benchmarks under limited-resource conditions, showcasing AdaGCRAG's robust generalization across various reasoning tasks and query complexities.

2 Related Work

LLM Prompting and RAG. Prompt engineering has become a key method to leverage the inherent abilities of LLMs without extensive fine-tuning [2,16]. Prompt-based approaches allow LLMs to perform various tasks such as QA, summarization, and translation by simply conditioning the model with natural language prompts. However, LLMs' parametric memory is inevitably limited by outdated or incomplete knowledge, leading to hallucinated or unfaithful outputs [20]. To mitigate this, RAG integrates non-parametric memory through retrieval from external corpora [11,13]. The standard RAG pipeline consists of two stages: (1) *retrieval*, where top-k relevant chunks are retrieved based on embedding similarity; and (2) *generation*, where the LLM generates answers conditioned on both the query and retrieved content. While effective in improving factual accuracy, these methods often suffer from shallow semantic matching [4].

Graph-Based RAG. To enhance entity-level precision and reasoning capabilities, recent research has integrated structured KGs into the RAG framework. ToG [21] treats the LLM as an agent that iteratively explores the KG via beam search to uncover reasoning paths. RoG [15] first generates relation paths grounded in the KG as faithful plans, which are then used to retrieve valid reasoning paths. SubgraphRAG [14] employs a lightweight multilayer perceptron with a parallel triple-scoring mechanism to retrieve subgraphs, encoding directional structural distances to enhance retrieval. AMAR [26] introduces a self-alignment module to align commonalities among entities, relations, and subgraphs, and a relevance gating module to determine the relevance of retrieved information. GNN-RAG [17] combines the reasoning abilities of Graph Neural Networks (GNNs) with the language understanding capabilities of LLMs. Despite improved factual consistency, these methods often depend on predefined schemas and high-quality KGs, limiting their adaptability in evolving environments. Additionally, many assume access to cloud-based LLMs, which poses challenges for privacy-preserving or local deployment.

Graph-Based RAG with Hybrid Retrieval. Graph-based RAG methods construct KGs from unstructured corpora to capture entity-centric relations and support multi-hop reasoning [28,29]. These approaches generally follow a three-stage pipeline: (1) *KG Construction*, where an LLM extracts nodes and edges from corpus D to build graph G; (2) *retrieval*, where relevant nodes/subgraphs are retrieved for query Q; and (3) *generation*, where an LLM generates the answer based on Q and the retrieved context. GraphRAG [5] pioneered entity-centric KGs using community detection to enable multi-hop reasoning and global semantic retrieval. LightRAG [9] optimized efficiency through dual-level indexing and incremental graph updates, reducing computational costs by 40%. While effective, these methods typically require significant resources for graph construction, multi-hop retrieval, and large-scale LLM inference [29]. MiniRAG [6] targeted resource-constrained environments with heterogeneous graph indexing and topology-aware retrieval, achieving 75% storage reduction while maintaining accuracy. However, its graph construction and entity retrieval are imprecise, lacking adaptive strategies for different queries, which can affect the reliability.

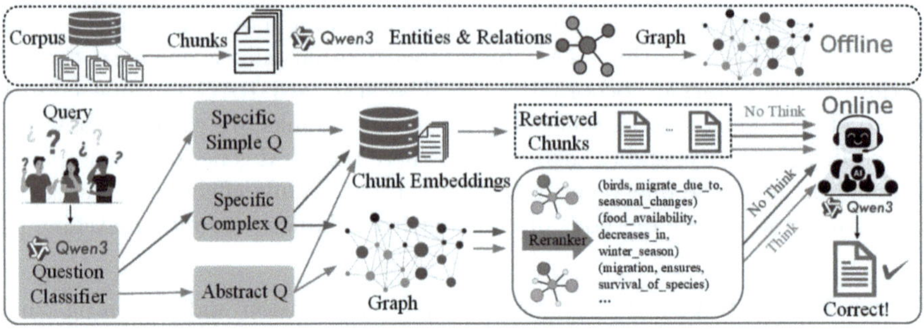

Fig. 2. AdaGCRAG consists of two phases: offline and online.

3 Preliminary

KGs store structured factual knowledge as triples $\mathcal{G} = \{(u, r, v) \mid u, v \in \mathcal{E},\ r \in \mathcal{R}\}$, where $\mathcal{E}$ and $\mathcal{R}$ denote the sets of entities and relations, respectively.

Reasoning Subgraphs are task-relevant subgraphs extracted from a KG to support multi-hop reasoning. A reasoning subgraph is a connected set of triples $\mathcal{S}_q \subset \mathcal{G}$ constructed by traversing relation paths relevant to a given query q.

Example 1. A reasoning subgraph for the query *"Where does Alice's step-son work?"* would be $\mathcal{S}_q = \{(\text{Alice}, \textit{marry to}, \text{Bob}),\ (\text{Bob}, \textit{father of}, \text{Charlie}),\ (\text{Charlie}, (\textit{work at}, \text{OpenAI})\}$

Hybrid Retrieval-Augmented QA extends traditional KGQA by incorporating both structured knowledge from KGs and unstructured evidence from chunks. Given a natural language question q, the system retrieves a reasoning subgraph $\mathcal{S}_q$ from $\mathcal{G}$ and a set of relevant text chunks $\mathcal{C}_q = \{c_1, c_2, \ldots, c_p\}$ from a corpus of documents $\mathcal{D}$. The final model input is the hybrid context $\text{Input}(q) = (\mathcal{S}_q,\ \mathcal{C}_q)$, enabling joint reasoning over graph-structured and textual knowledge to produce the answer $a = f(q, \mathcal{S}_q, \mathcal{C}_q)$.

4 Approach

We present the detailed architecture of our proposed AdaGCRAG framework, as illustrated in Fig. 2, it consists of two phases: *offline* indexing and *online* retrieval. *Offline*, we use the LLM to extract entities and relations from raw texts to construct the KG, and create embedding indexes for both text chunks and KG entities and relations. *Online*, given a query, the LLM first performs question classification to guide adaptive retrieval. Retrieved information is then combined with the question and fed into the LLM to generate the final answer. The key steps of AdaGCRAG are summarized in Algorithm 1, which we will elaborate on in the following sections.

Algorithm 1: AdaGCRAG:Adaptive Graph-Chunk RAG Pipeline

Input: Corpus $\mathcal{D}$, Query q, Embedding model Embed$(\cdot)$, LLM
Output: Answer to query q
Offline Indexing: ;
foreach *document* $D \in \mathcal{D}$ **do**
  Segment into chunks $C = \{c_i\}$;
  Compute embeddings $\mathbf{e}_i = \text{Embed}(c_i)$;
  Extract entities/relations via LLM; embed and store in $\mathcal{V}_{\text{KG}}$ and graph DB ;
Online Retrieval: ;
Classify query q into type $t \in \{\text{Simple, Complex, Abstract}\}$ via LLM ;
Retrieve top-n text chunks using $\mathbf{e}_q = \text{Embed}(q)$;
if $t \neq$ *Simple* **then**
  Extract query entities $\mathcal{E}_q$; retrieve top-k entities from $\mathcal{V}_{\text{KG}}$;
  Expand h-hop subgraph $\mathcal{G}_q$; re-rank triples to get top-m set $\mathcal{T}_q$;
Evidence Combination: Combine $\mathcal{T}_q$ and chunks based on t ;
Answer Generation: ;
if $t =$ *Abstract* **then**
  return $\text{Qwen3}_{\text{think}}(q, \text{Evidence}(q))$;
else
  return $\text{Qwen3}_{\text{no-think}}(q, \text{Evidence}(q))$;

4.1 Offline Indexing

We process raw text documents to generate chunk embeddings and construct the KG. Let D represent a raw document, and $C = \{c_1, c_2, \ldots, c_p\}$ the resulting set of text chunks. The segmentation begins with splitting the document by sentences, followed by further partitioning any long segments using a length threshold L. After obtaining the chunks, we generate embeddings for them and extract entities and relations from the raw text to construct the KG. This step enables the system to effectively combine both the unstructured text (chunks) and the structured knowledge (KG) for later retrieval.

Chunk Embedding Generation. Each chunk $c_i \in C$ is passed through a pre-trained text embedding model Embed(c_i) to obtain a dense vector representation $\mathbf{e}_i \in \mathbb{R}^d$, where d is the dimensionality of the embedding space. The embeddings of all chunks are then stored in a vector database $\mathcal{V}_{\text{chunks}}$ for fast retrieval.

KG Construction. Given a chunk c_i, the LLM extracts entities $\mathcal{E}(c_i)$ and relations $\mathcal{R}(c_i)$ using a few-shot prompt P, adapted from prior work [5,6]:

$$\mathcal{E}(c_i), \mathcal{R}(c_i) = \text{LLM}(c_i, P) \tag{1}$$

To ensure compatibility with lightweight models and reduce noise, we shorten the demonstration examples and refine the instructions. The prompt guides the model through three main steps: (1) identify all entities of specified types from the text; (2) extract all meaningful relations between entity pairs; and (3) return a unified list of extracted entities and relations in English. Each extracted entity $e_j \in \mathcal{E}(c_i)$ and relation $r_k \in \mathcal{R}(c_i)$ is then embedded using the same embedding model Embed$(\cdot)$:

$$\mathbf{e}_e = \text{Embed}(e_j), \quad \mathbf{e}_r = \text{Embed}(r_k) \tag{2}$$

The embeddings for entities and relations are stored in a separate vector database $\mathcal{V}_{\text{KG}}$. Additionally, the text-based entities and relations of the KG are stored in a graph database, such as Neo4j, to support efficient topological search and retrieval of reasoning subgraphs.

4.2 Online Retrieval

The online retrieval adaptively adjusts to the complexity and abstraction level of the user query, enabling efficient retrieval and accurate response generation. It consists of four modules: *LLM-based Question Classification*, *Hybrid Graph-Chunk Retrieval*, *Triple Re-ranking*, and *Graph-Augmented Reasoning with Hybrid Thinking*. This modular design allows our system to handle both factual and conceptual questions with a unified yet adaptive strategy.

LLM-Based Question Classification. To enable efficient and low-cost selection of retrieval and reasoning strategies for user queries, we first classify each query q into one of three predefined categories: *Simple SQ*, *Complex SQ*, and *Abstract Q*.

Prompt for Question Classification P_{cls}

—**Goal**—
Given a single question, classify it into one of the following categories:

0 – **Simple Specific**: The question asks for a specific fact or detail that can typically be answered using one or two text chunks. No reasoning across chunks is required.
1 – **Complex Specific**: The question asks for specific information but requires reasoning across multiple text chunks to find or synthesize the answer.
2 – **Abstract**: The question is conceptual in nature, possibly asking for summaries, high-level insights, themes, or general ideas. It does not focus on specific factual retrieval.

Respond only with one label: `0`, `1`, or `2`./no_think

Examples:

- Question: What is Herman A. Barnett's occupation?
  Answer (0, 1, or 2): 0
- ......
- Question: What are the potential challenges of adopting biodiversity-friendly techniques in market farming?
  Answer (0, 1, or 2): 2

Now classify this one:
Question: `{question}`
Answer (0, 1, or 2):

The LLM performs the classification using a structured few-shot prompt P_{cls}, and the predicted label guide the downstream retrieval and reasoning modules. We conducted an evaluation on a manually annotated set of 60 questions, where Qwen3-4B and GPT-4o achieved comparable near-perfect accuracy, both outperforming LLaMA3.1-8B. Considering efficiency and integration, we adopted the Qwen3 series models in our pipeline.

Hybrid Graph-Chunk Retrieval. We implement a dual-source hybrid retriever that combines the advantages of dense chunk retrieval with structured graph-based retrieval to cover both semantic similarity and knowledge-driven relevance.

Dense Chunk Retrieval. The user query q is encoded into a dense representation $\mathbf{e}_q \in \mathbb{R}^d$ using the Embed$(\cdot)$ function. We retrieve the top-u most relevant chunks $\{c_1, c_2, \ldots, c_u\}$ by computing cosine similarity with stored embeddings in $\mathcal{V}_{\text{chunks}}$:

$$\text{Sim}(\mathbf{e}_q, \mathbf{e}_i) = \frac{\mathbf{e}_q \cdot \mathbf{e}_i}{\|\mathbf{e}_q\| \|\mathbf{e}_i\|}, \quad e_i \in \mathcal{V}_{\text{chunks}} \tag{3}$$

Graph-Based Subgraph Retrieval. For more complex queries (*Complex SQ* and *Abstract Q*), we further extract a reasoning subgraph. We first use the LLM to extract entities from the query:

$$\mathcal{E}_q = \text{LLM}(q, P_{\text{ent}}) \tag{4}$$

P_{ent} instructs the model to identify all relevant entities of predefined types (e.g., organization, person, location, event) mentioned in the query. Each extracted entity $ent_i \in \mathcal{E}_q$ is embedded and matched against the entity vector database $\mathcal{V}_{\text{KG}}$. For the top-k matches, we apply a h-hop topological expansion on the graph database to retrieve the connected reasoning subgraph $\mathcal{G}_q$:

$$\mathcal{G}_q = \text{Expand}_h\left(\text{TopK-Match}(\mathcal{E}_q, \mathcal{V}_{\text{KG}})\right) \tag{5}$$

Triple Reranking over Subgraphs. To reduce noise in the topology-derived subgraph, we re-rank the triples in $\mathcal{G}_q = \{(u_j, r_j, v_j)\}$ based on their semantic relevance to the query, filtering out redundant information and enhancing reasoning precision. Each triple is linearized into a plain-text sequence using a simple concatenation scheme: `"u r v"`, where the head, relation, and tail are joined with spaces. For re-rank scoring, we utilize a compact cross-encoder model to directly estimate the semantic similarity between the query q and each concatenated triple string.

$$s_j = \text{Score}(q, (u_j, r_j, v_j)) = \text{CrossEncoder}(q, \texttt{str}(u_j, r_j, v_j)) \tag{6}$$

We select the top-m triples with the highest scores to construct $\mathcal{T}_q \subset \mathcal{G}_q$, a filtered set of the most semantically aligned knowledge statements for downstream reasoning.

Conditional Graph-Augmented Reasoning with Hybrid Thinking. To balance efficiency and reasoning capability, we leverage the hybrid inference architecture of Qwen3, which supports two distinct modes: *non-thinking* mode for rapid responses and *thinking* mode for step-by-step reasoning. This dual-mode design enables dynamic control of computational effort, governed by a query-specific reasoning budget. Before performing inference with the Qwen3 model, we conditionally integrate the unstructured and structured knowledge as follows:

$$\text{Evidence}(q) = \begin{cases} \text{Top-}n_s \text{ chunks}, & \text{if } \text{cls}(q) = \text{Simple SQ} \\ \text{Top-}k_c \text{ triples} + \text{Top-}n_c \text{ chunks}, & \text{if } \text{cls}(q) = \text{Complex SQ} \\ \text{Top-}k_a \text{ triples} + \text{Top-}n_a \text{ chunks}, & \text{if } \text{cls}(q) = \text{Abstract Q} \end{cases} \tag{7}$$

Here, k_* and n_* denote the number of triples and chunks retrieved for each query type, respectively. For reasoning-heavy tasks, triples are placed before chunks to emphasize graph-based reasoning. The final answer is generated as:

$$\text{Answer}(q) = \begin{cases} \text{Qwen3}_{\text{think}}(q, \text{Evidence}(q)), & \text{if } \text{cls}(q) = \text{Abstract Q} \\ \text{Qwen3}_{\text{no-think}}(q, \text{Evidence}(q)), & \text{otherwise} \end{cases} \tag{8}$$

We selectively activate Qwen3's *think mode* based on the predicted query type. For *Specific* queries, the model uses *no-think* to provide fast answers without step-by-step reasoning. For*Abstract* queries, the model switches to *think* to enable multi-hop or conceptual reasoning over retrieved evidence.

5 Experiments

Our experiments aim to answer following research questions (RQs):

- *RQ1: Comparative Performance.* How does AdaGCRAG perform compared with existing baselines on specific and abstract QA tasks?
- *RQ2: Component Analysis.* What is the contribution of key components to AdaGCRAG's overall effectiveness?
- *RQ3: Case Studies.* How effectively does AdaGCRAG respond to different types of complex queries?

5.1 Experiment Settings

Datasets. We evaluate AdaGCRAG on both *Specific* and *Abstract* QA tasks.

Specific QA involves fact-based questions grounded in explicit chunks or entities, and is divided into two types. *Simple* questions can be answered from one or two chunks without complex reasoning; we use HotpotQA [27]. *Complex* questions require multi-hop reasoning across documents and understanding of implicit relations; we use Multihop(RAG)QA [22] and MusiqueQA [24].

Table 1. Datasets used in our experiments.

Dataset	# Tokens	# Passages	# Questions	# Nodes	# Edges	QA Type
HotpotQA	1,284,956	9,221	1,000	43,809	48,714	Specific QA
MultihopRAG	1,426,396	609	2,556	45,310	51,831	Specific QA
MuSiQue	3,280,174	29,898	3,000	131,112	138,192	Specific QA
Mix	611,602	61	125	18,869	12,609	Abstract QA
MultihopSum	1,426,396	609	125	45,310	51,831	Abstract QA

Abstract QA requires high-level synthesis and conceptual understanding. We use Mix [18] and MultihopSum [22], which feature questions focused on broader themes, summaries, and topic-level reasoning.

The statistics of these datasets are reported in Table 1. As LLM-based graph construction is inherently non-deterministic, repeated inputs may yield variations in extracted triples. Thus, all reported node and edge statistics are derived from the KG generated by our AdaGCRAG(Qwen3-4B).

Baselines. We compare our AdaGCRAG against several representative model configurations.

- **Zero-Shot (Inference-only):** The LLM directly answers the question without any external retrieval.
- **Vanilla RAG (Chunks-only):** The top-ranked text chunks retrieved from the corpus are provided to the LLM for answer generation.
- **Graph-based RAG:** To ensure a fair and efficient comparison, we select graph-augmented methods that emphasize lightweight design and retrieval efficiency, including *LightRAG* [9], *HippoRAG* [10], and *MiniRAG* [6]. Among these, *LightRAG* supports local, global, and hybrid retrieval strategies (denoted as *LightRAG-L*, *LightRAG-G*, and *LightRAG-H*).

Evaluation Metrics. For Specific QA tasks, we evaluate model performance using *Accuracy* and *Recall*, where a prediction is considered correct if it contains the gold answer, without requiring exact string matches [3]. For Abstract QA, we adopt a head-to-head comparison approach following prior work [29], using GPT-4o as the evaluator. Specifically, we assess responses along four evaluation dimensions: *Comprehensiveness*, *Diversity*, *Empowerment*, and *Overall* for Abstract QA tasks.

Implementation Details. For text preprocessing, we first split documents by paragraph using newline characters (`\n`). If a paragraph exceeds a predefined chunk size L, it is further divided into smaller segments. We set the $L = 1200$ tokens with a 100-token overlap and store the resulting embeddings in the *nano*

Table 2. Comparison of methods on different datasets, where Red denotes the best result, and Orange denotes the best result excluding the best one.

Method	HotpotQA		MultihopRAG		MuSiQue	
	Acc.	Rec.	Acc.	Rec.	Acc.	Rec.
ZeroShot (Llama3.1-8B)	27.39	28.79	50.98	39.27	4.37	6.04
ZeroShot (Qwen3-4B w/o think)	22.68	22.74	53.99	38.44	2.90	7.54
VanillaRAG (Llama3.1-8B)	50.16	53.05	52.23	41.93	16.78	24.87
LightRAG-L (Llama3.1-8B)	33.47	38.16	45.14	38.01	8.37	19.85
LightRAG-G (Llama3.1-8B)	26.84	32.62	50.14	40.97	6.22	18.60
LightRAG-H (Llama3.1-8B)	34.94	40.31	52.42	43.09	10.03	20.36
HippoRAG (Llama3.1-8B)	50.65	54.13	54.76	45.35	17.42	26.04
LightRAG-H (Qwen3-4B w/o think)	36.18	38.76	53.90	39.17	9.70	22.49
MiniRAG (Qwen3-4B w/o think)	43.09	47.43	55.37	40.63	14.15	25.88
AdaGCRAG (Qwen3-4B)	52.61	54.97	62.28	60.89	20.94	29.26

vector base. For all retrieval-based methods requiring top-K selection (e.g., for chunks or entities), we default to $K = 4$ to stay within the context length limits. Our method supports query-adaptive retrieval, enabling more fine-grained control. Specifically, for *Simple SQ*, we perform chunk-based retrieval only and select the top-4 relevant chunks. For *Complex SQ*, we retrieve the top-4 chunks and the top-4 similar entities, expand to 2-hop neighbors in the KG, and select 25 candidate triples after reranking. For *Abstract Q*, we retrieve the top-6 chunks and the top-6 similar entities, apply a 2-hop graph expansion, and retain 30 triples after reranking for multi-hop reasoning. All hyperparameter choices, such as chunk size and expansion depth, are aligned with commonly adopted settings in prior studies [9,29].

To maintain a lightweight system design, we use *all-MiniLM-L6-v2* [25] for embedding and *ms-marco-MiniLM-L6-v2* [25] for reranking. While larger models often improve retrieval quality, our focus is on evaluating the retrieval diversity of lightweight RAG systems rather than maximizing performance through heavier components. For generation, we use *Qwen3-4B* as the primary experimental model, and include *LLaMA3.1-8B*, *Qwen3-1.7B* and *Qwen3-0.6B* as additional comparison baselines. *Qwen3*-based experiments are conducted on a single RTX 3070 GPU to emulate local deployment scenarios, while *LLaMA3.1-8B*, due to its higher computational demands, is evaluated on an RTX 4090.

5.2 Evaluation for Specific QA

We report the metric values of various RAG strategies on Specific QA tasks in Table 2. We can make the following observations and analyses.

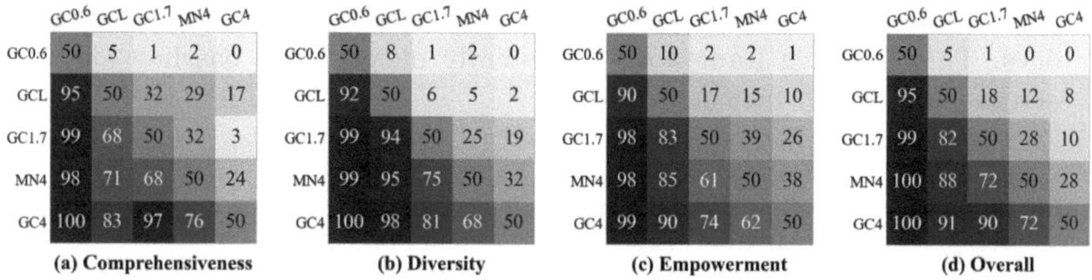

Fig. 3. The abstract QA results on MultihopSum dataset.

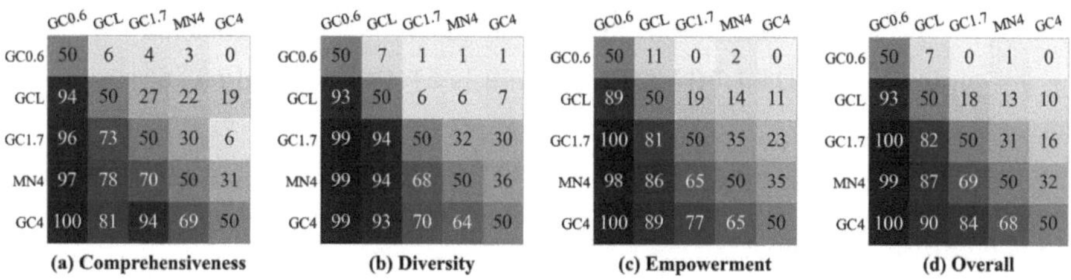

Fig. 4. The abstract QA results on Mix dataset.

(1) Model Efficiency. Qwen3-4B, with only half the parameters of LLaMA3.1-8B, achieves comparable performance in both ZeroShot and LightRAG-H settings. Its ability to run on a single 3070 GPU underscores the potential of lightweight LLMs for cost-sensitive and resource-constrained deployments.
(2) Retrieval Design. Using KG retrieval generally enhances the reasoning ability of LLMs. However, in frameworks such as LightRAG and MiniRAG, the KG functions primarily as an indexing mechanism: only passages linked to extracted entities are retained. In our experiments, we observe that both entity extraction and graph construction are inherently non-deterministic—regardless of whether LLaMA3.1-8B or Qwen3-4B is used. Consequently, the resulting KG structures vary across runs even with identical input, compromising retrieval consistency. Therefore, in lightweight RAG systems, preserving chunk-level retrieval is essential to ensure both coverage and stability.
(3) Graph-Augmented Reasoning. HippoRAG achieves strong performance across benchmarks by leveraging semantic retrievers such as Contriever or ColBERTv2 to identify paraphrastic entities and augment graph connectivity with synonym edges. It further applies Personalized PageRank (PPR) for evidence aggregation. While this pipeline improves reasoning capability, its complex graph construction and reranking mechanisms introduce considerable overhead, which may be unnecessary for simpler questions.
(4) Adaptive Strategy. For simple questions, introducing KGs may unnecessarily complicate the retrieval and suppress critical evidence, as evidenced by the inferior performance of LightRAG and MiniRAG on HotpotQA compared to Vanilla RAG. In contrast, our AdaGCRAG dynamically routes queries: it uses direct chunk retrieval for simple questions, and hybrid retrieval combin-

ing multi-hop KG reasoning with full-context chunk information for complex ones. This adaptive framework consistently outperforms baseline methods across multiple QA benchmarks.

Table 3. Ablation results of AdaGCRAG on MultihopRAG, showing accuracy and recall after removing reranking, triple-based, or chunk-based retrieval.

Model	AdaGCRAG		-Rerank		-Triples		-Chunks	
	Acc.	Rec.	Acc.	Rec.	Acc.	Rec.	Acc.	Rec.
Qwen3-4B	**62.55**	**60.35**	60.17	56.42	59.97	51.38	46.56	38.24
Qwen3-1.7B	**54.56**	**53.32**	51.03	49.17	51.43	45.19	40.12	32.65

5.3 Evaluation for Abstract QA

We evaluate the performance of various methods on abstract QA tasks as shown in Fig. 3 and Fig. 4, each cell indicates the proportion of questions for which the method in the row produces more accurate answers than the method in the column. Since MiniRAG is the only existing graph-based RAG specifically designed for deployment under resource-constrained environments, we use it as a strong baseline. For clarity, we denote *GC0.6*, *GCL*, *GC1.7*, *MN4*, and *GC4* as *AdaGCRAG (Qwen3-0.6B)*, *AdaGCRAG (LLaMA3.1-8B)*, *AdaGCRAG (Qwen3-1.7B)*, *MiniRAG (Qwen3-4B)*, and *AdaGCRAG (Qwen3-4B)*, respectively.

We highlight several observations: (1) When enabling the *thinking* mode in Qwen3, the reasoning ability improves significantly with model size, following the trend *Qwen3-4B* > *Qwen3-1.7B* > *LLaMA3.1-8B* ≫ *Qwen3-0.6B*. Combined with the ablation results in Sect. 5.5, we find that Qwen3-1.7B serves as a strong trade-off in severely resource-constrained environments. (2) Compared to MiniRAG, which retrieves chunks through entity-anchored graph traversal, AdaGCRAG performs dual-path retrieval by separately indexing and retrieving both graph-structured triples and raw text chunks. This allows AdaGCRAG to capture a broader range of relevant evidence and better support complex reasoning. When coupled with Qwen3's internal reasoning capabilities, AdaGCRAG is able to more effectively integrate heterogeneous knowledge and generate more comprehensive responses. To the best of our knowledge, our method is the first to systematically explore abstract QA under constrained-resource settings in graph-based RAG. These results demonstrate the potential of scaling down both retrieval and generation while retaining robust multi-hop reasoning performance.

5.4 Detailed Analysis

To answer the question *RQ2* and assess the contribution of each core component in AdaGCRAG, we conduct the ablation study on MultihopRAG using two backbone LLMs: *Qwen3-4B* and *Qwen3-1.7B*. As shown in Table 3, we evaluate three major variants by selectively removing key modules from the full framework:

- *-Rerank*: Disables the graph-based reranking stage by directly truncating the top-m retrieved triples based on retrieved subgraphs.
- *-Triples*: Disables the KG retrieval, using only chunk-level retrieval.
- *-Chunks*: Disables chunk-level, using only the reranked triples from the KG.

The results yield several insights into AdaGCRAG's design:

1. **Model Scalability.** Despite its smaller size, *Qwen3-1.7B* maintains strong retrieval and reasoning performance. This demonstrates its viability for deployment in resource-constrained local environments, offering a competitive trade-off between performance and efficiency.
2. **Component Contributions.** Both triple-based and chunk-based retrieval significantly impact overall performance. However, the absence of chunk information leads to a more severe degradation, highlighting the indispensable role of unstructured context even when structured KG evidence is available.
3. **Complementary Roles.** Triples and chunks serve complementary functions: triples enable precise multi-hop reasoning via topological query-to-entity path matching, while chunks provide detailed, unstructured descriptions that supplement the often sparse KG facts. Their synergy allows the LLM to balance structured reasoning with rich contextual grounding, enhancing the overall effectiveness.

5.5 Case Study Analysis

Before conducting the case study, we first analyzed the distribution of question types in each dataset. The statistics are summarized as follows:

- *HotpotQA*: 263 Simple SQ, 729 Complex SQ, and 8 Abstract Q.
- *MultihopRAG*: 17 Simple SQ, 2,448 Complex SQ, and 91 Abstract Q.
- *MuSiQue*: 146 Simple SQ, 2,823 Complex SQ, and 31 Abstract Q.

Based on dataset statistics, each dataset covers all three types of retrieval strategies, corresponding to the different question types. To illustrate AdaGCRAG practical advantages, we use two representative examples from Multihop, which targets both Specific and Abstract QA tasks, to perform case studies. As shown in results, it demonstrates AdaGCRAG selectively applies retrieval and structured reasoning depending on the question types.

Complex SQ. This case illustrates the limitations of Qwen3-4B: 1) Although the output was constrained to be brief, Qwen-4B (ZeroShot-nothink) frequently ignores the instruction, producing verbose and often inaccurate content. By contrast, AdaGCRAG benefits from targeted prompts and adaptive retrieval to provide accurate, faithful responses. 2) Even with step-by-step reasoning, Qwen-4B (ZeroShot-think) fails to identify the correct entity without external knowledge. However, AdaGCRAG retrieves relevant facts and integrates them into its reasoning to accurately identify the correct answer.

Abstract Q. Although Qwen3-4B shows stronger performance than LLaMA 3.1-8B on abstract questions in the *thinking* mode, it often relies on vague or speculative prior knowledge, producing responses that are fluent but not grounded. In contrast, AdaGCRAG makes use of retrieved evidence during its reasoning process, producing answers that are both coherent and factually reliable.

Case study for Complex SQ and Abstract Q

· **Complex SQ:**
Who is the individual that not only convinced a former Jane Street employee to join his trading and development ventures but also planned for a specialized board for his company, while facing allegations of fraud and conspiracy in court, as reported by Fortune, CNBC, and TechCrunch?

· **Ground-Truth:**Sam Bankman-Fried

· **ZeroShot w/o think Response:**
The individual in question is Peter Thiel. He convinced a former...

· **ZeroShot think Response:**
Rajon R. Suri

· **AdaGCRAG Response:**
Sam Bankman-Fried

· **Abstract Q:**
How does the dataset cover rumors about OpenAI's potential chip production?

· **ZeroShot think Response:**
<think>
Okay, the user is asking how the dataset covers rumors about OpenAI's potential chip production. First, I need to recall... including the GPT series, but I don't remember them having a significant focus on chip production...
</think>
The dataset covering rumors about OpenAI's potential chip production would likely be structured to track...

· **AdaGCRAG Response:**
<think>
Okay, the user is asking how the dataset covers rumors about OpenAI's potential chip production. Let me start by recalling the information provided... mention the rumors about OpenAI developing their own chips...
</think>
The dataset addresses rumors about OpenAI's potential chip production through... the dataset frames the rumors as part of a larger narrative about OpenAIâĂŹs strategic positioning in AI...

Summary. The case study analysis showcases AdaGCRAG's ability to adapt its retrieval strategies to a wide variety of question types. Without modifying system-level logic, changes in the input question alone are sufficient to trigger distinct and appropriate RAG pipelines, underlining the flexibility and robustness of our hybrid retrieval-augmented framework.

6 Conclusion

We present AdaGCRAG, a lightweight yet effective retrieval-augmented generation framework that combines dense chunk retrieval and structured KG reasoning in a query-adaptive manner. By classifying questions into simple, complex, and abstract categories, AdaGCRAG dynamically selects appropriate retrieval and reasoning strategies to balance efficiency and accuracy. Extensive experiments across both specific and abstract QA tasks demonstrate that AdaGCRAG significantly outperforms existing lightweight baselines, particularly under resource-constrained settings. Through a modular pipeline and conditional inference using Qwen3, our method achieves flexible, interpretable, and high-performance RAG without requiring cloud-based LLMs or costly graph construction.

Supplemental Material Statement. Our datasets, source code, and other details are available online at https://anonymous.4open.science/r/AdaGCRAG.

References

1. Achiam, J., et al.: Gpt-4 technical report. arXiv preprint arXiv:2303.08774 (2023)
2. Agarwal, R., et al.: Many-shot in-context learning. Adv. Neural. Inf. Process. Syst. **37**, 76930–76966 (2024)
3. Asai, A., Wu, Z., Wang, Y., Sil, A., Hajishirzi, H.: Self-rag: learning to retrieve, generate, and critique through self-reflection. In: The Twelfth International Conference on Learning Representations (2023)
4. Cheng, M., et al.: A survey on knowledge-oriented retrieval-augmented generation. arXiv preprint arXiv:2503.10677 (2025)
5. Edge, D., et al.: From local to global: a graph rag approach to query-focused summarization. arXiv preprint arXiv:2404.16130 (2024)
6. Fan, T., Wang, J., Ren, X., Huang, C.: Minirag: towards extremely simple retrieval-augmented generation. arXiv preprint arXiv:2501.06713 (2025)
7. Grattafiori, A., et al.: The llama 3 herd of models. arXiv preprint arXiv:2407.21783 (2024)
8. Guo, Q., Xie, X., Liu, S., Hu, M., Li, X., Bu, L.: Intention is all you need: refining your code from your intention. arXiv preprint arXiv:2502.08172 (2025)
9. Guo, Z., Xia, L., Yu, Y., Ao, T., Huang, C.: Lightrag: simple and fast retrieval-augmented generation. arXiv preprint arXiv:2410.05779 (2024)
10. Gutiérrez, B.J., Shu, Y., Gu, Y., Yasunaga, M., Su, Y.: Hipporag: neurobiologically inspired long-term memory for large language models. In: The Thirty-eighth Annual Conference on Neural Information Processing Systems (2024)
11. Izacard, G., Grave, E.: Leveraging passage retrieval with generative models for open domain question answering. In: Merlo, P., Tiedemann, J., Tsarfaty, R. (eds.) Proceedings of the 16th Conference of the European Chapter of the Association for Computational Linguistics: Main Volume, pp. 874–880. Association for Computational Linguistics, Online (2021). https://doi.org/10.18653/v1/2021.eacl-main.74. https://aclanthology.org/2021.eacl-main.74/
12. Ji, Z., et al.: Survey of hallucination in natural language generation. ACM Comput. Surv. **55**(12), 1–38 (2023)
13. Lewis, P., et al.: Retrieval-augmented generation for knowledge-intensive nlp tasks. Adv. Neural. Inf. Process. Syst. **33**, 9459–9474 (2020)
14. Li, M., Miao, S., Li, P.: Simple is effective: the roles of graphs and large language models in knowledge-graph-based retrieval-augmented generation. In: International Conference on Learning Representations (2025)
15. Luo, L., Li, Y.F., Haffari, G., Pan, S.: Reasoning on graphs: faithful and interpretable large language model reasoning. In: The Twelfth International Conference on Learning Representations (2024)

16. Luo, M., Xu, X., Liu, Y., Pasupat, P., Kazemi, M.: In-context learning with retrieved demonstrations for language models: a survey. arXiv preprint arXiv:2401.11624 (2024)
17. Mavromatis, C., Karypis, G.: GNN-RAG: graph neural retrieval for large language model reasoning. arXiv preprint arXiv:2405.20139 (2024)
18. Qian, H., Zhang, P., Liu, Z., Mao, K., Dou, Z.: Memorag: moving towards next-gen rag via memory-inspired knowledge discovery, **1** (2024). arXiv preprint arXiv:2409.05591
19. Sarmah, B., Mehta, D., Hall, B., Rao, R., Patel, S., Pasquali, S.: Hybridrag: integrating knowledge graphs and vector retrieval augmented generation for efficient information extraction. In: Proceedings of the 5th ACM International Conference on AI in Finance, pp. 608–616 (2024)
20. Shi, W., Han, X., Lewis, M., Tsvetkov, Y., Zettlemoyer, L., Yih, W.t.: Trusting your evidence: Hallucinate less with context-aware decoding. In: Proceedings of the 2024 Conference of the North American Chapter of the Association for Computational Linguistics: Human Language Technologies, vol. 2: Short Papers, pp. 783–791 (2024)
21. Sun, J., et al.: Think-on-graph: deep and responsible reasoning of large language model on knowledge graph. In: The Twelfth International Conference on Learning Representations (2024)
22. Tang, Y., Yang, Y.: Multihop-rag: benchmarking retrieval-augmented generation for multi-hop queries. arXiv preprint arXiv:2401.15391 (2024)
23. Team, Q.: Qwen3: Think deeper, act faster (2025). https://qwenlm.github.io/blog/qwen3/. Accessed 02 May 2025
24. Trivedi, H., Balasubramanian, N., Khot, T., Sabharwal, A.: musique: Multihop questions via single-hop question composition. Trans. Assoc. Comput. Linguist. **10**, 539–554 (2022)
25. Wang, W., Wei, F., Dong, L., Bao, H., Yang, N., Zhou, M.: Minilm: deep self-attention distillation for task-agnostic compression of pre-trained transformers. Adv. Neural. Inf. Process. Syst. **33**, 5776–5788 (2020)
26. Xu, D., et al.: Harnessing large language models for knowledge graph question answering via adaptive multi-aspect retrieval-augmentation. In: Proceedings of the AAAI Conference on Artificial Intelligence, vol. 39, pp. 25570–25578 (2025)
27. Yang, Z., et al.: Hotpotqa: a dataset for diverse, explainable multi-hop question answering. arXiv preprint arXiv:1809.09600 (2018)
28. Zhang, Q., et al.: A survey of graph retrieval-augmented generation for customized large language models. arXiv preprint arXiv:2501.13958 (2025)
29. Zhou, Y., et al.: In-depth analysis of graph-based rag in a unified framework. arXiv preprint arXiv:2503.04338 (2025)

The Graph Language: How Knowledge Graphs Speak to Large Language Models

Giuseppe Pirrò(✉)

DeMaCS, University of Calabria, Arcavacata, Italy
giuseppe.pirro@unical.it

Abstract. Large Language Models (LLMs) excel at reasoning but benefit from grounding provided by Knowledge Graphs (KGs). However, integrating these paradigms is challenging. We introduce GRALAN, which enables KGs to "speak;; directly in the LLM's semantic space through relational tokens that preserve graph structure. GRALAN's trainable *language mediator* generates structured tokens for any frozen LLM, creating a foundation for knowledge-intensive applications. We demonstrate its effectiveness in question-answering by re-framing the task as entity classification over question-focused subgraphs. Experiments show that GRALAN significantly outperforms existing methods, particularly on complex multi-hop reasoning tasks, establishing a new paradigm for KG-LLM integration that maintains structural fidelity while leveraging LLMs' reasoning capabilities.

Keywords: Knowledge Graphs · Large Language Models

1 Introduction

Knowledge graphs (KGs) have emerged as a powerful formalism for organizing structured information across numerous domains, including large-scale encyclopedic resources (e.g., DBpedia, Wikidata) and specialized scientific databases (e.g., drug-gene interactions) [37]. Their graph-based representations encode entities as nodes and relations as edges, enabling the discovery of rich relational patterns and the execution of symbolic (e.g., SPARQL) queries. Meanwhile, the rise of large language models (LLMs)—such as the GPT-family [5], BERT [10], and T5 [7]—has yielded impressive progress in natural language processing, with applications ranging from open-domain question answering to dialogue systems [46]. The question we address in this paper is: *can we enable KGs to speak the LLM language?* Achieving this would allow us to combine the structured, precise, and interconnected nature of KGs with the versatile reasoning and generative capabilities of LLMs. This integration is essential to enhance LLM performance by reducing hallucinations and enabling complex reasoning tasks.

This work was supported by STROKE 5.0. Progetto, sviluppo e sperimentazione di una piattaforma tecnologica di servizi di intelligenza artificiale a supporto della gestione clinica integrata di eventi acuti di ictus. CUP: B29J23000430005.

D. Garijo et al. (Eds.): ISWC 2025, LNCS 16140, pp. 611–628, 2026.
https://doi.org/10.1007/978-3-032-09527-5_33

Research Challenges. While KGs excel at capturing structured, factual relationships, and LLMs demonstrate remarkable linguistic understanding, their fundamentally different knowledge representations create a semantic gap that hinders effective integration. Current approaches either compromise the rich structural information in KGs through flattening or serialization [1,39], or require expensive fine-tuning that risks catastrophic forgetting [31,40,42]. Parameter-efficient methods [6,11] and iterative reasoning approaches [30] have made progress but still struggle with complex multi-hop reasoning tasks over heterogeneous graphs. Bridging structured KGs and powerful but text-oriented LLMs remains a nontrivial task [32].

Our Proposal. We introduce GRALAN (The Graph Language), a framework that bridges the gap between KGs and LLMs through semantic alignment rather than structural transformation. GRALAN treats a frozen LLM as a universal reasoning engine and allows KGs to "speak" directly in the LLM's semantic space through *relational tokens* - learned representations that encode the semantics of node, relation, and task-specific information. These tokens are composed into structured LLM input sequences that integrate KG-derived embeddings with task-specific context. The LLM processes these sequences to generate hidden states that function as neural workspaces where KG information and reasoning processes seamlessly merge. These distributed representations simultaneously encode both factual knowledge and logical relationships, enabling the model to generate responses that harmoniously blend structured information with task-specific reasoning within a unified computational architecture. GRALAN reimagines the KG-LLM integration problem as semantic alignment rather than structural transformation. Instead of forcing KGs to conform to LLM input formats as in prior work [36,44], GRALAN teaches KGs to communicate using a *language* that preserves their structural integrity while remaining fluently interpretable by frozen LLMs. Unlike methods that use fixed graph extraction [13] or rely on prompt engineering [35], our approach enables zero-loss knowledge transfer between symbolic and neural representations, combining the precision of graph structured reasoning with the flexible inference capabilities of language models. By establishing a bidirectional communication channel between KGs and LLMs via the *language mediator*, GRALAN creates opportunities for structured knowledge extraction, fact verification, multi-modal reasoning, and continuous knowledge integration—all while maintaining computational efficiency through its modular, parameter-efficient design. These capabilities address the hallucination challenges [2,15,47] and factual inconsistencies that plague current LLMs when reasoning over structured knowledge. This enriched representation supports diverse downstream applications while preserving the LLM's general-purpose language capabilities and ensuring computational efficiency.

1.1 Application to Question Answering

We show GRALAN in the task of natural language question answering (QA). The approach is outlined in Fig. 1. Consider the following question from the GraptextQA dataset [27] using Wikidata as underlying KG and Flat-T5 [25] as LLM: *"Which American presidents followed in their father's footsteps and became president?"*. GRALAN operates through three key components:

(1) Question-Focused Subgraph: rather than considering the entire KG, our framework first processes the natural language question to identify relevant seed entities and relations. This can be done via an LLM (with a carefully crafted prompt) or entity recognition. In this case (using ChatGPT) identified relevant entities are *USA President* while relevant relations are *father* and *position held*. Then, GRALAN uses a novel *question-focused* breadth-first search algorithm on the underlying KG, which starting from the seed entities, *USA President* in this case, *biases* the traversal toward relations most related to *father* and *position held*. Part of the extracted subgraph is shown in Fig. 1. There are several USA presidents along with their parents and the *occupation* or *position held*. We observe that *occupation* is included in the subgraph because its related with the seed relation *position held*. Less-relevant relations like *part-of* or *base salary*, that would have been considered by a traditional BFS, have been discarded thus reducing noise in the subsequent phases.

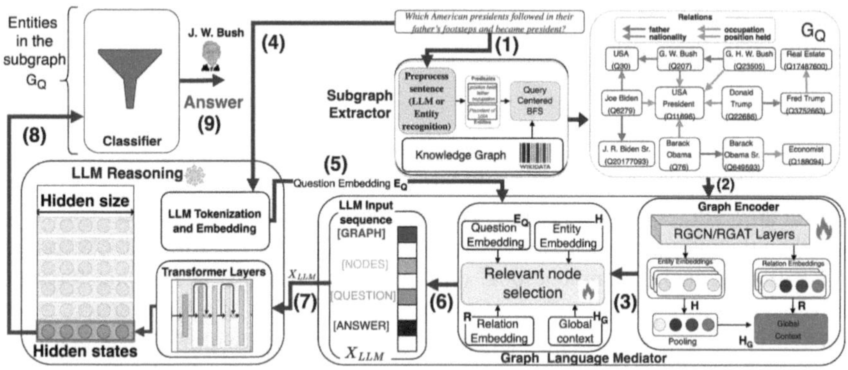

Fig. 1. GRALAN's end-to-end architecture for graph-language reasoning. Given a natural language question (1), GRALAN extracts a question-relevant subgraph (2) and processes it through RGCN/RGAT layers to obtain node (H), relation (R) and global context (H_G) embeddings (3). The question and graph representations are aligned in a shared semantic space through the Graph Language Mediator (4–6), which identifies the most related nodes to the question and creates a structured input sequence with special tokens [GRAPH], [NODES], [QUESTION], and [ANSWER] (during training). This sequence is processed by a frozen LLM (7) whose hidden states are used by a classifier (8) to predict the final answer, enabling reasoning without fine-tuning.

(2) Alignment: the *Graph Language Mediator* is responsible for transforming the structured information from the extracted subgraph into relational tokens that can be effectively utilized by the LLM. First, a *graph encoder* uses a GNN-architecture (e.g., RGCN) to embed entities (e.g., *George H. W. Bush*) and their relations (e.g., *father*, *position held*) thus capturing their semantics in the subgraph. Besides entities and predicate embeddings, the encoder computes a *global graph representation and a relation context embedding*. These embeddings encapsulate the overall structure of the subgraph and the specific relations *pertinent to the query*. Through a cross-attention mechanism, entities dynamically align with the question's semantics (e.g., *B. Obama*, *J. W.*

Bush, and *D. J. Trump* nodes attend strongly to *USA President* than *Economist*) all in the LLM's native embedding space. Then, the mediator assembles a specialized input sequence X_{LLM} by concatenating delimiter embeddings, a bird's-eye view of the entire subgraph (capturing global context around *USA President*), embeddings of the most relevant nodes (e.g., *J.W. Bush*), and the question representation itself.

(3) LLM reasoning: GRALAN treats the LLM as a general reasoning engine by keeping its parameters frozen. The frozen LLM processes the input sequence $\mathbf{X}_{\text{LLM}}$ and generates *hidden states* for each token. The hidden state corresponding to the final token (denoted by [ANSWER]) encapsulates the necessary contextual information. In GRALAN, the QA task is recast as *predicting which entity in the subgraph* correctly answers the question. The LLM is guided to reason over our structured input and select *J.W. Bush* as the answer directly from the subgraph entities through a classification layer. This formulation provides direct alignment between graph structure and LLM reasoning while remaining scalable to large KGs. By predicting entities rather than generating text, GRALAN bypasses vocabulary constraints while maintaining the LLM's powerful reasoning capabilities.

1.2 Contributions and Outline

Our approach advances the state of the art through six key innovations: (1) *Preserving Structural Integrity* by directly *encoding* question-relevant subgraphs with GNNs rather than flattening them into text; (2) *Parameter-Efficient Integration* by keeping the LLM frozen, reducing computational costs while preventing catastrophic forgetting; (3) *Reconceptualizing QA as Entity Classification* in the LLM's latent space, *bypassing* token-vocabulary constraints and enabling linear scaling with KG size; (4) *Unified Reasoning* through a relation-aware cross-attention mechanism that bridges symbolic KG structure and neural LLM reasoning; (5) *Enhanced Scalability and Interpretability* via relatedness-based prioritization that efficiently scales to large KGs while ensuring explainable reasoning paths, and (6) A novel *Graph Language Framework* where the Graph Language Mediator transforms graph structures into specialized relational tokens that serve as a semantic bridge between KGs and LLMs.

GRALAN offers flexibility, extending beyond question answering to support diverse applications including recommendation systems, knowledge discovery, and multimodal reasoning without requiring architectural modifications to either system.

The remainder of the paper is organized as follows. We review related work (Sect. 2), then introduce the GRALAN framework (Sect. 3). Then, we report on an extensive experimental evaluation (Sect. 4) and conclude (Sect. 5).

2 Related Work

Integrating KGs with LLMs presents significant challenges due to their fundamentally different knowledge representation paradigms. We categorize existing approaches and highlight how GRALAN advances the state of the art. Recent *parameter-efficient* approaches with frozen LLMs have shown various limitations. GraphToken [11] serializes graphs into specialized token sequences but loses higher-order structural relationships, while GraphLLM [6] creates "graph-enhanced prefixes" that capture only local neighborhood features. Both approaches overlook the inherent heterogeneity of real-world knowledge graphs (KGs). Task-specific approaches present additional constraints. GNP [36] and Q-KGR [44] remain limited to multiple-choice questions, while HiGPT [35] requires carefully crafted hierarchical prompts impractical for complex queries. Other approaches like InstructGLM [41] and GraphGPT [34] focus primarily on instruction tuning rather than semantic alignment. LangGraph[1] uses static, hand-crafted text templates to inject graph facts and treats graphs as input data processed through text workflows. In contrast, GRALAN learns dense relational embeddings end-to-end via back-propagation from the QA loss, dynamically adapting to each query. GRALAN treats graphs as first-class semantic objects communicating directly in the LLM's representation space, where learned tokens outperform fixed templates.

While G-Retriever [13] shares similarities with GRALAN, it differs fundamentally in architectural philosophy. G-Retriever operates as a retrieval-augmented framework using Prize-Collecting Steiner Tree optimization and employs a dual-pathway approach combining textual serialization with Graph Attention Networks. In contrast, GRALAN achieves true neural-symbolic integration through its Graph Language Mediator, establishing fundamental semantic alignment between graph structures and language understanding. GRALAN's relation-aware tokens create a cohesive shared semantic space where graph structures and language coexist with minimal transformation loss, while its hybrid cross-attention classification mechanism operates directly in the LLM's latent space. Unlike GRALAN's modular approach, JAKET [42] requires complete joint pre-training of both KG and language components, increasing computational costs and complexity. Its bidirectional architecture fundamentally differs from GRALAN's Graph Language Mediator, which preserves the LLM's capabilities while creating a specialized semantic alignment layer. While JAKET focuses on adapting to unseen KGs through extensive pre-training, GRALAN offers greater versatility through its transparent task encoding mechanism without resource-intensive LLM re-training.

GRALAN's Key Advantages. GRALAN's advantages derive from a synergistic combination of innovations. Its parameter-efficient design keeps the LLM frozen, preventing catastrophic forgetting while reducing computational overhead. By reconceptualizing QA as entity classification in the LLM's latent space, GRALAN transcends token-vocabulary limitations and scales linearly with KG size. The Graph Language Mediator introduces three fundamental innovations that enable true neural-symbolic integration. First, unlike RAG approaches that flatten graphs into text, GRALAN creates relational tokens that preserve graph structure while operating in the LLM's native semantic space, maintaining relational patterns through direct GNN encoding. Second, the mechanism enables bidirectional neural-symbolic communication through relation-aware cross-attention, going beyond simple concatenation or retrieval augmentation. Third, unlike G-Retriever's dual-pathway serialization or ToG's iterative exploration, GRALAN maintains complete structural fidelity through direct graph-language integration without intermediate transformations. Beyond question answering, this approach

[1] https://github.com/langchain-ai/langgraph.

serves as a universal translator between structured knowledge and language understanding, maintaining a consistent interface between KGs and LLMs across different domains while preserving task-specific semantics. This represents a paradigm shift from adaptation-based to alignment-based KG-LLM integration, fundamentally changing how knowledge graphs and language models interact and communicate.

3 The Graph Language Framework

Let G= (V, E, R) be a knowledge graph, where $V = \{v_1, \dots, v_{|V|}\}$ is the set of entities, $R = \{r_1, \dots, r_{|R|}\}$ is the set of relation types, and $E \subseteq V \times R \times V$ is the set of edges (triplets); $\mathcal{N}_i^r$ is the set of neighbors of node i linked by the relation r. Each triplet $(v_i, r, v_j) \in E$ indicates a directed relational link $r \in R$ from entity v_i to v_j. Despite the versatility of GRALAN, in this paper we focus on a concrete use case: natural language question answering combining KGs and LLMs. The problem can be stated as follows:

Problem: Given a natural language query Q, a knowledge graph G= (V, E, R), and a LLM, the task is to predict the correct target entity $v^* \in V$ that answers the question.

Our framework combines the KG's relational structure with linguistic information from Q, ensuring an effective utilization by the LLM. GRALAN includes three primary modules: (i) task-focused subgraph extraction (§3.1); (ii) graph language mediator (§3.2); and (iii) LLM reasoner (§3.3).

3.1 Task-Focused Subgraph Extractor

Given a knowledge graph $\mathcal{G} = (V, E, R)$ and a natural language question Q, we propose a two-stage process for extracting a task-relevant subgraph. There are three main reasons to focus on a local subgraph when answering questions over KGs. First, most entities and relations are irrelevant to a specific query. For instance, the question, "o manages the department where Alice works?" only involves exploring Alice's department and its managerial relations. Second, LLMs and GNNs have input size constraints; subgraphs make the input manageable while improving interpretability. Third, focusing on a smaller subgraph improves efficiency and accuracy by reducing processing time and irrelevant information [16].

(1) Question Analysis: the first stage involves mapping the natural language question Q to seed entities and relevant relations. This is achieved through a function Map(Q) = $(E_{\text{seed}}, P_{\text{rel}})$. Here, $E_{\text{seed}} \subseteq V$ represent the entities identified as most relevant to the question (e.g., through Named Entity Recognition or using a carefully prompted LLM), and $P_{\text{rel}} \subseteq R$ are the relations most aligned with the question's relations. The alignment is part of a question-focused BFS.
(2) Question-Focused Breadth-First Search: the second stage extracts the relevant subgraph $\mathcal{G}_{sub}$=$(V_{sub}, R_{sub}, E_{sub})$ based on the identified seed entities and relations. The

subgraph is computed as[2]:

$$\mathcal{G}_{\text{sub}} = \text{QuestionFocusedBFS}(G, E_{\text{seed}}, P_{\text{rel}}, \theta)$$

where θ is a relevance threshold that determines how closely edges in the graph must align with the question's context. The edge expansion priority during BFS is determined by a similarity function *sim*:$R \times R \rightarrow [0,1]$, which measures the alignment between the relation r in the edge $e = (v_i, r, v_j)$ and the question's seed relations P_{rel}. The similarity function can be defined using either co-occurrence statistics within the KG [23] or embeddings of the relations. The algorithm maintains a priority queue $\mathcal{Q}$, prioritizing edges with higher similarity scores. This ensures that the algorithm explores only the most relevant paths, focusing the subgraph around the seed entities while emphasizing edges (relations) most pertinent to the question relations. Furthermore, if multiple relevant relations or seed entities are identified during the Question Analysis stage, multiple BFSs can be initiated simultaneously with a final merge phase.

3.2 Graph Language Mediator

The Graph Language Mediator enables KGs to communicate with LLMs through three components:

Graph Encoder. Using RGCN [26], it encodes the subgraph structure by initializing node embeddings $\mathbf{x}_i \in \mathbb{R}^d$ and relation embeddings $\mathbf{r}_k \in \mathbb{R}^d$. Through L message-passing layers, we compute:

$$\mathbf{h}_i^{(l)} = W_0^{(l)}\mathbf{h}_i^{(l-1)} + \sum_{r\in R}\sum_{j:(j,r,i)\in\mathcal{E}_{\text{sub}}} \frac{1}{|\mathcal{N}_i^r|} W_r^{(l)}\mathbf{h}_j^{(l-1)} \tag{1}$$

This produces node embeddings $\mathbf{H}$ and relation embeddings $\mathbf{R}$. The global subgraph embedding $\mathbf{z}_{\text{graph}}$ is obtained via attention-weighted pooling [19] over the embeddings:

$$\alpha_i = \text{softmax}(W_p\mathbf{h}_i), \tag{2}$$

$$\mathbf{z}_{\text{graph}} = \sum_i \alpha_i \mathbf{h}_i \tag{3}$$

where $W_p \in \mathbb{R}^{1\times d}$ is a learnable parameter matrix.

Question Encoding. The natural language question Q is tokenized and embedded using the LLM vocabulary:

$$\mathbf{E}_Q = \text{LLM.embed}(Q) \in \mathbb{R}^{M\times d_{\text{lm}}} \tag{4}$$

where M is the number of tokens in the question, and d_{lm} is the embedding dimension of the LLM.

[2] The complete pseudocode is available from the GRALAN website https://github.com/giuseppepirro/gralan

Semantic Alignment. To enable graph-question interaction, we employ a sequential process:

1.*Relation-Aware Node Interaction:* For nodes i, j connected by relation r, we first compute attention scores considering their relational context:

$$\mathbf{A}_{i,j} = \text{softmax}\left(\frac{\mathbf{H}_i \mathbf{R}_r \mathbf{H}_j^\top \mathbf{E}_Q^\top}{\sqrt{d_{lm}}}\right) \tag{5}$$

It's important to note that $\mathbf{A}_{i,j}$ in Equation (5) serves a different purpose than the aggregation mechanism in Equation (1). While Equation (1) performs message passing based on predefined graph structure using the fixed neighborhood set $\mathcal{N}_i^r$, the attention scores $\mathbf{A}_{i,j}$ capture semantic relevance between connected nodes in the context of the question. These attention scores are used to enhance node representations before the question space projection, but do not directly replace the structural aggregation in the initial RGCN layers.

2. *Question Space Projection*: The relation-enriched representations are then projected into the question's semantic space via cross-attention:

$$\mathbf{Q} = [\mathbf{H} \parallel \mathbf{R}]W_Q, \tag{6}$$

$$\mathbf{K} = \mathbf{E}_Q W_K, \tag{7}$$

$$\mathbf{V} = \mathbf{E}_Q W_V, \tag{8}$$

$$\mathbf{Z} = \text{softmax}\left(\frac{\mathbf{Q}\mathbf{K}^\top}{\sqrt{d}}\right)\mathbf{V} \tag{9}$$

where W_x are matrices. Each node-relation pair becomes:

$$\mathbf{h}_i^{\text{final}} = \text{LayerNorm}\left(\mathbf{h}_i + \text{FFN}_g([\mathbf{h}_i; \mathbf{R}_i; \mathbf{z}_i])\right) \tag{10}$$

where FFN_g is a feed-forward network of g layers.

LLM Input Construction. Then, GRALAN additionally selects top-K nodes embeddings $\mathbf{z}_{\text{top-}K}$ based on relevance to the question embedding $\mathbf{E}_Q$ and assembles the final sequence with special delimiters ($\mathbf{e}_{[\cdot]}$):

$$\mathbf{X}_{\text{LLM}} = \left[\mathbf{e}_{[\text{GRAPH}]}; \mathbf{z}_{\text{graph}}; \mathbf{e}_{[\text{NODES}]}; \mathbf{z}_{\text{top-}K}; \mathbf{e}_{[\text{QUESTION}]}; \mathbf{E}_Q; \mathbf{e}_{[\text{ANSWER}]}\right] \tag{11}$$

Note that in Eq. (6), $\mathbf{Q}$ refers to the query matrix in the attention mechanism obtained by projecting node and relation embeddings, rather than the original question embedding $\mathbf{E}_Q$. This distinction allows the model to compute attention between graph elements and the question's semantic representation.

3.3 LLM-Based Reasoning

After obtaining the input sequence $\mathbf{X}_{\text{LLM}}$, GRALAN leverages a LLM for the reasoning and answer prediction phase.

LLM Processing. The LLM processes the input sequence $\mathbf{X}_{\text{LLM}}$ through its transformer layers. This sequence allows us to bypass the usual token embedding lookup and directly leverage our graph-aligned representations. The LLM generates contextual representations:

$$\{\mathbf{h}_{\text{LLM}}^{(t)}\}_{t=1}^{L} = \text{LLM}(\mathbf{X}_{\text{LLM}}) \tag{12}$$

where $\mathbf{h}_{\text{LLM}}^{(t)} \in \mathbb{R}^{d_{\text{LLM}}}$ represents the hidden state at position t. Importantly, since the LLM remains frozen, all adaptation happens through the upstream graph mediator.

3.4 End-to-End Training

To predict answer entities from LLM outputs, we adopt a scalable classification approach. We extract the final hidden state corresponding to the [ANSWER] token:

$$\mathbf{h}_{\text{answer}} = \mathbf{h}_{\text{LLM}}^{([\text{ANSWER}])} \in \mathbb{R}^{d_{\text{LLM}}} \tag{13}$$

This representation is mapped to probabilities over subgraph entities:

$$P_{\text{cls}}(v \mid X) = \text{softmax}\left(W_{\text{cls}}\mathbf{h}_{\text{answer}}\right)_{id(v)} \tag{14}$$

where $W_{\text{cls}} \in \mathbb{R}^{|V| \times d_{\text{LLM}}}$ projects to the entity space. The predicted entity is selected as:

$$v_{\text{pred}} = \text{argmax}_{v \in V} P_{\text{cls}}(v \mid X) \tag{15}$$

Multiple Answer Handling: While our core formulation focuses on single-answer prediction, GRALAN can be extended to support multiple answers. Instead of selecting a single entity with arg max in Eq. (15), we apply a threshold τ to the entity probabilities:

$$V_{\text{pred}} = \{v \mid v \in V_{sub}, P_{\text{cls}}(v|X) > \tau\} \tag{16}$$

The threshold τ can be optimized on the validation set or set dynamically based on the distribution of probabilities. We implement this functionality by modifying the classifier to handle multi-label classification with independent binary decisions for each entity rather than a single decision.

Training Process. For each batch of subgraph-query pairs, we compute both classification and LLM losses:

$$\begin{aligned}
P_{\text{cls}} &= \text{softmax}(W_{\text{cls}}\mathbf{h}_{\text{answer}}) \\
P_{\text{LLM}} &= \text{LLM}(X_{\text{LLM}})_{\text{output}} \\
\mathcal{L}_{\text{total}} &= \lambda_{cls}\mathcal{L}_{\text{cls}}(P_{\text{cls}}, v^*) + (1 - \lambda_{cls})\mathcal{L}_{\text{LLM}}(P_{\text{LLM}}, v^*) + \alpha\mathcal{L}_{reg}
\end{aligned}$$

where v^* is the ground truth answer and $\mathcal{L}_{reg} = \|W_{\text{cls}}\|_F^2 + \beta\text{KL}(P_{\text{cls}}\|P_{\text{LLM}})$ is the regularization loss, where the first term is standard L2 regularization on the classification weights. The LLM loss $\mathcal{L}_{\text{LLM}}(P_{\text{LLM}}, v^*)$ is computed as the standard cross-entropy loss between the LLM output probabilities and the ground truth answer, encouraging the LLM component to assign high probability to the correct entity $\mathcal{L}_{\text{LLM}}(P_{\text{LLM}}, v^*) = -\log(P_{\text{LLM}}(v^*))$. The second term uses Kullback-Leibler (KL) divergence to measure the difference between classification probabilities P_{cls} and LLM probabilities P_{LLM}. This encourages the classification layer's predictions to stay semantically aligned with the LLM's understanding while allowing for graph-specific specialization. The hyperparameter β controls this alignment strength while α and λ_{cls} balance between classification learning, LLM-guided learning, and regularization strength.

GRALAN's approach offers key advantages: (i) Scalability through decoupling from LLM vocabulary size; (ii) flexibility via independent training of the classification layer; (iii) interpretability through classification probabilities; (iv) synergy between graph structure and LLM reasoning through balanced training objectives.

Table 1. Dataset statistics across different question-answering tasks.

Datasets	Task	KG	Underlying KG Stats			Question Sets		
			#Entities	#Relations	#Triples	#Train	#Valid	#Test
PQ-2h	Open QA	Freebase	1,056	13	1,211	1,526	190	192
PQ-3h	Open QA	Freebase	1,836	13	2,839	4,158	519	521
PQL-2h	Open QA	Freebase	5,034	363	4,247	1,276	159	159
PQL-3h	Open QA	Freebase	6,505	411	5,597	825	103	103
MetaQA 1-hop	Open QA	WikiMovies	43,234	9	134,741	96,106	9,992	9,947
MetaQA 2-hop	Open QA	WikiMovies	43,234	9	134,741	118,980	14,872	14,872
MetaQA 3-hop	Open QA	WikiMovies	43,234	9	134,741	114,196	14,274	14,274
ZEROshotRE	Open QA (LLM comparison)	Wikidata 5M	~4.8M	822	20.6M	147,909	3,724	4,966
ComplexWebQuestions	Open QA (LLM comparison)	Wikidata 5M	~4.8M	822	20.6M	27,734	3,480	3,531
OBQA	Multiple-choice QA	ConceptNet	~2M	17	~2.4M	4,957	500	500
ARC	Multiple-choice QA	ConceptNet	~2M	17	~2.4M	2,590	299	1,172
RIDDLE	Multiple-choice QA	ConceptNet	~2M	17	~2.4M	3,510	1,021	1,184
PIQA	Multiple-choice QA	ConceptNet	~2M	17	~ 2.4M	16,113	1,838	3,084

4 Experiments

Given the vast amount of literature in KG-based QA, we evaluate the effectiveness of GRALAN along two main lines: Open (Sect. 4.1) and multiple-choice (Sect. 4.2) question answering. Then, we discuss an extensive ablation study (Sect. 4.3).

Datasets. As for *Open QA*, we considered PathQuestion (PQ) and PathQuestion-Large (PQL) [48] built on Freebase [4]. PQL presents a more challenging scenario with reduced training data and larger KGs. MetaQA [45], derived from WikiMovies [21], focuses on movie-domain queries of varying complexity. Each dataset organizes questions by the number of reasoning hops required, enabling systematic evaluation of multi-hop reasoning capabilities. To benchmark against ToG [30], the current state-of-the-art LLM-based approach, we additionally include ZEROshotRE [22] and ComplexWebQuestions [33]. For these additional datasets, we utilize Wikidata 5M [39] as

KG. As for *multiple-choice QA*, we considered four benchmarks, OBDA [20], ARC [8], RIDDLE [18] and PIQA [3], all utilizing ConceptNet [29] as the underlying knowledge graph[3]. Moreover, as done in [44] we use all answer nodes and question nodes to extract a single subgraph (re-grounded) as the knowledge source for the LLM. the datasets are summarized in Table 1. Further details are available in the Supplemental Material.

Experimental Setting. GRALAN is implemented in PyTorch(Geometric)[4]. To establish relation relatedness, we precomputed a TF-IDF-based relation relatedness matrix [23]. All experiments were conducted on a MacStudio with 192GB shared memory and are the average of 10 runs where the relatively low standard deviation is omitted.

Hyperparameters. For each task-specific dataset, we tune hyperparameters using a validation set. For model architecture, we set the relational token dimension to match the LLM's hidden size, use 2 GNN layers with 5 attention heads, and employ a dropout rate of 0.1. The node selection mechanism considers the top-5 most relevant nodes for each question. We use the AdamW optimizer with a learning rate of 3e-5, batch size of 32, and weight decay of 0.01. We train for 100 epochs. The graph encoder's hidden size is 200, edge dimension of 64, and uses batch normalization. Details about hyperparameter tuning are available in the Supplemental Material.

LLMs Used. While we conducted extensive experiments with various LLMs like BERT and GPT-2 (as detailed in our ablation studies Sect. 4.3), we focus our discussion on FLAN-T5-XXL as the LLM reasoning engine, as it consistently outperformed other language models in our preliminary studies.

Dataset splits. For both Open and Multiple-choice QA, we used the original splits.

Metric. Exact match accuracy (Hits@1) is used following previous work [30,38].

4.1 Results on Open Questions

We mainly choose reasoning-based QA methods as baselines: MINERVA [9]: uses RL to learn paths through knowledge graphs, IRN [48]: employs an interpretable reasoning framework with RL, SRN [24]: leverages structured reasoning networks with policy learning, TransferNet [28]: uses iterative label transfer, NSM [12]: neural state machine approach, JAKET [42], G-Retriever [13], and QAGCN [38] currently representing the most recent approach we are aware of. Table 2 presents the performance comparison between GRALAN and existing state-of-the-art approaches across different multi-hop reasoning tasks. Several key observations emerge from these results. First, on the PathQuestion datasets, GRALAN consistently outperforms existing approaches across all configurations. The performance gap becomes particularly evident in the more challenging PQL dataset, where GRALAN achieves substantial improvements of 3.25% and 15.7% over the previous best results for 2-hop and 3-hop reasoning, respectively. Notably, while other models show significant performance degradation when moving

[3] Preprocessed from DRAGON [40].

[4] Code is available from GitHub https://github.com/giuseppepirro/gralan/.

Table 2. Results on open questions based on multi-hop reasoning.

Model	PathQuestion				MetaQA		
	PQ-2h	PQ-3h	PQL-2h	PQL-3h	1-hop	2-hop	3-hop
MINERVA	75.9	71.2	71.8	65.7	96.3	92.9	55.2
IRN	91.9	83.3	63.0	61.8	85.9	71.3	35.6
EmbedKGQA	90.1	86.2	79.2	61.2	97.5	98.8	94.8
SRN	96.3	89.2	78.6	77.5	97.0	95.1	75.2
TransferNet	91.1	96.5	54.7	62.1	97.5	**100.0**	**100.0**
NSM	94.2	97.1	74.2	67.0	97.3	99.9	98.9
QAGCN	98.5	90.6	87.5	70.9	97.3	99.9	97.6
JAKET	93.5	91.2	83.1	67.6	93.5	73.4	71.2
G-Retriever	96.8	97.1	83.1	83.3	96.8	96.2	99.4
GRALAN	**98.9**	**97.3**	**90.75**	**86.6**	**97.8**	**100.0**	**100.0**

from PQ to the more complex PQL, GRALAN maintains robust performance, demonstrating its superior ability to handle larger knowledge graphs with reduced training data.

On the MetaQA benchmark, GRALAN achieves comparable or superior performance to state-of-the-art methods. Particularly noteworthy is its consistent performance across all hop lengths, matching TransferNet's perfect score on 2-hop queries and NSM's near-perfect performance on 3-hop queries. This consistency across varying reasoning depths demonstrates GRALAN's robust multi-hop reasoning capabilities. A distinguishing feature of GRALAN is its ability to maintain high performance across both datasets without task-specific architectural modifications. This generalization capability, combined with its strong performance on both simple and complex queries, suggests that GRALAN's graph language integration approach effectively captures both local and global graph structures while leveraging the language model's semantic understanding.

Moreover, when compared specifically to G-Retriever and JAKET, GRALAN demonstrates clear advantages in both benchmarks. On PathQuestion, GRALAN improves over G-Retriever by +2.1 points on PQ-2h (98.9% vs. 96.8%) and +7.65 points on PQL-2h (90.8% vs. 83.1 %), and outperforms JAKET by +5.4 points (93.5 % → 98.9%) and +7.65 points (83.1% → 90%) on the same splits. Moreover, GRALAN edges out G-Retriever on PQL-3h and surpasses JAKET by a substantial margin of 19 points (67.6% → 86.6%). On MetaQA, GRALAN consistently beats G-Retriever—e.g. by +3.8 points on 2-hop (100.0% vs. 96.2%) and +0.6 points on 3-hop (100.0% vs. 99.4%)—and outperforms JAKET by over 26 points on 2-hop (73.4% → 100.0%) and nearly 29 points on 3-hop (71.2% → 100.0%). These comparisons underscore that our semantic alignment approach not only rivals but often exceeds the performance of both retrieval-based and joint-attention methods (Table 3).

Comparison with LLM-Only. We compared GRALAN with Think-on-Graphs (ToG) taking the best results reported in [30]. ToG enhances LLM reasoning by integrating structured knowledge from KGs, enabling iterative exploration of reasoning paths. It treats the LLM as an agent that interactively explores related entities and relations within a KG. Our experiments demonstrate GRALAN's effectiveness compared to state-of-the-art LLM-KG approaches.

Table 3. GRALAN vs iterative LLMâĂŞKG approaches.

Model	ZeroShotRE	ComplexWebQ
ToG w/GPT-4 [30]	88.3	67.6
GRALAN	**89.45**	**70.23**

The table shows that GRALAN with FLAN-T5-XXL outperforms ToG using GPT-4 across both evaluated datasets. GRALAN achieves improvements of +1.15% on ZeroShotRE (89.45% vs. 88.3%) and +2.63% on ComplexWebQuestions (70.23% vs. 67.6%). These gains are particularly noteworthy given that ToG utilizes GPT-4, which is generally considered more powerful than FLAN-T5-XXL. This suggests that our hybrid architecture's structured approach to knowledge integration is more effective than purely iterative exploration strategies.

4.2 Results on Multiple-Choice Questions

We compare GRALAN with several state-of-the-art approaches including methods that combine KGs with LLMs: KG Flattening [40], which flattens graph nodes into a sequence via relevance score (REL) ranking; KAPING [1], which injects important KG triples from one-hop (OH) and two-hop (TH) neighborhoods; and GNP [36], which uses GNNs to model retrieved subgraphs as soft prompts to augment LLMs.

Table 4. Results on multiple-choice questions. Results marked with * are taken from Q-KGR [44], which also uses FLAN-T5-XXL as the underlying LLM.

Method	OBQA	Riddle	ARC	PIQA	Average
LLM-only*	76.80	61.37	68.93	56.58	65.92
REL*	72.80	53.53	66.78	56.80	62.48
KAPING TH*	60.60	48.43	57.25	53.21	54.87
KAPING OH*	60.00	47.65	56.65	51.69	54.00
Prompt Tuning*	78.80	61.37	74.85	61.26	69.07
Full Fine-tuning*	89.40	80.78	76.82	65.61	78.15
LoRA*	88.60	74.90	78.54	65.61	76.91
LoRA+GNP*	89.60	76.67	78.71	65.94	77.73
LoRA+Q-KGR*	**90.00**	80.98	79.78	**90.08**	85.21
GRALAN	89.87	**81.03**	**80.56**	89.65	**85.26**

We also consider LLM adaptation approaches: Prompt Tuning [17], which treats embedded knowledge as soft prompts prefixed to text questions; LoRA [14], which updates partial LLM parameters; and standard Full Fine-Tuning. Finally, we compare with Q-KGR [44], the current state-of-the-art that extends GNP with parameter-efficient KG-LLM integration. Our experimental results shown in Table 4 demonstrate GRALAN's effectiveness compared to existing approaches. The baselines LLM-only (65.92% average) and REL (62.48% average) show the limitations of pure language modeling or pure relational approaches. Similarly, KAPING variants (TH: 54.87%, OH: 54.00%) underperform, suggesting that their graph-to-text transformation strategy loses crucial structural information. Parameter-efficient tuning methods show improved performance. Prompt Tuning achieves 69.07% accuracy, while LoRA reaches 76.91%. Adding neural processing (LoRA+GNP: 77.73%) provides modest gains, indicating the value of structural information. LoRA+Q-KGR, achieves strong results (85.21% average) via graph-question alignment.

GRALAN achieves state-of-the-art results with 85.26% *average accuracy*, offering several key improvements. *First*, GRALAN shows consistent strong performance across all datasets, with particularly notable gains on complex reasoning tasks. On ARC, which requires multi-hop scientific reasoning, GRALAN achieves 80.56% accuracy compared to the previous best of 79.78%. On Riddle, which tests abstract conceptual understanding, GRALAN's 81.03% accuracy surpasses the previous 80.98%. *Second*, GRALAN maintains competitive performance on simpler tasks like OBQA (89.87% vs 90.00% previous best) while significantly improving on challenging scenarios. This suggests that our relation-aware attention mechanism effectively captures both straightforward and complex reasoning patterns. Most notably, GRALAN approaches or matches the best results on PIQA (89.65% vs 90.08%), despite PIQA's focus on physical commonsense reasoning—a traditional challenge for graph-based methods. This underlines GRALAN's ability to combine structured knowledge with the LLM's reasoning.

Efficiency Considerations. While full fine-tuning achieves strong results (78.15% average), it requires extensive computational resources and risks catastrophic forgetting. GRALAN matches or exceeds these results while keeping the LLM frozen, offering a more practical solution for real-world applications. The performance gains over other parameter-efficient methods like LoRA (76.91%) and LoRA+GNP (77.73%) validate our approach of teaching the graph encoder to communicate directly in the LLM's semantic space. These results demonstrate that GRALAN's novel approach to graph-language integration offers meaningful improvements over existing methods while maintaining efficiency (Fig. 2).

4.3 Ablation Studies

We conduct extensive ablation studies to understand GRALAN's performance and validate our design choices.

Subgraph Selection Threshold. The *relation similarity threshold* (θ) controlling subgraph extraction significantly influences model performance, with optimal values around 0.7 across all datasets. This finding contrasts with previous approaches like Q-KGR [44] and GraphLLM [6], which rely on fixed-size neighborhood extraction. Our adaptive threshold enables more precise context selection, leading to 3–5% accuracy improvements on complex queries.

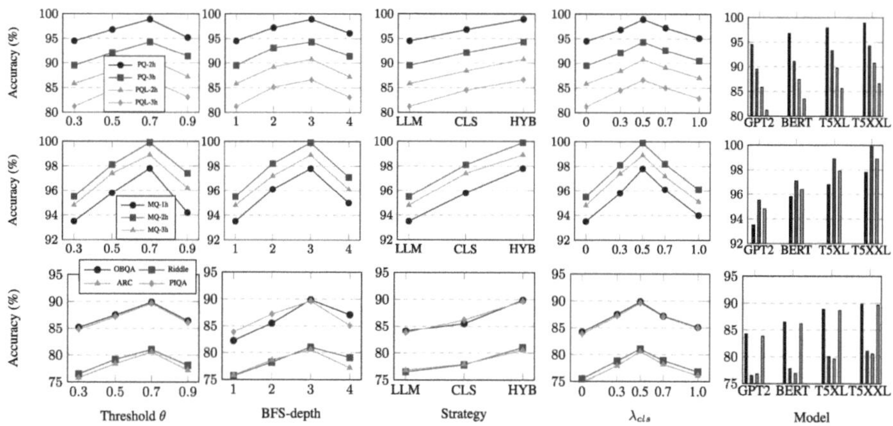

Fig. 2. Ablation studies. Top row: PathQuestion (PQ), middle row: MetaQA (MQ), and Bottom row: Multiple-choice datasets. From left to right: (1) Impact of subgraph selection threshold, (2) Effect of BFS exploration depth, (3) Comparison of prediction strategies (LLM/CLS/Hybrid), (4) Loss weighting influence (λ_{cls}), and (5) Performance across different language models (GPT2 through T5-XXL).

BFS Exploration Depth. We observe that a *BFS depth* of 3 consistently yields optimal results, achieving peak performance of 98% on MetaQA and 90% on multiple-choice tasks. The performance degradation at depth 4 indicates that controlled graph exploration is crucial for effective reasoning.

LearningStrategy Comparison. Our experiments compare three distinct entity prediction strategies: pure LLM reasoning (LLM), classification-based prediction (CLS), and our hybrid approach (HYB). While recent works like HiGPT [35] focus on enhancing LLM capabilities through specialized prompting, our hybrid strategy demonstrates that combining structured graph information with LLM reasoning yields superior results. This is particularly evident in complex scenarios like PQL-3h, where HYB achieves a 5% accuracy gain over the pure LLM approach.

Loss Balancing. The classification *loss weight* (λ_{cls}) shows consistent optimal values between 0.5–0.7 across datasets, indicating an ideal balance between classification accuracy and LLM reasoning. Unlike methods that rely solely on either classification (e.g., QAGNN [38]) or language modeling objectives, our balanced approach enables more robust learning. The sharp performance drop at $\lambda_{cls} = 1.0$ validates the importance of maintaining LLM influence in the final prediction.

LLM choice. While larger LLMs generally yield better performance, with T5-XXL achieving the highest accuracy, GRALAN demonstrates strong results even with smaller models. This contrasts with approaches like GraphToken [11] that show performance degradation with smaller LLMs. Our results suggest that GRALAN's structured graph integration effectively leverages model capabilities, making it more practical for resource-constrained settings.

5 Concluding Remarks and Future Work

This paper introduced GRALAN (The Graph Language), a novel framework that enables knowledge graphs to "speak" directly in the semantic space of large language models. Our comprehensive analysis of GRALAN demonstrates the effectiveness of bridging KGs and language models through semantic alignment rather than structural transformation. Through extensive experimentation, we have validated several key design principles that advance the state of the art in knowledge-intensive reasoning tasks. Our ablation studies reveal that controlled graph exploration (optimal at 3-hop depth) consistently outperforms both shallower and deeper alternatives across all datasets. The adaptive threshold mechanism for subgraph selection proves more effective than fixed neighborhood approaches, while our hybrid learning strategy demonstrates superior performance compared to pure LLM or classification methods. Notably, GRALAN maintains robust performance across different model sizes, making it practical for various deployment scenarios.

Building on these foundations, we identify several promising directions for future research: (i) extending GRALAN to support self-evolving knowledge graphs where the system can predict new edges and update reasoning paths dynamically. This could enable continuous knowledge acquisition and refinement through interaction; (ii) developing GNNs that can effectively fuse visual and textual node features, expanding GRALAN's applicability to rich multi-modal knowledge representations; (iii) investigating cross-domain transfer of reasoning patterns to leverage knowledge across different types of graphs and application domains.

Supplemental Material Statement: Source code for GRALAN along with further dataset description and the complete pseudocode are available from GitHub[5].

References

1. Baek, J., Aji, A.F., Saffari, A.: Knowledge-augmented language model prompting for zero-shot knowledge graph question answering. In: Proceedings of NLRSE, pp. 78–106 (2023). https://doi.org/10.18653/v1/2023.nlrse-1.7
2. Bang, Y., et al.: A multitask, multilingual, multimodal evaluation of chatgpt on reasoning, hallucination, and interactivity. In: Proceedings of AACL-IJCNLP, pp. 675–718 (2023). arXiv preprint arXiv:2302.04023
3. Bisk, Y., Zellers, R., Le Bras, R., Gao, J., Choi, Y.: Piqa: reasoning about physical commonsense in natural language. In: Proceedings of AAAI, pp. 7432–7439 (2020)
4. Bollacker, K., Evans, C., Paritosh, P., Sturge, T., Taylor, J.: Freebase: a collaboratively created graph database for structuring human knowledge. In: Proceedings of SIGMOD, pp. 1247–1250 (2008)
5. Brown, T., et al.: Language models are few-shot learners. In: Proceedings of NeurIPS, pp. 1877–1901 (2020)
6. Chai, Z., et al.: Graphllm: boosting graph reasoning ability of large language model. arXiv preprint arXiv:2310.05845 (2023)

[5] https://github.com/giuseppepirro/gralan.

7. Chen, Y.T., Ku, L.W.: Exploring the limits of chatgpt for query or aspect-based text summarization. arXiv preprint arXiv:2304.03516 (2023)
8. Clark, P., et al.: Think you have solved question answering? try arc, the ai2 reasoning challenge. arXiv preprint arXiv:1803.05457 (2018)
9. Das, R., et al.: Go for a walk and arrive at the answer: reasoning over paths in knowledge bases using reinforcement learning. In: Proceedings of ICLR (2018)
10. Devlin, J., Chang, M.W., Lee, K., Toutanova, K.: BERT: pre-training of deep bidirectional transformers for language understanding. In: Proceedings of NAACL-HLT, pp. 4171–4186 (2019)
11. Fatemi, B., Halcrow, J., Perozzi, B.: Talk like a graph: Encoding graphs for large language models. In: Proceedings of ICLR (2024)
12. He, G., Lan, Y., Jiang, J., Zhao, W.X., Wen, J.R.: Improving multi-hop knowledge base question answering by learning intermediate supervision signals. In: Proceedings of WSDM, pp. 553–561 (2021)
13. He, X., et al.: G-retriever: retrieval-augmented generation for textual graph understanding and question answering. In: Proceedings of NeurIPS, pp. 132876–132907 (2024)
14. Hu, E.J., et al.: LoRA: low-rank adaptation of large language models. In: Proceedings ofI-CLR (2022)
15. Ji, Z., et al.: Survey of hallucination in natural language generation. ACM Comput. Surv. **55**(12), 1–38 (2023)
16. Jiang, J., Zhou, K., Zhao, X., Wen, J.R.: UniKGQA: unified retrieval and reasoning for solving multi-hop question answering over knowledge graph. In: Proceedings of ICLR (2023)
17. Lester, B., Al-Rfou, R., Constant, N.: The power of scale for parameter-efficient prompt tuning. In: Proceedings of EMNLP, pp. 3045–3059 (2021)
18. Lin, B.Y., Chen, Z., Lee, C.H., Ren, X.: Riddlesense: reasoning about riddle questions featuring linguistic creativity and commonsense knowledge. In: Proceedings of ACL-IJCNLP, pp. 1855–1865 (2021)
19. Liu, C., et al.: Graph pooling for graph neural networks: progress, challenges, and opportunities. In: Proceedings of IJCAI, pp. 6712–6722 (2023). https://doi.org/10.24963/IJCAI.2023/752
20. Mihaylov, T., Clark, P., Khot, T., Sabharwal, A.: Can a suit of armor conduct electricity? a new dataset for open book question answering. In: Proceedings of EMNLP, pp. 2381–2391 (2018)
21. Miller, A., Fisch, A., Dodge, J., Karimi, A.H., Bordes, A., Weston, J.: Key-value memory networks for directly reading documents. In: Proceedings of EMNLP, pp. 1400–1409 (2016)
22. Petroni, F., et al.: KILT: a benchmark for knowledge intensive language tasks. In: Proceedings of NAACL-HLT, pp. 2523–2544 (2021)
23. Pirrò, G.: Reword: semantic relatedness in the web of data. In: Proceedings of AAAI, pp. 129–135 (2012). https://doi.org/10.1609/AAAI.V26I1.8107
24. Qiu, L., et al.: Structured attention for unsupervised dialogue structure induction. In: Proceedings of EMNLP, pp. 1889–1899 (2020). https://doi.org/10.18653/v1/2020.emnlp-main.148
25. Raffel, C., et al.: Exploring the limits of transfer learning with a unified text-to-text transformer. J. Mach. Learn. Res. **21**(140), 1–67 (2020)
26. Schlichtkrull, M., Kipf, T.N., Bloem, P., Van Den Berg, R., Titov, I., Welling, M.: Modeling relational data with graph convolutional networks. In: Proceedings of ESWC, pp. 593–607. Springer, Heidelberg (2018)
27. Shen, Y., Liao, R., Han, Z., Ma, Y., Tresp, V.: GraphextQA: a benchmark for evaluating graph-enhanced large language models. arXiv preprint arXiv:2310.08487 (2023)

28. Shi, J., Cao, S., Hou, L., Li, J., Zhang, H.: TransferNet: an effective and transparent framework for multi-hop question answering over relation graph. In: Proceedings of EMNLP, pp. 4149–4158 (2021). https://doi.org/10.18653/v1/2021.emnlp-main.341
29. Speer, R., Chin, J., Havasi, C.: ConceptNet 5.5: an open multilingual graph of general knowledge. In: Proceedings of AAAI, pp. 4444–4451 (2017). https://doi.org/10.1609/AAAI.V31I1.11164
30. Sun, J., et al.: Think-on-graph: deep and responsible reasoning of large language model on knowledge graph. In: Proceedings of ICLR (2024)
31. Sun, Y., et al.: ERNIE 3.0: large-scale knowledge enhanced pre-training for language understanding and generation. arXiv preprint arXiv:2107.02137 (2021)
32. Sung, M., Lee, J., Yi, S., Jeon, M., Kim, S., Kang, J.: Can language models be biomedical knowledge bases? In: Proceedings of EMNLP, pp. 7163–7180 (2021)
33. Talmor, A., Berant, J.: The web as a knowledge-base for answering complex questions. In: Proceedings of NAACL-HLT, pp. 641–651 (2018)
34. Tang, J., et al.: GraphGPT: graph instruction tuning for large language models. In: Proceedings of SIGIR, pp. 491–500 (2024). https://doi.org/10.1145/3626772.3657775
35. Tang, J., et al.: HiGPT: heterogeneous graph language model. In: Proceedings of ACM SIGKDD Conference on Knowledge Discovery and Data Mining, pp. 2842–2853 (2024)
36. Tian, Y., et al.: Graph neural prompting with large language models. In: Proceedings of AAAI (2024)
37. Wang, Q., Mao, Z., Wang, B., Guo, L.: Knowledge graph embedding: a survey of approaches and applications. IEEE Trans. Knowl. Data Eng. **29**(12), 2724–2743 (2017)
38. Wang, R., Rossetto, L., Cochez, M., Bernstein, A.: QAGCN: answering multi-relation questions via single-step implicit reasoning over knowledge graphs. In: Proceedings of ESWC, pp. 343–359. Springer, Heidelberg (2024)
39. Wang, X., et al.: KEPLER: a unified model for knowledge embedding and pre-trained language representation. Trans. Assoc. Comput. Linguist. **9**, 176–194 (2021)
40. Yasunaga, M., Leskovec, J., Liang, P.: LinkBERT: pretraining language models with document links. In: Proceedings of ACL, pp. 8003–8016 (2022)
41. Ye, R., Zhang, C., Wang, R., Xu, S., Zhang, Y.: Natural language is all a graph needs. In: Proceedings of EACL, pp. 1716–1729 (2024)
42. Yu, D., Zhu, C., Yang, Y., Zeng, M.: JAKET: joint pre-training of knowledge graph and language understanding. In: Proceedings of AAAI, pp. 11630–11638 (2022)
43. Zhang, X., et al.: GreaseLM: graph reasoning enhanced language models for question answering. In: Proceedings of ICLR (2022)
44. Zhang, Y., Chen, K., Bai, X., Kang, Z., Guo, Q., Zhang, M.: Question-guided knowledge graph re-scoring and injection for knowledge graph question answering. In: Proceedings of EMNLP, pp. 8972–8985 (2024)
45. Zhang, Y., Dai, H., Kozareva, Z., Smola, A.J., Song, L.: Variational reasoning for question answering with knowledge graph. In: Proceedings of AAAI, pp. 6069–6076 (2018)
46. Zhao, W.X., et al.: A survey of large language models. arXiv preprint arXiv:2303.18223 (2023)
47. Zhao, Z., Wallace, E., Feng, S., Klein, D., Singh, S.: Calibrate before use: improving few-shot performance of language models. In: Proceedings of ICML, pp. 12697–12706 (2021)
48. Zhou, M., Huang, M., Zhu, X.: An interpretable reasoning network for multi-relation question answering. In: Proceedings of COLING, pp. 2010–2022 (2018)

KROMA: Ontology Matching with Knowledge Retrieval and Large Language Models

Lam Nguyen(✉), Erika Barcelos, Roger French, and Yinghui Wu

Case Western Reserve University, Cleveland, OH 44106, USA
{ltn18,eib14,rxf131,yxw1650}@case.edu

Abstract. Ontology Matching (OM) is a cornerstone task of semantic interoperability, yet existing systems often rely on handcrafted rules or specialized models with limited adaptability. We present KROMA, a novel OM framework that harnesses Large Language Models (LLMs) within a Retrieval-Augmented Generation (RAG) pipeline, to dynamically enrich the semantic context of OM tasks with structural, lexical, and definitional knowledge. To optimize both performance and efficiency, KROMA integrates a bisimilarity-based concept matching and a lightweight ontology refinement step, which prune candidate concepts and substantially reduce the communication overhead from invoking LLMs. Through experiments on multiple benchmark datasets, we show that integrating knowledge retrieval with context-augmented LLMs significantly enhances ontology matching—outperforming both classic OM systems and cutting-edge LLM-based approaches—while keeping communication overhead comparable. Our study highlights the feasibility and benefit of the proposed optimization techniques (targeted knowledge retrieval, prompt enrichment, and ontology refinement) for ontology matching at scale. Our code and experimental dataset has been made available at: https://github.com/lamng3/kroma

Keywords: Ontology Matching · Large Language Models · Retrieval Augmented Generation

1 Introduction

Ontologies have been routinely developed to unify and standardize knowledge representation to support data-driven applications. They allow researchers to harmonize terminologies and enhance knowledge and sharing in their fields. Ontologies can be classified according to their level of specificity, ranging from more abstract, general-purpose ontologies such as Basic Formal Ontology (BFO) [35] or DOLCE [5] down to more domain-oriented 'mid-level" ones, such as CheBi [14] in chemistry, Industrial Ontology Foundy (IOF) [17] or Common Core Ontology (CCO) [26]. Domain ontologies are data-driven, task-specific "low-level" ontologies, containing concepts from domain-specific data, such as

D. Garijo et al. (Eds.): ISWC 2025, LNCS 16140, pp. 629–649, 2026.
https://doi.org/10.1007/978-3-032-09527-5_34

Materials Data Science Ontology (MDS-Onto) [42]. To achieve broad usability, ontologies need to be effectively aligned for better interoperability using ontology matching.

Ontology matching has been studied to find correspondence between terms that are semantically equivalent [50]. It is a cornerstone task to ensure semantic interoperability among terms originated from different sources. Ontology matching methods can be categorized to rule-based or structural-based (graph pattern or path-based) matching [10], matching with semantic similarity, machine learning-based approaches and hybrid methods. Linguistic (terminological) methods are often used for ontology matching tasks, ranging from simple string matching or embedding learning to advance counterparts based on natural language processing (NLP). Nevertheless, conventional rule- or structural-based methods are often restricted to certain use cases and hard to be generalized for new or unseen concepts. Learning-based approaches may on the other hand require expensive re-training process, for which abundant annotated or training data remains a luxury especially for *e.g.*, data-driven scientific research.

Meanwhile, the emerging Large Language Models (LLMs) have demonstrated remarkable versatility for NL understanding. LLMs are trained on vast and diverse corpora, endowing them with an understanding of language nuances and contextual subtleties. Extensive training enables them to capture semantic relationships and abstract patterns that are critical for aligning concepts across different data sources. A missing yet desirable opportunity is to investigate whether and how LLMs can be engaged to automate and improve ontology matching.

This paper introduces KROMA, a novel framework that exploits LLMs to enhance ontology matching. Unlike existing LLM-based methods that typically "outsource" ontology matching to LLMs using direct prompting (which may result in low confidence and risk of hallucination), KROMA maintains a set of conceptually similar groups that are co-determined by concept similarity and language models, both guided by their "augmented context" obtained via a runtime knowledge retrieval process. Moreover, the groups are further refined by a global ontological equivalence relation that incorporate structural equivalence.

Contributions. Our main technical contributions are summarized below.

(1) We propose a formulation of semantic equivalence relation in terms of a class of bisimilar equivalence relation, and formally define the ontology structure, called concept graph, to be maintained (Sects. 2 and 3). We justify our formulation by showing the existence of an "optimal" concept graph with minimality and uniqueness guarantee, subject to the bisimilar equivalence.
(2) We introduce KROMA, an ontology matching framework leveraging the power of LLMs (Sect. 4). KROMA fine-tunes LLMs with prompts over enriched semantic contexts. Such contextual information are obtained from the knowledge retrieval process, referencing high-quality, external knowledge resources.
(3) KROMA supports both offline and online matching, to "cold-start" from scratch, and to digest terms arriving from a stream of data, respectively. We

introduce efficient algorithms to correctly construct and maintain the optimal concept graphs (Section 5). (a) Offline refinement algorithm performs a fast grouping process guided by the bisimilar equivalence property, blending the concept equivalence tests co-determined by semantic closeness and language models. (b) Online refinement algorithm effectively incrementalizes its offline counterpart with fast delay time for continuous concept streams. Both algorithms are in low polynomial time, with optimality guarantee on the computed concept graphs.

(4) Using benchmarking ontologies and knowledge graphs, we experimentally verify the effectiveness and efficiency of KROMA (Section 6). We found that KROMA outperforms existing methods using large languge models by 10.95% on average, and the optimization of utilizing knowledge retrieval and refinement processes improves KROMA's accuracy by 6.65% and 2.68%, respectively.

Related Work. We summarize the related work below.

Large Language Models. Large language models (LLMs) have advanced NLP by enabling parallel processing and capturing complex dependencies [44, 51], which have scaled from GPT-1's 117M [40], GPT-2's 1.5B [41] to GPT-3's 175B [6] and GPT-4's 1.8T parameters [34]. Open-source models like Llama have grown to 405B [49], with Mistral Large (123B) [30] and DeepSeek V3 (671B) [13] also emerging. Recent advances in specialized reasoning LLMs (RLLMs) such as OpenAI's O1 and DeepSeek R1 have further propelled Long Chain-of-Thought reasoning—shifting from brief, linear Short CoT to deeper, iterative exploration, and yielded substantial gains in multidisciplinary tasks [8, 12, 29, 33, 38, 43, 46, 54].

Ontology Matching with LLMs. Several methods have been developed to exploit LLMs for ontology matching. Early work focused on direct prompting LLMs for ontology matching. For example, [36] frame product matching as a yes/no query, and [31] feed entire source and target ontologies into ChatGPT—both achieving high recall on small OAEI conference-track tasks but suffering from low precision. Beyond these "direct-prompt" approaches, state-of-the-art LLM-OM systems fall into two main categories: (1) retrieval-augmented pipelines, which first retrieve top-k candidates via embedding-based methods and then refine them with LLM prompts (e.g. LLM4OM leverages TFâĂŞIDF and SBERT retrievers across concept, concept-parent, and concept-children representations [20], while MILA adds a prioritized depth-first search step to confirm high-confidence matches before any LLM invocation [45]); and (2) prompt-engineering systems, which generate candidates via a high-precision matcher or inverted index and then apply targeted prompt templates to LLMs in a single step (e.g. OLaLa embeds SBERT candidates into MELT's prompting framework with both independent and multi-choice formulations [24], and LLMap uses binary yes/no prompts over concept labels plus structural context with Flan-T5-XXL or GPT-3.5 [23]).

2 Ontologies and Ontology Matching

Ontologies. An ontology O is a pair (C, E), where C is a finite set of concept names, and $E \subset C \times C$ is a set of relations between the concepts. An ontology has a graph representation with a set of concept nodes C, and a set of edges E. In this paper, we consider ontologies as directed acyclic graphs (DAGs).

In addition, each concept node (or simply "node") c in O carries the following auxiliary structure. (1) The *rank* of a node $c \in C$ is defined as: (a) $r(c) = 0$ if c has no child, otherwise, (b) $r(c) = \max(r(c') + 1)$ for any child c' of c in O. (2) A *ground set* $c.\mathcal{I}$, refers to a set of auxilary entities from *e.g.,* external ontologies or knowledge bases, that can be validated to belong to the concept c.

Ontology Matching. Given a source ontology $O_s = (C_s, E_s)$ and a target ontology $O_t = (C_t, E_t)$, an *ontological equivalence relation* $R_{\simeq} \subseteq C_s \times C_t$ is defined as an equivalence relation that contains pairs of nodes (c, c') that are considered to be "semantically equivalent". The relation $R_{\simeq}$ induces an equivalence partition

Table 1. Summary of Notations.

Notation	Description
$\mathcal{O} = (C, E)$	ontology $\mathcal{O}$, C: set of concepts, E: set of relations
$\vert\mathcal{O}\vert$	size of ontology $\mathcal{O}$; $\vert\mathcal{O}\vert = \vert C\vert + \vert E\vert$
r(c)	rank of concept node c
$c.I$	ground set of concept node c
$\mathcal{O}_s = (C_s, E_s)$, $\mathcal{O}_t = (C_t, E_t)$	source and target ontology, respectively
$R_{\simeq}$	ontological equivalence relation
$\mathcal{C}$	equivalence partition of concept set $C_s \cup C_t$
$\mathcal{G}_O = (V_O, E_O)$	concept graph $\mathcal{G}_O$, V_O: set of nodes, E_O: set of edges
$\Delta\mathcal{G}$	newly arrive edges; edge updates in $\mathcal{G}$
$[c] \in V_O$	an equivalence class in $\mathcal{C}$
M	a language model
$\mathcal{M}$	set of Large Language Model(s)
q	a prompt query
$q(M)$	a natural language answer from language model M
$F(c, c')$	concept similarity between two concepts c and c'
$q(c, c', \mathcal{M})$	a natural language answer to $\mathcal{M}$ asking if $c \simeq c'$
$\alpha \in (0, 1]$	threshold for asserting concept similarity
$W = (O_s, O_t, F, \mathcal{M}, \alpha)$	configuration input for ontology matching
z_c	embedding of concept c
$\mathbb{S}$	set of candidate concept pairs with similarity scores
$\mathbb{C}$	top-k pairs with highest similarity scores

$\mathcal{C}$ of the concept set $C_s \cup C_t$, such that each partition is an equivalence class that contains a set of pairwise equivalent concepts in $C_s \cup C_t$.

Consistently, we define a *concept graph* $\mathcal{G}_O = (V_O, E_O)$ as a DAG with a finite set of nodes V_O, where each node $[c] \in V_O$ is an equivalence class in $\mathcal{C}$, and there exists an edge $([c], [c']) \in E_O$ if and only if there exists an edge (c, c') in E_s or in E_t. A concept graph $\mathcal{G}_O$ can be a multigraph: there may exist multiple edges of different relation names between two equivalent classes.

Given O_s and O_t, the task of ontology matching is to formulate $R_{\simeq}$ and $\mathcal{C}$ induced by $R_{\simeq}$ and compute the concept graph $\mathcal{G}_O$ accordingly.

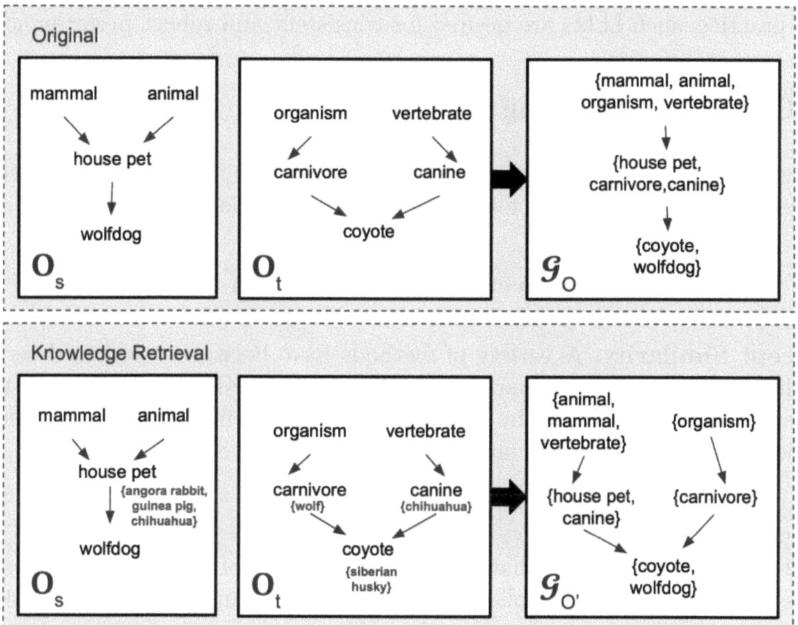

Fig. 1. Ontologies with ground sets, Ontology Matching and Concept Graphs.

Example 1. Fig. 1 depicts two ontologies O_s and O_t as DAGs with 9 concept nodes. An equivalence relation may suggest that "mammal", "animal", "organism" and "vertebrate" are pairwise similar; and similarly for the sets {"house pet", "carnivora" and "canine"}, and {"wolfdog, "coyote"}". This induces a concept graph $\mathcal{G}_o$ as a result of ontology matching, with three equivalence classes.

Language Models for Ontology Matching. A language model M takes as input a prompt query q, and generate an answer $q(M)$, typically an NL statement, for downstream processing. Large language models (LLMs) are foundation models that can effectively learn from a handful of in-context examples, included in a prompt query q, that demonstrate inputâĂŞoutput distribution [52].

Prompt Query. A prompt query q is in a form of NL statements that specifies (1) a task definition $\mathcal{T}$ with input and output statement; (2) a set of in-context examples $\mathcal{D}$ with annotated data; (3) a statement of query context Q, which describe auxiliary query semantics; and optionally (4) specification on output format, and (5) a self-evaluation of answer quality such as confidence. An evaluation of a prompt query q invokes an LLM M to infer a query result $q(M)$.

We specify a prompt query q and a large language model M for ontology matching. A prompt query q is in the form of $q(c, c')$, which asks "are c and c' semantically equivalent?" An LLM M can be queried by $q(c, c')$ and acts as a Boolean "oracle" with "yes/no" answer. An LLM is *deterministic*, if it always generate a same answer for the same prompt query. We consider deterministic LLMs, as in practice, such LLMs are desired for consistent and robust performance.

3 Ontology Matching with LLMs

In this section, we provide a pragmatic characterization for the ontological equivalence relation $R_{\simeq}$. We then formulate the ontology matching problem.

3.1 Semantic Equivalence: A Characterization

Concept Similarity. A variety of methods have been proposed to determine whether two *concepts* are semantically equivalent [7]. KROMA by default uses a Boolean function F defined by a weighted combination of a semantic closeness metric sim[1] and the result from a set of LLMs $\mathcal{M}$ (see Sect. 4).

$$F(c, c') = \gamma \mathsf{sim}(c, c') + (1 - \gamma) q(c, c', \mathcal{M})$$

where q is a prompt query that specifies the context of concept equivalence for LLMs, and γ be a configurable parameter. KROMA supports a built-in library of semantic similarity functions sim, including (a) string similarity, feature and information measure [37], or normalized distances (NGDs) [27]; and (b) a variety of LLMs such as GPT-4o Mini [34], LLaMA-3.3 [21], and Qwen-2.5 [39].

Ontological Bisimilarity. We next provide a specification of the ontological equivalence relation, notably, *ontological bisimilarity*, denoted by the same symbol $R_{\simeq}$ for simplicity. Given a source ontology $O_s = (C_s, E_s)$, and a target ontology $O_t = (C_t, E_t)$, we say a pair of nodes $c_s \in C_s$ and $c_t \in C_t$ are *ontologically bisimilar*, denoted as $(c_s, c_t) \in R_{\simeq}$, if and only if there exists a non-empty binary relation $R_{\simeq}$, such that: (1) c_s and c_t are conceptually similar, *i.e.*, $F(c_s, c_t) \geq \alpha$, for a threshold α; (2) for every edge $(c'_s, c_s) \in E_s$, there exists an edge $(c'_t, c_t) \in E_t$, such that $(c'_s, c'_t) \in R_{\simeq}$, and vice versa; and (3) for every edge $(c_s, c''_s) \in E_s$, there exists an edge $(c_t, c''_t) \in E_t$, such that $(c''_s, c''_t) \in R_{\simeq}$.

[1] We adopt similarity metrics that satisfy transitivity, *i.e.*, if concept c is similar to c', and c' is similar to c", then c is similar to c". This is to ensure transitivity of ontology equivalence, and is practical for representative concept similarity measures.

Lemma 1. *The ontological bisimilar relation $R_{\simeq}$ is an equivalence relation.*

We can prove the above results by verifying that $R_{\simeq}$ is reflexive, symmetric, and transitive over the concept set $C_s \cup C_t$, ensured by the transitivity of concept similarity and by definition. Observe that two entities that are conceptually similar may *not* be ontologically bisimilar. On the other hand, two ontologically bisimilar entities must be conceptually similar, following the definition.

3.2 Problem Statement

We now formulate our ontological matching problem. Given a *configuration* $W = (O_s, O_t, F, \mathcal{M}, \alpha)$ that specifies as input a source ontology O_s, a target ontology O_t, a Boolean function F and threshold $\alpha \in (0, 1]$ that determines concept similarity, and a set of LLMs $\mathcal{M}$, the problem becomes computing a smallest concept graph $\mathcal{G}_O$ induced by the ontologically bisimilar equivalence $R_{\simeq}$.

We can justify the above characterization by proving that there exists an "optimal", invariant solution encoded by a concept graph $\mathcal{G}_O$. To arrive at this, we provide a *minimality* and *uniqueness* guarantee on $\mathcal{G}_O$ as below.

Lemma 2. *Given a configuration W and semantic equivalence specified by the ontological bisimilar relation $R_{\simeq}$ property, there is a unique smallest concept graph $\mathcal{G}_O$ that captures all semantically equivalent nodes in terms of $R_{\simeq}$.*

Proof Sketch: We show that the above result holds by verifying the following. (1) There is a unique, maximum ontological bisimilar relation $R_{\simeq}$ for a given configuration $W = (O_s, O_t, F, \mathcal{M}, \alpha)$, where any LLM in $\mathcal{M}$ is a deterministic model for the same prompt query q generated consistently from W. This readily follows from Lemma 1, which verifies that $R_{\simeq}$ is an equivalence relation. (2) Let

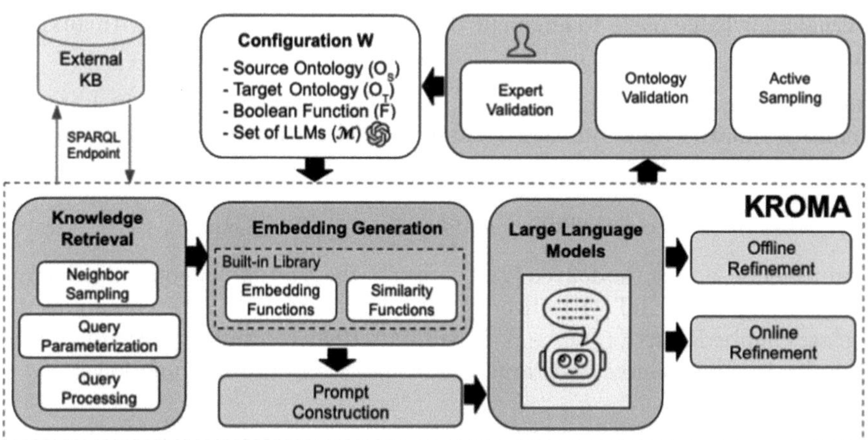

Fig. 2. KROMA Framework Overview: Major Components and Dataflow.

the union of O_s and O_t be a graph $O_{st} = \{C_s \cup C_t, E_s \cup E_t\}$. By setting $\mathcal{G}_O$ as the quotient graph induced by the largest ontological bisimilar relation $R_{\simeq}$ over O_{st}, $\mathcal{G}_O$ contains the smallest number of equivalent classes (nodes) and edges. This can be verified by proof by contradiction. (3) The uniqueness of the solution can be verified by showing that $R_{\simeq}$ induces only one unique partition $\mathcal{C}$ and results in a concept graph $\mathcal{G}_O$ up to graph isomorphism. In other words, for any two possible concept graphs induced by $R_{\simeq}$, they are isomorphic to each other.

The above analysis suggests that for a configuration W, it is desirable to compute such an optimal concept graph as an invariant, stable result with guarantees on sizes and uniqueness on topological structures. We next introduce KROMA and efficient algorithms to compute the aforementioned optimal concept graphs.

4 KROMA Framework

4.1 Framework Overview

Given a *configuration* $W = (O_s, O_t, F, \mathcal{M})$ where $\mathcal{M}$ is a set of pre-trained large language models $\mathcal{M}$, KROMA has the following major functional modules that enables a robust and effective multi-session ontology matching process.

Concept Graph Initialization Upon receiving two ontologies $O_s = (C_s, E_s)$ and $O_t = (C_t, E_t)$ as the inputs, KROMA initializes the concept graph $\mathcal{G}_O = (V, E)$ with $V = C_S \cup C_T$ and $E = E_S \cup E_T$. For each concept $c \in V$, KROMA then globally computes the structural *rank* $r(c)$ as described in Sect. 2.

Knowledge Retrieval. To assemble a rich, yet compact, context for each concept $c \in V$, we perform: (1) *Neighborhood Sampling*: traverse up to its two hops in $\mathcal{G}_O$ to collect parents, children, and "sibling" concepts of c, creating a node induced subgraph centered at c; (2) *Subgraph Parameterization*: Sample and substitute constant values from the subgraph with variables to create SPARQL queries $\mathcal{S}_q$, and (3) *Ground Set Curation*: Apply the generated SPARQL queries $\mathcal{S}_q$ onto external knowledge bases to augment the concept's ground set $c.\mathcal{I}$ with auxiliary information (*e.g.*, relevant entities, definition, labels, synonyms, etc.).

Embedding Generation. In this phase, KROMA leverages a built-in library of semantic similarity functions $\mathsf{sim}(\cdot,\cdot)$ and embedding functions $\mathsf{embd}(\cdot)$. For each concept $c \in V$, KROMA computes the joint textual and structural embedding:

$$z_c = \alpha\ \mathsf{embd}_{graph}(c) + (1 - \alpha)\ \mathsf{embd}_{text},$$

where embd_{graph} (e.g. node2vec [22]) captures the c's topology information and embd_{text} (e.g. SciBERT [4]) encodes c's textual context. After obtaining the necessary embeddings ($z_c\ \forall c \in V$), KROMA then computes pairwise concept similarity between source and target ontologies using the sim functions:

$$\mathbb{S} = \{(c_s, c_t, score_{s,t}) \mid c_s \in C_S, c_t \in C_T, score_{s,t} = \mathsf{sim}(\mathsf{z}_{\mathsf{c_s}}, \mathsf{z}_{\mathsf{c_t}})\}$$

From $\mathbb{S}$, we select the top-k pairs with the highest similarity scores (i.e. in descending order of $score_{s,t}$), yielding the best candidate list $\mathbb{C}$ to ask LLMs.

Example 2. We revisit Example 1. (1) A knowledge retrieval for node "house pet" samples its neighbors and issues a set of "star-shaped" SPARQL queries centered at "house pet" to query an underlying knowledge graph KG. This enriches its ground set with a majority of herbivore or omnivorous pets that are not "carnivore". Similarly, the ground set of "carnivore" is enriched by "wolf", unlikely a house pet. Despite "coyote" and "wolfdog" (house pet) alone are less similar, the ground set of "coyote" turns out to be a set of canine pets *e.g.*, "husky" that are "coyote-like", hence similar with "wolfdog". (2) The embedding generation phase incorporates enriched ground sets and generate embeddings accordingly, which scores that distinguishes "house pet" from "carnivore" due to embedding difference, and assert "coyote" and "wolfdog" to be conceptually similar, allowing the candidate pair to be "double checked" by LLMs in the following phase.

Prompt Querying LLMs. For each candidate pair $(c_s, c_t) \in \mathbb{C}$, KROMA generates an NL prompt that includes: (1) Task description $\mathcal{T}$ (e.g. "*Given two ontology concepts and their metadata, decide if they are related or not.*"), (2) In-context examples $\mathcal{D}$ containing both positive and negative matches, (3) Query context for c_s and c_t including their ground sets, (4) Output format and confidence (e.g., "Answer Yes or No, and provide a confidence score between 0 and 10."). KROMA then calls (a set of) LLMs $\mathcal{M}$ to obtain a matching decision with confidence. Low-confidence or conflicting outputs are routed to validation module.

A query template and a generated example is illustrated in Fig. 3.

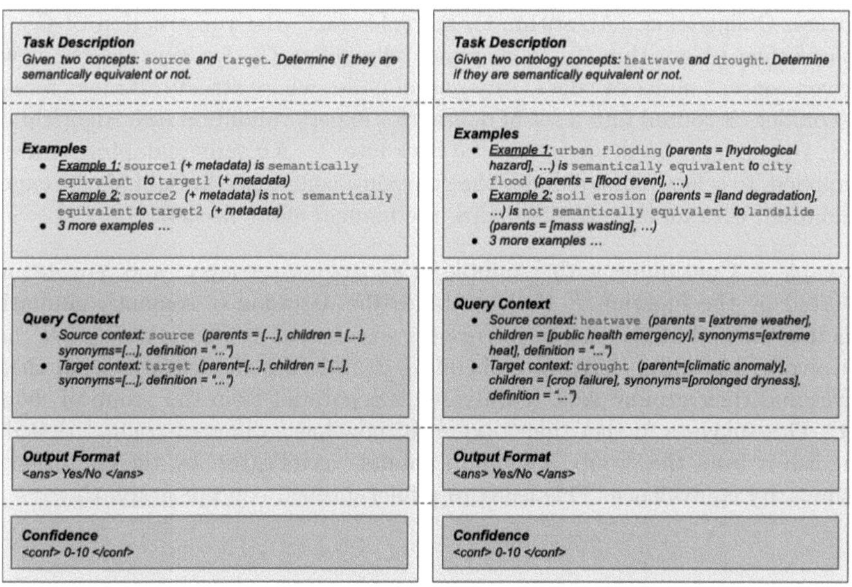

Fig. 3. KROMA Prompt Query Template and Query Example.

Algorithm 1: Offline Refinement

Input: Source ontology $O_S = (C_S, E_S)$, target ontology $O_T = (C_T, E_T)$
Output: Concept graph $\mathcal{G}_O$.

set $V \leftarrow C_S \cup C_T$; set $E \leftarrow E_S \cup E_T$;
Initialize concept graph $\mathcal{G}_O = (V, E)$;
foreach $c \in V$ **do**
  compute rank $r(c)$ as in Section 2;
$\rho \leftarrow \max_{c \in V} r(c)$;
for $i \leftarrow 0$ **to** ρ **do**
  $B_i \leftarrow \{c : r(c) = i\}$;
$P \leftarrow \{B_0, \ldots, B_\rho\}$;
for $i \leftarrow 0$ **to** ρ **do**
  $D_i \leftarrow \{X \in P : X \subseteq B_i\}$;
  foreach $X \in D_i$ **do**
    $G \leftarrow \mathsf{collapse}(G, X)$;
  foreach $c \in B_i$ **do**
    foreach $C \in P$ *with* $C \subseteq \bigcup_{j>i} B_j$ **do**
      Split C into C_1, C_2 by adjacency to c;
      $P \leftarrow (P \setminus \{C\}) \cup \{C_1, C_2\}$;
return $\mathcal{G}_O$;

Ontology Refinement and Expert Validation. KROMA next invokes a refinement process, OfflineRefine (Algorithm 1), to "cold-start" the construction of $\mathcal{G}_O$, or OnlineRefine (Algorithm 2), to incrementally refine $\mathcal{G}_O$ for any unseen, newly arrived concept nodes or edges. Any pair of nodes whose structural ranks remain in "conflict" is routed into a set of queries for expert validation (see Algorithm 2, Sect. 4); once approved, are integrated back into $\mathcal{G}_O$. An active sampling strategy is applied, to select pairs of nodes that have low confidence from LLMs for expert validation, with an aim to minimalize the manual effort needed.

Example 3. Continuing with Example 2, as "golden retriever" and "coyote" are asserted by the function F that combines the descision of semantic similarity function sim and LLMs, an equivalence class is created in $\mathcal{G}'_O$. As "house pet" and "carnivore" has quite different embedding considering the features from themselves and their ground sets, "carnivore" is separated from the group of "house pet". This suggests further that "organism" now has a different context that distinguish it from the group {mammal, animal, vertebrate}, by the definition of bisimilarity equivalence. This leads to a finer-grained concept graph $\mathcal{G}'_O$.

5 Ontology Refinement

We next describe our ontology refinement algorithms. KROMA supports ontology refinement in two modes. The offline mode assumes that the source ontology O_s and the target ontology O_t are known, and performs a batch processing to compute the concept graph $\mathcal{G}_O$ from scratch. The online refinement incrementally maintains $\mathcal{G}_O$ upon a sequence of (unseen) triples (edges) from external resources.

The offline refinement algorithm is outlined as Algorithm 1. (1) It starts by initializing $\mathcal{G}_O$ (lines 1-6) as the union of O_s and O_t, followed by computing the node ranks. At each rank, it initializes a "bucket" B_i (as a single node set) that simply include all the concept nodes at rank i (lines 7-8), and initialize a partition $\mathcal{P}$ with all the buckets (line 9). It then follows a "bottom-up" process to refine the buckets iteratively, by checking if two concepts c and c' in a same bucket B_i are concept similar (as asserted by LLM and embedding similarity), and have all the neighbors that satisfy the requirement of ontological bisimilar relation by definition (lines 10-13). If not, a procedure collapse is invoked, to (1) split the bucket B_i into three fragments: $B_i^1 = B_i \setminus \{c, c'\}$, $B_i^2 = \{c\}$, and B_i^3=$\{c'\}$, followed by a "merge" check to test if c and c' can be merged to B_i^1; and (2) propagate this change to further "split-merge" operators to affected buckets at higher ranks (lines 14-17). This process continues until no change can be made.

Correctness. Algorithm 1 correctly terminates at obtaining a maximum bisimilar ontological equivalence relation $R_{\simeq}$, with two variants. (1) As ontologies are DAGs, it suffices to perform a one-pass, bottom-up splitting of equivalence classes following the topological ranks; (2) the collapse operator ensures the "mergable" cases to reduce unnecessary buckets whenever a new bucket is separated. This process simulates the correct computation of maximum bisimulation relation in Kripke structures (a DAG) [15], optimized for deriving ontology matching determined by LLM-based concept similarity and bisimilar equivalence.

Time Cost. The initialization of concept graph $\mathcal{G}_O$ is in $O(|O_s| + |O_t|)$. Here $|O_s|$=$|V_s|$+$|E_s|$; and $|O_t|$ is defined similarly. The iterative collapse (lines 10-17) takes in $O(|O_s| + |O_t|)$ time as the number of buckets (resp. edges) is at most $|C_s| + |C_T|$ (resp. $|E_s|$+$|E_t|$). The overall cost is in $O(|O_s| + |O_t|)$.

Overall Cost. We consider the cost of the entire workflow of KROMA. (1) The knowledge checking takes $O((|C_s| + |C_T|)|KG|)$ time, where $|KG|$ refers to the size of the external ontology or knowledge graph that is referred to by the knowledge retrieval via *e.g.*, SPARQL access. Note here we consider SPARQL queries with "star" patterns, hence the cost of query processing (to curate ground sets) is in quadratic time. (2) The total cost of LLM inference is in $O(|C_s||C_t|T_I)$, for a worst case that any pair of nodes in $C_s \times C_t$ are concept similar in terms of $\sim$. Here T_I is the unit cost of processing a prompt query. Putting these together, the total cost is in $O(|C_s||C_t|T_I + (|C_s| + |C_t|)|KG| + (|O_s| + |O_t|))$ time.

Online Refinement. We next outline the online matching process. In this setting, KROMA receives new ontology components as an (infinite) sequence of triples (edges), and incrementally maintain a concept graph $\mathcal{G}_O$ by processing the sequence input in small batched updates $\Delta\mathcal{G}$. For each newly arrived concept (node) c in $\Delta\mathcal{G}$, KROMA conducts knowledge retrieval to curate $c.\mathcal{I}$; and consult LLMs to decide if c is concept similar to any node in $\mathcal{G}_O$. It then invokes online refinement algorithm to enforce the ontological bisimilar equivalence.

The algorithm (with pseudoscope reported in [1]) first updates the buckets in $\mathcal{G}_O$ by incorporating the nodes from $\Delta\mathcal{G}$ that are verified to be concept similar, as well as their ranks. It then incrementally update the buckets to maintain the bisimilar equivalence consistently via a "bottom-up" split-merge process as in Algorithm 1 (lines 6-15). Due to the unpredictability of the "unseen" concepts, the online refinement defers the processing of two "inconsistent" cases for experts' validation: (1) When a concept c is determined to be concept similar by function $\sim$ but not LLMs with high confidence; or (2) whenever for a new edge $(c, c') \in \Delta\mathcal{G}$, $(c, [c_1]) \in R_{\simeq}$, $(c', [c_2]) \in R_{\simeq}$, yet $r(c_1) < r(c_2)$ in $\mathcal{G}_O$. Both require domain experts' feedback to resolve. These cases are cached into a query set $\mathcal{Q}$ to be further resolved in the validation phase (see Sect. 4). We cache these cases into a query set by using an auxiliary data structure (*e.g.,* using a priority queue ranked by LLM confidence scores) to effectively manage their processing.

Analysis. The correctness of online refinement carries over from its offline counterpart, and that it correctly incrementalize the split-merge operator for each newly arrived edges. For time cost, for each batch, it takes a delay time to update $\mathcal{G}_O$ in $O(|\mathcal{G}_O| + |\Delta G| \log |\Delta G| + |\Delta G| \log |V_O|)$ time. This result verifies that online refinement is able to response faster than offline maintenance that recomputes the concept graph from scratch. We present detailed analysis in [1].

6 Experimental Study

We investigated the following research questions. **[RQ1]**: *How well* KROMA *improves state-of-the-art baselines with different* LLMs *?* **[RQ2]**: *How can knowledge retrieval and ontology refinement enhance matching performance?* and **[RQ3]**: *What are the impact of using alternative* LLM *reasoning strategies?*

6.1 Experimental Setting

Benchmark Datasets. We selected five tracks from the OAEI campaign [32], covering various domain tracks. For each track, we selected two representative ontologies as a source ontology O_s and a target ontology O_t. The selected tracks include Anatomy [16] (Mouse-Human), Bio-LLM [23] (NCIT-DOID), CommonKG (CKG) [19] (Nell-DBpedia, YAGO-Wikidata), BioDiv [28] (ENVO-SWEET), and MSE [25] (MI-MatOnto). To ensure a fair and comprehensive evaluation of KROMA, we adopted the standard benchmarks from the Ontology Alignment Evaluation Initiative (OAEI), enabling direct comparison with prior LLM-based methods. Despite the high cost of LLM inference, we tested KROMA across five diverse tracks to demonstrate its robustness and effectiveness across domains.

LLMs **Selection.** To underscore KROMA's ability to achieve strong matching performance even with smaller or lower-performance LLMs, we selected models with relatively modest Chatbot Arena MMLU scores [9]: Gemma-2B (51.3%) and Llama-3.2-3B (63.4%), compared to the baseline systems Flan-T5-XXL (55.1%) and MPT- 7B (60.1%). We have selected a diverse set of LLMs, ranging from ultra-lightweight to large-scale—to demonstrate KROMA's compatibility with models that can be deployed on modest hardware without sacrificing matching quality. Our core evaluations use DeepSeek-R1-Distill-Qwen-1.5B [48] (1.5B), GPT-4o-mini [34] (8B), and Llama-3.3 [21] (70B), each chosen in a variant smaller than those employed by prior OM-LLM baselines. To further benchmark our framework, we include Gemma-2B [11] (2B), Llama-3.2-3B [47] (3B), Mistral-7B [3] (7B), and Llama-2-7B [2] (7B) in our ablation studies. To run inference on the aforementioned models, we used TogetherAI and OpenAI APIs, treating them as off-the-shelf inference services on hosted, pretrained models. We are not performing any fine-tuning or weight updates to the models.

Confidence Calibration. Our selection of LLMs is justified by a calibration test with their confidence over ground truth answers. The self-evaluated confidence by LLMs align well with performance: over 80% of correct matches fall in the top confidence bins (9âĂŞ10), while fewer than 5% of errors are reported. Gemma-2B shows almost no errors above confidence 8, and both Llama-3.2-3B and Llama-3.3-70B maintain $\geq$ 95% precision at confidence thresholds of 9 or greater. We thus choose a confidence threshold to be 8.5 for all LLMs to accept their output.

Test Sets Generation. Following [20,23], for each dataset, we arbitrarily designate one concept as the "source" for sampling and its target counterpart. We remark that the source and target roles are interchangeable w.l.o.g given our theoretical analysis, algorithms and test results. We randomly sample 20 matched concept pairs from the ground truth mappings. For each source ontology concept, we select an additional 24 unmatched target ontology concepts based on their cosine similarity scores, thereby creating a total of 25 candidate mappings (including the ground truth mapping). Finally, we randomly choose 20 source concepts that lack a corresponding target concept in the ground truth and generate 25 candidate mappings for each. Each subset consists of 20 source ontology concepts with a match and 20 without matches, with each concept paired with 25 candidate mappings, totaling 1000 concept pairs per configuration.

Concepts and entities not selected as test sets are treated as external knowledge base for **knowledge retrieval**. All models operate with SciBERT [4] for **Embedding Generation**, leveraging its strength in scientific data embedding.

Baselines. Our evaluation considers **four** state-of-the-art LLM-based ontology matching methods: LLM4OM [20], MILA [45], OLaLa [24], and LLMap [23]. For RQ2, we also developed KROMA-NR, which skips the knowledge retrieval process, and KROMA-NB, which disables the use of bisimilarity-based clustering, allowing only the use of concept similarity to determine concept clusters.

Naming Convention. Each configuration uses a pattern `[Method][Optional Suffix][LLM Version]`, where the initials (K, M, O, L) specify the method

(KROMA, MILA, OLaLa, LLM4OM). Suffixes "NKR" and "NR" denote "no knowledge retrieval" and "no ontology refinement", respectively, and the trailing version number (e.g., 3.3, 2.0, 4mini) specifies the underlying LLM release.

6.2 Experimental Results

Exp-1: Effectiveness (RQ1). In this set of tests, we evaluate the performance of KROMA compared with baselines, and the impact of factors such as test sizes.

Table 2. kroma Performance vs. Baselines.

Model	MH	ND	NDB	YW	ES	MM
KL3.3	94.94	98.63	97.08	95.54	-	61.25
KNR3.3	91.25	95.01	94.26	91.98	-	59.95
KNB3.3	86.59	90.91	93.58	89.74	-	55.00
KL3.1	94.50	98.24	-	-	91.43	-
KL2.0	93.24	-	96.02	-	85.06	-
KG2	-	85.53	-	-	-	-
KM7	-	-	-	-	92.98	-
ML3.1	92.20	94.80	-	-	83.70	32.97
OL2.0	90.20	-	96.00	-	51.10	-
L4G3.5	89.11	83.01	94.26	-	-	-
K4mini	-	-	-	-	93.18	-
LLFT	-	72.10	-	-	-	-
L4L2	-	-	-	92.19	-	-
L4M7	-	-	-	-	55.09	-
L4MPT	-	-	-	-	-	32.97

KROMA *vs. Baselines: Overall Performance.* Across all six datasets in Table 2 (abbreviated by their first capitalized letters), the full KROMA configuration (KL3.3) achieves the highest F_1 on every task, substantially outperforming competing baselines. For MouseâĂŞHuman, KL3.3 delivers 94.94 F_1, eclipsing MILA's best (ML3.1) at 92.20, OLaLa (OL2.0) at 90.20, and LLM4OM (L4G3.5) at 89.11. On NCITâĂŞDOID, KL3.3 reaches 98.63 versus 94.80 for MILA, 83.01 for LLM4OM, and 72.10 for Flan-T5-XXL. Similar gaps appear on NellâĂŞDBpedia (97.08 vs. 96.00/94.26), YAGOâĂŞWikidata (95.54 vs. 92.19/93.33), ENVOâĂŞSWEET (93.18 vs. 92.98/85.06), and MIâĂŞMatOnto (61.25 vs. 59.05/32.97). These cumulative results verify the effectiveness of KROMA over representative benchmark datasets. More details (*e.g.*, Precision and Recall) are reported in [1].

Impact of Different LLMs. Across six ontology-matching tracks, KROMA equipped with Qwen2.5-1.5B outperforms the best existing baseline on five out of the six datasets (see Table 3). In the Anatomy's Mouse-Human track, Qwen2.5-1.5B achieves $F_1 = 83.58$ (versus 92.20 for the OM-LLM baseline), while GPT-4o-mini reaches $F_1 = 91.96$. On NCITâĂŞDOID both models surpass the baseline with F_1 of 97.44 and 97.56 (baseline: 94.80), and similar gains appear on Nell-DBpedia (95.02, 95.67 vs. 96.00), YAGO-Wikidata (95.45, 95.44 vs. 92.19), and MI-MatOnto (61.25, 60.88 vs. 32.97). Only on ENVO-SWEET does the smallest model dip below the baseline (79.80 vs. 83.70), whereas GPT-4o-mini (93.18) and Llama-3.3-70B (91.95) still lead. These results show that KROMA (with both knowledge retrieval and ontology refinement) delivers strong performance even on relatively "small" LLMs, and scales further with larger LLMs.

Table 3. Performance with different LLMs.

Dataset	Qwen2.5	GPT-4o-mini	Llama-3.3
MouseâĂŞHuman	83.6	92.0	**94.9**
NCITâĂŞDOID	97.4	97.6	**98.6**
NellâĂŞDBpedia	95.0	95.7	**97.1**
YAGOâĂŞWikidata	95.5	95.4	**95.5**
ENVOâĂŞSWEET	79.8	**93.2**	92.0
MIâĂŞMatOnto	61.3	60.9	**62.2**

Impact of Test Sizes. We next report the impact of ontology sizes to the performance of KROMA in performance (detailed results reported in [1]). For each dataset, we varied test sizes from 200 (xsmall) to 1,000 (full) pairs. KROMA's performance is in general insensitive to the change of test sizes. For example, its F_1 stays within a 1.90 variance on NCITâĂŞDOID and a 1.10-point range on YAGOâĂŞWikidata. This verifies the robustness and effectiveness of KROMA in maintaining desirable performance for large-scale ontology matching tasks.

Exp-2: Ablation Analysis (RQ2). In this test, we perform ablation analysis, comparing KROMA with its two variants, KROMA-NKR and KROMA-NR, removing knowledge retrieval and ontology refinement, respectively.

Impact of Ontology Refinement. Table 4 (Left) shows that by incorporating Ontology Refinement (KROMA vs. KROMA-NR), KROMA improves F_1 score across 6 datasets: MouseâĂŞHuman (+3.69), NCITâĂŞDOID (+3.62), NellâĂŞDBpedia (+2.82), YAGOâĂŞWikidata (+3.56), ENVOâĂŞSWEET (+1.06), MIâĂŞMatOnto (+1.30). By pruning false candidate pairs using offline and online strategies on the concept graph, KROMA is able to retain true semantical connections between concepts.

Impact of Knowledge Retrieval. Table 4 (Right) shows that ablating Knowledge Retrieval (KROMA-KNR vs. KROMA) results in significant F_1 drop

Table 4. kroma performance under different scenarios: with/without Ontology Refinement (Left); and with/without Knowledge Retrieval (Right).

Dataset	Model	P	R	F1
MouseÃćâĆňâĂIJHuman	KL3.3	90.78	99.50	**94.94**
	KNR3.3	92.34	90.16	91.25
NCIT-DOID	KL3.3	97.59	99.69	**98.63**
	KNR3.3	93.20	96.90	95.01
Nell-DBpedia	KL3.3	94.32	100.00	**97.08**
	KNR3.3	97.46	91.27	94.26
YAGO-Wikidata	KL3.3	91.80	99.60	95.54
	KNR3.3	93.50	90.50	91.98
ENVO-SWEET	K4mini	87.23	100.00	**93.18**
	KNR4mini	86.90	98.00	92.12
MI-MatOnto	KL3.3	45.74	92.69	**61.25**
	KNR3.3	44.80	91.40	59.95

Dataset	Model	P	R	F1
MouseÃćâĆňâĂIJHuman	KL3.3	90.78	99.50	**94.94**
	KNKR3.3	100.00	76.36	86.59
NCIT-DOID	KL3.3	97.59	99.69	**98.63**
	KNKR3.3	83.33	100.00	90.91
Nell-DBpedia	KL3.3	94.32	100.00	**97.08**
	KNKR3.3	91.17	96.12	93.58
YAGO-Wikidata	KL3.3	91.80	99.60	95.54
	KNKR3.3	90.50	89.00	89.74
ENVO-SWEET	K4mini	87.23	100.00	**93.18**
	KNKR4mini	82.00	88.00	84.89
MI-MatOnto	KL3.3	45.74	92.69	**61.25**
	KNKR3.3	42.00	85.00	55.00

across all six benchmark datasets: MouseâĂŞHuman (âĂŞ8.35), NCITâĂŞDOID (âĂŞ7.72), NellâĂŞDBpedia (âĂŞ3.50), YAGOâĂŞWikidata (âĂŞ5.80), ENVOâĂŞSWEET (âĂŞ8.29), MIâĂŞMatOnto (âĂŞ6.25). By enriching concepts with external, useful semantic context that are overlooked by other baselines, knowledge retrieval helps improving the performance.

Exp-3: Alternative LLM Reasoning Strategies. We evaluated KROMA's performance with two alternative LLM reasoning strategies: "Debating" and "Deep reasoning" to further understand their impact to ontology matching.

Table 5. KROMA Performance with/without "Debating" (Left); and with/without "Deep reasoning" (Right).

Dataset	Model	P	R	F1
MouseâĂŞHuman	D2A3R	100	70	82.35
	D2A5R	100	74	**85.06**
	D4A3R	100	66	79.52
	D4A5R	100	68	80.95
NellâĂŞDBpedia	D2A3R	97.83	90	93.75
	D2A5R	95.91	94	**94.95**
	D4A3R	95.55	86	90.53
	D4A5R	93.88	92	92.93
YAGOâĂŞWikidata	D2A3R	100	92	95.83
	D2A5R	100	96.9	**98.41**
	D4A3R	100	86	92.47
	D4A5R	100	90	94.73

Dataset	Model	P	R	F1
NCITâĂŞDOID	L3.3Short	97.59	99.69	**98.63**
	L3.3Long	97.66	96.31	96.98
NellâĂŞDBpedia	L3.3Short	94.32	100.00	**97.08**
	L3.3Long	94.67	95.48	95.07
YAGOâĂŞWikidata	L3.3Short	91.80	99.60	**95.54**
	L3.3Long	92.31	94.80	93.53

Can "Debating" help? We implemented an LLM Debate ensemble [18], where multiple agents propose alignments with their chain-of-thought and then iteratively critique one another. To bound context size, we drop 50% of historic turns and keep only each agent's latest reply. Due to its expense, we tested this on Mouse-Human, Nell-DBpedia, and YAGO-Wikidata using four permutation of configurations: 2 or 4 agents over 3 or 5 debate rounds, denoted as `D[Number Of Agent]A[Number Of Round]R`. From Table 5 (Left), on MouseâĂŞHuman dataset, extending rounds in the 2-agent setup raised F1 from 82.35 to 85.06, whereas adding agents degraded performance (4 agents: 79.52 at 3 rounds, 80.95 at 5). Similar trends follow for Nell-DBpedia and YAGO-Wikidata. This interestingly indicates that "longer debates" help small ensembles converge to accurate matches, but larger groups introduce too much conflicting reasoning. In contrast, a single-agent, single-round KROMA pass attains F1 = 90.78, underscoring that a well-tuned solo model remains the most efficient and reliable choice.

Can "Deep reasoning" help? Building on DeepSeek-R1's "Aha Moment" [12], we extended KROMA to include a forced long chain-of-thought for self-revision. Noting that vanilla DeepSeek-R1 often emits empty "`<think>`\n" tags (i.e. "`<think> \n \n </think>`"), we altered our prompt so every response must start with "`<think>`\n", ensuring the model spells out its reasoning. We then compared standard Llama-3.3 (70B) ("short" reasoning, noted as L3.3Short) to DeepSeek-R1-Distill-Llama-3.3 (70B) ("long" reasoning, noted as L3.3Long), finding that the added"`<think>`\n " tag inflated inputs by 20% and outputs by 600% but delivered only tiny precision gains (e.g., NCITâĂŞDOID: 97.59% → 97.66%) while slashing recall (99.69% → 96.31%), dropping F1 by 1.65-2.01 points, based on Table 5 (Right). This suggests that verbose self-reflection may improve transparency but consumes crucial context and can overly filter valid matches—especially in binary tasks, where lengthy chains of thought have been shown to harm recall, which has been consistently observed in [53].

Can "Active Sampling" Help? In the semi-supervised experiments on the Bio-LLM NCIT-DOID benchmark, KROMA paired with Llama-3.3-70B matches or exceeds the performance of MILA + Llama-3.1-70B. Under an active-learning regime with few-shot demonstrations, our method scores 1.90 F1 points higher than MILA and surpasses the previous state of the art by over 6 points. As Table 6 shows, combining bisimilarity-guided refinement with selective querying delivers a substantial boost in KROMA's alignment performance.

Table 6. Active Learning on NCIT-DOID.

Dataset	Model	P	R	F_1
NCIT-DOID	KROMA + Llama-3.1-70B	97.85	98.15	**98.00**
	MILA + Llama-3.1-70B	96.70	92.80	94.67

7 Conclusion

We have presented KROMA, an ontology matching framework that exploits the semantic capabilities of LLMs within a bisimilar-based ontology refinement process. We show that KROMA computes a provably unique minimized structure that captures semantic equivalence relations, with efficient algorithms that can significantly reduces LLMs communication overhead, while achieving state-of-the-art performance across multiple OAEI benchmarks. Our evaluation has verified that LLMs, when guided by context and optimized prompting, can rival or surpass much larger models in performance. A future topic is to extend KROMA with more LLM reasoning strategies and ontology engineering tasks.

Supplemental Material Statement. Our code and experimental dataset has been made available at https://github.com/lamng3/kroma, including an extended version of the paper [1], providing further details for KROMA.

Acknowledgements. This material is based upon research in the Materials Data Science for Stockpile Stewardship Center of Excellence (MDS3-COE), and supported by the Department of Energy's National Nuclear Security Administration under Award Number(s) DE-NA0004104. This material is based upon work supported by the U.S. National Science Foundation, Office of Advanced Cyberinfrastructure (OAC), Major Research Instrumentation, under Award Number 2117439. This work made use of the High Performance Computing Resource in the Core Facility for Advanced Research Computing at CWRU.

References

1. Full version (2025). https://github.com/lamng3/kroma/full.pdf
2. AI, M.: Llama 2 7B Chat Model Card. Technical Blog (2023). https://www.llama.com/llama2/
3. AI, M.: Mistral 7b. Technical Blog (2023). https://mistral.ai/news/announcing-mistral-7b
4. Beltagy, I., Lo, K., Cohan, A.: SciBERT: a pretrained language model for scientific text. In: Proceedings of the 2019 Conference on Empirical Methods in Natural Language Processing and the 9th International Joint Conference on Natural Language Processing, pp. 3615–3620 (2019)
5. Borgo, S., Ferrario, R., Gangemi, A., Guarino, N., Masolo, C., et al.: DOLCE: a descriptive ontology for linguistic and cognitive engineering. Appl. Ontol. **17**, 45–69 (2022)
6. Brown, T.B., Mann, B., Ryder, N., Subbiah, M., Kaplan, J.D. et al.: Language models are few-shot learners. In: Proceedings of the 33rd Neural Information Processing Systems, pp. 1877–1901 (2020)
7. Chandrasekaran, D., Mago, V.: Evolution of semantic similarity—a survey. ACM Comput. Surv. **54**, 1–37 (2021)
8. Chen, A., Song, Y., Zhu, W., Chen, K., Yang, M., Zhao, T., zhang, M.: Evaluating o1-like LLMS: Unlocking reasoning for translation through comprehensive analysis (2025)

9. Chiang, W.L., Zheng, L., Sheng, Y., Angelopoulos, A.N., Li, T. et al.: Chatbot arena: an open platform for evaluating LLMs by human preference. In: Proceedings of the 41st International Conference on Machine Learning, pp. 1–13 (2024)
10. Cruz, I.F., Sunna, W.: Structural alignment methods with applications to geospatial ontologies. Trans. GIS **12**, 683–711 (2008)
11. DeepMind, G.: Gemma 2b model card. Technical Blog (2024). https://blog.google/technology/developers/gemma-open-models/
12. DeepSeek-AI, Guo, D., Yang, D., Zhang, H., Song, J. et al.: Deepseek-r1: incentivizing reasoning capability in LLMs via reinforcement learning. Online (2025). https://arxiv.org/abs/2501.12948
13. DeepSeek-AI, Liu, A., Feng, B., Xue, B., Wang, B., et al.: DeepSeek-V3 technical report. Tech. Report (2023). https://arxiv.org/abs/2412.19437
14. Degtyarenko, K., Hastings, J., Matos, P., Ennis, M.: ChEBI: an open bioinformatics and cheminformatics resource. Curr. Protocols Bioinf. **14**, 14.9.1–14.9.20 (2009)
15. Dovier, A., Piazza, C., Policriti, A.: A Fast Bisimulation Algorithm. In: Berry, G., Comon, H., Finkel, A. (eds.) CAV 2001. LNCS, vol. 2102, pp. 79–90. Springer, Heidelberg (2001). https://doi.org/10.1007/3-540-44585-4_8
16. Dragisic, Z., Ivanova, V., Li, H., Lambrix, P.: Experiences from the anatomy track in the ontology alignment evaluation initiative. J. Biomed. Semantics **8**, 56 (2017)
17. Drobnjakovic, M., Ameri, F., Will, C., Smith, B., Jones, A.: The industrial ontologies foundry (IOF) core ontology. In: Proceedings of the 12th International Workshop on Formal Ontologies Meet Industry (2022)
18. Du, Y., Li, S., Torralba, A., Tenenbaum, J.B., Mordatch, I.: Improving factuality and reasoning in language models through multiagent debate (2023)
19. Fallatah, O., Zhang, Z., Hopfgartner, F.: A gold standard dataset for large knowledge graphs matching. In: Proceedings of the 19th International Semantic Web Conference (2020)
20. Giglou, H.B., D'Souza, J., Engel, F., Auer, S.: LLMs4OM: matching ontologies with large language models. In: Proceedings of the 21st European Semantic Web Conference (2024)
21. Grattafiori, A., Dubey, A., Jauhri, A., Pandey, A., Kadian, A. et al.: The Llama 3 Herd of Models. Tech. Report (2024). https://arxiv.org/abs/2407.21783
22. Grover, A., Leskovec, J.: node2vec: scalable feature learning for networks. In: Proceedings of the 22nd ACM SIGKDD International Conference on Knowledge Discovery and Data Mining, pp. 855–864 (2016)
23. He, Y., Chen, J., Dong, H., Horrocks, I.: Exploring large language models for ontology alignment. In: Proceedings of the Posters and Demos Track of the 22nd International Semantic Web Conference (2023)
24. Hertling, S., Paulheim, H.: Olala: Ontology matching with large language models. In: Proceedings of the 12th Knowledge Capture Conference, pp. 131–139 (2023)
25. Huschka, M., Nasr, E.: Evaluation of automatic ontology matching for materials sciences and engineering. Master's Thesis (2020). https://ad-publications.cs.uni-freiburg.de/theses/Master_Engy_Nasr_2020.pdf
26. Jensen, M., Colle, G.D., Kindya, S., More, C., Cox, A.P., Beverley, J.: The Common Core Ontologies. In: Frontiers in Artificial Intelligence and Applications (2024)
27. Jiang, Y., Wang, X., Zheng, H.T.: A semantic similarity measure based on information distance for ontology alignment. Inf. Sci. **278**, 76–87 (2014)
28. Karam, N., Khiat, A., Algergawy, A., Sattler, M., Weiland, C., Schmidt, M.: Matching biodiversity and ecology ontologies: challenges and evaluation results. Knowl. Eng. Rev. **35**, e9 (2020)

29. Li, X.: A Survey on LLM Test-Time Compute via Search: Tasks. Search Algorithms, and Relevant Frameworks. Transactions on Machine Learning Research, LLM Profiling (2025)
30. Mistral-AI: Mistral Large 2. Technical Blog (2023). https://mistral.ai/news/mistral-large-2407
31. Norouzi, S.S., Mahdavinejad, M.S., Hitzler, P.: Conversational ontology alignment with ChatGPT. In: Proceedings of the 18th International Workshop on Ontology Matching collocated with the 22nd International Semantic Web Conference ISWC (2023)
32. OAEI: Ontology Alignment Evaluation Initiative (2024). https://oaei.ontologymatching.org
33. OpenAI, : Jaech, A., Kalai, A., Lerer, A., et al.: Openai o1 system card. Tech. Report (2024). https://arxiv.org/abs/2412.16720
34. OpenAI: GPT-4 Technical Report. Technical Report (2024). https://cdn.openai.com/papers/gpt-4.pdf
35. Otte, J.N., Beverley, J., Ruttenberg, A.: Bfo: basic formal ontology. Appl. Ontol. **17**, 17–43 (2022)
36. Peeters, R., Bizer, C.: Using ChatGPT for entity matching. In: Proceedings of the 27th International Conference on Advances in Databases and Information Systems (2023)
37. Pirró, G., Euzenat, J.: A Feature and Information Theoretic Framework for Semantic Similarity and Relatedness. In: Patel-Schneider, P.F., Pan, Y., Hitzler, P., Mika, P., Zhang, L., Pan, J.Z., Horrocks, I., Glimm, B. (eds.) ISWC 2010. LNCS, vol. 6496, pp. 615–630. Springer, Heidelberg (2010). https://doi.org/10.1007/978-3-642-17746-0_39
38. Qin, L., Chen, Q., Zhou, Y., Chen, Z., Li, Y. et al.: Multilingual large language model: a survey of resources, taxonomy and frontiers (2024)
39. Qwen, Yang, A., Yang, B., Zhang, B., Hui, B. et al.: Qwen2.5 technical report. Technical Report (2025). https://arxiv.org/abs/2412.15115
40. Radford, A., Narasimhan, K., Salimans, T., Sutskever, I.: Improving language understanding by generative pre-training. Tech. Report (2018). https://cdn.openai.com/research-covers/language-unsupervised/language_understanding_paper.pdf
41. Radford, A., Wu, J., Child, R., Luan, D., Amodei, D., Sutskever, I.: Language models are unsupervised multitask learners. Tech. Report (2019). https://cdn.openai.com/better-language-models/language_models_are_unsupervised_multitask_learners.pdf
42. Rajamohan, B.P., Bradley, A.C.H., Tran, V.D., Gordon, J.E., Caldwell, H.W., et al.: Materials data science ontology (MDS-Onto): unifying domain knowledge in materials and applied data science. Sci. Data **12**, 628 (2025)
43. Sun, J., Zheng, C., Xie, E., Liu, Z., Chu, R., et al.: A survey of reasoning with foundation models (2024)
44. Sutskever, I., Vinyals, O., Le, Q.V.: Sequence to sequence learning with neural networks. In: Proceedings of the 28th Conference on Neural Information Processing Systems, pp. 3104–3112 (2014)
45. Taboada, M., Martinez, D., Arideh, M., Mosquera, R.: Ontology matching with large language models and prioritized depth-first search. Inf. Fusion **123**, 103254 (2025)
46. Team, K., Du, A., Gao, B., Xing, B., Jiang, C., et al.: Kimi k1.5: Scaling reinforcement learning with LLMs. Tech. Report (2025). https://arxiv.org/abs/2501.12599

47. Team, M.A.: Llama 3.2 3b instruct model card (2024). https://huggingface.co/meta-llama/Llama-3.2-3B-Instruct
48. Team, Q.: Introducing qwen1.5. Tech. Report (2024). https://qwenlm.github.io/blog/qwen1.5
49. Touvron, H., Martin, L., Stone, K., Albert, P., Almahairi, A. et al.: Llama 2: open foundation and fine-tuned chat models. Technical Report (2023). https://arxiv.org/abs/2307.09288
50. Trojahn, C., Vieira, R., Schmidt, D., Pease, A., Guizzardi, G.: Foundational ontologies meet ontology matching: a survey. Semantic Web **13**, 685–704 (2022)
51. Vaswani, A., Shazeer, N., Parmar, N., Uszkoreit, J., Jones, L., et al.: Attention is all you need. In: Proceedings of the 31st Conference on Neural Information Processing Systems, pp. 6000–6010 (2017)
52. Wei, J., Tay, Y., Bommasani, R., Raffel, C., Zoph, B., et al.: Emergent abilities of large language models. Trans. Mach. Learn. Res. **1**, 1–21 (2022)
53. Wei, J., Wang, X., Schuurmans, D., Bosma, M., Ichter, B., et al.: Chain-of-thought prompting elicits reasoning in large language models. In: Proceedings of the 36th Conference on Neural Information Processing Systems (2022)
54. Xu, Y., et al.: A survey on multilingual large language models: corpora, alignment, and bias. Front. Comp. Sci. **19**, 1–23 (2025)

Author Index

D. Garijo et al. (Eds.): ISWC 2025, LNCS 16140, pp. 651–654, 2026.
https://doi.org/10.1007/978-3-032-09527-5

Xie, Yuexiang I-462
Xie, Yuzhang I-328
Xu, Chuan II-3
Xu, Ran I-328
Xu, Zhen I-594

MIX
Papier aus verantwortungsvollen Quellen
Paper from responsible sources
FSC® C105338

If you have any concerns about our products,
you can contact us on
ProductSafety@springernature.com

In case Publisher is established outside the EU,
the EU authorized representative is:
Springer Nature Customer Service Center GmbH
Europaplatz 3, 69115 Heidelberg, Germany

Printed by Libri Plureos GmbH
in Hamburg, Germany